PLATINUM EDITION
USING
Microsoft®
Windows XP

Robert Cowart

Brian Knittel

que®

201 W. 103rd Street
Indianapolis, Indiana 46290

Contents at a Glance

PLATINUM EDITION USING MICROSOFT® WINDOWS XP

Copyright © 2004 by Que

International Standard Book Number: 0-7897-2790-0

Library of Congress Catalog Card Number: 2002103978

Printed in the United States of America

First Printing: July 2003

06   05   04   03   4   3   2   1

Que Publishing offers excellent discounts on this book when ordered in quantity for bulk purchases or special sales. For more information, please contact

U.S. Corporate and Government Sales
1-800-382-3419
corpsales@pearsontechgroup.com

For sales outside of the U.S., please contact

International Sales
1-317-581-3793
international@pearsontechgroup.com

Trademarks

Warning and Disclaimer

Publisher
Paul Boger

Associate Publisher
Greg Wiegand

Executive Editor
Rick Kughen

Development Editors
Mark Cierzniak
Jim Minatel
Rick Kughen

Managing Editor
Charlotte Clapp

Project Editor
Tricia Liebig

Production Editor
Benjamin Berg

Indexer
Tom Dinse

Proofreader
Juli Cook

Technical Editors
Mark Reddin
James F. Kelly
Ben Schorr

Team Coordinator
Sharry Lee Gregory

Multimedia Developer
Dan Scherf

Interior Designer
Anne Jones

Cover Designer
Anne Jones

Page Layout
Michelle Mitchell
Susan Geiselman
Tim Osborn

Graphics
Tammy Graham

TABLE OF CONTENTS

VI Management, Maintenance, and Repair

ABOUT THE AUTHOR

Robert Cowart has written more than 40 books on computer programming and applications, with more than a dozen on Windows. His titles include *Windows NT Unleashed*, *Mastering Windows (3.0, 3.1, 95, 98, and Me)*, *Windows NT Server Administrator's Bible*, *Windows NT Server 4.0: No Experience Required*, and *Special Edition Using Windows 2000 Professional*. Several of his books have been best sellers in their category, and have been translated into more than 20 languages. He has written on a wide range of computer-related topics for such magazines as *PC Week*, *PC World*, *PC Magazine*, *PC Tech Journal*, *Mac World*, and *Microsoft Systems Journal*. He has taught programming classes at the University of California Extension in San Francisco and has appeared as a special guest on the PBS TV series *Computer Chronicles*, CNN's *Headline News*, ZD-TV's *The Screen Savers*, and ABC's *World News Tonight with Peter Jennings*. He is president and co-founder of Brainsville.com, a company specializing in creating multimedia training courses. Robert resides in Berkeley, California.

In his spare time he is involved in the music world, presenting chamber-music concerts and playing classical piano. He also is a teacher of the Transcendental Meditation technique.

Brian Knittel has been a software developer for more than 20 years. After doing graduate work in nuclear medicine and magnetic resonance imaging technologies, he began a career as an independent consultant. An eclectic mix of clients have led to long-term projects in medical documentation, workflow management, real-time industrial system control, and most importantly, 20 years of real-world experience with MS-DOS, Windows, and computer networking in the business world. He is the author of *Windows XP Under the Hood: Hardcore Windows Scripting and Command Line Power*, and with Bob Cowart wrote three titles in Que's *Special Edition Using* series, covering Windows 2000 Professional, XP Professional, and XP Home Edition. Brian lives in Albany, California, halfway between the tidal wave zone and the earthquake fault. He spends his free time restoring antique computers (check out `www.ibm1130.org`) and trying to perfect his wood-fired pizza recipes.

ABOUT THE CONTRIBUTORS

Anil Desai, MCSE, MCSD, MCDBA, is an independent consultant in Austin, TX. He specializes in evaluating, developing, and managing solutions based on Microsoft technologies. Anil is the author of several technical books, including: *Windows 2000 Directory Services Administration Exam Guide* (Sybex), *Windows NT Network Management: Reducing Total Cost of Ownership* (New Riders Press), and *SQL Server 2000 Backup and Recovery* (Osborne/McGraw-Hill). He has made dozens of conference presentations at national events and is also a contributor to magazines. For more information, please see `http://home.austin.rr.com/akdesai` or contact him at `anil@austin.rr.com`.

Jeffrey A. Ferris, MCSE, is a systems architect for Dell Computer Corporation in Austin, Texas, where his current responsibilities focus on the engineering and management of the desktop environment. Jeff has held key roles in both the infrastructure upgrade to Windows 2000 and in the desktop migration to Windows XP. Before his move to Texas, Jeff was an associate consultant with Celeritas Technologies in Overland Park, KS. While in Kansas, Jeff fulfilled a critical role in the development and implementation of the first nationwide rollout of a Windows NT 4.0 domain architecture for the Call Center Services division of Sprint. Jeff has authored or co-authored eight titles covering various topics including Windows NT 4.0, Windows 2000, Windows XP, networking, and information systems security. Jeff can be reached online at `jeff@ferristech.net`.

Jim Foley, a.k.a. The Elder Geek, owns and operates a small consulting and Web design firm in Cambridge, NY that specializes in the integration of Windows XP technology into home and business environments. He is also the creator and owner of The Elder Geek on Windows XP (`www.theeldergeek.com`) Web site that strives to provide relevant information related to Windows XP, including a notification service to keep readers informed of the latest XP tips, troubleshooting, and update developments.

Arthur Knowles is president and founder of Knowles Consulting, a firm specializing in systems integration, training, and software development. Art is the author of *High Performance Windows NT 4 Optimization & Tuning*, *Microsoft BackOffice 2 Administrator's Survival Guide*, *Microsoft Internet Information Server 3 Unleashed*, and has served as a contributing author to several books, including *Designing and Implementing the Microsoft Internet Information Server 2*, *Windows 3.1 Configuration Secrets*, *Windows NT Unleashed*, and *Mastering Windows 95*.

Terry William Ogletree is a consultant currently working in New Jersey. He has worked with networked computer systems since 1980, starting out on Digital Equipment PDP computers and OpenVMS-based VAX systems. He has worked with Unix and TCP/IP since 1985 and has been involved with Windows NT and Windows 2000 since they first appeared, as well as the newest addition to the family, Windows XP. Besides being the lead author of the third edition of this book, he is the author of *Windows XP Unleashed*, *Practical Firewalls*, *The Complete Idiot's Guide to Creating Your Own CDs* (with co-author Todd Brakke) and has contributed chapters to many other books published by Que, including *Microsoft Windows 2000 Security Handbook* and *Special Edition Using Unix, Third Edition*. He is also the author of *Fundamentals of Storage Area Networking*. When not writing for Que he has on occasion contributed articles to *PC Magazine*.

Will Schmied (BSET, MCSE, CWNA, MCSA, Security+, Network+, A+), consultant and author, is a partner with Area 51 Partners, Inc. Will holds a bachelor's degree in mechanical engineering technology from Old Dominion University in addition to his various IT industry certifications. Will currently resides in Newport News, Virginia, with his wife, Allison; their children Christopher, Austin, Andrea, and Hannah; and their two dogs, Peanut and Jay. You can visit Will at www.area51partners.com.

Robert Sheldon has worked as a consultant and technical writer for a number of years. As a consultant, he has managed the development and maintenance of Web-based and client-server applications and the databases that support those applications. He has written or co-written eight books on various network and server technologies, one of which received a Certificate of Merit from the Puget Sound Chapter of the Society for Technical Communication.

Mark Edward Soper has been a PC user for 18 years, and has been a computer trainer and technical writer since 1988. Author of more than 150 magazine articles and several books, including *PC Help Desk in a Book*, *The Complete Idiot's Guide to High-Speed Internet Connections*, and *TechTV's Upgrading Your PC*, he also has written frequently about Windows from version 3.1 to Windows 2000. He also has contributed to multiple editions of *Upgrading and Repairing PCs*, and co-authored *Upgrading and Repairing PCs, Field Manual*, and *Upgrading and Repairing PCs, A+ Certification Study Guide*. He lives in Evansville, Indiana, where he enjoys researching the history of transportation.

DEDICATION

To my friends and family who have been so supportive over the past year, and especially to Frank, Viki, Kathy, and Mokie. —Bob

To my mother. —Brian

ACKNOWLEDGMENTS

We wish to thank the incredible editors at Que who kept this project afloat, and provided great leadership and guidance: Rick Kughen, Greg Wiegand, Mark Cierzniak and Jim Minatel. Also, this book wouldn't have been possible without our team of contributors who provided great expertise and enthusiasm.

Finally, huzzahs and kudos to the entire Que production staff. These talented folks labor away unseen and largely unthanked and squeeze our scribblings and fevered rants into the tidy package you're holding.

WE WANT TO HEAR FROM YOU!

As the reader of this book, *you* are our most important critic and commentator. We value your opinion and want to know what we're doing right, what we could do better, what areas you'd like to see us publish in, and any other words of wisdom you're willing to pass our way.

As an associate publisher for Que, I welcome your comments. You can email or write me directly to let me know what you did or didn't like about this book—as well as what we can do to make our books better.

Please note that I cannot help you with technical problems related to the *topic* of this book. We do have a User Services group, however, where I will forward specific technical questions related to the book.

When you write, please be sure to include this book's title and author as well as your name, email address, and phone number. I will carefully review your comments and share them with the author and editors who worked on the book.

Email: feedback@quepublishing.com

Mail: Greg Wiegand
          Que Publishing
          201 West 103rd Street
          Indianapolis, IN 46290 USA

For more information about this book or another Que title, visit our Web site at www.quepublishing.com. Type the ISBN (excluding hyphens) or the title of a book in the Search field to find the page you're looking for.

INTRODUCTION

Thank you for purchasing or considering the purchase of *Platinum Edition Using Microsoft Windows XP*.

When we published our first Windows book about 15 years ago, our publisher didn't even think the book would sell well enough to print more than 5,000 copies. I remember asking a stock broker to purchase some Microsoft stock for me back in 1995, and he asked me who Microsoft was, and what they did. Who could have imagined that a decade and a half later, anyone who hoped to get hired for even a basic IT job would have to be highly conversant in networking Windows-based PCs or that an MCSE (Microsoft Certified System Engineer) certificate could prove as lucrative as a medical or law degree, or that a typical Windows OS would be assembled from over 30 million lines of programming code as XP is. As you might know, Windows 1.0 was nothing more than a dinky application interface tacked on top of DOS. Windows XP is a brobdignagian beast with support for many complex technologies: CD-ROM, CD-R and CD-RW, DVD, TCP/IP, MP3, MPEG, DV, USB, IEEE 1394, APM, ACPI, RAID, UPS, PPOE, 802.11b, fault tolerance, disk encryption and compression...the list goes on.

Whether Microsoft's corner on the PC OS market was won unethically through monopolistic practices we'll leave up to you to decide. The evolution of Windows to what we have in XP today represents a lot of work, by anyone's accounting. And even though Gates and company are rarely on the bleeding edge of technology, a lot can be said from the end user's perspective for the standardization that Microsoft has imposed on the industry. In 1981, when we were building our first computers, the operating system (CP/M) had to be modified in assembly language and recompiled, and hardware parts had to be soldered together to make almost any new addition (such as a video display terminal) work. Average folks simply didn't have the techno-chops to build a computer, much less do something with it. The creation and adoption (and sometimes forcing) of hardware and software standards that have made the PC a household appliance the world over can largely be credited to Microsoft, like it or not. The unifying software glue of the PC revolution has been Windows, which is one reason it's been exciting to chart its evolution and document it all these last 15 years.

WHY THIS BOOK?

As you certainly know, these fat computer books make good door stops (or antidotes to occasional insomnia) in a couple of years. (We should know, since we've written more than a few of them and have stacks of extra copies them in our personal libraries.) Still, there's nothing like a good reference book when you need it. Although we've written two lengthy books on Windows XP (*Windows XP Home Bestseller Edition* and *Windows XP Professional Bestseller Edition*), we had a bunch of advanced material that didn't make it into those books for a couple of reasons. First, the target readership of those books wasn't advanced users or IT professionals, and second, we felt compelled to cover some of the more elementary XP topics in those titles, which necessarily consumed some of the limited number of book pages allotted to us. The book you're holding is thus the mental repository of many months of research and experimentation which had no home until Que suggested we write a higher-level title on Windows XP, containing more complex XP issues for a more advanced readership. Portions also grew out of our experiences writing Que's *Special Edition Using Windows 2000 Professional*.

As an experienced Windows user, you know that ever since Windows 95, Windows has come with negligible written documentation. Of course, online Help files abound, but they are written by Microsoft's contractors and staff. You won't find criticisms, complaints, workarounds, or talk of third-party programs there, let alone explanations of *why* you have to do things a certain way. For that, you need a book not written or published by Microsoft. Although we produced two separate titles for our Special Edition and Bestseller Edition XP books from Que (one for Home Edition and one for Professional), this book covers both. Since this is more of a reference manual than a tutorial text, we've covered both versions in this one volume, and simply noted the differences in features between the two versions where appropriate.

In this book's many pages, we focus not just on the gee-whiz side of the technology, but why you should care, what you can get from it, and what you can forget about. The lead author on this book has previously written 15 books about Windows, all in plain English (several bestsellers), designed for everyone from rank beginners to full-on system administrators deploying NT Server domains. The co-author has designed software and networks for more than 20 years. We work with and write about various versions of Windows year in and year out. We have a clear understanding of what confuses users and system administrators about installing, configuring, or using Windows, as well as (we hope) how to best convey the solutions to our readers.

While writing this book (and our other books, actually), we tried to stay vigilant of four cardinal rules:

- Keep it practical.
- Keep it accurate.
- Keep it concise.
- Keep it interesting, and even crack a joke or two.

We believe that you will find this to be the best book available on Windows XP Professional and Home Edition for the advanced user. While writing it, we targeted an audience ranging from the power user at home or the office to the support guru in a major corporation. Whether you use a Windows XP PC or support others who do, we firmly believe this book will address your questions and needs.

We're also willing to tell you what we don't cover. No book can do it all. This book is about Windows XP. We don't cover setting up the Server operating systems called Windows 2000 Server or Windows Server 2003. However, we do tell you how to connect to and interact with these servers using Windows XP. And, due to space limitations, there is only passing coverage in Appendix A of Windows XP's command-line utilities, batch file language, and Windows Script Host. For more, check out Brian's book *Windows XP Under the Hood: Hardcore Scripting and Command Line Power*.

Even when you've become a Windows XP pro, we think you'll find this book to be a valuable source of reference information in the future. Both the table of contents and the very complete index will provide easy means for locating information when you need it quickly.

How Our Book Is Organized

Although this book advances logically from beginning to end, it's written so that you can use the index or table of contents to jump in at any location, quickly get the information you need, and get out. You don't have to read it from start to finish, nor do you need to work through complex tutorials.

This book is broken down into seven major parts. Here's the skinny on each one:

Part I, "Installation," introduces Windows XP and explains its features, architecture, and new graphical user interface (GUI) elements. It then explains how to ready your hardware and software for installation of XP and describes the installation process itself under several different scenarios: basic XP installations, workstations that must be able to boot several different operating systems, and large-scale deployment in the enterprise.

Part II, "System Configuration and Setup," covers the additional setup and management steps needed to turn a "vanilla" XP installation into a fully functioning system. The chapters in this section tell how to manage user accounts, set up Internet connections (including shared and broadband Internet connections), add printers and fax modems, install applications, and configure system services. Additionally, a chapter is devoted to the tweaks and adjustments you can—and in some cases, should—make to the Windows user interface; that is, the desktop, taskbar, and Start menu. You'll also want to refer back to this chapter later when you need to modify or change these basic system settings.

Part III, "Windows XP Applications," covers the built-in applications and services provided with Windows XP. Readers of this book don't need tutorials, but want a comprehensive guide to the applications' features, options, and settings, as well as a repertoire of handy tips and tricks. So, with that in mind, this section shows you the deeper and darker sides of Windows Explorer, multimedia and imaging applications, and Internet applications such as Internet Explorer and Outlook Express. The last chapter in this section tells how to set up the Web, FTP, SMTP, and telnet servers provided with Windows XP.

Part IV, "Networking," deals with networking on the LAN. Here, we explain the fundamentals of Windows networking and, in case you don't have a corporate networking department to do this for you, we walk you through planning and installing a functional LAN for your home or office. We cover the use of a Windows XP network; give you a chapter on dial-up and remote access networking; show how to internetwork with Unix and other operating systems; and finish up with a chapter on the troubleshooting tools provided with XP.

Part V, "Security," covers a crucial aspect of Windows setup and management: keeping your system safe from unauthorized access. Since intruders can come in over the Internet or your local area network, or they can walk into your office, you'll want to read this part to find out how to lock down your system against all three types of attack. One chapter covers local security measures built into the operating system, one chapter covers user-specific security on the NTFS file system, and a final chapter covers network and Internet security measures.

Part VI, "Management, Maintenance, and Repair," dives even deeper into system administration and configuration. One entire chapter is devoted to disk management, while others cover hardware and device driver installation, the Windows Registry database, and the Microsoft Management Console (MMC) and its plug-ins. This section also shows you how you can use scripting, batch files, and the Task Scheduler to automate management tasks, and has a chapter devoted to special considerations and tools available managing XP in an enterprise setting. Finally, there are chapters devoted to troubleshooting and to XP's system recovery features that can help you in the event of a hardware or software disaster.

Finally, the Appendixes provide reference information that you may find helpful as you navigate through Windows's darker recesses. Appendix A covers the Windows XP command-line interface, including the command shell and batch file commands and the MS-DOS emulation subsystem. Appendix B lists all of the executable programs provided with

Windows XP, including system services and drivers, not only to help you find helpful tools you may never have known about, but also to help identify the various applications and tasks that Windows runs on your behalf. Appendix C lists troubleshooting resources for Windows XP. The appendixes are included as PDFs on the CD with this book.

WHAT'S ON THE CD?

We've made a 45-minute CD-ROM-based video presentation covering several Windows management and networking skills:

1. Windows Explorer (7 minutes)
   - Copying and moving files easily between distant folders
   - Finding and removing old chkdsk files
2. Taskbar and Multitasking (8 minutes)
   - Customizing toolbars on the taskbar
   - Tricks for switching between running applications
   - Adding toolbars, folders, and shortcuts to the Quick Launch bar
3. Viewing Photos (4 minutes)
   - Getting photos into your computer
   - The camera and scanner wizard
   - Creating slideshows
   - Changing the orientation of photos
4. Editing Photos (14 minutes)
   - Using Microsoft's photo editing tools *(requires Microsoft Office)*
   - Applying stylistic filters
   - Modifying contrast, brightness, gamma
5. Printing Photos (5 minutes)
   - Using the photo printing wizard to print your photos
   - How to use expensive photo paper efficiently
6. Setting Up a Shared Internet Connection (13 minutes)
   - Sharing one Internet connection between several computers on a LAN
   - Using a connection sharing router instead of Internet Connection Sharing (ICS)
   - Choosing which computer will act as host
   - Sharing a dial-up connection
   - Sharing a DSL or cable connection
   - Using the Network Setup Wizard
   - How to include computers running earlier versions of Windows
   - Ensuring security when sharing Internet connections

7. Doing Your Own Network Wiring (10 minutes)

- Choosing the right kind of CAT-5 cable
- Stripping the cable
- Arranging the wires in the correct order
- Using a crimping tool

8. Setting Up a Wireless Network (11 minutes)

- Wireless overview
- 802.11b versus other standards
- Choosing wireless gear
- Infrastructure versus ad hoc setups
- Installing the access points
- Installing wireless cards in laptops and desktops

You'll want to be sure to check this out, and meet the authors. Also, included on the CD as PDFs are Chapter 33 and the Appendixes.

CONVENTIONS USED IN THIS BOOK

Special conventions are used throughout this book to help you get the most from the book.

TEXT CONVENTIONS

Various typefaces in this book identify terms and other special objects. These special typefaces include the following:

Type	Meaning
Italic	New terms or phrases when initially defined.
`Monospace`	Information that appears in code or onscreen, or information you type.
Words separated by commas	All Windows book publishers struggle with how to represent command sequences when menus and dialog boxes are involved. In this book, we separate commands using a comma. Yeah, we know it's confusing, but this is traditionally how Que does it, and traditions die hard. So, for example, the instruction "Choose Edit, Cut" means that you should open the Edit menu and choose Cut. Another, more complex example would be "Click Start, Settings, Control Panel, System, Hardware, Device Manager."

Key combinations are represented with a plus sign. For example, if the text calls for you to press Ctrl+Alt+Delete, you would press the Ctrl, Alt, and Delete keys at the same time.

SPECIAL ELEMENTS

Throughout this book, you'll find Tips, Notes, Cautions, Sidebars, and Cross-References. These items stand out from the rest of the text so you know that they're of special interest.

TIPS

TIP

> These tips give you down-and-dirty advice on getting things done the quickest, safest, or most reliable way. Tips give you the expert's advantage.

NOTES

NOTE

> Notes are a visual "heads-up!" Sometimes they just give you background information on a topic, but more often they're there to point out special circumstances and potential pitfalls in some of Windows's features.

CAUTIONS

CAUTION

> Pay attention to cautions! They could save you precious hours in lost work.

CROSS-REFERENCES

Cross-references are designed to point you to other locations in this book (or other books in the Que family) that will provide supplemental or supporting information. Cross-references appear as follows:

➔ For more information on resizing disks, **see** "Resizing Basic Disks," **p. 1010**.

SIDEBARS

Sidebars

Sidebars are designed to provide information that is ancillary to the topic being discussed. Read this information if you want to learn more details about an application or task.

PART

I

INSTALLATION

CHAPTER 1

INTRODUCING WINDOWS XP

In this chapter

A WINDOWS OVERVIEW

Windows XP is the first family of Windows to break down the long-standing barrier between home-oriented and business-oriented releases of Windows. Originally code-named Whistler, Windows XP is the product of a development process that began with a consumer operating system code-named Neptune in late 1999 and a separate business-oriented operating system code-named Odyssey, which was planned as a successor to Windows 2000. In January 2000, Microsoft decided to integrate both Neptune and Odyssey into a single operating system family code-named Whistler, which you now know as Windows XP.

Thus, Windows XP was to be the first Windows family to combine a complete line of home-oriented and business-oriented releases of Windows into a single product continuum while sharing an identical code base. The release of Windows XP in Home and Professional versions (as well as some heavier-duty versions) was a big move for Microsoft, which has offered separate home-oriented (Windows 3.x/9x/Me) and corporate-oriented (Windows NT/2000) versions with drastically different internal designs since 1993. The common code base of all primary versions of Windows XP also is a big benefit for both users and developers. It makes program and device driver development much easier, because device drivers and software programs need to be created just once, rather than twice. But let's step back a bit and look at a little Windows history, in order to put XP into context, and to better frame the subsequent discussion of XP's features covered in this chapter.

Where did Windows comes from, anyway? Work on a Windows-like product began at Microsoft in 1981. However, the original Windows first appeared in 1985 (two years late) and was considered buggy and slow. In addition, it wasn't much to look at. As the saying goes, it had an (inter)face only a mother could love. Figure 1.1 shows a screenshot. It was quite primitive, compared with what we think of as Windows, and ran only on 640×480 resolution screens. It was essentially a very crude shell on top of DOS, allowing you to move files around and to click on program names to run them. There were also a few utility applications thrown in, such as a Notepad, Calculator, and Clock. The complete list was MS-DOS Executive, Calendar, Cardfile, Notepad, Terminal, Calculator, Clock, Reversi, Control Panel, PIF (Program Information File) Editor, Print Spooler, Clipboard, RAMDrive, Windows Write, and Windows Paint.

The originally-planned name for the product was Interface Manager, but Microsoft's marketing head, Rowland Hanson, convinced Bill Gates that Windows would be a superior name for the product. Competitors at the time consisted of VisiCorp's VisiOn, released two years earlier (which did have a GUI), and IBM's Top View (which didn't). Then there was GEM (Graphics Environment Manager), released by Digital Research in early 1985. The real issue wasn't which was better (actually GEM was way faster than Windows, and I used it quite a bit to run Ventura Publisher, one of the first desktop publishing programs), but how many apps and drivers were available for it.

When Windows first hit the market in 1985, it actually was a shell that sat upon the increasingly shaky foundations of MS-DOS. Early versions were frequently used as menuing systems for launching MS-DOS programs, because programs that actually required Windows were quite scarce for several years. In fact, to help promote Windows as a platform for programs, Microsoft distributed a "runtime" version of Windows with some of the early Windows-based programs such as Aldus PageMaker (now an Adobe product). Users who didn't have a full version of Windows needed to install the runtime version before using the program. The runtime version of Windows was launched when the application (such as PageMaker) was started, provided Windows menuing and print services, and closed when the application was closed.

Figure 1.1
Windows 1.01 was a far cry from today's Windows XP.

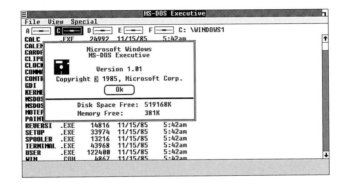

TABLE 1.1   WINDOWS RELEASE TIMELINE OVER 16 YEARS—ROUGHLY ONE MAJOR RELEASE PER YEAR, ON AVERAGE

Windows Version	Release Date
Windows 1.01	November 1985
Windows 2.0	December 1987
Windows 286 (same as 2.0)	Late 1987
Windows 386	Late 1987
Windows 3.0	May 1990
Windows 3.1	April 1992
Windows for Workgroups 3.1	October 1992
Windows for Workgroups 3.11	November 1993
Windows NT 3.1	August 1993
Windows NT 3.5	September 1994
Windows NT 3.51	June 1995
Windows 95	August 1995
Windows NT 4.0	August 1996

continues

TABLE 1.1 CONTINUED

Windows Version	Release Date
Windows 98	June 1998
Windows 2000	February 2000
Windows Me	September 2000
Windows XP	October 2001

Microsoft released a much-improved Windows 2.0 in 1987. Among other additions, this version introduced icons (much like those on the Mac), to represent programs and files. This prompted Apple Computer to file a 1988 lawsuit against Microsoft, alleging that Microsoft had broken the Macintosh's 1985 licensing agreement. Four years later Microsoft prevailed, and Windows development rolled ahead. Had the judge decided otherwise, Windows would likely not be the household word it is today.

Windows 386 offered more of a true multitasking environment, but Windows didn't really take off until the introduction of Windows 3.0 in 1990. Windows 3.0 could multitask both DOS and Windows programs if you used a 386 or 486 processor. Windows 3.1, in 1992, introduced TrueType scalable fonts. Windows for Workgroups 3.1 (1992) and 3.11 (1994) pioneered the built-in networking features that would typify all subsequent versions of Windows up to the present. Windows for Workgroups 3.11 was the last version of Windows to require that MS-DOS or a comparable non-GUI operating system be present at installation time.

While Windows 95, Windows 98, and Windows Me no longer required MS-DOS, they still used an improved form of DOS for some operations. This dependence upon MS-DOS made for an increasingly unstable operating system because the management tricks necessary to keep MS-DOS, old 16-bit Windows applications, and new 32-bit Windows programs running on the same hardware simultaneously led to frequent reboots and system lockups.

Gates and company realized that the Windows 3.x and 9x platforms were severely wanting in the areas of system reliability, security, true multi-processing, and networking, and got to thinking. For the enterprise to migrate onto the PC platform to any significant extent, Windows simply had to mature. It had to more thoroughly incorporate some of the characteristics of serious operating systems that were running on minis and mainframes. This realization lead to the procurement of a new team of programmers mandated to produce a version of Windows based on completely new technology, coded from the ground up; it was not to rely on the previous code base of Windows and DOS.

The programming team was headed by Dave Cutler, who joined Microsoft in 1988. Cutler had gained a name for himself by developing the VMS (Virtual Memory System) operating system for Digital Equipment (DEC)'s line of VAX multitasking and multiuser computers.

Designing NT was a tall order, considering it was to run reliably on the ubiquitous, yet infinitely varied IBM-compatible PC platform. With an almost incalculable number of hardware configurations (including a handful of CPUs, hundreds of motherboards from numerous makers, and literally thousands of add-in cards and peripherals), the job promised to be no walk in the park. With a background in semi-pro competitive auto racing, maybe Cutler was the right guy. What's more, the spec that Gates and team came up with for the new OS (to be called Windows NT) had some pretty stiff requirements. It was to be fully 32-bit, had to be multithreaded, had to support symmetrical processing (multiple CPUs), and had to be capable of smooth multitasking. The original specification document was more than 600 pages, and in October of 1999 story has it that Cutler presented the spec to The Smithsonian Institute where it will be displayed proudly as an important part of Microcomputing history.

OS/2 Still Exists

Actually, the Windows NT family (which includes Windows 2000 and XP, as described below) is a descendant of a Windows family that has some contentious roots. Microsoft's development of a non–DOS-based operating system goes back to 1987 and the joint development (with IBM) of a Windows replacement called OS/2. OS/2 was aimed squarely at the emerging corporate network world, then dominated by Novell and its NetWare network operating system.

Unlike NetWare, Microsoft and IBM's OS/2 was designed to handle both the server and the desktop sides of network computing. Unfortunately for OS/2 (and IBM), the IBM-Microsoft partnership broke up in 1991 after a series of ugly disagreements about the direction of OS/2. In the end, IBM kept OS/2, while Microsoft hung onto Windows. Although OS/2 Warp client and server operating systems are still being sold and used by IBM shops (try doing a Web search on it, you might be surprised), they've been eclipsed by Microsoft operating systems in sheer numbers of installed units.

NT first hit the shelves as Windows NT 3.1 (there was no version 3.0) in July 1993. Windows NT introduced a large number of new key features common to all the successors in the "NT" line of product, including Windows 2000 and Windows XP. Due to the significance of these to the XP product line, we'll enumerate:

- A brand new, journaling hard-disk file system called NTFS, featuring greatly increased security, more robustness, long filenames, automatic error correction, and support for a variety of RAID arrangements.

- Support for multiple file systems, including the old FAT16 file system used by MS-DOS and Windows 9x, and NTFS.

- Preemptive multitasking—Poorly written apps won't hog the CPU, so the user doesn't need to wait for one task to finish before starting another one.

- Client/server model for computing—The operating system is divided up into two parts, just as with mainframe systems. This protects core portions of the OS.

- Support for DOS, Windows 3.x, OS/2, and POSIX apps, and support for x86, MIPS, and Alpha processors.

- Dynamic disk caching/virtual memory—The operating system can use more than one drive as virtual memory (using disk space in place of RAM); desktop Windows versions up through Windows Me can use only one drive for virtual memory.

- Fault tolerance features—The capability to handle power outages and disk crashes.

- Capability to start and stop network services without rebooting.

- Fully 32-bit architecture—Windows NT and its successors are free from the limitations of 16-bit Windows (and MS-DOS!) instructions.

- An "Advanced Server" version of the system designed for secure, domain-based networking.

Unfortunately, NT was hungry. It needed what was then considered a *huge* amount of RAM—128MB—at a minimum. You had to be serious about computing to drop that much dough in those days. (RAM is way cheaper now.)

Next, Windows NT 3.51 hit the streets in June of 1995, adding PCMCIA (now called PC-Card) support and some other goodies such as faxing and improved networking, but nothing truly substantial. Windows NT 4.0, introduced in July of 1996, was upgraded to the Windows 95 user interface (replacing the Windows 3.1-sytle interface), but of course provided stability superior to Windows 95. However, it lacked support for Plug and Play, and many Windows 95–compatible hardware devices wouldn't work with Windows NT 4.0. This forced many serious Windows geeks to dual-boot between Windows 95 and NT in order to have it all. Windows NT 4 was offered in several flavors—Workstation, Server, and Internet Information Server (for serving up Web pages and the like).

NOTE

> While Windows NT was being developed and improved, Microsoft was also developing its Windows 9x product family, which culminated in the release of Windows Me in 2000. We'll skip detailed discussion of Windows 9x variants such as Windows 98, 98 Second Edition, and Me. They are all essentially refinements of Windows 95. Though pretty to look at (when not crashing), they continued to incorporate portions of 16-bit legacy code. Thus, you could think of them as a patchwork quilt of software (or a Frankenstein if you're feeling less generous). Although Windows 95, Windows 98, and Windows Me no longer required MS-DOS, per se, they still used an improved form of DOS for some operations. This dependence upon MS-DOS made for an increasingly unstable operating system because the management tricks necessary to keep MS-DOS, old 16-bit Windows applications, and new 32-bit Windows programs running on the same hardware at the same time led to frequent reboots and system lockups.
>
> Windows Me, like Windows 9x, is a hybrid operating system with some features inherited from MS-DOS as well as some 32-bit code, so its internal architecture is nothing like Windows NT, 2000, or XP. Instead, the most significant fact about Windows Me from a Windows XP viewpoint is Windows Me's introduction of a wide variety of built-in multimedia and imaging features. Windows XP features such as the Scanner and Camera Wizard, the slideshow features in the My Pictures folder, and Movie Maker are all descended from

Windows Me. Another significant feature of Windows XP that Windows Me pioneered is System Restore, which allows the user to get around tricky OS problems by resetting the system configuration to what it was on a previous day.

Apparently bored with the current lackluster naming convention, the term "NT" was scuttled just before release of NT 5, in favor of "Windows 2000." Don't ask why. Often confused with Windows Millennium Edition (though with almost nothing in common under the hood), Windows 2000 (a.k.a. Win2K) owns much of the same base code and architecture found in NT4, but with millions of lines of code (and resulting functionality) packed on top. Unlike the Win9x products, this could be achieved without jeopardizing system stability, owing to the NT's modular architecture and the fact that the core portions of the operating system (the "kernel" or "system executive") are run in protected mode, preventing errant applications from trouncing them and pulling down the system.

Unlike prior Windows NT versions, Windows 2000 (often called Win2K by users) introduced in early 2000, adopted the well-liked Windows 95 GUI, melded with a number of other features pioneered by the consumer-side OSes. Windows 2000 sports Plug and Play, ACPI power management, multiple-monitor support, a later version of Internet Explorer (IE), and PC-Card and multimedia support. There was also support for USB and IEEE-1394 ports and devices, AGP video, Internet Connection Sharing, and enhanced system management. Hard disk improvements included improved drive support by adding support for FAT32, the file system introduced by Windows 95 OSR 2.x that shatters the 2.1GB limit per drive letter imposed by FAT16. It also introduced a more advanced version of NTFS that supports file encryption, file compression, and support for mounting and dismounting drives to allow them to be accessed through folders on another drive.

Windows 2000 exemplified Microsoft's strong intention to move out of it's aging 16-bit "legacy" code base and merge the eye candy and user niceties of the Win9x products into a single, stable core of NT-based products. Since the price of PCs, RAM, and hard disk space continued to plummet, even home users could afford to run Windows 2000, where in the past they'd stayed away from NT due to the hardware requirements.

Windows 2000 Picking Up Steam

Even though XP is now getting most of the limelight, Windows 2000 is very much alive and well as of this writing. (Happily for us, since we also authored *Special Edition Using Windows 2000*!) Uptake of Windows 2000 has been a bit sluggish, but as of this writing is picking up steam. The business sector has been a bit slow to embrace Windows primarily because of deployment and support costs. Most corporations change course about as fast as oil tankers, and it takes a couple years to evaluate, deploy, and train support personnel on a given system platform and suites of applications. But as cost-benefit analyses (and employee demands) warrant it, and machines are depreciated and replaced, the next iteration of an operating system is introduced. That is, if it's reliable enough. Many cautious corporations (including the one that publishes this book) are running a generation or more back. Our editor still has Windows 95 on his computer!

ENTER XP

In October of 2001, Windows XP made its debut. The goal that Microsoft had set for the Windows XP line was ambitious: to create a reliable, easy-to-use family of operating systems whose features would meet the needs of PC users spanning a wide range of environments, whether in the home, the small office, or the demanding corporate enterprise. It had to provide state-of-the-art corporate network and security, management, and deployment features, while also including features popular with users who might have previously used Windows 9x or Windows Me. Windows XP also had to provide application and hardware compatibility with products made for older versions of Windows, and even MS-DOS game and graphics applications.

Windows XP actually meets these requirements pretty well. Windows XP (Professional and above) combines the reliability and corporate networking/security features of Windows 2000 with improved versions of the multimedia and crash-recovery features that Windows 98 and Windows Me pioneered. To make it more enticing to upgrade to Windows XP, it's designed to work much better than Windows 2000 did with older Windows (and even DOS-based) software, while still supporting the latest productivity, educational, recreational, and gaming programs from Microsoft and other publishers.

New PCs of every variety—whether sub-notebooks, office desktops, network servers, or Internet commerce servers—today typically ship with XP installed. Garden-variety portable or desktop PCs will come set up at the factory with one of the two most popular XP variants—XP Home Edition or XP Professional. Oddly, the Professional version isn't called Professional *Edition*. Go figure.

NOTE There are other XP versions, as well, discussed later in this chapter.

Like Windows 2000 before it, Windows XP is a highly extensible operating system. Windows XP uses a microkernel derived from Windows 2000, featuring an object-oriented, modular design that enables various types of services, file systems, and other subsystems to be attached to the core operating system, just as various types of hardware can be attached to a PC. This is achieved through what are called "environment subsystems,"—a little like plug-ins on a browser or in Photoshop, and so on. The result is that Windows XP can emulate other operating systems and support applications originally designed for other operating systems such as DOS, 16-bit Windows, older 32-bit Windows versions, and some Unix applications.

NOTE POSIX (Portable Operating System for Unix) support has been dropped in Windows XP. (The actual POSIX standard is ISO/IEC/9945-1/1990, is also known as POSIX.1, and was issued jointly by the International Standards Organization [ISO] and the International Electrotechnical Commission [IEC].) Windows NT and 2000 both could run strictly conforming POSIX apps via the POSIX environment subsystem. Likewise, OS/2 1.x will not run in XP.

1

> I guess the demand for running these apps didn't warrant the investment to program the subsystem. Interestingly, the POSIX subsystem has been replaced with a more Unix-like (but still POSIX-ish) environment called Interix. Interix is a superset of the original POSIX subsystem with more functionality. Since the environment subsystem is NT-based, Microsoft Windows NT Workstation or Server version 3.51 or higher; Windows 2000 Professional, Server or Advanced Server; and XP Home Edition or XP Professional will all support it. For additional information about Interix, check the following Microsoft Web site:
>
> `http://www.microsoft.com/windows2000/interix`

Whereas Windows 2000 provided a "one-size-fits-all" approach to running older Windows programs, which didn't always work, Windows XP goes beyond Windows 2000 by providing a customizable emulation feature that enables you to select which version of Windows it should emulate to run a particular program. See Chapter 32, "Crash Recovery," for details.

Many of Windows 2000's features have become part of Windows XP, including *Plug-and-Play* hardware support, *ACPI* power management, support for *USB* and *IEEE-1394* ports and devices, *AGP* video, *Internet Connection Sharing*, and enhanced system management. Windows XP can be fairly described as a combination of the security and stability of Windows 2000 and the multimedia and entertainment features of Windows Me.

Windows XP has been in the public eye longer than any other Windows version during its development process, and the final product has received a great deal of user feedback, thanks to its unprecedented public beta-testing process. Although some pundits derided Microsoft for charging users for the "privilege" of using a beta product, the decision to allow users to try beta versions with the Windows XP Preview Program, starting in April 2001, has helped make Windows XP a better product. The public scrutiny of Windows XP has forced controversial features such as Smart Tags (which added Microsoft-generated URLs to Web pages) to be dropped and others such as Hardware Activation (required before Windows XP can be used for the first time) to be modified in the favor of users.

Technically, XP is Windows NT 6. If you are willing to judge based mostly on appearance, it's the answer to Apple's OS X (the latest Mac OS, although OS X is really Unix), but running on the PC platform. It's hard to say who started this GUI-upgrade trend—we've all probably been influenced by the fashion or auto industry more than we want to admit—but it appears that PC operating systems look radically different every several years. Thus, in XP, we have yet another GUI facelift, which introduces somewhat of a problem for users and computer trainers (and another book-writing opportunity for us authors).

XP has garnered a lot of attention—both good and bad—for it's new interface. True, XP is cute and cuddly, with rounded corners, big goofy buttons, cartoonish wizards, a puppy-dog search assistant, and other features you'd expect to find in a kid's computer game. What were they thinking, putting this happy face atop an industrial-strength operating system aimed at Fortune 500 companies, you ask? Beats us. Perhaps Gates and Co. thought it

1

would help differentiate it from Windows 2000 or Windows Me to spur sales, or reduce computer phobia and ease the way for greater penetration of PCs into all environments, from homes to offices. In any case, our attitude is that the GUI difference is essentially a non-issue—if you don't like the way it looks, you can revert to the "classic" Windows 2000 look with a few clicks (see Chapter 10).

THE MANY FLAVORS OF XP

Like its predecessors Windows NT and Windows 2000, Windows XP comes in multiple flavors, at differing price-points, and aimed at different markets. Here's the breakdown, from least complex (and expensive), to most:

- Windows XP Home Edition (32-bit CPUs)
- Windows XP Professional (32-bit CPUs)
- Windows XP 64-bit Edition (for Intel Itanium CPUs)
- Windows Server 2003, 4 versions (32-bit and 64-bit CPUs)

Now let's break this down a bit more with a little discussion of each version. Following that you'll find several tables comparing features of the various versions.

HOME EDITION (32-BIT CPUs)

As the name suggests, Windows XP Home Edition is the home-oriented member of group. The idea of Home Edition is an ambitious one: to create an easy-to-use, *reliable* operating system whose features would appeal to home users with the latest PCs. It was also to provide application and hardware compatibility with products made for older versions of Windows—even MS-DOS game and graphics applications. And, to stop the wasteful and confusing development of two distinctly different versions of Windows that required different device drivers, Windows XP Home Edition had to share the same underlying software instructions as the rest of the Windows XP family.

To put it more succinctly, Home Edition is the natural upgrade for anyone using any of Microsoft's Windows 9x and Windows Me product lines. As said earlier, it consolidates all Windows users to the NT code base, which is what Microsoft has wanted for some time. Think of Home Edition as the primary consumer Windows OS. All the basic features of the entire Windows 9x line have been rolled into XP Home Edition. In addition, Home Edition has more sufficient Internet Security options (built-in Internet Connection Firewall, for example), and more robust multiuser support than Win9x versions, which will prove quite handy for homes with more than one user. Multiple users can log on and off at will, leaving each other's apps and documents open, for example. Since so many users are singing up for DSL and cable ISPs, functionality for those types of connections are built in. There is no need to run a PPoE client program such as EnterNet to sign on to your DSL service.

The main differences between Home and Pro center on networking. XP Home Edition...

- Doesn't allow a user to be a member of a domain network because Active Directory isn't supported.
- Doesn't support offline folders, very useful for people wanting to synchronize their documents between, say, a laptop and a desktop, for off-line viewing.
- Doesn't offer remote desktop management (access to administrator account).
- Only supports "simple file sharing" (see the following).

But other, non-network considerations are

- Doesn't support multiple CPUs.
- Doesn't support dynamic disks.

Second, because Active Directory isn't supported in Home Edition, there are no group policies. This leads to the exclusion of what's called "roaming users." Roaming users can log in from any computer on the domain and have all their desktop items and settings appear on whatever computer they log in from. Some other issues caused by lack of domain support are the inability to do remote installation of the OS, and remote software install and maintenance. However, from a home user perspective, most of these issues really would not matter, as the likelihood of home users being in a domain environment is rather small.

Professional (32-bit CPUs)

This version has power users and corporate users in mind. It's essentially a superset of Home Edition, and includes all integrated applications and multimedia features of Home Edition, yet also includes corporate network support, backup, and security features similar to those found in Windows 2000 Professional.

So, to put it succinctly, XP Professional is intended as the natural upgrade path for NT Workstation and Windows 2000 Professional users. Most power users and corporate IT jocks will likely want XP Professional rather than Home Edition. The primary advantage to the corporate user is security, since Simple File Sharing isn't very robust. XP Pro has full-scale user authentication, as opposed to Home Edition's simple file sharing which does not require user authentication for access to network resources. (Read: bad for security.) Support for multiple processors is another big plus. Reports are that many companies have been quickly making the switch to Windows XP on desktops and laptops, bypassing Windows 2000 totally.

Another big plus, especially for the road warrior, is the Remote Desktop feature. This is not dissimilar to programs such as PCAnywhere or Timbuktu, or you could also think it as a lighter version of Terminal Server or Citrix. Likewise, NetMeeting has a similar feature called Remote Desktop Sharing, but it was linked to NetMeeting (which has been dropped from XP). In any case, Remote Desktop allows you to access and control your computer from another computer. From a remote location and XP Professional, you'll be able to connect to your computer, see your desktop in a window, and interact just as if you were sitting right at your desk (so long as you're using a computer that can run MS's Terminal Client).

This is not to be confused with Remote Assistant—even though Remote Desktop and Remote Assistance sound almost identical, they are not. Both Home Edition and Professional include Remote Assistance, which simply allows someone to see your desktop, and with your permission, take limited control. Remote Assistance is designed for technicians or sys admins, for example, to help a user with a tech support problem, so the tech doesn't have to be present, or explain over the phone every detail of how to check settings or perform a task. It could also be used for training, if someone were to get creative with it. Remote Assistance doesn't allow remote dial-in or unattended usage. Remote Assistance is triggered by a user at the machine, either by sending an email or a special message via Windows Messenger.

NOTE Since the bulk of the readers of this book will be running XP Professional, we'll look more closely at Windows XP Professional later in this chapter.

ITANIUM VERSIONS (64-BIT)

The 64-bit Itanium processor from Intel has its own 64-bit versions of Windows XP. Windows XP 64-bit Edition is the workstation version, shipping at the same time as 32-bit versions of Windows XP. It supports up to 16GB of physical RAM and up to eight terabytes (8TB) of virtual memory, and takes full advantage of the superior floating-point performance of the Itanium processor. The recommended hardware platform is an 800MHz or faster Itanium processor with 1GB of RAM onboard; one or two Itanium processors can be used. Windows XP 64-bit Edition can run 32-bit Windows programs in a subsystem. The user interface is very similar to Windows XP Professional but the features will vary. The idea of this product is to support settings such as these:

- 64-bit qualified applications (*qualified applications* shall mean third-party applications which have been designed and tested on Windows Advanced Server, Limited Edition)
- 64-bit database applications
- 64-bit Web servers that serve HTML pages
- Scientific computing environments for performing numerical analysis
- File and print server cluster environments

The first server version of Windows XP, Windows Advanced Server Limited Edition, is available from hardware OEMs of Itanium-based servers such as HP, IBM, and Compaq before the official release of Windows XP. Free upgrades to Windows Server 2003 (the name for XP-based server products) will be available to users who license the product. Windows Advanced Server, Limited Edition, supports up to eight Itanium processors and 64GB of memory.

Both 64-bit versions use an emulation layer called WOW64 to run Win32-based applications, although for best performance, Microsoft recommends using 32-bit software on 32-bit Windows systems. The emulation feature enables organizations to use their Itanium-based systems with existing Windows applications until 64-bit versions are created internally or purchased from software vendors.

NOTE

Windows XP 64-Bit Edition will be available only in English, French, German and Japanese language versions.

WINDOWS SERVER 2003 (32-BIT AND 64-BIT VARIETIES)

Microsoft has multiple server editions of Windows XP, although the products are called Microsoft Windows Server 2003. These are the replacements for Window NT Server and Windows 2000 Server. The editions will be distinct, based on differences in the total amount of memory used by each version, the number of processors supported, and the number of domains that can be controlled. Otherwise, the concept is the same.

The Microsoft Windows Server 2003 product family includes four versions:

- **Windows Web Server 2003**—For Web serving and hosting, providing a platform for rapidly developing and deploying Web services and applications. The Web Server version is new in the Windows Server Family. It's what Microsoft is calling a "function-focused" Web server. It's optimized for Web serving and hosting that is easy to deploy and manage. Based on Microsoft's ASP.NET, part of the .NET Framework, this server provides developers with a platform for rapidly building and deploying XML Web services and applications.

- **Windows Server 2003**—This version is similar to Windows NT Server or Windows 2000 Server. Intended for the basic daily needs of any size business, it provides file and printer sharing, secure Internet connectivity, and centralized desktop application deployment. Windows Server member of supports two-way symmetric multiprocessing and up to 4GB of memory.

- **Windows Enterprise Server 2003**—Windows Enterprise Server 2003 is also a general-purpose server for businesses of all sizes, but supports more CPUs and memory. It supports up to eight processors and provides enterprise-class features such as four-node clustering and up to 32GB of memory. It is also available for 64-bit (Itanium) computing platforms.

■ **Windows Datacenter Server 2003**—Windows Datacenter Server 2003 is the operating system for the business-critical and mission-critical applications demanding the highest levels of scalability and availability. It is the most powerful and functional server operating system Microsoft has ever offered, supporting up to 32-way symmetric multiprocessing (SMP) and providing both eight-node clustering and load balancing services as standard features. The Datacenter Server is also available for 64-bit (Itanium) computing platforms.

Each of these networking OSes can be customized with features and functionality to meet users' specific business and IT needs. They can also integrate easily with Windows 2000–based servers. According to Microsoft, businesses that deploy Windows 2000 Servers today will be ready to easily upgrade to Windows Server 2003, and immediately benefit from improved manageability, reliability, security, performance, and integrated XML Web services. Time will tell, but upgrading will probably be pretty easy.

NOTE

> How soon we'll see uptake in the enterprise setting remains to be seen. Only now as of this writing do we see Windows 2000 servers gaining ground over NT4 server, and Windows 2000 has been out for approximately two years.

TABLE 1.2 WINDOWS SERVER 2003 FEATURES COMPARED

KEY: YES = Feature included. P = Feature partially supported. NO= Feature not included

Feature	Web Server	Standard Server	Enterprise Server	Datacenter Server
.NET Application Services				
.NET Framework[1]	Yes	Yes	Yes	Yes
Internet Information Services (IIS) 6.0	Yes	Yes	Yes	Yes
ASP.NET[1]	Yes	Yes	Yes	Yes
Enterprise UDDI Services	No	Yes	Yes	Yes
Clustering Technologies				
Network Load Balancing	Yes	Yes	Yes	Yes
Cluster Service	No	No	Yes	Yes
Communications & Networking Services				
Virtual Private Network (VPN) Support	P	Yes	Yes	Yes
Session Initiation Protocol Service (SIP)	No	Yes	Yes	Yes
Internet Authentication Service (IAS)	No	Yes	Yes	Yes

Feature	Web Server	Standard Server	Enterprise Server	Datacenter Server
Network Bridge	No	Yes	Yes	Yes
Internet Connection Sharing (ICS)	No	Yes	Yes	No
IPv6	Yes	Yes	Yes	Yes
Directory Services				
Active Directory	P	Yes	Yes	Yes
Metadirectory Services (MMS) Support	No	No	Yes	No
File & Print Services				
Distributed File System (DFS)	Yes	Yes	Yes	Yes
Encrypting File System (EFS)	Yes	Yes	Yes	Yes
Shadow Copy Restore	Yes	Yes	Yes	Yes
SharePoint Team Services	No	Yes	Yes	Yes
Removable and Remote Storage	No	Yes	Yes	Yes
Fax Service	No	Yes	Yes	Yes
Services for Macintosh	No	Yes	Yes	Yes
Management Services				
IntelliMirror	Yes	Yes	Yes	Yes
Resultant Set of Policy (RSoP)	Yes	Yes	Yes	Yes
Windows Management Instrumentation (WMI) Command Line	Yes	Yes	Yes	Yes
Remote OS Installation	Yes	Yes	Yes	Yes
Remote Installation Services (RIS)	No	Yes	Yes	Yes
Multimedia Services				
Windows Media Services	No	Yes	Yes	No
Scalability				
64-bit Support for Intel Itanium-Based Computers	No	No	Yes	Yes
Hot add memory[2]	No	No	Yes	Yes
Non-Uniform Memory Access (NUMA)[2]	No	No	Yes	Yes
Datacenter Program	No	No	No	Yes

continues

TABLE 1.2 CONTINUED

KEY: YES = Feature included. P = Feature partially supported. NO= Feature not included

Feature	Web Server	Standard Server	Enterprise Server	Datacenter Server
Security Services				
Internet Connection Firewall	No	Yes	Yes	No
Public Key Infrastructure, Certificate Services, and Smart Cards	P	Yes	Yes	Yes
Terminal Services				
Remote Desktop for Administration	Yes	Yes	Yes	Yes
Terminal Server	No	Yes	Yes	Yes
Terminal Server Session Directory	No	No	Yes	Yes

1 Not supported in Windows Server 2003, 64-bit edition operating system.

2 May be limited by lack of support by OEM hardware.

TABLE 1.3 WINDOWS SERVER 2003 SYSTEM REQUIREMENTS[1]

Requirement	Web Server	Standard Server	Enterprise Server	Datacenter Server
Minimum CPU Speed	133MHz	133MHz	133MHz for x86-based computers; 733MHz for Itanium-based computers	400MHz for x86-based computers; 733MHz for Itanium-based computers
Recommended CPU Speed	550MHz	550MHz	733MHz	733MHz
Minimum RAM	128MB	128MB	128MB	512MB
Recommended Minimum RAM	256MB	256MB	256MB	1GB
Maximum RAM	2GB	4GB	32GB for x86-based computers; 64GB for Itanium-based computers	64GB for x86-based computers; 128GB for Itanium-based computers

Requirement	Web Server	Standard Server	Enterprise Server	Datacenter Server
Multi-Processor Support	1 or 2	1 or 2	Up to 8	Minimum 8 required; Maximum 32
Disk Space for Setup	1.5GB	1.5GB	1.5GB for x86-based computers; 2.0GB for Itanium-based computers	1.5GB for x86-based computers; 2.0GB for Itanium-based computers

[1]System requirements are shown for Beta 3 only. Final system requirements are subject to change.

NOTE

> Windows Server 2003 and Windows 2000 Server provide many of the same support functions for networks. In this book, when there's no need to distinguish between the two server families, we'll just refer to "Windows 200x Server."

SECURITY DIFFERENCES BETWEEN XP HOME AND XP PRO

Since Windows Server versions are not going to be discussed to any great degree in this book, let's get back to a more relevant task at hand—comparing XP Home and Pro. As we discussed previously, there are a few software features that differentiate the two, such as Remote Desktop. But there are also some salient hardware and security issues worth some scrutiny. Let's look at these a little more closely.

HARDWARE-RELATED DIFFERENCES BETWEEN HOME EDITION AND PROFESSIONAL

As mentioned in a list earlier, XP Professional supports Symmetric Multi-Processing (SMP for up to two processors), whereas Home Edition doesn't. Since there are many dual-processor systems around these days, and prices have dropped (SMP-capable Athlon- and Intel-based motherboards can be found at well under $300 and a couple of speedy processors for about the same), this is a serious consideration. Actually, Microsoft did a bunch of research on this issue and decided that since so many of its older consumer-based products didn't support multiple CPUs—not DOS, not Windows 3.x, and none of the Windows 9x product line—they'd continue the trend. The moral here is that if you have a dual system, or see one in your future (either AMD or Intel are supported), XP Professional should be your natural choice.

Also as noted earlier, only XP Pro offers Dynamic Disk management. Debuting with Windows 2000, Dynamic Disks are very cool, indeed. The Dynamic Disk scheme is a very flexible method of using hard drives. Logical drive mappings are still used (for example, c:, d:, and so on), but the actual size and location of such logical disks becomes fluid (dynamic). The end result is that Dynamic Disks allow you to do such things as manage your disks sizes on-the-fly, and aggregate drives or folders from different disks to create larger and more complex logical drives. XP Professional achieves this by dropping the old partition and logical pointers stored in the Master Boot Record (MBR) in favor of a disk-management database stored at the end of a disk.

Since consumers have become used to multiple-monitor support (for example in Windows 98 and Me), both XP Home and XP Pro do support it. The maximum number of monitors supported is 10! Of course you'll need some pretty amazing hardware (such as 5 PCI-based dual-head cards) to support 10 monitors. Not likely. Two monitors is more the de-facto arrangement these days. Even many laptops support dual monitor arrangements.

NOTE When a laptop is used with a second monitor, Microsoft calls this arrangement *DualView*, not *Multiple Monitors*. The difference is that when using DualView on a laptop, your primary display must always be the laptop's LCD screen, whereas with the multiple monitors feature, you can choose a primary monitor on which to log in and start your programs.

SECURITY DIFFERENCES BETWEEN HOME EDITION AND PRO—SOME DETAILS

Security is a major issue, one that we're all more and more concerned with, for obvious reasons. Anecdotes about corporate and personal information being hacked into abound. We'll focus on this topic in Part V of this book, with three entire chapters devoted to security issues. Here's a short course on the security differences between Home and Pro, in the meantime.

As mentioned earlier, Home Edition doesn't have much in the way of networking security because it only supports so-called Simple File Sharing. That's a euphemism for saying that just about anyone can have access to resources you share from an XP Home computer. The complex array of access and security options that NT-based "domains" normally offer are not available. Home Edition is "workgroup" oriented, much like Windows for Workgroups was. It does have some support for domain or Active Directory integration, but not much. (Administration from a central location is gone, for example.) Actually, XP Home has even less in the way of domain integration than previous versions of the consumer Windows

Oses. With Win9x versions it was possible to set up the system so that Access Control Lists (ACLs—the database that controls access privileges) and security policy could be garnered from a domain controller. However, XP relies on something called Active Directory in lieu of Domain Controllers for gatekeeping. Since XP Home doesn't support Active Directory, taking advantage of a centralized security policy scheme won't wash.

Two more important items missing in Home Edition are EFS (encrypting file system) and the capability to control and restrict access to files, folders, and programs. The loss of EFS and access control can be quite a major blow to Home Edition, as it prevents Home Edition users from truly securing their profile folders, which can contain private bookmarks, documents, and images, from other local users. Without these two features, locking down individual accounts becomes very difficult. This is a feature we feel should have been left in Home Edition, as there are many uses for this in family computing systems for securing such items as tax documents and the like. Without access control, one unruly user can view, alter, or delete another user's important documents, or snoop around your favorite Web sites.

Table 1.4 compares Windows XP Home Edition and Windows XP Professional to other versions of Windows.

TABLE 1.4 VARIOUS CAPABILITIES OF WINDOWS XP HOME EDITION AS COMPARED TO EARLIER VERSIONS OF WINDOWS

Feature	Windows 9x/Me	Windows NT 3.xx	Windows NT 4 Workstation	Windows NT 4 Server
Virtual memory management (paging file on hard disk)	Yes	Yes	Yes	Yes
Multitasking type	Preemptive	Preemptive	Preemptive	Preemptive
Multithreading	Yes	Yes	Yes	Yes
Number of CPUs (maximum)	1	2 native, 4 with OEM-modified HAL	2	4
Maximum RAM supported				
Access security	No	Yes	Yes	Yes
Kerberos security	No	No	No	No
Runs real-mode device drivers	Yes	No	No	No
Runs 16-bit DOS and Windows applications	Yes	Yes	Yes	Yes
Runs 32-bit Windows applications	Yes	Yes	Yes	Yes
Runs OS/2 applications	No	Yes	Yes	Yes
Runs POSIX applications	No	Yes	Yes	Yes
Supports DOS FAT16	Yes	Yes	Yes	Yes
Support DOS FAT32	95 OSR2 and 98/Me only	No	No	No
Supports OS/2 HPFS	No	Yes	No	No

1

Windows 2000 Professional	Windows 2000 Server	Windows 2000 Advanced Server	Windows 2000 Datacenter Server	Win XP Home	Win XP Pro
Yes	Yes	Yes	Yes	Yes	Yes
Preemptive	Preemptive	Preemptive	Preemptive	Preemptive	Preemptive
No	Yes	Yes	Yes	Yes	Yes
2	4	8	32	1	2
4GB	4GB	64GB	64GB	64GB	64GB
Yes	Yes	Yes	Yes	No	Yes
Yes	Yes	Yes	Yes	No	Yes
No	No	No	No	No	Yes
Yes	Yes	Yes	Yes	Yes	Yes
Yes	Yes	Yes	Yes	Yes	Yes
Yes	Yes	Yes	Yes	No	No
Yes	Yes	Yes	Yes	No	No
Yes	Yes	Yes	Yes	Yes	Yes
Yes	Yes	Yes	Yes	Yes	Yes
No	No	No	No	No	No *continues*

TABLE 1.4   CONTINUED

Feature	Windows 9x/Me	Windows NT 3.xx	Windows NT 4 Workstation	Windows NT 4 Server
Supports NTFS	No	Yes	Yes	Yes
Supports disk compression	Yes	No	Yes	Yes
File encryption	No	No	No	No
RAID support/ levels	No	Yes	No	Yes
Built-in networking	Yes	Yes	Yes	Yes
Built-in email	Yes	Yes	Yes	Yes
Minimum Intel CPU required	386	386	Pentium	Pentium
Supports RISC chips	No	Yes/MIPS R4000 Alpha	Yes/ R4000 Alpha	Yes/ R4000 Alpha
Supports Active Directory	Planned	No	No	No
Supports clustering	No	No	No	Yes, only in Enterprise Edition
Supports load balancing	No	No	No	No
Supports Novell NDS	No	No	Yes	Yes
Includes Web server/Maximum number of connections	Yes/10	No/umlim	Yes/10	Yes/unlim

WHAT'S NEW IN WINDOWS XP PROFESSIONAL?

Now that you know Windows XP's family history and the differences between Home Edition and Professional, we'll cover in more detail the new features Windows XP Professional brings to the Windows family. One of the questions people ask me as I write books about each new version of Windows is whether the new version is different enough to justify upgrading. The Windows XP family is a major upgrade from any previous version

1

Windows 2000 Professional	Windows 2000 Server	Windows 2000 Advanced Server	Windows 2000 Datacenter Server	Win XP Home	Win XP Pro
Yes	Yes	Yes	Yes	Yes	Yes
Yes	Yes	Yes	Yes	Yes?	Yes
Yes	Yes	Yes	Yes	No	Yes
No	Yes	Yes	Yes	No	Yes
Yes	Yes	Yes	Yes	Yes	Yes
Yes	Yes	Yes	Yes	Yes	Yes
Pentium	Pentium	Pentium	Pentium	Pentium	Pentium
Yes/ DEC Alpha	Yes/ DEC Alpha	Yes/ DEC Alpha	Yes/ DEC Alpha	No	No
Yes	Yes	Yes	Yes	No	Yes
			Yes	No	No
No	No	Yes	Yes	No	No
Yes	Yes	Yes	Yes	No	Yes
Yes/10	Yes/unlim	Yes/unlim	Yes/unlim	No	Yes/10

of Windows, and the jump from Windows 98 or Windows Me to Windows XP Professional is as massive a jump as the one from Windows 3.1 to Windows 95 was a few years ago. Windows XP Professional isn't just a much-improved version of the Windows 2000 family, preserving Windows 2000 Professional's corporate networking and security features, but is also a superset of Windows XP Home Edition, which integrates improved versions of multimedia and recreational features originally introduced by Windows 98 and Windows

Me. Thus, whether you want an operating system ready for the corporate desktop or are looking to add multimedia and recreational features to your corporate operating system, Windows XP Professional can do the job. Thus, Windows XP Professional can be used to replace both Windows 2000 and the long-lived Windows 9x family on corporate desktops.

How big a change is Windows XP? Estimates are that by the time it was released, it contained about 40 million lines of code (see Table 1.5). That's more than one-third more code than its immediate predecessor, Windows 2000, and plenty of room for its new and enhanced features.

TABLE 1.5   LINES OF CODE COMPARISON

Operating System	Lines of Programming Code
Windows NT 3.1	6.5 million
Windows NT 3.5	10 million
Windows 95	10 million
Windows 98	13 million
NT 4	16.5 million
Windows 2000	~29 million
Windows 2000 Advanced Server	~33 million
Windows 2000 Datacenter	>40 million
Windows XP	~40 million

Windows XP is much bigger than Windows 2000 because it adds new multimedia and entertainment features absent from Windows 2000 Professional, and because it also contains improvements to features carried over from Windows 2000.

Because Windows XP Professional offers so many improvements and new features when compared to Windows 98, Windows Me, and even Windows 2000, in this section we'll highlight some of the new and improved features and what each feature does. Table 1.6 highlights some of the key improvements found in Windows XP Professional, and points you to the chapter in which it is covered.

TABLE 1.6   COVERAGE OF NEW AND IMPROVED WINDOWS XP PROFESSIONAL FEATURES

Feature	Covered in Chapter
New setup process	3, 4, 5
New interface: My Documents, My Pictures, My Music, custom toolbars, intelligent Menus, new help system, search function	10
Multimedia improvements: DVD, DirectX 8.1, image color management, scanner and digital camera support, Windows Movie Maker, Windows Media Player 8, CD burning, Web Publishing Wizard	13
Hardware support: Plug and Play, multiple monitors, FireWire	27
Active Directory	16
Enhanced Web browsing with IE 6	14
Better email and news reader with Outlook Express 6	14
Improved mobile support and power management	19
New Microsoft Management Console (MMC)	26
Improved Installer/Remover	9
Kerberos security	23
Internet Connection Sharing	8
Fast User Switching	11
Windows Messenger, NetMeeting	14
Remote Assistance	14
Files and Settings Transfer Wizard	3
System Restore	6, 32
Network Setup Wizard	17
System File Protection	23
Internet Connection Firewall	24
Task Manager	10
Personalized Welcome Screen	11

continues

TABLE 1.6   CONTINUED

Feature	Covered in Chapter
Taskbar Grouping	10
File Management	12
Compatibility Mode	32
ClearType	10
Device Driver Rollback	27, 32
Network Bridging	16, 17

INTERFACE IMPROVEMENTS

Although some might disagree, Windows XP really is the best-looking version of Windows ever, but the improvements are more than just skin deep. Windows XP takes full advantage of today's widespread support for high-resolution, 24-bit (16.8 million color) displays to provide subtle shading and animation effects to make working easier, but it also provides a more intelligent and customizable interface compared to previous Windows versions.

STARTUP AND START MENU IMPROVEMENTS

After you get to the splash screen, Windows XP Professional looks like no other Windows version. Before the splash screen loads, pressing F8 brings up a troubleshooting options menu that most closely resembles the one provided for Windows 2000, although Windows 9x/Me users will also find it familiar. This Advanced Options menu lets you boot into alternative modes such as "Safe Mode" to do troubleshooting (see Figure 1.2). Normal boot processes display a splash screen that is more compact than the previous full-screen one used by Windows 9x/Me and has an easy-to-see progress bar in the middle of the screen.

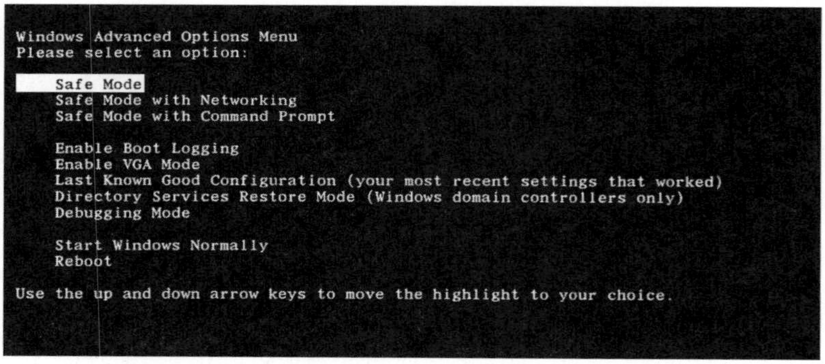

Figure 1.2
New startup options in Windows XP Professional offer various troubleshooting options if you simply press F8 at boot time.

```
Windows Advanced Options Menu
Please select an option:

    Safe Mode
    Safe Mode with Networking
    Safe Mode with Command Prompt

    Enable Boot Logging
    Enable VGA Mode
    Last Known Good Configuration (your most recent settings that worked)
    Directory Services Restore Mode (Windows domain controllers only)
    Debugging Mode

    Start Windows Normally
    Reboot

Use the up and down arrow keys to move the highlight to your choice.
```

NOTE

If you upgraded from an earlier version of Windows, your system will also display a "Return to OS Choices Menu" option after the Reboot option when looking at the troubleshooting options.

Windows XP shortens the startup time by using a technique called *prefetching*, which loads major portions of the operating system at the same time that devices are being initialized, rather than performing loading and device initialization in series, as with earlier versions of Windows. And, Windows XP learns which hardware and software you use during the first few times you boot your system, and moves the files used by your hardware and software to the fastest parts of your drive to further improve boot time.

If you're bringing up your system from a sleep mode, standby and hibernation are both much faster with Windows XP Professional. Newer notebook computers can restart from Standby, which shuts down power to peripherals but maintains power flowing to your RAM, in as little as two seconds. Hibernation, which stores the state of your system (open files and programs) on the hard disk before powering down, is also faster. Newer systems can emerge from Hibernation in as little as 20 to 30 seconds. After you've booted your system, the Windows XP Professional Start menu makes it easier to use the most popular programs. It shows you the major new features, and a link called All Programs displays the rest of the programs ready for your use.

If you need help through the Internet or email, or with your system's configuration, the Start menu items Control Panel, Help and Support, Internet Explorer, and Outlook Express are all available as soon as you click the Start button.

Right-click on the taskbar, select Properties, Start Menu, and then Customize, and you can control the appearance of the Start menu and the programs and features that will be displayed (see Figure 1.3).

Figure 1.3
Customize your Start menu by selecting the number of popular program shortcuts, icon sizes, and default Web browser and email programs.

Select large icons for better visibility, or small icons to show more programs at a time. By default, the Start menu displays six programs you use most often, but you can set the number yourself or clear the list of programs. By default, Internet Explorer is displayed as the standard Web browser, and Outlook Express is the standard email program, but you can remove them from the Start menu or choose alternatives you've installed. Service Pack 1 (see more details later in this chapter) includes a menu choice right on the Start menu, in fact, for removing these (and other) Microsoft "middleware" programs so they may be more easily replaced by competitor's programs such as Netscape Navigator, Pegasus mail, and so on.

Click Advanced to specify other Start menu features (see Figure 1.4), including

- Disabling features such as submenus opening when you pause over them

Figure 1.4
The Advanced tab of the Customize Start Menu dialog box lets you choose which Windows XP folders and tools to display on the Start menu, which display options to use, and other customizations.

- Disabling the highlighting of newly installed programs until you run them for the first time
- Whether to display the Control Panel, Favorites menu, Help and Support, My Computer, My Documents, My Music, My Network Places, My Pictures, Network Connections, Printers and Faxes, Run command, Search, and System Administration tools

You also can select whether to scroll the Programs menu, select how to display some menu items, and select whether to display recently opened documents. Figure 1.5 shows a typical menu on a Windows XP Professional system.

As you can see in Figure 1.5, the menu also adapts to your recent selections, placing shortcuts to the last six programs you've run into the blank space at the left side of the Start menu, as discussed earlier in this section.

Windows XP also launches your favorite programs up to 50 percent faster after you've run them a few times. It stores information about frequently used programs for faster loading in the future.

Figure 1.5
The Windows XP Professional main menu on a typical system. As you use different programs, the contents of the lower left side of the menu will vary.

The following is the rundown of a few other interface niceties that are new or improved, especially if you previously used Windows 9x or Windows Me:

- **New wizards**—Several new wizards have been added to simplify common tasks such as printing photos, copying photos to a CD-R or CD-RW drive, running older programs under Windows XP, and others.

- **Easier-to-use multiple-tab menus and properties sheets**—As you move your mouse from tab to tab, the tab currently under the mouse pointer is highlighted with a colored bar across the top of the tab. This feature makes it easier to click the correct tab on properties sheets such as the System properties and many others.

- **My Music**—A new My Music folder has been added for MP3 and WMA digital music files you download or create. You can play the music in this folder by clicking the Play All button, and shop for more music online. This complements the My Documents and My Pictures folders for unified storage of all types of media files.

- **Customizable toolbars**—You can drag toolbars, such as the Web address toolbar, around on the desktop or add them to the taskbar at the bottom of the screen. Additional personalized Start menu and taskbar settings are available from the Taskbar Properties dialog box shown in Figure 1.6 (right-click the Taskbar and choose Properties).

- **Media toolbar**—In all Explorer windows, you can add a Media toolbar. From this toolbar, you can easily choose music or radio stations to listen to while you work, and you can view current movie previews.

- **Taskbar icon grouping**—If you have multiple instances of the same program running (such as several Internet Explorer windows), Windows XP saves room in the taskbar by displaying a single icon for the program with a number listing how many instances are stored under the icon. Click on the icon and scroll to display the instance you want to display. You also can close an entire group of windows at the same time.

Figure 1.6
In this dialog box, you can choose new options for taskbar properties.

- **Smarter Open dialog boxes**—Many dialog boxes, such as the ones you use to open and save files, now remember the most recently entered filenames. Open dialog boxes also sport an iconic representation of the common locations in a new left pane, called the *Places Bar* (see Figure 1.7). Not all applications support the Places Bar, but those that do make it easier to save files to different local or network drives.

Figure 1.7
New Open dialog boxes include the Places Bar at the left side of the window.

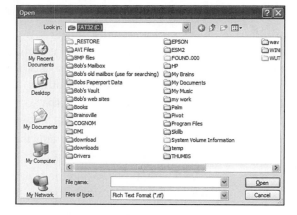

- **Customizable Explorer toolbars**—The toolbars are customizable, just like in IE or Office.

- **Improved topic-based help system in enhanced HTML**—The Windows XP Help and Support Center most closely resembles the hugely remodeled help system introduced in Windows Me. To save search time, major topics are displayed on the left side, and common tasks are listed on the right side. The index is a click away on the top of the screen, and a Favorites button makes it easy to collect help pages you use frequently, and display them instantly. Click the Home button to return to the main Help and Support Center menu at any time.

- **New display options in Windows Explorer**—You can group related files in Windows Explorer with the Show in Groups option, view Thumbnails of picture files, use a Tiled view to combine large icons with file detail, and use Filmstrip view in picture folders to see a larger view of the selected picture and navigate with directional arrows to other pictures in the folder.

- **New balloon help tips**—Novice users will appreciate the new balloon help tips that pop up, such as when you let your mouse pointer hover over certain icons, when network connections are made, reporting the connection speed, or to report immediate problems that require quick action.

ENHANCED SEARCH FEATURE AND HISTORY

The Windows XP Search option is familiar to users of Windows 2000 and Windows Me, but is greatly enhanced compared to the Find feature used by Windows 9x; you can search from any and all Windows Explorer windows. When you search the Internet, the LAN, or your local hard disk, you use the same dialog box now. You can search for a file, folder, network computer, person, Web topic, help topic, or map. You can display a thumbnail view of search results to see what files or other items have been found. If the network you're on uses the MS Index Server, the discovered items are also ranked according to closeness of match, just like search engines do. A friendly animated dog provides minimal levels of entertainment during Search, but you can banish the dog offscreen by changing your search preferences.

Pressing the Windows key + F or choosing Search from the Start menu brings up the box you see in Figure 1.8. This integrated, easier-to-use search feature helps you find information on your computer, your network, or on the Web. Select the type of search you want to perform, enter all or part of the name, and start the search. If you search the Internet with plain-text questions, Windows XP will choose a search task and Web site best suited to your search.

Figure 1.8
The Windows XP search tool works within Explorer and supports file, media, computer, Internet, and Help searches.

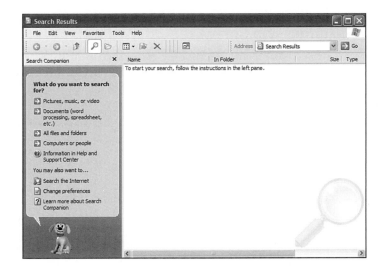

ENHANCED ACCESSIBILITY SUPPORT

Using computers is hard enough for those of us who have full mobility and physical abilities, considering how cryptic and idiosyncratic Windows is. For many folks, just the physical act of using a computer poses an additional challenge. Windows XP Professional provides the following accessibility features through the Accessibility Options icon in Control Panel:

- **Onscreen keyboard**—Allows text entry via the mouse
- **StickyKeys**—Allows keyboard combinations to be entered one keystroke at a time
- **FilterKeys**—Adjusts repeat rate and helps Windows ignore brief or repeated keystrokes
- **ToggleKeys**—Plays tones when keys such as Caps Lock are pressed
- **SoundSentry**—Displays your choice of visual alerts when your computer plays a sound
- **ShowSounds**—Provides captions for programs' speech and sounds
- **High-Contrast displays**—Choice of a variety of extra-large text sizes and high-contrast Windows desktops
- **Adjustable cursor blink rate and cursor width**—Makes it easier to find the text cursor onscreen
- **MouseKeys**—Enables the numeric keypad to run the mouse pointer
- **Serial keys**—Enables alternative keyboard and pointing devices to be attached through serial ports

The following accessibility features can be started from the Accessibility folder (Start, All Programs, Accessories, Accessibility) or by pressing the Windows key + U:

- Magnifier—Provides an enlarged view of the area under and near the mouse cursor
- Narrator—A simple text-to-speech program (English only) for onscreen events and typed characters
- Onscreen keyboard

INTERNET CONNECTIONS AND SOFTWARE

Windows XP Professional makes Internet use easier than ever. Its New Connection Wizard provides a one-stop interface for setting up Internet, home networking, direct serial/parallel/infrared connections (Direct Cable Connection for you Windows 9x fans), and remote office network connections through either dial-up or virtual private networking (VPN) connections. If you have an IEEE-1394 (FireWire) adapter, you also can use it for networking with this wizard.

Windows XP Professional also supports Internet Connection Sharing, using either a conventional modem (for the Internet) and a network card (for the rest of the network) or two network cards (the second one is for use with broadband connections) in the host system. And, if you're already running ICS on a Windows 9x/Me/2000 system, you can connect your Windows XP computer to it easily.

Internet Explorer 6.0, an improved version of the browser Microsoft has used to take over the browser market from one-time leader Netscape, is standard in retail and upgrade versions of Windows XP; hardware vendors who preinstall Windows XP on new computers can choose to omit it, although it's unlikely that most will. It now offers 128-bit encryption straight out of the box, meaning that you no longer need a strong encryption upgrade before you can go to some online banking, stock brokerage, or shopping sites.

Internet Explorer 6.0 is visually different than IE 5.5 in its icon display. For example, the Stop icon is now a red X in a page, rather than in a circle. The Favorites icon is a star instead of a folder. Beneath the surface, more significant differences include

- Integrated MSN Messenger support
- New Privacy tab in Internet Options to control cookies and personal data
- New Clear SSL State option on the Content tab to flush SSL (Secure Sockets Layer) certificates from the SSL cache for security
- Automatic resizing of images too large to be displayed in the browser window without scrolling
- Enhanced Internet setup options
- New Reset Web Settings option on the Programs tab

IE 6.0 also retains the integrated search tool used in previous versions of IE, integrates it with the Explorer Search tool, and offers a much wider variety of search engines from which to choose. IE's Search acts as a front end to popular search tools. Initially, it searches using the default search tool (MSN) or your preferred replacement (I like Google.com). After completing that search, you can send the search to other major search engines, one at a time. Type in two or more words, and the Search tool treats it as a phrase to get you more accurate results in most cases and fewer irrelevant hits. You can remove IE 6.0 from your system if you absolutely prefer another browser, but even if you're more of a Netscape or Opera fan, you'll probably want to keep IE 6.0 around for its tight integration to Windows Update, the online feature Microsoft uses to keep Windows up to date.

Windows XP Professional provides these enhancements and brand-new features to its networking and Internet feature set:

- An integrated Internet Connection Firewall—This feature, which is controlled from the network connection properties sheet, helps protect your connection from hacking by outside users, and is especially useful for full-time, always-on broadband connections such as cable modem, DSL, and LAN-based.
- Automatic adjustment of receive window size to achieve better performance on ICS when a dial-up connection is being shared.
- Support for Point-to-Point Protocol over Ethernet (PPPoE), an increasingly popular connection method for broadband modems.
- A protocol stack that supports IP version 6, which enables Windows XP to be used to develop applications that will support IPv6 when it is introduced (IPv6 will use a larger universe of IP addresses and have other benefits).

HARDWARE IMPROVEMENTS

Although Windows XP Professional is built upon the foundation of the "all-business" Windows NT 4.0 and Windows 2000 versions, it is still designed to be a replacement for the consumer operating systems (Windows 9x/Me). Therefore, Microsoft is determined to support a much broader range of hardware in Windows XP than in previous versions. Windows XP ships with drivers for hundreds of hardware devices not supported by Windows 2000, making it easier to install a broad range of hardware with Windows XP than with Windows 2000.

Drivers for many popular devices are supplied on the Windows XP Professional CD-ROM or are available from the vendor; Windows XP Professional will check Microsoft's Windows Update Web site for new drivers if it doesn't locate the right driver for your hardware. Both Windows XP Professional and Home Edition use the same Windows driver model (WDM) technology originally developed for hardware drivers in Windows 98/Me/2000. Thanks to the widespread preinstallation of Windows XP on new PCs, however, users should have a wider assortment of drivers to choose from initially than Windows 2000 users did.

If you can't get a Windows XP-specific driver for your hardware, most Windows 2000 device drivers will work with Windows XP Professional. And, because Windows XP Professional and Windows XP Home Edition share a common code base and have common multimedia and imaging features, the same device drivers will work on either version.

In the meantime, if you have rare, discontinued, or otherwise nonstandard hardware, be sure to check Microsoft's Hardware Compatibility List at `www.microsoft.com/hcl` before upgrading.

→ To learn more about hardware support issues, **see** Chapter 2, "Installation Prep."

The following is the lowdown on the newly added hardware support, help, and troubleshooting:

- The Device Manager can be launched as a part of the Microsoft Management Console (MMC) and offers online help, more ways to view devices, and easier driver updates.

- The Add Hardware Wizard has been enhanced to make installing drivers for new hardware easier and more reliable, and to make it harder to install drivers for "phantom" devices not already installed in or connected to your system.

- The Scanner and Camera Wizard introduced in Windows Me has been included and now supports flash memory card readers used by digital cameras, using a new technology called Windows Imaging Architecture (WIA). WIA is a Component Object Model (COM)-based architecture that incorporates device drivers supplied by the manufacturer and imaging applications supplied by third-party software vendors into its design. WIA supports both older TWAIN-based imaging devices as well as newer imaging devices supported specifically by WIA drivers.

- Enhanced audio playback is supported with separate volume controls for each speaker in a multichannel configuration, Acoustic Echo Cancellation (AEC) to improve signal processing with USB microphones in particular, and Global Effects (GFX) to add support for newer USB-based audio technologies such as USB array microphones.

- The latest DirectX (8.1 at the time of XP's initial release) is included for full support of the newest 3D games and multimedia programs. It supports USB, digital joysticks, more realistic 3D graphics effects, and better sound than previous DirectX versions.

- After you install a third-party DVD decoder, you can use the Windows Media Player as your DVD playback program.

- Support for both CD-R and CD-RW drives without the need to install third-party software for both data storage and music CD copying.

- An enhanced version of multiple-monitor support called DualView, which enables separate video displays on multi-monitor video cards as well as the built-in screen and external video ports of notebook computers.

- Improved power management, with support for wake-on-event, an improved user interface, and support for power management in applications.

- USB 2.0 support, speeding up USB to 480Mbps (see the section on SP1 [Service Pack 1]), later in this chapter.

Bluetooth, Bluetooth...Where Art Thou?

Don't look for Bluetooth in XP—it's not there.

There may be deeper issues with Bluetooth support for Windows XP than Microsoft wants to discuss: Bluetooth is seen as interference to an 802.11b wireless network, and can completely prevent it from functioning properly. The problem lies in the design of Bluetooth—it hops between frequencies in its 2.4GHz band about 1600 times per second, which is enough to all but completely disrupt other 2.4GHz based wireless traffic—such as that of an 802.11b network.

PLUG AND PLAY AND OTHER GOODIES

Windows XP Professional supports *Plug and Play (PnP)*, meaning you can add new stuff to your computer, such as a printer, video card, USB port, and so on, and Windows will attempt to automatically assign it resources and add drivers. It does so, assuming the add-on hardware is Plug and Play–compatible and the computer's BIOS is Plug and Play–compliant. Windows XP Professional's version of Plug and Play works better than the Windows 9x/Me flavor, locating new hardware faster and mapping more PCI-based hardware to the same IRQ than Windows 9x/Me could do. This reduces hardware conflicts considerably.

Windows XP Professional also supports ACPI's enhancements to Plug and Play, USB devices, IEEE-1394 (FireWire/i.Link) devices, AGP video cards, DVD, and CD-ROM drives on a par with Windows 98/Me and Windows 2000.

New hardware supported in Windows XP Professional includes

- Portable audio players
- CD-R and CD-RW drives

Windows XP Professional offers wizards to make copying files to these devices very easy.

FILE SYSTEM IMPROVEMENTS

Realizing the inherent security and efficiency limitations in the old DOS (FAT 16) file system, Microsoft has developed two improved file systems over the last several years—FAT32 and NTFS. NTFS was introduced with NT 3.1; FAT32, with Windows 98. Each has its strengths and weaknesses. FAT32's big advantage is that it's highly compatible with FAT16 yet supports larger disk drive partitions and divides the drive into smaller clusters than FAT16, thus economizing on disk space. However, it's not nearly as secure as NTFS.

Microsoft's updates and tweaks to NTFS in NT 4 service packs pushed NTFS's security even further, and Windows XP Professional uses the same enhanced NTFS 5.0 version originally introduced with Windows 2000. Now file caching for networked and shared drives is an option, and 128-bit file and folder encryption is built in. Caching speeds up access to the files as well, and allows users to work with them offline.

NOTE

> You can still use FAT16 and FAT32 file systems with Windows XP Professional, but you might want to convert to NTFS either during the installation process or later for more efficient and more secure file storage. You can convert either FAT file system to NTFS, but you cannot convert FAT16 to FAT32 with Windows XP (as you could with Windows 98/Me).

MORE STABILITY

Windows XP Professional inherits its stability in performance from Windows NT and Windows 2000. What makes the Windows NT/2000/XP family more stable than consumer Windows (3.x/9x/Me)?

Windows XP Professional is more stable than Windows 9x/Me (not to mention old Windows 3.1!) because its internal design protects the system kernel, which is the core of the operating system. Windows XP Professional's system kernel never interfaces directly with applications or hardware, which could corrupt the kernel and crash the system. Instead, applications and hardware make requests to subsystems, which then request attention from the kernel.

Windows XP Professional's stability also comes from its use of *preemptive multitasking*, which uses a scheduler to tell each program running how much CPU time it can use. Windows XP Professional divides tasks into four priority rankings and provides the most CPU time to real-time processes, followed by high-priority processes, normal-priority tasks, and, finally, idle tasks. While Windows 9x and Me also support preemptive multitasking, their reliance on old 16-bit code made multitasking a much riskier process.

To make multitasking work even better, Windows XP Professional also uses *multithreading*, which enables a single program to be divided up into separate *threads* (or subprocesses) which can be managed and run separately for greater efficiency.

Finally, Windows XP Professional is more stable because it prevents "DLL Hell," that all-too-common problem for Windows 9x/Me users who installed different programs that used different versions of the same DLL (Dynamic Link Library) program files. When programs used the wrong DLL files, they crashed, and sometimes took the whole operating system down with them. Microsoft has been aware of "DLL Hell" for some time, but fixes to this problem have been slow in coming.

Windows 98 Second Edition provided for a feature called "side-by-side DLLs." This allowed a developer to use the particular version of DLLs required by a particular program without overwriting system DLLs (those stored in the \Windows\System folder). This feature worked *only* on Windows 98SE and only if the program developer took advantage of the feature.

Windows 2000 introduced Windows File Protection, which restored system files automatically if they were overwritten by an application when you installed it or ran it. This protected Windows from crashing, but didn't do a thing about a program which needed a particular system file version to run. Microsoft's solution in Windows XP is called *Fusion*, which enables programs to install whatever system files (DLLs and others) they need, and redirects any files which would replace system files to the program's own folder. When such a program is run, Windows XP creates a memory-protected virtual machine to run the program with its own DLLs. The end result is that even if two or more programs are running at the same time, using different versions of DLL or other system files that would "break" the system in past versions of Windows, both programs will now run properly. No other programs can touch the area of memory granted to each program. Nor can that program or other programs gain access to the area of memory in which the basics of the operating system are running. This prevents the kinds of crashing well-known to Windows 9x/Me users.

Other Windows XP features which promote stability include

- **Shutdown Event Tracker**—This optional feature can be enabled to allow you to enter the reasons for a shutdown or restart of Windows XP, and takes a detailed technical snapshot of the system's condition. The snapshot records the processes running on the system, system resource usage, pagefiles, and drives. You can use this information to determine causes for problems and their solutions. The Shutdown Event Tracker is enabled via editing the Registry; see Windows XP Help and Support for details.

- **Easier shutdown of unresponsive applications**—You no longer need to open the Task Manager to shut down a program that's not responding; just click on the window (which states if the program is not responding) and click the Close button, just as with a normally responding application.

- **Windows Driver Protection**—This feature prevents installation of defective drivers and provides an online link for more information and possible updates. It also blocks defective drivers that are installed via Registry keys or the CreateService API set.

- **Device Driver Rollback**—You can return to the previous version of a device driver with all devices except printers. This feature is accessed through the Driver tab of a device's properties sheet in Device Manager.

- **Automatic updates**—Provides background updates for Windows, with the capability to resume an interrupted download. You can choose whether or not to install the update once it's been downloaded.

- **Dynamic updates**—This setup option, if selected, checks online for newer drivers and fixes than those available on the Windows XP CD-ROM, assuring you of an up-to-date version of Windows when first installed. A Dynamic Update package is available for network administrators, to ensure that all users get updated files when they install Windows XP in a corporate environment.

- **New Shadow Copy feature in Backup**—The Windows XP Backup program can back up open files and create volume snapshots while users are working. This prevents open files from being skipped during a backup.

- **Enhanced Last Known Good Configuration**—The Windows XP version of this startup option restores the device drivers used by the last known good configuration as well as the registry information. This enables you to recover from defective device drivers without the need to reinstall the originals.

- **Automated System Recovery (ASR)**—ASR enables the Windows XP Professional backup tool to back up applications, the current condition of the system, and critical boot and partition files and restore them. ASR replaces the Emergency Repair Disk used by Windows NT 4.0 and Windows 2000, and supports PnP devices.

- **Enhanced System Restore feature**—Originally developed for Windows Me, System Restore (which enables a user to return the system to a preset past condition) has many enhancements in Windows XP, including better performance and better use of disk space, support for NTFS compression, warning messages when disk space is running out, and the capability to remove all but the latest restore point to save disk space.

- **Better error handling**—Windows XP's error messages are easier to understand than those in previous versions of Windows, and provide better help for recovering from the error without rebooting the system. Also, Windows XP has a new Online Crash Analysis feature that logs details about a shutdown or "blue screen" crash to a file. When you restart the system, you can open an Internet connection and send the log to Microsoft Product Support Services for help within 24 hours. A companion Web site (oca.microsoft.com) allows you to check the status of your report.

IMPROVED SYSTEM MANAGEMENT

Now let's look briefly at what Windows XP Professional has to offer you as a manager of either a single computer or hundreds of machines in a large office setting. Will your work life really be less complicated, and should your company's operating costs be lower? Most likely, because Windows XP Professional provides you with centralized control over all the PCs in your organization. You'll also be able to use a new class of applications that are easier to deploy, more manageable, and more reliable. As a result, you will be able to provide better service with less hassle. Following are a few examples of Windows XP Professional's features that can improve an IT administrator's work life.

The most important management tool in Windows XP Professional is called the Microsoft Management Console (MMC) or Computer Management.

Computer Management provides a single interface for managing hardware (System Tools), drives (storage), and services such as indexing. It replaces the hodgepodge of programs and features found in Windows 9x and Me with a single interface (see Figure 1.9). It's also extensible with new "snap-in" modules provided by Microsoft or other companies.

Figure 1.9
Windows XP Professional's Computer Management tool offers many different system services under one roof, and accepts plug-in modules.

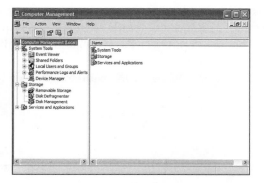

The Microsoft Management Console is a one-stop shop that you can use from your own desk to do the following:

- Check the status of remote machines
- Automatically install new applications
- Upgrade old applications
- Repair damaged applications
- Manage devices
- Manage security
- Prepare new hard drives for use

In addition to MMC, an improvement to the Windows Management Architecture alerts administrators to possible impending hardware or software problems. Microsoft has implemented industry standards called WBEM (Web-based Enterprise Management) and WMI (Windows Management Instructions) that empower help-desk teams to diagnose problems using a variety of third-party management tools. These tools gather information about a workstation to aid in diagnosing problems.

Another big area of annoyance for administrators is keeping track of updates for deployment across a whole sea of users. This is version control management. Management tools have been added to Windows XP Professional to help you with service-pack slipstreaming, so a company can keep one master image of the operating system on a network and deploy it to individual PCs as necessary.

Windows XP Professional also uses the Windows Update feature introduced by Windows 98, enabling managers and users to keep their systems up-to-date via a simple connection to the Web. Just click Start, All Programs, and choose Windows Update. Windows Update now supports both individual users—with automatic gathering of device information and immediate downloads—and corporate users—who can manually specify the updates needed and download an assembled package of desired updates.

The Windows XP Control Panel now offers a choice of Classic View (resembling its default in previous Windows versions) or the new default, Category View. Category View groups Control Panel options by typical uses in a task-centric approach, and provides quick links to other related Control Panel options in its Other Places window (see Figure 1.10).

Figure 1.10
The default Category View of Windows XP's Control Panel is designed to display the most common tasks.

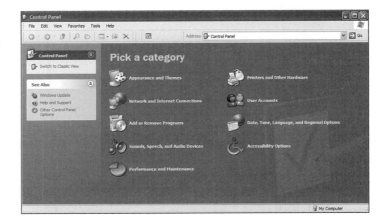

NEW AND IMPROVED WIZARDS

Windows XP Professional features improved versions of wizards originally found in Windows 9x, Windows Me, or Windows 2000, including

- **New Connection Wizard**—This wizard lets you start up network connections on-the-fly, whether in the office or at home (phoning into the Internet via your ISP), creating a Virtual Private Networking (VPN) connection to a LAN in another location, or whatever. The Network Connection Wizard is also used to set up direct connections to other computers, directly through infrared, parallel, or serial connections (see Figure 1.11). Note that infrared connections between computers are now supported for an ad hoc instant (slow-speed) cable-less LAN.

- **Add Printer Wizard**—This wizard makes it easy to set up and connect to local and network printers, even from an application, right from the Print dialog box (see Figure 1.12). No more fishing around for the Printers folder. The wizard automatically tries to determine the make and model of your printer without forcing you to scroll through a list of options.

Figure 1.11
You can use the New Connection Wizard to create several different types of connections.

Figure 1.12
You can choose or create a new printer without opening the Printers Control Panel.

- **Files and Settings Transfer Wizard**—This wizard helps you move settings for Internet Explorer, Outlook Express, desktop and display, dial-up connections, and document folders (such as My Documents and My Pictures) to a different computer running any 32-bit version of Windows; you can also use it to transfer settings from your old computer to a computer running Windows XP. While you still need to install matching applications on the target computer, this wizard saves valuable setup time and helps you get back to work faster with your new system.

WHAT IS NOT IN WINDOWS XP PROFESSIONAL

Windows XP Professional is almost completely a superset of Windows XP Home Edition. In other words, virtually every feature found in Windows XP Home Edition is also part of Windows XP Professional. Thus, it's no longer necessary to decide between multimedia features and corporate networking as you would with Windows Me and Windows 2000 Professional.

About the only major feature missing from Windows XP Professional is Windows XP Home Edition's simplified user configuration. Because Windows XP Professional is designed for corporate networking, it uses, as you learned earlier in this chapter, corporate-style security settings that are much more comprehensive than those used by Windows XP Home Edition. Otherwise, every feature in Windows XP Home Edition is present in Windows XP Professional.

Like Windows 2000 Professional, Windows XP Professional is limited to 10 simultaneous connections when it's used as a Web server, and it supports either one or two processors. You will need to use Windows 2000 Server or Windows Server 2003 if you need support for more users or more processors.

SERVICE PACK UPGRADES

In the fall of 2002, Service Pack 1 (SP1) was released for Windows XP. As with service packs for previous Microsoft operating systems such as NT, SP1 wasn't worthy of being dubbed a new version of XP, although it did extend the functionality of XP into new key areas. More importantly, it consisted of many bug fixes and attempted to placate the U.S. Department of Justice on the issue of monopolistic business practices. Your version of Windows may already incorporate SP1, or you may need to upgrade to SP-1 through Windows Update or another method (such as a CD from Microsoft). Some of the features of SP1 include

- **Windows CE for Smart Displays (Mira)**—Support for smart display devices running Windows CE .NET that interact via 802.11 wireless with a Windows XP base station.

- **Freestyle**—Support for a simple, graphical front-end to the most often used Windows XP digital media tasks that allows you to interact with your Windows XP computer by using a remote control instead of a mouse.

- **USB 2.0**—An enhancement to USB 1.x increases maximum transfer rates to 480Mbps.

- **IPv6**—Support for the next version of the IP protocol, created due to the need for more publicly addressable IP addresses.

- **Consent Decree compliance**—Allows users to "hide" links to Microsoft middleware products such as Internet Explorer and Outlook Express, and have other options shown instead.

- **Windows .NET Messenger 4.7**—New version of Messenger that features enhanced security and compliance with the DOJ Consent Decree.

- **Tablet PC**—Support for full-featured "baby" laptop computers with touch screens and handwriting recognition that can be picked up and taken on the go. A new version of Windows XP (Tablet PC Edition) will power these devices that allow for new and unusual ways to use Windows (see Figure 1.13).

- **Microsoft Product Activation**—Changes Product Activation to disable certain pirated versions of Windows XP. The changes should have no effect on legally obtained copies of Windows. Activation was also loosened, to allow a three-day grace period (in which to phone in to Microsoft for an exception) in the case of installation of XP on two different computers using the same activation key. This will prove to be a great benefit to those users who have a system experience a non-recoverable disaster and need to reinstall Windows XP onto a new computer.

- **Security Fixes and Improvements**—Includes all patches and hot fixes that have been released for Windows XP since it was released to manufacturing last year.

Figure 1.13
An example of a
Tablet PC.

How Does Windows XP Professional Compare to Unix and Linux?

Windows XP's kernel, like Windows 2000's, has its roots in Unix. Unix is a very popular multitasking operating system developed at Bell Labs in the early 1970s. It was designed by programmers for programmers. In fact, the language C was developed just to write Unix. Even though Unix has become a friendlier operating system with the addition of Windows-like interfaces such as MOTIF, it's still relatively user-unfriendly, requiring cryptic commands much like DOS.

Unix

Because it is written in C, Unix can run on any computer that has a C compiler, making it quite portable. AT&T gave away the Unix source code to universities and licensed it to several companies during its early years. AT&T no longer owns Unix; the Unix trademark is now owned by OpenGroup, though the source code is owned by the Santa Cruz Operation (SCO).

Unfortunately, to avoid paying the licensing fees to AT&T, Unix lookalikes sprung up over the years. Without the proper license, these versions could not call themselves Unix, only Unix-like. And as these clones proliferated, cross-compatibility became an issue. More than a handful of versions (dialects) of Unix have appeared, the primary contenders being AT&T's own, known as *System V*, and another developed at the University of California at Berkeley, known as *BSD4.x*, *x* being a number from 1 to 3. Other popular brands of Unix these days are HP-UX from HP, AIX from IBM, Solaris from Sun, and SCO's version, UnixWare.

In 1984, industry experts were brought together to create guidelines and standards for Unix clones, in hopes of creating a more coherent market. The result was a single Unix specification, which includes a requirement for POSIX (Portable Operating System Interface for Unix) compliance. Accepted by the IEEE and ISO, POSIX is a standard that makes porting applications and other code between variants of Unix as simple as recompiling the source code.

> **NOTE**
>
> Another popular version of Unix that runs on the PC platform is called FreeBSD. Briefly, FreeBSD 4.x is a Unix-like operating system based on U.C. Berkeley's 4.4BSD-lite release for the Intel 386 platform. It is also based indirectly on William Jolitz's port of U.C. Berkeley's Net/2 to the Intel 386, known as 386BSD, though very little of the 386BSD code remains. You can find a fuller description of what FreeBSD is and how it can work for you at `www.freebsd.com`.

Unix has been the predominant operating system for workstations connected to servers, mostly because of its multiuser capabilities and its rock-solid performance. Windows NT and its successors, Windows 2000 and Windows XP, have been making inroads due to the extensive number of development tools and applications for the Windows platform. However, a low-cost Unix variant called Linux is revitalizing Unix across all platforms.

LINUX

Linux is a Unix lookalike. Linux isn't a port of a preexisting operating system, but rather it was written from the ground up by Linus Torvalds, a Finnish-born computer scientist who wanted to develop a Unix-like operating system for computer students to run on low-cost Intel computers. Torvalds wrote the kernel with the help of a handful of computer programmers. Like all variants of Unix, Linux has many of the features of NT/Windows 2000/Windows XP, such as true multitasking, virtual memory, shared libraries, intelligent memory management, and TCP/IP networking.

Linux is an open system, and programmers worldwide are invited to participate in its building and refinement. Unlike other flavors of Unix that were based on licensed source code, Linux is based on Minix, which mimics Unix in a way that does not infringe on the Unix license. That's why Linux distributions are practically free.

> **NOTE**
>
> Actually, the term *Linux* pertains only to the kernel. What people have come to refer to as Linux is actually a collection of separate pieces of code, the majority of which are GNU. It was not until Linux came together with GNU that the full power of the Linux OS (what GNU enthusiasts would call GNU Linux) crystallized.

The several popularly distributed Linux versions are differentiated mostly by the selection of tools and utilities bundled with them. The most popular package at this point is Red Hat Linux. If you want to go it alone, you can acquire Linux for free, but buying some commercially bundled packages makes the job of installation and support easier because you get support. Technically, the distribution of the software must be free, in accordance with the GNU General Public License (GPL) agreement governing the distribution of Linux and the collected modules that accompany it.

Linux now runs on a wide variety of systems, including Sun JavaStations, the IBM RS/6000, and the Alpha chip originally developed by DEC and later sold by Compaq, MIPS, SPARC, Open VMS, Digital Unix, and other platforms.

Windows Application Compatibility with Linux

IT professionals willing to get under the hood and poke around and learn Linux's ways are impressed with its solidity. Though Linux is not commonly used as a business productivity workstation, it is embraced by some for back-end Web servers or transaction servers where reliability is a high priority.

WINE, a DOS, Windows 3.1, and 32-bit Windows emulator, is a popular program used by a number of vendors to move their Windows programs to the Linux platform. For more information, see the WINE Web site at www.winehq.com. However, even the most recent versions of WINE are limited, especially in their multimedia support. To get full Linux and full Windows XP support on a single system, set up a dual-boot system. The only reliable way to run Windows programs on a Linux system is to dual-boot.

→ To learn more about dual-booting Linux, **see** "Windows XP and Linux," **p. 154**.

Mainstream applications for Linux have taken a long time to arrive, but Corel's WordPerfect Office 2000 for Linux and Sun's StarOffice 5.2 provide powerful office suites with many of the features of recent Microsoft Office releases. CorelDRAW for Linux includes Linux-compatible versions of CorelDRAW 9 and PhotoPaint 9, and there are, of course, many downloadable freeware and shareware programs for Linux available online.

Microsoft, of course, doesn't want to develop Linux versions of either its programming languages or applications such as Office, for obvious reasons.

Obviously, as a capitalistic enterprise, Linux doesn't cut it for the entrepreneur, unless he or she is willing to look at the world through a radically new set of glasses. Giving away your software doesn't net you much. Then again, people are giving away PCs to sell the advertising, so go figure. The world of computing might be changing more than we know. But because applications developers for the Linux environment are supposed to distribute their source code along with the applications, this is a daunting shift of worldview for a behemoth such as Microsoft, which works overtime to protect its intellectual property. The upshot is that you're out of luck if you want to run Word, Excel, Access, Internet Explorer, or any other Microsoft programs on a Linux box.

Windows XP Versus Linux

Trying to compare Windows XP versus Linux is difficult for several reasons, including

- Windows XP requires a relatively recent computer with at least 128MB of RAM to function, while Linux can run successfully on even 486-based systems long obsolete for use with Windows
- Windows XP is available in just two versions (Home Edition and Professional), while Linux is available in numerous distributions

■ Windows XP is primarily a GUI-based operating system, while Linux is primarily command-line–driven (although KDE and Gnome, the two most common GUIs, are increasingly popular)

Although Linux has made great strides in so-called "back end" uses such as Web servers, network servers, and embedded devices, Windows XP is a better choice for desktops for several reasons, including

■ Journaling file system for higher reliability and crash recovery.

■ Compatibility testing and guarantees for operating system and applications.

■ Wide availability of commercial applications at retail and online stores.

■ Clustering and base-load balancing.

■ Long-term roadmap of operating system deployment plans.

■ Larger hard disks and maximum file sizes. Linux's maximum file size is 2 Gigabytes; Windows XP's limit is 18.4 quintillion bytes (Petabytes).

■ "Synchronous I/O," which allows smoother running in Windows XP when multiple threads are being processed and waiting for input or output. It improves SMP scalability as well.

■ Consistent GUI across all tools—Linux has no single standard GUI at present.

■ A single version which can be installed for most major languages and countries.

■ Dedicated support network, with close to one-half million Microsoft-certified trained professionals and engineers.

We believe that the entire Linux/Windows controversy comes down to this: Microsoft offers lots and lots of powerful stuff (which you can use to build very sophisticated software), from the C++ compiler, to the component-nature of Excel and other apps, to the ASP scripting language, COM, and so on. These tools let you leverage everything Microsoft offers to make very powerful applications. As people used to say in the sixties and seventies, nobody ever lost his job buying IBM. Now it's safe to say nobody ever lost his job buying Microsoft. True, you're locked into Windows because the stuff you build on Windows systems can't be ported to Unix variants, but that's the price you pay for the tools, the user base, and the support and training. Although increasing support options are available for Linux (see www.linuxcare.com), enterprise-level support for Linux is still not as widespread as for Windows.

Linux might be a decent choice for the small-business owners or IS professionals who need to build low-cost servers for Web, email, or file sharing. This operating system is designed for those uses, and the popular Red Hat and Caldera Linux packages make installation relatively painless (not as easy as Windows XP Professional, though, mind you). If you're thinking of using Linux on your desktop PC, beware—you might be biting off more than you can chew. The manuals that come with Linux—even the commercial versions—are dense. It is not always headache-free. But if you have a good understanding of computer technology and insist on switching from Windows to something more stable and more flexible, Linux might be the choice for you. If nothing else, using Linux will be a learning experience. However, for the foreseeable future, Linux will be primarily a server and embedded-device operating system, rather than a desktop operating system.

WINDOWS XP PROFESSIONAL ON THE CORPORATE NETWORK

Windows XP Professional, because it's designed as a replacement for Windows 2000 Professional, is designed to work well on corporate networks. Thus, it contains all the network and security features of Windows 2000 Professional, including

- Support for IP Security (IPSec) to protect data being transmitted across VPNs
- Kerberos v5 support for authentication
- Group Policy settings for administering networks and users
- Offline viewing of network data when not connected to the network
- Synchronization of local and network files
- Remote access configuration wizard
- Microsoft and Novell NetWare network clients
- Support for Active Directory (Microsoft's directory service feature which helps to manage users and resources on large networks)
- Disk quotas to prevent a few storage-hog users from running the server out of space
- Internet Information Services, including FTP, FrontPage 2000 Server Extensions, SMTP (Simple Mail Transport Protocol) service, World Wide Web service, the management snap-in for the Microsoft Management Console, remote deployment support, and documentation
- Fax services for sending and receiving faxes
- Simple Network Management Protocol (SNMP) support
- Print services for Unix

NEW NETWORKING FEATURES

Windows XP also adds many new network features specially designed to make corporate networking easier and more reliable, including

- Networking has been integrated into the Task Manager to display real-time network usage and connection-speed information.
- An enhanced Netdiag.exe command-line diagnostics tool is provided on the Windows XP CD-ROM.
- An enhanced version of Network Driver Interface Specification (NDIS), version 5.1, with support for PnP and Power Event Notification, send cancellation, better statistics capability, and better performance.

1

- A new version of the Windows Telephony API (TAPI), version 3.1, with support for H.323-compatible IP telephony and IP multicast A/V conferencing, recording of streaming A/V data for playback, USB phones, automatic discovery of telephony servers, and support for H.323 services such as call hold, call transfer, call diversion, call pack, and call pickup.

- Support for newer network devices, including HomePNA phoneline networks, USB-connected network devices, software-based (also called controllerless or "Winmodem") modems, and infrared-enabled cell phones (as modems).

- Support for Universal Plug and Play (UPnP) devices on a network, and use of UPnP to detect Internet Connection Sharing (ICS) hosts on a network.

- Network bridging—One computer can run two different types of networks (such as Fast Ethernet and IEEE 802.11b [Wi-Fi] wireless Ethernet) and act as a connection between them. You need a network card for each network type you're bridging.

- Auto-configuration of IEEE 802.11b Wi-Fi networks—Wi-Fi (wireless Ethernet) networks are harder to configure than wired networks such as Fast Ethernet, because you must synchronize the card to the wireless access point that allows your PC to talk to others. Windows XP Professional detects the correct settings automatically.

- Capability to store and recall settings of various wireless networks the user has connected to in the past for automatic configuration when the same network is encountered again. This feature simplifies moving between multiple wireless networks, such as home and office or different offices.

- An enhanced Connection Manager with new management options, split tunneling (secure VPN and public Internet access at the same time), Favorites feature for storing connection settings for different locations (useful for business travelers), client-side logging for troubleshooting, and support for ICS.

- The enhanced Network Troubleshooter feature, available from the menu on the left side of the Network Connections menu, provides one-stop access to network-related tools in the Help and Support center. You can start Ping and Net View commands to diagnose and check Internet and LAN connections, as well as run troubleshooters for Internet Connection Sharing, Modems, and other home and corporate network configurations. A new Network Diagnostics tool scans the network and tests your network card. As shown in Figure 1.14, at the end of the testing process, it displays the results of its tests for Internet service settings, computer information, and network adapters (including modems).

- Support for encrypted folders with multiple users.

- Remote desktop support via Remote Desktop Protocol (RDP), enabling users to access their computers remotely from anywhere with network access, including other offices, at home, or airport kiosks.

- Improved Group Policy feature with hundreds of new policies provided, making it easier to choose a pre-defined policy instead of needing to modify one.

■ Remote Assistance to allow network or Internet-based help desk personnel to view a user's display and provide training or technical assistance. This feature can be centrally enabled or disabled as desired.

Figure 1.14
The Network Diagnostics tool displays the configuration of both hardware and software components on your network.

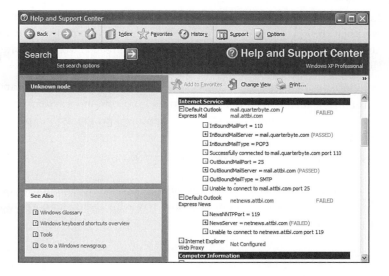

IMPROVED NETWORK SECURITY

Windows XP Professional, like Windows NT 4.0 and Windows 2000, is a high-security operating system designed for corporate networks. While many of its security features are carryovers from its predecessors, Windows XP Professional also features new and enhanced tools for network security, including

■ Standard access control list settings, standard security groups, and predefined security templates offering Basic, Compatible, Secure, and Highly Secure group policies. All of these security settings can be modified as needed, and can be controlled with tools such as the Microsoft Management Console or those provided with the optional Windows XP Professional Resource Kit.

■ Default guest-level access for network, Internet access, and simple security (non-domain) networks. This feature limits the ability of intruders to gain access to private information.

■ Limited access for users who don't password-protect their accounts. User accounts without passwords can't be used for any purpose other than to log on to their own systems; remote logons are no longer permitted.

■ Support for the Encrypted File System (EFS). You can encrypt data with your choice of the expanded Data Encryption Standard (DESX) or Triple-DES (3DES), and all contents of an encrypted folder are also encrypted. Encryption also works with offline files and folders and with Web folders, and is designed to be managed through Group Policy and command-line programs.

- User certificates are stored in a subfolder of each user's Documents and Settings folder, and private keys are stored in a different subfolder. Private keys are automatically encrypted when stored.

- A Credential Manager Key Ring feature which stores multiple credentials (username/password) used on the system. As you navigate from one secured network to another, the correct credential to log in is selected automatically, based on criteria such as the server name and domain name. This feature also works with Remote Access and Virtual Private Networking.

- Support for digitally signed software. This feature allows an administrator to block unsigned or unapproved ActiveX controls from running a system, prevent Windows Installer from installing unsigned or unapproved programs, and prevent unsigned Visual Basic Scripts from being run.

- Built-in support for smart card authentication.

Windows XP Professional builds on the already-strong corporate network features of Windows 2000 Professional to provide more powerful and easier corporate networking, security, and management.

CHAPTER 2

INSTALLATION PREP

In this chapter

BACKGROUND

There is a little known rule called the five P's that goes like this: Proper Preparation Prevents Poor Performance. Keep this rule in mind as you read this chapter. Before undertaking the installation of Windows XP Professional, there are several factors that you need to consider regardless of the scope and size of the deployment. Whether you are rolling out 5,000 copies of Windows XP Professional to an entire organization using sophisticated deployment methods such as ghosting or Remote Installation, or simply installing it on your home computer, the same things still require your attention *before* the installation process begins.

In this chapter, we will be spending our time looking at each of the following items in more depth, getting a feel for how they affect an installation of Windows XP Professional and how they will impact the computer, both now and into the future.

- System requirements
- Hardware and software compatibility
- Network configuration
- File system considerations
- Type of installation to perform
- Transferring files and settings

When working through this chapter, it might be helpful to build a checklist. For an example, see Figure 2.1.

Figure 2.1
My Windows XP Professional installation notes page.

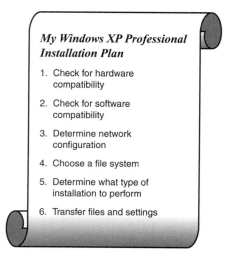

My Windows XP Professional Installation Plan

1. Check for hardware compatibility
2. Check for software compatibility
3. Determine network configuration
4. Choose a file system
5. Determine what type of installation to perform
6. Transfer files and settings

Without any further ado, let's get right into the meat of this chapter and start off by looking at the system requirements for installing Windows XP Professional.

SYSTEM REQUIREMENTS

Windows XP Professional combines the best and worst parts of Windows 2000 Professional and Windows Millennium Edition. On the good side, Windows XP Professional has the robust security, stability, and manageability of the Windows 2000 code-base, as well as the robust built-in multimedia and graphics support that Windows Millennium Edition touted. On the bad side, Windows XP Professional is very demanding of system resources, especially so on older or underpowered systems. You wouldn't dare run Windows 2000 Professional or Windows Millennium Edition in a production environment on less than 64MB of RAM, and so you shouldn't try it with Windows XP Professional.

The official system requirements to support installation of Windows XP Professional are presented in Table 2.1.

TABLE 2.1   HARDWARE REQUIREMENTS TO INSTALL WINDOWS XP PROFESSIONAL

Minimum Requirements	Recommended Requirements
Pentium (or compatible) 233MHz or higher processor.	Pentium II (or compatible) 300MHz or higher processor.
64 megabytes (MB) of RAM.	128MB (4GB maximum) of RAM.
2 gigabyte (GB) hard disk with 650MB of free disk space.	1.5GB of free disk space.
Video graphics adapter (VGA) or higher display adapter.	Super VGA (SVGA) display adapter and Plug and Play monitor.
Keyboard, mouse, or other pointing device.	Keyboard, mouse, or other pointing device.
CD-ROM or DVD-ROM drive (required for CD installations).	CD-ROM or DVD-ROM drive (12¥ or faster).
Network adapter (required for network installation).	Network adapter (required for network installation).

NOTE

> Windows XP Professional, like its predecessor Windows 2000 Professional, is capable of handling up to two CPUs and provides support for symmetric multi-processing.

Of course, knowing the hardware requirements to support a successful installation (and later operation) of Windows XP Professional is just one small part of the battle. Sticking to our plan of action, as outlined in the list in the first section of this chapter, we need to look at hardware and software compatibility issues, both of which can bring your installation of Windows XP Professional to a screeching halt at worst, or at best, cause you some annoyance and lack of functionality.

CHECKING HARDWARE AND SOFTWARE COMPATIBILITY

Verifying that your current hardware will support an installation of Windows XP Professional is critical to getting Windows XP correctly installed and running smoothly. Verifying the existing software installed on your computer when performing an upgrade installation is just as vital—Windows XP can get pretty particular when it comes to dealing with previously installed software.

There are a couple of means at your disposal when it comes to verifying hardware and software compatibility for the installation of Windows XP Professional. The first of these is the Hardware Compatibility List (HCL).

THE HARDWARE COMPATIBILITY LIST

The Windows Hardware Compatibility List, which can be found online at `http://www.microsoft.com/hcl/default.asp`, is shown in Figure 2.2. The HCL is a fully searchable database listing all hardware devices that have been tested for compliance with the Windows logo requirements. In some cases, these hardware devices may have drivers available on the Windows Setup CD-ROM. In Figure 2.3, you can see the results of a search I did for a network adapter installed in one of my computers, the NetGear FA310TX Fast Ethernet PCI adapter.

Figure 2.2
The Windows Hardware Compatibility List makes it easy to locate compatible hardware for your Windows XP installation.

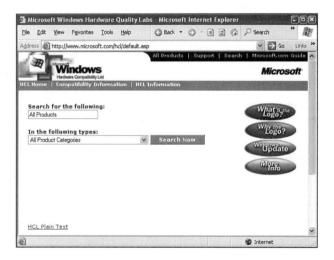

TIP

Interpreting the HCL

If you are curious as to what the specific symbols mean in regard to logo testing compliance, see `http://www.microsoft.com/hcl/legend.asp` for more information.

Figure 2.3
Locating a specific
piece of hardware.

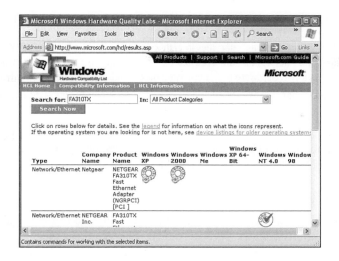

Of course, you can also browse the Hardware Compatibility List by category in an attempt to find hardware devices that are compatible with Windows XP Professional. This may be helpful in cases where you are looking to buy new hardware to add onto an existing Windows XP Professional installation, or are making preparations to acquire some new hardware to support the installation of Windows XP Professional.

A text copy is available for download from ftp://ftp.microsoft.com/services/whql/hcl/winxphclx86.txt, should you want to use it offline. The text file could easily be opened in Microsoft Excel or Microsoft Word for advanced search and sorting capabilities.

So, what do you do if you have a hardware device that is not listed? This by itself does not mean that you cannot use the hardware device. If the hardware manufacturer has developed device drivers for use with Windows XP Professional then you are probably going to be able to use the device without any troubles—other than possibly getting a warning about a driver not being digitally "signed," which simply means that Microsoft hasn't given the driver a seal of approval for working properly with the operating system. Of course, there is no guarantee that the hardware will work, so take the appropriate precautions ahead of time and prepare for the worst when experimenting with non-HCL hardware devices. If the hardware manufacturer does not make a device driver for Windows XP Professional, you may consider using one written for Windows 2000 Professional, but again there is no guarantee that you will have success using this method. In this situation, you may need to look for a newer device—your system will thank you.

→ To learn more about driver signing, **see** "System," **p. 1163**.

TIP

> **Non-HCL Hardware**
>
> Be prepared for difficulties in getting technical support in cases where you've used hardware devices that are not listed on the HCL. Most organizations, including Microsoft, do not support hardware that is not listed on the HCL. In this case, your only recourse is usually the manufacturer or vendor of the hardware in question.

If you prefer not to use the Hardware Compatibility List to locate your devices and desire to instead just plunge right into the installation process, take just a minute and run the Windows Upgrade Advisor, which is the topic of the next section.

USING THE WINDOWS UPGRADE ADVISOR

The Windows Upgrade Advisor is a nifty utility that takes some of the pain out of preparing for an installation of Windows XP Professional. The Windows Upgrade Advisor can be run at any time from one of two ways, and also runs as part of the Windows XP Professional setup routine.

The first, and easiest, way to start the Windows Upgrade Advisor is to run the Windows XP Professional Setup CD-ROM and select Check System Compatibility from the menu of items shown in Figure 2.4.

Figure 2.4
The Welcome to Microsoft Windows XP screen presents you with the option to run the Windows Upgrade Advisor by clicking Check System Compatibility.

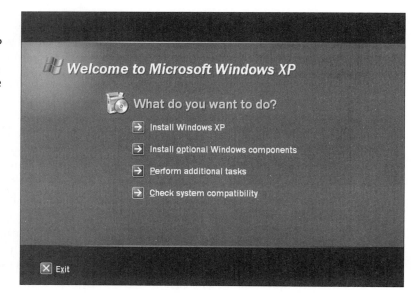

TIP

If Your CD-ROM Does Not Autoplay

If your Windows XP Professional Setup CD-ROM does not autoplay and display the welcome screen of Figure 2.4 automatically, don't despair. Simply navigate to the root of the Windows XP Setup CD-ROM from within Windows Explorer and double-click on the file named SETUP.EXE.

After a second or two, you will be prompted to update the Windows Upgrade Advisor files that are used in the compatibility analysis. If you have an Internet connection, you should select Yes and click Next. The message "Performing Dynamic Update" will appear briefly as your computer contacts the Microsoft servers and downloads the most recent set of configuration files.

If the connection to the Microsoft servers could not be made, an error will be displayed and you will be prompted to try the connection again. After the Windows Upgrade Advisor has completed its interrogation of your computer's hardware and software components, it will display an output similar to that shown in Figure 2.5.

Figure 2.5
Windows Upgrade
Advisor results.

As you can see in the output of Figure 2.5, there is one software item installed on the computer that has been deemed incompatible with Windows XP Professional and should be uninstalled before attempting an upgrade. Don't take these results lightly—they are serious items that require your attention. In some cases, the Windows XP Professional setup routine will actually remove or disable certain software installations. This will be discussed shortly in the "Known Upgrade Issues" section that follows.

You can also run the Windows Upgrade Advisor from the command line using the syntax `x:\i386\winnt32.exe /checkupgradeonly`, where x is the location of the Windows XP Professional Setup CD-ROM.

No matter which way you decide to run the Windows Upgrade Advisor, the results are automatically saved by default into a text file named UPGRADE.TXT, which is located in the %systemroot% directory—that is to say the location where Windows is currently installed on that computer.

TIP

> **Download the Microsoft Upgrade Advisor**
>
> If you have not yet acquired Windows XP Professional, or would like to easily distribute the Windows Update Advisor to multiple computers, it is available for download at `http://www.microsoft.com/windowsxp/pro/howtobuy/upgrading/advisor.asp`.

KNOWN UPGRADE ISSUES

When it comes time to upgrade an existing installation, there are some known issues that you will want to pay attention to; however, there are two main issues that occur most often and will be examined here. These issues deal with CD recording software, such as Roxio Easy CD Creator, and the NetBIOS Extended User Interface (NetBEUI) network protocol.

EASY CD CREATOR

If you upgrade a computer from Windows NT 4.0, Windows 98, Windows 98 Second Edition, Windows Millennium Edition (Me), or Windows 2000 to Windows XP, you may receive the following error message when you first attempt to run Easy CD Creator:

> Easy CD Creator 4 has a known compatibility issue with this version of Windows. For an update that is compatible with this version of Windows, contact Roxio, Inc.

You may also receive this error message when attempting to run Direct CD:

> A driver is installed that causes stability problems with your system.
>
> This driver will be disabled, please contact the driver manufacturer for an update that is compatible with this version of Windows.
>
> To run the program, click Continue. For more information, click Details.

This issue is due to a program incompatibility between Easy CD 5.0 and earlier and Windows XP due to Windows XP's native CD-RW burning support in Windows Media Player 7. To correct this issue, upgrade Easy CD Creator to version 5.02d or later by downloading the required updates from the Roxio Web site, located at `http://www.roxio.com/`.

CAUTION

> **Easy CD Creator Dangers**
>
> The types of errors that you can receive may be even more serious than the ones detailed here. On occasion, computers have suffered STOP errors (Blue Screen of Death) and random rebooting problems—directly as a result of mixing Easy CD 5.0 and Windows XP. Remove any version of Easy CD Creator before installing Windows XP Professional to avoid these problems.

NETBEUI

Should you attempt to upgrade your computer to Windows XP and NetBEUI is installed, you will receive the following message from the Compatibility Wizard:

The currently installed driver for the NETBEUI Transport Protocol is not compatible with Microsoft Windows XP and will be uninstalled during the upgrade. This protocol is removed from this new version of Windows.

For more information about this driver, visit the manufacturer's Web site at `http://www.microsoft.com`. Web addresses can change, so you may be unable to connect to this Web site.

For a list of protocols supported by Windows XP, see the Microsoft Windows Whistler protocols Compatibility List at the Microsoft Web site.

The venerable NetBEUI protocol has been effectively put out to pasture with the introduction of Windows XP. Microsoft has moved away from a NetBIOS environment with all of its operating systems and recommends a purely TCP/IP environment. This change first appeared with Windows 2000 and the introduction of Active Directory. Active Directory is based on the DNS domain model, and thus NetBIOS (and WINS) had to go. While Windows 2000 still provides NetBEUI support natively, Windows XP does not. The best option is to move away from NetBIOS on your network.

Should you, for some reason, still need the NetBEUI protocol, it is still available—on the Windows XP Professional Setup CD-ROM. You can find it located in the Valueadd\MSFT\Net\NetBEUI folder. MSKB# Q301041, located at `http://support.microsoft.com/default.aspx?scid=kb;en-us;Q301041` has more information on installing NetBEUI onto a Windows XP computer.

OTHER KNOWN ISSUES

Of course there are more than two compatibility issues that you may experience with an upgrade to Windows XP, as is the case with every version of Windows. To this end, Microsoft periodically releases packages they call Application Compatibility Updates which are available for download from the Windows Update Web site located at `http://windowsupdate.microsoft.com/`. As of the printing of this book, there have been three Application Compatibility Updates issued for Windows XP as listed:

- Windows XP Application Compatibility Update (October 25, 2001) deals with issues that arose between the release to manufacture of Windows and the release data of October 25, 2001. Among its various fixes is the fix for the infamous incompatibility issue of the Snow White and Seven Dwarfs DVD. Read more about this Update in MSKB# Q308381, located at
  `http://support.microsoft.com/default.aspx?scid=kb;en-us;Q308381.`

- Windows XP Application Compatibility Update (December 17, 2001) dealt with many issues, including issues with several well known applications such as ZoneAlarm, PCAnywhere, and Norton AntiVirus. Read more about this Update in MSKB# Q313484, located at
  `http://support.microsoft.com/default.aspx?scid=kb;en-us;Q313484.`

- Windows XP Application Compatibility Update (April 10, 2002) addresses issues with dozens of games and Works 2001. Read more about this Update in MSKB# Q319580, located at `http://support.microsoft.com/default.aspx?scid=kb;en-us;Q319580`.

TIP

> **Who's the Most Incompatible of All?**
>
> To read more about the infamous Snow White DVD issue, see `http://www.theregister.co.uk/content/archive/22472.html`.

The best place to keep on top of new updates for Windows is the Windows Update Web site.

As we work our way down the pre-installation preparation path, our next stop is network configuration information—we will look at this in the next section.

GETTING THE NETWORK CONFIGURATION

After you've determined what your hardware and software compatibility picture looks like, you are well on your way to being ready to install Windows XP Professional on your computer. There are only three more major areas to consider and we will be looking at the network configuration here.

If the computer that you will be installing Windows XP Professional on is not connected to a network, then you can skip this section. By network, I mean a formal (managed) network consisting of servers and client workstations that has a common naming system, uses an IP address assignment system, and uses network user accounts for access to resources. Does this sound exactly like your Windows NT 4.0 or Windows 2000 domain–based network? It is.

If your network instead uses a peer-to-peer arrangement without using a centralized database for the storage of user accounts and permissions, then you are operating in what is called a workgroup. The first piece of network information you need is either the workgroup name (for example, `dontpanic`) or the domain name (such as `netserverworld.com` or `netserverworld.local`). You can always install Windows XP Professional initially in a workgroup arrangement and then join the domain after installation.

If you are upgrading a computer that is already participating in a network environment, the following list of items should be recorded on your checklist *before* starting the upgrade process:

- The computer name.
- The domain or workgroup name, as previously mentioned.
- The TCP/IP address configuration, if not using a DHCP server for automatic TCP/IP address management.
- The user name and password of an account with permissions to add or create computer accounts.

- If you are using connection-specific DNS suffixes in addition to a primary DNS suffix, you will want to record all DNS suffixes. For example, if your primary DNS suffix is `netserverworld.com` and you ping a computer by machine name `server01`, your computer will look for `server01.netserverworld.com`. If you are also using connection-specific DNS suffixes, such as newportnews on a connection, the computer will look for `server01.netserverworld.com` and `server01.newportnews.netserverworld.com`. This can affect how your computers locate other computers in the network, so pay close attention to these settings. Figure 2.6 shows this information.

Figure 2.6
The connection-specific DNS suffix affects how your computer searches out other computers on the network.

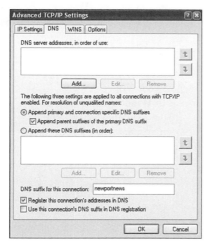

Of course, you will need all of the appropriate hardware and cabling as well...but that's kind of a given here! Once you have all of the network configuration information you need, be sure to write it down in a safe place so it will be available during the installation process.

Now that we've gotten the network configuration information we need for the installation, let's take some time to look in depth at choosing your file system, including the pros and cons of each file system.

CHOOSING A FILE SYSTEM: FAT32 OR NTFS

The choice of a file system is not one to be taken lightly. Unlike most other configurable items in your Windows XP installation, the file system is one that can only be changed one time after installation, and only in one direction.

→ Okay, every rule has to have an exception, so of course the rule about file system conversion has one. To learn more about converting file systems, **see** "Converting the NTFS File System to FAT16/FAT32," **p. 1014**.

For a clean installation of Windows XP Professional, you will have to make a choice between using the FAT32 or NTFS file system. On an upgrade installation from Windows 98, you could possibly even face an existing FAT16-formatted partition, as Windows 98 supported the FAT32 file system but did not automatically invoke it—you had to convert to FAT32 after the fact.

Table 2.2 provides a quick comparison of the FAT16, FAT32, and NTFS file systems.

TABLE 2.2   FILE SYSTEM COMPARISON

	FAT16	FAT32	NTFS
Supported operating systems	All versions of Windows, MS-DOS, and OS/2.	Windows 95 OSR2, Windows 98, Windows Millennium Edition, Windows 2000, and Windows XP.	Windows NT 4.0 SP4 or later can access files and folder. Windows 2000 and Windows XP can take full advantage of NTFS 5.0.
Volume sizes	Maximum size is limited to 4GB. In MS-DOS, Windows 95, Windows 98 and Windows Me the maximum size is 2GB due to the smallest "largest cluster" size being 32KB.	Minimum size is 512MB, maximum size is 2TB. In Windows XP Professional (and Windows 2000), the maximum size a FAT32 volume can be is 32GB.	Minimum volume size (recommended) is 10MB. Maximum volume size (recommended) is 2TB, although much larger sizes are possible.
Floppy disk usage?	No	No	No
Removable storage usage?	Yes	Yes	Yes, but not recommended.
Maximum file size	Maximum file size is 4GB minus 1 byte.	Maximum file is size 4GB.	Maximum file size 16TB minus 64KB.
Files per volume	65,536 (2^{16} files).	Approximately 4,177,920.	4,294,967,295 (2^{32} minus 1 files).
Supports NTFS 5.0 features?	No	No	Windows 2000 and Windows XP fully support the advanced features of NTFS 5.0. Windows NT 4.0 SP4 supports access only, but not the advanced features.

→ To learn more about the different file systems, **see** "Choosing Your File System: NTFS or FAT," **p. 997**.

During the installation process, you may be asked to make a file system selection from the menu shown in Figure 2.7.

Figure 2.7
Selecting a file system during setup; you can convert FAT to NTFS later if you want.

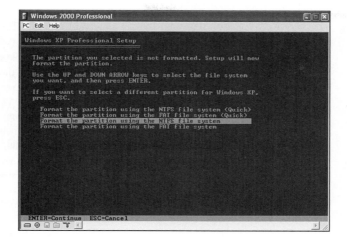

You will only be given this choice when dealing with an unformatted volume. If you have a volume that is currently formatted with FAT16 or FAT32, you will be given the opportunity to convert or format it to the NTFS file system.

TIP

> **Take the Easy Road**
>
> If you are concerned about system stability, you can always make use of the FAT file system during installation of Windows XP Professional. Once you've verified that the installation has taken without any stability problems, you can then convert the file system to NTFS.
>
> By installing Windows XP Professional in this way, you can still make use of a variety of DOS boot disks and utilities—some of which you probably have. On a new installation using new hardware certified for Windows XP Professional, this is probably not going to be a required step.

You cannot change your file system after Windows XP Professional has been installed unless you are converting from FAT16 or FAT32 to NTFS. You cannot (within Windows capabilities at least) revert the file system back to FAT32, although this is possible using a third-party application such as PartitionMagic, and is also discussed in depth in Chapter 25. The real question you must answer when making the decision about which file system to use is this: Will this computer be used to multi-boot another operating system that requires the FAT file system? If your answer is yes then you will need to keep at least the System partition (the partition that holds the system files needed to start the computer) formatted as FAT16 or FAT32, depending on what other operating system you will have installed on the computer. You can format your Boot partition that will hold Windows XP Professional with NTFS if you like, but any data on it will be inaccessible to the other operating systems installed on the computer.

NOTE

File System Misconception

A common misconception that people have about using the NTFS file system is that their files will not be available for access over the network when using a client operating system such as Windows 95 or Windows 98. The only time files on an NTFS volume are inaccessible to a legacy client is when the files reside in a different volume on the same computer in a multi-boot arrangement, and the legacy operating system is running. When files are accessed across the network, File and Printer sharing for Microsoft networks performs the magic in the background that allows FAT16 and FAT32 based operating systems access to files located on an NTFS volume.

It's always preferred to use the NTFS file system as often as possible, except where you must make the Windows XP Professional volume available to other operating systems installed on the same computer. Should you decide against using NTFS, you will miss the following features, just to name a few:

- **NTFS file and folder permissions**—Using NTFS permissions you can control access to every file on an NTFS volume. Thanks to permissions inheritance (a default option), permissions applied at the root of a volume will flow downward to all child objects. You can configure permissions at each level of the directory structure to meet your needs for allowing and/or preventing access to files and folders. However, don't get NTFS permissions confused with share permissions—they are two entirely different items, each requiring consideration both individually and as a pair.

- **The Encrypting File System**—Using a public/private key pair, EFS provides strong cryptographic encryption of files and folders that is extremely resistant to attack and compromise. EFS is completely transparent to the user, and in Windows XP supports multiple user access to an encrypted file. The only down side to using EFS is that its usage is mutually exclusive with NTFS compression.

- **File compression**—The NTFS file system supports encryption on both files and folders. NTFS uses a lossless compression algorithm which ensures that no data is lost when compressing and decompressing data. This is in contrast to lossy compression algorithms (such as those used in graphics and audio/video files), in which some data is lost each time data compression and decompression occur. Lossy compression cannot be used with files that require exact data, such as spreadsheets or document files—losses in compression will render the file corrupt and unusable. As previously mentioned, compression is mutually exclusive with EFS encryption.

- **Disk space quota management**—Using disk quotas enables you to control the amount of data that users can store on your NTFS volumes. Quota control is on a per-volume basis and can be configured with custom quotas for select users as desired. The disk quota system enables you to determine when users are nearing their limits and automatically prevent usage after a user has reached their defined quota limitation.

- **Volume mount points**—You can finally escape the 26 volume limit on a computer by using volume mount points. Think of it as mapping a path to a hard drive or CD-ROM to a folder on an NTFS volume; thus a new hard drive you've installed to hold user data can be mounted as C:\UserDocs or whatever name you choose.

→ To learn more about volume mount points, **see** "Choosing Your File System: NTFS or FAT," **p. 997**.

> **TIP**
>
> **Dealing with the Data Recovery Agent**
>
> On a Windows XP Professional computer that is not participating in a Windows 2000 Active Directory domain, there is no Data Recovery Agent defined. EFS encryption can still be carried out, however, due to the differences in the way the Certificate Services function in Windows 2000 Server and Windows Server 2003.
>
> For more information on using EFS encryption in Windows XP Professional, *see* "The Encrypting File System," *p. xxx,* (Chapter 25) and also the TechNet article "Data Recovery and Data Recovery Agents" at `http://www.microsoft.com/technet/prodtechnol/winxppro/reskit/prnb_efs_1nfx.asp`.

With your file system choice made, you are now ready to move onto the next item of consideration: the decision about what type of installation to perform.

INSTALLATION TYPES

Deciding on the type of installation to perform is the last planning step before installing Windows XP Professional. The type of installation that you perform is dictated by many factors, such as

- Is there an operating system currently installed? If so, do you want to preserve settings and configurations, or start from scratch?
- Will the installation be performed interactively or remotely?
- How many computers are to be installed at a single time?
- Is your network arranged in a domain model using Active Directory?

Once again, there are many questions that lead to a larger question: What type of installation will you be performing? There are three distinct possibilities and each of them is explored in the following sections.

UPGRADE INSTALLATIONS

Windows XP Professional supports direct upgrades from Windows 98, Windows Millennium Edition, Windows NT 4.0 Workstation, Windows 2000 Professional, and Windows XP Home Edition. If you are currently running any other operating system, including Windows NT 3.x Workstation, Windows 95, or Windows 3.x, you will need to perform a clean installation as upgrading is not supported.

NOTE

Although we assume most readers of this book are using Windows XP Professional, you might want to note that you can also upgrade Win98 and Me (but not Win2K Pro or NT4) to XP Home Edition.

An upgrade installation is most useful in cases where you have customized user settings that you want to preserve. This option, however, does not always work flawlessly, especially if you are upgrading from an operating system other than Windows 2000 Professional or Windows XP Home Edition due to the differences in the registry structure and the startup process.

Should you decide to upgrade an existing Windows 98 or Windows Millennium Edition installation to Windows XP Professional (and you allow a backup to made during installation), you will be able to later uninstall Windows XP Professional and effectively revert your computer back to the state it was in immediately preceding the Windows XP Professional upgrade. The ability to uninstall is contingent on the following things, however:

- The volume on which Windows XP Professional is installed cannot be converted from the FAT32 file system to the NTFS file system.
- You cannot create or delete any volumes on the computer.
- You must not delete the backup files that are created during Windows XP Professional installation. Thirty days after installation, you will be prompted to delete these files.

When upgrading from an installation of Windows 2000 Professional or Windows NT 4.0 Workstation, the process will be the easiest. Windows XP Professional shares a common operating system structure and core with these two operating systems, including device driver requirements and registry structures. If you upgrade a Windows NT 4.0 Workstation installation that is installed on an NTFS formatted volume, the file system will be automatically upgraded from NTFS 4.0 to NTFS 5.0 as part of the installation process. If the file system is FAT, you will be presented with the option to upgrade to NTFS during the installation.

UPGRADE ISSUES

When upgrading from older Microsoft operating systems, there are a few *gotchas* to be aware of. The following list details some items of concern when upgrading from Windows 98 or Windows Millennium Edition to Windows XP Professional:

- System tools such as ScanDisk and DriveSpace will not be upgraded in Windows XP Professional. Windows XP Professional brings along its own version of ScanDisk, and NTFS compression replaces legacy compression utilities such as DriveSpace.
- Client software for other network types cannot be upgraded during an upgrade to Windows XP Professional. The only exception to this rule is that if Novell Client32 is installed, the setup routine will detect it and replace it with a newer version of Client32 from the Windows XP Professional Setup CD-ROM.

- Some applications might not run properly under Windows XP Professional due to the fact that the Windows XP Registry is arranged differently than the Windows 98 or Windows Millennium Edition registry. In some cases, *migration packs* can alleviate this problem. A migration pack (or upgrade pack) is simply a set of new application and library files for a specific application that enables it to run in a newer, more advanced, environment then it was originally designed for.

- Some applications might not run properly under Windows XP Professional if they attempt to make calls to APIs that don't exist in Windows XP. In some cases, migration packs can alleviate this problem. In other cases, you will need to remove the application from your computer. The Windows Upgrade Advisor typically identifies these applications for you.

- Some applications might not run properly under Windows XP Professional if they install different files under different operating systems. In this case, you reinstall the application following the upgrade to attempt a fix.

- Applications that directly access hardware or use custom file filters will most likely not run correctly under Windows XP. The most common cases of these types of problems are related to CD-ROM–burning software and anti-virus software. You will need to obtain updated versions of these types of applications for use with Windows XP Professional.

Of course, there are some things to watch out for when upgrading from Windows NT 4.0 Workstation as well:

- File system filters written for Windows NT 4.0 will not work with Windows XP Professional due to the upgrade in NTFS. This is commonly seen in anti-virus software.

- Networking software written for Windows NT 4.0 will not run on Windows XP Professional if it attempts to use the Windows NT 4.0 TCP/IP or IPX/SPX protocol stacks.

- Custom power management solutions written for Windows NT 4.0 are not compatible with Windows XP and are not required due to Windows XP's native support for ACPI (Advanced Power Configuration Interface) and APM (Advanced Power Management).

- Custom Plug-and-Play solutions written for Windows NT 4.0 are not compatible with Windows XP and are not required, as Windows XP provides full Plug and Play support natively.

- Fault-tolerant disk arrangements, such as disk mirrors, are not supported in Windows XP. Windows 2000 Server and Windows Server 2003 support disk mirroring and striping.

Should you have an unsupported upgrade path or decide that you would rather perform a clean installation, but do not want to lose all of your personalized settings, don't despair! You can transfer a large majority of your personalized settings (and even your document files) by using either the Files And Settings Transfer Wizard (FSTW) or the User State

Migration Tool (USMT). Both options will be discussed later in this chapter, in the "Migrating Files and Settings" sections. One last point about upgrade installations before we move onto clean installations: You cannot perform upgrade installations over the network using Remote Installation Services—RIS only supports clean installations.

CLEAN INSTALLATIONS

Clean installations are the easiest to perform and should result in the least amount of work at installation time. A clean installation is required in any of the following situations:

- You have an unsupported upgrade path, such as from Windows 95.
- There is no operating system currently installed on the computer.
- The computer has more than one partition, and you want to configure the computer to support multi-booting.
- You are performing installations across the network using Remote Installation Services.
- You prefer to perform a clean installation—so as to "start over with a clean slate."

When performing a clean installation, there are really no problem areas to watch for in general. The most common problem that people run into is trying to install Windows XP Professional onto a computer in which the CD-ROM is not El Torito–compliant and thus does not support booting from the CD-ROM drive. In this case you will need to acquire the Windows XP Setup Boot Disk creation utility (makebt32.exe) by visiting MSKB# Q310994, at `http://support.microsoft.com/default.aspx?scid=kb;EN-US;q310994`. The makebt32.exe utility will enable you to create a setup of setup boot floppy disks; however you will need to have six disks in Windows XP Professional instead of the four disks you needed for Windows 2000 Professional.

NOTE

> **About the El Torito Specification**
>
> For more information about the El Torito specification, be sure to visit `http://www.netserverworld.com/infocenter/files/eltorito.pdf`.

MULTI-BOOTING WITH OTHER OPERATING SYSTEMS

Your last installation option is to install Windows XP Professional in a multi-boot situation with one or more other operating systems, including other instances of Windows XP. Installing in a multi-boot situation encompasses either an upgrade installation or clean installation as well—the same rules and caveats apply. The chief difference is in the formatting of the System partition—the place where the files required to start up the computer are loaded. If you are planning on multi-booting with an older operating system that does not recognize the NTFS file system, such as Windows 98, you will need to ensure that the System partition is never formatted or converted to the NTFS file system.

The only real trick to successfully installing Windows XP Professional into a multi-boot arrangement is that it must be the last operating system installed. As a rule, you should always install Microsoft operating systems from oldest to newest, so if you had a new computer for example and you wanted to install Windows XP Professional, Windows 2000 Professional, and Windows 98 on it, you would first install Windows 98, then next install Windows 2000 Professional, and lastly install Windows XP Professional. Of course, you must place each operating system instance in its own separate partition and you cannot set up a multi-boot system using dynamic disks, as only one operating system can own a dynamic disk or dynamic disk set. Lastly, do not install Windows XP Professional on a disk that is compressed using a third-party compression utility—it is not supported and the installation will most likely fail.

Of course, there is one big exception to the rule concerning the order in which you must install the operating systems (remember, oldest to newest). If you are using some sort of third-party boot loader, such as BootMagic from Power Quest, its files will create and control the boot menu and operating system selection process. You also gain the capability to install more than one instance of a Windows 9*x* operating system when using a third-party boot loader.

TIP

> **Power Boot**
>
> BootMagic is part of the PartitionMagic application and provides an enhanced boot menu. Read more about PartitionMagic on the Power Quest Web site, located at `http://www.powerquest.com/`.
>
> For information on installing BootMagic onto an NTFS partition, visit the Power Quest Technical Support site at `http://www.powerquest.com/support/primus/id2619.cfm`.

NOTE

> **Multi-booting with Windows 3.*x* or Windows 9*x***
>
> You can only install one instance total of Windows 3.x, Windows 95, Windows 98, or Windows Millennium Edition on a computer without using a third-party boot menu application.

Now that we've examined the options available for installation types, let's switch topics and look at something that Windows XP really improves: the capability to easily transfer files and settings from an old installation to a new one.

NOTE

> If Microsoft has released service packs past the one integrated into your Windows XP installation disc, or if you are using a Windows XP installation disc produced before Service Pack 1 was released, you should install the most recent service pack after completing your initial installation. You can do that before or after using the Settings Transfer Wizard described below.

MIGRATING FILES AND SETTINGS WITH THE FILES AND SETTINGS TRANSFER WIZARD

In the days of old, if you wanted to transfer files and settings from an existing installation of Windows, you had two choices: You could either perform an upgrade installation and take your chances with compatibility issues and other problems, or you could procure a third-party utility to perform this task for you. While both of these options are still available, there are some other options available to you as well. The Files and Settings Transfer Wizard (FSTW) and the User State Migration Tool (USMT) are two migration tools that are provided with Windows XP Professional which can be used to make your operating system migration a more enjoyable experience. In this section we will look at the Files and Settings Transfer Wizard. In the next section we will examine the User State Migration Tool.

The Files and Settings Transfer Wizard (FSTW) is a fantastic new utility that is provided on the Windows XP Professional Setup CD-ROM. This allows you to run the Files and Settings Transfer Wizard on any computer, or create a Files and Settings Transfer Wizard floppy disk if you want and use that instead. The Files and Settings Transfer Wizard can migrate a user's files and settings from any of the following operating systems to Windows XP:

- Windows 95
- Windows 98
- Windows 98 Second Edition
- Windows Millennium Edition
- Windows NT 4.0 Workstation
- Windows 2000 Professional
- Windows XP Home Edition
- Windows XP Professional

WHAT GETS TRANSFERRED?

By design, the Files and Settings Transfer Wizard is built to transfer settings for Microsoft applications, such as Internet Explorer, Outlook, Outlook Express, and the Office suite. The settings that are migrated fall into these four major groups:

- **Appearance**—Items such as wallpaper, colors, sounds, and the location of the taskbar.
- **Action**—Items such as the keyboard key repeat rate, double-click settings, and so on.
- **Internet**—Settings that control how your browser behaves, including home page, favorites or bookmarks, cookies, security settings, proxy settings, and dial-up settings.
- **Mail**—Settings for Outlook or Outlook Express, such as mail servers, accounts, signature file, views, mail rules, contacts and your local mail file.

The Files and Settings Transfer Wizard can migrate the following types of items, plus several others:

- Internet Explorer settings
- Outlook and Outlook Express settings
- Dial-Up connections
- Screen saver settings
- Folder options
- Taskbar settings
- Mouse and keyboard settings
- Network drives and printers
- Desktop, My Documents, My Pictures, Favorites, and Cookies folder

Files can be selected for movement by type, such as .DOC or .XLS; by folder; or specifically by name. The Files and Settings Transfer Wizard automatically moves many of the most common file types for you during the process; however, you can add or remove folders, file types, or specific files from the transfer should you want to.

The Files and Settings Transfer Wizard can also transfer settings for selected third-party applications, as listed in Table 2.3. Files and Settings Transfer Wizard only transfers the user's settings; it will not transfer or install the applications themselves. In order for these settings to be successfully transferred, the applications must be installed on the target computer *before* the settings are migrated to it using the Files and Settings Transfer Wizard.

TABLE 2.3   APPLICATIONS SUPPORTED BY THE FILES AND SETTINGS TRANSFER WIZARD

Application	Minimum Version Supported
Adobe Acrobat Reader 4	4
Adobe Acrobat Reader 5	5
AOL Instant Messenger (AIM)	4.3.2
Command Prompt	5.1
CuteFTP	4.2.2
Eudora Pro	5.1
FrontPage	4.02
GetRight	4.3
GoZilla	3.92
ICQ 2000b	4.60 b #3278

continues

TABLE 2.3   CONTINUED

Application	Minimum Version Supported
Lotus Smart Suite	9.6
Money 2001	9
MSN Explorer	1
MSN Messenger	3.5
MusicMatch Jukebox	6.00.0270
NetMeeting	3.01 SP2
Odigo	3
Photoshop 6.0	6.01
Prodigy Internet	5
Publisher	2000
Quicken 2001 Suite	1
Quicken Home and Business 2001	2001
QuickTime	4.1.2
Real Jukebox 2 Basic	1.0.2.340
Real Player 8 Basic	6.0.9.450
Roger Wilco	Mk1c Mod1
Sidewinder Game Voice	1.1
Sonique	1.9
Winamp v2.73	2.73
Windows Media Player	8
Windows Movie Maker	1.1
WinZip	8
Word Perfect Office	Office 2002
Works 2001	6
WS_FTP LE	6.6
Yahoo! Messenger	3.5
Zone	None

BEFORE STARTING THE TRANSFER

Before you go to start the transfer process using the Files and Settings Transfer Wizard, you should pay particular attention to the following list of potential trouble spots...it makes for a happier day!

- Before attempting to transfer files to the target computer, ensure that the appropriate user account has been created and configured with the required NTFS permissions to allow access to the location where the transfer image will be located. If the transfer image is to be located on a network share, ensure that the share permissions are also correctly configured to support access.

- Before attempting to transfer files to the target computer, ensure that any special or specific folder paths that exist in the user's profile on the old computer are created on the new computer. This will help to alleviate problems with orphaned folders and files during the transfer process. Make sure that these folders have the required NTFS and share permissions applied to them as well.

- When performing the transfer process, ensure that you are logged as the user whose files and settings you are transferring. While a minor annoyance on the source computer, this can be a great catastrophe on the target computer if you are logged in under the wrong user account.

- Ensure that the location where the transfer image file will be located has enough available space to support the operation. You will need between 50 to 600 MB per user that you migrate using the Files and Settings Transfer Wizard. Table 2.4 gives some recommended guidelines for space availability.

- After the transfer process is complete, you will have to manually delete the transfer image file and folders.

N O T E

> **Space Race**
>
> The estimates given in Table 2.4 are fairly realistic. I used more than 700MB to transfer my primary user profile and about 6MB to transfer a new (and unused) user profile. Plan ahead and ensure you have plenty of empty disk space before starting to use the Files and Settings Transfer Wizard!

TABLE 2.4   ESTIMATED SPACE REQUIREMENTS WHEN USING THE FILES AND SETTINGS TRANSFER WIZARD

Type of User	Space Required
Desktop user storing email on server	50–75MB
Desktop user with local email storage	150–400MB
Laptop user	150–300MB

The best practice is to pad these values somewhat as well, just for safety, by adding 25%–50% to them depending on the average user type in your organization.

RUNNING THE FILES AND SETTINGS TRANSFER WIZARD

The process to use the Files and Settings Transfer Wizard is broken down into two separate phases, as you might expect. You will need to first gather the files and settings from the source computer and then apply them to the target computer.

TIP

> **Musical Windows**
>
> It is possible to use the Files and Settings Transfer Wizard to transfer a user's files and settings from a Windows XP computer and then apply these settings back to the same computer, either following a new installation of Windows XP or into a new user account.

COLLECTING FILES AND SETTINGS FROM THE SOURCE COMPUTER

To transfer files and settings from the source computer, follow this procedure:

1. Log in to the source computer using the user account that you want to transfer files and settings from. If this computer is not a Windows XP computer, insert the Windows XP Professional Setup CD-ROM and proceed to step 2. If this computer is a Windows XP computer, you can launch the Files and Settings Transfer Wizard by clicking Start, Programs, Accessories, System Tools, Files and Settings Transfer Wizard; jump to step 4 of this procedure.

2. If this computer is not a Windows XP Professional machine, click Perform Additional Tasks on the Welcome To Microsoft Windows XP screen.

3. From the screen shown in Figure 2.8, select Transfer Files and Settings. Alternatively, you can navigate to the Support\Tools folder on the Windows XP Professional Setup CD-ROM and double-click the FASTWIZ.EXE file.

Figure 2.8
Starting the FSTW from the Windows XP Professional Setup CD-ROM.

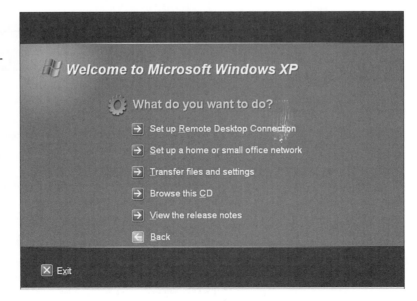

4. After making your selection, the Files and Settings Transfer Wizard will open, as shown in Figure 2.9.

Figure 2.9
The Files and Settings Transfer Wizard introductory screen.

5. Click Next to dismiss the opening screen of the Files and Settings Transfer Wizard.

6. If prompted, select Old Computer and click Next.

7. On the Select the Transfer Method page, shown in Figure 2.10, configure the transfer method you want to use, and click Next to continue. In most cases, you will want to use a network location for your transfer image, as the size can quickly grow past the capability of most removable storage media. Should you desire to use the direct cable connection, you will need to connect a null modem serial cable between the old computer (source) and the new computer (target) and follow through the prompts given in the wizard.

Figure 2.10
Selecting a location to place the transfer image.

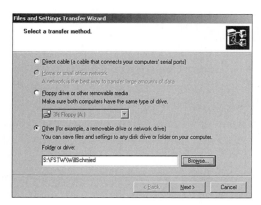

8. On the What Do You Want to Transfer? page, shown in Figure 2.11, select to transfer Settings Only, Files Only, or Both Files and Settings. If you want to configure additional transfer settings, place a check in the Let Me Select a Custom List of Files and Settings when I Click Next check box. Click Next to continue. If you are not custom-configuring your transfer settings, skip to step 10 of this procedure.

Figure 2.11
Selecting the transferred items: files, settings, or both.

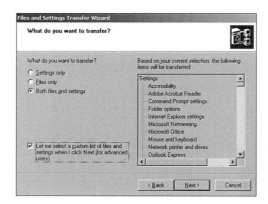

9. If you are custom-configuring your transfer settings, you can use the buttons shown in Figure 2.12 to modify the transfer settings. After you have customized the transfer settings, click Next to continue.

Figure 2.12
Customizing the transfer process ensures you get exactly what you want.

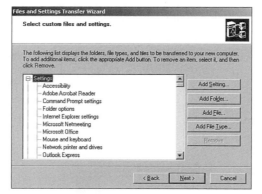

10. The Install programs on your new computer will show you a listing of what the Files and Settings Transfer Wizard thinks you need to install on the target computer before applying the transfer image. Click Next to continue.

11. The Files and Settings Transfer Wizard will now collect data and write it to the transfer image file. While this occurs, you can monitor the progress on the Collection in progress page.

12. After the Files and Settings Transfer Wizard has completed, a summary page will appear telling you to now move to the new computer and apply the transfer image. Click Finish to close the Files and Settings Transfer Wizard.

APPLYING FILES AND SETTINGS TO THE TARGET COMPUTER

After you have successfully completed the installation of Windows XP Professional onto your new computer, you can then apply the transfer image to regain your files and settings. However, before you jump back into the Files and Settings Transfer Wizard, you *must* install all of your applications that you transferred settings for—FSTW only transfers files and settings, not applications. If you transfer your settings and then install the application, you stand a good chance of having your settings overwritten during the install process.

→ To learn more about installing Windows XP Professional, **see** Chapter 3, "Installation."

To apply your files and settings to the target computer, follow this procedure:

1. Log in to the target computer using the user account that you want to restore the files and settings for.

2. If you've placed your transfer image on a network drive, map the network drive to the local computer and ensure that the user account has the required NTFS and share permissions.

3. Launch the Files and Settings Transfer Wizard either from the Start Menu or from the Windows XP Professional Setup CD-ROM.

4. The Files and Transfer Settings Wizard opening page will be displayed, as shown previously in Figure 2.9. Click Next to continue.

5. On the Which Computer Is This? page, shown in Figure 2.13, select New computer and click Next to continue.

Figure 2.13
Selecting the computer: This time around we are working with the New computer.

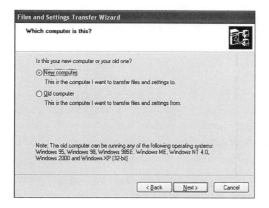

6. Since we have already collected our transfer files and settings, select I Don't Need the Wizard Disk on the Do You Have a Windows XP CD? page, shown in Figure 2.14. Click Next to continue.

7. On the Where Are the Files and Settings? page, shown in Figure 2.15, select the location where you placed your transfer image in the previous procedure. Click Next to continue.

7. The Files and Settings Transfer Wizard will now transfer and apply the files and settings to the target computer. You can monitor the progress on the Transfer in Progress page.

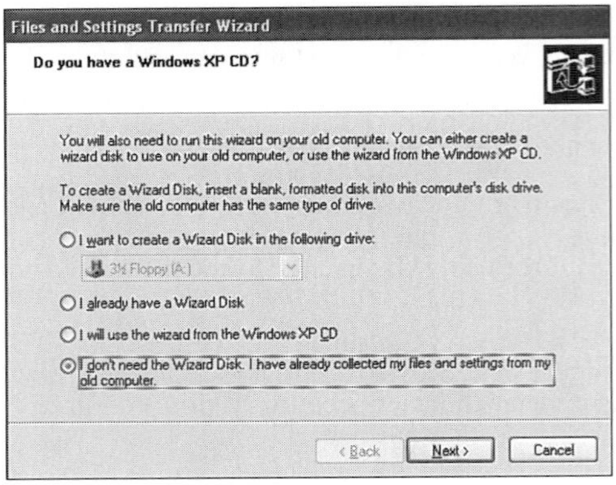

Figure 2.14
Telling the Files and Settings Transfer Wizard how to do its job!

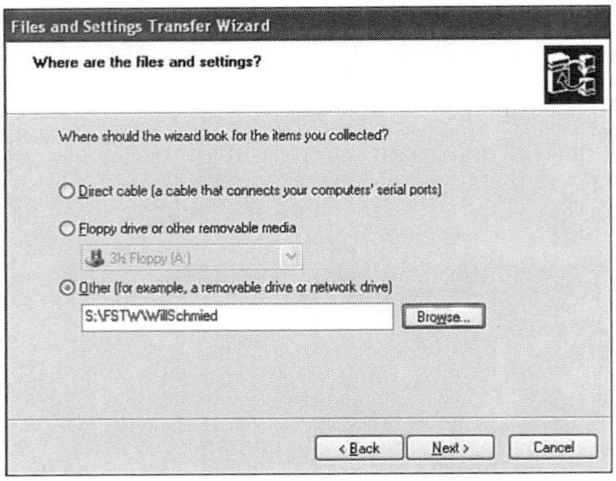

Figure 2.15
Locating the Files and Settings Transfer Wizard image.

8. After the Files and Settings Transfer Wizard has completed, a summary page will inform you of any errors or orphaned files that have been created during the process. Click Finish to close the Files and Settings Transfer Wizard.

9. You will receive the following message: `You need to log off for the changes to take effect. Do you want to log off now?` Select Yes and log back on to the account to see the transferred files and settings have taken effect.

If you have only one user or a small number of users to migrate settings for, the Files and Settings Transfer Wizard is the best way to go. Should you, however, need to migrate settings for a large number of users, or need extremely granular control over what gets transferred, then the User State Migration Tool is for you.

MIGRATING FILES AND SETTINGS WITH THE USER STATE MIGRATION TOOL

If the Files and Settings Transfer Wizard is like a shiny new Porsche 911 sitting in your driveway, the User State Migration Wizard (USMT) would be a HUMMV. The Files and Settings Transfer Wizard is sleek, easy to get along with, and can be used by end-users. The

User State Migration Tool is powerful, complex, and intended for administrators and advanced support personnel. The same thing that makes the User State Migration Tool so powerful is what makes it so complicated to most people: its arcane command-line interface that relies on .INF files to control the migration process.

The User State Migration Tool can be found on the Windows XP Professional Setup CD-ROM in the \VALUEACC\MSFT\USMT folder. The User State Migration Tool comes with predefined .INF files that you can use to perform a default migration; however the whole point of the USMT is to have granular control over what gets migrated and how the migration is applied to the target computer, so you may well want to modify the files to suit your needs.

The User State Migration Tool consists of two executable files, four migration rule .INF files, and various .DLL files. Table 2.5 explains the primary files and their purposes in some detail.

TABLE 2.5 THE CORE USMT FILES EXPLAINED

File	Description
ScanState.exe	Collects user data and settings based on the information contained in Migapp.inf, Migsys.inf, Miguser.inf, and Sysfiles.inf.
LoadState.exe	Applies the collected user state data on a computer that has a clean installation of Windows XP Professional.
Migapp.inf	Used to collect application settings; can be modified to customize a migration.
Migsys.inf	Used to collect system settings, such as fonts, accessibility settings, and Internet Explorer settings, among others; can be modified to customize a migration.
Miguser.inf	Used to collect personal settings and files from the My Pictures, My Documents, and other user specific folders; can be modified to customize a migration.
Sysfiles.inf	Used to specify files specific to each version of Windows that USMT can migrate settings from; not normally modified unless the version of Windows that you are migrating settings from is not supported.

NOTE

> **USMT and Upgrade Installations**
>
> The User State Migration Tool does not support the application of collected settings to computers that have been upgraded from a previous operating system. Install Windows XP Professional in a clean installation before attempting to use the USMT.

WHAT USMT TRANSFERS

As mentioned previously, the User State Migration Tool's .INF files are highly customizable and can be modified to fit your particular migration needs and requirements. Using the default .INF files will result in the USMT migrating the following items, plus many others:

- Internet Explorer settings
- Outlook and Outlook Express settings
- Dial-Up connections
- Screen saver settings
- Folder options
- Taskbar settings
- Mouse and keyboard settings
- Network drives and printers
- Desktop, My Documents, My Pictures, Favorites, and Cookies folder
- Common Office file types

TIP

Customizing the .INF Files

For information on customizing the .INF files that control the migration process in the USMT, see "User State Migration in Windows XP: Modifying the Migration Rule INF File," located at `http://www.microsoft.com/technet/prodtechnol/winxppro/deploy/usermigr.asp`.

USING THE USMT TO MIGRATE SETTINGS

As mentioned previously, the User State Migration Tool consists of two executable files, four migration .INF files, and several supporting .DLL files. The migration process takes place in just four major steps, just the same as when using the Files and Settings Transfer Wizard. Additionally, the information provided for the Files and Settings Transfer Wizard in the "Before Starting the Transfer" section of this chapter apply to using the USMT as well.

With no modification of the migration .INF files, the process to use the User State Migration Tool is summarized here.

1. On the source computer, logged on as the user in question, run the ScanState file to copy the settings to an intermediate storage location. This can be done via script, shortcut, or manually.

2. Prepare the target computer with a clean installation of Windows XP Professional. There are no restrictions on performing Remote Installations or other automated deployment methods.

3. On the target computer, logged on as the *local* administrator, run the LoadState file to apply the user's settings. This, again, can be done using a script, a shortcut or a scheduled task using the local administrator's credentials.

4. The user logs on to their account and the process is completed.

The ScanState file has the following syntax, which is explained in Table 2.6.

```
scanstate [/c /i input.inf]* [/l scanstate.log]
 [/v verbosity_level] [/f] [/u] [/x] migration_path
```

TABLE 2.6   SCANSTATE SWITCHES

Switch	Description
/c	Instructs ScanState not to stop on filename_too_long errors. These errors will be logged in the Longfile.log log file for later analysis.
/f	A troubleshooting switch that specifies that files will be migrated; not normally used.
/i	Specifies the .INF file (or multiple .INF files) that is to be used with ScanState to define the settings that are to be collected for transfer.
/l	Specifies the file to log errors that may occur during the collection process.
/u	A troubleshooting switch that specifies that user settings will be migrated; not normally used.
/v	Enables verbose output. Use the format: /v #, substituting 1 (least verbose) to 7 (most verbose) for the # symbol.
/x	A troubleshooting switch that specifies that no files or settings will be migrated; not normally used.
migration_path	Specifies the path to the location where files should be written to. You must have the appropriate NTFS and share permissions to this location.

The LoadState file has the following syntax, which is explained in Table 2.7.

```
loadstate [/i input.inf]* [/l loadstate.log] [/v #]
 [/f] [/u] [/x] migration_path
```

TABLE 2.7   LOADSTATE SWITCHES

Switch	Description
/i	Specifies the .INF file (or multiple .INF files) that are to be used with LoadState to define the settings that are to be migrated.
/f	Specifies that files will be migrated. This is a switch for troubleshooting only.
/l	Specifies the file to log errors that may occur during the collection process.
/u	A troubleshooting switch that specifies that user settings will be migrated; not normally used.

continues

TABLE 2.7   LOADSTATE SWITCHES

Switch	Description
/v	Enables verbose output. Use the format: /v #, substituting 1 (least verbose) to 7 (most verbose) for the # symbol.
/x	A troubleshooting switch that specifies that no files are settings will be migrated; not normally used.
migration_path	Specifies the path to the location where files should be read from. You must have the appropriate NTFS and share permissions to this location, as appropriate.

TIP

> Change and Configuration Management
>
> See the "Change and Configuration Management Deployment Guide: User State Migration", at http://www.microsoft.com/windows2000/techinfo/reskit/deploy/CCM/ for more information on migration user's settings.

SUMMARY

If we've done all of our homework, we should be ready to deploy Windows XP Professional in the most common scenarios at this point. A quick check of my installation notes page reveals that we've visited all of the major areas that need to be addressed before starting the installation process.

If your installation is a normal one (by normal, I mean not utilizing exotic procedures such as Remote Installation or disk imaging), you should be ready to move on to the installation phase as discussed in Chapter 3. If you are planning on using Remote Installation or disk imaging, you will find a wealth of information in Chapter 5.

CHAPTER

3

INSTALLATION

In this chapter

BACKGROUND

After you've completed the work detailed in Chapter 2, "Installation Prep," you are finally ready to get down to the business of actually installing Windows XP Professional. With Windows XP, Microsoft has made the installation process fairly simple and foolproof, but it will be a bit of a difference to those who have never installed Windows NT or Windows 2000 before. As discussed in Chapter 1, "Introduction to Windows XP," Windows XP Professional acts like Windows 2000 on the inside, as it is built on the ever-stable Windows 2000 code-base, but it's friendlier and easier to get along with on the outside. With the exception of the activation process (which some folks find invasive or at best annoying) the installation procedure and related options benefit from Microsoft's friendly XP approach.

In this chapter, we'll be looking at four major areas concerning installation:

■ **Installing Windows XP Professional**—Possible installation scenarios include clean installations and upgrade installations. Multi-booting Windows XP Professional is discussed extensively in Chapter 4.

■ **Uninstalling Windows XP Professional**—A great feature previously unheard of in Windows—but it has limitations. We will look at uninstalling Windows XP Professional in depth.

■ **Understanding Microsoft Product Activation**—A not too welcome addition to the Windows world, Product Activation has caused quite a stir. We will be taking an in-depth look into Product Activation, including how it works, what it does, and how it affects you.

■ **Setup switches**—Powerful ways exist in which to modify and customize the behavior of the Windows XP Professional Setup routine. By using various switches and combinations of switches with the setup commands, winnt32.exe and winnt.exe, you truly can have it your way.

■ **Automated System Recovery**—Although not properly part of installing and setting up a Windows XP Professional installation, ASR is a valuable and important part of Windows XP that should not be overlooked—the sooner you understand it the sooner you can make it work for you.

→ To learn more about installing Windows XP Professional by using unattended installation methods, **see p. 171**.

PERFORMING A CLEAN INSTALLATION

The process to perform a clean installation of Windows XP Professional is easy to carry out and will require 30–90 minutes of time, depending on your particular hardware. The Setup process consists of several steps which fall into two phases: the text-mode phase and the GUI-mode phase.

To perform a clean installation of Windows XP Professional, follow the process outlined here.

NOTE

For more information on customizing an installation using Setup switches, see the section "Using Installation Switches," later in this chapter.

1. Power on your computer and insert the Windows XP Professional Setup CD-ROM into the CD drive. If your computer is not capable of booting from the CD drive, you will need to create and use the Windows XP Professional Setup floppy disks.

NOTE

Making and Using Setup Floppy Disks

If you have a computer that does not support booting from the CD-ROM (that is, it does not support the El Torito specifications), then you will need to create and use a set of Windows XP Professional Setup floppy disks.

To download the executable to create the disks, see MSKB# Q310994 located at `http://support.microsoft.com/default.aspx?scid=kb;EN-US;q310994`.

For more information on the El Torito specification, see `http://www.netserverworld.com/infocenter/files/eltorito.pdf`.

3

2. When prompted onscreen, press any key (or the specific key required) to boot the computer from the CD-ROM.

3. After Setup briefly examines your computer's hardware, you will be prompted to press F6 if you have any third-party drivers that require loading, such as RAID device drivers.

4. At the next screen, you will be prompted to press F2 if you are performing an Automated System Recovery (ASR). Just sit on your hands and let Setup do its thing here.

5. For the next few minutes, Setup will load the files required to perform the installation. If you have an older, slower computer, this is a good time to grab a cup of coffee!

6. When you are presented with the Welcome to Setup screen as shown in Figure 3.1, press Enter to continue on with the setup process.

7. Before you can install Windows XP Professional, you must accept the End-User License Agreement. Press F8 to accept the EULA and continue forward with the installation process.

8. From the screen shown in Figure 3.2, you can create and delete partitions on your hard drives. Additionally, you will need to select the partition that you will install Windows XP Professional on. After selecting the partition to install Windows XP Professional on, press Enter to continue on.

Figure 3.1
Welcome to Setup.

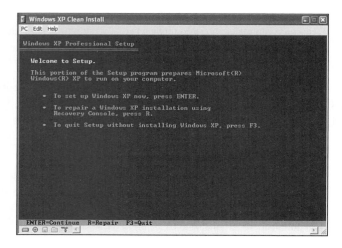

Figure 3.2
Selecting the installation partition.

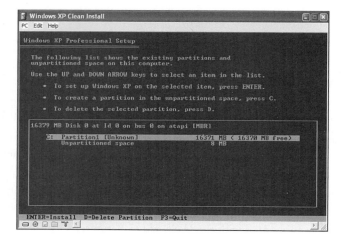

9. On the screen shown in Figure 3.3, you will need to select what file system to format the selected partition with. If you are installing on a partition that was previously formatted with FAT16 or FAT32, options to convert the file system will also be present. In most clean installations, the NTFS file system is preferable, so consider using it. After making your file system selection, press Enter to continue on.

> **NOTE**
>
> **MBR Versus GPT**
>
> MBR (Master Boot Record) and GPT (Globally Unique Identifier Partition Table) refer to types of hard disk arrangement. The MBR method is the old standby…it's been around since the days of old. The GPT method is new to Windows with the 64-bit edition of Windows XP Professional. Chapter 25, "Managing Your Hard Disks," discusses GPT disks at length, as does the TechNet article located at `http://www.microsoft.com/technet/ prodtechnol/winxppro/reskit/prkb_cnc_ywwc.asp`.

Figure 3.3
Selecting a file system.

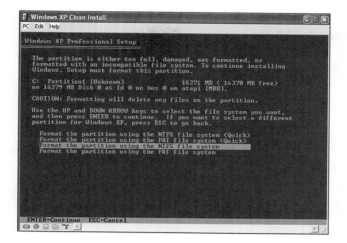

10. After the formatting process is complete (see Figure 3.4), Setup will examine your hard drives and then progress to copying the required installation files.

Figure 3.4
Formatting the partition.

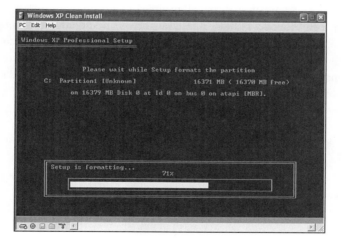

11. After the files have been copied from the installation source to their correct locations on the hard drive, the installation must be initialized.

12. After initialization has completed, the computer will prompt you for a restart. This is the last step of the text-mode phase. If you are prompted to "hit any key" to boot from your CD-ROM on the subsequent startup, *do not* do so; your installation will continue from the hard drive.

13. After the computer restarts, you will be presented with the GUI phase of Setup, as shown in Figure 3.5. Your screen may flash or go blank several times during the GUI phase—this is normal.

Figure 3.5
The GUI phase of
Setup begins.

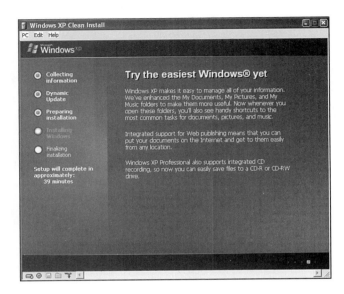

14. After some time (and after the small progress bar at the bottom-left side of the screen moves to 100%), you will be presented with your first configuration opportunity: the Regional and Language Options page. In most cases, you will want to simply click Next to accept the default values. Should you need to perform a custom configuration, you can change many settings, such as numbers, dates, and currencies, as shown in Figure 3.6, or Text Input Languages and keyboard layouts. When you have finished with your selections, click Next to continue.

Figure 3.6
Configuring standards
and formats.

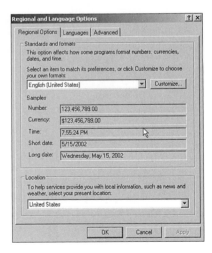

15. From the Personalize Your Software page, you can enter your name and organization. At a minimum, you must enter a name. You cannot use the name "Guest" or "Administrator." You do not have to enter an organization. After entering your information, click Next to continue on.

16. From the Your Product Key page, enter your 25-digit CD key. Click Next to continue on after entering your CD key.

17. From the Computer Name and Administrator Password page, shown in Figure 3.7, you will need to enter a unique computer name (that is, no other device on the network should have the same name) and the Administrator password. After entering this information, click Next to move ahead.

Figure 3.7
Configuring the computer name and administrative password.

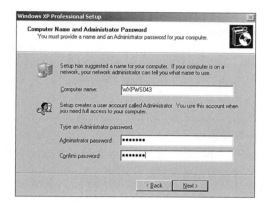

18. From the Date and Time Settings page, configure the appropriate date, time, and time zone settings. If you are in a Daylight Savings area, be sure to place a check in the Automatically Adjust Clock for Daylight Savings Changes box. Click Next to continue.

19. After Windows XP Professional Setup performs some more work, you will be presented with the Network Settings page, as shown in Figure 3.8. If this computer is participating in a domain-based network with DNS servers, DHCP servers, and/or WINS servers, you will want to select the Custom Settings radio button. If you are setting up this computer to participate in a workgroup or as a standalone computer, you can pretty much rest safely with the default selection of Typical settings. Either way, click Next to move on.

Figure 3.8
Configuring the network settings.

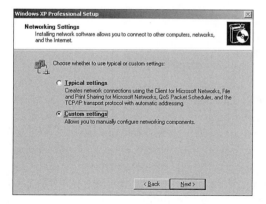

20. If you selected the Custom Settings option in Step 19, you will be presented with the Networking Components page. From here you can install, uninstall, and configure protocols, services, and clients. Since most configuration centers around the TCP/IP protocol, we will look at that. Selecting Internet Protocol (TCP/IP) and clicking Configure will open the Internet Protocol (TCP/IP) Properties page shown in Figure 3.9. Clicking the Advanced button opens the Advanced TCP/IP Settings page, shown in Figure 3.10, which lets you specify many TCP/IP related settings, including DNS servers, DNS suffixes, WINS servers, NetBIOS over TCP/IP, and TCP/IP filtering among other settings. After you've made your advanced configuration, click OK to close the Advanced TCP/IP Settings page. Click OK to close the Internet Protocol (TCP/IP) Properties page and then click Next after making all configuration entries. (You can change network properties at any time after installation completes, should you need to, so you needn't worry about it now.)

NOTE

Alternate Configuration

New in Windows XP Professional, the Alternate Configuration tab of the Internet Protocol (TCP/IP) Properties page enables you to configure an alternate (secondary) TCP/IP setup for those times when a DHCP server is not found. This is a great benefit to portable computer users who would like their portable computer to default to a second set of preconfigured TCP/IP settings when not connected to the corporate network.

Figure 3.9
The Internet Protocol (TCP/IP) Properties page.

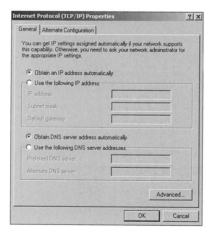

21. From the Workgroup or Domain page (see Figure 3.11), you will need to supply either the workgroup name or domain name you will be placing this computer into. If you are installing a standalone computer, you can pick any name you want for the workgroup. If you are installing a computer in a workgroup, ensure you enter the correct workgroup name. Either way, you will want to select the No option. If you want to join the computer to a domain at this time, you will need to supply the user name and password of a user who has privileges to add computers to the domain. You can also add the computer to a domain after installation is complete (which is what we will do later). Whatever your selection is, click Next to continue on.

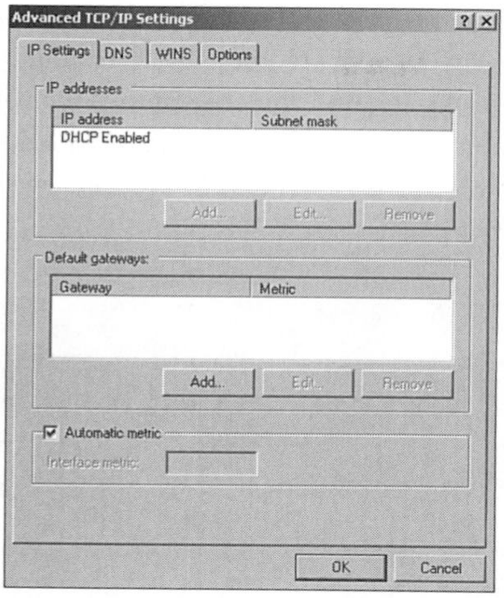

Figure 3.10
The Advanced TCP/IP
Settings page.

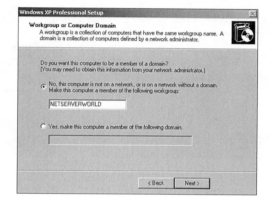

Figure 3.11
The Workgroup or
Domain page.

3

22. Windows Setup performs more configuring and file copying at this point, including installing the Start menu, registering components, saving settings, and lastly, removing temporary files. After Setup completes this phase, the computer restarts once again.

23. After the restart, the Windows XP Professional splash screen appears while Setup completes the installation process.

24. On the Welcome to Microsoft Windows page, click Next to get down to the last stages of Setup.

25. After Windows quickly checks your Internet connectivity status, it progresses to the Will This Computer Connect to the Internet Directly or Through a Network page. If you are using a modem for a dial-up Internet connection, you will most likely want to select the No, This Computer Will Connect Directly to the Internet option. If you are part of a network, then you should select the Yes, This Computer Will Connect Through a Local Area Network or Home Network option. Click Next after making your selection to continue on. (Here, we will select the Yes option.)

26. From the Ready to Activate Windows? page, seen in Figure 3.12, you will need to decide whether or not you are going to activate your installation at this time via the Internet. This is the easiest option by far, and thus the option we will use here. For more information on Product Activation, see the "Product Activation" section, later in this chapter. After making your selection, click Next to continue on. If you will not be activating at this time, skip to Step 28.

Figure 3.12
Preparing to activate Windows XP.

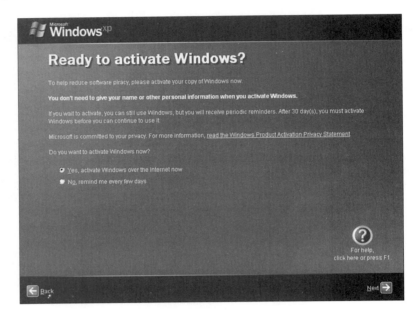

27. From the Ready to register with Microsoft page, select either to register or not register your Windows XP Professional software. You do not have to register your software to perform Product Activation. After making your selection, click Next to continue on.

28. After activation completes, you will be presented with the Who Will Use This Computer? page. Enter at least one user account, as shown in Figure 3.13, and click Next to continue on.

29. When all is said and done you will receive a Thank You! page informing you of what has been accomplished, such as installing Windows XP Professional, activating it, and so on. You've just completed the installation of Windows XP Professional! Click Finish to complete the process.

30. After a few moments of disk activity, the first user you configured in Step 28 will be logged in to the computer. At this time, you *need* to configure a strong password for this user account since the password box is empty. Do this before doing anything else. The password can most easily be changed by using the User Accounts applet located in the Control Panel. To change the password from the User Accounts applet, simply select the user and choose Create a Password.

Figure 3.13
Configuring a user account.

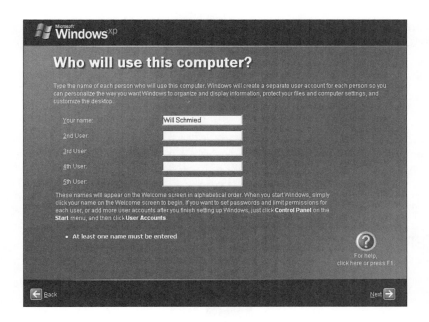

31. At this point, you are done. You can go on to add the computer to a domain, as detailed in Step 32, or stop here...the choice is up to you.

32. From the System applet in the Control Panel, switch to the Computer Name tab. Click the Change button to bring up the Computer Name Changes page, as shown in Figure 3.14. From here you can change the computer name and workgroup or domain membership. Enter the domain name information and click OK. You will need to supply the username and password for an account that is authorized to add computers to the domain. The username should be in the user@domain.com format. After you have joined the domain, a restart will be required to complete the process.

Figure 3.14
Joining a domain.

PERFORMING AN UPGRADE INSTALLATION

Upgrading an existing Windows installation to Windows XP Professional is a fairly straightforward and simple task. Windows XP Professional supports upgrades from the following operating systems; this is the first step of the upgrade process: determine upgrade capability.

- Windows 98
- Windows 98 Second Edition
- Windows Millennium Edition
- Windows NT 4.0 Workstation
- Windows 2000 Professional
- Windows XP Home Edition

There are no supported upgrade paths for the following list of operating systems. Installations performed from these operating systems will require a clean installation, as detailed previously in the "Performing a Clean Installation" section of this chapter.

- Windows 3.x
- Windows 95
- Windows NT 3.51 Workstation
- Windows NT 3.51 Server
- Windows 2000 Trial Edition
- BackOffice Small Business Server

If you have an upgrade path available to you, the second step you must complete is preparing for the upgrade. Installation preparation was covered extensively in Chapter 2. If you skipped over it, now would be a good time to go back and make sure you're ready for the upgrade!

Once you are sure you are ready to upgrade, the process is very similar to that of performing a clean installation; the chief difference being that there is no text-mode phase of Setup.

The process to perform an upgrade installation is outlined here (in this case from an installation of Windows Millennium Edition operating in a workgroup arrangement).

NOTE

For more information on customizing an installation using Setup switches, see the section "Using Installation Switches," later in this chapter.

1. Insert your Windows XP Professional Setup CD-ROM into your computer. If it does not auto-start, you can start the Setup program by double-clicking the SETUP.EXE file located in the root directory, or by typing x:\I386\winnt32.exe, where x is the location of your Windows XP Professional Setup CD-ROM.

2. From the What Do You Want to Do? screen, you should click the Install Windows XP icon to continue on. If you need to verify whether your system is ready to support Windows XP Professional, you can use the Windows Upgrade Advisor by clicking on Check system compatibility. The Windows Upgrade Advisor was discussed in Chapter 2.

3. When prompted to choose what type of installation you are performing, as shown in Figure 3.15, choose Upgrade (Recommended) and click Next to continue on.

Figure 3.15
Choosing the installation type.

4. On the License Agreement page, click to accept the End-User License Agreement and click Next to continue on. If you do not accept the EULA, Setup will not continue.

5. On the Your Product Key page, enter your 25-digit CD key and click Next to continue on.

6. On the Upgrade Report page, as seen in Figure 3.16, you have the option to view a limited compatibility report, a full compatibility report, or no compatibility report at all. Make your selection and click Next to continue on. In this example, we are going to get a full compatibility report.

Figure 3.16
Choosing the compatibility report.

7. From the Get Updated Setup Files page, shown in Figure 3.17, you will need to make a choice as to whether or not you want Setup to contact the Windows Update Web site and download files that are newer than those on your CD-ROM. In most cases, it's best to let Dynamic Update run unless you don't have an active Internet connection. If you do not let Dynamic Update occur, you can go back later and update your installation manually from the Windows Update Web site. Make your selection and click Next to continue on.

Figure 3.17
Choosing to Dynamic Update or not to Dynamic Update.

NOTE

Defining Dynamic Update

As we all know, Microsoft regularly updates its products for various reasons, ranging from security fixes to compatibility improvements. These updates are made available from the Windows Update Web site. Dynamic Update queries the Windows Update Web site during setup and downloads new and updated files as required.

8. Setup will work away for a while, downloading files if you selected Dynamic Update and performing various other tasks such as analyzing your computer and copying the installation files.

9. After Setup has finished copying the installation files it needs, it will prompt you for a restart.

10. Figure 3.18 shows the first noticeable change due to our Windows XP Professional upgrade: the Windows XP Professional boot menu. To continue with the installation, press Enter or let the timer time out to force the default selection of Microsoft Windows XP Professional Setup.

Figure 3.18
A new boot menu appears.

11. After your computer has restarted, Windows XP Professional Setup continues. You can expect to spend between 15–30 minutes at this step while Setup prepares the installation.

12. The next phase of the installation involves Setup actually performing the installation.

13. After a while, you will see your progress bar move all the way to the right during the Finalizing Installation phase of Setup. You're home free now.

14. After a restart, things are starting to look a lot more like home. The familiar Windows XP Professional splash screen is finally seen.

15. After Setup completes a few remaining tasks, Windows XP finally comes to life. The Welcome to Microsoft Windows screen appears, prompting you to complete the installation. Click Next to continue on.

16. From the Ready to Activate Windows? page, seen in Figure 3.19, you will need to decide whether or not you are going to activate your installation at this time via the Internet. This is the easiest option by far, and thus the option we will use here. For more information on Product Activation, see the "Product Activation" section later in this chapter. After making your selection, click Next to continue on.

Figure 3.19
Preparing to activate Windows XP.

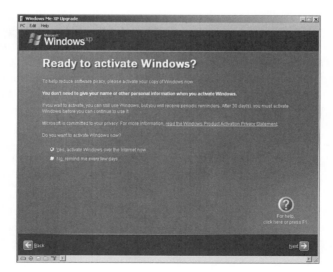

17. From the Ready to Register with Microsoft page, select either to register or not register your Windows XP Professional software. You do not have to register your software to perform Product Activation. After making your selection, click Next to continue on.

18. After activation completes, you will be presented with the Who Will Use This Computer? page. Enter at least one user account and click Next to continue on.

19. When all is said and done you will receive a Thank You! page informing you of what has been accomplished, such as installing Windows XP Profession, activating it, and so on. You've just completed the installation of Windows XP Professional! Click Finish to complete the process.

20. After a few moments of disk activity, you will be prompted to set a password for all users created on the computer, as seen in Figure 3.20. This will be Administrator and any additional users you configured in Step 18. After entering your password twice, click OK to continue on.

Figure 3.20
Setting an initial password.

21. You will (finally) come to the login screen shown in Figure 3.21 if the computer is not part of a domain. If your computer is part of a domain, you will see the standard login dialog box as shown in Figure 3.22. Note that you cannot access the local built-in Administrator account unless you use the standard login box. To bring up the standard login dialog box, simply press the Ctrl+Alt+Del key combination twice.

22. The last step you must perform is to change the user passwords for any users you have created on your computer. The password configured in Step 20 is for all users—not a very secure configuration. User account maintenance can be performed from the User Accounts applet in the Control Panel, shown in Figure 3.23. To change a user's password, click the user from those listed in the User Accounts applet and then click Change the password, which opens the page shown in Figure 3.24. Enter the new password (and hint if desired) and click Change Password to confirm.

Figure 3.21
The "new" Windows XP login screen.

Figure 3.22
The old standby login dialog box.

Figure 3.23
The User Accounts applet.

23. If you have a domain that you would like to join a workgroup computer to, you can do so from the System applet of the Control Panel. Switch to the Computer Name tab and click the Change button to bring up the Computer Name Changes page, shown in Figure 3.25. Enter the domain name information and click OK. You will need to supply the username and password for an account that is authorized to add computers to the

domain, as shown in Figure 3.26. The username should be in the `user@domain.com` `format`. After you have joined the domain, a restart will be required to complete the process.

Figure 3.24
Changing the password for Will Schmied's user account.

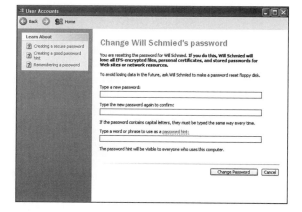

Figure 3.25
Joining a domain.

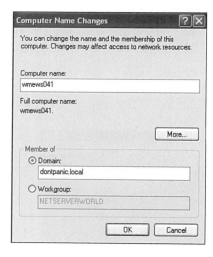

Figure 3.26
Providing the required credentials.

Your computer has now been upgraded from its previous operating system to Windows XP Professional. Before you perform any other actions on your newly upgraded computer, you need to be aware of the uninstall capabilities that are part of Windows XP Professional. The next section of this chapter addresses this new feature.

UNINSTALLING A WINDOWS XP UPGRADE

The ability to uninstall Windows XP Professional from your computer is a completely new one to the Windows world. For many years now, smart installation routines have existed (now perfected by the Windows Installer and its MSI packages) that allowed you to effortlessly uninstall, modify, repair, or roll-back installed applications on your computer. Now in Windows XP Professional, Microsoft has delivered this same functionality to the operating system—almost. Yes, as is the case with everything too good to be true, there is a catch to this as well.

Your ability to uninstall a Windows XP Professional upgrade installation hinges on several requirements which must not change from the time of the upgrade to the time of uninstallation. These requirements are

- The installation must have been an upgrade from one of the following operating systems: Windows 98, Windows 98 Second Edition, or Windows Millennium Edition.
- You cannot convert a volume to NTFS.
- You cannot convert a volume to a dynamic disk.
- You cannot create or delete a volume.
- You must have at least 300MB of empty space available for the uninstall files.
- You must not delete the uninstall files from your computer (even though you'll be prompted to do so by the Disk Cleanup Wizard 30 days after the upgrade).

If the day comes when you need to uninstall Windows XP Professional, and you meet all of the stated requirements, you can uninstall Windows XP as follows. Note, however, that there's one gotcha: You'll have to reinstall your applications after the reversion to the previous operating system.

CAUTION

Back Up for Safety!

Always back up your data before performing any major disk-intensive evolution—including uninstalling Windows XP Professional. See Chapter 25 for more information on using Windows XP's ntbackup.exe utility.

1. Open the Add or Remove Programs applet in the Control Panel.
2. Select Windows XP Professional from the list of currently installed programs, as shown in Figure 3.27.

Figure 3.27
Locating the Windows XP Professional uninstallation.

3. Follow the onscreen prompts to complete the uninstallation. You will be prompted at least two times before actually starting the uninstall process. This is a one-way process, hence the extra confirmation page before being committed to the uninstallation.

Alternatively, if you want to uninstall Windows XP Professional from the command line, you can do so using the following procedure.

1. Restart the computer using the Safe Mode with Command Prompt option. You will need to log in with local administrative privileges.

2. From the command line, enter the following command:
   `x:\windows\system32\osuninst.exe`, where x is the location of the Windows XP Professional uninstallation.

3. Follow the onscreen prompts to complete the uninstallation process.

After the uninstallation is complete, you will need to reinstall any applications that you had installed since the time of the upgrade.

PRODUCT ACTIVATION

Product Activation, or Microsoft Product Activation (MPA) as it has become known, was not exactly a welcome addition in Windows XP. It was, however, not introduced in Windows XP, as it existed in late versions of Office 2000, all versions of Office XP, and Visio 2002. MPA works to stop casual copying of software by tying the hardware profile of a computer to software installation.

In the next sections, we are going to take a in-depth look at Product Activation, including the different activation scenarios that exist, how Product Activation works including what information it transmits to Microsoft, and how Product Activation will affect you.

When dealing with Product Activation, there are three scenarios that can occur. Without exception, you should fall into one of these three scenarios:

- Retail box purchases
- OEM installations
- Volume licensing

RETAIL BOX PURCHASES

Retail box purchases of Windows XP Professional present the most complex and confusing situation when it comes to dealing with Product Activation. Product Activation depends on submission of the Installation ID to Microsoft. The Installation ID is a unique number generated from two different pieces of information about a computer: the Product ID number and a hardware hash. The Installation ID has been designed to ensure anonymity in that no personally identifying information is ever transmitted to Microsoft. Instead, the Installation ID serves to deter and prevent software piracy by preventing installations of Windows XP Professional that violate its license.

The Product ID uniquely identifies one and only one copy of Windows XP Professional, and is created from the Product Key used during the installation of Windows XP. Each retail copy of Windows XP Professional has a unique Product Key, and thus every Product ID generated from a valid Product Key is also unique. Additionally, as in the past, the Product ID is used by Microsoft for support calls. You can view your Product ID (see Figure 3.28) by looking at the General tab of the System applet in the Control Panel (alternatively, you can access this applet by right-clicking on My Computer and selecting Properties from the context menu).

Figure 3.28
Viewing the
Product ID.

NOTE

> **Product Keys and Product IDs**
>
> The practice of using Product Keys and Product IDs is not new to Windows XP. Microsoft, like many other software vendors, has been using Product Keys for many years to license software. Likewise, the practice of using a Product ID to validate an installed product has been around for a while as well.

The hardware hash is an eight-byte value that is created by taking information from 10 different components inside the computer and running this information through a mathematical calculation. The hash process is one-way and thus this information cannot be reverse-engineered to yield any specific details about the computer from which it was obtained. The hardware hash also only uses a portion of each individual component hash value, thus further increasing user anonymity and preventing Microsoft from collecting any personally identifying information during the process of implementing Product Activation. Hardware hashes will be discussed at greater length in the "How Product Activation Works" section later in this chapter.

OEM INSTALLATIONS

A large majority of users acquire Windows XP Professional in the process of purchasing a new computer. For these customers, since Windows XP Professional is pre-loaded onto the new computer already, no activation will be required by the consumer. OEMs can pre-activate Windows XP Professional as part of the setup and configuration process before the new computer ever leaves the manufacturer. The overwhelming majority of new computers that feature Windows XP Professional will be pre-activated by the OEM before shipping. The chief difference between how OEMs license Windows XP Professional comes in how they choose to implement Product Activation.

SYSTEM LOCKED PRE-INSTALLATION

Many OEM computers come with a system restore CD-ROM that allows the user to perform a complete reinstallation or repair of the installed software components, including the operating system. In this way a specific CD-ROM can be tied to a specific system BIOS, thus preventing the CD from being used to install Windows on any other computer. Although OEM CD BIOS locking is not new, it has been expanded and now features integrated Product Activation. This method of protecting the software product is called *System Locked Pre-installation*, or *SLP*.

When SLP is implemented, the information stored in the BIOS is what protects against casual piracy such as installing the product on another computer. No communication is required with the Microsoft activation center, and thus the hardware hash value is required to be calculated. This form of Product Activation relies entirely on the BIOS information matching the SLP information at boot time. Since no hardware hash is calculated, you could thus change out every piece of hardware in the OEM computer without the need for reactivation of Windows XP Professional. In cases where the motherboard must be replaced, this could also be done without reactivation as long as the replacement motherboard was from the same OEM and contained the proper BIOS. Should a different motherboard be installed in the OEM computer that has non-matching BIOS information, the Windows XP Professional installation would then require reactivation within 30 days via the Internet or telephone call.

USING STANDARD PRODUCT ACTIVATION

If desired, an OEM can also activate a Windows XP Professional installation in the same way that retail purchase versions are activated. OEM computer installations activated using the standard Product Activation methods have all of the same restrictions that retail purchase versions of Windows XP Professional do.

NO OEM PRODUCT ACTIVATION

Some OEMs may choose to not activate Windows XP Professional at all. New OEM computers that are purchased which fall under this category will require Product Activation by the consumer using the standard Product Activation methods, either via the Internet or by telephone call to Microsoft.

VOLUME LICENSING

The simplest of all scenarios occurs when dealing with Windows XP Professional licenses acquired through one of the Microsoft volume licensing agreements, such as Microsoft Open License, Enterprise Agreement, or Select License. Such installations will not require activation.

Windows XP Professional installations that are performed using volume licensing media and volume licensing keys (VLK) have no Product Activation, hardware checking, or limitations on product installation or disk imaging.

TIP

> **Licensing Lingo**
>
> For more information on Microsoft volume licensing and the various programs, see the article "Microsoft Licensing Madness" located at `http://infocenter.cramsession.com/techlibrary/gethtml.asp?ID=1409` and also the Microsoft Licensing home page located at `http://microsoft.com/licensing/`.

HOW PRODUCT ACTIVATION WORKS

As mentioned previously, the hardware hash and the Product ID are the two parts that make up the Installation ID. The Product ID is directly tied to the Product Key that is supplied with the Windows XP Professional retail product. OEMs will usually supply the Product Key with media they ship with new computers. Of the Product ID and the hardware hash, only the hardware hash truly identifies a particular computer—enough so for Product Activation's purposes anyhow. Thus, the hardware hash is of some concern to us, as it ultimately controls how Product Activation functions and whether or not activation is required on an installation.

Table 3.1 lists the hardware components that are utilized in calculating the hardware hash and the length of the data (in bits) that makes up the hardware hash. The hardware hash value is comprised of two 32-bit double words, for a total of 64 bits (or eight bytes) worth of data.

TABLE 3.1 HARDWARE HASH COMPONENTS

Component	Length of Hash Value (in Bits)
Volume serial number	10
Network adapter MAC address	10
CD-ROM/DVD-ROM/CD-RW identifier	7
Graphics display adapter	5
Amount of installed RAM (various ranges)	3
CPU type	3
CPU serial number	6
Hard drive serial number	7
SCSI controller serial number	5
IDE controller serial number	4
Docking capability	1
Hardware hash version (version of algorithm used)	3

The first four components make up the first double word value, with the rest of the list making up the second double word value. With the exception of amount of installed RAM and the hardware hash version, all other values are calculated using selected bits of an MD5 hash.

The value for a docking-capable computer also includes PCMCIA cards, as using either a docking station or PCMCIA cards can lead to hardware appearing and disappearing. This can lead to the appearance of devices being changed when they are simply not present at that time—such as when a portable computer is undocked.

The possible values for the installed RAM value are listed in Table 3.2. As of the time of writing, the hardware hash value is always set to a value of 001 decimal, which is a hex value of 0x01. If a component is not installed, such as a SCSI host adapter, then the value returned in the hardware hash will be a zero value.

NOTE

> **Hex, Huh?**
>
> Hexadecimal, or more commonly Hex, uses the numbers 0–9 and the letters A–F to form a base-16 numbering system. The 0x in front of a Hex value simply notates it as a Hexadecimal value.
>
> For a great primer on Hexadecimal numbering, see the Intuitor Hexadecimal Headquarters located at http://www.intuitor.com/hex/.

TABLE 3.2   RAM AMOUNTS AND CORRESPONDING HASH VALUES

Amount of RAM Installed	Value
Less than 32MB	1
32MB–63MB	2
64MB–127MB	3
128MB–255MB	4
256MB–511MB	5
512MB–1023MB	6
More than 1023MB	7

As an example, the processor serial number is 96 bits in length. When Product Activation performs the hash calculation on that 96-bit value, it returns a 128-bit long value. Of these 128 bits in the hash value, only six bits of data is actually used in the hardware hash value that forms part of the Installation ID.

Six bits provides 64 different combinations (2^6), thus for the millions of computers in existence, only 64 possible processor hash values are possible. As only a fraction of the original data is used in the Product Activation calculation, the data cannot be reverse engineered, as previously mentioned. The processor serial number can never be determined from these six bits of data; the same holds true for all of the other components that Product Activation performs hashes on. In this way, the hardware hash has purposely been designed by Microsoft to ensure the user's privacy is respected at all times.

NOTE

> **Perfect Privacy?**
>
> Although Microsoft has gone to great lengths to ensure that your private information stays private at all times, no process is perfect, and Product Activation is no exception. For more alternative views on the security of Product Activation, see the Fully Licensed FAQ on Product Activation at `http://www.licenturion.com/xp/fully-licensed-faq.txt`.

During the installation of Windows XP Professional, the hardware hash is calculated. This eight bytes of data, when combined with the Product ID (nine bytes) makes up the Installation ID. When Product Activation is conducted via the Internet, this seventeen bytes of data is sent to the Microsoft activation servers in binary format, along with header information, over a secure sockets (SSL) connection.

The activation process requires three steps when completed over the Internet:

1. A handshake request, which establishes the connection between the Windows XP Professional computer and the Microsoft activation servers.
2. A license request, in which the Windows XP Professional computer asks for a PKCS10 digital certificate from the Microsoft activation servers.

3. An acknowledgement request, in which the Microsoft activation servers transmit a signed digital certificate activating the installation.

If the Internet activation succeeds then Product Activation is complete and will not again become an issue unless you exceed the maximum number of allowed changes, as detailed in the "Number of Changeable Items" section.

Should Internet activation not be feasible or desirable, telephone activation is possible as outlined in the following process.

1. Locate the appropriate telephone number by selecting the country from which you are calling.

2. Provide the 50 decimal digit Installation ID to the Microsoft representative.

3. Enter in the corresponding 42 decimal digit Confirmation ID as supplied by the Microsoft representative.

NOTE

> For more information on Product Activation, including how the hardware hash values are calculated for each hardware component, see the Fully Licensed Web site at
> `http://www.licenturion.com/xp/`.

NUMBER OF CHANGEABLE ITEMS

Once Windows XP Professional has been activated, the hardware hash will be rechecked at every user logon event. This serves to reduce another prevalent form of software piracy—that of disk cloning. *Disk cloning* is an asset to administrators looking to quickly deploy multiple copies of Windows XP Professional, but is illegal without having the required Product Keys. In most legal cases, disk cloning is done using a volume license copy of Windows XP Professional using a Volume License Key, which does not require Product Activation in the first place.

When Windows XP Professional performs its hardware check, it is looking for changes in the hardware configuration of the computer. If a substantially different configuration is detected then reactivation is required. The actual number of components that will result in a reactivation scenario is discussed shortly. The hardware check at login is done after the SLP BIOS check should the SLP BIOS check fail. As long as an OEM computer is using a genuine replacement motherboard from the OEM containing the correct BIOS data, all other components in an OEM computer activated using the SLP BIOS method can be changed out without requiring reactivation of Windows XP Professional.

The number of hardware items that it takes to achieve "substantially different" (in Microsoft speak) is dependent upon two things: whether or not the computer has a network adapter at the time of Windows XP activation, and whether or not the computer is dockable (this also includes the presence of PCMCIA slots), as outlined in Table 3.3.

TABLE 3.3 NUMBER OF CHANGED COMPONENTS TO REQUIRE REACTIVATION

Network Adapter Status	Docking Capability	Number of Changed Components to Require Reactivation
None installed at the time of Windows XP activation	No	4 or more
Installed at the time of Windows XP activation and subsequently changed	No	4 or more
Installed at the time of Windows XP activation and not changed	No	6 or more
None installed at the time of Windows XP activation	Yes	7 or more
Installed at the time of Windows XP activation and subsequently changed	Yes	7 or more
Installed at the time of Windows XP activation and not changed	Yes	9 or more

To help explain Table 3.3, a couple scenarios might be helpful.

1. A computer has a network adapter installed at the time of Windows XP Professional activation. You later change the motherboard, CPU, video adapter, and CD-ROM drive. Additionally, you add more memory and a second hard drive.

   Reactivation is not required in this instance because only five components have been changed: motherboard, CPU, video adapter, CD-ROM and RAM (amount). The addition of a second hard drive is not of significance to Product Activation. If you were to change six or more hardware components, reactivation would be required.

2. A computer has no network adapter installed at the time of Windows XP Professional activation. You later change the motherboard, CPU, video adapter, and CD-ROM drive. Additionally, you add more memory and a second hard drive.

   Reactivation is required in this instance because five components have been changed: motherboard, CPU, video adapter, CD-ROM, and RAM (amount). When you change four or more hardware components, reactivation is required.

If a single device is changed repeatedly, such as a video adapter that is changed from the original one to new adapter A then later to new adapter B, this is evaluated only as one change. Either the current hardware is the same as when activation was completed or it's not. Windows XP doesn't care how many changes have been made in the interim. Adding components after activation that were not present at the time of activation also has no impact on the hardware hash and is ignored by Windows XP Professional during its check to determine whether reactivation is necessary. Microsoft has also built in two additional loopholes into Product Activation for power users who frequently reinstall Windows XP Professional or who frequently change the hardware configuration of their computers. Windows XP Professional can be reinstalled and subsequently reactivated on the same computer an infinite number of times. In cases where the hardware configuration has changed enough to require reactivation, Microsoft allows a maximum of four reactivations per year on "substantially different" hardware—this should be enough to keep most power users happy as they continually tweak their systems. Both of these reactivation events can occur over the Internet instead of requiring a phone call.

USING INSTALLATION SWITCHES

Depending on your needs and the type of installation you are performing, you can modify the behaviors and actions of the Windows XP Professional Setup routing by using various switches. Depending on how you are installing Windows XP Professional, there are two methods you can use to call the Setup routine: by using the winnt.exe command or by using the winnt32.exe command. Some typical reasons to use switches include unattended installations, using Dynamic Update, installing the Recovery Console, and changing the location for the installation source files, to name a few.

WINNT32.EXE

Let's look first at the more useful, and likely, winnt32.exe command. The winnt32.exe command can be used to perform a clean installation or an upgrade installation of Windows XP Professional. You can run the winnt32.exe command at the command prompt from any computer running one of the following operating systems:

- Windows 95
- Windows 98
- Windows 98 Second Edition
- Windows Millennium Edition
- Windows NT 4.0
- Windows 2000
- Windows XP

NOTE

> **Using winnt32.exe from Windows 95**
>
> You cannot upgrade from Windows 95 to Windows XP Professional. An installation started from Windows 95 using the winnt32.exe command will be a clean installation only.
>
> For more information about support upgrade paths, see the "Performing an Upgrade Installation" section earlier in this chapter.

The winnt32.exe command has the following syntax and switches as detailed in Table 3.4.

```
winnt32 [/checkupgradeonly] [/cmd:command_line] [/cmdcons]
[/copydir:{i386|ia64}\FolderName] [/copysource:FolderName]
[/debug[Level]:[FileName]] [/dudisable]
[/duprepare:pathname] [/dushare:pathname] [/m:FolderName]
[/makelocalsource] [/noreboot] [/s:SourcePath]
[/syspart:DriveLetter] [/tempdrive:DriveLetter]
[/udf:id [,UDB_file]] [/unattend[num]:[answer_file]]
```

TABLE 3.4   WINNT32.EXE SWITCHES

Switch	Description
/checkupgradeonly	Checks your computer for upgrade compatibility with Windows XP. When used with the /unattend switch, no user input is required. If used without the /unattend switch, the results are displayed on the screen and you can save them as desired. The default location is a file named upgrade.txt located in the %systemroot% folder.
/cmd:command_line	Instructs Setup to carry out a specific command before the final phase of Setup.
/cmdcons	Installs the Recovery Console as a startup option on a functioning x86-based computer. You can only use the /cmdcons option after normal Setup is finished.
/copydir:{i386|ia64}\FolderName	Creates an additional folder within the folder in which the Windows XP files are installed. You can use /copydir to create as many additional folders as you want.
/copysource:FolderName	Creates a temporary additional folder within the folder in which the Windows XP files are installed. Unlike the folders /copydir creates, /copysource folders are deleted after Setup completes.
/debug[Level]:[FileName]	Creates a debug log at the level specified. The default log file is C:\systemroot\Winnt32.log, and the default debug level is 2. The log levels are as follows: 0 represents severe errors, 1 represents errors, 2 represents warnings, 3 represents information, and 4 represents detailed information for debugging. Each level includes the levels below it.
/dudisable	Prevents Dynamic Update from running. This option will disable Dynamic Update even if you use an answer file and specify Dynamic Update options in that file.
/duprepare:pathname	Carries out preparations on an installation share so that it can be used with Dynamic Update files that you downloaded from the Windows Update Web site.

continues

3

TABLE 3.4   CONTINUED

Switch	Description
/dushare:*pathname*	Specifies a share on which you previously downloaded Dynamic Update files (updated files for use with Setup) from the Windows Update Web site.
/m:*FolderName*	Specifies that Setup copies replacement files from an alternate location. Instructs Setup to look in the alternate location first, and if files are present, to use them instead of the files from the default location.
/makelocalsource	Instructs Setup to copy all installation source files to your local hard disk. Use /makelocalsource when installing from a CD to provide installation files when the CD is not available later in the installation.
/noreboot	Instructs Setup to not restart the computer after the file copy phase of Setup is completed so that you can run another command.
/s:*SourcePath*	Specifies the source location of the Windows XP files. To simultaneously copy files from multiple servers, type the /s:SourcePath option multiple times (up to a maximum of eight). If you type the option multiple times, the first server specified must be available, or Setup will fail.
/syspart:*DriveLetter*	On an x86-based computer, specifies that you can copy Setup startup files to a hard disk, mark the disk as active, and then install the disk into another computer. When you start that computer, it automatically starts with the next phase of Setup. You must always use the /tempdrive parameter with the /syspart parameter.
/tempdrive:*DriveLetter*	Directs Setup to place temporary files on the specified partition. For a new installation, Windows XP will also be installed on the specified partition.
/udf:*id* [,*UDB_file*]	Indicates an identifier (id) that Setup uses to specify how a Uniqueness Database (UDB) file modifies an answer file (see the /unattend entry). If no UDB file is specified, Setup prompts the user to insert a disk that contains the $Unique$.udb file.

Switch	Description
`/unattend`	Upgrades your previous version of Windows 98, Windows Millennium Edition, Windows NT 4.0, or Windows 2000 in unattended Setup mode. All user settings are taken from the previous installation, so no user intervention is required during Setup.
`/unattend[num]:[answer_file]`	Performs a fresh installation in unattended Setup mode. The specified answer_file provides Setup with your custom specifications. *num* is the number of seconds between the time that Setup finishes copying the files and when it restarts your computer.

→ To learn more about using the Windows Upgrade Advisor, **see** "Checking Hardware and Software Compatibility," **p. 64**.

NOTE

Winnt32 on Itanium-based Computers

If you run the winnt32.exe command on an Itanium-based computer, the command must be run from the Extensible Firmware Interface (EFI) or from Windows XP. Also, the `/cmdcons` and `/syspart` switches are not available, and options relating to upgrades are also not available.

For more information on EFI, see the TechNet article "Managing GPT Disks in Itanium-based Computers," located at `http://www.microsoft.com/technet/prodtechnol/winxppro/reskit/prkb_cnc_ywwc.asp`.

WINNT.EXE

The second, and less often used, way to invoke startup is by using the winnt.exe command. The winnt.exe command can be used from the command prompt of even the oldest operating systems, such as Windows 95, Windows 3.x, and MS-DOS. These operating systems are not upgradeable to Windows XP Professional.

The winnt.exe command has the following syntax and switches as detailed in Table 3.5.

```
winnt [/s:SourcePath] [/t:TempDrive] [/u:answer file]
[/udf:ID [,UDB_file]] [/r:folder][/rx:folder][/e:command]
[/a]
```

TABLE 3.5   WINNT.EXE SWITCHES

Switch	Description
`/s:SourcePath`	Specifies the source location of the Windows XP files. The location must be a full path and can use UNC locations.
`/t:TempDrive`	Directs Setup to place temporary files on the specified drive and to install Windows XP on that drive.

continues

TABLE 3.5   CONTINUED

Switch	Description
/u:answer file	Performs an unattended Setup using an answer file. If you use /u, you must also use /s.
/udf:ID [,UDB_file]	Indicates an identifier (ID) that Setup uses to specify how a Uniqueness Database (UDB) file modifies an answer file (see /u). If no UDB_file is specified, Setup prompts you to insert a disk that contains the $Unique$.udb file.
/r:folder	Specifies an optional folder to be installed. The folder remains after Setup finishes.
/rx:folder	Specifies an optional folder to be copied. The folder is deleted after Setup finishes.
/e:command	Specifies a command to be carried out just before the final phase of Setup.
/a	Enables accessibility options.

AUTOMATED SYSTEM RECOVERY

Automated System Recovery is a new feature in Windows XP that adds another way to perform a system recovery should things go bad. ASR, shown in Figure 3.29, replaces an older tool from Windows 2000 and Windows NT 4.0: the Emergency Repair Disk (see Figure 3.30).

Figure 3.29
Locating ASR in
Windows XP.

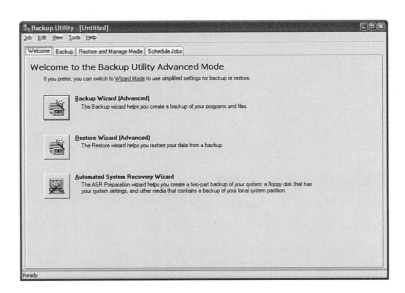

Figure 3.30
ERD from Windows
2000.

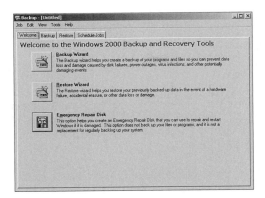

Automated System Recovery (ASR) uses the Windows XP Professional Backup utility and consists of two parts: a backup of critical files that is made to a local (recommended) or remote storage device, and a floppy disk containing three files critical to the restoration phase.

The files that are backed up include the system state data and all files stored on the system volume. System state refers to all of the components that determine the current state of the operating system (hence the clever name) and includes such things as user accounts, hard drive configuration, network configuration, video settings, hardware configuration, software settings, and various other critical files that are required to run Windows XP Professional properly. Additionally, the system state includes files that are required to start the operating system properly, including those that are found in the %systemroot% directory and boot files such as ntldr and ntdetect.

The floppy disk contains three files: asr.sif, asrpnp.sif, and setup.log. If you're thinking that the .SIF extension sounds familiar—you're right! .SIF files are used for answer files to customize unattended installations of Windows XP Professional. The functions of these three files are outlined as follows.

- **Asr.sif** contains information about your computer's storage devices including hard drives, partitions, volumes, and removable storage devices. A portion of the asr.sif file is shown in Figure 3.31.
- **Asrpnp.sif** contains information about the Plug and Play information installed in your computer.
- **Setup.log** contains a listing of all system state and critical files that were backed up. It aids in the restoration of these files when you invoke ASR recovery.

→ To learn more about Answer Files, **see** "Using Interactive Answer Files for Installation," **p. 175**.

Figure 3.31
Asr.sif contains information about hard drives and removable storage.

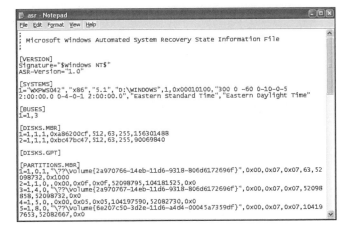

NOTE

Using asr.sif and asrpnp.sif

Although not the intended purpose of asr.sif and asrpnp.sif, they provide a great wealth of information about installed devices and configurations for exploration into Microsoft Product Activation.

USING AUTOMATED SYSTEM RECOVERY

The Automated System Recovery process is one that is not to be taken lightly. You should not consider using ASR until you have unsuccessfully tried to use other recovery methods, such as Driver Rollback, System Restore, Parallel installations, Last Known Good Configuration, Recovery Console, Safe Mode, or restoration using Windows XP Professional Backup. ASR will restore the system state and other critical files that were backed up at the time of its creation.

TIP

Backup Frequency

The frequency at which you make your ASR backups is critical to having a good experience when using ASR for recovery. Make them regularly, at least weekly—more often if you make frequent changes to the computer.

The process to create an Automated System Recovery set is outlined here.

1. Start the Windows XP Professional Backup utility by clicking Start, All Programs, Accessories, System Tools, Backup.

2. If the Wizard view appears, as shown in Figure 3.32, click Advanced Mode to switch to Advanced Mode as seen previously in Figure 3.29.

Figure 3.32
The Windows XP
Professional Backup
utility in Wizard mode.

3. Click the Automated System Recovery Wizard button.

4. Click Next to dismiss the opening page of the ASR Wizard.

5. From the Backup Destination page, shown in Figure 3.33, configure the location for the backed up files to be placed. For best results, a local storage location is preferred over a network location that may not be available later. After configuration your location, click Next to continue on.

Figure 3.33
Configuring the back-up destination.

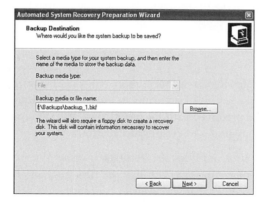

6. On the Completing the Automated System Recovery Preparation Wizard page, click Finish to initiate the ASR creation process.

7. When prompted, insert a blank 3-1/2 inch 1.44 MB floppy disk in the A: drive of your computer. Click OK to create the floppy disk portion of the ASR set.

8. Label and store the floppy disk in a safe, secure location for future use.

Should the day come when you need to use ASR to recover your computer, proceed as outlined here.

1. Start your computer with the Windows XP Professional Setup CD-ROM.

2. When prompted to press a key to boot from the CD-ROM, do so. If your computer does not support booting from a CD-ROM, you will need to use Setup floppy disks to start the process.

3. When prompted to press F2 to start Automated System Recovery, as shown in Figure 3.34, do so. You will be prompted to supply your ASR floppy disk.

Figure 3.34
Starting ASR.

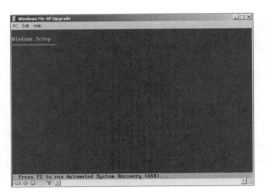

4. Follow the onscreen prompts to complete the Automated System Recovery process.

SUMMARY

Installing Windows XP Professional is a much improved process over previous versions of Windows—although not necessarily a faster one. In most cases, a clean installation using the NTFS file system is the preferred path for installation, but Windows XP Professional is flexible and allows for easy upgrades of existing installations.

The User State Migration Tool and Files and Settings Transfer Wizard, discussed previously in Chapter 2, aid you in migrating your settings and files from an old computer to a new computer. Should you decide later that you want to take advantage of the NTFS file system on an upgrade installation, you can easily convert the file system—without losing a single file. Chapter 25 discusses advanced disk management issues, including conversion and reversion of file systems.

Although about 99% of all installations should go smoothly, problems can and will happen. Some of the more common issues that you may see during an installation of Windows XP Professional include

- You see "Stop 0x0000000A irql_not_less_or_equal" appear on the screen. This error is usually due to hardware or hardware drivers that are not compatible with Windows XP Professional. Ensure that all of your hardware is listed on the Hardware Compatibility List and that you have the most up-to-date drivers for your installed hardware. MSKB# Q311564, located at http://support.microsoft.com/default.aspx?scid=kb; en-us;Q311564 has more information on this error.

- You get an error such as "Setup cannot copy the file file_name. Press X to retry, Y to abort" when attempting to perform the installation. This error can be caused by many problems such as a dirty CD-ROM, a damaged CD-ROM, viruses, or damaged RAM installed on your computer. If possible, attempt to perform the installation using a different CD-ROM, verify that all installed hardware in your computer is working properly, and that you do not have any viruses. Also, certain third-party applications that may be installed (if performing an upgrade installation) can cause this error to appear. MSKB# Q310064, located at `http://support.microsoft.com/default.aspx?id=kb;en-us;Q310064` has more information on this type of error.

- You receive this error: "NTLDR is missing. Press any key to restart." This error is usually caused by upgrading over a Windows 9*x* installation that resides on a FAT32 hard drive with an incorrect geometry configuration. To fix this error, you will need to correct the hard drive geometry configuration. MSKB# Q314057, located at `http://support.microsoft.com/default.aspx?scid=kb;en-us;Q314057` has more information on this error.

Should you encounter problems during your installation of Windows XP Professional, a quick search on the Microsoft Web site will usually turn up the required information. To perform advanced searches, visit the Microsoft Advanced Search page at `http://search.microsoft.com/advanced_search.asp`.

CHAPTER 4

INSTALLING WINDOWS XP FOR MULTI-BOOTING

In this chapter

WHY MULTI-BOOT?

In today's world of numerous PC-based operating systems and amazingly low hard-disk prices, it's pretty tempting for users to want to experiment with different operating systems. With the proliferation of the Internet and its accompanying high-bandwidth needs, whole operating systems are available for free download via many commercial distributors' FTP sites. Aside from simple curiosity and experimentation, there are some good, solid reasons for needing to switch between operating systems on the same computer.

- Many users use two or more operating systems because of application compatibility issues. Hardware support issues arise too: Windows 98 might have drivers for old hardware that Windows XP doesn't support.

- Some users want to run specific applications or games in the most well-suited environment possible.

- A developer might swap between Windows XP Professional and NT 4.0 to test application compatibility.

- Web site developers may need to use different OS versions to see how their pages look with the corresponding different Web browser versions, such as a Linux-based browser versus a Windows-based one.

- As an author, I need several operating systems functioning on a single computer to meet my testing and writing needs.

- As a user or administrator, you might need a way to test out potentially destructive programs or drivers on your production Windows XP system before committing to running them under XP officially.

Of course you can buy multiple computers, devoting one to each operating system you plan to run, or you can install and use pop-out hard drive bays to switch between OSes, but those are less-efficient approaches than multi-booting. With multi-booting under Windows, at boot time you're presented with a character-based menu of the operating systems you've installed. You simply choose the one you want, press Enter, and the desired OS loads.

NOTE

> You should read, or at least skim, this entire chapter before beginning to implement a complex multi-boot arrangement because we've saved pages by not reiterating some cautions under each multi-booting scenario. Pay particular attention to the issues of file systems, as well as applications and data sharing between operating systems. Then be sure to see the tips at the end of the chapter which cover some third-party multi-boot solutions.

Windows XP Professional directly supports multi-booting with the following operating systems:

- Windows XP Home Edition
- Windows 2000 Professional

- Windows NT 3.51 or Windows NT 4.0
- Windows 95, Windows 98 and Me
- Windows 3.1 or Windows for Workgroups 3.11
- MS-DOS
- OS/2

Multi-booting with Linux is also possible, although it takes some extra effort.

NOTE

Although this chapter provides some solid fundamentals for dual-booting operating systems, an in-depth discussion of the topic could—and in fact does—fill an entire book. For additional details on setting up multi-boot scenarios, we recommend that you pick up a copy of *The Multi-Boot Configuration Handbook*, published by Que.

CAUTION

Installing a new operating system is not always a smooth procedure, as you probably know. I strongly recommend that you create a backup, or at least an emergency repair disk, before you install another operating system on your computer. That way, you can revert to it in case of catastrophe.

Depending on your current or planned system, running multiple operating systems can be as simple as installing your new copy of Windows XP alongside your pre-existing operating system. But if you're like me, that will not be the perfect choice. Either way, I'll try to cover all the common methods so you can make the choice that's right for you.

4

FILE SYSTEM SPECIFICS

Your goal in creating a multi-boot system is to have all the operating systems coexist in such a manner that they will be capable of sharing files with each other. Nothing is more frustrating than realizing that you must reboot to retrieve a file, copy it to a floppy, and reboot again to copy it into your other operating system. A little bit of knowledge about file systems can save you many headaches down the road.

Install Apps Separately

This is a really important point. Do not attempt to install two Windows operating systems on the same partition. Just as Microsoft says, you really do need separate partitions for each OS. You should also install all your apps separately for each OS, typically on the same partition as the OS itself. Here's why this kind of cautious isolation is imperative:

- As a default, Windows installs apps in the ***Program Files*** folder on the boot partition. (The boot partition is the partition that contains the bulk of the Windows files of the OS in question.) So, if you have more than one OS on the same partition, application installers can overwrite one another's files by dumping them on top of one another. In some cases, this can cause major issues, since some applications come in different versions for each of the Windows operating systems.

- Most program preferences are stored in each operating system's registry files. If you change the prefs for an app under one OS and then boot another OS, the prefs can collide, which can cause the apps to act erratically, or at the least, unexpectedly.

- Control Panel's Add/Remove Programs lists and your Start menus' shortcuts can get confused. When you remove an app from one OS, the other OS's Start menu shortcuts are still there, but the apps they point to have been removed, so they become dead shortcuts.

As explained later in this chapter, it's certainly okay to store your data files on the same partition, and you probably should, so that you don't duplicate data and confuse yourself over what is the latest version of documents and such. This works so long as any apps that will be on multiple OSes can share the same data files. If you're running Word version 2 or something ancient like that under one OS, and Word XP on another, well, you will run into trouble trying to open the newer .doc files under the older version. But typically this will not be a problem, and I encourage you to store your data files in a central location. You can make it easy to keep your data in a central location by tweaking each OS's My Documents folder to point to that central location. On later Windows operating systems you can right-click My Documents, choose Properties, and then click Move.

As you most likely know there are several different *file system* formats supported by XP, determining how file space is allocated, where directory information is stored, and so forth. The problem is that each operating system has its own list of supported file system types. Table 4.1 lists the various file systems supported by the operating systems discussed in this chapter. (RO stands for read-only, RW stands for read/write, and NS stands for not supported.) Be sure to read the footnotes for any operating system you want to use.

TABLE 4.1   RELATIONSHIPS BETWEEN FILE SYSTEMS AND OPERATING SYSTEMS

OS	FAT16	FAT32	NTFS4	NTFS5	Extended2
Windows 95	RW	NS	RO[1]	RO[1]	RO[2]
Windows 95b	RW	RW	RO[1]	RO[1]	RO[2]
Windows 98	RW	RW	RO[1]	RO[1]	RO[2]
Windows NT 4.0	RW	NS[3]	RW[4]	RW[4]	RO[6]
Windows 2000	RW	RW	RW[7]	RW	RO[6]
Windows XP	RW[5]	RW	RW[7]	RW	RO[6]
Linux	RW	RW	RO[8]	RO[8]	RW

1. Windows Me/9x can read the NTFS file system via a free utility called NTFS for Windows 98. Although NTFSWIN98 is read-only, it works very well and is highly recommended. A version with limited write capability can be purchased. You can obtain these products from http://www.sysinternals.com.

2. Windows Me/9x can gain read-only access to Linux's extended2 file system by using the free utility FSDEXT2. This utility can be found at http://www.yipton.demon.co.uk.

3. You can use the FAT32 utility for Windows NT 4.0 to read and write to FAT32 file systems from Windows NT 4.0. This utility can be obtained from http://www.sysinternals.com. *This utility is not free. However, there is a free version of the FAT32 utility also at the same site that provides Read-only capability.*

4. If an NTFS partition is to be shared with Windows 2000 or XP, you must use Windows NT 4.0 Service Pack 4 or later.

5. You can't format a new partition with FAT16 during XP's installation process or disk manager. Another OS must create it.

6. Windows NT 4.0, Windows 2000, and Windows XP can read extended2 file systems by using the free utility Explore2FS. This utility can be found at `http://uranus.it.swin.edu.au/~jn/linux/explore2fs.`

7. Windows 2000 and XP automatically convert NTFS version 4 volumes to NTFS version 5.

8. Although the 2.2.x Linux kernel does contain a read/write driver for NTFS, you should use the driver only in read-only mode. The write portion of the NTFS driver is still in the very early stages of development and might damage your partition. You can enable read-only support when recompiling your kernel for NTFS support.

NOTE

Paragon Software (`http://www.partition-manager.com/n_ext2fs_main.htm`) sells a version of Ext2FS that allows read/write access to Extended2 for all of the versions of Windows listed in this table.

→ See Chapter 25 for an in-depth discussion of file system tools, commands, and techniques for managing your hard drive.

Understanding the interplay between these various file systems is key in creating an efficient multi-boot system. To the greatest extent possible, you should choose a format that's compatible with all the operating systems you'll want to use, on at least one disk partition. This will provide a place to store files that can be read no matter which OS you're using.

When you have the choice of several different candidate file systems, you must decide which is best, based on your hardware and the application for which you are creating your multi-boot system. The following sections quickly recap file system descriptions, with an eye toward multi-booting issues.

FAT16

FAT16 is the oldest file system mentioned in this chapter. It was originally intended for file systems based on the DOS operating system. As such, it is quite antiquated and not often used today. But FAT16 might be your only choice in some situations due to its two major advantages:

- FAT16 is supported by almost all operating systems, including all versions of Windows, OS/2, MS-DOS, and Linux.

- The structure of the FAT16 file system is much simpler than the others, giving it much less software overhead. This gives FAT16 increased speed on volumes less than 1GB in size.

Aside from not being as resilient as newer file systems, one big limitation of FAT16 is the fact that it can't be installed in primary partitions greater than 2GB in size with MS-DOS and Windows 9x/Me; 4GB is the limit for FAT16 with Windows NT/2000/XP. To use the full capacity of a disk beyond those limits, an extended partition can be created, but it must be broken into non-bootable logical drives of no more than 2GB/4GB in size each. For example, a 10GB drive prepared as a FAT16 drive for use with both Windows Me and Windows XP would need to be divided into five drive letters, C: through G:. Also, the larger the partition, the less efficient FAT16 is in allocating space to small files—more disk space is wasted. As explained later in the chapter, this limitation has been overcome by FAT16's newer brother, FAT32.

NOTE

> If you are using the first edition of Windows 95, you can use only the FAT16 file system. Versions of Windows 95 prior to Windows 95 OSR2 cannot read FAT32 partitions. A prompt upgrade to Windows 98 is recommended for this as well as for many other reasons.
>
> Also, keep in mind that Microsoft frequently uses the term FAT to refer to both FAT16 and FAT32 file systems, which can be rather confusing. (I think they secretly just want us all to upgrade to NTFS.)

FAT32

The FAT32 file system was introduced with Windows 95 OSR2. FAT32 was essentially the answer to most of the shortcomings of FAT16. The following are among FAT32's strengths:

- FAT32 supports partitions up to 2TB in size (that's 2,048GB to you and me). Actually, the practical limit is somewhat less. Win2K's Format tool, for example, won't format a FAT32 partition larger than 32GB.

- FAT32 increased the number of clusters (decreasing the cluster size) on the hard disk, making the storage of small files take up less room than it did previously with FAT16. Since there are often hundreds of small files on the average hard disk, this can amount to a significant space savings.

- The structure of FAT32 remains very small, providing a notable speed increase over FAT16 (but only on partitions larger than 1GB in size. Under that size, FAT16 is faster).

Of course, with all changes come pain and compatibility issues. To this day, Windows NT 4.0 does not natively support FAT32. The addition of FAT32 file support into Windows 2000 and XP is a welcome one, especially for multi-booting users. However, neither FAT version supports the advanced security and reliability features of NTFS, as explained in the following section.

NTFS

The New Technology File System, or NTFS, brought with it many welcome additions to the world of Microsoft computing, including the following:

- Permissions—NTFS brought with it a concept used in the Novell and Unix worlds for quite some time. Permissions enable you to configure files and folders to be accessible only by specific users, user groups, or both. This is imperative for networked multiuser operating systems. Importantly, permissions also allow you to specify the level of access: read-only, read/write, no access, and so on.

- Compression—You can transparently compress folders or files on an NTFS volume.

- Reliability—NTFS is much more reliable, and as such is suited to a server environment. Disk repair applications seldom need to be run on an NTFS file system.

- Large volumes are accessed much quicker with NTFS—Although FAT still rules the below-1GB world, NTFS excels at accessing files and folders in very large disk partitions.

- Encryption came with the version of NTFS supplied with Windows 2000 and XP (also known as NTFS 5). Now you can lock individual files or folders for high levels of security.

- Dynamic disk arrangements enable you to group separate physical drives into one large virtual drive (see Chapter 25, "Managing Your Hard Disks," in the section "Storage Types" for a full discussion).

CAUTION

> Be careful with dynamic disks—only Windows 2000 and XP Professional support them, and other operating systems can't boot from a drive that's been set up for dynamic disk partitions. Also, converting a basic disk that already contains multiple installations of Windows 2000 or XP to a dynamic disk can cause startup problems.

4

A disadvantage of NTFS when considering multi-booting scenarios, however, is that it can't be read directly by DOS, OS/2, Unix, or Windows Me/9x. You can download a free utility to read NTFS disks from `http://www.sysinternals.com`, and you can purchase a program with limited writing ability. Still, this isn't as straightforward as having support built in to the operating system. Likewise, Linux has only limited support for NTFS—reading works but writing is dangerous. So, NTFS is not a generally useful format for a *shared* partition on multi-boot systems.

To muddy the waters a little more, we now have two versions of NTFS: versions 4 and 5. Version 4 was used by Windows NT version 4.0. The updated version 5 is used by Windows 2000 and XP and supports additional capabilities such as encrypted files and dynamic disk partitions that can be rearranged while Windows is running. (Note that these last two capabilities aren't available with XP Home Edition, even though Home Edition still uses the newer disk format. Weird but true.) The version difference will only affect you if you share an NTFS-formatted disk volume between Windows NT 4.0 and Windows XP or 2000. The newer OSes will update your NTFS partitions to version 5, so you must update Windows NT 4.0 to Service Pack 4 or later so that it can read the new format.

THE WINDOWS XP BOOT LOADER

As mentioned earlier in this chapter, one of the great advantages of the approaches we're advocating in this chapter is that we're using the Windows XP boot loader. The primary asset it gives us is a *menuing* system that lets you choose which OS to start every time you boot up your computer. The following sections explain how the boot loader works.

THE MASTER BOOT RECORD

The *master boot record (MBR)* is the portion of the disk that tells your computer where to find the partition boot sector. All operating systems must be started up by some type of master boot record, whether this contains the system's native code or a multi-boot utility. When your system is booted, a chain of events ensues, based on your currently installed operating systems. The following is a simplified version of this chain of events for an installation containing Windows XP:

1. After POST (power-on self test), the system BIOS reads the master boot record (MBR).
2. Control is passed to the master boot record, which then looks for the partition listed as the "active partition" in the partition table of the startup disk, as defined in your BIOS.
3. After the active partition is found, the master boot record loads sector 0, the partition's boot sector, into memory and executes it.
4. The partition boot sector points to NTLDR (NT loader) in the root of the partition and executes that.
5. NTLDR reads the contents of BOOT.INI, located in the partition's root folder. BOOT.INI lists the locations and names of the computer's bootable operating systems. If more than one OS is listed, NTLDR displays a menu of OS choices. If only one is listed, which is usually the case, NTLDR fires it up directly.

At this point, the user can select the operating system to boot up. Windows 2000 and NT use this same system. In the next few sections, we'll explain how to set up multiple operating systems so that they all end up as choices in BOOT.INI.

THE BOOT.INI SETTINGS FILE

BOOT.INI handles many options for booting your system. For now, you can see your current BOOT.INI by selecting Start, Run and entering `C:\boot.ini`, which opens the BOOT.INI file with Notepad.

The BOOT.INI file has two sections.

THE [boot loader] SECTION

This section defines two specific settings:

- **Timeout**—This setting defines how long the system will wait until it boots into the default operating system. This value is in seconds. A value of -1 makes the system wait indefinitely until you make a manual selection. A value of 0 makes the system boot immediately into the default operating system.

- **Default**—This is the default operating system that will boot up, unless there is user intervention. The value of the Default entry must match the *location* part of one of the operating systems entries, which are described in the next section.

THE [operating systems] SECTION

This section contains a list of operating systems installed on your computer. You can see the option for Windows XP in your BOOT.INI file if you've successfully completed an installation.

Each entry in this section is of the form

```
location="OS Name" /options
```

where *location* specifies the drive, partition, and folder on which the operating system is stored, `"OS Name"` is a text description of the OS, and *options* is an optional list of operating system load modifiers. For Windows NT, 2000, HP Home Edition, and the 32-bit version of Windows XP, an entry might look like this:

```
multi(0)disk(0)rdisk(0)partition(1)\WINDOWS="Windows XP Professional"
```

(This strange format is a throwback from the days when Windows NT ran on the Alpha and MIPS processors. The format for the 64-bit Itanium processor version of Windows XP Professional is different, and equally obtuse.) In most setups, the rdisk number indicates the physical hard drive (0 = first), and partition indicates the partition number on the drive (1 = first). The entry is followed by a folder name.

> **TIP**
>
> For a listing of the options permitted in boot.ini, check out http://www.labmice.net/Windows2000/install/bootini.htm and http://appdeploy.com/tips/bootiniswitches.shtml.

Non–NT-based operating systems are loaded through files that contain images of the master boot record that the OS is usually loaded. For example, when you install Windows XP on a system that was previously running MS-DOS, the original MS-DOS boot sector is saved in a file, and the resulting BOOT.INI entry is

```
C:\ ="MS-DOS"
```

MULTI-BOOT SCENARIOS

The possibilities for multi-booting are nearly endless when you consider that a system can have multiple drives, each drive can have multiple partitions, and each partition can have an operating system on it. However, the scenarios discussed next represent the most common and usable configurations. When you understand the scenarios offered here, you should be able to effectively conquer any multi-boot setup.

We recommend that you at least read through the first scenario fully, regardless of your own designs. This will give you a better understanding of the overall process. We'll also refer to that scenario so we can reduce repetition. All these configurations assume that you already have a working computer with at least a CD-ROM drive and hard disk.

NOTE

Always be careful to consider file system compatibility between all these operating systems. Use Table 4.1 as a reference before forging ahead with your installations. This will save you from many of the common problems associated with setting up a multi-boot system.

TIP

All the following scenarios work on the assumption that you are able to boot from your CD-ROM drive. Most modern computers have this capability. A little-known fact is that some of the older operating systems in these examples are capable of booting from their respective CD-ROM installation discs. Windows NT 4.0, 2000, and XP can and will boot from your CD-ROM drive, as will OEM versions of Windows 98 and most modern versions of Linux. This method is much quicker and less error prone than the traditional method of booting from a floppy disk.

Booting from the CD-ROM is usually enabled simply by changing the boot sequence from within your system's BIOS so that it checks the CD for an operating system before checking the hard drive. Consult your computer's operating manual for the proper method to enable this feature for your specific system BIOS. Chapter 3 has more ideas on how to boot from a CD-ROM in case you're having trouble in this department. Look for the troubleshooting tip at the end of the chapter titled "DOS Won't Recognize the CD-ROM Drive."

TIP

If you want to know how the multi-booting system works, it's really quite simple. The boot record on the primary drive points to the NTLDR file (if an NT-based OS has been successfully installed). When NTLDR runs, it loads the Operating System selections from the Boot.ini file. If you select Windows NT, 2000, or XP, NTLDR will run Ntdetect.com. If you are running on an Alpha-based machine, control then passes to Osloader.exe (this only applies to NT, since Windows 2000 and XP were not released in Alpha versions). If you choose NT, 2000, or XP on an Intel-based machine, Ntdetect.com passes control to NTLDR. If Windows 9x, MS-DOS, or another DOS-based operating system is chosen, then NTLDR will pass off control to Bootsect.dos and the startup process will begin. (Note that some of these files are marked as hidden system files, so you won't be able to see them listed in an Explorer or Search window without adjusting the folder options.)

DUAL-BOOTING WINDOWS XP PROFESSIONAL AND WINDOWS ME/9X

Many people want or need to run Windows XP and Windows Me, 95, or 98 on the same computer. Because Windows 95, 98, and Me behave almost identically in this situation, for the remainder of this section, I'll use 9x to refer to all three of these older versions.

The following sections discuss two ways of dual-booting:

- In the same partition
- In separate partitions

PUTTING WINDOWS XP PROFESSIONAL AND WINDOWS 9X IN THE SAME PARTITION (NOT SUGGESTED)

If you already have a Windows 95/98 installation, you *can* simply install Windows XP beside it for a dual-boot arrangement from the same partition. As mentioned previously in the sidebar, I really don't recommend this setup, however.

Despite this, if it's absolutely necessary, you can follow these steps to install both Windows XP and 9x on the same partition:

1. Assuming you have successfully installed Windows 9x on your system, begin the Windows XP Professional installation wizard by inserting the CD-ROM.

2. If the wizard does not autorun, you can initialize it by choosing Start, Run and then typing `D:\i386\winnt32`, where D: is the letter of your CD-ROM drive.

3. After Windows Setup has launched, choose New Installation as the Installation Type. This will install Windows XP into a new system folder called \WINNT. From here, simply continue the Windows XP installation as usual.

4. When asked if you want to update your hard drive to use the NTFS format, choose No (leave the partition alone). If you upgraded to NTFS, Windows 9x would not be able to read the disk.

5. When the Windows XP installation has concluded, you should be able to successfully boot into either Windows XP or Windows 9x via the Windows XP boot menu presented at system startup.

At the risk of sounding redundant, I'll remind you that although this configuration used to be common (before Windows 2000), it can have its pitfalls. The following are some important things to keep in mind with this configuration:

- Both operating systems will use the same Program Files folder, which can result in version conflicts.

- Registry settings for an application on Windows 9x will not follow you into the Registry of Windows XP, and vice versa. You might have to reinstall some applications in order for them to function correctly in both operating systems. In some instances, you might even have to purchase separate Windows 9x- or Windows XP-specific versions of some applications. Finding out which ones you need to do this with is simply a matter of experimenting with each respective operating system. If you have to install two different versions of an app (one for each OS), be sure to install them into different folders so they don't overwrite one another.

TIP

> If there is one saving grace, it's that the Registry files from Win9x and XP won't overwrite one another. Windows 9x stores user Registry info in \Windows or \windows\profiles, while Windows XP stores user Registry data in \Documents and Settings\<username>.

PLACING WINDOWS XP PROFESSIONAL AND WINDOWS 9X IN SEPARATE PARTITIONS

As you have no doubt gathered by now, the preferred approach uses separate partitions. This arrangement is more flexible, imminently more stable, and foolproof in the long run.

First, you must plan the installation from a file system standpoint. This will give you a better foundation from which to proceed:

- The Windows 9x partition should be a FAT32 file system with C:\WINDOWS (the system directory), along with C:\Program Files contained in it.

- Windows XP will reside on the second partition, containing the Windows XP %SystemRoot% directory (typically D:\WINNT), along with D:\Program Files. You can format this partition with NTFS or FAT32.

- You might want to reserve a third and final FAT32 partition solely for sharing data between the two operating systems. You can use drive C for this, too, of course.

NOTE

> Wherever I suggest that you might want multiple partitions, remember they don't all need to be placed on the same drive. Regardless of the physical location of the target partition, the setup procedure remains the same. Just point to the target partition when prompted during the XP installation.

If you format the Windows XP partition with NTFS during installation, remember that it will not be visible to Windows 9x. Any FAT16 or FAT32 partitions located *after* the NTFS partition *will* be visible to Win9x. This can have the odd effect of making these extra partitions appear with different drive letters in the different operating systems, as each OS assigns letters to the partitions it recognizes, in order. I'll give you a concrete example of this later in the chapter under "Avoiding Drive Letter Madness."

USING FDISK TO DEFINE PARTITIONS

Chapter 3, "Installation," covered the fact that Setup will enable you to use unpartitioned free space to create a second partition (either NTFS or not) for installing Windows XP. You also learned about using a third-party program such as PartitionMagic to help in that process, especially if you don't have any "free" (meaning unpartitioned) space on your hard disk, which is likely the case. If you already have a free partition or two for installing Windows XP after Windows 9x/Me, you can skip ahead to the section titled "Installing Windows XP Professional into the Second Partition." If you need to define partitions before starting the Windows XP setup process (for example, to set up versions of Windows 9x or other operating systems), this section will give you an overview of the FDISK partitioning program that comes with DOS and Windows 9x.

CAUTION

> Using the FDISK editor is a permanent process. If you have any disk partitions currently defined on your system, be sure to have a backup of all your important data, because it will be trashed in this process. Unless you are partitioning your disk for the first time, I strongly suggest you use PartitionMagic if you want to save your data. PartitionMagic also has the added advantage of being able to actually resize your existing partitions for a maximum amount of flexibility.
>
> More information on PartitionMagic can be found at
>
> `http://www.powerquest.com/partitionmagic/`

If you need to set up partitions on a new disk, in lieu of using PartitionMagic (for whatever reason), you can opt to use the trusty old Microsoft-supplied FDISK program to do the job. It works okay in a pinch (especially on an unpopulated drive or one you're going to wipe), and knowledge of FDISK can sometimes come in handy.

4

The following discussion shows how to start with a blank hard disk, use FDISK to create the partitions, and then install Windows 9x and Windows XP. The following explains how to define partitions for each operating system:

1. First, boot from the Windows 9x CD-ROM and select the second option, Boot from CD-ROM. If you are booting from a Windows 9x installation floppy, just proceed to step 2.

2. Select Start Computer with CD-ROM Support.

3. After finally booting into DOS, run the FDISK program, which will give you the opportunity to partition your disk so that each operating system can occupy a different partition. This is simply done by typing **fdisk** at the prompt:

   `A:>fdisk`

4. When FDISK is loaded, you are asked whether to enable large disk support. Select Yes, which enables you to later format the disk with the FAT32 file system. (If you selected No here, you would only be able to create a partition of 2048MB or less using the FAT16 file system.)

5. Next, you will be presented with a menu of options for partitioning your hard disk, as shown in Figure 4.1. For the purposes of this installation, select option 1, Create DOS Partition or Logical DOS Drive. This option enables you to create the first partition for installing Windows 9x.

Figure 4.1
The FDISK main
menu screen.

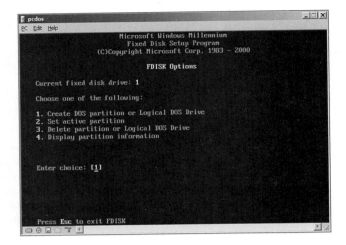

6. Select Create Primary DOS Partition to create a bootable primary partition.

> **NOTE**
> All Microsoft operating systems must be bootable from the first primary partition on the primary IDE bus. The only exclusion to this is a SCSI-based system, which must be bootable from the first primary partition of the SCSI controller–assigned boot disk. This does not mean the system and other files must be installed here; it only means that the Windows boot information must be installed in the MBR (master boot record) of this partition.

7. When asked whether you would like to use the maximum available size for this partition, select No. You will need additional space to be left on the disk for the other two partitions that will house the Windows XP system and the shared data.

8. Next you are asked for the size of the first partition. This particular setting will vary depending on the operating systems involved and the amount of disk space available.

   Table 4.2 (immediately following this set of steps) shows the minimum and recommended sizes for each operating system. You can make the partition larger than the recommended size, if you have the space.

9. Use the backspace key to erase the size that FDISK has filled in. Using the information in Table 4.2, enter the desired size for your first primary partition, in MB. For a 2GB partition, enter 2048.

10. Next, you must define the first partition as being the active partition so that the computer knows which partition it should try to boot from. Press Esc to return to the main FDISK menu. Select option 2, Set Active Partition, to pick the first partition and set it as active.

> **CAUTION**
> If more than one primary partition is listed (as might be the case with some Compaq models that use a special diagnostic partition for their BIOS setup program and testing software), make sure you select the partition you just created.

11. If you want to create the XP and data sharing partitions during the XP install procedure, you can leave the remainder of the disk unpartitioned and skip ahead to step 15.

   Otherwise, you may now create the logical partitions to house your remaining two file
   systems. This can be done by selecting option 1, Create a DOS Partition or Logical
   DOS Drive, and then selecting option 2, Create Extended DOS Partition.

12. FDISK adds all additional FAT partition entries inside what it calls an Extended DOS
partition. Therefore, you should allocate enough space for the Extended DOS Partition
to hold your Windows XP volume *and* your shared data volume. If you need no other
partitions, you can allocate all remaining space to the Extended Partition. Select a size,
press Enter, and then Esc.

13. FDISK will prompt you for the size of the first FAT partition to create inside the
extended partition—FDISK calls this a Logical DOS Drive. Select a size in MB for the
Windows XP partition, and then press Enter and Esc.

14. FDISK will prompt you for the size of the next Logical DOS Drive. Allocate the
remaining space to your data drive and press Enter.

15. Press Esc to exit FDISK. Finally, press Ctrl+Alt+Delete to restart the computer.

TABLE 4.2   RECOMMENDED HARD DRIVE CAPACITY FOR EACH OPERATING SYSTEM

Operating System	Minimum Size	Recommended Size
Windows 98	225MB to 400MB	2048MB
Windows NT 4.0	124MB	1024MB
Windows 2000 Professional	650MB	2000MB
Windows XP Home Edition	1500MB	2000MB
Windows XP Professional	1500MB	2048MB
Linux (Red Hat 6.1)	135MB to 1.2GB	2048MB

NOTE

Microsoft and others' discussions of disk space requirements in particular and hard disk storage in general are often confusing because MB (Megabyte) and GB (Gigabyte) each have two different meanings. Hard drives and similar storage devices are normally rated in decimal MB, in which 1MB equals one million bytes, and decimal GB, in which 1GB equals one billion bytes. However, disk utilities such as FDISK and most system BIOSes rate drives in binary MB/GB; a binary MB is 1,024×1,024 (the value of a kilobyte times a kilobyte), for a total of 1,048,576 bytes, and a binary GB is 1024×1024×1024, for a total of 1,073,741,824 bytes. Thus, there are substantial differences in the size of decimal versus binary MB/GB. Recently, the term Mebibyte (Mi) has been developed to refer to binary MB and Gibibyte (Gi) to binary GB, but this usage is not yet widespread.

INSTALLING WINDOWS 9X INTO THE FIRST PARTITION

After you've defined at least two partitions, you are ready to install Windows 9x into the first one. After that you'll install Windows XP in the second one.

1. If you are installing Windows 9x (and you have a bootable version of the installation CD) you can install it by booting from its installation CD-ROM. Select Start Windows 9x Setup from CD-ROM.

> **NOTE**
>
> If you're having trouble accessing the CD-ROM drive, check the BIOS settings; or as a good trick, many systems will boot up from a Windows 98 emergency startup disk with CD-ROM support (even one made on another machine). You can boot into DOS this way, with CD-ROM drivers loaded. Then run the Setup program located on the CD.

2. When you're in the Windows 9x installation program, you will be given the option to format drive C: and continue with the installation. Setup may also require that you format partition D:. It's okay to do this.

3. Continue with the Windows 9x installation, making sure that Windows is placed in the \WINDOWS folder on the C: partition by accepting the default.

> **CAUTION**
>
> If you've been booting from your CD-ROM installation disc, be sure to change the boot sequence in your BIOS so that your hard disk boots before your CD-ROM. This is essential for a successful installation.

> **TIP**
>
> Windows 9x is installed first for a very important reason. Windows 9x will always write its own master boot record to make the system boot into it after an installation. You'll want to make sure that Windows XP has the last say in what gets installed at the master boot level so that you can take advantage of its versatile boot loader.

INSTALLING WINDOWS XP PROFESSIONAL INTO THE SECOND PARTITION

Continue your multi-boot pursuit with the installation of Windows XP. Per Microsoft's recommendations, you should run the Windows XP installation program from within Windows 9x.

1. Insert the Windows XP disc. The Windows XP Installer should auto-run. If it doesn't, select Start, Run, and type **D:SETUP**, where D: is your CD-ROM drive letter.

2. Select Install Windows XP. When asked what type of installation you want to perform, select New Installation (Advanced) and click Next, as shown in Figure 4.2.

Figure 4.2
Choose New
Installation here to
install XP into a sepa-
rate partition.

3. Proceed through the License Agreement and Product Key pages to the Setup Options page. Click Advanced Options and check I Want To Choose the Install Drive Letter and Partition During Setup. This gives you the opportunity to select the D: partition as well as convert it to the NTFS file system later on in the setup. Click OK, and then Next.

4. After the Windows Setup Wizard copies some files to your hard disk, it will reboot your system and continue the installation from a text-based setup. From this setup, you will have the option to select where you'd like to install your Windows XP system, as shown in Figure 4.3. If you didn't create the XP and data partitions earlier, you can use this menu to create new partitions by pressing C. Finally, select the second partition as the Windows XP install procedure and press Enter.

Figure 4.3
Selecting the partition
for the \WINDOWS
install directory from
within the text-mode
Windows XP Setup.
Windows 2000 and
NT Setup offer a simi-
lar choice.

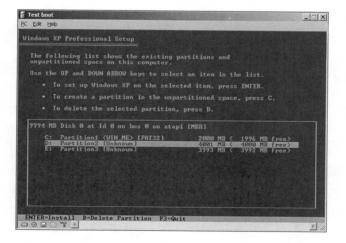

5. Next, you will be given the option to select the type of file system to use. You can keep your already formatted partition intact, or select a new file system format, as shown in Figure 4.4.

Figure 4.4
Here, you can choose to leave the original file system intact, or select a different file system for the Windows XP partition.

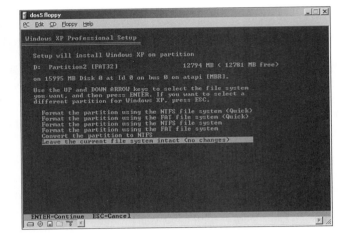

The "Quick" versions of these choices do not test the drive as it formats. Testing takes some time but it's worthwhile, so I recommend that you not use the Quick format options.

TIP

> Remember, you can convert a FAT partition to NTFS at any later time using a Windows command-line utility. Windows can't convert NTFS back to FAT, however. If in doubt, use FAT for now.

6. After making your choice, Setup will proceed to do its thing and install Windows XP. During setup, there will be one or two restarts and you'll see the multi-boot menu. Ignore it and let the default "Windows XP Setup" choice start up. This choice will be removed when Setup has completed successfully.

7. When you subsequently restart your computer, you should see the options shown in Figure 4.5.

Figure 4.5
The final result–the Windows XP boot loader now shows both operating systems at boot time.

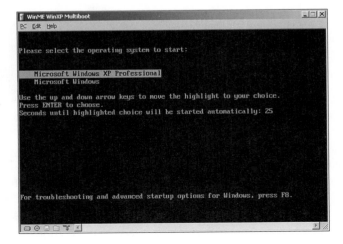

FORMATTING THE DATA-SHARING PARTITION

On some of our machines, we're quite content with two partitions only, with data placed either on the Windows 9x partition if it is nonsensitive, or on the Windows XP NTFS partition (and optionally in an encrypted folder) if it is sensitive. However, I recommend using a third partition to give you a place to store files that you want to keep while installing and uninstalling operating systems on the other two. I used such a partition while writing this book to hold my screen-capture program and notes; the main OS partitions needed to be erased and reinstalled dozens of times.

If you did create an extra data partition as I described in the previous section, the final installation step is to format this remaining partition. This can be done by using the Windows XP Disk Administration program, or the FORMAT command from a Command Prompt window in either OS.

➔ **See** Chapter 25 under the section "Disk Management" for more about formatting partitions with Disk Management.

AVOIDING DRIVE LETTER MADNESS

As I mentioned earlier, when you use file formats that are not compatible among all the operating systems you're using, logical drive letters will likely shift around based on which operating system you're booting.

The reason for this is that on bootup, Windows scans your disk controllers in the following order looking for fixed or removable hard disks:

1. Primary IDE Controller, Master Drive
2. Primary IDE Controller, Slave Drive
3. Secondary IDE Controller, Master Drive
4. Secondary IDE Controller, Slave Drive
5. SCSI Controllers, in SCSI ID order
6. Additional controllers (such as USB, IEEE-1394 drives)

(If your computer boots from a SCSI drive, the SCSI drives are scanned first.) Only the compatible partitions on these drives are scanned and assigned drive letters in the order found. This means that Windows 9x will skip over NTFS partitions, and will assign different drive letters to any subsequent FAT partitions it finds than Windows XP, 2000, or NT will.

For example, if I had one hard drive with three partitions, defined as follows:

#1 FAT32, Windows 98 Boot partition

#2 NTFS, Windows XP Boot partition

#3 FAT32, Data only

and a CD-ROM drive, Windows 98 and Windows XP will assign the default drive letters shown in Table 4.3.

TABLE 4.3 LOGICAL DRIVE LETTER ASSIGNMENTS

Drive	Partition	Drive Letter Assigned by Windows 98	Drive Letter Assigned by Windows XP
Hard Drive	#1, FAT32	C:	C:
	#2, NTFS	(none)	D:
	#3, FAT32	D:	E:
CD-ROM	CDFS	E:	F:

Notice that under Windows 98 the data partition is D:, whereas under Windows XP it is E:. This is not a problem if you store only data on the drive. However, it becomes more complicated if your applications expect to find support files on a given drive letter under any OS.

You might have already thought about using Windows XP Disk Management to reassign the drive letters while Windows XP is running. Although it is true that Disk Management can set drive letters in any way you please, you can't change the boot drive's letter. In our example, this means that we can't reverse the D and E drives letters under XP to match Windows 98 so that hard drive #3 is always logical drive E, regardless of operating system. However, there is another way. Retail copies of PartitionMagic include a program called DriveMapper that can remap the drive letters under Windows 98. You can run PartitionMagic in Windows 98, use the DriveMapper option, and reassign the data drive to E:, skipping D: altogether when you're running Windows 98. Then make your CD-ROM drive F:. Now, you can have the same logical drive assignment in both operating systems.

CAUTION

> If possible, reassign letters before you install applications; otherwise, Registry settings, shortcuts, and support files can point to the wrong drive. Consult the PartitionMagic user's guide or Help file for more about considerations when reassigning drive letters.

WINDOWS XP HOME EDITION AND WINDOWS XP PROFESSIONAL

Installing both the Home Edition and Professional version of Windows XP on the same system is popular for many people who need to test applications in both environments.

Because both operating systems use the same boot loader and compatible file systems, installation and setup are simple. However, you *must* ensure that the two versions are installed onto different partitions or hard drives.

To set up dual-booting of Windows XP Home Edition and XP Professional, simply install them both one after the other, taking care to select the Advanced Options button on the Special Options page during setup. Check I Want to Choose the Install Drive Letter and Partition During Setup, and then click OK. This will let you select the partition on which each version gets installed.

WINDOWS XP PROFESSIONAL AND WINDOWS 2000 OR NT

Installing both Windows XP and earlier NT versions on the same system is also something you might want to do. This configuration is popular for many people already running Windows NT 4.0 who want to try Windows XP before completely canning their previous installation. This is a worthwhile pursuit and can be obtained with a little care and planning.

If you already have Windows NT 4.0 installed, you are probably using either the FAT16 file system or NTFS. Looking at Table 4.1, you can see that Windows XP supports both of the file systems supported by Windows NT 4.0. When installing Windows XP Professional, you simply select a new installation, as opposed to an upgrade, and the installer will handle the rest. As with the previous configuration, Windows XP will save your Windows NT 4.0 installation and give you the choice of selecting it at boot time.

This setup also can suffer from the same sort of problems as the Windows 98/Windows XP configuration. You must be careful to not overlap your new and old installation directories. And although you can have them coexist on the same partition, you'd be installing files from two different versions of Windows into the same "Program Files" folder. It's much more prudent to have them occupy separate partitions or drives.

CAUTION

> Windows XP uses an updated version of the NTFS file system: NTFS5. XP Installation will upgrade any NTFS partitions to this new version of the file system. Therefore before installing Windows XP, you must be sure that you've first updated your installed version of Windows NT 4.0 with service pack 4 or greater. This will ensure that your NT 4.0 installation will be capable of reading your NTFS disk after adding Windows XP to your system. Service pack 6a is the current (and final) version.
>
> Even with the service pack, however, NT Version 4 won't be able to read XP's encrypted or compressed files. In fact, Microsoft recommends *against* using NTFS as the only file system on a shared XP Professional and NT system.

If you want to test or use Windows XP's advanced file system features, or if the NTFS version issue worries you, you can use this setup on a dual Windows XP/Windows NT installation.

Partition 1   Windows NT, NTFS version 4

Partition 2   Windows XP, NFTS version 5

Partition 3   Shared files, FAT16

Because Windows NT can't read FAT32 disks, you have to use a FAT16 partition as a shared file volume.

To dual-boot NT and XP, do the following:

1. Install Windows NT 4.0. Chances are good that you already have it installed, in which case this portion of the job is already complete.

2. You're going to want to have another partition to house Windows XP. Unless you have free, unpartitioned space available, you'll need to install an additional disk drive, or use PartitionMagic to insert a new partition on an existing drive. If you do have unpartitioned space, you can install Windows XP directly into that. You can leave the new partition unformatted. It will get formatted during the XP installation process.

3. Boot up Windows NT, insert the Windows XP setup disc, and choose Install Windows XP from the menu. (If the menu doesn't start automatically, look on the CD's root directory for Setup.exe and run it.)

4. Choose New Installation from the wizard's first page; otherwise, you'll wipe out Windows NT 4.0.

5. Accept the agreement, enter the serial number, and follow the wizard.

6. From the Select Special Options page of the Windows XP Setup Wizard, select the Advanced Options button. Check I Want to Choose the Install Drive Letter and Partition During Setup, and then click OK.

7. After the Windows Setup Wizard copies some files to your hard disk, it will reboot your system and continue the installation from a text-based setup. From this setup, you will have the option to select where you'd like to install Windows XP. Choose the partition you created in step 2, or choose any unformatted free space (if you have any).

8. Next, you will be given the option to select how you want the target partition formatted. Select Format as NTFS or Convert to NTFS.

9. The Setup process will continue normally. When it's finished, you'll be able to choose either Windows NT 4.0 or Windows XP when your computer boots up.

> **TIP**
>
> See the earlier section titled "Formatting the Data-Sharing Partition" for some thoughts about creating a third partition to store data that can be shared between the two operating systems.

WINDOWS XP, WINDOWS NT 4.0, AND WINDOWS 9X/ME

Although it might be uncommon, it is possible to create a setup using all three of these operating systems. Take the following approach:

1. Create three partitions (or four if you want a separate data partition). You can create these partitions on one or two hard drives, or three if you have that many.

2. If you decide you want a data partition, make it FAT16 because NT 4.0 can't see FAT32. FAT16 is the one common denominator. See Table 4.4 for a suggested layout. As you can see from the table, we're suggesting using FAT16 for all the partitions to ensure maximum compatibility and the least amount of drive letter shifting.

3. Install Windows 9x/Me in the first partition. If asked whether you want to upgrade to FAT32, say no unless you don't mind having the first partition invisible to Windows NT 4.0.

4. Install Windows NT in the third partition (unless you're not going to have a separate data partition, in which case it should go on the second partition) and upgrade it to at least Service Pack 4. This system will dual-boot. Check it to see that it works acceptably.

5. Install Windows XP in New Installation mode, into the last partition. This should add the third operating system to the boot loader.

6. Format the data partition however you like, but remember that for maximum compatibility between all three operating systems, you'll want to use FAT16.

   When you're finished, the Windows XP boot loader will give you the option of booting into each of the three operating systems. Remember to heed the cautions explained earlier in this chapter regarding sharing data and applications between operating systems.

TABLE 4.4   BOOTING WINDOWS XP, NT 4.0, AND WINDOWS 9X

Partition #	Operating System	Format	Notes
Partition 1	Windows 95 OSR2 Windows 98 or Windows Me	FAT16	Can use FAT32 if you don't mind thispartition not being seen by NT 4.0.
Partition 2	Optional Data Partition	FAT16	We've put it second so its drive letter stays the same under all three OSes.
Partition 3	Windows NT 4.0 SP4 or later	FAT16	Can use NTFS if you are aware of the consequences.
Partition 4	Windows XP	NTFS	

NOTE

> You can't multi-boot more than one version of Windows 95, 98, and Me even if they're on different partitions. The only way to have more than one Windows 9x on a single machine is with a third-party boot manager such as BootMagic or System Commander.

WINDOWS XP AND LINUX

Using both Windows XP and Linux on the same system is a very rewarding multi-boot scenario. This gives you two very powerful operating systems that can work in harmony on the same system. Linux can be booted from any type of partition on any installed disk, be it primary or logical. This enables you to create a Linux partition anywhere you have enough space to put it.

One of the great advantages of this configuration is Linux's capability to read, and sometimes write, nearly every file system under the sun. You'll be able to share files between your two systems with a minimal amount of hassle. Be sure to see Table 4.1 (earlier in this chapter) to properly plan for file sharing between both operating systems.

NOTE

> Linux can read NTFS partitions quite well. But with the current level of NTFS support, when Linux writes to an NTFS partition, it causes some repairable damage to the file system that Windows XP has to fix the next time it boots. Any intentional damage to a partition's file system makes me nervous, so I'd suggest that you avoid the need to have Linux write to an NTFS disk. Install Windows XP in a FAT32 partition, or use a third FAT16 or FAT32 partition to store common files.

LILO, THE LINUX LOADER

Just as Windows XP uses the Windows loader to select an operating system and boot up, Linux uses LILO—the LInux LOader. LILO has a comparable ability to select among several OSes in different locations. It's possible to use LILO as your primary boot program and to configure it to select between Linux and Windows XP.

However, configuring LILO is beyond the scope of this book. I'll only discuss how to set up multi-booting with the Windows loader, so if you're following these instructions it's important that whatever process you use to set up your system, you end up with the Windows loader on your primary disk's Master Boot Record, rather than LILO.

There are two ways to make sure this happens:

- If you install Linux first, and then Windows XP, the XP loader will replace LILO. Then you can use the procedure described later in this section to create a Linux boot file for the Windows loader.

- If you install XP first, then Linux, you'll have to take care to tell the Linux installation system not to put LILO on your computer's Master Boot Record (MBR). If it does, the XP loader will be overwritten. How you specify this differs from one Linux distribution to another, and may even differ between versions of the same distribution. In the instructions later in this section, I'll describe how to do this for Red Hat Linux version 7.1, but the procedure may be different for your copy of Linux. If the XP boot loader does get overwritten, you'll find out quickly: You won't get a boot choice menu. You'll have to follow the procedure in the following note.

Clearly, it's easiest and safest if you can install Linux first. If you can't, please read your Linux distribution's installation instructions carefully, and select an installation mode that does not automatically put LILO on the Master Boot Record. The scenario we discuss in the next section assumes that you've already installed Windows XP before installing Linux.

> **NOTE**
>
> If you do accidentally overwrite the Windows Loader with LILO, when you start up your PC, you won't get a choice of operating systems. Instead, an operating system boots up directly. What has happened is that an installation program overwrote the normal XP boot loader (for example, Linux may have installed the Linux Loader LILO). To restore the Windows loader, boot your computer from your Windows XP installation CD and follow the instructions to repair a damaged Windows XP installation. The only repair options you need to select at this point are the options to repair the startup environment and the boot sector. Your emergency disk will come in handy as the repair mechanism uses it to find your Windows XP partition.

INSTALLING LINUX

This section deals with the task of installing Linux in a multi-boot situation with Windows XP. Although a complete tutorial on the installation of Linux is out of the scope of this chapter, we will try to cover the essential points needed to make your system multi-bootable.

The procedures in this chapter are based on version 7.1 of Red Hat Linux. Adjust as necessary for later versions. For the purposes of this example, you will be installing Linux onto a separate partition on the same disk as your Windows XP installation. Refer to Table 4.2 to be sure you have enough free space to install both Windows XP and Linux.

> **NOTE**
>
> Although the following information provides the basics for dual-booting Windows XP with Linux, you'll find much more detailed coverage in *The Multi-Boot Configuration Handbook*, published by Que. You should also search the Web for information. Check out `http://www.linuxdoc.org/HOWTO/mini/Linux+NT-Loader.html` and `www.linuxdoc.org/HOWTO/mini/Multiboot-with-LILO.html`.

You can install Linux and Windows XP in either order. Just be sure to read the previous section titled "LILO, the Linux Loader." If you want to use NTFS for Windows XP, be sure to leave additional room for a FAT32 partition on which to store Linux and files you want to share between the two operating systems. Refer to Table 4.2 to find the minimum amounts of space needed. If you can, allow 3 or more GB for each partition.

Now, let's cover some of the important aspects of the Red Hat Linux installation procedure.

1. Boot from the Red Hat Linux installation CD-ROM. This will bring you to the Red Hat Linux installation program. Press Enter to begin a graphical-interface installation.

If your machine can't boot from the CD, then it's likely too old to run XP anyway. Almost all recent computers will boot from the CD, though sometimes it requires enabling that function in the BIOS.

2. After some preliminary questions about your keyboard and mouse, you will be prompted for what type of installation you would like. In the examples shown here, I chose the Custom System class (see Figure 4.6) so that I could specify that LILO not overwrite the Master Boot Record. This is very important if you're installing Linux after Windows XP! If you're installing Linux first, you can select a Workstation install, which will simplify your choices during the setup.

Figure 4.6
Selecting the Custom System installation type from within the Red Hat installation program.

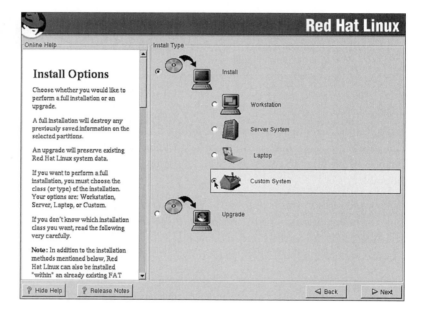

3. The next option offered by the Red Hat installation is whether you'd like automatic partitioning. Select the option to manually partition with Disk Druid and click Next. This step is necessary to create a multi-boot system with Windows XP, using the Windows boot loader.

4. On the following screen, the Disk Druid tool gives you the option of creating your Linux partitions. Although there are many options for partitioning and mounting Linux partitions, you can make it much easier on yourself simply by creating a root and swap partition. These are all that is needed to successfully install Linux. On the bottom pane, you can see a representation of your disk, as well as the used and free space available on it (see Figure 4.7).

Figure 4.7
The Red Hat Disk Druid disk partitioning tool.

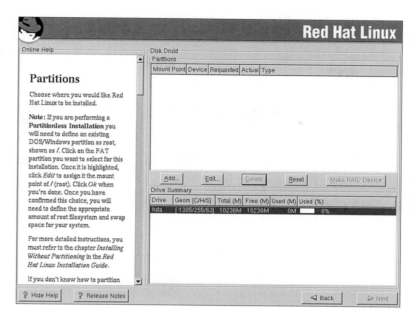

5. Click the Add button, and you can now add a partition for your Linux system. (If you have already installed Windows XP, you'll add the Linux partitions in addition to any already used for XP.) Because you will need to create two partitions, one each for / (or root) and swap, you must plan the sizes of each beforehand.

> **TIP**
>
> A good rule of thumb is to create a swap file that is at least the size of your installed memory. Twice the size is even better. This will be enough for most workstation applications. For example, if you're allowing 2GB of disk space (2048MB) for Linux on a system with 128MB of RAM, you could create a 1920MB root partition and a 128MB swap partition.

6. First, click the Add button to define the / (root) partition.

7. Type / into the Mount Point field and make sure the Partition Type (referred to as "Filesystem Type" in some newer versions of Red Hat) is the default Linux Native.

8. In the size field, add the size in megabytes for your root partition.

9. Select OK to create the partition. Notice now that the Free column on the second pane has changed to reflect the remaining space on the partition. This is the space left for your swap partition.

10. Next, click Add and define the swap partition. In the size field, enter the desired size in MB for the swap partition.

11. For the Partition Type, select Linux Swap, and the Mount Point field will automatically change to reflect that you are creating a swap partition.

Click OK to create the partition. At this point, if you haven't yet installed Windows XP, there should be a big chunk of unpartitioned space still available, as shown in Figure 4.8. Otherwise, you should end up with little or no unused space left.

12. After you have created these two partitions, click Next to continue the installation.

Figure 4.8
Root and swap partitions as defined in the Red Hat Disk Druid tool.

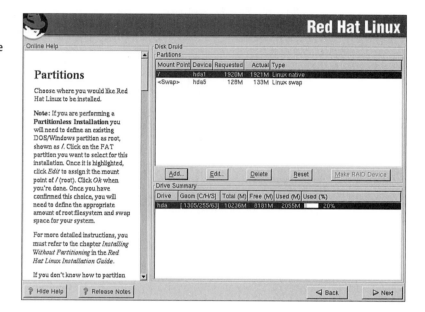

13. You will be asked whether you'd like to format your Linux root partition. This is perfectly safe so leave the option checked and continue by clicking Next.

14. On the next screen, Under LILO Configuration, check Create Boot Disk and Install LILO. Under Install LILO Boot Record On, select On First Record (sector) of Boot Partition, as shown in Figure 4.9. (If you've installed Windows XP already, it's important that you make these choices no matter which Linux distribution you are using.)

Write down the name of the partition that contains LILO. It will be named something such as /dev/hda1. You'll need to know this later when I discuss locating the Linux boot sector.

15. The bottom part of this screen sets which partitions show up in LILO's boot menu, as well as how you want to label the partitions. If you've already installed Windows XP, LILO will add an entry for your Windows XP partition and label it **dos**. This will actually enable you to boot into Windows XP's boot sector from within LILO by simply typing dos at the LILO prompt. Most likely, you'll want to leave this at its default setting.

16. Click Next and proceed through the setup menus to configure networking and other peripherals, user accounts, and so on. Follow the instructions in your Linux distribution manual because this will vary from version to version.

Figure 4.9
Boot disk and LILO
configuration from
the Red Hat Linux
installer.

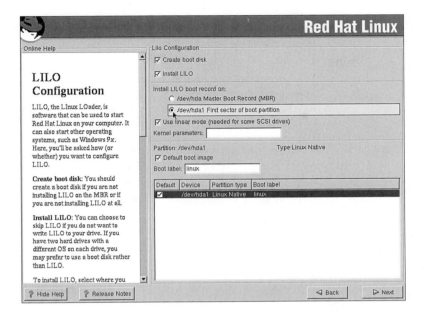

17. The installation will finally create and format your Linux file system and install system packages to complete the installation.

18. When prompted, insert your disk and the installer will create the boot disk for you. This boot disk will enable you to boot into Linux in case of an emergency (such as in case the Windows XP loader fails you!).

19. After LILO is installed, the Red Hat installation will finish and you may reboot your system.

GETTING THE LINUX BOOT SECTOR

After you install Linux, you'll need to create an image or file dump of the Linux boot sector. You need this to configure the Windows XP boot loader to boot into Linux. Here's how to get it:

1. Get a blank, formatted 1.44MB floppy disk.

2. Shut down and reboot your computer with the Linux boot disk discussed in the previous section.

3. When Linux has finished booting, log in as root using the password you supplied during installation. All the following steps must be performed as root.

4. Remove the boot disk, insert the formatted MS-DOS floppy into your disk drive and type the following command:

```
mount -t msdos /dev/fd0 /mnt/floppy
```

This will make the disk available to you by mounting it in the directory /mnt/floppy.

> **TIP**
>
> If you need to format the floppy from within Linux, you may do so by typing the following command from the prompt:
>
> `fdformat /dev/fd0; /sbin/mkfs -t msdos`
>
> This command will give you a freshly formatted MS-DOS disk in Linux. From there you can simply mount the disk to get access to it. Also, as a little reminder, you use the syntax /dev/fd0D720 for a double-density drive or /dev/fd0H1440 for a high density drive.

5. The next step is to write the Linux boot sector to the disk. The most important part of this step is to make sure you take the boot sector from the correct partition. This partition is the one that was installed in LILO during the Linux installation. If you're unsure which partition contains the Linux boot sector, issue the following command:

   `more /etc/lilo.conf`

   which will give you output similar to the following:

   ```
   boot=/dev/hda1
   map=/boot/map
   install=/boot/boot.b
   prompt
   timeout=50
   image=/boot/vmlinuz-2.4.2-2
       label=linux
       root=/dev/hda1
       read-only
   ```

6. The `boot=` entry at the top of the file tells us that LILO is installed in /dev/hda1. Using the dd program, issue the following command:

   `/bin/dd if=/dev/hda1 of=/mnt/floppy/bootsect.lnx bs=512 count=1`

   This command will copy the Linux boot sector at /dev/hda1 to a file called bootsect.lnx on your disk.

7. Before you eject a diskette, you have to unmount it. So unmount the floppy disk using the following command:

   `umount /dev/fd0`

8. Finally, remove the floppy disk from your computer and reboot the system:

   `/sbin/reboot`

   If you haven't already installed Windows XP, do this now. If you created an extra partition to use for shared file storage, you can create it now as well.

ADDING LINUX TO THE WINDOWS XP BOOT LOADER

After both Linux and Windows XP are installed, you can add Linux to the Windows XP boot loader from any version of Windows you have installed. The steps are exactly the same and are not operating system–dependent.

1. First, copy the bootsect.lnx file, which you created in the previous section, from your floppy disk to the root of your C: drive. This can be done from a command prompt or from the Windows Explorer. This file must be located in the root folder.

2. Modify the BOOT.INI file to add an entry for Linux. The easiest way is to open the System applet in Control Panel, view the Advanced tab, select Settings under Startup and Recovery, and click Edit.

3. Next, add the following line at the end of the BOOT.INI file:

```
C:\bootsect.lnx="Red Hat Linux 7.1"
```

4. You can now save BOOT.INI, reboot, and select Red Hat Linux 7.1 as one of your boot menu options. It's a long and complex procedure, but that's one of the reasons we love Linux!

MOUNTING WINDOWS DISKS WITHIN LINUX

Next, you'll want Linux to mount your Windows disks so that you can share files between both operating systems. This will enable you to copy files back and forth without using external media such as floppy disks. All the following steps must be performed as root because they are system-sensitive procedures:

1. First, create the directories within which you will mount the Windows file systems. The normal Linux convention is to create these directories in the /mnt tree.

2. Issue commands to create the directories for your Windows FAT16 or FAT32 partitions:

```
mkdir /mnt/windisk1
mkdir /mnt/windisk2
(etc).
```

NOTE
These directory names are a matter of taste. You can use whatever name you feel comfortable with at this point. As long as these directories exist, your Windows partitions should mount easily.

3. To test the first mount point, attempt to mount the first FAT32 partition using this command:

```
mount -t vfat /dev/hda1 /mnt/windisk1
```

4. You can examine the contents (with the exclusion of hidden files) of this partition by simply executing

```
ls /mnt/windisk1
```

5. If the mount was successful, you will see a familiar list of files and directories found on your first Windows partition.

6. Likewise, you can mount an NTFS partition with the following command:

```
mount -t ntfs /dev/hda2 /mnt/windisk2
```

using the correct hard drive number, of course.

NOTE

> By default, the NTFS file system driver is not enabled in Red Hat Linux. You must consult your documentation to enable this driver. As stated previously, if you use this driver, it is recommended that you use the read-only version. The current read/write version of the NTFS driver is still in the alpha stages as of this writing.

Enabling these file systems to automatically mount in Linux involves a procedure that is out of the scope of this discussion. Although it is possible, only experienced Linux users should attempt to modify the system's boot time mount parameters. Typically, the changes needed to auto-mount foreign file systems are made in /etc/fstab. Red Hat Linux includes a GUI utility, called linuxconf, that makes this task much more simple. Consult the documentation that came with your Linux distribution. (If linuxconf didn't come with your version of Linux, it's still available for download, of course.)

THE VIRTUAL MACHINE APPROACH

If you need access to multiple operating systems primarily for testing purposes, rather than for long periods of work, there's a way to enjoy the use of multiple operating systems like any of the hassle of multi-boot setups. In fact, you can even use multiple operating systems simultaneously on the same computer. It's done with a setup called a *virtual machine*. It's an old concept (IBM used it on its mainframes back in the 1970s) that's making a big comeback thanks to today's fast processors and huge hard disks.

A virtual machine program emulates (simulates) in software all of the hardware functions of a PC. It lets an entire operating system (called a *guest* operating system) run as an ordinary application program on a *host* operating system such as Windows XP. Since all of the hardware functions are emulated, the guest OS doesn't "know" it's not in complete control of a computer. When it attempts to physically access a hard disk, display card, network adapter, or serial port, the virtual machine program calls upon the host operating system to actually carry out the operation. Services supplied to the guest operating system (the virtual machine) typically include access to ports, floppy disks, CD-ROM drives, even networking (including access to the Internet).

Even though the software may need to execute several hundred instructions to emulate one hardware operation, the speed penalty is only 5 to 10 percent. And if a guest OS crashes, it doesn't take down your system. You can simply click a Reset menu choice and "reboot" the virtual machine. Check out Figure 4.10, where I have DOS, Linux, and Windows Me running in separate virtual machines.

Another advantage of the virtual machine programs currently on the market is that they don't allow the guest OS unfettered access to your real disk drives. Instead, you create a *virtual disk*, a single large file on your host operating system that contains the contents of what the virtual machine sees as a hard drive. With today's large hard drives, it's no big deal to create a 1 or 2GB file to serve as a virtual hard drive to host Windows 95, and another for Windows NT, and another for Linux…you get the picture.

Figure 4.10
Virtual PC running Windows Me, Linux, and DOS on three virtual machines simultaneously.

If you make a backup copy of the file after installing a guest operating system on one of these virtual disk drives, you can return the guest OS to its original, pristine state just by copying the backup over the virtual disk file. You can even boot up a guest OS, start a bunch of applications, and save the virtual machine in this exact state. When you want to use it again, you can just fire up the whole system starting right from this point. A typical startup from a saved state takes only about 5–10 seconds on a reasonably quick machine. If you're a tester or experimenter, a virtual computer can save you many, many hours of time installing, reinstalling, and rebooting.

Of course, you still need separate licenses for all of the extra operating systems you install, but the virtual machine can let you run as many OSes and as many configurations of these OSes as you like, separately or simultaneously. And all of this comes without the need to hassle with BOOT.INI or worry about partitions.

NOTE

Have you wondered how operating system book authors get screen pictures of the bootup and installation process? In the old days, we had to use film cameras or video recorders. Now, we just use virtual PC programs, and use screen capture software to get images of our desktop. It's a walk in the proverbial park.

If this sounds interesting, there are two products you should check into:

- VMWare, sold by VMWare. Check out www.vmware.com. VMWare was the first commercial system to emulate a PC on a PC. (Previous PC emulators ran on other computing platforms.) The advantage of VMWare is that the virtual machines can network among themselves, so it's a good platform for testing networking applications between multiple clients without requiring multiple physical machines.

- Virtual PC, sold by Connectix. These folks created Virtual PC for the Macintosh some time ago, and recently released Virtual PC for the PC. Check out www.connectix.com/products/vpc4w.html. This program I find easier to use. Creating new virtual machines for different operating systems is effortless, using a wizard. Pre-installed Virtual Machine "images" for popular operating systems (including license) are available from Connectix to make the process even easier.

Both vendors have trial versions that you can download and test before buying. Both also support networking, device and file sharing, and cut-and-paste capability between the host OS and several types of guest OS.

MIXING MACINTOSH AND WINDOWS OSES

As a system admin or just a power user type, you may have the need to work with Mac software or files in addition to the usual plethora of PCs you most likely administer. This section discusses means by which you can transfer files between Mac and XP, and even a way you can essentially "dual-boot" between XP and the Mac operating systems, using Mac OS emulation software.

MAC-TO-PC FILE CONVERSION

Let's start with file conversion, which is a common need if you work with data files created in both environments. As you probably know, the Mac can read and write PC disks, so that is one way around the hassle of file exchange. Just give the colleague a formatted PC disk and ask him or her to copy the files you want onto the floppy. Then stuff the floppy back into your PC and read the file(s).

An alternative approach works from the PC side alone. Suppose someone gives you a Mac-formatted disk that you need to read in the PC. A program called Mac-In-DOS made by Pacific Micro can skin that cat. We've tried that and like it. It works in the PC and reads, formats, and writes Mac disks in the PC floppy drive. It also supports CD-ROM, SyQuest, Bernoulli, and IOmega Zip and Jaz disks. Search for it on the Web. As of this writing, the product was in limbo to some degree. An older (DOS-based) version is available at

`http://www.netspace.net.au/~magainc/download.html`

For the newer Windows-based version (as shown in Figure 4.11), check www.softwareshelf.com or send email to info@softwareshelf.com to inquire.

Figure 4.11
Mac-In-DOS Serves as a disk format translator between Mac OS and Windows operating systems.

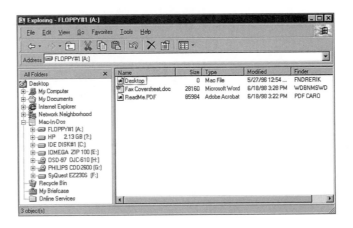

Another similar program that allows you to read and write disks cross-platform is a program called Gemulator Explorer. This is a free utility that empowers a Windows-based computer to read Mac (and Atari ST) diskettes. Gemulator Explorer can read Macintosh-formatted high-density (1.44MB) floppy disks as well as other Macintosh-formatted removable media such as ZIP, Syquest, Jaz, and CD-ROMs. Gemulator Explorer can also read externally connected SCSI hard disks formatted in either Macintosh HFS or Atari ST GEMDOS format, and 720KB, 800KB, and 1.44MB Atari ST/TT formatted floppy disks.

Gemulator Explorer also doubles as a disk imaging and backup tool. Using Gemulator Explorer, you can create a disk image from a physical disk, then write the entire disk image back onto a disk. Disk images can then be used by other Mac emulators such as SoftMac or Gemulator (see more about those, later in this chapter). Files can be copied off the Macintosh disks and saved as regular MS-DOS files on the PC. Files are displayed as icons in a familiar Explorer-like window.

http://www.emulators.com/explorer.html

RUNNING PC AND MAC PROGRAMS ON THE SAME MACHINE

If you want to actually *run* Mac programs on the PC, well, that's a little more complicated, but still possible. With some limitations, you can force a PC to emulate a Mac. Just as there are PC-on-a-PC virtual machine programs, and PC-on-a-Mac programs such as VirtualPC, SoftPC, and SoftWindows, several Mac emulators can run Mac programs on your PC. Here's a short description of emulators you should check out if you have the need.

> **NOTE**
> For links to all the emulators discussed here (and a few more), visit http://mes.emuunlim.com/software/macemu/.

ARDI EXECUTOR

One such program we've been experimenting with and are impressed with is called Executor, from ARDI. Executor is a virtual Macintosh machine for reading and writing Macintosh-formatted media and running Macintosh programs.

ARDI has implemented the core of the Macintosh operating system independently from Apple Computer, Inc. In order to legally sell software that will allow Mac applications to run on a PC, ARDI has written its own OS and tool box that implement a large portion of Macintosh System 7.0 OS software. As such, Executor requires no software (or ROM chip) from Apple, which makes it the only solution for many customers who need to run Macintosh programs who don't already have a Macintosh. (Some of the other emulators require you to have an actual Mac ROM chip taken out of a Mac and installed on a ROM card that plugs into the PC bus, or at least a legitimate soft copy of the ROM firmware code stored in a hard disk file.)

Executor runs as a native Windows application, either in full-screen mode or in a window (see Figure 4.12). You can print from Executor to any printer that your system can talk to (local printers, remote printers, faxes, and so on). However, font support is limited. You can cut and paste text and graphics between Executor and other applications. You can create shortcuts for a Macintosh application so that Executor will start up and run that application.

Figure 4.12
Executor runs many
Mac programs on the
PC under Windows
9x, NT, 2000, and XP.

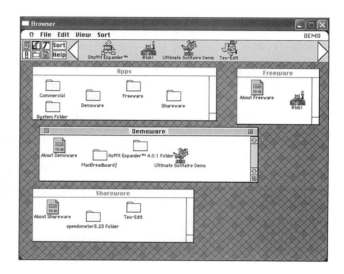

Unfortunately, Executor (like virtually all Mac emulators) won't support applications that are "PowerPC-only," which is an increasing proportion. Additionally, although ARDI supports most core operating system services, newer services are not supported. Macintosh programs are capable of querying the operating system to determine which services are supported and which aren't, but programmers often make assumptions that are valid for real Macintoshes but that are not valid under Executor. Executor doesn't yet support the system services that were added after Macintosh System 7.0 (Apple is now shipping 9.0 and X), nor does it yet support networking or system software extensions (known as INITs and CDEVs). ARDI has a compatibility database on its Web site at http://www.ardi.com, which you should check if you're interested in running a particular program.

SOFTMAC

SoftMac, made by Emulators Inc., is an example of a Mac emulator that does require an ISA-based ROM (computer memory) card that holds the Macintosh ROM, or that you have a working Mac from which to make a ROM BIOS "dump" file. The advantage of using a card is, according to the maker, that it's more likely to run "unruly" programs that make direct calls to hardware rather than passing off all service calls to the operating system. Although perhaps more stable, SoftMac, like Executor, doesn't emulate the PowerPC, so you can't use Mac OS versions 8.5 and higher, which means you can't run OS X either. But unlike Executor, at least SoftMac does support OS 7 and OS 8.

Figure 4.13
SoftMac runs many Mac programs on the PC under Windows, but requires that the user have Macintosh ROMs.

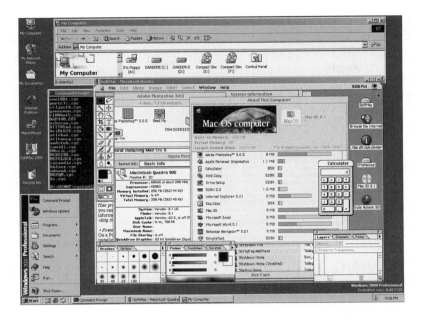

In April 2002, the company released their XP-compatible version which supposedly put a little more tiger in the tank of this emulator, doubling its speed. SoftMac XP comes with some additional software, including an MS-DOS–based Mac emulator called Fusion PC 3.0, and the Gemulator Pro program mentioned previously. Softmac is a capable tool, with some nice frills. It supports Windows XP, Windows 2000, Windows Me, Windows 98, Windows NT 4.0, and Windows 95, emulating Mac Classic, Mac II, Mac LC, and Quadra. It supports up to 1GB of Mac memory using a swap file. It supports CD-ROM, DVD-ROM, Mac floppy, LS-120, and Zip drives. You can easily drag and drop between PC and Mac disks, and it'll support high-res graphics displays, up to 1900×1080. Like Virtual PC described previously, SoftMac can save the system state via a Windows-like "Hibernate" command.

For more information, see

www.emulators.com/softmac.html

BASILISK II

Basilisk II is an Open Source Macintosh emulator that lets you run Mac OS software on your PC. Where SoftMac is marketed commercially, Basilisk II is an open source project, distributed under the GNU General Public License. In other words, it's freely available and not crippled.

However, as with SoftMac, you'll need a copy of MacOS and a Macintosh ROM image to use Basilisk II. The program requires genuine Mac ROMs (from a 32-bit clean '030/'040 Mac or from a Mac Classic) either on a permanent basis, installed into SoftMac's hardware card, or long enough to capture to a disk image file. (Legally, you should own the Mac you're using in this way).

Like many open source projects, versions have been developed for a variety of operating systems. In this case, Basilisk II is available for BeOS R4 (both PowerPC and x86), x86 Unix (tested with Linux, Solaris 2.5, FreeBSD 3.x, and IRIX 6.5), AmigaOS 3.x, and Windows NT/2000/XP/9x. Note that most (but not all) features work under Windows 95 and Windows 98. Source code is available for downloading.

The Windows versions are maintained by Lauri Pesonen. Check this site:

```
http://www.nic.fi/~lpesonen/BasiliskII/
```

More information can be found at the Basilisk II Web site:

```
http://www.uni-mainz.de/~bauec002/B2Main.html
```

Also check this site for a review, and installation tips:

```
http://www.lowendmac.com/mac2win/02/0501.html
```

REMOVING THE WINDOWS XP BOOT LOADER

There are times when you might want to remove the Windows XP Boot Loader. For example, this might be needed if you have incorrectly installed an operating system and want to remove it to start over. If you choose to remove the loader, however, you must be sure that you have an operating system to boot into. For this example, assume you have Windows 9x installed and want to return to a state in which it is the only operating system available.

First, while you are booted into Windows 9x, you must create a bootable system disk. This can be accomplished by selecting the Add/Remove Programs control panel. Then select the Startup Disk tab.

After creating a startup disk, reboot your system using the new disk. After you have fully booted into MS-DOS, simply enter the following command from the command prompt:

sys C:

This will install the Windows 9x startup boot sector onto drive C: and remove the Windows XP boot loader. Now that you're able to boot back into Windows 9x, simply remove the Windows XP directories.

You can optionally remove the following files to clean up the rest of the Windows XP boot loader files:

```
C:\boot.ini
C:\ntldr
C:\ntdetect.com
```

You might also want to remove

```
bootsect.dos
pagefile.sys
ntbootdd.sys,
```

if they're there.

Install Multi-boot Systems from Old to New

Something to keep in mind when installing multi-boot systems with Microsoft OSes is that their setup programs don't know about OSes *newer* than the one you're installing. This is why it's imperative to install these systems from oldest to newest. This is the golden rule of multi-boot installations. If you don't do this, boot files can be overwritten, disabling the newer OSes. So, for example, you should install Windows 98, then Windows 2000, then Windows XP, *in that order!* If you don't, you could see an error message such as this one:

```
Starting Windows... Windows 2000 could not start because the following file is
missing or corrupt: \WINDOWS\SYSTEM32\CONFIG\SYSTEM startup options for Windows
2000, press F8.
```

```
You can attempt to repair this file by starting Windows 2000 Setup using the
original Setup floppy disk or CD-ROM. Select 'r' at the first screen to start
repair.
```

Suppose you installed Windows 2000 *after* installing Windows XP. You'll suddenly not be able to start up Windows XP. The solution is to just copy back the boot files from the XP CD or perform a repair installation of XP. So if you don't fix the problem, you can't boot a newer OS. The fix is still going to cost you about an hour of your day.

1. Simply rerun the Windows XP Setup program from your bootable CD-ROM (or your shiny new startup disks).

2. Select the option to Repair your installation.

Don't worry, Windows XP is not reinstalling itself completely. Although Setup goes through the entire installation process, it's only looking for missing files, in this case the boot files. After the Setup process completes, you should be pleasantly surprised when you reboot the computer and your Windows XP installation once again starts up properly.

4

TIP

Microsoft has put together a some good technical documents on multi-booting that can be found at

```
http://www.microsoft.com/windowsxp/pro/using/howto/gettingstarted/
multiboot.asp
```

```
http://support.microsoft.com/support/kb/articles/q283/4/33.asp
```

```
http://support.microsoft.com/support/kb/articles/Q249/0/00.ASP
```

USING A THIRD-PARTY MULTI-BOOT LOADER

Even with all the advice in this chapter, managing more than one operating system on the same machine at the same time can be a daunting task. Fortunately, some special tools can save you at your darkest moments. (You never expected to find purple prose in a computer book, did you?)

The Windows XP multi-boot loader is capable of supporting a large number of multi-boot situations—probably more than will fit on the screen in a list. Still, editing the BOOT.INI file is an intimidating process, and you must remember quirky rules about the order of operating system installation.

If you're interested in loading a killer system with three or more operating systems, we recommend using a program designed specifically for the job. I'll describe a couple of them for your consideration.

Once again, the PowerQuest people come to the rescue with their offering, called BootMagic, which is bundled with PartitionMagic (not available separately, though it used to be). This program uses a graphical interface to help you set up and run multiple operating systems in the same machine, with a minimum of compatibility problems. You can run the setup interface from DOS, Windows 9x, or Windows NT/2000/XP. The program supports Windows XP/2000, Windows 95/98, Windows NT 4.0 (server and workstation), Windows NT 3.51 (server and workstation), Windows 3.x (must be installed with DOS 5 or later), MS-DOS 5.0 or later, PC-DOS 6.1 or later, Open DOS, OS/2 3.0 or later, Linux, BeOS, and most other versions of DOS and PC-compatible OSes (check their site at www.powerquest.com for more info).

Another similar program is System Commander 7, from V Communications. This product has received rave reviews from some magazines. System Commander Deluxe enables you to install and run any combination of PC-compatible operating systems, including Windows 95/98, Windows 3.x, Windows NT, DOS, OS/2, and all of the PC-compatible Unixes including Linux. Like BootMagic, this program also has a graphical user interface. In addition, it does partition management such as resizing, creation, and deletion. It's available from V Communications, Inc. (check their site at www.v-com.com).

4

CHAPTER **5**

AUTOMATED INSTALLATION AND NETWORK DEPLOYMENT

In this chapter

AUTOMATED DEPLOYMENT OVERVIEW

If you're planning to deploy Windows XP to a number of systems, you're probably considering automating the installation process. And if you're not, you should be. Automating a deployment may take a bit of development time up front, but it saves time in the long run when compared to manually installing a large number of systems. Automation ensures consistency by removing most of the opportunities for human error.

So who should use automated deployment? Well, if you're a home user, and you're only planning on installing Windows XP Home Edition on that old machine your kid uses to surf the Web, you probably just want to run with the standard out-of-the-box install process. But if you happen to have 50 such kids, if you need to frequently install the same base configuration on a system or two for testing purposes, if you configure Windows XP systems for resale, or if you're developing a deployment scenario for an organization's IT department, then you'll definitely want to consider automating.

A number of options are available when automating the installation of Windows XP, which are listed below and illustrated in Figure 5.1:

- **Scripted install from CD or Distribution Share**—This is the most basic type of automated install. Setup runs using the usual WINNT.EXE or WINNT32.EXE installer, and a preconfigured answer file is passed in from a command-line switch. The answer file supplies the information that would normally have to be entered manually.

- **Scripted install using boot CD**—In this process, the system boots from the install CD, and Windows XP Setup reads an answer file from the A: drive.

- **System image prepared with Sysprep**—With this scheme, you install and configure one system to your exact specifications, then use a *disk image* (an exact duplicate of a system drive) to deploy identical copies to a large number of systems.

- **Remote Installation Services (RIS)**—This more sophisticated method for deploying Windows XP over the network involves booting from a network interface card (NIC), ROM, or ROM emulator disk.

5

Figure 5.1
Four scenarios for automatic deployment of Windows XP.

Scripted Install from CD or Distribution Share

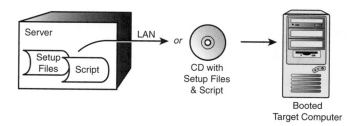

Scripted Install Using Boot CD

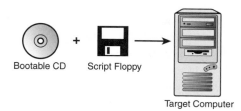

Scripted Install prepared with Sysprep

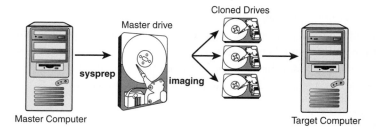

Remote Installation Services (RIS)

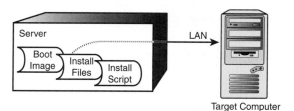

LICENSING ISSUES

Whether you choose to automate using the bootable Windows XP CD with an answer file, using a disk image, or using a scripted install over the network, the first thing you'll want to do is make sure you're properly licensed. If I had a dollar for every time I'd created an image using the wrong media for my licensing, I'd have exactly one dollar…because after the first time I screwed it up, I've always remembered to double-check my media before starting development on a new automated install.

> **NOTE** Microsoft revises its licensing policies almost as often as it releases Service Packs. For the latest twists and turns, check out
>
> `http://www.microsoft.com/licensing`

Under Microsoft's current licensing model, retail Windows XP media cannot be used for multiple installations. Using a scripted install with a separate retail CD for each system is still an option, as long as you aren't trying to fully automate the install. To script installs from retail media, though, you'd need one retail CD with a retail product key for each system, and you'd still need to prompt for the unique retail product key on each machine. Additionally, you'd need to run through the product activation wizard on each system. This method wouldn't be practical for most organizations, but if you're only worried about a handful of systems—in a very small office or in your home, perhaps—it is a valid option. Using an answer file to simplify individual installations is exactly like using an answer file for large-scale installations, except you won't need to spend nearly as much time on development and testing. I prefer the scripted install using the bootable Windows XP installation CD when developing a setup process for a small-scale environment.

→ For more details on product activation, refer back to "Product Activation," **p. 112**.

If you're planning to install Windows XP on five or more systems, you're eligible for one of Microsoft's Volume Licensing programs. There are four basic programs available for Windows XP volume licensing, listed in Table 5.1. Machines loaded with Windows XP using media acquired through one of these programs and using a valid volume license product key are not required to run the product activation wizard.

TABLE 5.1   WINDOWS XP VOLUME LICENSING

Program	Description
Open License	For academic institutions, charities, corporations, or government organizations needing licenses for five or more systems.
Select License	For academic institutions, charities, corporations, or government organizations with decentralized purchasing, needing licenses for 250 or more systems.
Enterprise Agreement	Software *purchasing* agreement for corporate customers with centralized purchasing, needing licenses for 250 systems or more. In this type of agreement, the company pays for the licenses needed, after which it can use those licenses as long as it wishes.
Enterprise Subscription Agreement	Software leasing agreement for corporate customers with centralized purchasing, needing licenses for 250 systems or more. In the leasing agreement, companies pay less for the OS licenses up front, but they pay additional fees to renew their subscriptions yearly to continue using the operating system. This type of agreement usually includes future OS upgrades as part of the deal.

If you've ever used the Select or MSDN media to install a previous version of a Microsoft operating system, you might have noticed that the product key was preconfigured on the CD. With XP, this feature is no longer there. Additionally, the Worldwide Fulfillment media no longer includes a product key on the CD packaging. For these media, you must use the unique Volume License Product Key assigned to your organization.

Adding and Using the Deployment Tools

As with Windows 2000, the deployment tools are in the DEPLOY.CAB file under the \SUPPORT\TOOLS directory of the installation CD. Extract these files to a directory of your choice. For the sake of future reference, we'll assume the files have been extracted to C:\DEPLOYTOOLS

NOTE

> While in this directory, it wouldn't hurt to install the Support Tools by running SETUP.EXE. Select Complete Installation for the full toolset. The Support Tools are unsupported utilities included to provide support personnel and experienced users with handy tools for diagnosing and resolving computer problems. About 70 executables and half a dozen script files are documented in the supporting files included with the install.
>
> Not all the included support tools are listed in the Support Tools Help (this Help file shows under the Support Tools program group after installing the tools). For a full list, be sure to read \SUPPORT\TOOLS\README.HTM.

Let's look at some of the key files we've got under C:\DEPLOYTOOLS:

- DEPLOY.CHM—Windows Help file for the Microsoft Windows XP Corporate Deployment Tools User's Guide. This Help file contains a great deal of useful information. To view it, double-click its icon, or type **start deploy.chm** at the command prompt.
- SYSPREP.EXE—Executable used to prepare a system for disk imaging.
- SETUPCL.EXE—When preparing a system for disk imaging, this executable must be included in the SYSPREP folder with the SYSPREP.EXE and SYSPREP.INF files.
- SETUPMGR.EXE—This is the Windows Setup Manager wizard. It will run through a series of questions, resulting in a properly formatted answer file suitable for framing.
- REF.CHM—This Windows Help file provides full documentation for all sections used in answer files. In addition, you can find a couple of sample answer files under both the Unattend.txt and the Sysprep.inf sections. Many of the sections listed in this Help file are not exposed by the Windows Setup Manager Wizard.

Using Interactive Answer Files for Installation

The answer file is the cornerstone of any automated installation routine. If you used answer files under Windows 2000, the concept and purpose haven't changed: The answer file provides the answers for both the text mode setup and GUI mode setup portions of the install, relieving end users or technicians from manually completing this repetitive task. Naturally, this speeds up the install process, increases the accuracy over manual data entry, and serves as a form of documentation. The basic structure of the file is the same for a CD-based unattended install, an over-the-network scripted install, an RIS-based install, or an OS image using SYSPREP.

CREATING AN ANSWER FILE

Creating an answer file can be as easy as running a wizard or as complex as manually creating the entire file in Notepad. Personally, I prefer the wizard to create the initial file and Notepad for post-wizard tweaking. To start the Windows Setup Manager Wizard, go to the `C:\DEPLOYTOOLS` directory and run `SETUPMGR.EXE`.

> **NOTE** You do not have to run the Setup Manager Wizard under Windows XP. It will run on Windows 2000, allowing you to create distribution share points and answer files for Windows XP without having XP installed.

Let's walk through using the wizard to create a complete answer file for a fully automated CD-based installation of Windows XP Professional. If you're following along in the wizard, this should take about 30 minutes to complete. I'm not going to take up space with screen shots, but I will identify and explain all the screens you should expect to see:

1. The first screen is the welcome screen for the wizard. Click Next.

2. The second screen, New or Existing Answer File, lets you select between creating a new file or modifying an existing file. Select Create a New Answer File and click Next.

> **NOTE** The Help button becomes active once you reach the second screen of the Setup Manager Wizard. The Help files in the Windows XP Setup Manager are very well developed and provide excellent on-the-spot information if you find yourself questioning the intricacies between multiple options.

3. Next is the Product to Install screen. On this screen, select whether to create a file to use with a Windows Unattended Installation, a Sysprep Install, or an install using Remote Installation Services. For our purposes, select Windows Unattended Installation and click Next.

4. The fourth screen, Platform, is where you select between Windows XP Home Edition, Windows XP Professional, and Windows 2002 Server. Note that the wizard was released before the server family officially changed names to Windows .NET Server and then to Windows Server 2003. Select Windows XP Professional and click Next.

5. On the screen titled User Interaction Level, decide how automated the automated install process should be. Table 5.2 details the different options for this screen. After

reviewing the table, select Fully Automated and click Next. If using retail media, you actually need to select Hide Pages or Read Only for the user interaction level, which I'll explain further in step 11.

TABLE 5.2 AUTOMATED INSTALL INTERACTION LEVELS

Interaction Level	Description
Provide defaults	Questions posed by Windows Setup are filled in with defaults provided by the answer file, but the user is able to review or change any answers you have supplied.
Fully automated	If you select this option, you must supply all required answers in the answer file. Windows Setup will not prompt the user for any answers, and setup will complete with no action required from the user. If you select this option, the wizard will require you to answer all necessary questions.
Hide pages	Any page for which all answers are provided by the answer file will not be displayed. If an answer is missing, the page will be displayed and the user will be prompted to fill in the blanks.
Read only	If you provided answers for questions posed by Windows Setup, the page will still be displayed, but the end user cannot change the answers you have provided. The user will be prompted for any answers left out of the answer file.
GUI attended	The text mode portion of install is automated, but the user must manually complete the graphical portion of Windows Setup.

6. On the sixth screen, select whether to create a distribution folder or run the installation from a CD. If you select the option to create a distribution folder, the Setup Manager Wizard will prompt you to insert a Windows XP CD from which it can copy the required files. For now, select No, This Answer File Will Be Used to Install from a CD.

7. On the License Agreement screen, check the box to accept the EULA. Click Next.

8. The remainder of the screens will prompt for answers to the questions normally presented by the graphical portion of setup. The first of these asks for a name and organization. Enter your name and organization, and click Next.

NOTE

> If you plan to use the option for automatic computer naming (see step 12), you must enter an organization name at this screen.

9. You should see the Display Settings panel. Here, configure the default colors, screen area, and refresh frequency. Sticking with the Windows default for all three options is the safe bet, but if you want different options and know your target hardware will support the exact configuration you select, feel free to adjust accordingly. When done, click Next.

5

10. Select your time zone and click Next.

11. The next screen is Providing the Product Key. If you're using retail media, you won't really get much use out of this screen; leave it blank and manually enter the product key at this point in each installation. In addition, you'll probably need to go back and select Hide Pages or Read Only for the user interaction level on step 5. If you have your volume license media and volume license product key (refer to the first section of this chapter), this is where you enter it. Enter a product key, and click Next.

12. In the Computer Names screen, click the check mark, Automatically Generate Computer Names Based on Organization Name, at the bottom of the screen. This lets you use the same answer file for any number of systems without naming conflicts. Automatically generated computer names are composed of the first word of the organization name, followed by a hyphen and a randomly generated alphanumeric string.

13. The next screen prompts you for the Administrator password. Unlike previous versions of Windows, you have the option of encrypting the password in the answer file. In Windows 2000 and earlier, the password was stored as clear text, which meant that anyone who found your answer file could compromise your local administrator passwords. Enter your password in both boxes, select the option to encrypt, and click Next.

> **NOTE**
>
> When using with a disk image, you must clear the Administrator account's password on the system used to make the master image. If you do not, setting the password in the answer file (SYSPREP.INF, in this case) will have no effect, and the target systems will retain the same local administrator password as on the master system.

14. In the Networking Components screen, select Typical Settings to configure your machine for standard settings (TCP/IP using DHCP for addressing, File and Print sharing for Microsoft Networks, and the Client for Microsoft Networks). Click Next.

> **NOTE**
>
> If you are in a small office or home office environment, rather than setting up a server just to use as a DHCP server, I recommend the Etherfast Cable/DSL Router from Linksys (www.linksys.com). It offers one-port, four-port, and eight-port versions, all of which can uplink into a hub. Not only do these devices provide full DHCP services for up to 253 clients, but they act as both an Internet gateway to a broadband connection and as a hardware-based firewall to protect your internal network from outside influences. For more information about Internet connection sharing hardware, see Chapter 17, "Building Your Own Network."

15. On the Workgroup or Domain screen, select the option for Windows Server Domain. During mass-production installations, you probably won't want to manually set up domain computer accounts in advance, so enter your domain name in the requisite blank, and select the option to create a computer account in the domain during installation. Enter a username and password with rights to add a computer to the domain. If

you do not have an accessible domain to use for this, are setting up standalone worksta-tions, or use workgroups instead of domains in your organization, you can select the option for Workgroup and provide a workgroup name.

NOTE

> Strangely enough, even though you can use encryption for the local administrator account password, it is not an option for this area. That means the account information you enter here will be stored in the answer file in clear text. For this reason, it is recommended that you do *not* use a domain administrator's account to join computers to the domain. You might wish to create a special domain account that does not have permission to log on as an interactive user but does have permission to create computer accounts in the domain, and enter the account information in these spaces.

16. On the Telephone screen, fill in your country, area code, and the number to access an outside line. Select whether your phone system uses pulse or touch-tone, and enter any number sequence required to access an outside line. When you've filled out all the boxes, click Next.

17. On the Regional Settings screen, select Use the Default Regional Settings for the Windows Version You Are Installing. Click Next.

18. The Languages screen provides an opportunity to install additional default language groups. For now, stick with the defaults and click Next.

19. On the Browser and Shell Settings screen select Use Default Internet Explorer Settings and click Next.

20. On the Installation Folder screen, specify where to install Windows XP. By default, Windows XP uses `Windows` as the folder name. If you want Windows to install to the same location as Windows NT 4.0 or Windows 2000, select the option labeled This Folder and enter `Winnt`. For now, let's stick with the default, a folder named Windows, and click Next.

21. If you want, you can automatically install network printers after the first user logon. You'll configure the default printers at this screen, the Install Printers screen. To use this feature, enter a network printer UNC in the form `\\servername\printername`, and click Next. If you don't have any network printers, leave this blank. It is not required for a successful fully automated setup.

22. The next screen, Run Once, lists commands to run after the user logs in for the first time. Any printers you added on the previous screen will show up here as `AddPrinter \\server\share`. Do not change anything on this screen; click Next. Any additional commands can be manually added to the script later.

23. The final screen in this section, Additional Commands, allows you, after installation, to run commands that do not require a user to be logged on. Commands entered here will execute before the Windows Logon screen shows up the first time. For the purposes of this walk-through, do not add anything at this screen; click Finish.

24. Windows Setup Manager prompts you for the location and filename under which to save your answer file. Save your file somewhere you can find it, with the filename `Winnt.sif`.

5

25. In the final window, Setup Manager Complete, if the Next button is not available, click the *X* in the upper right to close the dialog.

You should now have a complete answer file named `Winnt.sif`. If you open the file in a text editor, it should look a little like the following:

> **NOTE**
>
> If you copy the following example file for your own use, I strongly recommend changing the product key I've used to a valid product key for the media you are planning to use. The listing shows a Microsoft-provided generic product key that's suitable for testing purposes only. Refer to `http://www.microsoft.com/windowsxp/pro/techinfo/deployment/activation/productkeys.asp` for a full list of generic Windows XP product keys. These keys are blocked from activation at the Microsoft clearinghouse. If you use one of the generic keys, you will have approximately 14 days to experiment with and test your system before Windows will require activation.

```
;SetupMgrTag
[Data]
    AutoPartition=1
    MsDosInitiated="0"
    UnattendedInstall="Yes"

[Unattended]
    UnattendMode=FullUnattended
    OemSkipEula=Yes
    OemPreinstall=No
    TargetPath=\WINDOWS

[GuiUnattended]
    AdminPassword=eadb1736119939abdd99a9b993edc9a87a44c42236119ae1893bd142a2bbaead
    EncryptedAdminPassword=Yes
    OEMSkipRegional=1
    TimeZone=20
    OemSkipWelcome=1

[UserData]
    ProductID=DR8GV-C8V6J-BYXHG-7PYJR-DB66Y
    FullName="Jeff Ferris"
    OrgName="Ferris Technology Networks"
    ComputerName=*

[TapiLocation]
    CountryCode=1
    Dialing=Tone
    AreaCode=512

[GuiRunOnce]
    Command0="rundll32 printui.dll,PrintUIEntry /in /n \\printserver01\laser"

[Identification]
    JoinDomain=FERRISTECH
```

```
        DomainAdmin=ComputerAddAccount
        DomainAdminPassword=ferristechCA

[Networking]
        InstallDefaultComponents=Yes
```

CUSTOMIZING THE ANSWER FILE

To modify an existing answer file, you have two options: First, you can take the easy way out by rerunning the Setup Manager Wizard. After starting the wizard, select Modify an Existing Answer File on the second wizard screen. The rest of the process is the same as in the walk-through under the "Creating an Answer File" section in this chapter. Answers already provided by the existing answer file will show up in the proper locations as you go through the wizard. Change what needs changing, resave the file, and you're good to go. You'd probably want to use the wizard when making major changes to your answer file, such as when changing from a domain to a workgroup model.

Your second option is to modify the answer file using a text editor. Most of the answer file options are fairly self-explanatory, and the REF.CHM file from the DEPLOY.CAB contains full documentation for all sections, keys, and options in case you need additional guidance. I'd document everything for you here, but it would translate to about 150 pages of text that wouldn't be indexed and couldn't be searched (unlike the Help file), and you'd probably fall asleep reading through it all anyway. You'd probably prefer using a text editor to modify an answer file when changing things like the user name (FullName=<answer>), the organization name (OrgName=<answer>), or the username and password used to join a computer account to the domain (DomainAdmin=<answer> and DomainAdminPassword=<answer>).

If you are going to use the answer file installation method with standard retail Windows XP licenses, you will need to either edit the product ID in the answer file each time you use it, or you must delete the product ID line from the answer file so that the setup program will prompt for a unique product ID for each installation.

Changing the Answers in a SYSPREP.INF **File**

Once you've created a SYSPREP.INF file, saved it in the SYSPREP directory, executed Sysprep, and created your image, the SYSPREP.INF file becomes a permanent part of that image. So, if you need to make changes to something in the answer file, you must create a new image, update the SYSPREP.INF file, and rerun Sysprep.

Suppose you only need to change the answer file for a couple of systems. You wouldn't want to go through the whole reimaging process just to change some of the options in the answer file. Fortunately, there's a rarely documented out. Simply make the changes to your SYSPREP.INF file, and save SYSPREP.INF to the root of a floppy disk. Apply your image to a target system and boot the target system. As soon as the system starts to boot, insert the floppy disk containing the updated SYSPREP.INF in the A: drive. The Windows XP Setup Wizard will use the answer file on the floppy disk to override the settings specified in the Sysprep file stored with the image.

5

PUTTING AN ANSWER FILE TO USE

Four main types of installations can be performed using an answer file. The name of your answer file will be different depending on the type of install you intend to use it for. Table 5.3 lists the four standard file names for answer files, as well as their purpose and location.

TABLE 5.3 TYPES OF ANSWER FILES

File Name	Purpose
RISETUP.SIF	Automate the setup wizard for RIS-based installs. You'll put this file in the \I386\Templates subdirectory of the folder created for any RIS image.
SYSPREP.INF	Provides answers for the SYSPREP Mini-Setup Wizard. SYSPREP.INF should be placed in the C:\SYSPREP directory before running SYSPREP.EXE to prepare a drive for imaging.
UNATTEND.TXT	Provides responses for the installation process when running an install using WINNT or WINNT32 from a network share or from a command-line–initiated installation from the CD. This file can actually have any name and can be saved in any location that you will be able to access while running the install.
WINNT.SIF	Provides answers for the setup wizard when installing by booting to the Windows XP CD. Save this file to the root of a floppy, and insert the disk right after the installation starts from the bootable Windows XP CD.

LOCAL AND NETWORK-BASED UNATTENDED INSTALLATION

With the answer file created in the "Creating an Answer File" section earlier in this chapter, you might have noticed that the Setup Manager Wizard created a batch file in the same directory as your answer file. This batch file can kick off a Windows XP install from a machine that is already running Windows 95, Windows 98, Windows Me, Windows NT, Windows 2000, or Windows XP. The install will take advantage of the answer file as long as you leave both the batch file and the answer file in the same directory. By default, answer files created to install from the Windows XP CD expect to find your Windows XP CD in the D: drive. If your CD-ROM uses a different drive letter, you must edit the batch file using Notepad to reflect the correct drive letter.

You may remember a point in the walk-through under "Creating an Answer File" (step 6) where the Setup Manager Wizard asked whether to create an answer file to install from CD, or to create or modify a distribution folder. We selected the option to install from CD. Had we selected the distribution folder option, the batch file would point to the UNC to which the install files were copied. Additionally, from within Windows 95/98/Me/NT/2000/XP, you could manually run the installation using the answer file with the WINNT32.EXE command and the optional /unattend switch, using the following syntax:

```
<path_to_install_files>\winnt32 /unattend:filename
```

If you wish to complete an over-the-network installation from a system without an operating system, you need to create a DOS-bootable disk capable of connecting to the network and map a drive to the location of the shared Windows XP install files. Instead of running WINNT32.EXE as when running a local or network install from Windows 95/98/NT/2000/XP, use the WINNT.EXE command. To use the answer file, the full command will be

```
Winnt /s:install_source_directory /u:answerfile_name
```

UNATTENDED INSTALL FROM THE BOOTABLE WINDOWS XP CD

CAUTION

> The following paragraph starts a fresh unattended install of Windows XP Professional. This *will* wipe your drive clean. And once you've started, you can't go back. **Do not** attempt to run the bootable CD setup process unless you are willing to clear the primary drive on the target machine.

In the walk-through in the "Creating an Answer File" section of this chapter, the answer file was named WINNT.SIF, allowing it to be used to run a fully automated installation simply by booting from the Windows XP Professional install CD. To make this work, you don't need to worry about the batch file. Just copy WINNT.SIF to the root of a floppy disk. Go to your target system, insert the Windows XP Professional CD in the CD-ROM drive, and boot to the CD.

As discussed in "Licensing Issues" earlier in this chapter (*p. 173*), you must use volume license media and a volume license product key to use the same product key on multiple systems. If you're not using volume license media with a volume license product key, you must either update the Product ID line in the WINNT.SIF file before loading each different system or leave the Product ID line out of the WINNT.SIF so the system will prompt for the key during the mini-setup wizard.

NOTE

> If setup isn't starting when you attempt to boot to the CD, check two things: First, ensure that your system boot order is configured with the CD-ROM as the first boot device under your system BIOS. Second, pay close attention while booting your system. If you have no operating system, Windows Setup will start on its own. If, however, an active partition with a bootable OS exists, at one point booting to the CD will prompt you with "Press any key to continue booting from CD." Hit the Any key at this point. Look closely, the label for the Any key—usually the long key at the bottom center—frequently falls off before a keyboard leaves the factory.

As soon as your system starts to read the CD and recognizes it as bootable, insert the floppy disk containing the answer file into the A: drive. After a few minutes, setup will prompt you to partition and format the drive. This is a safety mechanism to give you one last chance to back out of the install before wiping out your system. After partitioning the disk, you should

5

be able to sit back and relax for about 45 minutes while Windows XP Professional completes installation to your system without prompting you to answer any additional questions.

NOTE

> *Hey! Wait a minute! I thought you said this would be a fully automated process…so why is setup asking for my input before it partitions and formats the disk?*
>
> Although you selected Fully Automated in the Setup Manager Wizard, the partitioning and formatting of the disk does not complete without user interaction…unless you know about this rarely documented trick: Open your `WINNT.SIF` file in Notepad, and add the following two lines under the (Unattended) section header:
>
> ```
> FileSystem = ConvertNTFS
> Repartition = Yes
> ```

NOTE

> *So what do you do when you try to run an automated install by booting to the Windows XP CD and the system still runs a normal setup?*
>
> If this happens, make sure you've named your answer file `WINNT.SIF` and saved it to the root of the A: drive. Windows Setup will not check for any other filename, and it will not check in any other location. In addition, double-check that you're getting the disk inserted as soon as the system starts to boot from the CD, or Windows Setup will not read the answer file.
>
> If you're having difficulty getting the disk inserted at the right time, you could go into your system BIOS and disable booting from floppy, or move the floppy drive to the end of your boot order. You should then be able to leave the floppy disk containing the `WINNT.SIF` file in your drive from the beginning of the boot process.

AUTOMATING INSTALLATION USING DISK IMAGING

Disk imaging when used in automating Windows XP deployment is the process of creating a master system, duplicating the files, and distributing the resulting system image to additional machines. The master image can be distributed using a disk-to-disk copy or by using disk-imaging software to create a disk image file. Most currently available disk-imaging software allows you to create a compressed image file, which can then be distributed from a shared network location or by copying the image file to CD-Rs.

NOTE

> Just to be clear about this, the Windows deployment tools provided by Microsoft only take you as far as configuring the master system disk. You'll need to get a third-party program to make copies (images) of the master disk. When a copy is installed in a new computer and booted up, a mini-setup program will ask a couple of questions, and the new system—an exact copy of the master system you configured—will be up and running.

A big advantage of disk imaging is that the imaged installation can include more than just the Windows XP operating system. With a disk-image–based install, you can wrap fully installed applications, data documents, directory structures, and configuration settings into a single package. So, although somewhat more complicated to debug, deploying systems using a disk image is usually the fastest of the Windows XP mass-deployment options.

For example, it might take 45 minutes to install Windows XP Professional using a scripted install and an additional 45 minutes to install a common application suite including the full installation of Microsoft Office XP, Adobe Acrobat reader, and Norton Antivirus Corporate Edition. But, if you create a master disk image containing all of these additional components, you should be able to deploy the fully configured operating system image with all three applications in about 45 minutes total, installing over a LAN-based connection. Of course, your mileage may vary depending on your network speed, additional applications wrapped into your image, and the disk imaging tool you use.

You'll have the best luck with disk imaging if you use somewhat similar hardware on all target computers. Specifically, all targets must have compatible hardware abstraction layers (HALs) and identical mass-storage controllers. The target computer's drive must also be the same size or larger than the master computer's drive.

→ If you wish to use a single image for systems with different types of mass-storage controllers, **see** the "Creating a SYSPREP.INF File" sidebar later in this chapter on **p. 188**.

So what constitutes a compatible HAL? There are six HALs available under Windows XP, listed with their compatible system types in Table 5.4.

TABLE 5.4 HALs AND THE MOTHERBOARDS THAT LOVE THEM

HAL Description (HAL filename)	Compatible System Types
Non-ACPI PIC HAL (*HAL.DLL*)	■ Non-ACPI PIC computers ■ Non-ACPI APIC UP and MP computers ■ ACPI PIC computers ■ ACPI APIC UP and MP computers
Non-ACPI APIC UP HAL (*HALAPIC.DLL*)	■ Non-ACPI APIC UP computers ■ ACPI APIC UP Computers
Non-ACPI APIC MP HAL (*HALMPS.DLL*)	■ Non-ACPI APIC MP and UP computers ■ ACPI APIC UP or MP computers
ACPI PIC HAL (*HALACPI.DLL*)	■ ACPI PIC computers ■ ACPI APIC UP and MP computers
ACPI APIC UP HAL (*HALAACPI.DLL*)	■ ACPI APIC UP computers
ACPI APIC MP HAL (*HALMACPI.DLL*)	■ ACPI MP and UP computers

Acronyms:

ACPI: Advanced Configuration and Power Management

APIC: Advanced Programmable Interrupt Controller   *MP: Multiprocessor*

PIC: Programmable Interrupt Controller   *UP: Single processor*

5

If you plan to use a disk image, you must prepare the disk for imaging using the Sysprep program from the Windows XP deployment tools. Sysprep only *prepares* a system for disk imaging—it is the last thing you must do before creating an image. To actually *create* the disk image, you must have a third-party disk-imaging utility or hardware-based disk duplicator, such as

- PowerQuest Drive Image (www.powerquest.com/driveimage)
- Symantec Ghost (www.symantec.com/ghost)
- Altiris RapidDeploy (www.altiris.com/products/rapideploy)
- Cyber-Pro hardware duplicator (www.cyber-pr0.com/hard_disk_duplicator.asp, and that's a zero, not the letter O in cyber-pr0)
- Aberdeen Omniclone hardware duplicator (www.aberdeeninc.com/abcatg/modular.htm)

Automating installation using a disk image can be broken down into three major components:

- Preparing the system
- Creating the image
- Applying the image

We'll examine these three components in the following sections.

PREPARE A SYSTEM FOR IMAGING

To prepare a system for imaging with Sysprep, follow these steps:

1. Install Windows XP Professional on a representative machine. Apply any applicable Service Packs and hotfixes.
2. Log on to the system using the default local administrator account (username: administrator).
3. On the system, create a local user account named...well, let's say Sillyputty, and add this account to the local Administrators group. Do not log on to this new account yet: that's in step 10. (Note: Silly Putty is a registered trademark of Binney & Smith Inc. While Silly Putty can be used to temporarily duplicate your favorite newspaper-based cartoon strip, Binney & Smith Inc. does not support or endorse the use of Silly Putty for creating duplicate images of computer systems.)
4. Configure your preferred OS options, such as default wallpaper, screensaver settings, taskbar options, or anything else that tickles your fancy.
5. Install and configure third-party applications such as virus protection, office suites, or company-specific applications.

NOTE

> Just as the OS has different product key requirements depending on the licensing model, many applications, including Microsoft Office, are similar. Be careful not to include any software requiring unique product keys per licensed user, lest you have to uninstall and reinstall applications after deploying the image.

6. Add any required shortcuts, favorites, documents, or directories to the system. However, do not use File Encryption to encrypt any files or folders—they will be unreadable on the deployed copies.

7. Right-click the Internet Explorer icon (either on the desktop or in the start menu) and select Internet Properties from the pop-up menu. On the General tab, select Delete Files and confirm, then select Clear History and confirm. This process cleans up unnecessary temporary Internet Explorer files.

8. Select Start, Run, and type `%temp%` in the Open box to open the temp directory for the currently logged-on profile. Clear all files in the temp directory.

9. If using the new Windows XP start menu, right-click Start and select Properties, Customize to open the Customize Start Menu dialog. Select Clear List on both the General tab and the Advanced tab. This resets the usage data and clears recently accessed documents from My Recent Documents. If you've selected to use the Classic Start Menu, right-click on the Start button, and select Properties, Customize, Clear.

10. Log off as Administrator and log on as Sillyputty, the local user account created in step 3.

11. Copy the Administrator profile folder, found at `<systemroot>\Documents and Settings\Administrator`, to the Default User profile folder, found at `<systemroot>\Documents and Settings\Default User`. (If you cannot see the Default User profile folder, you might need to enable the display of hidden files. Open any Explorer window, and select Tools, Folder Options, View, Show Hidden Files and Folders.)

    Now new users will receive the same desktop settings and program groups you configured under the Administrator account.

CAUTION

> If your disks are formatted using NTFS, you must remove the user-specific security on the Default Users directory and the Read & Execute right to the Everyone group. Users do *not* need the Modify right, since the settings will be used to create the unique user profiles, under which users will have the proper permission for modifications automatically. If you do not make this change, users will not successfully receive the default user profile upon first logon.

12. Create a folder named SYSPREP off of the root of the system volume. Place SYSPREP.EXE and SETUPCL.EXE from the deployment tools folder into \SYSPREP. If you know exactly how the systems need to be configured—for example, if you are the desktop engineer in charge of developing the install process for your company—you might want to use an

5

answer file here. For Sysprep-based installs, the answer file will be named SYSPREP.INF (see the "Creating a SYSPREP.INF File" sidebar). If you create a SYSPREP.INF file, copy this file into the SYSPREP folder as well. If you do not have a SYSPREP.INF file, the user must complete a mini-setup wizard to complete the installation of any disk-image–based installs. If you do not know how the system will ultimately be configured—for example, if you build machines, install software, and send them out to users over whom you have no administrative control—you should not include a SYSPREP.INF file. This will allow the users to configure systems to their liking.

Creating a SYSPREP.INF **File**

SYSPREP.INF is an optional answer file that can be used to provide answers to the questions asked by the mini-setup wizard that runs on the first boot after running SYSPREP.EXE. If you wish to create an answer file for the SYSPREP install, run the Setup Manager Wizard and select Sysprep Install on the Product to Install screen. You saw most of the wizard screens when running through the Setup Manager Wizard in the "Creating an Answer File" section earlier in this chapter.

At the end of the wizard you will encounter one new screen titled the OEM Duplicator String. Any data entered in this text box can be used later to identify systems that were created using your SYSPREP-prepared image. This is just a free-form text string, so you can enter anything you want. But you might want to ensure that it isn't offensive or personally embarrassing because after a system built with SYSPREP completes the mini-setup wizard, the OEM Duplicator String in the Windows Registry will be under the subkey HKEY_LOCAL_MACHINE\System\Setup\OemDuplicatorString.

The default SYSPREP.INF file created using the Setup Manager Wizard can only be used on systems with identical mass-storage controllers. If you plan to apply the disk image to systems with different mass-storage containers, open the SYSPREP.INF file in Notepad, and add the following entries to the end of the file:

```
[Sysprep]
BuildMassStorageSection = Yes
[SysprepMassStorage]
```

Adding the previous lines automatically populates the [SysprepMassStorage] section with all mass-storage Plug and Play hardware IDs specified in Machine.inf, Scsi.inf, Pnpscsi.inf, and Mshdc.inf. Windows will then test for the presence of each of these drivers when it boots up for the first time on the new computer. If you need to include an additional mass-storage driver that is not available from one of those four INF files, copy the new device's driver files into the \SYSPREP folder and manually add a line for the device after the [SysprepMassStorage] section. The format of a manually entered line under this section should be

```
Hardware_id = "path_to_device_inf"[,
disk_directory[,disk_description[,disk_tag]]]"
```

Refer to the Sysprep.inf section of the Ref.chm Help file from the Windows XP deployment tools for full documentation of the sections and entries available in the Sysprep.inf file.

---

13. Run a disk check and a disk defrag to reduce the potential for problems with disk imaging.

14. Reboot.

15. Log on with the local Administrator account.

16. Delete the Sillyputty user account created in step 3. (You may need to do this from the Computer Management Local Users and Groups tool rather than the User Accounts

control panel, as the control panel may not let you end up with just one Administrator account.) Delete the Sillyputty folder under C:\Documents and Settings.

17. Clear the Event Viewer log files.

18. If you want the end users of the copied systems to be able to set their Administrator password themselves, set the password on the local Administrator account to blank. This will allow SYSPREP to set a new administrator password during the mini-setup wizard. If you leave the master system with a non-blank Administrator password, any target systems created from the master will have this same password, regardless of a password specified in the SYSPREP.INF file.

19. Open the SYSPREP folder and run SYSPREP.EXE. The initial screen states that execution of Sysprep may modify security parameters of the system and warns you to click Cancel if you're not preparing the system for duplication. Since we *do* want to prepare the system for duplication, click OK. You should now see the Sysprep Options screen shown in Figure 5.2. As shown in the screen shot, select MiniSetup so that install will run the mini-setup wizard after the next reboot.

NOTE

> Remember, you can provide answers for any or all of the questions from the mini-setup wizard by creating a SYSPREP.INF file. Refer to the sidebar, "Creating a SYSPREP.INF File," on **page 188**.

If you will be applying this image to a target system with significantly different hardware, it may be beneficial to select the PnP option as well. If you are using a volume license product key and have already activated the system from which you are creating the master image, you can select Pre-activated. If you are only testing the Sysprep process and will not be moving the image to a different machine, select NoSIDGen to prevent the machine from generating a new SID. Select Reseal to complete Sysprep. After clicking the button, it may take 30 seconds to one minute before you see anything happening.

Using the Audit Boot option is similar to the Reseal option, except Windows will not delete the Sysprep directory after the next boot. This allows you to test a boot cycle and then run Sysprep again with the Reseal button (in this scenario, you should also use the NoSIDGen option) without copying the Sysprep files to the system multiple times.

Using the Factory option pauses the first reboot just before mini-setup to allow you to copy additional drivers from a network source to the target computer.

20. If the system is ACPI-compliant, it will shut down automatically. If not, it will prompt you when it is ready to be turned off.

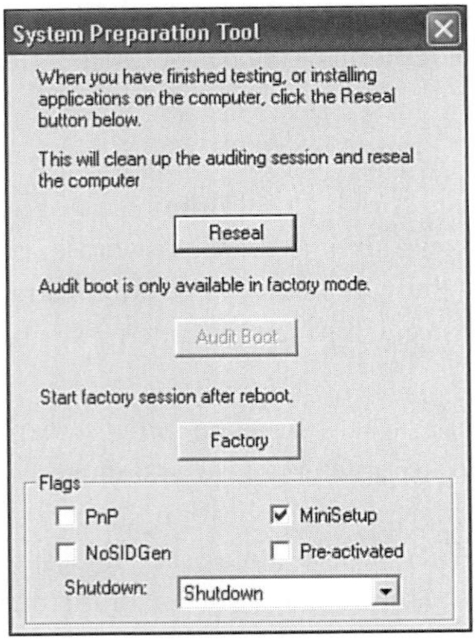

Figure 5.2
Interface for the
System Preparation
Tool.

CAUTION

Do not boot again from the hard drive until after making a disk image of the system. Booting from the hard drive will run the setup wizard, apply a new security identifier (SID), and prepare the system to run Windows XP. The SID is a theoretically unique identification number associated with all Windows XP security principals (users, groups, and machines). To maintain that uniqueness on machines created from a disk image, running Sysprep will cause a system to generate a new SID the next time it boots. If you do accidentally boot to the hard drive before creating the disk image, you must run SYSPREP again before imaging the system.

CREATE A DISK IMAGE

Again, Sysprep is only used to prepare a system for imaging. Do not boot the system on the prepared hard drive until after you have successfully created the master image. Creating the disk image is the process in which you make a copy of the master drive, either by doing a disk-to-disk copy or by copying all information on the disk to a single disk image file. To create a disk image file, follow the instructions provided with your disk-imaging application. If using a hardware-based disk-imaging solution, remove the system drive from your computer at this time.

APPLY A DISK IMAGE

To apply a disk image to a new target system, follow the instructions provided with your disk-imaging solution. If you are shipping these computers to others, you probably want to test at least one copy before you ship others off. Here's an overview of what happens when an imaged, Sysprepped Windows system is first started up:

On the first boot of a newly imaged system, SYSPREP will present the mini-setup wizard. If you have provided answers to all questions via the SYSPREP.INF file, no interaction will be required. If you did not provide a SYSPREP.INF file, however, you'll see the following mini-setup screens upon first boot (the same screens you may have seen if you purchased a Windows XP computer from a retail vendor):

1. On the Windows XP Setup screen there's nothing to do but follow the instructions: Please wait.

> **NOTE** If you selected the PnP option when running Sysprep, an additional screen will appear in this area while setup detects and installs Plug and Play devices.

2. Next, you should see the Welcome to the Windows XP Setup Wizard screen. Click Next.

3. The next screen, License Agreement, prompts you to accept or decline the EULA. Here, the end user is supposed to read carefully and agree to all the terms. Click the button signifying your acceptance, and then click Next.

4. You should now be at the Regional and Language Options screen. Click Next.

5. On the Personalize Your Software screen, enter your name and organization in the corresponding spaces, and click Next.

6. Enter a valid Windows XP product key on the Product Key screen. Remember, if using volume license media, you must use your organization's assigned volume license product key. Click Next.

7. You are now prompted to enter Computer Name and Administrator Password, and then click Next.

8. Next, you'll see the Date and Time Settings screen. Make sure it has the correct date, time, and time zone information, and then click Next.

9. The next screen is titled Networking Settings. Just wait for Windows to install the networking components.

10. You should now see the Networking Settings screen. Choose whether to use typical or custom settings. If following along on a real system, select Typical settings, Next.

11. On the next screen, Workgroup or Computer Domain, select Yes, Make This Computer a Member of the Following Domain, enter a valid domain that you can access from the network on which you are currently attached, and click Next.

12. If all has gone as expected, you'll be prompted for a username and password of a user authorized to join this computer to the domain. Enter a valid account and password and click OK.

13. On the Performing Final Tasks screen, mini-setup goes about its business, installing start menu items, registering components, saving settings, and removing any temporary files used during setup (which will include the SYSPREP directory).

5

14. Finally, you should see the Completing the Windows XP Setup Wizard screen. Remove any CDs or floppy disks and click Finish.

The computer will now reboot, and you should see a system that looks remarkably similar to the machine used to create the master image.

CAUTION

> When you deploy a system using Sysprep and disk imaging, files that were previously encrypted using the Encrypting File System (EFS) are no longer accessible.
>
> Before imaging a system containing files encrypted using the EFS, you must decrypt the files. As a security function, by design any encrypted files contained in a master disk image will be inaccessible and completely unrecoverable when applied to a new target system. No way exists to override this behavior. The lesson is not to create any encrypted files when preparing a Sysprep image.

After testing the prepared image on at least one clean target system and finding it sound, you can start replicating other image disks and deploying Windows XP computers. Original equipment manufacturers and computer resellers usually want to ship SYSREP-imaged computers to their customers without having gone through this first boot-up process. In a corporate environment, it may be expected that the IT department will perform this task; it's up to the organization's administrative policies.

REMOTE INSTALLATION SERVICES

If you are familiar with using RIS under Windows 2000, not much has changed with the upgrade to Windows XP. RIS is an optional server-side service provided with Windows 200x Server that enables you to deploy Windows XP to a new system by booting to the NIC using an NIC with a Preboot Execution Environment (PXE) boot ROM enabled.

Other than booting client systems using a PXE boot ROM rather than a network boot disk, installing Windows XP using RIS is similar to installing over the network from a network share point. All files are copied over the network to the client station, and Windows XP runs a full install.

From an infrastructure perspective, RIS requires a TCP/IP-based network that uses a DHCP server, a Windows 2000-compliant DNS service conforming with both RFC 2052 and RFC 2136, and Active Directory to provide client authorization and configuration information to the RIS server during the client install process. If you are still using Windows NT 4.0 Server DNS, it does *not* support the required protocols. If using Unix BIND, versions 8.1.2 and above support the required protocols.

To add a Windows XP Professional installation to your RIS server, follow the same procedure as adding a Windows 2000 Professional image, but using the source files and answer file for Windows XP. Remember, you can create the `RISETUP.SIF` answer file using the Setup Manager Wizard and selecting the option to create an install for RIS on the third screen of the wizard.

NOTE

> For full details on setting up and configuring RIS under Windows 2000, see the Remote Installation Services chapter excerpt from the New Riders title, *Windows 2000 Deployment and Desktop Management*, available online at `http://www.microsoft.com/technet/prodtechnol/windows2000serv/deploy/remote.asp`.

SYSTEMS MANAGEMENT SERVER

If so inclined, you can use Microsoft Systems Management Server (SMS) to deploy a Windows XP upgrade. The question is, should you? To be honest, I've tried it, and I don't like it. Part of the problem is that you can only deploy Windows XP via SMS if doing an upgrade. You cannot use SMS to deploy a clean installation of Windows XP. So rather than telling you *how* to use SMS to deploy a Windows XP upgrade, I'm going to tell you why you probably *shouldn't*.

NOTE

> If, after reading the rest of this section, you still wish to attempt an upgrade to Windows XP using Microsoft SMS, refer to the Microsoft-provided documentation at `http://www.microsoft.com/windowsxp/pro/techinfo/deployment/implementing/sms.asp`.

When planning for a mass-scale operating system upgrade, I usually opt to develop a single clean install process to use for all systems in an environment, rather than developing one install process for people who need a clean install and an additional upgrade process for systems that can handle the upgrade. Upgrading an operating system tends to result in a number of difficult-to-diagnose technical inconsistencies; a clean install does away with any questions. I'm sure if you've been working with any Microsoft operating system for very long, you've eventually re-installed just to improve system performance, get rid of unneeded files, and start with a clean slate. Major operating system upgrades provide an excellent opportunity for a wide-scale cleanup of all systems in an organization.

USER STATE MIGRATION TOOL

Unless you're lucky enough to be running in a fully managed environment with roaming user profiles and all unique user data stored on the network, you need to find a way to migrate the settings and documents from the old systems to the new. The User State Migration tool (USMT) helps with this endeavor. USMT is the IT Administrator's version of the File and Settings Transfer Wizard. USMT can perform all the functions of the File and Settings Transfer Wizard, but USMT is made to run from the command line, in environments where you will be migrating a number of users. In contrast, the File and Settings Transfer Wizard runs with a graphical wizard interface, and is only intended for one-off, user-driven migrations.

→ For a refresher on the File and Settings Transfer Wizard, refer to the section "Migrating Files and Settings with the Files and Settings Transfer Wizard," **p. 80**.

USMT will be on your Windows XP media, under the \VALUEADD\MSFT\USMT directory. You need the entire directory to successfully use the USMT. Two executable files are in the directory: SCANSTATE.EXE is used to collect user data and settings; LOADSTATE.EXE is used to apply the data and settings to a new target system.

Out of the box, USMT migrates the following files and settings:

- Accessibility
- Classic desktop
- Cookies folder
- Dial-Up connections
- Folder options
- Fonts
- Internet Explorer settings
- Mouse and keyboard settings
- My Documents folder
- My Pictures folder
- Network drives and printers
- Office settings
- Outlook Express settings and store
- Outlook settings and store
- Phone and modem options
- Regional options
- Screen saver selection
- Sounds settings
- Taskbar settings

By modifying the INF files in the USMT directory, you can change the files and settings that USMT will migrate. For full details, please refer to Microsoft's online documentation.

NOTE

> You can find the complete online documentation for the USMT on Microsoft's Web site:
>
> http://www.microsoft.com/windowsxp/pro/techinfo/deployment/userstate/default.asp

Let's run through a quick data and settings migration using the default INF files. You need a "used" system with a configured user profile directory, a server (or a workstation on which you can create a data share), and a clean system to which to copy the user state.

1. On the server, create a shared directory called USMT, and copy the entire USMT directory from the `\VALUEADD\MSFT\` directory of the Windows XP Installation CD into this directory. Create a subdirectory named DATA.

2. Log on to the "used" system and map the U: drive to the USMT share on your server.

3. Open the command prompt. Switch to the `U:\USMT` directory, and type the command **SCANSTATE U:\DATA.**

4. You will see the line `ScanState is running....` Wait. When ScanState finishes, you will see the line `The tool completed successfully.`

5. Move to the clean system and map the U: drive to the USMT share on your server.

6. Open the command prompt. Switch to the `U:\USMT` directory, and type the command `LOADSTATE U:\DATA.`

7. You will see the line `LoadState is running....` Wait. When LoadState finishes, you'll be back at the command prompt, and you should have the same data and settings as on the system from which SaveState was run.

MULTILINGUAL ISSUES

With every release, products in the Windows NT family line have been made available in a variety of localized versions. With the advent of Windows 2000, Microsoft made available a Multilingual User Interface (MUI) Pack, enabling any of 24 localized user interfaces to be used on a single English-language installation. Windows XP extends MUI support on top of the English installation to a total of 33 localized interfaces. Also, localized Windows XP media is available in 24 language versions in addition to English. Table 5.5 lists the language options available for Windows XP, and whether the option is available in localized media, or as part of the Multilingual User Interface.

TABLE 5.5   WINDOWS XP MULTILINGUAL OPTIONS

Language	Localized	MUI
Arabic	✓	✓
Bulgarian	—	✓
Chinese (Hong Kong)	✓	—
Chinese (Simplified)	✓	✓
Chinese (Traditional)	✓	✓
Croatian	—	✓
Czech	✓	✓
Danish	✓	✓
Dutch	✓	✓

continues

TABLE 5.5   CONTINUED

Language	Localized	MUI
English	✓	✓
Estonian	—	✓
Finnish	✓	✓
French	✓	✓
German	✓	✓
Greek	✓	✓
Hebrew	✓	✓
Hungarian	✓	✓
Italian	✓	✓
Japanese	✓	✓
Korean	✓	✓
Latvian	—	✓
Lithuanian	—	✓
Norwegian	✓	✓
Polish	✓	✓
Portuguese (Brazil)	✓	✓
Portuguese (Portugal)	✓	✓
Romanian	—	✓
Russian	✓	✓
Spanish	✓	✓
Slovak	—	✓
Slovenian	—	✓
Swedish	✓	✓
Thai	—	✓
Turkish	✓	✓

5

The Multilingual User Interface Pack is available as an add-on to the English version of Windows XP and is available *only* to customers taking advantage of one of the volume license programs. The MUI is comprised of six CDs—the English install of Windows XP Professional on one CD, and five CDs containing MUI-localized resources with the MUISETUP program. If you are not licensed via a volume license program, you must use localized media to enable a non-English interface. The MUI cannot be installed on a localized edition of Windows XP other than English. Since the MUI is an add-on, it can also be uninstalled through Add/Remove Programs. Uninstall requires a reboot, after which the interface will return to the native English interface.

So what if you need to deploy the MUI as part of an automated installation? Remember, MUI is add-on software, just like Office or an antivirus program. It can be pre-installed as part of an image-based installation, but for scripted installs from network shares or from the XP CD, the MUI language packs must be installed after completing the install of the English Windows XP operating system.

NOTE

If you do wish to automate the application of Windows XP language packs to different language regions within your company, you could wrap the installs into Microsoft Installer (MSI) software packages and deploy the packs to the proper target systems using the software distribution feature of Active Directory.

→ **See** Chapter 9, "Installing and Configuring Applications," **p. 321**, for general information on automating application deployment using Active Directory.

5

PART II

SYSTEM CONFIGURATION AND SETUP

CHAPTER 6

SETTING UP IMPORTANT SYSTEM SERVICES

In this chapter

AUTOMATIC UPDATE AND UPDATE NOTIFICATION OPTIONS

Like a few previous versions of Windows such as Windows 98, Me, and 2000, XP Home and Professional both have a built-in service called Windows Update. You're probably familiar with this feature. This is an Internet-based service for updating your OS, hosted by Microsoft. Using a combination of "pull" and "push" technology, Windows Update can send operating system *hot fixes*, security patches, device drivers, Internet application upgrades, language support, the latest Help files and other such upgrades to your computer.

NOTE

> Windows Update in the enterprise setting is covered in Chapter 33, "Managing Windows XP in an Enterprise Setting." If you are setting up a corporate machine, you should check that chapter for considerations that apply to you. We'll cover Windows Update briefly here, as it's something everyone should adjust prior to getting going with their XP machines.

Microsoft claims that the update technology is minimally invasive, but the process does probe your computer for information about its current state, to determine what updates are applicable to the target machine, which have been installed already, and which are most advisable (for example, security fixes). In order to give you an appropriate and accurate list of updates that apply to your computer, the following info is probed:

- Operating-system version number and serial number
- Internet Explorer version number
- Version numbers of some "other" software (what "other" means not explained by Microsoft in their literature, however)
- Plug and Play ID numbers of hardware devices

Update locates the Windows XP serial number to confirm that you're running a legit copy of Windows. If you aren't, some major updates (this is true of big service packs, for example) won't download, or will download but won't install. (We have seen smaller updates work on invalid copies of XP, though I wouldn't be surprised if Microsoft gets increasingly heavy handed about this.) What's not sniffed out are items such as your name, address, email address, or other forms of personally identifiable information. Microsoft claims, additionally, that the configuration information they collect is used only for the period of time that you are visiting the site, and is not saved.

You might find it interesting that the Windows Update site's back end also tracks whether your updates are successful, and notes how many uniquely identified computers access the service. Each computer is tracked via a unique number called a Globally Unique Identifier (GUID) that Windows XP itself generates. This number is stored on the local computer.

To set up the Windows Update settings for your computer

1. If you're running Windows XP Home Edition, make sure you're logged in as an administrator. In XP Professional, you'll have to be logged on as an administrator or a member of the Administrator's group.

2. Open Control Panel and choose the System icon. On the Automatic Updates tab (see Figure 6.1), you'll want to choose one the following settings:

   - **Keep My Computer Up to Date**—This check box is for turning on or off the automatic updating. If you don't want to be bothered with updates, clear the check box. This could be advisable in systems that you want to have complete lockdown control over, with no unexpected variables in software stability (other than taking the risk of bumping into bugs that are already present in the installed OS). If you want to run Windows Update only manually, clear this box, then initiate Windows Update by clicking Start, All Programs, Windows Update. As a general point, we suggest leaving this box checked and taking advantage of one of the automatic update options because it's only human to forget to check for updates.

   - **Notify Me Before Downloading Any Updates and Notify Me Again Before Installing Them on My Computer**—This option gives you more control over when Windows XP will search for and download updates. If you are using a costly Internet connection, or if you have limited bandwidth, you may want to select this option.

   - **Download the Updates Automatically and Notify Me When They Are Ready to Be Installed**—This option sets up Windows XP to regularly check with Microsoft for updates and to automatically download any that are available. When updates have been downloaded and are available for installation, a balloon message will pop up from the system tray (near the clock). Figure 6.2 shows a typical list.

   - **Automatically Download the Updates and Install Them on the Schedule That I Specify**—This schedule will apply regardless of who is logged on to the machine. You just set the days and time when you want Windows to install updates. Downloading of appropriate updates is done invisibly as a background task. A message balloon *does* appear near the system tray letting you review the updates that are scheduled for installation. But if you don't have the proper administrator privilege, or if you choose not to install at that time, the installation will occur according to the schedule. Since some updates might require that your computer be restarted, this could be a bit of a surprise if you don't know updating is even happening, but the user will see a message explaining the situation and alerting her to save work and restart, or to delay the restart.

6

Figure 6.1
Viewing Windows
XP's Automatic
Update settings.

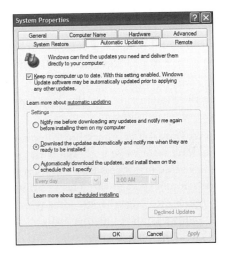

Figure 6.2
A sample list of
downloaded updates
ready to be installed.

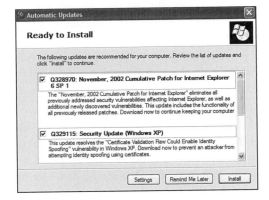

NOTE

> The first time you run Windows Update, you might be alerted to the need to install new Windows Update files. After all, the service depends on a program that runs on your local computer. As the Windows Update technology evolves, it will be prompted to update itself first, and then update other aspects of the OS. It's a bit like bootstrapping.

What happens if you have opted for the system to download all available updates, yet you opt out of certain ones? The updater will remove any related files from your hard disk to free up disk space. If you later reconsider what you'd like to have on your machine, no biggie. Notice the Declined Updates button in the dialog box (Figure 6.1). If any of the updates you previously declined still apply to your computer, they will appear the next time Windows notifies you of available updates.

NOTE

> Sometimes automatic downloading of updates is one of those mysterious CPU-hogging activities that makes you wonder what in blazes your computer is up to. Your hard disk is active and your apps are running slowly. Well, it just might be doing a Windows Update in the background. During the download process, there will be an indication in the notification area (near the system tray). Click the icon that appears there, and then click Pause. When you want Windows to start downloading again, click the automatic updating icon, and then click Resume.

RESTORE-POINT OPTIONS

First introduced with Windows Me, System Restore is a feature that was long overdue. While Windows Update and the temptation to update your drivers and install apps (that often overwrite system DLLs) is all fine in the name of progress, we all know that sinking feeling when Windows suddenly takes a nosedive after you've just made some so-called improvement. System Restore comes to the rescue, saving you the hassle of the tried, true, and incredibly time-wasting format and reinstall ritual. At least that's the idea. System Restore isn't a panacea, but along with driver rollback (see Chapter 27's section called "Using Driver Rollback") and parallel DLLs, the need for total reinstalls is going to be lower than it used to be. System Restore will probably save you once or twice, if you do much with your systems at all.

There are two essential setting areas you should check out with System Restore before you get working with Windows XP. To get to the settings, choose Control Panel, System. Then click on the System Restore tab. The first option, a check box, determines whether you want System Restore turned on at all, but by default it is on. Secondly, you can alter the default amount of disk space (on each logical drive) allocated for storage of *restore point* information. Restore points are explicit points in time to which you can revert the system, in case Windows XP begins to malfunction (typically after an application installation or some other kind of update scenario). By choosing a restore point, you can even undo a restore after you've tried it, in case it doesn't fix your problem. Then you can try another restore point.

NOTE

> System Restore is a bit of a shotgun method of repair. You should know also that there are more focused options for troubleshooting a whacked-out system, such as driver rollback (to undo a specific driver update you may have just performed), or the ability to undo a Windows Update. See Chapter 27 for more about driver rollback.

6

Click the Settings button in the dialog and notice that you'll see a slider for the drive, maxing out at 12% of the drive's capacity for restore points (see Figure 6.3). Similar to the Recycle Bin, the Restore Point repository is an amalgamated resource that is normally spread across all the logical drives in the system. You can remove a specific drive from the restore point resources if you like, using the Turn off System Restore on This Drive check box.

Figure 6.3
Checking and setting
Windows XP's System
Restore feature.

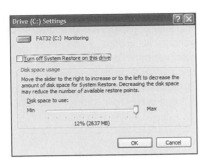

Next, you may want to take a look at the current System Restore points, and learn how to make a new, specific restore point.

INSTALLING AND CONFIGURING A UPS

Electricity is that unseen resource that we pretty much take for granted. It's an invisible, yet critical part of every computer. Not only is it essential in some form for the computer to work, the quality of the power that is being used can affect how a system performs. And, of course, in the case of sudden disruption of a power source, serious damage to both hardware and software can ensue. Most users just rely on power that comes through the wall outlet, but a Uninterruptible Power Supply (UPS) can be a lifesaver when the power goes off, giving you the time to back up files and close programs in a manner that will protect against such data loss and system corruption.

Windows XP, like Windows NT and Windows 2000, has built-in support for Uninterruptible Power Supplies. They are relatively cheap and provide a good measure of protection from power outages, but all Uninterruptible Power Supplies are not created equal. The most basic UPS should give you a few minutes of time that it will support system operation after a power failure. As the price of the UPS goes up, the amount of time you have available increases. The number of devices you have connected to the UPS and how much power they draw also plays a large role in this timeframe.

The tendency is to think that all electric power sources are equal in quality and that if there is a wall plug with the approximate voltage your computer requires, then all will be well. However, that's not the case. Just because there is power going to the machine it doesn't mean it's the best possible power or what is commonly referred to as "clean" or "filtered" power. Power is cyclical by nature and these cycles or variations in the supply of power can impact the stability of a computer. Today's computers have switching power supplies and voltage regulators in them that do their best to filter and to keep voltages stable within the box, but if you've ever seen the monitor display shrink momentarily and then expand to fill the screen again, chances are good it may have been due to a power fluctuation. A computer's power supply doesn't have the necessary circuitry or power reserves to supply unwavering voltages to compensate for sizable spikes or dips in voltage from the wall outlet.

However, due to the internal battery and circuitry in a UPS, it can filter the incoming electricity and can supply a higher quality power and result in a more stable operating environment.

UPS systems come in a huge range of sizes and capacities. Generally, the larger and more expensive the unit, the longer it will run your computer. Since CRT monitors suck up the bulk of the current in computers, for maximum operating time during power failure, you'll want to consider using an LCD monitor, since they're miserly on power draw. Shop carefully for your UPS, and ideally get one that is guaranteed to work with Windows XP. Simple UPS systems don't have an interface for the computer, but better ones do. The interface allows the UPS to signal the computer about the state of the power source, send alerts to the operating system in case of power outage, and indicate how long the UPS's internal battery power is going to last before shutting down.

When setting up a UPS, follow the manufacturer's instructions for connecting the unit, most commonly by attaching it to a serial or USB port. Most units will also come with a CD containing software that provides additional functionality to the UPS. Even if additional software isn't included, it's likely that XP will automatically detect the presence of the UPS. Once it's been installed it needs to be configured to suit your particular situation.

INSTALLING AN UNINTERRUPTIBLE POWER SUPPLY

1. The first step is physically installing the UPS device. Follow the manufacturer's instructions and connect the cables appropriately depending on whether you selected a Serial port (RS-232) or USB model.

2. Power up the computer and let it complete the boot process. In all likelihood the UPS will be detected by XP.

> **NOTE**
>
> It's necessary to be logged on as Administrator or a member of the Administrator Group to perform a UPS installation and configuration. Network installations can be affected by network policy settings that are already in place. Check with the Administrator if you encounter any difficulty.

3. Navigate to Start, Control Panel, Performance and Maintenance, Power Options to open Power Options Properties. Select the UPS tab. Click Select.

4. In the UPS Selection dialog box (see Figure 6.4), click the manufacturer of the UPS device.

5. In Select Model, click the model of the UPS device attached to the computer.

6. Click the serial port where the UPS device is attached to the computer.

7. Click Finish.

6

Figure 6.4
Choosing a UPS
brand.

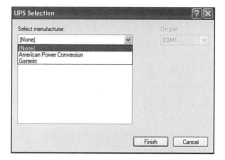

NOTE

It's possible there may not be a UPS tab in Power Options when XP automatically detects the UPS after it has been connected to the computer and the system is booted. If the UPS tab *is* visible, the UPS was probably not detected and will need to be selected using the Select button in the Details section. If the UPS tab does not exist, check for the Power Meter and Alarms tab to confirm UPS detection.

CONFIGURING THE UPS

Unlike many devices attached to computers, Uninterruptible Power Supplies really don't need to be configured to perform the basic operation of supplying battery power to the computer during a power outage. However, if you're like most XP users, when there are additional configuration options available it's likely you'll want to play with them.

A number of different monitoring tools that keep track of how much battery power is available and when power outages occur may be set from the same Power Options section of Control Panel. One of the handiest tools for a computer that is not constantly attended allows the ability to set a specified amount of time after a power outage occurs for the computer to shut down automatically.

Different Uninterruptible Power Supplies will support a varying number of options. Windows XP will try to detect only those options supported by the installed UPS, but it's wise to check the manufacturer's Web site for the latest software to ensure you are getting the full benefit of your UPS purchase. An example of the dialog box for UPS settings is shown in Figure 6.5.

If you are content to use the UPS as nothing more than a battery backup, there is no need to explore the advanced settings, but you would be missing some of the most useful features. Navigate to the Power Options Properties dialog box and select the Alarms tab. The options found here allow you to set an alarm point based on the remaining charge available in the UPS battery. The alarms are divided into two categories, Low Level and Critical Level, the difference being in the amount of battery power remaining before the alarm is activated. Use the sliders to make adjustments if you disagree with the default settings of 50% for Low Level and 10% for Critical Level alarms.

Figure 6.5
More advanced UPS settings.

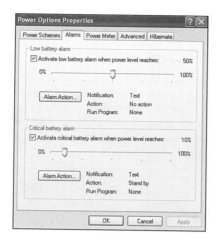

Once the levels have been finalized, click the Alarm Action button to open the Low Battery Alarm Actions (see Figure 6.6) dialog box. Neglecting the settings here may not be critical provided you are always in front of the computer whenever it's powered on to immediately deal with a power loss. However, if you leave the computer running while you are away and don't utilize these settings, you've accomplished nothing more than having the UPS battery extend the up time of the system for a few minutes before it dies.

Figure 6.6
More advanced UPS settings—Low Battery Alarm Actions.

Use the check boxes to determine whether you'd prefer to be notified of the low power situation visually or audibly. If you want to be extra cautious, select both. Taking action after an alarm has been given isn't essential, but the Alarm Action section allows the system to automatically go into Standby or to shut down. To be sure a pesky app that hangs occasionally doesn't prevent the system from shutting down, there is also an option to force the system into standby or shutdown if a program stops responding.

The last section allows you to specify a program you'd like to run if the alarm conditions are met. Simply check the box and use the Browse button to navigate to the executable. Once you have everything set up, run a test to make sure things behave as you expect. Yank the power cord and let the UPS take over. It's better to know now that the batteries don't have enough power to sustain the settings, or the program you selected doesn't run as you'd intended, rather than when you walk back in after a real power failure.

TIP

You can turn off or on the UPS service from the command prompt using the command `net start UPS` or `net stop UPS`. Also note that if you configure the Uninterruptible Power Supply service to execute a command file upon shutdown, the command file must finish running in 30 seconds. A run time that is greater than 30 seconds threatens the capability of a graceful system shutdown completing successfully.

THINKING ABOUT BACKUPS

There are few things that elicit as big an "Uh-Oh" as when a computer dies and the realization hits home that all your data may be at risk. Unfortunately, it's human nature to ignore this aspect of responsible computing until it's too late to do anything other than re-create the lost data.

NOTE

Detailed discussion of backups can be found in Chapter 25, "Managing Your Hard Disks." However, we'll discuss some backup strategies here, since it's wise to do some advance backup planning before you begin using a system. Do see Chapter 25 for more thorough discussion of the backup program provided with Windows XP.

As I think back to the very first backup I did of a computer, memory serves that it took about 50 floppy disks to back up everything; operating system, programs, and data. I won't even go into how long it took to complete the procedure or how boring it was shuffling diskettes in and out of the drive and applying the little adhesive labels. If I were to use the same methods today it would take approximately 98,000 diskettes to back up the computer I'm using to type this chapter. While we don't use diskettes for major backup procedures anymore, a lot of the thinking that goes into a backup is pretty ancient, more attuned to the days when backing up meant copying everything on a hard drive. Today, it's more prudent to concentrate on protecting the data that's user created and not worry as much about the basic operating system. XP is a prime example of operating systems that have become much more stable with fewer crashes and glitches that require reinstalling the operating system.

I don't believe any users actually set out on a given day to destroy a functional operating system, but you know as well as I do that it happens. A little tweak here, a registry edit there, a power surge or perhaps a badly behaved application that trashes the computer or hard disk. We've all been there and when it happens I can almost guarantee you that if you listen closely you'll hear something approximating, "Damn. I meant to _____." Fill in the blank with whatever task related to backup you put off until another day.

6

In this section we'll take a look at the different aspects related to backing up and restoring a computer. Some of the items you'll find in this article have been touched on in different sections of this book, but I wanted to gather them all together in one place for easier reference. Just skip over the sections that don't apply in your situation.

When pondering backup strategies, you may want to consider the idea of separating the operating system and programs from the data when it's backed up. As you know, all three components—operating systems, programs, and data—have become huge over the years. In most cases, lumping them into a single backup is a waste of time, especially for home users.

MAP OUT A BACKUP PLAN

Before you actually back up anything, you need to ask yourself some questions. The answers you give will determine in large part your backup line of attack.

One of your first questions should be about where the backup will be stored. Many of today's computers come with devices that are suitable for backups; 3.5" floppy drives, CD-R and CD-RW drives, DVD writers, tape drives, removable cartridge drives, and even a second hard drive can be used to store backups. With the exception of the second hard drive, any of those mentioned can be removed from the site where the system is located, and even the hard drive can be relocated by using specialty cradles that allow it to be plugged in and removed easily, or external drives. Personally, I use external FireWire- and USB2-based drives for backups. They are relatively inexpensive, are fast, and can easily be shifted between computers without installing removable drive bays. Business users normally back up to a company server, be it local or remote, and the IS department takes over from that point.

Which of these options is best? Each option has its weak and strong points, but human nature being what it is, the best system is the one that you're going to actually use, even if it's not the most sophisticated or flashy. If you have the discipline to mess with the disks, cartridges, or burning CDs or DVDs, then a local machine solution will work fine depending on how much data you need to back up. For those who prefer not to deal with the mechanics of backing up, the offsite solution (which can easily be automated) might be the best choice. If you travel and generate data on the road, the offsite backup solution is ideal. Of all the options mentioned, the only one I really don't endorse for home users is tape. It's cheap, but it does require a dedicated tape drive that is better suited to business situations. Also, tape drives tend to be slow, since access is sequential, meaning the tape has to be wound and rewound (spooled) to find files. It can be quite annoying.

PHYSICAL LOCATION OF BACKUPS

Another pivotal question: Where will you physically store the backup media once it's created? The theory is that if fire, flood, or theft should strike where the system is located, the backup should be available from another location to restore the system and data files. Unfortunately, storage of the backup, especially for home users not using an offsite service, is a little unwieldy. Safety deposit boxes are often mentioned as being an ideal place to store backups, but let's be realistic. Are you going to take a backup to a safety deposit box every

6

week? No, and neither am I. In the last few years, a number of Web-based hosting services that can be used for offsite storage for a monthly subscription fee have emerged, charging as little as $15 or $25 a month. This is great idea, because you don't have to bother relocating your backups to an off-site location yourself. Even if your office or house burns to the ground five minutes after you've made a backup, you still have your data. If you don't use an off-site service, consider storing your backups in one of the small fireproof chests that can be purchased at most any department or office supply store. Everything will be in one place and if disaster does strike you can grab the chest and take it with you if you have to flee (assuming it's light enough to lift).

WHAT FILES SHOULD BE BACKED UP?

Here's where the discussions about backing up usually get heated. At the beginning of this chapter I mentioned the 50 floppy disks I used years ago and the 98,000 it would take to do a full backup of everything on my system today. At one time, it was accepted, if not almost reasonable, to back up everything on a system at one time. But the amounts of data and the size of applications make that procedure very outdated. Perhaps the best way to look at backing up is to break it into two distinct categories, the first being System Files.

SYSTEM FILES

For the average user there is no need to back up your operating system files. What *is* important is to protect the original media, that is, the Windows XP CD and all of your program installation discs. Windows XP comes with System Restore that backs up all of your system files automatically, or you can create a restore point whenever you'd prefer. (System Restore is covered elsewhere in this chapter.)

Would I place exclusive trust in System Restore to restore a damaged or malfunctioning XP installation and ensure all my data was also going to be available afterward? No, and neither should you, but what I am willing to do is give System Restore a chance at getting XP back to that previous state. With some registry tweaking, you can save restore points for a year or more, eliminating the ones of lesser importance along the way. For those who don't like or trust System Restore, there are a number of programs available that create an exact "image" of a hard drive and allow you to replicate a crashed drive on a new or reformatted drive in a fraction of the normal time. Ghost by Symantec is one of the popular choices. Drive Image by PowerQuest is another.

The second category is Data Files, and I like to break that into Archive Files and Current Data Files.

DATA FILES

Archive Files—These are files acquired through any number of methods, either downloaded or created by you, that don't change once they have been created. Image and audio files are good examples in this category. They are looked at and listened to for enjoyment but as a rule they seldom if ever receive any modification once they have been added to your system. To back up these same files repeatedly is a waste of time and storage space.

Current Data Files—Of everything on your system, these are the files you want backed up and protected on a regular basis. The list of included files will vary by user, but a few examples are text documents, spreadsheets, financial records, databases, email, Internet favorites, Personal Information Managers (PIMs), Web site projects, and generally any type of data you create and work with or modify on a regular basis.

AIDING THE BACKUP PROCESS BY SYSTEM ORGANIZATION

How you organize the system can make backup a relatively painless process. Structuring the system so the data files discussed previously are organized in one area facilitates pointing the backup program to one area rather than having to gather files from widespread locations. In Windows XP, the My Documents folder is an excellent choice for this purpose. Many programs default to saving created files in this location, Office XP being a good example.

Programs that don't use My Documents by default can often be redirected through their Preferences option to save files in a new location. If that's not possible, using the Save As command will allow selection of any location on the system or creating a new location. If My Documents isn't your preferred choice, create a folder anywhere on the system and use it as your default data storage location. Whatever location you choose, the important point is to use it for all the data you create and work with or modify on a regular basis that will be a part of the backup. You can create subfolders under My Documents for each subcategory of documents you create, just to help organize them. Direct the backup program to store My Documents and all child folders.

TIP

A system administrator managing automatic or manual backups may want to back up each user's My Documents folder. Look under *system root\documents and settings* to find each user's folders, including ones for Favorites, and so on. A slightly simpler and more inclusive solution in the case of an admin managing backups for multiple users would be to back up the entire Documents and Settings folder and all of its subfolders. You'll have to be logged in as an administrator to do this.

TIP

Systems with multiple hard drives are becoming quite common. The extra space they afford can also be used for backing up any of the three categories mentioned above. If you have a second hard drive and still want to use My Documents, it can be relocated to the second drive. Right-click My Documents, select Properties, and click the Target tab. Click the Move button and select the drive where it's to be relocated.

6

I mentioned disk imaging and the Ghost program earlier. On my personal system I use a small (20GB), fast (7200RPM) drive for C:\ and load it only with the system files and programs. Nothing else. I keep a Ghost image of that drive and if anything does happen to the system it can be reloaded in a matter of minutes. The data is in no way compromised because it resides on a totally different drive. Even if you don't add additional drives, the principle can be applied to a system with one drive that is partitioned to keep system/program and data files separated.

It's a fact of life that some users simply don't need to back up their system. If you surf the Web and send a few occasional emails that you'll never refer to again, there really isn't much point in backing things up. That's not to say you don't want to consider a program such as Ghost that will create an image of your system for a quick reinstall, but establishing a routine data backup isn't always necessary.

One of the first things I hear when discussing backups is how long the process takes. Sure it does, especially when you're backing up things that have no reason to be backed up. Take Quicken for example, a very popular personal financial management program. Most people just check off the Quicken directory and forget about it after that. Why? Why would you back up the entire program when the only relevant items are the files that hold your personal data? Lack of planning, pure and simple. As a matter of fact, there are very few programs that require much backup other than for the data specific to your personal use.

What it all boils down to is how much losing your data scares you. If the thought of losing one day's work makes the hair on the back of your neck stand upright then you'd better have a tightly structured backup plan and ensure that it's adhered to without fail. If you have a computer full of spam and FreeCell stats, it doesn't make much difference when or if you back up.

INSTALLING THE BACKUP UTILITIES IN WINDOWS XP

As discussed more thoroughly in Chapter 25, while it isn't absolutely essential to have a utility specifically designed for backing up a computer system, it can make life easier. Both Windows XP Home and Professional come with what Microsoft calls the Backup and Restore Utility, better known as *NTBackup*. Unfortunately for Home users, Backup and Restore is not installed by default nor is it as fully functional as the version installed by default in XP Professional. Supposedly, the reason it's not installed by default in Home is because Home does not support Automated System Recovery (ASR), which is a part of Backup and Restore. This in no way prevents you from making a full backup in Home Edition, but it does limit the recovery or restore options. Bottom line: If you have Pro you're ready to go. If you have Home, follow the directions below:

To manually install the backup utility in Windows XP Home Edition

1. Insert the CD-ROM and navigate to *CD-ROM Drive*:\VALUEADD\MSFT\NTBACKUP.

2. Double-click the Ntbackup.msi file to start the wizard that installs Backup.

3. When the wizard is complete, click Finish. The Backup Utility will now appear in the System Tools group, from the Start button.

A Rant About Restore CDs

A few years ago I wouldn't even have had to add this paragraph, but a trend I heartily dislike has been gaining a foothold in the computer industry. That trend is the supplying of "Restore CDs" by PC manufacturers. These useless little CDs are used to restore a PC to factory specifications. What does that mean, factory specifications? It means it basically wipes your system clean and reinstalls XP along with all the other garbage (read: commercial sweetheart deals) that PC manufacturers use to augment their coffers while depriving you of an unadulterated copy of a Windows XP installation CD.

Unfortunately, if you fall into this group and have XP Home, you may have to buy a third-party backup program. Short of that, borrow a real Windows CD from a friend and install Backup on your system. The backup utility is something you should have received to begin with.

Okay, kicking my soapbox back under the desk and moving on...

THIRD-PARTY BUTT-SAVING TOOLS

There are some third-party programs you might consider installing on any new system—programs that go beyond what Microsoft has seen fit to include in XP. While it's true that Microsoft, in its usual gameplan of feature expansion, has seen fit to co-opt many operating system improvement ideas developed by other vendors (System Restore is a good example), there are still a few tricks they haven't packed under XP's hood. Here we'll discuss briefly a few of them you might consider installing. We're not actually endorsing them for mission-critical enterprise settings, because we know that you'll probably want to keep system installs down to a bare minimum and not invite possible bugs by installing programs that fiddle with the registry or that insert themselves somewhere in the system internals to any degree, but you may want to know that these programs exist or might even give some of them a whirl.

WinRescue

WinRescue is a 4-in-1 Backup and Recovery tool that addresses a number of issues necessary for maintaining, protecting, and recovering a XP installation. It contains CrashFixer, File BackUp, RegPack, and Troubleshooter sections. The user interface is straightforward and easy to understand, providing a number of different ways to back up files and also the registry, a very nice addition. Over time, as programs are added and deleted, the registry tends to grow in size and contain stray entries. RegPack addresses this issue, compacting the size and removing useless entries. The only weak section is Troubleshooting, as it links directly to the XP troubleshooters that are included in the XP Help and Support Center for free, but it does provide a convenient interface for accessing each of the troubleshooters. At the current price of $25, WinRescue is worth a look for those who prefer a suite approach rather than individual programs, and it comes highly recommended by a number of respected computer industry journalists and Web sites. More information is available at the Super Win Software Web site (www.superwin.com).

6

ANTIVIRUS PROGRAMS

It's essential in today's computing climate to install and use a quality antivirus product. Running a connected system without one is an invitation to disaster, and it probably won't take long before the system picks up a nasty infection. Norton and McAfee are the best known providers of antivirus products, both standalone versions and suites that contain other products such as firewalls, parental controls, and system maintenance utilities. When considering a product, it's critical to select one that is vigilant in providing frequent updates. New viruses and variants appear alarmingly fast. A product that doesn't counter the newest developments quickly will leave the system exposed and at risk. There are also a number of free online virus scanners available. A search of the Internet or download.com will point you toward them, but again, make sure they are updated frequently.

ROXIO GOBACK

GoBack, from Adaptec (well, actually Roxio.com, which is Adaptec's software spinoff) is a potentially very useful butt-saving utility. I've discussed it in more detail in Chapter 32, but basically it is a rollback utility. Once installed, it works transparently and continuously, tracking every write to the hard disk. It does continuous tracking of hard disk files and lets you roll them back to re-create the content of your hard disk as it was at virtually any moment in recent history—five minutes, five hours, even five days ago. GoBack is inexpensive (about $50) and keeps a journal of all modified hard disk files in a separate pre-allocated area of the HD (defaulting to 10% of the total HD size). "Safe points" are created during your working day, allowing a range of choices if recovery should be necessary.

GHOST AND DRIVE IMAGE

As mentioned in the section on backup strategies, Norton Ghost and Power Quest Drive Image are worthy contenders in the disaster-proofing arena. Like "mirroring" (also known as RAID-1, but only available on computers running Windows 2000 Server, Windows 2000 Advanced Server, or Windows 2000 Datacenter Server), these programs make a carbon copy of a hard disk or partition, and store it away for safe keeping. Should your actual drive or partition get clobbered, you simply boot up with a special floppy, and restore the entire drive from the backup. This is especially cool in the case of your operating system drive crashing, because unlike making file-by-file backups, these programs re-create an exact replica of your drive, including the boot track (track zero), operating system, and so forth.

TURNING ON THE INDEXING SERVICE

Put two experienced Windows XP users together and mention Indexing Service. Chances are good that you will get one that loves it and another that despises the service. Both of them may have valid reasons for their feelings but there is no doubt that Indexing Service is one of the most misunderstood features of XP.

Microsoft provides a description of Indexing Service as follows: "Indexes contents and properties of files on local and remote computers; provides rapid access to files through flexible querying language." As a brief bit of history, Indexing Service became a part of Windows 2000 core components after first being developed for use with Microsoft's Internet Information Services, aimed toward enhancing Web searches. Expanding its use to normal disk-based storage was a natural progression and in XP it's integrated into the XP Search Companion. If you have the need to search files on your computer for specific phrases or words (for example, a law firm may require the ability to sift through titanic numbers of briefs or depositions in search of specific phrases pertaining to case law), Indexing Service would enable more detailed searches than would the standard search assistant.

I mentioned earlier that Indexing Service generates strong love/hate feelings among proponents and detractors, but a few highlights of what is possible with Indexing Service may provide the insight necessary to decide if you want it enabled.

On the positive side

- Normally there will be a dramatic increase in search speed.

- Searches aren't limited to a minimal set of file properties when Indexing Service is enabled. For example, a search can be initiated on when a file was last saved, document author name, or even the number of words in a document.

- Boolean operators are supported that greatly expand the chance of finding what's being sought by allowing inflected word forms rather than merely the entered word form.

On the minus side:

- The single biggest complaint I hear from Indexing Service detractors is it causes a huge system performance hit when working on other tasks. This simply isn't true. It works in the background during system idle time, but the myth is so widespread it has almost reached urban legend status.

- The service does consume disk space when it indexes and creates the catalogs where the information is stored. A lot of numbers have been tossed about relative to how much space is consumed, but 20–40% of the size of the indexed files seems to be fairly common. Your mileage may vary.

- The ability to perform case-sensitive searches is unavailable when Indexing Service is activated.

- A "noise" filter list is created and used to filter searches that contain common words. The list is stored in the System32 folder and can be edited with Notepad if you find the default list impacts your particular type of search.

- Filters are used to instruct Indexing Service how to extract meaningful, useful information from the file types it supports. By default, the supported types are text, HTML, Internet mail and news, and Microsoft Office documents. Other document types are easily added to the index through the installation of additional filters. For example, you might want the indexing service to be able to search through PDF and Zip files.

- Two notes on security: An NTFS-formatted drive will prevent users from seeing documents listed in search results unless they have permission to access those files. (Indexing

6

Service never indexes encrypted files, incidentally.) Secondly, don't store your catalog on a Web site because a catalog stored in a virtual directory or Web root may be locked by Windows XP or 2000's Internet Information Service, causing Indexing Service to bog down your computer's processor while it tries in vain to update the catalog.

→ **See** Chapter 12, "Windows Explorer Power Users' Guide," for more information about using the Indexing service, **p. 437**.

NOTE

A thorough discussion of filters and how they are applied and used is available at MSDN Online at the Microsoft Web site. Additional information can be found at

```
http://support.microsoft.com/default.aspx?scid=KB;EN-US;
Q309173&ID=KB;EN-US;Q309173
```

Adding Search Filters

Before the Indexing Service will index a file, it will look to see whether it has a filter that will allow it to read the file. If it doesn't, then it skips the file. Unfortunately XP comes with filters for only a small number of file types, such as text files. ZIP or PDF files, for example, won't be searched. One solution suggested by Microsoft is a registry hack that tells the indexing service to treat all unknown files as text files. Or you can search for filters and install them. To add a new filter, you should do a search of the Web. For example, for adding PDF filters, check the Adobe site. Zip filters are available from various vendors. For serious searching capabilities, also search the Web for a program called mnoGoSearch Pro. It runs about $700, but is very powerful and flexible.

If you don't mind using the command-line interface, you might want to know that Windows XP has included a command similar to the grep command found in Linux and Unix that can find a needle in a haystack of files. The findstr command does essentially the same thing as grep: It will accept regular expressions, search case sensitive or otherwise, and can process a file containing file names or search queries.

Another solution is the actual grep utility itself, just as found in Unix and Linux systems. There is actually a Windows grep that has been ported to Windows and operates just like its Linux cousin. You can download grep and several other very useful Unix tools that have been ported to Win32 at

```
http://unxutils.sourceforge.net/
```

If you would prefer not to use a command-line interface, there is a GUI version called Wingrep that is a shareware tool.

```
http://www.wingrep.com/
```

ENABLING THE INDEXING SERVICE

Is Indexing Service something you want enabled? Truthfully, it depends on the type of system you run, how it's organized, what type of work you do, and how you intend to use the search capabilities. If you do lots of searches for files during your work day using the standard Start, Search command (Fido the dog) and find it rather slow and limited in its abilities, then give the Indexing Service a try and see if it's to your liking.

To activate Indexing Service

1. Click Start and select Search on the Start Menu.
2. Select Change Preferences.
3. Click With Indexing Service, as seen in Figure 6.7.

Figure 6.7
Enabling Indexing
Service in Search
Results.

That's it. The service is now running and will run at system startup. It does need idle time to generate a catalog before it's usable, however. The quickest way to do this is to leave the system on overnight. Its search capabilities should be ready to go by morning. If you wonder what your otherwise idle computer is doing during the day when hitting the hard disk continually, it's probably sifting through every new or altered file and generating an index of the collective content.

To terminate the Indexing Service, the easiest way is again from the Search Assistant. However, since it's a service, you could also control when it starts and stops by right-clicking My Computer and choosing Manage. Open Services and Applications. Then Click on Indexing service. Next, right-click on Indexing Service. A context menu gives you some options, such as starting, stopping, and pausing indexing. You can also see which directories are being (or have been) added to the index (see Figure 6.8). Some people have noted that it can take forever to shut down. If your computer has been sitting for a while and is indexing, you'll have to wait for it to close all of its threads and shut down before it returns control to you. Incidentally, you should stop indexing every time you run your backup software or perform a virus scan, because these programs can lock files and cause Indexing Service to abandon its update.

6

Figure 6.8
Indexing Service
options in Computer
Management.

> **TIP**
>
> To control whether an individual drive is indexed, open Windows Explorer, right-click the hard drive, and select Properties. On the General tab at the bottom, remove the checkmark from Allow Indexing Service.

> **TIP**
>
> For more tips on indexing, see Chapter 12, on searching for files.

FINE TUNING INDEXING SERVICE A TAD

Before letting the indexing service rip, you might want to fine tune it a bit. For example, you can tell it to exclude or include certain directories. The amount of memory used by the service is proportional to the number of files it indexes, so excluding directories can aid system performance.

> **NOTE**
>
> Microsoft suggests that you'll want 64MB of RAM for indexing up to 100,000 files, and 256MB or more to index around 500,000 files.

You can create your own catalogs that contain only those directories you name, or easier, you can customize the default System catalog so it doesn't waste time indexing folders you never search.

1. In Computer Management's tree pane, select the System catalog under Indexing Service, and double-click the Directories icon in the right pane.
2. Now you simply double-click the directory icons of folders you don't want indexed, select No under Include in Index?, and click OK.

Next, you can increase indexing speed:

1. Right-click Indexing Service in Computer Management's tree pane and choose Properties.
2. Uncheck Index Files with Unknown Extensions to limit indexing to files whose three-letter extensions match Windows's known filters (for example, .txt, .doc, and .htm). Click OK.

3. You can also right-click Indexing Service and choose All Tasks, Tune Performance. Select a usage level (Used Often for frequent updates, and so on). Or click Customize, set the Indexing slider to the desired levels for Windows index updates, and set the Query slider to indicate how frequently you make searches. Drag the slider to the left to use the least system resources, or to the right for more up-to-date indexes and faster searching.

4. Click OK as required to close all dialog boxes.

5. Restart the service to apply your changes: Right-click Indexing Service and choose Start. With Indexing Service selected in the Computer Management tree, the right pane will show how many documents you've designated for indexing and the number of documents that remain to be scanned.

INSTALLING THE RECOVERY CONSOLE

Sooner or later it's going to happen. You power on the computer and instead of getting the XP splash screen with the scrolling blue or green bars you see…nothing. You punch the reset button and wait, hoping that Safe Mode will appear to allow the machine to start. Still nothing. Now what do you do? A few deep breaths calm the nerves but the Recovery Console is more likely to solve the immediate problem.

First introduced in Windows 2000, Recovery Console is a set of tools run from a command-line environment that helps to diagnose and repair problems in Windows XP. The true value of Recovery Console is in its ability to be used when Safe Mode is inaccessible. One of the primary reasons for XP failing to load is file corruption. While Recovery Console is an excellent tool to help repair corrupted files, it's not limited to that one function. Other areas where it can be utilized quite successfully are

- Creating and format drives.
- Copying, renaming, and replacing XP system files and folders.
- Repairing the XP boot menu.
- Repairing the Master Boot Record (MBR) and the boot sector of the XP system drive.
- Initiating changes to devices and services, enabling or preventing them from loading.

LOADING RECOVERY CONSOLE FROM THE XP CD

1. Insert the XP CD and reboot the computer. It may be necessary to adjust the BIOS settings so the computer boots initially from the CD.

TIP

> If the computer has already been powered off without the CD being inserted and you don't want to turn it back on to open the CD tray, straighten a paper clip and insert it in the small hole on the front of the CD drive. Pushing the clip straight in will engage the tray mechanism and force it open enough for it to be grasped and opened fully. Insert the XP CD and gently push the tray closed. (Not all drives have a manual eject feature, but many do.)

6

2. Watch the bottom of the screen until you see "Press any key to boot from CD" appear; then whap any key to get the process started.

3. Basic XP startup files will load, eventually bringing you to the Welcome To Setup screen. Press **R** to load the Recovery Console.

4. On systems that have multiple operating systems installed, you may have entries displayed for W2K or NT4 as well as the current XP installation. Type the number of the Windows installation you want to access in Recovery Console.

CAUTION

> When selecting the XP installation, it's important to note that you need to type the actual number of the installation even if it's the only one listed. Tapping the ENTER key at this point will initiate a system reboot rather than loading Recovery Console.

5. Enter the Administrator password when prompted. This is the password you created during the initial XP installation, not necessarily the one you use with the everyday logon that was created during the XP Out Of Box Experience setup screens where you were first greeted by the little Microsoft Wizard. On XP Home Edition installations the password is blank; hit the Enter key to continue.

Once the correct password has been entered, you will be deposited at the C:\Windows prompt with the Recovery Console ready for use. You're in command-line territory, where there is no fancy GUI available. A list of the commands available for use with Recovery Console can be pulled up by typing **help** at the current prompt.

Here's how to add the Recovery Console to the Boot Menu:

1. Making Recovery Console a permanent part of the boot menu is initiated from inside Windows XP. Insert the XP Installation CD and close the splash screen that appears if you have AutoRun enabled.

2. Click Start, Run and in the Open line type **G:\i386\winnt32.exe /cmdcons**, substituting the letter of your CD drive for *G* in the example.

3. The Windows Setup dialog box (see Figure 6.9) will open. Click Yes to confirm the Recovery Console installation.

Figure 6.9
Recovery Console
Setup.

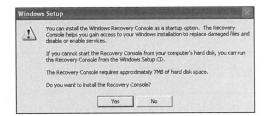

4. Setup will attempt to access the Internet and perform a Dynamic Update to the installation files. If you don't wish to perform the update, press Esc to interrupt the Dynamic Update process and use the existing setup files.

5. Once the Dynamic Update is completed, a setup screen will track the installation progress of Recovery Console as the files are copied and system files updated to place the Recovery Console on the Boot Menu.

6. Upon completion of the Recovery Console install, a dialog box is displayed to confirm a successful installation. Click OK and restart the computer. Now you'll have a startup option that includes the Recovery Console, as shown in Figure 6.10.

TIP

If you had a single operating system installation prior to installing Recovery Console, you didn't have a Boot Menu screen. While Recovery Console will normally be installed as the second, non-default option on the new menu, you may find the delay while the timer counts down annoying. This delay can be minimized by right-clicking My Computer, Properties, Advanced tab and then clicking the Settings button in the Startup and Recovery section. Use the spinner options at the top to set how long the startup options will be displayed.

Figure 6.10
Boot menu now includes recovery console.

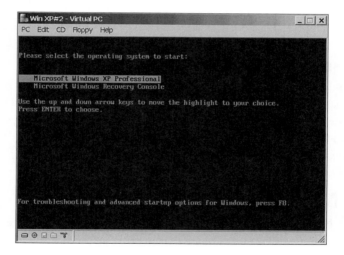

NOTE

Chapter 32 discusses the use of the Recovery Console in the case of a crashed system.

6

Removing the Recovery Console

If for some reason you'd rather not have the Recovery Console as part of the Boot Menu after it's been installed, the following steps will remove it and allow you to modify the Boot Menu back to the original state.

1. Restart your computer, click Start, click My Computer, and then double-click the hard disk on which you installed the Recovery Console.

2. On the Tools menu, click Folder Options, and then click the View tab.

3. Click Show Hidden Files and Folders, click to clear the Hide Protected Operating System Files check box, and then click OK.

4. At the root folder, delete the Cmdcons folder and the Cmldr file.

5. At the root folder, right-click the Boot.ini file, and then click Properties.

6. Click to clear the Read-only check box, and then click OK.

7. Open the Boot.ini file in Microsoft Windows Notepad and remove the entry for the Recovery Console. It looks similar to this:

```
C:\cmdcons\bootsect.dat="Microsoft Windows Recovery Console" /cmdcons
```

8. Save and close the file.

9. Reboot the system.

CAUTION

Modifying the Boot.ini file incorrectly may prevent your computer from restarting. Be sure to delete only the entry for the Recovery Console. Also, it is recommended that you change the attribute for the Boot.ini file back to a read-only state after you complete this procedure.

LIMITATIONS WHEN USING RECOVERY CONSOLE

A common misconception about Recovery Console is once it's installed you pretty much have the keys to the XP kingdom. The reality is that you are very limited in what can actually be accessed. The console is a repair tool, and as such, the files and operations it needs to perform the job can be utilized while still maintaining security measures. The limitations that are imposed are discussed in more detail in Chapter 32.

RUNNING NETWORK SETUP WIZARD

Running the Network Setup Wizard is necessary because even if you enter the information, file sharing will not work until you've run the network setup wizard once.

A few years ago it was uncommon to have more than one computer in a home and networking wasn't nearly the issue it has become today. With more and more perfectly good computers being replaced solely because they are slower and not capable of supporting the latest technologies, many homes now have two, three, or even more computers. It was only natural that as XP developed, an easy method of connecting or networking machines to allow them to communicate would be included. The Network Setup Wizard is the result of that development process. It has greatly simplified what used to be a task reserved for those with pocket protectors and bad eyesight.

How you connect to a network depends on the type of connection you have between the individual computers, your Internet connection, whether you are using a router, and a number of other factors. The Network Setup Wizard will sort through them, providing excellent help documentation and graphical representations of different connection possibilities. The Network Setup Wizard was designed as a tool to help small office and home users set up a network with the least amount of fuss possible. It will not run on computers that are joined to a domain.

To open Network Setup Wizard

1. Click Start, Control Panel, Network and Internet Connections.
2. Under Pick a Task, click Set Up or Change Your Home or Small Office Network.
3. The Network Setup Wizard (see Figure 6.11) will open.

Figure 6.11
Network Setup
Wizard.

There have been many complaints that after running the Network Setup Wizard, the local machine was still unable to connect to the network and share files and printers. In most cases, this is because the wizard has either activated the Internet Connection Firewall (ICF), or the name of the network workgroup has been entered incorrectly. All the computers on the network must be a part of the same workgroup to be visible to the other computers. How you connect to the Internet and the network will determine whether ICF is needed, but as a general rule, if you connect through a Local Area Network (LAN) that uses a hardware router (such as LinkSys products) or a software router (such as Internet Connection Sharing) you do not want ICF enabled.

To disable Internet Connection Firewall

1. Click Start, Control Panel, Network and Internet Connections, Network Connections.
2. Right-click the LAN or High-Speed Internet connection and click Properties.
3. On the Local Area Connection Properties sheet, select the Advanced tab.
4. Remove the checkmark from the box in the Internet Connection Firewall section and click OK.

One popular misconception about Internet Connection Firewall is that disabling ICF allows programs on your machine to call home without your knowledge, or allows Trojan Horse

6

programs to connect to outside machines without you being aware of the outbound traffic. The truth is that ICF will not prevent this even if enabled; ICF protects only against inbound traffic and connections. It has no ability at all to monitor or guard against outbound traffic. To do this you need a third-party firewall. A search of the Internet will turn up many offerings, many free for non-commercial use. Zone Alarm, Symantec, and many other companies market excellent firewalls.

→ Please **see** Chapter 17, "Building Your Own Network," for more information about the Network Setup Wizard, **p. 637**.

POWER MANAGEMENT

Earlier in this chapter, Uninterruptible Power Supplies were discussed as an excellent way to improve the power coming into your system and guard against the problems that can occur when a power outage strikes. Having power available is only one part of the equation. Windows XP has a number of options that allow managing the available power. These options are available from Control Panel in the Performance and Maintenance section by clicking Power Options. A number of different property sheets are available in Power Options. A brief discussion of each one follows (see Figure 6.12).

Figure 6.12
Checking and setting Windows XP's Power Schemes and settings.

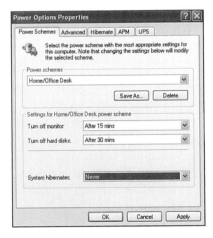

Power Schemes—Microsoft likes to group similar functions in XP. The principle behind Power Schemes is very similar to what is done with Themes: Take the different settings and group them under a heading that makes it quick and easy to select a number of settings. The available Power Schemes are

- Home/Office Desk
- Portable/Laptop
- Presentation
- Always On

- Minimal Power Management
- Max Battery

Each scheme has a different set of defaults to alter how XP handles power functions. If none of the preset schemes seems suited to your method of operation, select the closest scheme and use the individual settings to make modifications. Once the settings have been selected they can be saved as a custom scheme using the Save As button.

Advanced—The Advanced tab contains settings for controlling what function will be selected when the power button is pressed, special power keys that are available on some keyboards, and whether or not a password is necessary when resuming from standby mode.

Hibernate—Enables or disables hibernation, the ability for the computer to write all data (including the system state) in memory to hard disk and then shut down. Upon startup, all this data is read back into RAM, and the CPU and other system hardware is reinitialized to the state it was in when hibernation ensued. Hibernation is very handy for those who always use the same set of applications on startup, or who want to leave their applications and documents open between computing sessions. The amount of hard drive space required to place the machine into hibernation mode is also displayed.

> **TIP**
>
> I use hibernation a lot, and to invoke it, I press Windows+U, followed by H. It's very quick. I also have a computer with a softkey on it for either putting the computer into standby or hibernation. This option is set on the Advanced tab of the Control Panel, Power Properties dialog. Whenever I press this key or close the lid of my laptop, it hibernates without even using the key sequence above.

APM—Whether or not the Advanced Power Management (APM) tab is present depends on hardware component detection during the XP installation. If all installed components and the BIOS support power management, Advanced Configuration and Power Interface will be installed and the APM tab will not be present. Any non-compliant devices or BIOS will cause the APM tab to appear where you can enable Advanced Power Management support.

UPS—This property was discussed previously in the Uninterruptible Power Supply section.

6

SETTING SHUTDOWN AND RESTART OPTIONS

A lot of conversation centers on getting XP booted up and running. Just as important are the settings that close XP down properly. It makes me chuckle a bit whenever I write a little piece about XP and note that the first step in shutting down XP is clicking the Start button. It just seems totally incongruous, but as you know, improper shutdown is an invitation to lost data and a corrupt operating system.

By default, clicking Start will present the Log Off and Turn Off Computer options at the bottom of the Start Menu. Log Off is a new XP feature associated with Fast User Switching.

Clicking Turn Off Computer presents a more familiar dialog box with the Turn Off and Restart buttons. Depending on how the system is configured, there may also be a Stand By or Hibernate button. If Hibernation is enabled and the option isn't visible in the shutdown dialog box, press the Shift key and it should become visible, replacing the Standby icon.

CONFIGURING FOR PROPER SHUTDOWN AND SUSPEND BEHAVIOR

The Power Options properties accessible via Control Panel that were discussed earlier in this chapter are used to set the Stand By and Hibernation options. But notice that there are a couple important options in that dialog that pertain to automatic shutdown of a laptop computer in case of battery power running low. There is a System Standby option and a System Hibernates option. You will want to check your computer first, to ensure that these options actually work as expected. On one of our laptop machines, hibernation functions as expected, but although standby is listed as an option, the system will not properly power back up from the Standby state. This is probably due to an incompatible driver being installed, but tracking such things down is not always easy.

CRASH RECOVERY OPTIONS

It's inevitable that sooner or later you will have to deal with a system crash. That's not a slam against Windows, just a fact of life with any operating system. Crash recovery is especially important for machines running server-like apps, because other users on the LAN who are running apps from the server require the system to be fully functional to get their work done. Setting up some crash options on a newly installed app server is something to consider.

By default, XP is configured so that when a system failure is encountered, the system automatically restarts. This behavior may at times be desirable, especially if a system is unattended and a reboot is necessary to restore a system to operation.

Unfortunately, it also makes it very difficult if not impossible for a user to read the messages that are presented that may provide clues to a shutdown problem. To prevent the system from automatically restarting so that an error message may be read:

1. Right click My Computer, click Properties, and select the Advanced tab.
2. Click the Settings button in the Startup and Recovery section.
3. Remove the checkmark from Automatically Restart in System Failure section.

On systems that are unattended, the default setting is probably the best, but for everyday-use systems I'd make sure the auto-restart functionality is disabled to make troubleshooting more convenient.

MAKING AN ASR DISK

Windows XP users fortunate enough to be running the Professional rather than Home version have another crash recovery tool available called Automated System Recovery or ASR.

Using ASR is a two-step process as explained on the opening screen (see Figure 6.13) of the ASR Preparation Wizard.

Figure 6.13
The Automated System Recovery Preparation Wizard.

To make use of ASR it's essential that both steps in the process be completed. One without the other leaves you defenseless in a crash situation. Open the XP Backup utility in Advanced Mode and click the Tools menu. Select the ASR Wizard and follow the directions for completing the backup.

The first step is creating the system backup. The backup file can be saved to a hard disk, a floppy disk, or to any other removable or non-removable media accessible by the system. After the creation process is finished you'll be prompted for the floppy diskette that will be used to start the system recovery process. Store it in a safe place or the entire process is worthless.

It's worth noting that to use ASR to recover the system, you will need to boot from the original XP installation CD. Make sure that both the CD and the floppy diskette are available and then boot from the CD. Press F2 when prompted and insert the floppy to begin the restoration process.

NOTE

Chapter 32 covers in detail issues pertaining to crash recovery.

6

ADDING HARDWARE PROFILES

The days of a simple system with a floppy and hard drive are long gone. Today there are multiple devices on every system, and while it's nice to have all the extras that allow us increased connectivity and functionality, there are times when it's better to not have everything available. Portable computers are an excellent example where hardware profiles come in very handy. Setting up different profiles for different locations where the computer is used allows you to specify what devices will be loaded to match the intended use.

To set up multiple hardware profiles, navigate through Start, Control Panel, Performance and Maintenance, System, and click the Hardware tab followed by the Hardware Profiles button. You'll see Profile 1 (Current), the default hardware profile established by XP on the initial operating system installation. It contains all the devices listed in Device Manager and is used as the basis for a new hardware profile.

Here's how to create a new hardware profile:

1. Click Profile 1 (Current) and then click the Copy button.

2. Give the new profile a descriptive name and click OK.

3. Open Device Manager and enable/disable devices as desired for the new hardware profile.

CAUTION

Once a new hardware profile has been created, the default Profile 1 (Current) will no longer be available from the list of available profiles shown at startup. Name the first Profile 1 (Current) copy that's created something like "Default Hardware Profile" then make another copy that will be altered to use an alternative hardware configuration.

Once the new profiles have been created, set the options controlling which profile will be selected by default if no choice is made from the hardware profiles menu. The length of time the choices are displayed before the default is selected can be controlled from the same screen.

PROFILES FOR LAPTOPS AND DOCKING STATIONS

A desktop situation is normally static in relation to what devices are used and the method of connectivity employed to access remote services. By contrast, laptops and docking stations constantly encounter a variety of situations where devices may or may not be available, needed, or desired.

This is where the true value of hardware profiles becomes apparent. Each time you find yourself in a unique or different situation that is likely to be encountered on a recurring basis, create a new hardware profile so that it will be available each time the situation is encountered.

The procedure for setting up a hardware profile on a laptop varies just a bit from a desktop computer. To set up hardware profiles

1. Click Start, Control Panel, Performance and Maintenance, and then click System.

2. Select the Hardware tab and click Hardware Profiles.

3. Select a profile and click Copy. Assign a distinctive name that will allow the profile to be easily identified to its function.

4. Select the new profile and click Properties to open the Profile Property Sheet shown in Figure 6.14.

5. Click This Is a Portable Computer, and then use the radio buttons to set the appropriate docking state.

6. Click Always Include This Profile When Windows Starts.

Figure 6.14
Hardware Profile
Settings for portable
computers.

CHAPTER

7

PRINTING AND FAXING

In this chapter

PRINTER SETUP

When it comes to printing, Microsoft got Plug and Play right. If you had a printer connected to your computer and powered up during Windows setup, it should have been detected and installed automatically at that time. In addition, Windows checks for new locally attached printers whenever a Computer Administrator or Power User-level user is logged on, and by default, on workgroup networks, it also periodically scans the network for shared printers, and automatically creates printer icons for these printers as well. So, in most cases, you should be able to print from Windows applications without having to lift a proverbial finger.

In an ideal world, then, there would be no need for a chapter on printer setup and management. However, if your printer isn't Plug and Play compatible, or if Windows doesn't have the proper printer driver already loaded, you'll have to install your printer manually. And, once your printer is configured, you'll probably want to control your print jobs, print to network-based printers, share your printer for others to use, and fine-tune the Windows Fax system for sending and receiving faxes through your modem. This chapter covers these topics. Before we get started, though, let's cover some of the basic terms used to describe the Windows printing system.

When you print from an application, the application passes the data stream--a list of characters, lines, and picture pixels to be drawn—off to Windows, which in turn *spools* this data to a specified printer. Spooling is the process of temporarily stuffing onto the hard disk the data to be transmitted to a printer, and then delivering it at the relatively slow pace with which the printer can receive it. Windows passes the information from the queue through a *printer driver* program, which determines the specific codes and commands that your printer needs in order to *render*, or draw, your document. Finally, a software driver called a *port monitor* handles the communication between the Windows printer drive and the printer's hardware or network connection.

The Windows printing system takes control of all printing jobs, whether from Win32, Win16, OS/2, POSIX, or DOS applications. In cases of trouble (for example, ink or paper outage or paper jams), it also displays pop-up balloon notification messages.

THE PRINTERS AND FAXES FOLDER

Windows gives you control over the printing system through the Printers and Faxes folder, shown in Figure 7.1. You can add printers, check the status of the queue, and manage print jobs by clicking Start, Control Panel, Printers and Other Hardware, Printers and Faxes.

> **TIP**
>
> If you use Printers and Faxes frequently, you can add it to your Start Menu. Right-click the Start button and select Properties. View the Start Menu tab and click Customize. Select the Advanced tab, and check Printers and Faxes under Start Menu Items.

After you open the folder, you can view the Task menu for a particular printer by clicking that printer's icon.

Figure 7.1
The Printers and Faxes folder is the starting point for printer setup and management.

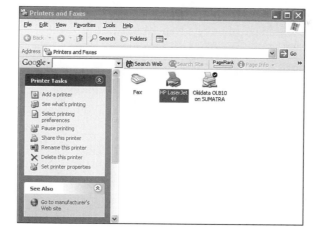

Throughout the rest of this chapter, I'll refer to the Windows printing system and its windows GUI, taken as a whole, as the *Print Manager*.

The Print Manager in Windows XP has the following features:

- It lets you easily install, configure, and remove printers through the Add Printer Wizard and through each printer icon's right-click context menu.

- The intuitive user interface uses simple icons to represent printers that are installed (available to print to) on the workstation. You don't need to worry about the relationships of printer drivers, connections, and physical printers. You can simply add a printer and set its properties. After it is added, it appears as an icon in the Printers and Faxes folder.

- Multiple users and applications can send print jobs to the same printer, from the local computer and across the LAN. Additional documents are simply added to the queue and are printed in turn.

- You can set your own preferred settings for such options as number of copies, paper tray, page orientation, and so forth as the printer's default settings, so you don't have to manually set them each time.

- If you want, you can create multiple icons for the same physical printer, each with different default settings. You can then choose between several different setting regimes just by selecting an alternate printer name in your application.

- You can easily view the document name, status, owner, page count, size, time of submission, paper source and orientation, number of copies, and destination port of jobs. You can pause, resume, restart, and cancel jobs, rearrange the order of the print queue, and temporarily pause printing without causing printer time-out problems.

7

- You can set color profiles for color printers, ensuring accuracy of output color. Associating the correct color profile with all your publishing tools helps to ensure consistent color application throughout the publishing process.

LAN users can take advantage of more advanced features:

- Browsing for LAN-based printers to which to connect has been made very simple. On a workgroup network, in fact, Windows scouts for and installs icons for shared printers automatically.
- Groups of users (administrators, guests, and so forth) can be assigned rights for printing, sharing, and queue management.
- The priority level of print jobs can be increased or decreased. This is handy when you have an urgent need to print a document on a busy network printer. You can also limit times of day when a network printer is available for use.
- In a busy LAN environment, you can attach a group (pool) of printers to a single queue, so that output automatically goes to the first available printer.
- You can easily share a printer over the LAN by modifying a few settings on the printer's Properties sheet. Your computer then acts as a print server for other computers.
- The system can track the use of network print servers locally or remotely for later review or for billing purposes.

→ To learn more about sharing and managing printers on the network, **see** "Sharing Printers," **p. 723**.

- With the Web printer feature (Internet Printing Protocol, or IPP), printers can be shared securely over the Internet, without using *Virtual Private Networking (VPN)*.

→ To learn more about IPP, **see** "Using Printers Over the Internet with IPP," **p. 709**.

INSTALLING AND CONFIGURING PRINTERS

If your printer is already installed and operational at this point, you can skip this section and skim ahead for others that may be of interest. However, if you need to install a new printer, modify or customize your current installation, or add additional printers to your setup, read on.

You might want to add a printer in a few different instances, not all of which are obvious:

- You're connecting a new physical printer directly to your computer. In this case, follow the instructions in the next section, titled "Adding a New Locally Attached Printer."
- You're connecting to a printer that's shared by some other computer on the network. Connecting to a shared printer is under "Using a Network (Shared) Printer."
- You're installing a printer that connects directly to the network. Network-attached printers are discussed in Chapter 18, "Using the Network."

- You want to set up multiple printer configurations (preferences) for a single physical printer, so that you can switch among them without having to change your printer setup before each print job. This process is described later in this chapter under "Adding Alternate Configurations for One Printer."

- You want to print to formatted disk files that can later be sent to a particular type of printer. This is described in this chapter under "Printing to Disk."

TIP

> This borders on the obvious, but before you buy any new piece of hardware, it's always a good idea to check the Microsoft Hardware Compatibility List (HCL) on the Web, or use the compatibility tool on the Windows XP CD. You should at least check the manufacturer's Web site or the printer's manual to ensure that it's compatible with Windows XP or at least Windows 2000. Bargain-basement and used printers might not be supported by XP.

ADDING A NEW LOCALLY ATTACHED PRINTER

The basic game plan for installing and configuring a printer that is to be directly connected to your computer is as follows:

1. Read the printer's installation manual and follow the instructions for Windows XP, or if XP-specific instructions are not provided, for Windows 2000. Some printer manufacturers ask you to install their driver software *before* you plug in and turn on the printer for the first time. If your printer's instruction manual says this, *heed this advice*.

2. In the absence of more specific instructions, log off and connect the printer to your computer. For parallel port or USB connections, just attach the printer's cable to the appropriate connector on your computer. For Infrared or wireless connected printers, be sure the printer is within range of your computer's infrared eye or wireless antenna.

3. Turn the printer on, and log on as a Computer Administrator or Power User. In most cases, Windows XP will identify and install the drivers for your printer automatically, and you can proceed to the section titled "Configuring Printer Preferences."

4. If the printer doesn't configure itself, you can run the Add New Printer Wizard (or use a setup program, if one is supplied with your printer). We'll go over this procedure in detail in the next section.

In most cases, Windows XP automatically detects and installs printers. If it doesn't, you can add the printer manually.

IF THE PRINTER ISN'T FOUND OR IS ON A SERIAL PORT

If your printer isn't automatically installed when you log on as a Computer Administrator user, if the printer is connected via a COM port, or if you want to add an alternate printer icon, you have to fake out Plug and Play and go the manual route. To do so, just follow these steps:

7

1. Open the Printers and Faxes folder, and select Add a Printer from the Printer Tasks list.
2. Click Next.
3. Click Local Printer, make sure that Automatically Detect My Printer is *not* checked, and then click Next.
4. Select the port that the printer is connected to in the resulting dialog. Figure 7.2 shows the printer port dialog box; the options and what they mean are as follows:

Figure 7.2
Choosing the port for a printer.

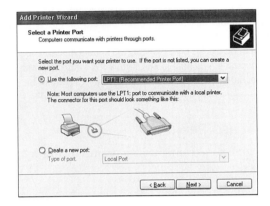

Options	Notes
LPT1:, LPT2:, LPT3:	The most common setting is LPT1 because most PC-type printers hook up to the LPT1 parallel port.
COM1:, COM2:, COM3:, COM4:	If your printer uses a serial interface, it's probably connected to the COM1 port. If COM1 is tied up for use with some other device, such as a modem, use COM2. If you choose a COM port, click Settings to check the communications settings in the resulting dialog box. Set the baud rate, data bits, parity, start and stop bits, and flow control to match those of the printer being attached. Refer to the printer's manual to determine what the settings should be.

7

Options	Notes
other ports	If you already have a USB or network-based printer attached, you may see additional ports listed; these represent the connection between your computer and the existing printer. If you're adding an additional, alternate icon for an existing printer, select the same port that is used by the existing printer's icon. (You can have multiple printer icons all directing output to the same port, each with different preference settings.)
File	This is for printing to a disk file instead of a printer. When you use the resulting printer icon, you will be prompted to enter a filename. (See the section "Printing to Disk.") Later, you can send a file to a printer or to someone via floppy disk or email.
Create a New Port	Create a New Port is used to make connections to printers that are directly connected to your LAN and are to be controlled by your computer. Its use is covered in Chapter 18.

5. Select the manufacturer and model of your printer in the next dialog, as shown in Figure 7.3. You can quickly jump to a manufacturer's name by pressing the first letter of the name, such as E for Epson. Then use the up- and down-arrow keys to home in on the correct one.

   If you can't find the appropriate model, you have two choices: You can choose a similar compatible model, and risk getting less-than-perfect output, or you can try to obtain the correct driver. If you have an Internet connection, click Windows Update to see if Microsoft has a driver available. Otherwise, get the manufacturer's driver on a floppy disk or CD-ROM or download it via the Internet, and then click Have Disk. Locate the driver (look for an INF file, the standard type for driver setup programs) and click OK.

→ For more information on dealing with unlisted printers, **see** the next section, "If Your Printer Isn't Listed."

7

Figure 7.3
Choose the make and model of your printer here.

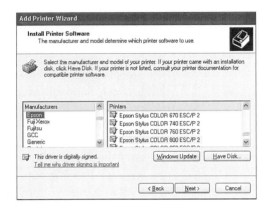

If the wizard finds that the appropriate driver is already installed on your machine, you can elect to keep it or replace it. It's up to you. If you think the replacement will be newer, go for it. By contrast, if no driver is listed on the machine, you may be prompted to install it or insert a disk, such as the Windows XP setup disk.

6. Name the printer. The name will appear in LAN-based users' browse boxes if you decide to share this printer. Some computers have trouble with filenames longer than 31 characters if you share the printer, so keep the name short and sweet.

7. Choose whether you want this printer to be your default printer.

8. Click Next. Choose whether you want to share the printer on the LAN. If not, skip to step 10. If so, click Share As and enter a name for sharing—this name will also be visible to network users. In the unlikely case that your network still has DOS, OS/2 or Windows 3.x computers, you might want to limit this name to 12 characters because that's the maximum name length those computers can handle.

→ To learn more about sharing your printer on a network, **see** Chapter 18.

9. Click Next. Now you can fill in additional information about the printer that people can see when browsing for a printer over the LAN. Something like Joe's Laser Printer in Room 23 would be useful. Although these fields are optional, by filling in the location, you at least let users know where to pick up their documents.

10. Click Next. You then are asked whether you want to print a test page. Doing so is a good way to confirm that the printer is now operational. Choose Yes or No, and then click Next.

11. Assuming that everything looks good, be sure your printer is turned on and ready to print and click Finish. Some files will be copied between directories. You might be asked to insert disks again.

12. If you chose to print a test page, your printer should start up and print a single page. You will be asked whether it printed okay. If it did, click Yes and you're finished. If it didn't print correctly, click Troubleshoot, and follow the wizard's instructions to identify the problem.

7

When you're finished, the icon for the printer appears in your Printers and Faxes folder and you can configure its default settings and preferences.

IF YOUR PRINTER ISN'T LISTED

If your printer isn't detected with Plug and Play, and isn't listed in the selection list, you'll have to find a driver elsewhere.

First of all, your printer probably came with a floppy disk or CD-ROM with driver software. On the printer manufacturer selection dialog (shown earlier in Figure 7.3), click Have Disk and then click Browse to find the Windows XP or Windows 2000 driver files for your printer. Select the appropriate INF file and click OK.

If you can't find the disk or it doesn't contain a Windows XP or 2000 compatible driver, don't worry; there's still hope.

Many off-brand printers or models are designed to be compatible with one of the popular printer types, such as the Apple LaserWriters, Hewlett-Packard LaserJets, or one of the Epson series. Also, many printer models are very similar and in a pinch can use the same driver.

Make your first stop Microsoft's online Hardware Compatibility List to see whether the printer in question has been tested with Windows XP or 2000. If it has, check the Microsoft drivers site, call the manufacturer, or check the manufacturer's Web site for the latest driver and download it. If the printer isn't on the HCL, determine whether the printer has a compatibility mode in which it can emulate a particular brand and model of printer that is. For example, some offbeat printers have an HP LaserJet compatibility mode.

Assuming that you have obtained a printer driver, follow these instructions to install it:

1. Open the Printers and Faxes folder, and run the Add Printer Wizard.
2. Click Next, choose Local Printer, and then turn off the check box for autodetecting the printer type.
3. Choose the correct port, and click Next.
4. Click Have Disk.

> **TIP**
>
> If you're online, you can click the Windows Update button to query the Microsoft site for additions to the list of printers that are supported. If your printer isn't already on the standard list, connect to the Internet, and try this approach. Your printer driver might be newly available over the Net from Microsoft.

5. Click the Have Disk button. You're now prompted to insert a floppy disk or CD. Insert the disk and select the appropriate drive letter, or click Browse to get to a disk or network volume that contains the driver. The wizard is looking for a file with an .INF extension, which is the standard file extension for manufacturer-supplied driver files.

7

6. Click OK. You might have to choose a driver from a list if multiple options exist.

7. Continue through the wizard dialog boxes as explained previously.

USING A NETWORK (SHARED) PRINTER

Windows XP really excels at network printing. Windows can directly attach to printers shared via Microsoft Networking services, whether from Windows XP, 2000, NT, 95, 98, Windows for Workgroups, OS/2, or even the Samba service from Unix or Mac OS X, and also to printers managed by Novell NetWare.

On Workgroup networks (that is, on home and small office networks without Windows 2000 Server or Windows Server 2003), Windows automatically searches for and sets up icons for all printers shared on the network. If this describes your network, there should be nothing you need to do. Within a few minutes of logging on, you should be able to see all of the available printers in your Printer and Faxes folder, as shown in Figure 7.4. Select and use them as you would a local printer.

Figure 7.4
By default, on a Workgroup network, Windows XP seeks out shared printers and automatically installs icons for them. The word "Auto" indicates printers that were discovered by Windows.

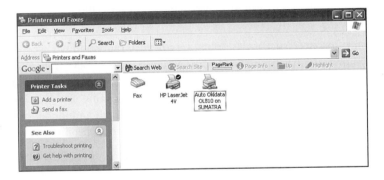

TIP

> The printer discovery feature is controlled from the Folder Options dialog. In Windows Explorer, choose Tools, Folder Options. Select the View tab. The first item in the Advanced Settings list is Automatically Search for Network Folders and Printers. If you don't like Windows populating your Printers folder with other people's networked printers, you can uncheck this item, and then delete the unwanted network printers.

On a domain network, or if you have disabled the automatic printer discovery feature, you must add shared printers to your Printer and Faxes folder manually. One way to do this is to browse or search your network for shared printers, through My Network Places. If you locate an appropriate printer, right-click its icon and select Open to set it up for your computer.

However, a more straightforward way to prepare to use network printers is to use the Add Printer Wizard in Printers and Faxes as you would to install a locally attached printer. To use the wizard, click Start, Printers and Faxes, and select the Add a Printer task. Click Next. Select Network Printer rather than Local Printer, and choose Next.

Now, you have to identify the shared printer. If you know its network name already, click Connect to This Printer, and enter the share name into the Name box in UNC format—for example, \\sumatra\laserjet—as shown in Figure 7.5.

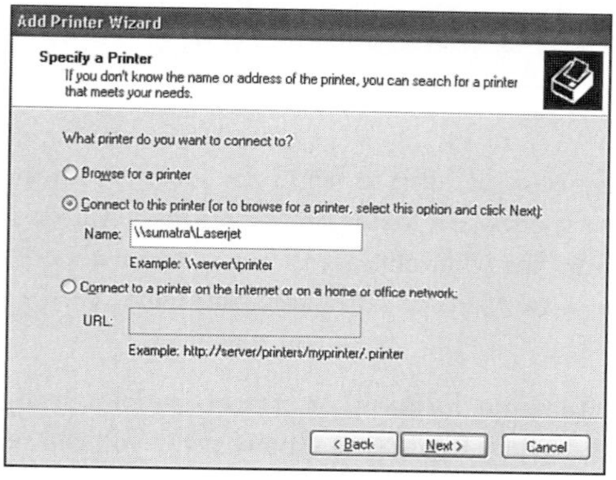

Figure 7.5

You can enter a UNC shared printer name if you know it, or you can leave the Name field blank and choose Next to browse the network for a shared printer.

After you've identified the shared printer, click Next to finish installing it. From this point, the installation process proceeds much like the installation of a local printer, as described earlier in this chapter.

If you don't know the printer's share name, or if you're on a large network, you might need some help identifying the printer you want you use. Windows provides a nifty find-a-printer feature for users of an Active Directory network; it lets you find shared printers based on features such as location and capabilities. To use it, select Find a Printer in the Directory, and click Next. I'll describe the process for searching the directory in the next section.

If you don't have an Active Directory network, skip ahead to the section "Browsing for a Suitable Printer."

SEARCHING FOR PRINTERS IN ACTIVE DIRECTORY

If your computer is connected to a domain-type network, the Active Directory can help you locate networked printers in your organization. This feature is very handy if you're a business traveler using the network in an unfamiliar office, or if you're in such a large office setting that you aren't familiar with all the printing resources on your network.

You can search for printers three ways: by name and location, as shown in Figure 7.6; by printer capabilities; or by more advanced attributes.

7

Figure 7.6
Using the Printers tab in the Active Directory printer search tool, you can search for printers by printer name, location, and model.

You can choose a major organizational unit to begin the search from the "In" drop-down list, search the entire directory, choose a major organizational unit, or select Browse to select a more regional subunit. See what choices In has on your network to see whether restricting the search makes sense for your company; otherwise, let the search use the Entire Directory.

Searching by the printer share name, location, or printer model is straightforward; just type a name or part of a name, and select Find Now. At any time, you can refine or expand your search by changing your selection criteria and selecting Find Now.

You can view *all* the printers in the directory by entering no information in the Find Printers dialog box: Just click Find Now.

TIP

> The first time you search for printers, I suggest that you view the entire directory. This will give you an idea of how location and printer names are organized in your company. If too many names are listed, you can click Clear All to clear the search listing and then restrict your search using an appropriate location name.

To search for printers based on capabilities you need, select the Features tab, as shown in Figure 7.7. Here, you can limit the directory display to just printers with required color and finishing capabilities, speed, resolution, and available paper sizes.

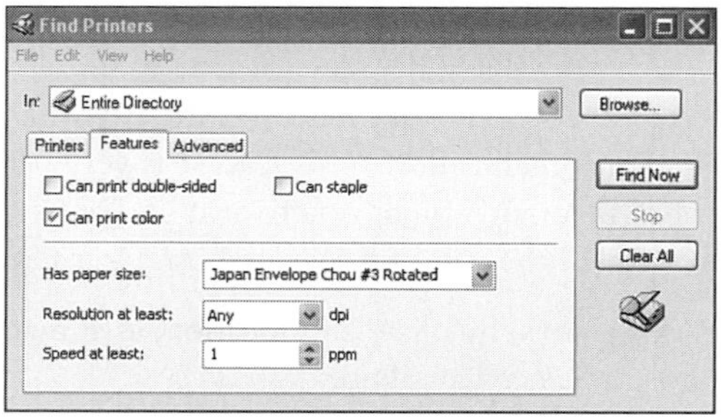

Figure 7.7
Using the Features tab, you can select printers based on printing capabilities such as speed, resolution, and color capability.

![Find Printers dialog box showing the Features tab with options: Can print double-sided, Can staple, Can print color (checked), Has paper size: Japan Envelope Chou #3 Rotated, Resolution at least: Any dpi, Speed at least: 1 ppm]

NOTE

The name and location attributes you select on the Printers tab, the capabilities you select on the Features tab, and any advanced search restrictions on the Advanced tab all operate together to limit the final result, even though you can see only one of the tabs at a time.

If these selections aren't specific enough for you, you can really nail down what you want on the Advanced tab, as shown in Figure 7.8.

Figure 7.8
Using the Advanced tab, you can select printers based on the full range of information stored in the Active Directory.

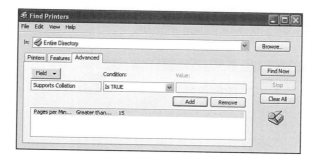

This tab lets you list your requirements in no uncertain terms. To perform an advanced search, follow these steps:

1. Select Field, and choose a criterion from the list. The searchable attributes include Asset Number, Input Trays, Installed Memory, and Printer Language; you can choose from 27 different attributes.

2. Under Condition, select an appropriate comparison type: Starts With, Greater Than or Equal To, and so on. You can also choose Present and Not Present to test whether an attribute is blank.

3. Under Value, enter the desired asset number, number of trays, megabytes of memory, printer language, and so on. Then click Add.

4. Enter more filtering items, or select Find Now to begin the search.

Remember, anything you entered on the Printers or Features tabs factors into this search as well.

TIP

If you get the message "No Printers Match the Current Search," you might be specifying the criteria too precisely and missing some close but inexact matches. Instead of specifying Postscript Level 2 as a Printer Language, for example, try searching for "Post". You might be missing a printer that was entered PostScript Lvl 2. If this doesn't help, remove a criterion or two and repeat the search.

7

After you've found a printer, what do you do with it? Right-clicking a printer in the search results list gives you two action options: You can connect to it or open it. Connecting installs the printer on your computer; in other words, it adds the printer to the list of those your computer can use. Open displays the printer's current print jobs without installing it.

BROWSING FOR A SUITABLE PRINTER

If you don't know the name of the printer you want to use, you can browse through the network. In this case, choose Connect to This Printer. Leave the Name field blank, and choose Next.

The network display appears, as shown in Figure 7.9, to let you probe into domains or workgroups, computers, and their shared printers.

Figure 7.9
You can browse your network for shared printers by opening the list view of networks, domains, workgroups, and computers. Shared printers are found listed under each computer. The list includes only computers with shared printers.

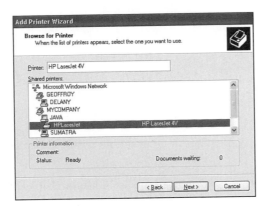

From here, just select the printer you want, and click Next to finish the installation.

FINISHING THE INSTALLATION

When you've chosen a shared printer, Windows automatically looks to the computer sharing that printer for the correct software driver. If it finds the driver, that driver is instantly downloaded to your PC, and the installation completes without your having to look up the printer's model number, hunt for the right driver diskettes, or otherwise lift a finger.

You might hit a snag, though, if the sharing computer doesn't have the correct Windows XP printer driver for you. You might have this problem if the remote computer isn't running Windows XP. In this case, Windows pops up a message saying: "The server on which the printer resides does not have the correct printer driver installed. If you want to install the driver on your local computer, click OK."

If you want to use the printer, well, now you will have to lift a finger. Click OK, and Windows displays the Add Printer Wizard with its list of known printer manufacturers and models, as discussed earlier in this chapter. Choose the correct make and model from the list, and then click OK. If you can't locate the correct printer model in this list and need more detailed instructions on installing printer drivers, see "If the Printer Isn't Found or Is on a Serial Port."

NOTE

> If you install an icon for a shared printer under one user account, it won't appear for other users as a local printer's icon would.
>
> If you want shared printer icons to appear for all users, you should use a system logon script to ensure that the icon is always installed at every logon. For more information on logon scripts, see Chapters 29, "Automating Routine Tasks," and 33, "Managing Windows XP in an Enterprise Setting."

CONFIGURING PRINTER PREFERENCES

Once you've added a new printer icon, you might want to make alterations and customizations to the printer setup. For example, you can do the following:

- Choose the default printer if you have more than one printer installed.

- Set job defaults pertaining to paper tray, two-sided printing, scaling, type of paper feed, halftone imaging, printer setup information (such as a PostScript "preamble"), and paper orientation.

- Check and possibly alter device-specific settings such as DPI (dots per inch), memory settings, and font substitution.

- Share the printer, and specify its share name so that other network users can use your printer.

- Declare a separator file, usually one page long, that prints between each print job with the user's name, date and so on. (These are handy on busy networked printers so users can find their own output among stacks of printouts.)

- Arrange security for the printer by setting permissions (if you have Computer Administrator privileges).

NOTE

> Printer security issues such as setting permissions, conducting printer access auditing, and setting ownership are covered in Chapter 18.

CHANGING A PRINTER'S PROPERTIES

Each printer driver has a Properties sheet of associated settings—typically, enough to choke a horse. The basic settings are covered in this chapter, whereas you'll find those relating to network printer sharing in Chapter 18. Printer drivers dictate, among other things, the particular options available on their Properties sheet. Because of the variations possible, the following sections describe the gist of these options without necessarily going into detail about each printer type.

If you are logged on with Computer Administrator privileges, or if the Administrator has granted your account permission to manage a given printer, you can then alter the properties as follows:

7

1. Open the Printers and Faxes folder by clicking Start, Printers and Faxes; if this choice is not available, select Control Panel, Printers and Other Hardware, View Installed Printers or Fax Printers.

2. Select the printer's icon and choose Set Printer Properties from the task list. Or, right-click the printer icon and select Properties. The printer's Properties dialog box then appears, as shown in Figure 7.10.

Figure 7.10
A typical printer's Properties dialog box. The settings available vary between printers. Some have more or fewer tabs.

3. Change any of the text boxes as you see fit. (Their significance was explained earlier in this chapter.)

Any printer's Properties sheet can have as many as eight tabs: General, Sharing, Ports, Advanced, Color Management, Security, Device Settings, and Utilities. Table 7.1 shows the general breakdown. Keep in mind that the tabs can vary depending on the capabilities of your printer.

TABLE 7.1   PROPERTIES SHEET TABS

Tab	What It Controls
General	This tab lists the name, location, model number, and features of the printer. From this tab, you can print a test page. You also can set default printing preferences, including the paper size, page orientation, paper source, pages per sheet (for brochure printing), affecting all print jobs. (You should rely on your application's Print Setup commands to control an individual print job's choice of paper orientation, paper source, and so on, which will override these settings.) Some color printers may have settings for paper quality, color control, and other utilities on this tab.

Tab	What It Controls
Sharing	On this tab, you can alter whether the printer is shared and what the share name is. You also can add drivers for other operating systems by using the Additional Drivers button (see Chapter 18).
Ports	On this tab, you can add and delete ports; set time-out for LPT ports; and set baud rate, data bits, parity, stop bits, and flow control for serial ports.
Advanced	This tab controls time availability, printer priority, driver file changes, spooling options, and advanced printing features such as booklet printing and page ordering. The first two settings are pertinent to larger networks and should be handled by a server administrator. The Advanced settings vary from printer to printer, depending on its capabilities. Booklet printing is worth looking into if you do lots of desktop publishing. Using this option, you can print pages laid out for stapling together small pamphlets.
Color Management	On this tab, you can set optional color profiles on color printers, if this capability is supported. (See "Color Management" later in this chapter.)
Security	If you have disabled Simple File Sharing (discussed in Chapters 16 and 18), this tab will appear to let you control who has permission to use, delete documents from, and manage this printer.
Device Settings	The settings on this tab vary greatly between printers. For example, you can set paper size in each tray, indicate the amount of RAM in the printer, and substitute fonts.
Utilities	This tab contains options for nozzle cleaning, head cleaning, head alignment, and so on, depending on printer driver and printer type.

I discuss the most important of the settings in more detail in the next section.

TIP

> Each time you add a printer, Windows creates an icon for it in the Printers and Faxes folder. Although each is called a printer, it is actually a "virtual" printer, much the way a shortcut represents a document or application in the GUI. A given physical printer can have multiple icons, each with different default settings. For example, one could be set to print in landscape orientation on legal-size paper, whereas another printer would default to portrait orientation with letter-size paper. Of course, you can always adjust these settings when you go to print a document, but that can get tedious. With multiple printer icons, you can choose a setup by just selecting the appropriate printer icon. See "Adding Alternate Configurations for One Printer" to see how to take advantage of this.

7

COMMENTS ABOUT VARIOUS SETTINGS

Table 7.2 describes the most common settings from the Properties dialog box for both PostScript and HP-compatible printers.

TABLE 7.2   THE OPTIONS IN THE BASIC SETUP DIALOG BOX

Option	Description
2 Sides	This option enables or disables double-sided printing for printers that support this feature.
Configure Port, LPT Port Timeout	This option specifies the amount of time that will elapse before you are notified that the printer or plotter is not responding. If printing from your application regularly results in an error message about transmission problems, and retrying seems to work, you should increase the setting. The maximum is 999,999 seconds.
Configure Port, Serial Port Settings	Settings here pertain to the serial port's communications settings, such as baud rate and parity. The serial port's baud rate, data bits, parity, stop bits, and flow control must match that of the printer's, or you're in for some garbage printouts. If you have trouble, check the printer's DIP switch or software settings and the printer manual to ensure that the settings agree.
Default Datatype	The default is RAW. The EMF data types can result in faster transmission over slow networks (for example by modem); see the sidebar "RAW versus Metafile Spooling" for more information.
Enable Advanced Printing Features	When this option is checked, metafile spooling is enabled, and options such as Page Order, Booklet Printing, and Pages Per Sheet may be available, depending on your printer. For normal printing, you should leave the advanced printing feature set to the default (Enabled). If compatibility problems occur, you can disable the feature.
Enable Bidirectional Support	This option lets the computer query the printer for settings and status information.
Font Cartridges	For this option, you choose the names of the cartridges that are physically installed in the printer. You can select only two.
Font Substitution	TrueType Font Substitution Table: Used for PostScript printers to declare when internal fonts should be used in place of downloading TrueType fonts to speed up printing.
Form-to-Tray Assignment	For this option, you click a source, such as a lower tray, and then choose a form name to match with the source. When you choose a form name (such as A4 Small) at print time, the printer driver tells the printer which tray to switch to. You don't have to think about it. You can repeat the process for each form name you want to set up.
Hold Mismatched Documents	This option directs the spooler to check the printer's form setup and match it to the document setup before sending documents to the print device. If the information does not match, the document is held in the queue. A mismatched document in the queue does not prevent correctly matched documents from printing.

Option	Description
Keep Printed Documents	This option specifies that the spooler should not delete documents after they are printed. This way, a document can be resubmitted to the printer from the printer queue instead of from the program, which is faster.
New Driver	Use this button to install an updated driver for the printer. It runs the Add Printer Driver Wizard.
Orientation	This option sets the page orientation. Normal orientation is Portrait, which, like a portrait of the Mona Lisa, is taller than it is wide. Landscape, like a landscape painting, is the opposite. Rotated Landscape means a 90-degree counterclockwise rotation of the printout.
Page Order	This option determines the order in which documents are printed. Front to Back prints the document so that page 1 is on top of the stack. Back to Front prints the document so that page 1 is on the bottom of the stack.
Page Protect	If turned on, this option tells the printer to forcibly reserve enough memory to store a full-page image; some intense graphics pages otherwise might not be able to print if the printer gives too much memory over to downloaded fonts and macros.
Print Directly to the Printer	This option prevents documents sent to the printer from being spooled. Thus, printing doesn't happen in the background; instead, the computer is tied up until the print job is completed. There's virtually no practical reason for tying up your computer this way, unless your printer and Windows are having difficulty communicating or you find that printing performance (page per minute throughput) increases significantly when this option is enabled. When a printer is shared over the network, this option isn't available.
Print Spooled Documents First	This option specifies that when deciding which document to print next, the spooler should favor documents that have completed spooling even if the completed documents are of a lower priority than documents that are still spooling.
Printer Memory	This option tells Windows how much memory the printer has installed.
Printing Defaults	You click this option to view or change the default document properties for all users of the selected printer. If you share your local printer, these settings are the default document properties for other users.

continues

7

TABLE 7.2 CONTINUED

Option	Description
Priority	Printers can have a priority setting from 1 to 99. Print jobs sent to a printer that has a priority level of 2 always print before a job sent to a printer with a level 1 setting if both setups use the same physical printer. The default setting is 1.
Resolution	Some printers can render graphics in more than one resolution. The higher the resolution, the longer printing takes, so you can save time by choosing a lower resolution. For finished, high-quality work, you should choose the highest resolution. (On some printers, this choice is limited by the amount of memory in the printer.)
Separator File	A preassigned file can be printed between jobs, usually just to place an identification page listing the user, job ID, date, time, number of pages, and so forth. Files also can be used to switch a printer between PostScript and PCL (HP) mode for printers that can run in both modes. Separator pages are discussed in Chapter 18.
Use Printer Halftoning	Because virtually no printer can print shades other than black and solid primary colors, photographic images must be converted into a series of dots called a halftone. Normally, Windows determines the necessary pattern of dots; this option instructs Windows to let the printer hardware generate the dot pattern.

NOTE

If you can't figure out what an option does, you can always click the Help button in the upper-right corner of the Properties dialog box and then click an option. A description of the option should appear.

TIP

You can access the Printing Defaults dialog through two paths: One is by choosing Printing Defaults from the Advanced tab, and the other is by choosing Printing Preferences from the General tab. There's a significant difference between the two:

Printing Defaults are the default settings initially offered to each user. If you're configuring a printer connected to your own computer or for your corporate network, use Printing Defaults to set sensible baseline defaults for all of your users.

The Printing Preferences option sets individual preferences for each user account. Use Printing Preferences to customize a given printer icon for your personal needs.

TIP

Another set of properties is available for shared printers. To locate it, right-click an empty spot within the Printers and Faxes folder, and choose Server Properties. The Server Properties dialog lists ports and shows the collective list of all installed drivers in use. Here, you can define form and paper sizes, and set events and notifications. The last tab is covered in Chapter 18 because it's a network topic.

RAW Versus Metafile Spooling

When you're configuring printer properties, you may run into the Default Data type option in the Print Processor setting dialog. This option determines where in the printing process Windows translates graphics and text output into printer-specific commands. Windows can translate document output into printer commands either before or after spooling the data. In "RAW" mode, Windows translates your document to printer commands immediately, and spools the resulting data to the hard disk or through the network to a remote printer queue. In Enhanced Metafile (EMF) mode, Windows spools the high-level graphics instructions. The actual printer commands are generated only when the document is actually being printed.

If the printer is attached to a remote computer, in EMF mode the remote computer will do the work of translating the graphics instructions into printer codes. This can make printing go faster, as the remote computer takes some of the load off of yours, and less data must be transmitted over the network. However, it's just as likely that the remote printer's driver will be out of date, so compatibility problems can arise.

If you are printing to a network printer, you might try spooling in EMF mode. Start with the highest numbered EMF version available. If print jobs fail, however, you may need to go back to RAW mode so that your computer's printer driver will be used to generate printer commands.

ADDING ALTERNATE CONFIGURATIONS FOR ONE PRINTER

If you tend to use your printer in several different ways, you may find yourself frequently changing printer properties from within your applications. For example, if you have a color inkjet printer, you may print most text documents in black-and-white in order to conserve the more expensive color inks, but may print most graphics jobs in color. Or, you might frequently print certain documents with the manual-feed option selected so that you can insert special papers.

If you do this often, changing the printer settings can get tiresome. There is something you can do about this: It's not an obvious thing to do, but you can create more than one icon for any locally attached or network shared printer. Each icon can be given different default settings, so that you can select a group of predefined settings simply by selecting an alternate printer name when you go to print certain jobs. By selecting an alternate printer, you benefit by inheriting that icon's default preference settings.

This is no problem for Windows—several printer icons (and thus several queues) can all point to the same physical connection or port. The port monitor software takes care of selecting print jobs from one queue at a time.

To create an alternate printer icon for an existing local or network printer, right-click the existing icon and select Properties. Select the Ports tab and note the name of the checked port currently used by this printer. Then close the properties dialog.

Next, create a new printer icon. For a network printer, use the standard procedure. For a locally attached printer, follow the instructions given earlier under "If Your Printer Isn't Listed." You'll have to manually select the printer make and model. In step 4, select the same port as you found selected on the original printer icon. In step 6, select an alternate name for the printer (for example, something like "Epson, B-W mode").

7

When the new printer icon appears in the Printer and Faxes folder, right-click it, select Properties, and configure the alternate default print settings, as discussed earlier under "Configuring Printer Preferences."

TIP

If you share your printer on the network and find that your printer becomes too busy for you to use yourself, create an alternate icon for your printer that is not shared. Configure this icon with a high default Priority value on the Advanced properties page, say 99, and use this as your default printer. This way, your print jobs will have a higher priority than those submitted by network users and your jobs will print ahead of theirs.

COLOR MANAGEMENT

Color management is the process of producing accurate, consistent color among a variety of input and output devices. In Windows, the color management system (CMS) maps colors between devices such as scanners, monitors, and printers; transforms colors from one color space to another (for example, RGB to CMYK); and adjusts tints displayed or printed for correctness. For most of us, this kind of precision isn't very important, but for graphic artists and designers, it's an essential part of preparing proofs and professional output.

To manage colors, each display and printer device has its own *color profile*. A profile is a file made by the hardware manufacturer (or Microsoft) specifically for the device, and it contains information about the color characteristics of the hardware and a specific set of inks, dyes, or phosphors. You simply associate the profile with the device via the device's Properties sheet, and the color system does the rest. Only if a device supports color management does its Properties sheet have a Color tab on it, however.

Even though some profiles are included with Windows XP, you might need to obtain a profile for your particular hardware. Check with the manufacturer. You can use the following procedure to add a color profile to a printer:

1. If you obtain a custom color-profile file from your manufacturer, copy it to *%systemroot%*\system32\spool\drivers\color, where *%systemroot%* is your Windows folder.

2. Open the Printers and Faxes folder.

3. Right-click the printer that you want to associate with a color profile, click Properties, and then click the Color Management tab. Notice that the tab has two settings: Automatic and Manual. Normally, Windows uses the Automatic setting, in which case it assigns a color profile to the printer from those it has on hand. If you want to override the default, click Manual.

4. Click Add to open the Add Profile Association dialog box.

5. Locate the new color profile you want to associate with the printer. You can right-click a profile and choose Properties to read more about the profile. Because the filenames are cryptic, this is the only way to figure out what device a color profile is for.

7

6. Click the new profile, and then click Add. Keep in mind that you can associate any number of profiles with a given piece of gear. Only one can be active at a time, however. After you open the profile list, select Manual and click the one you want to activate. For sophisticated setups, you may have reason for multiple profiles, but it's not likely that many users who are not designers or artists will bother.

You can use the same approach to add profiles for other hardware pieces, such as displays and scanners. Just bring up the Color Management tab of each item through its Properties sheet.

NOTE

For a video display, open the Settings tab, click Advanced, and then click the Color Management tab.

TIPS FOR PRINTING FROM WINDOWS AND DOS APPLICATIONS

When you print from 16-bit or 32-bit Windows applications, the internal Print Manager kicks in and spools the print job for you, adding it to the queue for the selected printer. The spooler then feeds the file to the assigned printer(s), coordinating the flow of data and keeping you informed of the progress. Jobs are queued up and listed in the given printer's window, from which their status can be observed; they can be rearranged, deleted, and so forth. All the rights and privileges assigned to you, as the user, are applicable, potentially allowing you to alter the queue (as discussed later in this chapter), rearranging, deleting, pausing, or restarting print jobs.

If the application doesn't provide for a specific printer (typically through a Print Setup dialog box), then the default printer is used. You can set the default printer from the Printers and Faxes folder by right-clicking a printer and choosing Set as Default Printer.

PRINTING BY DRAGGING FILES INTO THE PRINT MANAGER

As a shortcut to printing a document, you can simply drag the icon of the document you want to print either onto an icon of a printer or into the printer's open window (from the Printers and Faxes folder). You can drag the file from Explorer right onto the chosen printer's icon or open window to see it added to the print queue for that printer.

When you drop the document, Windows realizes you want to print it, and the file is loaded into the source application, the Print command is automatically executed, and the file is spooled to the Print Manager. Figure 7.11 shows an example of dropping a Word document on a PostScript printer.

7

TIP

> Documents must have associations linking the filename extension (for example, .doc or .bmp) to the application that handles that file type; otherwise, printing by dragging them to Print Manager doesn't work. Also, you obviously don't have the option of setting printing options when you print this way. The default settings are used.

→ For more information about file associations, **see** "Tweaking Folder Options," **p. 453**.

Figure 7.11
You can print a document or a number of documents by dragging them onto a destination printer in the Printers and Faxes folder. The files must have application associations.

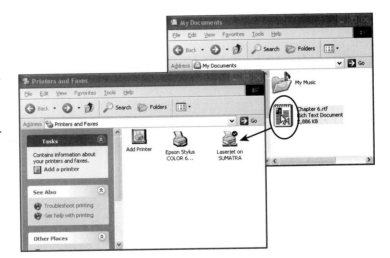

DIAGNOSING PRINTER PROBLEMS

If you're getting garbage characters in your printouts, check the following:

- You might have the wrong driver installed. Print a test page and see whether it works. Open the Printers and Faxes folder (by choosing Start, Control Panel, Printers and Other Hardware, View Installed Printers or Fax Printers), open the printer's Properties sheet, and print a test page. If that works, then the problem could be an out-of-date driver or a bad printer cable. If the test page doesn't work, try removing the printer and reinstalling it. Log on as a Computer Administrator user. Right-click the printer icon in the Printers and Faxes folder, and choose Delete. Then add the printer again, and try printing.

- If the printer uses plug-in font cartridges, you also might have the wrong font cartridge installed in the printer, or your text might be formatted with the wrong font.

- Some printers have emulation modes that might conflict with one another. Check the manual. You may think you're printing to a PostScript printer, but the printer could be in an HP emulation mode; in this case, your driver is sending PostScript, and the printer is expecting PCL.

- If you have a laser printer that prints only part of a page and then stops with an error indication, your printer may need additional memory. Try printing with a lower resolution (fewer dots per inch); if that fixes the problem, you need more memory.

- If you have a printer connected via a serial port (it's an antique), suspect a problem with the printer cable, or suspect a problem with the flow control settings on the port properties page. Serial printers often required software (XON/XOFF) flow control.

Printing from DOS Applications

A DOS application will try to print to a DOS LPT port, usually LPT1, regardless of what port your default printer is installed on. If your printer is out there somewhere on a LAN, nothing will come out! To direct a DOS program's output to a network printer, issue the command

```
net use lpt1: \\server\sharename
```

from the Command Prompt window.

NOTE

> If Windows prompts you to enter a username and password and gives an "Access denied" error even though you know the username and password are correct, it could be that the LPT device you are attempting to map is already being used by a locally installed printer. Try using a different LPT device, for example, try LPT2:.

The same situation applies if your printer is connected via some technology other than a standard PC parallel port, such as USB or Wireless. To use such a printer from DOS applications, share the printer as a network printer to give it a share name, and then type the command

```
net use lpt1: \\computername\sharename
```

where *computername* is the name of your computer, and *sharename* is the share name that you've assigned to your printer.

→ For more information about the `net use` command, **see** "Mapping from the Command Line," **p. 705**.

Remember also that a DOS program must be told directly what make and model of printer it's using, as it will generate the required printer control codes, and Windows will pass them directly to the printer.

Print jobs from DOS applications will appear in the printer queue with the title "Remote Downlevel Document."

Printing Offline

If your printer is disconnected, you can still queue up documents for printing. You might want to do this while traveling, for instance, if you have a laptop and don't want to drag a 50-pound laser printer along in your carry-on luggage.

If you simply unplug your printer, however, you'll quickly find that the Print Manager will beep, pop up messages to tell you about the missing or nonresponsive printer, and otherwise

7

make your life miserable. You can silence it by right-clicking the printer's icon in the Printers and Faxes folder and selecting Use Printer Offline.

NOTE

> Offline printing is a nifty feature, but unfortunately, it's only available for locally connected printers, not networked printers.

Windows will now quietly and compliantly queue up anything you "print." Later, when you've reconnected the printer, uncheck Use Printer Offline (with the same steps used previously) and the output will flow forth. Just don't forget this last step, or else you'll be wondering why your printer is "broken."

PRINTING TO DISK

Printing to disk creates a file of the data and command codes that normally would be sent to the printer. This file isn't a copy of the file you were printing; it is the series of formatting codes necessary to render your document on a specific make and model of printer. Print files destined for PostScript printers typically include their PostScript preamble, too. The primary use of print-to-disk files is to send documents formatted using PostScript to a service bureau for professional printing.

In some applications, this option is made available in the application's Print dialog box. If it isn't, you will need to temporarily modify your printer's configuration to print to a file rather than to a port, or, if you plan on doing this often, you can set up an alternate printer icon specifically configured to print to disk. To make a printer send its output to disk, follow these steps:

1. In the Printers and Faxes folder, right-click the printer's icon, and choose Properties.

2. Click Ports.

3. Set the port to File, and close the dialog box.

   The next time you or another user prints to this printer, you'll be prompted to enter a filename, as illustrated in Figure 7.12. You should specify the full path with the filename. The file will be stored on the machine where the print job originated.

Figure 7.12
Enter the full path and filename for the printer output file.

TIP

> If you want to create an encapsulated PostScript (.EPS) file, you can select a printer that uses a PostScript driver (the Apple LaserWriter or the QMS PS-810, for example) or set up a phony printer that uses such a driver—in which case you don't even need to actually have a PostScript printer at all. Modify the properties of the printer to print to a file by selecting

the Ports tab and choosing Print to File. In the Printing Preferences or Printing Defaults dialog, view the Layout tab and click Advanced. In the list of options, locate the item Document Options, PostScript Options, Postscript Output Option. Click on this item and select Encapsulated PostScript (EPS) from the drop-down list. Now, print your document. When you are prompted for an output filename, enter a name with the extension .EPS.

WORKING WITH THE PRINTER QUEUE

After you or other users on the network have sent print jobs to a given printer, anyone with rights to manage the queue can work with it. If nothing else, it's often useful to observe the queue to check its progress. This way, you can better choose which printer to print to, or whether some intervention is necessary, such as adding more paper. By simply opening the Printers and Faxes folder, you can see the basic state of each printer's queue, assuming you display the window contents in Details view.

For each printer, the window displays the status of the printer (in the title bar) and the documents that are queued up, including their sizes, status, owner, pages, date submitted, and so on.

TIP

You can drag a printer's icon from the Printers and Faxes window to your desktop, for easy access. Click Yes when Windows asks if you want to create a shortcut.

Figure 7.13 shows a sample printer's folder with a print queue and related information.

Figure 7.13
A printer's folder showing several print jobs pending.

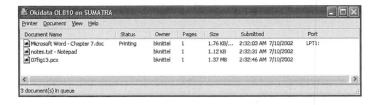

TIP

When print jobs are pending for a workstation, an icon appears in the system tray, near the clock. You can hover the mouse pointer over it to see the number of documents waiting to print. Right-click it to choose a printer's queue to examine in a window.

To keep network traffic down to a dull roar, Windows doesn't poll the network constantly to check the state of the queue, but updates it every several seconds. If you are printing to a network printer and want to check the current state of affairs on the network printer, choose View, Refresh or press F5 to immediately update the display.

7

T I P

> By default, all users can pause, resume, restart, and cancel printing of their own documents. However, to manage documents printed by other users, your system administrator must give you the Manage Documents permission.

→ To learn more details about managing print jobs as a system administrator, **see** "Tracking Printer Users," **p. 726**.

VIEWING AND ALTERING DOCUMENT PROPERTIES

Like everything in Windows, each document in the printer queue has its own properties. For a more detailed view of information pertaining to each document, you can open the Properties sheet for a given print job entry by right-clicking it and choosing Properties. You can change only two settings from the resulting dialog box (see Figure 7.14):

- The print priority. Documents with higher priority numbers get printed ahead of documents with lower numbers.
- The time of day when the document can be printed.

Figure 7.14
Altering the properties for a print job on the queue.

N O T E

> As a shortcut, you can open a document's properties by just double-clicking it.

DELETING A FILE FROM THE QUEUE

After sending a document to the queue, if you decide you don't want the document to print, you can simply remove it from the queue. To do so, right-click the document and choose Cancel, or choose Document, Cancel from the menu. The document is then removed from the printer's window.

If you're trying to delete the job that's currently printing, you might have some trouble. At the very least, the system might take some time to respond. Occasionally, canceling a laser printer's job while it's printing in graphics mode necessitates resetting the printer. You may need to use its Reset option (if available), or power the printer off and back on.

NOTE
> When you cancel the printing of a lengthy document, pages may continue to print out for a while. You may be tempted to turn the printer off and back on to stop the extra output, but you'll probably find that it doesn't help—you'll just get more pages of gibberish than you would have gotten otherwise. It's best to just let Windows print the last couple of pages it wants to print before stopping.

CANCELING ALL PENDING PRINT JOBS ON A GIVEN PRINTER

Assuming you have been given the privilege, you can cancel *all* the print jobs on a printer. In the Printers and Faxes folder, right-click the printer, and choose Cancel All Documents. A confirmation dialog appears to confirm this action.

PAUSING, RESUMING, AND RESTARTING THE PRINTING PROCESS

If you need to, you can pause the printing process for a particular printer or even just a single document print job. This capability can be useful in case you have second thoughts about a print job, want to give other jobs a chance to print first, or you just want to adjust or quiet the printer for some reason.

To pause an individual print job, right-click it and choose Pause. Pretty simple. The word Paused then appears on the document's line. The printing might not stop immediately because your printer might have a buffer that holds data in preparation for printing. The printing stops when the buffer is empty. When you're ready to resume printing, just right-click the job in question, and choose Resume.

TIP
> Pausing a document lets other documents later in the queue proceed to print, essentially moving them ahead in line. You can achieve the same effect by rearranging the queue, as explained in the section titled "Rearranging the Queue Order."

In some situations, you might need to temporarily prevent any jobs from printing, for example, to add paper or just to shut up the printer while you take a phone call. To pause all jobs, open the Printer's window and choose Printer, Pause Printing. You have to choose the command again to resume printing, and the check mark on the menu goes away.

Should you need to restart a print job from the beginning—due to a paper jam or other botch—just right-click the document and choose Restart.

7

REARRANGING THE QUEUE ORDER

When you have several items on the queue, you might want to rearrange the order in which they're slated for printing. Perhaps a print job's priority has increased because you need it for an urgent meeting, or you have to get a letter to the post office. Whatever the reason, as long as a given document hasn't yet started to print you can easily rearrange its position in the print queue like this:

1. Click the file you want to move, and keep the mouse button pressed.

2. Drag the file up or down to its new location. A solid line moves to indicate where the document will be inserted when you release the mouse button.

3. When you release the mouse button, your file is inserted in the queue, pushing the other files down a notch.

REMOVING A PRINTER

You might want to remove a printer setup for several reasons:

- The physical printer has been removed from service.

- You don't want to use a particular network printer anymore.

- You have several definitions of a physical printer using different default settings, and you want to remove one of them.

- You have a nonfunctioning or improperly functioning printer setup and want to remove it and start over by running the Add Printer Wizard.

In any of these cases, the approach is the same:

1. Be sure you are logged on with Computer Administrator privileges.

2. Open the Printers and Faxes folder.

3. Be sure nothing is in the printer's queue. You have to clear the queue for the printer before deleting it. If you don't, Windows will attempt to delete all jobs in the queue for you, but it unfortunately isn't always successful.

4. Select the printer icon you want to kill, and choose File, Delete (or press the Del key).

5. Depending on whether the printer is local or remote, you see one of two different dialog boxes. One asks whether you want to delete the printer; the other asks whether you want to delete the connection to the printer. In either case, click Yes. The printer icon or window disappears from the Printers and Faxes folder.

TIP

> The removal process removes only the printer icon; the related driver file and font files are not deleted from the disk. Therefore, if you ever want to re-create the printer, you don't have to insert disks or respond to prompts for the location of driver files.

7

SETTING UP FOR FAXING

Faxing is a function that Microsoft has added to and taken out of Windows with practically every version. We're on the "added to" part of the cycle now: Windows XP has faxing capability built in, and it's quite nice. If your computer has a compatible modem installed, you can use it to send and receive faxes.

To send a fax from Windows XP, you can write a document using your favorite application, choose the Fax icon from the printer folder, and print. Or, you can use the Scanner and Camera Wizard to scan and fax hardcopy documents. In either case, Windows prompts you for the appropriate fax phone number and makes the call. The fax service can even add a cover sheet to your document on the way out. To receive faxes, your modem can be set to answer calls. When a fax arrives, you can view its image onscreen or print it, or even have it printed automatically.

NOTE

> I should tell you that while computer-based faxing is great for documents you're typing up in your word processor, it's not so great for hardcopy documents. Scanning and faxing from a flatbed scanner is cumbersome. A multifunction fax/printer/copier makes this much easier. And there's a lot to be said for the good old inexpensive standalone fax machine.

Third-party Fax software such as Symantec's WinFax Pro has more bells and whistles, and can provide fax services for the whole network, but the basic version that comes with Windows will take care of most home and small office users' needs. Windows XP faxing can't be shared among a number of users on the LAN the same way you can share regular printers, though. If you want to provide a shared fax modem for your LAN, you should look for a third-party product.

NOTE

> Microsoft seems of two minds about allowing its fax service to be shared across the network. The standard software is definitely capable of it, and you can see on the Fax printer's properties dialog that it's called the "Microsoft Shared Fax Driver." And at one point during the Windows 2000 beta program, I was able to enable fax sharing, although I've not been able to repeat that accident with the commercial release of Windows 2000 or XP. We'll have to see if there is a way to turn it back on!

INSTALLING THE FAX SERVICE

All you need to get started faxing is a fax device, such as a fax modem; it cannot be just a plain data modem. Because all modems sold these days have fax capability, the odds are slim that you'll have to buy a replacement. There also are some combination scanner/printer/faxing machines that can serve as a Windows Fax device.

7

NOTE

> For more information on modem compatibility with faxes, see the Microsoft Windows Hardware Compatibility List at the Microsoft Web site (`http://www.microsoft.com/hcl`). Not all fax modems are supported by the Fax service. I've poked into the fax service software and found that it is hard-coded to work with specific modem types.

In this day of Plug and Play, installing a modem or attaching a fax device will probably prompt Windows into installing the fax service and a fax printer automatically. If, for some reason, Windows doesn't sense that you've attached a modem even when you reboot and log on with a Computer Administrator or Power User account, you can use the Add/Remove Hardware Wizard. (See Chapter 27, "Installing, Removing, and Managing Hardware Devices," for coverage of the Add/Remove Hardware applet and the Modem applet, both in the Control Panel.)

When a functioning fax modem or multifunction printer has been installed, check to see whether a Fax icon has appeared in your Printers and Faxes folder (you get there from Start, Control Panel, Printers and Other Hardware). If it's not there, you'll need to install the fax service by following these steps:

1. Log on as a Computer Administrator or Power User.

2. Open the Printers and Faxes folder by clicking Start, Control Panel, Printers and Other Hardware, and then View Installed Printers or Fax Printers.

3. Click Install a Local Fax Printer or Set up Faxing in the Printer Tasks list.

4. You may need to insert your Windows XP installation disc if Windows needs to copy the Fax service files.

NOTE

> If you inadvertently delete the Fax icon later on, just repeat this procedure.

NOTE

> If nothing happens when you click Install a Local Fax Printer, be sure you're logged on with a Computer Administrator or Power User account.

When the fax service has been installed, a Fax icon will appear in your Printers and Faxes folder, and a set of Fax management programs will be installed under Start, More Programs, Accessories, Communications, Fax. Table 7.3 lists these commands and their purposes.

TABLE 7.3   FAX-RELATED COMMANDS

Command	Action
Fax Console	Displays a queue of outgoing faxes and lists received faxes.
Fax Cover Page Editor	Lets you design custom cover pages for your faxes.
Send a Fax...	Used by itself, sends only a cover page. Use the Print function in Windows applications to send whole documents.

In addition, there is a Fax Configuration Wizard that asks you for setup information to be used in cover sheets and selects devices to be used for sending and receiving faxes, and a more sophisticated setup program called the Fax Service Manager. We'll discuss all of these programs in the following sections.

CONFIGURING FAX SETTINGS

After you install your fax hardware, you can get started by entering your fax-related settings using the Fax Configuration Wizard, shown in Figure 7.15. Open it by clicking Start, More Programs, Accessories, Communications, Fax, Fax Console, and then Tools, Configure Fax.

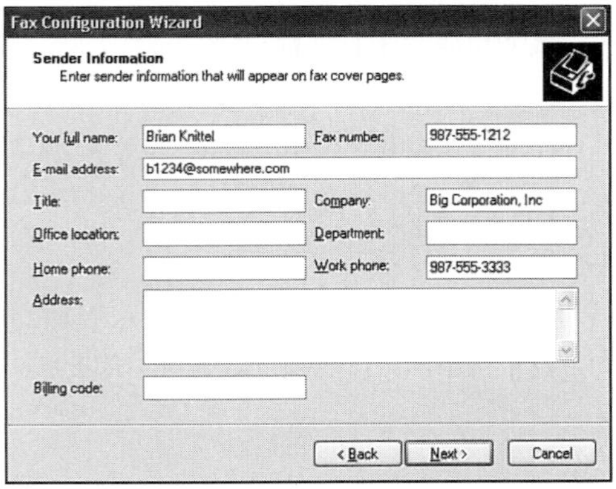

Figure 7.15
The Fax Configuration Wizard sets up your cover page particulars.

1. Enter your particulars into the User Information tab. You can skip any fields that are not relevant. This data will be printed on your cover pages. Click Next.

2. Select the modem(s) and/or other fax device(s) you wish to use. If there are more than one, you can prioritize them with the arrow buttons. Click Next when done.

3. Enter an identifying string (TSID) for your fax transmissions, usually your fax number or company name. This is displayed by receiving fax machines. Enter up to 20 characters and click Next.

4. If you'd like to receive faxes automatically, check the box corresponding to your fax modem. However, if you do, your modem will answer all incoming calls on its line (you can select the number of rings before it answers). If you leave the box unchecked, your computer won't automatically receive faxes.

5. If you decide to receive faxes, enter a Called Station Identifier, usually your fax number or company name. This will display a sender's fax machine. Click Next.

6. If you chose to receive faxes, indicate what you'd like done with them as they arrive. You can choose to print them automatically by checking Print It On and selecting a printer. You can also ask that Windows save an extra copy of each incoming fax in a designated folder. (I say *extra* because by default, Windows keeps a copy of each received fax; more on this in a moment.)

7. Finally, click Finish.

NOTE

By default, Windows automatically keeps a copy of each fax it sends and receives. To alter this, open the Printers and Faxes folder, right-click the Fax icon, select Properties, and view the Archives tab. Here, you can select where and whether to store copies of incoming and outgoing faxes.

IMPORTING FAXES FROM WINDOWS 9X/ME

If you used Personal Fax for Windows in Windows 95, 98, or Me, and you want access to the archived faxes you sent and received with it, you can import these faxes into the new Fax service. Follow these steps:

1. Open the Printers and Faxes folder and double-click the Fax icon. This opens the Fax Console.

2. Select File, Import, and then select either Sent Faxes or Received Faxes.

3. In the Browse dialog, locate the folder containing your sent or received faxes. When you have selected the folder, click OK.

The imported faxes are not deleted from their original location. If the import is successful and you're happy with the new setup, you can delete the old archives later on to recover disk space.

TIPS FOR USING THE FAX SERVICE

To send a fax from a Windows application, follow these steps:

1. Open the document you want to send.

2. Choose File, Print. From the standard Print dialog box, choose the Fax icon as the printer. Set up the particulars as necessary (page range, and so on), and click OK.

3. The Send Fax Wizard then begins and walks you through the process of preparing the fax. (If you haven't run the Fax Configuration Wizard yet, you'll get the pleasure of going through it now.)

4. Fill in the recipient and dialing information as prompted, as shown in Figure 7.16. You can add multiple names to the list. If you set up your area code and Dialing Rules when you installed your modem, just enter the fax recipient's area code and number. If you didn't, uncheck Dialing Rules and enter the recipient's number including a 1 and area code if needed. Click the Add button to add the first recipient, and repeat the process for each additional recipient.

→ Windows can automatically manage area codes and special features like outside-line access by setting up Dialing Rules. This is really handy when you're on the road. For more information, **see** "Dial-Up Internet Connections," **p. 276**.

If you select recipients from the Address Book, the fax numbers stored there *must* contain all necessary dialing prefix numbers and area codes; dialing rules are not applied to these numbers in any case.

When you've entered all of the recipients, click Next.

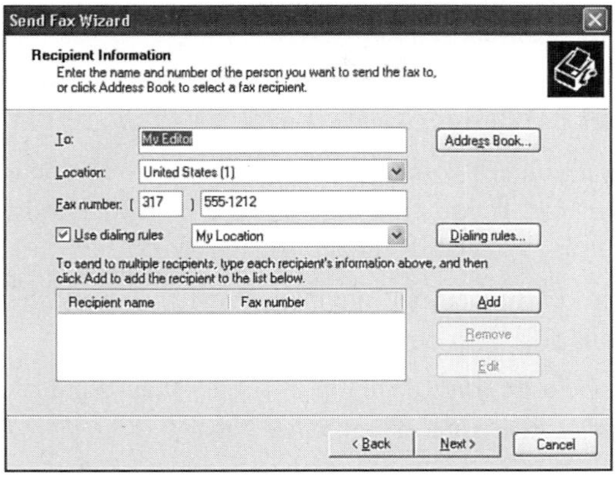

Figure 7.16
Adding recipients to the fax transmission list.

5. If you'd like to add a cover page to your fax, check Select a Cover Page and choose one of the predefined formats from the drop-down list. Enter the subject and any notes you want to appear on the cover page. If you'd like to alter your personal information, click Sender Info.

6. Click Next. Choose when you'd like to send the fax. Typically, this is Now, but the When Discount Rates Apply option is interesting. (See the section titled "Detailed Fax Device Properties" near the end of the chapter to see how to set the timing.) Alternatively, you can specify a time in the next 24 hours.

7. Click Next. If you'd like to preview the fax before it's sent, click Preview, otherwise click Next.

Windows then will prepare the print job for faxing. You can follow its progress by watching the Fax Console, which I'll discuss in the next section.

TIP

You can send a quick note via fax without using a word processor at all. Just click Start, All Programs, Accessories, Fax, Send a Fax. This sends a cover sheet only, and you can type your message into the Send Fax Wizard's Note field.

SENDING A FAX FROM YOUR SCANNER

If you need to send a fax from hardcopy documents, my first suggestion is that you save yourself some time and trouble, and use a standard inexpensive fax machine. If you have a special-purpose combination scanner/printer/fax device, it should also be easy to use; just follow the instructions provided by the manufacturer.

If you have neither of these, you can use a standard flatbed scanner and standard Windows XP software. It's not convenient, but it will work. Here's the procedure:

7

1. Open the Scanner and Camera Wizard from Start, All Programs, Accessories, Scanner and Camera Wizard.

2. If necessary, choose the desired scanner device.

3. Click Custom Settings and set the Resolution to 100DPI for a standard resolution fax, or 200DPI for a "fine" resolution fax.

   Under Picture Type, if you are going to fax a normal printed document, select Black and White Picture or Text. If you are going to fax a picture, choose Grayscale Picture. Then, click OK.

4. Position the first page on the scanner and click Preview. Check the resulting image to be sure that the page is correctly positioned.

5. Drag the corners of the cropping rectangle in the Preview pane to cover the entire page, not just the text on the page. Then, click Next.

6. Choose a unique name for the fax scan set, set the file format to TIFF, and select a folder. You can leave the folder at the default setting, which will be a subfolder of My Pictures. Click Next to start the scan.

7. When the scanning process finishes, if you have more than one page to scan, click Back, replace the sheet, and click Next. Repeat this as many times as necessary. Each image will be saved in a numbered file.

8. When you have finished scanning pages, leave the default selection on Nothing and click Next, then Finish.

9. Windows will display the folder containing the new scans. Select Print Pictures from the Picture Tasks list.

10. Click Next, and then check all of the images that belong to the set of documents you just scanned. Click Next to proceed.

11. Choose the Fax printer, and proceed to select recipients as described in the previous section.

As I said, it's cumbersome, but it works.

TIP

> To send a fax that combines hardcopy pages with electronic documents, scan the hardcopy pages, and pull the page images into your document. Then, print the document through the Fax printer.

MANAGING THE FAX SYSTEM

7

For detailed control of how the Fax service sends and receives faxes, and to set up shared cover sheets that can be used by all of the computer's users, there's a management tool called Fax Console. You use this application to do the following:

- Set up your fax devices to receive a fax
- Change security permissions for fax users
- Declare how many rings must occur before a fax device answers a fax
- Determine how many retries are allowed before the fax device aborts the fax send
- Specify where to store the sent or received faxes
- Set the amount of detail for the event log
- Suppress personal cover pages, to force the use of your organization's cover page design

To run it, double-click the Fax icon in Printers and Faxes, or choose Start, More Programs, Accessories, Communications, Fax, Fax Console.

You then see the window shown in Figure 7.17.

Figure 7.17
Fax Console lets you manage outgoing and received faxes.

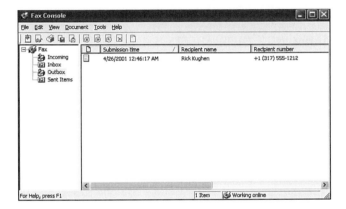

Poke around in this application to familiarize yourself with it. As you can see, you can browse through sent, outgoing, and received faxes by opening their Explorer folder views. You can right-click faxes in any of these lists and select one of the following functions:

- View, to view the fax with the Windows Picture and Fax viewer.
- Delete, to remove the fax.
- Save As, to store a copy of the fax in another location. Faxes are stored as TIF files, with one or more page images in a single file.
- Mail To, to send a copy of the fax as an email attachment using your default email program.
- Print, to print a hardcopy of the fax. You can also forward the fax to another recipient by selecting your Fax printer.
- Properties, to view the fax's date, time, and user information.

The most common use of Fax Console is to cancel an outgoing fax if you change your mind. To do this, just highlight the entry in the Outbox listing and press the Del key.

7

The Tools menu also offers several management options, as listed in Table 7.4.

TABLE 7.4   FAX CONSOLE TOOLS

Tools Menu Item	Lets You...
Sender Information	Change your contact information used on cover sheets
Personal Cover Pages	Edit personal cover sheets not shared with other users of your computer
Fax Printers Status	(Not terribly useful)
Configure Fax	Run the Fax Configuration Wizard again
Fax Printer Configuration	Edit Fax Printer Properties
Fax Monitor	Monitor the progress of outgoing faxes

CREATING AND MANAGING COVER SHEETS

Windows XP comes with several fax cover sheet forms predefined for typical business use: Generic, Confidential, Urgent, and so on. You can modify these cover sheets using the Fax Cover Page editor from the Fax menu or from Fax Console, as noted in Table 7.4. I can't go into much detail on this program, except to give you few hints:

- From the Fax Console, select Tools, Personal Cover Pages to start the Cover Page Editor. You can select an existing cover sheet, or you can click New to create a new one.

- It's easiest to start with one of the predefined cover sheets and modify it as desired. Click New to start the Cover Sheet Editor. Use File, Open, and browse to one of the files in \Documents and Settings\All Users\Application Data\Microsoft\ Windows NT\MSFax\Common Coverpages.

- Use the text button (labeled "ab1") and graphics button to draw items that never change, such as a labels or a confidentiality clause. Use the Insert menu to drop in information specified when each fax is sent, such as the recipient name.

- When you've finished editing, use Save, or Save As to store the personalized cover sheet in My Documents\Fax\Personal Coverpages. To make a new cover sheet available to everyone, save it in the folder named two bullets up.

DETAILED FAX DEVICE PROPERTIES

There are several Fax service fine-tuning settings buried so deeply that they're easily overlooked. To view these additional settings, follow these steps:

1. Log on as a Computer Administrator user.
2. Open the Printers and Faxes folder, right-click the Fax icon, and select Properties.

3. View the Devices tab and select your fax modem from the list of installed modems. (If you have several fax modems installed, you can configure them each separately. For example, you might configure one to receive faxes only, and another to send faxes only.)

4. Click Properties.

The resulting dialog box has three tabs: Send, Receive, and Cleanup. Some of the properties can be set by the Configure Fax Wizard and the Fax console, but this dialog includes additional important properties. Table 7.5 lists the properties and their use.

TABLE 7.5   FAX DEVICE PROPERTIES

Tab/Property	Description
Send	
Enable Device to Send	Check to permit this modem to send faxes.
TSID	This is the identification text sent to the fax recipient's fax machine.
Include Banner	Check to have the TSID, page count, date, and time printed at the top of each fax page sent.
Retries	The number of times to attempt sending each fax.
Retry After	The interval in minutes between send attempts.
Discount Rate Start	The time of day to begin sending faxes that were marked "Send when discounted rates apply."
Discount Rate End	End of discount rate period; if same as start time, there is no discount period.
Receive	
Enable Device to Receive	Check to let this modem answer incoming calls.
CSID	This is the identification text sent to the fax sender's fax machine.
Answer Mode	Select Manual or Automatic After *n* Rings.
Print It On	If checked, you may select a printer on which all incoming faxes are automatically printed.
Save Copy in Folder	If checked, you may select a folder in which copies of incoming faxes are saved, *in addition* to the fax archive folder.
Cleanup	
Automatically Delete Failed Faxes After	This setting controls how long failed faxes are stored in the Sent Items archive folder.

I'll discuss automatic fax printing in more detail in the next section.

7

INCOMING FAXES

When you configure the Fax system to receive faxes, it will answer incoming calls on your Fax modem.

Each fax is converted to a file using the TIF file format when it arrives. Because TIF is a nonproprietary format, you can view or edit it with almost any graphics program. However, using the default Windows Picture and Fax viewer and editor is easy enough.

There are two ways to set up the fax service for receiving faxes: It can answer your modem's phone line whenever it rings, or you can do a one-time receive.

To set up auto-answering, follow these steps:

1. Log on as a Computer Administrator user.
2. Open the Printers and Faxes folder, right-click the Fax icon, and select Properties.
3. Select your fax modem on the Devices tab and click Properties.
4. View the Receive tab. Check Enable Device to Receive. You can enable auto-printing here as well, as I'll discuss later in this section.

If you don't want the fax modem to answer every call, you can enable a one-time receipt this way:

1. Open the Printers and Faxes folder. Double-click the Fax icon to open the Fax Console.
2. Wait for the phone line to ring, or use a telephone handset to call the sender and tell him to press the Start button on his fax machine.
3. In the Fax Console, choose File, Receive a Fax Now.

> **TIP**
>
> If you have pending outgoing faxes or if you have enabled your fax modem to receive faxes, the fax icon appears in the system tray. Double-clicking it brings up the Fax Monitor.

By default, incoming faxes are converted to TIF files and are dumped into the Fax Console's Inbox. But you can configure a fax setup to actually print your documents on paper as they come in. To shunt all incoming faxes to a physical printer for automatic printing, follow these steps:

1. Log on as a Computer Administrator user.
2. Open the Printers and Faxes folder, right-click the Fax icon, and select Properties.
3. Select your fax modem on the Devices tab and click Properties.
4. View the Receive tab. Check the Print and/or Save a copy options, as shown in Figure 7.18, and click OK. Use Save a Copy only if you want to store an *extra* copy of received faxes, as they'll also be stored in the Fax console's inbox.

7

Figure 7.18
Use this dialog box to configure automatic printing of received faxes. You can have incoming faxes printed automatically, and/or store a copy in a folder.

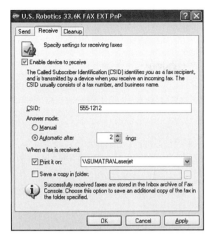

Fax Resolutions

With all the talk about digital cameras and scanners these days (and their respective resolutions), you might be wondering about fax resolution. Here's the skinny on that: The standard resolution for faxes is 3.85 scan lines/mm (approximately 98dpi vertically) with 1728 pixels across a standard scan line of 215mm (approximately 204dpi horizontally).

An additional, popular setting on many fax machines is called "fine" resolution. This setting scans 7.7 lines per millimeter (approximately 196dpi vertically) with the same resolution horizontally as with the normal setting.

Can some fax machines go higher? Yes. Many so-called Group III fax machines use nonstandard frames to negotiate higher resolutions. Some go as high as 300×300dpi (similar to older laser printers) and even 400×400dpi, but have to be talking with other fax machines made by the same manufacturer for this scheme to work. Manufacturers are working to set standards to support this level of resolution between machines of dissimilar manufacture.

The resolution you get on your printouts or as viewed on your computer screen depends on many factors. First, the screen resolution depends on the resolution of the source fax machine or computer. Second, it depends on the type of fax your system is employing and, finally, on the resolution of your display or printer. If what you intend to send someone is a high-resolution picture, you should always try to acquire a good color or grayscale scan of the image. Then you can attach it to an email as a GIF, TIF, or JPEG file. Generally speaking, it will look better than sending it as a fax.

When scanning a document that you intend to fax, in most cases you'll get the best results if you scan it at 100 or 200dpi.

7

CHAPTER 8

CONFIGURING YOUR INTERNET CONNECTION

In this chapter

8

DIAL-UP INTERNET CONNECTIONS

The Windows XP New Connection Wizard provides an easy way to create an Internet connection with an analog modem or broadband connection. You can launch the New Connection Wizard in the following ways:

- Click Start, All Programs, Accessories, Communications, New Connection Wizard.
- Open the Network Connections icon and click Create a New Connection.

After the Wizard opens, click Next to see the screen shown in Figure 8.1.

Figure 8.1
The Windows XP New Connection Wizard offers a choice of connection types.

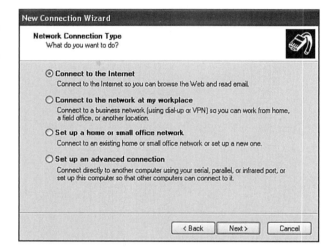

As Figure 8.1 demonstrates, you can also use the wizard to connect to a business network with a VPN, configure a home or office network, or set up a direct parallel, serial, or infrared connection with another computer.

➔ To learn more about virtual private networking, **see** "Virtual Private Networking," **p. 782**.

OPTIONS FOR CREATING A DIAL-UP CONNECTION

If you select Connect to the Internet, you can choose to

- Choose from a list of ISPs; choose this option if you want to configure the MSN Explorer browser or select MSN or another ISP.
- Set up your connection manually to use an existing dial-up account (if you know your settings).

NOTE

You don't need to use the wizard at all if you have a setup CD from your ISP, although this is the third option listed. Selecting this option from the wizard simply displays a message telling you to close the wizard and run the setup CD.

CONFIGURING A DIAL-UP CONNECTION MANUALLY

If you already have a dial-up Internet account, choose Set Up My Connection Manually and click Next. On the next screen, choose Connect Using a Dial-up Modem and click Next.

The wizard prompts you for the following information:

- The name of the ISP; this is the name which will be displayed in your Network Connections folder when the connection is completed.
- The ISP's access number, including 1 and the area code if necessary; try the number on your telephone without 1 or the area code to determine if you will need to dial the call as a long-distance call.
- Your user name; provide the user name assigned by your ISP.
- Your password; provide the password assigned by your ISP and confirm it.

You can also enable or disable (default is enable) any of these three options for your dial-up connection:

- Use This Account Name and Password When Anyone Connects to the Internet from This Computer; disable this option you don't want your account to be available to every user.
- Make This the Default Internet Connection; disable this option if you primarily use a broadband or LAN Internet connection.
- Turn on Internet Connection Firewall for This Connection; disable this option if you use third-party firewall software.

→ For more information on how Windows XP's built-in Internet Connection Firewall compares to third-party firewalls, **see** "Securing Your Internet Connection," **p. 310**.

When you complete the configuration of your dial-up connection, a digest of the settings is displayed onscreen (see Figure 8.2). Click Back to change any settings, click the box to add a desktop shortcut, and click Finish when you are satisfied with the settings.

Figure 8.2
A typical dial-up networking connection at the end of the New Connection Wizard process.

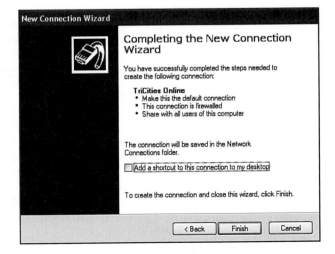

8

TIP

You can also use the File and Settings Transfer Wizard to transfer existing dial-up networking settings from another computer to your current computer.

Once you click Finish, the new connection is opened up for immediate use. Click Dial to make the connection from the dialog box shown in Figure 8.3.

Figure 8.3
Connecting to a dial-up ISP.

Note that the first time you use your connection, you can set up the connection for use only by yourself (Me) or for anyone who uses the computer. Change the setting to Me if you want each user to configure a separate Internet account.

NOTE

It's not always easy to determine if a particular Internet access number is a local call. Call the seven-digit number with your telephone so you can hear any error messages such as "please dial one plus the area code" (which would indicate the number is long distance) or a modem's answering tones (which indicates the number is local and is ready for your modem to connect to it).

SETTING UP AN MSN CONNECTION

If you want to sign up for MSN Internet access or use the MSN Explorer Web browser with your existing online service, select Choose from a List of Internet Service Providers, and then select Get Online with MSN. When you click Finish, the New Connection Wizard closes and an MSN connection wizard starts.

After you select MSN, a dialog box appears asking you if you want to use MSN Explorer to get on the Internet and write email. Whether you select Yes or No, a dialog box appears, welcoming you to MSN Explorer. Click Continue after you have verified that your modem is connected to your telephone line.

On the screens that follow, select the correct options for

- Country or Region
- MSN Internet access with an existing MSN or Hotmail email address
- MSN Internet access with a new MSN email address
- Use the MSN Explorer with an existing Internet account

TIP

If you don't have a properly installed modem in your system or it's not connected to a telephone line, you won't be able to proceed with the process beyond this point.

If you select MSN Internet access, complete the questions about access codes and tone dialing, and then click Continue to connect to the MSN sign-up site. The computer will dial the MSN server and prompt you for your name and other personal information. After you provide your address, the MSN server will check to see if MSN Broadband is available in your area.

The MSN server displays the available MSN services for your selection; broadband is displayed only if it's available in your area. Once you select a service type, you will need to provide billing information to complete the setup process.

CHOOSING FROM OTHER SERVICES

If you choose Select from a List of Other ISPs, Windows XP opens a folder called Online Services which contains two shortcuts, one for MSN and one called Refer Me to More Internet Service Providers; Windows XP no longer includes third-party ISP client software as part of its installation. Open the Refer Me icon, and your computer will dial the Microsoft Internet Referral Service's toll-free number and display a list of national ISPs who serve your area.

NOTE

This option will not display regional or local ISPs. If you want to use a regional or local ISP (which is often less expensive per month), contact the ISP directly for setup instructions or a setup CD.

Scroll through the list of providers for current pricing and service details, and then click Next to start the signup process for the selected provider.

Complete the personal information (name, address, and phone number) and click Next to continue. Select from the service offer(s) listed and click Next. Provide payment information and follow the instructions onscreen to complete account setup.

VIEWING YOUR EXISTING CONNECTION(S)

Windows XP stores all types of network connections, including LAN and dial-up Internet connections, in the Network Connections folder (see Figure 8.4). Open this folder to view the properties for an existing connection, to create a new connection, or to start a dial-up or broadband Internet connection.

Figure 8.4
The Network Connections folder for a computer, which has both dial-up (top) and LAN-based (bottom) network connections.

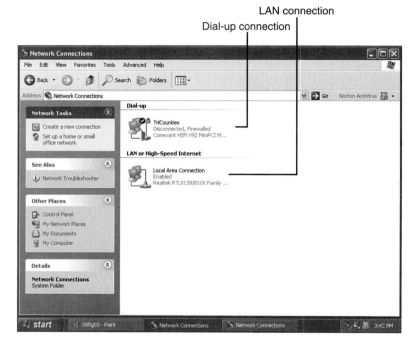

If you need to adjust the user name, password, telephone number, or other settings for a connection, right-click the connection's icon and select Properties.

CONFIGURING YOUR BROWSER FOR DIAL-UP ACCESS

Normally, Windows XP automatically configures Internet Explorer or MSN Explorer to dial your ISP connection if it is the only Internet connection you have on your computer. If you need to view or change the connection settings in Internet Explorer, choose Tools, Internet Options, and click Connections to display the connection options screen (see Figure 8.5).

If your computer can connect to the Internet only through a dial-up connection, select Always Dial My Default Connection. If you have used dial-up connections in the past, but now access the Internet only through a LAN or broadband connection, select Never Dial a Connection. If you travel away from a home or office network which offers a LAN/broadband connection and sometimes use a modem while on the road, select Dial Whenever a Network Connection Is Not Present, as shown in Figure 8.5.

Figure 8.5
The Connections tab for a computer that can connect to the Internet through either a dial-up or LAN (broadband) connection.

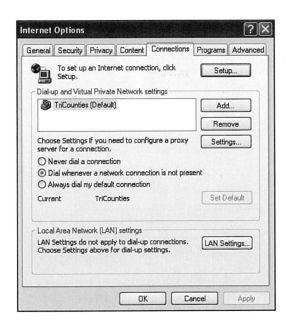

8

ADJUSTING PROXY SERVER SETTINGS

Click the Settings button in the Dial-Up and Virtual Private Networks Settings section of the Connections tab shown in Figure 8.5 if you need to specify a proxy server or other specialized settings, or need to change the username and password for your connection.

Some specialized Internet resources, such as newsgroups and specialized databases which are provided by universities only for use by university students and staff, might require you to configure your Internet connection to use a proxy server if you connect to the resources through a normal ISP.

You can enable a proxy server or other specialized settings by using automatic detection, referencing an automatic configuration script, or by specifying an IP address and TCP port setting (see Figure 8.6).

If you specify a proxy server and TCP port setting for a proxy server, the same proxy server and port setting is used for all types of Web protocols by default. However, if you need to specify different proxy servers or port settings for different types of protocols, click the Advanced button next to the Proxy Server information to display the dialog box shown in Figure 8.7.

In most cases, all servers use the same proxy server settings. However, if you must specify different proxy server or TCP port settings for different protocols, clear the Use the Same Proxy Server for All Protocols box shown in Figure 8.7. Once you clear this box, you can enter the proxy addresses or TCP port addresses needed for each type of protocol.

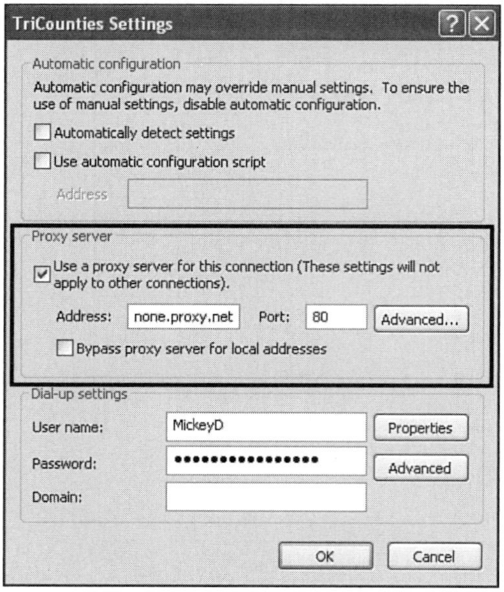

Figure 8.6
Specifying a proxy server for access to specialized content.

Figure 8.7
Specifying proxy server settings for different types of protocols and exceptions (sites and IP addresses which don't need the proxy server settings).

If some types of resources (such as local Intranet servers or certain IP address ranges) don't need to be accessed through a proxy server, type the IP address ranges or names into the Exceptions field. Click OK when you are finished specifying proxy servers or exceptions to return to the main Settings screen.

ADJUSTING DIAL-UP PROPERTIES

You can change the user name, password, and domain settings for your dial-up connection from the main Settings dialog (see Figure 8.6). If you need to change other settings, click the Properties button next to the User Name field to display a multi-tabbed properties sheet.

- General tab—Use to change the modem, adjust its settings, change the telephone number, add alternate numbers to call if the normal telephone number is busy, and change the dialing rules (to specify access codes for outside lines, area codes, and so forth) (see Figure 8.8).

- Options tab—Use to change dialing options such as the number of redial attempts, how long to keep an idle connection open, password prompts, and X.25 settings (see Figure 8.9).

- Security tab—Use to change password types, configure security protocols, or to enable interactive or script-based logins (see Figure 8.10).

- Networking tab—Use to switch dial-up server types (the Windows and Internet default PPP or Unix's SLIP) and to install or change properties of network components (see Figure 8.11).

- Advanced—Use to enable or disable the Internet Connection Firewall or Internet Connection Sharing (see Figure 8.12). To enable remote users to access services such as FTP server, remote desktop, and others on your computer, click Settings and enable the services shown in Figure 8.13.

Figure 8.8
The Dial-Up Properties' General tab.

Figure 8.9
The Dial-Up
Properties' Options
tab.

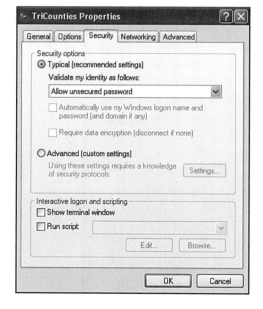

Figure 8.10
The Dial-Up
Properties' Security
tab.

Figure 8.11
The Dial-Up
Properties'
Networking tab.

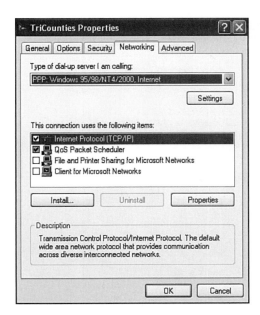

NOTE

You need to enable the services shown in Figure 8.13 only if you want your computer to act as a server. Generally, this makes sense only if your computer has a full-time (LAN or broadband) connection to the Internet rather than a dial-up connection. Keep in mind that, with any type of Internet connection, running these services on your computer creates a potential security risk.

Figure 8.12
The Dial-Up
Properties' Advanced
tab.

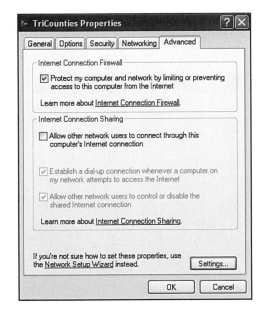

Figure 8.13
The Settings dialog for enabling remote access to services on this computer.

Generally, if you have configured your connection with a setup CD provided by your ISP or if you have carefully followed manual configuration instructions, you shouldn't need to work with these dialogs. However, if your ISP changes its access numbers, if you move to another city or take your notebook computer on the road, or if your ISP changes its server configuration, you might need to troubleshoot your connection using these tabs.

→ To learn more about using Dial-Up Networking features with your notebook computer, **see** "Dial-Up Networking," **p. 767**.

TROUBLESHOOTING YOUR DIAL-UP CONNECTION

The extensive customization that is available through the dial-up connection's properties sheets enables you to solve many common problems. Table 8.1 provides an overview of common problems you might encounter with your dial-up connections and their solutions.

TABLE 8.1—DIAL-UP CONNECTION PROBLEMS AND SOLUTIONS

8

Symptom	Problem	Solution
You can't connect to the service.	Incorrect username and password.	Provide correct username and password and retry connection.
You can't dial out from a hotel room.	You're not using the correct dialing prefix.	Open the General tab, check the Use Dialing Rules box, and adjust the dialing rules as needed.
	You might not have your modem plugged into a working data jack.	If the data line is not built into the phone, it might not be connected to a working phone line. Plug the modem into the data jack on the phone, or call the maintenance department for help.
You can't connect to the remote computer because it's constantly busy.	You need to set up an alternate telephone number (if available).	Open the General tab, click Alternates, and add alternate phone numbers.
You can't connect after installing a new modem.	Your dial-up connection is still using the old modem.	Open the General tab, click the Connect Using drop-down menu, and select the correct modem; if you still have problems, open the Device Manager and delete the old modem. If the old modem used configuration software listed in Add/Remove Programs, uninstall that software.
	An external modem might not be connected to a working port.	Use the Modem Diagnostics feature in Windows XP.
	The new modem might not be working properly.	Check the modem status (see Figure 8.16) and use the Troubleshoot button if problems are reported by the modem.

continues

8

TABLE 8.1—CONTINUED

Symptom	Problem	Solution
The connection is not reliable.	The modem might not be configured correctly.	Open the General tab, click the Configure button, and enable hardware flow control, modem error control, and modem compression (see Figure 8.14).
	An external modem might not be connected properly to the computer.	Check the cables between the external modem and the computer. Use the thumbscrews on the serial cable to tightly connect the cable used with a serial-port modem.
	The RJ-11 telephone cable might be loose or damaged.	Check the cable for cracks and make sure the ends of the cable are snapped into place at the wall jack and the modem; if the retaining clips on the cable are broken, replace the cable.
	The modem's drivers might be damaged or outdated.	Install new drivers through the modem's properties sheets (see Figure 8.24).
	The transmit and receive buffers might be set too high.	Reduce the size of the transmit and receive buffers (see Figure 8.21).
	The maximum port speed might be set too high.	Reduce the maximum port speed (see Figure 8.17).
You can't hear the modem dial or negotiate the connection.	The modem's speaker may be turned off.	Open the General tab, click the Configure button, and enable the modem speaker.
	The volume control for the modem speaker may be set too low.	Adjust the volume through the modem's properties sheet in Device Manager (see Figure 8.17) or, on a notebook computer with a built-in modem, through the computer's volume control.

8

Symptom	Problem	Solution
The modem drops the connection while you are writing a reply to an email or while you read a long document on a Web site.	The idle time before hanging up is too short.	Open the Options tab, click the Idle Time Before Hanging Up pull-down menu, and select a longer interval.
The modem stops redialing a busy connection after a few tries.	The number of redial attempts is set too low.	Open the Options tab, click the Redial Attempts pull-down menu, and select a larger number.
The connection doesn't prompt you for a telephone number, making it hard to use the connection from different locations with different access numbers.	The prompt for phone number option isn't checked.	Open the Options tab and enable Prompt for Phone Number.
The modem doesn't reconnect after the line is dropped.	The Redial if line is dropped option is not enabled.	Open the Options tab and enable this option.
You can connect to the remote computer, but it will not accept your password.	You might not be using the correct security settings.	Contact the ISP and determine if you need to use a secured password or other special security settings. To configure the settings, open the Security tab and make the settings needed.
You can connect to the remote computer, but you can't run the correct script to complete the logon process.	Your connection isn't configured to use a logon script.	Open the Security tab, click Run Script and select the correct script from the pull-down menu, or browse to a custom script provided by the ISP.

continues

TABLE 8.1—CONTINUED

Symptom	Problem	Solution
You can connect to the remote computer but can't view its contents.	You might not have the correct network components installed.	Contact the ISP or remote computer help desk and determine what components are needed. To add a component, open the Networking tab and click Install. To configure a component, select it and click Properties.
	You might not have the correct TCP/IP settings configured.	Contact the ISP to determine the correct TCP/IP configuration. Open the Networking tab, click Internet Protocol (TCP/IP), and click Properties. Make the changes needed and click OK (see Figure 8.15).

Figure 8.14
The modem configuration dialog box.

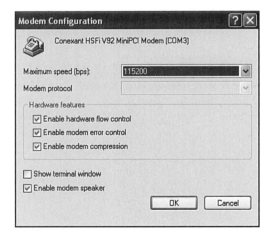

The connection properties sheets shown in Figures 8.8 through 8.15 can be used to solve some basic problems with your connection, but if your modem's configuration needs to be adjusted beyond the settings shown in Figure 8.14, you will need to open the Modem Properties sheets.

Figure 8.15
The Internet Protocol (TCP/IP) properties sheet.

USING THE MODEM PROPERTIES SHEETS

You can use the Modem Properties sheets to troubleshoot your dial-up modem connection, adjust your modem's speaker volume, update the modem driver, and configure the modem. These features can be very useful if you need to diagnose connection problems caused by your modem.

To access the properties sheet for your dial-up modem

1. Open the Windows Control Panel.
2. Open the Phone and Modem Options icon.
3. Click the Modems tab to see the modem(s) attached to your system.
4. Select a modem and click Properties to display the General tab shown in Figure 8.16.

The General tab displays modem status and enables you to fix problems listed by clicking the Troubleshoot button. You can also use the General tab to disable the modem and to view the modem type and location.

The properties sheet for an external modem doesn't feature the Resources or Power Management tabs shown in Figure 8.16, but is otherwise similar.

TIP

To determine if a resource conflict is preventing your external modem from working, open the Device Manager and check the properties sheet for the port used by the modem.

Figure 8.16
The General tab for a typical internal modem.

Click the Modem tab (see Figure 8.17) to adjust the speaker volume (useful to determine if you're dialing a wrong number or to determine if you have a good connection; some internal modems only offer on and off options), view and adjust the maximum port speed, and select whether to wait for a dial tone before dialing.

Adjusts speaker volume

Figure 8.17
The Modem tab for a typical external modem.

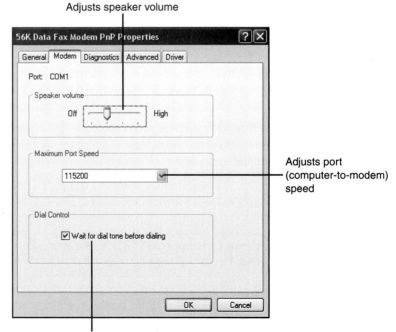

Adjusts port (computer-to-modem) speed

Clear the checkbox to enable manual dialing

8

For most 56Kbps internal and external modems, the maximum port speed of 115200bps shown in Figure 8.17 should provide reliable performance. While you can reduce it to improve reliability, reducing the maximum port speed reduces your connection speed. Try these other options first:

- Connect a serial-port external modem to another serial port (if available)
- Make sure the modem cable is connected tightly to your modem and to your serial port
- With all types of modems, update the modem driver (refer to Figure 8.24)
- If the modem is connected to the serial or USB port, update the serial or USB drivers; use Windows Update or check with your motherboard or system vendor to see if newer drivers are available

Click the Diagnostics tab and click Query Modem to send commands to your modem. If your modem replies, you have a working connection to your modem (see Figure 8.18). If the modem displays an Error dialog box stating your modem failed to respond (see Figure 8.19), follow the instructions in the dialog box to solve the problem with your modem.

Figure 8.18
The Diagnostics tab after querying the modem and receiving replies.

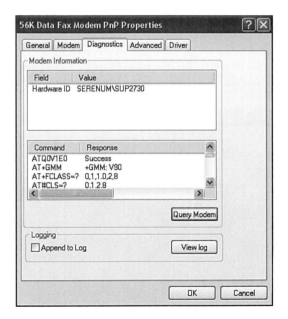

The modem need not be connected to a telephone line during the Diagnostics process. However, if an internal modem has a resource conflict with another device, or if an external modem isn't powered on or connected to a working port, the Error dialog shown in Figure 8.19 will be displayed.

Figure 8.19
The Error dialog displayed if the modem fails to respond when queried with the Diagnostics tab.

TIP

> You can click on the General tab and use the Troubleshoot button (see Figure 8.16) to solve problems with modem or port resource conflicts.

Use the Advanced dialog (see Figure 8.20) to send additional initialization commands (also called initialization strings) to the modem. While your modem driver software controls all your normal modem functions, sending extra commands when you use the modem can fix various problems modem users might have, including

- Inaccurate reporting of the actual connection speed
- Better volume control
- Preventing your modem from answering the telephone
- Disabling V.90 (56Kbps) support when connecting to Internet services that don't support V.90 technology
- Enabling your modem to work with specialized devices such as call alert hardware (which notifies you when you're receiving a call on the line used by your modem)

Figure 8.20
Adding extra initialization commands recommended by an Internet call alert notification device.

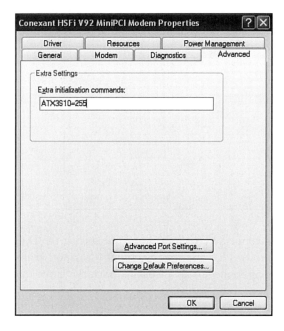

The documentation provided with your modem might indicate that you need to add initial-ization commands and provide the correct commands for your modem. You can also check with your modem vendor's Web site or the documentation provided with hardware or soft-ware add-ons you might use with your modem.

To determine exactly what a particular initialization string will do, you can look up each command in the documentation for your modem or in a generic modem AT command ref-erence manual. For example, the initialization commands used in Figure 8.20 have the fol-lowing meanings:

- ATX3 shuts off the modem's ability to detect a dial tone
- S10=255 prevents the modem from detecting loss of carrier signal and hanging up

> **TIP**
>
> The 56K.com Web site has a useful list of initialization strings by modem brand and model, as well as links to Web sites. Go to `http://www.56k.com/inits/` for details.
>
> The Modem Mechanic Web site also offers a list of initialization strings by modem brand and model as well as a reference to AT commands. Go to `http://supportmech.virtualave.net/init-index.htm` for details.

Click the Advanced Port Settings button to adjust the size of the transmit and receive buffers used by your modem (see Figure 8.21). By default, the maximum number of receive and transmit buffers are used (14 and 16) with your modem to provide the best perfor-mance, but you might have a more stable connection if you reduce the size of the buffers. Adjust the buffers as desired and click OK to return to the Advanced tab.

Figure 8.21
Adjusting send and receive buffers.

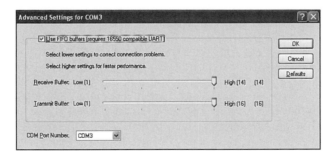

If you need to change how long the modem tries to connect before canceling a call, the port speed, the compression type, the data protocol, or the type of flow control, click the Change Default Preferences button (refer to Figure 8.20) to display and change these options (see Figure 8.22). You should change these options only if your ISP recommends changes.

Figure 8.22
The general connection preferences for a typical internal modem.

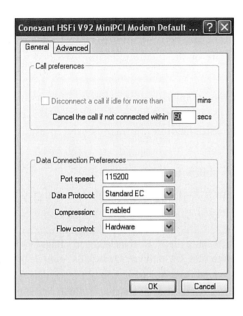

Click the Advanced tab shown in Figure 8.22 if you need to adjust the settings your modem uses for data bits, stop bits, and parity. Most remote computers use the settings shown in Figure 8.23, but a few remote systems might require you to change these settings.

Figure 8.23
The advanced connection preferences for a typical internal modem.

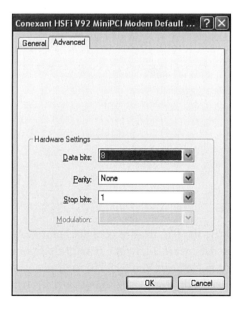

If you see garbled text onscreen after you connect to a remote computer, you might need to change these settings. Contact your ISP or remote computer IS department for the correct settings.

If your modem indicates that you need to reinstall the driver on its General tab (see Figure 8.16) or it reports other problems on the General or Diagnostics tabs, you should download and install a new driver. Click the Driver tab to display the Driver dialog (see Figure 8.24).

Figure 8.24
The Driver dialog for a typical modem.

For more information about installing and updating drivers, **see** "Understanding Device Drivers," **p. 1104**.

The Driver tab lists the modem name, driver date, version, and driver provider. Click Details to see the driver files by name, location, and version. Click Update Driver to search your computer for a better driver; use this option if you download a driver; specify the location of your driver file. Click Roll Back Driver to return to the previous driver if your update fails. Click Uninstall to remove the driver.

Internal modems also feature a Resource tab, which provides the same view of the hardware resources used by the modem as the Device Manager does. *See* "Troubleshooting Hardware Failures and Configuration Problems," *p. xxx*, this chapter, for details.

Some Internal modems also feature a Power Management tab. If you use the modem when your computer is likely to be on standby, you should click the check box next to Allow This Device to Bring the Computer Out of Standby and click OK. This allows the modem to "wake up" the computer.

HIGH-SPEED AND BROADBAND INTERNET CONNECTIONS

Windows XP supports all types of high-speed and broadband Internet connections using the same New Connection Wizard you learned about earlier in this chapter. To get started, open the New Connection Wizard, select Connect to the Internet, Set Up My Connection Manually, and choose from one of the following:

- Connect Using a Dial-Up Modem
- Connect Using a Broadband Connection That Requires a User Name and Password
- Connect Using a Broadband Connection That Is Always On

NOTE

> Connect Using a Dial-Up Modem is used with one-way broadband systems. These systems use a high-speed connection for downloads but a conventional dial-up modem for uploads. Broadband Internet services such as one-way cable modem, one-way fixed-base wireless, and one-way DirecWay (satellite-based) use a dial-up modem, but most broadband services are two-way services.

If you use a two-way cable modem or fixed-base wireless Internet connection, select Connect Using a Broadband Connection That Is Always On. If you use a DSL connection, you might be able to use the always on option, but many DSL (and some cable modem) broadband ISPs require you to use the user name and password option because they use the *Point-to-Point over Ethernet (PPPoE)* protocol; contact your broadband vendor for details.

CREATING A PPPoE CONNECTION

After you click the option to create a broadband connection that requires a user name and password, the wizard asks you for the name of the ISP. Provide this information (to identify your connection) and click Next to continue. On the following screen, provide your user name and your password (both are provided by your ISP). You can also choose to make the account and password available to all users of your computer, make this connection the default connection, and enable the Internet Connection Firewall (see Figure 8.25). Make your selections and click Next to continue.

The wizard displays a digest of the settings and provides you with the opportunity to click Back to make changes, Cancel to cancel the process, or Finish to save the changes. After you click Finish, the connection dialog is displayed onscreen so you can test your connection right away (see Figure 8.26). If you need to alter the connection properties, click the Properties button. Otherwise, click Connect to log on to the service and begin to use it.

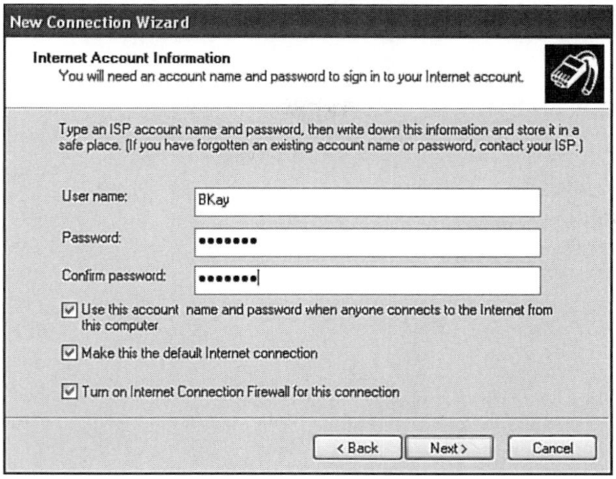

Figure 8.25
Providing user name, password, and optional settings for a PPPoE broadband account.

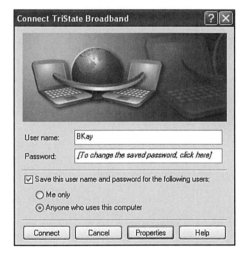

Figure 8.26
The connect dialog for a PPPoE connection.

Windows XP lists PPPoE connections as "Broadband" connections in its Network Connections folder, while cable modem and other types of connections which don't require a login are listed as "LAN or High-Speed Internet Connections."

TROUBLESHOOTING A PPPoE CONNECTION

You can open the properties sheet for a PPPoE connection from the Connect dialog or by right-clicking on the icon in the Network Connections folder and selecting Properties. The properties sheets for a PPPoE connection are similar to those used by a dial-up connection. And, they can be used in similar ways to fix problems with a PPPoE connection.

Table 8.2 helps you solve common problems you might encounter with a PPPoE connection.

TABLE 8.2—PPPoE CONNECTION PROBLEMS AND SOLUTIONS

Symptom	Problem	Solution
You can't connect to the service.	Incorrect username and password.	Provide the correct username and password and retry the connection.
You can't connect to the service, although the password, username, and security settings are correct.	Incorrect settings for the PPPoE protocol.	Contact the ISP and determine the correct settings for PPPoE. Click Networking, make sure PPPoE is selected, and click Settings to select the correct values for LCP extensions, software compression, and multilink.
The remote computer won't recognize your password, although you have supplied the correct username and password.	You might not be using the correct security settings.	Contact the ISP and determine if you need to use a secured password or other special security settings. To configure the settings, open the Security tab and make the settings needed.
Remote users can't connect to games or other services you are trying to host on your computer.	You have the Internet Connection Firewall enabled.	Click Advanced and disable the Internet Connection Firewall. If you want to use a firewall to protect your computer while still hosting games or providing other server functions, see "Securing Your Internet Connection," p. 310.

CONFIGURING A BROADBAND CONNECTION (ALWAYS-ON OR PPPoE)

If you select Connect Using a Broadband Connection That Is Always On in the New Connection Wizard, the system displays a screen which offers you a link to more information if the connection isn't working. To determine if your connection is working, open your browser and see if you can display a remote website. If your connection is working, click Finish to close the wizard.

In most cases, you don't need to perform any configuration for a broadband or high-speed/LAN connection beyond setting up the username and password for a PPPoE connection. The reason is that most broadband connections are designed to use a *dynamic* (changing) IP address, rather than a *static* (fixed) IP address. Normally, the IP address is provided by your broadband (cable, DSL, or fixed wireless) modem. By default, the TCP/IP protocol used by Windows XP is configured to receive an IP address from a Dynamic Host Configuration Protocol (DHCP) server, and such a server is normally built in to broadband modems.

NOTE

Static IP addresses for individual Internet users have become less common today because the Internet has become so popular that there aren't enough static IP addresses to go around. By using dynamic IP addressing, ISPs can provide IP addresses only to users when they're actually connected to the system, enabling a range of IP addresses to serve more users. Because dynamic IP addressing is the default in Windows, it's also easier for ISPs to provide self-install kits for DSL and cable modem Internet access.

Thus, you might need to adjust the properties of your broadband connection only if your provider has assigned you a static IP address; generally, static IP addresses are used primarily for business accounts which need to run FTP or other types of servers. If you need to configure a static IP address, follow this procedure:

1. Open the Network Connections folder.
2. Right-click on the connection you need to change.
3. Select Properties from the right-click menu.
4. Click Networking.
5. Select Internet Protocol (TCP/IP) from the list of components.
6. Click Properties.
7. Enter the following information as provided by your ISP:
   - IP address
   - Preferred and alternate DNS servers; DNS servers translate IP addresses into domain names (see Figure 8.27)

   Click the Advanced button if you also need to provide the following information for your connection:
   - Enable or disable use of default gateway on remote network
   - Enable or disable IP header compression
   - Additional DNS server information
   - WINS servers
   - NetBIOS traffic over TCP/IP

   Contact your ISP for details.
8. Click OK when you're finished.

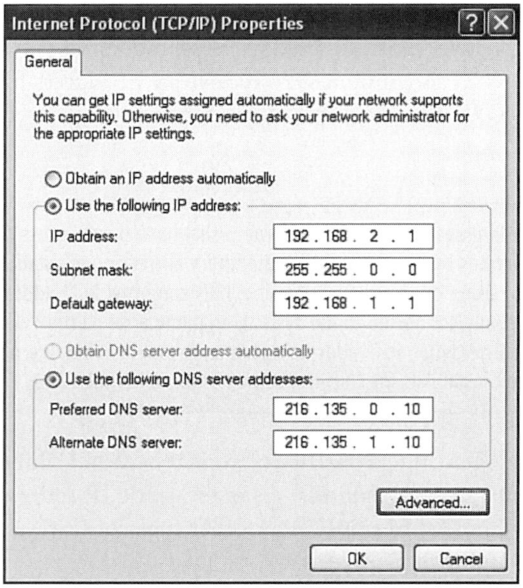

Figure 8.27
Configuring a connection with a static IP address; static IP addresses normally require that DNS server IP addresses also be provided

Internet Protocol (TCP/IP) Properties

General

You can get IP settings assigned automatically if your network supports this capability. Otherwise, you need to ask your network administrator for the appropriate IP settings.

○ Obtain an IP address automatically
⦿ Use the following IP address:

IP address:	192 . 168 . 2 . 1
Subnet mask:	255 . 255 . 0 . 0
Default gateway:	192 . 168 . 1 . 1

○ Obtain DNS server address automatically
⦿ Use the following DNS server addresses:

Preferred DNS server:	216 . 135 . 0 . 10
Alternate DNS server:	216 . 135 . 1 . 10

Advanced...

OK   Cancel

REPAIRING A HIGH-SPEED INTERNET CONNECTION

Windows XP treats broadband connections which use a USB or Ethernet port and don't require a username and password as LAN or High-Speed Internet connections. If you have problems with this type of connection, you can use the Repair option to try to fix the problem.

To start the repair process

1. Open the Network Connections folder.
2. Right-click on the connection you need to repair.
3. Select Repair from the right-click menu.
4. The Repair process runs and displays a Repair Connection dialog box when it is finished. Click OK.

What does the Repair option do? Repair runs a series of commands which are designed to fix common problems with connections that use dynamic IP addresses. Repair performs the following tasks, all of which can also be run manually from the Windows XP command line, according to the Microsoft Knowledge Base article #289256:

- Repair renews the DHCP address lease with the command IPCONFIG/RENEW
- Repair flushes the Address Resolution Protocol (ARP) cache, which stores IP addresses and their corresponding Ethernet or Token Ring hexadecimal addresses, with the command ARP -D *
- Repair reloads the NetBIOS name cache, which matches NetBIOS computer names with IP addresses, with the command NBTSTAT -R

8

- Repair releases and refreshes NetBIOS names with the command NBTSTAT -RR
- Repair flushes the DNS cache to remove any incorrect DNS entries with the command IPCONFIG /FLUSHDNS
- Repair re-registers DNS names and IP addresses with the command IPCONFIG / REGISTERDNS

If you suspect that you are having problems with a static IP address, Repair cannot help you with that specific problem, since it is designed to fix problems with a DHCP-based IP address. However, you can run Repair to fix other problems you might encounter with a system which has a static IP address, such as DNS, ARP, and NetBIOS issues.

Sharing Your Internet Connections

Windows XP supports the following types of Internet sharing:

- Internet Connection Sharing
- Sharing via a router and hub or router and switch
- Sharing via third-party gateway or proxy server software such as Ositis WinProxy, Sygate Home Network, or Deerfield WinGate

Both Internet Connection Sharing and sharing via a router with a switch or a hub are easy to implement with Windows XP's default TCP/IP configuration, because both of these normally use dynamic IP addresses.

➜ To learn more about installing network hardware for Internet sharing, **see** "Building Your Own Network," **p. 637**.

Configuring and Using Internet Connection Sharing

To use Internet Connection Sharing (ICS) with Windows XP, you need the following:

- A connection to a dial-up or broadband Internet provider
- A connection to a home or small office network

Before you enable ICS, you need to verify that the computer with the Internet connection is working properly and can connect to the Internet.

➜ If you are using ICS to share a broadband connection, you might need to install two network adapters in the ICS host computer. To learn more about installing network adapters, **see** "Installing Network Adapters," **p. 642**.

To enable ICS on a Windows XP computer that has an Internet connection, follow this procedure:

1. Connect the computer with the Internet connection to a home or small-office network. If necessary, install a network adapter to make this possible.

2. Open the Network Connections folder and right-click on the connection you want to share.

3. Select Properties.

4. Click Advanced.

5. Click the box next to Allow Other Network Users to Connect Through This Computer's Internet Connection to enable ICS (see Figure 8.28).

6. If you connect to the Internet through a dial-up modem, click the box next to Establish a Dial-Up Connection Whenever a Computer on My Network Attempts to Access the Internet to enable any computer on the network to activate the Internet connection.

7. If you want to allow other computers to control or disable the shared Internet connection, click the box for this option.

8. Click OK.

Figure 8.28
Configuring ICS on an always-on broadband connection.

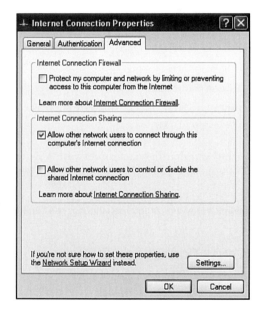

CONFIGURING ICS CLIENTS

There are several ways to configure ICS clients, including

- Manual configuration
- Using the Windows XP Network Setup Wizard on other Windows XP computers
- Using the Windows XP Network Setup disk on older versions of Windows
- Using the Windows XP CD-ROM on older versions of Windows

MANUAL CONFIGURATION OF ICS CLIENTS

If you have already configured your system with the following network components:

■ Client for Microsoft Networks

■ Internet Protocol (TCP/IP)

And if the Internet Protocol uses the default setting of Obtain an IP Address Automatically, you don't need to run a wizard to connect to the ICS host. Instead, follow this procedure with Windows XP or Windows 2000:

1. Make sure the computer is connected to a hub or switch that is also connected to the ICS host.
2. Click Start.
3. Click Run.
4. Type **CMD** and click OK; this opens the Windows XP command prompt window and starts the command interpreter.
5. Type **IPCONFIG /RELEASE** and press ENTER to release the existing IP address.
6. Type **IPCONFIG /RENEW** and press ENTER to obtain a new IP address from the DHCP server built in to the ICS host.
7. Type **EXIT** and press ENTER to close the command prompt window and return you to the Windows XP desktop.
8. Open your Web browser and your default home page should appear; if you use a local file or a blank page as your default page, type in a new URL or select a Favorite to make sure your Internet connection is working correctly.

Once you have established a connection to the Internet via ICS on a Windows XP client, the Network Connections folder displays the name of the computer under the Internet Gateway category (see Figure 8.29).

Follow this procedure with Windows 9x or Windows Me:

1. Make sure the computer is connected to the hub or switch which is also connected to the ICS host.
2. Shut down the computer.
3. Turn on the computer.
4. The DHCP server built in to the ICS host will automatically provide an IP address to each computer as it starts up.
5. Open your Web browser and your default home page should appear; if you use a local file or a blank page as your default page, type in a new URL or select a Favorite to make sure your Internet connection is working correctly.

Figure 8.29
COMPAQ is the ICS host that provides this computer with shared Internet access.

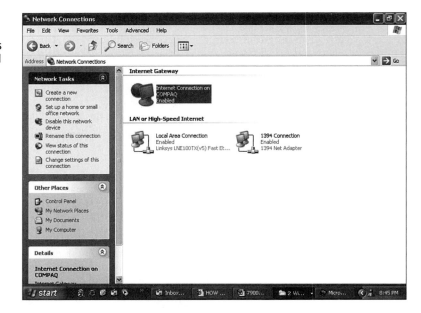

If the manual process doesn't work, you can use the Windows XP Network Setup Wizard to configure other computers on the network.

CONFIGURING WINDOWS XP COMPUTERS WITH THE NETWORK SETUP WIZARD

To run the Network Setup Wizard on other Windows XP computers, follow this procedure:

1. Click Start, All Programs, Accessories, Communications, Network Setup Wizard.
2. Click Next to continue.
3. Follow the steps given on the next screen to connect the computer to the network, and then click Next to search for a shared Internet connection.
4. If the wizard finds a shared connection, you can use it or you can choose another way to connect to the Internet (see Figure 8.30). Click Next to continue.
5. If you have two network connections, you can choose to let the wizard bridge them (which allows computers connected to your computer to access the Internet through your computer) or you can choose your own connections. Select an option and click Next to continue.

TIP

> If you have an IEEE-1394a (FireWire, i.Link) port on your computer, Windows XP can use it as a network connection with the wizard. However, if you have such a port and prefer to use it for connecting drives, DV camcorders, or scanners, select Let Me Choose My Connections to My Network to prevent Windows XP from using it for network connections.

8

Figure 8.30
Detecting an existing shared Internet connection with the Network Setup Wizard.

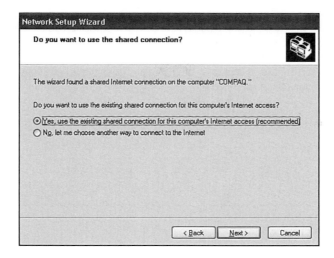

6. If you select Let Me Choose My Connections, the next screen displays the network connections that Windows XP has detected on your computer. Clear the check box for any connection that provides direct Internet access, or for an IEEE-1394a connection you use for storage or multimedia tasks (see Figure 8.31). Click Next to continue.

Figure 8.31
Selecting the Fast Ethernet Adapter connection as the connection to the network.

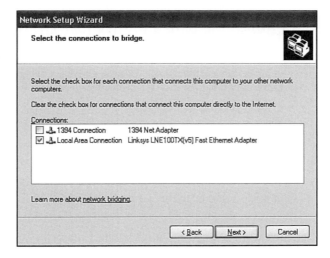

7. Enter a description and name for the computer and click Next to continue.

8. Enter the workgroup name. Microsoft defaults to MSHOME, but if you have already created a network, use the workgroup name you have already selected for the other computers on the network.

8

N O T E

> If you enter the wrong workgroup name, you can still access the Internet, but other shared resources (files, folders, drives, and printers) won't be available to your computer until you enter a workgroup name which matches the workgroup used by the rest of the computers. You can correct an error in the workgroup name through the Computer Name tab of the System Properties sheet.

The wizard displays the selections you made in a scrolling window (refer to Figure 8.24). Review it before you click Next to complete the wizard. An animation runs while the wizard completes the setup.

Once the wizard has completed configuring the computer, it displays a dialog box that enables you to create a network setup disk, use an existing network setup disk, or use the Windows XP CD-ROM to configure other computers on the network. Select the setup option you want to use for other computers, click Next, and the instructions for that setup option are displayed for your reference.

N O T E

> You can use the Windows XP CD-ROM to set up home networking on other Windows computers that have a CD-ROM or compatible drive. Create a network setup disk only if you need to add computers to the network which don't have a CD-ROM drive.

SHARING AN INTERNET CONNECTION WITH A ROUTER OR GATEWAY

Some broadband Internet modems contain a built-in router, a device that directs network and Internet traffic to the correct destinations, but most do not. Routers that combine wireless support or a multiport switch can be connected to broadband modems to allow multiple users to share an Internet connection. The major differences between ICS and router-based Internet sharing include

- ICS requires separate connections to the modem and to the network, while routers have separate connections to the broadband modem and to each computer on the network.

- ICS requires two network connections on the computer which has a broadband modem (one to the modem, and the other to the network), while routers require a single network connection to each computer.

- The ICS host is not protected against outside attacks unless the Internet Connection Firewall is enabled on the network connection to the Internet, but computers that share the network are protected because their IP addresses aren't visible to the outside world. All computers that use a router are protected by the router from incoming attacks, and can also use Internet Connection Firewall or third-party firewalls for additional protection.

- The ICS host computer must be completely booted before its Internet connection can be shared with other users. Computers connected to a router can be powered up in any order; as long as the router is working, all computers can access the Internet.

- If the ICS host computer goes into standby or suspend mode, no computer in the network can connect to the Internet. You must disable power management features (except for screen blanking) on the ICS host to permit full-time Internet access. Routers don't use power management, so power management features on individual computers don't affect any other computer's ability to access the Internet on a router-based network.

You can use the Network Setup Wizard to configure a router-based network, or you can configure it manually.

Figure 8.32 compares typical ICS configurations to typical router-based configurations.

While Figure 8.32 portrays wired networks, you can also use wireless gateways to share Internet access among multiple computers. Some wireless gateways can also act as bridges to wired networks.

→ To learn more about wireless networks, **see** "Wireless Networking," **p. 790**.

I recommend router-based sharing because the low cost of broadband routers makes this option not much more expensive than ICS. Router-based sharing is more secure and offers less chance for failure than ICS.

Figure 8.32
A typical broadband Internet network using ICS (top) and using a router (bottom).

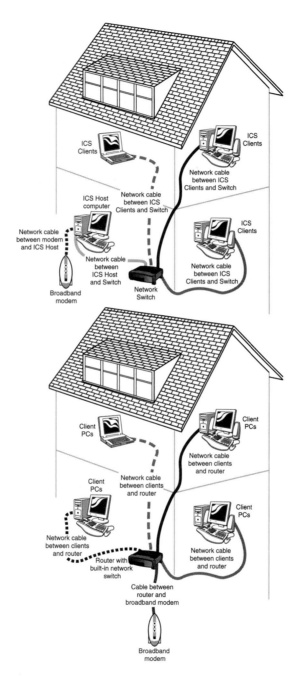

SECURING YOUR INTERNET CONNECTION

Internet connections are vulnerable to attacks from outside users, and always-on connections, such as those that use a cable modem, fixed-base wireless, or some types of DSL connections, are extremely vulnerable to being hacked and compromised by other users. Computers that are connected to routers and computers that are ICS clients are protected against most types of incoming threats because their actual IP addresses are not visible to the Internet. However, an ICS host is vulnerable, because it must be connected directly to the Internet. To block incoming threats, computer experts recommend using a firewall appliance or firewall program. The simplest firewalls work by examining incoming data packets and blocking those that are not requested by the computer or are attempting to perform unauthorized actions (such as activating a Trojan Horse program).

Windows XP is the first version of Windows to incorporate a built-in firewall, the Internet Connection Firewall. The Internet Connection Firewall works with all types of Internet connections, including dial-up, broadband, and LAN. It is enabled from the Advanced tab of the properties sheet for the connection, as shown in Figures 8.12 and 8.28. ICF might already be enabled if you installed Windows XP on a standalone computer with an Internet connection, and it is automatically enabled when you run the Network Setup Wizard or New Connection Wizard on systems with a direct connection to the Internet.

NOTE

For more details about how ICF works, see Microsoft's Internet Connection Firewall Feature Overview available online at

`http://www.microsoft.com/windowsxp/pro/techinfo/planning/firewall/`
`default.asp.`

ICF uses a stateful packet filter that bases its filtering on its analysis of the connection flows currently occurring in your system. By default, ICF permits traffic that matches established connection flows. ICF also sets up new connection flows for outbound (sent) packets. ICF blocks all incoming TCP/IP traffic that didn't originate with the computer running ICF. However, if you need to run services such as file transfer, mail, or others that require the computer to accept incoming traffic, click the Settings button on the Advanced tab to display a list of services you can enable (see Figure 8.33).

If you want to add a service not listed (including online gaming, video chatting, and others), click the Add button to display a dialog box that enables you to provide ICF with the information needed to permit the service (see Figure 8.34).

As Figure 8.34 shows, you need to supply a description plus two pieces of technical information if you want to add a service:

- The IP address of the computer running the service—You can use IPCONFIG or WINIPCFG, depending upon the version of Windows the client is using, to display this information.
- The external (incoming) and internal (outgoing) TCP or UDP ports used by the service.

Figure 8.33
The computer's ICF has been configured to permit the FTP and Web server services to run.

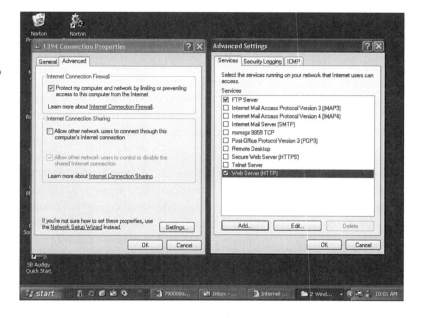

Figure 8.34
Configuring ICF to permit an online game to run on the network.

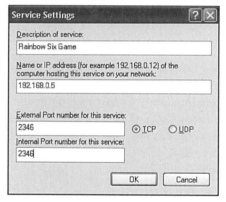

Click OK when all information is completed to add the service to the list of enabled services.

NOTE

The most difficult part of the process of adding a new service is determining the correct values for the TCP or UDP ports used by the service. Here are some Web sites that provide this information:

- Port Numbers for Common Applications— `http://www.fulton.net.au/port_numbers.htm`

- Search `http://whatis.techtarget.com` with the phrase "Port numbers" to find several links

> ■ Practically Networked's list of ICS configuration mappings (originally developed for use with the Windows 98/Me version of ICS) can be viewed with a text editor and manually added to the Windows ICF configuration as described in this section—
> `http://www.practicallynetworked.com/sharing/ics/`
> `icsconfig_maps.htm`

SHORTCOMINGS OF THE INTERNET CONNECTION FIREWALL

The Internet Connection Firewall (ICF) blocks all TCP/IP traffic that wasn't requested by the computer running the firewall. Unfortunately, this means that it can't be used by computers that have shared resources because ICF can't distinguish between true Internet traffic and traffic coming from another IP address on a home or small-office network.

For example, I have configured a computer on my network to be a Windows ICS host. Because this computer is connected to the Internet, I have enabled the ICF on this computer to provide protection for the connection and the computers sharing the connection. However, my network also has another computer that has shared printers and folders. If I enable ICF on that computer, no other computers on the network can access its shared resources; ICF sees all traffic from another IP address as Internet traffic, and blocks it, even though the traffic is coming from another computer on the same network.

A second limitation of ICF is its inability to stop unauthorized outbound traffic, such as mass emailings or remote connections triggered by Trojan horse programs such as BackOrifice, Klez, and many others, and the transmission of your surfing habits as gathered by Spyware programs such as Alexa, Gator, Comet Cursor, and others. While ICF provides basic incoming security, these limitations have caused many Windows XP users to continue to use third-party personal firewall programs and the new breed of firewall appliances.

→ For more information about ICF, **see** "Internet Connection Firewall," **p. 977**.

THIRD-PARTY PERSONAL FIREWALL PROGRAMS

The increasing numbers and escalating nature of attacks against personal computers, particularly those that have an always-on broadband connection, has fueled the rise of a new type of utility software, the personal firewall. Programs such as Zone Alarm, Zone Alarm Pro, Sygate Personal Firewall, McAfee Firewall, BlackICE PC Defender, Norton Internet Security, and others are a necessity for protecting your individual PC or your network from Internet attacks, whether they originate from the Internet or from software installed on your PC.

While the exact features of these programs vary, the programs mentioned in the previous paragraph generally have several distinct advantages over the free Windows XP ICF:

■ They create a list of programs which are permitted to access the Internet based on your responses; most programs of this type will *not* permit any program, even your Web browser, to access the Internet unless you grant explicit permission.

8

- They intercept unauthorized outgoing traffic: for example, traffic sent by a spyware program, a Trojan, or a virus. Programs that have not been permitted to access the Internet are not allowed to send data or otherwise access the Internet.

- They distinguish between incoming requests from another computer on your network and a request from the Internet, enabling you to use firewall software on all computers on your network, including those which have shared resources.

NOTE

> Leading vendors of personal firewall software include:
>
> Symantec (Norton Internet Security, Norton Internet Security Professional and Norton Personal Firewall)—`http://www.symantec.com`
>
> Zone Labs (Zone Alarm and Zone Alarm Pro)—`http://www.zonelabs.com`
>
> Sygate (Sygate Personal Firewall and Sygate Personal Firewall PRO)—`http://soho.sygate.com`
>
> Internet Security Systems (BlackICE PC Protection [formerly called BlackICE Defender] and BlackICE Server Protection)—`http://www.iss.net/products_services/hsoffice_protection/`
>
> McAfee.com (McAfee Firewall)—`http://www.mcafee.com`

Some products, such as Zone Alarm and Sygate Personal Firewall, are free for home and educational use. Free firewalls provide good basic protection against intrusions and outbound traffic. Commercial products often add several additional features, such as tracking of hackers, privacy controls, protection against hostile active script content on Web sites, and additional protection against email viruses, worms, and Trojans.

NOTE

> The best single Web site for firewall security issues, personal firewall comparisons, and security testing continues to be Steve Gibson's Shields Up! and LeakTest site, available at `http://grc.com`.

To achieve the maximum level of protection at a low cost for your network

- Connect a router between your broadband modem and your computer, even if you only have one computer for now—Routers use a method called *network address translation (NAT)* to shield the actual IP address of your computer from being detected by potential Internet snoops. Look for routers that also feature the ability to block WAN (Internet) requests. When this feature is enabled, the router will not respond to pings (a common method for discovering the IP address of a device). The popular LinkSys 4-port router with Integrated 10/100 Ethernet switch is a low-cost router with this feature. Most low-cost routers support a single VPN connection to a corporate network, but more expensive router/firewall appliance devices often support multiple or unlimited VPN connections, which are useful if two or more people at home need to connect to their company's network.

NOTE

> Some of the leading vendors of routers and gateways for home and small-office use include
>
> - 2wire—http://www.2wire.com
> - Asanté FriendlyNet—http://www.asante.com
> - D-Link—http://www.dlink.com
> - Linksys—http://www.linksys.com
> - Netgear—http://www.netgear.com
>
> Contact these vendors for details of their current products.

- Use a reliable personal firewall program—Even if you use a router, you still need firewall software. Routers can protect your system against snooping and unauthorized incoming traffic, but third-party personal firewalls can protect your system against unauthorized incoming and outgoing traffic.

- Update the firewall software when improved versions are available—Just as firewall software has improved to stop newer types of security problems, creators of Trojans and other malicious programs are developing counterattacks.

- Update the firmware in your router if an update will improve security, add features you need, or improve the router's general reliability—Just as computers and other peripherals get bug fixes and improved features through firmware updates, so do routers. Router firmware updates are available from the router vendors' Web sites.

NOTE

> Upgrade your router's firmware only if you absolutely need to. Because a firmware upgrade reprograms the device, a failed firmware upgrade will render your router useless. Follow the manufacturer's instructions carefully to avoid problems and make sure you download the correct file for your router.

FIREWALL APPLIANCES

The newest type of protection for your network is a device called a firewall appliance. While firewall appliances typically range in price from $300 to as much as $500 or more for a typical ten-user appliance (most offer upgrades to as many as fifty users), they provide much more protection than the combination of routers and personal firewall software can.

Typical features of firewall appliances include

- Support for virtual private network (VPN) connections between one or more computers on the network and a remote computer
- Packet inspection for both incoming and outgoing network traffic
- Options for content filtering and networkwide antivirus protection

8

- Router support for shared Internet access; attach a switch to the firewall to handle more than one user
- Automatic software updates

At first glance, the cost of a firewall appliance for a small home-office or office network might seem excessive, but when you start to calculate the cost of providing antivirus and personal firewall software for each user, and the hidden costs of maintaining the software and training each user to properly set up and use the software, a firewall appliance makes more and more sense, especially if you have four or more PCs on the network.

NOTE

> Some of the leading firewall appliances include
>
> Watchguard SOHO—http://www.watchguard.com/products/fireboxsoho.asp
>
> SonicWALL SOHO3—http://www.sonicwall.com/products/soho/index.html
>
> SofaWare Safe@Home—http://www.sofaware.com/html/consumer_info.shtm
>
> D-Link DFL 300—http://www.dlink.com/products/broadband/dfl300/
>
> NexLand Pro100 and Pro400 series—http://www.nexland.com
>
> Symantec Firewall VPN appliance series—
> http://enterprisesecurity.symantec.com/

TROUBLESHOOTING

Problems with your Internet connection have several potential causes, including

- Hardware failure
- Incorrect hardware configuration
- Incorrect TCP/IP configuration
- Incorrect ICS configuration
- Incorrect ICF usage or configuration

Use this section to get your connection working again.

→ For additional troubleshooting tips and tools, **see** Chapter 21, "Troubleshooting Your Network," **p. 851**.

TROUBLESHOOTING HARDWARE FAILURES AND CONFIGURATION PROBLEMS

Hardware failures can affect network adapters, cables, dial-up and broadband modems, routers, firewall appliances and entire systems. Fortunately, hardware failures are rare and can be detected if you know what to look for.

To detect failures with network adapters, cables, broadband modems, routers, and firewall appliances, check the following

8

- The device's signal lights—Most network hardware is based on the 10/100 Ethernet or 10BaseT Ethernet standard. These standards use one or more signal lights to indicate the device and its cabling are working correctly. When a router/switch or switch is connected to a computer and both are turned on, you should see signal lights on the network adapter and the router/switch or switch indicating the connection is working (see Figure 8.35).

Both broadband and dial-up modems also have signal lights to indicate when they are sending or receiving data from the Internet or from your computer. Cable and fixed-base wireless broadband modems also have signal lights that indicate when the modem is receiving a signal from the network or transceiver. If you see an unusual pattern of signal lights on the front of your modem or router, check the documentation for a list of signal light patterns and their meaning. You might be able to reset the device to fix a momentary problem, but if the device fails its self-test, it should be repaired or replaced. If the device passes its self-test but cannot connect to the Internet, your ISP might be having a service outage.

Loose network cable connector   Connection light

Figure 8.35
A loose or failed network cable (top) compared to a properly secured and working network cable (bottom). The connection light will work only when both ends of the cable are connected to working network ports and the cable itself is working.

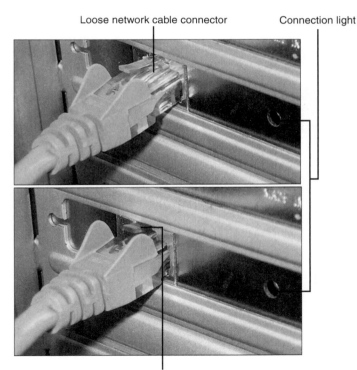

Properly inserted cable connector

■ The cable connectors—If the dial-up or broadband modem isn't properly connected to the outside signal source, or the serial, USB, or Ethernet cable from the computer to the modem is properly connected, the device won't work.

To determine whether a cable has failed when the cable connectors appear to be okay, check the cable itself for damage. If possible, replace a suspect cable with another cable. If only one computer has lost its Internet connection but others continue to work, a single port on a router or switch may have failed. Try connecting the cable to another port. If another port works, the original port was bad and the router or switch should be replaced.

■ The Windows XP Device Manager—The fastest way to open the Device Manager is to

1. Click Start.

2. Right-click My Computer.

3. Select Properties.

4. Click Hardware.

5. Click Device Manager.

A modem or network adapter that has stopped working will be displayed with a yellow circle with an exclamation point (!) inside it (see Figure 8.36).

Figure 8.36
The Linksys network card (highlighted) has a problem. Double-click the icon to view its properties sheet to start the troubleshooting process.

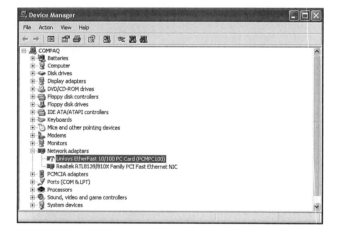

Some of the typical reasons for an installed device to stop working include

■ Hardware resource conflicts—Although the use of Plug-and-Play system BIOS chips and hardware has minimized this once all-too-common problem, it's still possible to install hardware with a conflicting setting. To avoid this problem, don't use manual resource settings, since they can interfere with Plug-and-Play's ability to change settings dynamically. On desktop computers, change a card which has a conflict to a different PCI slot, and avoid the use of ISA cards completely unless you have no

8

satisfactory PCI or built-in substitute. Disable ports you don't use; for example, if you no longer use devices which connect to the serial or parallel ports, disable these ports to free up resources.

- Device driver failure—Although Windows XP features protection against the deletion of some system files, this doesn't usually extend to device drivers. And, while Windows 2000 drivers can be used in a pinch for some devices that lack Windows XP–specific drivers, other devices won't work at all without Windows XP drivers.

→ To learn more about rolling back to a previous version of a device driver, or about returning the system to a previous configuration in the event of device problems, **see** "Using Driver Rollback," **p. 1137**.

- Power failure—If you don't turn on an external device, or if a bus-powered USB device needs more power than a USB port can provide, it will fail; some devices might not even show up in the Device Manager at all.

TIP

> Use the Power tab on the properties sheet for a USB root hub or generic (external) hub to see how much power per port is available and the power requirements of the devices attached to the port. Whenever possible, attach bus-powered devices to a self-powered hub so that the full 500mA power level is available to each port. Root hubs (hubs built into the computer) are self-powered, and you can also purchase external hubs which use an AC adapter for power.

To determine the reason for a device's problem in Device Manager, open its properties sheet. A device with a problem will display an error message similar to the one shown in Figure 8.37.

Figure 8.37
This device has a hardware conflict with another device in the system.

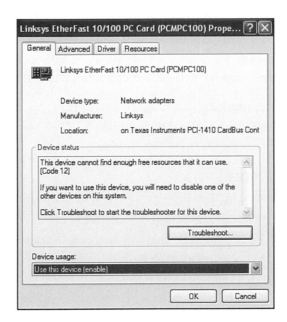

If a device has a hardware conflict such as the one shown in Figure 8.37, the Windows Device Manager will advise you to disable another device in the system to resolve the conflict. This isn't always necessary. First, I recommend that you open the properties sheet for the device that has the conflict and view the Resources tab. If the device is using manual resource settings, check the box Use Automatic Settings, click OK, and restart the computer. This will solve most problems. If the problem persists, determine which other device uses the same setting and make sure it is also using automatic settings (automatic enables Plug-and-Play to work correctly). If this fails, then disable a device you don't need.

→ For more information about using Device Manager, **see** "Using Device Manager," **p. 1111**.

TROUBLESHOOTING INCORRECT TCP/IP AND ICS SETTINGS

Since most ISPs use dynamically assigned IP addresses for both dial-up and broadband connections, and ICS and router-based connection sharing also normally uses server-assigned IP addresses, it's easier to get TCP/IP configuration working today than it was several years ago when static IP addresses were used. To fix TCP/IP and ICS problems, check the following:

- Open a command prompt window and enter the command **IPCONFIG** to view your current TCP/IP configuration. If the IP address displayed is 0.0.0.0, you don't have a valid IP address. To obtain a valid IP address from the DHCP server in the broadband modem, ICS host, or router, enter the command **IPCONFIG /RENEW**.

- Run the Repair option if it's available. See "Repairing a High-Speed Internet Connection," earlier in this chapter.

- Rerun the Network Setup Wizard on the computer with the shared Internet connection and on each client. Make sure that each computer has a unique name, but specify the same workgroup name for all computers.

- Use a router rather than ICS if possible. While Windows XP's version of ICS is more reliable and robust than previous versions, a router is still more reliable.

For additional tips on fixing dial-up connections, see "Troubleshooting Your Dial-Up Connection," in this chapter. For additional tips on fixing a PPPoE connection, see "Troubleshooting a PPPoE Connection," in this chapter.

TROUBLESHOOTING ICF PROBLEMS

To see if ICF is causing problems, disable it. If connection or sharing problems go away, ICF is being used on the wrong computer or is not configured correctly.

The Internet Connection Firewall must be used *only* on a computer that acts as an ICS host for other computers, not on ICS clients.

If basic Web surfing works, but other services don't work, you need to configure ICF to enable those services. See "Securing Your Internet Connection," earlier in this chapter, for details.

CHAPTER 9

INSTALLING AND CONFIGURING APPLICATIONS

In this chapter

ADD/REMOVE PROGRAMS

One of the first things that you'll want to do with your Windows XP system is to install—and customize—your own favorite applications. In all probability, you're already accustomed to doing this—whether under Windows 9x, NT, or 2000—and adding or removing programs under Windows XP is not drastically different from before.

Thus, depending on the source, installing an application may be as simple as inserting a disc in the CD-ROM drive—or, given a network or DSL connection, downloading the installation to a local or network drive—and then following the onscreen prompts.

In general, most applications are distributed with a wizard or installation program which is designed explicitly to make installing and configuring the application as simple and painless as possible, and only rarely do modern software installations require some more complex sequence of tasks.

Given that most CD-distributed applications are self-launching when the CD is placed in the drive—see the following note—and that most downloads are either similarly self-extracting and self-launching or, if they must be unzipped manually, usually contain a setup or install program, there is normally very little need to invoke the Add/Remove Programs utility found in the Control Panel (see Figure 9.1).

NOTE

> To prevent a CD from automatically playing, hold either Shift key while inserting the disk in the CD-ROM drive.

Figure 9.1
Invoking the
Add/Remove Program
utility from the
Control Panel.

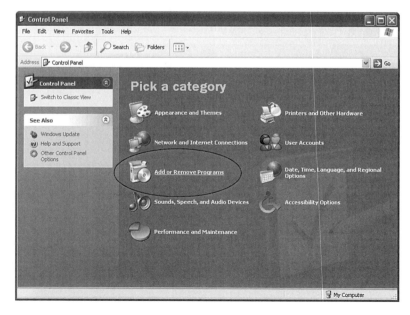

USING AUTOPLAY TO INSTALL FROM CD-ROM

In most cases, when you insert a CD, and if there is an AutoRun executable on the CD, the installation program will be launched automatically and will begin the install process without any further action. If, however, a CD with an AutoRun executable does not automatically respond—if, for example, the AutoPlay feature is disabled or if the CD was in the drive before the system was booted—then you can

1. Open My Computer from the desktop.
2. Right-click on the drive icon to bring up an option menu.
3. Select AutoPlay from the menu as in Figure 9.2.

This will invoke the AutoRun executable and start the installation process.

Figure 9.2
Accessing a CD-ROM with AutoPlay directly.

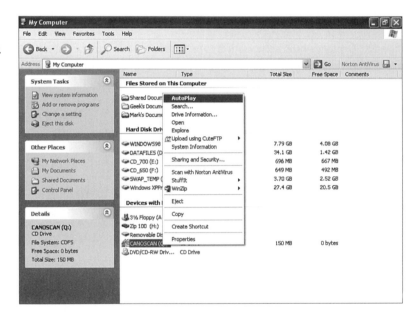

NOTE

Most AutoRun or Setup installation programs assume a target directory using the form C:\Program Files*program_name*. If you prefer to install applications to another drive or directory location, you may change the drive and/or path as desired. Any changes, however, may be answered by a dialog explaining that the requested directory does not exist and asking for confirmation before creating the directory. Unless you want to make a further change, a simple Yes or OK will allow the installation to proceed in the location specified.

Note that AutoPlay does not appear in the right-click menu if the CD-ROM doesn't contain an AutoRun program. To install CD-based programs which don't use AutoRun, see the next section.

USING A SETUP PROGRAM

Quite often when applications are downloaded over the Web, and sometimes when they are distributed by CD or diskette, the programs are provided in the form of a ZIP file or other compressed format. Windows XP Explorer treats ZIP files as if they were folders and, in the example in Figure 9.3, the compressed ed27.zip file shows a Setup.exe file within the contents.

Figure 9.3
Opening a ZIP file to launch an application's Setup utility.

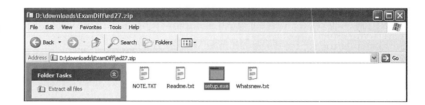

The XP Explorer offers the option (see the left taskbar) to extract all files, or you can simply launch the Setup.exe file directly without extraction from the ZIP file.

Once the Setup utility has been launched, the setup wizard should guide you through finishing the installation process.

INSTALLING AND UNINSTALLING APPLICATIONS

When the Add/Remove Programs application opens, three options are offered:

- **Change or Remove Programs**—Removes installed applications or makes changes in the application configuration.

- **Add New Programs**—Used to install a new application from a CD-ROM or floppy disk; to install new Windows XP features, device drivers or system updates by download over an Internet connection; or to install published programs available on your corporate network.

- **Add/Remove Windows Components**—Used to modify (add or remove) Windows XP components; installs components from the original CD.

Each of these options serves a different purpose and each is detailed in the following sections, beginning with the Add New Programs screen.

If the computer is not connected to an Active Directory domain network, the Add New Programs screen offers two options, installing from a CD-ROM or floppy disk, or downloading a new Windows XP feature, device driver, or system update as shown in Figure 9.4.

The CD or Floppy button will prompt you to insert the first floppy disk or CD-ROM disc. The installation process will then check the floppy drive (if a disk is present) or will check the CD-ROM drive, looking for an AutoRun.exe, Setup.exe, or Install.exe utility program.

Figure 9.4
Invoking the Add New Program utility.

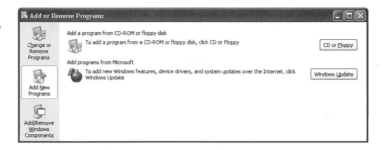

Once any of these are found and launched, the installation process proceeds just as if the installation utility had been launched manually or by the AutoPlay feature.

The Windows Update button launches Internet Explorer to connect to Microsoft's Windows Update site via the Internet and to check for the latest versions of the Update software and the latest versions of any Windows components (see Figure 9.5).

Figure 9.5
Use the Windows Update service to install important security patches and other Windows software.

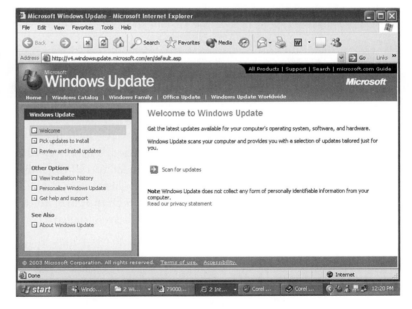

NOTE

If you are using a dial-up connection to the Internet, the size of the downloads may cause the update process to be relatively slow and, for example, downloading the Windows XP Service Pack 1 may require six to eight hours to complete installation. Thus, if at all possible, a cable, DSL, or other high-speed connection is recommended.

The Windows Update service offers two options; you may either scan for updates or use the automatic update option.

The Scan for updates option—see Figure 9.6—presents a list of available updates.

Figure 9.6
Windows Update provides a list of updates available for downloading and installation on your computer.

In Figure 9.6, a host of updates are listed, most of which are actually relatively small and could be installed easily even over a dialup connection. The first update listed is Windows XP Service Pack 1, which requires an initial download of 1.9MB. This initial download, however, is only a utility to determine which components are needed, and the total download required to complete the upgrade can run as high as 30MB. You will be prompted to confirm acceptance before downloaded components are installed.

Still, installing this initial service pack is recommended and, once completed, repeating the scan for updates will show a much shorter list of components needing updating.

NOTE

Service Packs, such as Service Pack 1 released in fall of 2002, are packages combining a variety of patches and updates. If a Service Pack is available, it should always be installed before proceeding with individual updates.

While you are performing a Windows XP Update, the Automatic Updates Setup Wizard will also appear in your taskbar, offering you the opportunity to schedule unattended and automatic updates for system, software, and driver applications.

The settings dialog for automatic updates—see Figure 9.7—begins with an option to allow the Windows Update software itself to be updated prior to downloading and installing system, software, or driver updates.

Figure 9.7
You'll see this window first, which allows you to set up how updates are handled.

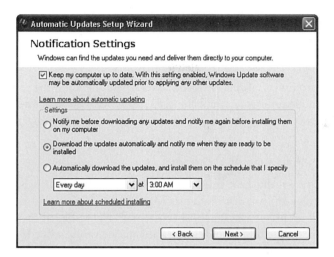

For the updates themselves, the wizard offers three choices:

- **Notify the user prior to downloading or installing any updates**—Essentially a manual update process.

- **Download updates automatically but notify the user before installation (default)**—Updates are retrieved automatically when an Internet connection is available but installation requires the user's permission before proceeding.

- **Schedule automatic download and installation of updates on a daily, weekly, or monthly basis at a regular time**—Both downloads and installation are carried out automatically at regularly scheduled intervals.

N O T E

> When you are installing a service pack or a large update, if you are warned that your system drive lacks sufficient space to back up the files necessary to undo the upgrade, you can select another drive as the backup location. Alternatively, you may choose not to keep the backup files.

INSTALLING PUBLISHED APPLICATIONS

If your computer is connected to an Active Directory domain network, the Add or Remove Programs' Add New Programs submenu displays an additional option: Add Programs from Your Network. Programs listed in this category are called *published programs*.

A published program is a program which is made available through the group policy settings for your user or group account. In other words, users in group A might see different programs available than users in group B.

To select a program to install

1. Click Category and select the program category to browse.

2. Click the program you want to install and click Add.

3. Follow the prompts to install the program. Depending upon the settings made by the network administrator when publishing the program, you might not be able to customize the installation as you normally would with a normal program installation.

ASSIGNED VERSUS PUBLISHED APPLICATIONS

A published program is different than an assigned program, although both are provided by group policy settings and are distributed through the corporate network. As you see from the description given previously, a published program is installed at the user's discretion. An assigned program, on the other hand, is installed automatically when the user selects the shortcut from the program menu, opens an application which is handled by the assigned program, or starts an OLE/COM application which also uses the assigned program.

UNINSTALLING VERSUS MODIFYING APPLICATION SETUPS

The most common reason for invoking the Add/Remove Programs utility is to change or modify an installed application or to uninstall an application entirely. For this reason, the Change or Remove Programs screen—see Figure 9.8—opens showing an alphabetical list of currently installed programs.

NOTE

The Sort By option (upper right) offers a choice of how the list is sorted, including sorting by Name, Size, Frequency of Use, and Date Last Used.

Figure 9.8
Selecting a program to change or remove.

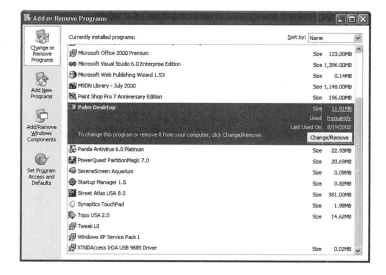

As an item is highlighted on the list of installed programs—the Palm Desktop in Figure 9.8—the display for the selected item expands to show the application size (file size), how frequently the application has been used, and the date the application was most recently used.

The Change/Remove button—in the highlighted listing, below the application statistics—will bring up one of the following options:

- An uninstall dialog which requests user confirmation before proceeding to remove the application.
- A dialog with options to add or remove features (such as import/export filters, additional programs in an office suite, or optional program components) or uninstall the program. Some programs, such as Microsoft Office XP, also provide an option to repair an existing installation that has been damaged.

CAUTION

While most applications request confirmation before uninstalling themselves, some applications are known to very abruptly remove themselves without confirmation. This behavior is entirely the responsibility of the application designer and is not mandated by the Windows XP operating system.

The Last Used On date for some applications might refer to the last time the program's installer was run, rather than the last time the program itself was run. For example, the Microsoft Office XP Professional entry on my computer lists its last-used date as the day it was installed, even though I use Microsoft Word XP almost every day. Thus, you should not rely on the Last Used On date information to be an accurate indicator of how recently a particular program was used.

Cannot Locate Application

If you receive an error message indicating that the application you want to uninstall cannot be located, this is an indication that the selected application is not installed or that the uninstall utility for the application has been damaged or deleted. Of course, as an alternative cause, the application files might have been moved to another location.

If you're using the Add/Remove utility (from the Control Panel), you should also see a prompt offering to remove the application from the list. As a first step, yes, go ahead and remove the application from the list.

Next, check the application directory and, if necessary, manually delete the directory and contents.

If you can't find the application files, use the Search/All Files and Folders facility from the Start menu.

Finally, as a last resort, open RegEdit, search for entries referring to the application and delete as required. Be careful, however, since you can seriously compromise your system by altering the registry. And always create a backup (export) of the registry before making alterations.

ADDING AND REMOVING WINDOWS COMPONENTS

The Add/Remove Windows Components option—on the taskbar at the left in Figure 9.8—invokes the Windows Components Wizard, which lists the system components by categories (see Figure 9.9).

Functionally, the Windows Component Wizard works the same as it did under Windows 2000, 9x, and NT. Thus, an empty check box indicates that a component is not installed or, for a category, that no components in that category are installed; a gray check box with a check mark indicates that one or more components in the category are installed; a clear check box with a check mark indicates that a component is installed or that all components in a category are installed.

Figure 9.9
The Windows Components Wizard allows you to add or remove basic Windows components.

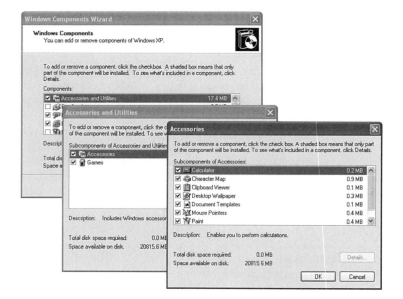

The components list is similar to a directory tree where top-level categories may contain subcategories and/or individual components. In Figure 9.9, the top-level window has highlighted the Accessories and Utilities category, which appears in the next window as two subcategories: Accessories and Games. The Accessories category, in turn, is opened in a third window to show a list of individual components ranging from the Calculator utility to the Paint application.

Categories can be opened either by a double-click on the category or by selecting the Details button. Alternatively, if a component rather than a category is highlighted, the Details button will be disabled.

Windows components can be added or removed either as individual components or as entire categories. To add a component or category, simply click on the check box next to the entry until a checkmark appears and the check box is clear.

Conversely, to remove a component or category, click on the checkbox until the box is empty.

HIDING AND UNHIDING WINDOWS COMPONENTS FROM THE COMPONENT WIZARD

A careful examination of the Windows XP Components Wizard's list of programs reveals that many Windows components are not listed and therefore cannot be uninstalled with the wizard. It is possible, however, to unhide programs which are not listed by the wizard so they can be uninstalled. And, it is equally possible to hide normally visible programs to prevent their being uninstalled through the wizard.

Windows XP maintains a list of components in a file called sysoc.inf. This file is located in the Inf folder beneath the default Windows XP installation location (\Windows\Inf or \WinNT\Inf). To unhide a component so it is displayed by the Components Wizard:

1. Close the components wizard and Add/Remove Programs.
2. Make a backup copy of sysoc.inf.
3. Open sysoc.inf with a plain-text editor such as Notepad.
4. To unhide a listed component so it can be uninstalled, replace the word HIDE (or hide) in the settings listed for the component with a comma. See Figure 9.10.
5. Make the same change in step 4 for each component you want to unhide.
6. Save the file.
7. Restart the Add/Remove Programs wizard, select the Windows XP Components Wizard, and select the unhidden component.

To hide a component, follow the same instructions, but in step 4, replace a comma with the word HIDE.

Figure 9.10
Unhiding the Pinball component by modifying sysoc.inf.

Pinball entry after replacing HIDE with comma

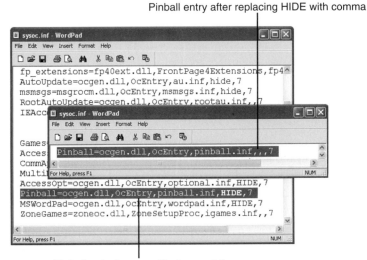

Pinball entry in unmodified sysoc.inf

THIRD-PARTY AND ADD-ON PROGRAMS YOU CAN'T LIVE WITHOUT

Everybody has their own private list of essential tools and no single list is likely to satisfy everyone. There are some tools, however, which are likely to appeal broadly and we hope the following selection of utilities and applications will, to some degree, fall within this broad category.

POWERTOOLS (POWERTOYS)

You might know the PowerTools set of utilities better as "PowerToys." PowerToys have been around in one form or another since Windows 95. However, when you install and use these Microsoft-provided-yet-unsupported utilities, you are likely to agree with the many users who have found PowerToys to be much more useful than the name implies.

NOTE The PowerTools will only work with the US-English regional settings.

The PowerTools set can be downloaded from `http://www.microsoft.com/windowsxp/pro/downloads/powertoys.asp` and consists of ten utilities:

- Alt-Tab Replacement
- CD Slide Show Generator
- HTML Slide Show Wizard
- Image Resizer
- Open Command Window Here
- Power Calculator
- Taskbar Magnifier
- Tweak UI
- Virtual Desktop Manager
- Webcam Timershot

Unlike some previous versions of PowerToys, each utility is a separately downloaded program.

The ten utilities in the PowerTools set are described in the following sections.

ALT-TAB REPLACEMENT

The TaskSwitch.exe utility replaces the familiar Alt-Tab response showing icons for the open applications with a large display combining the application icons with a thumbnail (preview) of the selected application's main window—useful when multiple sessions of an application are open. This preview change aside, the Alt-Tab key combination continues as before to provide a convenient means of switching between open applications.

CD SLIDE SHOW GENERATOR

The Slide Show Generator allows images burned to a CD to be presented as an autorun slideshow which can be executed from any Windows computer. The Slide Show Generator is backward compatible with Windows 9x systems.

HTML SLIDE SHOW WIZARD

The HTML Slide Show Wizard is useful for managing digital images as a Web-ready HTML slide show. The wizard will assist you in selecting and arranging images and choosing a size for presentation, saving the product ready for uploading to a Web site. While not the most sophisticated slide show utility, the Slide Show Wizard does a smooth job of creating a basic presentation.

IMAGE RESIZER

The Image Resizer is very useful if you need to batch-process a group of files you want to use on a Web site or a hand-held PC.

The Image Resizer is invoked by right-clicking on an image or group of images and selecting the Resize Pictures option from the context menu. In response, a dialog offers four standard image sizes—240×320, 640×480, 800×600 and 1,024×768—as well as a custom size. By default, Image Resizer saves a resized image with (Small) in the filename, preserving the original. However, if you click the Advanced button, you can select two options: Make Picture Smaller but Not Larger, and Resize the Originals. Don't select the Resize the Originals option unless you have backup copies of your images.

OPEN COMMAND WINDOW HERE

The CmdHere.exe utility adds a context menu option on file system folders. Labeled "Open Command Window Here", the new menu option provides a quick way to open a command window (cmd.exe) with the current path pointing to the selected drive and directory.

POWER CALCULATOR

The Power Calculator provides an onscreen calculator with the ability to evaluate and graph functions. In addition to the basic arithmetic operations, the Power Calculator also offers Trig, Log, and user-defined functions as well as conversion capabilities for length, mass, temperatures, time, and velocity.

TASKBAR MAGNIFIER

The Taskbar Magnifier is similar to the Magnifier utility found on the Start menu under Programs/Accessories/Accessibility. The difference is that the Taskbar Magnifier remains in the taskbar with a small view window (the height of the taskbar and a fixed width). Like the conventional Magnifier, the Taskbar Magnifier shows an enlarged view of the portion of the screen centered on the mouse pointer.

To invoke the Taskbar Magnifier, right-click on the taskbar, select Toolbars from the menu, and then click on Taskbar Magnifier.

TWEAK UI

This "Swiss Army knife" of utilities is the one item you simply can't do without in the PowerToys collection. Tweak UI provides access to system settings which—perhaps in the interests of protecting the average users—are not exposed through the default user interfaces. The Tweak UI utility provides access to settings for the mouse, desktop shortcuts, taskbar settings, Control Panel contents, repair options, paranoia settings, and a variety of other options which would be otherwise difficult to find/modify.

TIP

The Paranoia tab in the TweakUI utility provides control options for the autoplay for both audio and data CDs.

VIRTUAL DESKTOP MANAGER

The Virtual Desktop Manager allows up to four separate desktops to be managed from the Windows taskbar. Each desktop can run a different application (or applications) and can have its own individual background.

You may switch between desktops by selecting the button for the desired desktop from the taskbar or all four desktops can be displayed simultaneously at quarter-size. To select a desktop from the quartered display, simply click on the desired desktop.

To invoke the Virtual Desktop Manager, right-click on the taskbar, select Toolbars from the menu, and then click Desktop Manager.

WEBCAM TIMERSHOT

The Webcam Timershot allows snapshots to be taken from a Webcam connected to the computer at scheduled intervals with the snapshots saved to a specified location and name. By default, only the most recent snapshot is saved, but the Options menu provides settings to capture each snapshot to a separate file which can be stored on a local drive, a network share, an FTP share, or an HTTP webdav share.

This last PowerToy will probably appeal to *agent du espionage* in all of us…but could also be just the thing to find out who—or what—is snacking on your cheese crackers when you're out.

RESOURCE KIT TOOLS

Windows XP Resource Kit consists of documentation to help IT professionals deploy, manage, and support the Windows XP operating system. This information is available both in a free, online version at `http://www.microsoft.com/WindowsXP/pro/techinfo/productdoc/resourcekit.asp` and in print from Microsoft Press.

The Windows XP Resource Kit is a comprehensive technical resource for installing, configuring, and supporting Windows XP Professional and Windows XP 64-Bit Edition in networks that use Windows 2000 Server, Windows NT Server 4.0, and other server systems.

The provided documentation consists of

- **Deployment and Installation**—Discusses customizing the Windows XP Pro installation, planning deployment, automating and customizing installation, multilingual solutions, and supporting installations.

- **Desktop Management**—Discusses managing desktops, managing files and folders, support for mobile users, configuring remote desktops, managing device and digital media, enabling printing and faxing, managing disk and file systems, and backing up and restoring systems.

- **Security**—Covers logon and authentication, authorization and access control, and encrypting file systems.

- **Networking**—Topics include connecting to Windows networks, configuring TCP/IP, IP address and name resolution, configuring remote offices, and configuring telephony and conferencing.

- **Interoperability**—Discusses interoperability issues with Unix, NetWare, and IBM Host Systems.

- **System Troubleshooting**—Provides support for computers running Windows XP with an introduction to troubleshooting techniques, troubleshooting disks and file systems, and troubleshooting problems encountered during startup.

- **Appendices**—The appendices provide references and supplemental information for
  - System files references
  - User rights
  - Common stop messages for troubleshooting
  - Security event messages
  - Device manager error codes
  - Differences with the Home and 64-bit Windows XP editions
  - Accessibility for disabled individuals
  - Well-known security identifiers

MICROSOFT SCRIPT DEBUGGER

The Microsoft Script Debugger can be used to debug .htm, .html, and .asp scripts within Web pages viewed with Internet Explorer. Click View, Script Debugger, Open. It can also be started as an independent program from the Internet Information Server to debug selected programs, started automatically during program development, or started when a script error is displayed during script operation. Figure 9.11 shows the script debugger working with a Web page.

CAUTION

> You should not install the Windows Script Debugger if you use Microsoft Visual Studio, which contains its own debugger. If you install the Windows Script Debugger, it disables the Visual Studio Debugger.

The Microsoft Script Debugger can be downloaded from the Microsoft MSDN site (`http://msdn.microsoft.com/library/default.asp?url=/downloads/list/webdev.asp`). Be sure to select the Windows XP/2000/NT 4.0 version.

Note that the Script Debugger doesn't create an icon accessible with the Windows Start menu. Its default location is \Program Files\Microsoft Script Debugger on the default Windows system drive.

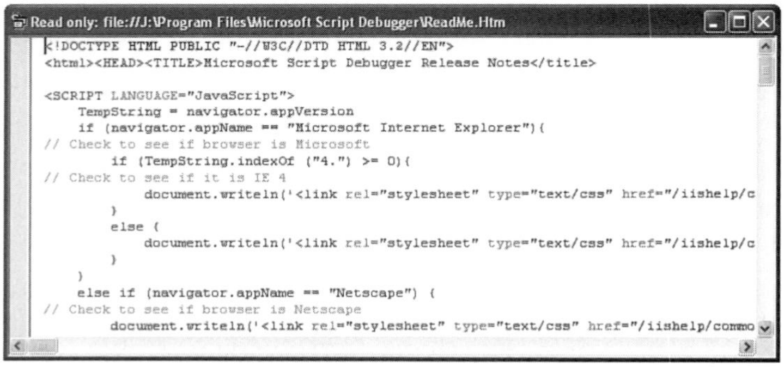

Figure 9.11
Debugging a Web page with the Microsoft Script Debugger.

POWERQUEST TOOLS

Once the OS has been installed and configured and the various applications are functional, the biggest maintenance headache—and the one we definitely don't want to manage at all—involves the hard drive(s).

Windows XP provides the Disk Management snap-in as part of the Microsoft Management Console to partition, format, and adjust drive letters (see Chapter 19, "Windows Unplugged: Remote and Portable Computing"). While Disk Management is far better than the fdisk/format disk tools used by Windows 9x/Me, all of these tools are destructive to data. If you decide to change the size of a disk partition to make room for another operating system or to create a logical drive just for data, these tools require you to back up or copy the data to another location, change the drive's partitions (wiping out the data in the process), and copy the data back. Even when much smaller hard drives than today's drives were in use, this process could consume many hours and provided many risks to data. While drive imaging utilities allow us to create backups of the operating system we can restore without reinstalling Windows, when it comes to managing a new or existing hard drive, we usually prefer to rely on third-party tools: specifically on PartitionMagic and DriveImage from PowerQuest.

While the PartitionMagic and DriveImage programs are sold as separate packages, they are best used in combination with each other. Therefore, we'll describe each application briefly and then discuss how they can be employed in combination to maintain your drive(s). For additional information or to download free evaluation versions, see the PowerQuest Web site at www.powerquest.com.

PARTITIONMAGIC

PowerQuest's PartitionMagic (version 7.0 or later) is the preferred tool for managing hard drive partitions. Unlike the Disk Management utility—which does permit managing drives and creating partitions but only by destroying existing data—PartitionMagic makes it possible to "see" how a physical drive is organized, to create, delete, move, resize, or manage primary and logical partitions without destroying existing data. In addition, partitions can be converted from one type to another—such as converting a FAT32 drive to an NTFS drive—for more efficient use of space or greater security. The latest version, PartitionMagic 8.0 (see Figure 9.12), adds support for Linux Ext3 partitions, GRUB, USB2 and FireWire, making it useful with non-Windows operating systems and the latest types of external hard drives.

Figure 9.12
PartitionMagic (v8.0) resizing the J: (Windows XP) logical drive to provide more space on D: (data) logical drive.

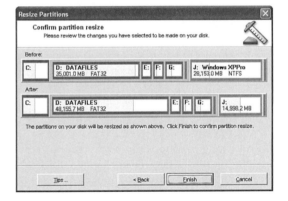

More importantly, by creating partitions on a physical drive, we can better organize our applications, where our data is kept and, perhaps most important, how we maintain backups of critical data.

As Figure 9.12 makes clear, even if you create multiple partitions to organize your hard disk, sooner or later the partitions might be the wrong size. If the partition used for the operating system files is too small, for example, Windows could become less reliable because it doesn't have enough room for temporary files or paging files (swapfiles). If the logical drive used for data becomes too small, data would usually need to be transferred to other storage media (such as CD-R, CD-RW, rewritable DVD, or tape) and then deleted, or be stored on another drive letter, making backup more difficult.

Instead of backing up the drive letters on the hard disk, deleting them, re-creating new partitions, and restoring the information—which might even involve reinstalling the operating system, applications, user accounts, and settings—you can use PartitionMagic. PartitionMagic resizes partitions, moves partitions around, and adjusts free space allocations as in Figure 9.12 without destroying the data on the drive. In extreme cases, you can even add or remove one or more partitions or logical drives and then use the DriveMapper utility to search for and correct drive letter references throughout your system.

Supported operations provided by PartitionMagic include

- **Create partitions**—You can create both primary and extended partitions and create logical partitions within an extended partition. Note that there is a limit of four primary partitions on a physical drive. In the drive shown in Figure 9.12, there is one FAT32 primary partition used for Windows 98 and a second primary partition (NTFS) used for Windows XP.

- **Delete partitions**—Deleting a partition frees space for other uses such as enlarging one or more other partitions. You may delete logical partitions to make space within an extended partition, and then resize the extended partition to free space to resize a primary partition or create an additional primary partition.

- **Resize or Move partitions**—Any existing partition can be resized and/or moved. When resizing a partition, the partition can be enlarged if there is available free space or can be reduced but cannot be made smaller than required by the data present on the partition.

NOTE

PartitionMagic 8.0 provides improved support for NTFS partitions and allows changes to NTFS partitions—including the system partition—without requiring a reboot.

- **Copy partition**—A partition can be copied to create a duplicate of the partition on the same drive or on a separate physical drive.

- **Merge partitions**—Two existing partitions can be merged to create a single partition, with the contents of one becoming a folder in the combined partition. The two partitions to be combined must be adjacent and you will be prompted to determine which partition becomes a folder of the other.

CAUTION

Do not try to merge two operating system partitions or two compressed partitions. This can cause data loss or prevent the system from rebooting.

- **Split partitions**—A single partition can be split to become two new partitions. The Split Partition operation will allow you to determine which folders of the original partition are placed on each of the new partitions.

- **Format partitions**—Both new and existing partitions can be formatted to prepare them for use. Formatting an existing partition, of course, will destroy any files on the partition.

- **Changing drive formats**—While formatting a drive includes the option of choosing a format—FAT, FAT32, NTFS, Linux, NetWare, HPFS, and so on—PartitionMagic also offers the opportunity to covert an existing drive from one format to another (with some limitations) without destroying the existing folders and files.

Other operations include redistributing free space among existing partitions, checking drives for errors, and defragmenting drives.

With the release of PartitionMagic 8.0, PowerQuest's DataKeeper is now included while two new options have been added:

- **Create a backup partition**—A backup partition is a partition used to store copies of your personal data files and is ideal for use with the DataKeeper utility (discussed following).

- **Install another operating system**—The OS installation wizard makes it easy to install a second (or third, and so on) operating system on a computer while still keeping the original operating system(s). While an OS installation wizard does check locations and confirms suitable file systems and boot code on the selected location, the wizard does not place the new OS in the boot menu of any boot manager. This latter provision must still be configured through the boot manager selected.

BootMagic

BootMagic is included with PowerQuest's PartitionMagic and allows creation of a multiboot system where the desired operating system is selected at boot time. BootMagic functions by hiding one or more bootable partitions, leaving only one boot partition visible at startup.

While BootMagic is functional, there are other boot managers which are more flexible in operation and which do not hide partitions to function. For example, if you install Windows XP on a different disk drive or disk partition than your previous version of Windows, the NTLDR program sets up a dual-boot configuration so you can choose to load Windows XP or your previous version of Windows at start time.

Another popular choice for boot management, System Commander 7, is available from VCom (www.vcom.com).

DriveImage

PartitionMagic's DriveImage 2002 or newer is another essential utility. While it has many of the functions of a traditional backup utility, its primary reason for being is to help you create working images of your drives to another physical drive or CD-R/CD-RW media for restoration in the case of a system or disk crash (see Figure 9.13).

If the system crashes, you can restore the image to the same drive to get back to work quickly. If the drive crashes, you can install a new drive and still restore the same image. Since the image contains your operating system, installed applications, and data, you are able to get back to work very quickly. In essence, DriveImage is a disaster-recovery utility. While disaster recovery *should* be part of every backup program, it is missing from many of the simpler third-party backup programs. And, because DriveImage supports CD-R and CD-RW drives and media as well as other drive partitions, you don't need an expensive tape backup to create a restorable image of your system.

Figure 9.13
Creating an initial backup to CD-R/RW media with Drive Image 2002.

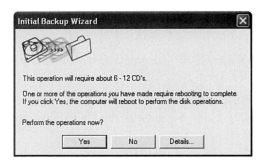

DriveImage is used to

- Create system backups
- Transfer system and application drives to new physical hard drives or to a new computer
- Restore system files after corruption, virus attack, or other catastrophic failures

DriveImage can be used to create compressed images, commonly taking about 50% of the original size, allowing primary drives to be backed up to smaller secondary drives or to CD-R/RW drives.

DATAKEEPER

PowerQuest's DataKeeper is distributed with DriveImage and, in several respects, is more important than DriveImage.

DataKeeper is a data protection utility that continuously monitors one or more drives and creates backup copies of data files as they are revised.

DataKeeper is quite flexible and can be set to monitor only certain types of files—such as documents, spreadsheets, and project files—and create copies of these as they are modified or revised.

DataKeeper can

- Include or exclude files by type or by wildcard file specifications
- Maintain multiple backup versions (up to 99 versions of each document or file)
- Create daily/weekly/monthly archives
- Create compressed backup files
- Create password-protected backup files

MANAGING HARD DRIVES INTELLIGENTLY

Having introduced the PowerQuest tool set as individual components, it now seems appropriate to discuss how these programs are used in combination to maintain reliable data backups and ensure against accidental—or even malicious—data losses.

In the early days of personal computers, hard drives were both small and expensive and making backups to stacks of floppy disks was inconvenient but initially practical.

Then, as hard drives grew in capacity—and as the essential data expanded to match—using floppies for backup became impractical and tape drives became the option of choice.

Tapes, however, are slow, linear, and awkward while, today, hard drives are both large and cheap! For example, a typical 80GB hard drive will probably run you less than $100. However, a tape drive capable of backing up the drive when it's just half-full (40GB) is at least $500 or more. Thus, for a standalone system, the ideal backup for a hard drive can be—very simply—a second physical hard drive. If you have a computer with a built-in ATA RAID adapter, you can configure two identical drives to work in a mirrored (RAID 1) configuration. However, while this protects against drive failure, any other changes to data, including user error, are immediately carried out on both drives.

A smarter way to proceed is to perform a multi-step procedure to help guard against both equipment failure and other types of data loss.

For a desktop or a network system, PowerQuest's PartitionMagic is the first tool in your arsenal and provides the ideal means for managing multiple partitions on your primary (working) drive.

The first step is to create several partitions, beginning with a primary boot partition for your operating system. For a Windows XP (or Windows 2000) installation, a 4GB partition should be more than generous, including space for the system's swapfile, backups following the service pack upgrades, and general utility.

Your second step is to create a partition for your applications. Here, the space requirements are more flexible and will depend on which applications you plan to install. For a start, a 4 or 5GB drive should be adequate but, if you find later that more space is required, PartitionMagic can be used to resize the partition as necessary. Some users might prefer to use a single larger partition for both the operating system and applications. This is also acceptable; however, data should never be stored on the operating system or operating system/applications partition.

The third step is to create one or more drives for your workspace. If you are a developer, you'll probably want to dedicate one drive—drive E:, for example—for your projects. And, perhaps, you will want a fourth drive—F:—for general documents and data storage. Alternatively, you may want to create additional drives for personal documents or reserve a drive just for audio or video files for editing, and so forth. If you create CDs or DVDs, you might want to create a 650MB or 700MB drive to hold the contents of a CD or a 4.7GB drive to hold the contents of a DVD.

For the moment, however, we'll assume that four drives are sufficient:

- C: [System]
- D: [Applications]
- E: [Development]
- F: [Documents]

Note that, for convenience, we've also named the drives appropriately.

NOTE

> By default, virtually every application you install is going to try to install itself to drive C: in the Program Files directory. Unfortunately, there is no simple setting to tell applications that you prefer them to default to D: and you will need to explicitly redirect them during installation.

Now, once we've installed our operating system and applications, the next step is to use PowerQuest's DriveImage to create an image of C: and D:, placing the compressed image on a separate physical drive which we have reserved for our backups. This can be a separate local drive or a directory on a network drive. In either case, we'll want to re-create this backup image at regular or irregular intervals to ensure that we have backed up any new applications we've installed and that we've preserved any changes to the system configuration we've made.

NOTE

> It is preferable to back up the system and application files together—even though we've installed these on separate drives—because many, if not all, applications write settings and installation information to the registry (on the system drive) and may copy dynamic link libraries or other files to the system drive. For this reason, some users might prefer to use a single partition for the operating system and applications.

Also, assuming that we have adequate backup space, we'll probably want to keep more than one backup version and we'll name the drive images to indicate the date the backups were made. For example, an image created on September 17th might be named WXP_917.pqi while the earlier image created on the 2nd might be named WXP_902.pqi.

In this fashion, you can choose how many—and which—backup images to keep and, if you later need to restore your system, you'll be able to choose which system configuration to restore. If you don't have a physical drive large enough for the image, you can use CD-R or CD-RW media. DriveImage will name the data file on each CD in sequence. Or, if you have enough room on a second physical drive for the backup image, but prefer to copy the image to a CD later, you can break the image file up into sections small enough to fit on CDs.

While doing this, you need to remember that DriveImage does not execute as a Windows application but will reboot the system using the DRDOS OS to perform the operation and then reboot to Windows XP when the images are complete. This is not a shortcoming in DriveImage but a requirement to exit the Windows OS so that all of the system files can be copied in a static format. Attempting to copy system files while the system is active would be thwarted by the Windows OS, which restricts access to critical files.

Relocating the Paging File

By default, Windows installs the pagefile.sys file on the boot drive. Because this file can be rather large and because the contents of the file are transient and do not need to be backed up, it can be a good idea to locate your swapfile somewhere else on the system. And, if you already have a second local drive available, placing the swapfile on this second physical drive not only removes it from the backup image but also offers some advantages in access times if it is handled by a separate IDE controller.

To relocate the swapfile, open the Control Panel. If the Control Panel is set to the default Category View, select the Performance and Maintenance option, select System, and click on the Advanced tab (in Classic view, System is displayed as soon as you open the Control Panel). From the Advanced tab, under Performance, click the Settings button. Next, from the Performance Options dialog, select the Advanced tab and click on the Change button under the Virtual Memory section.

In the Virtual Memory dialog, begin by selecting the drive where you want the swapfile to be located, click the Custom size button, set the initial and maximum sizes, and click the Set button. Use the same initial and maximum sizes as shown for the existing swapfile.

Next, after creating a new swapfile on the selected drive, select the original drive from the list, select No paging file and click on Set.

Finally, click OK. You will be advised that your system will need to reboot before the changes can take effect.

Now that you've created backups for your system and application files, the next step is to provide for a continuous backup—rather than a scheduled or incremental backup—of your documents, data, and development files.

Since we've specifically decided to keep our development and document files on drives E: and F:, we'll set up DataKeeper to only monitor these two drives and to ignore drives C: and D:, which were backed up using DriveImage.

Now, if you're accustomed to using the Documents and Settings folder on the Windows XP drive (drive C:), you might want to change the default location of the My Documents folder for each user on the computer. To make this change for the current user:

1. Click Start.
2. Right-click My Documents on the Start menu.
3. Click Properties to display the current path to the folder.
4. Highlight the current path and press the Ctrl+C keys to copy it for safekeeping.
5. Change the drive letter in the current path to F: and click Apply.
6. If you are asked if you want to create this path, click Yes. This creates the same folder path to your documents on F: as existed on your default drive.

9

7. Click Yes to move the files and folders in the former My Documents folder and sub-folders to the new location. After the files are moved, the new My Documents folder is used whenever you click on My Documents.

8. Continue to specify My Documents as the location for data files and they will be saved to the new location.

By using PowerQuest's DataKeeper to manage backups of the My Documents folder and other folders and file types you specify, you can ensure that all work is backed up immediately as you make changes or revisions. In this fashion, a drive crash (or other catastrophe) doesn't mean that you've lost critical data or even that you've lost what work you've done since your last backup. Using DataKeeper, everything you've done—assuming that you have saved your files recently—is included in the backup sets.

Conversely, depending on what type of work you are doing, there are probably a lot of files that you don't really want to waste space backing up. For example, every time you open a Word document—to use a simple example—there are one or more temporary files created which, quite frankly, just aren't worth preserving.

Happily, since most of these have names which begin with a tilde (~) or use the extension .tmp, we can include wildcard exclusions in our DataKeeper specifications as "~*.*" and "*.tmp" to ensure that these "trash" files are not included in our backups. Furthermore, since most of these files are written to the \Documents and Settings*Your Name*\Local Settings\Temp directory and since we have not included the C: drive in our DataKeeper backup, these files would not normally be included anyway.

However, if you are accustomed to using the \Documents and Settings*Your Name* folder to keep important files—and many people do simply because this is the default location used by many applications—then you should explicitly include the drive and directory where the My Documents folder is located. The default for Windows XP installed on C: is C:\Documents and Settings*Your Name*\My Documents. If you change this location as outlined earlier in this section, be sure to change the configuration of DataKeeper to back up the new location.

N O T E

> The default inclusion and exclusion wildcards supplied by DataKeeper on installation are rather broad and should be carefully checked to ensure that you are backing up all of the appropriate data files. For example, "*.exe " appears in the exclusion list and means that any executables copied to the monitored drives will not be included in the backups. You might want to change this setting since many utility programs and other downloads are self-installing .EXE files and you might want DataKeeper to maintain backups of them.
>
> Likewise, the exclusions apply to .zip files and may result in the backed up ZIP file only possessing part of the original contents. Check carefully to ensure that you know which files are being included.

CONTROLLING WHICH PROGRAMS START AUTOMATICALLY

In a perfect world, very few applications would start automatically when you boot your Windows XP system; some would argue that the only really important programs would be antivirus auto-protection and Windows Update. Unfortunately, many program developers assume that you want to use the software they create every time you turn on your computer. As a consequence, much of the software installed on the typical computer also adds itself to the system's startup process, even though there's little time savings and no real advantage to launching the program at startup instead of at your convenience.

Fortunately, we can control which applications and utilities are permitted to remain in the startup folder.

STARTUP: ALL USERS AND CURRENT USER; REGISTRY: HKLM AND HKCU; WIN.INI

There are several ways for applications and utilities to place themselves in the startup process. These include the StartUp program group(s), the HKeyLocalMachine and HKeyCurrentUser registry hives, and, although obsolete, the venerable win.ini file.

THE STARTUP PROGRAM GROUP(S)

Originally, the StartUp program group—on the Start menu under Programs—was the preferred location for loading application or service automatically. Essentially, any program or program shortcut could be added to the StartUp group and, equally, users were free to remove programs from the StartUp group.

Today, the StartUp group is actually two folders, both located under the Documents and Settings folder. The first is found under ..\Documents and Settings\All Users\ Start Menu\Programs\Startup while the second is found under ..\Documents and Settings*Your Name*\Start Menu\Programs\Startup.

The first folder, in the \All Users branch, contains entries which will be loaded for any user logging on to the machine, while the second, in the *Your Name* branch, is loaded only when the named user logs on.

Of course, if there are several users with accounts on a machine, there will be separate named subdirectories for each under the \Documents and Settings folder and, consequently, each user may have quite different services and applications auto launching on startup.

Keep in mind that the Startup folder might be empty for a particular user or for all users, although programs are running at startup. As discussed in the following sections, these programs could be started because of registry entries or entries in the Win.ini file.

REGISTRY ENTRIES: HKLM AND HKCU

Following the Startup program group(s), the next location where programs can be set for auto-launch is in the HKeyLocalMachine registry hive and, to a lesser degree, in the HKeyCurrentUser registry hive.

In either branch, the location is HK..\Software\Microsoft\Windows\CurrentVersion, where six relevant keys may be found:

- **\Run**—An application or process is executed on startup.

- **\RunServices**—A service such as an antivirus monitor is loaded on startup.

- **\Run (Disabled)**—An application was previously executed on startup but has been disabled (perhaps by Startup Manager or similar).

- **\RunOnce or \RunOnceEx**—An application is executed on startup but the entry is then deleted and the application is not executed again.

- **\RunServicesOnce**—A service is loaded on startup but the entry is then deleted and the service is not executed again.

The same keys may be found under HKeyCurrentUser where they would be specific to the currently logged on user.

Following is an example of the \Run and \RunServices keys:

```
[HKEY_LOCAL_MACHINE\SOFTWARE\Microsoft\Windows\CurrentVersion\Run]
    "Synchronization Manager"="mobsync.exe /logon"
    "Matrox Powerdesk"="C:\\WINNT\\System32\\PDesk.exe /Autolaunch"
    "Tweak UI"="RUNDLL32.EXE TWEAKUI.CPL,TweakMeUp"
    "APVXDWIN"="\"D:\\Program Files\\Panda Software\\Panda Antivirus
➡6.0\\APVXDWIN.EXE\" /s"
    "ScanInicio"="\"D:\\Program Files\\Panda Software\\Panda Antivirus
➡6.0\\Inicio.exe\""
    "3c1807pd"="C:\\WINNT\\SYSTEM32\\3cmlink.exe RunServices
➡\\Device\\3cpipe-3c1807pd"
[HKEY_LOCAL_MACHINE\SOFTWARE\Microsoft\Windows\CurrentVersion\RunServices]
    "PandaScheduler"="\"D:\\Program Files\\Panda Software\\Panda Antivirus
6.0\\Pavsched.exe\""
```

WIN.INI

The WIN.INI file is essentially obsolete but, for purposes of backward compatibility, is still recognized and, consequently, may still be the source of an autoexecute instruction.

The WIN.INI file is located in your \Windows directory and is an ASCII text file divided in several sections identified by labels enclosed in brackets. In the section identified as [windows], look for lines reading:

```
[windows]
run=application.exe
run=H:\QBWIN\DITTO.EXE
run=hpfsched
load=C:\subdir\application.exe
load=C:\MOUSE\POINTER.EXE
```

Either the run or load commands may indicate one or more applications delimited with semicolons, and each instruction may include parameters or flags. In general, the run instruction was used to launch applications while the load instruction was used for software drivers and similar utilities.

NOTE

These instructions may also appear as disabled entries:

```
run (Disabled)=application.exe
load (Disabled)=application.exe
```

USING THE SYSTEM CONFIGURATION UTILITY

While startup programs can be loaded from various parts of the Windows XP configuration, you can use a single tool, the System Configuration Utility, also known as msconfig, to disable or enable most startup programs.

To start the System Configuration Utility

1. Click Start, Run.

2. Type `msconfig` and click OK.

The System Configuration Utility for Windows XP has six tabs:

- **General**—Selects startup type and files to process (see Figure 9.14)
- **SYSTEM.INI**—Enables or disables hardware settings
- **WIN.INI**—Enables or disables software settings
- **BOOT.INI**—Adjusts boot options
- **Services**—Enables or disables system services
- **Startup**—Enables or disables startup programs

Figure 9.14
The Selective Startup option in System Configuration.

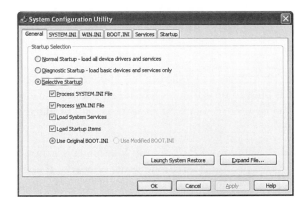

If you choose the Selective Startup option shown in Figure 9.14, you can disable all startup commands located in SYSTEM.INI, WIN.INI, System Services, or Startup Items. Clear the check box next to each category to disable the entire category. To disable a particular item instead, click on the tab and select the option to disable (see Figure 9.15).

Figure 9.15
Disabling Acrotray.exe from starting automatically.

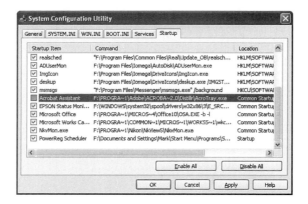

The changes made by the System Configuration Utility don't take effect until you restart your computer. Unlike other methods of disabling startup programs or services such as Registry editing or uninstalling programs, you can easily restore a disabled item back to the startup process by rerunning System Configuration.

TIP

It isn't easy to determine which programs are useful, useless, or might even be harmful from the list provided by System Configuration. I recommend using Paul Collins' Startups page (also known as Pacman's Portal – Startups) for both Windows XP users and users of other recent Windows versions. It provides a comprehensive list of startup programs; recommendations to help you determine if they're necessary at startup, can be run manually or should be uninstalled; and excellent links to startup managers, spyware detection and removal sites, and other startup resources.

Find it online at `http://www.pacs-portal.co.uk/startup_content.htm`.

DISABLE WINDOWS MESSENGER

Windows Messenger is built in to Windows XP and runs automatically in the taskbar, but because it can compromise user privacy, system security, and productivity, many business users prefer to disable it.

In the original version of Windows XP, Windows Messenger was not listed in the Add/Remove Programs list of Windows components. However, if you have installed Windows XP Service Pack 1, Windows Messenger Service can be disabled through Add/Remove Programs.

Even if you have not installed Windows XP Service Pack 1, there are several other ways to disable Messenger. I recommend this simple method:

1. Start Windows XP in Safe Mode.

2. Double-click My Computer to display the drives on the system.

3. Double-click the drive used by Windows XP. If a warning dialog is displayed, click as prompted to display the contents of the drive.

4. Double-click the Programs folder.

5. Right-click the Messenger folder. This is the folder which contains the Windows Messenger program.

6. Select Rename from the right-click menu and enter a new name. I recommend **MessengerDisabled**.

7. Shut down Windows XP, restart it, and Messenger does not start. The process can be reversed by renaming the MessengerDisabled folder back to its original name.

Because the folder name has been changed, Messenger cannot be started by Outlook, Outlook Express, or by Web pages.

THIRD-PARTY STARTUP PROGRAM MANAGERS

There are quite a few startup program managers available either as freeware or as inexpensive shareware, and an Internet search (use www.google.com and the keywords "startup manager") should provide you with leads to far more than you could possibly need. Links for several are included in the following text.

For the moment, the Advanced Startup Manager (see Figure 9.16) from Rayslab.inc will serve as a good example of how a startup manager functions.

Figure 9.16
Advanced Startup Manager allows you to manage the programs automatically launched when Windows is started.

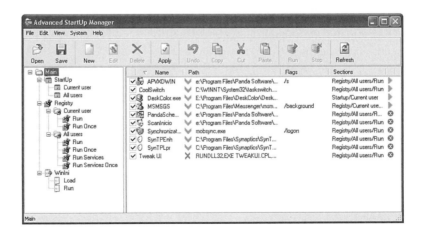

The Advanced Startup Manager is a rather nice example because, in the left pane, you can see the several locations where startup entries may occur. Further, by highlighting a branch or location in the left pane, the manager will show exactly which entries appear under that heading and location.

In the right pane, since the Main (root) entry is highlighted on the left, all of the various start entries are listed and individual items can be temporarily disabled by clearing the check box (left), or permanently removed by selecting and deleting the entry.

In particular, in this example, notice that the Advanced Startup Manager shows a breakdown by entry type, showing which items apply to all users in the startup group or in the registry and what type of entry is being executed.

Other versions of startup managers function in different ways but all should provide similar capabilities.

The following list provides links to several usable startup managers:

- `http://www.rayslab.com/startup manager/startup manager.html`
- `http://www.busterboy.org/startupmanager/`
- `http://www.startupmgr.com/startupmgr_desktop.htm`
- `http://www.pcworld.com/downloads/file_description/0,fid,5018,00.asp`

DOS APPLICATION COMPATIBILITY SETTINGS

Previously, the AUTOEXEC.BAT and CONFIG.SYS files—normally found in the root directory on your boot drive—were used to initialize the DOS environment. Today, the venerable AUTOEXEC.BAT file is replaced by AUTOEXEC.NT and the CONFIG.SYS file by a new configuration file CONFIG.NT, both of which are located in your \Windows\ system32 directory. Unless a different pair of startup files are specified in an application's .PIF (Program Information File), the AUTOEXEC.NT and CONFIG.NT files will be used to initialize the MS-DOS environment.

TIP

When a DOS program is executed by clicking on the application's .PIF icon, the pif settings take effect and control the application's DOS environment. If, however, a DOS application is executed from the command line (typing a command in a DOS box or using the RUN command from the start menu), settings in the .PIF file are not observed at all.

To ensure that the application's environmental settings are observed, instead of running the application directly from a command line entry—that is, instead of entering `appname`—enter the name of the .PIF file—for example, enter `appname.pif`—to launch the program.

AUTOEXEC.NT

The default AUTOEXEC.NT file provides a few basic configuration options such as:

```
REM  Install CD ROM extensions
lh %SystemRoot%\system32\mscdexnt.exe

REM  Install network redirector (load before dosx.exe)
lh %SystemRoot%\system32\redir

REM  Install DPMI support
lh %SystemRoot%\system32\dosx
```

As needed, additional configuration entries can be added to the AUTOEXEC.NT file following the same format as the previous AUTOEXEC.BAT file.

CONFIG.NT

The CONFIG.NT file has essentially the same structure and purpose as the earlier CONFIG.SYS file and can be edited to include any special configuration directives needed. There are, however, a few new entries which you may need to be aware of. These include

- **ECHOCONFIG**—When the DOS environment is initialized, by default, no information is displayed. If you want to display the CONFIG.NT and AUTOEXEC.NT settings instructions, add the command **echoconfig** to the CONFIG.NT startup file.

- **NTCMDPROMPT**—When execution returns to the command prompt from a TSR or while running a DOS-based application, Windows runs COMMAND.COM, allowing the TSR to remain active. To run CMD.EXE—the Windows command prompt—rather than the DOS COMMAND.COM, add the command **ntcmdprompt** to the CONFIG.NT startup file.

- **DOSONLY**—After opening a DOS window by executing COMMAND.COM, any type of application can be launched from the prompt. However, if an application other than a DOS-based application is executed, any running TSRs may be disrupted. Adding the command **dosonly** to the CONFIG.NT startup file ensures that only DOS-based applications can be launched.

> **NOTE**
>
> Both COMMAND.COM and CMD.EXE open DOS windows. COMMAND.COM, however, opens a Microsoft Windows DOS window while CMD.EXE opens a Windows XP DOS-emulation window. While both of these appear similar, the environment variables, EMM support, and path information for each can be quite different.

- **EMM**—The EMM command line can be used to configure EMM (Expanded Memory Manager), taking the form

  ```
  EMM = [A=AltRegSets] [B=BaseSegment] [RAM]
  ```

  AltRegSets sets the total Alternative Mapping Register Sets the system supports. The default value is 8 but the permissible range is 1 <= AltRegSets <= 255.

BaseSegment sets the starting segment address (in the DOS conventional memory) where the system allocates EMM page frames. The argument must be specified in hexadecimal format where 0x1000 <= BaseSegment <= 0x4000. All assignments are rounded down to 16KB boundaries while the default address is 0x4000.

RAM specifies that the system should only allocate 64KB address space from the Upper Memory Block (UMB) area for EMM page frames and leave the rest (if available) for DOS to support loadhigh and devicehigh commands. By default, the system will allocate the entire UMB for page frames.

The EMM size settings for an application are determined by the .pif file (either the specific .pif file associated with the application or the _default.pif file). If memory settings in the .pif file are zero, EMM will be disabled and the EMM settings in CONFIG.NT will be ignored.

Using .pif settings are discussed in the section "Configuring the DOS Emulation Environment."

SETTING ENVIRONMENT VARIABLES AND THE PATH

The default CONFIG.NT file contains three settings:

```
dos=high, umb
device=%SystemRoot%\system32\himem.sys
files=40
```

These three specifications, respectively, instruct the system to load DOS in high memory, to use the himem.sys memory manager in the \Windows\system32 directory, and set the maximum number of open files to 40. These settings, of course, apply only to the DOS environment used by the application.

The most common configuration changes required are to increase the number of file handles (files=nn) and to add a device specification such as device=ansi.sys.

You may also add additional environmental variables—although many of these can better be included in the application's .pif specification—as well as adding additional path information.

To add an additional path specification, use the form

```
path=%path%;d:\newdir\
```

The %path% argument preserves the existing path specification, appending the added specification to the end of the path.

Alternatively, the existing path specification can be replaced by simply assigning a new path as, for example

```
path=d:\newdir\
```

CONFIGURING THE DOS EMULATION ENVIRONMENT

In most cases, the preferred method of customizing the DOS emulation environment is to make changes to the .pif file for the application.

Originally, an application's .pif file was automatically created the first time the DOS application was executed and was located in the same directory where the application was placed. Today, however, the .pif file is placed in the \Windows\PIF directory and, since the directory is hidden, will not appear when you do a search.

The simplest way to edit the .pif file is to right-click on the application itself, and then select Properties from the pop-up menu to enter the pif editor as shown in Figure 9.17.

Figure 9.17
The PIF settings
General tab allows
you to customize the
DOS emulation envi-
ronment.

The General tab in the settings editor provides the usual file information maintained for all files and isn't really relevant to customizing the emulation environment.

The Program tab, seen in Figure 9.18, however, is where we can begin customizing the environment.

The Program tab provides options to set the command-line argument, set the working directory, set a batch file argument, assign a shortcut key, select a window type (normal, maximized, or minimized), and set the Close on exit option.

The Advanced button on the Program tab allows you to choose custom Autoexec and Config files (the defaults are AUTEXEC.NT and CONFIG.NT) while the Change Icon button allows selection of a new icon to represent the application.

Next, the Font tab—Figure 9.19—provides settings for the font used for the DOS display.

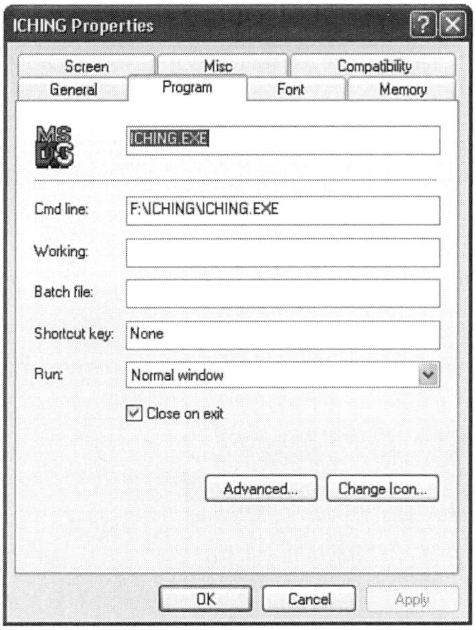

Figure 9.18
The PIF Settings
Program tab provides
options for setting the
command-line argu-
ment as well as other
customizations to the
DOS emulation envi-
ronment.

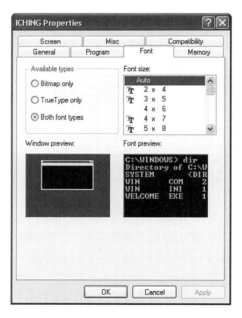

Figure 9.19
The PIF Settings Font
tab allows you to alter
the font used in the
DOS display.

Figure 9.20 shows the Memory settings tab where the amount of conventional, EMS, XMS, and protected mode (DPMI) memory allotted for the application can be specified.

Conventional memory is memory below 640KB. The Auto setting provides the maximum amount of conventional memory available. However, if a program requires a specific amount of conventional memory, you can choose from a wide number of values.

XMS memory is the specification for Extended memory (memory above 1MB). Recent Windows versions as well as Windows XP use XMS memory. DPMI memory is an older memory standard used to control memory above 1MB. Normally, leaving both of these settings at the default of Auto will work properly, but the values for both can be set to None or to a specified value as needed.

EMS memory is also known as Expanded memory, which was a method for accessing additional memory through a 64KB page frame located between 640KB and 1MB. This is normally set to None. If your program needs to use EMS memory (very common with older DOS games), you can select Auto or a specified value. However, you also need to specify EMM=RAM as discussed in the section "CONFIG.NT" earlier in this chapter.

Figure 9.20
The PIF Settings Memory tab allows you to modify the amount of Extended Memory used by older DOS games.

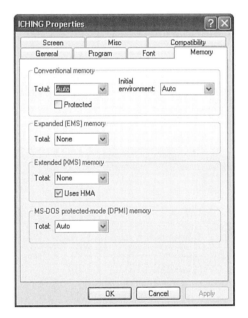

In Figure 9.21, the Screen tab offers a choice between Full-screen and Window for the DOS application, but also controls a couple performance options. When Fast ROM emulation is checked, the video driver emulates the video card's ROM features for additional speed. Dynamic memory allocation should be enabled for programs that use text and graphics memory; enabling this feature provides more video memory to other programs.

Figure 9.21
The PIF Settings
Screen tab allows you
to change the window
size in which DOS
applications appear.

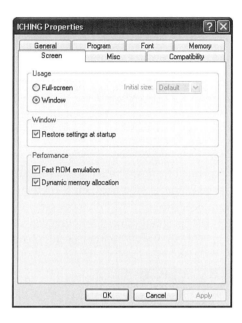

The Misc settings tab—Figure 9.22—covers a variety of options including the Foreground and Background performance, Mouse capture, Termination, Idle sensitivity, Fast pasting, and shortcut keys.

Figure 9.22
The PIF Settings Misc
tab allows you to futz
with a variety of PIF
settings.

Last, the Compatibility tab—Figure 9.23—allows the DOS app to be run in compatibility mode for Win95, Win98/Me, WinNT 4.0, or Win 2000. For more information about compatibility mode, see Chapter 32, "Crash Recovery."

Figure 9.23
The PIF Settings Compatibility tab allows DOS applications to run in compatibility modes for Windows 9x, Me, NT, and 2000.

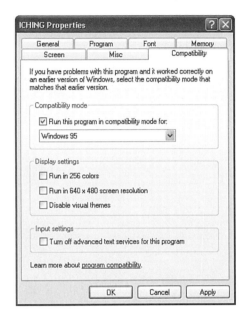

In addition, the Compatibility tab offers options for the display settings and advanced text services. Refer to the program compatibility link for more information on compatibility settings.

CHAPTER **10**

USING AND TUNING THE USER INTERFACE

In this chapter

10

MANAGING THE START MENU

The first thing I did after I installed Windows XP was click Start. When I saw that the familiar landscape of the Start menu had changed—a discovery that always fills me with at least some apprehension—I set out to discover just what the redesign was all about and what it would take to adapt, and I have to say, within a few minutes I began to appreciate these changes and found that the new menu made maneuvering through the Windows environment easier, helped to reduce desktop clutter, and could be better customized than the *classic* Start menu in previous versions of Windows.

But don't despair if you're one of those diehard classic Start menu fans. Windows has preserved the legacy configuration and allows you to switch back to the good old days with a few clicks of the mouse. Just right-click the Start menu, click Properties, and select the Classic Start Menu radio button on the Start Menu tab of the Taskbar and Start Menu Properties dialog box.

For the rest of you, read on to learn more about the new Start menu and how it can be customized to meet your personal needs.

TIP

> You can open the Start menu by clicking the Start button, by pressing the Windows logo key on your keyboard, or by pressing Ctrl+Esc.

DIVING IN TO THE NEW START MENU

The default Start menu is divided into two columns, as shown in Figure 10.1.

Figure 10.1
Default Start menu in Windows XP.

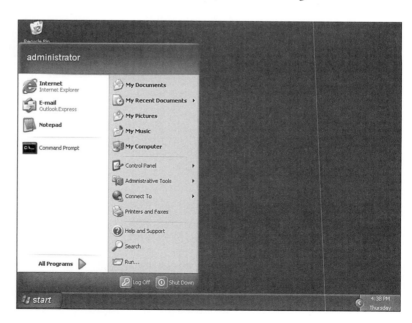

The left column includes shortcuts to various applications installed on your computer. The top section lists those shortcuts that you specifically want to appear here and the order that you want them in. Items in this section are referred to as *pinned* items. You can pin or unpin any application. By default, Internet Explorer and Outlook Express are added to this section.

The bottom section of the left column includes shortcuts to your six most frequently used applications. You cannot add shortcuts to this section or change their order. Only Windows XP can. However, you can remove shortcuts, and you can change the default number. When you first install Windows XP, several applications are already included in the list, such as MSN Explorer and Windows Movie Maker. Feel free to remove them as you like, or wait until they disappear through natural attrition.

I'll explain how to add and remove shortcuts from this column and change default settings later in this section. In the mean time, let's move on to the All Programs button at the bottom of the left column.

The All Programs button allows you to access the rest of the Start menu. You'll probably recognize this configuration from working with the Programs link in the Start menu in previous versions of Windows. In much the same way, you can enter the hierarchy of programs installed on your system. As with any link on the Start menu, just click or hover over All Programs to move to the next level in the hierarchy. To launch an application, simply click the icon.

The right column of the main Start menu includes shortcuts to Windows XP utilities and links to default folders created when you installed the OS. Windows allows you to display only certain shortcuts in this column. You can set which shortcuts these are by customizing the Start menu's properties, which I discuss later in this section.

The final items on the Start menu are the Log Off button and Shut Down button at the bottom of the menu. The Log Off button allows you to close your programs and log off, or leave your programs running and switch to another user. The Shut Down button also allows you to log off in addition to shutting down the computer, restarting the computer, or putting the computer in Standby mode or Hibernate mode.

NOTE

If you are running Windows XP Home Edition, you will see the Turn Off Computer button rather than the Shut Down button.

MANAGING ITEMS ON THE START MENU

Not all Start menu items are created equal. Some you can move, some you can pin, some you can delete. Others you can manage only through the Start menu's properties. In this section, I discuss those items that can be manipulated directly. For those items that you set up in the Start menu's properties, see the "Customizing the Start Menu" section.

PINNING AND UNPINNING APPLICATIONS

As I discussed earlier, pinning is the process of identifying which items should appear in the left column. You can *pin* almost any shortcut that is listed in the Start menu except My Recent Documents.

> **NOTE**
>
> My Recent Documents is a special folder that contains a list of the documents you opened most recently. This folder, which was referred to as Documents in the classic Start menu, is located in Documents and Settings*<username>*\\Recent.

You can use any of the following methods to pin an application listed in the Start menu:

- To pin an application in the frequently used applications section or in the All Programs menu, right-click the shortcut and click Pin to Start Menu.

- To pin an application listed in the frequently used applications section, drag the shortcut to the pinned section. When you pin an application that is listed in this section, it's removed from the list and appears only in the pinned section.

- To pin an application listed in the All Programs menu, drag the shortcut to the pinned section. This will pin the application without removing the shortcut from its original location.

You can also pin any program on the desktop, in Windows Explorer, or in My Computer by right-clicking the program file or shortcut and then clicking Pin to Start Menu. In addition, you can drag a program or shortcut to the Start button, which automatically adds a shortcut to the list of pinned applications.

> **NOTE**
>
> Internet Explorer and Outlook Express are added to the pinned section when you install Windows XP. Notice that the applications are labeled "Internet" and "E-mail," respectively. Although these items appear in the pinned section, they are handled differently from other pinned items. I'll discuss them in more detail in the "Customizing the Start Menu" section.

As you continue to use Windows XP, you'll no doubt want to unpin certain applications. Windows XP supports several methods for unpinning an item from the Start menu:

- You can unpin an item directly in the list of pinned applications by right-clicking the shortcut and then clicking Remove from This List, or clicking Unpin from Start menu.

- You can unpin an application from anywhere that the application is listed. For example, if you have a shortcut on your desktop for a pinned application, you can unpin the application by right-clicking the shortcut on the desktop and selecting Unpin from Start Menu.

- You can unpin the Internet or E-mail shortcuts from the pinned list by right-clicking the shortcut and then clicking Remove from This List.

ADDING ITEMS TO THE START MENU

The easiest way to add an application to the Start menu is to drag and drop the application file or shortcut from Windows Explorer, My Computer, or the Desktop and maneuver through the All Programs hierarchy. To add the item, drag and drop the icon over the Start button until the Start menu appears, then over the All Programs button until the programs menu appears, and through the layers of the All Programs menu until you reach your destination. This process creates the shortcut in the Start menu but leaves the program file in its original location.

NOTE
If you drag and drop the item in the pinned section rather than the All Programs menu, the application will be pinned. You cannot drag and drop an item to any sections other than the pinned applications section and the All Programs menu.

MANIPULATING ITEMS

Windows XP allows you to move and copy items within the Start menu, remove items from the menu, rename items, and sort items within the All Programs menu and the list of pinned applications.

TIP
You can manage items in the All Programs menu by accessing the folder in Windows Explorer and working with the shortcuts directly. Remember, though, that there are two folders that define the Start menu: the Documents and Settings\<*username*>\Start Menu folder and the Documents and Settings\All Users\Start Menu folder. The contents of the two folders are merged together to form the All Programs menu.

Your ability to move or copy items within the Start menu depends on the specific type of item:

- You can copy an item from the most frequently used applications list to the All Programs menu by dragging the item to the new location.
- You can copy an item from the pinned list to the All Programs list by dragging the item to the new location.
- You can move an item anywhere within the All Programs list by dragging it to its new location.
- You can move an item anywhere within the list of pinned applications by dragging it to its new location.
- You can copy an item anywhere within the All Programs list by dragging it while pressing the Ctrl key.
- You can copy items in the right column to the All Programs menu by dragging it to its new location.

Like moving and copying items, the procedure for removing an item depends on the type of item:

- You can remove an item in the left-hand column by right-clicking the item and then selecting Remove from This List.

- You can remove an item in the right column only by accessing the Start menu's properties, which is discussed later in this chapter.

- You can remove an item from the All Programs menu by right-clicking the item, clicking Delete, and then clicking Yes when prompted to confirm the deletion.

Often when you install a program, you'll find that you want to change the name that was assigned to the shortcut in the Startup menu. Windows XP makes this process very simple. Just right-click the shortcut, click Rename, and type in the new name. You can rename any of the following shortcuts in the Start menu:

- All shortcuts in the All Program menu
- All shortcuts in the most frequently used applications section
- All shortcuts that you added to the list of pinned applications
- My Documents, My Pictures, My Music, Favorites, and My Computer

Windows XP also allows you to sort listings in the All Programs menu. All you do is right-click the specific submenu that you want to sort, and click Sort by Name. The list for that particular submenu will be sorted alphabetically. You can also sort the list of pinned applications by dragging the shortcut from one place in the list to another.

CUSTOMIZING THE START MENU

I have found that I'm rarely satisfied with the default settings that are loaded with a new OS. My first task is to eliminate any marketing hype I come across (usually in the form of icons), and my second task is to customize the interface to suit my needs. And the Start menu is as good a place to begin as any.

Windows XP makes customizing the Start menu a very straightforward process. Simply access the Customize Start Menu dialog box and make the appropriate changes.

To access the dialog box, right-click the Start button and click Properties. On the Start Menu tab of the Taskbar and Start Menu Properties dialog box, click the Customize button next to the Start menu radio button. The Customize Start menu appears, with the General tab selected, as shown in Figure 10.2.

As you can see, the General tab includes several options that allow you to configure a number of items that appear in the Start menu. Table 10.1 describes each of these options.

Figure 10.2
General tab of the
Customize Start Menu
dialog box.

TABLE 10.1   OPTIONS ON THE GENERAL TAB

Option	Description
Select an Icon Size for Programs	You can choose the size of the icons that appear next to shortcut names. Using small icons saves space in the various lists.
Number of Programs on Start Menu	You can designate how many programs you want to have appear in the most frequently used applications list. If you pick zero, no application will appear.
Clear List	This button clears the list of shortcuts that appear in the most frequently used applications list.
Show on Start Menu	You can designate which application is tied to the Internet icon and which application is tied to the E-mail icon on the list of pinned applications. You can also remove either of these icons by deselecting the Internet check box or E-mail check box.

In addition to the options that you can set on the General tab, there are a number of additional options on the Advanced tab, as shown in Figure 10.3.

There's nothing really advanced about the options shown on this tab. They're just a different set of options and there's more of them. Table 10.2 provides an overview of many of these options.

Figure 10.3
Advanced tab of the
Customize Start Menu
dialog box.

TABLE 10.2   OPTIONS ON THE ADVANCED TAB

Option	Description
Open Submenus When I Pause on Them with My Mouse	If you deselect this item, you'll have to click on certain menu items for them to open submenus. However, this applies only to items in the main part of the Start menu, not to submenus. For example, if you deselect this option, you'll have to click the All Programs button to open the Programs menu, but you can hover over Administrative tools to open its submenu.
Highlight Newly Installed Programs	By default, newly installed menu items are highlighted, which makes them easier to find within the All Programs hierarchy. However, if you find this feature annoying (which I do), you can remove these highlights by deselecting this option.
Start Menu Items	For the most part, this section lists the items that are displayed in the right column of the Start menu. You can choose whether the item is displayed and how the link works. For example, you can set up Control Panel to link to the Control Panel folder or to open the folder contents as menu items. This section also includes the Enable Dragging and Dropping check box and the Scroll Programs check box, which are described next.
Enable Dragging and Dropping	This option serves two purposes. As its name suggests, it allows you to drag and drop menu items. However, it also determines whether a shortcut menu will appear when you right-click an item. This option must be selected to view the shortcut menus.

Option	Description
Scroll Programs	By selecting this option, you can display the contents of a submenu in a scrolling list, rather than columns.
List My Most Recent Opened Documents	When this box is checked, the My Recent Documents link appears on the menu and allows you to access your most recently used files.
Clear List	This button allows you to clear the list of documents that appear in My Recent Documents. It also clears the document shortcuts from the Documents and Settings\ <i>username</i>\Recent folder.

TIP

> You can customize the classic Start menu by opening the Taskbar and Start menu properties dialog box and clicking the Customize button next to the Classic Start menu radio button. The Classic Start menu option must be selected in order to customize the classic Start menu.

10

MANAGING DISPLAY PROPERTIES

Now that you have a good understanding of the Start menu, we can move on to display properties. In Windows XP, you can configure a wide variety of desktop settings by accessing the display properties. The process of configuring display properties is similar to previous versions of Windows. In fact, many of the settings are identical.

To access these properties, right-click anywhere on the desktop and select Properties. The Display Properties dialog box will appear and display the Themes tab. (You can also open this dialog box by selecting Display in Control Panel.) The dialog box includes five tabs, which I'll discuss individually.

CONFIGURING THEMES

The Themes tab is selected whenever you open the Display properties dialog box. The Themes tab, shown in Figure 10.4, allows you to select an existing theme or create a new theme based on your desktop configurations.

A *theme* forms the foundation for the look and feel of your desktop environment. It can be made up of such settings as your background, color scheme, windows and buttons style, fonts, icons, or screen saver. You can define most of the elements in a theme through the other tabs in the Display Properties dialog box.

By default, the desktop environment is configured with the Windows XP theme, which is the new *Luna* display scheme that was designed for Windows XP. For a journey down memory lane, you can choose the Windows Classic theme so that your systems looks like you're still living in the days of Windows 2000.

Figure 10.4
Themes tab of the
Display Properties
dialog box.

10

If neither of these themes are to your liking, Windows XP provides several other options:

- Define your own theme by configuring the display properties and saving these settings in their own file. This allows you to preserve any settings that you've configured should you want to switch between themes.

- Browse your computer or network directories for additional themes.

- Connect to the Microsoft Plus! Web site for additional themes.

- Search the Internet for third-party themes that you can apply to your display properties.

NOTE
> You might want to check out the WinCustomize Web site (www.wincustomize.com). They offer an online library that includes themes, icons, and skins, among other programs. A skin is a program add-on that applies a visual style, such as a window blind effect.

CONFIGURING THE DESKTOP

The next stop on the road to display nirvana is the Desktop tab, as shown in Figure 10.5.

On the Desktop tab, you can define which background you want to have appear on your desktop. You can choose a picture or a color. If you choose a picture, you can then choose its position. This, of course, depends on the size of the picture. If it takes up the full screen, you don't have to worry about whether to center, tile, or stretch the graphic across the screen. However, for those smaller pictures, you'll want to determine how to position the picture, and if you center the picture, you'll want to choose a background color to surround it.

Figure 10.5
Desktop tab of the
Display Properties
dialog box.

NOTE

If you choose the Stretch option, Windows XP enlarges the picture until it fills the screen. This can greatly distort the picture. Although the effect might be interesting, it might not be what you're looking for. However, if the picture is larger than the size of the screen, using the Stretch option will shrink the picture to fit into the desktop. If stretching is turned off and the picture is larger, the outer portions of the picture will be cut off.

CUSTOMIZING THE DESKTOP

The Desktop tab also includes the Customize Desktop button. If you click this button, the Desktop Items dialog box appears, as shown in Figure 10.6.

Figure 10.6
General tab of the
Desktop Items dialog
box.

The Desktop Items dialog box includes two tabs: the General tab and the Web tab. The General tab allows you to set up certain desktop icons and run the Desktop Cleanup Wizard.

→ We'll be discussing the Web tab later in this chapter; **see** "Adding Web Content to Your Desktop," **p. 376**.

At the top of the General tab, you can choose any of four shortcuts (My Documents, My Computer, My Network Places, and Internet Explorer) to appear on your desktop.

Notice anything missing from this list of available shortcuts? That's right: the Recycle Bin icon. It's not included with the four icons on the General tab and you can't delete it directly on the desktop. However, there is a workaround for getting rid of the shortcut; you can modify one of the local group policies:

1. Select Run from the Start menu. The Run dialog box appears.

2. In the Open text box, type `gpedit.msc` and then click OK. The Group Policy console appears.

3. In the policy tree, open User Configuration\Administrative Templates\Desktop.

4. In the preview pane, double-click Remove Recycle Bin Icon from Desktop. The Remove Recycle Bin icon from desktop Properties dialog box appears.

5. Select the Enabled radio button and click OK. The policy will take effect next time you log on to the computer.

CAUTION

> Enabling the Remove Recycle Bin Icon from Desktop policy removes the icon not only from the desktop, but from Windows Explorer and programs that use Windows Explorer. In addition, changes to local group policies affect all users on your computer.

SHORTCUTS DON'T APPEAR ON THE DESKTOP

It's possible that the option that controls whether icons appear on the desktop has been deselected. If your icons are not appearing, right-click anywhere on the desktop, point to Arrange Icon By, and select Show Desktop Icons. Note that the Show Desktop Icons option will have a checkmark next to it if it is selected.

Once you've selected this option, the Recycle Bin icon and any other icons you've added to the desktop should now appear. (The Recycle Bin icon will not appear if it's been disabled in Group Policy.)

If any of the My Documents, My Computer, My Network Places, or Internet Explorer icons are missing, open the Display Properties dialog box, select the Desktop tab, and click Customize Desktop. On the General tab of the Desktop Items dialog box, select the icons that you want to have appear on the desktop.

NOTE

> Here's another option you might want to check out as a way to remove the Recycle Bin icon—Tweak UI. Tweak UI is one of the PowerToys for Windows XP utilities that you can download from Microsoft (www.microsoft.com). The PowerToys tools are a collection of programs that enhance the functionality of Windows XP, and best of all, they're free (although Microsoft doesn't support them). Tweak UI allows you to access and modify system settings that are not exposed in the Windows XP interface.

Let's return to the General tab of the Desktop Items dialog box. In addition to being able to add shortcuts to the desktop, you can change icons for My Documents, My Computer, My Network Places, and Internet Explorer. You can also change the Recycle Bin (full) and Recycle Bin (empty) icons.

At the bottom of the tab is another new Windows XP feature, the Desktop Cleanup Wizard. The wizard allows you to choose which shortcuts to remove from your desktop. The shortcuts are then placed in the Documents and Settings*username*\\Desktop\\Unused Desktop Shortcuts folder. A shortcut to the folder is added to your desktop. You can then delete any shortcuts from the folder or use them when necessary.

The Desktop Cleanup Wizard is scheduled to run every 60 days. You can deselect this option, or you can leave it selected but change the number of days in the registry. Open the Regedit tool and go to HKCU\\Software\\Microsoft\\Windows\\CurrentVersion\\Explorer\\Desktop\\CleanupWiz. Double-click the Days Between Cleanup value. Change the Base to Decimal and enter in the number of days in the Value data text box.

CAUTION

> You should use great care whenever editing the registry. An incorrect value can conflict with other settings and affect overall performance, damage your system, or prevent your system from starting.

Whether or not you schedule the Desktop Cleanup Wizard to run at regular intervals, you can still launch the wizard at any time by clicking the Clean Desktop Now button at the bottom of the General tab.

CONFIGURING THE SCREEN SAVER

Moving on to the next tab...the Screen Saver tab is almost identical to how it appears in Windows 2000. You can select a screen saver, choose not to use a screen saver, configure screen saver settings, preview the screen saver, and enable password protection.

NOTE

> Here's a fun little screen saver you might want to check out—CubeShow, which you can download from the PC Magazine Web site (www.pcmag.com). The utility allows you to display your own images in a tumbling, three-dimensional cube.

The tab also allows you to launch the Power Options Properties dialog box, which is the same dialog box that opens when you launch the Power Options utility in Control Panel, as shown in Figure 10.7.

Figure 10.7
The Power Schemes tab of the Power Options Properties dialog box.

The Power Options Properties dialog box allows you to configure a number of power-related settings:

- You can define power schemes that determine when the monitor and hard disks should be turned off and when the system should be put into standby and hibernate modes.
- You can configure settings related to the low battery alarm and to the critical battery alarm.
- You can view the current power source and the amount of power remaining in the batteries.
- You can set up your options to display an icon on the taskbar or prompt for a password when the computer resumes from standby.
- You can determine which action Windows XP will take when you press the power button on the computer.
- You can enable hibernation on the computer.

You can probably tell from this list that the options available in the Power Options Properties dialog box will vary depending on whether you're using a laptop or desktop computer. For example, the battery-related options are unique to laptops.

CONFIGURING THE DESKTOP'S APPEARANCE

The Appearance tab in the Display Properties dialog box allows you to choose a style for your windows and buttons. You can choose Windows Classic style or Windows XP style. As I mentioned earlier, the Windows Classic style is similar to what you were used to in

Windows 2000, and the Windows XP style is the new Lunar look and feel that gives Windows a facelift.

As was the case in Windows 2000, the Appearance tab also allows you to select the color scheme and the font size. However, two additional options have been added: the Effects button and the Advanced button.

CONFIGURING EFFECT OPTIONS

When you click the Effects tab, the Effects dialog box appears, as shown in Figure 10.8.

Figure 10.8
Effects dialog box.

For the most part, the options in the Effects dialog box are self-explanatory. You either select them or you deselect them. However, a couple are worth looking at further.

In the first option, Use the Following Transition Effect for Menus and Tool Tips, you can choose how certain windows open and close. If you deselect this option, windows will pop open and close, without fading back into place. If you select this option, and then choose Fade Effect or Scroll Effect, the window will ease into place. However, on some displays, you might not see much of a difference between the two effects.

The next option, Use the Following Method to Smooth Edges of Screen Fonts, includes two options: Standard and Clear Type. In theory, Clear Type is supposed to improve the clarity of types running on LCD monitors. However, this was not my experience. I found that the Standard option was much clearer than the Clear Type option, and deselecting the check box produced the same results as selecting Standard.

Your best bet with any of the options on the Effects dialog box is to play around with them and see what results you come up with.

TOOL TIPS OR STATUS AREA MESSAGES DISPLAYED INCORRECTLY

On some displays, you might find that part of a tool tip or part of a message from the status area of the taskbar is only partially displayed, or the message remains after it should disappear. This problem can be caused by using a transition effect for menus and tool tips.

To resolve this problem, you should disable any transition effect options:

1. Open the Display Properties dialog box.

2. Select the Appearance tab and click Effects.

3. In the Effects dialog box, clear the option Use the Following Transition Effect for Menus and Tooltips.

4. Click OK, and click OK again.

CONFIGURING ADVANCED EFFECT OPTIONS

If you click the Advanced button on the Appearance tab of the Display Properties dialog box, the Advanced Appearance dialog box appears. This dialog box allows you to set the color and size of specific items in the interface, such as the active title bar or menu. You can also configure the font for the selected items. Remember to save these settings to your theme file if you want to retain them.

CONFIGURING THE DESKTOP'S SETTINGS

The Settings tab, like the Screen Saver tab, is nearly identical to how it appears in Windows 2000. You can set the screen resolution and color quality, and you can launch a troubleshooting tool that helps you determine what problems you might have with your screen settings. The Settings tab also includes an Advanced button, which opens the properties for your computer's monitor and video adapter. Figure 10.9 shows the dialog box that appears for my laptop computer when I click the Advanced button.

Figure 10.9
Default Monitor and Trident Video Accelerator 3D Cyber9397DVD Properties dialog box.

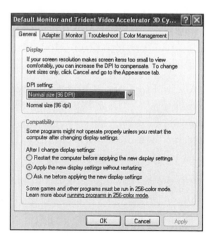

The dialog box includes five tabs that provide information about your monitor and video card and that allow you to modify display settings. The tabs are described in Table 10.3.

TABLE 10.3	TABS IN THE PROPERTIES DIALOG BOX
Tab	**Description**
General	You can change the DPI setting, which changes the size of items as they appear on the screen. You can also set when changes to display settings will take effect: after restarting your computer, without restarting your computer, or after you're prompted to apply the new settings.
Adapter	You can view information about your adapter and access your adapter's properties. The properties allow you to troubleshoot the device, update or roll back the driver, or uninstall the driver. You can also view the resources used and possible device conflicts. The Adapter tab also lists all valid modes that your adapter supports, such as 800×600, True Color (32 bit), 60 Hertz.
Monitor	You can change the screen refresh rate and access the monitor's properties. The properties allow you to troubleshoot the device and enable or disable the device. You can also update, roll back, or uninstall the driver.
Troubleshoot	You can set the hardware acceleration, which controls the level of video processing that is performed by the adapter, as opposed to the CPU. The more processing performed by the adapter, the better. You can also enable write combining, which speeds up your display and improves performance; however, increased speed can sometimes cause screen corruption.
Color Management	You can add color profiles to the monitor and set one as the default. Color profiles communicate with the color management system. The profile contains information about the color characteristics of the device. The color management system uses this information to ensure that colors will be consistently and accurately presented on all your devices, such as scanners, printers, and monitors.

CAUTION

Be certain not to set the refresh rate too high for your monitor. A rate that's too high could cause display problems or damage the monitor.

CONFIGURING VENDOR-SPECIFIC PROPERTIES

It is not uncommon for video drivers and display-related software to add tabs to the Display Properties dialog box. These tabs provide additional options that help you configure or refine your display beyond what is supported in Windows XP. When additional tabs are installed, be sure to read the documentation that accompanies the software. It should provide you with specific information about the new options.

You'll want to make sure you don't choose options that mess with your video monitor in untoward ways. For example, you might have options in your Display properties dialog that tweak the refresh rate beyond what the monitor can handle (such as high refresh rate) or reposition or resize the image off the edges of the monitor. Since monitors also have their own positioning controls, there might be some interactions to consider. Some tabs might also control the use of external secondary monitors and/or TV output on the video card. For example, the later ATI Rage chipsets have some pretty complicated (and confusing) tabs that let you declare which monitor is primary, which is secondary, and set individual refresh rates, scaling, sync method, and resolutions for each one.

NOTE

> Third-party applications are available to enhance and expand your display. For example, Pivot software from Portrait Displays, Inc. allows you to rotate your computer's display from landscape to portrait on monitors that support rotating displays. This is especially handy for individuals who want to be able to view an entire document, rather than having to scroll up and down to see the whole page.

ADDING WEB CONTENT TO YOUR DESKTOP

As with earlier versions of Windows, Windows XP allows you to add Web content to your desktop. The content is displayed in small windows which are essentially mini browsers that can be resized and moved around just like your Internet Explorer browser. These windows are sometimes referred to as Active Desktop components, although I'm seeing the term *Active Desktop* used less than it used to be. Even Windows XP Help refers to these items simply as Web content.

In addition to adding content that displays Web pages, you can add pictures (.bmp, .gif, .jpg, .jpeg, .dib, .png) or HTML documents (.htm, .html, .mhtml, .url, .cdf) that are located on your computer or network. The process is basically the same whether adding content from the Web or from your network. You can also add items from the Microsoft Desktop Gallery, which provides Web content that includes such things as weather reports, stock ticker reports, and satellite tracking.

ADDING A DESKTOP ITEM

Adding Web content to your desktop is pretty straightforward. Open the Display Properties dialog box, select the Desktop tab, and click Customize Desktop. When the Desktop Items dialog box appears, select the Web tab, which is shown in Figure 10.10.

The Web tab includes the Web pages list, which contains the links to content sources. The My Current Home Page link is created by default. You can add new links, delete current ones, activate or deactivate links, synchronize their content, or view the properties for those links that are actual Web pages, as opposed to files on your network.

To add a new link, click the New button. This opens the New Desktop Item dialog box, as shown in Figure 10.11.

Figure 10.10
Web tab of the
Desktop Items dialog
box.

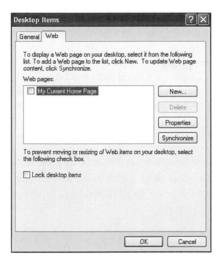

Figure 10.11
New Desktop Item
dialog box.

You can add a link by taking any of the following steps:

- Click the Visit Gallery button to go the Microsoft Desktop Gallery Web site. Once at the site, click the Add to Active Desktop button next to the item you want on your desktop. Follow the prompts. The Web content is automatically added to your desktop.

- Add a URL or file path to the Location text box. The file path can be either the complete path and filename, or you can enter the path for just the folder, in which case that folder will appear on your desktop in one of the browser windows. Once you've added the URL or path, click OK. The new link will be added to the Web pages list on the Web tab of the Desktop Items dialog box.

- Click the Browse button to select a picture or HTML document from your computer or the network. You cannot use this method to add just a folder. Once you've selected the file, click Open. The path is added to the Location textbox in the New Desktop Item dialog box. Click OK to add the link to the Web pages list.

NOTE

> You may have noticed that when you clicked View Gallery, you were linked to the Internet Explorer 4.0 Desktop Gallery site; at least that is what was happening during the writing of this book. This alone should have alerted you to a problem, given that Windows XP comes equipped with Internet Explorer 6.0. I found that I could download some items but not others. I also found that Microsoft documentation had little to say about the Desktop Gallery as it relates to Windows XP. Perhaps in the near future there will be more information available.

You must be connected to the Internet to add an active link to your desktop. An *active* link is any link that connects to a live Web site, as opposed to links to files and pictures on your computer or network. When you add an active link, the page is synchronized with the live content and then added to the Web pages list.

By default, a new link is enabled when it's added to your list of Web pages. You can disable the link by deselecting the check box. You can also synchronize the contents of a Web page by selecting the link and then clicking the Synchronize button. Again, you must be connected to the Internet to synchronize a Web page.

You can also lock desktop items. If you select the Lock Desktop Items check box (on the Web tab of the Desktop Items dialog box), you will not be able to move or resize the browser window on your desktop.

CONFIGURING A WEB PAGE'S PROPERTIES

You can configure the properties of any active link in your list of Web pages, whether or not the link is disabled. To configure the properties, highlight the link and click Properties. This will launch the Properties dialog box for that link. Table 10.4 describes each of the tabs in the dialog box.

TABLE 10.4   TABS IN THE PROPERTIES DIALOG BOX

Tab	Description
Web Document	You can view information about the link and download history as well as set whether this page is available offline. By default, the page is available offline.
Schedule	You can schedule when you want to synchronize the Web page. You can set it for manual only, or you can set up a synchronization schedule based on days and times.
Download	You can define which content to download (how many links deep from the page) and limit hard disk usage for the page. You can also send an email notification when the page changes. If the originating site requires a password, you can configure it through this tab. In addition, you can configure which items to download (for example, images) and whether to follow links only to HTML pages.

WORKING WITH THE WEB CONTENT WINDOWS

All enabled links will appear on your desktop. As long as you haven't locked the desktop items, you can move them and resize them as necessary.

Figure 10.12 shows a desktop with three Web content windows displayed: the MSNBC Weather site, the NASDAQ home page, and a picture on the local hard disk.

Figure 10.12
Desktop with three Web content windows displayed.

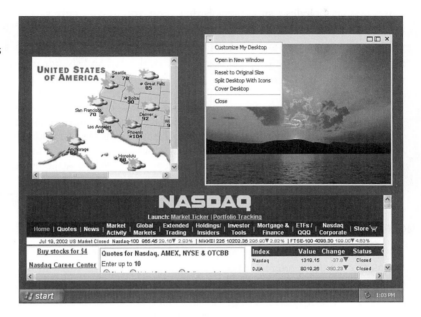

When you point to one of these windows, a border appears. The size and type of border depends on where you point in the window:

- If you point in the center of the windows, a small border appears around the image.
- If you move your cursor toward the edge of the image, the border thickens, and you can then resize the window.
- If you move your border toward the top of the image, a menu bar appears. The menu bar includes icons that allow you to expand the window, close it, or view a drop-down menu that contains additional options. Active content will include more options than windows connecting to local files.

TIP

The drop-down menu includes the same options represented by the icons as well as options specific to that link. However, it also includes the Customize My Desktop option, which opens the Desktop Items dialog box, with the General tab selected. It might seem strange to you that the General tab is selected, rather than the Web tab, but getting this far will still save you a couple steps.

I recommend that you experiment with the various options and try resizing the windows to see how it affects your displays. If your image contains links, you can click on one and the new page will be displayed in Internet Explorer, assuming you're connected to the Internet.

CONFIGURING ACCESSIBILITY FEATURES

Windows XP includes a suite of tools that allow you to configure various levels of accessibility on your computer. For example, you can magnify areas of the screen, display messages in place of warning tones, and filter repeated key strokes. With the Windows XP accessibility tools, you can configure your keyboard, mouse, display, and sounds in a way best suited to meet your individual needs.

NOTE

> The Windows XP accessibility tools provide only a minimal level of accessibility to users with certain types of disabilities. These users often require functionality more advanced than what the Windows XP tools can support. For this reason, this section references other products that might be useful to users with disabilities. At the very least, they're worth checking out.

USING THE MAGNIFIER TOOL

The Magnifier tool provides a window (at the top of the screen by default) that magnifies the portion of the screen near the pointer or cursor. Figure 10.13 shows the tool as it appears when the cursor is on a Notepad document.

Figure 10.13
Using the Magnifier tool in Windows XP.

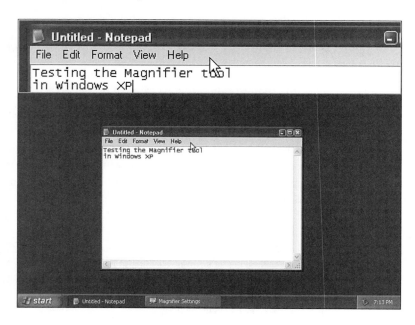

The tool is easy to implement and use. Click Start, point to All Programs, then Accessories, then Accessibility, and click Magnifier. When the Magnifier Settings dialog box appears, select or deselect the appropriate options, and minimize the dialog box.

You can resize the Magnifier window by dragging down the bottom bar. You can also move the window and then resize it by clicking it and dragging it to another place on your desktop.

NOTE

> PowerToys for Windows XP also includes a desktop magnifier tool called Taskbar Magnifier. Taskbar Magnifier is similar to Magnifier, only the window can sit only on the taskbar and is very small. However, for some users, this might be ideal. You might also want to check out ZoomText Xtra from AI Squared (www.aisquared.com). ZoomText supports different zoom windows and partial-screen enlargement.

USING THE NARRATOR TOOL

The Narrator tool is a text-to-speech utility (screen reader) that reads the contents of the screen out loud. The Narrator can read such things as menu commands, dialog box options, or characters as you're typing them. To launch the Narrator tool, click Start, point to All Programs, then Accessories, then Accessibility, and click Narrator. When the Narrator dialog box appears (and starts to speak), select or deselect the appropriate options, and minimize the dialog box.

NOTE

> Freedom Scientific (www.freedomscientific.com) offers scanning and reading applications that convert a printed page into electronic information. This information can then be read out loud through the included voice synthesizer or displayed for people with low vision. IBM (www-3.ibm.com/able) offers Home Page Reader, a text-to-speech application that provides an interface for Web navigation and manipulation.

USING THE ON-SCREEN KEYBOARD TOOL

There's really not any trick to working with the On-Screen Keyboard tool. To start using it, Click Start, point to All Programs, then Accessories, then Accessibility, and click On-Screen Keyboard. A graphical representation of a keyboard appears on the desktop, as shown in Figure 10.14.

Once the keyboard is launched, you can configure the keyboard in the Keyboard menu and the Settings menu. The Keyboard menu allows you to set the size and layout, whereas the Settings menu allows you to configure how you want the keyboard to work. For example, you can choose a typing mode that allows you to hover over a key to select it.

Figure 10.14
Using the On-Screen
Keyboard tool in
Windows XP.

USING UTILITY MANAGER

Utility Manager is a handy little tool that allows you to start, stop, and set up administrative options for Magnifier, Narrator, and the On-Screen Keyboard tools. To launch Utility Manager, press the Windows logo key + U, or click Start, point to All Programs, then Accessories, then Accessibility, and click Utility Manager. The Utility Manager dialog appears on your desktop, as shown in Figure 10.15.

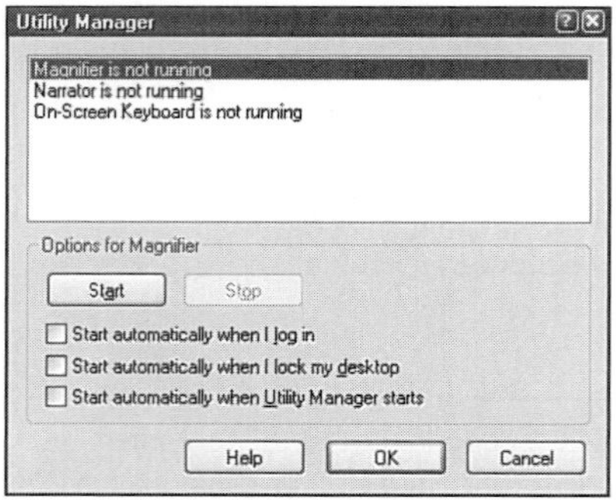

Figure 10.15
Utility Manager dialog
box.

The administrative options in Utility Manager allow you to start a selected tool automatically when you log in, when you lock your desktop, or when Utility Manager starts. By default, Narrator is configured to start when Utility Manager starts.

TIP

> You can use the Windows logo key + U shortcut to launch Utility Manager before you log in to Windows XP, when the Welcome to Windows screen appears. Of course, you won't be able to configure any of the administrative options at the bottom of the screen until you're logged in, but you can start or stop any of the three accessibility tools.

If you start an accessibility tool from Utility Manager, it is immediately launched, or if you stop a tool it immediately closes. Any tool that you start or stop outside of Utility Manager is reflected in the list of tools within Utility manager.

ADMINISTRATIVE OPTIONS IN UTILITY MANAGER CAN'T BE CONFIGURED

If you start Utility Manager through the start menu, the administrative options might not be available. The administrative options are the three options at the bottom of the dialog box. If this occurs, close Utility Manager and launch it by using the Windows logo key + U shortcut key combination. When Utility Manager appears, all three options should be available. You can then open Utility Manager by using the shortcut key or by using the start menu, as long as you're running within the same session.

If you find that the first two options are available, and the third option—Start Automatically When Utility Manager Starts—is grayed out, then you are not logged on as an administrator. You must log out and then log back in as an administrator or run Utility Manager under the context of an administrator account by using the Run As command or the Runas command-line utility. See the "Running Programs as Another User" section for more information about running an application as another user.

USING THE ACCESSIBILITY OPTIONS UTILITY IN CONTROL PANEL

The Accessibility Options dialog box includes a number of tools and settings that you can use to configure accessibility settings. To access the Accessibility Options dialog box, click Start, point to Control Panel, and click Accessibility Options. From there, you can configure the following tools and settings:

- **StickyKeys**—Allows the Shift, Alt, Ctrl, and Windows logo keys to act as if they're being held down when pressed once.

- **FilterKeys**—Causes Windows to ignore accidentally repeated keystrokes. A key must be held down for several seconds for that key to register.

- **ToggleKeys**—Sounds a high-pitched tone when Caps Lock, Num Lock, or Scroll Lock are pressed.

- **SoundSentry**—Causes a portion of the normal Windows screen to blink in place of a sound generated by events such as errors. Usually it is the window or application generating the error that blinks.

- **ShowSounds**—Causes a text caption or special icon to appear on your screen in place of a generated sound.

- **High Contrast**—Increases the screen contrast by altering the display properties.

- **Cursor Options**—Controls the speed that the cursor blinks and the width of the cursor.

- **MouseKeys**—Allows you to control the mouse by using the numeric keypad on your keyboard.

- **Automatic Reset**—Turns off the accessibility features after your system has been idle for a specified amount of time.

- **Notification**—The first option provides a warning message when a feature is turned on. The second option makes a sound when turning a feature on or off.

- **SerialKey Devices**—Allows you to connect a special input device to a free serial port.

- **Administrative Options**—The first option applies accessibility settings to the logon desktop, which is the desktop you see when you're logging on. The second option applies settings to new users.

10

NOTE

A number of third-party tools are available to enhance accessibility in a Windows XP environment. For example, Dragon Naturally Speaking from ScanSoft (`www.scansoft.com`) is a voice recognition program that comes in several versions that can be used in personal and professional environments. ViaVoice, from IBM (`www-3.ibm.com/software/speech/`), is also a voice recognition program that can support both personal and professional. Another useful product, Liquid View from Portrait Displays, Inc. (`www.portrait.com`), improves the legibility of the Windows XP interface by manipulating the display registers and preference settings.

USING THE ACCESSIBILITY WIZARD

The Accessibility Wizard guides you through the process of setting up the various accessibility settings on your system. To run the wizard, click Start, point to All Programs, then Accessories, then Accessibility, and click Accessibility Wizard. Follow the screens to configure your system.

Depending on the options you configured in the wizard, changes might have occurred in the Accessibility Options utility, the display properties, or one of the accessibility tools. It's not always easy to tell where properties might have been changed after running the wizard, and you might find yourself searching through various settings to modify a property that you would have preferred not to have had changed. In the long run, I think you're better off learning the tools that are specific to your needs and configuring them manually.

MANAGING MULTIPLE APPLICATIONS

Here's what Windows operating systems do: multitask. That means the computer can run more than one program at a time, a feature I (and most of us, no doubt) take full advantage of. At any one time, I might have several Word files open, maybe one or two text files, my browser (multiple instances!), the Command Prompt window, and perhaps an administrative tool or two, just to keep life interesting. And then there's Explorer, Outlook, Visio, Excel, TechNet, Help, and on and on and on. What this amounts to is a desktop that looks more like a jigsaw puzzle than a powerful interface to a sophisticated operating system that can run many applications simultaneously.

The question, then, is how do you handle these numerous applications and maneuver painlessly through your desktop jungle so you're not incapacitated by a display crammed with windows and icons? Luckily, Windows XP provides a number of options that allow you to move smoothly from application to application, manage your programs, and organize your desktop so you're not spending all your time just trying to figure out what's running and where it is.

USING THE TASKBAR

One way to work with multiple applications is by using the taskbar. The taskbar in Windows XP works much the same way it did in Windows 2000. When you launch an application, a button is added to the taskbar. You can then click the button to restore or minimize the window. You can also right-click the button to access additional options that allow you to perform such tasks as restoring, minimizing, maximizing, or closing the window. Which options are available depends on the state of the window when you access the menu. For example, if the window is already displayed on your desktop, the Restore option is grayed out.

The great thing about the taskbar is that it makes switching from one application to another as simple as a click of the mouse. However, the simplicity continues to diminish each time you launch another application, leaving you with a taskbar that looks like the one in Figure 10.16.

Figure 10.16
Taskbar without grouping enabled.

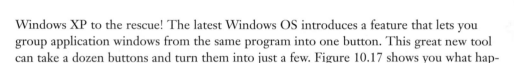

Windows XP to the rescue! The latest Windows OS introduces a feature that lets you group application windows from the same program into one button. This great new tool can take a dozen buttons and turn them into just a few. Figure 10.17 shows you what happens when you group the buttons from the previous figure into their application families.

Figure 10.17
Taskbar with grouping enabled.

Now all you do is click the tiny down arrow on the group button to view the list of files associated to that button. You can then treat each item in the list as you did a nongrouped button on the taskbar: Click the item to minimize or restore the window, or right-click the item to view other options, as shown in Figure 10.18.

Figure 10.18
The shortcut menu for the Local Security Setting icon.

TIP

> You can minimize all the windows at the same time by pressing the Windows logo key + M, or restore them all at the same time by pressing the Windows logo key + Shift + M. If you're using the Quick Launch toolbar, you can click the Show Desktop button to minimize all the windows.

To enable grouping on your taskbar, right-click a clear area of the taskbar and select Properties. The Taskbar and Start Menu Properties dialog box appears. On the Taskbar tab, select the Group Similar Taskbar Buttons check box and click OK.

NOTE

> If you open the Taskbar and Start Menu Properties dialog box by right-clicking the taskbar, the Taskbar tab will be selected. If you open the dialog box by right-clicking the Start menu, the Start Menu tab will be selected. You can also open the dialog box by selecting Taskbar and Start Menu in Control Panel, in which case the Taskbar tab will be selected.

SWITCHING APPLICATIONS WINDOWS

Okay, so you have your taskbar icons all grouped together in nice neat little packages and can easily move from one application to the next. However, you might find that even this is a little too cumbersome for your lightning speed operations and you would prefer to use the keyboard, rather than the mouse, to switch applications. Here's where the Alt+Tab keyboard shortcut comes in.

If more than one application is open on your desktop, the simplest way to switch between them is to press Alt+Tab. When you press this key combination, a small window appears that displays icons representing each of the application windows, as shown in Figure 10.19.

Figure 10.19
The Alt+Tab window displaying icons for the open application windows.

The icon that's highlighted is the one that will open when you release the keys. If you want to select a different window, continue to hold down the Alt key and re-press the Tab key. This will move the highlight one icon to the right. Press the Tab key as many times as necessary until the icon you want is highlighted. The application will open when you release the Alt key.

You can reverse the direction that the highlight moves by pressing Alt+Shift+Tab. Again, the highlight will move one icon each time you press Tab.

You can also switch between open application windows by pressing Alt+Esc. An icon window is not displayed when you use this method; instead, you merely switch from window to window. If you hold down the Alt key and re-press the Esc key, you will cycle through the application windows. You can reverse the order that you cycle through the windows by pressing Alt+Shift+Esc.

TIP

> PowerToys includes the Task Switcher utility, which works with the Alt+Tab functionality to switch between applications. The tool displays a thumbnail preview of the windows, in addition to the icons.

USING TASK MANAGER

I have found that one of the handiest administrative tools in Windows XP is Task Manager. In addition to allowing you to manage your applications and processes, you can also monitor your system's performance, local area connection, and users. It's a sort of one-stop shopping utility that gives you a quick overview of what's going on with your system and where performance problems might exist. And best of all, it allows you to kill those applications that might be hanging up your system and causing you endless grief.

10

You can use any of several methods to open Task Manager:

- Press Ctrl+Alt+Delete.
- Press Ctrl+Shift+Esc.
- Right-click the taskbar and select Task Manager.

CTRL+ALT+DELETE DOESN'T OPEN WINDOWS SECURITY DIALOG BOX

If your computer is configured to support Fast User Switching, you can use the Ctrl+Alt+Delete method to open Task Manager. Otherwise, the Ctrl+Alt+Delete method works a little differently. Instead of the Welcome screen appearing, the Windows Security dialog box appears, and from there you can open Task Manager.

To enable Fast User Switching, you must meet the following criteria:

- Your system must be a standalone computer or a member of a workgroup. It cannot be a member of a domain.
- User accounts must be configured to use the Welcome screen.
- Offline files must be disabled.

➔ For more information about Fast User Switching, **see** Chapter 11, "Creating and Managing User Accounts," **p. 407**.

The Windows Task Manager dialog box, shown in Figure 10.20, contains five tabs and a number of menus that allow you to perform such tasks as controlling how you view information in Task Manager, running applications, logging off, or shutting down the computer. Although the menus appear separate from the tabs, the options available in each menu vary according to the tab that is selected.

Figure 10.20
Applications tab in
Task Manager.

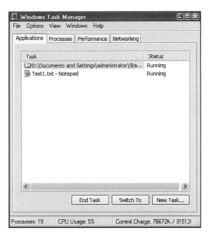

TIP

> A particularly useful command to know about in Start menu is the Always On Top item in the Options menu. By default, this option is selected, which means that Task Manager will always sit on top of any other application windows open on your desktop. Deselecting this option might save you a lot of frustration as you're switching between applications.

MANAGING APPLICATIONS

The Applications tab in Task Manager (see Figure 10.20) lists all the applications you have running on your desktop and the status of each application. This can be very handy information to have if you find that applications are slow and hanging. Usually, but not always, if an application is hung, the status will be listed as Not responding. If this occurs, you can select the application from the Task list, and then click End Task. This will close the application.

TIP

> It's possible that Task Manager appears not to be responding to stopping or starting applications. The problem might be because Task Manager has been paused. To verify this, click the View menu, select Update Speed, and verify that Paused is not selected. If, for some reason, you want to keep Paused enabled, select Refresh Now from the View menu. Keep in mind that it can take time to stop some applications. The best approach is sometimes just to wait a bit to allow the issue to resolve itself.

Before giving an application the old heave ho, you might want to wait a bit to see whether it's just being slow to process everything it needs to process or it's waiting for a response from another resource on your intranet or the Internet. For example, sometimes your browser will appear not to be responding if it's waiting to download a page. If you can avoid it, try not to end an application because this can cause instability in the operating system (although it usually doesn't). In addition, if you end an application unnecessarily, you could lose data.

TIP

Sometimes a macro within an application will hang and cause the program to stop responding, even though the application itself is fine. Try pressing Esc within the application before terminating it in Task Manager.

The Applications tab also allows you to switch to the selected application by clicking the Switch To button or double-clicking the application. Using Task Manager for this purpose alone would be a long-about way to get from one application to another, but if you're already within Task Manager, it can be a handy feature.

You can also launch a new program from the Applications tab by clicking the New Task button. When the Create New Task dialog box appears, enter the executable name of the application in the Open textbox or search for the application by clicking Browse. This process is the same as launching an application from the Run dialog box, even though the names of the dialog boxes are different.

MANAGING PROCESSES

As you can guess from its name, the Processes tab, shown in Figure 10.21, lists the processes running on your system. If there are multiple users on your computer, you can list the processes for all users. Notice that Task Manager in Windows XP now displays the security context (user, service, or system object) under which the process is executing. You can also select other types of information to display, such as I/O reads and I/O writes.

Figure 10.21
Processes tab in Task Manager.

In the Processes tab, you can end almost any process by selecting that process and clicking the End Process button. (You can also right-click the process and select End Process.) There are some system-level processes that you cannot end, even if you're logged in as an administrator. In addition, you can end the process tree by right-clicking the process and clicking End Process Tree.

When you end a process, it is stopped immediately. For example, if you ended the notepad.exe process, the Notepad application would immediately close, and you would lose any data that had not been saved. If you close Notepad from the Applications tab, it would close just like it did if you were to close it from within the application, which means you would have an opportunity to save any unsaved data. Whenever possible, close a program from the Applications tab, rather than from the Processes tab.

TIP

> You can also use the Taskkill command-line utility to end a process. (Taskkill is a replacement for the old Kill tool.) The easiest way to use the tool is to run it with the process identifier (PID) as one of its parameters. The Tasklist command-line utility allows you to view running processes and their PIDs. See Help and Support Center for more information about both of these utilities.

Task Manager also allows you to set the priority of each process. There are six priority levels: Realtime, High, AboveNormal, Normal, BelowNormal, and Low. Typically, it's not necessary to change the default priority, but if you decide to do it, right-click the process, point to Set Priority, and select the new priority level. You should avoid setting processes to High that might interfere with essential operations.

CAUTION

> Processes running under the SYSTEM security context are used by the kernel. You should avoid altering the priority of any of these processes. Altering one of these processes could make your system stop working. Fortunately, changed priority levels do not persist across a reboot, so if you get yourself in trouble, restart your computer and start over.

In some cases, raising the priority level of a process can improve an applications performance. If you think that it might be useful to do this, make your changes in small increments (one priority level at a time). Don't jump from Low to High without testing your changes at each level to see what the hits are on performance and system stability.

MONITORING PERFORMANCE

The Performance tab is my favorite one because it's got all those cool graphs about CPU and page file usage and history (see Figure 10.22). The tab also gives you information about memory, threads, processes, and handles. Together, this information provides a dynamic overview of your system's performance.

The graphs themselves on the Performance tab are pretty self-explanatory. You might have noticed that the two lower graphs now display page file usage, rather than memory usage, as was the case in earlier versions of Windows. What is of particular note here are two options available on the View menu. The CPU History option allows you to display different graphs for each CPU (assuming you have more than one), and the Show Kernel Times option changes the CPU graphs to display kernel activity in red and all other activity in green.

Figure 10.22
Performance tab in
Task Manager.

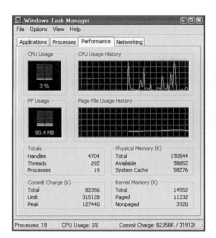

The Totals section is another self-explanatory area. This section lists the number of handles, threads, and processes that are currently running on the computer.

The Commit Charge (K) section displays the amount of virtual memory that your system uses. The Total figure is the amount being used by all processes, the Limit figure is the amount that can be committed (without enlarging the paging file), and the Peak figure is the maximum amount used in the session. The Peak amount can sometimes exceed the Limit amount if virtual memory is expanded.

The Physical Memory (K) section provides total amount of memory installed on your computer, the amount of memory available for applications before disk caching begins, and the amount of memory the system is using for caching.

The Kernel Memory (K) section provides the information about the memory used for kernel operations. The nonpaged memory can be used only by the operating system, whereas the paged memory can be used by other programs when necessary.

MONITORING YOUR NETWORK CONNECTION

The Networking tab displays a history graph of and other information about the activity on your local area connection, as shown in Figure 10.23. The tab is handy to provide you with a quick look at what's going on with your network connection in case you suspect a problem.

The main portion of the screen is devoted to the graph. You can display it as is, or you can configure it to show bytes sent (red), bytes received (yellow), and total bytes (green). To change the information displayed on the graph, open the View menu, point to Network Adapter History, and select the appropriate options.

At the bottom of the Network tab is a table that provides information on each network adapter configured on your system. You can customize the type of information that's displayed in the table by selecting the Select Columns option from the View menu. From there, you can choose the information you want to display.

Figure 10.23
Networking tab in
Task Manager.

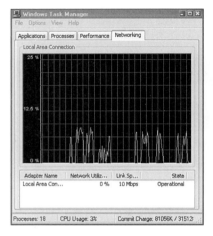

MONITORING YOUR USERS

The Users tab (shown in Figure 10.24) provides a list of users on your system or connected via a network.

Figure 10.24
Users tab in Task
Manager.

By default, the list includes the user's ID, status, client name, and session; however, you can modify what information is displayed by selecting the Select Columns option from the View menu. From this tab, you can also disconnect a user, log off a user, or send a user a message.

USERS TAB DOESN'T APPEAR IN TASK MANAGER

The Users Tab is available in Task Manager only if Fast User Switching is enabled. To use Fast User Switching, you must meet the following criteria:

- Your system must be a standalone computer or a member of a workgroup. It cannot be a member of a domain.

- User accounts must be configured to use the Welcome screen.
- Offline files must be disabled.

→ For more information about Fast User Switching, **see** Chapter 11, "Creating and Managing User Accounts," **p. 407**.

Using Advanced Features in Windows XP

Windows XP includes a number of advanced features that allow you to better utilize its powerful interface and work with applications within that interface. This section takes a look at several of the features and techniques that you can use to take better advantage of the OS and its environment.

Using the Open and Save As Dialog Boxes

The Open and Save As dialog boxes in Windows XP applications include a number of great features that go way beyond simply opening or closing a file. The dialog boxes are essentially Windows Explorer windows that allow you to perform such tasks as searching folders, deleting files, viewing folder properties, setting up shares, or almost anything else you can do in Explorer.

For the most part, the dialog boxes are pretty similar to one another and from application to application, at least within those applications that ship with Windows XP. Other applications, such as Office XP, support more functionality than the Windows XP applications; however, even among the built-in applications there are differences. For example, the Save As dialog boxes for Notepad and Internet Explorer include an Encoding drop-down list, but WordPad and Paint do not.

One of the nice features about the Open and Save As dialog boxes is the ability to resize them just like any other window. The only limitation is that the dialog box has a set minimum size, and you can't make it any smaller than that.

In some cases, such as with Internet Explorer, when you select Open from the File menu, the Open dialog box that appears is just a simple dialog with few options. However, if you click Browse, the dialog box that opens will be more like what you would expect in a Windows XP application.

You can group the options in the Open and Save As dialog boxes into three categories: the window options, the places bar, and the folder and file list.

Window Options

When you look at an Open or Save As dialog box, you'll notice that the window includes several options, as shown in Figure 10.25.

10

Figure 10.25
The Open dialog box
for Notepad.

The Places bar is the column of icons on the left. The folder and file list, to the right of the Places bar, is the list of files and folders contained within the selected folder. (The Places bar and folder and file list are discussed in the following sections.) Above and below the folder and file list are a number of icons and drop-down lists that allow you to move around, change views, or open or save a file. All these options are the same as they were in Windows 2000, except for the Encoding drop-down list.

The Encoding drop-down list provides a list of encoding schemes (character sets) for a particular application. For example, Notepad supports several encoding schemes, including ANSI and Unicode. With this option, you can convert a file to a particular character set when you open it or when you save it, which gives you greater flexibility when working with documents that use different character sets.

NOTE

Earlier I mentioned that WordPad doesn't include the Encoding drop-down list; however, you can open or save WordPad documents as Unicode text documents, which you do by selecting the Unicode Text Documents option from the Files of type drop-down list.

You probably noticed that one of the icons at the top of the dialog box is the View Menu icon, which opens a drop-down list that contains options for viewing the folder and file list. By default, the List view is selected, but you can change the view to Thumbnails, Tiles, Icons, or Details. Unfortunately, you can't make your change persistent. Whenever you open an Open or Save As dialog box, the List view will be selected.

PLACES BAR

The Places bar provides some handy links to several folders, including My Recent Documents, Desktop, My Documents, My Computer, and My Network. This configuration is similar to how the Places bar appears in Windows 2000, except that now the My Documents folder is included. Unfortunately, you can't customize or remove the places bar unless you use a third-party tool, such as Tweak UI, to configure the interface.

Folder and File List

As in Windows 2000, you can view a list of the folders and files that are contained in the selected folder. For example, if you refer again to Figure 10.25, you'll see that the selected folder is My Documents, which contains three folders—My Music, My Pictures, and My Received Files—and a number of text files.

You can open a folder or file by double-clicking the name or icon, or you can right-click the file or folder and select from a number of options in the shortcut menu. For example, if you right-click a folder, you can open it, search its contents, rename it, or take one of many other actions, just like you would do in Windows Explorer. Some folders support options unique to their type of folders. The My Music folder, for instance, includes an Add to Playlist option and a Play option. You can also share a folder from within the Open or Save As dialog boxes.

The shortcut menus for files provide many of the same options as folders, such as cut, copy, or delete. You can also specify that the file be opened in a specific application. For example, you can open a text file in WordPad, rather than the default Notepad.

You should spend time playing with all the options in the shortcut menus as well as all the other options to become familiar with the Open and Save As dialog boxes. The more comfortable you are with the various features, you more you'll be able to utilize the power of each of these windows.

Using the Taskbar to Move Objects

As you're no doubt aware, you can use drag-and-drop techniques in a variety of ways to move or copy objects from one place to another. For example, you can drag a picture from a folder in Windows Explorer to your desktop, or you can drag an application file to the Start menu to create a shortcut.

Another useful drag-and-drop technique is to drag an object from one application window to another through the buttons on the taskbar. This is especially useful if you have a number of windows open and you don't want to have to search for the target window before you can drag an object to it. For example, suppose you have several WordPad documents open on your desktop, along with a number of other applications. The first document has a .jpg file attached to it that you want to copy to one of the other documents. Rather than trying to display both windows side-by-side so you can drag the picture from one to the other, you can drag the object to the taskbar button and then to the target document.

The simplest way to illustrate how you do this is to walk you through the steps:

1. In the first application window, drag the object to the taskbar button for the target window.

2. Hover over the button until the application window appears. If multiple instances of an application are open and your toolbar buttons are grouped, hover over the button until the list of open windows appears, and then hover over the specific link until the application window appears.

3. Drag the object to the target window and release the mouse button. The object will be inserted in the target document.

Throughout this process, remember to keep the mouse button depressed until you reach the target window. You'll have to experiment with different applications to see which ones allow you to use this process and how the process might differ from one to the next. You'll find that different effects will occur depending on where you drop the object. In some applications, you must drop the object in the document window, whereas in other applications, you must drop the object in the title bar. In some cases, such as Photoshop, dropping the object on the title bar opens a new document, while dropping it within the document window pastes the item to that document.

CHANGING THE DEFAULT LOCATION OF MY DOCUMENTS

Windows XP, like Windows 2000, allows you to change the destination folder where the contents of My Documents are stored. By default, these contents are stored in the \Documents and Settings\<*username*>\My Documents folder. However, you can change the default folder and move the contents from that folder to the new one.

You must use the My Documents properties to change the target folder. You can access the properties through the My Documents icon in the Start menu, on the desktop, or in Windows Explorer. If you access the properties through Explorer, you must use the icon at the top of the folder tree, just beneath Desktop. You cannot use the properties of the actual target folder (\Documents and Settings\<*username*>\My Documents).

Follow the steps below to change the target folder for My Documents.

1. Right-click the My Documents icon in the Start menu, on the desktop, or in Windows Explorer, and then select Properties. The My Documents Properties dialog box appears.

2. On the Target tab, take one of the following steps:

   • Enter the target folder in the Target text box, and then click OK. If the folder doesn't exist, you'll be prompted to have it created. Click Yes.

   • Click Move, and then select the folder where you want to store the My Documents contents. You can also choose to make a new folder at this point. When you're returned to the Target tab, click OK.

3. When you're prompted to move all documents into the new location, click Yes.

When you create a new target folder and move all the documents over, the \Documents and Settings\<*username*>\My Documents folder is deleted. However, you can restore the default properties by once again accessing the Target tab:

1. Right-click the My Documents icon in the Start menu, on the desktop, or in Windows Explorer, and then select Properties.

2. On the Target tab, click Restore Default, and then click OK.

3. When you're prompted to move all documents back to the default location, click Yes.

RUNNING PROGRAMS AS ANOTHER USER

It's generally considered good practice to log on to your system as a regular user (for example, a member of the Power Users group) when performing day-to-day tasks, and to log on as an administrator only when you need to perform tasks that require administrative privileges. This is especially true when working in a networked environment in which you might be the administrator for more than one computer on the domain or, more importantly, a domain administrator. Yet no matter what reward you might reap from being a good network citizen, it can still be a bit of an inconvenience if, when logged on as one type of user, you want to run a program that requires the privileges of another type of user.

Windows XP provides several methods that allow you to run that program in a security context other than the one you're logged on as. You can use the Run As utility, the Runas command-line utility, or the Fast User Switching feature.

USING THE RUN AS UTILITY

The Run As utility is very straightforward to use. When you go to launch the program—whether from the Start menu, a desktop icon, or in Windows Explorer—right-click the program name or icon and select Run As. This will launch the Run As dialog box, as shown in Figure 10.26.

Figure 10.26
The Run As dialog box.

In the Run As dialog box, select the The Following User radio button, enter the appropriate user name and password, and click OK. The program will open under the new security context. When you enter your user name, you must include the name of the domain or computer name. For example, if you want to run a program using the Administrator account in the Domain01 domain, you must enter domain01\administrator as the user name. You can also enter a user principal name (UPN) when logging in, which in this case would be administrator@domain01.com.

The Run As functionality does not work with all programs. For example, you can't use it to open Windows Explorer or any of the Explorer folders, such as Printers and Faxes and My Documents. In most cases, it's easy to tell that you can't use Run As to open an application; when you right-click the program name or icon, the shortcut menu doesn't include a Run As option. Unfortunately, Windows Explorer includes this option, and when you click it, the Run As dialog box appears. But if you enter your user name and password and then click OK, nothing happens (other than the dialog box disappearing). After a few seconds you're likely to realize that the program isn't going to launch, but you never receive any sort of notification or error message.

PROGRAM WON'T RUN UNDER DIFFERENT USER

There are several reasons why a program might not run under the context of another user:

- The user account must have a password. Both the Run As command and the Runas command-line utility require that a password parameter be passed when launching a program in the context of another user. If a password is not received, even if the user has a blank password, the application will not run.

- If you're using the Run As command to run a program, you must include the domain name or computer name as part of the user name (for example, domain01\administrator). If you're using the Runas command-line utility, you need to supply a domain name if you're using a domain account, but you don't have to supply a computer name for a local account.

- Security policies and permissions might prevent the new user from accessing the program. Be sure that the domain and local policies as well as permissions permit access.

- The Secondary Logon service must be running to use the Run As command and the Runas command-line utility. To verify whether the Secondary Logon service is started, view the service in the Services administrative tool.

USING THE RUNAS COMMAND-LINE UTILITY

The Runas command-line utility is similar to the Run As utility, except that you run the command-line utility from the Run dialog box, a Command Prompt window, or in a shortcut. Regardless of which location you choose, the syntax is the same:

```
runas /user:<username> <program>
```

There are, of course, a number of additional parameters that you can set. For a complete description of each of these parameters, look up the utility in the Help and Support Center.

If you want to run an application in the context of a domain account, you must include the name of the domain in the user parameter:

```
runas /user:domain01\administrator notepad
```

This example opens an instance of Notepad in the context of the domain's Administrator account. If you want to open Notepad in the context of the local administrator account (on a computer named xppro05), you can use either of the following commands:

```
runas /user:xppro05\administrator notepad
```

```
runas /user:administrator notepad
```

As soon as you run one of these commands, you'll be prompted for a password. You'll notice that, as you type your password, nothing happens on the screen. It will seem as though your keyboard is not working. However, Windows XP is still recording your password, so type it as you normally would and click Enter. If you've entered the correct information, your program will be launched.

You can also create a shortcut on your desktop and launch the Runas utility from there. This is a handy way of making a program always ready to run in the context of another user. For example, suppose you regularly log in as a standard user but you just as regularly need to open a Command Prompt window in the context of the local administrator. The easiest way to handle this is to create a shortcut that contains the Runas command with the appropriate parameters.

To create the shortcut, follow the steps below:

1. Right-click your desktop, point to New, and select Shortcut.
2. In the Create Shortcut screen, type the Runas command and parameters in the Type the Location of the Item text box. Click Next.
3. In the Select a Title for the Program screen, type a name for your shortcut in the Type a Name for This Shortcut text box.
4. Click Finish. The shortcut is added to your desktop.

You can then double-click the shortcut to launch your program. The only information you'll need to provide is your password.

Using Fast User Switching

As you probably know, Fast User Switching allows you to switch between users without logging them off the system. If, for example, you're logged on with a standard account, you can easily switch to an administrator account without having to log off or close out your applications. All you need to do is click Log Off on the Start menu, and then click Switch User. When the Welcome screen appears, click the name of the administrator account, and you'll be switched to that user. When you're finished with whatever tasks you wanted to perform, simply switch back to the original user.

→ For more information about Fast User Switching, **see** Chapter 11, "Creating and Managing User Accounts," **p. 407**.

WORKING WITH DOS APPLICATIONS

In 1981, Microsoft released MS-DOS for IBM and IBM-compatible PCs. A single-tasking operating system with a command-line interface, MS-DOS managed program execution, oversaw file maintenance, and controlled operations such as disk I/O and keyboard input. By tech age standards, this might seem like ancient history and of little relevance to the world of Windows XP. Yet DOS has not been totally relegated to the annals of electronic history, and Windows XP makes room for those legacy DOS applications through the Virtual DOS machine (VDM) environment subsystem.

The VDM mimics the hardware and software of an MS-DOS computer. When you run a DOS application, Windows XP runs it through the VDM, which allows Windows XP to emulate the DOS operation and translate the program's requests into Windows XP commands.

The nice part about the DOS environment is that you can configure a number of settings that determine how Command Prompt windows are displayed and how DOS applications run. Windows XP allows you to configure properties within a Command Prompt window that affect either that window or all subsequent instances of Command Prompt, as well as change an application's properties, modify environment variables, configure startup files, or use environment-altering commands.

YOU CAN'T INSTALL A DOS PROGRAM

When you install a DOS program, you might receive an error message that says that an installable virtual device driver failed DLL initialization, or a message that says that the virtual device driver format in the registry is invalid. Sometimes all you need to do is to click Ignore, and the program will run properly.

However, it's possible to receive one of these messages if a virtual device driver registry value is corrupt. This can sometimes happen when you install a 16-bit application. It can also occur if you install an application that uses a 16-bit installation program that is not Windows XP-compliant.

To resolve this issue, you must edit the registry:

1. Start the Regedit registry editor utility.
2. Delete the VDD value in
   `HKEY_LOCAL_MACHINE\SYSTEM\CurrentControlSet\Control\VirtualDeviceDrivers`.
3. Create a new multi-string value and name it VDD.
4. Quit Regedit.

CONFIGURING PROPERTIES IN A COMMAND PROMPT WINDOW

A Command Prompt window is a good place to start configuring your DOS environment. Command Prompt (cmd.exe) is a 32-bit Windows application that provides a DOS-like command-line environment in which you can run DOS programs and other types of programs from the command line. The process of running a program is the same as it was in previous versions of Windows; you type the command at the command prompt—along with the appropriate parameters—and press Enter.

Windows XP also includes the Command.com program, which is DOS's old command shell. For the most part, Cmd.exe replaces Command.com unless you're running a legacy DOS application that requires the old shell. Otherwise, it's generally recommended to go with Cmd.exe because of its enhanced functionality.

To open a Command Prompt window, select Run from the Start menu, type **cmd** in the Open text box, and click OK. You can open as many instances of Command Prompt windows as you like. You can also open a new Command Prompt window from within another Command Prompt window by typing **start** or **start cmd** at the command prompt.

TIP

> If you open a Command Prompt window and it's running in full-screen mode, you can switch to a regular window display by pressing Alt+Enter. You can switch back to full-screen mode by using the same key combination.

Once the Command Prompt window is open, you can configure its properties or run a program. Property settings affect not only the window itself, but any DOS programs that you run within it.

To access the window's properties, open the control menu (by clicking the Command Prompt button in the upper left corner) and click the Defaults option or the Properties option:

- If you click Defaults, the Console Windows Properties dialog box appears. Any settings you change here affect all future Command Prompt sessions except those launched from a shortcut whose properties have been modified or those DOS-based applications with a configured program information file (PIF). (PIFs are discussed a little later in this section.)

- If you click Properties, the *<pathname>* Properties dialog box appears. If you change any settings you can choose whether to have those settings affect only the current window or affect future windows with the same title.

Both dialog boxes include the same options. Figure 10.27 shows the dialog box that appears when you click the Defaults option.

Each of the Properties dialog boxes includes four tabs: Options, Font, Layout, and Colors:

- **Options**—Cursor size, display size, buffer size, and number of processes that can have history buffers. You can also set options that eliminate duplicate commands in the buffer, enable you to use a pointing device to cut and paste, and enable you to insert text at the cursor.

- **Font**—Available fonts and font sizes.

- **Layout**—Screen buffer size, window size, and window position.
- **Colors**—Available colors for screen text, screen background, pop-up text, and pop-up background.

Figure 10.27
Options tab of the Console Windows Properties dialog box.

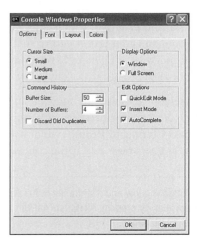

TIP

For a description of each of the options in the dialog boxes, click the question mark (?) icon and then click the option. A pop-up menu will appear with a description of the selected option.

MODIFYING AN APPLICATION'S PROPERTIES

In addition to modifying Command Prompt properties through its windows, you can modify properties for the individual DOS application's executable file. When you modify the executable's properties, Windows XP creates a PIF for that file. The PIF contains properties such as memory allocation, screen settings, and font size.

An application's PIF is displayed as a shortcut, usually in the same folder as the executable file. The shortcut has the same name as the executable file. You can modify the properties of the application file or the PIF shortcut. Changes made in either place are applied to the PIF. If you create a different shortcut to the executable—for example, on your desktop—you can modify the properties for that shortcut as well; however, those changes affect the application only when you run it through that particular shortcut. The beauty of this is that you can create multiple shortcuts (with different names) that allow you to open an application with different settings, should this need ever arise.

Which properties are applied to the application when you run it depends on where and how it is launched:

- If you double-click the application file or PIF shortcut, the PIF settings are used.
- If you double-click a shortcut (other than the PIF shortcut), the settings specific to that shortcut are used.

- If you launch the application in a Command Prompt window, the window's settings are used.

- If you launch the application in a Command Prompt window, but use the Start command (for example, `start pictview`) to start the program, the PIF settings are used.

- If you launch the application from the Run dialog box, the PIF settings are used.

NOTE
If Windows XP cannot find a PIF for an application, it uses the default PIF file. You can view and modify the default PIF setting by accessing the properties for the _Default shortcut in the Windows folder. Any properties that you modified by selecting the Defaults option in a Command Prompt window are reflected in the _Default PIF shortcut. When you open a Command Prompt window, it uses the properties of the default PIF. Any application that you run from that window uses the default settings unless they are overwritten by an application PIF file, a shortcut, or properties that you modified after you opened the window.

TIP
To change the properties in the _Default PIF shortcut, you need to be logged on as an administrator. If you're logged on as a user who is not an administrator, you'll have to log off and then log on with an administrator account. You cannot use the Run As command or the Runas command-line utility to change shortcut properties.

Whichever properties you modify, the configuration process is the same: Right-click the application file, the PIF shortcut, or any other shortcut, and select Properties. When the Properties dialog box appears, modify the settings as necessary. Figure 10.28 shows the properties for the PictView shortcut. PictView for DOS is a freeware image viewer and converter that reads and writes files in a number of different formats.

As you can see, there are a variety of property settings that you can configure, such as conventional and expanded memory usage or font size and screen preferences. You should review each tab and its options so that you're comfortable with how the settings can be configured. Remember, if you don't understand one of the options, click the question mark (?) button and then click the option to view an explanation. Also be certain to check any documentation that might have come with your DOS applications for instructions on how to set up the environment.

SETTING ENVIRONMENT VARIABLES

I want to touch briefly on the issue of environment variables. An environment variable is a string that consists of environment-related information, such as a file or folder, associated with a variable name used by Windows XP. For example, Windows XP, by default, includes an environment variable named %windir%. On my system, the value for %windir% is D:\Windows. Whenever the %windir% variable is used, Windows XP knows that it refers to the D:\Windows folder.

Figure 10.28
General tab of
PictView Properties
dialog box.

In most cases, you won't have to be concerned with environment variables, as they relate to running DOS applications; however, you might find that you want to add a folder to the system's search path or that the DOS application requires that a specific environment variable be set.

To access the environment variables, double-click the System icon in Control Panel to open the System Properties dialog box. On the Advanced tab, click Environment Variables. The Environment Variables dialog box is shown in Figure 10.29.

Figure 10.29
Environment Variables
dialog box.

In this dialog box, you can edit, add, or delete user variables and system variables. The user variables apply only to the logged on user. Note that the variables are listed without the percentage signs.

CONFIGURING STARTUP FILES

When you launch a DOS program, a VDM is created and two configuration files— Config.nt and Autoexec.nt—are loaded into the VDM. This process is repeated for each DOS application that you launch. The two files, like their legacy counterparts Config.sys and Autoexec.bat, contain system startup information that defines certain parameters related to how your application runs.

You can create custom startup files based on Config.nt and Autoexec.nt and then point your application to these files so they're loaded into the VDM when the program is launched. Basically, you must create the files and modify the program's properties, as outlined in the following steps:

1. Copy the Config.nt and Autoexec.nt files to a new folder, or copy the files to within existing folder (%SystemRoot%\System32), but give the copies new names.
2. Use a text editor such as Notepad to edit the new files.
3. Open the properties for the specific application or one of its shortcuts.
4. On the Program tab of the Properties dialog box, click Advanced. The Windows PIF Setting dialog box appears, as shown in Figure 10.30.
5. Enter the paths and filenames for the new files, and click OK.

Figure 10.30
Windows PIF Settings dialog box.

Now whenever the application is launched, it will use the settings from the new Config and Autoexec files. Remember, though, that you can't launch the application from just any-where. For example, if you add the new files to a shortcut's properties, the application won't use these settings if it's launched from the Run dialog box. Refer to the "Modifying an Application's Properties" section earlier in this chapter for more information.

USING ENVIRONMENT-ALTERING COMMANDS

There is one other method that you can use to affect how a DOS application will run, and that is to run subsystem commands at the command prompt. For example, you can use the Loadfix command to load a program above the first 64KB of conventional memory, or you can use the Device command to load a device driver into memory. For a complete list of the commands available in Windows XP, go to the Help and Support Center.

TIP

Most commands provide an online reference that you can access by typing the command name, a space, and then /?. For example, to view the reference for the Set command, type `set /?`, and information about the command will be displayed in the Command Prompt window.

CHAPTER **11**

CREATING AND MANAGING USER ACCOUNTS

In this chapter

SIGNING ON AND OFF

Unlike its Windows 9x and Windows Me predecessors, Windows XP is built from the ground up to support multiple user accounts. XP requires each user to log on before using the computer so that it can apply the user's security privileges and desktop preferences and locate the user's personal files and folders (the user's *profile*).

When you sign on locally--which means you are physically at the keyboard of the machine--six possible scenarios exist:

1. You loaded this system on your own and this is the first boot, so you'll access the machine using the local Administrator account and password that you'd assigned during setup.

2. You've previously created usernames and passwords for this system, and you currently have the required credentials needed to access the local machine.

3. This system is part of a domain, and you access it using your domain authentication information.

4. This system is part of a domain, and you access it by logging on using a Smart Card with a stored PIN number.

5. This system uses no security and boots straight to a usable desktop. (Actually, Windows does use user-level security in this scenario; it just automatically logs you on with a stored username and password.)

6. You do not have access to this system, and you're hoping I'll tell you some sneaky way to get into it without knowing the password.

Depending on the applicable scenario, you'll see one of four screens. If this system uses an automatic logon and boots straight to the usable desktop, you'll be at the desktop, Start bar at the bottom, ready to go. Non-domain systems display a Welcome screen, and systems joined to the domain--as well as standalone systems that have been so configured--display a familiar Windows NT/2000 family logon screen. I'll discuss these scenarios in the following sections.

THE LOGON DIALOG

If the system is a domain member or a standalone member configured to use the classic-style logon screen, you'll see the good ol' Press Ctrl-Alt-Delete to Begin message box shown in Figure 11.1. If you're reading this book, you should already know the basics of what to do next.

CAUTION

Many people are unaware that two different ways exist to specify your domain when you're using the classic Windows logon interface. The common method is to enter the username and password in the spaces with those labels and then select the domain in the Log on To drop-down box. But did you know that you can also specify your username as *username@domain*, to disable the Domain selection box? For example, if my username in the FerrisTech domain were jferris, I could enter my username as `jferris@ferristech`.

Figure 11.1
This is the classic style Windows XP logon screen.

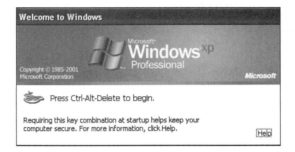

A minor variant to the previous classic-style logon screen, a system enabled for Smart Card-based logon, will display a slightly different logon screen including an icon of a Smart Card reader and the text `Insert card or press Ctrl-Alt-Delete to begin`. You can see this slightly different dialog in Figure 11.2. I'll delve into Smart Cards in a little more detail in the section "Smart Card and Biometric Authentication" (**p. 413**), but I wanted to include it here so you could easily compare the screenshots of the different logon dialogs.

Figure 11.2
Here's the classic style Windows XP logon screen with Smart Card login enabled.

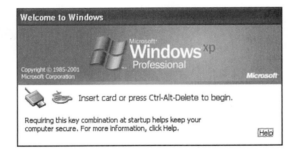

HIDING THE LAST LOGGED-ON USER

One potential downside to the classic logon dialog is a feature by which the system remembers the last logged-on username through a reboot. This might not sound like a bad thing at first--in fact, you might appreciate the convenience of not retyping your name each time. But imagine if a hacker were to sit down at your machine. If the system comes up totally blank, he has to guess both a username and a password. If the user name is already displayed, then half his work is done. And if your company uses an easily guessable scheme for determining usernames, then the hacker would have an easy way to generate a list of valid usernames, making the likelihood of finding a weak password even higher.

So how can you configure your system to conceal the last logged-on user? The easiest way to make this change on an individual machine is through the local group policy manager. Remember: This only works for systems that are running the classic logon interface.

NOTE

> If the Administrative tools don't show up under your Start menu, you can get to them by going into Control Panel and selecting Switch to Classic View, Administrative Tools. Optionally, you can add the Administrative Tools link to your Start menu by right-clicking Start, selecting Properties, Customize, Advanced, Display, and selecting Start Menu under the System Administrative Tools category.

Click Start and select Administrative Tools, Local Security Policy. Under Security Settings, expand Local Policies. Then expand Security Options, and find the policy named Interactive Logon: Do Not Display Last User Name. Enable the policy to blank the display for the local system by right-clicking the policy and selecting Properties, Enable, OK. You can set this same policy at the domain level to blank the last logged on username for every computer joined to your domain without requiring a local policy change at each local system.

NOTE

> When you're using the classic logon interface, if you would rather change this setting directly in the registry than by using group policy, set the following registry key to a value of 1:
>
> ```
> HKLM\Software\Microsoft\Windows NT\CurrentVersion\Winlogon\
> DontDisplayLastUserName
> ```

→ To read more about configuring Windows XP using the group policies, please **see** "Policy Construction on an Active Directory Network," **p. 893**.

→ Editing the registry is covered in detail in Chapter 30, "Registry Maintenance and Repair."

THE WELCOME SCREEN

If this is a standalone or workgroup network system that uses multiple user profiles and the fancy new Windows XP logon screen, you'll see an entry with an icon for each user, as illustrated by Figure 11.3. I'd worked with Windows XP for about three months before I ever tried setting it up as a standalone system, so imagine my surprise when I reloaded a system without joining it to a domain and saw this new sign-on interface. In Figure 11.3, you see four local user accounts available on the system. In addition, notice that the guest account has been enabled.

All you need to do on this screen is click your name. If you have not set a password, you'll be taken to your desktop. If you have previously configured this account to require a password, the password entry box will magically phase in right below your name, as shown in Figure 11.4. Type your password, press Enter, and you're off and running.

Figure 11.3
The snazzy new standalone Windows XP Welcome screen.

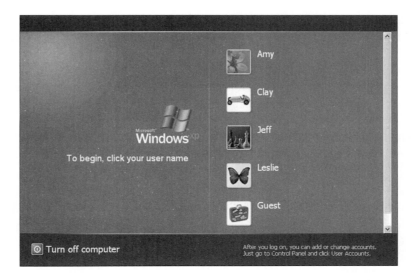

Figure 11.4
Local accounts can be password-protected on a standalone system.

NOTE

By default (and by design), there is no password for the guest account.

I leave the guest account enabled so that after visitors to my secret underground computer lab have made it past the vicious dogs and found their way through the hedge maze, they can easily access the Internet without bugging me to set up an account for them. You probably don't want to enable guest access on systems connected to a corporate network, but in the home I've found it to be a useful amenity to visitors. Besides, after someone has physical access to my home, either I trust him, or he's there to steal my computer anyway. As a bonus, guest users cannot install new hardware or software, so I don't have to worry too much about someone mucking up my machine configuration.

Unfortunately, there is no way to use the Welcome screen with a system that belongs to a domain. If the cool interface were all you'd lose by joining a domain, it would be no big deal. Unfortunately, you also lose the ability to perform fast user switching, described later in this chapter in the section "Fast User Switching," on **p. xx**. In fact, I find the fast user switching and Welcome screen interface so useful that I no longer join my primary home workstation to my home domain--it's just that cool.

LOGGING ON AS ADMINISTRATOR FROM THE WELCOME SCREEN

The Windows XP Welcome screen does not normally list the local Administrator account as an available account. If you don't know the passwords to any of the accounts displayed on the Welcome screen, or if none of the displayed accounts have administrative privileges but you need to perform some administrative function, you can bypass the Welcome screen to log on with the "standard" logon dialog, using any valid local account by pressing Ctrl+Alt+Del twice.

NOTE

On Windows XP Home Edition, the Administrator account is only available when you boot Windows in Safe Mode, and by default, a password is not set for the Administrator account.

Then, simply enter the local administrator username and password, make whatever changes to the system you need to make, and log out. You'll be back at the Welcome screen.

Remember, though, that you can often use the `runas` command to perform administrative tasks to save yourself the bother of switching users. I'll discuss `runas` later in this chapter.

➔ Refer to Chapter 10, (**p. 359**) for more information on the `runas` command.

SHOWING AND HIDING ACCOUNTS ON THE WELCOME SCREEN

By default, the Administrator account and several system service accounts are not shown on the Welcome screen. You can instruct Windows to display the Administrator account or to remove specific user accounts by editing the registry key `HKEY_LOCAL_MACHINE\SOFTWARE\Microsoft\Windows NT\CurrentVersion\Winlogon\SpecialAccounts\UserList`. This key holds values that determine which accounts are omitted from the Welcome screen.

The `UserList` key contains values that name the accounts to be hidden, such as Administrator, HelpAssistant, and NetShowServices. The associated values determine how the account is displayed:

Value	Result
0	Account will not be shown
1	Account will be shown
0x00010000	Any account whose name starts with the same letters as the value name will not be shown

To add the Administrator account to the Welcome screen, log on as Administrator and run `regedit`. Open the key indicated earlier and change the Administrator value from 0 to 1. To hide a user account, add a new DWORD value with the name *names* as the user's logon name, and enter the numeric value 0.

You can log on to a hidden account by pressing Ctrl+Alt+Del twice at the Welcome screen to display the Logon dialog.

CAUTION

> You already know this, but our attorneys insist that we warn you anyway: Be careful when editing the registry because a mistake could render your system inoperative. It's best to make a backup before hacking on the registry!

SMART CARD AND BIOMETRIC AUTHENTICATION

Smart Cards are hardware tokens used in a public key infrastructure environment to store a user certificate. A user certificate has many uses, including Windows authentication, email encryption, and email signing. *Biometric authentication* refers to the use of a guaranteed unique physical characteristic to validate a user's identity. Examples of biometric authentication include voice recognition, fingerprints, retinal scans, face recognition, or even DNA testing for the true extremist.

A few marketing-induced misconceptions surround Windows XP, Smart Cards, and Biometric authentication technologies. Many people expect Windows XP to provide built-in mechanisms for locally available Smart Card- and biometrics-based authentication, but in reality, XP only supports Smart Cards in a domain environment, including a public key infrastructure (PKI) with a certificate authority (CA). Using Smart Cards or biometrics on a standalone system requires a third-party utility. Windows XP only provides the framework for these third parties, so they can easily plug in to the authentication mechanics of the Windows XP operating system.

For a full background on user authentication using PKI and Smart Cards, check out Microsoft's Smart Card Deployment Cookbook at

```
www.microsoft.com/technet/treeview/default.asp?url=/TechNet/security/prodtech/
smrtcard/
smrtcdcb/smartc00.asp
```

All of the software components needed to implement Smart Cards on your domain are included out of the box with Windows 2000 Server and Windows Server 2003 (which, for the remainder of this chapter, we'll call Windows 200x Server). For the physical card readers and Smart Cards, take a look at

Gemplus: `www.gemplus.com`

Schlumberger: `www.slb.com/smartcards`

Xiring: `www.xiring.com`

Windows XP login supports biometric login as well, but unlike Smart Card security, you must purchase the software components as well as the hardware from a third party. Take a look at the following biometric vendors for some possible solutions:

DigitalPersona: www.digitalpersona.com

Identix: www.identix.com

SecuGen: www.secugen.com

Visionics: www.visionics.com

Iridian Technologies: www.iridiantech.com

Ethentica: www.ethentica.com

Polaroid: www.polaroid-id.com/biosmart/

Saflink: www.saflink.com

FAST USER SWITCHING

We've already discussed the new Welcome screen in the earlier section "The Welcome Screen," and I told you I've stopped adding my primary workstation to my home domain to take advantage of the new logon interface. Now, I'm the first to admit, I'm a pretty big geek...so this seems strangely superficial, doesn't it? Ah! But wait! There's a bit more I didn't tell you about this configuration: If your workstation is not joined to a domain and you're using local accounts, you get the additional bonus of Fast User Switching.

So how do you use Fast User Switching? Even if you didn't know Fast User Switching existed, but you'd set up local accounts on your system using the Welcome screen, the default screensaver configuration under Windows XP in a standalone environment would drop back to the Welcome screen after 10 minutes of idle time. Sounds inconvenient at first--who wants to get logged out every 10 minutes? But take a look at Figure 11.5, and you'll notice that two of the user account names now look a little different than before. Both of these users were at some point logged on to the machine, but they got distracted as users often do, and they wandered away. Unlike an environment in which the screensaver is configured to automatically lock the system until the user returns or an administrator overrides the lock, another user can still log on without needing to reboot or override the locked screen.

In Figure 11.5, you can see that Amy is currently logged on, and Jeff is logged on with two programs running. Either user can resume right where he left off simply by signing on to his accounts. Any of the other users can log on here as well, without affecting the current workspaces of Jeff or Amy. Finally! A simultaneous multiuser environment that doesn't require Windows Terminal Services! Just don't go clicking that friendly looking Turn Off Computer button without letting Jeff and Amy know; the environment of a logged-on user is not persistent through a reboot or power loss. That means that if Amy or Jeff have open documents that haven't been saved, their work will be lost if the system is rebooted. (You can do it if you have to, of course.)

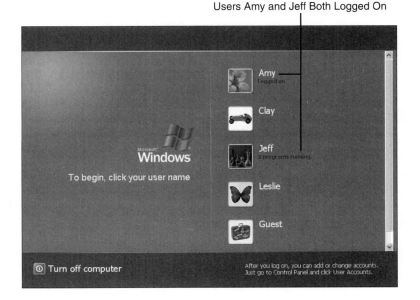

Users Amy and Jeff Both Logged On

Figure 11.5
The Windows Welcome screen shows users still logged on in the background.

When using Fast User Switching, keep these few trade-offs in mind: You already know that running multiple applications requires more system resources. Well, running multiple applications under multiple users takes even more. Any programs that are running under a different user account are still using system resources, and if you're planning to run multiple applications as multiple users on a regular basis, things will run more smoothly if you have a fast processor and a lot of RAM. If the application you are using was written to the Microsoft Windows XP Logo standards (see www.microsoft.com/winlogo for details), it should behave properly in a multiuser environment.

If you happen to be using the remote desktop feature to control your system via Windows XP desktop terminal services, you can remotely connect to a session that you had been working on locally. Your programs will be just how you left them, no different than if you'd resumed the connection from the local console. If you're currently logged on using the same credentials when you attempt a terminal services connection, your local connection will drop you back to the Welcome screen. Likewise, if you are connected to a system remotely and someone tries to sign in locally, your remote terminal session will be disconnected.

NOTE

Note that, although both features are based on the same Terminal Services technology, the Remote Desktop feature is significantly different when it comes to logon than the Remote Assistance feature. Connecting to the Remote Desktop is meant to be a single-user environment, and multiple people cannot be logged on to the session. With the Remote Assistance feature, two people (one local and one remote) are viewing and interacting with the same desktop environment.

11

So waiting 10 minutes for the user session to idle out doesn't seem particularly fast, does it? Then why are they calling it fast user switching? The key to fast user switching is that Windows XP does not close your active programs when a new user logs in. As a result, you don't have to spend all that time getting back to where you were if you let someone else use your system. But that still doesn't mean you should wait 10 minutes for the convenience. You need only select Start, Log off, Switch User.

TIP

You can also perform an instant Fast User Switch by pressing the hotkey combination of Windows key + L.

Either way, I recommend saving any open documents before switching users. If another user accidentally shuts down (or manages to crash) the system, your data could be lost if you have not saved.

CAUTION

Not all applications will run properly in a Fast User Switching environment. For example, older versions of McAfee's Virus Scan would alert users to an incompatibility with Fast User Switching at the time of install, and PCAnywhere version 10.5 will disable Fast User Switching during install. If you have questions about your applications, check the vendor's Web site for support information or application updates.

When Fast User Switching is enabled, you lose the following features:

- **Serial Keys**—This accessibility feature will be *disabled* if Fast User Switching is enabled. Serial Keys provides support for alternative input devices such as puff and sip devices, switch-driven input devices, and other serial-based keyboard or mouse alternatives.

- **Domain Membership**—If your system is joined to a domain, you can't use Fast User Switching. You must use the classic logon interface.

- **Offline File Caching**—Network files cannot be synchronized and made available offline when you're using Fast User Switching.

- **Secure Login**—Fast User Switching uses the Welcome screen, meaning that you lose the secure Ctrl+Alt+Del-required Login dialog associated with the classic logon interface.

If you need any of these features, disable the Fast User Switching feature. To do this, go into the User Accounts applet under the Control Panel, and click the task titled Change the Way Users Log On or Off. On the resulting dialog, clear the option to Use Fast User Switching. You will not be able to change this option if multiple users have active sessions on the machine.

CREATING AND MANAGING USER ACCOUNTS

You can choose from three general categorized approaches to creating user accounts. The tried-and-true GUI method is for all you mouse-lovers out there. Then there's the old-school command-line method for those who want to look cool in front of the mousers. And finally, for the true power users and the hard-core lazy, there's the scripted method.

LOCAL ACCOUNTS VERSUS DOMAIN ACCOUNTS

Before you begin working with user accounts, be sure you're clear on the difference between local accounts and domain accounts. A local account exists only on the computer on which it was created. You will most often find local accounts used for home systems, and local accounts are always used for machines that do not participate in domain security. Although local accounts can exist on systems joined to a domain, they can belong only to local groups. Out of the box, all computers have two local accounts: the Administrator account and the disabled Guest account.

Domain accounts exist on domain controllers and can be used to log on to machines that participate in domain security of the same domain or of a trusted domain. Domain accounts can be added to domain groups or to local groups on a particular system. Domain accounts cannot exist on computers that are not joined to a domain.

USER PRIVILEGES

In a standalone, workgroup, or domain-based environment, all kinds of rights and privileges can be assigned to user accounts. But pulling back to a functionalist vantage point, you really only need to worry about three high-level categories of privileges:

- **Limited users**—These are the common end users who are not able to install new applications or hardware, cannot create new user accounts, have no special rights, and really have to work to mess something up.

- **Power users**—This group, which is not available on Windows XP Home edition, can create local user accounts and groups and modify or delete accounts they created. Power users can add or remove users to the Power Users, Users, or Guests groups but cannot modify membership of the Administrators group. Power users cannot take ownership of files, which prevents them from viewing other users' files and folders. They cannot load or unload device drivers, back up or restore directories, or manage security or auditing logs. Power users can, however, install software. This group is a great compromise between the rights of administrators and the limitations of users.

- **Administrative users**—These users can manage user accounts, add or remove hardware and software, and have some form of special permission to perform higher-level tasks than a normal end user or power user would have.

Because accounts with administrative privileges can do pretty much anything to a system, I strongly recommend creating multiple accounts for anyone in your environment that will have administrative rights. One account should be a limited account, used for all day-to-day

11

functions such as checking email, creating documents, surfing the Web, and other standard tasks. The Administrative account should *only* be used when you're performing administrative tasks.

> **NOTE**
>
> With the ability to run commands as a different user with the `runas` command, you can remain logged in as a regular user account but execute administrative programs using your elevated privileges, without needing to log out. For details, refer to Chapter 10, "Using and Tuning the User Interface."

→ In a domain environment, you will likely need to break down administrative functions into more manageable chunks. You might want to specifically restrict or grant specific user rights and permissions. For more detailed coverage of user privileges and local computer policies, please **see** Chapter 22, **p. 889**.

MANAGING USERS THROUGH THE MICROSOFT MANAGEMENT CONSOLE INTERFACE

If you used Windows NT or Windows 2000 in the past, you're probably familiar with the Microsoft Management Console (MMC) GUI. XP Professional comes with an MMC snap-in that you can use to manage users and security groups. Although the Control Panel user management tool is also available on Windows XP Professional and is quite useful for some management tasks, the MMC interface is important because it gives you access to the Power Users security group. However, MMC can be used to manage users and groups only on Windows XP Professional, not XP Home Edition. (So, Home Edition users, don't even read this. It will just frustrate you, so skip ahead to the next section.)

You can get to the GUI-based user management screen in a couple of different ways--and you're going for a different application shortcut depending on whether you're creating a local account or a domain account. Let's start with local accounts. For home and small office users, this is the place to start.

The MMC tool for local users and groups was lifted straight from Windows 2000 and dropped into Windows XP Professional. The MMC is the primary GUI interface by which you perform advanced user management functions, such as creating special groups or moving users in and out of groups other than Administrators or Users. To find the Local Users and Groups MMC interface, do the following:

1. Right-click My Computer. If the icon isn't on your desktop, right-click the icon on your Start menu.
2. Select Manage from the pop-up menu.
3. The Local Computer Management console opens, where you'll find Local Users and Groups about five lines down.
4. Double-click Local Users and Groups to expose the individual Users and Groups folders, as shown in Figure 11.6. I'll leave it to you to figure out which of these folders contains local user objects and which holds local group objects.

Figure 11.6
This is the Local Users and Groups MMC interface.

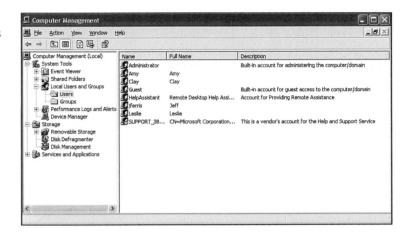

When you're in the MMC, you can right-click on either the Users or Groups folders to create new users and groups. You can double-click an individual user or group to manage properties related to that object, and you can right-click a user or group to rename or delete the object.

For instance, in a home or small office environment, you might find it easiest to create most of your local user accounts with the Control Panel user management tool, but you'll then want to assign most of your users to the Power Users group. To do this, follow these steps:

1. Log on as a Computer Administrator user.

2. If you created the user accounts using the Control Panel User Manager, be *sure* to make the users Limited Users, and not Computer Administrators. If you create the user accounts with the Local Users and Groups tools, they'll be Limited Users by default, so you'll be all set.

3. Open the Groups list and double-click the Power Users entry.

4. Click Add, and under Enter the Object Names to Select, enter the desired usernames separated by semicolons.

5. Click OK, and then click OK again to save the changes.

6. Open the Administrators group, and ensure that the accounts you selected are not also in the Administrators group. However, be *absolutely* sure that the Administrator account remains a member!

If you want to connect to a different computer to manage local users and groups, simply right-click Computer Management on the screen depicted in Figure 11.6, select Connect to Another Computer, and enter the computer name. Now all options in the Computer Management MMC reflect the configuration of the remote system, and you can manage the users and groups in the same way as on the local system.

User and group management for domain accounts is similar to local account management. But then again, after a while, pretty much anything you do through the MMC will smack of déjà vu. To manage accounts or groups on the domain, you'll need to be logged on as a Domain Administrator. Click Start, go to Administrative Tools, and run Active Directory Users and Computers.

NOTE

> Again, if the Administrative tools don't show up under your Start menu, you can get to them by going into the Control Panel, clicking Switch to Classic View, and selecting Administrative Tools. Optionally, you can add the Administrative Tools link to your Start menu by right-clicking on Start, selecting Properties, Start Menus, Customize, Advanced, Display.

NOTE

> If you don't see Active Directory Users and Computers under the Administrative Tools, you can install the tool from the ADMINPAK.MSI file, which you can find on the Windows 200x Server installation CD under the i386 directory. You can also find the tools on Microsoft's Web site, as described in the Knowledge Base article Q304718:
>
> `http://support.microsoft.com/default.aspx?scid=kb;EN-US;q304718`

The Active Directory Users and Computers interface is displayed in Figure 11.7.

Figure 11.7
Here is the Active Directory Users and Computers MMC interface.

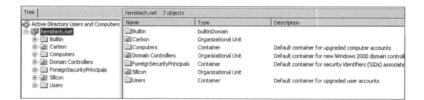

As you can see, account management with the MMC under Windows XP is identical to account management with the MMC under Windows 2000. You will find some interesting changes in the next section, however, so please read on….

MANAGING USERS THROUGH THE XP USER MANAGEMENT CONTROL PANEL

If you're not planning to get too fancy with group membership, you might want to manage the accounts using the slick, super-simple, XP User Management interface. Even "Limited" users can use this control panel to manage some aspects of their own user account, such as their picture, password, and .NET Passport.

To get to this interface, simply select Start, Control Panel, User Accounts to open the User Management applet. You should see something similar to Figure 11.8.

Figure 11.8
This is the Windows XP gee-wizard Local Account Management interface.

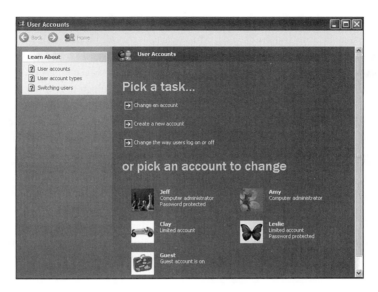

In Figure 11.8, the links on the left side under Learn About open help documentation for the listed tasks. On the top of the main panel is a list of basic tasks that can be performed at this screen, including these:

- Change an Account
- Create a New Account
- Change the Way Users Log On or Off

The bottom section of the main panel lists all local user accounts that exist on this system. You can see details about each of the user accounts, including whether the user has administrative rights and whether the account is password protected. Accounts described as a Limited Account are really just standard user accounts. You might also notice that the guest account is enabled. By selecting it at this screen, you can change the enabled or disabled status of the account. Holding the mouse pointer over one of the accounts brings up a pop-up with additional information about what you can change by going into the account.

You must be an administrator to create or modify another user's account. If you click on another user account to manage it, you will see quick-click actions to do the following:

- **Change the Name**—This option changes the user's sign-on account name.
- **[Create | Change] a Password**—This option changes depending on whether an account already has an assigned password. If the password is blank, you have the option to create a password. If the password is non-blank, you have the option to change it.
- **Remove the Password**—This option only shows up if a non-blank password is currently assigned to the account. If the account has no password, this action is not displayed.

11

■ **Change the Picture**—This option changes the 48×48 pixel graphic associated with the user's account. You can select from a variety of included icons or browse to any other graphic. Windows will store a thumbnail-sized copy of whatever picture you select in `C:\Documents and Settings\All Users.WINDOWS\Application Data\Microsoft\ User Account Pictures\`*accountname*`.bmp`. If the selected graphic is too large to fit in the 48×48 pixels, it will be scaled to fit. Full-sized, full-color, high-detail photos are, therefore, not recommended. And, as goofy as it sounded at first, I've found having a favorite picture or cartoon associated with my user account is kind of delightful.

■ **Change the Account Type**—This option allows you to change the account from a Limited account to an Administrative account. This is equivalent to adding the user account to the local Administrators group for users with administrative rights, or removing it for users with Limited rights. Users with Limited rights are only members of the local Users group. When you're managing users through the Control Panel Wizard, you cannot add or remove the account from groups other than Administrators or Users.

> **TIP**
>
> As I mentioned earlier, XP Professional has a third account type called Power User, which is a compromise between Limited User and Administrator. Power Users can install some hardware and software and make some system settings, but they can't access the most sensitive areas of Windows. For most home and small office users, the Power User account type is the most appropriate for day-to-day use--but you can't select this account type from this Control Panel. After you've created and configured your user accounts, make the users "Limited Users," and then run the Local Users and Groups Management tool, which I discussed in the previous section, to add the users to the Power Users group.

■ **Delete the Account**—This option deletes the account, including the user's preferences. Don't delete an account unless you're sure you don't need the associated settings. It is always safer to *disable* an account at first, using the MMC interface described in the previous section.

In Figure 11.9, I'm modifying the same account that I am logged in with. This not only modifies the voice of the quick-click actions to the first person (for example, "Change *my* password"), but as you'll notice from the illustration, you have an additional action:

■ **Set Up My Account to Use a .NET Passport**—This option associates a Microsoft .NET Passport account to your local user account, relieving you from manually entering the Passport username and password for .NET services that require authentication through the Passport service. Clicking this option will start a wizard, and if you do not currently have a passport, the wizard will allow you to create one on the spot. You must have an active connection to the Internet for this wizard to complete successfully.

NOTE

Carefully consider the privacy implications before you configure your account to use the Passport feature.

Figure 11.9
This is the screen for modifying your own Windows XP local user account.

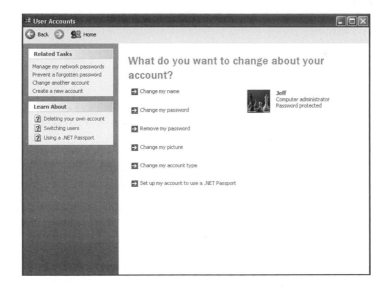

→ For more information about .NET Passports, **see** ".NET Passport," **p. 533**.

LOCAL ACCOUNTS AND PASSWORD RESET DISKS

Administrators have a hefty responsibility. They have access to reset the password for any user account, meaning they could potentially change a password, log on as a user, and see all the user's preferences and files. With pre-Windows XP systems, resetting a password would give a user carte blanche access to everything in the user's profile, including saved passwords, encrypted files, and more. Windows XP changes things a bit. If a local administrator forces a password change of a local user account, Windows XP erases all other passwords associated with the user account, including the security key required to decrypt files encrypted using the included Encrypting File System (EFS). This means that a local administrator can't see your encrypted files, but if you lose your password and need to have your password reset, you'll lose these files, too.

→ See Chapter 23 for more information on EFS.

For local accounts, Windows XP provides a mechanism so that you can protect yourself from this consequence of a forgotten password by creating a *password reset disk*. This floppy disk lets you log on to your user account without the password and without losing any other associated passwords or EFS keys. Think of it as a physical "key" to your computer account.

To create a password reset disk, follow these steps:

1. Insert a blank, formatted floppy into your A: drive.
2. Click Start, Control Panel, User Accounts.
3. Select your user account and click Prevent a Forgotten Password from the Related Tasks list.
4. Follow along with the wizard.
5. Store the completed password reset disk in a secure location.

Remember: Someone who gets hold of this disk has access to your account, so keep it somewhere safe and secure. Each user must create his own password reset disk. Users will not need to re-create this disk when their password changes.

Do the following to use the password reset disk:

1. Attempt to sign on using the Windows XP Welcome Screen.
2. After the unsuccessful attempt, click the link marked Did You Forget Your Password?
3. Click Use Your Password Reset Disk.
4. Follow the wizard to reset your password.

You do not need to re-create the password reset disk after using it. Just store it away for the next time you need it.

For domain users, you still must contact a domain user administrator to reset a password or unlock an account. On domain accounts, EFS keys are not destroyed when the account is reset, so the password reset disk mechanism is not needed.

MANAGING USER ACCOUNTS FROM THE COMMAND LINE

I tend to use this method when doing quick, simple changes to user accounts. I like it because it does away with superfluous mouse moving and pointing and clicking and takes us back to the way things used to be, before we had all these wimpy "icons" and "windows" and "user friendliness." It's fast, it's easy, and it makes a paper-MCSE sweat. These all execute from the command line, so first you need to get yourself to one of those by clicking Start, All Programs, Accessories, Command Prompt, or by pressing Window+R, cmd, Enter.

The command you want to use is net, with the user, group, or localgroup options. Here are some examples. These are by no means complete; check out the net help *command* for more details:

For quick help with any of these commands:
```
net [user | group | localgroup] /?
```
For complete help with any of these commands:
```
net help [user | group | localgroup]
```

To show all local users:

```
net user
```

To list all local security groups:

```
net localgroup
```

To show all members of a local group:

```
net localgroup groupname
```

To create a local user account:

```
net user userid password /add
```

To add a local user to a local group:

```
net localgroup groupname userid /add
```

To modify an existing local user's password:

```
net user userid newpassword
```

To deactivate (disable) a local user account:

```
net user userid /active:no
```

To reactivate a disabled local user account:

```
net user userid /active:yes
```

To delete a local user account (but not the profile folder):

```
net user userid /del
```

To add a domain user:

```
net user userid /add /dom
```

To show all members of a domain group:

```
net group groupname /dom
```

To add a domain user to a domain group:

```
net group groupname userid /add /dom
```

To add a domain user to a local group:

```
net localgroup groupname domain\userid /add
```

To deactivate (disable) a domain user account:

```
net user userid /active:no /dom
```

To reactivate a disabled domain user account:

```
net user userid /active:yes /dom
```

To delete a domain user:

```
net user userid /del /dom
```

MANAGING USER ACCOUNTS THROUGH SCRIPTS

You have a couple of options when doing scripted user management. You can use classic batch files, or you can use Windows Script Host (WSH). WSH is by far the more flexible of the two options. By tying in to the Active Directory Service Interfaces (ADSI), you can create, read, or modify any information or configuration options available for a user account.

BATCH FILES

Batch files have been around since the early days of DOS. Some excellent enhancements have been available since Windows 2000 to allow batch files to loop through lines of a text file, processing the file by defining arguments as tab- or character-delimited portions of the file. In this section, I'll look at using these commands to allow scripted bulk account management.

Let's consider a common scenario: The first of every month, your company hires 50 new employees. The new hires show up for training at 8 a.m., and they expect to be able to log in. Almost without fail, your HR liaison forgets to forward you the spreadsheet containing their account information until 7:50 a.m., leaving you 10 minutes to get 50 accounts entered manually. That's only 5 accounts per minute, so you could probably pull it off. But you'd rather not cut it that close, so you write a batch file to handle the issue.

Each line of your comma-delimited spreadsheet of user data should be laid out like the following:

```
UserID,Badge,Full Name,Department,Shoe size,group1, ... , groupn
```

We'll pretend this is how you requested the spreadsheet, and the HR staffer actually delivers it properly formatted every week. More likely, however, you'll get the spreadsheet in Excel format and export it to a text file with the correct delimiters and columns in the proper spots. UserID will be the login name. Badge will be used for the initial password in the format *pass<badge>word*. Full Name is the first and last name of the user. Department is the user's department, which should be included in the Comments field for the user account. Shoe size is not used in the creation of the employee's account, but the HR staffer has a foot fetish and includes the data regardless of what you tell him. Finally, the last part of the line could be any number of groups. We're only handling a maximum of four with the script. The line is terminated with a single hard return, and no spaces should be between the lines. So, for some sample data, let's use the following four entries:

```
jferris,42,Jeff Ferris,Engineering,9.5,Monkey_Trainers,Tech_Writers
aferris,43,Amy Ferris,Engineering,7,Project_Managers,People_Managers
lboyd,44,Leslie Boyd,Consulting Services,6.5,Consultants,Corp_Card_Users,VPN_Users
criddle,45,Clay Riddle,Board of Directors,10,Board_Members,Executives,VPN_Users
```

We'll assume all the group names specified here already exist. To use this data with a batch file, save the data file to C:\usernames.txt.

Now create a new batch file at C:\loadusers.bat. This will be the file you use to kick off the user creation script. The file should contain the following two lines of code:

```
@echo off
```

```
for /F "tokens=1-9 delims=," %%i in (c:\usernames.txt) do _
    procusers.bat %%i %%j "%%k" "Dept: %%l" %%n %%o %%p %%q
```

The final required file for this script will be named procusers.bat. It should contain the following lines:

```
@echo off
net user %1 %2 /fullname:%3 /comment:%4 /add /dom

:nextgroup
    if """" == ""%5"" goto end
    net group %5 %1 /add /dom
    shift /5
goto nextgroup
:end
echo User %1 added.
```

To execute the script, simply run the `loadusers.bat` file. *Voilà*! Instant users.

WINDOWS SCRIPT HOST

Batch files are cool, but they're only as flexible as the utilities available from the command line. There is quite a bit more you can do using WSH. With WSH and ADSI, you can query or modify any aspect of a user account or group.

WSH is a complex topic. I've included a couple of basic scripts in this section, but for full coverage, consider some of these excellent references:

> *Windows XP Under the Hood* by Brian Knittel; ISBN 0789727331 (our favorite, of course!)
>
> *Windows NT/2000 ADSI Scripting for System Administrators* by Thomas Eck; ISBN 1578702194
>
> *Windows 2000 Script Host* by Tim Hill; ISBN 1578701392

You'll also find some downloadable examples of administrative scripts at the following Web sites:

> Swink.com (`http://www.swynk.com/winscript/`)
>
> InformIT (`http://www.informit.com`)

I also recommend taking a look at Andrew Clinick's administrative scripts from Microsoft TechEd 2000. This was the presentation that first got me addicted to WSH. The article and source code are available for download on MSDN Online at

`http://msdn.microsoft.com/library/en-us/dnclinic/html/scripting06122000.asp`

The following script will present a pop-up box for a domain name and password. You must have account management permissions on the target domain to use this script. It will fill in your current user domain as the default domain name in which to create the account. If you want to create an account on the local machine, use the computer name when you're prompted for a domain.

```
Set WshNetwork = WScript.CreateObject("Wscript.Network")

CurDomName=WshNetwork.UserDomain
DomainName = InputBox("Enter the Domain Name","Domain",CurDomName)
UserName = InputBox("Enter the new user name","Username")

Set myDomain = GetObject("WinNT://" & DomainName)
Set myUser = myDomain.Create("User", UserName)
```

11

```
myUser.fullname = InputBox("Enter the user's full name","Full Name")
strPassword = InputBox("Enter the user's password","Password")
call myUser.SetPassword(strPassword)
myUser.SetInfo

set myDomain = Nothing
set myUser = Nothing
set WshNetwork = Nothing
```

A common task that help desk personnel often require is the ability to easily unlock user accounts. The following script prompts for an account name and unlocks the account. Again, note that the user who is running the script must have the rights to unlock the target account.

```
Set WshNetwork = WScript.CreateObject("Wscript.Network")

CurDomName=WshNetwork.UserDomain
DomainName = InputBox("Enter the Domain Name","Domain",CurDomName)
UserName = InputBox("Enter the account name to unlock","User ID")

Set myUser = GetObject("WinNT://"& DomainName &"/"& UserName &"")
wscript.echo myuser.IsAccountLocked
If myUser.IsAccountLocked = -1 then myUser.IsAccountLocked = 0
wscript.echo myuser.IsAccountLocked
myUser.SetInfo

If myuser.IsAccountLocked = 0 Then
    msgbox UserName & " is unlocked."
Else
    msgbox "An error occurred. Make sure you have permission to " & _
        "unlock the specified account."
End if
set WshNetwork=nothing
set myUser = Nothing
```

→ For more information about automating tasks with scripts, please **see** "Windows Script Host," **p. 1183**.

MANAGING USER PROFILES

A *user profile* is a folder that contains all of a user's personalized information: the registry file that contains their customized settings, their Desktop and My Documents folders, and application data such as Outlook Express's address list and email database. By default, profiles are stored under C:\Documents and Settings, in folders with the same name as the user account. User-customized settings can include desktop layout, program shortcuts, icon layout, wallpaper, default screen resolution, screensaver settings, program customizations, Outlook configuration and messages, words added to the custom dictionary in Word, Internet Explorer favorites, printers, dial-up network connections, and so on. Most settings are stored in the NTUSER.DAT file, which is loaded into the HKEY_CURRENT_USER hive of the Registry upon user logon.

→ **See** Chapter 30, **p. 1239**, for more information on the Registry.

You'll find an interface for simple local user profile management by right-clicking My Computer, selecting Properties, Advanced, and then clicking the Settings button in the User Profiles box. You should see something similar to Figure 11.10.

Figure 11.10
This is the User Profile Management screen.

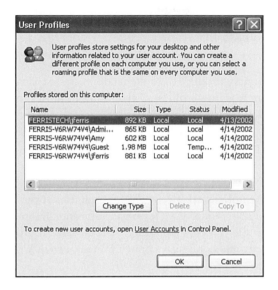

Notice the three buttons:

- **Change Type**—This configures whether the selected user will use the network-stored roaming profile or the locally cached copy of the profile.
- **Delete**—This permanently deletes the selected profile.
- **Copy To**—This copies the selected profile to another profile directory, overwriting the settings in the destination profile with those in the selected users' profile.

ROAMING VERSUS LOCAL PROFILES

The local user profile stores all the aforementioned profile-related settings on the local system. A local profile is created the first time you log on to a computer in an environment that does not use roaming profiles. Changes made to your profile are available only on the local system.

Roaming profiles are created by a system administrator and stored on a server. The profile is available any time you log on to the network from a computer that participates in domain security. When you log on using a domain account that is configured with a roaming user profile, the profile folders are copied from the domain server to the local computer you are using. When you log out, any changes to your documents or profile settings are copied back to the domain server, so those changes will be available on subsequent logins from different systems.

> **NOTE**
>
> Some relatively unimportant folders are *not* copied back and forth between the domain server and a local computer to save time and network traffic. By default, these folders include Local Settings, Temp, Temporary Internet Files, and the History folder. The list of ignored folders is stored in the Registry under `HKEY_CURRENT_USER\Software\Microsoft\Windows NT\CurrentVersion\Winlogon\ExcludeProfileDirs`, which can be configured per user.

In addition to standard roaming profiles, the system administrator can create mandatory roaming profiles. These are roaming profiles in which the administrator has specified settings that the user cannot change.

→ For more information about creating and implementing roaming user profiles, please **see** "Roaming User Profiles," **p. 34** on the CD.

CONFIGURING A DEFAULT USER PROFILE

If you aren't happy with the initial settings created for each user at the time of logon, you can configure a profile and copy it into the Default User profile. Subsequently, newly created users will receive the profile you created, rather than the default profile provided out of the box. If you have to create and configure a bunch of user accounts, you'll want to know how to do this! Here's how:

1. Create a new user account (someone without an existing personal profile on the system) and log on to that account.

2. Make all the changes you want included in the default profile. For example, you can set a default screen saver configuration, add some default favorites, drop some shortcuts on the desktop, reorganize the shortcuts on the Start bar, and add a default background. You can also delete the sample files in My Documents and My Pictures or create new files and folders.

3. Log off as this user and log in as an account with local administrative privileges. Note that you *must* be logged in as a different user to free all files for a successful copy. Doing a fast user switch does not work.

4. Under My Computer, click Tools, Folder Options, and go to the View tab. Check Show Hidden Files and Folders and click OK. Otherwise, you will not be able to see the Default User folder.

5. Right-click My Computer, select Properties, Advanced, and click the Settings button in the User Profiles box.

6. Select the profile of the user you just configured, and click the Copy To button.

7. Click Browse, and browse to `C:\Documents and Settings\Default User`. Click OK.

8. Click the Change button under Permitted to Use, and select the Everyone group. This ensures that all new users have permission to read the default profile. Click OK.

9. Log out, and log back in as a user who has not logged on to this machine before. You should see the same configuration as the account you used when you originally created the default user profile.

If your users are not receiving the settings you expect from the default user profile, it is usually the fault of one of two situations: In the first, the user has already logged in to this system once before, in which case the default profile will not be applied without first deleting the user's existing profile. To fix this situation, simply back up any of the user's important files and delete the user's profile. The user should then receive the proper default profile at the next login.

In the second situation, the user does not receive the default profile because he does not have the permission required to read the profile. To fix this problem, go to `C:\Documents and Settings`, and grant Read & Execute, List Folder Contents, and Read permissions to the Everyone group for the Default User directory. In addition, select the option to replace permissions on all child objects under the Default User directory. Again, any users who received the wrong default profile must have their profiles deleted to receive the proper profile at their next login.

COPYING PROFILES

If you need to copy a user profile from one user to another or from a local user's profile directory to a domain user's profile directory, you'll follow similar steps as in the previous section.

CAUTION

> Be careful when performing a profile copy procedure. All files and settings under the target user profile will be replaced with the files and settings from the origin profile. This includes files under the user's My Documents directory and Outlook Express email and address book data. When you overwrite a profile, you destroy any existing account data!

1. Ensure that the target user has previously logged on to the system so that his default profile directory already exists.

2. Log on to the computer as an administrator, but do not log on as either account involved in the copy procedure.

3. Right-click My Computer, select Properties, Advanced, and click the Settings button in the User Profiles box.

4. Select the profile of the user you want to copy, and click the Copy To button.

5. Click Browse, browse to the `C:\Documents and Settings\<target user account>` directory, and click OK.

6. Click the Change button under Permitted to Use, and enter the target user's account. This ensures that the target user has permission to read files and settings in the duplicated profile. Click OK, and you're done.

11

The target user account now has the same files and settings under its profile as the origin profile.

BREAKING THROUGH TO A SYSTEM THAT HAS LOST ITS WAY

If you work with Windows NT-based domains long enough, it'll eventually happen...Someone will bring you a system, protected with NTFS. The system was previously a member of the domain but has a long-forgotten local administrator password and no other local accounts. Somehow, either through computer account corruption or improper user interaction, the system is no longer accessible. The ensuing conversation usually goes something like this:

> User: I need this system working in 10 minutes for a critical presentation to the board. I can't log in.

> You: So what did you do?

> User: Nothing.

> You: Riiiight. Anyway, so what do you want me to do about it?

> User: Get me all my files back.

> You: No problem, I'll just load the system drive in another machine, take ownership of the files, burn them to CD, and you'll have all your data. I should be able to have that for you in about 3 hours.

> User: No, now I only have 9 minutes. Did I mention that I'm the VP of the Department of People Who Can Fire You for Not Fixing My Problems?

> You: No, you hadn't mentioned that. Get out of my cube so I can perform my miracle.

So now what do you do? Well, hopefully, you had already read this tip, and you'd already gone out to www.winternals.com and picked up at least NTFSDOSPro, if not the entire Administrator's Pak, making you ready for any data recovery or lost-password–related activities you might need to perform on an NTFS-formatted drive.

Personally, I've used the Administrator's Pak since Windows NT 4.0, and it is probably the single most useful utility package I've ever owned in all my years of working with computers. With the tools included in the Administrator's Pak, you can perform such miracles as the following:

- Recovering data from an NTFS-formatted disk after booting to DOS
- Changing an unknown local administrator password to a known local administrator password
- Booting a corrupt NT/2000/XP install to a DOS disk, connecting to the network, and remotely recovering files from the corrupt system
- Repairing errors in the partition table or boot sector

So if the preceding scenario were to happen to you, you'd be able to boot the lost system to DOS, connect to the network, reset the local administrator password, reboot the system, log in as the local administrator, and access all of the users' data files, most likely in under 10 minutes. Of course, the VP of the Department of People Who Can Fire You for Not Fixing His Problem will have completely forgotten your name by the end of his presentation to the board...but in the end, shouldn't that be thanks enough?

11

PART III

WINDOWS XP APPLICATIONS

CHAPTER 12

WINDOWS EXPLORER POWER USERS' GUIDE

In this chapter

CHANGING VIEWING OPTIONS IN WINDOWS EXPLORER

The Windows Explorer interface is used in many parts of Windows XP, including My Computer, My Documents, and My Network Places. Windows Explorer is the main interface for creating and managing folders and files stored on a computer; it is used whenever you open or save a file within a 32-bit Windows application. You can make file and folder management more intuitive for your users, and more effective and efficient for you, by learning how to adjust the configuration of Windows Explorer.

This chapter covers many of the advanced options in Windows Explorer, including how to select and configure the different file and folder views available, efficiently perform searches, change file associations, and troubleshoot some of the common problems you might encounter.

MENU BAR

The menu bar and the toolbars are the basis for all configuration, customization, and navigation functions within Windows Explorer.

The menu bar is not customizable; however power users and administrators rely heavily upon it as the means for completing tasks mouse-free. You can navigate within any Windows application, including Windows Explorer, by using the Alt key in combination with specific *underscored* letters on the menu bar. Menu bar navigation can also be triggered by pressing specific menu keys (also underscored) or using the arrow keys to highlight the specifics. Tried and true menu keys that will work for nearly every application are Alt+F for the file menu; Alt+E for Edit; and Alt+V for view. A few of the more commonly used in-depth combinations within Explorer would be: Alt+F, R for properties, ALT+E, C for copy, ALT+E, P for paste, Alt+F, P for print.

To enhance your mouse-free experience, you can use the Tab key to move between sections and panes of Explorer (or any Windows application). Arrow keys will navigate within the pane, and hotkeys such as Ctrl+C and Ctrl+V will copy and paste highlighted files and folders respectively.

TOOLBARS

Toolbars are the items that exist between the menu bar and the folder and file panes of Windows Explorer. There are three standard toolbars within Explorer:

- Standard Buttons
- Address Bar
- Links

The Standard Buttons toolbar is enabled by default and can be accessed from View, Toolbars on the menu bar. It consists of the main navigation buttons that have been around since Windows 95. Microsoft has standardized the code for the Standard Buttons in such a manner that much of the same functionality and interface are shared with Internet Explorer.

NOTE

Windows Explorer and Internet Explorer are really the same utility in two different guises. You can view a LAN resource or Web page within Windows Explorer if you enter the UNC for the resource or URL for the Web page. Similarly, you can open a local text, HTML, or other file within Internet Explorer.

The Standard Buttons toolbar buttons are displayed with large icons by default, and can be changed via View, Toolbars, Customize from the menu bar. Button sizes, along with individual displayed buttons, can be enabled within this interface.

Figure 12.1 shows some of the optional toolbar buttons you can add to the standard interface. These buttons perform the same task as the menu bar equivalent. For example, the Map Drive button highlighted in Figure 12.1 performs the same task as the menu option Tools, Map Network Drive or as the keystrokes Alt+T, N.

Figure 12.1
Adding the Map Drive button to the toolbar buttons in Windows Explorer. Separators can also be added to create groups of related buttons.

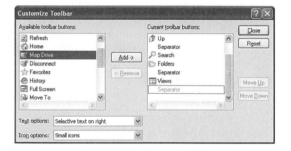

The address bar is used to allow quick navigation to LAN-based or Internet resources. It is accessed via the View option on the menu bar, followed by Toolbars, Address bar. Most of the time end users do not need the address bar because of the potential confusion that can occur if they enter a Web address on the address line. It can easily be disabled by selecting Toolbars, Address Bar from the menu bar.

The links bar is not enabled by default within Windows Explorer, but it is an option that is usually used in one of two environments. The first is a situation where a power user chooses to use Windows Explorer for all of their local file management as well as their default Web browser of choice. The second is a similar situation where security may be in place that restricts users from using Internet Explorer without completely eliminating Web access altogether.

TIP

All settings and customizations for Windows Explorer are stored in a user's profile. If you need to restrict or impose certain settings, you can implement a mandatory profile locally on the system or over the network by using Mandatory Roaming Profiles. Profile management is discussed in Chapter 22, "Locking Down Your Computer."

12

By default, toolbars are anchored to the top of the window. They can be configured by selecting View, Toolbars, Lock the Toolbars from the menu bar.

Graphics programs frequently use unlocked toolbars that float within the editing window for faster access to specific buttons, as in Figure 12.2.

Figure 12.2
Floating toolbars in use with Corel PhotoPaint v9. The user can also drag toolbars to the top of the screen and rearrange them as desired.

Windows Explorer does not float its toolbars when they are unlocked. Instead, the toolbars appear with a series of dots to the left of each toolbar. Clicking on these dots will allow the menu bar and toolbars to be shuffled or combined with other toolbars on in the same area. Menu bars and toolbars can be compressed and displayed on the same row in this manner, as shown in Figure 12.3. Once changes have been made, the toolbars should be locked again in order to prevent accidental movement.

Figure 12.3
Standard (top) and undocked toolbars (bottom) in Windows Explorer. The undocked toolbars can use less screen space than the standard arrangement.

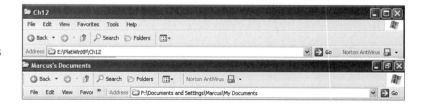

If you try this, be very careful: It's easy to move the toolbars and menu bar around, but not always so easy to get them back the way they were when you started. If this occurs, you should disable the address bar, make your changes, and then re-enable the address bar: It's much easier to navigate with only two elements available rather than three.

EXPLORER BARS

On the View Menu under Explorer Bar, you'll find several options that can customize the appearance of Windows Explorer and add more functionality. Explorer bars appear in the left pane of the main Explorer window and provide the gateway for several functions of Windows Explorer.

Explorer bars can be accessed via the View Menu, but they also can be configured as a standard toolbar button. By default, the Search and Folders Explorer bars are already configured as toolbar buttons. Adding or removing other Explorer bars from the toolbar is done through toolbar customization.

Explorer bars can be turned on or off. This is an advantage for the person who doesn't wish to permanently have a particular Explorer Bar displayed in the left pane. This is also a *huge* comfort factor for prior Windows 9x, Me, and 2000 users who are accustomed to seeing folders in the left pane. To display folders in the left pane, click the Folders button in the toolbar. To display the Explorer bar again, click the Folders button again.

When the Explorer bar is displayed, the default background Common Tasks are displayed with options for File and Folder Tasks, Other Places, and Details. This is intended as the default working environment for users when Common Tasks is selected as the default folder option. Similar to the functionality of Microsoft Outlook, users will recognize this background pane as similar to the Outlook bar within that program. Unlike Outlook, it is not possible to customize sections of the Common Tasks pane. The exact features of the Common Tasks bar vary when different resources are viewed. For example, when My Network Places is viewed with Explorer, Network Tasks replaces File and Folder Tasks.

Novice computer users will find the default background pane ideal for their standard working environment. Veteran users may, however, find it annoying and wish to have the "old" Windows default Folders view be their default. To set the default view for a particular folder:

1. Display the folder in Windows Explorer.
2. Click Tools, Folder Options.
3. On the General tab, click Show Common Tasks to select the Windows XP default, or click Use Windows Classic Folders to display a folder list in the left pane. Click Apply to make the change, and then OK.

The following Explorer Bars are available from the View Menu:

- Search—Selecting the Search option brings up the Search Companion from which you can search for folders, files, pictures, music, computers, and people (see Figure 12.4).

12

Figure 12.4
Select the search type from the Search Companion bar. Additional options are displayed after you select a search type.

- Favorites—Clicking on the Favorites option displays all your favorite Internet links.
- Media—The media bar makes it easy for you to play your favorite music, videos, and multimedia files (see Figure 12.5).

Figure 12.5
The media bar uses Windows Media Player to play audio and video.

- History—Clicking the History option displays a list of all the Internet sites that have been visited recently.
- Folders—The Folders option returns you to the default view displaying the hierarchy of folders and files in Windows Explorer.

SEARCH

The most common way to search for folders and files is by using the Search Companion, formally known as Windows Search, which is accessible off the Start menu or through Windows Explorer. Aside from noticing significant differences from prior versions of Windows, you'll also notice that the search functionality within the Start Menu, Search is identical to that shown within the Search Explorer bar. The Search Companion allows you to search for the following types of items:

- Files and folders
- Pictures, music, and videos
- Documents
- Computers and people

Microsoft has used, for many years in the Microsoft Office suite, animated "companions" to provide assistance and help. Most power users choose to turn this feature off in the interest of overhead and processor efficiency, not to mention sheer annoyance. You can similarly turn off and customize the Search Companion in several different ways. The first is done by right-clicking the companion itself, and choosing whichever option you prefer. You also have the ability to change the overall search preferences by opening the search bar, and clicking on the Change Preference option (see Figure 12.6). Table 12.1 summarizes the configurable options.

Figure 12.6
Customizing the Search Companion. Click an option to choose from the settings shown in Table 12.1.

How do you want to use Search Companion?

- Without an animated screen character
- With a different character
- With Indexing Service (for faster local searches)
- Change files and folders search behavior
- Change Internet search behavior
- Don't show balloon tips
- Turn AutoComplete on

[Back]

12

TABLE 12.1   OPTIONS FOR CONFIGURING THE SEARCH COMPANION

Option	Description
With/without an animated screen character	Hides or shows the animated character you see when performing searches.
With/without Indexing Service	Allows you to enable or disable the indexing service for faster searches.
Change files and folders search behavior	Allows you to configure the default search behavior. The Standard option provides step-by-step help for refining a search. The Advanced option provides fields to manually enter search criteria.
Change Internet search behavior	Allows you to change how Internet searches are performed. By choosing the Search Companion option, your searches will be automatically sent to other search engines. The Classic option allows you to specify the search engine to be used.
Don't show balloon tips	This option allows you to disable or enable balloon tips.
Turn off/on autocomplete	Allows you to enable and disable autocomplete for searches.

Just in case you're wondering, the default search preferences are the opposite of what appear in these Search Preferences options.

NOTE   The default Internet search engine that Windows XP uses is MSN.

FILENAME SEARCH   If you are searching for a file and you know all or part of the file name, you can perform a file name search. Click on the Search button within Windows Explorer and click the option to search for files and folders (see Figure 12.7).

If you know the exact name of the file, you can type it in (see Figure 12.7). If not, you can type in part of the filename. The search results will display all folders and files containing the filename characters you specified. For example, if you know the filename contains the word "my," you can have the Search Companion search for all files containing this word in the filename (see Figure 12.8).

TIP   Windows XP does not by default display the details of a file. Highlight the file in the results pane and press F3 to have the file details displayed.

Figure 12.7
Searching for a specified filename on the local hard drives.

Figure 12.8
Results of a search using a portion of the filename (my).

When performing a file search, you can also specify other criteria outlined below.

■ Look In—Using this option you can specify where you want the Search Companion to look for the file. For example, to search only in a particular drive, click the Look in menu and select the drive to search. You can also select a particular user's folder, all local hard drives, and other options that vary by system.

■ When Was It Modified—To narrow the search criteria, you can specify when the file was last modified (see Figure 12.9).

Figure 12.9
Specifying a date range. Enter the exact dates to search, or choose ranges such as last week, past month, or past year.

■ What Size Is It—If you know the approximate size of the file you can choose one of the options shown in Figure 12.10.

12

Figure 12.10
Specifying a file size range. Enter the minimum or maximum file size, or choose from small, medium, or large files. Configuring the approximate size of the file being searched for.

- More Advanced Options—Using the Advanced options you can configure the Search Companion to include system folders, hidden folders and files, and subfolders in the search. You can mark the search as being case sensitive and have a tape backup included in the search (see Figure 12.11).

Figure 12.11
Configuring advanced search options. The more options you check, the longer the search will take.

TEXT SEARCH   If you are unsure of the filename or want to further narrow a search, you can search by including a word or phrase within the file. For example to search for files containing the name "Windows XP", use the Search option in Windows Explorer and type in the name under A Word or Phrase in the File. The Search Companion will search the contents of all folders and files and display all those containing the name (see Figure 12.12).

NOTE

If you find that files that contain the text you specified are not being returned in the search results, you may have to download and install the Windows XP Compatibility Update. For more information review the following article: http://support.microsoft.com/default.aspx?scid=KB;EN-US;Q309173&.

TIP

To increase text search performance, precede the text with an exclamation mark.

12

Figure 12.12
Performing a text
search. The locations
and text searched for
appear in the
progress window at
left.

USING THE INDEXING SERVICE FOR ADVANCED SEARCHING The indexing service indexes files and their properties and places them into a catalog, similar to the index you may find in the back of a book, thereby increasing your search performance. Once the catalog is created, you can perform queries against it searching by key word, phrases, or properties.

When indexing is enabled, files are indexed when your computer is idle. The service is designed to run automatically and requires little maintenance and administration.

TIP

> If performance is an issue you may want to disable the Index Service. There may be times when your computer assumes you are doing nothing and will begin indexing your files thereby consuming CPU cycles. If search performance is not a concern, consider disabling the service.

By default the Indexing Service startup type is manual. You can set it to automatic using the Computer Management console (see Figure 12.13).

You can also use the following procedure in Windows Explorer to enable the Indexing Service:

1. Click the Search button within Windows Explorer to open the Search Companion.

2. Click the Change Preferences option.

3. Click the With Indexing Service option and click the Yes, Enable Indexing Service option (see Figure 12.14).

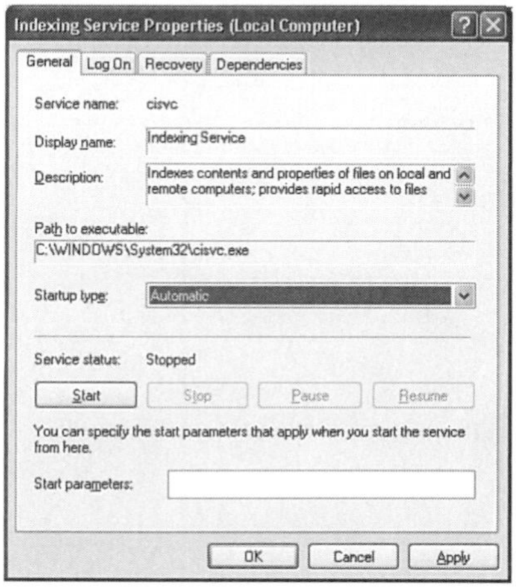

Figure 12.13
Configuring the
Indexing Service to
start automatically
when you start the
computer. Use the
same dialog to pause
or stop the service if
desired.

Figure 12.14
Enabling the Indexing
option for searches
through Windows
Explorer.

Once indexing is enabled it may take several hours before the initial index is complete. You shouldn't need to make any changes to the default settings for the service, although more advanced users may want to monitor and customize indexing on their computer. To do so, open the Computer Management console, right-click the Indexing Service, and choose Properties from the shortcut menu (see Figure 12.15).

By default all filenames are indexed for searches but it will only index the content of those files that are indexed for context searches. To have the content of files with unknown extensions indexed as well, you must enable the option Index files with unknown extensions.

Figure 12.15
Configuring the
Indexing Service.
Specifying these
options requires addi-
tional indexing time,
but can make the
index more useful.

TIP

An unknown extension is a file extension not matched to a particular program in the
Windows Registry. If users specify their own file extensions for different types of files rather
than using the default extension used by the application, the non-standard file extension is
unknown. For example, the default file extension for Corel WordPerfect files is .WPD, but
many WordPerfect users specify their own extensions such as .LTR (letter), .MEM (memo),
and so on. By indexing files with unknown extensions, you can discover information you
might have overlooked.

Selecting the option to generate abstracts will increase the size of the index. What this
option does is enable the search results to display a description or a portion of the contents
along with the file name. One thing to keep in mind is that this information cannot be displayed using the Search Companion. Use the Tracking tab to configure whether the
Indexing service will add or remove network share aliases.

A sure way to check the status of the Indexing Service is to use the Query the Catalog
option under the Indexing Service folder in the Computer Management console. Enter in a
query, click the Search button, and the results should appear.

When you click on the Indexing Service, the right pane displays the default location of the
catalog. To add a new catalog, right-click the Indexing Service, point to New, and select the
Catalog option (see Figure 12.16). Type in the name of the catalog and the location and
click OK. The new catalog will not be brought online until the Indexing Service is restarted.
To add a new directory to a catalog, right-click the catalog in the right pane, point to New,
and click Directory. Type in the path to the directory or provide the UNC if the directory is
on another computer. If the directory is not on the local computer, type in a username and
password with permission on the remote computer.

Figure 12.16
Creating a new cata-
log on the C: drive.

There are two different ways to perform searches against the catalog. You can use the
Search Companion or query the catalog (refer to Figure 12.17).

Figure 12.17
Querying the index
catalog. Select options
to change how the
query is performed
and how the results
are sorted.

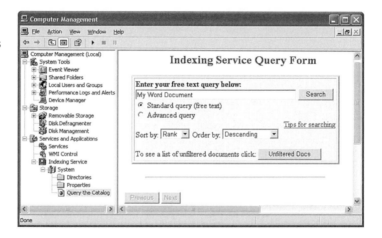

The following lists some general tips to use when searching the index:

- When finding files by filename, precede the query with @filename or #filename.
- If you are sure about part of the filename, place asterisks around that portion of the
  search.
- Be as specific as possible to limit search results. For example, if you are looking for a
  file named WindowsXP.doc, try searching as @filename*WindowsXP*.doc.
- You can also use Boolean operators (AND, OR, NOT). For example, if you are looking
  for a word document called MYDOC, you can search using the criteria
  #filename"MYDOC" AND NOT #filename*MyDOCS*. This search retrieves files
  with names such as MYDOC.DOC, but does not retrieve files with names such as
  NotMyDOCSDog.DOC.

FOLDERS

The Folders Explorer bar displays what veterans will recognize as the "traditional" view for
Windows Explorer. While it may take awhile to become accustomed to the newer configuration, this is actually a huge advantage. Now, instead of using multiple mouse clicks to use

features such as Search and those made available through the default Explorer bar, you can now quickly switch from any view that you've chosen as your standard to any other Explorer bar available.

CHOOSE DETAILS

Windows XP provides a number of different ways to view information in Windows Explorer; some are similar to previous versions of Windows and some are new.

THUMBNAILS

The Thumbnail view displays the images a folder contains as a folder icon so you can quickly and easily identify the contents.

TILES

The Tiles view is similar to the Large icons view in previous version of Windows. It displays the contents of a folder as tiles with detailed data about each tile below.

The remaining views are Details, Icons, and List, all of which remain unchanged from previous versions.

FILE DETAILS

Another new option is Choose Details. Previous versions of Explorer were limited in the details they provided about files. Now with XP there are a number of new details available that you can choose from. Clicking on the View menu and choosing the Choose Details option brings up a window that allows you to pick and choose the type of information you want displayed for files.

NOTE Configuring the view type displayed for files only pertains to the current folder. If it is necessary to apply these view changes to all folders, you can select Tools, Folder Options, View tab, and select to view all folders with the same configuration as the current one.

A NEW ARRANGEMENT

Files and folders can be arranged differently depending upon which type of view (icons, details, thumbnails, and so on) is selected. Files and folders can be arranged alphabetically by name, by file size, by file type (this is the extension of the file), or by how long ago they were modified. These arrangement options can be customized to display in groups (by name, file size, file type, or date modified) where each group is separated by a group header. For example, icons arranged by name will be grouped alphabetically: Files and folders beginning with A will have a group header labeled A. Another example would be grouping by date modified, where files are grouped by date with easy-to-read headers such as "Two months ago." Auto-Arrange is another option for items that are viewed as icons.

File and folder view and arrangement options are done via the View window, but there are two other ways of configuring these settings that may be faster (other than using the Alt hotkeys). Right-clicking on a blank area of the pane will display a pop-up menu with most, if not all of the same options as you would see from the View option on the menu bar. Additionally, items that are viewed in List or Details mode can be arranged by clicking on the column headers right above the pane itself.

TWEAKING FOLDER OPTIONS

Folder Options are used to customize the way your folders function and how the content is displayed. You can access the Folder Options by using the Tools menu in Windows Explorer or by clicking the Folder Options icon within the Control Panel.

The Folder Options window automatically opens to the General tab. From here you can configure the behavior of Windows Explorer. You can choose between different views, whether folders are opened in the existing window or a separate window, and whether items are opened with a single click or a double click.

COMMON TASKS VERSUS CLASSIC FOLDERS

A new feature with Windows XP Explorer is the ability to display Common Tasks versus Classic Folders. By default, the Common Tasks view will be displayed. This results in the Common View default pane on the left side of the window. The Classic Folders structure is basically the same as it has been for several versions of Windows.

By and large, Common Tasks is more flexible than Classic Folders because it offers all of the features of Classic Folders (with the Folders Explorer bar) along with the ability to use the Common Tasks pane for specific details that are easily accessed from that particular spot.

INSIDE THE FOLDERS

Clicking on the View tab brings up a number of advanced settings (see Figure 12.18). The options are described in Table 12.2.

12

TABLE 12.2   FOLDER OPTIONS ADVANCED SETTINGS

Advanced Setting	Description
Automatically search for network printers and folders	Specifies that Windows periodically search for network printers and folders and display them in My Network Places.
Display file size information in folder tips	Select this option if you want information about the size of the file displayed.

continues

TABLE 12.2 CONTINUED

Advanced Setting	Description
Display simple folder view in Windows Explorer's folder list	Windows Explorer will automatically display the contents of a folder and its subfolders when it is clicked.
Display the contents of the system folders	The contents of system folders are hidden by default. Click this option to have the contents dis played.
Display the full path in the address bar	The complete path of the folder or file is displayed in the address bar of the window.
Display the full path in the title bar	The complete path of the folder or file is displayed in the title bar of the window.
Do not cache thumbnails	Thumbnails will not be cached in a cache file. Caching thumbnails can improve performance on a slow network.
Hidden Files and Folders	Specifies whether to show or hide hidden files and folders.
Hide extensions for known file types	The file extensions for known files are hidden and only the filename appears. Choose this option if you want to reduce clutter.
Hide protected operating system files	Operating system files will not appear in Windows Explorer. It's a good idea to leave this option checked to avoid the possibility of a critical file being deleted.
Launch folder windows in a separate process	Specifies that each window is opened in a separate memory space. Checking this option can increase stability but decrease performance.
Managing pairs of web pages and folders	Refers to HTML pages saved complete with graphics from Explorer. Default (show and manage as a single file) keeps the HTML code and graphics folder together and is recommended.
Remember each folder's view settings	Individual folder settings are retained when a folder is opened and closed.
Restore previous folder windows at logon	Specifies that the folder window left open when you log off is restored the next time you log on.
Show Control Panel in My Computer	Displays the Control Panel when you open My Computer.
Show encrypted or compressed NTFS files in color	Encrypted and compressed files are displayed in color making them easy to identify.

12

Advanced Setting	Description
Show popup description for folder and desktop items	A descriptive pop-up window is displayed when a folder or desktop item is selected. This is a handy feature for beginners but more advanced users will want to turn this off.
Use simple file sharing (recommended)	Allows all users in a workgroup to access shares on your computer. Clear this option if you want to set permissions for users and groups.

Figure 12.18
Specifying advanced display options for the current folder. Click the Apply to All Folders button to apply the specified settings to all folders on your system.

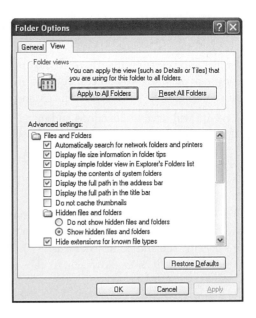

UNDERSTANDING FILE TYPES AND ASSOCIATIONS

The File Types tab within the Folder Options window displays all the registered file types for Windows and allows you to configure file associations. File associations allow you to control certain aspects of different file types, including

- The application that is launched when a user double-clicks a file
- The icon that appears for a file type
- The commands that appear in the file's shortcut menu

A file association basically makes an application take ownership of a certain file type. Referring back to Figure 12.4, when a user clicks on the file My Word Doc.Doc, the application that is automatically launched is Microsoft Word. A .doc file is normally associated with Microsoft Word.

CREATING A FILE ASSOCIATION

What happens when a file association is lost or there is no application currently associated with the file type? For example, troubleshooting problems sometimes means having to reinstall applications. After you reinstall an application you may find that some of the file associations are gone. The problem is easy to fix and requires you to reassociate the file type with the application. The same thing occurs when you have a file that has no association, meaning Windows XP cannot find a program to open it with. In both cases, you must create an association.

Use the following procedure to create a file association for an unassociated file type:

1. Right-click a file you want to associate an application with and click Open. Or you can also double-click the file.

2. Windows XP will display a dialog box stating that there are no applications associated with the file type and presenting you with two choices. You can use Web services to search for a program on the Internet or you can select a program from a list.

3. If you select the first option, you will have to download and install the program. Once complete, you can select it from the list of available programs to associate with the file type.

EXAMINING AN ASSOCIATION

Using Windows Explorer or My Computer you can view the application that is associated with a file type. You can use the Folder Options from the Tools menu to view all file associations or you can right-click on a specific file and point to Opens With. This shows you all the programs currently associated with the file and allows you to choose which program you want to open it with.

EDITING ASSOCIATIONS

Using Windows Explorer, you can change the application that is associated with a file type. To reassociate a file type, you can perform the following procedure:

1. Within Windows Explorer, click Tools and then click Folder Options.

2. Click the File Types tab. Windows XP will register all known files types and display the application associated with each one.

3. To change an association, highlight the file type from the list of extensions and click Change.

4. Click the program you want to launch when a file with that extension is clicked. Click OK. If you don't see the application you are looking for, you can use the Browse button to locate it.

NOTE

> When you click the File Types tab, all filename extensions and the associated file types registered with Windows are displayed. Clicking the New button allows you to associate a new file name extension with a file type.

Once you've changed the file association and returned to the Folder Option window, you can use the Advanced button to further tweak the settings for files with a certain extension. Click the Advanced button, which brings up the Edit File Type window. From here you can change the icon associated with a file type. This is mainly for customizing the user's interface. You can also edit the commands that have been defined for a specific file type. This is useful for extending or modifying the commands available on a file's shortcut menu. Once a new command is added it will then appear as an available command when you right-click on a file.

CAUTION

> When you create a new file association or change an existing file association, make sure the program you associate with a particular file type can open the specified file type. With some program and file type combinations, you might need to perform a custom installation of the program first to install the needed import/export filters so the program can open and save the specified file type. For example, Microsoft Word's default installation has limited compatibility with WordPerfect files. A custom installation of Microsoft Word or Microsoft Office lets you select the necessary import/export filters for WordPerfect files.

DISPLAYING SPECIFIC FILE EXTENSIONS

Displaying all file extensions can clutter the Windows Explorer view. Some file types are easily identified by distinct icons without having the extension visible. By default, Windows XP hides the file extensions for registered file types.

However, if you prefer to see the file extensions (displaying them makes it easier to select an alternative program to use to open and edit a file), you can configure Windows Explorer to display them.

You have two options for displaying file extensions. The first option is to configure the Folder Options so the extensions for all known file types are displayed. The second option is to configure only specific file extensions to be displayed.

Use the following procedure to display specific file extensions:

1. From the Tools menu, click Folder Options.
2. Click the File Types tab.
3. From the list of registered file types, highlight the extension type you want displayed and click the Advanced button.
4. Select the option to Always show extension (see Figure 12.19).

12

Figure 12.19
Specifying the option to display the file extension used by Microsoft Word at all times.

MODIFYING AUTOMATIC DOWNLOAD BEHAVIORS

Another thing you can do when configuring file types is change the way in which files with a specific extension are downloaded. If you refer back to Figure 12.24, you will see an option that allows you to specify what Windows should do after downloading a file with a specific extension. The default setting is to have Windows confirm before it opens a file that has been downloaded (regardless of the extension). Clearing this option means that all files with that specific extension will be automatically opened.

OFFLINE FILES AND FOLDERS

Clicking on the Offline Files tab brings up a dialog box, as shown in Figure 12.20. Offline Files is a great tool for mobile users or if your network temporarily goes down. It allows you to continue to work on files that are normally stored in a shared folder on a network. When the network is up again or you dock a mobile computer, the cached offline files stored on your computer are synchronized with those on the network.

SETUP AND CONFIGURATION

Windows XP enables Offline Files by default. You can also choose when to have the files synchronized with those on the network when you log on or when you log off.

TIP

Keep in mind what happens when you enable Offline Files and Folders for a specific user. If the data is large, the user could be stuck waiting for synchronization when they log in, or worse...when they're waiting to go home. When you implement Offline Files and Folders, make sure that only the *most essential* data is synchronized.

You can also configure the amount of disk space to use for caching files. The default is set to 10% of the drive. Depending on the amount of space you have and the number of files being cached, you may want to increase or decrease this setting.

Figure 12.20
Configuring Offline
Files.

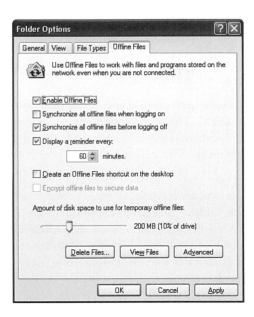

At the bottom of the Offline Files tab, you will see three buttons:

- **Delete Files**—Deletes the offline files stored in the cache. This option is handy if you are running low on disk space. Only the files in the cache are deleted, not the files stored on the network.

- **View Files**—Displays a list of files that are currently available offline.

- **Advanced**—Allows you to configure how your computer behaves when it becomes disconnected from the network (see Figure 12.21).

Figure 12.21
Configuring advanced
settings for offline
files. Click the Add
button to specify a
computer used for
synchronization and
the action to take
when the connection
is lost.

12

Flagging Files and Folders for Offline Synchronization

Offline files and folders are somewhat annoying to administer because, unlike the Briefcase, there is no single place to simply view and administer the feature. Then again, we're talking about a tool that has more features than Briefcase, too.

Once Offline Files and Folders have been enabled and configured, you need to define which files and folders will be synchronized. The process for doing this is easy: Simply use Explorer to navigate to the file location, right-click on it, and select the Make Available Offline option from the pop-up menu. This option will not appear if offline files and folders are not enabled.

Once files have been flagged for synchronization, all other administrative tasks can occur from the Tools, Folder Options, Offline Files tab in Explorer. Synchronized files can be viewed and accessed from the View Files button, or from the Offline Files shortcut on the desktop, if that particular option is enabled. Synchronized files themselves can be deleted from this interface, but they will reappear when synchronization occurs again. If it becomes necessary to remove an item from the synchronization list, the Delete button can be used to do so.

Once offline files and folders have been fully configured, here's the general idea of what happens when a network failure occurs:

1. A user is editing a network-based file that also is configured for offline file usage.
2. The network connection fails for any reason (NIC failure, cable failure, switch failure, power failure, and so on).
3. The Offline Status icon on the taskbar flashes a balloon indicating that all or part of the network server is unavailable.
4. The user continues working: Saves the file (apparently to the network), opens another file (from the same location), and so on.
5. The problem is resolved, and connectivity is restored.
6. The user saves the file to the network, and upon synchronization, any other unsynchronized files are updated.

The Bulk of Administration: Folder Properties

Throughout this chapter, we've discussed methods of configuring Windows Explorer. Now, we're going to investigate some of the advanced methods of file and folder management.

Indexing, Compression, and Encryption

When a folder's properties are accessed within Explorer, My Computer, or My Documents, the General tab contains location, file size, and attribute information for the folder. The Advanced button displays advanced attributes which can be toggled on and off.

By default, the system will enable the Indexing Service to index all folders in order to allow for speedier searches, as discussed earlier in this chapter.

Compression is an option that is available from both drive properties and folder properties. *Compression* uses advanced algorithms to physically reduce file sizes when they are written to the disk. Similarly, when a file is read from the disk, the processor must decompress the data before the user can view it. While this usually makes for a handy feature for saving disk space, it can spell disaster for any system where performance is a concern: specifically XP systems that may be running low on RAM, or whose processors are overloaded. Additionally, compression can only be enabled with NTFS-formatted drives, and is not available with FAT or FAT32 partitions.

Encryption is another handy feature that adds security on the local workstation. *Encryption* uses a set of public and private keys to encrypt data in such a manner that it can only be viewed by the person who encrypted it. Once a folder is encrypted, any new files that are saved within that folder are automatically encrypted also. Files that are copied from an encrypted folder will remain encrypted, provided that the destination is on an NTFS volume in a Windows XP, 2000, or Windows Server 2003 system. If the destination is FAT, or is located on a Windows NT system, the file will be decrypted after an alert message appears.

Generally, encryption is a good thing, but once in a blue moon, it can be the source of a problem. First, truly secure encryption can only occur locally, and not on the network. Yes, it is possible to encrypt a file that is located on a network server, but the data is *not* encrypted while it is in transit between Windows XP and the server. There are workarounds for this involving Windows .NET and 2000 IPSec and a strict network security policy, but these policies aren't really available for other networks such as Lotus or NetWare. It's important to keep this in mind if security is a priority in the environment.

Another encryption annoyance occurs when the encrypting user no longer has access to the data: His account has been disabled, he's forgotten his local password, or he's left the company. This isn't really a big deal if the system is on a Windows domain where an Administrator can simply change the password, log in as the user, and decrypt the data. The problem becomes a real concern when there is no administrative way to log in as the user. Encryption is keyed specifically for the user account's security identifier (SID) that is generated when the account is created. Data cannot be decrypted without the appropriate keys, which are linked to that SID. SIDs change from account to account, even when every other aspect of the account is identical. Luckily, Microsoft has provided a backdoor for decrypting data in just this situation. The backdoor involves using the Data Recovery Agent (DRA). The DRA is a designated account that has the ability to decrypt data. By default, this is the administrator. The administrator (or other account that is the designated DRA) can decrypt data on behalf of any other user account on the system.

Encryption and decryption are a part of the Microsoft Certificate Services, which includes a range of security options and features available at both the local and domain level.

12

→ It's recommended that prior to implementing encryption, you consider the full suite of security options described in Chapter 11, "Creating and Managing User Accounts."

FOLDER TEMPLATES

Windows XP allows you to customize the appearance of folders within Windows Explorer. With folder templates, you can customize a folder based on its contents. Choosing a specific template will apply special features to the folder. For example, if your folder contains pictures, you may want to choose the Pictures or Photo Album template.

TIP

> If you apply the Pictures or Photo Album template to a folder, you will then have another view added to the View menu called Filmstrip. The Filmstrip view adds toolbar buttons so you can view your pictures like a filmstrip.

Use the following procedure to apply a specific template to a folder:

1. Right-click a folder within Windows Explorer and click Properties from the shortcut menu.
2. From the properties window for the folder, click the Customize tab (see Figure 12.22).
3. Under What Kind of Folder Do You Want?, use the drop-down box to select a folder template.
4. Select the Also Apply This Template to All Subfolders option to apply the template to all folders within your customized folder.

Figure 12.22
Choosing the Photo Album folder template.

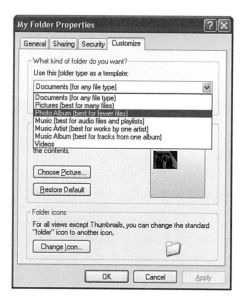

NOTE

> You cannot customize the My Documents, My Pictures, or My Music folders. You can, however, customize any folders within them.

You can further customize the appearance of a folder by changing the thumbnail icon identifying it (remember you must be in thumbnail view) for a helpful reminder of the contents of the folder.

To change the thumbnail for a folder, use the Customize tab for the folder properties and click the Choose Picture button. You can then browse and select the picture you want displayed on the folder. If you choose the Restore default button, the last images within the folder that were modified will be used as the thumbnails.

If you are not in thumbnail view you can use the Folder Icons options (again available on the Customize tab) to change the icon identifying the folder. Clicking on the Change Icon button brings up a window from which you can select a new folder icon (see Figure 12.23).

Figure 12.23
Selecting a new folder icon from the icons in the Shell32.dll file.

SPECIAL FOLDERS: MY DOCUMENTS, MY PICTURES, SHARED FILES, AND SO ON

Everyone likes to have their own personal space. This is kind of what the My Documents folder is for. It's your own personal folder for storing files, pictures, music, and more. By default, it contains two subfolders called My Pictures and My Music. You can share the contents of the folder with others or you can make it private so only you can view them.

TIP

> You can make the folders within My Documents folder private so no one other than yourself can view the contents (if the drive is formatted with NTFS). For more information see the following knowledge base article: http://support.microsoft.com/default.aspx?scid=KB;EN-US;Q298399&.

Each user that logs on to Windows XP has a personal folder named after their first name. When a user logs on, the same folder is displayed in My Documents.

If your computer is a member of a workgroup, Windows XP also creates another folder for each user called Shared Documents. It also contains two subfolders called Shared Pictures and Shared Music. This folder is intended as a storage place for content that you want to share with others on your network.

NOTE

> If you want to remove this folder from My Computer you can use the registry editor and create a Dword value named NoSharedDocuments under HKEY_CURRENT_USER\ Software\Microsoft\Windows\CurrentVersion\Policies\Explorer. Set the Dword value to 1.

WHERE USERS' MY DOCUMENTS FOLDERS ARE ACTUALLY LOCATED

When a user logs on to Windows XP, the My Documents folder appears on the desktop. The folders are actually stored in a user's profile on the C partition. To locate a user's personal folder, navigate to the Documents and Settings folder. In here you will find a folder for each user that logs on to the computer. Each of these folders will contain a My Documents folder. Keep in mind that it will only be named My Documents for the user that is currently logged onto the computer. Another user's folder will be assigned the user's first name: for example, DianaB's Documents (see Figure 12.24).

Figure 12.24
Viewing a user's personal folders.

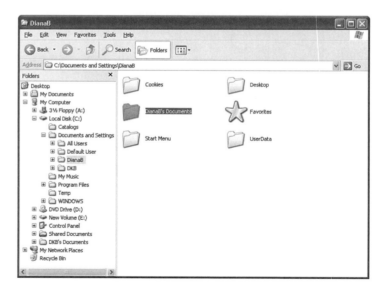

WHY YOU SHOULD USE NETWORK FILE SHARING

One of the nice things about Windows XP is that multiple users can use the same computer while still maintaining some level of privacy when it comes to personal data.

One of the easiest ways in which you can share content among multiple users is by storing it in the Shared Documents folder. The Shared Documents folder is kind of like a central repository where you can store files that you want everyone to be able to access. Instead of having to share individual folders to give others access, you can simply place them into the Shared Documents folder. All users who log on automatically have access to anything placed within this folder.

NOTE

If your computer is a member of a domain, the Shared Documents folder is not available.

If you have files you want to add to the Shared Documents folder use the following procedure:

1. Click the file you want to add to the Shared Documents folder.
2. From the File and Folder task list, select the option to Move this file (see Figure 12.25).
3. From the Move Item window select the Shared Documents folder (see Figure 12.26) and click Move. Once the file is moved into the Shared Documents folder it is accessible to all users that log on to the computer.

Figure 12.25
Selecting a file to move.

ALTERNATIVES TO USING SPECIAL FOLDERS

If you do not want to use the Special Folders, the alternative is to create your own folders and share those that you want to make available to others on the network.

Figure 12.26
Selecting the Shared Documents folder as the destination for the file being moved.

Once you've created a folder, you can use the following procedure to make it available to other users:

1. Right-click the folder you want to share and click Properties from the shortcut menu.
2. From the Properties window for the folder, click the Sharing tab.
3. Select the option to Share this Folder on the Network (see Figure 12.27).
4. Type in a share name for the folder, making it as descriptive as possible so other users can easily identify the contents.
5. If you want other users to be able to make changes to the files within the shared folder select the option to Allow Network Users to Change My Files. This is the same as full access. If you don't select this option, users have read-only access.

Figure 12.27
Sharing a folder with full access.

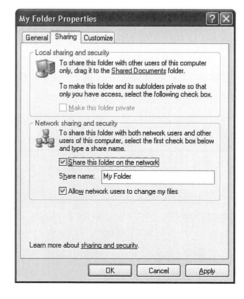

EMBEDDED FOLDERS IN THE START MENU

With Windows XP, you have the ability to embed entire folder structures within the Start Menu, Programs feature. This allows the ability to use the Start Menu for several navigation tasks that would otherwise require Windows Explorer.

The process for embedding folders is the same as adding any item to the Start Menu: Open Explorer, and drag the parent folder to the Start Menu and drop it in the desired location. Hovering over the closed Start button will open the menu, and similar hovering over any section will open the applicable subsections, such as All Programs.

Once a folder has been embedded within the Start menu, its contents can be viewed, opened within Explorer, deleted, or its properties sheet displayed. Folders containing subfolders will be displayed as cascading options that can be navigated from the Start menu ad infinitum.

TROUBLESHOOTING

The following table describes some of the common problems you may run into with Windows Explorer and some suggested resolutions.

TABLE 12.3   COMMON PROBLEMS THAT MAY ARISE IN WINDOWS EXPLORER

Problem	Resolution
System files are not displayed in Windows Explorer.	You must select the option to show hidden files and folders within the Folder Options window.
The option to make a folder private is not available.	The partition must be formatted with NTFS. Only folders within the My Documents folder can be made private.
File extensions are not displayed in Windows Explorer.	You must clear the option to hide extensions for known file types.
Every time you double-click a file with a certain extension it launches the wrong program.	You must edit the file association and change the program that is used to open the files.
The Filmstrip view is not available.	You must change the folder template to Pictures or Photo Album before the Filmstrip option is available.
File details are not automatically displayed.	This is the default behavior. To have the file details displayed, highlight the file and press F3.
Windows is unable to open files with a specific extension.	The file association is lost or there is no program installed to open files of that type. Re-create the file association or have Windows locate a program that can open the files.

CHAPTER **13**

MULTIMEDIA AND IMAGING

In this chapter

MANAGING AND EDITING IMAGES

When it comes to multimedia productivity and personal expression, XP excels significantly when compared to Windows 2000. Microsoft has rolled the multimedia home-user goodies originally developed for Windows 98 and Me into XP, as discussed in Chapter 1, "Introduction to Windows XP." To some, this might lead to misidentifying XP as a whimsical, end-user operating system, but as you know, that's not the case. XP has an NT engine under the hood, and simply has lots of bells and whistles integrated into it.

Even though this book concerns itself primarily with practical matters such as installation, fine tuning, and networking, we thought we'd also cover some of the multimedia issues here as well, especially since those seem to have crept into many folks' everyday work life. Whether for work or for fun, cutting audio CDs, managing and printing digital photographs, and even working with DVD burners have become fairly common activities.

In the early days of post-Windows 3.11, when Windows 95 was the newly crowned lord of the Microsoft manor, there was, as in the previous OS, no place to store documents or other files without the user making a directory themselves. Even Windows NT, Redmond's powerhouse enterprise-grade OS, made it harder to store documents by hiding user data in the system root. When Windows 2000 appeared on the corporate scene it offered a default location appropriately dubbed My Documents. Windows 2000 was a multiple user system that required a better way of organizing each users files and other data (see Figure 13.1). Also, users had complained.

Figure 13.1
Windows 2000 managed images and other media but not with much flair.

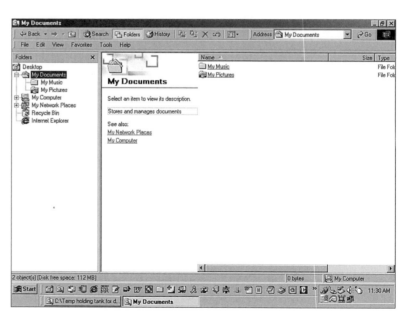

The My Documents directory soon showed up in Windows Me, the follow-up consumer version to Windows 98 Second Edition. Windows Me took the My Documents structure and added a My Pictures subdirectory and the My Music directory. Windows XP is smart enough to recognize what kind of files you are working with and sends these files to the correct directory. If you had a CD-R full of JPG files, XP would recognize that and give you the option of copying them to the My Pictures folder. See Figure 13.2 for a look at XP's improved My Documents folders.

Figure 13.2
Windows XP manages the same files with far more aplomb.

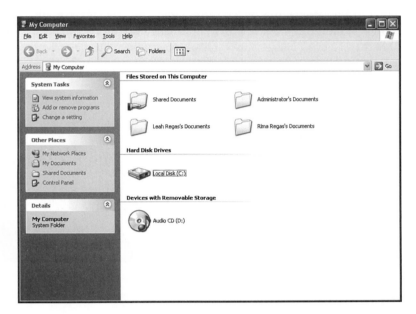

XP adds even more useful features to the My Pictures directory, including a deeply integrated image viewer with very rudimentary editing features. With this integration also comes a pair of new views: Filmstrip and Tiles. The Tiles view isn't very useful if you are interested in previewing the images, but Filmstrip is. Of course, the Thumbnails view is also present, but only Filmstrip offers the rotation buttons, as you can see in Figure 13.3, in the next section.

NOTE

Though XP will warn you, rotating the images using the built-in tools will cause the image to be resampled, often resulting in reduced quality. Try using a third-party tool such as the freeware IrfanVIEW (www.irfanview.com).

XP's ability to recognize file types and offer you logical choices for what to do with them forms the basis for all media file treatment throughout XP. First, though, let's take a look at working with images.

13

VIEWING THUMBNAILS AND PREVIEWS

My Pictures offers up the aforementioned views specifically designed for graphics: Thumbnails and Filmstrip. The Thumbnail view delivers previews in the form of 64×64-pixel resampled versions of the original file, but not much detail. In the Filmstrip view (see Figure 13.3), which only appears when there are graphic files present, these thumbnails appear in a horizontal row underneath a larger, resizable preview area. Selecting an image to preview in Filmstrip mode is as easy as clicking once on the intended image. If there are more than 10 or so images you will likely have to scroll to find what you are looking for.

Figure 13.3
The My Pictures directory in Filmstrip view mode. You can drag files around to rearrange them in a more logical order.

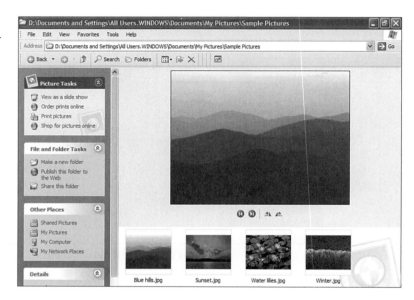

Filmstrip offers the ability to rearrange the order of the thumbnails by dragging and dropping each image where you'd like to have it on the filmstrip. Keep in mind that if you choose to show hidden files in the View tab of the Folder Options dialog found in most windows's Tools menus, they will also appear in the list. Trying to preview some of these files can cause the system to become unstable.

NOTE
Once you change views, the sorting returns to what is set as the default in the Arrange Icons By menu. What this means is that if you rearrange your images in Filmstrip view and then switch views, your customized arrangement will not be retained.

The drag-and-drop trick also works in Thumbnails mode, but the view mode change is limited. For example, switch to Small Icons and back again and the special order you applied will be gone. A better way to manage image files is by arranging them in separate directories. You can make the hierarchy as basic or deep as suits your style.

13

By default the image viewer for XP is Picture and Fax Viewer, a component of XP that is so deeply buried into the system that there's no way to call it directly from the command line or from a script. This behavior is an example of XP's enhanced MIME type system. See Figure 13.4.

Figure 13.4
Windows XP uses its own built-in imaging software to show images and other supported media. Adding codecs and other support files (such as DivX, Targa, Ogg Vorbis, etc...) allows these tools to show more file formats.

Previewing multiple images using the Picture and Fax Viewer, as can be seen in Figure 13.4, is simple. Open one of the images in the directory, and you can access all other images in that same directory by clicking on the Previous or Next buttons at the extreme left of the toolbar that runs across the bottom of the preview window. This method will skip any unsupported files.

IMAGE VIEWING FEATURES

The viewing modes in Explorer are limited, but the Picture and Fax Viewer tool has a few basic tools for simple image modification (see Figure 13.5).

Figure 13.5
The Picture and Fax Viewer's toolbar.

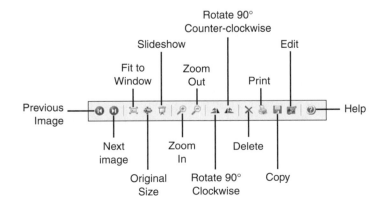

- **Previous Image**—Click to move one image back in the directory.

- **Next Image**—Click to open the next image in the directory.

- **Fit To Window**—Causes the image to be resized to fit in the window. Size is constrained by aspect ratio.

- **Original Size**—Resets the image zoom level to 100%.

- **Slideshow**—Starts the slideshow feature. Control tools appear in the top right corner and fade if the mouse is idle for 5 seconds. The Close button or ESC key quits.

- **Zoom In**—Zooms the image in increments of 10% original image size.

- **Zoom Out**—Zooms image out in the same increments.

- **Rotate 90° Clockwise**—This function redraws the image and saves it over the original, so be careful.

- **Rotate 90° Counterclockwise**—Same as above.

- **Delete**—Deletes the image from the storage media, unless the media is locked or read-only.

- **Print**—Prints the image on the default printer.

- **Copy**—Copies the image to a location of your choice.

- **Edit**—Opens the image in Microsoft Paint, an extremely simple and basic bitmap image editor.

- **Help**—Opens the program's help files.

As you can see, the Image and Fax Viewer is about as simple as you can get. There are other applications, such as the aforementioned IrfanView, which has far reaching abilities and is an invaluable tool for life for anyone who uses it just once.

MANAGING IMAGES WITH XP

Explorer in XP is rather well suited to media organization (see Figure 13.6). Windows Explorer modifies its appearance to visually indicate the directory's contents. Otherwise, organization of files and folders remains essentially the same as in Windows Me and Windows 2000. One of the benefits of the integration of Internet Explorer with Windows Explorer is that more visually adorned interfaces can be designed using existing Internet technologies. Media files are given special treatment in XP.

One way of managing media is by dragging and grouping files manually. This method, as mentioned earlier, allows you to modify the relative position of files to each other. Birthdays are common examples, so you could place all of Wendy's images at the top, Bob's below hers, and the office St. Patrick's Day party pictures on the bottom. Of course, changing view modes eliminates the custom sorting and reverts back to the mode you have specified as default, so it behooves one to not change it often, if at all.

Figure 13.6
Windows Explorer showing a directory full of images and the images watermark in the background. Note the Picture Tasks in the Tasks Pane on the left.

You can organize your images as XP imports them from your digital camera (see Figure 13.7). While it's not all that smart (it can't give nice names to each file individually), it can change the name from the completely incomprehensible mess digital cameras typically generate into something relatively readable. You can rename photos automatically when transferring them to the computer using the Scanner and Camera Wizard in Windows XP. This is the most convenient way to change the file names of a number of photos at once.

Figure 13.7
Installing a new camera on Windows XP is easy. It's even easier to get images off of the camera when its integrated with XP.

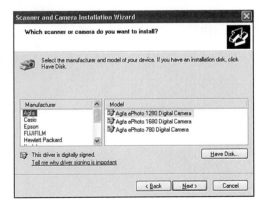

To start the Scanners and Cameras Installation Wizard, go to Start, Control Panel and open Scanners and Cameras. If XP didn't detect a camera or you haven't installed it yet, you will be prompted to have your camera automatically detected or select your camera from a list, as shown in Figure 13.7. Once the camera is installed (there are few that are not supported on XP) you may then access the Scanner and Camera Wizard by opening your camera or scanner's name that will now be in the Scanners and Cameras Control Panel.

Once you get to the Picture Name and Destination page of the wizard, you are offered two data entry opportunities. First is the Group Name, the static portion of the filename of each imported image. The wizard automatically adds the increasing numbers to make each image file unique. Of course, if you are into personal anguish you can change the names individually.

NOTE

If you are just starting to use a digital camera, do yourself a favor and develop an organizational system up front. Friends of ours did not and accumulated 25,000 images taking up 50GB of drive space and they spent weeks cleaning it up.

You can apply an image as desktop wallpaper. Simply select the image you want, click on the Set As Desktop Background link under Picture Tasks or right-click the image and select the same item, and wait a few seconds. You can also order prints from an online service, or even look for pictures to purchase over the Internet. You can order prints from Fuji Color, Shutterfly, or Kodak via Ofoto's online service. For additional images, XP offers stock from Microsoft's own Design Gallery Live, MSN's Photos service, BizPresenter.com, and GettyWorks (see Figure 13.8).

Figure 13.8
Go online to get images from a number of sources, including GettyWorks, a source for incredible stock photographs.

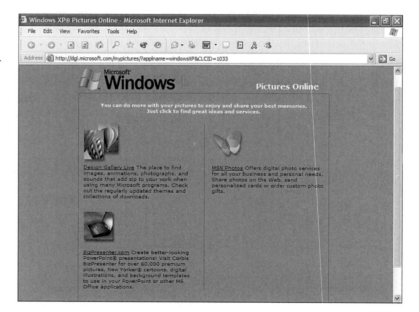

PRINTING IMAGES

Printing images is the same as printing other documents except you will use the Photo Printing Wizard.

The Photo Printing Wizard, seen in Figure 13.9, makes it easy to select numerous images to print sequentially. You can also select a printer if you have more than one or are using a specialty printer such as Adobe's PDF Writer.

Figure 13.9
Starting up the Printing Wizard and selecting images to include in the run.

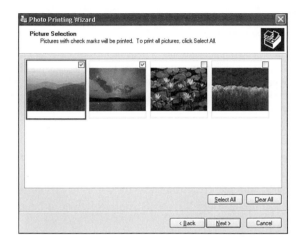

WINDOWS MEDIA PLAYER

In the past, Microsoft has ignored obvious trends and left the Media Player about as bare bones as you can get while Apple was busy working on QuickTime, and Real was already starting to establish its dominance in Internet audio and video streaming technologies. Microsoft did, however, start to get the idea and released Windows Media Player (WMP) 7.0, which also marked the first time Microsoft deliberately created an application that uses what are termed "skins" and offers "Visualizations" (see Figure 13.10).

Figure 13.10
Windows Media Player 9 Series showing a "visualization."

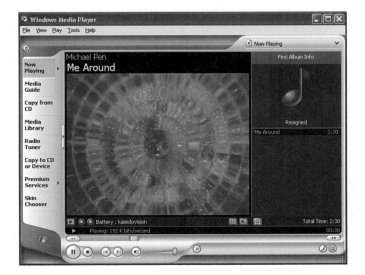

13

What Are Skins and Visualizations?

First skins. The term arose from the programmatic practice of laying a different appearance over the default user interface look. An example of this is StarDock's WindowBlinds, which can, along with hundreds of other skins, make Windows appear to be a Macintosh computer. The regular Windows look is still under the skin, which is why aficionados call them skins, but it is covered. Windows Media Player 7, 8, and 9 Series use skins to change the shape and appearance of the program itself.

Now visualizations. On the other end of the audio spectrum came the development of visualizations, which first appeared in the WinAmp software which is now owned by America Online. The most basic visualization is a pattern of colored lines that pulsate to the rhythm of the music, but they can get quite a bit more complex.

Of course, the key elements to WMP7 were streaming audio and video, access to the online Windows Media service, the introduction of several new codecs (many of which are proprietary), and rudimentary DVD playback capabilities. The final added attraction, though, was the ability to "rip" CD audio tracks into MP3 or WMA files, organize them using playlists, burn your own CD mixes, and even resample and copy files to mobile devices. The introduction of WMP7 was a huge leap for Microsoft and has helped it become a large contender in an area it had previous dismissed.

NOTE

> A codec is a made up word that is short for Compression/Decompression, and that's what a codec does. QuickTime uses, among others, the Sorenson codec for streaming internet video. Other common codecs are MP3; MPEG-1, which is common to Video CDs and Super Video CDs; MPEG-2 which is used for DVDs; and Real's series of video and audio codecs. There are literally hundreds more like the Ogg Vorbis codec which is gaining popularity, and DivX, which started its life as a mix of MPEG-2 video and MP3 audio and is now its own proprietary codec.

The current version of WMP is what Microsoft calls the 9 Series. While essentially the same as WMP7 in terms of capabilities and features, the key differences are shiny new codecs and the addition of premium fee-based features. WMP9S also takes on a series of new plug-in capabilities, allowing third-party software developers to more easily integrate new capabilities, much like AOL's WinAmp has been doing for years now. WMP9S also incorporates Roxio's CD-R burning technology more deeply (it first appeared as an add-on to WMP 7.2) and Microsoft's Super Codec, Windows Media Audio 9, which the company claims is their in-house developed MP3 killer.

WMA VERSUS MP3

WMA and MP3 have been squaring off for some time now, at least ever since WMP7 took center stage in Windows Me. Both codecs, however, are quite similar in how they go about reducing the size of your favorite music. The goal, not surprisingly, is to render listenable audio from "White Book" audio CD content and store it on your computer or other digital media. Having digital, portable versions of your media is convenient because you can load it to a portable player or PDA, make your music more accessible and organized, and make your own CD mixes. Whatever the reason, there are benefits but it also has to sound right.

MP3, more accurately know as MPEG-I Layer 3 audio encoding, was designed by Fraunhofer Laboratories to work with and around the human ear and how humans perceive sound in relation to the tolerances and frequency ranges of audio media. A dog whistle illustrates how dogs have the ability to hear higher pitched sounds compared to what we can hear. CD audio is like a dog whistle in that it can reproduce sounds that we as humans will never explicitly hear. MP3 encoding removes these sounds, and when you remove data from a file it gets smaller, allowing you to cram more onto a storage card for a portable MP3 player or PDA. How much gets removed depends on two factors, data rate measured in Kilobits Per Second (Kb/s) and bit depth measured in Kilohertz (KHz).

Windows Media Audio (WMA) works along similar lines, but since it's Microsoft's proprietary technology, we can only surmise how it works. In general, it works by not only removing ranges outside of our hearing but also re-encoding the remaining audio to then approximate the removed components. WMA encoding's ability to trick the human ear is finite, as we can see in matching MP3 and WMA files together in an impromptu test.

In general, MP3 audio encoded at 320Kb/s and 44.1KHz is indistinguishable from the original source. The same file reduced to 192Kb/s and left at 44.1KHz remains indistinguishable. Re-encode the digital source to 128Kb/s at 44.1KHz and you've reached the limit where anything less will sound like its being played in a can. Most people are happy with 128/44.1 MP3 audio, and this is the most common encoding for the codec. For audiophiles and aficionados, however, anything short of 256/44.1 is unthinkable. In comparison, FM radio falls in the 128Kb/s to 192Kb/s data rate range at 22.05 KHz where it sounds really good, but the halved KHz saps out the depth and timbre.

WMA encoding tries to rebuild the higher quality audio output by resampling the remaining frequencies using complex mathematical algorithms that are designed to fool the human ear. The WMA7 codec was about on par with MP3 at the time, but the WMA8 codec started to change that. WMA8 files encoded at half the data rate of MP3 files and were mostly indistinguishable from the larger MP3 version. This means that a 64Kb/s WMA file is, to the human ear, almost identical to the 128Kb/s in sound quality and at half the size. If you go below 64Kb/s second, however, you start to hear serious anomalies in audio quality and a periodic, odd channel-sliding effect where an artifact will move from one speaker to the next and back again.

It is because of the low bit rate problems WMA files exhibit that MP3 and RealAudio codecs remain the most popular over slow connections. As an example, you can encode the "This Too Shall Pass" track from Bruce Hornsby's *Big Swing Face* album at 320Kb/s and 44.1KHz, and it produces a 11.4MB MP3 file. Re-encode that in WMA7 at 64Kb/s and 44.1KHz and the file shrinks to 2.4MB in size and still sounds quite good. It would sound

13

even better in WMA9. This particular track has a strong, deep syncopated percussion pattern that destroys playback if recorded at higher gains, even in 320Kb/s MP3. This is why it's best to "rip" via digital extraction and not through a pre-amp or pre-processor.

In the end it's about which codec you prefer. There are audio players for most platforms that are capable of playing a wide range of formats. WMA files can even be played on a Mac using Microsoft's Windows Media Player for Mac OS X. Even Linux users aren't excluded. The general consensus says that MP3 encoding is more "pure," because it only removes elements from the source and leaves the rest untouched. WMA, on the other hand, rewrites the source to try and recapture the original sound quality in a smaller file, which is, in essence, cheating. Of course, file formats don't worry about ethics and its not an ethical dilemma.

Use the procedure in the next section to "rip" an audio CD using various encodings to see what you like best. Unfortunately, you'll have to purchase MP3 encoding capabilities for WMP9S but it's quite inexpensive. Other factors that will define audio quality is the system on which you play these files. If you have $10 speakers that shipped with your desktop you won't be hearing the best sound that even an old 16-bit audio card can offer. Try connecting your superior home stereo system to your soundcard using a two-headed stereo patch cable (Radio Shack Cat# 42-2551, $6.99, has 1/8th" phone tip on one end and stereo RCA jacks on the other) or, if your soundcard and system both support optical, get their nice patch cable (Cat# 15-1093, $59.99). If you're a real audiophile you might want to invest in a line leveler, if you don't already have one. If you have to ask what one is, you're not an Audiophile.

TIP

> If your aim is to convert your entire CD library to digital files (check your available hard drive space!) there are two options that you will find priceless. Go to Tools, Options and click on the Copy Music tab. Check the boxes marked Copy CD When Inserted and Eject CD When Copying Is Completed in the Copy Settings section. This will dramatically speed up conversion. Just make sure you're using WMP9S. WMP 8 does not offer this feature.

TIP

> You may or may not want to uncheck the Copy Protect Music option in the same locale. This depends on your equipment limitations. Some devices refuse to play copy protected files. Others won't play without copy protection. Most, however, are quite flexible. Try both settings on a few sample files in both MP3 and WMA encoding to see what works and what doesn't.

COPYING TRACKS FROM A CD

Copying tracks from a CD is a piece of cake:

1. Insert an audio CD into the first CD drive. It's the first drive that is digitally connected to the soundcard. If you have a CD-R/RW drive in addition to a CD or DVD drive, that one most likely has the digital audio connection. Referring to your manufacturer's documentation may or may not reveal whether your model supports digital audio connections. See Figure 13.11.

Figure 13.11
The Digital Extraction setting, shown here as Digital CD Playback, for the author's drive in the drive's Properties sheet. Some systems will crash if this is set on a drive that is not supported.

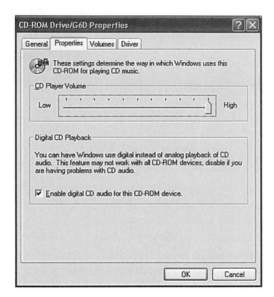

TIP

If you cannot determine which drive is connected to the soundcard for digital extraction, then you have two choices. You can try extracting data digitally. If it fails, the drive isn't connected. On some systems you can turn on digital extraction (go to the Properties tab in the devices Properties dialog for the drive located in the Device Manager) and watch the system crash if it doesn't support the setting (but most won't crash). Finally, you can open the case, find the back of the drives, and look for a thin little pair of loosely twisted wires that run from the drive to the sound card. That drive should have the feature enabled.

2. Select the Copy from CD item if it isn't already active. By default, all of the disc's tracks are selected. If this is contrary to what you want, uncheck the offending cuts. When you are done, click on the button near the top of the window labeled Copy Music. You can click Stop to end the playback of the disc being copied. It won't stop the copy operation. A completed copy operation can be seen in Figure 13.12.

Figure 13.12
The result of a CD copy operation. WMP9S downloads data on the CD, a cover image, song lyrics, and even a review. Note the "Buy CD" link in the top right corner of the window? Ironic, because in order to legally copy it you should already have it.

THE WMP9S MEDIA LIBRARY

It's hard enough maintaining thousands of digital media files without having to do it across several different applications. WMP9S's Media Library collects and organizes all media files on your drive and removable media. In older versions, such as WMP7, the Library was very dumb. If you kept all digital media in one directory and added some that were not cataloged already, you would have to add each item individually. It was easier to simply delete the WMP Media Library database and have it search anew. WMP9S fixes that and then some. If you add media, WMP 9S can scan the entire drive and only add the newest additions, ignoring the files already added. If you prefer, you can even have WMP9S check to see if what it has in the library matches what's in the file system. Slick.

The Media Library is divided into several hierarchical sections. The sections are

- All Music
- All Video
- Other Media
- My Playlists
- Auto Playlists
- Radio
- Premium Services

Under each of those sections are subsections. WMP9S uses online information and MP3 tag data to make several determinations about how the media should be entered into the library. By default these are Artist, Album, and Genre for music; Actor and Genre for Video; and Genre for other media. The Radio category is divided into My Favorites, Featured Stations, and Recently Played.

The My Playlists and Auto Playlists sections are catchalls for playlists that you create and special playlists created for WMP9S that are designed to "play" to your moods and listening patterns. Of course, the Auto Playlists aren't completely automatic. You have to spend time playing and rating your music with WMP9S before it can start to get a sense of what you like and when you listen to music (see Figure 13.13).

Figure 13.13
The rating system (see the column with the stars) allows you to rate what you like and what you don't, powering the new Auto Playlists system in WMP9S.

Most people pick a single application for something they want to do and stick with it. Multimedia, though, has so many facets that few single applications can command everything a media junkie needs. WMP9S aims to do away with that concept and provide organization and replay capabilities for all kinds of media file formats. A good number of file formats, like DivX 5.x, require downloading and installing additional files before WMP9S can play them back.

MANAGING CODECS

The word *codec* is nerd slang for Compression Decompression Algorithm, but Codecal didn't sound right, so codec was born. MP3, WMA, AVI, DivX, and MPEG are all codecs. WMP9S, like its predecessors, can automatically download the bulk of these common codecs and install them. If you are a broadband user, you might not even notice it happening. At least from that point of view there's nothing to manage. You can see a list of the installed codecs via Control Panel, Sounds and Audio Devices, Hardware tab. Choose Audio Codecs or Video Codecs, click the Properties button, and then the Properties tab. Figure 13.14 shows an example.

13

Figure 13.14
A list of the installed codecs available to Windows. Some deal with video and others handle audio. All of them are generally good about working together.

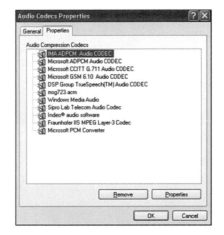

CREATING CDs WITH DIGITAL RIGHTS IN PLACE

XP makes it easy to burn media files onto a CD-R/RW or DVD-R/+R disc, depending on your hardware. Most of today's modern portable and auto CD players are capable of reading CD-R/RW media, but some cannot. There are even numerous portable CD players that can decode MP3 audio files burned onto a CD-R/RW disc. While all this copying of music, movies, and other media makes things more convenient for us, someone owns the copyright to that media and is trying to make a living off of it. This is why Microsoft has started incorporating digital rights into WMP9S.

WMP9S allows you to decide for yourself whether you are going to secure the copy or not (see Figure 13.15). If you do, WMP9S adjusts for conversion to a secure device. Limitations apply, such as you cannot copy the music to an Apple iPod for Windows and then deliver another copy to a friend's computer downtown.

Figure 13.15
Making the choice. Since there are no laws against fair use there should be no moral dilemma involved, but your values are important, so let them guide your choice.

To burn a CD with digital rights management enabled, do the following:

1. Go to Start, All Programs, and then select Windows Media Player.
2. Insert a blank CD-R/RW.
3. Switch to the Copy to CD or Device tab and select what you want to copy.
4. Click Copy Music in the top right corner.
5. In the dialog box that appears, select to encode the files.

This process causes the Roxio CD recording software that actually handles the burning to take over. Letting WMP9S encode the files, despite the fact that it is quite advanced, takes a very long time. Most of the time, once you've copied protected media to a single device, for example a portable MP3 player, they cannot be copied again. Of course, not all devices support this 100% so there are some loopholes.

NOTE

As was mentioned before, WMP9S does not have the ability to natively encode MP3 files, though it can play them. In order to encode in MP3 you'll have to acquire a third-party solution. Check out the Windows Media Web site for details. The two options offered at the 9 Series Web site (go to Tools, Plug-ins, Download Plug-ins when you are online) are CyberLink's MP3 PowerEncoder and InterVideo's MP3 XPack, both available to purchase and download. MusicMatch is another popular application that performs more or less like WMP9S and provides MP3 coding capability.

Ripping a store-bought CD onto your hard drive using Windows Media Player automatically creates a license for the version of that track on your computer, but the licenses are not updated automatically. That job is up to you. The assumption is that you will only need a single license because audio CDs never get updated like software. To ensure your license stays active:

1. Go to Tools, License Management.
2. Click Restore Now.

In order for this process to work, you need to have an active Internet connection. The process also sends unique data to Microsoft's DRM servers in order to validate the request. This helps prevent licenses from being swapped willy nilly.

Of course, on occasion you may want to enable another computer to play protected media. It's easy enough to back up license files to a floppy disk, but the machine that they will be moved to must also have an active Internet connection and validate the license files with Microsoft's DRM servers.

PROTECTING YOUR LICENSES

Using Windows of any variety is never perfect. Because of this, there are backup devices, recovery services, and a slew of related protection rackets. The basics, though, should never

13

be ignored, and it's annoying to re-rip your CDs to reinitiate the license after having ripped 5,000 tracks from your classical collection.

There are two things you should do:

1. Save a local copy of your licenses.
2. Save an off-site copy of your licenses.

The local copy is good for small disasters and the big one is for those periodic full recovery fests that come around when least wanted. Performing the backup, either one that is, is simple. Go to Tools, Licenses Management (see Figure 13.16). In the dialog you can select where to save to or restore from, the default being the License Backup subdirectory to your chosen newly copied media directory.

Figure 13.16
License management is easy for the end user, but it involves a lot of behind-the-scenes work.

> **NOTE**
>
> Every once in a while, change the directory to a floppy or other removable media drive and save a copy there.

The files that are produced are proprietary to WMP and are only useful to WMP users. If you enable protection *and* have hidden files shown in Folder Options, you would see the following:

- drmv1key.bak
- drmv1lic.bak
- drmv2key.bak
- drmv2lic.bak

COPYING FILES TO CD-R/RW DRIVES

CD-R/RW discs are the most common casual backup media these days, long overshadowing ZIP disks and the now ancient floppy disks. XP offers probably the easiest way of copying files to and from CD media of any operating system right out of the box. In fact, XP comes with the ability to write to CD-R/RW discs where most systems require the purchase of a third-party solution. This is really good because the CD-R is likely the most perfect mass storage medium, despite its seemingly limited 700MB capacity.

13

Other popular aspects of CD-R/RW media are ease of storage, relative durability, and rock-bottom prices. There are also dozens of suppliers, many of them well known and respected among consumers (such as, Sony, 3M, TDK, and so on). Combine these aspects with the fact that nearly every new PC that ships comes with a CD-R/RW burner and you can see why they are so popular. XP makes it very easy to use CD-R/RW media to copy files. All you need is a CD burner, and XP recognizes a huge number of available drives.

The process of copying files is very easy:

1. Place a blank disc in the CD-R/RW drive.
2. Open My Computer and navigate to the files you want to copy (see Figure 13.17).

Figure 13.17
Selecting files for
inclusion on the disc.

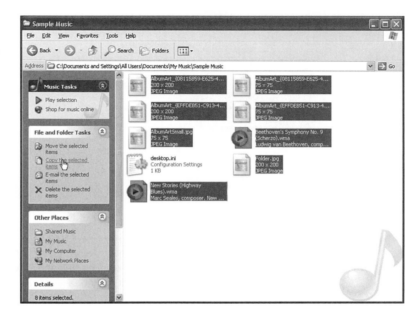

3. Select the files you want to copy (see Figure 13.17) and select the most appropriate option in the File and Folder Tasks pane. Images and audio files skip a step, as this interim step is automated for these file types. A dialog will open asking where to copy (see Figure 13.18). Select the burner and click OK.
4. In the Copy Items dialog box, click the CD recording drive, and then click Copy.

Once you're done and you're ready to burn the actual disc, you need to tell XP to burn it (see Figure 13.19). Go to My Computer and right-click on the burner's drive letter. Select Write Files to Disc and you're off. You can send various files from all over the file system to the disc for burning when you're done. This also conveniently removes the need for a formal interface, eliminating a step from the process. If you want to start over, you can select the Delete Files from Cache option. No actual files will be deleted, though, even if you chose to move them instead of copy.

13

Figure 13.18
Selecting the CD-R/RW drive to store the files.

Figure 13.19
In the My Computer root, you select the burner and choose the Write Files to Disc option in the contextual menu. This action burns the files.

NOTE

> Pay close attention to capacities. If you exceed the capacity of your media the write will fail and you'll have a nice, new coaster. If you require overburning, look to a third-party utility such as Nero Burning ROM (www.ahead.de) or Roxio's gear (www.roxio.com). All CD-Rs and CD-RWs have more room than they state. Overburning can take advantage of that extra space, but it's more an art than science.

13

There are two additional options to look at. First is related to XP's new insertion notification capabilities. XP actually scans the CD to see what is stored on it. By default, XP asks what you want to do, but you can change that behavior to suit your needs. The second is controlling whether XP ejects the CD after burning or not. If you burn a lot of CDs, you might find it annoying. You can access both of these options here:

1. Open My Computer.
2. Right–click on the CD recording drive. Select Properties.

The insertion behaviors are on the AutoPlay tab (see Figure 13.20) and ejection is on the Recording tab (see Figure 13.21).

Figure 13.20
The AutoPlay tab.

Figure 13.21
The Recording tab.

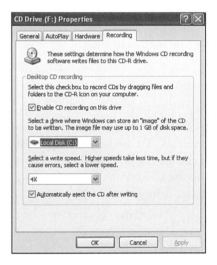

13

CD-R/RW TROUBLESHOOTING

Usually problems center on a driver mishap, or the drive mechanism has failed. Check the drive's properties sheet for details (see Figure 13.22).

The chances that it is anything other than a faulty driver is unlikely. Because of Windows XP's architecture, which tries to accommodate as many past architectures as possible, the backward compatibility can often get more complicated than what it was meant to run on. Additionally, most device drivers are still not "signed" as per Microsoft's requirements, meaning compatibility will not be guaranteed. What this really says is that Microsoft recognizes how complex the system is and steps back away from responsibility, leaving compatibility to the driver makers.

Figure 13.22
A typical removable optical media drive's Properties sheet. XP allows a number of options for managing drivers and makes it easier to handle faulty drivers than previous versions of the operating system.

What does this mean for you? It means that you can break anything every time you install something new. How can you prevent problems? You can't, but you can be careful. A general rule that I try to follow is to install each piece of new software one at a time, with restarts in between. If something fails, remove the last install and check for updates. For more culprits, check the following list:

- Stick a blank CD-R or CD-RW in the drive.

- The blank disc may be damaged. Try another one.

- You may have exceeded your available cache. Regular CD-Rs need around 700MB of cache space; high capacity discs need 1GB. Check your Recycle Bins to make sure they aren't full. You may also want to change the drive the cache is on if you have more than one drive. In My Computer, go to the CD burner, get the drive's Properties, switch to the recording tab, and select another drive letter.

- XP may be trying to burn at a speed greater than is supported by the drive. You can force it to burn slower. In My Computer go to the CD burner, get the drive's Properties, switch to the recording tab, and select either the maximum your drive can burn at or a lower speed.

- Something else may be using the drive. With multitasking one never knows.

- Try a different brand of media. Some of the lesser quality media doesn't work well in most drives.

- Your drive might not work. You may have to install additional drivers for your device to work properly with XP.

- The files you want to write to the disc may be damaged. Try burning other files.

- Update to the latest firmware, though this is not suggested. Rarely does a drive require a firmware update and updates can fail to the point where it cannot be recovered, rendering the drive useless.

DVD Troubleshooting

DVD drives have their own set of issues, but can be susceptible to CD-R problems. Run through the list in the CD-R/RW section and then come back here. You should know, though, that DVD media is far denser than CD media, meaning it is also more susceptible to physical damage. If your errors are related to a single DVD and everything else works fine, replace the DVD. Primarily the problem lies with software and/or hardware. The biggest software culprit is the software decoder. The biggest hardware culprit is usually an older system. Nothing much short of a 633MHz Pentium III/Celeron system with 256MB of RAM will run DVDs without hardware decoding, and it's less expensive to get a new computer.

One thing to keep in mind is that WMP9S is the middleman, relying on third-party software to actually decode the DVD media. Try playing the disc in the player that ships with your decoder. If that doesn't work then you know it's not WMP. At that point you need to check with your vendor about patches and other updates. You could try removing the software and reinstalling it, but that rarely works. Also, don't bother trying the compatibility tools. Those are designed for applications that came before the rise of DVD.

DVD playback relies on a lot of system resources to work, so the problem might also come from a driver for another component or even a hardware incompatibility. The error might even come from a legacy component such as DirectShow or from Microsoft's own DirectX multimedia layer. For DirectShow, you can run the older mplayer32.exe file located in the Windows Media Player directory. For DirectX problems, upgrade to the latest version of DirectX *and* upgrade your video card's drivers.

Finally, if you have to reduce display resolution, reduce color depth, or reduce video acceleration performance then the problem is with your hardware. At this point you should strongly consider upgrading certain hardware components to catch up with the obsolescence that seems to closely follow Windows versions.

13

INTERNET APPLICATIONS

In this chapter

Windows XP contains updated versions of Microsoft's popular Internet programs, including Internet Explorer 6, Outlook Express 6, and command-line tools for troubleshooting. This chapter provides advanced uses for these programs and third-party enhancements you can add to get the most out of your online experience.

INTERNET EXPLORER

Internet Explorer version 6, the browser included in Windows XP, provides powerful and easy-to-use Web navigation features. Striking a balance between easy Web surfing and system security requires that you understand how vulnerable IE's default settings can make your system and how you can adjust them. From Autocomplete forms to cookie management, IE's convenience features often need adjusting to properly safeguard your system's contents.

NOTE

> The changes you make to Internet Explorer's settings apply to the current user only; each user of a computer can make changes to the IE settings unless the Administrator of the computer or network uses the group policy tool, GPEDIT.MSC, to create a group policy that sets security zones and content rating settings for all users.

URL PROTOCOLS AND APPLICATIONS

When you type a URL such as `http://www.microsoft.com`, Internet Explorer (or your chosen Web browser) looks at the first word to determine the protocol or format to be used. Besides `http:`, there are other URL types such as those listed in Table 14.1.

TABLE 14.1 PREDEFINED URL PROTOCOLS

Protocol Specifier	Description
`callto:`	NetMeeting call
`file:`	Local file display
`ftp:`	FTP file transfer
`gopher:`	Gopher database lookup
`hcp:`	Window Help and Support Center
`http:`	Hypertext Transfer Protocol (Web pages)
`https:`	Secure HTTP
`ldap:`	Address Book Entry via Lightweight Directory Access Protocol

Protocol Specifier	Description
mailto:	Email
mms:	Windows Media content
mmst:	Windows Media content
mmsu:	Windows Media content
msbd:	Windows Media content
news:	Newsgroups
nntp:	Newsgroups (alternate URL form)
pnm:	RealAudio content (Progressive Networks Metafile)
rlogin:	Unix remote login
shell:	Windows Explorer folder view
snews:	Secure news
telnet:	Telnet (remote terminal) protocol
tn3270:	IBM 3270 terminal emulation
vnd.ms.radio	Windows Media player radio
wmtcontent:	Windows Media content
wmtmedia:	Windows Media content

Additional formats may be added if you install additional applications on your computer. For example, installing AOL Instant Messenger adds an aim: protocol entry. Viewing the URL aim: opens Instant Messenger.

After the protocol type, the rest of a URL is protocol-specific information. For example, http: is followed by a path name, mailto: is followed by an email address, and telnet: is followed by a hostname.

Whenever you type a URL into your Web browser or Windows Explorer's address bar, if the URL begins with a word followed by a colon, Windows looks for this word in the Registry as a key under HKEY_CLASSES_ROOT. If it is found and the key contains a value named URL Protocol, Windows activates the associated application and passes this application of the entire URL as addressing information.

So, the configuration information for each URL protocol is stored in the Windows Registry by name as a key under HKEY_CLASSES_ROOT. Under each key, several subkeys and values store configuration information. The following values may be defined:

14

Value	Value	Significance
URL Protocol	(empty)	Always present; indicates that the key name is a valid URL Protocol name
EditFlags	2	If present, indicates that the Web browser should offer an Edit context menu choice
Source Filter	(various)	If present, indicates the CLSID of the filter used to decode files of type .wav, .avi, .mov, and .mpeg.

Under each protocol name, the Shell subkey specifies the command line of the application used to display the URL content. In most cases, the subkey `shell\open\command`'s default value is a command line. Table 14.2 lists the default command lines for several common protocols.

TABLE 14.2 DEFAULT PROTOCOL COMMAND LINES

Protocol	Command Line
callto:	rundll32.exe msconf.dll,CallToProtocolHandler %l
file: *	(none)
ftp: *	"C:\Program Files\Internet Explorer\iexplore.exe" %1
gopher: *	"C:\Program Files\Internet Explorer\iexplore.exe" -nohome
hcp:	"C:\WINDOWS\PCHealth\HelpCtr\Binaries\HelpCtr.exe" -url "%1"
http:	"C:\Program Files\Internet Explorer\iexplore.exe" -nohome
https: *	"C:\Program Files\Internet Explorer\iexplore.exe" -nohome
ldap: *	"C:\Program Files\Outlook Express\wab.exe" /ldap:%1
mailto:	"%ProgramFiles%\Outlook Express\msimn.exe" /mailurl:%1
mms:	"C:\Program Files\Windows Media Player\wmplayer.exe" "%L"
mmst:	"C:\Program Files\Windows Media Player\wmplayer.exe" "%L"
mmsu:	"C:\Program Files\Windows Media Player\wmplayer.exe" "%L"
msbd:	"C:\Program Files\Windows Media Player\wmplayer.exe" "%L"
news:	"%ProgramFiles%\Outlook Express\msimn.exe" /newsurl:%1
nntp:	"%ProgramFiles%\Outlook Express\msimn.exe" /newsurl:%1
rlogin:	rundll32.exe url.dll,TelnetProtocolHandler %l
shell: *	%SystemRoot%\Explorer.exe /idlist,%I,%L
snews:	"%ProgramFiles%\Outlook Express\msimn.exe" /newsurl:%1
telnet:	rundll32.exe url.dll,TelnetProtocolHandler %l
tn3270:	rundll32.exe url.dll,TelnetProtocolHandler %l
vnd.ms.radio	"C:\Program Files\Windows Media Player\mplayer2.exe" "%L"

Protocol	Command Line
wmtcontent:	`C:\PROGRA~1\WINDOW~2\wmplayer.exe "%L"`
wmtmedia:	`C:\PROGRA~1\WINDOW~2\wmplayer.exe "%L"`

* These protocols use DDE to communicate the URL data to the application program. The `ddeexec` *subkey specifies the DDE topic and data format.*

NOTE

> The command line `rundll32.exe url.dll,TelnetProtocolHandler` runs the default telnet.exe application.

Netscape Navigator provides a user interface to make changes to the applications associated with URL protocols, but Internet Explorer does not. If you use IE, you can control the application used to display each URL type by editing the command-line key. For example, to specify an alternate telnet application named putty.exe, you could change the value `HKEY_CLASSES_ROOT\telnet\shell\open\command` to something like `c:\program files\putty\putty.exe "%1"`.

SECURITY ISSUES

The default configuration of Internet Explorer 6 presents many challenges to the security-minded user. By default, IE 6 presents few barriers to potentially hostile code and makes it easy for unauthorized users to pretend to be someone else online. Fortunately, most of these shortcomings can be overcome by proper configuration of these browser features:

- Properties for security zones (Internet, Trusted Sites, others)
- Settings for Internet privacy (cookies)
- Certificates for authentication of Web sites and installable programs
- Personal information
- Browser responses to invalid URLs

NOTE

> Because Internet Explorer 6 is the gateway to the Internet, the prime source of attacks on computers today, using Windows Update frequently to install the latest critical updates and security patches is essential. Since Internet Explorer also incorporates Outlook Express, the email client supported by most ISPs, using Windows Update is essential to stop both browser- and email-based security flaws as they are uncovered.

CONFIGURING AND SELECTING SECURITY ZONES

To configure security zones in Internet Explorer, click Tools, Internet Options, Security. IE divides browsable entities into four zones. With a typical installation of IE 6, all four zones

14

start out with custom security settings. However, if you select the default security settings for each zone, the default setting will be the one listed as follows:

- Internet Zone—This is the default zone used for computers not on your Intranet, and for sites not assigned to any other zone. Its default setting is Medium (see Table 14.1).

- Local Intranet—This is the default zone used for computers on your network. Its default setting is Medium-Low (see Table 14.3).

- Trusted Sites—You can assign Web sites you trust completely to this zone (no sites are placed there by default). Its default setting is Low (see Table 14.3).

- Restricted Sites—You can assign Web sites that you believe to be dangerous to this zone (no sites are placed there by default). You can still browse these sites, but IE will prevent virtually any other type of interaction with sites in this zone. Its default setting is High (see Table 14.3).

You can customize the settings for each zone, and after reviewing the information in Table 14.3, you may want to do so for additional protection.

Table 14.3 provides an overview of all 23 security settings used by Internet Explorer 6 and the default settings for each level.

TABLE 14.3   INTERNET EXPLORER 6 DEFAULT SECURITY SETTINGS, BY SECURITY LEVEL

Setting	High	Medium	Medium-Low	Low	Notes
ActiveX Controls & Plug-ins					
Download Signed ActiveX Controls	Disable	Prompt	Prompt	Enable	Prompt is recommended for all security levels, since many online sites try to install "adware" and "spy ware" programs you may not want on your computer.
Download Unsigned ActiveX Controls	Disable	Disable	Disable	Prompt	Prompt enables you to decide whether you want to install the ActiveX control; some software demos found online from reputable firms may use unsigned controls but are safe to install.

14

Setting	High	Medium	Medium-Low	Low	Notes
Initialize and script ActiveX controls not marked as safe	Disable	Disable	Disable	Prompt	If your organization uses Windows Script Host (.wsh) files, set to Prompt to give the user the option to run the script (.wsh files appear to be unsafe scripts to IE).
Run ActiveX controls and plug-ins	Disable	Enable	Enable	Enable	Other options include Administrator Approved (suitable for Intranets) or Prompt (see earlier discussions).
Script ActiveX controls marked safe for scripting	Disable	Enable	Enable	Enable	Prompt option also available.
Downloads					
File download	Disable	Enable	Enable	Enable	Recommend setting to Disable because of IE's known vulnerability to file extension spoofing exploit; if Disabled, right-click and Save File As option still works to save files.
Font download	Prompt	Enable	Enable	Enable	Pages with embedded fonts will trigger warnings if Prompt is selected; Disable option is also available.
Microsoft VM					
Java permissions	Disable Java	High Safety	Medium Safety	Low Safety	Custom setting (Figure 14.1) is also available; it's highly customizable (Figure 14.2).

continues

14

TABLE 14.3   CONTINUED

Setting	High	Medium	Medium-Low	Low	Notes
Miscellaneous					
Access data sources across domains	Disable	Disable	Prompt	Enable	Can allow dangerous content to come from an apparently trustworthy site.
Allow META REFRESH	Disable	Enable	Enable	Enable	No known security risks to this setting.
Display mixed content	Prompt	Prompt	Prompt	Prompt	Enable (displays both secure/nonsecure content without prompt) and Disable (can't display secure/nonsecure content on a page) options also available.
Don't prompt for client certificate selection when no certificates or only one certificate exists	Disable	Disable	Enable	Enable	
Drag and drop or copy and paste files	Prompt	Enable	Enable	Enable	I recommend using Prompt for all levels to improve security.
Installation of desktop items	Disable	Prompt	Prompt	Enable	Using Prompt will warn you of spyware programs such as Comet Cursor when they try to install on your system.
Launching programs and files in an IFRAME	Disable	Prompt	Prompt	Enable	
Navigate sub-frames across different domains	Disable	Enable	Enable	Enable	Prompt is also available; use in place of Enable to improve system security.

14

Setting	High	Medium	Medium-Low	Low	Notes
Software channel permissions	High Safety	Medium Safety	Medium Safety	Low	Controls automatic Safety updates of software; medium allows automatic downloads but requires the user to install the program update manually.
Submit nonencrypted form data	Prompt	Prompt	Enable	Enable	Applies only to sites which don't use SSL (Secure Socket Layer) encryption.
Userdata persistence	Disable	Enable	Enable	Enable	Enable allows Web sites to store identifying data on your system so you don't need to log in every time.
Scripting					
Active scripting	Disable	Enable	Enable	Enable	To make using Enable safer, make sure you use an up-to-date antivirus program (such as Norton AntiVirus 2002) which can intercept hostile scripts.
Allow paste operations via script	Disable	Enable	Enable	Enable	Should be set to Disable to prevent changes to your system files.
Scripting of Java Applets	Disable	Enable	Enable	Enable	Prompt option is also available. It provides better security if you don't use a program which can block hostile Java applets.

14

continues

TABLE 14.3 CONTINUED

Setting	High	Medium	Medium-Low	Low	Notes
User Authentication	Prompt for user name and password	Automatic login only in Intranet zone	Automatic login only in Intranet zone	Automatic login with username and password	Automatic login with username and password is very unsafe and should be changed, even for low security.

Figure 14.1 displays the Java permissions after editing the default High Safety setting used for the Internet Zone's default Medium security level. Normally, High Safety shows green lights (safe operation) for all settings, but increasing permissions for Java operations (see Figure 14.2) will change some settings to yellow (possible danger) or red (very dangerous) settings. Changes to default Java permissions should be performed only when absolutely necessary; for example, for a Java developer's test system or the rollout of a Java-based internal application.

Figure 14.1
Seen here is a customized Java Permissions screen in Internet Explorer 6.

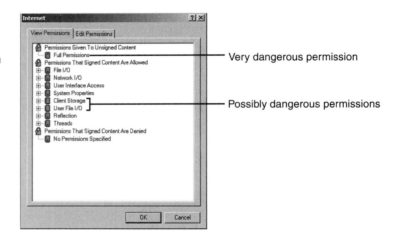

Very dangerous permission

Possibly dangerous permissions

 Use the following Web site to display the current security settings for the Internet Zone in text form:
`http://www.nextgenss.com/typhon/reports/10.1.1.2/browser.html`

CONFIGURING AND ADJUSTING PRIVACY CONTROLS

The Security tab in IE helps protect your system from unauthorized programs but is not the only adjustment you should make to your browser. The IE Privacy control (see Figure 14.3), which adjusts how your browser handles *cookies* (small text files stored on your hard disk by Web sites), is also important to protecting your identity online. Previous versions of IE incorporated cookie controls into the security settings discussed earlier in this chapter.

Figure 14.2
You can edit Java permissions in Internet Explorer 6.

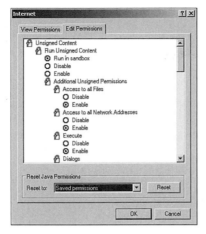

Figure 14.3
The Privacy slider in IE 6 adjusts cookie settings for the Internet zone.

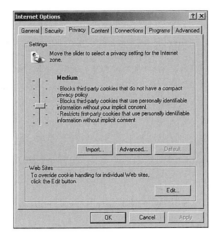

IE 6's new Privacy control is designed to work with the Platform for Privacy Preferences (P3P) specification, a specification developed by the World Wide Web Consortium (W3C). The P3P Web site is located at http://www.w3.org/P3P/.

The P3P specification enables organizations to put their privacy practices into a standardized machine-readable format (also called a *compact privacy statement*) that can be read by Web browsers such as IE 6. Depending upon the contents of the compact privacy statement and the privacy settings configured by the user, IE 6 might allow or disallow the storage of new cookies on your system or allow or disallow access to existing cookies.

There are two types of cookies:

■ Session

■ Persistent

14

Session cookies are stored on your system for the duration of a computing session and are deleted when you close your browser. They are generally used to make navigating interactive sites such as travel, hotel, or other types of sites easier; they are deleted at the end of each session.

Persistent cookies stay on your system between sessions. They can be used simply to store your username and password to make future access to password-restricted content easier, but they can also be used to collect information about how you use the Internet.

There are two sources for cookies:

- First-party
- Third-party

First-party cookies are stored on your system by the Web site you are visiting.

Third-party cookies are stored on your system by Web sites other than the one you are visiting, such as advertising companies that provide ads within a Web site.

IE 6 places more restrictions on third-party cookies than on first-party cookies.

Before IE 6, you could allow or disallow cookie storage and use, but to do so effectively for a particular site might require you to read and understand a Web site's cookie policy. For example, the Alaska Airlines Web site's page explaining its use of cookies is located at `http://www2.alaskaair.com/help/site/cookies.asp`.

The P3P specification enables companies to condense their cookie policy into a custom HTTP response header that can be interpreted by IE 6's Privacy control.

IE 6 categorizes cookies with a compact privacy specification as either satisfactory or unsatisfactory. An unsatisfactory cookie has all four of these characteristics:

- The cookie contains information that can personally identify you or allows access to that information. Includes cookie category codes PHY (physical), ONL (online), GOV (government), and FIN (financial).
- The information contained in or accessed by the cookie is used for unstated purposes. Includes cookie purpose codes IVA (individual/analysis), IVD (individual/decision), CON (contact), TEL (telemarketing), OTP (other purpose).
- The information contained in or accessed by the cookie is provided to unstated recipients. Includes cookie recipient codes SAM (same), OTR (other recipient), UNR (unrelated), and PUB (public forums).
- The cookie doesn't provide you with a way to opt in or out of its intended action; the cookie's action will take place without your consent. If the Web site provider enables an opt-in option (adds an *i* to the recipient code, as in *PUBi*) or an opt-out option (adds an *o*, as in *SAMo*), the cookie might be accepted by IE 6, depending upon the current privacy setting.

A further refinement to IE 6's Privacy control is its capability to modify the default behavior of a cookie based on your system's current privacy settings.

First-party cookies (cookies stored by the Web site provider) are accepted by most IE 6 privacy settings. However, even after IE 6 accepts a first-party cookie, the cookie is treated as a third-party cookie if the cookie's source tries to access the cookie through third-party content, such as an advertisement on another company's Web site. IE 6 refers to this as a *leashed cookie*.

A *downgraded cookie* is a cookie that was designed to be a persistent cookie but will be deleted at the end of the computing session because of the current IE 6 privacy setting. This type of cookie is also called a *restricted cookie*.

A cookie that cannot be stored on or accessed from your system because of your browser's privacy settings is referred to as a *blocked cookie*. A leashed cookie will be blocked if its creator tries to access it through another Web site.

IE 6's Privacy control enables you to control your system's acceptance of cookies with six settings as described in Table 14.4.

TABLE 14.4 IE's 6 PRIVACY SETTINGS AND THEIR IMPACT ON COOKIE STORAGE

Setting	Use
Block All Cookies	**Denies:** Persistent and session first- and third-party cookies regardless f compact policy or per-side privacy settings.
	Accepts: None.
High	**Denies:** Persistent or session first- and third-party cookies with no ompact policy or with an unsatisfactory or no opt-out policy.
	Accepts: Persistent or session first- and third-party cookies with an acceptable compact policy.
Medium High	**Denies:** *Persistent*—third-party cookies with no compact policy; first- and third-party cookies with unsatisfactory or no opt-out policy.
	Session—third-party cookies with unsatisfactory or no opt-out policy.
	Leashes: First-party cookies with no compact policy.
	Accepts: *Persistent*—First- and third-party cookies with acceptable compact policy.
	Session—First-party cookies of all types; third-party cookies with an acceptable compact policy.
Medium (default setting)	**Denies:** Third-party persistent or session cookies with an unsatisfactory or no compact policy.

continues

14

TABLE 14.4 CONTINUED	
Setting	**Use**
	Accepts: First- and third-party persistent or session cookies with an acceptable compact policy.
	Leashes: Persistent cookies with no compact policy.
	Downgrades: First-party persistent cookies with unsatisfactory compact policies.
Low	**Denies:** No cookies are denied.
	Accepts: First- and third-party persistent cookies with acceptable compact policy; first-party persistent cookies with unsatisfactory compact policy; first-party session cookies.
	Leashes: First-party persistent cookies with no compact policy.
	Downgrades: Third-party persistent cookies with an unsatisfactory or no compact policy.
Accept All Cookies	**Denies:** No cookies are denied.
	Accepts: All first- and third-party cookies regardless of policy or per-site settings.
	Leashes: No cookies are leashed.
	Downgrades: No cookies are downgraded.

To determine how a particular Web page handles privacy issues, display it, then click View, Privacy Report. See Figure 14.4 for a privacy report from a typical commercial Web site that uses advertising banners. Every component on the Web page has a separate listing.

Figure 14.4
The privacy report for a newspaper Web site's home page shows that both the newspaper and an advertiser have stored cookies on this system.

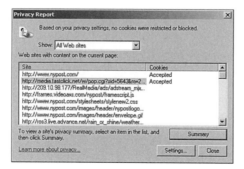

To determine the details about a particular Web page component's privacy policy, select it and click Summary. Sites that lack a compact privacy summary will display a screen similar to that in Figure 14.5, directing you to contact the Web site directly.

Figure 14.5
This screen is displayed for Web pages that lack a compact privacy summary.

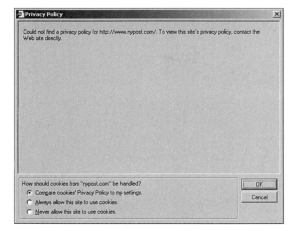

Web content that has a compact privacy policy will display a screen similar to the one in Figure 14.6 when you click its Summary button. If your system has blocked, restricted, or accepted a cookie, read all portions of the privacy policy before deciding how to handle cookies from that site.

Figure 14.6
Here is a portion of the compact privacy summary for a Web advertiser.

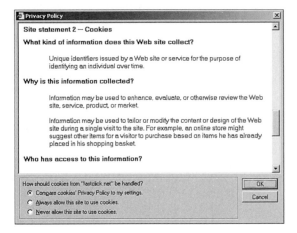

Note that in Figures 14.5 and 14.6 you have three options for how to handle cookies from the provider:

- Compare cookies' privacy policy to my settings (default)
- Always allow this site to use cookies
- Never allow this site to use cookies

14

I recommend using the default setting to receive a warning whenever a Web content provider tries to place a cookie on your site that is blocked by your privacy settings (see Figure 14.7).

Privacy Report icon

Figure 14.7
IE 6's Privacy Report icon in the IE status bar indicates that one or more cookies on the site were blocked or restricted. Double-click the icon to display the Privacy Report of Restricted Web Sites. Click the Summary button to determine why the cookie was blocked or restricted.

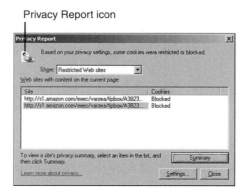

Because of the wide variety of Web sites you are likely to encounter, you might discover that the default privacy setting is too restrictive or permissive for a given provider. For example, the Web site cookies blocked in Figure 14.7 belong to Amazon.com. and are needed to help you shop at that online bookstore.

To handle problems like this, you can use the Always Allow Cookies button shown in Figures 14.5 and 14.6. To display and manage individual sites' use of cookies, click the Settings button to go to the Privacy control shown in Figure 14.3. Click Edit to go to the Per Site Privacy Actions screen. Enter the Web address of the site you want to manage, then click Allow to permit the site to store cookies, or click Block to stop the site from storing cookies, regardless of your privacy settings. You can also see a list of sites you are managing (see Figure 14.8). Sites you are managing with the Allow or Block Cookies options on the Summary screen are also displayed here.

Keep in mind that using the privacy settings Block All Cookies or Accept All Cookies will override per-site settings.

If you have upgraded to Windows XP from a previous Windows version (as opposed to a clean Windows XP installation), access to existing cookies on your system isn't controlled by the privacy settings unless you select Block All Cookies, even though the cookies might not match the privacy settings IE 6 uses. If you are concerned about the potential impact of these legacy cookies on your online privacy, your only option is to delete them. To delete all cookies, click Tools, Internet Options, Delete Cookies. When you visit a site which stores cookies, IE 6's Privacy control will evaluate the new cookies used by that site.

14

Figure 14.8
The Per Site Privacy
Actions screen lets
you add sites for cus-
tom cookie control
and displays settings
for sites you are
already managing.

> **NOTE**
>
> Cookies left over from older Windows versions (9x/Me) might be lost when you upgrade to
> Windows XP. To avoid the possibility of cookie loss before you upgrade, each user on a sys-
> tem should open IE, click File, Import/Export, and select the option to export cookies to a
> file. Each user's cookie file can be imported into IE 6 after the upgrade is complete and
> users are configured.

If you want to delete only selected cookies, close all browser windows first to delete session
cookies. Then, restart IE, and click Tools, Internet Options, Settings. From the Settings
window, click View Files. Right-click the file listing and select Arrange Icons by Type to
group the cookies together. Scroll down through the list and select the cookie(s) you want to
delete (see Figure 14.9). Note that many cookies have expiration dates years or even decades
into the future. Press the Del key to delete the selected cookies.

> **NOTE**
>
> If you delete a cookie required by a site you visit in the future, you must allow the site to
> store a new cookie on your system, or some site features might not work.

LOCAL PASSWORD STORAGE AND AUTOCOMPLETE

If you fill out a lot of online forms, IE 6 will probably offer to help you out with its
Autocomplete feature. Autocomplete can help you enter names, addresses, passwords, and
other commonly entered data. Autocomplete is enabled if you answer Yes to the question,
"Would you like to turn Autocomplete on?"

Autocomplete will also memorize user names and passwords if you answer Yes to the question, "Do you want Windows to remember this password, so that you don't have to type it
again the next time you visit this page?" You can also select Don't Offer to Remember Any
More Passwords to disable this feature.

14

Figure 14.9
You can delete selected cookies from the Temporary Internet Files folder.

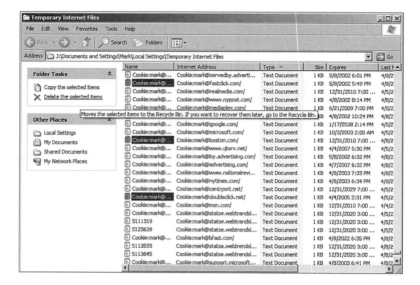

You can control how Autocomplete works through the Internet Options' Content tab. Click the Autocomplete button to display the Autocomplete Settings button. You can enable or disable Autocomplete for the following:

- Web addresses
- Forms
- User names and passwords on forms

An option to prompt you to save passwords is also offered. If you turn off this option, it has the same effect as if you'd selected Don't Offer to Remember Any More Passwords.

If you share a computer with others and don't use separate accounts for each user, Autocomplete represents a potential security risk; others could "borrow" your IE 6 identity by using your Autocomplete information. Click the Clear Forms button to delete information such as telephone numbers and street addresses; click the Clear Passwords button to dump Autocomplete's record of usernames and passwords.

For a balance of security and usability, I usually leave the Web addresses option enabled but disable the forms and user names options.

One problem with Autocomplete is that it's not always easy to get rid of out-of-date or incorrect information or add new information. You can delete items from each list when an Autocomplete list is displayed, but the only way Autocomplete will let you load new information is during the completion process for each new form. Autocomplete isn't designed to let you view all the field values it stores for you at the same time, either. To make Autocomplete more powerful and easier to maintain, *PC Magazine* offers a free utility called AutoWhat? 2, which can be used to view, edit, or add Autocomplete values. Learn more about it at http://www.pcmag.com/article/0,2997,s=1478&a=23587,00.asp.

AUTHENTICODE AND CERTIFICATES FOR NON-ROOT CERTIFIED SITES

IE 6, like IE 5, uses Authenticode technology for digital certificates, which are used by software developers to assure you that a program you are downloading into your browser is from a known, reliable source. VeriSign is one of several certification authorities that provide digital certificates. When a public certification authority creates the digital certificate, it is referred to as a *non-root certificate*; a *root certificate* is one created by the software vendor itself. Periodically, certificates go out of date (they are good for a given length of time) or are revoked by the certification authority.

Generally, certificates issued by a non-root certification authority (CA) such as VeriSign are trustworthy. However, in January 2001, VeriSign was tricked into issuing Microsoft digital certificates dated 1/30/2001 and 1/31/2001 to an imposter. Microsoft Security Bulletin MS01-017 discusses this case in detail and provides a patch for Windows users that installs a Certificate Revocation List (CRL) onto systems. It also adds an installable revocation handler to check certificates missing valid CRL Distribution Point information, and enables checking in IE for software publisher's certificates. These changes have been implemented in the version of IE 6 installed with Windows XP.

While the changes instituted by Microsoft with Security Bulletin MS01-017 will help keep systems safer than they would be otherwise, it might still be possible for digital certificates to be abused in the future.

Whenever a security warning about a new Java or ActiveX control is displayed as in Figure 14.10, click the company name under "distributed by." Carefully read the details of the certificate, including its effective date (General tab), Revocation status (Extended Error Information on Details tab), and Certification Path, which should lead back to the certification authority.

Figure 14.10
The application (left) has a valid digital signature (right) as attested to by its Certification Path and by information on the General and Details tabs (not shown).

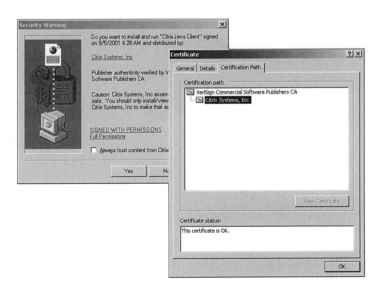

14

Due to the possibility of certificate compromise, and because you should always know what programs are being installed on your system, I recommend that you do **not** click the Always Trust Content from *(Vendor)* option shown in Figure 14.10. However, even if you click this option, software from the same company that uses a different digital certificate will still prompt you for permission to install itself.

CONFIGURING IE 6 SEARCH FROM THE ADDRESS BAR (AUTOSEARCH) FEATURE

Several versions of IE have supported Search from the Address Bar, which enables you to run a search when you type a word into the Web address field in IE. The default behavior for IE 6 is to pass entries that aren't working URLs to the selected IE 6 search engine. By default, this is MSN Search.

NOTE

> Originally, IE 6 treated entries other than URLs as RealName searches for a keyword before passing the search to the default IE 6 search engine. However, RealNames, which provided keyword matches to site URLs under a contract with Microsoft, was shut down as of June 28, 2002.

What if you enter a URL that isn't recognized by the Microsoft domain name system? MSN Search will try to find a related Web site.

If you prefer a search engine other than the default MSN Search, you might disable MSN Search or specify a different default search engine for IE 6 to use. To modify the behavior of RealName or MSN Searches, make changes in the Advanced tab of the Internet Options menu (Tools, Internet Options).

Use Table 14.5 to make the changes desired. The default setting is Just Display the Results in the Main Window.

TABLE 14.5 SEARCH FROM THE ADDRESS BAR OPTIONS

Option	Entry into Address Window	MSN Search
Display Results, and Go to the Most Likely Site	Single word or phrase	Opens MSN Search window on left and displays site matches in condensed form and in main window
	Invalid URL	Displays We Can't Find (Web site); provides related sites and a link to MSN Search
Do Not Search from the Address Bar	Phrase	Opens MSN Search in main window and displays site matches; resets search option to Just Display the Results in the Main Window
	Single word or invalid URL	MSN Search is disabled

Option	Entry into Address Window	MSN Search
Just Display the Results in the Main Window (default)	Phrase or single word	Opens MSN Search in main window and displays site matches
	Invalid URL	MSN Search displays an error message that it can't find the Web site and offers the option to search the Web, use MSN search, or register the domain name
Just Go to the Most Likely Site	Phrase or single word	MSN Search looks for a matching Web site and displays it in the main window; if no exact Web site match is found, the default search window is displayed with search results
	Invalid URL	Displays We Can't Find (Web site); provides related sites and link to MSN Search

Note that the option Do Not Search from the Address Bar disables only single-word searches; search for a phrase, and IE 6 will ignore your wishes and use the default search engine configured for this option. If you use the default MSN Search, IE 6 will even change the Do Not Search from the Address Bar setting to Just Display the Results in the Main Window.

You can change this infuriating bug/feature by customizing the IE 6 Autosearch function.

SELECTING YOUR PREFERRED AUTOSEARCH PROVIDER

To start the customization process, click the Search icon (the magnifying glass). If the Search Companion Natural Language Search window appears instead of the Search menu, select Change Preferences, click Change Internet Search Behavior, With Classic Internet Search, and click OK. Close the browser window. Reopen the browser and the Search menu will be displayed.

To customize Autosearch options with IE once Classic Search has been enabled, click Search on the menu bar, Customize from the Search menu, and the Autosearch settings button.

By default, MSN is used for all four types of Autosearches described in the previous section.

To change the search provider used for Autosearches from the default (MSN), click When Searching and select the search type, then click Choose a Search Provider to choose from the providers listed, which include Google Sites, Yahoo!, and even Netscape Search, among others. You can have a different search provider for each of the four search options. Note that you must still select a search provider, even for the misleadingly named Do Not Search from the Address Bar option. Depending on the search engine highlighted in the Choose a Search Provider window, you might not be able to select from all four of the When Searching options. Select MSN as your Search Provider to choose the When Searching

14

option you want; then choose the Search Provider you prefer for this option. Click OK when finished.

While you can't disable Do Not Search from the Address Bar, you can select a different search engine than the default (MSN). One benefit of selecting a different search engine than MSN is that a phrase search, while it will display results from the search engine you select, won't reset this option as MSN Search does.

CUSTOMIZING SEARCH TOOLS USED BY THE SEARCH ASSISTANT

To change the search tools used for the many different types of searches you can perform with IE 6, click Use Search Assistant from the Customize Search Settings menu. You can add or remove search tools from each of the categories displayed. To change the order of search tools, clear all check marks in a category, then click the search tool you want to use first. Continue until you have selected the search tools you want to use in the order you prefer (see Figure 14.11).

Figure 14.11
Customize the default search tools and search order with the IE 6 Search Assistant.

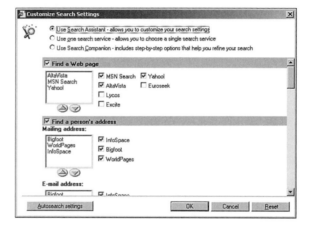

When you select New Search, the first search tool on the list for the category you select will be used. To try the search with your other search tools, click Next and select the search tool you want to use.

ACTIVEX MANAGEMENT

ActiveX is Microsoft's name for reuseable program components that can be run anywhere on a network using Windows. ActiveX controls can be used for many tasks, but one of the most common uses for ActiveX is for Web programs and animations. Depending upon the privacy settings used by IE 6, ActiveX controls can be automatically downloaded and installed by your browser, or you can be prompted to grant or deny permission for the browser to download and install the control.

Because ActiveX components are used by many parts of Windows, damaged or corrupt ActiveX components can cause programs on your system (IE or others) to crash. Frequent

IE crashes during use or when closing the browser are probably due to problems with ActiveX, especially if they persist after you delete temporary files and the browser history (which can also cause browser crashes if corrupted).

To determine whether ActiveX components are damaged, and to see what ActiveX components have been installed in your browser, start IE, and click Tools, Internet Options, Settings. Click the View Objects button to open the ActiveX Explorer (see Figure 14.12). Unlike My Computer/Windows Explorer, which displays individual files, the objects displayed in the ActiveX Explorer may have multiple components.

Figure 14.12
One of the components displayed in the Downloaded Program Files (ActiveX components) browser is damaged.

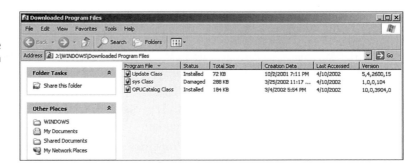

ActiveX controls can be listed as Installed or Damaged. A damaged control might be missing one or more component files (such as .dll, .ocx, or .inf), or one of its component files might have been replaced by an incompatible file during another program's installation process.

To learn more about a particular control, right-click on it and select Properties. The General tab displays its ID, location, and other information.

The ID field in the General tab is the name used by the control in the Windows Registry.

To see the components in a control, click Dependency. This lists the files and Java packages used by the control. A file marked Damaged has been deleted or replaced.

Click the Version tab to determine the version number, company, and copyright information for the control.

To fix a damaged control, you have three options:

- You can check the Recycle Bin to see if the component file was stored there for deletion. If you locate the file, you can restore it and see if the control status changes to Installed.

- You can right-click on the control and select Update. IE will attempt to locate an updated copy of the control. If IE locates an updated version of the control, it will download and install it or prompt you for permission, depending upon its security settings. If IE cannot locate an updated copy of the control, the program file status will remain Damaged. In that case, use the remaining option.

14

- Remove; this will delete the control's components and Registry entry. If you get an error message indicating that some files are currently in use, close all browser windows and retry this operation; you might need to restart Windows before you can remove the control.

If you remove the control, the next time you visit a Web site that requires the component, IE will download it or prompt you for permission to download it, depending upon its security settings.

Because ActiveX represents a potential threat to your computer's security by permitting Web sites to store and run programs on your computer, take the following steps to keep ActiveX working safely for you:

- Use the Automatic Updates feature in Windows XP to check for Critical Updates, some of which are designed to protect you against ActiveX-based vulnerabilities; so that you know what's being downloaded, configure Automatic Updates to notify you of updates.

- Check the status of your ActiveX controls periodically to verify that they're working properly as described earlier in this section.

- Use the Version tab on the control's Properties sheet to determine which components were provided by Microsoft. Use the Update feature to check for updates to these controls.

STOPPING POP-UP ADS AND SPYWARE WITH IE6

The online experience today is as full of advertisements as an AM talk radio station; everywhere you surf, you are bombarded with pop-over, pop-under, banner, and other types of ads. And, even if you resist the Click Here to Learn More message, companies that have provided you with "free" software might be analyzing your every click or borrowing your computer during idle times for their own purposes.

Unfortunately, IE 6 by itself isn't designed to stop pop-up ads or detect spyware. However, fed-up programmers have developed a variety of free and low-cost services and routines to stop the pops and put spyware on the shelf.

If you want to stop pop-up advertising, check out these programs:

- Stop Pops—http://www.stoppops.com/
- PopUpStopper—http://www.popupstopper.net/
- Super Popup Killer—http://www.popup-stopper.net/

Technoerotica.net's list of major pop-up ad providers enables you to contact them directly and opt-out of their ads:

http://technoerotica.net/mylog/optouts.html

To detect and stop spyware such as Aureate, Comet Cursor, Gator, and others, carefully read the user agreement provided with free software and refuse to install programs that track your Web surfing or borrow unused computing power without compensating you. To find and stop spyware that's already on your computer, try these products:

- SpyStopper—http://www.itcompany.com/spystop.htm
- Ad-aware—http://www.lavasoft.nu/
- ZoneAlarm and ZoneAlarm Pro—http://www.zonelabs.com

These Web sites also provide tools and techniques for detecting and stopping spyware:

- Gibson Research's OptOut—http://grc.com/optout.htm
- The Ongoing Proactive fight for your box —http://www.searchlores.org/adsuc_1.htm

OUTLOOK EXPRESS

Outlook Express 6 (OE 6) is the default Windows XP email and newsgroup client. It's integrated with Internet Explorer 6 and looks almost identical to its previous version, Outlook Express 5, which was integrated with IE 5.x.

SETTING UP ACCOUNTS WITH OE 6

When you start OE 6 for the first time, you are prompted to create mail and newsgroup accounts, which will then be displayed in the OE 6 Folder view along the left side of the OE 6 interface.

To create a mail account, you need the following information:

- Your name as you wish it to appear in outgoing messages
- Your email address
- Your mail server type—HTTP: used for Hotmail and other Web-based mail services, POP3: used for most ISP-based and some corporate mail services, or IMAP: used for some corporate mail services.
- Incoming mail server name—OE 6 enters this information automatically for you if you are a Hotmail or MS Passport email user, but you must enter this manually for other email services
- Outgoing (SMTP) mail server name—Not used for Hotmail, but required for most other email services
- User name and password
- Whether your mail provider uses secure password authentication (SPA) logons

To create additional email accounts, click Tools, Accounts, Add, Mail, and supply the information required.

14

To create a news server account, click Tools, Accounts, Add, News and provide the following information:

- Your name as you wish it to appear in outgoing messages
- Your email address
- The name of your news service (NNTP) server
- Whether or not you need to log on to receive news

To create an Internet Directory Service account, click Tools, Accounts, Add, Directory Service and provide the following information:

- The name of the Internet directory (LDAP) server
- Whether you need to log on to the server
- Whether you want to check email addresses with the directory server

Each account you create will be displayed in the left window of OE 6. You can scroll this window as needed to view different accounts and folders.

ADJUSTING OE'S DEFAULT MAIL FOLDER LOCATION

By default, OE 6's mail folder is located on the default boot drive (normally C:) in a subfolder of your personal folder in \Documents and Settings. Storing your email on your boot drive is potentially risky; for example, if you ever need to rebuild your drive with a system recovery CD, all data, including your email, would be wiped out.

Depending upon your situation, you might prefer to change your *message store* (OE's name for the folder containing your email) to a location such as a different hard drive letter on your system. (You can shrink your primary partition to make room for an extended partition containing additional drive letters with programs such as Power Quest Partition Magic or V Communications Partition Commander.)

→ For more information on resizing drives, **see** "Resizing Basic Disks," **p. 1010**.

To make this change, follow this procedure:

1. Create a new folder on the target drive.
2. Click Tools, Options, Maintenance.
3. Click Store Folder.
4. Click Change.
5. Select the folder you created in step 1 and click OK.
6. Verify that the new location is displayed in the folder path and click OK.
7. Close OE and reopen it.

Your email folders will be copied to the new location.

14

NOTE

> Unfortunately, especially given the ease and power of networking with Windows XP, it's almost impossible (and extremely dangerous!) to store your OE message store on a networked or removable-media drive. You *can* do it if you map a drive letter to the network folder, but if the mapped drive is not available for any reason when you start OE, Windows will rewrite the Registry key to point to a local folder. If you want to store email on a network folder, use Outlook 2000 or later, or a third-party email client that supports network use.
>
> For more details on why OE is network-unfriendly, see Tom C. Koch's excellent discussion of OE storage issues at
> `http://www.tomsterdam.com/insideOE/files/wab.htm#netwab`.

SHARING OE ON A DUAL-BOOT COMPUTER

If you dual-boot your computer with Windows XP Professional and another recent Windows version, you can share the same email accounts no matter which version of Windows you boot with by using the following method. Note that the email folder must reside on a drive that uses a file system compatible with the other version of Windows. For example, I'm dual-booting Windows 98SE with Windows XP Professional. Because Windows 9x/Me versions don't understand the NTFS file system, I need to use a drive that is partitioned as a FAT16 or a FAT32 as my mail store (mail folders) location.

→ For more information on file systems, **see** "Choosing Your File System: NTFS or FAT," **p. 997**.

1. Back up your existing email folders (.dbx files) first.
2. Note the location of your email folder.

   NOTE

   > I recommend moving the folder to a friendly folder name instead of the knuckle-breaking ID number folder used by Windows by default. Because Windows 9x/Me and Windows XP have differences in their Registry keys, the default location used in one version won't work in another version unless you're willing to do a bit of Registry fiddling as described at
   > `http://web.ukonline.co.uk/cook/dualshare.htm`.

3. Shut down Windows XP and restart your computer, booting to the other version of Windows.
4. If necessary, upgrade this installation to IE 6/OE 6.
5. Open OE 6.
6. Click Tools, Options, Maintenance.
7. Click Store Folder.
8. Click Change.
9. Browse to the folder you are using for the Windows XP version of OE.
10. OE will notify you that a mail store already appears to be in this folder. *Keep* the existing mail store.

14

No matter which Windows version you boot from, you can access the same email (a feature I'm using right now!).

OUTLOOK EXPRESS 6 VERSUS MICROSOFT OUTLOOK 2002

OE 6 and Microsoft Outlook, despite their similarity in names, are very different products. As you've seen, OE is an email/newsgroup reader that can also use directory services. Microsoft Outlook, while it can also be used for email and newsgroup access, is a fully integrated information management tool which also includes calendar and contact management. Outlook is available as part of Microsoft Office XP, as a standalone product, or with the Microsoft Exchange Server email server. Compared to Outlook, OE has the following email limitations:

- No message preview
- Limited view of attachments in preview pane
- No auto archive
- No auto-save of unsent messages
- No follow-up reminder tagging
- Can't track delivery and read receipts with original message
- Can't recall or resend a message
- Can't send or receive Rich Text messages (though OE does do HTML)
- Doesn't support auto spell correction feature of WordMail
- Doesn't support message templates
- Doesn't support AutoText feature of WordMail
- Doesn't support message expiration
- Doesn't support deferred delivery
- Doesn't support redirected replies
- Can't use Exchange Server Global Address List
- Can't print address cards
- Doesn't support network folders for mail storage
- Doesn't let you use Microsoft Word for composing email
- Doesn't allow removal of attachments from stored emails

If you need these features, you should upgrade to Outlook. When you install and start Outlook, it will prompt you to import your OE email and address information, which makes moving to Outlook from OE quite simple.

You can see a more detailed comparison of Outlook, Outlook Express, and other members of the Outlook family at

```
http://www.microsoft.com/office/outlook/evaluation/compare.asp
```

IMPORTING MAIL AND ADDRESS BOOKS WITH OUTLOOK EXPRESS

If you switch to Outlook Express from another email client, you will usually want to import your existing email and address books into Outlook Express. Similarly, if you decide to switch to a different email client, you will probably want to export email and address books in a format that can be used by the other email client (Outlook will automatically import OE mail and address books if you specify this when you start Outlook). You can also use import and export to help you transport information between home and office copies of OE.

To import address books, messages, or email/news account settings into OE, click File, Import, and select the import type you wish to perform:

- Address book—Imports addresses in the Windows Address Book (.WAB) format used by OE, NetMeeting, Internet Explorer, and Microsoft Phone System
- Other address book—Imports addresses from Eudora Pro/Light (up to version 3.0), LDIF-LDAP Data Interchange Format, MS Exchange Personal Address Book, MS Internet Mail for Windows 3.1, Netscape Address Book (V. 2 and 3), Netscape Communicator V. 4.x Address Book, and CSV (Comma Separated Values) Text file (a common export file option you can use to import address books from programs not directly supported)

Depending on the address book type you want to import, OE might locate the address book automatically or might ask you for its location; a Browse tool helps you locate the file and displays its extension.

After the import process is complete, you can use the addresses with OE.

To import messages, select the message type you wish to import. OE can import messages from Eudora Pro/Light (up through V. 3.x), MS Exchange, MS Internet Mail (32-bit or Windows 3.1), MS Outlook, OE 4, OE 6, Windows Messaging, Netscape Communicator, or Netscape Mail (V. 2 or 3). In most cases, you must supply the location of the messages. If you select OE 6 as the import source, you can import messages from a particular identity (a feature in OE 6 that lets multiple users of a computer log on to OE with unique OE identities) or from a store directory (a folder containing OE messages).

You can also import email or news account settings from other email programs already on your system with the Import Wizard.

EXPORTING AND RELOCATING THE OUTLOOK EXPRESS ADDRESS BOOK

OE doesn't store the address book (.wab file) in the same folder as the message store, so even if you move the message store to a different folder, the OE address book remains in its default location:

```
System drive letter:\Documents and Settings\username\Application Data\
Microsoft\Address Book\username.wab
```

14

N O T E

> If you use the Multiple Identities feature of Outlook Express, the address book is named after the main identity. Separate folders within the address book are used for the main identity's contacts, each additional identity's contacts, and shared contacts; by default, only MSN Messenger contacts are shared with other identities. If you search for .WAB files and open them outside of OE, you can see which contacts are stored in each folder.

You can export the address book to a different file with File, Export, Address Book. You can choose from two formats:

- Outlook Personal Mail Storage (.pst)
- Comma-separated text file (.csv), a format supported by most email programs

The option to export messages to Outlook will work only if

- Outlook is already installed
- Outlook is the default email handler

N O T E

> Only the contacts used by the current identity on a multiple-identity installation of OE will be exported. To export all contacts, switch to each identity, export the address book, and continue until all address books have been exported.

If you want to move the location of the OE address book to a different folder or drive, no feature built in to OE can perform this task. Follow this procedure:

1. Close OE if it is open.
2. Click Start, Search, and look for .wab files to determine the location of your OE Address Book (.wab) file.
3. Note the current location of each file.
4. Copy the .wab file for the current user (you might find more than one if multiple user accounts are configured on your computer) to the desired location.
5. Edit the Windows XP Registry to point to the new location.

To edit the Registry:

1. Click Start, Run.
2. Type REGEDT32 and click OK to start the Registry Editor.
3. Navigate to the following registry key:
   HKEY_CURRENT_USER\Software\Microsoft\WAB\WAB4\Wab File Name
4. Change the value in the right pane (the filename and location) to match the location and name of the .wab file you copied.

5. Close the Registry Editor and restart the computer; log back on to the same user account you were logged in during the editing process.

6. Restart OE, and it will use the .wab file in its new location.

If more than one user account is using OE, log off the system, select each user when you restart the system and repeat both sets of instructions; make sure you use a unique location for each OE Address Book you copy to a new location.

After you verify that the address book is working correctly in its new location, delete the original address book file(s) or keep them as backups.

To make sure OE is using the new address book, open OE, close it, and run Search again to display the .wab files. The .wab file with the date and time closest to the current date and time should be the one in the new location.

Note that each user account in Windows XP has a unique address book and mail store folder locations *unless* OE identities are used. In that case, all identities using the same user account share a common mail store folder, although each identity has a separate address book.

BACKING UP AND RESTORING OUTLOOK EXPRESS FOLDERS

Backing up the entire OE message store is fairly simple, especially if you have transferred the message store to an easier-to-access folder than the usual location. The OE help systems tells you to

1. Compact each folder

2. Copy each folder to a removable-media drive

I like to use a CD-RW drive with CD media formatted with Roxio's DirectCD for this task, since I can use the XCOPY command from a command prompt to back up both the folders and other files I create on a particular day. However, you can also drag and drop the files or use a CD mastering program for your backup. To restore the files, I can copy them back to the original mail store folder or to another folder and tell OE to use the new folder for its mail store.

> **NOTE**
>
> If you use CD-R or other recordable (not rewriteable) media for your backup, your files will be marked as read-only when you restore them to the hard disk. Use the Windows Explorer to remove the read-only attribute, or OE can't read them.

The issue is trickier if you're trying to back up just certain folders. If you back up certain folders and you want to restore the backup using OE alone, you must ensure that you don't change the folder structure. Here's why: The folder structure is stored in the folder.dbx file. If you create new folders or change the parent-child relationship of folders, the folder you back up might not be restorable. Thus, it's best to back up all your folders at once.

14

However, if you want to back up and restore a single folder, this procedure will work for you:

1. Create a folder for messages you want to back up. Call the folder Backup; it will be stored as Backup.dbx.

2. Copy the Backup.dbx folder to your backup media.

3. Delete the Backup.dbx folder in OE.

To restore Backup.dbx

1. Start OE and create a new folder called Backup.dbx.

2. Open the folder and close it.

3. Close OE.

4. Delete the Backup.dbx folder located in your default OE message store folder.

5. Copy Backup.dbx from your backup media to your default OE Mail Store folder.

6. Restart OE, and your Backup.dbx messages can be viewed.

You can also create a new Identity called Backup and import folders from your default OE message store folder into this identity, and then back it up.

To restore the entire Outlook Express backup folder without deleting any messages that have not been backed up, follow this procedure:

1. Click File, Import, and select Messages.

2. Select Microsoft Outlook Express 6 as the message type and click Next.

3. Select Import Mail from an OE 6 Store Directory as the source of the messages and click OK.

4. Click Browse and navigate to the folder that contains the backup of your OE mail store folders. Click OK.

5. To restore all the backed-up folders, select All Folders and click Next. To restore only certain folders, select the folders you want to restore; hold down the Ctrl key and click the folders you want to restore. Click Next.

6. Click Finish after the messages have been imported.

The Microsoft Knowledge Base articles referring to Outlook Express Backup include

- "How to Back Up and Recover Outlook Express Data" (Q270670)
- "How to Backup and Restore Outlook Express Blocked Senders List and Other Mail Rules" (Q276511)

14

NOTE

Get more details about the backup identity backup/restore process from Tom C. Koch's "Outlook Express Partial Backup" page at
`http://www.tomsterdam.com/insideOE/backup/bu_partial.htm`.

See a visual tutorial of the Import restore process from "Site Developer's Outlook Backup Tutorial" at `http://www.sitedeveloper.ws/tutorials/outlook.htm`.

You might also want to try AJSystems.com's Express Assist backup program. Designed especially for backing up Outlook Express, it can create compressed backups of your message store; allow selective or full restoration of backed-up files; back up accounts, rules, and preference files for email handling; and also back up your OE Address Book. You can try it free for fifteen days from `http://www.ajsystems.com/oexhome.html`. Registration is $29.95 U.S.

BACKING UP INDIVIDUAL OUTLOOK EXPRESS EMAIL MESSAGES

You can save individual OE email messages for backup in three ways:

- .Ttxt—Plain-text files can be read by WordPad, Notepad, and other text-editing and word-processing programs
- .eml—Outlook Express email messages are designed to be read by Outlook Express only
- .htm—HTML email messages can be viewed in Web browsers

To save a file in one of these formats:

1. Open the message in Outlook Express.
2. Click File, Save As.
3. Enter the name you want to use for the message.
4. Select the file type and location; by default, OE will store the message in the current user's My Documents folder unless you specify another location.
5. Select the file format you want to use to save the file.
6. Click Save to save the file.

NOTE

To keep the message in its original form including any attachments, save the file as Mail (.eml). To save a message without its attachment, save the file as Text (.txt) or HTML (.htm).

CREATING OUTLOOK EXPRESS .EML FILES WITH DRAG-AND-DROP

To create .eml files from your Outlook Express messages by using drag-and-drop

1. Shrink the Outlook Express program to a window.
2. Click Start, My Computer and open the folder where you want the messages.

14

3. Click the Outlook Express icon in the taskbar to make it the active program.

4. Select the message(s) you want to drag. To select multiple messages, hold down the Shift or Ctrl key while you click on each message.

5. Drag the selected message(s) to the target folder.

6. Each message (including any attachments) will be stored as a separate .eml file in the target folder. The subject of each message is used as the name of each .eml file.

When you open an .eml message in any folder, Outlook Express is used to read the message and extract any attachments it contains.

To drag and drop .eml files back into Outlook Express

1. Open My Computer and navigate to the folder containing the message(s) you want to transfer back into an Outlook Express folder.

2. Start the Outlook Express program and shrink it to a window if necessary.

3. Make sure the target folder is visible in Outlook Express.

4. Click the folder icon in the taskbar to make it the active program.

5. Select the mail message file(s) you want to drag and drop.

6. Drag the files into the Outlook Express folder where you want to place them.

SAVING OE MESSAGES WITHOUT SAVING THE ATTACHMENTS

As you learned in "Backing Up Individual Outlook Express Email Messages," *p. 525*, saving Outlook Express Email messages as Text or HTML files will not save file attachments. However, you cannot drag and drop messages back into Outlook Express folders in any format other than .eml.

If you want to save a particular message without its attachment but keep it in .eml format, you will need to use one of the following tricks.

If you are primarily concerned about the message's contents

1. Forward the message to yourself.

2. Remove the attachment.

3. Click File, Copy to Folder.

The disadvantage is that the message now appears to have come from you, not the original sender.

If you want to keep the original headers, use this procedure instead:

1. Select the message and click File, Save As and save the message as type *.eml, or just drag the message onto your desktop.

2. Start Notepad and open the file.

14

3. Scroll down to the beginning of the encoded attachment and delete everything below that area.

4. Save the file, then drag the *.eml and drop it in an OE folder.

To save time opening the file once you have created an .eml file from your message, add Notepad to your SendTo folder. Here's how:

1. Search for the SendTo folder for each user; click Start, Search, SendTo. Each user's SendTo folder is located in the Documents and Settings*username* folder.

2. Open the SendTo folder for each user and right-click. Select New, Shortcut.

3. Click Browse and navigate to the location of Notepad.exe (the default Windows folder). Select Notepad and click OK; click Next to continue.

4. Click Finish to accept NOTEPAD as the shortcut name, or enter another name and click Finish.

To use this shortcut, right-click on the .eml file and select Send To, then select Notepad.

NOTE

> If you start Outlook Express and don't see any of your email folders, they might still be on your hard disk but not in Outlook Express anymore. Use these steps to locate them (ensure you have Administrator privileges before you start):
>
> 1. Start OE and click Tools, Options, Maintenance. Click Store Folder to determine the location of the store folder. Select the entire path displayed and press Ctrl+C to copy it.
> 2. Click Start, Run, and then press Ctrl+V to paste in the name of the store folder. This displays a window with all your message store files in it.
> 3. Rename the folders.dbx file as folders.xxx.
> 4. Restart OE. Your folders should reappear, but will now be on the same level instead of being listed as subfolders. Drag and drop folders as desired to create the folder layout you want. If you use message rules for routing messages to particular folders, verify that the message rules correctly reference your destination folder, or modify the rules to match the new destination folder. Verify that settings such as Identities, Signatures, and Newsgroup Synchronization are also correct.

CONFIGURING OUTLOOK EXPRESS SECURITY SETTINGS

With most viruses, worms, and Trojan horses traveling between computers via email, keeping your email secure is even more important today than ever. To view or adjust OE's security settings (see Figure 14.13), click Tools, Options, Security.

14

Figure 14.13
Shown are OE's
default Security set-
tings.

By default, OE uses the Restricted Sites Zone setting from IE for its Virus Protection setting. To verify that restricted site settings are configured for maximum safety, open the
Internet Options icon in Control Panel and click Security. Select Restricted Sites, click the
Custom button, and verify that the following active content and scripting options are **disabled**:

- All items in the ActiveX Controls and Plugins category
- File download
- Disable Java
- The following items in the Miscellaneous category:
  - Access Data Sources Across Domains
  - Allow META Refresh
  - Don't Prompt for Client Certificate Selection
  - Installation of Desktop Items
  - Launching Programs and Files in an IFRAME
  - Navigate Sub-frames Across Different Domains
  - Software Channel Permissions
    User Data Persistence
  - All items in the Scripting category

Also, user authentication should be set to Prompt for User Name and Password.

NOTE

One problem with the default security settings for OE 6 is that disabling Active Scripting will
prevent email stationery messages you might receive from scrolling. My advice: *Don't*
change this setting (and thus avoid a security risk); instead, inform your stationery-
obsessed friends to cut out the fancy email and send you plain-text messages.

OE also prevents other programs from sending email under your name. While this can stop external programs from taking over OE, this won't stop Visual Basic scripts executed within OE from spamming the contents of your address book. To completely stop OE script attacks, supplement these default settings with an up-to-date antivirus program that includes script blocking, such as Norton AntiVirus 2002.

The option Do Not Allow Attachments to Be Saved or Opened That Could Potentially Be a Virus is disabled by default. If you've had problems with viruses, worms, or Trojans in email attachments, enable this feature. When you receive email with attachments, you can see the attachment when you click on the paperclip icon, but you can't download or open the attachment until you disable this security setting.

USING DIGITAL CERTIFICATES WITH OUTLOOK EXPRESS

If you want to send an encrypted message or a digitally signed message with Outlook Express, you must obtain a digital certificate. If you attempt to send a digitally signed message without having a digital signature, a warning box pops up prompting you to Get Digital ID. Click this box to be routed to a Microsoft Web page that displays a list of approved sources for digital certificates. Click any of the links listed to purchase a digital certificate.

If you attempt to send an encrypted message without a digital certificate, OE will warn you that you won't be able to read the message you send. A digital certificate will enable you to send both encrypted and digitally signed messages. When you purchase a digital certificate, you will be sent an email explaining how to install the digital certificate into OE. Once you have installed the digital certificate, you need to associate it with your email accounts

1. Click Tools, Accounts, and select your email account.
2. Click Properties.
3. Click Security.
4. To use your digital certificate to sign documents, click the Select button next to the Certificate field in the Signing Certificate section of the Security Properties sheet. Select the certificate from those listed and click OK.
5. To use your digital certificate to encrypt documents, click the Select button next to the Certificate field in the Encrypting Preferences section of the Security Properties sheet. Select the certificate from those listed and click OK.
6. To change the encryption algorithm, click the Algorithm pull-down menu and select from the options available. The default, 3DES, is widely supported and should not be changed unless some of your email recipients can't read email encrypted with this algorithm.
7. Click Apply to accept your settings, then OK.

To encrypt a message, click Tools, Encrypt from the message menu. To add a digital signature, click Tools, Digitally Sign from the message menu.

14

> **NOTE**
>
> If you use multiple email accounts (such as a POP3 account and a Hotmail or other Web-based email account) and want to use digital signatures or encryption with each account, you must purchase a separate digital signature for each account.

→ For more information on digital certificate management, **see** "The Certificate Snap-in," **p. 1088**.

MSN MESSENGER

While it's still below the radar of many computer users over thirty, younger users have made instant messaging (IM) software the 21st-century replacement for the party line. Pioneered by Netscape (now AOL) Instant Messenger and ICQ, IM software is also part of Microsoft's Internet strategy with its Windows Messenger IM client.

Windows Messenger 4.6 is installed by default with Windows XP, and can interconnect with the MSN Messenger IM client used by other Windows versions. Like MSN Messenger, Windows Messenger requires you to set up a .NET (Microsoft) Passport or have a Hotmail email address.

Windows Messenger provides text and voice chat, video camera support for USB and IEEE-1394 WebCams, file transfers, Remote Assistance, Whiteboard, drop-down emoticons for text chat, and support for contact groups. .NET Alerts support lets you receive stock alerts and other information through Messenger, your mobile device, or your email inbox.

To download add-ins that support MSN Messenger features such as Hotmail incoming mail notification, mobile text messaging, profiles, and daily links, visit

`http://messenger.microsoft.com/download/addin.asp`

INTERCONNECTING WITH OTHER IM CLIENTS

Unfortunately, a universal standard for IM that would enable AOL, Microsoft, Yahoo, and ICQ users to connect with each other does not yet exist; AOL is the main stumbling block in this effort. However, if you're willing to sacrifice some of the more exotic IM features such as video chat, some third-party clients are available which can connect with the major IM services. Using one of these interoperable clients instead of installing multiple clients can help you save memory, disk space, and system resources. Some of these include

- Trillian—Download it from Cerulean Studios' Web site at `http://www.trillian.cc`.
- Jabber Instant Messenger—Download it from Jabber, Inc. at `http://www.jabber.com`.
- imici.M3 Messenger 3.0—Download it from Budokan, LLC's Web site at `http://www.imici.com`.

WINDOWS MESSENGER AND CORPORATE NETWORKS

Traditionally, IM clients have worked very well between individual users' home PCs or between PCs on small home/office networks. Depending upon the task you want to perform with Windows Messenger, you might have no difficulties, or you might need to make changes to your router or firewall configuration to make a particular feature work correctly.

Table 14.6 describes the tasks that might cause problems for Windows Messenger and some typical solutions. Universal Plug and Play (UPnP) support, an optional feature for Windows XP, enables Windows Messenger to work in a wider variety of network configurations than with older versions of Windows. If you use the Windows XP Network Setup Wizard disk or Windows XP CD-ROM to configure other Windows systems on a network, they will also be able to use UPnP.

TABLE 14.6 TROUBLESHOOTING WINDOWS MESSENGER ON NETWORKS

Task	Solution
Can't call another computer with Windows XP Pro IM when the Windows XP Internet Connection Firewall is enabled	Set up user with administrator privileges.
Can't establish an IM session when connecting from a network address translation (NAT)-based network via an ISP that also uses NAT	When NAT is used by an ISP, the actual public address of the computer connected to the Internet cannot be determined; Windows Messenger needs to know this address to work.
	Contact the ISP to determine whether you can use a static IP address, or whether the ISP has a special configuration to allow IM clients such as Windows Messenger to work.
Can't connect because the NAT device on the home network doesn't support UPnP NAT	Use a UPnP-enabled gateway such as Windows XP Internet Connection Sharing (ICS), or upgrade to a router/gateway which supports UPnP.
Can't connect because non-UPnP firewall/router won't permit IM traffic as needed.	Upgrade firewall/router to UPnP, or configure firewall to allow User Datagram Protocol (UDP) traffic on the following ports:
	Voice & Video: open UDP ports 5004–65535 to incoming traffic
	File transfer: open ports starting with 6891; add a port for each simultaneous file transfer you want
	Application sharing/Whiteboard sharing: open port 1503
	Remote assistance: open port 3389
	If you cannot open all the ranges desired on an individual basis with a given firewall/router, you can use the demilitarized zone (DMZ) setting to disable all port controls, but this exposes the system in the DMZ to all Internet traffic, including potential hostile access.

14

continues

TABLE 14.6   CONTINUED

Task	Solution
Session initiation protocol (SIP) servers are used on both sides of an Internet Security and Acceleration (ISA) firewall on a corporate network.	If only one side of the connection is connected via an SIP server, calls can go through, but if both sides of a potential connection connect through separate SIP servers, the connection can't be completed.

Windows XP doesn't install UPnP support by default; to install it

1. Open the Add/Remove Programs icon in Control Panel.
2. Click Add/Remove Windows Components.
3. Scroll down to Networking Services and select it.
4. Click Details.
5. Click Universal Plug and Play.
6. Click OK to install it.

SECURING UNIVERSAL PLUG AND PLAY

As Table 14.6 makes clear, many potential problems with Windows Messenger support are eliminated when UPnP-aware gateways, routers, and firewalls are used. However, the implementation of UPnP in Windows XP as shipped is not limited in how far it will search for UPnP-aware devices. This creates a significant security risk described in detail in Microsoft Knowledge Base article Q315000.

To prevent UPnP from becoming a way for hostile remote users to take control of your computer, install the patch referred to in Microsoft Security Bulletin MS01-059, "Unchecked Buffer in Universal Plug and Play Can Lead to System Compromise."

You can download this patch through Windows Update for Windows XP, or directly from this URL:

`http://www.microsoft.com/Downloads/Release.asp?ReleaseID=34951`

By default, a patched machine will search only the same subnet or a private IP address for UPnP device descriptions, and only up to four router hops. Once you have installed this patch, you can add special Registry values to adjust the scope of UPnP device description searches, as described in Table 14.7. For additional details about the effects of the patch, see Microsoft Knowledge Base article Q315056.

Click Start, Run. Type **Regedt32.EXE** and click OK to start the Windows XP Registry Editor to make the following changes if desired.

14

TABLE 14.7   NEW REGISTRY VALUES FOR ADJUSTING UPnP OPERATION

Existing Registry Key	New Value to Add	Data Type	Value Data	Limits Search to
HKEY_LOCAL_ MACHINE\SOFTWARE\ Microsoft\UPnP	DownloadScope	REG_ DWORD	0	Same subnet
			1	Same as 0 or a private address
	Control Point		2	Same as 1 or within four router hops
			3	No limits (anywhere)
HKEY_LOCAL_ MACHINE\ SYSTEM\ CurrentControlSet\ Services\SSDPSRV\ Parameters	TTL	REG_ DWORD	Any number 0 or higher	Value entered equals maximum number of hops between the com puter and the UPnP device

.NET PASSPORT

Windows XP strongly encourages users to get a .NET Passport (previously referred to as a Microsoft Passport). A .NET Passport provides one login name and password for access to all Passport-enabled Web sites and services such as Windows Messenger, MSN Mail, Hotmail, MSN Money Central, and e-commerce sites which support the optional Passport Wallet feature.

HEY, WHO'S AFRAID OF MICROSOFT PASSPORT?

Microsoft Passport is a simple way to sign on and purchase items and services from a growing number of sites affiliated with (read "owned by") Microsoft. Because people are so darned tired of having to remember tens of passwords (maybe even hundreds if you're a Web addict like me), the idea of using a simple MS Passport that stores your username, password, credit card info, and so forth, and promises to effortlessly log you on to all types of Web sites and services, might sound pretty alluring. I mean, I forget my passwords all the time, don't you? In fact, I keep a Notepad file on my computer of nothing but my passwords and other such stuff. If I don't have access to this file when I'm traveling and I want to, say, purchase a plane ticket, I'm out of luck, because I can't remember how to log in to Travelocity. (Of course, I keep this file in an encrypted file folder running under Windows XP, so it's not going to be easy for someone to liquidate my IRA. After the "substantial penalty for early withdrawal," it's not going to amount to that much anyway!)

But I'll suggest to you that Passport isn't all it's cracked up to be: It's a whole lot less. In fact, if you were concerned about cookies, you'll really be scared of Passport. As mentioned earlier, cookies are small text files stored locally on your computer used to store a bit of info about you. When you go to a Web site that uses cookies, the Web server and your computer

14

agree to exchange a little information, based on what you do on the Web site. Suppose you set up an account at Jack's Pizza with your name and address, or just that you like pepperoni pizza. Only the information you give to that site, along with possibly when you viewed the site, what you purchased, and what server you were coming in from will be stored in the cookie. The idea is to make it easier for the site to recognize you the next time you visit. This is why you can go to some sites and the Web page says "Hi Karen!" It simply looks in your cookie directory on your hard disk (the cookie jar) and looks for the one it stored there. It opens the cookie, sees that your name is Karen (because you typed that into its site the last time you visited), and displays it. It also knows that last time you bought an extra-large pepperoni pizza and a bag of fries. This time it automatically suggests an extra-large pepperoni pizza and fries. Neat. Convenient. It's like going into your favorite restaurant, and the waiter knows what you like.

The important point to remember is this: The agreement is that this information is only transacted between you and the Web site you're visiting. You have some privacy of informa-tion. Jack's Pizza's Web server is not talking to Jill's Soda Pop Company's Web server and then generating email to you trying to sell you a soda to wash your pizza down with. (Okay, so maybe you want a soda with your pizza, but this can get out of hand. Keep reading.)

The idea of Passport is totally different. Although it contends otherwise, I don't think Microsoft is just trying to offer a better "user experience" on the Web by offering you a Passport to keep your passwords and stuff all tidy. With Passport, you sign on in one place, essentially Microsoft, even if you're clicking the "Sign in through Passport" link on your favorite Web site. Really, you're signing in at Microsoft's Passport, which in turn links you back to the site you wanted. Then, you start hopping around between sites. Although most of the Passport sites are now MS sites like Hotmail, they hope to entice other vendors to become Passport-enabled. (With any luck on Microsoft's site, Jack and Jill will both fall down this slippery slope.) When that happens, the Web servers are linked to one another. Lots of valuable customer information (such as your buying patterns, net worth, geographi-cal location, age, sex, hobbies, medical history, and other such private info) can be more and more easily aggregated into one large database. Do you think that type of information is valuable? You bet it is, and Microsoft knows it!

Let's consider some examples. Log in to Microsoft's Investor site (`http://www.investor.com`) and look in the upper-right corner. There's a logon button for Passport. Now, I'm not say-ing this is happening now, but it's possible. Suppose you're buying a house, refinancing your current one, or buying a new car, through a Passport-affiliated site. It is possible using today's technology that the selling agent can determine your net worth by checking your portfolio on Investor.com and bargain harder with you. This type of thing actually hap-pened with Amazon, who raised its prices on DVDs for people who regularly bought DVDs from them. The practice was based only on cookies (and was stopped, by the way, after cus-tomers discovered what was going on).

If you want to read that story, here's a brief quote and URL: "Amazon customers on DVD Talk reported that certain DVDs had three different prices, depending on which so-called cookie a customer received from Amazon."

`http://news.cnet.com/news/0-1007-200-2703210.html?tag=st.ne.1002.tgif.ni`

In essence, the Passport is circumnavigating the idea of cookies being private. What's particularly scary is that one entry point (or gatekeeper) exists to all Passport sites—Microsoft. Over time, look to see more and more sites (and even IE itself) incorporating Passport. I think we should be wary of the aggregation of information about us and wary of allowing that information to be passed around freely between corporations. Even umpteen-page-long privacy statements can't protect you when a Web company goes bankrupt and the court orders sale of its valuable database with your buying patterns or other private information in it.

NOTE

> Once you've enabled Passport, when you activate Outlook Express, MSN Messenger starts up. However, even though you can't prevent it from starting, you can prevent it from automatically logging you on. To do so:
>
> 1. Start OE and click Tools, Options.
> 2. Click the General tab and uncheck the box, Automatically Log On to Windows Messenger.

OBTAINING A .NET PASSPORT

Assuming that didn't scare you off, and you want to create a .NET Passport account, here's how (if you don't already have a .NET Passport account. If you have ever signed up for a Hotmail or MSN email address, you have a .NET Passport. However, you can also obtain a .NET Passport or configure your system to use an existing email address with a .NET Passport through the User Accounts icon in Control Panel.): Click Set Up My Account to Use a .NET Passport to start the process.

If you don't want to use an existing email account, you can use the wizard to create a new MSN Mail account. To use an existing Hotmail, MSN Mail, or other email account, select that option and enter the email address you want to use when prompted.

If you enter a third-party email address (not MSN Mail or Hotmail), you will be prompted for a password, a secret question/answer combination in case you lose your password, and your location information. After you agree to the terms of the service, you can optionally share your email address or other registration information with participating sites. Keep in mind that while third-party sites must agree to disclose to you how they use .NET Passport information, what they do with that information is not controlled by Microsoft.

To add additional information to your .NET Passport profile, go to the .NET Password Member Services Web site at

`http://memberservices.passport.com`

Click Edit My .NET Passport Profile.

14

CREATING AND USING THE .NET PASSPORT WALLET

If you want to use .NET Passport to make your online shopping easier at Web sites that display the Passport Express Purchase button, go the Member Services page on the .NET Passport Web site and click Create or Edit My .NET Passport Wallet.

When you select this option, you can select the option to sign yourself in automatically after you provide your username and password. Select the credit card type and provide credit card and billing information for that card to set up your wallet. Passport stores this information, enabling you to purchase items at participating Web sites without requiring you to provide your actual credit card details to the site.

When you access a site that uses .NET Passport login, click on the Login .NET Passport button. Your Passport username will appear; enter your password to log in. When it's time to pay for your purchase, select the card, billing, and shipping address you stored in Passport to make your purchase and check out.

Some sites don't use Passport until it's time to pay for a purchase. These sites are referred to as .NET Passport Express Purchase sites, and the login button is not displayed on these sites until you've selected your purchases and are starting the checkout process. Click the .NET Passport Express Purchase button and provide your password. Select the credit card you want to use and accept or edit the shipping and billing information to complete your purchase.

.NET PASSPORT SECURITY WITH WINDOWS XP

While .NET Passport accounts work with both Windows and other operating systems, Windows XP's implementation of .NET Passport security is better than other systems', especially when the latest patches to IE 6 are installed. Even if you store your .NET Passport setting with MSN Messenger, you typically must log in again to use your .NET Passport wallet. However, security experts continue to be concerned about some aspects of .NET Passport, as in this Web article by Marc Slemko, who discovered problems with the .NET Passport function in October 2001:

```
http://alive.znep.com/~marcs/passport/index.html
```

While the specific vulnerability discovered by Mr. Slemko has been patched, Microsoft's efforts to make Passport easier to use can lead to big security headaches if your computer isn't secured properly. While Microsoft encourages Windows XP users to associate their .NET Passport with their Windows XP login account, I don't recommend it. If you do, anyone who "borrows" your computer while you're logged in will see your basic contact information (email address and other contact information, but not your password) just by going to the .NET Passport site and clicking Edit the Information on Your .NET Passport. And, if you used your true country, state, and ZIP code when filling out your profile, a hacker who knows you might find it fairly easy to reset your password and take over your account, including your Wallet. They'd just have to guess the answer to one of the secret questions such as "favorite dog" and know your credit card numbers. To protect yourself, maybe you should lie a little when you fill out your Passport profile—and don't leave credit card statements or receipts in your office.

REMOTE ASSISTANCE

The remote assistance feature in Windows XP enables you to ask another Windows XP user for help with your computer, or to provide help to another user without using third-party software. To request help, start Remote Assistance from the Help and Support menu: Click Invite a Friend to Help You with Remote Assistance, and Invite Someone to Help You.

You can invite anyone on your Windows Messenger (WM) buddy list who's currently online to help you, or send an email message. If you send an email message, you specify a maximum length of time for the invitation to be valid (one hour is the default); this helps to prevent unauthorized users from hacking your system. You are strongly encouraged, although not required, to set up a password for your helper to use. You must provide the password to the user separately; I recommend that you agree on a password in advance, or call your helper by phone or WM to send along the password.

It's easier to invite a WM buddy who's currently online; you can even do it from the WM interface; click I Want To, More, and Ask for Remote Assistance. Select the user from the list to send the invitation.

If your network's group policy allows you to offer Remote Assistance to another user, and if you are listed as a member of the Administrators Group on that computer or listed as a helper under the Offer Remote Assistance policy setting, you don't need an invitation to offer help to that user. This option is available only for Windows XP Professional users; if you have Windows XP Home users on your network, they must initiate the request for assistance.

To offer Remote Assistance without an invitation to another user on your LAN, open the Help and Support Menu, click Tools, click Offer Remote Assistance, and enter the name or IP address of the computer.

In either case, once the invitation/offer to help has been sent, the WM Conversation box appears on both the requesting (Novice) and helping (Expert) systems. The Expert system can click Accept [Alt+A] to start the help process, or Decline [Alt+D] to reject the request for assistance. A similar screen on the Novice side allows the user who asked for help to cancel the request if desired.

During Remote Assistance, the Novice controls the process; the requester must specifically grant permission for the Expert to view the screen and use text chat. A two-column toolbar appears on the Novice's screen during the entire help process: The left column is used for displaying both sides' chat messages; the lower left corner provides a message entry area. The right column contains controls for file transfer, audio chat and quality settings, disconnecting, and stop control, as shown in Figure 14.14.

14

Figure 14.14
Shown is a Novice's control panel during a typical Remote Assistance session.

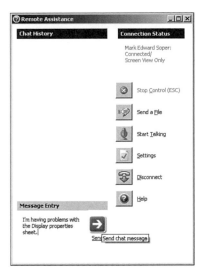

Figure 14.15 shows the Expert's view of the requester's screen. The left side shows the chat process, with the lower left corner used for message entry. The larger window shows a scaled or scrollable actual-size view of the requester's display.

Figure 14.15
Shown is an Expert's control panel during a typical Remote Assistance session. Note the chat window indicates that the Expert has taken control of the system.

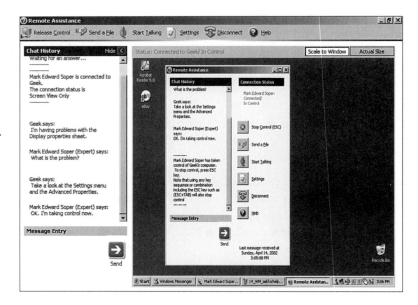

Until the Expert takes control, the Novice controls the system; as before, the Novice must specifically permit this to take place. This enables the Expert to watch the Novice try a process, or allows the Expert to take over if necessary. During the process, either side can initiate a file transfer and start or stop voice chat to help solve the problem.

14

Whenever desired, the Novice can click Esc to stop remote control of the system. Either side can click Disconnect to stop the process.

MANAGING OR DISABLING REMOTE ASSISTANCE

Remote Assistance will work on most networks unless both the Novice's and Expert's computers are connected to a non-UPnP NAT device; see "Windows Messenger and Corporate Networks," later in this chapter, for details.

Remote Assistance uses the Remote Desktop Protocol, which uses TCP port 3389. While the Windows XP Internet Connection Firewall doesn't block this port, third-party firewalls or routers might block this port by default; configure the firewall/router to leave this port open.

If you want to control or eliminate Remote Assistance on a network that uses an Active Directory Windows 2000 Server, use the Solicited Remote Assistance policy snap-in. You can also enable or disable Remote Assistance invitations through the System properties sheet in the Control Panel. Click the Remote tab and check the Allow Remote Assistance Invitations check box. To prevent a user from taking over your system with Remote Assistance, click the Advanced button on this tab and clear the Allow This Computer to Be Controlled Manually check box.

ALTERNATIVES TO WINDOWS XP REMOTE ASSISTANCE

Windows XP Remote Assistance provides good, basic, one-to-one remote control features but lacks the security features and support options that are useful for a help desk in a corporate setting, such as support for multiple network types, server remote control, file synchronization, drive cloning, and support for non-Windows XP systems.

If you need these types of features, consider these products:

- PCAnywhere 10.5—Symantec (`http://www.symantec.com`); about $180; supports all 32-bit versions of Windows from Windows 9x & NT 4.0 through XP
- LapLink Gold 11.0—LapLink, Inc (`http://www.laplink.com`); about $140 to $180; supports all 32-bit versions of Windows from Windows 9x & NT 4.0 through XP
- VNC—AT&T Laboratories Cambridge (`http://www.uk.research.att.com/vnc/`); free; supports 32-bit Windows, x86 Linux, Macintosh, DEC Alpha, Windows CE 2.x, and Solaris

PCAnywhere can be used to control multiple systems, includes a Host Assessment Tool to check security, and works with firewalls. It supports seven different types of authentication, making it a good choice for both Windows-based and Novell networks.

LapLink Gold 11.0 provides very strong file transfer services and can also be used in a direct-connect situation with parallel, serial, or USB cables. It works behind firewalls and supports folder-based user privileges.

14

VNC (Virtual Network Computing) requires that Windows XP's Fast User Switching be disabled, and can't work with some firewall configurations. Two types of programs are used with VNC: the server (which hosts remote connections) and the viewer (installed on the client PCs). VNC also supports Java-based remote control via Web browsers.

→ For more information about Remote Assistance, Remote Desktop and other remote control packages, **see** "Accessing Computers Remotely," **p. 794**.

TCP/IP Tools

Windows XP provides a suite of TCP/IP tools that can help you diagnose problems with your connection, make Telnet or terminal-style connections to other users, and perform FTP. This section covers the uses of these tools.

Using TCP/IP Diagnostic Tools

Windows XP includes the following command-line tools for diagnosing TCP/IP problems:

- Ping
- Tracert
- Pathping
- Nslookup

NOTE

> To open a command-prompt window in Windows XP, click Start, Run, type **CMD**, and click OK. Press ENTER after you type each command. Type **EXIT** and press ENTER to close the window.

→ To read more about the TCP/IP diagnostic programs, **see** Chapter 21, "Troubleshooting Your Network," **p. 851**.

Using Ping

Ping has many options, but this is the most common form of the command:

```
ping hostname
```

With this option, Ping resolves the IP address used by the specified host name, sends four 32-byte packets, and displays the round trip time (also called site latency), the host's IP address, and the time to live (TTL) value for that site (in milliseconds).

Use this command:

```
ping 127.0.0.1
```

to ping your own system; if this fails, you need to reinstall the TCP/IP protocol.

You can also use ping to determine the host name for a particular IP address:

```
ping -a IPaddress
```

If the speed of the connection to particular IP addresses has dropped, and you know the routing that your company networks use to reach those IP addresses, you can use this command to determine the performance bottleneck in the routing used:

```
ping -j FirstIPaddress SecondIPAddress DestinationIPAddress
```

NOTE

To determine the routing used to reach a given IP address, use `Tracert`.

For additional help with `ping`, open Help and Support, search for Ping, and click on the entry for Ping under Overviews, Articles, and Tutorials.

If `Ping` displays "Unknown Host," verify that you specified the correct host name and check your TCP/IP settings to verify that you can reach a DNS server. You can use this command

```
ipconfig /all
```

to display your current DNS server and other TCP/IP configuration information. If you see invalid IP addresses such as 0.0.0.0 and your computer uses dynamic IP addressing, use this command

```
ipconfig /release
```

to release current IP addresses, followed by this command

```
ipconfig /renew
```

to obtain new IP address information for your system.

USING Tracert

`Tracert` is the Windows equivalent of the Unix command `traceroute`; use it to determine what path a request to a particular host follows. With the default command

```
tracert hostname
```

each router in the path between your system and the destination system is displayed by its IP address and host name, up to a maximum of 30 hops. Figure 14.16 shows typical output from a `tracert` command.

To create a cleaner display, specify

```
tracert -d hostname
```

to suppress the hostnames of each router. If `tracert` cannot complete tracing the route to the specified hostname because it exceeded 30 hops, use `tracert -h` to specify the number of hops:

```
tracert -h MaxNoHops hostname
```

You can use `Pathping` along with `Tracert` to learn more about the performance of the routers between your computer and your destination host.

14

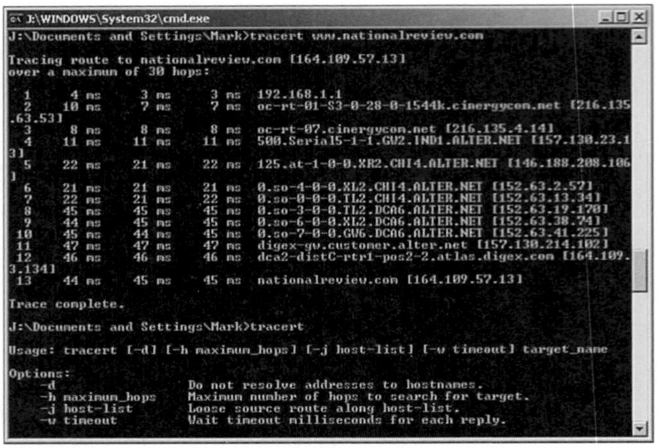

Figure 14.16
Tracert determines that there are 13 hops between the author's PC and the destination host (www.nationalreview.com).

USING Pathping

`Pathping` acts as a combination of `ping` and `tracert`. `Pathping` provides output similar to that of this command:

```
tracert -d hostname
```

`Pathping` displays the number of hops and the names and IP addresses of routers between your system and the destination host. It also calculates the efficiency of each router along the way, as shown in this sample output:

```
C:\Documents and Settings\Howard>pathping http://www.nationalreview.com

Tracing route to nationalreview.com [164.109.57.13]
over a maximum of 30 hops:
   0  Tosh_P2000.insightbb.com [192.168.0.104]
   1  192.168.0.1
   2  10.10.32.1
   3  12.220.7.129
   4  12.220.0.50
   5  gbr5-p40.sl9mo.ip.att.net [12.123.25.26]
   6  tbr2-p013501.sl9mo.ip.att.net [12.122.11.121]
   7  tbr2-p013701.cgcil.ip.att.net [12.122.10.9]
   8  ggr1-p3100.cgcil.ip.att.net [12.122.11.210]
   9  POS5-2.BR5.CHI2.ALTER.NET [204.255.169.145]
  10  0.so-6-0-0.XL2.CHI2.ALTER.NET [152.63.68.194]
  11  0.so-1-0-0.TL2.CHI2.ALTER.NET [152.63.67.121]
  12  0.so-3-0-0.TL2.DCA6.ALTER.NET [152.63.19.170]
  13  0.so-6-0-0.XL2.DCA6.ALTER.NET [152.63.38.74]
  14  0.so-7-0-0.GW6.DCA6.ALTER.NET [152.63.41.225]
  15  digex-gw.customer.alter.net [157.130.214.102]
  16  dca2-distC-rtr1-pos2-2.atlas.digex.com [164.109.3.134]
  17  nationalreview.com [164.109.57.13]

Computing statistics for 425 seconds...
                Source to Here   This Node/Link
Hop   RTT     Lost/Sent = Pct   Lost/Sent = Pct   Address
   0                                               Tosh_P2000.insightbb.com
```

14

```
➡[192.168.0.104]
                                  0/ 100 =   0%   |
   1    1ms    0/ 100 =   0%      0/ 100 =   0%   192.168.0.1
                                  0/ 100 =   0%   |
   2   11ms    0/ 100 =   0%      0/ 100 =   0%   10.10.32.1
                                  0/ 100 =   0%   |
   3   11ms    0/ 100 =   0%      0/ 100 =   0%   12.220.7.129
                                  0/ 100 =   0%   |
   4   20ms    0/ 100 =   0%      0/ 100 =   0%   12.220.0.50
                                  0/ 100 =   0%   |
   5   20ms    0/ 100 =   0%      0/ 100 =   0%   gbr5-p40.sl9mo.ip.att.net
➡[12.123.25.26]
                                  0/ 100 =   0%   |
   6   21ms    0/ 100 =   0%      0/ 100 =   0%   tbr2-p013501.sl9mo.ip.att.net
➡[12.122.11.121]
                                  0/ 100 =   0%   |
   7   28ms    0/ 100 =   0%      0/ 100 =   0%   tbr2-p013701.cgcil.ip.att.net
➡[12.122.10.9]
                                  0/ 100 =   0%   |
   8   27ms    0/ 100 =   0%      0/ 100 =   0%   ggr1-p3100.cgcil.ip.att.net
➡[12.122.11.210]
                                  0/ 100 =   0%   |
   9   29ms    0/ 100 =   0%      0/ 100 =   0%   POS5-2.BR5.CHI2.ALTER.NET
➡[204.255.169.145]
                                  0/ 100 =   0%   |
  10   31ms    0/ 100 =   0%      0/ 100 =   0%   0.so-6-0-0.XL2.CHI2.ALTER.NET
➡[152.63.68.194]
                                  0/ 100 =   0%   |
  11   30ms    0/ 100 =   0%      0/ 100 =   0%   0.so-1-0-0.TL2.CHI2.ALTER.NET
➡[152.63.67.121]
                                  0/ 100 =   0%   |
  12   44ms    0/ 100 =   0%      0/ 100 =   0%   0.so-3-0-0.TL2.DCA6.ALTER.NET
➡[152.63.19.170]
                                  0/ 100 =   0%   |
  13   44ms    0/ 100 =   0%      0/ 100 =   0%   0.so-6-0-0.XL2.DCA6.ALTER.NET
➡[152.63.38.74]
                                  0/ 100 =   0%   |
  14   45ms    0/ 100 =   0%      0/ 100 =   0%   0.so-7-0-0.GW6.DCA6.ALTER.NET
➡[152.63.41.225]
                                  0/ 100 =   0%   |
  15   46ms    0/ 100 =   0%      0/ 100 =   0%   digex-gw.customer.alter.net
➡[157.130.214.102]
                                  0/ 100 =   0%   |
  16   47ms    0/ 100 =   0%      0/ 100 =   0%   dca2-distC-rtr1-pos2-2.atlas.digex.
➡com [164.109.3.134]
                                  0/ 100 =   0%   |
  17   46ms    0/ 100 =   0%      0/ 100 =   0%   nationalreview.com [164.109.57.13]
Trace complete.
```

NOTE

The amount of time displayed by `pathping` in the "computing statistics for xxx seconds" varies with the amount of time needed to complete the trace to the specified Web site.

14

If any packets were lost, the percentage would increase from 0% (perfect transmission). Thus, `pathping` shows you which routers are causing a bottleneck in your ability to connect with a remote host.

Because pathping sends much more data than ping (100 packets by default, instead of 4 with ping), some hosts that respond to ping might not respond to pathping, discarding all data.

Pathping, unlike ping, can also be used to check the route from a different IP address to the destination. Thus, you can use Pathping to troubleshoot TCP/IP connectivity on a remote computer.

To check the connection between a remote computer and destination host, use this pathping command:

```
pathping -i remotecomputerIP Hostname
```

For more information about pathping and its options, look up pathping in Windows XP Help and Support.

USING NSLOOKUP

NSLookup is a command-line tool that can be used to display all types of IP-related information about the specified DNS server. To view the name and IP address of the default DNS server for your computer, type this command:

```
nslookup
```

The NSLookup prompt (>) is displayed after the DNS server name/IP address, allowing you to query the server for additional information, such as the DNS resource records needed to join an Active Directory domain. For a list of additional commands you can use at the NSLookup prompt, type **help** or **?** and press ENTER. Some NSLookup commands you might find particularly useful include

- NAME—Displays the name and IP address of the current server.
- *servername*—Displays the IP address of the specified server.
- *IP address*—Displays the server name of the specified IP address.

See Windows XP Help and Support for additional details about NSLookup, including a list of subcommands and how to perform the steps necessary to use NSLookup to join an Active Directory domain.

> **NOTE**
>
> Nslookup is a complex diagnostic tool. If you're interested in really delving into the Internet's Domain Name System, the "bible" on this topic is *DNS and Bind*, by Paul Albitz and Cricket Liu (O'Reilly).

TELNET

While IE 6 is the Windows XP tool of choice for Web browsing, some types of computer access require different types of clients.

Before the World Wide Web, the Internet was accessed through the use of a client/server technology called Telnet, which treats the client computer as a dumb terminal. Internet sites designed to be accessed with Telnet are referred to as Telsites. Compared to Web access,

Telnet is faster because all processing is performed on the host computer, and the connection is maintained continuously until the user or the host breaks the connection.

Windows XP includes a command-line Telnet client for access to Telnet servers, and a two-connection Telnet server is included with Windows XP Professional.

To enable the Telnet Server on Windows XP Professional

1. Right-click My Computer and select Manage to open the Computer Management interface.
2. Click the plus (+) sign next to Services and Applications.
3. Double-click Services to display a list of services.
4. Scroll down to Telnet.
5. Click Start the service.

To view the properties for the Telnet Server, double-click it. The General tab lists the path to the executable file, the service status, and its description. You can add Start parameters if necessary.

The Log On tab is used to select which accounts can log on to Telnet Server and whether the service can interact with the desktop.

The Recovery tab sets up options for handling service failures, such as Take No Action (default), Restart the Service, Run a Specified Program, or Restart the Computer.

Use the Dependencies tab to determine what system components are used by Telnet.

If a Telnet client's group hasn't already been configured, you will need to add this group to the Local Users and Groups, Groups folder in Computer Management. For maximum security, each user should be assigned a password.

→ For more information on creating user accounts, see "Creating and Managing User Accounts," **p. 417**.

To start the Telnet client on Windows XP

1. Click Start, Run.
2. Type Telnet and click OK.
3. Enter the Telnet commands desired. To see a list of commands, type `?/h`.

To log into a Telnet server after you start Telnet, type

```
o servername
```

You might need to enter your username and password manually to complete the login process.

14

ENABLING NTLM AUTHENTICATION OF USERS

Windows XP's built-in Telnet server supports NTLM Authentication, which enables Windows users to connect with the Telnet server without logging in again; NTLM passes through the username and password used on initial system login to the Telnet Server. However, logins from all users are treated as Guest logins by the Telnet client by default, which disables this feature.

Windows 9x/Me don't support NTLM authentication, so these users need to log in manually anyway. However, Windows 2000 and XP clients will appreciate the ability to log in as themselves. To make this option work correctly

1. Make sure you have created a TelnetGroup as discussed in the previous section.
2. Configure each member of the TelnetGroup with the username and password provided by the system administrator.
3. Each user in the TelnetGroup should configure their system's account to require login with the same username and password as that stored in the TelnetGroup on the Telnet Server. You can use the User Accounts icon in Control Panel on each computer to make this change.
4. The security policy on the Telnet Server must be modified to allow users to log on with their own identities:
    1. Open the Administrative Tools icon in Control Panel.
    2. Open Local Policies.
    3. Open Security Options.
    4. Scroll down to Network Access: Sharing and security model for local accounts.
    5. Change the setting from the default of Guest Only to Classic Model—users log on as themselves.
    6. Click OK.
    7. Close the Administrative Tools window.

USING HYPERTERMINAL AS A TELNET OR TERMINAL EMULATION CLIENT

Before the World Wide Web was popular, most computer users connected to remote computers by dialing up the telephone number of the remote computer and running a terminal emulation program. HyperTerminal can be used for direct computer-to-computer connections, can be used to emulate several popular terminals, and can also be used as your default Telnet client in place of the command-line Telnet client.

When you start HyperTerminal, it offers to make itself the default Telnet client. You can use HyperTerminal as a dial-up or TCP/IP client application.

If you haven't configured your telephone location information (country/region, area code, carrier code, and outside line code), HyperTerminal will prompt you to set this information before you continue.

14

HyperTerminal prompts you to create a connection the first time you use it; select an icon, provide a name, and select a connection type. Provide the following information based on your connection type:

- Modem connection—Country/region, area code, telephone number
- TCP/IP connection (LAN or broadband device)—host address (URL or IP address), port number (23 is the default for Telnet)
- The COM port option (for direct cable connection) has no options

Once you make the connection, the resizable HyperTerminal window displays the process of your session. Use the Transfer menu to capture the text to a file or to a printer as seen in Figure 14.17.

Figure 14.17
Capturing a Telnet session in HyperTerminal.

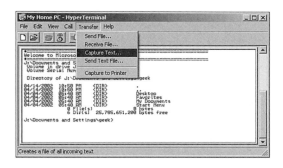

To change the default font and size used by HyperTerminal, click View, Font, and select from the menu. To resize the window to match the font size selected, click View, Snap.

To change the keyboard or other terminal behavior used for the current session, click File, Properties, Settings. If you have scrambled text or incorrect line lengths, you might need to select a particular terminal emulation type from the Emulation window instead of the default Auto detect setting. If every line is "printed" over the previous line, or if there are blank lines between each line onscreen, click ASCII Setup and adjust the Sending or Receiving settings as appropriate. By default, you can scroll back 500 lines during a session; if this is too large a setting, adjust it with the Backscroll Buffer Lines control.

Because HyperTerminal supports the Windows GUI and provides easy text capture, file transfer, and print options, you might prefer it over the command-line Telnet client.

USING THE WINDOWS XP FTP CLIENT

Windows XP includes the same command-line FTP client, FTP.EXE, used in previous 32-bit versions of Windows. While IE 6 enables downloading from FTP sites, you can use FTP.EXE to upload, download, delete, and rename individual files or groups of files. FTP can also be used to create or delete folders. FTP works interactively or in batch mode under the command of an ASCII text file called a script.

14

To start FTP

1. Click Start, Run.

2. Type `ftp` and click OK.

To see a list of FTP commands, type `?` and press ENTER at the FTP prompt `ftp>`.

SCRIPTING FTP COMMANDS

The contents of a script file used to automate FTP commands are simple: Each FTP command should be on a separate line. Create the file with Windows Notepad and save it as a .txt file. If you use Microsoft Word, WordPad, WordPerfect, and so forth, be sure to save the file as an ASCII or ANSI plain-text file.

Here's an example of a script file:

```
open ftp.mywebsite.com
user myname mypassword
lcd webgraph
cd pub/graphics
mput *.gif
mput *.jpg
close
```

To run this script (which logs you on to an FTP site, changes to a local folder called webgraph, changes to a Web folder called pub/graphics, uploads all .gif and all .jpg files from webgraph to the pub/graphics folder, and closes the connection) use this command:

```
ftp -s:scriptname.txt
```

OTHER THIRD-PARTY SOFTWARE TOOLS

You can greatly enhance the already-strong Internet support built into Windows XP by adding third-party tools to your system. Some of the major software types to consider adding include

- GUI-based TCP/IP diagnostics
- GUI-based FTP clients
- Open SSH, which provides encrypted-transmission replacements for Telnet and FTP, which don't encrypt transferred data
- MIB browsers to view network management data structures

REPLACEMENTS FOR Ping, Tracert, AND FTP

There are a number of commercial alternatives to Windows XP's built-in TCP/IP diagnostics and FTP tools. Among the best-known are

- IPSwitch WS_Ping ProPack—Runs within the Windows GUI, tabbed interface for Ping, Traceroute, Finger, Lookup, Whois, and other tests and diagnostics features. See `http://www.ipswitch.com/Products/WS_Ping/index.html` for details and pricing. Free 30-day evaluations available for download.

- IPSwitch WS_FTP32—Runs within the Windows GUI, stores site information (user-name, password, connection type), tutorials and wizards, auto retry/resume, and transfer manager, as well as supports 128-bit SSL encryption. See `http://www.ipswitch.com/Products/WS_FTP/index.html` for details and pricing. Free 30-day evaluations available for download.

- Globalscape CuteFTP—Runs within the Windows GUI, supports drag-and-drop file transfers, can build a list of files (transfer queue) from different folders for batch trans-fers, directory comparison, and transfers between remote sites. See `http://www.globalscape.com/products/cuteftp/index.shtml` for details and pricing. Free 30-day evaluations available for download.

- Globalscape CuteFTP Pro—Runs within the Windows GUI, supports classic or Pro interface, automatic .zip/.cab file compression, scripting, accelerated file transfer engine, scheduler, and advanced security features. See `http://www.globalscape.com/products/cuteftppro/index.shtml` for details and pricing. Free 30-day evaluations available for download.

Because these programs run in the Windows GUI and provide more features than the Windows command-line programs they replace, you will find it much easier to perform management, troubleshooting, and file transfer tasks with these programs.

SSH Tools

As network security woes increase, more and more users of utilities such as FTP and Telnet are realizing that the lack of encryption support provided by the standard Windows XP clients makes these types of connections vulnerable. As an alternative, the Unix Secure Shell (SSH) command interface protocol provides support for digital certificates and encrypted passwords.

SSH is supported on Windows XP by a variety of commercial, shareware, and open-source programs, including the following commercial GUI-based programs:

- SecureCRT from VanDyke Software Inc—See `http://www.vandyke.com/products/securecrt/index.html` for details and pricing. Free 30-day evaluations available for download.

- SSH Secure Shell from SSH Communications Security—Available for Windows, Unix, Solaris, HP/UX, Linux, and AIX in workstation and server versions. See `http://www.ssh.com/products/ssh/` for details and pricing.

14

Freeware SSH tools are available from many sources. Two of the most recommended include

- PuTTY—Freely downloadable from
  `http://www.chiark.greenend.org.uk/~sgtatham/putty/`
- WinSCP—Freely downloadable from `http://winscp.vse.cz/eng/`

Go to the following Web sites for links to additional SSH tools:

- Freeware SSH and SCP for Windows 9x, NT, Me, 2000, and XP—
  `http://www.jfitz.com/tips/ssh_for_windows.html#Introduction`
- Open SSH Windows and Mac [clients]—`http://www.openssh.com/windows.html`

MANAGEMENT INFORMATION BASE BROWSERS

Network devices that can be managed by the Simple Network Management Protocol (SNMP), such as routers, switches, servers, and firewalls, include Management Information Base (MIB) files, which describe the characteristics of the device and might allow the characteristics (which are stored in Object ID [OID] fields) to be changed via SNMP. To view MIBs, you need a management program that contains an MIB browser, which might be a standalone program or part of a network management suite. Many network management programs include an MIB browser. The following products are some of the leading standalone MIB browsers now available:

- MG-Soft Corporation—MG-Soft MIB Browser includes an MIB compiler which can be used to compile a vendor-specific MIB file into a format which can be read by the MIB Browser. Available in versions for SNMP through V. 2c or for SNMP through V. 3. For more information or a free evaluation, see `http://www.mg-soft.si`.
- Network View—Low-cost network discovery and management program including MIB Browser. Accepts .csv import of additional OIDs. For more information or a free evaluation, see `http://www.networkview.com`.
- Getif—A freeware MIB browser written by Phillipe Simonet. It's available from the SNMP for the Public Community Web site of Williams Technology Consulting Services. Learn more about it and find a download link at `http://www.wtcs.org/snmp4tpc/testing.htm`.

14

INTERNET INFORMATION SERVICES

In this chapter

15

IIS

Microsoft's Internet Information Services (IIS) is one of the most popular Web servers on the Internet today. Market share surveys, for example www.netcraft.com/survey, indicate that IIS is behind roughly 30% of all Web sites on the Internet, and is second in popularity only to the Apache Web server, which runs on Linux, Windows, and several versions of Unix. IIS is actually more than just a Web server, however. Included in the package is an FTP server, an SMTP mail transport server, and other features that assist in the support and development of Web sites rich in content and presentation. IIS is also closely integrated into the Windows operating system. This enables IIS to make use of services offered by Windows, such as the security features of the NTFS file system and the Indexing Service, among others.

In this chapter you'll learn how to install IIS on a Windows XP Professional computer (IIS is not available on the Windows XP Home Edition). You'll also learn how to configure IIS components, and get a quick overview of some of the programming features that can be used with IIS, including scripting in ASP and other languages. If you are already familiar with using a Web browser, this chapter will take you behind the scenes to show you how it's all done.

IIS on Windows XP Professional is the same industrial-strength Web server provided with the Server version of Windows. However, under XP Pro, it has some restrictions placed on it:

■ Under Windows 2000 Server and Server 2003 (which, from now on, I'll refer to collectively as Windows 200x Server), IIS can support any number of simultaneous visitors. Under XP Pro, there is a limit of 10 concurrent connections. Since many Web browsers maintain their connection to a server for several minutes even after they've received the requested content, this means that XP Pro can host only low-traffic sites. Extra visitors over the 10-connection limit will receive an error message through their Web browser.

■ Under Windows 200x Server, one computer can be given any number of names, such as "www.onecompany.com" and "www.anothercompany.com", and IIS can be told to deliver different pages depending on the name used by remote visitors. This is called "hosting multiple virtual domains." On Windows XP Pro, IIS can host only one domain.

Despite these limitations, it's perfectly reasonable to use IIS on XP Professional in many situations. For example:

■ To create a "intranet" Web server for your small office, or on a corporate LAN that allows departments to have a Web presence.

■ To create a personal or special-interest Web site for the Internet when you expect to have only a small amount of traffic. (As long as you aren't written up on slashdot.com, you'll probably be fine.)

■ As a test-bed to help you develop and test Web sites or Web software before installing them on a production server.

If you want to allow for more connections, or if you need to host multiple domains on one computer, you'll have to install one of the Windows 200x Server versions.

You can also install other manufacturer's Internet service software. For example, you can download a free version of the RealAudio server from www.real.com. There are other Web and FTP server packages besides IIS, and a host of email servers as well. However, according to the Windows End User License Agreement, the 10-connection limit applies to *any* software you might run on your computer, so even with non-Microsoft server programs you'd be faced with the same issue. With a different Web server program you *could* host multiple virtual domains, though.

A QUICK OVERVIEW OF IIS COMPONENTS

The term *information services* covers a broad territory. The most often thought-of feature of IIS is its Web server component, provided by the WWW Service. The WWW Service delivers Web pages to visitors on your LAN or on the Internet. It can deliver static (preformatted) pages, but also includes support for dynamic content generated by server-side includes, Common Gateway Interface (CGI) programs, and scripts. These are covered in more detail later in this chapter. You will also find that there are many third-party add-ons you can use with IIS.

Before you install IIS, consider whether you want to install the entire package, or just some of the components. In addition to the World Wide Web (WWW) Service, IIS includes the following components:

- **Documentation**—IIS comes with a great deal of helpful, online documentation in the form of Web pages.

- **FrontPage 2000 Server Extensions**—This optional component provides a secure way for remote users running Microsoft FrontPage, Office XP, or other compatible applications to update or "publish" files to your Web site. It makes it possible to securely share files with other Windows users over the Internet, using the Web Folders feature in Internet Explorer. Finally, it provides CGI programs that make it easy for your Web pages to process forms, send email, and maintain a guestbook.

- **File Transfer Protocol (FTP) Service**—The FTP server lets remote users transfer files to and/or from your computer. FTP can be put to good use in letting your employees or customers download files. It can also provide a way for others to send files to your computer. Later in this chapter we'll look at the pros and cons of using FTP, especially as they relate to network security.

- **SMTP Service**—The Simple Mail Transfer Protocol service allows your computer to receive and deliver mail destined for other mail servers. However, IIS does *not* provide a complete email solution, as it does not provide a Post Office (POP3 or IMAP) service to allow users to retrieve mail.

- **Internet Information Services Snapin**—This is a Microsoft Management Console snap-in that is needed to configure and manage IIS.

15

- **Support for the Internet Printing Protocol (IPP)**—This lets you access printers attached to your computer over the Internet. (IPP is discussed in Chapter 19, "Windows Unplugged: Remote and Portable Computing.")

- **Support for Remote Desktop access to your computer from a Web page**—This can let you access your computer or other Remote Desktop-enabled computers over the Internet, from Windows computers that don't have the Remote Desktop client program installed.

- **Visual InterDev RAD Remote Deployment Support**—Visual InterDev is Microsoft's software development system for sophisticated Web-based services that access corporate database and multitier transactional systems. The Remote Deployment Support service lets VID developers install and test software on-the-fly.

Its best to install only those components you need and intend to use. IIS, like all large programs, certainly has some undiscovered bugs in it, and some of those bugs will undoubtedly result in security risks. The fewer Internet services that are running on your computer, the less chance that you'll be running one whose security flaws will be discovered and exploited by a hacker.

NOTE

> If you had the FrontPage Extensions installed under an earlier version of Windows that you upgraded to Windows XP Professional, you must still manually choose to install the FrontPage Extensions, and reconfigure them afterward. They are not automatically upgraded during the Windows XP installation process.

SAFETY FIRST: WEB SERVER SECURITY

Making your computer accessible over the Internet opens up many security risks. After all, the whole point is to let random people all over the world run software on and retrieve information from *your* computer. In the corporate world, Web server computers are placed outside of the enterprise firewall, run *only* a web server program and nothing else, and have *only* the documents and files that they need to deliver, so that in the event that they're hacked, no more information than necessary is exposed.

If you're using your personal computer to host a Web site, you're potentially exposing your entire machine and all of your files to the Internet. Windows has many security safeguards built in, but still you must take responsibility for keeping your computer safe. So, here are some steps you should take before we even start to talk about installing IIS:

- Read Chapter 22 "Locking Down Your Computer" and Chapter 24, "Network Security."

- Use the NTFS file system for your computer. At the very least, be sure that your Web site folders and/or FTP directory are placed on an NTFS disk volume, so that Windows can enforce user-specific file security.

- Ensure that *every* account on your computer has a good password: one with letters *and* numbers or punctuation characters.

- Keep up-to-date with Windows Service Packs and Hotfixes, by enabling Automatic Updates (see "Automatic Update and Update Notification Options" in Chapter 6, "Setting Up Important Systems and Services"), and regularly logging on as a Computer Administrator user and visiting Windows Update.

- Subscribe to a Windows security mailing list at `www.microsoft.com/security`, `www.sans.org`, and/or `www.ntbugtraq.com`.

- Be sure that there is a firewall between your computer and the Internet: either a corporate firewall, a broadband connection sharing router, a third-party firewall program, or the Windows Internet Connection Firewall option for your Internet connection.

DETERMINING WHICH IIS SERVICES YOU NEED

IIS is a sophisticated suite of programs. These applications require forethought and oversight to make them useful and to manage the security risk that comes with global accessibility.

So, to minimize the headaches and risks, you should install only the components that are necessary to run your Web site. If you only want to present Web pages, and you can access the computer locally, then you probably don't need the FTP Service and its attendant security issues. The same goes for the Indexing Service. If you are only going to present a few static Web pages and have no need to allow for a search of your Web site's files, then you don't need to install this service.

Let's look briefly at the optional services, and discuss some of their pros and cons.

FTP SERVICE

FTP is not as secure a file transfer protocol as the FrontPage Extensions, but its client software is available on almost every operating system in the world, so it provides a way to make file transfers available to people who are not using Windows.

The problem is that the FTP protocol sends passwords over the Internet as clear-text *without encryption*, where they could be intercepted by hackers. So, ironically, permitting password-controlled FTP access is a security risk!

It's best to install the FTP server *only* if you absolutely must have a way for users who can't use FrontPage or Internet Explorer's Web Folders to post files to your computer. If you do need this, you might consider setting up user accounts just for people to use for FTP access, so that standard user accounts won't be compromised if a password gets intercepted.

SMTP SERVICE

The SMTP service can be used to deliver outgoing mail. It does *not* provide a way to process incoming mail, and doesn't give you mailboxes or a Post Office server. The only

15

good reason to install the SMTP service is if your Internet connection is intermittent. In this case, the SMTP service can be used to receive mail from your network (tell your mail programs to use your computer as their SMTP host). It will hold this mail until it can be forwarded.

Except in this case, it's better not to install the SMTP service at all. Configure your email program and the FrontPage extensions to send email through your ISP or your network's main mail server.

FRONTPAGE 2000 EXTENSIONS

You should install the FrontPage 2000 Extensions if you want to do any of the following:

- Use FrontPage (any version) or Microsoft Office to develop Web pages.
- Use your WWW service to use FrontPage's searching or form extensions.
- Copy files to and from your computer via the Internet, using Internet Explorer and Web Sharing.

FrontPage Extensions provide a way for Web-enabled applications to *publish* the composed HTML file and graphics to the Web server's online folders. Thus, the author doesn't have to manually place files into the WWW folders or use the FTP service to copy them there. FrontPage Extensions also provide HTML Form processing services, in the form of some special CGI (*Common Gateway Interface*, or Web server extension) programs that can record or email form responses, and index or searching services that let Web site viewers search your Web site for keywords or phrases. They also include as standard equipment a CGI-based Web page system to manage your printers.

VISUAL INTERDEV RAD REMOTE DEPLOYMENT SUPPORT

You'll want this component only if you're setting up an InterDev development and test computer. This is a Windows XP component you can install separately after you've installed IIS.

INSTALLING IIS ON WINDOWS XP PROFESSIONAL

Installing IIS is a simple matter of using the Add/Remove Programs applet in the Control Panel to add additional components to Windows XP Professional. Before you start the installation, however, check the following prerequisites:

- Your computer should have at least 256MB of memory, but the more the better. I would want to have at least 512MB.
- You will need approximately 16MB of disk space if you install all of the IIS components. (If you're so tight on disk space that this matters, you've bigger things to worry about than installing IIS).
- The TCP/IP network protocol must be installed on the computer. (It *is* installed by default on Windows XP.)

■ You must be running Windows XP Professional, not Home Edition.

To begin the installation, log in to the computer using a Computer Administrator account. Open the Control Panel and double-click the Add/Remove Programs icon. Then, select the Add/Remove Windows Components icon on the left.

NOTE

> If you are using the new Category View of the Control Panel, then select Add or Remove Programs from the Pick a Task menu.

In Figure 15.1 you can see the Windows Components Wizard that pops up.

Figure 15.1
Choose Internet Information Services (IIS) in the Windows Components Wizard.

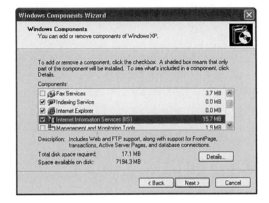

If you select the check box for Internet Information Services (IIS) you will notice that the check box has a gray background. This means that only some of the components of the service will be installed. To see the full listing of available components, and to see which are selected for installation, click the Details button. Figure 15.2 shows the dialog box that can be used to select or deselect IIS components.

Figure 15.2
Use this dialog box to indicate which components of IIS you want to install.

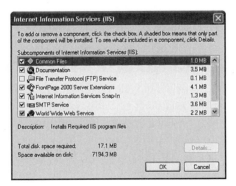

15

In addition to the basic Web site components described earlier, you will also find other choices in this dialog box, such as Common Files (leave this selected, it's required by other components) and Documentation. Provided you have no space constraints on your computer, installing the documentation is recommended. Updated documentation can also be found at Microsoft's Web site.

The World Wide Web Service (WWW) check box also allows you to further select subcomponents of the service. If you select this check box, it will be gray. Click on the Details button to find out which components of the WWW Service are selected. The options are

- **Printers Virtual Directory**—Installs IPP printing support, which lets you access printers attached to your computer over the Internet.
- **Remote Desktop Web Connection**—Installs sample Web pages that let you access your computer via Remote Desktop from Windows computers that don't have the Remote Desktop client installed.
- **Scripts Virtual Directory**—Sets up a virtual directory named /scripts to hold ASP or other scripts you create.
- **World Wide Web Service**—The WWW service itself.

After selecting the IIS components you want to install, click the OK button. When the Windows Components Wizard reappears, click the Next button. The wizard will build a list of files and then copy them to your computer. You may be prompted for the original Windows XP Professional CD during this step, and if you installed a Service Pack from a CD, you may be prompted for that CD as well.

When the wizard has finished, click the Finish button and then exit the Add/Remove Windows Components dialog box.

CAUTION

Immediately after installing IIS, visit Windows Update by clicking Start, All Programs, Windows Update. With IIS installed, one or more new Critical Updates may be indicated. Download and install them now! You *must* keep IIS up-to-date as IIS bugs tend to give random strangers the ability to rampage through your system.

CONFIGURING AND MANAGING THE WWW SERVICE

The basic WWW Web service comes with a default Web page already installed in folder `c:\inetpub\wwwroot`. By default, if you use the NTFS file system, only Computer Administrators have write access to this folder. If you will be maintaining the Web site using a different user account, you may wish to start by granting that account write permission in this folder, using Windows Explorer. (If you will only ever manage the Web site using FrontPage or Office XP, you can let the Permissions Wizard take care of this when you configure the FrontPage 2000 Server Extensions later on.)

→ To learn more about setting folder permissions, **see** "Managing File Permissions," **p. 954**.

Now, you can use the Computer Management utility found in the Control Panel to administer the WWW Service.

To do this, log on as a Computer Administrator user. Right-click My Computer and select Manage. Expand Services and Applications, and select Internet Information Service in the left pane, as shown in Figure 15.3. (You can also open this MMC utility from the Administrative Tools menu.)

Figure 15.3
Use the MMC interface to manage IIS services.

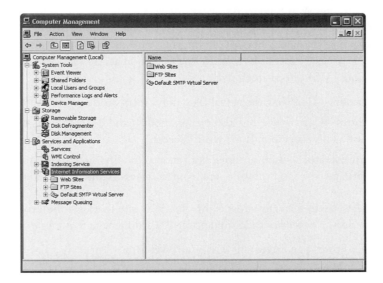

Using this interface you can manage any of the installed IIS services: Default Web Site, FTP Site, and the default SMTP server.

To start with, if you click on Internet Information Services, and then click on the Action menu at the top of the window, you can select All Tasks from the menu that appears. Here you can back up or restore the configuration for this Web site. You can also restart the IIS service using this menu.

Open the Internet Information Services item, and then the entry for your computer, and under this you'll see entries for the specific services you installed: Web Site; FTP Site, if you installed the FTP service; and Default SMTP Virtual Server, if you installed the SMTP service. Figure 15.3 shows the manager window with all three services installed.

From this point, you can manage properties for each service, as we'll explain later in this chapter.

In this Explorer-like view of the IIS components, you can take complete control of IIS's behavior, down to its treatment of individual files.

Configuring the FrontPage 2000 Server Extensions

If you plan on using the FrontPage 2000 Server Extensions to manage Web site publishing, to permit Web Folder access, to process forms or perform searches, or if you plan to send email from forms or scripts, you'll need to attach the Server Extensions to your Web site.

Before you do, you should consider how to manage security on the site. Among other things, the FrontPage Extensions make it possible for remote users to gain access to the folders using the Web Folders feature of Internet Explorer. This lets people directly peruse the file and folders that make up your Web site. This may be just what you want—you can use this feature to share files over the Internet. However, you do want to exercise strict control over this. The Extensions refer to three levels of access *above and beyond* the usual "anonymous" Web site visitor's rights:

- **Browsers**—Can view the actual files and folders inside your Web site content folders.
- **Authors**—Can browse but also create, modify, and delete files in the Web site content folders. This corresponds to "write" access.
- **Administrators**—Like authors, but can also modify the Extensions settings, create new FrontPage webs and subwebs, and control access rights for other users.

The easiest way to manage access rights in a Web site that uses the FrontPage Extensions is to let the Server Extensions Configuration Wizard manage them for you.

To use the FrontPage extensions with your Web site:

1. In the left pane, under Web Sites, highlight Default Web Site and select Action, All Tasks. If Check Server Extensions appears, the extensions are already installed. If Configure Server Extensions appears, select this item to start the Server Extensions Configuration Wizard. Click Next.

2. The wizard will ask if it can create Windows security groups to define which users get management, read, and write access to your site's Web folders. If you want to manage access permissions to your Web site folder manually, you can uncheck this and click Next. Otherwise, just click Next to let the wizard create three security groups: XXX Browsers, XXX Authors, and XXX Admins, where *XXX* is the name of your computer. You'll add users to these groups later.

3. Enter the name of the security group or user that should be the Web Administrator; the default value Administrators is best. This will let any Computer Administrator manage FrontPage. Click Next.

4. If you plan to send email from your Web pages or forms, select Yes to configure mail settings. There are three fields to enter:
   - **Author Email**—This will be the "From" email address that appears in any email sent automatically by the Web site.

- **Contact Email**—This email address will appear in Web pages that FrontPage generates in the event of an error; it should be the address of the person responsible for managing and fixing your Web server. You might want to have your ISP or email administrator set up a special account for this purpose, perhaps named "webmaster". If your Web site will be visible on the Internet, I recommend that you enter the address in the form "name at domain" rather than as "name@domain," to help thwart address harvesters who sell names to spammers.

- **SMTP server**—This is the fully qualified domain name of the outbound SMTP server you use on your network, the server that will be used to deliver outgoing mail. This might be something like "smtp.myhost.com". If you have also installed the SMTP Service and want the SMTP service to forward the messages, you can enter "localhost". I don't recommend doing this if you can help it, however; it just gives you one more thing to manage, configure, and worry about. Instead, have IIS route outgoing messages through your ISP's or company's mail server.

5. Click Next, and then Finish.

When the wizard is finished, if you chose to let it manage security settings, it will have created three security groups and will have granted these groups the appropriate rights to the folders that will contain your Web site content. You'll next want to add users to these groups:

1. Right-click My Computer, select Manage, and in the left pane select Local Users and Groups.

2. Select Groups, and under Groups, double-click the XXX Authors group. Click Add, and enter the name or names of users who should be able to add, modify, and delete files on your Web site, as shown in Figure 15.4. These would be users who are Web site content authors, or users with whom you want to use the site as a Web Folder to share files over the Internet. In other words, these are users who should be allowed to add, edit, and delete files in the Web site's folders.

Figure 15.4
Use the Select Users dialog to add users to the Authors security group.

15

Separate multiple names with semicolons. (You can click Advanced and Find Now to get a list of names, if you want to just click to select them.) Click OK to save the group.

3. The names should now appear in the group list.

You can leave the XXX Admins group alone; by default, it already contains Administrators, giving all Computer Administrators management rights. And, you can leave the Browsers group alone unless you want to name specific users who should have the ability to directly peruse the lists of files in your Web site folder. (You don't have to add anything to grant permission for anonymous users to view your Web site in the normal way.)

NOTE

> As useful as they are, the FrontPage Extensions are pretty squirrelly. If you are publishing from FrontPage to the Web server on your own computer, you must enter `http://computername` as the name of the computer to publish to, where `computername` is your computer's network name. `Localhost` will not work.
>
> In my experience, even when using the correct name, about half of the time after first setting up a new system, when I attempt to publish FrontPage will say that the server has reported that the extensions are not installed.
>
> The solution is to remove them from the Web site and reinstall them. Open the Internet Information Services management tool, right-click Default Web Site, and under All Tasks, select Remove Server Extensions. Leave Preserve Web Meta-information checked and click OK. Now, right-click Default Web Site again, and under All Tasks, select Configure Server Extensions. Repeat the wizard process. This often remedies the problem.

CONFIGURING THE WEB SERVER

You can manage your Web server using the Internet Information Services management tool. As I said earlier, IIS is a complicated program and there are *many* settings. Entire books are written about managing IIS. To get a feel of what is possible, you can look at the Web server's default configuration settings. To view them, right-click the Default Web Site entry in the left pane and select Properties. You then are presented with a complex dialog with eight tabs (see Figure 15.5).

In my experience, you'll only need to consider a few items, and it's quite likely that you won't need to make any changes at all. I'll go through some of the more important settings in Table 15.1.

TABLE 15.1   IIS WEB SITE CONFIGURATION SETTINGS

Tab	Setting	Value
Web Site	Enable Logging	Lets you keep a record of all Web site visits. You'll find out more about this later in the chapter.
	TCP Port	You can change the TCP Port of your Web site from the usual 80 to another value; this is usually only done if you host several different Web servers. 8080 is a common alternate port number.

15

TABLE 15.1   CONTINUED

Tab	Setting	Value
Home Directory	Home Directory	Sets the home or "starting point" directory for the folders displayed on your Web site. By default, it's `c:\inetpub\wwwroot`. *The home directory should be on a disk partition formatted with NTFS.* You'll only need to change this if the default folder is on a partition using FAT and you can't update the drive. (If you do, be sure to update the Indexing service as well).
Documents	Default Document	Lets you select the names IIS tries when looking for a "default document" to return for a URL that names a folder but not a specific document.
HTTP Headers	File Types	Lets you specify MIME Types for file types not already registered with Windows.
Server Extensions	Settings	Under Performance, you should select the number of distinct pages your site will have, usually "fewer than 100."

You can also use this tab to modify the site's email address and mail server information.

Figure 15.5
On the Default Web Site Properties dialog, you can control the behavior of the Web server.

You can also manage the settings for specific folders listed under the Default Web Site entry, by right-clicking them and choosing Properties. On the Documents tab, you can specify that a given document or folder is to be obtained from a different URL on a different Web server, using a process called *redirection*. Complex CGI programs called *ASP applications* are configured here as well.

15

MANAGING THE FTP SERVER

If you have installed the FTP service, open the Internet Information Services management tool as described in the previous section, right-click Default FTP Site, and select Properties.

To establish a secure server, make the following settings:

- On the FTP Site tab, be sure to check Enable Logging (see the "Log Files" section).
- On the Home Directory tab, you can specify the folder in which FTP looks for files. If you want to let users use FTP to post files to the Web site, you can specify the same home folder for FTP as you use for the Web service, usually c:\inetpub\wwwroot.
- The FTP Home Directory should be on a hard drive formatted with the NTFS file system, so that Windows can enforce user-level file security. *Do not* point the FTP service at a drive formatted with FAT.

> **TIP**
>
> When a user connects to your computer with FTP, if the FTP server finds a folder with the same name as the user's account name under the FTP root folder, it will make this the default folder for the user. This is handy if you want to let several users store files on your FTP server; you can create a subfolder for each one using their account name, and FTP will automatically start them in the private folder. You may want to use NTFS permission settings to make each such folder readable and writeable only by its owner.

- On the Directory Security tab, you'll have to decide whether or not to permit access based on user account names and passwords. As I mentioned earlier, FTP sends passwords over the Internet as clear-text without encryption, so, it's best to permit only anonymous access, where passwords are not required, and allow only *read-only* access to files (you don't want to let people write files to your FTP server without a password). On the other hand, if you must let people post files to your computer with FTP, you must use password control to prevent your computer from being abused by others:
  - If you will use FTP only to let people pick up files, check Allow Anonymous Connections and check Allow Only Anonymous Connections. Be sure that Write permission is *not* checked on the Home Directory tab.
  - If you want to let people send you files with FTP, you should uncheck Allow Anonymous Connections and uncheck Allow Only Anonymous Connections. Select only specific directories to give Write permission. I would recommend adding a new drive or creating a new disk partition with the NTFS file system to contain the FTP root folder and nothing else.
- On the Messages tab under Welcome, you can enter a few lines of text that will be presented to the FTP user when they establish a session with your FTP server. For example, you might want to issue a warning like this:

```
All access to this server is logged. Access to this server is
allowed by permission only and unauthorized use will be prosecuted.
```

MANAGING THE SMTP SERVER

If you've installed the SMTP mail deliver service component, you'll need to take a moment to configure it so it can deliver mail generated by your Web site.

Open the Internet Information Services MMC Console. Open the Default SMTP Virtual Server entry. Right-click Default SMTP Virtual Server and select Properties, to display the configuration dialog shown in Figure 15.6.

Figure 15.6
Managing the SMTP Server.

There are four settings that you should consider:

- **Relaying**—Relaying is the process of receiving mail from another computer, and then sending it on to recipients in the outside world. You absolutely do *not* want to provide this service to the Internet at large: mail servers that do are quickly exploited by people who send "spam," or junk email messages. By default, your mail server will not accept outgoing mail from any other computer. To let it deliver mail for other computers on your network (*only*), select the Access tab, click Relay, and then Add. Select Group of Computers and enter your computer's IP address and subnet mask. Click OK to close the Add box. This will make the server relay mail for computers on your network but no others.

- **Message Size**—On the Messages tab, you can configure the maximum message size and maximum number of messages that someone can send at once. You can deselect all of the "Limit" check boxes if you trust the users on your network not to send spam.

- **Delivery**—By default, the SMTP server will attempt to deliver all mail to all recipients by itself. If you want to give this job to your ISP's mail server, you can tell SMTP to send all mail to a "smart host" for delivery. To do this, on the Delivery tab, click Advanced. Under Smart Host enter the name of your ISP's SMTP server name. If you have to authenticate with the server to send mail, click on the Outbound Security button to enter the required name and password.

■ **Receiving Domains**—If you want this SMTP server to receive mail, you'll have to tell it what domains are "local." Mail addressed to any other domains is considered "outside" mail and will be sent out to the Internet. As I mentioned, Windows XP Professional doesn't come with any means of handling mail that the SMTP service receives. If you devise one, you'll need to configure the local domain list. On the Internet Information Services manager window, select Domains in the left pane. Right-click the default name that appears in the right pane and select Rename. Change the name to your desired domain name, for example "mycompany.com". This way any mail received for "somebody@mycompany.com" will be stored rather than sent back out again. You can add additional domains by right-clicking Domains and selecting New, Domain.

CREATING YOUR WEB SITE CONTENT

Once you've installed the IIS services you want to use, you can set up a Web site. Before starting that process, let's review a few basics that you should know about before using any Web server.

Your IIS server should be reachable by either clients on your local network (a LAN or intranet), or from the Internet, or possibly both. In either case you will need to use a fixed IP address assigned by your own network administrator, so that other users can find your Web server by typing its name into their browser.

NOTE

Many company networks today use an internal network address scheme based on Network Address Translation (NAT). This technology is also used by Windows Internet Connection Sharing, and by the small broadband connection sharing routers that we discussed in Chapter 8, "Configuring Your Internet Connection." NAT allows a router to connect your network to the Internet, using just one public IP address. Within your internal LAN, you can use a group of "private" IP addresses such as those starting with the number 192.168. Users on your private LAN can access your Web server, but the Internet public at large—those outside your private network—won't be able to see your Web server unless you take special action. We'll discuss this shortly.

If you wish to offer a Web site on the Internet, then your Internet service provider (ISP) will need to assign you a unique IP address that can be used on the Internet. This unique IP address will be stored in a Domain Name System (DNS) server so that browsers can translate between your domain name (for example, www.mysite.com) and the IP address assigned to your domain. If your ISP can't provide DNS service for you, there are free domain name services available, for example, at www.granitecanyon.com.

Once you've installed IIS, the next thing to do is to create the content you want to offer from the Web site. You do this by placing files in folders that the IIS WWW Service can access.

15

A FOLDER BY ANY OTHER NAME IS...A VIRTUAL FOLDER

When someone visits your Web site, they type or click on a URL that names the content your Web server needs to deliver. This content is usually stored in a file on your hard drive. But, it may not seem obvious, at first, just what file `http://www.mysite.com/index.html` refers to. The first part of the name `http://www.mysite.com` just names your computer. The rest, `/index.html`, indicates the file that IIS is to return.

When you set up your Web site, you'll specify which directory contains the documents that you want to publish. The Web site has a *home directory*, which is the starting point for the translation of URL names into filenames. For example, if the home directory is `c:\inet-pub\wwwroot`, then the URL filename

`/index.html`

returns file

`c:\inetpub\wwwroot\index.html`

Any file or folder inside this home directory is available to Web browsers. For example, the URL

`http://www.mysite.com/sales/catalog.html`

would return the file

`c:\inetpub\wwwroot\sales\catalog.html`

You can also add other folders on your computer to the Web site mapping, even if they aren't in the home directory or its subfolders. They are called *virtual directories* because to Web visitors, they appear to be part of the home directory structure, but they aren't physically part of that structure. You could instruct IIS to share folder `c:\partlist` with the virtual URL name of `/parts`, so that the URL

`http://www.mysite.com/parts/index.html`

would return file

`c:\partlist\bullet.gif`

When IIS is installed, adding a virtual folder to your Web site is very simple. This process is integrated right into Explorer and is just a right-click away.

Web servers can also use a process called *redirection*, where the server is told to make a virtual directory whose content is stored on another Web server. When one user requests a file in a redirected virtual directory, the Web server tells the browser program to retrieve the file from the other server. Redirection is useful when you rearrange your site—it lets visitors using an old URL obtain the files they want even though they're stored in a new location. Redirection can also be useful when your site uses more than one computer, and data from multiple computers is offered through the single Web site interface.

15

DEFAULT DOCUMENTS—WHEN "NOTHING" JUST ISN'T ENOUGH

A *home page* is a URL that lists a server name but no filename, such as `http://www.brainsville.com`. It corresponds to just the name of the server's home directory:

`c:\inetpub\wwwroot`

But this doesn't tell the server what *content* to return to the browser. The Web server has to look for a *default document*. This is a file the WWW server should send out whenever a URL names a folder but not a full filename. IIS looks for a default file with any of the following names, in this order:

- `iistart.asp`—In the home directory only, IIS searches for an ASP script file with this name. ASP stands for Active Server Pages, which is discussed later in this chapter.
- `default.asp`—This is another common script file name used to return a default page.
- `default.html`—This is the most common name to give to a default page file that contains just HTML markup.
- `default.htm`—This is another variation on the standard home page name.

You can change this list and change the order in which IIS looks for the files on the Web site's Properties page on the Documents tab.

If no default document can be found, by default IIS returns an error message. You can instruct IIS to instead display a list of all files and subfolders in the URL's folder, by checking Directory Browsing on the Home Directory tab, or on the properties page for specific subfolders under the home directory. This can be useful when you want visitors to be able to select any of a bunch of files without you having to creating a Web page to link to each of the files.

> **TIP**
>
> If you're not writing scripts, but are creating a simple, basic Web site, here's what you want to do: Create your home page file with the name `default.htm` in folder `c:\inetpub\wwwroot`. You can put other pages in the same folder.
>
> If you want to create subfolders, put a `default.htm` file in each of them as well.

MULTIPURPOSE INTERNET MAIL EXTENSIONS (MIME)

Web browsers must be told how to interpret the content returned by the server. They don't know in advance whether they're going to get HTML text, a Microsoft Word document, an image, or something else. Windows determines a file's type from the filename's extension—the part of the filename following the last period. For example, `.doc` or `.html`. That technique isn't used by some other operating systems, so a standardized naming scheme was developed for the Web. This is called a file's *MIME type*. Web browsers get file type information from the Content-type field returned by the server as part of the response data.

MIME type names are agreed-upon Internet standards, and it's the Web server's job to know how to label each of the files it shares. When sending out files, IIS uses the Windows File Types Registry to map file types like .doc and .html into MIME types, and you can add to the list any special types of files you share.

In addition, you can configure IIS to recognize additional file extensions and supply the correct MIME type name to Web browsers. I'll discuss this later in the chapter.

EXECUTING PROGRAMS ON THE IIS SERVER OR THE BROWSER CLIENT COMPUTER

When a URL references a program file, a Web server can transmit the program file itself to the browser's computer, which you can then elect to save or run. Or, the Web server can run the program on *its* side and return the program's output to your browser. This capability enables the Web server to provide interactive, up-to-the-minute information. These are often called Common Gateway Interface or CGI programs, or scripts.

Programs run on the server's side can do virtually anything: search libraries, access your bank account, buy airline tickets, among other things, and then return the results to you as a Web page. This flexibility has helped make the Internet more useful over time. Programs such as "shopping basket" applications and credit card verification programs can be implemented using dynamically created Web page content.

For IIS, the distinction between "send the program file itself" and "run the program and return the output" is made by changing a Web folder's *read*, *script*, and *execute* attributes. Folders with the read attribute treat scripts and executable programs as data files to be returned directly. When the script or execute attribute is set, scripts and programs, respectively, are run on the server (your computer), and the output is sent back to the browser requesting information from the Web server.

IIS FOLDER ATTRIBUTES

You can set the read, script, and other attributes in the IIS Management application by selecting Default Web Site (or subdirectory names displayed under it) and right-clicking Properties. On the Home Directory (or Directory) tab, you can check any of the following properties:

- **Script Source Access**—Lets remote users read and write script files themselves, rather than running them and returning their output. It's best never to check this box; instead, copy script files into your Web site manually.
- **Read**—Lets visitors retrieve files from the folder.
- **Write**—Lets visitors post (write) files to the folder. *DO NOT* check this box.
- **Directory Browsing**—Lets IIS return a directory listing if a URL maps to a folder with no default document.
- **Log Visits**—Instructs IIS to write a line to a log file for each access to the Web server.
- **Index This Resource**—Instructs the Index Server to add the contents of this folder to the directories listed under "Web," as discussed earlier in the chapter.

15

Under Execute Permissions, the default setting, Scripts Only, means that IIS will only execute script programs. If you want to run standard CGI programs with the .EXE extension, you must change this setting to Scripts and Executables. You can also set this to None to prevent scripts from being run at all.

TAKING A QUICK TOUR OF IIS

After you've installed and configured IIS, you can take a quick tour of the major components that have been put into place. To do so, first start Internet Explorer, and enter the URL http://localhost. Localhost is shorthand for "the IP address of my computer" and will display IIS's default home page, shown in Figure 15.7. Internet Explorer will also fire up the online documentation for IIS in a separate browser window, shown in Figure 15.8.

Figure 15.7
IIS serves you a welcome page when first installed.

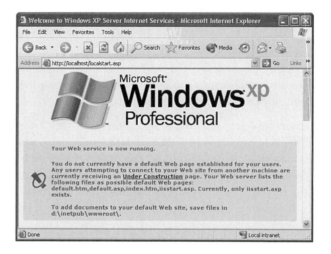

Figure 15.8
You can also view the documentation for IIS using a browser.

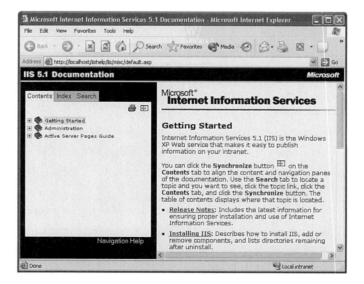

Congratulations! You now have your own Web server. Let's take a look at the built-in pages. If you find them useful you might want to add them to your Favorites folder.

ONLINE DOCUMENTATION

Type `http://localhost/iishelp` in the Address bar to display the IIS Online documentation, which has a built-in search and indexing feature. Check this documentation for the latest IIS news, release notes, and detailed instructions. (This documentation is a good place to spend a couple of hours.) Keeping up-to-date with this online documentation is important, especially if your site requires a high degree of security.

PRINTER MANAGER

If you chose the "Printers virtual directory" when you installed IIS, you now have a Web-based printer management console. When you type `http://localhost/Printers` in the Address bar, note that your installed printer(s) and any pending print jobs are listed on the page. Other Windows XP or Windows 2000 users on your network or on the Internet can view and use your printers.

NOTE

> The printing functionality built in to IIS uses the Internet Printing Protocol (IPP). This set of protocols was developed to enable using and managing printers via a browser, and to allow for connections to computers that may be geographically distant from your computer. For example, instead of using a fax machine to send messages to a remote branch office, you could set up printers so that you could simply connect using IPP and send the document directly to a printer at a branch office.

If you are viewing this page from a computer running Windows XP, 2000, or from a Windows 9x or NT 4 computer with the Internet Printing Protocol add-on (it's available from www.windowsupdate.com), you can select Connect and install this printer as a remote printer. You'll learn about Web printing in Chapter 19.

REMOTE DESKTOP

If you selected the optional Remote Desktop Web Connection component when you installed IIS, a subfolder named `tsweb` was created in `\inetpub\wwwroot`. This folder contains a sample Web page and the necessary files to let you use a Web-based version of the Remote Desktop client. The URL `http://localhost/tsweb` displays the page shown in Figure 15.9.

You can view this page from any computer and Web browser that supports and permits ActiveX controls; for the most part, this means just Windows computers running Internet Explorer. You can enter the hostname of any computer that accepts Remote Desktop connections (hint: yours), and click Connect to establish a Remote Desktop link.

Figure 15.9
The Remote Desktop
Web Connection page
lets you use Remote
Desktop from any
Windows computer.

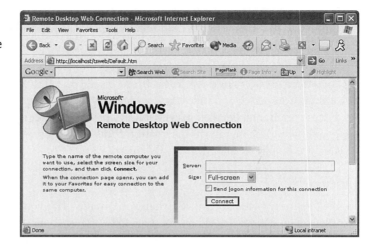

If you enable Remote Desktop access to your computer, install this page, and make your
Web server available from the Internet, you will able to securely log on to and use your own
computer from anywhere in the world—it's a pretty spiffy feature, and in my opinion, makes
Windows XP Professional worth the price just for this.

SETTING UP A SIMPLE WEB SITE

Right out of the box, IIS is ready to serve up static Web pages and images. If you have files
from an existing Web site, or if you can create and edit HTML files yourself, you can simply copy them into the home directory c:\inetpub\wwwroot and any subfolders you want to
create. The default page name is initially default.htm, so give this name to your home page
file.

With no further administration or fuss, other users on your network and/or on the Internet
can view your Web site, using your computer's Internet domain name or, on a Windows
LAN, by viewing http://machinename, where machinename is the Windows name of your
computer. (You can find that name by right-clicking My Computer, selecting Properties, and
viewing the Computer Name tab.)

If you are not already familiar with HTML, you can download many free guides from the
Internet—just do a quick search for "HTML Reference" or the like. If you are already
familiar with HTML coding, but need to see an example, you can just look at the source for
a Web page that's already on the Internet. Using Internet Explorer, just select the View
menu and then Source. The source text for the page will be displayed in the Notepad window that pops up. I've…um…borrowed many HTML ideas this way.

If you've installed the FrontPage 2000 Server Extensions, you can also post files to your
Web site using FrontPage or Office XP. Tell FrontPage to publish the files to whatever

15

URL you use to view your Web server, for example `http://machinename` if you're at your own computer or on your office LAN, or `http://full.domain.name` if you're offsite and sending files to your computer over the Internet.

SHARING FOLDERS WITH WEB SHARING

If you want to add to your Web site a folder that is not inside `c:\inetpub\wwwroot`, you can add it as a virtual folder through the Internet Information Services management tool, or through a shortcut feature called Web Sharing.

You can set up Web Sharing using Windows Explorer. It provides a quick and easy way to make a folder available to others through your computer's Web server. To do this, right-click a folder in the Explorer display, and select Properties. After IIS has been installed, you'll find that there is a new tab called Web Sharing. Select the Web Sharing tab, and select Share This Folder. The virtual directory or Edit Directory dialog appears, as shown in Figure 15.10.

Figure 15.10
Here, you can set alias properties for a new virtual directory. The Alias name is the URL name this folder will have.

Enter the URL name you want to use for this folder, and change the Access and Application Permissions check boxes if necessary. For a folder that will hold Web pages and images, check Read. If this folder will also contain scripts and/or CGI programs that you want to have run by the server, check Scripts or Execute (Including Scripts). If you want to let remote users see the contents of the directory in the absence of a default document, check Directory Browsing.

15

Remember that Windows file permissions will be in force in addition to the permissions you set for Web sharing. If you use Simple File Sharing, you should only use Web sharing on folders that are in your Shared Documents file, so that outside visitors can read the files. If you are on a Windows domain network or are not using Simple File Sharing, you'll need to be sure that you give read permission to the shared folder to Everyone or at least to user IUSR_*xxxx*, where *xxxx* is the name of your computer—this is the account that IIS uses when fetching files for anonymous visitors.

Log Files

By default, if you enable logging when you set up your WWW and/or FTP servers, IIS creates log files in the Windows directory, `\Windows\System32\LogFiles`. The Web service log files are in subdirectory `W3SVC1` and are named `exyymmdd.log`, where *yymmdd* are digits indicating the current date. A new log file is created on any day on which Web server activity occurs.

The FTP service follows a similar format, storing its log files in `\Winnt\System32\LogFiles\MSFTPSVC1`.

You can change the interval at which IIS starts new log files from daily to hourly, weekly, or monthly, or you can base this change on the size to which a log file is allowed to grow. To do so, you use the Default Web or FTP Site Properties dialogs. Locate the Enable Logging check box, and click the Properties button next to it.

The log files are plain ASCII text files that contain a line for each file or page retrieved from the Web server. Each line contains the time, the browser's IP address, the HTTP method used (usually `GET`), and the URL requested.

Simply scanning the log file data can let you see how your Web site is being used. If you are interested in further analyzing the use of your Web site, several free or shareware analysis tools are available.

Enabling Site Searching Using the Indexing Service

If you want to let remote browsers search your Web site for documents of interest, you can install and configure the Indexing Service. This service periodically scours selected

Web-shared folders and documents and maintains a list of all the words it finds in them. It actually maintains two separate indexes: one of your whole hard disk, for your use alone, and another of the Web folders for Internet searching. It's sophisticated enough not to show results for documents Web visitors don't have permission to download.

INSTALLING THE INDEXING SERVICE

While the Indexing Service is not a component of the IIS package, it is a helpful ancillary service that can scan and index all of your Web site's content, and provides the database back-end for a site search capability. If you want to offer this kind of feature on your Web site, then install and configure the Indexing Service on your Windows XP computer.

> **NOTE**
>
> The Indexing Service only builds a database of Web site content; you'll need additional software to actually search through the Index database and return the results as a Web page. The FrontPage Extensions have such a function built-in, and if you install the Extensions you can take advantage of the Indexing Service's enhanced searching power.

By default, the Indexing Service is installed on Windows XP, but is not activated. To turn it on

1. Log on as a Computer Administrator user, right-click My Computer, and select Manage. Click on Services and Applications in the left pane, and then Services (not Indexing Service).

2. Find Indexing Service in the list, as shown in Figure 15.11. (If it's not present, go to the Control Panel, choose Add or Remove Programs, select Add/Remove Windows Components, and check Indexing Service. Click OK, and insert your Windows CD if asked.)

3. In the Startup Type column, if the setting is not Automatic, right-click the Indexing Service line and select Properties. Under Startup Type, select Automatic. Click Start, and then OK.

Figure 15.11
Use the Services Management tool to enable the Indexing Service.

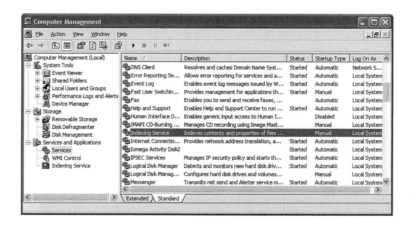

15

The Computer Management program is also used to configure the Indexing Service. In the left pane, under Services and Applications, select Indexing Service.

As installed, there are two main groups listed under Indexing Service: System and Web, as shown in Figure 15.12. You can specify properties for each of these on an individual basis. The System folder specifies the drives and folders that are indexed for use by the Windows Search utility. The Web folder specifies the drives and folders that will be indexed for use by Web site searches. Usually, the Web folder should list the folder used by IIS to hold your Web site contents, which by default is `c:\inetpub\wwwroot`, and a couple of folders of help files under the Windows folder.

Figure 15.12
The Indexing Service lists indexed Web site folders in the Web folder.

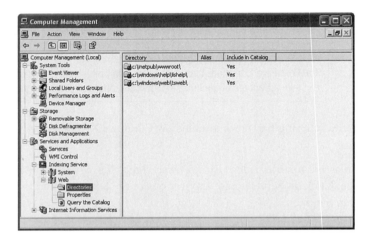

It's not necessary to manually enter folder names here, however. It's best to manage which folders will be indexed from the IIS Administration tool. On each folder's property page, on the Home Directory or Directory tab, you can check Index This Resource to instruct the Indexing Service to visit the folder.

NOTE

> The System and Web folders are only visible to Computer Administrator users. Other users can view the Indexing Service management screen, but it will be blank.

To configure the Indexing service to properly index your Web site content

1. Right-click the Web item, and select Properties.
2. Select the Generation tab to bring it to the front, and make the following choices:
   - Check Index Files with Unknown Extensions to include more than the expected .html and .txt files in the index. If you check this option, the Indexing Service will attempt to make sense of every file it finds in your Web folders.

- Check Generate Abstracts. This option increases the size of the index in a large Web site but lets the search results return not only a filename but a paragraph or so of text from the beginning of each matching file. You can set the maximum size of this abstract if you want or leave the default setting of 320 characters.

3. Click OK. From this point on, whenever you change your Web site contents, the Indexing Service will automatically update the index.

By default, the Indexing Service includes the IIS documentation in its index. You might find this information useful, but visitors to your Web site probably won't. You can open the Directories pane and remove the IIS documentation by selecting these IIS help folders, double-clicking them in the right pane, and checking No for Include in Index? You can also use this technique to exclude any folders in your Web site that you'd prefer to keep under wraps.

When you specify a folder, all its subfolders are included as well. You can prevent them from being included by specifying a subfolder and marking No under Include in Index.

You can use FrontPage to create search forms that take advantage of the Indexing service by adding a Web Search component from the Insert, Web Component menu.

NOTE

> The search function will only report files that were published through FrontPage. Files that are manually placed in your Web server home folder or one of its subfolders will not appear.
>
> Also, just to warn you, don't expect "Google" quality search results from the Indexing service. It works *most* of the time, but has problems. I've seen it omit documents and words for no apparent reason. To be honest, for this reason, I don't even bother to use the search function on www.microsoft.com. Google does a much better job of indexing Microsoft's site than Microsoft does.

CONFIGURING SHARED CONNECTIONS

If your computer uses a shared Internet connection—that is, one provided by Internet Connection Sharing or a connection-sharing router device—and if you want your Web site to be available to the Internet, you'll have to set up the sharing service to direct incoming Web server requests to your computers. Otherwise, the router or the computer with the Internet connection won't know to which computer to forward incoming requests.

To make your Web server accessible, you'll need to forward requests on TCP port 80 from the connection sharing machine to your computer. With Microsoft's Internet Connection Sharing service on a computer running Windows XP Professional, you can simply specify your computer's name as the target of the forwarded requests. To do this

1. On the computer that is providing Internet Connection Sharing, log on as a Computer Administrator.

2. Open the Network Connections window, right-click the icon for the connection that is being shared, and select Properties.

3. View the Advanced tab, and click the Settings button.

4. On the Services tab, check Web Server (HTTP). In the Service Settings dialog that appears, enter the name or fixed IP address of your computer, the computer that has IIS installed.

5. Click OK to close all of the dialogs.

If you have more than one Web server installed, you will need to use alternate ports for incoming users: Port 80 can only be forwarded to one computer. In step 4, you can click Add and enter a custom port number. 8080 is a common port to use for alternate Web servers. Enter 8080 as the "external" port, and 80 as the "internal" port. Outside users can then access your Web server by entering, for example, `http://www.yourcompany.com:8080`.

One interesting thing to note is that Internet Connection Sharing can find your computer by its name, even if its IP address changes due to dynamic address assignment.

If you use a hardware-based connection sharing router, you'll have to follow the manufacturer's instructions for forwarding incoming requests from the router to your computer. In this case, you can't use automatic IP address assignment (DHCP) for your Web server computer, because its IP address can change periodically, and forwarded requests would end up going to the wrong computer.

Instead, you will have to specify your computer's IP address explicitly, using an IP address outside the block of addresses that the router uses for automatic assignment. You'll also need to enter the network mask and DNS server addresses when you set up your computer's Local Area Connection. You can read more about configuring IP address information in Chapter 17, "Building Your Own Network."

NOTE

If you try to retrieve a non-HTML file from your Web server, such as a PowerPoint file, Word document, or music file, and see a bunch of apparently random letters and symbols, check the file-type to MIME-type mappings on the server computer.

First, note the file's extension, for example, ".mp3". On the server computer, click Start, Run, and type `regedit`. In the left pane, under HKEY_CLASSES_ROOT, find the extension. In the right pane, see if a "Content Type" entry appears, saying for example, "audio/mpeg".

If not, open the IIS Administration tool. Right-click Default Web Site, and view the HTTP Headers tab. Click the File Types button. Click New Type, enter the extension (such as `mp3`) and the correct MIME type for the file (such as `audio/mpeg`).

SCRIPTING FOR INTERACTIVE SITES

15

Earlier in this chapter you learned that creating dynamic Web pages is a valuable feature. This allows a Web server (such as IIS) to create Web pages based on information contained in databases or other files the server has access to. For example, you might want to check your account balance at your bank using an online application. After you supply the information necessary to authenticate you to the Web server, and then give it your account number, the server can look up the balance and construct a web page to return this information to you.

The original server-side programs, called CGI programs, were complex and difficult to write and debug, until bright people developed scripting languages for Web servers. Scripting systems put most of the complex stuff into one program that was provided with the Web server. Then, users could write short, easy-to-manage programs, or scripts, that leverage the power in the main program to do all sorts of interesting and interactive things.

The most common scripting languages are Perl and Python, which are very popular in the Unix and Linux world. Perl and Python can be added to IIS so that you can take advantage of the huge pool of already-written script programs that are available for free on the Internet. If you know Python or Perl, or want to learn, you can download free Windows versions at www.activestate.com. These folks have a Windows version of TCL as well, another popular scripting program, and have a huge library of documentation and free scripts.

NOTE

A version of ActiveState's Perl is included in Microsoft's Services for Unix product. This is an inexpensive package of applications that provide Unix-like functionality on a Windows platform. For more information, visit http://www.microsoft.com and do a simple search for Services for Unix.

Active Server Pages (ASP) is a scripting application that was developed by Microsoft. You can choose from several programming languages to use with ASP. Out of the box, you can choose between a JavaScript and a dialect of Visual Basic called VBScript. If you install the appropriate language interpreters, you can use Perl, Python, and other languages with ASP as well.

The advantage of ASP is that it allows you to mix HTML and your chosen script language in the same file. You don't have to use an external compiled program. You can use HTML to manage the formatting and static part of the page, and scripting to generate the dynamic part, and it's all there in one place.

ASP scripts can take full advantage of Microsoft COM and ActiveX programming objects. These objects provide a way for scripts to perform very complex functions such as manipulating databases and sending email. You can find a lot of useful pre-written ASP scripts on the Internet. For example, check out www.asp-help.com. Also, take a look at Microsoft's Developer's Web site at msdn.microsoft.com.

NOTE

> You can also use Microsoft's newest Web application development system called ASP.NET. ASP.NET comes with built-in support for scripting in VB .NET, Jscript .NET, and C#. For more information about ASP.NET and free downloads of the runtime and development software, visit www.asp.net.

As an example of what ASP scripting can do, use Notepad to create a file named `time.asp` in `c:\inetpub\wwwroot`, with this inside:

```
<HTML>
<HEAD>
<TITLE>What time is it?</TITLE>
</head>
<BODY>
You viewed this web page at
<% response.write time() %>,
<% response.write date() %>.
</BODY>
</HTML>
```

Then, view `http://localhost/time.asp` in Internet Explorer. The result should be something like this:

```
You viewed this web page at 11:08:25 AM, 12/10/2002.
```

Here's what's happening: IIS copies most of the file literally. But characters falling between `<%` and `%>` are treated as *script* code, which are commands written in Visual Basic or JavaScript. In this case, VBScript commands are used to insert the time and date into the HTML file at the server end, before it's sent to your browser. To see what I mean, right-click the displayed page in Internet Explorer and select View Source. You'll see what the ASP script generated and sent to you—there is no sign of the embedded script commands.

Consider the example of adding a feedback form to a Web site. Marketing researchers say that a fill-in form is over *five times* more likely to be used than an email link. Adding a form will give you five times as many responses to your Web page.

Sending email with form data used to require an EXE program, which you probably had to pay extra for, and it was hard to configure. Not so with ASP. You can just use the mail-sending objects already built in to Windows. As an example, here is a fairly simple Web page that lets viewers fill in information, and the text will be sent to you via email.

The file `feedback.asp` is shown here. First, edit this file to add your own email address and the name of your company's mail server. Then place the file into the directory `\inetpub\scripts`.

```
<HTML>
<HEAD>
<TITLE>Feedback Form</TITLE>
</HEAD>
<BODY BGCOLOR=White>

<% @ LANGUAGE="VBSCRIPT" %>
<%
```

```
    M_SendTo     = "brian@mycompany.com"
    M_Host       = "mail.mycompany.com"
    M_Subject    = "Feedback from web page"

    If request.ServerVariables("REQUEST_METHOD") = "POST" Then
        process_form        ' POST means form is being submitted
    else
        display_form        ' otherwise: GET, means form is to be displayed
    End If

sub display_form            ' send HTML codes to display the form
    response.write "<H1>Feedback</H1>"
    response.write "<P>We'd like to hear from you! Please fill in this form."
    response.write "<FORM NAME=FEEDBACK METHOD=POST ACTION='/feedback.asp'>"
    response.write "<P>Your email address: <INPUT NAME=EMAIL TYPE=TEXT
        SIZE=60>"
    response.write "<P>Your name: <INPUT NAME=NAME TYPE=TEXT SIZE=40>"
    response.write "<P>Comments: <TEXTAREA NAME=REMARKS ROWS=6
        COLS=60></TEXTAREA>"
    response.write "<P><INPUT TYPE=SUBMIT VALUE='Send!'>"
    response.write "</FORM>"
end sub

sub process_form        ' take data from Request.Form object and mail it
    if request.Form("EMAIL") <> "" then
        M_MailFrom = request.Form("EMAIL")
    else
        M_MailFrom = M_SendTo
    end if

    set msg  = CreateObject("CDO.Message")
    set conf = CreateObject("CDO.Configuration")

    with msg                            ' build the message
        .to       = M_SendTo
        .from     = M_MailFrom
        .subject  = M_Subject
        .textBody = request.Form("NAME") + " said: " + request.Form("REMARKS")
    end with

    prefix = "http://schemas.microsoft.com/cdo/configuration/"
    with conf.fields                            ' set delivery options
        .item(prefix & "sendusing")      = 2 ' Send the message with SMTP
        .item(prefix & "smtpauthenticate") = 0 ' Do not authenticate.
        .item(prefix & "smtpserver")     = M_Host
        .update
    end with

    set msg.configuration = conf        ' deliver the message

    on error resume next
    msg.Send
    sentok = err.number = 0             ' True if it went OK
    on error goto 0

    set msg = Nothing                   ' release message object
```

15

```
      if sentok then
          response.write "<H1>Thank You!</H1>"
          response.write "<P>We appreciate your comments."
      else
          response.write "<H1>Unable to send remarks</H1>"
          response.write _
              "<P>We're sorry, there was a problem recording your comments."
          response.write "Please try again later."
      end if
      response.write "<P><A HREF='/'>Click here to return to our home page</A>"
end sub
%>
</BODY>
</HTML>
```

View `http://localhost/scripts/feedback.asp` with Internet Explorer and fill in the form. When you click `Send!`, your Web server should send the form's contents to the specified email address.

TIP

> On a public Internet site, don't construct an email form that lets you specify the email address to which the form will be sent, either on the displayed form or in hidden fields in the HTML. Odds are it will be discovered by spammers and used to send thousands of advertisements for risqué photographs of the latest pop music stars and Viagra.

I hope this helps show what ASP can do, and I hope it encourages you to use it. There are many, many books and Web sites devoted to scripting, if you want to learn more.

PART **IV**

NETWORKING

CHAPTER 16

INTRODUCTION TO XP NETWORKING

In this chapter

WINDOWS XP NETWORK MODELS

Windows XP was designed from the ground up to work well on a network. Whether you have two computers at home or 20,000 computers in your organization, adding a network can help you move information, share resources, and simplify management tasks. It's virtually guaranteed to be a worthwhile investment.

In this chapter, I'll explain Windows XP networking concepts and the options available to you. Then, in Chapter 17, "Building Your Own Network," we'll cover the installation and setup of a small network for a home or small office, and we'll show how to join a Windows XP computer to a network of any size. Chapter 17 also covers network maintenance functions such as the addition and removal of network services and protocols.

As I've hinted already, Windows XP networking services were designed with two different environments in mind: the home or small office, and the large organization (enterprise). There are good reasons for considering these environments separately, as outlined in Table 16.1.

TABLE 16.1 DIFFERENCES BETWEEN HOME/SMALL OFFICE AND ENTERPRISE NETWORKS	
Home/Small Office	**Enterprise**
Small number of computers	Large number of computers
Computers in close proximity	Computers may be spread out geographically
All users are trusted	Security is a major concern, even within the organization
All users are peers	Hierarchies of responsibility and trust
Self-management	Management and maintenance performed by—and restricted to—specialists
Ease of use and cost are primary concerns	Reliability and security are primary concerns

These two environments have very different sets of goals and constraints, and so it's no surprise that Windows offers two distinct ways of building a network. You actually have to tell Windows which type of network you're using when you install Windows XP or when you add a network adapter for the first time. In Microsoft's terminology, the two models are called the Workgroup Network and the Domain Network.

WORKGROUP NETWORKS

A workgroup network is the appropriate model for a home or small office. Generally, in addition to the attributes listed in Table 16.1

- The network will connect ten or fewer computers.
- There is no centralized master or "server" computer.

- All computers are in the same location, more or less, and are served by a single Local Area Network.
- Computers may be running Windows XP Home Edition, XP Professional, and/or older version of Windows.

The primary attribute of a workgroup network is that there is no centralized list of authorized users and passwords. Each computer may be set up with one or more user accounts, but each computer is on its own. This makes the workgroup network terribly inconvenient for large businesses; it becomes very difficult to manage security when the number of computers grows, but it makes life much easier (and cheaper) for home and small office users.

There is technically no real restriction on the number of computers you can hook up with a workgroup-type network, although Microsoft's licenses (and the software) restrict you to interacting with at most 10 other computers at the same time.

SECURITY GROUPS

Windows uses a security database on each computer that holds a list of valid user names and passwords—it's called the Security Access Manager or SAM. Not only does the user database determine who can log on and use a given computer, it also provides the list of names users and managers can choose from when restricting access to files and folders on the hard disk. Windows also associates with each user a set of one or more system privileges, such as "Can log on locally," "Can access the computer over the network," "Can install device drivers," and so on.

When there are several users, though, it can get rather cumbersome to have to select each by name when selecting who is to have access to a given file. As an example, consider an office where you want all users to have access to the folder containing business correspondence, but only a selected few to have access to the folder containing payroll data. For each folder containing business data, you'd have to go through the list of users and select the appropriate user by name.

Then, if you hired a new payroll manager, you'd have to go back through all of the folders and add this user to the list—and if you forgot one folder, the new manager wouldn't be able to get to that folder's files.

Enter the *Security Group*. Windows permits you to create lists of users, and then to grant file and privilege access rights to the *groups*, rather than to the individuals. If a user is a member of a group with rights to a given file, the user can access the file. In the example we just discussed, we might create two groups, one named "Office Staff" and one named "Management." We'd put the appropriate users into each group, and we'd list the "Management" group as a member of the "Office Staff" group, as well. Now, access to folders could be granted to these groups. Adding a new hire would only involve adding the new user to the appropriate group; appropriate file access would then follow automatically.

This might sound trivial if you don't need this kind of compartmentalized security, but when networks grow, this kind of collective management is a crucial tool.

16

DOMAIN NETWORKS

A Domain Network is the appropriate model for a larger organization, or when any of the following requirements apply:

- Need for stringent security and centralized administrative control
- Need for centralized storage and backup
- A dozen or more computers working together
- Geographical distribution (two or more Local Area Networks, connected with some sort of Wide Area Networking medium)

In this case, the network must include one or more computers running one of Microsoft's Server operating systems, which include Windows NT 4 Server, Windows 2000 Server or Windows Server 2003 in one of the Server, Advanced Server, or DataCenter Server flavors.

> **NOTE**
>
> For the remainder of this chapter, I'll refer to Windows 2000 Server and Windows Server 2003 in their various Server, Advanced Server, and DataCenter Server versions collectively as "Windows 200x Server," except if there's a need to make a distinction.

This is called a *domain* network because all user and password security information is grouped together and managed by the server computer or computers (which, in Microsoft's terminology are dubbed Domain Controllers), and all of the other computers on the network (called *domain members*) pass logon requests to the domain controllers for verification. All security functions are thus centrally located, where they're easier to manage. The domain system lets network managers create user accounts and security groups that are automatically recognized by all of the computers on the network.

The domain system also makes it possible for users to *roam* around the organization: A computer on the fourth floor of your building should be able to recognize your username and password even though you primarily work on the second; likewise, a computer in the Los Angeles office should be able to recognize you even if you primarily work in New York.

> **NOTE**
>
> This use of the term "domain" is not related to the use of this word on the Internet. The concepts behind the terms are similar, in that both refer to ways of delegating responsibility on a large network. But, it's important to keep in mind that when you set up a Windows "domain," it doesn't involve the Internet, and there is no intrinsic relationship between the domain names used in Windows networking and those your organization may use on the Internet.

In the case of larger organizations, there may be a need to construct several independent domains; that is, separate security environments, reflecting divisions of responsibility and trust in the organization. When the number of domains grows beyond three or four, configuring Windows domain servers to recognize and trust each others' separate lists of users becomes very cumbersome. Microsoft's answer to this problem is called Active Directory.

ACTIVE DIRECTORY DOMAINS

Thus far, we've talked about domains in a fairly general sense. Now, we need to look at the specifics of how domains work. The purpose of this section is to provide a basic overview of how the Active Directory works.

The Windows domain system that we discussed in the previous section is managed by users with what's called *Domain Administrator* security rights. However, it's an all or nothing thing: A given user is either a domain administrator or not, and if so, can change any aspect of any computer in the organization, can view or edit any file, and so on. Simply put, this concentrates too much power in one place, and places the entire maintenance burden on a few individuals.

Active Directory extends the Windows Domain network model by providing a *hierarchical* security structure; it lets the network designers delegate management responsibility in a very fine-grained way. Specific users can be given permission to edit security information for other users and for network resources along the lines of the organizations' own management structure: Group leaders can manage their employee's accounts and files, division managers can manage their groups, and so on. It's completely flexible, and this sort of flexibility is essential in order to make management simpler (by delegating authority to more people) and more secure (by limiting each manager's scope of authority).

For example, let's say a company has East Coast and West Coast divisions and an accounting department in each (see Figure 16.1).

If the network manager grants read and write privileges to a shared network folder to the East Coast container, then all users anywhere in the East Coast structure (Jose, Sue, Bob, and Mary) get access rights to the folder. If Jose is granted "manager" rights to the East Coast Accounting group, then he can control the user accounts for Sue and himself.

Management of all East Coast printers could be granted to a network manager by granting him management rights to the East Coast container. He then would get the right to manage any printers within the entire container, across all its subdivisions.

Active Directory is a *distributed database*. "Distributed" means that information about separate parts of a geographically dispersed network are automatically copied from region to region, from server to server, so that the same information is available at all locations. Any of the information can be managed from any location, and the changes made automatically propagate throughout the network. This might not matter or make sense to the user of an eight-person network, but to the manager of a corporate network that spans several continents, the ability to manage a given computer just as easily from Canada as from Canberra is *very* appealing indeed.

Figure 16.1
Active Directory lets network managers define groups based on actual organizational structure. These groupings model the organization's chains of command. The resulting structure can then be used to sensibly control access privileges and to delegate management rights.

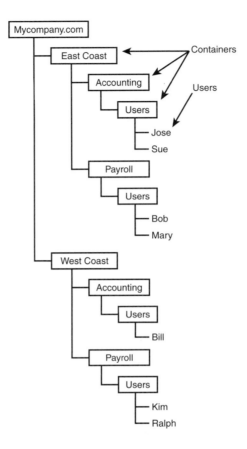

Active Directory is a true database: It can store any sort of information. Out of the box, it's used to store usernames, passwords, group membership, privileges and other security information, and feature-limiting controls called Group Policies, as well as the names and locations of computers and network printers. But it can also be used by software developers to store arbitrary information about software applications, such as the location and names of the nearest database servers—anything that would be useful to have spread throughout an organization's network.

Active Directory is integrated into the domain name system (DNS) for a company's network so that, for example, a computer in the East Coast accounting division could be named bigbox.accounting.eastcost.mycompany.com. Actually, Active Directory relies heavily on DNS. On an Active Directory network, Windows computers use DNS to locate the domain's controlling servers.

MULTI-DOMAIN ENVIRONMENTS: FORESTS AND TREES

Larger organizations may be divided into several major operating divisions. In many cases, each of these divisions will have its own management team and business requirements. For example, the overall company "Acme, Inc." may have divisions called "Acme Research" and "Acme Services". Businesses may also experience significant change through mergers, acquisitions, or reorganizations. The Active Directory supports all of these types of changes by giving systems administrators the ability to implement multiple, independently managed domains. That is, each domain has its own security and configuration database. This is an important feature for supporting distributed administration (where one group of IT staff might have access to control resources in only one domain or part of a domain), or where other stringent political or security requirements exist.

In these configurations, each of the organizations may have to exist as a separate entity. But, it's also likely that members of these different entities will want to access and share information between them. In order to accommodate these needs, multiple Active Directory domains can be given access to each other. An Active Directory *tree* is a collection of domains that share a contiguous namespace. For example, the following domains may all form a single tree:

- Acme.com
- Research.acme.com
- Sales.acme.com
- NorthAmerica.Sales.Acme.com

Domains that do not share a contiguous namespace can form Active Directory *forests*. For example, the following domains could be members of a single Active Directory forest:

- Acme.com
- A2ZHardware.com
- CleanAir.org

In keeping with the terms that the Active Directory uses, a forest can contain multiple trees. Figure 16.2 provides an example of how Active Directory domains, trees, and forests can interact.

Trust Relationships

In the real world, many different types of relationships are based on trust. Modern businesses are no exception. As we discussed earlier in this section, the purpose of trees and forests is to allow each of the member domains to remain independent (that is, they have their own security and configuration information), but also to allow them to share resources between them. The sharing of resources is configured through the use of relationships called *trusts*.

A trust is simply an agreement between one or more domains that allows for the sharing of resources. For example, an organization might create a trust between Acme.com and A2ZHardware.com in order to allow users to share resources (such as files, printers, and other information) between the two domains. Creation of a trust enables the sharing of resources by making it possible for one domain to grant access permissions to its files for the users of the other.

16

Figure 16.2
An Active Directory forest consisting of two trees.

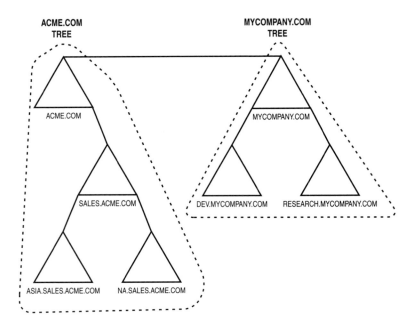

A trust relationship can have two different properties. First, the relationship can be *transitive*. What this means is that if DomainA trusts DomainB and DomainB trusts DomainC, then DomainA implicitly trusts DomainC. This is illustrated in Figure 16.3.

Figure 16.3
Transitive and two-way trust relationships.

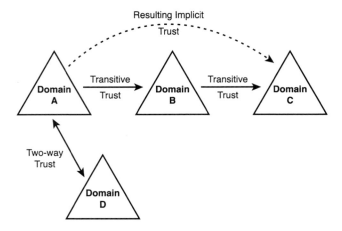

The second property determines whether a trust is one-way or two-way. A two-way trust, as you might expect, simply works in both directions. That is, if DomainA trusts DomainD, then DomainD also trusts DomainA.

BENEFITS OF ACTIVE DIRECTORY

Now that we have a basic understanding of the Active Directory, let's take a more detailed look at the actual benefits of using the Active Directory in an Enterprise environment. Microsoft has designed its newest domain model to be a very flexible method of meeting organizations' business requirements for security, configuration, and other details of running in a networked environment. It's likely that your organization has been divided into many different areas based on business goals. For example, most businesses have different departments (for example, Marketing, Sales, and Engineering). Each of these departments has employees, along with all of the necessary technology that these workers need to get their jobs done. The goal in creating these divisions within an organization is to help coordinate the various functions required for the success of the organization as a whole.

From an IT standpoint, departments are likely to have different requirements. For example, all employees in the Sales and Marketing departments might need access to a company database of customers, whereas members of the Engineering department should be the only ones that have access to a development server that contains source code. Furthermore, in many real-world environments, changes are frequent. Employees are often added, removed, or reassigned from within departments. A good directory service should be able to take all of this into account and make administration easy, yet secure.

The IT department in these companies is responsible for maintaining the security of the company's information. In modern businesses, this involves planning for, implementing, and managing various network resources. Servers, workstations, and routers are common tools that are used to connect users with the information they need to do their jobs. In all but the smallest environments, however, the effort required to manage each of these technological resources can be significant.

As we mentioned earlier, the overall design goal for the Active Directory is to create a single, centralized repository of information that securely manages a company's resources and models the company's own organizational structure. User account management, security, and applications are just a few of these areas. Let's took a more detailed look at some of the benefits of using the Active Directory:

- **Organizing Network Resources**—The Active Directory can be designed to contain multiple *Organizational Units (OUs)*. Each OU is simply a logical container that includes other objects such as users, computers, and groups. Furthermore, OUs can contain other OUs, allowing systems administrators to configure and manage groups of users based on their requirements.

  Figure 16.4 provides an example of an OU hierarchy that might represent a business environment. There are 12 containers shown, starting with "Sales.Acme.com" at the outside down to the innermost containers such as "China" and "CA." Administrative authorization for each can be controlled independently. To get the same granularity of control with traditional Windows NT domains, one would have to set up 12 separate domain databases, configure at least 11 separate trust relationships, and even then all cross-container security would have to be managed by the Administrator of one primary domain.

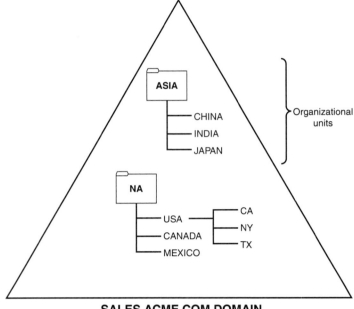

Figure 16.4
A hierarchical OU structure based on geography.

SALES.ACME.COM DOMAIN

Through the use of various organizational components, a company can create a network management infrastructure that mirrors its business organization. This structure can efficiently accommodate the physical and logical aspects of information resources such as databases, users, and computers.

- **Extensible Schema**—In addition to the default types of security and configuration information that are stored in the Active Directory, organizations may want to include additional attributes and data within their directory services. This might include anything from locator information for specialized database and messaging server resources to additional personnel details. The information stored within the structure of the Active Directory can be expanded and customized through the use of various tools. This allows the Active Directory to support special applications (such as Microsoft Exchange Server 2000, which depends on the Active Directory) and to store additional information, as needed.

- **Centralized Data Storage**—All the information within the Active Directory resides within a single data repository. This allows for easily accessing the information users and systems administrators need from throughout the company. And, it allows an easy method for backup and recovery, should the need arise.

- **Replication**—If server performance and reliability were not concerns, it might make sense to store the entire Active Directory on a single server. In the real world, however, reliability and speed of access constraints require the database to be replicated throughout the network. Through the use of replication technology, the directory's data store can be distributed between many different servers in a network environment. Logical "sites" allow systems and network administrators to limit the amount of traffic transmitted between remote locations (which are often connected by relatively slow and unreliable links) while still ensuring adequate performance and usability. Reliable data synchronization allows for "multi-master" replication—that is, all Domain Controllers can update information stored within the Active Directory and can ensure its consistency at the same time. If one of these machines fails, another can take over its responsibilities.

■ **Ease of Administration**—To accommodate various business models, the Active Directory can be configured for centralized or decentralized administration. This allows network and systems administrators to delegate authority and responsibilities throughout the organization while still maintaining security. Furthermore, the tools and utilities used to add, remove, and modify Active Directory objects are available from all Windows 200x Server domain controllers. They allow for making companywide changes with just a few mouse clicks.

■ **Network Security**—Through the use of a single logon and various authentication and encryption mechanisms, the use of the Active Directory can facilitate security throughout an entire Enterprise. Through the process of delegation, higher-level security authorities can grant permissions to other administrators. For example, I might specify that the Jane_Admin user has access to add and remove printers from within the Sales OU. For ease of administration, objects in the Active Directory tree inherit permissions from their parent objects. This feature can greatly simplify administration in large, complex environments.

■ **Client Configuration Management**—One of the biggest struggles for systems administrators is in maintaining a network of heterogeneous systems and applications. A fairly simple failure—such as a hard disk crash—can cause hours of work in reconfiguring and restoring a workstation or server. Or, when users are forced to move between computers, they may need to reinstall all of their applications and update the necessary system settings. Many IT organizations have found that these types of operations can consume a great deal of IT staffers' time and resources. New technologies integrated with the Active Directory allow for greatly enhanced control and administration of these types of network resources. The overall benefit is decreased downtime, a better end-user experience, and reduced administration. We'll cover these features in detail in the next section.

■ **Scalability and Performance**—Large organizations often have many users and large quantities of information to manage. The Active Directory has been designed with scalability in mind. Not only does it allow for storing up to millions of objects within a single domain, but it also provides methods for distributing the necessary information between servers and locations. These features relieve much of the burden of designing a directory services infrastructure based on technical instead of business factors.

■ **Searching Functionality**—When a lot of information is stored in one place, it can often be a challenge to find exactly what you need. Users often see network operating systems as extremely complicated because of the naming and location of resources. For example, if I need to find a printer, it's annoying to need to know the name of the domain or print server for that object. Using the Active Directory, users can quickly find information about other users or resources such as printers and servers, through an intuitive querying interface. Windows XP includes the ability to search Active Directory as part of the standard Windows Search Wizard, and a more sophisticated tool found on the My Network Places screen.

Clearly, Active Directory provides a huge advantage for enterprise IT support, over the original Windows NT domain structure that it supplants. In addition, all of the original Windows networking services are still available, as we'll discuss in the next few sections.

CHOOSING A NETWORK MODEL

If you're setting up a home or small office network, in most cases you'll want to set up a workgroup network. As your network grows to 10 computers or more, there are more advantages in using one of the Windows Server versions on your network instead of basing it entirely on XP Home Edition or Professional. Table 16.2 lists the primary differences between these two approaches.

TABLE 16.2 PRIMARY DIFFERENCES BETWEEN HOME/PRO ONLY AND WINDOWS SERVER NETWORKS

Network with Windows XP Professional Only	Network with Windows 200x Server
This network provides at most 10 connections to other computers.	Connections to the server are unlimited.
The cost is low.	This network costs a few hundred dollars more, plus additional fees for Client Access Licenses.
Configuration is simple (relatively, anyway!).	This network is complex to configure and administer.
Each machine must be administered independently.	Administration is centralized.
Provides rudimentary remote access, connection sharing, and WAN support.	The features are more sophisticated. For example, DHCP and DNS servers are included.
Managing file security is difficult when you have more than one user per computer.	Centralized user management eases the task of managing security.
A given computer can host at most one Web site (domain).	A single server can host multiple Web sites.
Can use files on Windows and NetWare servers, share files with Windows clients only.	Can serve files and share printers to Mac clients.
Unix NFS client available with purchase of add-on package.	Unix NFS client and server available with purchase of add-on package.

So, even if you don't want to take advantage of Active Directory, the Server advantages can add up pretty quickly.

NOTE

> If you decide you need or want to use a server-based network, you should get a copy of *Special Edition Using Microsoft Windows 2000 Server*, or *Special Edition Using Microsoft Windows 2003 Server* (both published by Que) and a big bottle of Alka-Seltzer before you go any further.

16

WINDOWS XP'S NETWORK SERVICES

Besides file and printer sharing, Windows XP provides many other network services. You might never interact with some of these services directly, but their presence makes Windows the amazing application platform it is.

Let's take a short tour of Windows network services. I'll describe what each service is, why it's useful, perhaps a bit about how it works, and I'll tell you where to find out how to install, configure, or use it, if appropriate.

FILE AND PRINTER SHARING

Networking software was developed to share and transfer files between computers (America Online Instant Messenger came later, if you can believe that). Windows XP comes with the following features:

- Client for Microsoft Networks, which gives access to files and printers shared by other Windows computers as well as OS/2, Unix, Linux, and so on.

- File and Printer Sharing for Microsoft Networks, which lets Windows XP Professional share files and printers with users of those same operating systems. Windows XP Pro is limited to 10 simultaneous connections from other computers; one of the Server versions is required for larger LANs.

- Web Sharing, which is a new technology that provides secure file copying to and from shared folders over the Internet, using the Web's Hypertext Transfer Protocol. The "new" part is that it uses full Windows security and the Windows Explorer user interface, while the underlying technology is based on the World Wide Web and Microsoft's Internet Information Server.

- Client for Novell Networks, which gives access to files and printers shared by Novell NetWare file servers.

- Unix Print Services, which lets you use and share printers with computers using the Unix operating system's LPR protocol.

Unlike Windows 200x Server, however, Pro has no tools to share files with Apple Macintosh computers or to use Macintosh shared folders.

→ For information about installing, configuring, and using Microsoft network software, **see** Chapters 17 through 19.

→ For information about interacting with Novell and Unix servers, **see** Chapter 20, "The Heterogeneous Network."

ROAMING USER PROFILES

When Windows XP Professional is connected to a Windows Server domain, besides simply validating usernames and passwords, servers can supply Pro computers with a *profile* for each user as he or she logs in.

A profile contains information that helps Windows XP Professional make its desktop and folders look the same no matter which physical computer you use. User profiles contain the following:

- Desktop icons and shortcuts
- The contents of your My Files and Documents folder
- Your configuration and preference settings for all the software you use, from your Word preferences to your choice of screen savers
- Management settings that control, for example, whether you are allowed to change Control Panel entries

User profiles are covered in more depth in Chapter 11, "Creating and Managing User Accounts."

DISTRIBUTED APPLICATIONS

Windows XP provides network protocols that let software application developers write programs that interact across a network. You will probably never have to install, configure, or even know such protocols exist; you'll just use the programs that use them and happily go about your business. But someone may mention them, so you should be familiar with their names: RPC and COM+.

RPC

Microsoft's remote procedure call (RPC) network protocol allows software to be split into pieces that run on different computers and interact across a network. The RPC mechanism is used, for instance, when a user on one Windows computer pauses print spooling on another. It's the basis of most of Windows's remote management capabilities; these are more sophisticated things than the authors of the basic file sharing protocols made allowances for.

COM+ (FORMERLY COM AND DCOM)

The former Component Object Model (COM) and Distributed COM (DCOM) services have been combined in Windows 2000 and XP to the upgraded COM+ service. COM+ provides software developers tools to build highly modular software in a variety of languages. You should be happy it exists and happier still if you never hear about it again.

To learn more about COM and DCOM, pick up a copy of *COM/DCOM Unleashed*, published by Sams Publishing.

.NET

The .NET (pronounced "dot net") initiative is Microsoft's most recent replacement for COM, DCOM, and RPC. .NET is an entire software framework for Internet-enabled software application development. It's designed to make possible a whole new generation of software applications.

VIRTUAL PRIVATE NETWORKING

Windows XP Professional can connect to remote LANs through the Internet using *Virtual Private Networking (VPN)*. This very secure technology makes it safe to use Microsoft networking over the Internet. Windows XP comes with built-in software supporting two VPN technologies: the *Point-to-Point Tunneling Protocol*, or *PPTP*, which was developed by Microsoft and the *Layer Two Tunneling Protocol*, or *L2TP*, an industry standard technology, which is faster and better than PPTP. There are also several third-party VPN hardware and software solutions that may be used by your business.

→ If you're interested in learning more about Virtual Private Networking, **see** "Virtual Private Networking," **p. 782.**

REMOTE ACCESS

If you travel with a laptop or often work from a location outside your physical LAN, you can still use RAS (Remote Access Service, also called *dial-up networking*) to interact with people and files on your network.

→ For more detailed information about RAS, **see** "Dial-Up Networking," **p. 767.**

CONNECTION BY MODEM

Windows XP Professional allows you to configure a modem for incoming connections as well as outgoing. You can provide access to your LAN via modem, for example, to retrieve files from your office while you are at home or in the field. At most, two incoming connections are permitted with Pro.

→ To configure Remote Access, **see** "Enabling Dial-In and VPN Access to Your Computer," **p. 779.**

INCOMING VPN

Windows XP Professional also allows you to connect to your LAN via the Point-to-Point Tunneling Protocol (PPTP); that is, it lets you create a Virtual Private Network. If your LAN has a full-time Internet connection, it will (or it should) have a firewall installed, thus preventing you from using file sharing directly from the outside world. A VPN connection lets you safely penetrate the firewall to gain access to your LAN over the Internet.

16

16

REMOTE DESKTOP AND WINDOWS TERMINAL SERVICES

Windows XP Professional and 200x Server provide a sort of remote-control system called, variously, Windows Terminal Services, Remote Desktop, and Remote Assistance. Terminal Services let you use a computer remotely. Your applications run on the remote computer, while you use your local computer's display, keyboard, and mouse. There are three names for what is basically the same piece of software, because it's used three different ways:

- **Terminal Services**—A Windows NT or 200x Server can be set up to host applications used by remote clients. For example, one beefy computer can run complex software, while the remote computers, which only need to provide a display and keyboard, can be relative lightweights. Terminal services is also great for remote administration of a server—a manager can sit in front of one computer, but can control and configure servers anywhere in the world.

  Although the service is provided only by Windows NT and 200x Server, the client software is available for Windows XP, 2000, 9x, and NT.

- **Remote Desktop**—Windows XP Professional has a Remote Desktop feature, which is a copy of the Terminal Services server limited to *one* incoming connection. It's intended, for example, to enable an employee to access his or her Windows XP Pro computer at the office from home. When a remote user is connected, the XP computer's screen blanks out, so only one person at a time can use the computer.

  > **NOTE**
  >
  > In my opinion, Remote Desktop alone is worth the price of Windows XP Professional. There's more about Remote Desktop in Chapter 19, "Windows Unplugged: Remote and Portable Computing."

- **Remote Assistance**—Windows XP Professional and Home Editions' Remote Assistance feature is based on—you guessed it—Terminal Services again, also limited to one connection. In this case, however, the desktop is *not* blanked out when the remote user attaches: It's intended for the remote and local user to work together to resolve a problem. Also, the remote connection can only occur when the computer owner emails the remote user an electronic invitation, which is good for one connection only. This makes the service useless for general remote-employee-type work, but handy for one-time assistance. (It also doesn't work when the person requesting assistance is behind a hardware Internet connection sharing router.)

CONNECTION SHARING

Windows XP Professional has a handy feature that first appeared in the Windows 98 Second Edition: Internet Connection Sharing. This feature lets one XP Pro computer with a modem or high-speed Internet connection provide Internet access to all users of a LAN. This access is somewhat limited, however. It requires that the LAN use the Windows built-in automatic IP address configuration system, so it's incompatible with WAN configurations. It also requires that the computer with the modem or high-speed connection be left turned on all the time.

Connection sharing is described later in this chapter, and is discussed in more detail in Chapter 8, "Configuring Your Internet Connection."

ACTIVE DIRECTORY

As discussed earlier in this chapter, Windows XP Professional can take advantage of a service called the *Active Directory (AD)*. Active Directory combines a name/address directory, management and security services, and wide-area replicated database technologies to provide a foundation for all of Windows's networking functions. If your network is managed by a Windows 200x Server with AD installed, this service is automatically and transparently made available to you. AD is entirely based on TCP/IP technology, and for this reason, all Windows XP computers should use TCP/IP as their primary, if not only, network protocol.

→ To learn how to use Active Directory services, **see** "Using Active Directory," **p. 733**.

Active Directory is used internally by Windows tools such as Explorer, My Network Places, and the Printer Manager. User-written programs can get access to the directory's contents through a programming interface called Active Directory Services Interface (ADSI) or more generally through an Internet protocol called Lightweight Directory Access Protocol (LDAP), which is an industry standard for directory queries and responses. Email programs, for example, can be designed to use LDAP to search for email addresses, regardless of the underlying network system, whether it's based on Windows, Novell NetWare, or other networking systems.

INTELLIMIRROR

You might hear the term IntelliMirror and wonder what sort of network feature it is. IntelliMirror actually is just Microsoft's name for several features and services provided by its domain networks based on Active Directory. These are as follows:

- **Remote Installation**—Windows XP can be installed from scratch onto an empty hard drive over a network.

- **Roaming User Profiles**—Your My Documents folder and your preferences settings are stored on the network servers and copied to the computers you use, so they're available anywhere on your enterprise network.

- **Group Policy**—Windows's capability to "force" preferences settings and restrict access to system configuration dialog boxes is based on Registry entries defined by the network administrators and copied to your computer when you log in.

- **Application Publication**—Application software such as Word and Excel can be installed automatically across the network, based again on Group policy settings.

16

Together, these features let network administrators give you the experience of walking up to any computer in your organization and having it be "your" computer with all your files, settings, and applications. You should, in theory, even be able to log off, throw your computer out the window, and replace it with a brand new, empty one, and in short order pick up your work where you left off. In theory, anyway.

INTRANET/INTERNET SERVICES AND TOOLS

Finally, Windows XP comes with a full complement of applications and tools that Internet and Unix users expect on a TCP/IP-based computer. They're not part of Windows Networking, technically speaking, because they don't use the Networking Clients. They communicate with other computers using TCP/IP directly. These tools include the following:

- Internet Explorer (Web browser)
- SNMP Agents
- Telnet client and server
- Ping
- FTP
- NetMeeting
- nslookup
- pathping
- tracert
- Outlook Express (SMTP/POP mail client)
- Internet Information Server (Web server)

SECURITY

Finally, Windows XP Professional, when it's part of a Windows Server-based network, supports the use of two very sophisticated network security systems to encrypt network traffic and to communicate passwords and information about user rights between computers.

Windows XP Professional supports the IPSec TCP/IP data encryption standard. IPSec provides a means for each of the data packets sent across a network to be encrypted—scrambled—so that an eavesdropper with a wiretapping device can't glean passwords or other sensitive information from your data while it flows through the wires of your building, through airwaves in a wireless network, or across the Internet.

Windows XP also supports the Kerberos network authentication protocol, which was developed at Carnegie-Mellon University and is now widely used in secure distributed network operating systems. Kerberos manages the identification of computer users on a network to eliminate many network security risks, such as the recording and playback of passwords.

TIP

Both IPSec TCP/IP data encryption and Kerberos network authentication protocol are activated under the control of the administrator of Windows 200x Server and are invisible to you as a Windows XP Professional user.

NOTE

If you're really into security—and I mean really into security—I recommend that you grab a copy of *Microsoft Windows 2000 Security Handbook*, published by Que (ISBN: 0-7897-1999-1). Better hang on to your hat, though....

16

How Windows Networking Works

In this section, I'll discuss some of the technology behind Windows networking. You may be familiar with many of these terms, and if you are, you can skip ahead to later sections. However, if you're new to networking, our hope is that this section will make sense of some of the "alphabet soup" of acronyms you'll encounter while constructing and working with a network.

Networking Protocols

Network transport protocols define how data is arranged and sent in a coordinated fashion between computers. There are three transport protocols commonly used on Windows-based computers:

- *TCP/IP (Transport Control Protocol/Internet Protocol)* forms the basis of the Internet, and is also used for Windows file and printer sharing. TCP/IP is actually a set of several related protocols that are used to provide the services that higher-level network components need: resolving computer names into network card and IP addresses, guaranteeing correct transmission, and inter-network routing. The *TCP* part, or *Transmission Control Protocol*, is the method an IP-based network uses to guarantee that data is sent end-to-end without errors. I'll go into more detail about TCP/IP in a little bit.

- *IPX/SPX (Internetwork Packet Exchange/Sequenced Packet Exchange)* was developed by Novell for its NetWare network software. Windows can use IPX/SPX for its file sharing services as well. Like TCP/IP, IPX/SPX is really a set of protocols that provide many services, including name resolution, guaranteed transport, and inter-network routing. Novell has transitioned away from IPX/SPX to TCP/IP in its recent server versions, so this can be considered a legacy protocol.

- *NetBEUI (NetBIOS Enhanced User Interface)* was developed by IBM for its original IBM PC Network; it provides similar services to TCP/IP and IPX/SPX, except that it doesn't have a mechanism to route data to remote networks. NetBEUI can transport data between computers only on the same physical LAN. NetBEUI was supported by previous versions of Windows, but its use is discouraged with Windows XP.

The following are some other protocols you might hear about:

- *AppleTalk* and its Ethernet-based counterpart *LocalTalk* are used in Apple Macintosh networking. Windows 2000 Professional provided LocalTalk support to facilitate using LAN-connected Apple printers, but it's been dropped from Windows XP.

- *DLC (Data Link Control)* is an IBM networking protocol, but you won't run into it directly unless you're working on a corporate network with IBM mainframes. In that case, if it's used, your company's network management staff will want to take care of this task for you. DLC is also used by some network-connected printers. Like AppleTalk, support for DLC has been dropped by Microsoft.

- *Point-to-Point Protocol*, or *PPP*, is used to carry Internet Protocol data packets across a modem connection. This protocol is used to establish almost all modem connections to Internet service providers. PPP is part of the TCP/IP suite and a standard part of Windows's Dial-Up Networking support.

- *Point-to-Point Protocol over Ethernet*, or *PPPoE*, is used by some DSL and cable modem Internet service providers to link your computer to the ISP's routing equipment. For previous versions of Windows, ISPs provided their own PPPoE software. PPPoE is now built into Windows XP as part of its Broadband Connection support.

- *Universal Plug and Play*, or *UPnP*, lets networked computers and networked devices such as printers and household appliances automatically configure themselves to join whatever network they find themselves plugged into. It can, for example, automatically configure your computer to use an Internet connection shared by another computer on the LAN. It's not yet widely supported, however.

- *Point-to-Point Tunneling Protocol*, or *PPTP*, is used to create *Virtual Private Networks*, or *VPNs*. PPTP takes data destined for a private, remote network, repackages the data for transmission across the Internet, and at the other end unpackages the data to be released into the private, protected network. I'll go into greater detail explaining VPNs in Chapter 19.

TCP/IP IN A NUTSHELL

Most networks for PC, Macintosh, and Unix/Linux computers use the TCP/IP protocol (officially known as TCP/IP version 4) which is also used as the basis of the Internet. As a bit of background, the abbreviations TCP/IP actually stand for two different protocols: TCP and IP. So what's the difference between these two protocols and how do they work together? To summarize succinctly

- IP stands for the *Internet Protocol*. IP defines the basic means through which computers can send information back and forth, and it defines a hierarchical address space that works for computer networks as ZIP codes and street addresses do for the postal network. The IP address space makes routing possible, whereby packets of information can be delivered to another computer on a distant network. IP is designed with the idea that the network on which its data rides is "unreliable"; that is, it's assumed that data sent with IP might never reach its destination, and IP doesn't by itself provide the means to provide any guarantees.

■ TCP stands for the *Transmission Control Protocol*. As the name implies, TCP manages the transmission of information sent from one network application to another. Since IP doesn't check to find out whether data packets ever actually get delivered, TCP provides a means to perform this function. Data sent by one computer is broken up into bite-sized packets, and TCP uses a system of receipt-confirmation messages and please-send-again requests to ensure that all of the pieces arrive at the other computer and can be reassembled into the original message. Thus, TCP is considered to be a reliable, connection-oriented protocol.

Another important protocol in the TCP/IP suite is the *User Datagram Protocol (UDP)*. This protocol, like TCP, uses IP as its basic transport mechanism. However, UDP doesn't require the acknowledgments that TCP does; it's used for applications such as streaming audio where speed and the ability to simply carry on is more important than fidelity.

Still another protocol called the *Internet Control Message Protocol (ICMP)* is used to communicate information about the state of the network, and it's employed by a number of utilities that are used to diagnose network problems. For example, ping and tracert make use of ICMP messages to test network connectivity and to map network routing paths.

Figure 16.5 shows the relationship between the different protocols mentioned in the previous paragraphs, and how they relate to getting your data transmitted on the network media.

IP Addressing

When one computer sends data via IP (or any of the subsidiary protocols like TCP or UDP), the sending computer constructs one or more *packets*, which are independent message units that contain the data to be transmitted. It's very similar to the way you'd send a letter: You insert the pages (your data) into an envelope (a packet), address it, and post it.

For IP data sent with the most commonly used IP version 4 system, packets are addressed using a number called an *IP address* or *IP number*, which is a 32-bit binary number most often written in *dotted decimal notation*, a form that looks like this: 73.165.202.47. Each of the four numbers represents 8 bits (one *octet*) of the IP address. Table 16.3 lists the correspondence between the possible decimal values and the corresponding octets. You can use this table to see that the sample IP address 73.165.202.47 mentioned previously represents the binary number 01001001 10100101 11001010 00101111.

16

Figure 16.5
The TCP/IP suite of protocols is made up of layers of protocols, each of which perform specific functions.

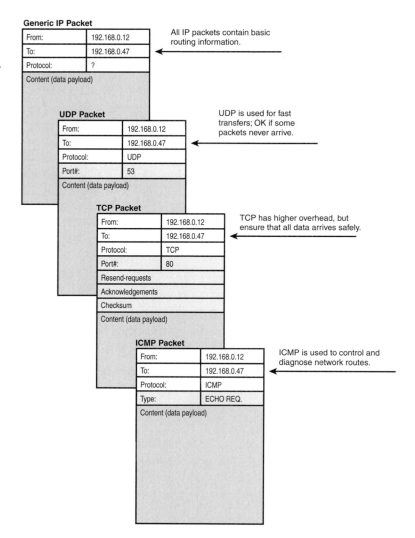

Generic IP Packet

From:	192.168.0.12
To:	192.168.0.47
Protocol:	?
Content (data payload)	

All IP packets contain basic routing information.

UDP Packet

From:	192.168.0.12
To:	192.168.0.47
Protocol:	UDP
Port#:	53
Content (data payload)	

UDP is used for fast transfers; OK if some packets never arrive.

TCP Packet

From:	192.168.0.12
To:	192.168.0.47
Protocol:	TCP
Port#:	80
Resend-requests	
Acknowledgements	
Checksum	
Content (data payload)	

TCP has higher overhead, but ensure that all data arrives safely.

ICMP Packet

From:	192.168.0.12
To:	192.168.0.47
Protocol:	ICMP
Type:	ECHO REQ.
Content (data payload)	

ICMP is used to control and diagnose network routes.

TABLE 16.3 DECIMAL/BINARY CONVERSION

Decimal	Binary	Decimal	Binary	Decimal	Binary	Decimal	Binary
1	00000000	64	01000000	128	10000000	192	11000000
1	00000001	65	01000001	129	10000001	193	11000001
2	00000010	66	01000010	130	10000010	194	11000010
3	00000011	67	01000011	131	10000011	195	11000011
4	00000100	68	01000100	132	10000100	196	11000100
5	00000101	69	01000101	133	10000101	197	11000101

Decimal	Binary	Decimal	Binary	Decimal	Binary	Decimal	Binary
6	00000110	70	01000110	134	10000110	198	11000110
7	00000111	71	01000111	135	10000111	199	11000111
8	00001000	72	01001000	136	10001000	200	11001000
9	00001001	73	01001001	137	10001001	201	11001001
10	00001010	74	01001010	138	10001010	202	11001010
11	00001011	75	01001011	139	10001011	203	11001011
12	00001100	76	01001100	140	10001100	204	11001100
13	00001101	77	01001101	141	10001101	205	11001101
14	00001110	78	01001110	142	10001110	206	11001110
15	00001111	79	01001111	143	10001111	207	11001111
16	00010000	80	01010000	144	10010000	208	11010000
17	00010001	81	01010001	145	10010001	209	11010001
18	00010010	82	01010010	146	10010010	210	11010010
19	00010011	83	01010011	147	10010011	211	11010011
20	00010100	84	01010100	148	10010100	212	11010100
21	00010101	85	01010101	149	10010101	213	11010101
22	00010110	86	01010110	150	10010110	214	11010110
23	00010111	87	01010111	151	10010111	215	11010111
24	00011000	88	01011000	152	10011000	216	11011000
25	00011001	89	01011001	153	10011001	217	11011001
26	00011010	90	01011010	154	10011010	218	11011010
27	00011011	91	01011011	155	10011011	219	11011011
28	00011100	92	01011100	156	10011100	220	11011100
29	00011101	93	01011101	157	10011101	221	11011101
30	00011110	94	01011110	158	10011110	222	11011110
31	00011111	95	01011111	159	10011111	223	11011111
32	00100000	96	01100000	160	10100000	224	11100000
33	00100001	97	01100001	161	10100001	225	11100001
34	00100010	98	01100010	162	10100010	226	11100010
35	00100011	99	01100011	163	10100011	227	11100011
36	00100100	100	01100100	164	10100100	228	11100100
37	00100101	101	01100101	165	10100101	229	11100101

16

continues

Table 16.3 Continued

Decimal	Binary	Decimal	Binary	Decimal	Binary	Decimal	Binary
38	00100110	102	01100110	166	10100110	230	11100110
39	00100111	103	01100111	167	10100111	231	11100111
40	00101000	104	01101000	168	10101000	232	11101000
41	00101001	105	01101001	169	10101001	233	11101001
42	00101010	106	01101010	170	10101010	234	11101010
43	00101011	107	01101011	171	10101011	235	11101011
44	00101100	108	01101100	172	10101100	236	11101100
45	00101101	109	01101101	173	10101101	237	11101101
46	00101110	110	01101110	174	10101110	238	11101110
47	00101111	111	01101111	175	10101111	239	11101111
48	00110000	112	01110000	176	10110000	240	11110000
49	00110001	113	01110001	177	10110001	241	11110001
50	00110010	114	01110010	178	10110010	242	11110010
51	00110011	115	01110011	179	10110011	243	11110011
52	00110100	116	01110100	180	10110100	244	11110100
53	00110101	117	01110101	181	10110101	245	11110101
54	00110110	118	01110110	182	10110110	246	11110110
55	00110111	119	01110111	183	10110111	247	11110111
56	00111000	120	01111000	184	10111000	248	11111000
57	00111001	121	01111001	185	10111001	249	11111001
58	00111010	122	01111010	186	10111010	250	11111010
59	00111011	123	01111011	187	10111011	251	11111011
60	00111100	124	01111100	188	10111100	252	11111100
61	00111101	125	01111101	189	10111101	253	11111101
62	00111110	126	01111110	190	10111110	254	11111110
63	00111111	127	01111111	191	10111111	255	11111111

Each computer participating in a TCP/IP network is assigned a unique IP address, just as every house has a unique mailing address. IP addresses used on the Internet are administered by an international organization called the Internet Assigned Numbers Authority (IANA). Large blocks of numbers are parceled out to national assignment registries, then to top-level Internet Service Providers, then to smaller ISPs, and ultimately to individual computers connected to the Internet.

N O T E

You can find out who "owns" any given IP address by consulting the *whois* service provided by the four Regional Internet Registries:

www.arin.net for the Americas and sub-Saharan Africa

www.apnic.net for Asia/Pacific region

lacnic.net for Latin America and the Caribbean

www.ripe.net for Europe, the Middle East, Central Asia, and Northern Africa

The whois lookup searches offered by these sites may provide a direct answer, or may direct you to search a specific National Internet Registry.

16

N O T E

Even with the 4,294,967,296 possible addresses afforded by the 32-bit numbering system used by IP version 4, we are running out of IP addresses. The "next generation" IP version 6 will solve this problem by using a 128-bit addressing scheme that offers more possible addresses than we're likely to ever need: 3 followed by 38 zeros. IPv6, as it's known, is gradually being introduced on the Internet but it will take quite a while to become commonplace, due to cost involved in replacing the enormous established IPv4 infrastructure. Windows XP has IPv6 networking software built in, though, should your organization be ready to use it.

Given an IP address, TCP/IP's network software determines how to route the data to its destination. There are two ways that the data could be sent:

- If the destination computer is on the same local area network as the sending computer, data can be delivered directly to the destination.
- If the destination computer is not on the same local network, it has to be *routed* there; that is, the data packets have to be passed from the sending computer through additional computers or hardware devices that are attached through additional networks, until they reach the network to which the intended recipient is connected.

How does TCP/IP know if the destination computer is on the same local network as the sender? It uses a second component of a computer's IP address setup called its *network mask*. The network mask is a number that in binary has all 1 bits at the left, and all 0 bits at the right. TCP/IP compares the first several bits of the sender's and receiver's IP addresses, those bits that correspond to the 1's in the network mask, which are called the *network number*. If sender's and receiver's network numbers are the same, the destination is local, and the data is sent directly. If the network numbers don't match, the destination is not local and the packet is forwarded to a *gateway*, which is a router or another computer on the local network that is presumed to know how to get the data where it's going. The bits in the IP address that correspond to the 0's in the network mask are called the *local address*.

The first two columns of Table 16.4 show the most commonly used values for the network mask, along with the corresponding network number bits.

16

TABLE 16.4 COMMONLY USED NETWORK MASK VALUES

Network Mask	Mask Bits	Subnet Size (Bits)	Usable IP Addresses
255.0.0.0	11111111 00000000 00000000 00000000	24	16,777,214
255.255.0.0	11111111 11111111 00000000 00000000	16	65,534
255.255.128.0	11111111 11111111 10000000 00000000	15	32,766
255.255.192.0	11111111 11111111 11000000 00000000	14	16,382
255.255.224.0	11111111 11111111 11100000 00000000	13	8,190
255.255.240.0	11111111 11111111 11110000 00000000	12	4,094
255.255.248.0	11111111 11111111 11111000 00000000	11	2,046
255.255.252.0	11111111 11111111 11111100 00000000	10	1,022
255.255.254.0	11111111 11111111 11111110 00000000	9	510
255.255.255.0	11111111 11111111 11111111 00000000	8	254
255.255.255.128	11111111 11111111 11111111 10000000	7	126
255.255.255.192	11111111 11111111 11111111 11000000	6	62
255.255.255.224	11111111 11111111 11111111 11100000	5	30
255.255.255.240	11111111 11111111 11111111 11110000	4	14
255.255.255.248	11111111 11111111 11111111 11111000	3	6
255.255.255.252	11111111 11111111 11111111 11111100	2	2

For the IP address we were discussing earlier, if the network mask was defined by the network administrator as 255.255.192.0, then the address breaks down as follows:

IP address:	73.165.202.47
in binary:	01001001 10100101 11001010 00101111
network mask:	11111111 11111111 11000000 00000000
network number:	01001001 10100101 11
local address:	001010 00101111

Let's check to see if a couple of other IP addresses are local or not. IP address 73.165.201.32 is local, because it has the same network number:

IP address:	73.165.201.32
in binary:	01001001 10100101 11001001 00100000
network mask:	11111111 11111111 11000000 00000000
network number:	01001001 10100101 11
local address:	001011 00100000

How about 63.193.114.1?

IP address:	63.193.114.1
in binary:	00111111 11000001 01110010 00000001
network mask:	11111111 11111111 11000000 00000000
network number:	00111111 11000001 01
local address:	110010 00000001

It's not local, because the network number is different. Our sample computer with IP address 73.165.201.32 would not try to deliver data directly to this address, but would instead forward it to its gateway.

To see a practical example of how this works, go to a computer that's connected to the Internet via a direct or dial-up connection. Open a Command Prompt window. On Windows XP or 2000, type the command **ipconfig**, or on Windows 9x/Me type **winipcfg**. This command will display the computer's IP address along with a network mask and a gateway address. You can check the bits of the IP address and gateway address and see that the gateway address is local—it has to be, as it's the only path through which your computer can send data to the Internet.

The second two columns in Table 16.4 show how many local addresses can be assigned on a local network given its network mask. The *subnet size* is the number of 0 bits in the network mask; in other words, the number of bits left over to use as the local address. The number of usable IP addresses is the number of unique addresses that can be constructed with this number of bits, less two. The local addresses with all bits equal to 0 and all bits equal to 1 cannot be used as IP addresses, so the number of usable addresses is calculated as $(2^{subnet\_size} - 2)$.

16

As I mentioned earlier, IP addresses used on the Internet are regulated, in order that the Internet's many data carriers can properly route information to the correct destination. There are specific ranges of numbers that are reserved for use behind network firewalls; these numbers are guaranteed never to be assigned to computers visible on the Internet. If you set up your own LAN, you should use one of the reserved address groups so local addresses will never conflict with Internet addresses. In the event that a local computer had the same IP address as a desired Internet host, your computer would always try to communicate with the local computer, rendering the Internet host unreachable. The private IP address ranges are listed in Table 16.5.

TABLE 16.5   IP ADDRESS RANGES FOR PRIVATE SUBNETS

IP Addresses	Network Mask
10.0.0.1 through 10.255.255.254	255.0.0.0
172.16.0.1 through 172.31.255.254	255.240.0.0
192.160.0.1 through 192.168.255.254	255.255.0.0

You can use smaller subnets than this, if desired. That is, you can use network masks with more 1's. For example, a common range used for home and small office networks is 192.168.0.1 through 192.168.0.254 with mask 255.255.255.0

ARP

When an IP data packet is to be transmitted to a computer on the local network, or has traveled through routers on a wide area network (or the Internet) and has reached the local network of its final destination, the network has to figure out how to get the packet to the actual destination computer. The networking hardware itself doesn't "know" about IP addresses. Instead, each network adapter has an address (like a phone number) that is actually built right into the hardware of the network card. It is called the *physical network address* or *media access control (MAC)* address. It's this physical address that's used to deliver data on a local network.

TCP/IP has a mechanism called the Address Resolution Protocol or ARP that is used to discover the MAC address of a computer on the local network. When a computer has to deliver a packet to a computer it hasn't previously communicated with, it transmits what's called a *broadcast* message that is received by every computer on the local network. An ARP broadcast in effect asks, "Will the computer that's been assigned IP address such-and-so please tell me where you are?" The computer with this address responds to the first computer, and in its reply sends its physical MAC address. This lets the first computer send the IP packet on its way.

Each computer keeps a list of IP addresses and MAC addresses that it's learned so that it doesn't need to repeat the ARP process for every transmission; it's called the *ARP cache*.

However, this information can grow stale. If you switch network adapters in a given computer, for instance, the new adapter will come with a new physical MAC address and any other computer on the network that "remembers" the old one won't be able to communicate with it. To keep this type of problem from lasting indefinitely, Windows drops an entry from the ARP cache if two minutes go by without any communication with the listed address, and keeps an entry for at most 10 minutes in any case.

TIP

> The arp command-line utility displays the contents of the ARP cache and lets you make permanent entries, if necessary.

DHCP (Automatic Configuration)

If networking hardware devices have built-in physical MAC addresses but they themselves know nothing about IP addresses, how do IP addresses get assigned in an orderly fashion to the computers on a network? There are several ways this can happen:

- The addresses can be assigned and entered into each computer's TCP/IP software manually.

- One of two automatic assignment systems can be used, the Dynamic Host Configuration Protocol (DHCP) or the Boot Protocol (BOOTP). Windows computers can only use DHCP, while Unix and Macintosh computers can usually use either. We'll discuss DHCP here.

- There can be a combination of the two: Some devices can be configured manually, and the rest configured using the automatic system.

- Dial-up Internet connections and PPPoE DSL connections are assigned IP addresses by the dial-up networking server on the other end of the connection using a mechanism similar to DHCP.

When a computer is set up to use DHCP to get its IP address, at boot time it sends a broadcast message that is received by every computer on the local network asking, in effect, "What's my IP address?" If one of the computers or routers on the network is set up to provide DHCP service, it responds with a message indicating what IP address, network mask, and gateway addresses the computer should use. DHCP can supply additional configuration as well: computer names, database servers, time-of-day servers, and other network resource locators can be delivered to a newly booting computer via DHCP.

DHCP service can be provided for a network by Windows 200x Server, by hardware Internet connection sharing router devices, and is automatically provided by any Windows 9x/Me/2000/XP system that is running Microsoft's Internet Connection Sharing service. However, there can be at most one DHCP server on a given network—otherwise duplicate addresses might get given out.

Since each computer on the network must have a unique IP address, and since the number of available addresses is limited by the subnet size assigned to the network (as noted in Table 16.4), a DHCP server must keep track of which addresses have been handed out and which are available for use. Therefore each DHCP server keeps a database of physical MAC addresses, which identify the computers it's dealt with, and the IP addresses that have been assigned. Servers only guarantee a computer the use of an assigned IP address for a fixed length of time, called a *lease*. DHCP client computers periodically tell the server that they're still alive and kicking, a process called *renewing* the lease; otherwise, when the fixed time has expired, the DHCP server has to assume that the computer using the address has disconnected from the network, and frees the IP address for use.

NOTE

Cable modem Internet services often use DHCP to dole out IP addresses. To help reduce fraud, these ISPs often keep track of which MAC addresses are authorized to plug in to their network, which is why you often have to call your cable ISP to reregister when you change computers or network adapters.

NOTE

If you unplug a computer that was configured with DHCP from its network and plug it into another network without rebooting, the computer will be using the wrong IP address setup for the new network. In this case, it's necessary to tell Windows to release its IP information and request a new configuration. Windows XP does this automatically when it detects that the network cable has been unplugged and reconnected. You can also force this to happen by selecting a connection icon and then clicking on the Repair This Connection button on the Network Connections screen.

If you have servers on your network that provide Internet services such as email, Web pages, and so on, it's often best to assign these server computers *static* (manually assigned, fixed) IP addresses so that other computers can more easily locate them by name (more about this later, when we discuss the Domain Name System, or DNS). This is done by reserving a range of IP addresses for static addressing, and another range for DHCP. On my office network, for instance, I assign servers addresses in the range 192.168.0.1 through 192.168.0.99, and my Internet Connection Sharing router is allowed to distribute up to 100 addresses using DHCP starting with 192.168.0.100.

Automatic Private Internet Protocol Addressing

Another feature offered by Windows 9x, Me, 2000, and XP is called Automatic Private Internet Protocol Addressing (APIPA). In this scenario, no DHCP server is needed. Instead, on a small network, APIPA allows the clients to configure themselves once they discover that no DHCP server is responding to their requests.

The address range that APIPA uses is 169.254.0.1 through 169.254.255.254. When a Windows XP computer that uses APIPA finds that no DHCP server is responding, it will simply pick an address from this range of addresses and probe the network using ARP requests to see if the address is in use. It will do this until it finds one that isn't being used. Thus, within a matter of a few minutes, a small network can automatically configure itself without manual intervention or the use of a DHCP server.

However, I've found that APIPA causes terrible slowdowns in Windows computers running versions from Windows 98 on up to Windows XP. I've never seen a satisfactory answer for this, but it could have something to do with Windows's need to wait to see if a DHCP server is present; it does this at bootup and every 15 minutes or so thereafter.

TIP

> If you are setting up a small network and aren't using an Internet Connection Sharing scheme so you don't have DCHP, manually assign IP addresses 192.168.0.1, 192.168.0.2, and so on, using a different address for each computer. Set the network mask to 255.255.255.0 and leave the DNS and gateway setup fields blank.

Name Resolution

While every computer on the Internet and on a Windows XP network has to be assigned an IP address, these numbers are not convenient to type nor are they easy to remember. When we're looking for information, we prefer to use meaningful names such as "sales_server" and "www.quepublishing.com". How this is accomplished depends on the transport protocol in use: (the now-retired) NetBEUI, or TCP/IP. The difference between the two is significant.

NetBEUI

I'm sure you've tried to find a friend in a crowded airport lobby. The quickest way to find him or her is to stand up on a chair and shout out his or her name. Works like a charm, even though it momentarily interrupts everyone around you. The old NetBEUI protocol resolved names this way. It would broadcast a request to every computer on the network: "Will the computer named Sales_Server please send me a message with your MAC address!"

This approach is fine when the desired computer is on the same physical LAN wire; in fact, it's great because it works without any configuration or additional servers. But when two LANs are separated by a slower wide area networking (WAN) link, NetBEUI's technique would require that the broadcast message be sent across the WAN. The WAN link would *have* to transmit every broadcast on every connected LAN to every other connected LAN to be sure that every computer could be found. Remember that WAN links were historically slow, on the order of 64Kbps, and with a few hundred computers sending a broadcast every minute or so, the WAN link would be fully occupied, carrying only broadcast messages and no useful data.

So, NetBEUI was a bad choice for networks with wide area links, and in fact, Microsoft has dropped support for NetBEUI in Windows XP as better ways have been developed.

Therefore, networks provide *name resolution* services that are used to map computers' names into their network addresses. Two distinct name resolution services can be involved in Windows networking: the Windows Internet Naming Service or WINS, which is used to look up Windows computers 'names, and the Domain Name Service or DNS, which is used for Windows computer names and for Internet hosts.

THE HOSTS FILE

For TCP/IP networking, before trying any network services to resolve computer names, Windows consults a file named `\windows\system32\drivers\etc\hosts`. If there is an entry in this file listing the desired computer name and listing an IP address, the listed address is used. Hosts file entries look something like this:

```
127.0.0.1     localhost              # self-test address
192.168.0.10  laserjet lj            # networked HP Laserjet
```

In the left hand column are IP addresses, followed by one or more names for the given address. The name "localhost" is always defined for the special address 127.0.0.1, which refers to your own computer. In this case I've added a definition for my networked HP Laserjet printer, which I can refer to as "laserjet" or "lj".

You can put entries in your computer's hosts file by editing it with Notepad. There are two good reasons to do so:

- If your network doesn't have a DNS server of its own, you can define entries for network devices that can't respond to any of the other name resolution services that I'll describe shortly. This includes printers, network routers, and so on. These devices *must* have fixed IP addresses, though; otherwise you'll have to constantly keep updating your hosts file.

- You can make entries for Web site names that you never want to actually contact, with a bogus IP address. For example, if you become irritated by Web pages that obtain banner ads and popup ads from a site named "www.annoyingads.net", the entry

  ```
  www.annoyingads.net    192.168.123.123
  ```

  will prevent Internet Explorer from ever being able to reach this host.

Even if you don't have a DNS server on your network, you don't need to use a hosts file to enter the names of the computers on your network, as Windows can automatically resolve these names by other means, as I'll explain shortly.

WINS

The *Windows Internet Naming Service*, or *WINS*, was introduced with Windows NT, which was the first Microsoft operating system that allowed Microsoft File Sharing to operate over the TCP/IP protocol. Windows users are used to using one-word names to identify computers, and networks can contain computers using NetBIOS and IPX/SPX as well as the TCP/IP protocol. Microsoft developed WINS as an integrated address resolution system. It learns the names of all the computers connected to each network connected to the server running WINS and makes these names available to TCP/IP-based computers on those networks. When a new computer appears on the network, the computer registers itself with the WINS server so that other computers can find it by name.

More importantly, WINS servers trade information across a WAN or the Internet, making name service available out of the reach of NetBEUI-based computers. The addition of WINS and TCP/IP to Microsoft networking made file sharing across a WAN a much more efficient operation, as it removed the requirement for bridging NetBEUI packets across a WAN link.

It works like this: A WINS server can respond to broadcasts ("Will a WINS server please tell me the address of the computer named Sales_Server?"), but on a large network, you can also tell Windows to direct its request to a specific WINS server at a particular IP address. This way, a TCP/IP-based client can find computers across a WAN link, through TCP/IP's capability to efficiently route directly addressed packets from network to network, without the need to send broadcast packets across the link as well.

16

> **TIP**
>
> Windows XP supports WINS, but it's no longer really necessary. When you use Windows 200x Server to manage the network, Windows can use the standard Internet-style DNS system to locate network resources.

DNS

Domain name service, or *DNS*, is the name resolution system used by all Internet-based software. The domain name service is a sort of distributed database system that looks up names such as www.quepublishing.com and returns IP addresses such as 198.70.146.70. It also provides *Inverse DNS* information, which tells you that IP address 63.69.110.193 is http://www.quepublishing.com.

You can use DNS-based naming with Microsoft Networking, too. For example, you can tell Windows Explorer to view \\server.mycompany.com. Windows tries the hosts file first. If no entry is found there, and a WINS server has been set up, it tries WINS. If WINS is not set up or doesn't recognize the name, Windows tries to resolve the name using DNS. If DNS fails, Windows broadcasts a request to the local LAN. If one of these methods succeeds, Windows can go ahead and use Microsoft File Sharing to connect to the computer.

> **CAUTION**
>
> I will warn you many times that you must somehow put up a barrier between the Internet access and Microsoft Networking on your computer, even if you only use a modem to connect to the Internet. When you're connected, your shared files are vulnerable to attack by hackers if you're not adequately prepared.

On Windows 200x Server-based networks, in fact, Microsoft is encouraging the use of DNS-like names (such as host.region.company.com) even inside a company's network, rather than the old-fashioned single-word computer names. Microsoft is making this use easier by tying the Windows 200x Server DNS service into the *Active Directory*, which identifies all of the network's computers, networks, users, and resources.

DNS was designed for the original 1970s Internet with its fairly static database; entering new computers and domains was time-consuming. The DNS server provided with Windows 200x Server, however, interacts with the Microsoft networking system on a dynamic basis to learn the names of computers as they plug into and leave the network. The DHCP service supplies IP address and name information to the DNS server, so that dynamically configured computers can appear in the DNS.

NAT (INTERNET CONNECTION SHARING)

Internet connections for a LAN can be made in either of two ways:

- Each computer on the network can have its own official, registered IP address, assigned by your ISP. The ISP sends data for all these IP addresses through your connection to your LAN.
- One connection and one public IP address can be used for all Internet traffic.

The first method can be costly—most ISPs charge a hefty extra fee to wire up a whole network, while single-access broadband and cable Internet service is fairly inexpensive. However the second idea has a technical problem: Since the Internet is based on TCP/IP networking that requires each computer to have its own IP address, which is used to route data to the correct computer, how does one create an Internet "party line"?

Windows XP's Internet Connection Sharing service and hardware connection sharing routers both use the same mechanism to solve this problem: It's called *Network Address Translation (NAT)*, *circuit proxying*, and also *IP Masquerading*. It works like the telephone receptionist in an office who answers every call from the outside and routes messages to each extension in the office.

NAT software running in a Windows XP computer or in a standalone hardware device allows your Internet connection to carry multiple conversations using just one IP address. NAT software carries on the conversations on your behalf, using the one public IP address (see Figure 16.6). NAT has some significant benefits and drawbacks.

The benefits of using NAT are as follows:

- You can use an inexpensive, single-user ISP account to provide Internet access for as many computers as you want.
- NAT conserves IP addresses, which are in short supply due to the worldwide growth of the Internet.
- NAT acts as a basic firewall, preventing hackers from probing your network. (Incoming data is simply discarded if it's not a direct reply to an outgoing request made by one of your computers.)

Figure 16.6
A NAT device or program carries on all Internet communications using one IP address. NAT keeps track of outgoing data from your LAN to determine where to send responses from the outside.

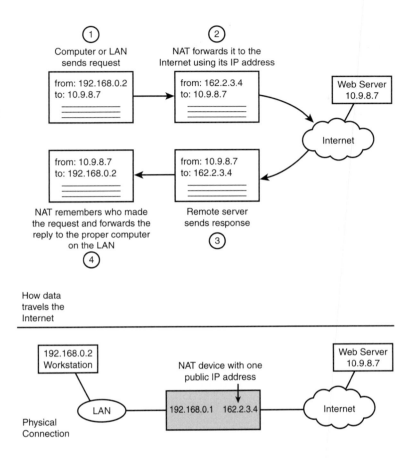

16

The drawbacks of using NAT are as follows:

- If you want to establish a public Web, FTP, or email server on your LAN, NAT has to be specially configured to direct incoming connection requests to the proper server on your network. Configuring NAT this way is not a big problem, but it means you can't have more than one public server of each type.

- NAT doesn't work with all network software. Some vendors' versions of NAT don't support RealAudio, Microsoft VPN software, or other protocols. NetMeeting audio and video and Windows Remote Assistance don't work with hardware NAT solutions, although they do work with Windows Internet Connection Sharing.

One significant drawback of Windows Internet Connection Sharing is that the computer with the connection must be powered up anytime anyone on the LAN wants Internet access. If you're sharing a modem connection, the computer has to remain logged in as well. If the computer with the connection is logged out or turned off, so is your connection.

As I mentioned, NAT software is built into inexpensive broadband connection sharing routers for DSL and cable Internet service, as well as the industrial strength routers used in enterprise networks. You can also buy external devices that will help share a dial-up connection. These hardware solutions cost between $30 and $300, and their cost is quickly recovered because you can use a less expensive single-IP address plan from your ISP.

BROWSER SERVICE (NETWORK NEIGHBORHOOD)

If you've used Windows 9x or Me, you're familiar with the "Network Neighborhood" display that shows the other active computers in your workgroup or domain. On Windows 2000 and XP, this display is reached from the My Network Places by clicking Display Entire Network or View Workgroup Computers. This display is made possible by a Windows networking service called the Browser service.

Here's how it works: One computer on the network is given the task of serving as the Browse Master: It's given the job of keeping track of all computers known to be up and running. When you open your Network Neighborhood or Entire Network display, Windows queries the Master Browser over the network, and with any luck the Master responds with the list of names that you ultimately see as icons on your screen.

It's a fascinating system, as the role of Master Browser is chosen by an election—all of the computers on the network decide which one is to get the job, with preference given to Windows 200x Servers, followed by NT servers, followed by Windows NT/2000/XP Professional workstations, followed by computers running Window 9x, and so on down the line.

Unfortunately, it's also a rather troublesome system. The display often comes up empty even when there are definitely other computers up and running on the network. The problem is that the Master Browser might get turned off unexpectedly, leaving the network without anyone who can supply this information; it can take about 20 minutes for the computers on the network to notice the disappearance and hold another election. Similarly, although each Windows computer is supposed to announce to the network that it has booted up or is about to shut down, sometimes the Master Browser misses the message, and its roster will be inaccurate.

The situation only gets worse when there are several network protocols in use, as elections and Browser services run independently for each network protocol (that is, for TCP/IP, NetBEUI, and SPX/IPX). Different computers can get the Browse Master job for each protocol. Unfortunately, when you ask for the Network Neighborhood display, you only see the result from the first Browser to answer your query, and so you may end up, again, seeing only a partial list.

Browser problems can be cured in any of several ways:

- *Use the same set of protocols in every computer on the network.* This will help ensure that the same computer gets the Master Browser job for all protocols together. Of course, if there is just one protocol installed, so much the better.

- If the display is inaccurate or empty, wait 20 minutes to see if it recovers. Sometimes you just have to wait for the system to notice that it's in trouble; if it does, it may fix itself.

- Reboot a Windows 2000 or XP computer; this may cause a new election and restore the browser service.

- Check the Event Log for messages saying that there are problems with your network adapter driver. Deleting and reinstalling the adapter from the Device Manager may fix the problem.

- Configure one computer that is always left on to be the designated master browser, and configure all other computers so that they will never offer to be browser masters. This is discussed in Chapter 17.

For more information about the Browser service, check out
www.microsoft.com/ntserver/techresources/commnet/browser/ntbrowser.asp.

ROAMING USER PROFILES

When your domain-network user account is set up to use a Roaming User Profile, Windows stores the *profile* on a network server. A profile is a folder that contains:

- Your Registry data, which contains personal preferences information such as desktop settings, email configuration, environment variables, network printer settings and drive mappings, and software preferences.

- Your My Documents, Desktop, and Start Menu folders, in most cases, although the domain administrator can designate that these will be kept on a network server rather than in your profile folder.

- Application-specific data such as the Outlook Express mailbox.

Normally, your user profile is kept in the \Documents and Settings folder, in a subfolder given your login name, optionally followed by the computer's name or the domain name of your account. Without a roaming profile, if you log on to two different computers, you will have two separate profiles, and documents stored in My Documents on one computer will not be available from the other.

If you have a domain user account with a roaming profile, when you log on, Windows will copy your profile folder from the domain network server to the computer that you happen to be using. Thus no matter which domain computer you use, you will see your usual desktop and settings. Your My Documents files will also be present, because they'll have been copied along with the profile folder, or because they're stored on a network folder that is reachable through the network.

When you log out, Windows uses its intelligent File Replication system to copy the changed files back to the domain server; new files you've created while working will also be copied back, and files you've deleted while working will be deleted on the server.

The next time you log on to a given computer, Windows will only have to update files that were modified elsewhere, thus if you use the same computer most of the time, the synchronization process will be fairly fast.

NOTE

Roaming User Profiles are only available when your Windows XP Professional computer is a member of a domain-type network. It's not available at all with Windows XP Home Edition.

ACTIVE DIRECTORY

We discussed the features and advantages of Active Directory earlier in the chapter. Here, I'll say a bit about how AD actually works.

Active Directory is tightly coupled with the Domain Name Service. DNS is used by member computers of an AD network to locate domain controllers and other network resources. On an AD network, Windows expects that it will be configured to refer to DNS servers can return records for the Windows domain name. It's a good fit, actually, as the DNS system was designed with goals very much in line with those of Active Directory: hierarchical trust relationships and distributed administration.

This reliance on DNS explains why, on an AD network, Windows domain names use the same naming hierarchy as the Internet: The company's primary domain might be named "mycompany.com", while subdivisions might be "eastern.mycompany.com" and "western.mycompany.com". A computer that is a member of the "western.mycompany.com" Windows domain will look to DNS to find server information using this domain name.

Information pointing to responsible domain servers is stored in SRV records in subzones of the master domain, and in each of divisional subdomains. For example, the master DNS zone `mycompany.com` will contain the zones listed in Table 16.6, each of which is populated with SRV records that point to domain controller directory servers that may be reached using the LDAP service over TCP:

TABLE 16.6   DNS SUBZONES USED BY ACTIVE DIRECTORY TO LOCATE DOMAIN CONTROLLERS

DNS Zone	SRV Records Locate
`_ldap._tcp.mycompany.com`	Domain Controllers (DCs)
`_ldap._tcp.SiteName._sites.mycompany.com`	DCs for designated geographic sites
`_ldap._tcp.pdc._ms-dcs.mycompany.com`	Primary domain controller of a mixed-mode (NT/AD) domain
`_ldap._tcp.gc._msdcs.mycompany.com`	Global Catalog server

DNS Zone	SRV Records Locate
`_ldap._tcp.`*SiteName*`._sites.gc.` `_msdcs.mycompany.com`	Global Catalog servers for specific sites
`_ldap._tcp.`*DomainGuid*`.domains._msdcs` `.mycompany.com`	Domain controllers, given the controller's GUID

Similar hierarchies exist for each of the divisional DNS subdomains, such as western.mycompany.com and eastern.mycompany.com. And within each of these domains, there are further subzones that use a comparable naming scheme to identify servers available via the UDP protocol, and to locate servers providing other services such as Kerberos authentication.

It's all quite complex, but the result is that the DNS system, which has over many years proven to be a robust, scalable distributed name resolution system, can be exploited to let AD network clients easily and efficiently locate appropriate nearby resources.

Once the servers are identified using DNS, the Active Directory system communicates directly with the located domain controller servers using the Lightweight Directory Access Protocol (LDAP). LDAP is the ultimate mechanism by which domain member computers query the domain for user and other resource information.

GROUP POLICY

There are many mentions of "Group Policy" in this book that speak to the ability of the network administrator to limit your ability to configure your computer. Of course, in a large organization this is a desirable thing, as it enforces uniformity and helps prevent self-inflicted configuration problems.

How does Group Policy actually work? It's actually rather straightforward. Most of Windows's configuration information is stored in the Registry, which is a sort of database system. The registry contains data organized in a hierarchical fashion much like the familiar file system of folders, subfolders, and files. Many Windows applications and system tools look to the registry not only for configuration information such as the name of the computer and its IP addresses, but also to determine what control panel applications and preference dialogs to permit you to use. A value can be stored in the registry that will prevent the Start menu from displaying the Run button, for instance.

Now, registry information is normally stored on your hard drive; machinewide settings are stored in files in `\windows\system32\config`, while user-specific settings are in each user's profile folder under `\Documents and Settings`. Stored on your computer, this is exposed and subject to potential alteration. So, when you log on to a Windows domain network, the domain controller computer can send a set of registry data—called *policy*—that *overrides* any settings stored in your computer. This information is automatically downloaded at each logon, and there's nothing you can do to override it. If, for instance, the policy data sent by the domain server contains the value that blocks the Run button, you don't get a Run button.

This sort of policy mechanism has been around on Windows domain networks for quite some time. However, it was cumbersome to set up, and difficult to administer.

The "Group" part of Group Policy comes as part of Active Directory. As I've said several times in this chapter, AD lets managers define information in a hierarchical fashion that matches the organizational structure of your enterprise. The innovation is that with AD, bits of policy information can be defined for each organizational unit and layer. When you log on, the AD domain server collects all the bits of policy that apply to the groups and organization units to which you belong.

Some policy settings might be defined for all members of the West Coast division, forcing the use of a particular mail server. Other policy settings might be applied if you're a member of the Accounting team: You might inherit from that the settings that automatically ensure that Excel and your accounting package are installed on your computer. The result, called the Resultant Set of Policy, is quite nicely custom-designed just for you, based on your needs and responsibility level.

DEMYSTIFYING "SIMPLE" FILE SHARING

Windows XP introduced a new network security model called Simple File Sharing. Before I explain this, I'll give you some background. In the original Windows NT/2000 workgroup network security model, when you attempted to use a shared network resource, Windows would see if your username and password matched an account on the remote computer. One of four things would happen:

- If the username and password exactly matched an account defined on the remote computer, you'd get that user's privileges on the remote machine for reading and writing files.

- If the username matched but the password didn't, you'd be prompted to enter the correct password.

- If the username didn't match any predefined account, or if you failed to supply the correct password, then you'd get the privileges accorded to the Guest account, if the Guest account was enabled.

- If the Guest account was disabled, and it usually was, you would be denied access.

The problem with this system is that it required you to create user accounts on each computer you wanted to reach over the network. Multiply, say, 5 users times 5 computers, and you had 25 user accounts to configure. What a pain! (People pay big bucks for a Windows Server-based domain network to eliminate just this hassle.) Because it was so much trouble, people usually would enable the Guest account.

The problem is that Guest is a member of the group Everyone, and usually Everyone has read/write or at least read privileges on the entire hard drive, and full privileges on FAT-formatted disks, which have no user-level security at all. This means the user account headache invited people to make their entire computers vulnerable to abuse over their LAN and the Internet.

Enter Simple File Sharing. On all Windows XP Home Edition computers, and as the default option on XP Professional, Simple File Sharing is enabled, and has the following effects:

- It treats anyone who attempts to use shared resources over the network as Guest. Network users are never prompted for a username and password; this information would simply be ignored if provided.

- The Guest account is enabled by default for network use. You can separately choose whether Guest can log on at your keyboard. This is disabled by default on both Home and Pro.

- If you check Allow Network Users to Change My Files, network users can read, write, rename, or delete the contents of the shared folder. If you don't check this option, network users can view but not modify the contents.

- When you share folders, Windows in most cases automatically applies the correct permissions to the shared folder so that Everyone (that is, Guest) can read and optionally write to the folder. For folders it knows aren't safe to share, it doesn't do this. For example, Windows removes Everyone from the permission lists for access to the Windows directory. This means that only authorized locally logged-on users can access the Windows directory.

- The Security properties tab that is normally used to assign per-user permissions to files and printers is not displayed.

16

This means that it's now very easy to set up shared files and folders for your LAN. You won't be called upon or able to select which individual users get access and which don't. If you share a folder, you share it with read-only or read/write access. It's very simple indeed, and it's perfectly appropriate for home and small office LANs. Microsoft's reasoning here is that it's better to configure a somewhat looser LAN *correctly* than a stricter LAN *poorly*. Of course, for stricter control, most corporations use Server-based networks.

There are two down sides to Simple File Sharing: First, and most important, it's crucial that you have a firewall in place. Otherwise, everyone on the Internet will have the same rights in your shared folders as you. That's one of the reasons for the Internet Connection Firewall, and why the Network Setup Wizard is so adamant about either installing the Firewall or disabling file sharing.

The second down side is less troublesome and probably less noticeable to most people: If you attempt to use a shared folder from another computer, even if you are using the Administrator account or your own username and password, you won't get the full rights that you'd have locally. You'll be a guest like anyone else.

On Windows XP Professional, if you want to use the old per-user permission scheme, you can disable Simple File Sharing. You'll have more control over permissions at the cost of lots more work in configuration.

NOTE

> Simple File Sharing applies only on a peer-to-peer workgroup network. Domain network users must live with the full, more complex security system.

NETWORK HARDWARE OPTIONS

As you know, a LAN consists of a group of computers connected together using some sort of electrical medium. The signals transmitted across a LAN are generated and interpreted by electronics in each computer. Some computers have built-in network interfaces; otherwise, each computer in a LAN needs a *network interface card*, or *NIC*. I also refer to them as network cards or network adapters.

These electrical signals have to be carried from computer to computer somehow. The original design for Ethernet used a *very* expensive 1/2-inch thick cable that could carry a 10Mbps Ethernet signal up to 500 meters. (It was named 10BASE5 for reasons that only make sense to an engineer.)

Today's network interface cards are designed to use one of several inexpensive varieties of network cabling, or use radio waves to avoid the need for wiring altogether. In the following sections, I'll list the various types of media you'll want to consider if you're building your own network.

ETHERNET

Ethernet was developed by Xerox, Intel, and Digital Equipment Corporation, and has grown so popular and common that you hardly need to use the word anymore: Most networks today are Ethernet networks using Unshielded Twisted Pair (UTP) cable.

UTP is so named because like-colored pairs of wires in the cable are gently twisted together for better immunity to electrical interference from fluorescent lights, radio signals, and so on. This inexpensive type of cable is also used for telephone connections, although the variety used for networking is of a higher quality, has more twists per inch, and is certified for its capability to carry high data rates. UTP cables are terminated with eight-wire RJ45 connectors, wider versions of the ubiquitous modular telephone connectors.

UTP cable quality is categorized by the highest data rate it was designed and certified to carry reliably. The most common cable types are shown in Table 16.7.

TABLE 16.7   UTP CABLE CATEGORIES

Designation	Highest Data Rate	Application
CAT-1	Less than 1Mbps	Telephone (voice)
CAT-2	4Mbps	IBM Token Ring

Designation	Highest Data Rate	Application
CAT-3	16Mbps	10Mbps Ethernet (10BASE-T)
CAT-4	20Mbps	16Mbps Token Ring
CAT-5	100Mbps	100Mbps Ethernet (100BASE-T), ATM, others
CAT-5E or -5x	250Mbps	Gigabit Ethernet* (1000BASE-T)
CAT-6	250Mbps	Gigabit Ethernet*

Gigabit Ethernet uses four pairs of wire each carrying 250Mbps

The thing to remember here is that you can't use just any old wiring you find in your walls to carry a network signal: You have to look for the appropriate "CAT-something" designation, which will be printed on the cable jacket every foot or so.

UTP cabling can be used for Token Ring networking as well, but is most commonly used for Ethernet. UTP Ethernet devices are connected to a central device called a *hub* in what is called a *star* network, as shown in Figure 16.7. (Alternatively, a router or switch can take the place of a hub.) If a cable in a star network fails, only the computer connected by that cable goes offline.

Figure 16.7
Unshielded twisted-pair network with a hub, forming a star pattern.

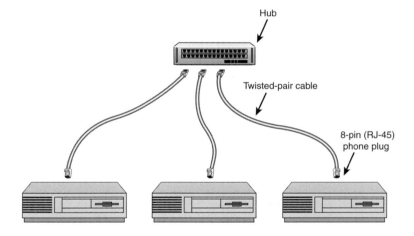

You can buy three varieties of UTP-based Ethernet hardware, denoted 10BASE-T, 10/100BASE-T, and 1000BASE-T in order of increasing speed. I'll discuss the 10BASE-T variety first.

10BASE-T

From the hint I dropped earlier, you might guess that the *10BASE* part means 10Mbps, but T? The T stands for twisted pair, and you just have to *know* that the maximum permitted cable length is 100 meters, or 330 feet.

The maximum cable distance from hub to computer of only 100 meters or 330 feet limits 10BASE-T's usefulness in a large building or campus LAN. Hubs can solve this problem by serving to connect several close-by computers. The hubs can then be connected to each either other with further lengths of UTP coaxial or fiber-optic cable, which forms a "backbone" connecting groups of computers, as shown in Figure 16.8.

Figure 16.8
In larger LANs, hubs are connected together to span larger distances. Hubs can be connected using UTP, ThinNet, or fiber-optic cabling.

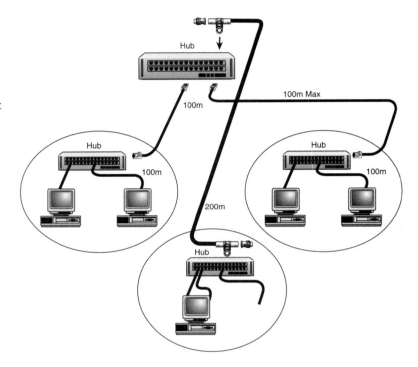

100BASE-T OR FAST ETHERNET

Fast Ethernet is a 100Mbps version of Ethernet over UTP cable. It is also called 100BASE-T or 100BASE-Tx. (The x stands for full-duplex, which means that a computer can both send and receive data simultaneously; this is standard with 100BASE-T networking hardware.)

The raw speed of 100Base-T hardware is (not surprisingly) 10 times faster than 10BASE-T hardware. In practice, it doesn't transfer data quite ten times as fast, but it's significantly better. On the other hand, the CAT-5 cable and connectors required to carry this high-speed signal are a *bit* more expensive and require more care in installation than CAT-3 cabling. 100Base-T hubs and network cards cost a bit more, as well.

However, the price difference between 10BASE-T and 100BASE-T equipment is so low these days that it doesn't make sense to buy new 10BASE-T parts now. Most new network cards work at either speed and are labeled 10/100 BASE-T. I recently purchased 10/100Base-T network adapters for $3 each. But even at $30, they'd be worth it.

TIP

> Hubs also come in 10/100 versions, and accept connections from either 10, 100, or 10/100 Base-T network adapters. If you're building a wired network, you want to buy a 10/100 hub, or switch, or a broadband Internet connection sharing router with a built-in 10/100 hub.

1000BASE-T OR GIGABIT ETHERNET

Gigabit Ethernet is a relatively new technology whose standards have not yet stabilized. Data is transmitted over all four pairs of wire in the cable (unlike 10 and 100Base-T which uses just two pairs), at 250Mbps per pair, half-duplex (one way at a time). It's expensive (now), but a tenfold increase in speed is nothing to sneeze at if you're involved in image processing or other such intensive communication work. It's also widely used for the backbones of large networks; that is, to connect hubs and switches that then connect to workstations with standard 10 or 100Base-T, and for fast server-to-server connections.

1000Base-T networking requires ultra-high quality Cat-5E or Cat-6 cabling and similarly rated connectors.

OPTICAL FIBER

Optical fiber is capable of gigabit (1000Mbps) and higher speeds and can also carry data over runs of several miles, quite a bit farther than standard UTP cable. Optical fiber is not generally run directly to individual computers, but between hubs and routers between buildings, to form the "backbone" of a campus network, as shown in Figure 16.9. Optical fiber cables can carry multiple 10 or 100Mbps Ethernet data signals, as well as more advanced, higher-speed data formats called *Fiber Distributed Data Interface (FDDI)* and *Asynchronous Transfer Mode (ATM)*.

Figure 16.9
Optical fiber cable linking two 100BASE-T hubs via a fiber "uplink" port. Cables contain pairs of fibers because each fiber can carry information in only one direction.

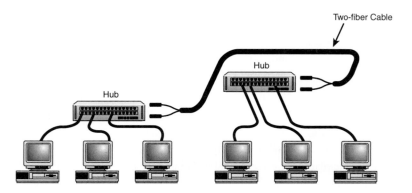

WIRELESS NETWORKING

With wireless network adapters, you can connect computers in a small area (such as a home or office) via radio signals, as illustrated in Figure 16.10. With modern equipment, the maximum data rate can range from 10 Mbps to 50 Mbps, depending on the type of equipment

16

you're using, although at distances of more than a few dozen feet the speed can fall to a tenth of that.

Equipment based on industry-wide wireless network hardware standards is available, and pricing is now very competitive with wired networking. You can get the equipment for under $75 per computer. With no wiring costs, and with minimal maintenance, wireless networking can be a good deal. For convenience, wireless can't be beat.

Figure 16.10
Wireless Access Point connecting computers to a standard twisted-pair network.

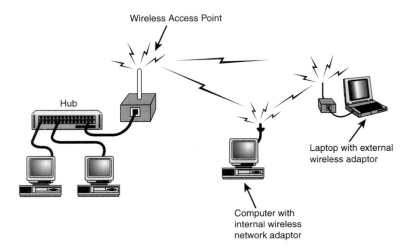

Wireless access is especially handy for users of laptop computers, Palm Pilots, and other mobile users who visit several offices in the course of a day. A device called an *access point* can be installed at each location to make the connection between wireless devices and a standard wired network or the Internet. Then, to quote Buckaroo Banzai, "Wherever you go, there you are." Several companies make inexpensive Internet connection sharing routers that include a wireless access point and ports for wired Ethernet connections, for under $200. Some even include a print server with a parallel printer port, so that you can connect a printer directly to the network.

Wireless technology has become so inexpensive that it's now the hip new thing in coffee shops. In fact, a certain big coffee chain from Seattle has installed wireless Internet access equipment in more than 2,000 of its outlets nationwide…they'll connect you to the Internet for a small hourly fee while you sip a latte! (Your humble authors would never set foot in one of these places, of course, preferring to patronize locally owned establishments and the original Peet's Coffee & Tea. But I digress.)

Windows XP contains built-in support for the extra security configuration required with Wireless networking; I'll discuss that in the Chapter 17.

As I mentioned, there are several standards for wireless equipment, offering different data rates and interoperating possibilities.

802.11B

The first widespread standard for wireless networking (also called Wi-Fi) was 802.11b, which delivers data at rates up to 11Mbps. Real-life data rates range from 1Mbps to 11Mbps. 802.11b equipment is almost ridiculously inexpensive and is available at almost every computer store. (If you want to buy wireless gear, shop around and wait for bargains to show up. Wireless is hot stuff these days, and loss-leader sales are common.)

802.11b equipment uses radio frequencies in the 2.4GHz band that are used by other sorts of consumer equipment as well, such as Bluetooth wireless devices and cordless phones. Unfortunately, this means that it's subject to interference by these consumer devices, and by some reports, microwave ovens.

I've found that 802.11b signals will reliably travel several hundred feet outdoors, if there are no obstructions—from my office, I can reliably link into a network in a house about a block away, with a line-of-sight view. Enterprising individuals have built interesting and possibly illegal highly directional antennas from potato chip and soup cans that can link networks several miles away; see for instance www.turnpoint.net/wireless/has.html. On the other hand, I've heard reports of signal problems between adjacent rooms of the same house, so, as they say, your mileage may vary.

N O T E

> 802.11b data rates are perfectly adequate for most Internet surfing; even cable modems rarely deliver Internet data at more than a few Mbps, and DSL service typically tops out at 1.5Mbps. As long as you're not trying to work 802.11b at its distance limits, the wireless link won't be a bottleneck for your Web surfing. However, the limited speed will be noticeable if you copy large files from computer to computer.

802.11B DOUBLE SPEED

Some manufacturers are producing 802.11b equipment with a rated speed of 22 Mbps; however this double-speed operation works, or is certified to work, only with other network adapters made by the same manufacturer. Otherwise, you get standard 11Mbps 802.11b operation.

If you're buying a bunch of gear at the same time, this may be a cheap way to double the potential data rate. Otherwise, if you're after speed, consider 802.11a or 802.11g.

802.11A

A higher-speed alternative for wireless networking is called 802.11a. This equipment transfers data at a maximum rate of 54Mbps on the 5GHz radio frequency band, so it's not susceptible to interference from Bluetooth devices and cordless telephones.

802.11a equipment is less common and more expensive than 802.11b, although the increase in price may be more than compensated for by the additional speed. Again, Internet traffic will typically be rate-limited by your ISP, not your wireless LAN, but 802.11a can definitely improve your server-to-computer or computer-to-computer transfer speed.

A downside to 802.11a is that since it uses a different frequency band, it cannot interoperate with 802.11b equipment. Some manufacturers sell dual-band equipment, but as you might guess, it's about twice as expensive as straightforward 802.11b or 802.11a equipment. However, there is yet another contender that may render this a moot issue....

802.11G

A promising new breed of wireless equipment is appearing that will offer 802.11a's speed (54Mbps maximum) on the 2.4GHZ radio band. 802.11g has the big advantage that it can interoperate with 802.11b equipment, so a "g" adapter or access point can work with both b- and g-compliant equipment at the same time. You get 11Mbps transfers when connecting to 802.11b computers or access points, and 54Mbps with other "g" devices. However, the hardware must be able to find a channel unused by 11Mbps equipment in order to achieve 54Mbps operation, so in the enterprise, 802.11a may prove to be the more realistic option when higher speeds are required.

Apple computer's new "AirPort Extreme" access point could be called an example of an 802.11g device, but for one thing, at the time this book was written, the standard was not yet finalized, so there is a possibility that equipment manufactured before the standard is ratified will not be compatible with future, standard-compliant gear.

When 802.11g is finalized—and it may well be by the time you read this—it will be the standard of choice for home and small office wireless networks.

> **TIP**
>
> Whichever type of equipment you choose, be *sure* to get equipment that is certified as meeting the requirements of one of the official wireless standards, so that you can be sure that your equipment will work correctly if you mix in hardware made by another manufacturer, or if you take your computer to a network based on another vendor's hardware.

WIRELESS NETWORKING TERMINOLOGY

Wireless networking comes with a whole slew of new acronyms and concepts. Table 16.8 lists the ones you're most likely to encounter.

TABLE 16.8   WIRELESS NETWORKING TERMS AND ACRONYMS

Term	Meaning
WEP	Wired Equivalence Privacy—An encryption technology whose name is meant to lull you into thinking that your data, which is radiating out in a 200 foot radius around your computer, is secure. It's nowhere near that good, but unless you're working on something of interest to spies and government agents, it's probably good enough.
Wi-Fi	Wireless Fidelity—A popular term for the 802.11b wireless networking standard.

Term	Meaning
SSID	Server Set Identifier—A name given to a set of wireless networking access points or wireless-linked computers. The SSID is used to select the appropriate network to which to connect when more than one is available at the same time.
Ad Hoc Network	A wireless network composed only of individual computers that communicate with each other in peer-to-peer fashion.
Infrastructure Network	A wireless network that contains one or more access points. Computers on an Infrastructure network communicate only through the access point(s).
Network Key	A password or number whose binary representation is used as the basis of the encryption key used by the WEP security system. In most cases, the Network Key must be manually entered into every computer and access point in a given wireless network. On some corporate networks, the key can be distributed automatically via the network.
War Driving	The practice of locating and exploiting unsecured Wi-Fi networks to gain free Internet access.
Warchalking	Drawings chalked onto the sidewalk in front of homes and offices with unsecured Wi-Fi networks, to indicate the availability of free networking to any random passerby. (See www.warchalking.org.)

Further distinctions are made with regard to the length of (the number of bits in) the encryption key used in WEP security. You will see the numbers 40, 64, 104, 128, 152, and 256 mentioned. More bits signifies a greater level of security, as each additional bit doubles the number of possible encryption keys, and hence doubles the amount of work a cracker should have to perform (on average) to break the system.

However, these numbers actually refer to just four levels of encryption. The reason is that WEP combines the configured Network Key, which is either 40, 104, 128, or 232 bits in length, with an additional 24 bits that vary with each data packet, but which are not secret. Thus, the lower number indicates the actual level of security provided by WEP.

It has been demonstrated that WEP is fairly easy to crack (see, for example, www.cs.umd.edu/~waa/wireless.pdf), hence if the KGB, the NSA, or your corporate competitors are after you, you should always use the highest security level supported by your hardware.

The Network Key that provides the basis of the encryption key can be specified as an alphanumeric phrase (using any of the keys and symbols on your keyboard), or as a series of hexadecimal digits (using the digits 0 through 9 and the letters A through F). Alphanumeric characters supply 8 bits each, while hexadecimal digits four each, so the pass phrase must fit in one of the forms listed in Table 16.9.

16

TABLE 16.9 NETWORK KEY FORMAT REQUIRED FOR VARIOUS WEP ENCRYPTION LEVELS

"Advertised" Encryption Level in Bits	Actual # of Bits	Alphanumeric Characters Required	Hexadecimal Digits Required
40	40	5	10
64	40	5	10
104	104	13	26
128	104	13	26
152	*128	16	32
256	*232	29	58

*The built-in WEP drivers provided with Windows XP support only 40 and 104-bit security; add-on drivers provided by equipment vendors may be able to provide 128 or 232-bit security.

For example, for a 104-bit Network Key you could use something like 6oS/RT3:^ImY5 (alphanumeric format) or F54DF488F230AC591DBB0572FB (hexadecimal format).

When making up a key for your own network, it's best if you generate the characters or digits randomly; if there is any predictability in your choice of a key (for example, if you use lowercase letters only), you lose randomness, and hence make for an easier cracking target. You can find Web sites that will help you generate truly random keys, if you want the added security. See, for instance, www.warewolf.net/portfolio/programming/wepskg/wepskg.html.

NOTE

> You can enter a key in either alphanumeric or hexadecimal format when configuring a Wireless connection in Windows. Windows uses the length of the key (5, 10, 13, or 26 characters) to infer the format. To configure access points and wireless routers, consult the manufacturer's instructions; the techniques vary.

OTHER NETWORK TYPES

There are several other networking technologies that you may encounter in business settings. They are either too old or too slow to consider installing now, or are esoteric enough that they are found mainly in telephone companies and corporate data centers. In either case it's not worth our discussing their merits and pitfalls in detail. These technologies include the following:

- **Phoneline Networking (HomePNA)**—HomePNA Networking sends data via radio signals through standard telephone lines. HomePNA network adapters can achieve speeds of up to 10Mbps and at one time was promoted for household networks. However, its appeal has faded now that the cost of wireless networking hardware has plummeted to the same range as HomePNA. Also, HomePNA networks require that the same telephone extension be run to each location where you want to place a networked computer. If you have these telephone lines and jacks in place, HomePNA networking might be a reasonable choice, but if you have to run new wires, you might as well run Ethernet cables to get ten times the data rate, or spend the same amount of money on hardware and set up a wireless network.

- **Powerline Networking**—Powerline networks send data on radio signals carried by—you guessed it—your home or office's power lines; the adapters plug into your wall sockets. Powerline networking was another promising home networking technology done in by the falling costs of Wireless and Ethernet hardware.

- **ThinNet Ethernet**—Thin Ethernet uses coaxial cable similar to television cable. It is also called 10BASE2 Ethernet, which indicates that the network runs at 10Mbps and has a maximum wiring length of 200 meters, or 660 feet. Thin Ethernet cables end in distinctive twist-on connectors called bayonet connectors, or BNC. Some coaxial cable is still around, but it's never used for new network installations, having been supplanted by the much less-expensive twisted-pair system.

- **Token Ring**—Developed by IBM and still used in businesses that are "blue" to the core, Token Ring is rarely installed now because it's slower and much more expensive than Ethernet.

- **ATM**—Asynchronous Transfer Mode or ATM is a network transport technology that is used widely in the telecommunications industry. One of its notable attributes is that it is well-suited for simultaneously carrying both voice and video traffic—which requires dedicated bandwidth and a stable end-to-end transfer time or *latency*—and network data, which tends to be "bursty" and can tolerate randomness in the transport time. It can carry point-to-point data connections as well as support many-to-many networks like the Internet.

BRIDGED NETWORKS

Windows XP has built-in support for creating *bridged* networks. Bridging is the process of retransmitting network traffic between two different network segments that may be (but don't have to be) based on different physical media; for example, between a wired Ethernet LAN and a wireless network. Figure 16.11 illustrates how bridging works. On a bridged network, both networks share a common set of IP addresses. Data broadcast on one network segment is simply repeated onto the other. A single DHCP server and Internet connection on either network can serve computers on both networks.

By default, when you install two different network adapters on Windows XP, Windows will ask you if you wish to bridge the networks. You can also choose to create a bridge from the Task list on the Network Connections menu. This can be used to save the expense of buying a wireless network access point; if you install both a wired Ethernet adapter and a Wireless network adapter in one of your Windows XP computers, you can bridge the two networks with Windows XP. This can be used not only to share files and printers between wired and wireless computers, but also to share an Internet connection made on one of the two networks.

Figure 16.11
Example of a bridged network.

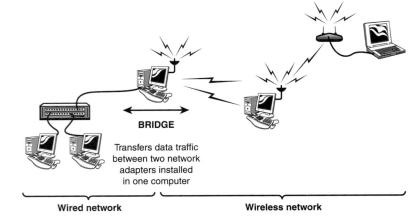

BRIDGE

Transfers data traffic between two network adapters installed in one computer

Wired network   Wireless network

However, if you use Windows to create a bridge, in order for computers on the bridged segments to communicate, the computer must be left on all the time; this is a disadvantage if you're concerned about conserving power. Alternately, bridging can be accomplished by small hardware devices such as wireless access points and network hubs that sport both UTP and coaxial cable connections.

CHAPTER 7

BUILDING YOUR OWN NETWORK

YOU DO NEED A NETWORK

If you have two or more computers and you don't already have a network, you need one—it's about that simple. A network offers many advantages, including

- The ability to share a single Internet connection; this is an especially big win if you use a broadband DSL or cable Internet service.

- Sharing of files and printers, so that you can get at your data and use any of your printers from any of your computers.

- The ability to quickly transfer files from one computer to another; this can help you move from an old to a new computer, and can also serve as the basis of a simple but effective backup scheme.

- Two words: *multi-user games*. (Or is that three words?)

In this chapter, we'll discuss how to construct and configure a network based on Windows XP. In addition, we'll show you how to add computers, adapters, and network services to an existing network.

Modern network hardware is a snap to install and set up. It's not expensive either—if you have only a few Windows computers, you can construct a network for as little as $25 per computer. All it takes is a bit of planning, and some careful shopping.

NOTE

> Chapter 8, "Configuring Your Internet Connection," shows how to use Internet Connection Sharing to let a single dial-up or broadband connection serve all of the computers on your LAN. It also shows how to share a connection with a small hardware device called a connection sharing router. There are many of these devices on the market today, most designed to share a broadband connection, although some work with an analog or ISDN modem to share a dial-up connection. If you want to use a shared Internet connection, read Chapter 8 as well as this chapter (the Internet Connection Sharing feature is not available in the 64-bit versions of Windows XP).

The first decision you have to make is what kind of network to install. As I discussed in the previous chapter, there are three types of Windows XP networks: the Workgroup network, which provides basic services for the home or small office; the Domain network, which is better suited for larger or spread-out organizations; and the Active Directory network, which is used in large enterprises and which allows very detailed control and delegation of management responsibilities.

If you decide that you need a Domain or Active Directory type network, you'll need to install Windows 2003 Server, 2000 Server, or NT Server. These Server operating systems are complex and covering them takes several entire books, so we can't go into the details of building this sort of network. Later in the chapter, though, we will show you how to configure Windows XP Professional if you are adding it to an existing Domain or Active Directory network.

NOTE

> In a corporate environment, you probably won't have to handle network setup yourself at all—your IT department will likely take care of all of this for you. In fact, on a tightly secured network, you might not even be able to view or change any of the network settings or control panels described in this chapter. If this is the case in your workplace, you can skip ahead to Chapter 18, "Using the Network."

However, if you want to build a Workgroup-type network for your home or office, read on. In this chapter, we'll show how to install and configure a network of two to ten computers.

PLANNING YOUR NETWORK

Some advance planning will go a long way toward making your network installation easier, and more likely to succeed. Some questions that you need to answer before you start are

- What type of networking hardware do you want to use: standard wired Ethernet, Wireless, power-line, or phone line? This will determine what sort of hardware you need to buy.

- If you plan on sharing a broadband Internet connection, do you want to use a hardware sharing router, or Windows Internet Connection Sharing? In the former case, you can get a connection sharing router with a built-in hub or wireless access point, so you don't need to buy one of these separately. In the latter case, you'll need two network adapters in the computer that will share the connection.

- Where do you want to locate your computers? If you're using a wired network, you'll have to decide how to route the network cables, and whether to lay down pre-built cables or use custom-installed wiring. If you're using wireless networking, you need to be sure that the signal will reach all of your computers. You may need to install and wire together one or more access points if your computers are widely spread out.

- Do you want to operate a Web server (or other type of server) that is to be accessible to the Internet? If so, you'll need to arrange for a *static* IP address and domain name hosting services from your Internet service provider. In addition, you'll need to configure your network so that service requests arriving over the Internet will be directed to the computer that is running the server software.

- Do you want to do the work yourself, or hire a consultant to do the work? In a business setting, it's especially worth considering hiring an expert not only to set your network up but to provide ongoing support.

17

Instant Networking

If your goal is to share printers, files, and maybe an Internet connection between a few computers that are fairly close together, and you don't want to make any decisions, here's a recipe for instant networking. Get the following items at your local computer store, or at an online shop like www.buy.com.

continues

continued

- For each computer that doesn't already have an Ethernet adapter built-in, you'll need to buy one 10/100BASE-T Ethernet adapter. These cost about $10 for internal PCI cards, and about $30 for PCMCIA (PC Card) or USB adapters. The buy.com categories are Computers-Networking-NIC Cards, PC Cards, or USB Networks. Choose one of the featured or sale items.

- A 10/100BASE-T dual-speed switch or hub with four or more ports—about $30—*or*, if you want to share an Internet connection, a DSL/Cable-sharing or a dial-up gateway router with a built-in four switch/hub— $40–100. (The buy.com categories are Computers-Networking-Hubs or Cable/DSL.)

  A switch, by the way, is a hub on steroids: While a hub simply repeats data transmitted by any one computer to all of the others, a switch tries to send the data on only to the computer to which it's addressed. It can thus pass several independent "conversations" at the same time, increasing overall network throughput. For a home or small office network, though, it's rare that this will make a big difference in performance.

  You'll also see that all modern network adapters and hubs indicate that they are capable of "full duplex" operation. This means that the equipment can send and receive data at the same time, at full speed in each direction.

- One CAT-5 patch cable for each computer. You'll place the hub next to one of your computers, so for that one you need only a short cable. The other cables need to be long enough to reach from the other computers to the hub. Pricing varies, but at the time I'm writing this, a 5-pack of 15-foot cables is selling for $17. (The buy.com category is Computers-Accessories-Cables.)

When you have these parts, skip ahead to the "Installing Network Adapters" section later in this chapter. By the way: I'm not getting a kickback from buy.com! I've just found that buying from them is a no-brainer. Their prices are low enough that it's hardly worth the time to shop around, and more importantly, their service is ultra-reliable and fast.

Let's discuss these decisions in a bit more detail.

CHOOSING A NETWORK AND CABLING SYSTEM

For a simple home or small office network, there are four reasonable network hardware alternatives:

- 10BASE-T Ethernet over unshielded twisted pair (UTP) wiring
- 100BASE-T or Fast Ethernet, over high-quality CAT-5 UTP Ethernet wiring
- Wireless networking using radio signals transmitted through antennas or carried through your telephone wiring
- Phone-line networking, which sends radio signals over the same wiring used by your telephones

Today, there is virtually no price difference between 10BASE-T and dual-speed 10/100BASE-T equipment, so it's easy to eliminate the slower 10BASE-T option from consideration.

The choice, then, is between wired 100BASE-T Ethernet, wireless, phone-line, and power-line networking. You might consider the following points in making your decision:

- Phone-line networking requires that you have a telephone jack next to each computer that you want to connect, and the jacks must all carry the same telephone extension. If you have this in place now, phone-line networking is a decent option. On the other hand, if you'd have to have one or more new phone jacks installed, you might as well spend the same money running wired Ethernet cables.

- The newest generation of "HomePlug" power-line networking supports an adequate 14Mbps maximum transfer rate and requires no additional cabling, as long as all of your home or office's power outlets are served by the same utility transformer. You can't roam about with power-line networking, but you don't have to worry about signal fade-out. HomePlug network adapters are about as expensive as wireless adapters.

- Wired Ethernet is the cheapest option, and it also provides the fastest data transfers. If you're going to copy a lot of data across your network, this is a big plus. On the other hand, if you're primarily adding a network to share your Internet connection, *any* of these network technologies will do.

- Wireless networking costs a bit more but saves the hassle of running cables. It works best if your computers are within, say, 50 feet of each other indoors, or 150 feet if separated by open space. If you choose wireless networking, you'll have to choose one of the three technologies currently in use: 802.11b, 802.11a, or 802.11g; the numbers refer to compatibility standards published by the Institute of Electrical and Electronics Engineers International (IEEE). See Chapter 16, "Introduction to XP Networking," for a discussion of these options.

You can also use a combination of these technologies in the same network. For example, you might use a wired network to attach several computers in close proximity, and add a wireless access point to extend your network to other areas of your home or office.

If you are only creating a network that will connect two computers so that you can perform some one-time file transfers, there are a few of other options you may want to consider:

- If your computers are both running Windows XP and both have FireWire adapters, you can simply connect the two computers with a "6-6" FireWire cable.

- If both computers have Ethernet adapters, you can connect the two adapters together directly, without using a hub, with what's called an Ethernet *crossover* cable.

- You can buy a parallel printer cable or serial data cable to use with Windows "Direct Cable Connection." This can cost as much as adding network hardware, but you still may want to check out Chapter 19, "Windows Unplugged: Remote and Portable Computing," for a discussion of this option.

For a one-time transfer, these techniques can save you the trouble of setting up a full-scale network.

INSTALLING NETWORK ADAPTERS

I've made this point before, but it's worth repeating: Before you purchase a network card, be sure to check the Windows XP Hardware Compatibility List (HCL). You should purchase cards that appear on the HCL or that are marked by the manufacturer certifying their compatibility with Windows XP or 2000. You can find the HCL at

`http://www.microsoft.com/hcl`.

CHECKING EXISTING ADAPTERS

If your adapter was already installed when you set up Windows XP, it may already be ready to go, in which case you can skip this section and jump down to "Installing Network Wiring." Follow these steps to see whether the adapter is already set up:

1. Right-click My Computer and select Manage.

2. Select Device Manager in the left pane, and open the Network Adapters list in the right pane.

3. Look for an entry for your network card. If it appears and does not have a yellow exclamation point (!) icon to the left of its name, the card is installed and correctly configured. In this case, you can skip ahead to "Installing Network Wiring."

   If an entry appears but has an exclamation point icon by its name, the card is not correctly installed and you'll have to fix this before proceeding. Most likely the problem is that no driver software was installed. See Chapter 27, "Installing, Removing, and Managing Hardware Devices," for more information on fixing this sort of problem.

4. If no entry exists for the card, the adapter is not fully plugged into the motherboard, it's broken, or it is not plug and play capable. Be sure the card is installed correctly. If the card is broken or non–plug-and-play, you should replace it; they're *very* inexpensive.

When you've confirmed that your existing adapter is functioning correctly, you can proceed to the section titled, "Installing Network Wiring."

INSTALLING A NEW NETWORK ADAPTER

If you're installing a new network adapter, follow the manufacturer's instructions for installing with Windows XP or Windows 2000. Even if it does not come with specific Windows XP instructions, the installation should be a snap. Just follow these steps:

1. If you have purchased an internal card, shut down Windows, shut off the computer, unplug it, open the case, install the card in an empty slot, close the case, and restart Windows.

If you've never worked inside your computer, **see** "Installing Hardware Devices," **p. 1107**.

   If you are adding a PCMCIA or USB adapter, be sure you're logged on with a "Computer Administrator" type account, and then just plug it in while Windows is running.

If you're using your computer's IEEE-1394 port, there's nothing to install or configure.

2. When you're back at the Windows login screen, log in as a Computer Administrator user. Windows displays the New Hardware Detected dialog when you log in.

3. The New Hardware Detected dialog might instruct you to insert your Windows XP CD-ROM. If Windows cannot find a suitable driver for your adapter from this CD, it may ask you to insert a driver disk that your network card's manufacturer should have provided (either a CD-ROM or floppy disk).

   If you are asked, insert the manufacturer's disk and click OK. If Windows says that it cannot locate an appropriate device driver, try again, and this time click the Browse button. Locate a folder named WinXP, WindowsXP, Windows2000, W2K, or NT5 (or some variation on these themes) on the CD or floppy, and click OK.

4. After Windows has installed the card's driver software, it automatically configures and uses the card. Check the Device Manager as described previously under "Checking Existing Adapters" to see whether the card is installed and functioning. Then you can proceed to "Installing Network Wiring" later in this chapter.

INSTALLING MULTIPLE NETWORK ADAPTERS

You might want to install multiple network adapters in your computer if one of the following applies:

- You simultaneously connect to two or more different networks with different IP addresses or protocols. You'd use a separate adapter to connect to each network.

- You want to share a broadband cable or DSL Internet connection with your LAN without using a hardware sharing router. I prefer the hardware solution, as I'll discuss later in this chapter, but you can do it using one adapter to connect to your LAN and another to connect to your cable or DSL modem.

- You have two different network types, such as wireless and wired Ethernet, or Phoneline and Ethernet, and want the computers on both LAN types to be able to communicate. You could use a hardware access point, but you could also install both types of adapters in one of your computers, and use the Bridging feature to connect the networks. I'll discuss bridging later in this chapter.

I suggest that you use the following procedure to install multiple adapters:

1. Install and configure the first adapter. If you're doing this to share an Internet connection, install and configure the one you'll use for the Internet connection first.

2. Click Start, Control Panel, Network and Internet Connections (if using category view), Network Connections. Select the icon named Local Area Connection and choose Rename This Connection in Network Tasks. Change the connection's name to something that indicates what it's used for, such as "Connection to Cable Modem" or "Office Ethernet Network."

3. Write the connection name on a piece of tape or a sticky label and apply it to the back of your computer above the network adapter, or on the edge plate of the adapter itself.

4. Shut down Windows and install the second adapter. Configure it and repeat steps 2 and 3 with the new Local Area Connection icon. Name this connection appropriately, for example, "LAN" or "Wireless Net", and put a tape or paper label on the computer, too.

If you follow these steps, you'll be easily able to distinguish the two connections, instead of having to remember which "Local Area Connection" icon is which.

Later in this chapter, I'll discuss how to configure Windows networking to use both of your adapters, under "Setting Up a Routed Network and "Setting Up a Bridged Network."

CAUTION

> Microsoft recommends that you do *not* install multiple network adapters in a computer that is a domain controller or master browser, unless you are bridging the adapters. Master browsers with multiple interfaces wreak havoc on the browser service.
>
> So, if you install multiple unbridged adapters in your computer, you should set the registry entry `MaintainServerList` to No, as described later in this chapter under "Designating a Master Browser," *page 665*.

INSTALLING NETWORK WIRING

When your network adapters are installed, the next step is to get your computers connected together. Installing the wiring can be the most difficult task of setting up a network. How you proceed depends on the type of networking adapters you have:

- If you're using wireless adapters, of course you don't have to worry about wiring at all. Just follow the manufacturer's instructions for configuring the wireless network adapters.

- If you're using phone-line networking, plug a standard modular telephone cable into each phone-line network adapter and connect them to the appropriate wall jacks. The adapter must be plugged directly into the wall jack, and then additional devices such as modems, telephones, and answering machines can be connected to the adapter.

- If you're using power-line networking, plug the adapters into wall sockets near your computers.

- If you're using IEEE-1394 networking, buy certified IEEE-1394 cables and plug your computers together as shown in Figure 17.1.

If you're using any of these three network types, make the connections and skip ahead to the "Configuring a Workgroup Network" or "Joining an Existing Network" section.

Otherwise, you're using UTP 10BASE-T or 10/100BASE-T Ethernet adapters and you have to decide how to route your wiring and what type of cables to use. The remainder of this section discusses UTP wiring.

Figure 17.1
Computers networked with IEEE-1394 (FireWire) can be connected in any convenient way. The maximum cable length of 15 feet limits the usefulness of 1394 for networking, however.

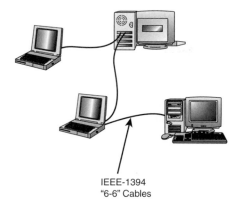

IEEE-1394
"6-6" Cables

If your computers are close together, you can use pre-built *patch cables* to connect your computers to a hub. (The term patch cable originated in the telephone industry—in the old days, switchboard operators used patch cables to temporarily connect, or patch, one phone circuit to another. In networking, the term refers to cables that are simply plugged in and not permanently wired.) You can run these cables through the habitable area of your home or office by routing them behind furniture, around partitions, and so on. Just don't put them where they'll be crushed, walked on, tripped over, or run over by desk chair wheels—this not only constitutes a safety hazard; it can cause network problems.

If the cables need to run through walls or stretch long distances, you should consider having them installed inside the walls with plug-in jacks, just like your telephone wiring. I'll discuss this later in this section. Hardware stores sell special cable covers you can use if you need to run a cable where it's exposed to foot traffic, as well as covers for wires that need to run up walls or over doorways.

GENERAL CABLING TIPS

You can determine how much cable you need by measuring the distance between computers and your hub location(s). Remember to account for vertical distances, too, where cables run from the floor up to a desktop, or go up and over a partition or wall.

CAUTION

> If you have to run cables through the ceiling space of an office building, you should check with your building management to see whether the ceiling is listed as a *plenum* or air-conditioning air return. You may be required by law to use certified *plenum cable* and follow all applicable electrical codes. Plenum cable is specially formulated not to emit toxic smoke in a fire.

Keep in mind the following points:

- Existing telephone wiring usually won't work. If the wires are red, green, black, and yellow: no way. The cable must have color-matched twisted pairs of wires, each with one wire in a solid color and the other white with colored stripes. Unless the cable jacket is clearly marked "CAT-5," "CAT-5E," or "CAT-6," don't use it. Install new wiring.

■ You *must* use CAT-5 quality wiring and components throughout: cables, RJ-45 jacks, RJ-45 plugs, terminal blocks, patch cables, and so on.

■ If you're installing in-wall wiring, follow professional CAT-5 wiring practices throughout. Be sure not to untwist more than half an inch of any pair of wires when attaching cables to connectors. Don't solder or splice the wires.

■ When you're installing cables, be gentle. Don't pull, kink, or stretch them. Don't bend them sharply around corners; you should allow at least a one-inch radius for bends. And don't staple or crimp them. To attach cables to a wall or baseboard, use rigid cable clips that don't squeeze the cable, as shown in Figure 17.2. Your local electronics store can sell you the right kind of clips.

Figure 17.2
Use rigid cable clips or staples that don't squeeze the cable if you nail it to a wall or baseboard.

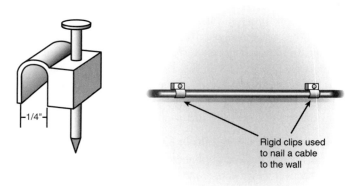

Rigid clips used to nail a cable to the wall

■ Keep network cables away from AC power wiring and away from electrically noisy devices such as fluorescent lamps, arc welders, diathermy machines, and the like.

NOTE

If you really want to get into the nuts and bolts, so to speak, of pulling your own cable, a good starting point is Que's *Practical Network Cabling*, which will help you roll up your shirtsleeves and get dirty (literally, if you have to crawl around through your attic or wrestle with dust bunnies under too many desks at the office).

WIRING WITH PATCH CABLES

If your computers are close together and you can simply run prefabricated cables between your computers and hub, you've got it made! Buy CAT-5 cables of the appropriate length online or at your local computer store. Just plug (click!), and you're finished. Figure 17.3 shows how to connect your computers to the hub.

Figure 17.3
In a UTP Ethernet network, each computer is connected to a hub or switch.

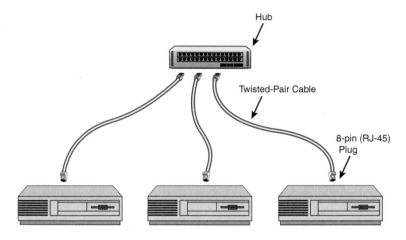

If you have the desire and patience, you can build custom-length cables from crimp-on connectors and bulk cable stock. Making your own cables requires about $75 worth of tools, though, so it's only sensible to do so if you have many cables to make, or if you need to run cables through holes that the pre-built cables' connectors won't fit through. Factory-assembled cables are also more reliable than homemade ones because the connectors are attached by machine.

For the ambitious or parsimonious reader, Figure 17.4 shows how to order the wires in the connector.

Figure 17.4
Standard wiring order for UTP Ethernet network cables.

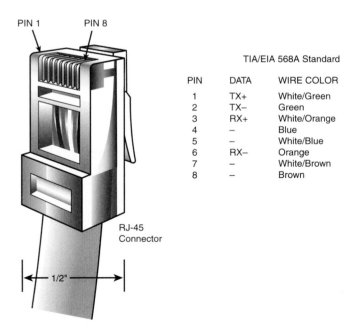

TIA/EIA 568A Standard

PIN	DATA	WIRE COLOR
1	TX+	White/Green
2	TX–	Green
3	RX+	White/Orange
4	–	Blue
5	–	White/Blue
6	RX–	Orange
7	–	White/Brown
8	–	Brown

N O T E

> Be sure to check out the Brainsville CD included with this book. In one of the lessons, I'll show you how to do this.

You might guess (correctly) that it really doesn't matter which pair of wires you use to connect pins 1 and 2 at each end of the cable, as long as pin 1 goes to pin 1, pin 2 goes to pin 2, and the wires that carry these two signals are twisted together. However, the color codes do matter if you're using wall-jack connectors or patch panels, for two reasons. First, jacks are often labeled with colors instead of pin numbers. Second, telecommunications professionals are used to seeing the wires in a particular order, and in fact there is an industry standard known as "586A" that specifies the color coding shown in Figure 17.4. It's best to stick with the standard.

T I P

> If you buy wall jacks or patch panels, it's best to use all "568A" hardware so that the color code-to-pin correspondence is consistent throughout your network.

INSTALLING IN-WALL WIRING

In-wall wiring is the most professional and permanent way to go. However, this often involves climbing around in the attic or under a building, drilling through walls, or working in an office telephone closet. If this is the case, calling in a professional is probably best. Personally, I find it a frustrating task and one I would rather watch someone else do while I sip coffee and eat pastries. Hiring someone to get the job done might cost $30 to $75 per computer, but you'll get a professional job, and if you consider that the price of network cards has gone down at least this much in the last few years, you can pretend that you're getting the wiring thrown in for free.

T I P

> Look in the yellow pages under Telephone Wiring, and ask the contractors you call whether they have experience with network wiring. The following are some points to check out when you shop for a wiring contractor:
>
> - Ask for references, and check them out.
> - Ask for billing details up front: Do they charge by the hour or at a fixed rate? Do they sell equipment themselves, or do you have to supply cables, connectors, and so on?
> - Ask for prices for parts and labor separately so that you know whether you're getting a good deal and can comparison-shop.
> - Find out what their guaranteed response time is, should problems or failures occur in the future.
> - Ask what the warranty terms are. How long are parts and labor covered?

In-wall wiring is brought out to special network-style modular jacks mounted to the baseboard of your wall. These RJ-45 jacks look like telephone modular jacks but are wider.

You'll need patch cables to connect the jacks to your computers and hub, as shown in Figure 17.5.

Figure 17.5
Connect your computers and hub to the network jacks using short patch cables.

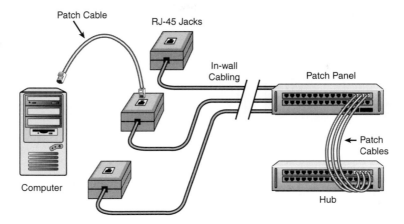

Patch Cable

RJ-45 Jacks

In-wall Cabling

Patch Panel

Patch Cables

Computer

Hub

OUT OF THE (PHONE) CLOSET

If you're wiring an office, running all your network wiring alongside the office's phone system wiring to a central location may be most sensible. You might be able to put your hub near the phone equipment in this case.

But this might require you to enter the phone closet for the first time. In most office buildings, telephone and data wiring are run to a central location on each floor or in each office suite. Connector blocks called *punchdown blocks* are bolted to the wall, where your individual telephone extension wires are joined to thick distribution cables maintained by the phone company or the building management.

These commercial wiring systems are a little bit daunting, and if you aren't familiar with them, it's best to hire a wiring contractor to install your network wiring.

CONNECTING JUST TWO COMPUTERS

If you're making a network of just two computers, you may be able to take a shortcut and eliminate the need for a network hub or additional special hardware. If you want to add on to your network later, you can always add the extra gear then.

If you're connecting two computers with IEEE-1394, you have the simplest possible cabling setup: Just plug one end of a "6-6" cable into a free IEEE-1394 socket on each computer.

If you are connecting two computers with Ethernet, yours is the second easiest possible network installation: Simply run a special cable called a *crossover cable* from one computer's network adapter to the other, and you're finished. This special type of cable reverses the send and receive signals between the two ends, and eliminates the need for a hub. You can purchase a crossover cable from a computer store or network supply shop, or make one as shown in Figure 17.6.

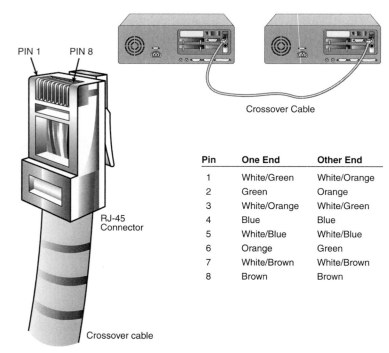

Figure 17.6
Wiring for a UTP Ethernet crossover cable. The cable reverses the send and receive wires so that two network cards can be directly connected without a hub. Note that the green pair and orange pairs are reversed across the cable.

Crossover Cable

PIN 1   PIN 8

RJ-45 Connector

Crossover cable

Pin	One End	Other End
1	White/Green	White/Orange
2	Green	Orange
3	White/Orange	White/Green
4	Blue	Blue
5	White/Blue	White/Blue
6	Orange	Green
7	White/Brown	White/Brown
8	Brown	Brown

Again, as I mentioned earlier, it really doesn't matter which colors are used, as long as pins 1 and 2 on one end of the cable go to pins 3 and 6 on the other. However, it's best to use the color scheme shown in the figure so that you can be sure it's correct without having to think about it.

TIP

> Be sure that your crossover cable is labeled as such, as it won't work to connect a computer to a hub and you'll go nuts trying to figure out what's wrong if you try. Factory-made models usually have yellow ends. When I make them myself, I draw three rings around each end of the cable with a permanent-ink marker.

EXTENDING THE NETWORK WITH MULTIPLE HUBS

Wired Ethernet hubs and switches come in several sizes with varying number of ports, or jacks, that can be used to connect computers. There are typically 4, 5, 8, 16, 24, or 32 ports. Many of the inexpensive Internet connection sharing routers have a five-port switching hub built in.

If you outgrow your hub, you don't need to completely replace it; you can simply connect a new hub to the old one and gain additional ports, as illustrated in Figure 17.7. You may also want to add an additional port to help you reduce the amount of network cabling you need: Instead of running long wires from a cluster of computers back to a central hub, you can a small hub near the cluster, and run just one wire back. Figure 17.7 shows this scenario as well.

Figure 17.7
Add an additional hub to gain extra ports, or to consolidate network wiring.

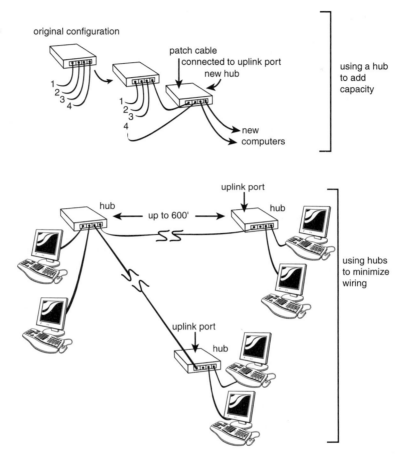

When you connect a hub to another hub, rather than to a computer, a special electrical connection is needed; one way or another, the send and receive signals from one hub have to be connected to the receive and send connectors on the other. There are three ways that this can be done:

- Many hubs have a special socket (port) called an *uplink port*. A standard UTP Ethernet patch cable can be used to connect an uplink port to a standard port on another hub, as shown in Figure 17.7 (a). If you're using a custom-built cable, use the standard wiring order.

- Some hubs have one port that can be used either as a standard or uplink port; a switch determines the port's function. To connect this sort of hub to another hub, set the switch to the uplink position and use a standard patch cable or standard wiring order in a custom cable.

- If the new hub doesn't have an uplink port, you can connect any of its ports to another hub by using a crossover cable, or a custom cable wired in the crossover style shown earlier in Figure 17.6.

Also, if you link hub to hub to hub, be careful how you arrange things. To meet Ethernet signaling specifications, there can be at most three hubs between any two computers on the network.

WIRELESS NETWORKING

Wireless networking adapters come in the same formats as standard Ethernet adapters: internal cards, PC Card (PCMCIA), and standalone boxes with USB attachments. They're installed and configured in the same way as standard Ethernet adapters. Installation was covered in the previous section, and protocol configuration will be covered in the next several sections.

However, wireless adapters require additional configuration for wireless security and wireless network type.

→ For an introduction to Wireless networking concepts, **see** "Wireless Networking," **p. 790**.

It's assumed that wireless-equipped computers can roam from location to location, and thus can be configured to connect to any of several wireless network groups, each of which may have its own security setup. But, whether you're roaming or not, you need to configure the network's Wired Equivalency Privacy (WEP) security settings.

CAUTION

> While it's possible to use wireless networking without it, we *strongly* recommend that you do enable encryption. Without encryption it's possible for neighbors and passers-by to tap into your network without you ever knowing it. At the very least, they can freeload on your Internet connection. At worst, if your network uses Simple File Sharing, random people will be able to access and modify shared files on your network.

If you're configuring your computer to work with an existing network set up by someone else, you just need to obtain the following information in order to get online:

- SSID (network name), a descriptive text string.
- If encryption is enabled, you will need a network key (password) that consists of 5 or 13 text characters, or an 8 or 26 digit hexadecimal number, depending on the security level in use. Hexadecimal numbers use the characters 0 through 9 plus A through F.
- Key index, a number between 1 and 4 (not all networks use this).
- Authentication mode: Shared Mode or Open System Mode. On corporate networks, you may be provided with additional information needed to configure wireless network authentication settings.
- Network Type: Infrastructure or ad hoc.

If you're setting up your own network, you'll need to select this information yourself. This is fairly straightforward:

- **SSID (wireless network name)**—You can use any short, descriptive text string, such as "Home Network" or "My Company". If you are using access points, you will have to enter the same SSID in each of your access points.

- **Network Key**—There are two levels of security currently used by wireless networks, although you'll see four numbers used to describe them: 40- and 64-bit security are actually the same thing, as are 110- and 128-bit security. You should use 110-bit security if all of your equipment supports it; otherwise, use 40-bit. For 110-bit security, choose a 13-character password that includes letters, numbers, and punctuation. For 40-bit security, choose a 5-character password.

- **Authentication Mode**—For homemade networks, the authentication mode will always be Open System Mode.

- **Network Type**—As mentioned in Chapter 16, there are two types of wireless networks: ad hoc and Infrastructure. Infrastructure networks include one or more access points or wireless routers. If you have no access points, you're building an ad-hoc network.

If you're building an Infrastructure network, the first step is to configure the access point(s) according to the manufacturer's instructions. This will make it easier to configure the network adapters; they'll "see" the access points and obtain the SSID automatically.

NOTE

> If the access point is packaged as part of a router, configure the router at the same time, following the manufacturer's instructions.
>
> If the access point requires an IP address for management purposes, see the discussion "IP Addressing Options" later in this chapter to help choose an appropriate address.

After you've set up any access points, configure the wireless adapters in each of your computers.

If your wireless adapter is an older one whose drivers don't support Windows's "Wireless Zero Configuration," you'll have to follow the manufacturer's instructions. However, most wireless adapters that are usable with Windows XP can be configured using the standardized setup system supplied with Windows, which I'll describe in the remainder of this section. To configure your wireless adapter, you'll need to log on as a Computer Administrator or Power User. Then, follow these steps:

1. If a wireless connection icon appears in the notification area, as shown in Figure 17.8, click it. Otherwise, open the Network Connections window from the Start Menu or My Network Places, and open the Wireless Network Connection item.

Figure 17.8
When a wireless network adapter is installed, an icon will appear in the notification area. A popup balloon will appear when a new network is encountered.

17

2. Available wireless networks will be displayed by their SSID names. Click the Advanced button.

3. The Wireless Network Connection Properties dialog will appear, as shown in Figure 17.9. (You can also reach this dialog by opening the Properties page for your wireless adapter from Network Connections, and selecting the Wireless Networks tab.)

Figure 17.9
The Wireless Network Connection Properties dialog lets you configure Windows to use one or more wireless networks.

4. Select your wireless network (which you can identify by its SSID name) in the top section under Available Networks and click Configure. If you're configuring the first member of an ad-hoc network, there will be nothing to choose from. In this case, click Add, and enter the SSID you wish to use.

5. In the Wireless Network Properties dialog, shown in Figure 17.10, enter the appropriate security configuration information. If your network was set up by your IT department, enter the setup information they provided. You may need to use the Authentication tab to add additional information supplied by the network manager.

Otherwise, if you are configuring your own network, follow these steps:

Figure 17.10
The Wireless Network Properties dialog lets you configure wireless encryption and authentication.

Following the figure, the steps:

a. Check Data Encryption (WEP enabled).

b. Uncheck Network Authentication (Shared mode).

c. Uncheck The Key is Provided For Me Automatically.

d. Enter your selected network key twice, under Network Key and under Confirm Network Key.

e. If you are not using an access point, check This Is a Computer-to-Computer (Ad Hoc) Network. In addition, click the Advanced button and select Computer-to-Computer (Ad Hoc) Networks Only.

6. Click OK.

If you have an access point or another ad-hoc network member up and running, you can check the wireless connection status by hovering your mouse over the connection icon in the task tray. This will display the current connection speed and signal strength. Double-click the connection to see a graphical display of this same information, as shown in Fgure 17.11.

Use the signal strength display to adjust your adapter's antenna to get the best possible reception. Try twiddling the antennae on your access point as well.

N O T E

You can change any of the wireless network properties except the Ad Hoc setting when you are logged on using a Power User or Computer Administrator. If you made the wrong choice for Ad Hoc, you'll need to delete the network entry from the Properties dialog and add it again from scratch.

Figure 17.11
The Wireless Connection Status display shows data rate and signal strength.

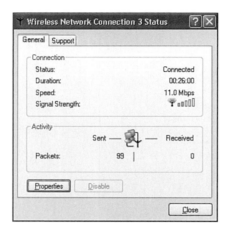

If your computer will be traveling between several wireless networks—for example, between home and the office—or if you visit Internet cafés and business centers with wireless access, you can add additional networks to the list shown earlier in Figure 17.9. Windows will choose whichever network is available as you roam from site to site.

NOTE

If you click the Advanced button, you can select which types of networks Windows will make available: Any, Infrastructure Only, or Ad-Hoc Only. If you find that you can't connect to a network that you know to be present in your area, check this setting.

Once your wireless adapters are configured and talking to each other and their access points, if any, you can proceed to configure the network itself.

CONFIGURING A WORKGROUP NETWORK

The first step to configuring a computer on a Workgroup network is to run the Network Setup Wizard. This isn't optional. For security reasons, Windows won't enable file and printer sharing until this wizard has been run at least once. Beyond the settings made by the Network Setup Wizard, there are several features that you should consider and adjust manually. After discussing the wizard, then, this section covers the following topics:

- IP addressing options
- Adding alternate network protocols
- Simple File Sharing
- Automatic share and printer discovery
- Designating a master browser
- Preparing for network printing

You may wish to review any or all of these topics. In addition, be sure to read the section "Managing Network Security."

NOTE

> If your computer is going to be a member of a domain network, you can skip ahead to "Joining a Domain Network" on *page 672*.

USING THE NETWORK SETUP WIZARD

Windows XP comes with a Networking Setup Wizard program that can automatically configure file sharing and Internet access for each of the computers on your network. The wizard lets you make a few basic choices, but otherwise takes care of all of the technical details for you.

NOTE

> If you're going to use Microsoft's Internet Connection Sharing, configure the computer that will be sharing its Internet connection first. Establish and test its Internet connection, and then configure the other computers. Otherwise, you can configure your computers in any order.

To start the wizard, click Start, Control Panel, Network and Internet Connections, and Set Up or Change Your Home or Small Office Network. Read the "Checklist for creating a network" if you wish, and then click Next. Follow the wizard through the following steps.

SELECT A CONNECTION METHOD

The wizard asks you to select a statement that best describes your computer. The choices can be confusing, so consider them each carefully. They are

- **This computer connects directly to the Internet. The other computers...connect...through this computer**—Choose this if your computer will be using Internet Connection Sharing to share its Internet connection with the rest of your LAN. This computer will connect to the Internet with its own dial-up modem, or through a cable/DSL modem that's either installed inside, or connected directly to a USB port or network adapter. In the last case, you'll have installed two network adapters in this computer: one for the LAN connection and one for the Internet connection. In either case, be sure that you've already configured and tested your Internet connection.

  With this selection, the wizard will enable Internet Connection Sharing on this computer. It will enable the Internet Connection Firewall (the Internet Connection Firewall feature is not available in the 64-bit versions of Windows XP) on the dial-up connection or LAN adapter that is used to connect to the Internet.

- **This computer connects to the Internet through another computer on my network or through a residential gateway**—Choose this if this computer will be using another computer's shared Internet connection, or if your network has a hardware Internet connection sharing router with Network Address Translation (NAT).

With this selection, the wizard will not enable the Internet Connection Firewall, as it is assumed that the sharing computer or router will provide firewall service.

■ **Other**—This choice (and a click on Next) leads you to three more alternatives:

• **This computer connects to the Internet directly or through a network hub. Other computers on my network also connect [this way]**—Select this if your computer uses its own dial-up or direct DSL/cable connection but you are *not* using Windows's Internet Connection Sharing to share this connection with your LAN. Also, use this choice if your LAN has routed Internet service, such as that provided by a DSL, cable, ISDN, or Frame Relay router connected to your network hub. (With this type of service, your ISP will have supplied a list of IP addresses for your computers.)

With this selection, the wizard will assume that you have no firewall protection in place and will enable the Internet Connection Firewall on your LAN adapter. This will prevent file sharing from working; see the following note for more information.

• **This computer connects directly to the Internet. I do not have a network yet**—This strange choice would be used if you have a direct Internet connection (that is, a cable or DSL modem that uses a network adapter), but no LAN.

With this selection, the Wizard enables the Internet Connection Firewall on your LAN adapter.

• **This computer belongs to a network that does not have an Internet connection**—Select this if your computer connects to the Internet using Dial-Up networking and neither provides nor uses a shared Internet connection, or if this computer will never connect to the Internet.

With this selection, the wizard will not enable the Internet Connection Firewall.

NOTE

If you have direct or routed Internet service and choose This computer connects to the Internet directly or through a network hub…, you must take special precautions to avoid attacks from Internet hackers.

If you make this choice, the wizard will assume that your Internet connection is insecure and will enable the Internet Firewall on your LAN adapter. *File sharing will be blocked* between your computer and the other computers on your own LAN. You will not be able to share files or access shared files from your computer.

Please read Chapter 24, "Network Security," for details on network and Internet security, and ensure that at least the services listed in Table 24.1 are blocked by your Internet router. Only when you are certain that the Internet connection on your LAN has adequate firewall protection, disable the firewall in your own computer as discussed under "Managing Network Security," *page 666*.

Make the appropriate selection and click Next.

SELECT YOUR INTERNET CONNECTION

If you chose one of the "This computer is directly connected to the Internet" choices, Windows will present a list of options for making that connection, listing your network adapters and your configured dial-up connections. Choose the connection that is used to reach the Internet and click Next. If you use a dial-up or PPPoE connection (a type of DSL service), choose the appropriate dial-up connection. Otherwise choose the network adapter that connects to your Internet service.

GIVE THIS COMPUTER A DESCRIPTION AND NAME

Enter a brief description of the computer (such as its location or primary user) and a name for the computer. Choose a name using just letters and/or numbers with no spaces or punctuation. Each computer on your LAN must have a different name.

If you're hard pressed to come up with names, try the names of gemstones, composers, Impressionist painters, or even Star Wars characters, as long as Mr. Lucas doesn't sue you over them. I use the names of islands in the Indonesian archipelago—with more than 25,000 to choose from there's little chance of running out of unique names!

Some Internet service providers, especially cable providers, require you use a name that they'll provide. (If you have a hardware connection sharing device hooked up to your cable modem, enter that name into the hardware device and use any names you want on your LAN.)

NAME YOUR NETWORK

Choose a name for your network workgroup. This name is used to identify which computers should appear in your list of network choices later on. All computers on your LAN should have the same workgroup name. If you have an existing network, enter the same workgroup name that the other computers use. Otherwise, you could pick a creative name like "WORKGROUP", or accept the wizard's default "MSHOME".

CAUTION

> Beware! If you run the wizard a second time, it will try to change your workgroup name to MSHOME. Re-enter the name you used the first time.
>
> Also: The workgroup name *must* be different from all of the computer names.

In the final step, "Ready to Apply Network Settings," review the list of selections you've made and either click Back to correct them or click Next to proceed.

RUNNING THE WIZARD ON LAN COMPUTERS

You'll need to run the wizard on all of the computers on your LAN at least once. If all the computers use Windows XP, select Just Finish the Wizard, and run the wizard on the other computers. If you have computers running versions of Windows 95, 98, Me, NT, or 2000, you can create a diskette that will let you run the wizard on these older machines, or you can use your Windows XP CD-ROM in these computers.

To use a diskette, choose Create a Network Setup Disk, and insert a blank, formatted floppy disk. If you ran the wizard earlier and just changed some of the settings, choose Use the Network Setup Disk I Already Have, and re-insert the setup disk you created earlier. Otherwise, choose Just Finish the Wizard; I Don't Need to Run the Wizard on Other Computers.

NOTE

> If you need to adjust the computer or workgroup name later, log on as a Computer Administrator, right-click My Computer, select Properties, and view Computer Name Tab. You can use a name-assignment wizard by clicking Network ID, or you can enter the information manually by clicking Change.

CONFIGURE OTHER COMPUTERS

Repeat the same setup procedure on your other computers.

If a computer is running a version of Windows earlier than XP, you'll need the Network Setup Diskette you created earlier, or use the Windows XP CD-ROM. To fire up the wizard from a diskette, insert the diskette into the older computer. Click Start, Run, type `a:setup`, and press Enter.

To use the CD-ROM, insert the CD-ROM in the older computer and wait for it to auto-run the Windows setup program. Choose Perform Additional Tasks, and then Set Up Home or Small Office Networking.

Now, continue with the next section to review the IP addressing choices made on your network.

IP ADDRESSING OPTIONS

Windows uses TCP/IP as its primary network protocol. So, each computer on the network needs to have an IP address assigned to it. There are three ways that IP addresses can be assigned:

- Manually, in what is called *static* IP addressing. You would select an address for each computer and enter it manually.

- Dynamically, through the DHCP service provided by Internet Connection Sharing, a Windows NT/200x Server, or a hardware router.

- Automatically, though Windows's Automatic Private Internet Protocol Addressing (APIPA) mechanism. If Windows computers are configured for dynamic IP addressing but there is no DHCP server present, Windows automatically assigns IP addresses.

I recommend that you do *not* rely on APIPA to configure your network. In my experience, it can cause horrendous slowdowns on your computers. If you don't have a device or computer to provide DHCP service, configure static TCP/IP addresses.

CONFIGURING DYNAMIC (DHCP) IP ADDRESS ASSIGNMENT

By default, Windows sets up new network adapters to use dynamic IP address assignment, so for new adapters, you don't need to take any additional configuration steps.

N O T E

> If you used static addressing in the past, just view the properties page for your network adapter, select Internet Protocol (TCP/IP), click Properties, and set both the IP Address and DNS settings to Obtain an Address Automatically.

You will need a computer or hardware device to provide DHCP service. This is provided automatically by any Windows computer that runs Windows Internet Connection Sharing (there can be at most one such computer on a network), or by a connecting sharing router device, which is discussed in Chapter 8 and later in this chapter. And, you can run the DHCP service on Windows NT or 200x Server; these operating systems can be used on workgroup networks as well as domain networks.

If you are using Windows Internet Connection Sharing, it will assign IP address 192.168.0.1 with a network mask of 255.255.255.0 to the network adapter in the sharing computer. Other computers should be configured for dynamic addressing and will receive addresses from 192.168.0.2 on up.

If you are configuring a hardware router, you will need to enable and configure its DHCP server. For the most part you can use the following settings:

DHCP Server: Enabled Server IP address: 192.168.0.1 DHCP Starting Address: 192.168.0.2 Number of addresses: 90 DNS Server(s): (as provided by your ISP) Some routers prefer to use a different subnet (range of network addresses), for instance 192.168.1.x. Whichever range you use, be sure to use the same subnet range for any static IP addresses you assign.

If you are planning on making services available to the Internet—that is, if you want to run your own Web or email server on your network—you must provide a way for incoming requests to be forwarded to the servers. See the "Making Internet Services Available" later in the chapter for more details.

If you want to assign static IP addresses to devices such as Web servers or print servers, use IP addresses 192.168.0.254 down to avoid conflicting with the DHCP assignments. Use the following static configuration settings:

IP address: 192.168.0.x where x is 254, 253, etc Network mask: 255.255.255.0 Gateway: 192.168.0.1 DNS Server: 192.168.0.1 if using Windows ICS, or as provided by your ISP, if using a router

N O T E

> If you have more than two DNS servers that you want to use, or if you have more than one possible gateway address, click the Advanced button, and select the IP Settings or DNS tabs. There, you can click Add to enter more than one or two addresses; you can also use the up and down arrow buttons to order the server addresses by preference.

CONFIGURING STATIC IP ADDRESSES

If you want to use static IP addresses on your network, use a range that's appropriate to the type of Internet connection you're using: values in your ISP-assigned subnet, if you are using routed Internet service; otherwise a range of private network addresses such as 192.168.0.2 through 192.168.0.254. Use the address range used by your Internet connection scheme.

Make a list of computer and other networked devices and assign an IP address to each. Generally, the number x.x.x.1 is given to your router or Internet Connection Sharing computer. It's best to use numbers from 100 and up for statically configured devices, so that DHCP, if it is used, can have the numbers 2 through 99 to pass out automatically.

To assign an IP address to a computer running Windows XP, use the following steps:

1. Log on as a Computer Administrator.
2. Open the Network Connections window. Right-click the entry or icon for your LAN adapter (usually labeled Local Area Connection) and select Properties.
3. Select Internet Protocol (TCP/IP) and click Properties.
4. On the General tab, enter the selected IP address, subnet mask, default gateway, and one or two DNS server IP addresses, as shown in Figure 17.12.

Figure 17.12
Enter static IP address information on the General tab.

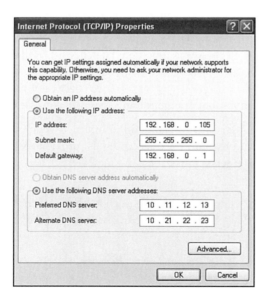

5. You can configure your preferred Internet domain name (called the *preferred DNS suffix*) on the Network Identification page in the System Properties dialog. To get there, right-click My Computer and select Properties, or select Advanced, Network

Identification in the Network Connections window. View the Computer Name tab, click Change, and then click More.

You can also enter a preferred Internet domain name for each individual network or Internet connection. You might want to use your company's domain name on the Network connection, and your ISP's domain name on a dial-up connection. To do this, view the network connection's properties dialog, click the Advanced button, select the DNS tab, and enter the domain name under DNS Suffix for This Connection, as shown in Figure 17.13.

Figure 17.13
Enter per-connection DNS information on the connection's Advanced Properties DNS tab.

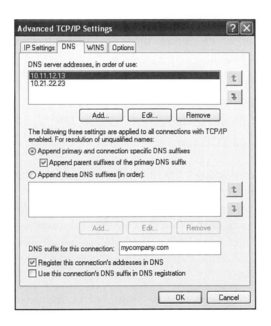

6. Unless your computer's DNS server supports dynamic IP address registration, uncheck Register This Connection's Addresses in DNS.

7. Click OK to close the dialogs.

INTERNET CONNECTION SHARING DISCOVERY AND CONTROL

If you are using Windows Internet Connection Sharing to share a dial-up or PPPoE ("dialed") DSL connection, you should install the Internet Connection Sharing Discovery and Control service on all of your computers. This service places an icon in each computer's Network Connections folder that lets users of all computers monitor and manage the Internet connection that is hosted on the sharing computer.

To install the Discovery and Control Service, follow these steps on each computer:

1. Log on as a Computer Administrator.

2. Open the Network Connections window.

3. From the menu, select Advanced, Optional Networking Components.

4. Select Networking Services and click Details.

5. Check both Internet Connection Sharing Discovery and Control and Universal Plug and Play, and click OK.

6. Click Next.

This service can be installed on Windows 98 and Me computers as well.

DISABLING NETBIOS OVER TCP/IP (NETBT)

Windows file sharing uses the Server Message Block (SMB) protocol, which can be carried by any of several network protocols:

- NetBEUI, whose use is being phased out
- Novell's IPX/SPX or Microsoft's IPX/SPX-compatible protocol
- NetBIOS over TCP/IP (NetBT), which uses TCP port 139
- Direct TCP/IP, which uses TCP port 445

Versions of Windows prior to Windows 2000 and XP use any of the first three protocols, Windows 2000 can use any of the four, and Windows XP prefers to use any of the last three (although, for the time being, NetBEUI is still available). When Windows 2000 or XP attempt to establish a file sharing connection with another computer using TCP/IP, by default they attempt connections using both 139 and 445 simultaneously. When the other computers responds to the connection request, Windows uses the first response and closes the other attempted connection.

If you are using TCP/IP as the sole protocol on your network and you do not need to support versions of Windows prior to Windows 2000, you can gain a small performance increase by disabling NetBT. To do this, follow these steps:

1. Open your network connection's Properties page.

2. Select Internet Protocol (TCP/IP) and click Properties.

3. Click the Advanced button and view the WINS tab.

4. Select Disable NetBIOS over TCP/IP.

5. Then, click OK to close the dialogs.

If you later need to internetwork with older versions of Windows, you'll need to restore this to the default setting.

ADDING ALTERNATE NETWORK PROTOCOLS

If your network has a Novell NetWare server or computers running older versions of Windows, you may wish to consider installing additional network protocols.

For NetWare connectivity, you'll need to install a NetWare client program, either Microsoft's or Novell's, and you may need to install the SPX/IPX protocol used by older versions of NetWare.

→ For more information about NetWare, **see** "Internetworking with Novell NetWare," **p. 834**.

If you are using older versions of Windows that rely on the NetBEUI protocol for networking, you'll need to either configure the older computers to use TCP/IP for their networking protocol, or add NetBEUI to Windows XP.

→ For a discussion about networking with older versions of Windows, **see** "Networking with Windows 95, 98, Me, and NT," **p. 813**.

SIMPLE FILE SHARING

By default, on a workgroup network Windows XP enables its Simple File Sharing mechanism (see "Demystifying "Simple" File Sharing" in Chapter 16, *page 624*).

You should consider the pros and cons of Simple File sharing, and if you choose to disable it, perform the following steps:

1. Log on as a Computer Administrator.
2. Open Windows Explorer.
3. Select Tools, Folder Options, and select the View tab.
4. Scroll to the bottom of the list of Advanced options and uncheck Simple File Sharing (Recommended). Click OK to close the dialog.

AUTOMATIC SHARE AND PRINTER DISCOVERY

On a Windows XP Workgroup network, Windows automatically locates and adds icons in the My Network Places window for all the shared folder and printers in your workgroup, without your needing to do anything.

You can disable this behavior if you wish. To do so, open My Computer, select Tools, Folder Options, and select the View tab. You can check or uncheck "Automatically search for network folders and printers."

DESIGNATING A MASTER BROWSER

As discussed in Chapter 16 under "Browser Service (Network Neighborhood)," Windows uses a database of known online computers to build the display known variously as Network Neighborhood, Computers Near Me, or View Workgroup Computers. The service runs on one primary computer called the *master browser*, which is determined by an automatic *election* held by the computers on the network. In addition, on a larger network some computers may be elected as backup browser servers.

When you are running a network with different versions of Windows, this service will not function correctly; the election goes haywire or the database is not filled in correctly or other problems occur, and the Network Neighborhood display won't function correctly even though the computers clearly can communicate with each other (for example, one can map network drives to folders shared by the invisible computers).

If you find that this occurs on your network, you may want to force the master browser service to run on a designated Windows XP computer that is always left on. This can help stabilize Network Neighborhood.

To make this work you have to (a) configure one computer to always be the master browser, and (b) configure all of the other computers never to offer to be the master.

To force the setting in Windows XP, 2000 and NT computers, you have to edit the registry key `HKEY_LOCAL_MACHINE\System\CurrentControlSet\Services\Browser\Parameters`. There are two values that can be altered:

Value	Possible Settings
IsDomainMasterBrowser	True—This computer is the master browser
	False—Master is determined by election
MaintainServerList	No—Never serve as the master
	Yes—Ask to be the preferred master
	Auto—Offer to be the master if needed

For Windows 98, the setting is made in the Control Panel. Open the Network applet, select File and Print Sharing for Microsoft Networks and click Properties. Under Browse Master, change the setting from Default to Disabled.

PREPARING FOR NETWORK PRINTING

If you're going to share a printer with LAN users running Windows 95, 98, Me, or NT 4 on Intel or Alpha platforms, they'll need different printer drivers than Windows XP and 2000 machines do. When you set up shared printers on your networked Windows XP computers, you can install drivers for the other operating systems to make it easier for users running older computers to use the shared printers.

→ For instructions, **see** "Installing Extra Printer Drivers," **p. 724**.

MANAGING NETWORK SECURITY

Simply put, you *must* take conscious steps to secure your network from hackers.

Chapter 24 discusses this topic in detail, but at the very least you must ensure that *every* point of contact between your computers and the Internet is secured by a firewall of some sort. The reason for this concern is that every computer exposed to the Internet will be subject to probing by unscrupulous people. These probes are automated, common and thorough, and they *will* find you and test you.

Simple File Sharing only makes this worse, because if your Internet connection is left unsecured, *everyone* on the Internet will have the same access to your network's shared files as you do. This is the reason that the Network Setup wizard is so adamant about either installing the firewall or disabling file sharing.

SECURING VARIOUS TYPES OF INTERNET CONNECTIONS

There are several ways that you can connect to the Internet. The following figures, 17.14 through 17.18, show the different ways that you can secure these connection styles.

- If you use Internet Connection Sharing (ICS), be sure that the Internet Connection Firewall is enabled on the connection (dial-up or LAN adapter) that connects to the Internet (see Figure 17.14).

    The Internet Connection Sharing and Internet Connection Firewall features are not available in the 64-bit versions of Windows XP.

Figure 17.14
Protection provided by Internet Connection Sharing and the Internet Connection Firewall on one computer.

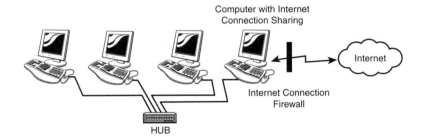

- If you use a hardware Internet connection sharing router, this device will provide significant protection. For additional protection, configure filtering on the TCP ports listed in Table 17.1 (see Figure 17.15).
- If you use routed Internet service (which provides a direct connection for all of the computers on your LAN), be *absolutely sure* that your router is configured to filter at least the TCP ports listed in Table 17.1 (see Figure 17.16).
- If you use a cable modem that provides several independent IP addresses for several computers, install two network adapters in each computer and set up two separate LANs. One should be used *only* for the cable Internet service, and the connections to this LAN must have the Internet Connection Firewall enabled. The other LAN is used for file sharing (see Figure 17.17). (Hint: You can save this difficulty and the expense of the extra connections by getting a connection sharing router, or by using ICS.)
- If you use a direct or dial-up Internet connection on your computer, be sure that the Internet Connection Firewall is enabled on the connection (dial-up or LAN adapter) that connects to the Internet (see Figure 17.18).

Figure 17.15
Protection provided by a sharing router and filtering.

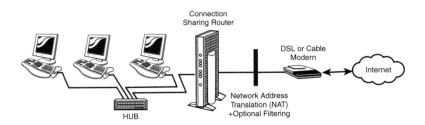

Figure 17.16
Protection provided by filtering in the router.

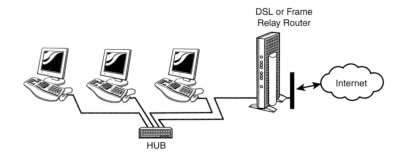

Figure 17.17
Protection provided by separate Internet and File Sharing networks, and the Internet Connection Firewall.

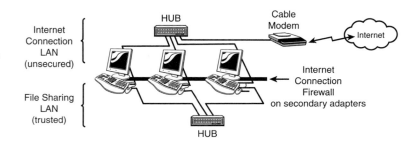

Figure 17.18
Protection provided by the Internet Connection Firewall on each direct connection.

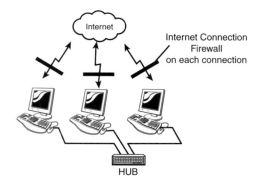

You can check the status of the Internet Connection Firewall on each of your computers' dial-up and LAN connections in the Network Connection window; the icons for each connection will show a small lock: and will carry the label "Firewalled."

To enable or disable ICF manually, view the properties page for a dial-up or local area connection and view the Advanced tab. ICF is enabled and disabled by a check box.

FILTERING TO PROTECT A ROUTER

If you are configuring a hardware router used for a shared or routed Internet connection, you should configure your router to block (filter out) several specific ports, which has the effect of blocking communication for several corresponding network services. Table 17.1 lists the minimum set of ports to block. You can find more information on filtering in Chapter 24.

TABLE 17.1	PORTS THAT SHOULD BE BLOCKED	
Protocol	**Port**	**Service Blocked**
UDP	137	NetBIOS Name Service
UDP	138	NetBIOS Datagram
TCP	139	File Sharing (SMB over NetBT)
UDP	161	Simple Network Monitoring Protocol (SNMP)
TCP	445	File Sharing (SMB over TCP)

You can usually accomplish this with three entries: block port range 137–139 for both TCP and UDP, port 161 for UDP and port 445 for TCP.

Each router make and model uses a different setup scheme, so you'll need to consult your router's instructions to find out how to set up filtering. If you have direct routed Internet service, your ISP will help you do this or may do it for you. If you use a connection sharing router, in most cases you will be on your own. The Web-based configuration page for a typical connection sharing router is shown in Figure 17.19.

Figure 17.19
Configuring Port Filtering in a typical connection sharing router.

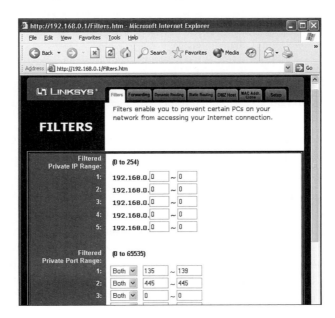

JOINING AN EXISTING NETWORK

If you're adding a new computer to an existing network, most of the difficult configuration decisions have already been made, so your task is greatly simplified.

The first step, of course, is to install your network adapter as discussed earlier in this chapter.

Then, you must be sure that your computer has the necessary drivers to support the file sharing protocol used on the network. TCP/IP is installed by default. If the computers on your existing network use IPX/SPX as the primary protocol for file sharing, you'll need to install IPX/SPX by following these steps:

1. View the Network Connections window, right-click the Local Area Connection icon, and select Properties.
2. Click Install, select Protocol, and click Add.
3. Highlight NWLink IPX/SPX/NetBIOS Compatible Transport Protocol and click OK.

If your network has old computers that require the use of the NetBEUI protocol for file sharing, you can install NetBEUI on Windows XP. You may wish to consider installing TCP/IP or IPX/SPX on the other computers, instead, as Microsoft may entirely withdraw support for NetBEUI in the future. As it is, you have to jump these hoops to install NetBEUI support on Windows XP:

1. Insert your Windows XP installation CD-ROM.
2. Open Windows Explorer, browse the CD-ROM, and locate the folder `\VALUEADD\MSFT\NET\NETBEUI`.
3. Copy file `nbf.sys` to the folder `\windows\system32\drivers` on the drive on which Windows is installed. (If you've installed Windows in a different folder, locate `system32\drivers` under that folder.)
4. On the Windows Explorer menu, click Tools, Folder Options, View and be sure that Show Hidden Files and Folders is selected.
5. Copy file `netnbf.inf` to the hidden folder `\windows\inf` on the drive on which Windows is installed.
6. View the Network Connections window, right-click the Local Area Connection icon, and select Properties.
7. Click Install, select Protocol, and click Add.
8. Highlight "NetBEUI Protocol" and click OK.

Once you are sure that the necessary protocols are installed, you can join your computer to the existing network. The steps you'll need to take differ depending on whether you are joining a workgroup or domain-type network. We'll cover the workgroup case first.

JOINING A WORKGROUP NETWORK

To add a new Windows XP computer to an existing network, you'll need to gather the following information:

- Workgroup name; should match the workgroup name used by all of the existing computers.
- Computer name; must be a name not used by any other computer, domain, or workgroup.
- IP addressing scheme used on network: dynamic or static? If static, you'll need to select an IP address and collect the following additional information: network mask, gateway address, and DNS server address(es). These last three items will be the same as used by the other computers on the network.

With this information in hand, perform the following steps:

1. Install Windows XP on the new computer, if necessary. If you do this, you'll be prompted to enter the workgroup name. When Windows installs the network adapter, if you are using a static IP address you can click Custom to enter this information during setup.
2. Install the network adapter, if it is not already installed.
3. Log on as a Computer Administrator, open the Network Connections window, view the properties page for the Local Area Connection icon, select Internet Protocol (TCP/IP), click Properties, and verify that the IP address and DNS information is entered correctly. It should be set to gather the information automatically if you are using DHCP; otherwise enter the correct static IP addressing information.
4. Open the My Network Places window and select Set Up a Home or Small Office Network from the Network Tasks list. Follow the instructions for the Network Setup Wizard given earlier in this chapter ("Using the Network Setup Wizard," *page 657*).

TIP

If you are going to use the same computer on several different networks, for example, at home and at work, be sure to check the section titled "Managing Multiple Network Configurations" in Chapter 19 (*page 807*).

This should complete the addition of your computer to the network.

NOTE

If you need to adjust the computer or workgroup name later, log on as a Computer Administrator, right-click My Computer, select Properties, and view Computer Name Tab. You can use a name-assignment wizard by clicking Network ID, or you can enter the information manually by clicking Change.

JOINING A DOMAIN NETWORK

If you are adding a new computer to a domain-type network you will need the cooperation of a Domain Administrator. You must either have the username and password of a domain admin account yourself, or a domain admin must preconfigure the network by adding a "computer account." You'll need to obtain the following information from your network administrator:

- Computer name.
- Domain name.
- IP address configuration information. In almost all cases you will be instructed to leave your network adapter set for automatic (DHCP) address assignment. In rare cases you may be supplied with an IP address, network mask, gateway address and DNS server address(es).

If you are installing Windows XP from scratch, you will be asked to supply the domain and computer names during setup; this should be all you need to do.

If you are adding an existing Windows XP computer to a domain network, install the network adapter. Then log on as a Computer Administrator.

In most cases, you can leave the adapter's IP address information set for automatic (DHCP) configuration, unless your network admin instructs you otherwise. To enter manual settings, open the Network Connections window, right-click the icon for your Local Area Connection, select Properties, select Internet Protocol (TCP/IP), and click Properties.

Then, run the Network Identification Wizard: On the Network Connection window's menu, select Advanced, Network Identification, and click Network ID. Enter the information supplied by your network administrator as requested by the wizard:

1. Click Next on the wizard's first screen.
2. Select This Computer Is Part of a Business Network, and I Use It to Connect to Other Computers at Work, and then click Next.
3. Select My Company Uses a Network with a Domain, and then click Next twice.
4. Enter your network login name, password, and the network domain name. Then, click Next.
5. You might be asked to enter your computer's name and its domain name. This information will also have been supplied by your network admin. If you're asked, enter the computer and domain names provided; then click Next.

   You also might be prompted for a domain Administrator account name and password. If this occurs the network administrator will have to assist you.
6. You should finally get the message "Welcome to the *xxx* domain." Close the Properties dialog and allow Windows to restart.

If an error message appears, click Details to view the detailed explanation of the problem. Report this information to your network administrator for resolution. The problem could be in your computer or in the network itself.

TIP

> If you are going to use the same computer on several different networks, for example, at home and at work, be sure to check the section titled "Managing Multiple Network Configurations" in Chapter 19 (*page 807*).

SETTING UP A ROUTED NETWORK

If configured with two or more network adapters using the TCP/IP protocol, Windows XP has the ability to serve as a router, and will pass traffic between the two networks. You may want to do this if you have a test network that you want to keep isolated from your office LAN.

Here's how routing works: If Windows receives a data packet whose IP address matches no network interface in the computer, it will try to forward the packet according to its routing table. In general:

- If the destination address belongs to the subnet of one of the installed network adapters, Windows will send the packet out that adapter (in the context of routing, it's more often called an *interface*).

- If the destination address belongs to a subnet that is listed in Windows's routing table, which lists known networks and the interface used to reach them, the packet will be sent to the gateway address associated with the designated interface.

- If the destination address belongs to no known subnet, Windows sends the packet to the default gateway address.

The trick to making a Windows computer act as a router is to get the computers on the two networks to send it packets destined for the other network.

This can be done in one of two ways. If one of the connected networks has no other outlet—that is, it has no Internet connection and no other routers—you can configure that network with the routing Windows computer's IP address specified as the default gateway. Traffic on that network that is bound for any other subnet will be sent to the Windows router, which will forward it either directly to a connected network, or to its own default gateway. This is illustrated in Figure 17.20. You'll most likely need to configure the computers on this subnet manually, as a computer Internet Connection Sharing or a sharing router would set themselves to be the gateway computer.

It's more difficult to configure a network that has additional connections. In this case you must make an entry in the routing table for each of the computers, to indicate that the routing computer is the gateway for the "other" network. The routing table is modified by running the "route" command-line program while logging on as a computer administrator.

Figure 17.20
Windows can serve as a default gateway for an isolated subnet.

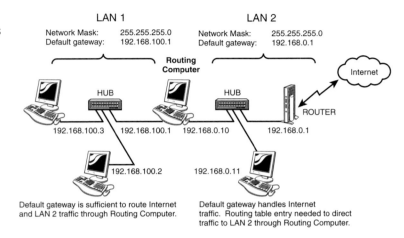

You can print the current routing table by typing the command route print. It will print something like this:

```
Active Routes:
Network Destination          Netmask           Gateway         Interface  Metric
        0.0.0.0              0.0.0.0       192.168.0.1    192.168.0.101     20
      127.0.0.0            255.0.0.0         127.0.0.1        127.0.0.1      1
    192.168.0.0        255.255.255.0     192.168.0.101    192.168.0.101     20
  192.168.0.101    255.255.255.255         127.0.0.1        127.0.0.1      20
  192.168.0.255    255.255.255.255     192.168.0.101    192.168.0.101     20
      224.0.0.0          240.0.0.0     192.168.0.101    192.168.0.101     20
255.255.255.255    255.255.255.255     192.168.0.101    192.168.0.101      1
Default Gateway:       192.168.0.1
```

When Windows needs to send a data packet that is destined for some other computer, it first checks to see if the target address is a member of a directly connected subnet. If so, Windows sends the packet directly to the destination computer.

Otherwise, it consults the routing table and compares the intended destination address to entries in the "network destination" column, looking for matches the bits indicated by the network mask.

As an example, if this computer needed to deliver a packet to IP address 192.168.0.100, it would find one match. This is the entry 192.168.0.0 with netmask 255.255.255.0. Converting these numbers to binary bits using Table 16.3, we see that all of the bits corresponding to the 1's in the netmask match:

Target address: 11000000 10101000 00000000 1100100

Route entry: 11000000 10101000 00000000 0000000

Netmask: 11111111 11111111 11111111 0000000

The most specific match is chosen; that is, the match with the most number of bits in the network mask. If several routes match, the one with the lowest metric (the greatest speed) is chosen. The entry 0.0.0.0 is the default route used if no other entry matches.

When a route entry has been chosen, Windows sends the packet to the associated gateway address, and it's that device's job to get the packet where it's going. (On a network that's connected to the Internet, the default gateway is usually the address of an Internet connection or a sharing router; this sends packets for all but local IP addresses to the router and eventually to your ISP.)

Now, what this means is that computers on a network that has an Internet router as their default gateway will need a specific route table entry added in order to send data destined for an additional local network to the Windows routing computer. The command will take this form

route add *destination_net* **mask** *network_mask* *gateway_address*

where *destination_net* is the subnet address of the secondary private network, *network_mask* is the subnet's network mask, and *gateway address* is the IP address of the Windows routing computer as seen by the computer whose routing table you are updating. In the example we presented earlier, the command would be

```
route -p add 192.168.100.0 mask 255.255.255.0 192.168.0.10
```

With the `-p` option, the Route command is persistent and the entry will remain even after the computers are rebooted. This command would need to be issued on all of the computers on LAN 2 except the routing computer, which already knows that it can send data to LAN 1 directly.

NOTE

> If the hardware router in Figure 17.20 can accept routing table entries, you can give it the job of routing data to LAN 1. In this case, you would not add routing table entries in any of the computers on LAN 2. Instead, their default gateway entry will automatically send traffic destined for LAN 1 to the hardware router, which will then send it to the routing computer for delivery.

SETTING UP A BRIDGED NETWORK

Windows XP can serve as a *bridge* between two or more networks (the Bridging feature is not available in the 64-bit versions of Windows XP.). A bridge forwards all traffic received from any one network to all of the others, and its main purpose is to join networks using disparate media. For example, you can use the bridging feature to join a wired Ethernet network with a phoneline network, a wireless network, or a FireWire network; you can join a slower 10BASE-T network with a 10/100BASE-T network, or you can join all of these types together. Figure 17.21 illustrates a bridged network.

To create a bridged network, install the necessary network adapters in one Windows XP computer, as described previously under "Installing Multiple Network Adapters." Do not bother configuring the adapters yet. When all of the adapters are installed, follow these steps:

17

1. Log on as a Computer Administrator.

2. View the Network Connections screen.

3. Select all the icons for the network adapters you wish to bridge by clicking with the Shift key held down.

4. Right-click any of the icons and select Bridge Connections.

Figure 17.21
Bridging joins physically separate networks into one virtual network.

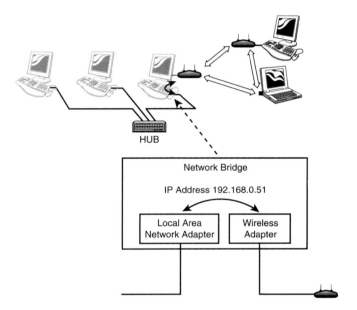

A new icon will appear that represents the bridge itself, as shown in Figure 17.22. Once established, the bridge will join the network connected to the linked adapters as if they were a single network.

Networking properties like TCP/IP address assignment are now associated with the bridge as a whole, rather than with individual adapters, as you can see in Figure 17.23. In effect, the bridge is the "adapter," and the linked network cards are its several physical ports. So, you must now right-click the Bridge icon and configure its TCP/IP properties.

CAUTION

Do not bridge a network adapter that is used to connect directly to the Internet, as this will bypass the Internet Connection Firewall.

Later, if needed you can modify the bridge from the Network Connection window:

■ To add an additional adapter to the bridge later on, right-click the adapter icon and select Add to Bridge.

■ To remove an individual adapter from the bridge, right-click the adapter's icon and select Remove from Bridge. You may need to reconfigure the TCP/IP properties for the newly removed adapter.

- To remove the bridge entirely, right-click the Bridge's icon and select Delete. You may need to reconfigure the TCP/IP properties of the adapters that were part of the bridge.

Figure 17.22
The Network Bridge icon appears when interfaces have been bridged.

Figure 17.23
Most network properties are associated with the bridge a whole, rather than with the individual adapters.

ADDING NETWORK SERVER APPLIANCES

It's often easier and sometimes less expensive to add network services in the form of purpose-built devices called *network server appliances*, rather than setting up servers of your own. You can get network server appliances that perform any of the following services:

- **File storage**—These devices have hard disks that are shared with the network. Examples include the Cobalt "Qube," the Network Appliance "NetApp Filer," and the GreenComputer "PowerElf."

- **Web and Email servers**—Examples of this type of device include the Intel InBusiness eMail Station, as well as most of the file storage devices mentioned previously. Many of these devices perform Internet connection sharing as well.

- **Print servers**—These devices connect a printer to your network so that any computer can send data directly to the printer. This avoids the need to keep a computer turned on all the time just to share its printer, and in the case of print servers that are installed directly inside the printer, can significantly speed up printing of complex graphics. Examples include the HP JetDirect series of print servers, and devices made by LinkSys, DLink, NetGear, Hawking, Siemens, and just about every other networking vendor.

These devices usually only need to have an IP address assigned to them, and from there a built-in Web server is used to walk through fairly straightforward configuration screens.

MAKING INTERNET SERVICES AVAILABLE

If you have an always-on Internet connection, you may be tempted to run your own Web or mail server. You may also wish to make your computer available over the Internet through the Remote Desktop service so that you can get at your computer from home, work or while traveling.

If you're using a shared Internet connection, though, there is a small problem: The shared connection uses one publicly visible IP address, and the computers on your LAN are essentially hidden. It's rather like a gated community: Visitors are stopped at the guard gate and can't proceed to the residences inside without permission and directions. In the equivalent case of the network, the connection sharing service or device must be told which Internet network IP address is to receive incoming requests on various TCP and UDP ports, which correspond to specific Internet services.

If you plan to run servers that will be accessible from the Internet, or if you want to use Remote Desktop to reach your computer from the 'net, you'll need to configure your shared or routed Internet connection to direct incoming service requests to the computer that is hosting the desired service. How this is done depends on the type of sharing system you're using.

PORT FORWARDING WITH INTERNET CONNECTION SHARING

If you are using the built-in Internet Connection Sharing service, see "Allowing Service Requests to Pass Through Internet Connection Firewall" in Chapter 24 (*page xxx*) for instructions on configuring the ICF service to forward requests in to the network.

A big advantage of using ICS when you are running services is that requests can be forwarded to your network's computers by name, rather than by IP address. Since the IP addresses on an ICS network are passed out dynamically, they can change from time to time, so the ability to forward requests by name is a big help.

PORT FORWARDING WITH A HARDWARE SHARING ROUTER

If you are using a hardware connection sharing router on your network, it too can be configured to forward incoming Internet requests to the appropriate computers on your network. However, you will have to direct the requests to your computers by their IP addresses. This means that computers which are to host services must be configured with static IP addresses; if these computers are set up to receive dynamic addresses there is no guarantee that the address won't change, and render the forwarding useless. Static IP addressing is discussed earlier in this chapter under "IP Addressing Options."

When you have configured static IP addresses for the computers that will be hosting services, Remote Desktop and so on, add port forwarding entries to your router's configuration. Table 17.2 lists the protocols and ports used by standard Internet-based services.

TABLE 17.2 PROTOCOLS AND PORTS FOR STANDARD INTERNET SERVICES

Protocol	Port Number	Service
TCP	20+21	FTP (File Transfer Protocol)
TCP	22	SSH (Secure shell)
TCP	23	Telnet
TCP	25	SMTP (Email)
TCP+UDP	53	DNS (Domain Name Service)
TCP	80	HTTP (Web)
TCP+UDP	88	Kerberos
TCP	110	POP3 (Post office protocol version 3)
TCP	119	NNTP (Network news)
TCP	143	IMAP4 (Internet Mail Access Protocol v4)
TCP	220	IMAP3 (Internet Mail Access Protocol v3)
TCP	443	HTTPS (Secure web)
TCP	3389	Remote Desktop
UDP	5361	Symantec PCAnywhere
TCP	5362	Symantec PCAnywhere

17

TIP

> If you want to connect to more than one Windows XP Pro computer through Remote Desktop, Chapter 19 shows you how you can make more than one computer accessible by changing the port number used by Remote Desktop.

Figure 17.24 shows the configuration page for port forwarding in a typical connection sharing router. On this network, several services are hosted on the computer with fixed IP address `192.168.0.4`. PCAnywhere connections are forwarded to the computer at IP address `192.168.0.123`.

Figure 17.24
Port Forwarding configuration for a typical hardware connections sharing router.

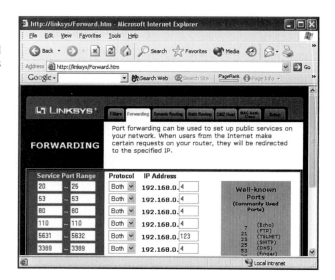

There are protocols other than TCP and UDP that may require forwarding. To permit incoming connections for a VPN connection using Microsoft's Point to Point Tunneling Protocol, for instance, you must be able to forward packets using protocol #47 (Generic Routing Encapsulation, or GTE) to the host computer. Most inexpensive routers do not permit you to forward protocols other than TCP and UDP, so it's generally not possible to establish a VPN connection to a computer behind a connection sharing router. You can, however, establish an incoming VPN connection to a Windows XP Professional computer running the Internet Connection Firewall.

OBTAINING DNS SERVICE

If you want to host an Internet accessible server on your own network, you will probably want to set up Domain Name service so that your servers can be reached by sensible names like www.mycompany.com, rather than by your IP address or the hostname provided with your broadband line—this will look something along the lines of adsl-60-193-168-192.dsl. snfc21.pacbell.net, a rather unfriendly name. DNS service is usually something you have to arrange independently of registering your domain name. Registering just establishes ownership. You must then provide, or pay someone to provide, domain name servers to turn names in your domain into your servers' IP addresses.

It will be difficult to do this with a standard dial-up Internet account as your connection's IP address—and the IP address that outside users need to use to connect to you—will be different every time a dial-up session is established. There are service providers that offer dynamic DNS service (DDNS); these providers set up domain name information that you can update when you go online. For a list of DDNS providers, check out the Google Web Directory page `Computers > Software > Internet > Servers > Address Management > Dynamic DNS Services`. For occasional use, you can just find your connection's current IP address and give it to an outside user. For the duration of the connection they can then connect to your Web server with a URL that uses this number, along the lines of `http://101.102.103.104`.

If you have cable Internet service, you may be prohibited by your terms of service from hosting a server on your connection. But it seems only fair to use the connection to reach your own computer via Remote Desktop or Web Folder sharing. If the service uses DHCP addressing, your IP address may change from time to time, and a DDNS provider will again be needed if you want to reach your network using a standard domain name.

If you use DSL service and want to host servers on your network, your ISP may be able to give you a static (fixed) IP address. This makes it possible for you to use any type of DNS service. Your ISP probably offers it for a fee, but there are also free DNS services; check out `www.granitecanyon.com` for instance. If you plan on running a serious although small-volume server, you may want to investigate getting Symmetric DSL (SDSL) service, which uses the same data rate for both incoming and outgoing connections. A higher outgoing data rate will help speed up transfers made to Web visitors.

ADVANCED NETWORK OPTIONS

There are several networking options not covered thus far because they're not usually needed in a standard network setup. In this section I'll discuss these options.

ADAPTERS AND BINDINGS

You can control which protocols and services are associated with each network adapter using the check boxes on each adapter's properties page. For example, you can uncheck Client for Microsoft Networking and File and Printer Sharing for Microsoft Networks on a network adapter that is used only to connect to a broadband Internet modem, to gain additional security above that provided by the Internet Connection Firewall.

You can also monitor and modify all network bindings in one place with the Adapters and Bindings dialog. To view this, open the Network Connections window and select Advanced, Advanced Settings.

PROVIDER ORDER

If you have installed clients for both the Novell NetWare and Microsoft networking (as discussed in Chapter 20), you can adjust the network provider order, which determines which computer name service, Novell's or Microsoft's, is queried first to find a given named file or print server. For example, if you choose a shared printer named \\munich\laserjet, Windows has to locate the machine named munich. It might need to query both the Windows computer name service (Active Directory or the browser service) and the NetWare naming service before it finds the name. When you use a mix of Microsoft and NetWare servers, you might be able to speed up network operations by setting the provider order so that the most likely name service is examined first.

In most cases, you won't need to make any changes to Windows's Provider Order list. If your network administrator suggests that you do, just follow these steps:

1. Open Network Connections by selecting Start, My Computer, My Network Place, View Network Connections.

2. From the Advanced menu, select Advanced Settings, and select the Provider Order tab. The dialog lists services used to find access to file servers and print servers, respectively.

3. Arrange the services so that the type you use most frequently is listed on top, followed by less-often-used services. Highlight a service type, and click the up- or down-arrow button to rearrange the types.

When finished, click OK to close the dialogs.

OPTIONAL NETWORKING COMPONENTS

Windows comes with several additional network services and components that are not installed by default. These components are

- **Network Monitor Driver**—Allows your computer's network communications to be recorded and monitored by a network supervisor, for diagnostic purposes. Install this only if requested by your network administrator.

  To install this driver, open the properties page for a selected network adapter, click Install, and select Protocols.

- **Simple Network Management Protocol (SNMP)**—Used on larger networks to monitor computer and router configuration. See the additional notes on SNMP later in this section.

- **WMI SNMP Provider**—Gives Windows Management Interface application software (for example, Windows Script Host programs) access to SNMP data.

  To Install SNMP or the WMI SNMP Provider, open the Network Connections window. Select Advanced, Optional Networking Components. Select Management and Monitoring Tools, and click Details.

- **Internet Gateway Device Discovery and Control Client**—Allows other computers on the network to monitor and control the dial-up or PPPoE Internet connection on the computer running Windows Internet Connection Sharing. Requires the Universal Plug and Play service as well. This service was discussed earlier in the chapter. (Not available on 64-bit versions of Windows XP.)

- **RIP Listener**—Lets Windows configure the TCP/IP routing table automatically when network routers broadcast path information using the Router Information Protocol.

- **Simple TCP/IP Services**—A set of primitive TCP/IP services such as character stream generation and data echo. They're rarely needed and can make you an easy target for Denial of Service (DOS) attacks by hackers if installed.

- **Universal Plug and Play (UPnP)**—Lets your computer automatically discover and connect to networked appliances and other new network devices. UPnP is a new technology that lets network hardware and future network-ready appliances communicate without manual setup

  To install the Discovery and Control client, RIP Listener, Simple TCP/IP Services or UPnP, open the Network Connections window. Select Advanced, Optional Networking Components. Select Networking Services, and click Details.

- **Print Services for Unix**—Lets Unix/Linux users use your computer's printers (and other shared printers on your network). Also installs the lpr and lpq programs so you can send print jobs to Unix/Linux printers.

  To install the Discovery and Control client, RIP Listener, Simple TCP/IP Services or UPnP, open the Network Connections window. Select Advanced, Optional Networking Components. Select Other Network File and Print Services, and click Details.

You must be logged on as a Computer Administrator to install these components.

MORE ON SNMP

SNMP should not be installed unless your network administrator requires its use, as there are some security risks attached to it. If you do choose to install SNMP, you should immediately configure the SNMP monitor to protect your computer's information with a secret "community name." This name is like a password that remote monitors need to supply before they can extract information from your computer. The default community name is `public`. Your network manager might supply you with an alternative community name. To set it, do the following:

1. Click Start, right-click My Computer, and select Manage.
2. Open Services and Applications, select Services, and locate SNMP Service in the right pane. Double-click it to open its Properties page.
3. Select the Security tab. Select Public, and then click Remove. Next, click Add to enter any community names provided by your network manager. Generally, assign only read-only community rights unless your network manager specifies otherwise.

4. You can additionally restrict SNMP access to specific network hosts (namely, management computers) by selecting Accept SNMP Packets from These Hosts and adding the appropriate IP addresses.

> **NOTE**
>
> SNMP can be a security risk because it reveals the names of user accounts on your computer and your computer's network routing information. A community name with write or create permission can alter network routing tables. For this reason, SNMP should be blocked by your network's firewall, and you should *not* install it unless it's necessary.

> **TIP**
>
> If you're a network manager and use SNMP to monitor equipment health, you might find it valuable to know that Windows XP and 2000's Professional and Server versions come with a utility that can turn specified Windows Event Log entries into SNMP traps (messages) as they happen. This feature is configured by the undocumented program `evntwin`, which is installed when you install SNMP. This utility can let your network monitor detect and report on full hard drives, security violations, and other significant events.
>
> `evntwin` can save a list of event-to-trap mappings to a file. Another undocumented utility, `evntcmd`, can instantly install this file on another Windows XP or 2000 computer, even remotely.

MULTIHOMING

In some instances it is desirable to assign multiple IP addresses to a single network adapter. You might do this if you are providing Internet services and need a single computer to take up the job of one that has gone offline.

To assign multiple IP addresses, open the adapter's Properties page. Select Internet Protocol (TCP/IP) and click Advanced. On the IP Addressing tab, you can click Add to enter multiple IP addresses and network masks, as well as multiple default gateways. The addresses you assign don't necessarily have to belong to the same subnet, although it is not recommended practice to run multiple TCP/IP subnets over the same wire.

> **NOTE**
>
> If you install multiple network adapters or multiple subnet addresses in one Windows XP computer, you should configure the computer never to be the Master Browser. This is discussed earlier in the chapter.

CHAPTER **18**

USING THE NETWORK

In this chapter

WINDOWS XP NETWORKS

Windows XP was designed pretty much from the ground up to work well on a network, whether in the home, small office, or enterprise. For the most part, using files and printers on the network is exactly the same as using files and printers located in your own computer. The "look and feel" are identical. You only need to learn how to locate and attach to resources shared by others, and how to make your own computer's resources available to others on the network.

In this chapter, I'll assume that you're familiar with the terms and concepts behind Windows networking. If you aren't, you may want to check Chapter 16, "Introduction to XP Networking," for an introduction to Windows network types, features, and functions.

USING XP HOME EDITION ON A DOMAIN NETWORK

This chapter discusses both workgroup and domain-type networks, which were defined in Chapter 16. If you use Windows XP Home Edition, your computer always behaves as if it is part of a workgroup network, even if attached to a domain-type network. Domain security, policy, and Active Directory will not be available. However, you can still use the network. You will probably be prompted to enter a valid domain logon name and password the first time you attempt to access a resource on a given domain server or member computer.

In this case, Windows will offer to "remember" the logon name and password and associate them with your XP Home Edition user account. This will make life easier. You can subsequently manage these memorized credentials from the User Accounts control panel applet—select your account and choose Manage My Network Passwords.

NETWORK PERMISSIONS AND SECURITY

From the standpoint of *using* resources shared by other computers, there's nothing you can do to change your ability to access the resources, other than to use an alternate username and password (we'll discuss this later in the chapter, under "Mapping Drives and Folders"). The person managing the computer that is sharing the resources determines which files, folders, and printers you can access.

Network security takes place at the point where a computer *sharing* resources decides whether to grant another user access to its shared files and folders. In a nutshell, here's how it works. Windows controls access to the files and folders it shares with the network in the same way that it controls access by users directly logged in at the computer: through the NTFS file permissions on the individual files and folders exposed through file sharing.

When Simple File Sharing is disabled, an additional level of security allows you to limit access for all of the files and folders in a given shared folder, with the option of granting read, change, and/or "full control" access to selected users and/or security groups. This mechanism works in *addition* to NTFS file permissions, and is the only user-level security mechanism for shared folders stored on a FAT-formatted drive:

- If a given user is denied access to read a file by NTFS permissions, they have no access to the file over the network either.

- If a user has read-only access to a file according to NTFS, and "full" or "change" access through the additional shared folder permission list, the user has read-only access to the file over the network.

- If a user has read/write access to a file according to NTFS, but read-only access according to the share permissions, the user has read-only access to the file.

- If NTFS grants the user read/write access *and* the share permissions grant "full" or "change" access, only then will the remote user have read/write access to the file.

For shared folders that reside on disks formatted with the FAT file system, NTFS permissions are not available, and can be considered to offer full read/write access to everyone. Thus, for shared folders residing on FAT disk partitions

- If the user is granted read-only access to the shared folder, the user gets read-only access to the files and folders inside.

- If the user is granted read/write access to the shared folder, the user will have read/write access to all of the files and folders inside.

NETWORK USERS AND SIMPLE FILE SHARING

The concept of a remote network "user" is not as straightforward as you might expect, depending on the type of network on which a networked computer resides. In a nutshell:

- For Windows XP Pro computers on a domain network, user accounts for network access are generally domain accounts and are thus recognized by all computers in the domain. Machine-specific accounts can be created and used, but this is rarely useful.

- For Windows XP Pro computers on a workgroup network on which the owner has disabled Simple File Sharing, requests for access to shared resources are validated against that computer's own list of user accounts. If the network user happens to be using an account with the same name and password as an account on the sharing computer, they'll be granted access according the rules described previously. Otherwise, they'll be prompted to provide a username and password valid on the sharing computer.

- For all Windows XP Home Edition computers, and for Windows XP Pro computers that have Simple File Sharing enabled, all access to the computer's shared folders is evaluated according to privileges granted to the Guest user account. There is no distinction made between one user and another, or even between authorized users and an intruder who has plugged into the network (or connected via an unsecured wireless link!) In effect, the computer's owner can only specify whether *everyone* gets full read/write access, or just read-only access to *all* files and folders shared by his or her computer.

18

Simple File Sharing makes a dramatic difference, and it's very important to understand the consequences it has on security and convenience. On workgroup networks before Windows XP, it was necessary to enter the same list of usernames and passwords in each of the network's computers, at least those that were sharing resources. This method can still be used if you're using Windows XP Professional on a Workgroup network.

With the Simple File Sharing feature—whose use is forced by Windows XP Home Edition (meaning that it cannot be disabled in Home Edition) and is optional on Windows XP Professional—since *all* access to shared folders and printers from other networked computers is handled through the Guest user account, there is no need to maintain user accounts for each user on each computer. The downside of this, however, is that there is no way to limit network access on a user-by-user basis.

UNC NAMES

You are familiar with the DOS-style pathnames used to identify files stored on your disk drives, which look like this:

```
c:\documents\roofing bids.xls
```

When referring to files stored on other computers on the network, Windows uses a syntax called the *Universal Naming Convention*, or UNC, which looks like this:

```
\\ambon\docs\roofing bids.xls
```

The initial double backslash indicates that the name ambon is the name of a computer on the LAN. docs is a *share name*, the name that one of ambon's folders was given when it was shared with the network. Everything past the share name is used to locate a file or folder inside this shared folder; that is, after the share name, a UNC path can list subfolders and a filename. Figure 18.1 shows how the UNC path \\ambon\docs\roofing bids.xls relates to the actual file roofing bids.xls stored on computer ambon.

Figure 18.1
The first part of UNC Path indicates a computer and shared folder, and the rest selects content in the shared folder.

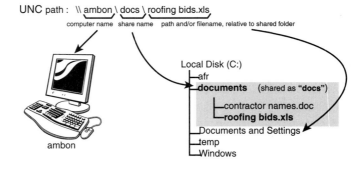

NOTE

While a folder's share name may be the same as the folder's name on the hard drive, it doesn't have to be.

If the computer whose files you want to use is on a LAN using Active Directory, or is part of a distant company network, you may also specify the remote computer name more completely, as in the following:

```
\\ambon.mycompany.com\docs\roofing bids.xls
```

Or, if you know only the remote computer's IP network address (which might be the case if you're connecting to a remote computer that's connected to the Internet with Dial-Up Networking), you can even use a notation like this:

```
\\11.22.33.44\docs\roofing bids.xls
```

> **NOTE**
>
> Elsewhere in this chapter, I'll use UNC names such as `\\server\folder` as a generic sort of name. In actual use, you'd replace `server` with the name of the computer that's sharing a folder, and `folder` with the folder's actual share name.

Shared printers are also given share names and can be identified by a UNC path. For example, if I share my HP LaserJet 4V printer, I might give it the share name *HPLaser*, and it would be known on the network as `\\ambon\HPLaser`.

LOCATING NETWORK RESOURCES

It's fairly easy to locate printers, files, and folders stored on other computers on your network; as you would expect, Windows can display the contents of your network in an Explorer-type view that's as easy to interpret as the My Computer display. In addition to this familiar point-and-click browsing model, however, there are some additional tools that make it possible to locate resources from the command line, and to search through very large networks.

The most straightforward way to locate resources on small networks is through the My Network Places display. My Network Places gives you a way to browse, search, and bookmark network resources, including shared folders, Web pages, FTP sites, and so on. To open My Network Places, you can

- View My Computer, and then select My Network Places from the Other Places menu.
- Open the Network Connections window and select My Network Places from the Other Places menu.

When you select My Network Places from the My Computer window, you get the "folder" view of My Network Places, as shown in Figure 18.2.

Figure 18.2
My Network Places is the starting point for searching and opening network resources. On a peer-to-peer network, Windows displays icons for all shared folders.

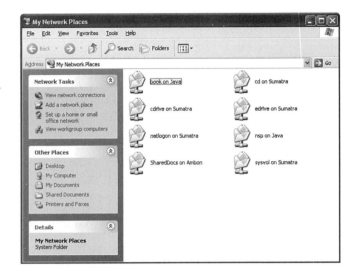

NOTE

When you open My Network Places from My Computer, you get a folder view. When you open it from the Network Connections window, the left pane displays a task list. As always, you can switch between the two views by selecting Tools, Folder Options, and choosing one of the Tasks options on the General tab.

If you find yourself using My Network Places frequently, you can save time by adding it to your Start Menu. Just right-click Start, select Properties, and Customize. Select the Advanced tab and scroll the Start menu items list down to My Network Places. Check it and click OK.

You also can drag a shortcut to My Network Places from your Start menu onto the desktop or the Quick Launch bar.

My Network Places is meant to be a place to collect shortcuts to commonly used remote network resources such as shared folders, Web Folders, FTP sites, and the like.

AUTOMATIC SHARED FOLDER DISPLAY

On a workgroup (peer-to-peer) network, by default Windows will automatically display an icon for each shared folder on your network. It does this by scanning the network at intervals of 10 minutes or so. On small networks, this is a great advantage, as you can quickly access every shared folder on the network from this window, without having to hunt around. On larger networks, however, this display can grow quite large and can be distracting. You can enable or disable this feature from Windows Explorer by selecting Tools, Folder Options. On the View tab, check or uncheck Automatically Search For Network Folders and Printers.

MANUALLY BROWSING THE NETWORK

On a domain network, automatic searching for shared folders isn't available, and you'll have to take some extra steps to manually browse through the network. You can use this method on a Workgroup network as well:

1. Open My Network Places in the Task List view, as described in the previous section.

2. If you are on a workgroup network, select View Workgroup Computers from the Network Tasks list. This will let you peruse all the computers with the same workgroup name as yours. Open the computers' icons to view the folders and printers they're sharing.

3. The Other Places list will display either Entire Network or Microsoft Windows Network. Select this item.

4. If you chose Entire Network, a list of network types will appear in the right pane. Select Microsoft Windows Network, or, if your organization uses Novell NetWare servers, you could select Novell NetWare Network.

5. After choosing Microsoft Windows Network, the right pane will list any workgroups or domains that your computer has observed on the network.

6. Browse into any of the listed workgroup/domain names to view a list of active member computers.

7. Double-click any of the listed computers to see the folders and printers they're sharing. You can open the shared folders to see the files inside, and you can open the shared printers to view and manage the print queues.

NOTE

> Windows will only display computers that have been up and running within the last 20 minutes or so. If the computer list is empty or is missing a computer you expect to see, wait 20 minutes for the Browser service to collect information, then select View, Refresh.

If you're on a domain-type network with Active Directory Network, you'll have an additional item in Network Tasks called Search Active Directory. I'll discuss AD searching later in this chapter.

You also can explore your network from the Folders view of Explorer, as shown in Figure 18.3. (You can bring up the Folders view in any Explorer window by clicking the Folders button.) This view lets you see that your network is as structured as the folders of your hard drive.

18

Figure 18.3
The Folders view in Explorer lets you browse through your network. This view shows the shared folder "cdrive" on the computer named Sumatra.

Computers and shared folders

As you can see, within Entire Network is a list of network types, which contain workgroups and domains, which contain computers, which contain shared resources, which contain folders and files.

COMMON SHARED FOLDER NAMES

Besides folders shared by each computer's owner, administrators, and users, Windows shares several folders automatically. In particular, and of most general interest, most Windows XP computers will have a folder with the share name SharedDocs. This is the folder c:\Documents and Settings\All Users\Documents, which appears in Windows Explorer as "Shared Documents" under My Computer.

NOTE

> Yes, it's very confusing. Explorer has a way of presenting certain special folders with "friendly" names rather than the folders' actual names. If your computer's local user accounts are set up to share their document folders, the accounts' "My Documents" folders will appear in Explorer as "Bob's Documents", "Susan's Documents", and so on. These folders are actually the "My Documents" folders under the users' profile folders.

Server computers on a domain network offer some network resources to member computers that are used by automatic services or for maintenance. Table 18.1 shows some of the shared resources you might see and what they do.

TABLE 18.1   TYPICAL ADMINISTRATIVE FOLDERS SHARED ON A WINDOWS 200X SERVER

Folder	Description
CertEnroll	Contains data used to provide Security Certificates to member computers, if your network has its own Certificate Authority. This share is used only by the Certificate Wizard.
NETLOGON	Used by the domain login system.
Published	Contains installation packages for published and assigned application software, which may be available to or forced into your computer. When using the Add/Remove Software Control Panel via the network, files are automatically retrieved from the Published folder.
SYSVOL	Used only by the domain login system; contains policy and script files.
Printers and Faxes	Mirrors the locally installed items in the computer's Printers folder; can be used by an administrator to install, manage, and control printers across the LAN. (This is not an actual shared folder; it's just the way Windows Explorer presents the list of printers shared by a given computer.)
Scheduled Tasks	Mirrors the computer's Scheduled Task list; can be viewed only by an administrator for remote maintenance. (This is not an actual shared folder; it's just the way Windows Explorer presents the list of tasks scheduled on a given computer; these are found under \Windows\Tasks, which is reached through the ADMIN$ share.)
ADMIN$	Used by remote administration software—contents of the Windows folder.
IPC$	Used for remote procedure calls, a network software system built into Windows.
print$	Shared folder containing print drivers for the computer's shared printers.
FxsSrvCp$	Folder containing shared Fax cover pages.
FaxClients	Shared Fax service client software.
C$, D$, and so on	Entire hard drives, shared for Administrators' use (only).

NOTE

Share names ending with $ are not displayed in Explorer's browsing lists, but you can view and map them by entering their UNC path name directly.

Of these folders, only Printers and Scheduled Tasks are of general interest, and then only to administrators. The operating system uses the others, which should not be modified.

SEARCHING FOR COMPUTERS

You can use the Windows XP Search wizard to locate computers by name. On an Active Directory network, your options are more sophisticated, as discussed later in this chapter under "Using Active Directory." But with or without AD, you can perform basic searches as follows:

1. Click Start, Search.

2. Select Computers or People.

3. Select A Computer on the Network.

4. Enter a computer name, or a partial computer name with a wildcard, such as s* or just *. Then, click Search. If you use a wildcard, Windows searches only the workgroup or domain to which your computer belongs.

5. Computers will be listed in the right pane by name and workgroup or domain name. You can double-click these entries to view shared printers and folders.

> **NOTE**
>
> After searching, the wizard offers the option Search This Computer for Files, but it appears that this *does not work*. As of Windows XP Service Pack 1, even if you select one of the located computers, a subsequent file search examines only your own computer (and drives mapped to network shares, as usual). It does *not* query the selected computer or computers.

LOCATING RESOURCES FROM THE COMMAND LINE

You can also browse your network from the command line, using the `net view` command. This is actually a rather convenient way to work, which I personally use more often than the graphical method described in the previous section.

At the command prompt, the command

```
net view
```

will display the list of up-and-running computers that are members of the same domain or workgroup as your computer. For example, on my network the command `net view` prints

```
Server Name           Remark
-------------------------------------------------------------------
\\AMBON
\\BALI
\\JAVA
The command completed successfully.
```

You can display the list of computers in another workgroup or domain by adding /domain:*name* to the command, as in

```
net view /domain:mycompany
```

If your network contains Novell NetWare servers, you can list the available NetWare servers with the command

```
net view /network:nw
```

To view the resources shared by a specific computer, use the command `net view \\computername`. For example, on my computer, the command `net view \\bali` prints the following:

```
Shared resources at \\bali

Share name  Type   Used as  Comment
-------------------------------------------------------------
bknittel    Disk   R:
bob         Disk
Laserjet    Print           Laserjet 4V via JetDirect
weblogs     Disk
www         Disk   W:
The command completed successfully.
```

This shows that there are four shared folders available on computer \bali, and one printer.

In addition, this display indicates that two of the shared folders are currently mapped to drive letters on my computer—more on the topic of mapping later in the chapter.

Finally, adding the option `/cache` displays the Offline Folder caching option set for each shared folder. For example, on my computer the command `net view \\bali /cache` displays the following:

```
Shared resources at \\bali

Share name  Type   Used as  Comment
-------------------------------------------------------------
bknittel    Disk   R:       Manual caching of documents
bob         Disk            Manual caching of documents
weblogs     Disk            Manual caching of documents
www         Disk   W:       Manual caching of documents
The command completed successfully.
```

→ To learn more about Offline Folder caching, **see** "Making Your Shared Folders Available for Offline Use by Others," **p. 752**.

CREATING BOOKMARKS IN MY NETWORK PLACES

My Network Places lets you organize shortcuts to commonly used shared folders, and also lists several commonly used tasks:

- **View Network Connections**—Displays and configures your dial-up connections or LAN adapter.

- **Add a Network Place**—Opens a wizard to create network or Internet shortcuts. I'll discuss the Add Network Place Wizard later in this section.

- **Set Up a Home or Small Office Network**—Runs the Network Setup Wizard. (For more information, see "Using the Network Setup Wizard" in Chapter 17, "Building Your Own Network".)

On a peer-to-peer-network, there is an additional choice:

- **View Workgroup Computers**—Provides a quick way to view the list of computers in your workgroup, and from there, shared folders and printers; this item was discussed previously.

18

On a workgroup network, by default Windows will automatically populate My Network Places with shortcuts to every shared folder on every computer in the workgroup, as it finds them through period scans. (This feature can be disabled, as discussed under Automatic Shared Folder Display later in the chapter.)

ADDING NETWORK PLACES

By using the Add a Network Place Wizard, you can add shortcuts in My Network Places to network shared folders, for a quick return when you need them in the future. These entries appear in the list of choices in every application's Save As dialog, as shown in Figure 18.4. This is very handy for saving files to a remote location.

Figure 18.4
Select network folders when you're saving files in any application.

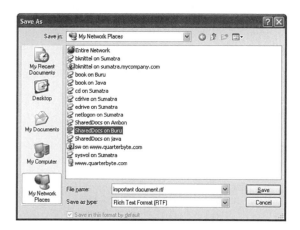

You might find that Windows automatically adds locations to Network Places whenever you open a remote folder by name using Windows Explorer or Internet Explorer's Web Folder view. If you want to add a network place shortcut by hand, do the following:

1. Open My Network Places and select Add a Network Place from the task list.
2. When asked where you want to create the network place, select Choose Another Network Location and click Next.
3. The Add Network Place Wizard asks for the name of the network resource, as shown in Figure 18.5. Enter one of these three types of network resource names:

   - A UNC name for a shared folder, such as `\\server\share`
   - A URL for a Web Sharing folder, such as `http://host/share`
   - The name of an FTP site, such as `ftp://host` or `ftp://host/subfolder`

You can also choose Browse to search through an Explorer-like view of the Entire Network.

4. Click Next, and enter a name for your Network Place shortcut. Then select Finish. A shortcut icon appears in My Network Places, and Windows pops up an Explorer window showing the contents of the remote shared folder or site.

Figure 18.5
The Add a Network Place wizard lets you enter a UNC name, a URL for Web folders, or an FTP site.

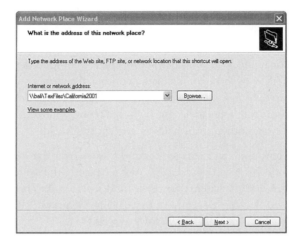

> **TIP**
>
> When you're browsing through your network or browsing the Internet using Internet Explorer, you can drag network folders or Web page addresses to My Network Places to instantly make a Network Place shortcut without the Add Network Place Wizard.
>
> Likewise, you can drag the address from the Explorer window's Address bar to your desktop or to a folder to make an instant network shortcut.

USING SHARED FOLDERS

When you have identified a shared folder that contains files you need to use, you can simply open the folder and use it as you would if the files were stored on your own hard drives. Here are a few tips to make your life on the network a bit easier:

- When you use Explorer to drag files between a network shared folder and your local drives or a different server's folders, by default Windows will *copy* the files rather than *move* them. If you hold down the Shift key when you drop the files, Windows will move the files; that is, it will copy the files and then delete the originals. As usual, the Ctrl key will force Windows to perform a copy (which it would anyway), and the Alt key will create a shortcut.

- If another user is currently using a file that you want to open, rename, or delete, you will receive an error message indicating that the file is in use. If the file is one stored on your computer, you can find out who is using it by using the management tools described later under "Viewing and Managing Shared Resources." If you get this error and you know nobody is using the file, wait about 10 minutes and try again.

- If you're using Windows XP Professional, you can keep up-to-date copies of network files on your own computer using Windows "Offline Folders" feature. See "Offline Folders" in Chapter 19, "Windows Unplugged: Remote and Portable Computing" (*page 743*), for more information.

USING WEB FOLDERS

Windows XP Professional and Windows NT4/200x Server computers running Internet Information Services (IIS) can share folders using another file sharing system called *WebDAV (Web Distributed Authoring and Versioning)*, or *Web Sharing*. Because it's based on the standard HTTP protocol, you can access Web folders on your office PC from home, over the Internet, or from another LAN halfway around the world.

Web Folders let you view, use, and manage files and folders over the Internet just as if you were using them on your PC or on your LAN. You get exactly the same look and feel. You can use Microsoft Office 2000 or later, FrontPage, and Internet Explorer version 5 or higher to access Web folders. You don't even have to be using Windows XP; you can use these three applications on earlier versions of Windows as well.

To use a folder that has been shared using Web Sharing, you need to know the folder's URL, which is set by the manager of the Web server you'll be using. In Internet Explorer, you can't use a link in a Web page to pop open a Web Folder. You have to use the following procedure instead:

1. Open Internet Explorer and select File, Open.
2. Enter the Web folder's URL, being sure to start with `http:`, and be *sure* to check the Open as Web Folder box, as shown in Figure 18.6.

Figure 18.6

3. Click OK.
4. You might be prompted to enter your login name and password. It's safe to do so, even over the Internet, as they will be encrypted.

An ordinary folder view will appear, as in Figure 18.7. You can treat it in the usual way: view its contents, drag files in and out, create new folders, and rename and delete files if you have the appropriate permissions. These operations take much longer than with LAN file sharing, however.

Figure 18.7
The Web Folder view looks just like an ordinary Explorer folder view.

One peculiar thing to note is that after you open a Web Folder from Internet Explorer, the window changes to Windows Explorer view. The File menu will no longer have an Open choice. If you want to open another Web folder, you'll have to start Internet Explorer again.

Windows will automatically add the Web folder address you used to My Network Places, and the Web Folders list in "other places." This is a convenient way to return to the folder later.

You can also view a Web folder using the Add Network Place Wizard in My Network Places. When you're asked for the location of the network place, enter the Web folder URL starting with http:.

18

NOTE

> After you open a Web folder, you might be tempted to create a shortcut to it by dragging the address from the Address bar in the Explorer window. This approach doesn't work if you opened the Web folder by choosing File, Open; you get a Web page shortcut instead.
>
> If you opened the Web folder by using the Add Network Places Wizard, however, or by opening an existing Web Folder icon, you'll get a working folder shortcut. Strange!

NOTE

> If you view a Web folder known to contain files and it appears to be empty, the Web server that is sharing the folder does not have Directory Listing (Directory Browsing) enabled on the shared folder. The manager of this Web server (who could be you) needs to set this property in the Web Sharing Properties dialog box for the folder.
>
> If you view a Web folder and see a columnar text listing of filenames, sizes, and dates instead of the expected folder view with icons, either
>
> - You did not view the folder using the Open dialog box with Open As Web Folder checked.
> - The Web site you visited does not have WebDAV, FrontPage, or Office server extensions installed.
> - You opened the folder using a shortcut you created by dragging the Address icon from Explorer when you first viewed this Web folder. Get your shortcut from My Network Places instead.

NAMING FOR WEB-BASED SHARING

Path names used for Web Folders technologies use the Web's traditional forward slash rather than the backslash. A Web folder path name looks just like a standard Web URL:

```
http://ambon/docs
```

or

```
http://ambon.mycompany.com/docs
```

It's very easy to enter backslashes, but these will not work.

USING A SHARED DISK DRIVE

Shared folders don't have to be subfolders. Computer owners can share the *root folder* of any of their disk drives, making the entire drive available over the network. This is especially useful with CD-ROM, floppy, and Zip disk drives. If an entire CD-ROM drive is shared, you can access the entire CD from any computer on the network.

Just so you know, Windows automatically shares your entire hard drive with the special name C$. (Any other hard drives would also be shared as D$, E$, and so on.) These shares don't show up when you browse the network—the dollar sign at the end tells Windows to keep the name hidden. But you can enter the share name directly, such as \\**ambon****c$**, in Explorer or other programs, to view the entire drive.

> **NOTE**
>
> You must have Administrator rights on the remote computer to use this feature. On a workgroup network with Simple File Sharing enabled, these administrative shares are never accessible, as all network users are treated as Guest.

> **TIP**
>
> If you need to install CD-ROM-based software on a computer with a broken CD-ROM drive but a good network connection, you can put the CD-ROM in another computer's drive, and share the entire drive. On the computer with the bad CD-ROM drive, map a drive letter to the shared drive. Then, use the mapped drive as if it was a local drive. We discuss mapping in the next section.

MAPPING DRIVES AND FOLDERS

If you are going to use a given shared network folder frequently, you can *map* the folder so that the remote folder appears as one of your computer's attached drives. In essence, mapping assigns an unused drive letter between A and Z to a remote folder. Then, the contents of the shared folder appear to be the contents of this new attached disk drive.

Mapping gives you several benefits:

- The mapped drive appears along with your computer's other real, physical drives in My Computer for quick browsing, opening, and saving of files, as well as in the Search Wizard.

- Access to the shared folder is faster because Windows maintains an open connection to the remote computer.

- MS-DOS applications can use the shared folder through its assigned letter. Most legacy DOS applications can't accept UNC-formatted names such as `\\server\shared\subfolder\file`, but they can use `j:\subfolder\file`.

- You can map a shared folder using an alternate username and password to gain access rights you might not have with your current Windows login name.

Mappings can be either *persistent* or *temporary*. The difference is that information about persistent mappings is stored in the registry so that the drive mappings can be restored each time you log on; temporary mappings are not remembered, and so will not automatically reappear when next you log on.

NOTE

> Persistent mappings can easily be deleted when no longer needed, or by accident. When drive mappings are required for correct operation of your application programs, you or your system administrator may wish to create the mappings in a logon script so that they will always be re-created at each logon, even if you or your users accidentally delete or change them during day-to-day use.
>
> The information for persistent mappings is stored in the Registry in keys named `HKEY_CURRENT_USER\Network\x`, where *x* is the drive letter for the persistent mapping. I'll discuss this further under "Mapping in Scripts."

18

As I mentioned earlier, drive mapping causes the contents of a shared folder to appear to be the contents of a hard drive with a selected drive letter. As an option, you can create a mapped drive whose contents are those of a *subfolder* in a shared folder. In other words, the mapped drive "sees" only part of the shared folder, and can't view any of the contents "above" the selected point. Novell NetWare users are familiar with this as the "map root" function.

See Figure 18.8, in which I'm mapping a drive to the folder `h02\images` inside the shared folder `\\java\book`. The mapped drive will appear to contain the contents of folder `\\java\book\h02\images`, and it can't be made to see up into `\\java\book\h02` or higher. The root, or top-level, directory of the drive will be the images folder.

Figure 18.8
You can map the root directory of a drive letter to a deeper point in the share.

This feature is especially useful in two situations:

- To set up personalized shared folders for each network user. On a server, a folder can be created with subfolders for each network user, and this single folder can be shared, perhaps with the share name "users". A user's logon script can map a drive to his or her private subfolder, (that is, to \\server\users\%username%). The advantage to the user is that the mapped drive will display only his or her own files. The advantage to the administrator is that only one folder need be shared, and application programs can be configured to use the selected drive letter in the same way for each user.
- Some old application programs—especially but not limited to DOS programs—insist that their data and application files be installed in or under the root folder of a local drive. These applications can often be fooled into running on a network shared folder by mapping a drive letter to a network shared folder. You can select a subfolder of a shared folder to use for this purpose.

CAUTION

> This won't make it safe for more than one user at a time to access this application's data, unless the application is specifically designed for multiuser use. It does, however, make it possible to locate the data on a server that has daily backups, and to get to the data from alternate locations.

In the following sections, we'll discuss several ways to create and delete network drive mappings.

MAPPING FROM WINDOWS EXPLORER

To map a drive, select Tools, Map Network Drive in any Explorer window (such as My Computer). Or you can right-click My Network Places and select Map Network Drive.

Next, select an unused drive letter from the drop-down list, as shown in Figure 18.9. If possible, pick a drive letter that has some association for you with the resource you'll be using: E for Editorial, S for Sales—whatever makes sense to you.

Figure 18.9
You can select an unused drive letter to use for the drive mapping.

Then select the name of the shared folder you want to assign to the drive letter. You can type the UNC-formatted name if you know it already—for example, \\servername\share-name—or you can click Browse to poke through your network's resources and select the shared folder. Find the desired shared folder in the expandable list of workgroups, computers, and share names, as shown in Figure 18.10, and click OK.

Figure 18.10
Browsing for a shared folder. You can open the list view to see network types, workgroups, computers, and shared folders.

PERSISTENCE AND ALTERNATE USERNAMES

After you select the shared folder and click OK, the folder name appears in the dialog, and you have two options:

- If you want this to be a persistent mapping that reappears every time you log in, check Reconnect at Login.

- If your current Windows username and password don't give you sufficient permissions to use the shared resource, or if your username won't be recognized at the other computer because your account name is different there, select Connect Using a Different User Name. Choosing this option displays a Connect As dialog, as shown in Figure 18.11. Here, you can enter the alternate username and password, and click OK. (On an AD network, you can select Browse to view valid usernames by location, if you need help.)

Figure 18.11

This is especially useful when you are on a domain network and are attaching to a computer in a different domain, or in a workgroup. Since Windows will send your current username to the remote computer in the form *yourdomain\yourname*, you will not be able to connect without specifying a name in the form *computername\username* or *otherdomain\username*.

NOTE

> You must use the same username for *all* connections to a given computer. If you have other drive letters already mapped to the other computer with your original username, you'll have to unmap those drives before you can make a drive mapping with a different username.

After you map a drive letter, the drive appears in your My Computer list along with your local disk drives. You might notice a couple of funny things with these listings:

- If you haven't accessed the network drive for a while, 20 minutes or so, it might turn gray, indicating that Windows has temporarily disconnected from the remote computer. When you attempt to use the drive again, it will reconnect and turn black.
- If the remote computer (or you) really goes offline, a red X appears through the drive.

To map a network drive with its root in a subfolder of the shared folder, specify the additional subfolder path after the server and share name when entering a UNC path in the Map Network Drive dialog. To obtain the drive mapping illustrated in Figure 18.8, you would enter `\\java\book\h02\images`.

MAPPING A SHARED FOLDER WITHOUT A DRIVE LETTER

You can make an established connection to a shared folder, keeping it readily available for quick response without assigning it a drive letter. Follow the procedure shown earlier for mapping a drive letter. When you select the letter to map, go all the way to the bottom of the Drive Letter drop-down list, and select (None), the last choice. Continue through the rest of the process as described.

Mapping a shared folder to (None) doesn't add a drive to your My Computer list, but it does make for speedier response from the server when you're accessing that folder. The shared folder will be visible, however, if you choose Disconnect Network Drive, or if you use the `net use` command from the command line.

DISCONNECTING MAPPED DRIVES

Delete network mappings when

- You no longer need to access a given network computer, especially if you are accessing it through a dial-up networking or VPN connection. This will prevent error messages from popping up later when the remote computer is no longer available.

- You want to change a mapped drive letter from one network folder to another. You must unmap before you can reuse a given drive letter.

- You have attached a removable drive that is configured in Disk Management to use the same drive letter as a network mapping. Windows won't let you map the letter of a drive that's online, but will let you map a drive that's disconnected or offline; you must unmap to make the removable drive visible.

- You want to attach to a given remote computer with an alternate username/password. You must delete all connections to the computer before you can reattach with an alternate username.

- You are finished using resources on the shared folder. Deleting the mapping will save a bit of time the next time you log on.

You can delete a drive mapping from Windows Explorer by selecting Tools, Disconnect Network drive. Select the icon for the drive mapping you no longer want, and click OK. You can also delete a mapping from the command line, as will be discussed in the next section, or by right-clicking the drive in the My Computer display and selecting Disconnect.

If the mapping was persistent, it will not be restored upon your next logon.

18

MAPPING FROM THE COMMAND LINE

You can map drives from the command line with the net use command. You can use the command line version in batch files to help automate routine tasks, or, if you're like me, as an alternate to the GUI method when you're mouse-challenged but a decent typist.

NOTE

> The net command comes to us virtually unchanged since the original PC network software developed by Microsoft and IBM back in the early 1980s. There are so many variations of the net command that I think of them as separate commands: net view, net use, net whatever. Each net command contains a word that selects a subcommand or operation type.
>
> You can get online help listing all the net subcommands by typing **net /?**, and detailed help by typing **net command /?**, where command is any one of the net subcommands.

The command-line syntax is

```
net use x: \\server\sharename
```

where you would replace x with the drive letter you wish to use, and \\server\sharename with the actual UNC path to the shared folder you wish to use.

You can add the option /persistent:yes or /persistent:no to control whether or not the mapping will be restored at the next logon.

You can set the default value for the persistent option by issuing the command net use /persistent:*xxx*, where *xxx* is yes or no. This is useful in logon script batch files to set the default environment for the user.

You can map the drive letter root to a subfolder of the shared folder by adding additional path information to the command; to create the mapping shown in Figure 18.8, the command would be

```
net use m: \\java\book\h02\images
```

MAPPING WITH AN ALTERNATE USERNAME

You can specify an alternate user account to use for a network mapping made with net use by adding one of the following options to the command line:

/user:*username*	Makes the connection using the specified user account. Windows will prompt for a password.
/user:*domainname\username*	(Alternate version, specifying a Windows Server domain name and username.)
/user:*user@domain.name*	(Alternate version, specifying an Active Directory-type domain name and username.)
/smartcard	Makes the connection using user credentials read from a smart card.

As an example, this command maps drive letter j: to \\sumatra\cdrive using the Administrator account:

```
net use j: \\sumatra\cdrive /user:Administrator
```

Windows will prompt you for the password to be used.

NOTE
> You can use at most one set of user credentials to attach to a given remote computer. Windows will not be able to create the drive mapping if there is already another drive mapped to the same computer using, for example, your default account information.

In a batch file that is expected to run unattended, it's not practical to have Windows prompt for a password. If you *must* use a net use command with an alternate credential in a batch file, you can store the password in the batch file by placing it just before the /user option, as in this example:

```
net use j: \\sumatra\cdrive x23aB42 /user:Administrator
```

However, this is a major security risk: Putting a password in a batch file means that anyone who can see the batch file will be able to read the password. Be *absolutely* sure that either (a) the user account and password you use in such a manner has very limited privileges, or (b)

the batch file is placed on an NTFS-formatted disk partition and is readable *only* by the Administrator and SYSTEM.

DELETING DRIVE MAPPINGS FROM THE COMMAND LINE

You can also use the `net use` command to delete a drive mapping from the command line, whether it was originally made with the Explorer GUI or from the command line. The syntax is

```
net use x: /delete
```

where you would replace *x* with the drive letter you wish to unmap.

You must delete any previous mappings before creating a new one with a given drive letter. If you are creating mappings in a batch file, then you should use `net use /delete` before attempting any new mapping.

However, the `net` command prints an error message if there was no previous mapping to delete. To prevent this unnecessary and confusing message from appearing, you can redirect the output of the command to the NUL file, which is a special filename that Windows recognizes as a "black hole," into which all that is written is discarded. Thus, in a batch file, the command

```
net use m: /delete >nul 2>nul
```

could be used to silently delete any old mapping for drive M: before attempting to make a new one.

For more information about working with batch files, **see** "Batch Files," **p. 1218**.

You can delete *all* drive mappings with the command

```
net use * /delete
```

This command is useful mostly in login script batch files to prepare a "clean" environment for the user; it can be followed by other `net use` commands to prepare standard drive mappings. Windows will prompt for confirmation before deleting drive mappings when using this wildcard option. You can add `/y` to the command to suppress this prompt and force the connections to be closed and the mappings to be deleted. However, this is a rather dangerous option.

CAUTION

> Forcing Windows to delete a drive mapping that is in use–that is, when application programs are using files on the mapped drive–can cause data loss and application crashes. Your author recalled this only after testing the `/y` option while writing this chapter, which was stored on a network drive, and…you can guess the rest of the story.

`net use` also maps network printers to the legacy DOS printer devices LPT1, LPT2, and LPT3. The `capture` printer setting found in Windows 9x is not available, and the only way to redirect DOS program output to a network printer is through `net use`.

The following command directs DOS application LPT1 printer output to the network printer:

```
net use lpt1: \\server\printername
```

The following command cancels it:

```
net use lpt1: /delete
```

MAPPING IN SCRIPTS

There are two types of scripts in which you may wish to map network drives: logon scripts, and general-purpose scripts written to use with Windows Script Host (WSH).

You can map network drives in WSH scripts using the WScript.Network object provided with Windows.

For more information about mapping drives from Windows Script Host, **see** "WScript.Network," **p. 1200**. (Chapter 29)

Logon scripts can be written as ordinary batch files that use the net use command described in the previous section, or as Windows Script Host scripts written using the techniques described in Chapter 29, "Automating Routine Tasks." Logon Scripts are discussed in Chapter 33, "Managing Windows XP in an Enterprise Setting," under "Using Logon Scripts to Enforce Consistency." Using a logon script can prepare a standard environment for users at each logon; if the user accidentally deletes a necessary drive mapping, a simple logoff and logon will fix the problem.

PERSISTENCE OPTIONS

You can use scripting to modify the information Windows stores for persistent network mappings by editing the registry with your script. The information for persistent mappings is stored in the Registry in keys named HKEY_CURRENT_USER\Network\x, where x is the drive letter for the persistent mapping. Under these keys Windows reads the values listed in Table 18.2 at every logon, in order to set up persistent mappings:

TABLE 18.2   REGISTRY VALUES FOR PERSISTENT MAPPINGS

Value	Type	Description
ConnectionType	REG_DWORD	1 for a drive mapping, 2 for a printer mapping.
DeferFlags	REG_DWORD	Normally 4, connection is temporarily closed after several minutes idle. Set to 1 to keep connection open permanently.
ProviderName	REG_SZ	Usually "Microsoft Windows Network."
ProviderType	REG_DWORD	Usually 0x00020000 (hexadecimal).
RemotePath	REG_SZ	UNC path of the mapping.
UserName	REG_SZ	Username used for the connection; blank (or DWORD value 0) to use current user.

You can use REG_EXPAND_SZ values for the UNC path and username, if desired. You can then insert the user's account name into the path with %USERNAME%, as in this example:

```
\\mainserver\users\%USERNAME%\homedir
```

The advantage of this format is that if your network share names are constructed using user names, you can use the same path definition for each user; the insertion can be made with a login script or group policy.

NOTE

> Persistent connections are restored *before* the login script is run, so changes made to this registry information by a login script will not take effect until the next login.

Using Shared Printers

Microsoft has done a remarkable job making network printing effortless. It's seamless and easy. In fact, given the low cost of network hardware, it's worth installing a network just to be able to share printers, even if you have only two computers.

Chapter 7, "Printing and Faxing," discussed most of the details of working with network printers. In this section, we'll go into extra detail on a few topics. Later in the chapter, we'll discuss how to share a printer on your computer with the rest of the network.

18

Locating and Connecting to Network Printers

To use any networked printer, you have to set up an icon for the printer in your Printers window. One way to do this is to browse or search your network for shared printers. If you locate an appropriate printer, right-click its icon and select Open to set it up for your computer.

Alternatively, you can use the Add Printer Wizard in Printers and Faxes as you would to install a locally attached printer. The wizard will walk you through locating and installing the printer. If your computer is a member of an Active Directory network, you can search for suitable printers in the directory. This feature is very handy if you're a business traveler using the network in an unfamiliar office, or if you're in such a large office setting that you aren't familiar with all the printing resources on your network.

For more information about installing and searching for printers **see** Chapter 7, "Printing and Faxing," **p. 233**.

Using Printers Over the Internet with IPP

A fairly recent addition to Windows is the ability to install and print to a shared printer through the Internet as easily as you can through a LAN.

The Internet Printing Protocol (IPP) was developed by a group of network and printer technology companies at the initiative of Novell Corporation and Xerox Corporation. The idea is that business travelers should be able to send reports back to their home offices via the Internet and use the same technology to print reports or presentations in a hotel's business center or a commercial copy service center. I use it myself to print to my office's laser printer from home. IPP is based on the Hypertext Transfer Protocol (HTTP), which runs the World Wide Web, so it's simple and it can pass safely through network firewalls. In Windows, IPP uses Windows's own safely encrypted username and password security, so your printers are protected from abuse by anonymous outsiders.

As with all the shared resources I'm discussing, using and providing these services are really separate things. You can use IPP to reach a printer without providing the service yourself, and vice versa. In this section, I'll talk about *using* the service.

The blessing of IPP is that once you've installed the printer icon, you can use the remote printer in exactly the same way as you use any Windows printer. The printer queue, management tools, and other operations are all exactly the same, as long as you're connected to the Internet or the appropriate intranet LAN.

SELECTING AN IPP PRINTER BY ITS URL

You can connect to a remote printer via IPP in either of two ways.

If you know the URL of the IPP-connected printer, you can use the Add Printer Wizard. Your network administrator should supply you with the URL, if the printer is on your company's intranet, or by a hotel or service bureau, after they've gotten your credit card number.

1. Follow the instructions in Chapter 7 for adding a network printer.
2. When you are asked to enter the printer name, instead of browsing the network, choose Connect to a Printer on the Internet or on a Home or Office Network.
3. Enter the URL provided by your administrator or the service you are using, as shown in Figure 18.12, and select Next.

Figure 18.12
Adding an Internet-connected printer using IPP.

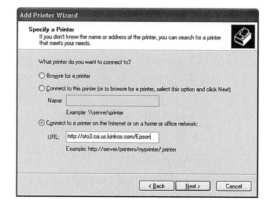

4. You might be prompted for a username and password. If so, enter the name and password supplied by the vendor or, if the printer is on your own network, your network username and password.

5. Continue with the installation procedure described previously; you might need to select a print driver if the remote print server doesn't provide it automatically.

When the new printer icon is installed, you have a fully functional Windows printer. You can view the pending jobs and set your print and page preferences as usual as long as you're connected to the Internet (or the LAN, in a service establishment).

TIP

> If you use a printing service bureau, remember to delete the printer from your Printers folder when you leave town; you don't want to accidentally print reports in Katmandu after you've returned home.
>
> Also, if you are printing to a different brand and model than you normally do, you should select the remote printer and scroll through your document to check for changes in page breaks or other options that could affect your output. If your document's layout has changed because you're about to use a different printer, save your document under a different name before you print it.

SELECTING AN IPP PRINTER VIA THE WEB

If you can reach the Web site of a service bureau or a Windows XP/2000 Professional or Server computer that sports both Internet Information Services (IIS) and a shared printer, Internet printing is a snap.

TIP

> If you use Windows XP Professional or Server at work, and Windows XP Home Edition at home, you can use this feature to print to your office printer from home, as long as the office computer's Web server is reachable over the Internet.

If you view the URL http://computername/Printers, replacing computername with the actual hostname of the remote computer, you get a display like the one shown in Figure 18.13.

Figure 18.13
Windows XP's Professional and Server versions provide a Web Interface for printer management. The home page gives a quick overview of all shared printers. You can select a printer to view or manage for more detail.

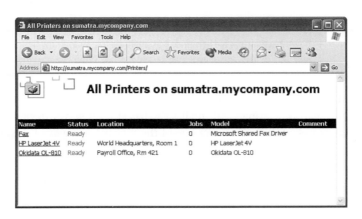

Selecting one of the printers brings up a detailed printer status page, as shown in Figure 18.14. The printer status page lists queued print jobs and current printer status. If you're using Internet Explorer as your Web browser and have IPP printing software installed in Windows, clicking Connect sets this printer up as a network printer on your computer, drivers and all. You can select the printer and use it immediately, right over the Internet.

Figure 18.14
The printer status page shows current print jobs; using it, you can manage the printer and queued documents. The Connect hyperlink installs the printer on your computer.

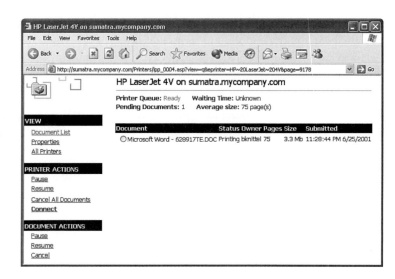

USING OTHER IPP PRINTERS

You can buy an IPP-capable printer and plug it directly into your LAN. An IPP-capable printer will probably provide Web-based management and status, which is a great way to monitor its health from across the country (or across the room).

USING UNIX AND LPR PRINTERS

In the Unix world, most shared printers use a protocol called LPR/LPD, which was developed at the University of California at Berkeley during the early years of Unix and the TCP/IP protocol.

NOTE

> If you have a Unix background, you might be happy to know that the familiar Unix lpr and lpq utilities are available as command-line programs in Windows XP.

Manufacturers such as HP make direct network-connected printers that accept the LPR protocol, and many companies sell small LPR-based print server devices that can attach to your printer as well. You can connect one of these printers to your LAN, configure its

TCP/IP settings to match your LAN, and immediately print without running a cable from a computer to the printer. This way, you can place a printer in a more convenient place than could be reached by a 10-foot printer cable. Better yet, you can use these networked printers without requiring a Windows computer to be left turned on to manage it.

You can install a Windows printer that directs its output to an LPR print queue or device as easily as you can install a directly connected printer. Follow these steps:

1. For the first LPR-based printer you use, you have to install LPR support. Open My Network Places and select View Network Connections. Select Advanced, Optional Networking Components. Check Other Network File and Print Services and click Next. You might need to insert your Windows XP Installation CD-ROM.

2. View Printers and Faxes and select Add a Printer.

3. Select Local Printer. (You choose Local because Network connects only to Windows and IPP shared printers.) Uncheck Automatically Detect and Install My Plug and Play Printer, and click Next.

4. Select the Create a New Port option, choose LPR Port in the Type of Port box, and click Next.

5. In the Add LPR Compatible Printer dialog, enter the IP address or hostname of the Unix or print server, and the name of the print queue on that server, as shown in Figure 18.15.

Figure 18.15
In this dialog box, enter the IP address or hostname of the LPR print server and the queue or printer name.

6. Select the manufacturer and printer model as usual, and proceed with the rest of the printer installation.

NOTE

If you enter the wrong IP address, hostname, or print queue name, Windows will not let you change this information. To correct the problem, bring up the printer's Properties page, select the Ports tab, highlight the LPR port, and select Configure Port. If Windows doesn't display a dialog to let you change the IP information, uncheck the LPR port. Delete the port, and add a new LPR port with the correct information. Then check the port to connect your Windows printer to the LPR server.

Using AppleTalk Printers

If your network has AppleTalk printers attached, you probably have Macintosh users on your LAN. If you want to share files with Macintosh users, you need to have Windows 200x Server on your network because it includes File and Printer Services for Macintosh Networks. These services let Macintosh and Windows users access shared printers and folders on each others' networks as if they were their own.

Windows XP Professional doesn't provide such services, so without the Server version you can't directly use AppleTalk-based printers. Regrettably, Windows XP Professional doesn't come with the AppleTalk Protocol and AppleTalk Printer port monitor components that were provided with previous versions of Windows. You may be able to obtain SMB protocol software to let your Macs use printers shared by Windows.

→ To learn more details about internetworking with Macintosh computers, **see** "Macintosh Connectivity," **p. 815**.

NOTE

> Before giving up, however, check the documentation on your networked printer. Some printers support access via all three standard protocols: AppleTalk, NetBIOS (SMB), and TCP/IP.

Using Other Network-Connected Printers

Windows XP can use other types of network-connected printers as well. Some printer models come with a built-in network connection, and others have a network adapter option. You can also buy network print servers, which are small boxes with a network connector and one to three printer connection ports. These devices let you locate printers in a convenient area, which doesn't need to be near a computer. Some broadband Internet connection sharing routers include a print server as well, for example, the D-Link DI-713p and DI-704P, the Siemens SS2602, the NetGear FR114P and so on. The installation procedures for various printer and server models vary. Your networked printer or print server will come with specific installation instructions.

When you install one of these devices, you have a choice about how the printer will be shared on your network:

- You can install the network-to-printer connection software on *one* of your Windows computers, and then use standard Windows printer sharing to make the printer available to the other computers on your network

- You can install the printer's connection software on *each* of your computers

With the first method, you will guarantee that print jobs will be run first-come-first-served (or you can set priorities for print jobs if you want), because one computer will provide a single queue for the printer. Another plus is that you'll only have to do the software setup once; it's much easier to set up the other workstations to use the standard Windows shared printer. However, the one computer will have to be left on for others to use the printer.

With the second method, each computer will contact the printer independently, so there may be contention for the printer. However, no computers need to be left on, since each workstation will contact the printer directly.

You can use either method. The first one is simplest, and is best suited for a busy office. The second method is probably more convenient for home networks and small offices.

Windows automatically makes your computer's Shared Documents folder available on the network. However, you might want to share other folders with your network cohorts. This capability is built right in to Explorer.

The procedure has some slight differences depending on the type of network you have. If you're using a workgroup-type network with Simple File Sharing enabled, follow the procedure in the next section. If you're on a domain-type network or you've disabled Simple File Sharing, skip ahead to "Sharing Folders on a Domain Network."

NOTE

As you start to select folders to share, you might notice that Windows has automatically already shared your entire hard drive with the name C$. Leave this share alone; it lets Administrators manage your computer. You can choose an additional, different name if you want to share your entire hard drive—for example, `cdrive` or `cdrive$`, although Microsoft discourages sharing entire hard disk drives.

SHARING FOLDERS WITH THE NETWORK

You can share folders on your own hard drive(s) with other users on your network. The procedures are described in the following sections. Be sure, though, to consider the security aspects of file sharing before you do this. In particular, you *must* have some sort of firewall present if you have Internet connectivity as well as a network.

NOTE

Unless your computer is a member of a domain network File Sharing will not work unless you've run the Network Setup Wizard at least once, even if you've configured your network manually! For more information about the Network Setup Wizard, see Chapter 17.

SHARING FOLDERS ON A WORKGROUP NETWORK

On workgroup networks with Simple File Sharing enabled, Microsoft provides a simplified user interface and security system for file sharing, which is discussed in detail in Chapter 23, "Managing File Security." It's the default method, so I'll describe it first.

NOTE

If you've disabled Simple File Sharing, skip head to the next section titled "Sharing Folders on a Domain Network."

To share a folder with Simple File Sharing enabled, just follow these steps:

1. Select a folder in Explorer, or select the name of the CD-ROM, floppy, Zip, or hard drive itself at the top of the Explorer view, if you want to share the entire disk.

   Microsoft recommends that you only share folders found inside your My Documents folder, but I think that's too restrictive. You can safely share any folder on your hard drive except Documents and Settings, Program Files, and your Windows folder. You should *not* share the entire hard drive that contains your Windows folder.

2. Right-click the folder, and choose Sharing and Security.

3. Select Share This Folder on the Network, as shown in Figure 18.16. Windows fills in the Share Name field with the name of the folder. If the name contains spaces, it may not be accessible to Windows for Workgroups users, so if you still have such ancient versions of Windows running, you might want to shorten or abbreviate the name.

Figure 18.16
To share a folder, check Share This Folder, and enter a share name. Comments are optional.

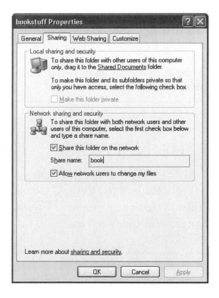

TIP

You can prevent other users from seeing your shared folder listed when they browse the network by adding a dollar sign to the end of the share name—for example, mystuff$. But note that this convention alone does *not* prevent them from seeing your files if they know the share name.

Before clicking OK to make the folder accessible, however, you should consider file security and the ability of other users to access your files. I'll continue this discussion in the next section.

NOTE

> You must run the Network Setup Wizard at least once to share any of your computer's files, even if you've set up your network manually. The Network Setup Wizard was discussed in Chapter 17.

SHARED FOLDER SECURITY

Sharing security is frequently misunderstood. You can specify the rights of remote users and groups to read or change (that is, write, delete, rename, and so on) the files in your shared folder when you enable sharing, as shown in Figure 18.16. On a workgroup network with Simple File Sharing enabled, it works like this:

- If you check Allow Network Users to Change my Files, remote users will be able to delete, edit, or rename files.
- If you don't check Allow Network Users they'll only be able to view and read files.

If you are sharing files on a FAT-formatted disk partition, these are the *only controls* you have at your disposal to manage access to your files, because *anybody* can read or write any of your files on a FAT-formatted disk.

CAUTION

> When you are on a LAN, it is not a good idea to share any folders from a FAT-formatted disk with Simple File Sharing enabled because there are no user-level controls to restrict access to your files. If you do enable sharing of a FAT-partition folder, be *sure* your network is secured by a firewall, and that you aren't concerned about people wandering into your home or office and poking around. Although share-level security is better than no security, it's not as good as other options. See Chapter 24, "Network Security," for more about securing your network.

Network security is a serious matter, and in a business setting, you should be very sure to understand the risks you're exposing your files to and the ways you can protect them.

After you've chosen whether or not to permit write-access by network users, click OK to make the share available on the network.

Finally, when you have shared a folder, its icon changes to a hand holding the folder like an offering. This is your cue that the folder is shared. You can right-click the folder later on to select Sharing and Security if you want to stop sharing or change the sharing permissions.

18

SHARING FOLDERS ON A DOMAIN NETWORK

If your computer is a member of a domain network, or if you've disabled Simple File Sharing, use the following steps to share a folder:

1. Select a folder in Explorer, or select the name of the CD-ROM, floppy, Zip, or hard drive itself at the top of the Explorer view, if you want to share the entire disk.

   Microsoft recommends that you only share folders found inside your My Documents folder, but I think that's too restrictive. You can safely share any folder on your hard drive except Documents and Settings, Program Files, and your Windows folder. You should *not* share the entire hard drive that contains your Windows folder.

2. Right-click the folder, and choose Sharing and Security.

3. Select Share This Folder on the Network, as shown in Figure 18.17. Windows fills in the Share Name field with the name of the folder. If the name contains spaces, it might not be accessible to Windows for Workgroups users, so you might want to shorten or abbreviate the name. You also can enter a comment to describe the contents of the shared folder.

Figure 18.17
To share a folder, check Share This Folder, and enter a share name. Comments are optional.

TIP

You can prevent other users from seeing your shared folder listed when they browse the network by adding a dollar sign to the end of the share name—for example, `mystuff$`. Although this convention alone does *not* prevent them from seeing your files if they know the share name.

Before clicking OK to make the folder accessible, you should consider file security and the ability of other users to access your files. I'll continue this discussion in the next section.

SHARED FOLDER SECURITY

By default, other network users will be able to add, delete, and edit files in the shared folder, *if they would have permission to do so when they were directly logged on at the computer*. That is, by default, user-level file security applies to network users as well as local users as long as your hard disk uses NTFS formatting. If your hard disk has FAT formatting, or if you want to restrict network access to shared files in *addition* to NTFS security settings, you can (further) restrict the rights of remote users and groups to read or change (that is, write, delete, rename, and so on) the files in your shared folder.

On the Sharing properties page, click Permissions. This displays the Share Permissions tab shown in Figure 18.18. Here, you can add or remove entries for Windows users and groups, and allow or deny access in three categories:

Figure 18.18
Sharing Permissions restrict access by network users in addition to any user-level security on the files themselves.

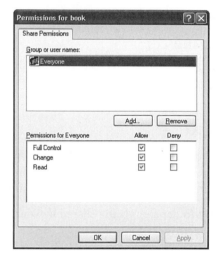

- **Read**—The ability to view the list of files in the folder and read files.
- **Change**—The ability to write, edit, delete, and rename files in the folder.
- **Full Control**—The ability to read AND change files, as well as take ownership and change file permissions.

To change sharing permissions, select a user or group name in the upper half of the dialog box, and check or uncheck this user's or group's permissions in the lower half.

If you are sharing files on a FAT-formatted disk partition, these are the *only* controls you have at your disposal to manage access to your files, because *anybody* can read or write any of your files on a FAT-formatted disk. In this case, you probably should uncheck Full Control and Change for group Everyone. Then, click Add to add specific users and groups for whom you want to grant Write access.

If your disk is formatted with the NTFS file system, Share Permissions apply in *addition* to the NTFS user-level permission system, so it's generally safe to leave the default Share Permissions set to Full Control by Everyone. However, network security is a serious matter, and in a business setting, you should be very sure to understand the risks you're exposing your files to and the ways you can protect them.

You should read Chapter 23 for more information about setting User and Group access to folders using NTFS permissions.

After you've chosen whether or not to permit write-access by network users, click OK twice to make the share available on the network.

Finally, when you have shared a folder, its icon changes to a hand holding the folder like an offering. This is your cue that the folder is shared. You can right-click the folder later on to select Sharing and Security if you want to stop sharing or change the sharing permissions.

SHARING FOLDERS FROM THE COMMAND LINE

You can use the command line program `net share` to create network shares. The syntax is

```
net share sharename=drive:\path
```

For example

```
net share project1=c:\files\project1
```

The `net share` command has other options that can be specified on the command line to limit the number of users who can attach to the shared folder at the same time, and to control how the folder will be cached for users who elect to use it as an offline folder.

You can delete a share—that is, stop a folder from being shared by your computer—with the command

```
net share sharename /delete
```

For example

```
net share project1 /delete
```

You can read more about the `net share` command by opening a Command Prompt window and typing **net share /?** and then **net help share**.

SHARING WEB FOLDERS

If you have installed Internet Information Services on your computer, then Web Folder sharing is available by default. When you view a folder's properties on a computer running IIS, the Web Sharing tab is displayed, as shown in Figure 18.19, and you can use it to make the folder available to people who access your computer using a Web browser. Then

- Visitors who use the shared folder's URL will be able to read and download the files—this is an instant way to publish Web pages.

- Visitors using Internet Explorer's "Open as a Web Folder" feature will be able to view and modify files in this folder, if they have permission.

→ To learn more about installing the Web services on your computer, **see** Chapter 15, "Internet Information Services."

Figure 18.19
Web Sharing appears as a folder property when you install IIS and configure the Server Extensions.

NOTE

> If Web Sharing does not appear as a tab in a folder's properties, either IIS is not installed or the Server Extensions are not configured for this Web site. Check to see that these services are properly installed, as explained in Chapter 15. If the Web Sharing tab is still not available, uninstall the Server Extensions and reinstall them.

TIP

> Enabling regular sharing on a folder does not make it available as a shared Web folder, or vice versa.

To make the folder available to Web visitors using Internet Explorer version 5 or higher, Microsoft Office, or FrontPage, select Share This Folder on the Web Sharing tab. A dialog box appears, as shown in Figure 18.20.

Now you can set a URL name or *alias* for the shared folder; the URL for Web access is http://hostname/aliasname, so it's best to enter the name without spaces or punctuation characters.

By default, the folder is set up for read-only access. Remote Web folder users with permission to view the folder will see the folder in a standard Explorer view and can copy and view the files in it, but cannot add or modify the files in it.

Figure 18.20
In this dialog box, you can control access to the Web-shared folder.

To enable read/write access to the shared folder, check Write in the Access Permissions section, *and* set Application Permissions to None.

CAUTION

If you enable Write access, you must set application permissions to None to prevent outside users from delivering arbitrary programs and scripts to your computer that they could then execute on your computer via the Internet.

By default, Windows *does not* grant anonymous access to Web folders set up using the Web Sharing dialog. If you grant Write access, though, you should confirm this by checking the virtual directory's properties page in the Internet Information Services manager, just to be on the safe side. See "IIS Folder Attributes" in Chapter 15 for more information.

These permission settings work in *addition* to NTFS permissions on an NTFS-formatted disk, so the same issues pertain to Web sharing as to standard sharing:

- Don't Web-share a folder on a FAT-formatted partition.
- Carefully check NTFS permissions on any folders you share.
- Read Chapter 24 for an important discussion of file and network security.

TIP

The most important thing to do after enabling Web sharing is to open a Web browser and attempt to access the shared folder using no username or password, and then with the username and password of a user account that you do not think should have access to the files. If either of these methods works, be sure you want it to. You might not have effective security in place.

NOTE

If you want to delete or rename the folder, it's best to first view the Web Sharing tab and disable Web Sharing. You can re-enable it after renaming, if desired.

The Web Sharing tab actually sets up a "virtual folder" under your computer's Internet Information Services Web site. When you delete or rename the folder pointed to by a virtual folder entry, Windows does not notify IIS of the change, and the virtual folder's URL will stop working. If this happens, you'll need to run the Internet Administration Services management tool to delete or modify the virtual folder information.

SHARING PRINTERS

You can share any local printer on your computer. It can be a printer directly cabled to your computer or one connected via the network using LPR or other network protocols.

To enable printer sharing, do the following:

1. Choose Start and view the Printers and Faxes folder.

2. Right-click the printer icon and choose Sharing, or select Properties and then select the Sharing tab.

3. Select Share This Printer, and enter a network name for the printer, as shown in Figure 18.21. Enter up to 14 characters, using letters, numbers, and hyphens. Avoid spaces if you have Windows 3.x computers on your network. 8.3 naming is recommended if Windows 3.x computers need to access the share.

Figure 18.21
Enabling sharing for a printer.

4. If your network has only Windows XP/2000 computers, click OK, and you're finished. Other network users can now use the shared printer.

Otherwise, continue to the next section to add extra printer drivers for other operating systems.

INSTALLING EXTRA PRINTER DRIVERS

If you have computers running other versions of Windows or other CPU types, you can load the appropriate printer drivers for those operating systems now, and network users will receive them automatically when they connect to your printer. This step is optional, but it's the friendly thing to do.

View the Sharing tab in your printer's Properties dialog box, and select the Additional Drivers button. Windows displays a list of supported operating systems and CPU types, as shown in Figure 18.22. (By the way, "Intel" refers to any Intel or compatible chips such as those made by AMD or VIA/Cyrix.)

Figure 18.22
You can install drivers for additional operating systems or CPUs to make it easy for network users to attach to your printer.

Check the boxes for the CPUs and operating systems you want to support, and click OK. Windows then goes through any additional operating systems you chose one-by-one and asks either for your Windows XP CD-ROM, or other operating system installation disks to locate the appropriate drivers.

You can find these drivers on the original installation disks for the alternative operating system, or often on disks provided with the printer, which might contain support for many operating systems on the same disk.

When installed, the alternative drivers are sequestered in your Windows folder and delivered to users of the other operating systems when necessary.

SETTING PRINTER PERMISSIONS

If you have a peer-to-peer network and have enabled Simple File Sharing, you don't need to worry about setting permissions for Printers. If you're on a domain network or have chosen to use detailed user-level permissions on your peer-to-peer network you can control access to your shared printers with three security attributes that can be assigned to users or groups, as shown in Figure 18.23:

Permission	Lets User or Group
Print	Send output to the printer
Manage Printers	Change printer configuration settings, and share or unshare a printer
Manage Documents	Cancel or suspend other users' print jobs

You can use the Security tab in the printer's Properties dialog box to alter the groups and users assigned each of these permissions.

Figure 18.23
The Security tab lets you assign printer management permissions for users, groups, and the creator of a networked printer.

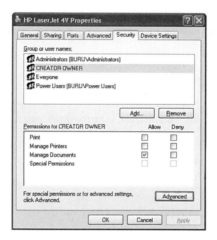

The CREATOR OWNER name applies to the user who submitted a given print job.

You probably don't have to change the default permission settings unless you want to limit use of the printer by outside users in a domain environment only. In this case, delete Everyone, and add specific groups with Print permission.

REDIRECTING OUTPUT TO AN ALTERNATE PRINTER

If you view the Ports tab on a local printer's properties page, you'll notice that the list of available ports includes all of the local computer's LPT and COM ports, as well as various entries for special printer devices such as "Print to File," Adobe Acrobat, and possibly network printer ports.

If a shared printer malfunctions or if you need to take it out of service, this can cause difficulties for network users who are used to sending output to the shared printer. To minimize inconvenience to other network users, you may be able to modify the Port settings to redirect print output to an alternate printer so that remote users can continue using the same shared print device. For this to work, you must have an alternate printer of the same make and model as the original shared printer, installed on and shared by another computer on your network. To redirect the original printer to the alternate printer, follow these steps:

1. Log on as a Computer Administrator.

2. On the computer that shared the original printer, view the printer's properties page and select the Ports tab.

3. Click Add Port.

4. Select Local Port and click New Port.

5. Enter the UNC name of the printer to which you want to redirect output, for example, `\\alternate\laserjet`. Then, click OK.

6. Be sure that the original printer port (usually LPT1) is unchecked.

Now, any output spooled to the original shared printer will be forwarded to the alternate printer.

NOTIFYING USERS WHEN PRINTING IS COMPLETE

You can have Windows send a pop-up message to remote users when print jobs they send to your printer have completed. By default, this feature is turned off when you install Windows XP.

To enable remote user notification, do the following:

1. Open the Printers and Faxes window.

2. Choose File, Server Properties.

3. Select the Advanced tab.

4. Check Notify When Remote Documents Are Printed.

5. If users on your network tend to use more than one computer at a time, check Notify Computer, Not User, When Remote Documents Are Printed. This option sends the notification to the computer where the print job originated rather than to the user who submitted the print job.

6. Click OK.

With remote notification enabled, when a print job has completed, a notification pops up on the sender's desktop. No message is sent if the print job is canceled, however.

TRACKING PRINTER USERS

If you want to track usage patterns of your printer, you can instruct Windows to record print job completion and maintenance alerts in the System Event Log, through settings on the Print Server Properties dialog box. Here's how:

1. Open the Printers and Faxes window.

2. Choose File, Server Properties.

3. Select the Advanced tab.

4. Check Log Events to record the degree of login required:

Log Spooler Error Events records the most severe printer errors.

Log Spooler Warning Events records less severe errors.

Log Spooler Information Events records successful print job completion.

5. Click OK.

I generally disable Log Spooler Information Events to prevent the system log from recording print activity, which I don't care to keep track of.

If you do care, though, more detailed recording of printer use and management activity is available through Auditing. Auditing provides a way to record printer activity in the Windows Event Security Log.

The Windows Auditing feature records an event when a specified permission has been either granted or denied. The granting or denying of permission implies that someone completed, or tried to complete, the action that the permission controls.

This situation sounds a little more complex than it is. In practical terms, if you audit success *and* failure of the Print permission, you'll see who submitted print jobs and who tried and was denied. If you audit just failure of the Manage Documents permission, you'll see who tried to delete another user's document and was prohibited.

You can add permissions in the Auditing tab by viewing a printer's Security properties, clicking Advanced, and selecting the Auditing tab. Select Add, choose a user or group of users to select for auditing, and then choose permissions and outcomes to audit, as shown in Figure 18.24.

Figure 18.24
Adding an Audit entry to record when Printing permission has been granted or denied to anyone.

Finally, click OK to add the permission to the Audit list, and add more if desired.

CHANGING THE LOCATION OF THE SPOOL DIRECTORY

When jobs are queued up to print, Windows stores the data it has prepared for the printer in the folder of the computer that's sharing the printer. Data for your own print jobs and that for any network users will all end up on your hard drive temporarily. If the drive holding your Windows directory is getting full and you'd rather house this print data on another drive, you can change the location of the spool directory.

To change the location of the Windows print spooler folder

1. View the Printers and Faxes folder.
2. Select File, Server Properties and select the Advanced tab.
3. Enter a new location for the Spool Folder and click OK.

PRINTER POOLING

If your network involves heavy-duty printing, you might find that your printers are the bottleneck in getting your work done. One solution is to get faster printers, and another is to add multiple printers.

If you have two printers shared separately, you'll have to choose one or the other for your printing, and you'll probably encounter bank-line syndrome: The other line always seems to move faster.

The way around this problem is to use printer pooling. You can set up one shared printer queue that sends its output to multiple printers. The documents line up in one list, and multiple printers take jobs from the front of the line, first-come, first served.

To set up pooled printers, follow these steps:

1. Buy identical printers; at least, they must be identical from the software point of view.
2. Set up and test one printer, and configure network sharing for it.
3. Install the extra printer(s) on the same computer as the first. If you use network-connected printers, you need to add the necessary additional network ports.
4. View the printer's Properties, and select the Ports tab. Mark Enable Printer Pooling, and mark the Ports for the additional printers.

That's all there is to it; Windows passes print jobs to as many printers as you select on the Ports pages.

SEPARATOR PAGES

Windows XP has a feature that lets you add a cover page to each print job sent to a given printer. The cover page can be configured to show the name of the user who sent the print job, his or her computer name, and so on. On a network with dozens of users sharing a given printer, these cover pages can be very helpful in sorting out whose printouts are whose. On the other hand, using cover pages is wasteful of paper and isn't a good "green" practice unless the confusion around your printers is really significant.

Separator pages have another very important use: They can be used to switch "multiple personality" printers into one language mode or another. For example, some Hewlett-Packard printers accept input in both the PostScript and PCL page description languages. These printers normally detect which format is being used and adjust automatically. They don't always, however, so setup information stored in separator page files can be used to force the issue.

You can set up the pages like this: Create two Windows shared printer icons in the Printers folder, both pointing to the same physical printer on the same LPT port. Configure one with the PostScript driver, and the other with the standard PCL driver. Name the printers appropriately—for example, LaserJet-PS and LaserJet-PCL. Configure each printer with a separator page that forces the printer into the correct mode. This way, you can select the printer driver you want, and the printer will never mistake the language being used. This is really handy if Unix or Macintosh users are sending output to your printers.

Windows ships with four predefined separator files:

pcl.sep	Forces a LaserJet printer into PCL mode and prints a separator page
sysprint.sep	Forces a LaserJet printer into PostScript mode and prints a separator page
pscript.sep	Forces a LaserJet printer into PostScript mode but doesn't print a separator page
sysprtj.sep	Contains a Japanese font version of sysprint.sep

Separator files are stored in your \Windows\system32 folder. You can use one of the predefined files, or you can create one of your own. These plain text files can be edited with Notepad. To assign a separator page to a given printer, follow these steps:

1. Open the printer's Properties box, and select the Advanced tab.
2. Click the Separator Page button and enter the desired filename, or click Browse to find the file manually.
3. Click OK.

The first line of a *.sep file contains only one character, which sets the "escape character" for the rest of the file. Subsequent lines are sent to the printer. Sequences starting with the escape character are interpreted as substitution commands; the sequence is replaced with other text before being sent to the printer. The command substitutions are shown in Table 18.3. In the table, I assume that backslash (\) is the escape character.

TABLE 18.3   SEPARATOR PAGE SUBSTITUTIONS

Sequence	Is Replaced With
\N	Name of the user who submitted the print job.
\I	Print job number.
\D	Date the job was printed.
\T	Time the job was printed.
\L*xxxxxx*	Text *xxxxxx* up to the next escape.
\F*filename*	Contents of file *filename*. This file is copied literally with no substitution. It can be used for a "message of the day."
\H*xx*	Hexadecimal value *xx*. Particularly useful is \H1B, which emits the ASCII <esc> character used in printer control commands.
\W*nn*	Limits the width of the page to *nn* columns.

You can create or modify separator page files using the predefined files as examples. Table 18.3 can help you interpret these files.

TIP

If you have a two-bin printer, you can put colored paper in the second bin and print the separator pages on it so they really stand out. To do so, add the appropriate printer control sequences to the .sep file. At the beginning of the file, have the sep file reset the printer and switch to bin two, print the separator page stuff, and then switch back to bin one.

SHARING PRINTERS ON THE WEB VIA IPP

If you have installed Internet Information Services on Windows XP, IPP printing is installed by default. Simply view the Web page http://hostname/printers.

NOTE

The built-in Web page support for IPP printing is installed only if you check the Printers Subfolder option when you install Internet Information Services; for details see "Installing IIS on Windows XP Professional," p. 556.

The Web pages are generated by a set of nearly two dozen ASP script files that are installed in \Windows\Web\printers. (They make fascinating reading, if you want to learn serious ASP programming!)

Windows XP users can access the shared printer across the Internet by viewing the /printers page, if your computer is reachable. Microsoft has made IPP printer drivers available for Windows 9x and Windows NT4 as well as Windows XP/2000, so you can print to an IPP printer from computers running any of these operating systems. The add-on software is available at http://www.windowsupdate.com.

You can print to the Windows IPP service from any other operating systems that support IPP. You need to know the correct URL for the printer, which is `http://`*computername*`/printers/`*sharename*`/.printer`. For example, my shared printer \\bali\laserjet is accessible over the Internet as `http://bali.mycompany.com/printers/Laserjet/.printer`. You also can specify the share name for the printer, such as `http://bali.mycompany.com/sharedlaserjet`. This URL can't be browsed as a Web page; it's meant to be used as the target of IPP software only.

You don't have to remember this URL, either; you can view the /printers Web page and select Properties. The resulting page lists the IPP network name and the printer's other printing capabilities.

VIEWING AND MANAGING SHARED RESOURCES

When your computer is sharing folders and files with other users of your network, you may from time to time want to know just what folders are being shared, and who is using them.

You can locate your computer in My Network Places and open its icon to see the list of shares offered by your computer, but there are two other tools that you should know about. The quickest is through the command line program net share. Net Share displays a list of all folders and printers that your computer is currently sharing. On my computer, opening a command prompt window and typing **net share** results in this printout:

```
Share name   Resource                    Remark
-------------------------------------------------------------------
IPC$                                     Remote IPC
C$           C:\                         Default share
D$           D:\                         Default share
print$       C:\WINDOWS\System32\spool\drivers
                                         Printer Drivers
cdrive$      C:\
ADMIN$       C:\WINDOWS                  Remote Admin
CDROM        E:\
lib          c:\lib
SharedDocs   C:\DOCUMENTS AND SETTINGS\ALL USERS.WINDOWS\DOCUMENTS
temp         c:\temp
HPLJ4        HPLaserJet4V        Spooled  HP LaserJet 4V Direct
Printer      C:\Documents and Setti Spooled  Acrobat Distiller
The command completed successfully.
```

COMPUTER MANAGEMENT SHARED FOLDERS SNAP-IN

You can view additional information about current shares and more importantly, who's using them, through the Shared Folders management console snap-in. To open this tool

1. Click Start, right-click My Computer, and select Manage.
2. In the left pane, select Shared Folders, as shown in Figure 18.25.
3. Select any one of the three views: Shares, Sessions or Open Files.

18

Figure 18.25
The Shared Folders Computer Management snap-in displays active shares, connections, and open files.

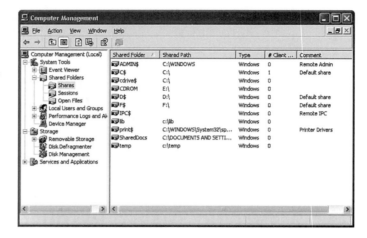

The Shared Folders management tool has three displays, which I'll outline in turn.

SHARES

The Shares display lists all of the folders shared by your computer, as shown in Figure 18.25. In this window, you can right-click any share and select Stop Sharing to cancel it, or Properties to change its parameter: comment, maximum concurrent users, share permissions, or the folder's NTFS security settings.

You can also right-click the word Shares in the left pane to create a new shared folder; Windows displays a rather handy wizard. On the wizards first page, you can enter the share name and file path. On the second page, you can select share permissions from the following list:

- All users have full control
- Administrators have full control; other users have read-only access
- Administrators have full control; other users have no access
- Customize share and folder permissions

SESSIONS

The sessions display shows the names of all remote users and computers that have attached to one or more of your computer's shared folders or printers. The information listed includes the number of files each user has open, and whether the user is connected as Guest (as is the case when Simple File Sharing is enabled).

You can right-click any username and select Close Session to disconnect the user. If they are actively using a file at the time, they will likely lose their work—be very careful when doing this. The only good reason to do so is to disconnect a phantom session left after the computer it represents has crashed.

You can right-click the word Sessions in the left pane and select Disconnect All Sessions to disconnect *all* remote users. You might do this in the event of an emergency if you had to repair a database file system, for example.

OPEN FILES

The Open File display lists all files currently open for reading or writing by other users on your network. In the event of an emergency, you can right-click any listed open file and select Close Open File to disconnect the file from its user; you can also right-click the phrase Open Files in the left pane and select Disconnect All Open Files. Again, this is a drastic measure, and best taken only when the computer that has opened the file has crashed.

COMMAND-LINE UTILITIES

In this chapter there are several sections discussing the use of the net command in its various incarnations: net use, net share, and net view.

There are actually 22 variations of the net command, which can not only manage file and printer sharing, but create user accounts, start and stop system services, and update the system clock.

The net commands are worth learning about. To get more information, open a command prompt window and type the command **net** to get a list of all 22 variations.

Then, type **net help** *xxx* where *xxx* is any of the subcommands; for example, net help start displays information about the start variation.

You can also get more online help through the Windows Help and Support Center.

→ For a discussion of the net use subcommnad, **see** "The net use Command," **p. 1228**.

USING ACTIVE DIRECTORY

If you are using Windows XP Professional on a domain network that uses Active Directory, additional network searching functions are available to you. In this section, we'll discuss how to search Active Directory for people, printers, computers, and more.

SEARCHING FOR PEOPLE

The basic Windows search tool lets you locate people by name or by email address. It can look in your personal address book (the one used by Outlook email), in various Internet directories, and in the Active Directory.

To search, click Start, Search, Computers or People, People In Your Address Book. The Find People dialog box will appear, as shown in Figure 18.26.

Figure 18.26
Using Find People, you can search by name or email address in the Active Directory or in any of several Internet Directory services.

Choose a directory under Look In. You can select from several choices, including Active Directory, Address Book, Bigfoot Internet Directory, Verisign Internet Directory, and WhoWhere Internet Directory. (I presume that the commercial directory companies have to pay to be placed in the list you see, so the list might change over time.)

Enter a name or part of a name, or email address or part of an email address and click Find Now.

Using the Advanced tab of Find People (shown in Figure 18.27), you can perform a more specific search.

Figure 18.27
Advanced searching properties let you specify multiple searching criteria.

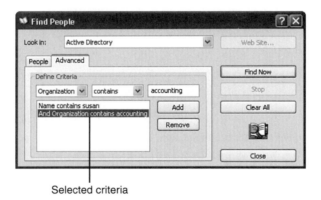

Selected criteria

To perform an advanced search from the Start menu, follow these steps:

1. Choose Start, Search, Computers or People, People In Your Address Book, and select the Advanced tab.

2. Select the first drop-down list (Name is the default value), and choose a criterion from the list. The searchable attributes include First Name, Last Name, Email, and Organization.

3. Under the second drop-down list ("contains" is the default value), select a comparison type. The choices are Contains, Is, Starts With, Ends With, or Sounds Like.

4. In the third box, which is empty by default, enter the name or address, or a fragment.

5. Choose Add to add a condition; highlight a condition and click Remove to delete a condition.

6. Enter more filtering items if you want, or select Find Now to begin the search.

The two search tabs on the Find People dialog operate independently of one another, so selections on one tab do not influence searches made with the other.

You can open any entries returned by the search to view comprehensive information about the user, as shown in Figure 18.28. The information is spread out over five tabs:

- **General**—Contains name, address and telephone number.

- **Address**—Contains complete postal address information.

- **Business**—Shows job title, department, the person's manager, and any managed employees.

- **NetMeeting**—Indicates direct connection information for NetMeeting chat/voice/videoconferencing, and includes a Call Now button.

- **Digital IDs**—Lists any digital email-signing certificates on store for the user; they contain public keys that can be used to encrypt or validate email messages.

Figure 18.28
Find People returns information about the user.

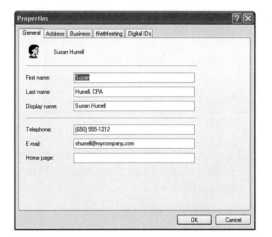

18

> **NOTE**
>
> You can change and update any of the information for your own account made available for user-level editing by the domain administrator. You also might be able to edit the information for employees you manage, if this is permitted on your network.

USING THE SEARCH ACTIVE DIRECTORY TOOL

You can also search for people with the Active Directory Search tool. Its advanced option provides much more fine-grained searching than the Find People tool discussed in the previous section. To use the Active Directory search tool, follow these steps:

1. Open My Network Places and select Search Active Directory.
2. Under Find, select Users, Contacts and Groups, as shown in Figure 18.29.
3. Under In, select a domain or sub-part of the Directory. (Searching the Entire Directory returns no results.)
4. Click Find Now.

Figure 18.29
Searching Active Directory for people in your organization.

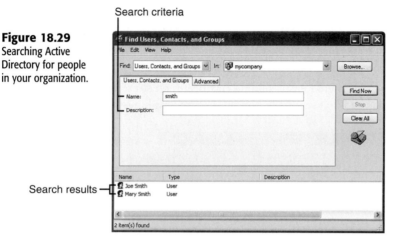

A list of matching names will appear at the bottom half of the window. You may select any name, right-click it, and select Open Home Page, Send Mail or Properties. The Properties page displays three tabs of contact information.

For more fine-grained searching, select the Advanced tab.

Advanced searches work by combining one or more selection criteria such as First Name, City, Fax Number, or Job Title with a criterion such as "Starts with", "Is (exactly)", or "Present", and a value to match.

This is the full-blown search system, and here you'll have 53 fields to choose from when searching for users, everything from Assistant to ZIP code: A to Z, if you need. To perform advanced searches

1. Select a criterion by clicking the Field button and selecting one of the dozens of available search parameters.
2. Select a matching condition, such as "Starts with" or "Present".

3. Enter a matching value or part of a value into the Value field. For names, upper/lower-case does not matter.

4. Click Add to insert the selection criterion into the list.

5. If you want to select based on several criteria, repeat steps 1 through 5 as many times as desired.

6. Click Find Now.

Again, you may select any name, right-click it and select Open Home Page, Send Mail, or Properties. If the search returns no results, try using fewer or less strict matching criteria.

NOTE The advanced criteria work in addition to any entered on the basic Users, Contacts and Groups tab. If you started with a basic search, be sure to clear its search fields before starting an Advanced search.

SEARCHING FOR PRINTERS

If your computer is connected to a domain-type network, the Active Directory can help you locate networked printers in your organization. You can search for printers three ways: by name and location, as shown in Figure 18.30; by printer capabilities; or by more advanced attributes.

Figure 18.30
Using the Printers tab in the Active Directory printer search tool, you can search for printers by printer name, location, and model.

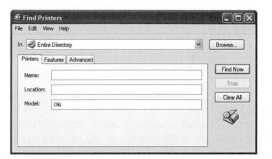

You can choose a major organizational unit to begin the search from the In drop-down list; you can search the entire directory, choose a major organizational unit, or select Browse to select a more regional subunit. See what choices In has on your network to see whether restricting the search makes sense for your company; otherwise, let the search use the Entire Directory.

Searching by the printer share name, location, or printer model is straightforward; just type a name or part of a name, and select Find Now. What works best when searching by Location depends on how your organization has set up the Active Directory. Yours may use cities, addresses, floors and room numbers, or another system. At any time, you can change your selection criteria and select Find Now again to update the search listing and refine or expand your search.

You can find all the printers in the directory by entering no information in the Find Printers dialog box: Just click Find Now.

TIP

> View the entire directory the first time you use Find Printers. This will give you an idea of how location and printer names are organized in your company. If too many names are listed, you can click Clear All to clear the search listing and then restrict your search using a location name that makes sense for your network. For example, if your company has put floor and room numbers like "10-123" in the Location column, you might restrict your search to printers on the 10th floor by searching for "10-" in Location.

To search for printers based on capabilities you need, select the Features tab, as shown in Figure 18.31. Here, you can limit the directory display to just printers with required color and finishing capabilities, speed, resolution, and available paper sizes.

Figure 18.31
Using the Features tab, you can select printers based on printing capabilities such as speed, resolution, and color capability.

NOTE

> The name and location attributes you select on the Printers tab, the capabilities you select on the Features tab, and any advanced search restrictions on the Advanced tab all operate together to limit the final result, even though you can see only one of the tabs at a time.

If these selections aren't specific enough for you, you can really nail down what you want on the Advanced tab, as shown in Figure 18.32.

This tab lets you list your requirements in no uncertain terms. To perform an advanced search, follow these steps:

1. Before clicking the Advanced tab, be sure that you've cleared out any selection criteria you entered on the basic search page. Then, select the Advanced tab.

2. Select Field, and choose a criterion from the list. The searchable attributes include Asset Number, Input Trays, Installed Memory, and Printer Language; you can choose from 27 different attributes.

Figure 18.32
Using the Advanced tab, you can select printers based on the full range of information stored in the Active Directory.

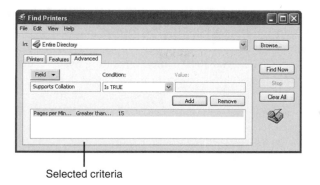

Selected criteria

3. Under Condition, select an appropriate comparison type: Starts with, Greater than or Equal to, and so on. You can also choose Present and Not Present to test whether an attribute is blank.

4. Under Value, enter the desired asset number, number of trays, megabytes of memory, printer language, and so on. Then click Add.

5. Enter more filtering items, or select Find Now to begin the search.

Anything you entered on the Printers or Features tabs factors into this search as well.

You can adjust the search results by double-clicking any of the filtering items you entered; just change the settings and select Add or Remove, and then click Find Now.

Using any of these three tabs, you should be able to quickly narrow down the possibilities enough to choose a suitable printer.

Right-clicking any printer in the search results list gives you two action options: You can connect to it or open it. Connecting installs the printer on your computer; in other words, it adds the printer to the list of those your computer can use. Open displays the printer's current print jobs without installing it.

SEARCHING FOR COMPUTERS

You can search the Active Directory for computers by name, operating system version, role (workstation versus server), owner or manager. To do this, follow these steps:

1. Open My Network Places and select Search Active Directory.

2. Under Find, select Computers, as shown in Figure 18.33.

3. Under In, select a domain or sub-part of the Directory. (Searching the Entire Directory for computer names returns no results.)

4. For a basic search by computer name or owner, enter all or part of a name in the input fields. To search by role, select Any, Servers and Workstations, or Domain Controllers. Then, click Find Now.

5. For an advanced search, clear any entries in the basic search form, and then select the Advanced tab. Select a criterion and selection value, and click Add. The advanced criteria are: Computer Name (pre-Windows 2000 or NetBIOS name), Description, Managed By, Name (Windows 2000 name), Operating System, and Operating System Version. You may add more than one criterion if you wish.

6. Click Find Now.

Figure 18.33
Active Directory lets you search for computers by name, role, operating system and more.

Search criteria

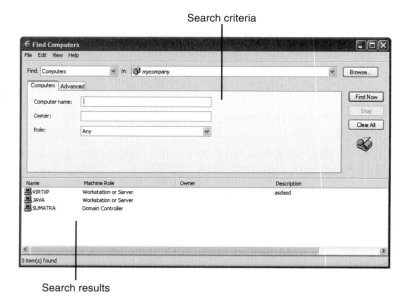

Search results

You can manage any of the listed computers by right-clicking its name and selecting Manage.

SEARCHING FOR PUBLISHED SHARED FOLDERS

On an Active Directory network, the domain administrator may choose to list, or *publish*, some shared folders in the directory; they might contain important resources that the company wanted to make widely accessible and easy to find. To search the directory for published shared folders

1. Open My Network Places and select Search Active Directory.

2. Under Find, select Shared Folders.

3. Under In, select a domain or sub-part of the Directory. (Searching the Entire Directory returns no results.)

4. For a basic search, enter all or part of a name in the share name or descriptive keywords that may have been used in the share's description. Then, click Find Now.

5. For an advanced search, clear any entries in the basic search form, and then select the Advanced tab. Select a criterion and selection value, and click Add. The advanced criteria are: Description, Keywords, Managed By, Name, and Network Path. You may add more than one criterion if you wish.

6. Click Find Now.

You may right-click any of the matched folders located by the search and select Open, Explore, Find, Map Network Drive or Properties.

ADVANCED AD SEARCHES

Active Directory contains information on many more objects than just users, computers, and printers. It includes records describing organizational units, certificate templates, containers (business groupings), foreign security principals, remote storage services, RPC services (used for advanced client/server software applications), and trusted domains. It can also contain information for other objects defined by your own organization. Most of this information is used only by domain administrators to configure Windows networks over vast distances; however, you can search for anything and can specify your qualifications based on more than 100 different criteria.

To make an advanced search, open My Network Places, and select Search Active Directory.

If you choose Custom Search, you have the whole gamut of fields to choose from, and in the Advanced tab, you can enter LDAP (Lightweight Directory Access Protocol) queries directly for submission to the AD service, as shown in Figure 18.34. This is the native query syntax for Active Directory, and it's available here mostly for system debugging. (Strangely, in Custom Search, any qualifiers set in the form-based search are applied along with a manually entered LDAP query; you should be sure to clear out the form if you are going to enter LDAP directly.)

Query

Figure 18.34
Querying the Active Directory Server directly with its native LDAP query syntax.

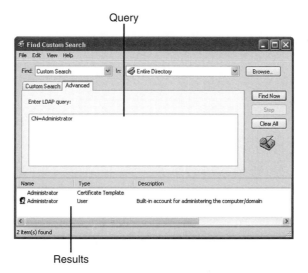

Results

CHAPTER **19**

WINDOWS UNPLUGGED: REMOTE AND PORTABLE COMPUTING

In this chapter

TOOLS FOR THE ROAD WARRIOR

Not too many years ago, phones were tethered to desks by wires, and when you left the office, it pretty much didn't matter whether you were at the deli or on the moon: You were out of touch, and that was it. Now, we carry our phones in our pockets and we can communicate whether we're at the office, in the car, or on the beach.

Likewise, not too many years ago, computers were islands unto themselves. Sharing files and data between computers in the same office was a pretty big deal; it was difficult, expensive, and mysterious. Nowadays, your computer can be as well-connected as you are. Whether you're in your office, at home, or overseas, and whether your computer came with you or stayed behind, you should be able to get at any information you want, from wherever you are.

In this chapter, I'll show you how you can have access to your files and programs when you're on the road, and how you can connect back to your home base. There are several strategies you can use to span the distance:

- **You *can* take it with you**—Windows XP Professional's "offline folders" feature can synchronize folders between a network server and your own computer. It's easy to take important files with you when you go, and copy back any updates and additions you've made while traveling upon your return.

- **Connect wherever you go**—Use Wireless, wired, or infrared networking connections to connect your computer at remote locations.

- **Network from afar**—Use Dial-Up or Virtual Private Networking to connect your computer to a distant network over phone lines or over the Internet.

- **Use the "next best thing to being there"**—Windows XP Professional's Remote Desktop and third-party remote control programs let you securely access your office's or your own computer from any other, over the Internet or by modem. You can even connect to your XP computer from a Mac.

- **Use the Web**—Windows's Web-based services let you access shared files and printers over the Internet. In addition, several companies provide "mobile" desktop services that let you store and retrieve files at home or on the road.

TAKING FILES WITH YOU: OFFLINE FOLDERS

You may have experienced the "Offline" problem: There are important files on a network server that you need when you're away from the network. So, you need to make copies to take with you. If you later make changes to your copies, the network's copies will be out of date. But, if someone changes the originals on the network computer, *your* copies will be out of date. Trying to remember where the originals came from and where the most recent copies are located is a painful job. The answer to the offline problem, of course, is automation. Computers can do anything, right?

I don't know if you ever tried to use My Briefcase in previous versions of Windows, but the answer to that question is "not always." My Briefcase was a tool that let you transfer files between computers by copying them to and from a special folder. Or something like that—the whole thing was so confusing I never really understood it. Whenever I tried to use it, it froze, lost files, or crashed my computer. Well, as the saying goes, "It's the thought that counts."

Windows XP Professional's Offline Folders feature takes care of these problems. Here's the skinny: When you mark a network folder for offline use, Windows stashes away a copy or *caches* the folder's files somewhere on your hard drive, but all you see is the original shared folder on your screen. When you disconnect, the shared folder appears to remain on your screen, with its files intact, because Windows has its backup copies. You can still add, delete, and edit the files. Meanwhile, network users can do the same with the original copies. When you reconnect later, Windows will set everything right again.

I was skeptical at first, but this time, Microsoft really did it right. You'll find that this feature works, and it's more powerful than it seems at first glance. The following are some of the applications of Offline Folders:

- Maintaining an up-to-date copy of a set of shared files on a server (or desktop computer) and a remote or portable computer. If you keep a project's files in an offline folder, Windows keeps the copies on all your computers up-to-date.

- "Pushing" application software or data from a network to a portable computer. If software or data is kept in an offline folder, your portable can update itself whenever you connect or dock to the LAN.

- Automatically backing up important files from your computer to an alternate location. Your computer can connect to a dial-up or network computer on a timer and refresh your offline folders automatically.

After I describe all the functions and settings for Offline Folders, I'll give you some scenarios and show how you can set up Offline Folders to help.

NOTE

If your computer is not a member of a domain network, to use Offline Folders, you must disable Fast User Switching (why this is, we don't know. Perhaps Microsoft felt that providing too many useful features at the same time might ruin their reputation). To disable Fast User Switching, click Start, Control Panel, and User Accounts. Select Change the Way Users Log On or Off, and uncheck Use Fast User Switching.

Then, you must enable Offline Folders. Open any Explorer window or My Computer. Select Tools, Folder Options. View the Offline Files tab, and check Enable Offline Files.

If your computer is a member of a domain network, these settings are the defaults, so you should not need to adjust them.

Offline Folders are not available on XP Home Edition. If you use XP Home Edition, you can still use the Briefcase feature discussed later in this chapter.

19

IDENTIFYING FILES AND FOLDERS FOR OFFLINE USE

You can mark specific files, subfolders, or even entire shared folders on a "remote" server for offline use.

> **NOTE**
> The server I'm talking about might be in the next room, which isn't very "remote" at all, but that's what I'll call it for simplicity's sake. In this section, a "remote" server refers to a computer other than your own, which you access via networking.

While you're connected to the remote network, view the desired items in Explorer, in My Network Places, or, if you've mapped a drive letter to the shared folder, you can select it under My Computer.

> **NOTE**
> The Offline Folders feature works with folders shared by any network server using Microsoft's standard SMB networking protocol, so you can use shares from Windows, OS/2, Samba, and so on, but not NetWare.
>
> However, you cannot take offline any folder whose full pathname is longer than 64 characters. Windows caches only files whose pathnames are shorter than 64 characters.

When you find the folder or folders you want, select them, and right-click Make Available Offline. Be cautious about marking entire shared drives or folders available offline, though, unless you're sure how much data they contain, and you're sure you want it all. You could end up with a few hundred gigabytes of stuff you don't need!

> **NOTE**
> If you select a shortcut to a file and mark it Make Available Offline, Windows does you a favor: It gets the file to which the shortcut points and makes the file available offline, too. But Windows *doesn't* do this with a shortcut to a folder. You'll be able to see the shortcut when you're offline, but unless you also explicitly select the folder for offline use, its contents won't be available.

USING THE OFFLINE FILES WIZARD

The first time you select a given folder for offline use, Windows starts the Offline Files Wizard. The wizard then asks you to make choices for three options:

- **Automatically Synchronize the Offline Files When I Log on and off My Computer**—Check this to have Windows automatically update or *synchronize* your cached copies with the network. If unchecked, you need to tell Windows to sync-up files manually.

- **Enable Reminders**—Check this to have Windows periodically pop up a reminder when you're offline and using cached files.

■ **Create a Shortcut for the Desktop**—Check this to put an Offline Files icon on your desktop. You can use this to see what you've made available offline.

When you've marked a folder for offline use, Windows immediately makes a local copy of it, and when the synchronization is finished, the network folder or file icon appears with a special "roundtrip" marker to indicate that it is now available when you're offline.

TROUBLE WITH OFFLINE AVAILABILITY

If you right-click a file or folder and Make Available Offline doesn't appear as an option, here are some possible reasons why:

■ You must be using Windows XP Professional. Offline Folders are not available with Home Edition.

■ You must disable Fast User Switching and enable Offline Folders, as described earlier in this section.

■ If you are working through My Network Places, you can select a subfolder for offline use, but not the whole top-level folder. To make an entire shared folder available offline, select it from Windows Explorer or My Computer.

If you try to select a file for offline use but receive the error "Files of this Type Cannot Be Made Available Offline," you have run into another Offline Folders glitch—well, maybe it's a glitch and maybe it's a good thing. Microsoft has deemed that some file types (for example, Access's .mdb database files) shouldn't be available offline. They assume that these files are in use by multiple LAN users, and there's no way to reconcile changes made by offline and online users. This can help you avoid database damage, but it's annoying if you really do want to take the file offline. There is a way to get around this if you are sure you won't take offline any files that might be edited by others while you have them.

If you're on a domain network, ask your domain administrator to modify the Group Policy entry `Computer Configuration\Administrative Templates\Network\Offline Files\Files not cached`.

If you are on a workgroup network, follow these steps:

1. Log in as a Computer Administrator and start the Microsoft Management Console with Start, Run, mmc.

2. Choose File, Add/Remove Snap-in, Add.

3. Highlight Group Policy and click Add.

4. Leave the Group Policy Object set to Local Computer. Click Finish, Close, and OK.

5. In the left pane, open Local Computer policy and drill down through Computer Configuration, Administrative Templates, Network, Offline Files.

19

6. In the right pane, double-click Files Not Cached.

7. Check Enabled, and enter any extensions that should be protected against offline sharing, such as `*.dbf`. Omit the file types you want to take offline.

8. Click OK and close the MMC console program.

9. Log out, and then log back in.

USING FILES WHILE OFFLINE

When you disconnect from the network by undocking or disconnecting a remote connection, the offline files and folders will remain visible in the Explorer display, as shown in Figure 19.1.

Figure 19.1
When you disconnect from the network, only offline folders and files remain.

Online   Offline

While offline, you can still use the remote folder. You can add, delete, or edit files in it. If you have a drive letter mapped to the offline folder, the drive letter still functions.

This process works so well that it's disconcerting at first because the effect is…well, because there is no effect at all. You can happily drag files into a network folder, and it seems to happen, except they won't show up on the remote server until you reconnect.

When you reconnect, you should synchronize your offline folders with the network folders so that both sets of files will be up-to-date.

THE SYNCHRONIZATION MANAGER

You can synchronize files anytime you are connected to the network containing the original shared folder, whether by LAN, modem, or VPN network connection. There are five ways to start a synchronization:

- Manually, from Explorer's Tools menu or by choosing Start, All Programs, Accessories, Synchronize. This method lets you synchronize all offline folders whose remote server is available.

- Manually, by right-clicking a specific shared file or folder and choosing Synchronize. This method synchronizes just the selected file or folder.

- Automatically, when your computer is connected and idle.

- Automatically, when you log on, off, or both.

- Automatically, at specified times and days of the week. For a scheduled synchronization, Windows can even automatically make a dial-up connection.

As wonderful as the Offline Folder system is, it can't help you if two people modify the same file from two different locations. Windows helps you avoid this problem while you're connected by using the online copy of the file (see the following tip for one teensy exception). This way, everyone uses the same copy, and Windows can use its standard file and record locking mechanism to control access to the file by multiple users.

> **TIP**
>
> Although Windows uses the online copy of the file whenever possible, there is one exception: If the person who shared the files made them available for offline use as "applications," Windows doesn't let you change them, and it uses your local, cached copy whenever possible. I'll talk about this topic under "Making Your Shared Folders Available for Offline Use" later in this chapter.

During offline use, though, it's possible for both the original and your copy to be changed. When you synchronize, you must pick a "winner," the version of the file that will be kept. One set of changes will be lost. If you are keeping copies only of your own files, shared from your own computer, losing one set probably won't be a big problem. If you're collaborating with others on a project and editing files offline, the best way to avoid problems is to talk with your colleagues and plan out who can edit which files when—and synchronize frequently.

19

MANUAL SYNCHRONIZATION

You can start synchronization manually after you've reconnected to a network whose files you took offline. You must synchronize manually if you connect to the remote server with a dial-up or VPN connection.

In Windows Explorer, choose Tools, Synchronize. Select the shared folders whose files you want to update, as shown in Figure 19.2, and select Synchronize.

Figure 19.2
For manual synchro-
nization, check the
network shares
whose folders you
want to update.

Windows copies updated files as necessary and then asks you to resolve any conflicts it encounters. The three types of conflict for any given file are as follows:

- A file on the server was deleted. Windows asks whether you want to delete your local copy, too, or put your copy back on the server.

- You deleted your copy of the file. Windows asks whether you want to pick up another copy or delete the original file on the server.

- Your copy of the file and the server's copy were both edited since you last synchronized. Windows asks who wins: Do you want to copy your file to the server, the server's copy to your computer, or keep both files under two different names? This dialog box is pretty nicely done; you can view either version with the click of a button. You can check a box to apply the same decision to all file conflicts.

I can't tell you a right or wrong answer for any of these situations. You'll have to determine which is the appropriate answer in each case.

After all files have been checked, Windows displays a summary. This synchronization summary indicates any significant problems encountered. If any problems occur synchronizing a folder, Windows stops updating that folder and continues with the next network share.

CAUTION

If the process fails because a file is in use, you should repeat the synchronization when no one is editing files in the shared folder; otherwise, you might lose changes to some files.

AUTOMATIC SYNCHRONIZATION

You can tell Windows to perform synchronization automatically upon logon, logoff, or when your computer is sitting idle while you are connected to the remote network. This feature is good for dockable mobile computers that spend a good deal of their time directly connected to a LAN.

If you bring up the Synchronization Manager (in Windows Explorer, by choosing Tools, Synchronize), you can select the Setup button to display the Synchronization Settings dialog, which is shown in Figure 19.3.

Figure 19.3
On the Synchronization Settings dialog, you can specify when automatic synchronization should occur.

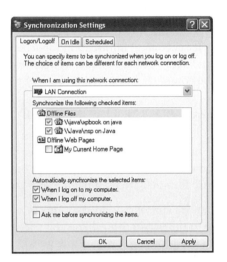

You can specify that Windows is to synchronize selected folders each time you log on or log off while connected to a network. You can check which offline files are to be updated (and which offline Web pages too, by the way; I've been ignoring them, but they are updated with the Synchronization Manager, too). You can also select different folders to update, depending on which connection is active, using the When I Am Using This Network Connection selection.

19

Update on Idle

You can instruct Windows to synchronize offline folders and cached Web pages when your computer is sitting idle by using the On Idle tab of the Synchronization Settings dialog. Here, you can also choose which folders to update, depending on which connection is in use. By default, Windows waits for 15 minutes of inactivity before starting an update, and it updates again every 60 minutes. You can change these times by choosing the Advanced button.

Updating when idle is useful for computers that spend a lot of time connected to a LAN, but it is less useful for a portable computer dialed in by modem.

Scheduled Synchronization

Finally, you can instruct Windows to begin synchronizations on a timed schedule. Enabling this feature makes sense only if your computer is *on* at the time of the scheduled update. It would be useful to get copies of large files from a LAN server or from a distant server through a VPN connection. The Scheduler can automatically establish a dial-up or VPN connection before synchronizing.

You can view scheduled synchronizations on the Synchronization Manager's Scheduled tab. The Synchronization Settings dialog lists any currently scheduled updates. To add a new entry, click Add, and the Scheduled Synchronization Wizard will walk you through the process.

Once configured, you can manage the scheduling information for scheduled synchronizations just like any other scheduled task. It's a rather complex system with many options (for example, don't synchronize while the computer is running on battery power).

Making Your Shared Folders Available for Offline Use by Others

When you've marked a network file for offline use, Windows makes a copy of the file on your hard disk. While you're still connected to the network, it's faster to use the local copy when you want to access the file. On the other hand, this would not be appropriate for files that change frequently or for database files that are used by multiple users concurrently.

Windows has to know whether or not it's appropriate to serve up the cached copy during online use, and leaves the choice up to the person who shares the network folder. When *you* share folders on your computer, you can specify the way Windows will make this folder available for offline use by others.

By default, Windows will *not* give users a cached file when the network copy is available. This is appropriate for database files and editable documents. It's only useful to change the default settings when you are sharing a folder that contains read-only documents and/or application programs. In this case, you may be able to give users faster access by following these steps:

1. Simple File Sharing must be disabled. If you are using Simple File Sharing on a workgroup LAN, open Explorer or My Computer and select Tools, Folder Options. Select the View tab and uncheck Simple File Sharing in the Advanced Settings List. Click OK, and then log off and back on.

2. Use Explorer or My Computer to locate the folder you're sharing. Right-click it and select Properties. View the Sharing tab and click the Caching button.

3. Select Automatic Caching of Programs and Documents, and click OK. Close the Properties window.

4. If you disabled Simple File Sharing in step 1, and don't need to use Offline Folders from this computer, you can now re-enable it.

You also can force Windows to make files available for offline use by specifying Automatic Caching. With automatic caching, when a network user accesses any file in your shared folder, the remote user's copy of Windows *automatically* marks it as available for offline use and makes a copy on their computer.

The complete list of caching options is described in Table 19.1.

TABLE 19.1 CACHING SETTINGS	
Option	**Description**
Allow Caching of Files in This Shared Folder	If this box is unchecked, the files cannot be copied for offline use. Use this setting to protect sensitive or fast-changing data.
Manual Caching of Documents	Users can select files and folders for offline use and are responsible for synchronizing them. This is the default setting and is appropriate for most cases.
Automatic Caching of Programs and Documents	Windows automatically makes any file accessed by the user available offline and uses the cached copy if it can. You should use this setting if your files are programs or are documents that cannot be modified by the remote users.
Automatic Caching of Documents	Windows automatically makes any opened file available offline, but Windows uses the net work copy if it can. You can use this setting to "push" documents to other users' computers for their offline use.

The amount of disk space allocated to "automatically" available offline files is limited to an amount set in the Offline Files properties page.

OFFLINE FILES PROPERTIES

You can control your computer's overall treatment of offline files from Windows Explorer. Select Tools, Folder Options, and then select the Offline Files tab, as shown in Figure 19.4. (If Fast User Switching is enabled, this tab will not appear as in the figure, but will tell you that the feature is not available.)

The settings are described in Table 19.2.

TABLE 19.2 OFFLINE FILES OPTIONS	
Option	**Description**
Enable Offline Files	Uncheck to disable the entire Offline Files system.
Synchronize All Offline Files When Logging On, Synchronize All Offline Files Before Logging Off	Check to force Windows to run he Synchronization Manager when you log on and off. These options also can be set individually for each folder.

continues

TABLE 19.2 CONTINUED	
Option	**Description**
Display A Reminder	Uncheck to disable the annoying balloon that pops up on the taskbar to remind you that you're offline. You can also set the time between annoyances.
Create an Offline Files Shortcut on the Desktop	The shortcut can let you view the cached file list; not too useful.
Encrypt Offline Files to Secure Data	Check to have Windows encrypt the cached files. Check this if the files you use are sensitive.
Amount of Disk Space to Use	Limits disk space used to cache temporary ("Automatic") offline files. Manually chosen offline files are *not* counted against this amount.
Delete Files	Deletes temporary and/or manually chosen offline files from the cache. Network copies are *not* deleted. Use this feature to force a refreshed copy of all files.
View Files	Displays the Offline Files folder, a listing of all cached files. It provides the same view as given by the desktop icon.
Advanced	Allows you to specify computers whose connection can be lost without triggering Offline mode.

Figure 19.4
The Offline Files properties page makes global settings for the handling of offline files.

You don't *need* to change any of these options to use Offline folders. However, after you've been using Offline Folders awhile, you might find that some of these settings will save you some time or trouble.

ADDITIONAL USES FOR OFFLINE FOLDERS

Earlier, I listed three uses of offline folders. Now that you've read all the details, you should be able to see how the Offline system handles these tasks:

- **Maintaining an up-to-date copy of a set of shared files on a server (or desktop computer) and a remote or portable computer**—If you manually select a network folder to be available offline, your computer will always have up-to-date files. If you typically connect to the LAN with a docking portable computer, you can synchronize automatically on logon and logoff. If you connect to the network by a dial-up or VPN connection, you must synchronize manually.

- **"Pushing" application software or data from a network to a portable computer**— If you put application software or seldom-changed read-only data on a shared network folder and enable Automatic Caching for Applications, remote users must copy the file across a slow network connection only once. The trick is to have the users always refer to the files by their network shared folder name, even when offline. Windows gives them the cached copy automatically. This capability is a boon for modem users.

- **Automatically backing up important files from your computer to an alternate location**—You can make a shared folder on a server or computer at your office and create an offline copy at home or on your portable. If you do all your work in the offline folder, the synchronization process will serve as an intelligent backup process. You can even schedule it automatically.

I don't get too enthusiastic about these things usually, but after struggling and suffering with My Briefcase and then working with offline folders, I'd say that they're probably one of the three neatest features I've found in Windows XP.

Remember, after you've marked folders for offline use, continue to use them in the normal way, referring to them using their full network path filenames or through mapped network drives.

Finally, you can uncheck Make Available Offline on a file or folder at any time to remove it from the cached file list. This will delete the local copies and recover the space they're taking on your hard disk.

19

> **NOTE**
>
> If you find that a file or files are missing from an offline folder, you may run into one of Offline Folders' unfortunate limitations: Files with pathnames longer than 64 characters are simply ignored and not copied for offline use. Check the name of the file you've found to be missing; if its full path is more than 64 characters long, this is the problem. The solution is to contact the manager of the computer sharing the folder and ask him or her to make a network share at a deeper level in the folder tree, so that the pathname will be shorter.

OTHER WAYS OF COPYING FILES

The Offline Folders system does a great job of transferring files to and from a computer that comes on and off of a network. However, there are other times that you may want to copy files from one computer to another, and other ways to accomplish it:

- Use an external high-capacity drive such as a FireWire- or USB-connected hard drive, or a Zip disk.

- Install network adapters in the two computers and connect them with a *crossover cable*, as described in Chapter 17, "Building Your Own Network." The cable will cost about $7.50, and if you need to buy network adapters, this might set you back another $5 to $50 per computer. You'll eventually want the network hardware anyway, though, and with this mini-LAN you can copy mega-files in minutes.

- If both computers have FireWire (IEEE-1394) ports and are running Windows XP, you can get a so-called "6-6" cable to directly connect the computers, and use the IEEE-1394 ports to set up a LAN. (The price of the cable might bring tears to your eyes, though.)

- You can use the Direct Connection networking feature to connect two computers through their parallel, serial or Infrared ports. Parallel or serial connections require special "Direct Connection" parallel or serial data crossover cables—these cables are needed to hook input wires to output wires on each computer and vice versa.

- If you want to synchronize files between a computer running Windows XP or 2000 and one running an older version of Windows, you can use the Briefcase feature, which I discuss later in the chapter.

In this section, I'll discuss these alternative connection techniques.

NOTE

If you are setting up a new computer and want to move both your files and your preferences and settings from an older computer, you can use one of these connection techniques with the "Files and Settings Transfer Wizard" discussed in Chapter 2, "Installation Prep."

TWO-COMPUTER NETWORK

If you need to copy files between two computers and don't have a network already in place—for example, if you've bought a new home computer and want to get files from your old computer—you can set up a temporary network just long enough to transfer your files. It may take a while to set up the network, but if you have a lot of data to copy, it can save you hours.

Chapter 17 and Chapter 20, "The Heterogeneous Network," tell how to set up a network and how to make Windows XP work well with older versions of Windows. Here's the process in a nutshell:

- You'll install a network adapter in each computer that doesn't already have one. Most newer computers have an Ethernet adapter built-in, but if yours doesn't, you can add one for about $10.

- If you don't have a network already set up, you can directly connect the two computers' network adapters with what's called a *crossover cable*. Most network cables are wired to connect an Ethernet adapter to a network hub. A crossover cable is wired differently, so that it can connect two adapters without requiring a hub. At the time this was written, buy.com was selling five foot crossover cables for $6.

- You'll install Windows File sharing, and at least one networking protocol on each computer. Both computers have to have at least one protocol in common. The "NWLink ISP/SPX Compatible Protocol" is the best one to use. Be sure that both computers have the same Workgroup name set.

- Share the entire hard drive (or drives) of one computer or the other by right-clicking the drive in My Computer, selecting Sharing (or Properties, Sharing tab), and selecting Share This Folder.

- On the other computer, view Network Neighborhood or My Network Places, find the other computer, and open the folder(s) that represent the shared drive(s).

- Drag files to copy them back and forth.

It takes 5–15 minutes to set up a two-computer network, and with it you can transfer data at between roughly one to five megabytes per second. Compare this with about one megabyte every two minutes with a floppy disk and you can see that it's definitely worth the trouble.

NOTE

> If both of your computers are running Windows XP and have FireWire (IEEE 1394) ports, you can connect them with a FireWire cable instead of using network adapters.

19

DIRECT CABLE CONNECTION

You can copy files between two Windows-based computers through a special cable that connects between two computers' parallel printer or serial ports. This is called a *Direct Cable Connection*, and while it's much slower than a network connection, it can be easier to set up and get working. The Direct Cable Connection system provided with Windows XP can connect to a computer running Windows XP, 2000, 95, 98, or Me, but not Windows 3.x, NT, or Windows for Workgroups.

I should point out that the special-cable approach dates back to a time when network adapters were costly. But networking equipment has gotten ridiculously inexpensive in recent years, so it no longer makes much sense to bother with these older, slower technologies. You can probably get a pair of real network adapters and a crossover cable for the same price or less than the cost of the special cable you'll need to use Direct Cable Connection. Still, if you have only a few megabytes to transfer and only need to do it once, you may want to consider this approach.

To make a Direct Cable Connection, you can use a serial port cable that has its transmit and receive data wires reversed between the two ends (often called a "null modem cable"). Serial data connections top out at about 110,000 bits per second (110 Kbps) which works out to 11,000 bytes per second (11KBps). This is not fast.

For faster data transfer you need a special cable that connects between the parallel printer ports of two computers, called a DirectParallel cable, which you can get from Parallel Technologies Inc at www.1pt.com, or from other vendors. There are different versions of the cable used depending on the type of parallel port in your computers, and the maximum transfer speed you can expect depends on the type of parallel ports you have. The port types are listed in Table 19.3 in ascending order of speed:

TABLE 19.3 PC PARALLEL PORT TYPES

Port Type	Transfer Speed (bytes/second)	DirectParallel Cable Required
Standard	40-60KBps	Basic 4-Bit or UniversalFAST
Bidirectional	80-120KBps	UniversalFAST
Enhanced (EPP)	120KBps	UniversalFAST
Extended (ECP)	500+KBps	UniversalFAST

The transfer speed will be limited by the slower of the two ports in use.

TIP

In most computers, you can set the parallel port mode in the computer's BIOS setup screen. You'll get the fastest Direct Cable Connection transfers if both ports are set for ECP mode.

NOTE

Several third-party programs also support serial, USB, and parallel port connections, including Carbon Copy, LapLink and so on. Parallel Technologies, which makes the DirectParallel cable used with Direct Cable Connection, sells a USB version as well. However, again, these solutions can end up being much more expensive than setting up a two-computer network.

To make a Direct Cable Connection, connect the serial null-modem cable to free COM ports on each computer, or connect a DirectParallel cable to the two computers' parallel printer ports. You'll need to use the Direct Cable Connection Wizard on both computers. You'll need to select one computer to be the "host," the computer whose hard drives will be shared with the other, which is called the "guest." You will do your copying work at the Guest computer, but it doesn't really matter which is which; you can copy files from the guest to the host or vice versa.

On the Windows XP computer, follow these steps:

1. Open Network Connections.

2. In the Tasks menu, select Create a New Connection.

3. Select Set Up an Advanced Connection.

4. Select Connect Directly to Another Computer.

5. Select Host or Guest.

6. If you choose Guest, you'll need to enter the name of the other computer. This is the name entered on the Identification tab of the Network control panel on Windows 9x and Me, or on the Computer Name tab of the System properties dialog on Windows 2000 and XP.

7. Choose the device for the connection: a parallel, serial, or infrared port. If you're using a serial connection, click the Properties button, and select a reasonable serial port speed (usually 19200, 38400, or 57600 bps).

8. On the Host computer, select the user account or accounts that will be granted access from the guest. On the Guest computer, enter the username and password of one of the selected accounts.

Once the connection is established, Windows will add one or more new entries to the list of drives in My Computer on the Guest computer; these represent the hard drive(s) of Host computer. You can drag and drop files to and from these drives.

If the other computer is not running Windows XP, you'll have to follow the instructions for establishing a Direct Cable Connection for the other version of Windows; use online help to find the description of this procedure.

When you're finished, close the connection by right-clicking on the connection icon in the notification area on the Guest computer. On the Host computer, you can disable incoming connections by opening the Network Connections page, right-clicking the Incoming Connection icon, and unchecking the connection device you chose earlier.

INFRARED CONNECTIONS

Most portable computers include an infrared data transmission device similar to that used on TV remote controls. Using a data transmission standard called IrDA (after the Infrared Data Association), computers, printers, and handheld organizers can communicate with each other without LAN wiring.

If you don't have or want a network connection, and if your two computers both have infrared data capability, you can establish a Direct Cable Connection without the cable, or if both computers are running Windows XP and/or 2000, you can use the special Infrared File Transfer feature. This is a reasonable—although slower—alternative to setting up a hardware network.

19

IrDA comes in two flavors: SIR (Serial InfraRed), which tops out at 112Kbps, and FIR (Fast Infrared), which runs up to 4Mbps. Most new portables support both protocols. The advantage of using SIR is that you can attach an (expensive) adapter to a standard serial port on your desktop computer and give it infrared capability.

NOTE

An FIR adapter connects to an SIR adapter by automatically adopting SIR's slower transfer rate. The two standards interoperate quite nicely.

SETTING UP AN INFRARED DEVICE

If your computer has IrDA-compatible hardware installed, Windows should have detected it and installed support for it during installation. You can tell by checking for a Wireless Link applet in the Control Panel under Printers and Other Hardware.

NOTE

In many cases, the IrDA adapters in a laptop are disabled by default. You may have to enter the computer's BIOS setup at boot time and enable it. The setting is usually under a title such as "Built-In Peripherals." You must enable IrDA 1.1 support. It might require a DMA and Interrupt port as well, so you might not be able to use infrared and ECP printing at the same time. When you restart Windows, it will detect and install support for the infrared connector.

If you've added an external serial port IrDA adapter to your desktop computer, choose Add/Remove Hardware in the Control Panel, select Add Hardware, choose the device manually, and select Infrared Devices. Finally, choose the proper IrDA device type and serial port information.

Open the applet, and view the Hardware tab to confirm that Windows thinks the device is operating properly (see Figure 19.5). If it's not, select Troubleshoot to diagnose and fix the problem.

Figure 19.5
Using the Wireless Link Control Panel applet, you can configure file transfer directories and the transfer speed.

The applet has three tabs. On the first two, you can enable transfers of files and images, and select the destination folder for files and images received from other computers and digital cameras. The default folder for received files is your desktop. The default folder for received images is the My Pictures folder inside your My Documents folder. You can change these defaults by clicking Properties and selecting a different folder.

On the Hardware tab, you can set the maximum speed for wireless transfers. If you experience a high error rate, click Properties and try changing the speed from the default 115200bps to 57600 or lower.

INFRARED "DIRECT CONNECTION"

To establish an infrared "Direct Cable Connection," point the two computers' infrared ports at each other. Then, follow the steps in the previous section for establishing a Direct Cable Connection. In step 7, select the Infrared port. This should work for any version of Windows from 95 on up.

If both computers are running Windows XP or 2000, you can take advantage of the built-in support for IRDA file transfers between capable devices such as laptops, digital cameras, and so on.

INFRARED FILE TRANSFER

When another infrared-capable Windows 2000 or XP computer is in range of your computer's beam, your computer will make an interesting sound, a Send Files to Another Computer icon will appear on the desktop, and a small control icon will appear in the notification area (see Figure 19.6).

Figure 19.6
When another infrared file transfer device is in range, the Send Files icon (left) appears on the desktop, and the Wireless control icon (right) appears in the notification area.

The wireless control icon appears in the notification area

19

The Send Files icon appears when another file transfer drevice is in range

If the Send Files icon doesn't appear, the problem could be with either computer.

The following are a few points to check:

- Be sure that the wireless optical ports are within a few feet of each other, pointed relatively directly at each other, with a clear line of sight between them.
- Check the Device Manager on both computers to be sure that both IrDA ports are working correctly.

- Be sure that both computers have wireless file transfers enabled.
- If all else fails, borrow a handheld video camcorder. These cameras can often "see" the infrared light emitted by IrDA ports. With the camcorder in "record" mode, look through the viewfinder and check to see that the ports on both computers are blinking. If you see one blinking but not the other, you know one computer isn't set up correctly.

When the Send File icon has appeared, you can use any of these three methods to send files:

- Drag and drop the files onto the Send Files to Another Computer icon on the desktop. What could be easier?
- Select and right-click a file, choose Send To, and select Infrared Recipient.
- Open the Send Files icon, or select Transfer Files from the control icon in the taskbar to bring up the Wireless Link dialog. This lets you browse for and select the files to transfer. Click Send to transfer the files.

NOTE

> The Wireless Link dialog box is a standard Open File dialog box; it's really a little Explorer window. If you drag a file into this dialog, you're moving it to the displayed folder on your own computer. To transfer a file via drag and drop, you must drag it to the Send Files icon.

After you've selected files to transfer via drag and drop, Send To, or the dialog, progress dialogs appear on both computers, indicating that a file transfer is taking place.

NOTE

> When infrared file transfers are enabled, anyone with an IrDA-equipped Windows XP or 2000 computer can zap files onto your computer's desktop—there is no security feature. Don't worry, though, because files are never overwritten. If someone sends you a file with the same name as an existing file on your desktop, it's named something like "Copy 1 of (Original File Name)".

DIGITAL CAMERA IMAGE TRANSFER

When you bring a digital camera with a compatible IrDA interface near your computer, the image transfer utility appears. Follow your camera manufacturer's instructions to copy images from the camera to your computer.

You can specify the directory for image transfers in the Wireless Link properties, from the Control Panel, or from the Wireless Link task tray icon. The default is the My Pictures folder inside your My Documents folder.

INFRARED PRINTING

When your computer has an IrDA interface, you can print to infrared-connected printers. To make a connection to an infrared printer, follow these steps:

1. Power up the printer and point your computer's IR beam at it. Windows may detect and install the printer automatically. If it doesn't, proceed with step 2.

2. In Printers, select Add Printer. Choose Local Printer, and uncheck Automatically Detect.

3. Under Use the Following Port, choose IR (Local Port).

4. Select the printer's manufacturer and model. If it's not listed, and you have a disk from the manufacturer, select Have Disk and locate the Windows XP printer drivers.

5. Supply a name for the printer, choose whether it will be the default printer, and choose whether to share the printer to your LAN.

Now you can use the printer whenever it's in visible range of your computer.

MY BRIEFCASE

The Briefcase feature provides a simplified, manual version of the Offline Files function—it lets you take copies of files from one computer to another, make changes, and reconcile the updated files with the original set.

Basically, a briefcase is just a folder into which you can drag copies of important files. What's different is that this folder remembers where the files came from originally. You can copy this folder to a floppy disk or across a network, work with the files somewhere else, and later, tell Windows to copy any new or changed files back to their original location(s).

Here are a couple of scenarios showing how you might use a Briefcase:

- At work, you can create a Briefcase folder, drag in copies of some important documents, and then move the Briefcase folder to a floppy disk or Zip disk. You can take this removable disk home or to another office and work on the files. Then, you can bring the disk back to your original computer and tell Windows to copy the updated files back to their original locations.

- You can connect from home or the road to your office network using Dial-Up Networking or a VPN. You can create a briefcase folder and drag files from the office network into it. You can work with these copies after disconnecting from the network. Later, when you connect again, you can tell Windows to copy any changed files from the Briefcase folder back to the their original locations on the office network.

19

My Briefcase is a decent idea and it works with all versions of Windows from 95 on up. The only problem is that it's a bit cumbersome, and it seems to be buggy. If you have Windows XP Professional and are interested mainly in the network file scenario, you're better off using the Offline Folders feature that I discussed earlier in the chapter. But, if you use XP Home Edition or want to carry files around on a removable disk, the Briefcase is not a bad way to go.

Creating a Briefcase Folder

To create a Briefcase folder, start at the computer that contains the files you want to work with, or in the case of network files, that has access to the network files. Follow these steps:

1. Right-click your desktop and select New, Briefcase.
2. Rename the Briefcase folder if you wish—use any name that makes sense, like "Briefcase", "Work Files", "XYZ Proposal", and so on.
3. Drag files into the Briefcase folder from your hard drive or from network locations.
4. If you want to bring the files to another computer using a removable disk, open My Computer and drag the Briefcase folder to the removable disk's icon while holding down the Shift key. This will move the folder, rather than making a copy. You only want one copy of the Briefcase folder.

Alternately, you can create the Briefcase folder on the removable disk to begin with.

> **NOTE**
>
> If you are moving a Briefcase folder from one drive to another and Windows asks "Are you sure you want to move the system file desktop.ini?", **be sure** to click Yes. Without this file, Windows won't recognize the copied folder as a Briefcase.

Now, you can remove the disk containing the briefcase folder, or disconnect from the network.

Using Briefcase Files

You can take the disk with the briefcase to another computer and work with the files there. Figure 19.7 shows the Briefcase display after changing a file. (You may need to click View, Refresh to update the Status display.)

Figure 19.7
The Briefcase folder shows where its files came from and whether they have been modified.

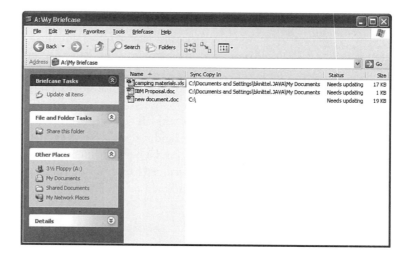

Be sure, though, that you *always* work with the files directly in the Briefcase folder. *Don't*, for example, drag a file from the Briefcase folder to your desktop, edit it there, and then drag it back to the Briefcase. The reason is that the Briefcase will then forget where the original copy of the file lives back on the original computer. If Windows asks you if you want to *replace* a file in the Briefcase with one you're dragging in, click Cancel, or you'll lose the original location information.

You can, however, add *new* files to the Briefcase folder at any time. It's best if you create them right in the Briefcase folder itself, where they'll be listed as "Orphan" files, ones for which Windows has no recollection of an original location. The reason for this is that when you return to the original computer, you probably want to choose where to store these new files, rather than store them in the same folder that was used on the second computer.

If working with files on a floppy disk is too slow and you want to use the Briefcase files from a hard drive, follow these steps:

1. Drag the Briefcase folder itself from the removable disk to your hard disk, say, to your Desktop.
2. Work with the files where they are, inside the Briefcase folder.
3. When you're finished, drag the entire Briefcase folder back to the removable disk while holding the Shift key, and replace the copy on the removable disk.

Now, you can bring the removable disk back to the original computer, or reconnect to the network.

SYNCHRONIZING THE BRIEFCASE

When you've brought the Briefcase folder back to the original computer, or when you've reconnected to the network, tell Windows to *synchronize* it; Windows will then copy any modified files that are listed with status "Needs Replacing" back to the original locations, overwriting the original, unedited copies.

To synchronize all of the files in the Briefcase, open the Briefcase folder and select Briefcase, Update All. To synchronize only a single file or set of files, left click them to highlight them (hold down the Ctrl key to select multiple files), and then select Briefcase, Update Selected.

The Update My Briefcase synchronization wizard will then run, and will show you the names of any files that have changed in the Briefcase, in the original location, or both, as shown in Figure 19.8.

The wizard will indicate which direction it thinks that files need to be copied, based on the dates and times the files were last modified. Carefully check each listed file to be sure that you'll end up with the version you want! You can right-click the arrow in the list to elect to copy a file either way, or to skip it and leave both copies alone, by choosing one of the icons listed in Figure 19.9.

19

Figure 19.8
Update My Briefcase lets you choose how files will be copied between the Briefcase and the original locations.

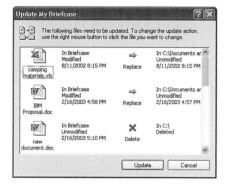

Figure 19.9
You can choose which way to copy any given file while updating the Briefcase.

NOTE

> An *orphan* file is one you created directly in the Briefcase folder. Windows doesn't know where it came from or where it goes, so it can't synchronize it. Manually drag any orphan files from the Briefcase to the desired location on your hard drive. If you want to keep them in your Briefcase, drag them back into the Briefcase so Windows remembers the location.

SALVAGING A DAMAGED BRIEFCASE

You don't need to worry about this during normal use of a Briefcase folder, but here's how the Briefcase works internally:

- A Briefcase is a normal folder that contains copies of the files that you've dragged to the Briefcase. This is how you can drag the briefcase to, say, a floppy disk and end up with copies that you can view on another computer.

- There are two hidden files in the Briefcase folder: desktop.ini and Briefcase Database. Desktop.ini contains a special entry that tells Windows Explorer to present the special Briefcase view. Briefcase Database contains the original full pathnames of the files copied in the folder, so Windows knows where to look during synchronization. This provides the information displayed by Explorer in the Briefcase view.

If the Briefcase Database file gets corrupted, Explorer may crash or fail to display the briefcase properly. If this happens, here's how you get to your files again:

1. View the folder or drive that *contains* the briefcase in Windows Explorer. Don't open the briefcase itself.

2. Select Tools, Folder Options and select the View tab. Check Display the Full Path in the Address Bar and click OK.

3. Select View, Toolbars and be sure that Address Bar is checked.

4. With your mouse, select the entire drive and path in the Address bar and type Ctrl+C to copy it to the clipboard.

5. Open a Command Prompt window from Start, All Programs, Accessories, Command Prompt.

6. Type **cd**, a space, and then press Alt+Space, E, P to paste the folder path onto the end of the command. This will look something like this:

```
cd c:\Documents and Settings\bknittel\Desktop
```

but with the path to the folder containing *your* briefcase. Press Enter.

7. Type **cd** and a space again, and then the name of the briefcase, for example, "New Briefcase" or "My Briefcase". Press Enter. The current folder should now be the Briefcase folder.

8. Type the command **dir** and press Enter. Windows should list the names of the files in your Briefcase.

9. Type the following commands:

```
attrib -h -s desktop.ini
attrib -h -s "briefcase database"
del desktop.ini
del "briefcase database"
```

10. Now, you can close the Command Prompt window and open the briefcase folder in Windows Explorer. It's now a plain, ordinary folder containing copies of your files. You'll have to drag any new or changed files back to their original location manually; you can't synchronize it anymore. Drag out any files for which you don't have original copies, or which were changed since you created the briefcase.

11. When the folder is empty or contains only duplicate copies of your original files, delete the briefcase folder.

12. If you still want to use the briefcase feature, create a new briefcase folder and drag your files into it from their *original* locations.

If the desktop.ini file is lost, Explorer will display the Briefcase as an ordinary folder. This isn't a problem really; you'll just have to manually drag its files to their original locations when you return to the original computer. You can follow steps 10 through 12 in the preceding list to reconstruct your Briefcase.

DIAL-UP NETWORKING

Thus far in this chapter, we've talked about ways of taking files with you when you're away from your network. Today, Internet connections are never very far away, and many companies set up dial-up modem banks for employees to connect while on the road, so in many cases, you don't *need* to take files with you; you can get at your files and office computers from just about anywhere in the world. In the next two sections, we'll talk about how this can be done with Dial-Up Networking and through Virtual Private Network (VPN) technology.

First off, Windows XP can connect to a remote Windows network via modem. All file sharing, printing, and directory services are available just as if you were directly connected, including any Novell, OS/2, and Unix file and print services provided on the network. Just dial up, open shared folders, transfer files, and email as if you were there, and disconnect when you're finished.

The receiving end of Dial-Up Networking can be handled by the Remote Access Services (RAS) in Windows 200x and NT4 Servers, or by third-party remote connection hardware devices manufactured by networking companies such as Cisco and Lucent.

Windows XP Professional and Home Edition come with a stripped-down version of RAS, so you can also set up your own Windows XP computer to receive a single incoming modem connection. You can do so, for example, to get access to your office computer and LAN from home, provided your company permits this access.

I'll discuss incoming calls later in the chapter. First, though, let me tell you how to connect to a remote Windows network.

SETTING UP DIAL-UP NETWORKING

To create a dial-up connection to a remote network or computer, you need an installed and configured modem.

You also must get or confirm the information shown in Table 19.4 with the remote network's or computer's manager.

TABLE 19.4   INFORMATION NEEDED FOR AN RAS CONNECTION

Information	Reason
Telephone number	You must know the receiving modem's telephone number, including area code.
Modem compatibility	You must confirm that your modem is compatible with the modems used by the remote network; check which modem protocols are supported (V.92, V.90, V.32, and so on).
Protocols in use	The remote network must use TCP/IP and/or IPX/SPX. Windows XP does not support the NetBEUI protocol.
TCP/IP configuration	You should confirm that the Remote Access Server assigns TCP/IP information automatically (dynamically) via DHCP. Usually, the answer is yes.

Information	Reason
Mail servers	You might need to obtain the IP addresses or names of SMTP, POP, Exchange, Lotus Notes, or Microsoft Mail servers if you want to use these applications while connected to the remote network.
User ID and password	You must be ready to supply a username and password to the remote dial-up server. If you're calling a Windows 2003, XP, 2000 or NT RAS server, then use the same Windows username and password you use on that remote network.

Armed with this information, you're ready to create a dial-up connection to the remote network. To do so, just follow these steps:

1. Choose Start, My Computer, My Network Places, and select View Network Connections. (Note: You might need to close the left Folders pane to see the Task list.)

2. Select Create a New Connection, and click Next.

3. Select Connect to the Network At My Workplace (see Figure 19.10) and then click Next. Choose Dial-Up Connection, and then click Next.

Figure 19.10
Choose Connect to the Network At My Workplace from the New Connection Type selections.

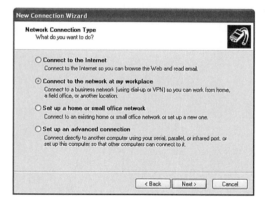

4. Enter a name for the connection, for example, Office LAN, and click Next.

5. On the Phone Number to Dial dialog box, enter the telephone number of the remote dial-in server. You can enter the number directly, including any necessary prefixes or area codes. Select Next. The final page asks if you want Windows to put a shortcut to this connection on your desktop. Check this if you wish, and select Finish.

> **NOTE**
> You can delete a connection shortcut later if you don't want it and can drag the connection icon from Network Connections to your desktop later if you do.

6. After you've clicked Finish, Windows immediately wants to open the connection. You must check the connection properties, so click the Properties button.

SETTING A DIAL-UP CONNECTION'S PROPERTIES

There are two ways you can edit the properties for a dial-up connection from the Network Connections window: You can open the connection icon and click the Properties button, or you can right-click the icon and select Properties.

The Dial-Up Connection's properties page has five tabs and a heap o' parameters. Most of the time, the default settings will work correctly, but you might need to change some of them. I'll walk you through the most important parameters.

GENERAL

On the General tab of the Properties dialog (see Figure 19.11), you can set your choice of modems if you have more than one installed. You also can set telephone numbers and dialing rules.

Figure 19.11
General Properties include dialing and modem settings.

The following are the significant parameters:

- **Connect Using**—If you have more than one modem installed, choose which modem to use for this connection. The Configure button lets you set the maximum speed (data rate) to use between the computer and the modem, and other modem properties.

- **Area Code, Phone Number, and Country/Region code**—If the remote server has more than one phone number (or more than one hunt group), you can specify alternative telephone numbers. It's a neat feature if your company has several access points or provides emergency-use-only toll-free numbers.

- **Use Dialing Rules**—Check to have Windows determine when to send prefixes and area codes. If you want to use this, enter the area code and phone number in their separate fields. This feature is useful if you call the same number from several locations with different dialing properties.

- **Show Icon in Notification Area**—This option lets you keep a small connection monitor icon in your task tray when you're connected to the remote network. Opening it lets you quickly disconnect the remote connection, so it's best to leave Show Icon checked.

OPTIONS

The Options tab of the Properties dialog (see Figure 19.12) includes dialing options, choices for being prompted for phone number and passwords, and redialing settings.

Figure 19.12
The Options tab includes dialing and prompting options.

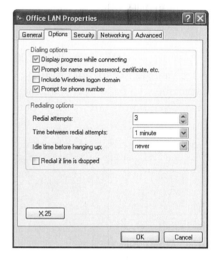

The important options are as follows:

- **Prompt for Name and Password**—If this box is checked, Windows always prompts for your remote connection user ID and password. If it is unchecked, after the first successful connection, Windows stores your password and uses it automatically later on. If you are worried that someone might dial the connection by gaining unauthorized access to your computer, leave this box checked; otherwise, you can uncheck it to skip the password step when connecting.

- **Include Windows Logon Domain**—Be sure to check this box if you are calling a Windows 2003/2000/NT4 domain-type network but your computer is not set up as a member of the same domain. When this box is checked, the dialing dialog box has a space for you to enter the remote domain's name.

- **Prompt for Phone Number**—If this box is checked, Windows displays the phone number it's about to dial. Leave it checked if you don't trust Windows to use the correct area code, prefixes, and so on. It's best to leave it checked until you're convinced.

- **Redialing Options**—If the remote server frequently gives you a busy signal, increase the number of attempts from 3 to, say, 20, and lower the delay from 1 minute to 15 seconds to get quicker redialing action.

19

- **Idle Time Before Hanging Up**—If you tend to wander off for hours with your modem still online, you can set this option to a reasonable time, and Windows will automatically disconnect you if no network traffic occurs for the specified time.

- **Redial If Line Is Dropped**—This option makes Windows redial immediately if your modem connection fails. It's good if you have lousy phone connections but bad if the remote computer disconnects you because its "idle time" runs out before yours does.

SECURITY

On the Security tab, you can select which encryption methods are required or permitted when you're logging on to the remote connection server.

- **Security Options**—If you are connecting to a Windows 2003, 2000, or NT Remote Access Server, select Typical and set Validate My Identity to Require Secured Password. If the Windows domain name, username, and password you'll use for the remote network are the same as those you use to sign in to your own computer, check Automatically Use My Windows Logon.

- **Advanced (Custom Settings)**—Select Advanced if you are calling a Shiva Remote Access Server. Click the Settings button, and then select Shiva Password Authentication Protocol (SPAP).

NOTE

> *Shiva* is shorthand for a user account/password verification system manufactured by Shiva Corporation (now owned by Intel). The Shiva system only validates a caller's right to connect to the modem; it doesn't grant rights to resources (such as file servers) on the network.

NETWORKING

The Networking tab of the Properties dialog (see Figure 19.13) defines which network protocols and network services are connected through the dial-up connection.

Usually, all protocols and services should be checked except File and Printer Sharing. This option should be disabled so remote network users cannot use your computer's shared folders and printers. If you want to let the remote network's users see them, check File and Printer Sharing.

Normally, a Remote Access Server automatically assigns your connection the proper IP address, DNS addresses, and other TCP/IP settings through DHCP, so you don't need to alter the Internet Protocol properties. In the very unlikely event that the network administrator tells you that you must set TCP/IP parameters yourself, select Internet Protocol from the Components list, and click Properties. Enter the supplied IP address and DNS addresses there.

Figure 19.13
On the Networking tab, you can choose which network protocols and services are enabled for the dial-up connection. Check everything, and set the TCP/IP protocol's properties if necessary.

ADVANCED

The Advanced tab configures Internet Connection Sharing and the Internet Connection Firewall. These utilities aren't used when you're connecting to a remote network.

Finally, after you've finished making any changes to the connection's options, select OK. The connection icon is then installed in Network Connections for use anytime.

MAKING A DIAL-UP CONNECTION

Making a remote network dial-up connection is no more difficult than connecting to the Internet. If you're a mobile user who moves between area codes, check your current location first, and then dial.

CHECK YOUR CURRENT LOCATION

If you've changed area codes or phone systems since the last time you made a modem connection, check your location setting by following these steps before dialing into the network:

1. Open the Control Panel, and select Printers and Other Hardware, and then Phone and Modem Options.

2. Check your current location in the list of configured dialing locations using the Dialing Rules tab.

3. Click OK to close the dialog.

Windows should now use the correct area code and dialing prefixes.

CHOOSE A PROFILE OPTION

If your computer is a member of a Windows XP domain network that offers roaming user profiles, you can decide whether to connect using your current local profile or use your remote "roaming" profile. Your network manager will tell you if the network provides roaming profiles. You have two options for making the connection:

■ If you connect while you're already logged on to your computer, you'll have access to the files, printers, and all other network resources on the remote network, but the My Documents folder and desktop will remain as they were before you made the connection. You'll be "here."

■ If you log off from Windows and then log on again using the Log On Using Dial-Up Connection option, you'll be connected with your user profile on the remote network. Your My Documents folder, home directory, desktop layout, and other preferences will be copied from the server to your mobile computer, and you'll be "there."

If you're not connecting to a Windows domain-type network, if you don't have a roaming profile, or if you don't need to use it, use the steps under "Connect to a Remote Network Without a Roaming Profile."

If you have an account with a roaming profile on the remote network, and you want to have access to the My Documents folder and settings you use on that network, follow the steps under "Connect to a Remote Network with a Roaming Profile."

CONNECT TO A REMOTE NETWORK WITHOUT A ROAMING PROFILE

To connect to a remote network using the profile you're already using in your own computer, make the connection directly, without logging out. Just follow these steps:

1. Open the connection from the Start Menu "Connect To" list, from Network Connections, or from a shortcut to the connection.

> **TIP**
>
> Windows puts a Connect To menu on the Start menu when you've defined a dial-up connection. You can select a connection to dial, or right-click it to edit its properties. This is a real timesaver.
>
> You can manually add or remove Connect To from the start menu with the start menu's Customize dialog.

2. Windows will open the connection dialog, as shown in Figure 19.14. Enter your login name, password, and domain (if any). You can also select Properties to adjust the connection's telephone number or dialing properties. (The Dialing From choice appears only if you checked Use Dialing Rules and have defined more than one dialing location.)

TIP

If you're connecting to a remote Windows 2003/2000 domain, you can enter DOMAIN\username or username@domain in the User name field.

Figure 19.14
In the Connect dialog box, you can enter your username and password for the remote network. If you're logged in, you can also tell Windows to remember your password and change the dialing properties.

3. You can choose to let Windows remember your password, if you're not worried that other people might use your computer to gain inappropriate access to the remote network. (Giving access to "anyone who uses this computer" is usually used only for a shared ISP connection, not remote networks.)

4. Select Dial. Windows shows you the progress of your connection as it dials, verifies your username and password, and registers your computer on the remote network.

If the connection fails, unless you dialed the wrong number, you'll most likely get a reasonable explanation: The password or account name was invalid, the remote system is not accepting calls, and so on. If you entered an incorrect username or password, you are usually given two more chances to re-enter the information before the other end hangs up on you.

If the connection completes successfully, a new connection icon appears in your taskbar, indicating the established connection speed, as in Figure 19.15.

Figure 19.15

You can now use the remote network's resources, as discussed next.

CONNECT TO A REMOTE NETWORK WITH A ROAMING PROFILE

To use the remote network under your user profile on that network, you must log in using the remote connection, using these steps:

1. Log off Windows if you are currently logged on. Choose Start and select Log off.

2. Press Ctrl+Alt+Del to display the logon dialog. Enter your network username, password, and domain. If Log on Using Dial-Up Connection isn't displayed, click the Options button. Check Log On Using Dial-Up Connection, and select OK.

3. Choose a network connection by selecting the name of the remote connection from the drop-down list, and select Dial. You can select VPN or modem dial-up connections.

4. When the Connect dialog appears, enter your remote access username and password and logon domain, as previously shown in Figure 19.14. This usually is the same as your network logon information. (You won't have the option to save your password or change the connection properties here, because you're not logged in.) Select Dial.

Windows then dials the remote network connection and logs in. After your profile settings have been copied, you're online and ready to use the network.

NOTE

If the connection fails because the telephone number was wrong, you may need to log on locally to change the number in the connections' properties dialog.

CALLBACKS

For security purposes, some networks don't permit you to just call in; they want to call you, so you not only need the right login name and password, but you also must be at the right location to gain access to the network. This type of access also generates an audit trail through phone company records.

When this type of security is in force, your network manager will contact you to arrange the predetermined telephone number to use to call you. You cannot access the network from any other location unless you arrange for call forwarding from the original number.

Callbacks can also be used to make the remote host pay for a long distance phone call. Some businesses use callbacks so that employees can dial in from the field at the company's expense.

When callbacks are in effect, you'll dial up the remote network as I described earlier, but as soon as the network accepts your password it will hang up. Within 30 seconds it will call back, and your modem will pick up the line and establish a connection.

If your network manager says that callbacks are optional, you can tell Windows how you want to exercise the option. In Network Connections, select the Advanced menu, choose Dial-Up Preferences, and select the Callback tab. You can indicate that you want callbacks on or off, or that you want to be asked each time you make a connection.

MANAGING DIAL-UP CONNECTIONS FROM MULTIPLE LOCATIONS

As you've seen already, Windows lets you enter your current telephone area code and dialing prefix requirements so that it can make modem calls using the customs appropriate for your local phone system. This capability is great if you use a portable computer. For example, at home, you might be in area code 415. At the office, you might be in area code 408 and have to dial 9 to get an outside telephone line. When you're visiting Indianapolis, you're in area code 317 and might need to use a telephone company calling card when making long-distance calls.

Windows offers great support for these variations by letting you define "locations," each with a separate local area code and dialing rules. When you use one of your Network Connections icons, as long as you've told Windows your current location, it can automatically apply the correct set of rules when making a dial-up connection.

However, if you use an ISP with access points in various cities, or your company has different access numbers in various regions, you'll find that this Locations system does not let you associate a different dial-up number with each location. It would be great if it did, but no such luck.

If you want to use different "local" dial-up numbers for the various locations you visit with your computer, you must set up a separate Network Connections icon for each access number and use the appropriate icon when making a connection at each location.

> **TIP**
>
> Set up and test the first access number you need. Then, when you need to add a new access number, right-click the first one, select Create Copy, rename it, and change its telephone number. I name my icons based on the location of the local number: Office-Berkeley, Office-Seattle, and so on.
>
> When you travel and want to make a dial-up connection, set your current location so Windows uses the right dialing rules; then select the appropriate dial-up icon so Windows uses the right access number.

19

> **TIP**
>
> If you travel, you'll find that having your Internet Options set to dial a particular connection automatically is not a great idea. It would dial the chosen connection no matter where you were (and remember, if there's a 50-50 chance of things going wrong, 9 times out of 10 they will). So, if you travel with your computer, you might want to open Internet Explorer and click Tools, Internet Options. Select the Connections tab, and choose Never Dial a Connection. This way, you won't be blind-sided by an inadvertent call to Indiana while you're in India.

USING REMOTE NETWORK RESOURCES

When you're connected, you can use network resources exactly as if you were on the network. My Network Places, shared folders, and network printers all function as if you were directly connected.

The following are some tips for effective remote networking by modem:

- Don't try to run application software that is installed on the remote network itself. Starting it could take hours!

- If you get disconnected while using a remote network, it's a bummer to have to stop what you're doing and reconnect. You can tell Windows to automatically redial if you're disconnected while you're working. In Network Connections, from the Advanced menu, choose Dial-up Preferences, and select the Autodial tab. Check any locations you work from where you would like Windows to automatically reconnect you.

- You can use My Network Places to record frequently visited remote network folders. You can also place shortcuts to network folders on your desktop or in other folders.

- If the remote LAN has Internet access, you can browse the Internet while you're connected to the LAN. You don't need to disconnect and switch to your ISP. You might need to make a change in your personal email program, though, as I'll note later under "Email and Network Connections."

- If you use several different remote networks, you can create a folder for each. In them, put shortcuts to the appropriate connection and to frequently used folders on those networks. Put all these folders in a folder named, for example, Remote Networks on your desktop. This way you can open one folder and be working within seconds.

EMAIL AND NETWORK CONNECTIONS

If you use your computer with remote LANs as well as an ISP, you must be careful with the email programs you use. Most email programs don't make it easy for you to associate different mail servers with different connections. And, this is a big problem.

Although most email servers allow you to retrieve your mail from anywhere on the Internet, most are very picky about whom they let send email. Generally, to use an SMTP server to send mail out, you must be using a computer whose IP address is known by the server to belong to its network. That is, you can usually pick up mail from any servers you use, but you can only send mail out through the server that serves your current connection.

See if your favorite email program can configure separate "identities," each with an associated incoming and outgoing server. If you send mail, be sure you're using the identity that's set up to use the outgoing (SMTP) server that belongs to your current dial-up connection.

MONITORING AND ENDING A DIAL-UP CONNECTION

While you're connected, note that the System Tray connection icon flashes to indicate incoming and outgoing data activity. It's a true Windows tool, which means you can have it do pretty much the same thing in about five different ways.

NOTE
If the connection icon is missing, open Network Connections. Right-click the connection you're using, select Properties, and check Show Icon in Notification Area When Connected.

- If you hover your mouse cursor over the connection icon, a box appears, listing the connection name, speed, and number of bytes sent and received.

- If you double-click it, the connection status dialog box appears, as shown in Figure 19.16. From the status dialog, you can get to the connection properties or disconnect.

- If you right-click it, you can select Disconnect, Status, or Open Network Connections. This is the way to go.

Figure 19.16
The connection status dialog box displays current connection statistics and lets you disconnect or change connection properties. Right-clicking the connection icon in the taskbar is a quicker way to disconnect.

Truthfully, all I ever do with the taskbar icon is make sure it blinks while I'm working, and right-click Disconnect when I'm finished.

When you disconnect a remote network connection, the taskbar icon disappears. If you logged in using a remote network profile, you remain logged in using the local copy of this profile until you log out.

ENABLING DIAL-IN AND VPN ACCESS TO YOUR COMPUTER

Windows XP Professional has a stripped-down Remote Access Server built in, and you can take advantage of it to get access to your own computer. You can also enable remote access temporarily so that a system administrator can maintain your computer.

CAUTION

> RAS is not too difficult to set up, but beware: Permitting remote access opens up security risks. Before you enable dial-in access on a computer at work, be sure that your company permits it. In some companies, you could be fired for violating the security policies.

To enable dial-in access, you must be logged on as a computer administrator. Then follow these steps:

1. In Network Connections, select the Create a New Connection Task in the New Connection Wizard. Click Next.

2. Choose Set Up An Advanced Connection, and click Next. Choose Accept Incoming Connections, and click Next.

3. Check the modem to be used for incoming connections.

> **TIP**
>
> Despite what the wizard dialog box seems to say, you can choose at most one modem. You *can* choose one of each different type of connection: for example, modem and direct parallel port.

4. If you want to disconnect incoming connections that sit idle (unused) for too long, click the Properties button and check Disconnect a Call If Idle More Than XXX Minutes, and then click OK.

5. You then are asked whether you want to additionally permit Virtual Private Network connections to your computer. I'll discuss Virtual Private Networking later in this chapter. You can read ahead to decide whether you want it or check Do Not Allow Virtual Private Connections now. You can always repeat this process to enable it later. It's best to not allow virtual private connections now if you're not sure.

6. Windows then displays a list of your computer's or domain's users. Select the ones who will be permitted to access your computer remotely, as shown in Figure 19.17. This step is very important: Check only the names of those users whom you really want and need to give access. The fewer accounts you enable, the less likely that someone might accidentally break into your computer.

Figure 19.17
Here, you can choose users who will be granted the right to remote access of your computer. Check only the names of those users really needing access, and don't check Guest.

> **CAUTION**
>
> Under no circumstances should you enable Guest, IUSR_*xxx*, or IWAM_*xxx* (where *xxx* is the name of your computer—for example, IUSR_AMBON) for remote access. The IUSR and IWAM accounts are used exclusively by Internet Information Server for access by Web site visitors, and Guest is used for general network access. There's no way you would ever want to give unprotected access to your network via modem or VPN!
>
> Check only the names of users who need access and who have good (long, complex) passwords.

7. You can enable or enforce callbacks for individual users if you like. Select the username, click Properties, and then select the Callback tab. If you do enable callbacks, you must enter any required dialing prefixes and area codes. Windows doesn't use dialing rules when making callbacks.

8. Windows displays a list of network protocols and services that will be made available to the dial-up connection. Generally, you can leave all protocols and services checked.

View the properties page for each checked protocol to specify whether callers have access only to your computer or have access to the LAN via your computer. Unless you have a reason to ban a remote caller (usually you) from reaching the rest of your LAN, you have no reason to disable these services.

NOTE

> If you use Internet Connection Sharing or a connection sharing router between the Internet and your computer, you'll have to forward incoming VPN connections to your computer. For details, see "Enabling Incoming VPN Connections with NAT," *p. 789*.

Access to Windows and NetWare servers through the IPX/SPX protocol is handled without difficulty.

However, the TCP/IP protocol presents a significant problem. Incoming callers must be assigned IP addresses valid on your LAN to be able to communicate with computers other than your own.

If your network has a DHCP server, or if you are using Internet connection sharing or a gateway device, then a caller will automatically receive a valid IP address. You don't have to worry about setting the TCP/IP address.

If your network does not have a true DHCP server on the network, you must manually assign a valid subnet of at least four IP addresses taken from the IP address range of your network. If you don't, incoming callers can access only your computer. (And if that's sufficient, you don't need to worry about this.)

NOTE

> You must provide a subnet with one IP address for the RAS server component on your computer and one for each incoming connection. Subnets have an overhead of two addresses, so the minimum subnet size is four addresses (two overhead, one for the server process inside your computer, and one for a caller). With an eight-address subnet, you could have five incoming connections (two overhead, one for the server, five for callers), although XP limits you to two or three incoming connections total.

Unfortunately, the process of assigning subnet addresses is more complex than I can go into here in any detail, and the articles on this topic in Windows XP's online help are worse than useless. You'll have to get a network manager to assign the subnet for you.

19

NOTE

You also can read more about TCP/IP networking in *Upgrading and Repairing Networks, 3rd Edition*, published by Que.

TIP

If you have a home or small-office LAN, look up your LAN adapter's IP address. If it starts with 192.168, you might try this trick for assigning IP addresses for incoming connections. For the starting and ending addresses, use the first three numbers of your IP address followed by .220 and .223, respectively. For example, my IP address is 192.168.0.34. I'd enter 192.168.0.220 and 192.168.0.223 as the From and To addresses.

When the incoming connection information has been entered, a new icon appears in your Network Connections window. You can edit its properties later or delete it to cancel incoming access. When someone connects to your computer, yet another icon appears in Network Connections showing their username. If necessary you can right-click this to disconnect them.

VIRTUAL PRIVATE NETWORKING

You know that you can use dial-up networking to connect to your office LAN or home computer from afar. But, with the Internet providing network connections and local modem access nearly all over the world, why can't you reach your network through the Internet instead of placing a possibly expensive long-distance call?

Well, in fact, you can. Microsoft networking can use the Internet's TCP protocol to conduct its business, so you can use an Internet connection to access shared files and printers, if the computer you want to reach has an Internet connection up and running.

But the Internet is not a friendly place. With tens of millions of people using it every day, you know that some of them are up to no good. Network break-ins are everyday news now. If your computer's file sharing services are exposed to the Internet, any number of people thousands of miles away could just try password after password in the hope of guessing one that will give them access to your files. How do you take advantage of the convenience of accessing network services over the Internet without, figuratively speaking, putting out a big welcome mat that says "Please Rob Me"?

The answer is by the use of firewalls and Virtual Private Networking. We'll describe these concepts in detail in Chapter 24, "Network Security," but in a nutshell, a *Virtual Private Network (VPN)* lets you connect to a remote network in a secure way. Access by random hackers is blocked by a network firewall, but an authorized user can penetrate the firewall. Authorized data is *encapsulated* in special packets that are passed through the firewall and inspected by a VPN server before being released to the protected network. VPNs create what is effectively a *tunnel* between your computer and a remote network, a tunnel that can pass data freely and securely through potentially hostile intermediate territory.

Figure 19.18 illustrates the concept, showing a Virtual Private Network connection between a computer out on the Internet and a server on a protected network. The figure shows how the computer sends data (1) through a VPN connection which encapsulates it (2) and transmits it over the Internet (3). A firewall (4) passes VPN packets but blocks all others. The VPN Server (5) verifies the authenticity of your data and transmits the original packet (6) on to the desired remote server. The encapsulation process allows for encryption of your data, and allows "private" IP addresses to be used as the endpoints of the network connection.

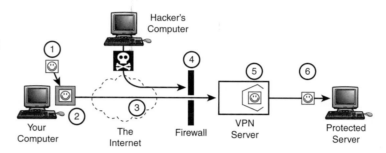

Figure 19.18
A Virtual Private Network encapsulates and encrypts data that is passed over the Internet.

On Windows XP, VPN connections work like dial-up connections. Once you have an Internet connection established (via modem or broadband service), an additional dial-up connection icon establishes the link between your computer and a VPN server on the remote network. Once connected, the VPN service transmits data between your computer and the remote network. In effect, you become part of the remote LAN.

You can use Windows XP's VPN service to allow incoming connections to your computer as well. You can use the Internet Connection Firewall or a firewall on your LAN to protect against hackers, yet still connect to your computer through the Internet to retrieve files from afar.

Windows XP supports two VPN encapsulation or repackaging technologies. The *Point-to-Point Tunneling Protocol*, or *PPTP*, was developed by Microsoft and was provided with previous versions of Windows. The *Layer Two Tunneling Protocol*, or *L2TP*, is an industry standard technology, and is faster and better than PPTP. L2TP requires a certificate for its IPSec-based encryption, so if you don't have Windows 200x Server, Windows will automatically use PPTP for VPN connections.

SETTING UP FOR VIRTUAL PRIVATE NETWORKING

To establish a VPN connection from your computer to another network, you must know the hostname or IP address of the remote VPN server. This information corresponds to the telephone number in a dial-up connection; it lets you specify the endpoint of the tunnel. VPN connections are set up by the New Connection Wizard. Just follow these steps:

1. Open Network Connections. You can view My Network Places and select the View Network Connections task, or, if Connect To appears on your Start menu, choose Connect To, Show All Connections.

2. Select Create a New Connection from Network Tasks.

3. Select Connect to The Network at My Workplace and click Next. (This is a poorly named choice—you might be connecting to your home computer!)

4. Select Virtual Private Network Connection, and click Next.

5. Enter a name for the connection, such as "VPN to Office."

6. If you use a dial-up connection to connect this computer to the Internet, you can select Automatically Dial This Initial Connection to ensure that your Internet connection is up before attempting the VPN connection, as shown in Figure 19.19. If you have a dedicated Internet connection, use a shared connection from another computer, or want to make a dial-up connection manually, choose Do Not Dial, and click Next.

Figure 19.19
You can have Windows automatically dial a selected Internet connection before making a VPN connection.

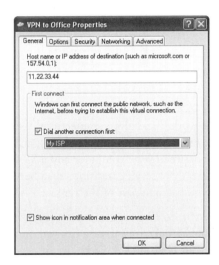

7. Enter the hostname or IP address of the remote dial-in server—for example, vpn.mycompany.com—and select Next.

8. Click Finish to close the wizard.

NOTE

You can delete a connection shortcut later if you don't want it and can drag the connection icon from Network Connections to your desktop later if you do.

Windows immediately opens the Dialer dialog. Before establishing the connection for the first time, verify the connections properties pages.

VPN Connection Properties

To modify a VPN connection's properties, click the Properties button on the dialer dialog, or right-click the connection icon in Network Connections and select Properties.

The properties page has five tabs. Most of the time, the default settings will work correctly, but you should check some of them. In this section, I'll walk you through the most important parameters.

GENERAL PROPERTIES

The General tab of the Properties dialog holds the hostname or IP address of your VPN connection server, and if needed, the name of a dial-up connection to use to carry the VPN connection. If you are establishing the VPN connection over a LAN or dedicated Internet connection, you can uncheck Dial Another Connection First.

OPTIONS

The Options tab includes dialing and redialing options. The two important options are

- **Prompt for Name and Password**—If you tell Windows to remember your username and password when dialing, and after you've made a successful connection once, you can uncheck this option to bypass the Dialing dialog. When you select the connection icon, Windows will just make the connection.
- **Include Windows Logon Domain**—If the VPN server is a Windows 200x or NT Server, you may need to provide your login domain name with your username. You can also enter *domain\username* or, with Windows 200x Servers only, *username@domain*.

SECURITY

It's unlikely that you will need to change any security settings. The data in a VPN connection is usually carried across the Internet, and a high level of security is required. Your password and data should be encrypted in the strongest fashion possible. Be sure that Require Secured Password and Require Data Encryption are set on the Security tab.

If you use the same logon name, password, and domain name on your local computer as you use on the remote network, you can check Automatically Use My Windows Logon Name and Password so that you don't have to enter it whenever you use the connection.

NETWORKING

It's likely that you want to participate as a full member of the remote network, so leave all Components checked on the Networking tab of the Properties dialog.

As I mentioned, Windows XP and 2000 use two types of VPN protocols. Generally, you can leave the Type of VPN server set to Automatic, and Windows will determine to which type it's connected when it makes each call.

If the remote network is a complex, multi-subnet network, or if you want to browse the Internet while you're using the VPN, you also must deal with the gateway issue, which I'll discus later in this chapter under "Routing Issues." To change the gateway setting

1. Select Internet Protocol, and choose Properties. Leave the IP address and DNS information set to Obtain Automatically, and click Advanced.

2. If the remote network has only one subnet, *or* you will set routes to multiple subnets manually, uncheck Use Default Gateway On Remote Network.

DIALING A VPN CONNECTION

Making a VPN connection follows the same procedure as making a dial-up connection:

1. Select the desired VPN connection icon from Network Connections.

2. If this VPN connection requires a dial-up connection, you are prompted with the username and password for your dial-up connection to your ISP. Check for the proper location and dialing rules, and then select Dial. After the connection has been made, Windows proceeds to make the VPN connection.

3. Enter the username and password for access to the remote network. Select Connect.

   Windows then contacts the remote VPN server, verifies your username and password, registers your computer on the network, and creates a connection status icon in the notification area, just as for a standard dial-up connection.

You can use the remote network now, access shared files and folders, access printers, synchronize offline folders, and so on.

When you're finished, right-click the connection icon, and select Disconnect.

ROUTING ISSUES

If the remote network you want to use is a simple, small network with only one subnet or range of IP addresses, you can skip this section. Otherwise, I must address an issue with TCP/IP routing here, as much as I fear it's a real can of worms.

When you establish a VPN connection to another network, your computer is assigned an IP address from that other network for the duration of your connection. This address might be a private, non-Internet-routable address such as 192.168.1.100. All data destined for the remote network is packaged up in PPTP or L2TP packets and sent to the remote host. But what happens if you want to communicate with two servers—a private server through the tunnel and a public Web site on the Internet—at the same time?

When you send data to an IP address that doesn't clearly belong to the private network's range, Windows has two choices: It can pass the data through the tunnel and let the network on the other end route it on, or it can pass the data without encapsulation and let it travel directly to the Internet host.

It would seem sensible that Windows should always use the second approach because any IP address other than, say, 192.168.1.xxx obviously doesn't belong to the private network and doesn't need protection. That's right as long as the remote network has only one such subnet. But some complex corporate networks have many, with different addresses, so Windows can't always know just from the address of the VPN connection which addresses belong to the private network and which should go direct.

If you plan to use a VPN connection and the Internet at the same time, you must find out whether your remote network has more than one subnet. Then follow this advice:

- If the remote network has only one subnet, tell Windows not to use the remote network as the gateway address for unknown locations. This is the easy case.

- If the remote network has more than one subnet, tell Windows to use the remote network as its gateway, so you can connect to all servers on the remote network. Internet access will go through the tunnel, too, and from there to the Internet. It slows things down, but it will work.

- Alternatively, you can tell Windows not to use the remote network gateway, but you'll have to manually set routes to other subnets while you're connected. It's tricky and inconvenient. I'll show you how I do it under "Specifying Routes to a Remote Network," later in this chapter.

When you know how you'll resolve the gateway issue, refer to the VPN Connection Properties earlier in this chapter to make the appropriate settings on the connection's Networking properties tab.

In the remainder of this section, I'll tell you how to take the third option and manually specify routes on the remote network. If you can get by without doing this, you can skip the rest of this section.

SPECIFYING ROUTES TO A REMOTE NETWORK

As I discussed previously (the bit about a can of worms), if you use Virtual Private Networking to connect to a remote network with more than one subnet, and you don't want to pass traffic to Internet sites through the tunnel, you have to disable the default gateway and manually add routes to any subnets that belong to the private network. You can do so at the command line by using the route command, which looks like this:

`route add` subnet `mask` netmask gateway

The subnet and netmask arguments are the addresses for additional networks that can be reached through the gateway address gateway. To add a route, you must know the IP address information for the remote subnets and your gateway address through the VPN.

You must get the subnet numbers from the network administrator on the remote end. You can find the gateway address from your own computer. Connect to the remote VPN, open a command prompt, and type **ipconfig**. One of the connections printed will be labeled PPP Adapter or L2TP Adapter. Note the IP address listed. This address can be used as the gateway address to send packets destined for other remote subnets.

Suppose you're connecting to a VPN host through a connection named VPN to Client and find these connection addresses:

19

```
PPP adapter VPN to Client:
        IP Address. . . . . . . 192.168.005.226
        Subnet Mask . . . . . . 255.255.255.255
        Default Gateway . . . . 192.168.005.226
```

Now, suppose you know that there are two other subnets on the remote network: 192.168.10.0 mask 255.255.255.0, and 192.168.15.0 mask 255.255.255.0. You can reach these two networks by typing two route commands:

```
route add 192.168.10.0 mask 255.255.255.0 192.168.005.226
route add 192.168.15.0 mask 255.255.255.0 192.168.005.226
```

Each route command ends with the IP address of the remote gateway address (it's called the *next hop*).

Check your work by typing **route print** and looking at its output. You should see only one destination labeled 0.0.0.0; if you see two, you forgot to disable the use of the remote network as the default gateway. See that the two routes you added are shown.

To avoid having to type all this every time, you can use another neat trick. You can put a rasdial command and route commands in a batch file, like this:

```
@echo off
rasphone -d "VPN to Client"
route add 192.168.10.0 mask 255.255.255.0 192.168.005.225
route add 192.168.15.0 mask 255.255.255.0 192.168.005.225
```

The rasphone command pops up the connection dialer. When the connection is made, the two routes will be added, and you're all set. With this setup, you'll need the network administrator to give you the real RAS gateway address of the remote VPN server to use as the "next hop" of the route commands, because your connection address will likely change every time you dial in. With a shortcut to this batch file you can connect and set up the routes with just a click.

When you disconnect the VPN connection, Windows removes the added routes automatically.

For more information about rasdial and route, click Start, Help and Support, and search for the commands by name.

ENABLING VPN ACCESS TO YOUR COMPUTER

You can enable incoming VPN connections to your computer if it has a dedicated Internet connection. Your Windows XP computer can act as a VPN server for one incoming connection at a time. You can connect to your computer through the Internet from home or in the field from a computer running Windows 9x, NT, 2000, or of course, XP.

To function correctly, however, your computer must have a known IP address, and if its Internet connection is made through a router, Internet Connection Sharing, or a connecting sharing device, then PPTP packets must be forwarded to your computer. I'll discuss this in more detail shortly, under "Enabling Incoming VPN Connections with NAT."

The process for enabling VPN access is exactly the same as for enabling dial-in access, so see the section "Enabling Dial-In Access to Your Computer" earlier in this chapter. Follow those instructions, being sure to enable an incoming VPN connection. You don't need to choose any modems to receive incoming modem calls.

When Incoming Calls is configured, your computer can be contacted as the host of a VPN connection. To connect to it, establish a VPN connection as you learned in the preceding section, using your computer's public IP address or hostname as the number to dial.

NOTE

> You must configure the Internet protocol to assign valid IP addresses for incoming connections. This topic, which was discussed in "Enabling Dial-Up Access to Your Computer," applies to VPN access, too.

ENABLING INCOMING VPN CONNECTIONS WITH NAT

Microsoft's Internet Connection Sharing and the commercial DSL/cable sharing routers known as *residential gateways* use an IP addressing trick called Network Address Translation or NAT to serve an entire LAN with only one public IP address. Incoming requests, as from a VPN client to a VPN server, have to be directed to a single host computer on the internal network.

This means if you use a shared Internet connection, only one computer can be designated as the recipient of incoming VPN connections. If you use Microsoft's Internet Connection Sharing, that computer should be the one sharing its connection. It will receive and properly handle VPN requests.

If you use a hardware sharing router, the VPN server can be any computer you wish to designate. (Remember that once the VPN connection is established, you can communicate with any of the computers on the LAN.) Your router must be set up to forward the following two packet types to the designated computer:

TCP port 1723

GRE (*protocol* 47…this is not the same as port 47!)

Unfortunately, some of the inexpensive commercial DSL/cable connection sharing routers (residential gateways) don't have a way to explicitly forward GRE packets. Some newer routers provide a configuration screen for a "VPN Endpoint." If your router doesn't have this feature, you may be able to upgrade its firmware to get it. If you use a router device without PPTP support, you will need to designate the VPN target computer as a DMZ host, which will receive *all* unrecognized incoming packets.

CAUTION

> If you designate a computer as a DMZ host, that computer is exposed to the Internet and vulnerable to hacker attacks. You *must* also configure your router to block Microsoft File Sharing packets, at the very least. Set up filtering to block TCP and UDP ports 135 through 139 and 445.

19

WIRELESS NETWORKING

One great way to work "unplugged" is to maintain your network or Internet connection with wireless networking. Radio-based networking technology has advanced rapidly in recent years, and it's being deployed in schools, universities, corporations, and, oddly enough, coffee houses. Whether you're at a branch office, a client's desk or in an overstuffed chair sipping a *café latte*, as long as you're within hundred feet or so of a network access point, you can be online.

→ For details on installing and configuring wireless networking, **see** "Wireless Networking," **p. 652**.

The configuration screens for wireless network adapters let you add name and security information for multiple wireless networks. As you move your computer from place to place, Windows can automatically select the correct network password and attach without your having to do anything. You might want to take advantage of this if you

- Travel between branch offices that each have wireless access points
- Visit airport lounges, Internet cafés or libraries that offer wireless access
- Carry your computer between home and the office
- Visit clients who use wireless networking

CONNECTING TO WIRELESS NETWORKS ON THE ROAD

By default, if you have a wireless network adapter and bring your computer into range of a wireless network access point that Windows hasn't already been in contact with, Windows will pop a dialog asking if you want to connect to the new network. It's pretty much plug-and-play; connecting to a new wireless network can be effortless. If the new network needs a password (also called a key), you'll have to click the Properties button to enter it.

NOTE

If you're not logged on as a Computer Administrator, Windows will complain that it cannot run the Network Setup Wizard. However, if you are using a "Power User" account, you can still configure the wireless connection. Double-click the notification area icon for your wireless adapter, click Properties, endure another privilege complaint, and then select the Wireless Networks tab.

You can also add network information in advance of visiting a new wireless-enabled site, or edit it after the fact. Log on with a Power User or Computer Administrator account and open the Network Connections window. Right-click the icon for your wireless adapter, click Properties, and select the Wireless Networks tab.

In either case you will see the dialog shown in Figure 19.20.

Figure 19.20
The Wireless
Networks tab lets you
enter information for
several "Preferred
Networks."

The Preferred Networks list itemizes wireless network groups in order of preference, so that Windows knows which network it should attach to if it should find itself in range of more than one network at the same time. Windows will display any networks it is currently able to reach in the Available Networks list, whether they've been entered in the Preferred List or not.

If you need to specify a wireless network password for a new network, or change the password for one that's already listed, you can bring up the configuration dialog shown in Figure 19.21 in any of three ways:

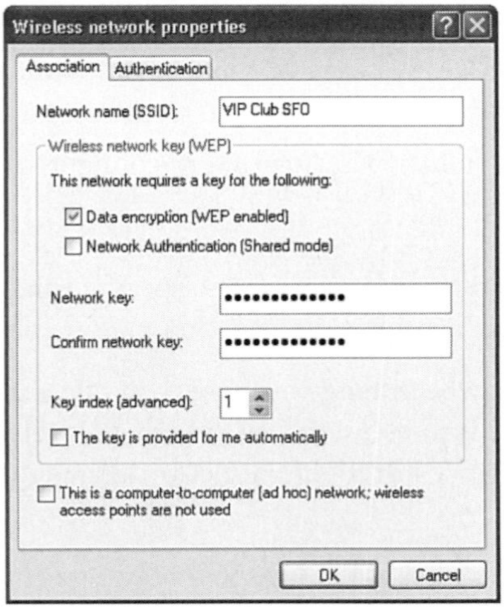

Figure 19.21
Wireless Network
Properties let you
specify a network
password (key), if one
is required.

19

- Select a currently "available" network and click Configure.
- Select an existing "preferred" network and click Properties.
- Click Add, to enter information for a new network before you bring your computer into range for the first time.

To configure security for a given wireless network, go through this checklist:

- If the network does *not* use WEP security, uncheck Data Encryption (WEP Enabled). In most cases, however, wireless networks should be secured, and you will need to check this box.
- If the network provides the encryption key automatically (this is sometimes the case with more expensive corporate networks), check The Key Is Provided for Me Automatically. Otherwise, uncheck the box and enter the network key.
- If you need to enter a network key, it will be provided by the network's manager in one of the following four forms, depending on the level of security the Wireless network uses:
  - A five character alphanumeric pass phrase (for example, "xY#1q")
  - An eight digit hexadecimal key (e.g. "01AE423F") for 40-bit security
  - A 13 character alphanumeric pass phrase
  - A 26 digit hexadecimal key for 104-bit security

  (As we mentioned in Chapter 17, 40-bit and 64-bit security are the *same thing*, as are 104-bit and 128-bit).

  In rare cases, you may also be instructed to choose an alternate key index.
- If the wireless network uses no access point but involves only the wireless adapters of individual computers, you will need to check This Is a Computer-to-Computer (Ad Hoc) Network. This will be unlikely to occur in the case of mobile network access unless you're connecting to another computer just to transfer a few files.
- On some corporate networks, you may be instructed to configure information on the Authentication tab.

The settings entered in this dialog are associated with one specific wireless network, and must be configured separately for each wireless network you may encounter.

If you expect that your computer may be in range of more than one wireless network at the same time, you can select which one is to be used over the others by changing the order of the items in the Preferred Networks list; just highlight network names and click Move Up or Move Down.

You can also control what types of networks Windows will offer up for connection. If you click the Advanced button, the dialog shown in Figure 19.22 appears.

Figure 19.22
The Advanced dialog lets you limit the types of wireless networks Windows will use.

By default, Windows will connect to any available network, but will select one supported by an access point to an ad-hoc network, and will automatically connect to a non-preferred network—that is, one that it "hears" but which isn't already listed in Preferred Networks dialog.

- If you want to use or test an ad-hoc network in the presence of access points, select Computer-to-Computer. If you want to avoid ad-hoc connections entirely, select Access Point. Otherwise the default setting Any Available Network is OK.

- If you want to avoid the possibility of inadvertently connecting to a new, possibly insecure wireless network, uncheck Automatically Connect to Non-Preferred Networks. If you do this, when you encounter a new wireless network, you'll have to go to the Wireless Networks dialog discussed earlier, select a new network from the Available list and click Connect.

SECURITY CONCERNS

Data sent on a wireless network isn't confined to a network cable. It can be received by any other wireless-equipped computer up to several hundred feet away. The current generation of wireless network cards employs an encryption technique called WEP (Wired-Equivalent Privacy), but the word "equivalent" has proven to be overly optimistic: Researchers have found that the encryption can be broken by a sufficiently determined eavesdropper. And if WEP encryption isn't enabled, your data is available to *anyone* nearby. Most email programs, Web sites, and FTP servers send passwords without additional encryption, so, on a wireless network without WEP, these passwords are at risk, and you have to weigh this risk against wireless convenience. Many coffee-house networks fall in this category, so beware. (Don't confuse the need to sign on with a password and/or pay for the service with the use of a network key.)

With WEP enabled, even though each user starts with the same basic network key, each computer adds additional random encryption so it's not *easy* for other computers on the same wireless LAN to eavesdrop on your communications. But, a diligent hacker or an NSA-type eavesdropper could conceivably glean your account information. You should think carefully about what you're transmitting across the airwaves, especially in public places. For the average home user, the risk is probably not too great. Businesses should be

19

more concerned about the possibility of eavesdroppers monitoring their network data. You should research the issue for yourself before you buy into this technology.

ACCESSING COMPUTERS REMOTELY

So far we've concentrated mostly on how to access remote files and networks when you're traveling. The techniques for remote networking give you access to files and folders that you've left behind. There's another way to get at information from afar, and it gives you not just your files and folders but your whole home-base computer, desktop and all. Generically, it's called Remote Control, and there have been commercial applications to support it for years. Windows XP Professional comes with built-in remote control software called the Remote Desktop Connection, and in my opinion, just this one feature is a good enough reason to buy XP Pro instead of Home Edition.

REMOTE DESKTOP CONNECTION

Windows XP Professional has a spiffy feature called Remote Desktop that lets you connect to and use your computer from another location. You'll be able to see your computer's screen, move the mouse, and type on the keyboard just as if you were there. This is just what you need when you're out of town and need to read a file you left on the computer back home, or if you have to catch up on work at the office while you're at home. I use this feature almost every day, and now I can't imagine not having it on every computer I work with.

You also can use the Remote Desktop client program to attach to computers running Windows NT Terminal Server Version and Windows 200x Server's Terminal Services. The client program lets you log on to these computers to access special applications provided by your company, or for administration and maintenance.

NOTE

> You don't have to be miles and miles away to take advantage of Remote Desktop, either. You can also use it to access other computers on your own LAN. For instance, you could use it to start a lengthy computing job on someone else's computer without leaving your own desk.

Third-party programs such as Carbon Copy, PC Anywhere, Timbuktu, and VNC have been doing this for years, and they have some more sophisticated features, but Remote Desktop is built into Windows XP and it's essentially free. It's a scaled-down version of Windows Terminal Services, a component of the Windows NT/200x Server program that lets multiple users run programs on one central server. By stripped down, I mean that only one person can connect to Windows XP Professional at a time, and it forces a local user off.

While the host computer (the computer you'll take control of) has to be running Windows XP Professional, the Remote Desktop Client software (that you use to view your XP computer) can run any version of Windows from 95 on up, and there's even a Macintosh version of the Remote Desktop client available for download from www.microsoft.com/mac. Figure 19.23 shows how this works. There's even an initiative to develop a Remote Desktop client for Unix, which you can read about at http://www.rdesktop.org.

Figure 19.23
You can use any Windows-based computer to connect to and control your Windows XP Professional computer.

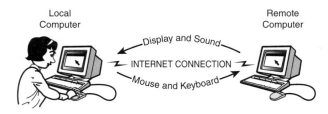

To use Remote Desktop, the host computer must be reachable over the Internet, and this means that it will need a dedicated Internet connection with a fixed IP address (or, you'll need someone to make an Internet connection at the computer and tell you what the IP address is). Furthermore, if your computer gets its Internet connection through a shared connection or a residential gateway, your sharing computer or router will have to be set up to forward incoming requests on TCP port 3389 to the computer you want to reach by Remote Desktop.

Making Your Computer Available for Remote Desktop Connection

To enable Remote Desktop connections to your computer, follow these steps:

1. Right-click My Computer and select Properties. Or, open the old-style System control panel applet.

2. Select the Remote tab and check Allow Users to Connect Remotely to This Computer.

3. If you want to grant Remote Desktop access to user accounts with Limited Access or Power User permission level, click Select Remote Users and check the boxes next to the user names. Computer Administrator users can connect without explicit permission.

   In any case, however, *only* accounts with passwords can be reached. Windows will not grant Remote Desktop access to any user account without a password.

4. Click OK to close the dialogs.

If you want to reach your computer through the Internet, and you use Internet Connection Sharing or a connection sharing router, you'll have to instruct your sharing computer or router to forward Remote Desktop data through to your computer, and you'll only be able to contact one selected computer from outside your network.

You'll have to set up your sharing computer or router to forward incoming requests on TCP port 3389 to the computer you want to reach by Remote Desktop.

19

CAUTION

If your computer is part of a corporate network, be sure that your organization's security policies permit you to enable Remote Desktop connection. On a Windows Domain network, Remote Desktop might even be disabled by the Group Policy feature.

PROVIDING ACCESS TO MORE THAN ONE COMPUTER

If you have more than one computer on your network that you want to reach through Remote Desktop Connection, and you use Internet Connection Sharing or a connection sharing router that uses Network Address Translation (NAT), you'll have to take some special steps.

By default, Remote Desktop uses TCP Port 3389 for its connection. Since a given port can only be forwarded from the sharing computer or router to one specific computer inside your network, only one computer can be reached using this default port. However, you can change the TCP port number that Remote Desktop uses, and thus make it possible to connect to any of several computers. Figure 19.24 illustrates how this works.

Figure 19.24
You can configure Remote Desktop to use alternate port numbers in order to access more than one computer behind a firewall.

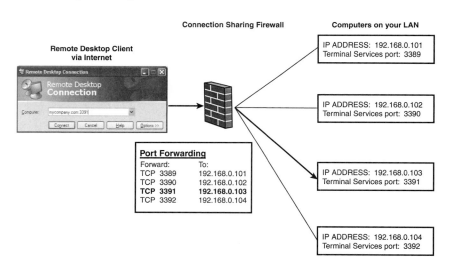

One computer is left in the standard configuration and accepts Remote Desktop connections on TCP port 3389. Other computers are configured to listen on alternate ports; for example, 3390, 3391 and so on. This makes it possible to direct incoming requests to more than one computer behind the NAT firewall.

To change the port that Remote Desktop Connection uses to receive incoming connections, log on as a Computer Administrator and follow these steps:

1. Choose a port number for each computer that you want to reach by Remote Desktop Connection, starting with 3389 and going up or down. Unless you're using Internet Connection Sharing, each of these computers must also be configured to use a fixed IP address, which you should also note along with the chosen port number.

Repeat steps 2 through 5 on each of the computers that won't be using the default port value of 3389.

2. Open the Registry Editor by clicking Start, Run, typing **regedit**, and pressing Enter.

3. In the left pane, view the key
   `HKEY_LOCAL_MACHINE\System\CurrentControlSet\Control\TerminalServer\`
   `WinStations\RDP-Tcp`.

4. In the right pane, double-click the value PortNumber. Select Decimal, and change the port number from 3389 to the chosen value for this particular computer.

5. Click OK, close the Registry editor and restart the computer.

6. If you're using Internet Connection Sharing, configure the sharing computer to forward incoming connections on ports 3389 and the other selected ports to your computers. You can specify the computers by name. If you are using a connection sharing router with NAT services, configure the router to forward ports 3389 and the other ports to the selected computers. Specify the computers by their IP addresses.

NOTE

> Some routers let you specify both a destination IP address *and* port in their forwarding configuration screens. If yours can do this, you don't have to reconfigure each of your computers. Instead, forward incoming connections on port 3389 to port 3389 on one computer, incoming connections on port 3390 to port 3389 on another computer, and so on.

CONNECTING TO OTHER COMPUTERS WITH REMOTE DESKTOP

To establish a connection to a computer that's been set up to receive Remote Desktop connections, you'll need a copy of the Remote Desktop Client, also called the Terminal Services Client. There are several ways you can get this program:

- It's preinstalled on Windows XP computers. Select Start, All Programs, Accessories, Communications, Remote Desktop Connection.

- It's on your Windows XP CD-ROM. Insert it in another computer, and from the setup program select Perform Additional Tasks, then Set Up Remote Desktop Connection. This will run the installation program.

- You can download it from www.microsoft.com. Search for "Remote Desktop Client". This is handy if you're traveling and don't have an XP disc with you. Microsoft makes a Macintosh version of the Remote Desktop client, so you can even access your Windows XP computer from a Mac.

When you run the Remote Desktop Client, you'll see the Remote Desktop Connection dialog, as shown in Figure 19.25.

19

Figure 19.25
The Remote Desktop Connection dialog lets you configure the connection and select the remote computer to use.

Enter the IP address or register DNS name of the computer you'd like to use. If you want to connect to a computer using an alternate TCP port number, enter a colon and the port number after the IP address or name, as in `mycompany.com:3391`.

Entering a username and password at this point is optional. If you don't enter them now, you'll be asked for them when the connection is established. Click Connect to establish the connection immediately, or click Options to adjust the connection properties first. The properties tabs are described in Table 19.5.

TABLE 19.5   REMOTE DESKTOP CONNECTION PROPERTIES

Tab	Properties
General	*Connection Settings* saves the configuration for a particular remote computer as a shortcut for quick access later.
Display	Sets the size and color depth of the window used for your remote connection's desktop. Display size can be set to a fixed window size or Full Screen.
Local Resources	Connects devices on the local computer so that you may use them as if they were part of the remote computer. (This feature does not work when connecting to Windows NT and Windows 2000 Terminal Services.)
	The Keyboard setting determines whether special Windows key commands such as Alt+Tab apply to your local computer or the remote computer.
Programs	Lets you automatically run a program on the remote computer upon logging on.
Experience	Lets you indicate your connection speed, so that Windows can appropriately limit display-intense features such as menu animation.

19

When you establish the connection, you'll see a standard Windows logon dialog. Enter your username and password to sign on. It may take a while for the logon process to complete, if Windows has to shut down a logged-on user.

When you're logged on, you'll see the remote computer's desktop, as shown in Figure 19.26, and can use it as if you were actually sitting in front of it. Keyboard, mouse, display and sound should be fully functional. If you maximize the window, the remote desktop will fill your screen. It all works quite well—it can even be difficult to remember which computer you're actually using!

In addition, any printers attached to your local computer will appear as choices if you print from applications on the remote computer, and the local computer's drives will appear in the list in My Computer. You can take advantage of this to copy files between the local and remote computers.

Printer on the local computer

Figure 19.26
When connected to Windows XP via Remote Desktop, your local computer's drives and printers are available for use.

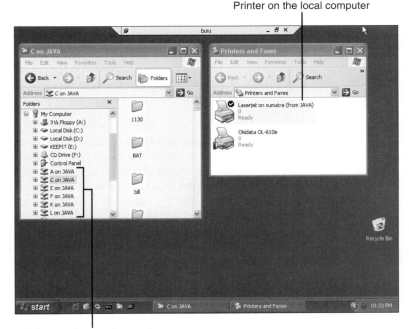

Drives on the local computer

Finally, your local computer's serial (COM) ports will also be available to the remote computer. (My friend Norm syncs his Palm Pilot to his Windows XP Professional computer from remote locations using this feature.)

While you're connected, you might want to use keyboard shortcuts such as Alt+Tab to switch between applications. This can confuse Windows, which won't know whether to switch applications on the local computer or the remote computer. You can specify where special key combinations should be interpreted on the Local Resources properties page, as I described earlier, or you can use alternative key combinations to ensure that the desired actions take place on the remote computer. The alternative keyboard shortcuts are shown in Table 19.6.

TABLE 19.6 SOME OF THE REMOTE DESKTOP KEYBOARD SHORTCUTS

Use These Keys:	To Transmit This to the Remote Computer:
Alt+PgUp, Alt+PgDn	Alt+Tab (switch programs)
Alt+End	Ctrl+Alt+Del (task monitor)
Alt+Home	(Displays the Start menu)
Ctrl+Alt+Break	Alt+Enter (toggle full screen)
Ctrl+Alt+Plus	Alt+PrntScrn (screen to clipboard)

When you've finished using the remote computer, choose Start, Log Off to end the connection. If you want the remote computer to continue running an application, though, you can simply close the Remote Desktop window or select Disconnect. Your account will stay active on the remote computer until you reconnect and log off, or until a user at that computer logs on.

N O T E

Windows XP Professional only permits one person to use each computer. If you attempt to connect to a computer while another user is logged on, you'll have the choice of disconnecting or forcing them off. If Quick User Switch is enabled, they'll be switched out; otherwise they're summarily logged off. This is somewhat brutal; the other user might lose work in progress. If you log on using the same username as the local user, though, you simply take over the desktop without forcing a logoff.

If someone logs on to the remote computer while you're connected from afar, *you'll* be disconnected. If Quick User Switch is enabled, you can reconnect later and pick up where you left off. Otherwise, the same deal applies: If they used a different username, your applications will be shut down.

THIRD-PARTY REMOTE ACCESS OPTIONS

Several software vendors provide tools that perform the same function as Remote Desktop Connection. You might want to consider these if you want to connect to a computer running Windows XP Home Edition, or if you want to gain remote access via modem. Here are some of the pros and cons of these programs:

- Most of them allow connections via modem, direct serial cable connections as well as network protocols such as TCP/IP, IPX/SPX, and NetBEUI.
- Most provide extras such as drag and drop file transfers and scripting.

- Some are available on several platforms. The free VNC program, for example, has both client and server versions for Windows, Macintosh, and most versions of Unix.

- The third-party programs tend to be slower than Remote Desktop Connection, which is tightly integrated with Windows and is very efficient.

- With the exception of VNC which is free, they are commercial programs that you must buy in addition to Windows.

- As far as I know, none of the third party packages extend the host computer's sound, serial, and parallel ports to the remote computer.

Some of the more common packages are

- pcAnywhere (www.symantec.com).
- Timbuktu Pro (www.netopia.com). Comes in both Windows and Mac versions.
- Magic Remote Desktop 32 (www.magicsolutions.com).
- LapLink Gold (www.laplink.com).
- NetOp Remote Control (www.netop.com).*
- Remotely Anywhere (www.remotelyanywhere.com).*
- Remote Administrator (www.famatech.com).
- Carbon Copy (www.altiris.com).
- VNC (www.uk.research.att.com/vnc and www.tridiavnc.com).*

> **NOTE**
>
> Packages marked with an asterisk (*) support connections via network or the Internet, but not direct modem connections.

19

There are also some Web-based remote control applications. These work by installing a server program on your computer, which you then access through a Web browser. They require that your computer be accessible through the Internet with an always-on connection, just as if you were running a Web browser. Check out www.gotomypc.com for an example of this type of service.

REMOTE ASSISTANCE

Remote Assistance lets two people work collaboratively on one Windows XP computer—one at the computer and one remotely, over the Internet. The feature is intended to let people get technical assistance from someone at a remote location, and it's based on the same technology as the Remote Desktop feature I described in the previous section. There are several significant differences, however:

- With Remote Assistance, both the local and remote users see the same screen at the same time, and both can move the mouse, type on the keyboard, and so forth.

- Remote Assistance doesn't make the local computer's drives appear in the drive list, nor does it transmit sound back, as Remote Desktop does.

- Remote Assistance connections can't be made *ad lib*. One Windows XP user must invite another through email or Windows Messenger. Or, one user can offer assistance to another using Messenger. In any case, the procedure requires the simultaneous cooperation of users at both ends of the connection.

- Remote Assistance can be used to connect to Windows XP Home Edition. Users of any version of Windows XP can assist each other.

- Remote Assistance allows you to use text chat or to establish voice communication while the desktop session is active.

If you're familiar with NetMeeting's Desktop Sharing function, this may all sound familiar. The difference is that Remote Assistance is based on the more modern Terminal Services technology that powers Remote Desktop, so it's only available to Windows XP users. Also, it just plain works better than Desktop Sharing.

NOTE

> If your computer gets its Internet connection through a residential gateway (hardware router), your friend won't be able to connect to you unless the router explicitly supports Remote Assistance. Simply forwarding TCP Port 3389 will not work, as the invitation message contains your local, unreachable IP address. Windows Internet Connection Sharing does support incoming Remote Assistance connections, because it modifies the invitation to use your public IP address.

REQUESTING REMOTE ASSISTANCE

To invite a friend or colleague to work with you on your computer, first contact your friend and confirm that they have Windows XP and are ready to work with you. If you want help making system or network settings, or installing software, you should log in with a Computer Administrator user account before going any further. Then, follow these steps:

1. Select Start, Help and Support.
2. Click Invite a Friend to Connect to Your Computer with Remote Assistance.
3. Select Invite Someone to Help You.
4. You can issue an invitation via Windows Messenger, if you and your friend both have accounts, or via email. Select your friend's name from the Messenger Online list, or enter her email address, as shown in Figure 19.27. Then, click Invite This Person.
5. If you have chosen to send the invitation by email, Windows will pop up a rather alarming message warning you that a program is attempting to send email. Choose Send (and thank the guy who wrote the Melissa virus for making this necessary).

NOTE

> If you use a dial-up Internet connection or a DSL service that requires you to sign on, your Internet IP address changes every time you connect. Remote Assistance invitations use this address to tell the other person's computer how to contact you, so they will only work if you stay connected from the time you send the invitation to the time your friend responds. If you have a fixed (static) IP address, this won't be a problem.

Figure 19.27
Select a Windows Messenger user ID or enter an email address to invite someone to connect to your computer.

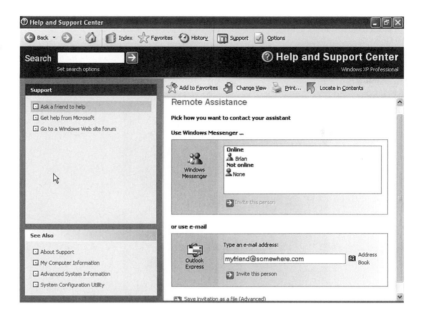

If you sent your request via Windows Messenger, you should get a response within a few seconds. If you sent the request by email, it could be some time before the other party reads and receives it.

You also can select Save Invitation as a File to transfer the invitation by other means such as a network or floppy disk. The invitation, whether sent by Messenger, email, or file, is actually an XML file containing the IP address of your computer and some encrypted information that specifies how long the invitation remains valid.

If you want to view the list of invitations you've sent by email, select View Invitation Status on the Remote Assistance page. You can then select invitations to delete, expire (disallow), or re-send.

When someone responds to your request for assistance, a dialog will appear on your screen asking if it's okay for them to connect. Click Yes, and after a minute or so a window will appear with which you can control the Remote Assistance session, as shown in Figure 19.28.

You can use this dialog to type text messages back and forth, initiate a voice connection or a file transfer, or terminate the connection. When the remote user wants to take control of your mouse and keyboard, you'll be asked and can permit or deny this. Even then you can still type and move the mouse yourself, and can end the remote user's control by pressing the Esc key or by clicking End Control on the Remote Assistance window.

RESPONDING TO AN ASSISTANCE REQUEST

When someone invites you to connect by Remote Assistance, you'll either see a pop-up box in Windows Messenger, or you'll receive an email, as shown in Figure 19.29.

19

Figure 19.28
When your Remote Assistant has connected, you can use this window to chat and control the connection.

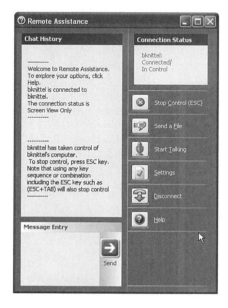

Figure 19.29
You might receive an email invitation (left) or an instant message (right) requesting Remote Assistance. To accept an email invitation, open the attachment.

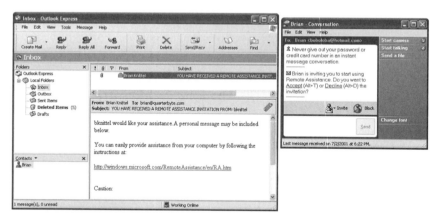

You can directly respond to an instant message invitation as indicated in the message window. To accept an email invitation, open the attachment. (How you do that depends on your email program—in Outlook Express 6, click on the paperclip icon, and select the attachment labeled rcBuddy.MsRcIncident. When the Attachment Warning dialog appears, select Open It.) Opening the attachment should activate the Remote Assistance connection.

NOTE

You can absolutely prevent others from manipulating your computer when they connect using Remote Assistance–they'll be able to see your screen but not control it. To do this, right-click My Computer and select Properties. View the Remote tab and click Advanced. Uncheck Allow This Computer to Be Controlled Remotely and click OK. In any case, you have to grant the other user permission to manipulate your computer each time a connection is made.

You will be asked if you wish to proceed with the connection, and when it's been established, the remote user will be asked if they want to permit you to connect. Assuming you both say yes, at this point patience is called for as it can take more than a minute for the required software to load up and for the other user's desktop to appear on your screen, as shown in Figure 19.30.

Figure 19.30
The Remote Assistance screen has a control panel on the left, and a view of the remote user's screen on the right. Click Take Control if you want to manipulate the remote computer.

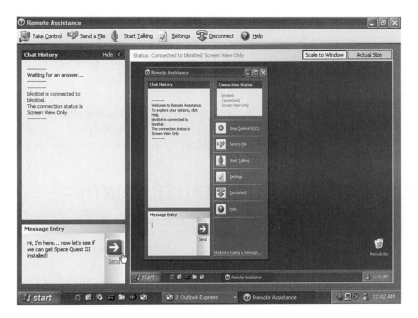

The Remote Assistance window has several sections. On the left is a text chat window through which you and the other party can type to each other. Enter messages in the Message Entry window.

Across the top is a menu of controls. The choices are

- **Take Control**—Click this to begin using the other computer's mouse and keyboard. The remote user will be asked to grant permission. Once you have control of the other computer, both of you can use your mouse and keyboard. The remote user can cancel your control at any time by pressing the Esc key.

■ **Send a File**—Brings up a dialog to let you transfer a file to the remote computer. You can select a file to send, and the remote user must select a place to store it, as shown in Figure 19.31.

Figure 19.31
File Transfers during Remote Assistance require the sender to select the file and the recipient to select a destination folder.

■ **Start Talking**—Establishes a voice connection. If both of you have a microphone, speakers, and a sound card, you will be able to speak to each other over your Internet or LAN connection.

■ **Settings**—Lets you change the audio settings for voice communication and the default screen scaling setting.

■ **Disconnect**—Ends the Remote Assistance connection.

Most of the window is devoted to a view of your friend's screen. You can click Scale To Window to fit his entire screen in this window, or click Actual Size to see a normal size view which you'll probably have to scroll up and down from time to time.

WEB FOLDERS AND INTERNET PRINTING

If a remote computer has Internet Information Services (IIS) installed, has enabled Web Sharing on any folders, and is accessible over the Internet or a corporate Internet, you can access its shared files through Internet Explorer version 5 or higher. This technology lets you copy files to and from a remote computer with a high degree of security, through firewalls that normally block access to file sharing protocols.

When IIS is installed, the computer's shared printers may also be used through the Internet using the Internet Printing Protocol, or IPP. IPP lets remote computers print to shared printers across the Internet, again through firewalls.

You can use these technologies to great advantage if your office or home computer has dedicated Internet access because you access its shared folders over the Internet without using a modem or VPN connection.

These applications are all described elsewhere in this book; I just wanted to be sure they were mentioned here as they're great resources for the "unplugged" user.

→ Installing IIS is covered in detail in Chapter 15, "Internet Information Services." Using Web folders and Web printing is covered in Chapter 18, "Using the Network."

MANAGING MULTIPLE NETWORK CONFIGURATIONS

Most desktop computers sit where they are installed, gathering dust until they're obsolete, and participate in only one LAN. But portable computer users often carry their computers from office to office, docking or plugging into several different local LANs. While Microsoft has made it easy for you to manage several different dial-up and VPN connections, it's difficult to manage connections to several different LANs if the network configuration settings are manually set.

Internet Protocol settings are the difficult ones. If your computer is set to use automatic TCP/IP configuration, you won't encounter any problems; your computer will absorb the local information each time you connect.

If your TCP/IP settings are set manually, things aren't so simple. Microsoft has come up with a partial solution called Alternate Configuration. You can configure your computer for automatic IP address assignment on most networks, and manual assignment on one. The way this works is that Windows looks for a DHCP server when it boots up, and if it doesn't find one it uses the Alternate Configuration. This can be a static IP address, or the default setting of Automatic Private IP address assignment, whereby Windows chooses a random address in the 169.254 subnet. (The automatic technique was the only option in Windows 98, Me, 2000, and XP.)

This means that your computer can automatically adjust itself to multiple networks, at most one of which requires manual IP address settings.

To set up Alternate Configuration, open Network Connections, view Local Area Connection's properties, and double-click Internet Protocol. Be sure the General tab uses the Obtain and IP Address Automatically setting. View the Alternate Configuration tab and choose User Configured to enter the static LAN's information.

If you need to commute between multiple networks that require manual configuration, you'll have to change the General settings each time you connect to a different network. I suggest that you stick a 3-by-5-inch card with the settings for each network in your laptop carrying case for handy reference.

NOTE

Although it appears that Microsoft isn't going to solve this problem for us, we can hope that third-party software developers will come up with a tool to manage multiple LAN connections properly. Back on Windows 95 I used a program called Network Hopper that let you choose from a list of multiple network setups. It changed not only the IP address info but even email setups, so that the appropriate mail servers were used on each network. A tool like that for Windows XP would be a real blessing. Developers, care to take this on?

19

CHAPTER 20

THE HETEROGENEOUS NETWORK

In this chapter

NETWORKING IN A MULTI-VENDOR ENVIRONMENT

Most networks today do not use a single network operating system or hardware platform. Indeed, the larger the business entity, the more likely you are to run into a network that includes NetWare, Unix, and Linux servers along with Windows NT and the Windows 2000 Server and Windows Server 2003 families, all supporting PCs running every version of Windows from 95 on up.

NOTE

In the remainder of this chapter, I'll refer to the Windows 2000 Server and Windows Server 2003 versions collectively as *Windows 200x Server*.

Apple Macintosh computers appear in many environments, especially when graphics or multimedia applications are a critical part of the business. In larger enterprises, mainframe computers have been in use for years—and they aren't going to go away anytime soon, because while PCs continue to increase in speed and capability, their security and reliability haven't improved at anywhere near the same pace.

The need to mix operating systems on a network isn't limited to the office, either. Many home users have several computers and want to use Windows-based PCs with Macs and computers running Linux.

So, in this chapter we'll show you how Windows XP can share files, folders, and printers with a myriad of other operating systems.

MIX AND MATCH OVERVIEW

There are four general strategies for letting Windows and other operating systems share files and printers, diagrammed in Figure 20.1:

- You can install software on Windows to let Windows client computers access shared resources offered by the other operating system.

- You can install software on the other computer systems to let them access resources shared by Windows.

- You can install "native" services on a Windows 200x Server computer to share file and print services to other operating systems through foreign protocols.

- You can install a proxy or "gateway" service on a Windows 200x Server computer. The gateway takes resources shared by the other operating systems, translates them on-the-fly, and presents them to Windows client computers as if they were being shared by the Windows server, and vice versa: A gateway service can serve as a proxy through which other operating systems can see and use Windows resources.

20

Figure 20.1
Four strategies for interplatform networking.

• *Install Alternate Client in Windows*

• *Install Windows Client in Other System*

• *Install Foreign Sharing Services on Windows Server*

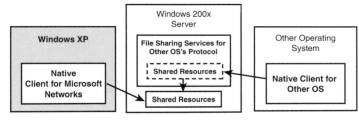

• *Install Gateway Service on Windows Server*

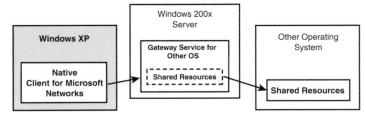

There are pros and cons to each approach. Gateway services require you to set up a server process, giving you one more system to manage on your network. In addition, they tend to be less efficient, as *two* computers—the computer sharing the resource and the proxy server translating it—are in between a given shared file and a client computer.

Gateway services let each client computer work with a single environment, and it need only deal with resources shared in its native format. This can minimize deployment, configuration, and maintenance headaches. Gateway services also provide a smooth path for eventually replacing the alternate operating system. Initially, the shared resources just *look* like they're part of a Windows server. Later, they can actually be located on the Windows server, and the clients don't have to be reconfigured.

20

On the other hand, providing a way for client computers to directly access resources provided by a different operating system frees you from having to set up a gateway server, and it tends to provide faster throughput. There are two ways to go about it: You can configure your Windows computers to access resources shared on other systems, or you can configure clients running under the other operating systems to use Windows shares. It usually doesn't make sense to use both approaches at once; your life will be simpler if you can locate all shared resources in just one environment.

Most other operating system vendors have made a point of making it much easier for their users to access Windows resources, but Microsoft isn't exactly bending over backward to make it easy for Windows users to access foreign systems in a seamless fashion. Support for other protocols and systems looks promising in Microsoft's whitepapers and executive summaries, but performance and implementation are spotty.

Unfortunately, there is no simple formula to choose which approach to take. You'll have to look at your current and expected future operating system mix and consider the alternatives. As an overview, here's a quick rundown; we'll discuss each them in more detail later in the chapter.

WINDOWS 9X AND NT

Older versions of Windows can internetwork quite nicely with Windows XP without additional hardware or software, but surprisingly, it usually doesn't work out-of-the-box. Later in the chapter, we'll discuss how to make Windows versions play well together.

NOVELL NETWARE

Both Microsoft and Novell provide client software that can be installed on Windows XP clients to access NetWare resources. Microsoft also offers Gateway Services for NetWare (GSNW) for Windows 2000 Server so that a single Windows 2000 server can operate as a gateway to access NetWare resources for a number of Windows XP clients, without the necessity of installing the client software on each Windows computer.

Microsoft's Services for NetWare (SFN) package provides tools to help integrate NetWare NDS and Microsoft Active Directory domain networks.

> **NOTE**
>
> Microsoft has dropped GSNW from Windows Server 2003.

UNIX AND LINUX

For Unix shops, Microsoft offers Services for Unix 3.0 (SFU), which provides an NFS client and gateway service; additional services such as NIS, Telnet, and User Mapping; and the *Interix* environment that lets you run Unix tools, applications, and shell scripts under Windows—SFU even comes with a host of Unix applications including sendmail, vi, and gcc. SFU provides both end-user client tools and server-based sharing services.

Alternatively, the Samba open-source code can be used by Unix, Macintosh, and Linux systems to access files and printers shared by Windows-based hosts and servers, and vice versa: Unix/Mac/Linux machines can share files and printers with Windows clients over TCP/IP.

APPLE MACINTOSH

While Windows XP does not provide any native protocols or services for connections to Apple's various network protocols, there are several internetworking options.

First, Windows 200x Server can be outfitted with File Services for Macintosh and Print Services for Macintosh to provide native Mac file sharing services to Macs.

On the Mac side, the Samba package is available for Mac OS X users, giving Macs access to Windows file and printer shares. In fact, Samba support is built into the OS X 10.1 GUI, making Windows internetworking a snap (even if all the work is done on the Mac side). For Macs running OS 9 and earlier, you can buy third-party applications to access Windows file shares.

IBM HOSTS

If your network contains IBM mainframe or AS/400 computers, your Windows 200x Servers can use Microsoft's Host Integration Server. It provides 3270 and 5250 terminal emulation, protocol gateway services, file sharing, and print services, as well as a host of application level gateways that enable developers to integrate host and Windows applications. If all you need is terminal and printer connectivity, there are many third-party and free applications available that let your PC function as a mainframe terminal and/or printer over Ethernet, Token Ring, or twinax connections.

In the next sections, we'll go over each of these operating system environments in more detail.

NETWORKING WITH WINDOWS 95, 98, ME, AND NT

If you have computers running older versions of Windows as well as XP, you'll very likely want to network them—if not permanently, at least long enough to transfer files from an old computer to a newer one. What most people quickly find out is that it's not as simple as you'd hope. While all versions of Windows use the same basic networking protocols to share files and printers, compatibility problems crop up more often than not. And while some of the problems are easily explained and fixed, others remain mysterious and intermittent. (We Windows users are used to that, aren't we?)

20

PROTOCOL ISSUES

The most significant issue facing would-be Windows networkers is that starting with XP, Microsoft has changed the default networking protocol from NetBEUI to TCP/IP. Windows XP doesn't overtly offer NetBEUI as an option, while older versions of Windows installed NetBEUI by default, and often didn't install TCP/IP at all. Unless you take steps to give all of your computers one common protocol, they won't be able to talk to one another.

There are three ways to get around this problem:

- You can install TCP/IP on your older computers.
- You can install NetBEUI on Windows XP (yes, it's there, it's just hard to find).
- You can use the IPX/SPX-Compatible Protocol as the common protocol.

The best route to follow won't be clear until you consider these other points:

- NetBEUI is not compatible with large, routed networks. In the future, NetBEUI may not be available at all. So, while it's an acceptable approach on small networks for the present, it's not a good long-term solution. It probably won't be usable at all with XP's successor.
- NetBEUI and IPX/SPX require no configuration, so they work "out of the box." TCP/IP has to be properly configured to work—you must either manually assign at least an IP address and network mask to each computer, or you must use a DHCP server, which is provided as part of the Windows Internet Connection Sharing and by hardware broadband connection sharing routers. (Don't rely on Windows's "autoconfiguration" scheme—it can cause huge delays and slowdowns in Windows 98 and perhaps other versions.)
- If your network includes Macs, Unix, and/or Linux and you want to share files with them as well, you'll definitely want to use TCP/IP for file sharing. TCP/IP is also the standard on all enterprise networks.
- Unfortunately, older versions of Windows, including Windows 2000, often have problems when TCP/IP is the sole networking protocol. In particular, the Browser service that underlies Network Neighborhood often doesn't work properly on TCP/IP-only networks.
- Windows networks definitely don't like to have different mixes of protocols installed on different machines. It's best to install the same protocol or set of protocols on every computer. It doesn't matter which, as long as every computer has the same mix.

With this in mind, I recommend that you follow one of these three plans:

- On a home or small-office network, if you plan on retiring the older Windows computers within the next couple of years, go ahead and install NetBEUI on Windows XP (as well as all of your older computers). In the next section, I'll tell you how to install NetBEUI on Windows XP. Install TCP/IP as well.

  For a one-time network copy from an old computer to a new one, this is probably the best option. After the old computer is gone, you can uninstall NetBEUI from Windows XP.

- If you have a larger number of computers and don't want to rely on NetBEUI remaining available, install the IPX/SPX-Compatible Protocol on all computers. Remove or disable NetBEUI from all computers on which it is installed. You can do this on each computer's Network control panel. Chapter 17, "Building Your Own Network," tells how to install protocols on Windows XP.

- On larger networks, or on networks that involve other operating systems, install TCP/IP on all computers. Disable or remove NetBEUI and IPX/SPX from all computers. You'll have to expect some flakiness and sensitivity to the order in which your computers are booted up. You may find that some computers see others but not vice versa. If possible, boot a Windows XP machine first and keep it running all the time.

INSTALLING NETBEUI ON WINDOWS XP

If you want to install the NetBEUI protocol on Windows XP in order to network with older versions of Windows, follow these steps. You'll need your Windows XP Installation CD.

1. Log on as a Computer Administrator user.
2. Insert the Windows Installation CD into your computer's CD or CD/DVD drive.
3. Open Windows Explorer and locate folder `\Valueadd\MSFT\Net\NetBEUI` on the installation CD.
4. Drag file `nbf.sys` to `C:\Windows\System32\Drivers` (or wherever Windows XP is installed on your computer).
5. Drag file `netnbf.sys` to `C:\Windows\inf`. Now, you can install the NetBEUI protocol using the usual procedure, which I'll recap here.
6. Click Start, Network Connections (or click Start, and then right-click My Network Places).
7. Open the connection corresponding to your network adapter (usually Local Area Connection). Click Properties.
8. Click Install. Select Protocol, and click Add.
9. Select NetBEUI and click OK.
10. Close all the dialogs by clicking OK.

You won't need to restart Windows XP, but it may take a few minutes for your Windows XP computer to appear in the Network Neighborhood lists of other computers on your network. If it doesn't appear within 20 minutes, restart all of your computers, starting with the XP machine.

MACINTOSH CONNECTIVITY

Like Novell, for many years Apple had gone its own way when it comes to networking protocols. Of these legacy Apple protocols, AppleTalk is predominant, and it was even

20

supported directly by Windows NT and Windows 2000 in order to connect Windows machines to networked Apple printers. Market pressures being what they are, today's Macs are able to use both the older proprietary protocols, as well as the standard Internet Protocol (IP).

You can use any of several approaches to integrate Macs with Windows on your network, as outlined in Table 20.1.

TABLE 20.1 WINDOWS/MACINTOSH INTERNETWORKING TECHNIQUES

Service	Hosted By	Used By	Technique
Print	Mac	Windows	Install AppleTalk protocol on Windows 200x Server; share network-connected Apple printer as a Windows print queue
	Windows	Mac	Install Print Services for Macintosh on Windows 200x Server; share Windows printers to Macs
File	Mac	Windows	Use Samba Server on Mac OS X
	Windows	Mac	Install File Services for Macintosh on Windows 200x Server; share files to Macs via AppleTalk
			Or, Mac OS X can use built-in SMB protocol support to access Windows file shares

NOTE

If you are going to use AppleTalk on a LAN that uses routers, be sure to check with your network administrator to see whether the routers have been properly configured to route the AppleTalk protocol.

APPLETALK PRINTER SUPPORT ON WINDOWS 2000

Windows 2000 Professional comes with direct support for AppleTalk-based printers (and only printers; file sharing isn't supported). For reasons of its own, Microsoft decided to remove direct support for AppleTalk from Windows XP. If you are upgrading to Windows XP from a previous version of Windows that has AppleTalk installed, you'll get the following message during the upgrade:

> The currently installed AppleTalk Protocol is not compatible with Microsoft Windows XP and will be required to be uninstalled for the upgrade to proceed.

You can, however, install the protocol on a Windows 2000 Professional computer, or on Windows 200x Server, in order to provide Windows users access to AppleTalk printers. To provide all of your network's Windows users access to files shared from Macs via AppleTalk, use the following steps in Windows 2000 Pro or Server:

1. Click Start, Settings, Network and Dial-up Connections.

2. On the connection you wish to use with AppleTalk (probably "Local Area Connection," if you haven't changed the default name), right click and select Properties.

3. When the Properties pages appear, select Install. From the next dialog box (Select Network Component Type), choose Protocol and click Add.

4. The next dialog box will list the network protocols that have not yet been installed on your system. Click once on the AppleTalk protocol and then OK.

5. Click Close to exit the protocol installation.

6. In the Printers window, add a new locally connected printer and deselect the check box labeled Automatically Detect My Printer. In the Select the Printer Port dialog, choose Create a New Port, and select AppleTalk Printing Device.

7. Select the printer from the AppleTalk Printing Devices browser.

8. If the printer will be used by Macintosh users as well as Windows users, click No when asked Do You Want to Capture This AppleTalk Printing Device? The printer itself will have to resolve contention for access from multiple Mac users and the Windows machine.

9. Continue to select the make and model of printer, and install print drivers as usual. If you have clients running older versions of Windows, you may wish to install additional print drivers for them. (See Chapter 17 for more information on installing alternate print drivers.)

10. Share the printer.

Other Windows users will now be able to access the printer by connecting to the shared printer on the Windows 2000 computer. Mac users can access the printer directly.

FILE AND PRINT SERVICES FOR MACINTOSH

Two additional components are included with Windows 200x Server that can be used to interoperate between Windows and Mac networks. These are File Services for Macintosh and Print Services for Macintosh. The print services component allows Windows clients to print to PostScript or LaserWriter printers on an AppleTalk network. Additionally, printers connected to Windows 2000 computers can be accessed by Macintosh clients, as the Service delivers native AppleTalk printer sharing.

PRINT SERVICES FOR MACINTOSH

To install Print Services for Macintosh on Windows 200x Server, use the following steps:

1. Use the Add/Remove Programs applet in the Control Panel. Select Add/Remove Windows Components. At the top of this window, a button named Components will appear. Click that button.

2. When the Components dialog box appears select Other Network File and Print Services (see Figure 20.2) and then click the Details button.

20

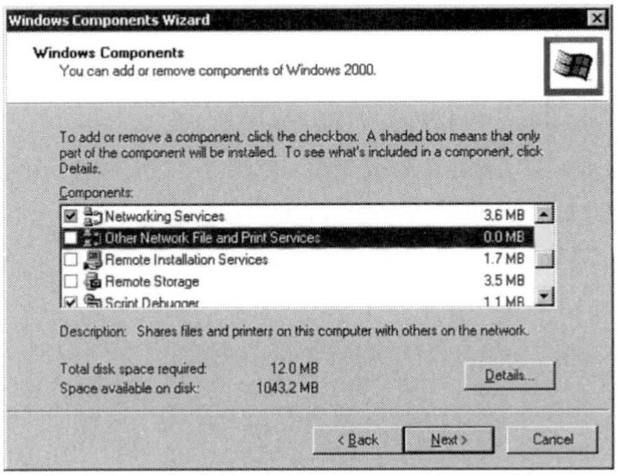

Figure 20.2
Select Other Network
File and Print
Services.

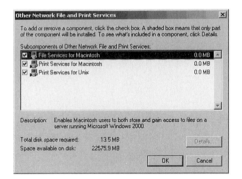

3. A list of services that have not yet been installed will appear. Select the check box labeled Print Services for Macintosh (as shown in Figure 20.3). Then click the OK button, and then the Next button. The component will be installed.

Figure 20.3
Select File Services for
Macintosh from the
dialog box that
appears.

Once you have Windows 2000 with Print Services for Macintosh installed on your network, then you can create a queue for an AppleTalk printer. Use the regular Add Printer Wizard on Windows 200x Server, following these steps:

1. Select Local Printer and deselect the check box labeled Automatically Detect My Printer. See Figure 20.4.

2. When the port dialog box appears, select Create a New Port. Under Type, select AppleTalk Printing Devices. Select the appropriate AppleTalk printer from the AppleTalk Network Browser dialog.

3. When prompted to "capture" the printer, select Yes. This will let the Server queue print jobs from both Windows and Mac users in a first-come, first-serve fashion. Mac users will have to connect to the printer as shared by the Windows 200x server, not directly to the printer.

20

Figure 20.4
Use the Add Printer Wizard to create a local printer.

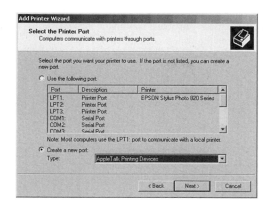

4. Continue to select the make and model of printer, and install print drivers as usual. If you have clients running older versions of Windows, you may wish to install additional print drivers for them. (See Chapter 17 for more information on installing alternate print drivers.)

5. Share the printer.

This will make the printer available to Windows and Mac users alike, thanks to Print Services for Macintosh.

FILE SERVICES FOR MACINTOSH

Microsoft's File Services for Macintosh provides native AppleTalk file sharing services to Macintosh client computers. These files can be offered as a standard share available to both Windows and Mac users, or as a Macintosh Volume, which can only be seen and accessed by Macintosh. To limit the files to which Macintosh clients can gain access, the administrator must explicitly designate each shared folder as Macintosh-accessible. When viewing files, Windows clients see them in the native Windows directory format, while Macintosh clients see them in their typical folder format.

First you should install the File Services for Macintosh on your Windows 200x Server, if you did not already install this feature during your original server installation. To install Print Services for Macintosh on Windows 200x Server, use the following steps:

1. Use the Add/Remove Programs applet in the Control Panel. Select Add/Remove Windows Components. At the top of this window a button named Components will appear. Click that button.

2. When the Components dialog box appears select Other Network File and Print Services.

3. A list of services that have not yet been installed will appear. Select the check box labeled File Services for Macintosh. Then click the OK button, and then the Next button. The component will be installed.

NOTE

> In order for Macintosh users to access files on a Windows 200x server, the Mac user requires an account on the Windows 200x domain.

To install File Services for Macintosh on Windows 200x Server, use the same steps you used to install Print Services for Macintosh, via the Add/Remove Programs Control Panel applet. Select File Services for Macintosh instead of the Print Services.

NOTE

> As an alternative to File Services for Macintosh, the open-source `Netatalk` program lets Sun, Linux, and BSD-based Unix servers provide native AppleTalk file sharing services to Macs, AppleTalk routing, and AppleTalk printer sharing via LPR/LPD. See `netatalk.sourceforge.net` for more information.

USING SMB IN OS X

Apple's newest operating system, OS X, comes with the capability to access Windows networks in a very transparent fashion—support for SMB/CIFS (Server Message Block/Common Internet File System) is included with the operating system. SMB was the original network messaging system used by Microsoft networks. CIFS is similar to SMB, but is an attempt to further extend the SMB protocols. Using SMB/CIFS, OS X can access files shared by Windows computers, Unix computers, and any other operating system that supports Samba. For this to work, all of these computers should be using TCP/IP as the networking protocol. OS X 10.1 even includes GUI support to browse for Windows file shares, and to share volumes to Windows users from the Mac.

CONNECTING TO SMB SHARES FROM THE MACINTOSH

To connect to a Windows file or print share from your Mac, you'll need to install the TCP/IP protocol on the Mac. Once you've done this, click on Go, then Connect to Server.

On OS X 10.0 and 10.1, you'll have to enter the UNC path name to the shared folder. In the Connect to Server dialog, enter the path to the Windows server using the syntax `smb://servername/sharename`. You can enter the host computer's IP address in place of `servername`.

When connecting to a network that uses the Workgroup method, you may have to specify the name of the Windows Workgroup. Use a semicolon to separate the Workgroup name from the server, using the syntax `smb://workgroup;servername/sharename`.

Click the Connect button to finish the process. The shared folder will now appear on your desktop.

On OS X 10.2 (Jaguar) and later, a Network Neighborhood-like browser is available, so that you can select a shared folder without having to know its UNC pathname. Figure 20.5 shows the Connect to Server dialog on OS 10.2. You can still enter a UNC pathname or computer name directly into the Address field, or you can select a workgroup or domain in the left pane and a computer in the right.

Figure 20.5
Select a Windows Computer in the Mac OS X 10.2 Connect to Server dialog.

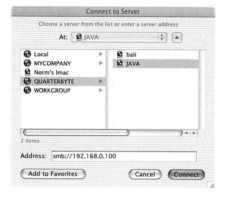

You may be prompted to enter a username, password, and domain name, as shown in Figure 20.6. You can enter anything at all if you are connecting to a Windows XP computer with Simple File Sharing enabled, as authentication information is ignored and all remote users are given Guest access. Otherwise, you'll need to enter a username and password valid on the host computer.

TIP

Check Add to Keychain to save the password so you won't have to re-enter it the next time you connect. Remember, though, that this is a potential security risk: It makes your Windows account accessible by anyone who can get into your Mac account.

Figure 20.6
Enter a Windows username and password in the Authentication dialog.

SMB/CIFS Filesystem Authentication
Enter username and password for JAVA:

Workgroup/Domain
QUARTERBYTE

Username
BKNITTEL

Password
••••••

☐ Add to Keychain

Cancel   OK

When the connection has been established, you'll be prompted to select one of the folders (volumes) shared by the Windows host, as shown in Figure 20.7. If the volume you need to use doesn't appear because your account doesn't have permission to access it, or because OS X is using a previously saved username and password, you can click Re-authenticate to enter a new set of credentials.

20

Figure 20.7
Select one of the volumes shared by the Windows host.

Finally, the Windows volume will appear as a desktop icon. You can disconnect by dragging the icon into the trash.

> **NOTE**
>
> Mac OS X users can also install the Network File System (NFS) protocol to mount remote Unix file systems. NFS can also act as a gateway, to provide older Mac clients access to Unix shares.

SHARING FILES OVER SMB ON THE MACINTOSH

OS X also includes Samba, a SMB/CIFS file sharing service. Samba is an open source software package that is licensed using the GNU General Public License. With Samba, Mac OS X computers can share files with Windows clients as well as any other operating system with SMB client support.

> **NOTE**
>
> The GNU license allows you to use the software and, if you wish, have access to its source code, for free. All software derived from GNU-licensed code must be made available by its authors under the same terms.

> **NOTE**
>
> You can learn more about Samba and the many operating systems it can be used on by visiting the Web site www.samba.org. From that page, select your country and you'll get the latest news about Samba projects and links you can use to download the software as well as sign up for mailing lists to keep up with Samba. You'll also find source code, documentation, and even t-shirts for sale if you want to support the cause!

To share files from Mac OS X computers to Windows clients with Samba, you're best off running OS X 10.2 (Jaguar) or better. Jaguar has seamlessly integrated Samba into the Mac GUI. (If you don't yet have OS X 10.2, you might want to download Samba X, at xamba.sourceforge.net. This is a free Samba server with a GUI configuration tool.)

To enable Windows sharing from Mac OS X 10.2, follow these steps:

1. In System Preferences, open the Sharing window. Check Windows File Sharing, as shown in Figure 20.8.

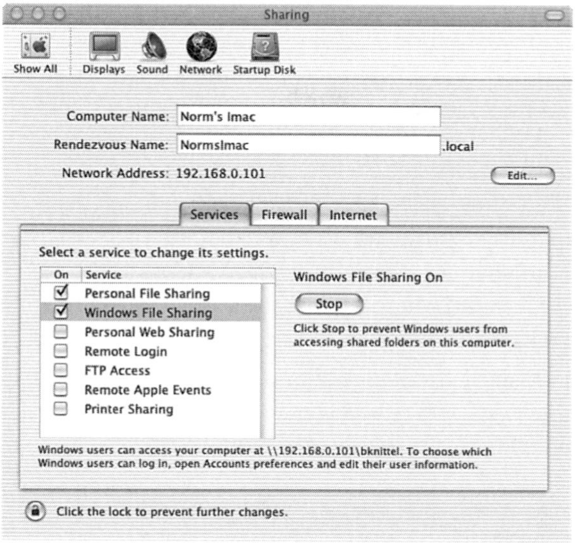

Figure 20.8
Enable Windows File Sharing to turn on the Samba server.

2. Create one or more user accounts for Windows users; each user attaching to the Mac will require a valid username and password. You can use one account that will be shared by all remote users, or you can create a Mac user account corresponding to each Windows user. On each of these accounts, check Allow User to Log On from Windows, as shown in Figure 20.9.

Figure 20.9
Check Allow User to Log On from Windows to permit Windows users to access files shared by the Mac.

3. Share volumes as usual. They will automatically be made available to Windows computers and SMB clients on any other operating system.

To use these shares from Windows computers, you will have to jump through some hoops. The Mac will not advertise itself through the Windows Browser service, so it will not appear in Network Neighborhood. You'll have to use Windows Explorer's Map Network Drive feature to enter a path to the Mac's shared folder, following these steps:

1. Open Explorer and click Tools, Map Network Drive.

2. Select a drive letter to associate with the shared folder.

3. If the Mac computer has a name registered in your network's DNS server (assuming you have one) or in your computer's hosts file, you can enter the UNC path \\ `computername`\`volumename`, where `computername` is the Mac's DNS host name and `volumename` is the name of the volume shared by the Mac.

    If the Mac's name isn't registered, you must enter the path \\`xxx.yyy.zzz.nnn`\ `volumename`, where `xxx.yyy.zzz.nnn` is the Mac's IP address and `volumename` is name of the shared volume. Figure 20.10 shows an example.

Figure 20.10
To use files shared by OS X, enter the UNC path to the Mac's shared volume using the Mac's DNS host-name or IP address.

4. Click OK to establish the connection. You may be prompted to enter a username and password if the Mac doesn't have an account to match your Windows logon or if you haven't set your computer or domain's Security policy to permit Windows to send unencrypted passwords over the network.

When the connection has been established, an Explorer window will pop up showing the files in the shared Mac folder, and the mapped drive letter will appear in the Folders pane with other local and mapped drives.

NOTE

> You should only have to enter your username and password the first time you connect to a given Mac; thenceforth Windows should remember the account information.
>
> If you really require seamless access to Mac shares and don't want to require Windows users to have to enter their username and password when attaching to the Mac even the first time, you'll have to create user accounts on the Mac to match each Windows user's logon name and password.

Also, modern versions of Samba can use the somewhat more secure NTLM authentication system, so it's no longer necessary to instruct Windows to permit unencrypted passwords to be transmitted on the network.

MACINTOSH FILE SHARING PITFALLS

The Windows and Mac file systems are quite different, and some special accommodations have to be made to make them play well together. This section touches on the differences.

FILENAME LENGTH

On old Macs using the original HFS file system, filenames cannot exceed 31 characters, including the extension (for example, .doc). However, Mac filenames can contain any character except the colon (:).

NOTE

A second-generation disk formatting system called HFS+ is available as an add-on for users of Mac OS 8 or higher. HFS+ solves many of HFS's limitations; for example, filenames can have up to 255 characters.

Windows permits filenames up to 256 characters in length but has a longer list of unacceptable characters: the colon (:), backslash (\), forward slash (/), question mark (?), asterisk (*), quotation mark ("), greater-than symbol (>), less-than symbol (<), and pipe symbol (|).

You must be careful when naming files that are to be visible to users in both camps. Stick with shorter names that use characters legal on *both* operating systems.

FILE STRUCTURE

Macintosh files actually consist of two separate parts called *forks*:

- The data fork, which contains data, document text, program code, and so on
- The resource fork, which can contain font and language information

The two parts can be read and written independently on the Macintosh; it's as if each file is composed of two bundled but separate files. Windows isn't aware of this two-part structure, which can lead to conflicts when Windows users and Mac users write to the same file. If a Windows user drags a file from a shared Mac volume to a Windows drive and then replaces the file on the Mac volume, or edits a file on a volume shared by Services for Macintosh, the file's resource fork will be lost.

FILE AND VOLUME SIZE LIMITATIONS

Macintosh computers running the Mac operating system (MacOS) versions prior to 7.6.1 can't see further than 2GB into any disk drive, local or networked. If your Windows network shares files from volumes larger than 2GB, your Macs must run OS 7.6.1 or higher.

20

PRINTING

With Services for Macintosh in place on a Windows 200x Server, Windows and Mac users alike can fully utilize any available PostScript printers. Services for Macintosh can also make non-PostScript printers available to Mac users. However, due to Windows printer driver limitations, Mac users can't print at greater than 300dpi resolution on these printers.

SPECIAL FILES

Windows users should take care not to delete or in any way fool with the hidden `.Trash` subfolder that is created in folders shared with Mac users, nor the hidden files `.DS_Store` and `.CFUsrTextEncoding`. The Mac desktop GUI uses these items.

Likewise, Mac users should leave alone the hidden file `desktop.ini` and `thumbs.db` files that Windows Explorer uses to manage its folder views.

LINUX AND UNIX

Microsoft makes it a fairly easy task to incorporate Unix and Linux computers into your network. Table 20.2 shows the basic strategies you can use.

TABLE 20.2 WINDOWS/UNIX INTERNETWORKING TECHNIQUES

Service	Hosted By	Used By	Technique
Print & File	Unix	Windows	Use Samba on Unix to share files to Windows using native Windows SMB
			Or, install the NFS Client from the Services for Unix (SFU) package on Windows XP to access NFS shares
	Windows	Unix	Use SMB client on Unix
			Or, install NFS Server on Windows 200x Server to share file via NFS

NOTE

> Services for Unix (SFU) provides a host of other Unix compatibility tools in addition to providing file and print services. I'll talk more about SFU later in this section.

USING SAMBA WITH UNIX AND LINUX

The open-source Samba package can provide file and print sharing between Windows and Unix or Linux hosts. Samba is continuously undergoing modifications, and is a great third-party, cost-effective solution (it costs nothing) for integrating multiple file and print sharing on a mixed-network. And, it allows your Windows XP computer to make connections to many other operating systems.

NOTE

> Samba is available for more than just Windows, Mac, and Unix clients. At the Samba Web sites you'll find implementations for other operating systems, such as VMS, OS/2, and—for the truly geeky—the Amiga. Check out www.samba.org for details.

NOTE

> Since the Samba commands for Unix and Linux are identical, for the remainder of this section I'll try to save wear and tear on your patience and my fingers by writing "Unix." I know it's heresy, but please accept this to mean both Linux and Unix.

Using Windows Shares from Unix or Linux

To access file services on a Windows server from a Unix host, you must know exactly what resources are available. Samba includes a command-line program called smbclient for just that purpose. This application enables you to list available Windows shares and printers from within Unix. The command

```
smbclient -L \\lombok
```

for example, lists all the folders and printers shared by the computer named lombok. (You may recognize that this is exactly what the Windows net view command does.)

When you know the name of the desired shared folder, the smbmount command allows you to mount the Windows share on the local file system. The command

```
smbmount //lombok/shareddocs /mnt/winshare -U brian
```

mounts the SharedDocs folder on computer lombok to the local directory /mnt/winshare. The -U switch tells smbclient what username to use when trying to mount the share. You'll be prompted for a password.

NOTE

> If the Windows computer is running Windows XP with Simple File Sharing enabled, you can use any username and password. With Simple File Sharing, all network access is made using Guest credentials regardless of the username and password supplied.

You also can use a Windows printer from a Unix client. The easiest way to configure a Windows printer on a Red Hat Linux system is to use the Red Hat GUI-based print tool while logged on as root. This way, you can set up an SMB-based printer with a minimal amount of hassle. If you are not using Red Hat Linux, you must edit your /etc/printcap file manually. The number of options involved are beyond the scope of this chapter. A thorough read of the SMB How-To, available from http://en.tldp.org/HOWTO/SMB-HOWTO.html, is recommended.

20

Samba Server Tools

Samba also includes tools and servers to make your Unix system look just like a Windows-based network server; this capability lets your Windows computers use files and printers shared by Unix systems. (In fact, Samba developers are trying to figure out how to make Samba function as a Windows Active Directory Domain Controller. If and when they succeed, it should draw an interesting response from Microsoft.)

The parameters for configuring Samba in a server capacity are contained in the file /etc/smb.conf on the Unix host. The default file included with Samba has comments that explain every parameter. Configuring the Samba server is beyond the scope of this book; in fact, it's the sole topic of several whole books. However, I can offer a few pointers:

- Samba is complex. You should read the documentation and FAQs for your Samba version before starting the setup procedure. A good place to start is http://en.tldp.org/HOWTO/SMB-HOWTO.html.

- There are several GUI Samba configuration tools. The Samba Web site www.samba.org lists several. If one is available for your operating system and GUI environment, by all means use it.

- You can configure Samba for share-level passwords (à la Windows 9x sharing) or user-specific passwords with the security option. User security is the usual way to go, although you'll have to set up Unix user accounts for each of your Windows users.

- If you do use user security, you should set encrypt passwords = yes in smb.conf, as Windows will not transmit unencrypted passwords without special configuration. You'll also need to set up a user and password file for Samba's use, which is usually specified as smb passwd file = /etc/smbpasswd. Your Samba documentation will explain how to do this.

- You can mimic Windows's Simple File Sharing by using share-level security without a password. However, in this case you *must* take care to prevent SMB access to your Unix computer over the Internet.

When you have finished editing the smb.conf file, you can test to see that the syntax is correct by using the Samba program testparm. testparm checks smb.conf for internal "correctness" before you actually use it in a production environment. The command

```
/usr/bin/testparm
```

gives a printout like this if all goes well:

```
Load smb config files from /etc/smb.conf
Processing section "[homes]"
Processing section "[printers]"
Processing section "[storage]"
Loaded services file OK.
Press enter to see a dump of your service definitions
```

You can press Enter to see a dump of all the parameters the server uses to configure itself. When the configuration file is complete and correct, you must stop and restart the smbd service to make the changes take effect.

SERVICES FOR UNIX (SFU) 3.0

Microsoft sells an inexpensive ($50 to $99 retail) set of tools that provides most all of the utilities you will need to seamlessly glue together a network that includes Windows, Unix, and Linux computers. While "vanilla" Windows XP comes with several of the TCP/IP tools that Unix gurus expect, SFU provides a much more complete toolkit for those who are used to Unix computers. For example, while Windows XP contains a basic FTP client and a Telnet Server, you'll find enhanced versions of both of these important utilities in SFU 3.0. While some components of SFU are applicable only to Windows 200x Server, most parts can be installed on Windows XP Professional and put to good use, as I'll explain shortly.

N O T E Services for Unix 3.0 does not work on Windows XP Home Edition.

The major components of Services for Unix Version 3.0 include

- **NFS**—This includes an NFS client, an NFS server, a gateway service for NFS, and a server for PCNFS. PCNFS enables Windows clients to access NFS servers on Unix boxes, by mapping the Windows SID to a Unix GID/UID (via user name mapping)

- **NIS**—Server for NIS (Sun's Network Information Service) allows a Windows 2000 Active Directory domain controller to act as a master NIS server. Unix NIS servers and clients can be managed from the Windows environment. A migration tool is also provided so that NIS data stored on Unix systems can be imported into the Windows-based NIS Server.

- **User Name Mapping**—This tool allows for mapping Windows user account names to Unix account names.

- **Password Synchronization**—Similar to User Name Mapping, this utility can be used to keep passwords for user accounts synchronized between Unix and Windows systems.

- **New Telnet Client and Server**—While Windows 2000 comes with a Telnet client and server, SFU 3.0 offers enhanced versions of these standard TCP/IP applications.

- **ActiveState PERL**—You can use this tool to run PERL scripts on Windows systems. (This is available separately, for free, from www.activestate.com.)

- **Interix**—The Windows NT kernel upon which Windows XP is built was designed to provide support for more than one operating system environment. The Interix subsystem overlays NT with more than 1,900 Unix APIs, to provide a nearly complete Unix environment that can run alongside Windows. With Interix, you can run real Unix applications from the familiar Korn and C shells, in an environment that even exposes a single-root file system.

- Utilities including the vi editor, the gcc C/C++ compiler, the GNU SDK, make, rcs, yacc, lex and more than 300 other Unix utilities.

20

NOTE

> You can obtain a time-limited demo version of the SFU package from the following URL to see if it suits your needs:
>
> `http://www.microsoft.com/windows/sfu/productinfo/trial/default.asp`
>
> It's also included with some Microsoft Developer's Network subscription categories.

Table 20.3 lists the components provided with Services for Unix. SFU can be installed on Windows 200x Server, Advanced Server, and Windows XP Professional. However, not all components will be installed on Windows XP, as shown in the table.

TABLE 20.3   SERVICES FOR UNIX SYSTEM COMPATIBILITY

SFU Component	Windows 200x Server	Windows XP
Basic Utilities	Yes	Yes
Unix Perl	Yes	Yes
Interix GNU Utilities	Yes	Yes
Interix GNU SDK	Yes	Yes
Interix SDK	Yes	Yes
ActiveState ActivePerl	Yes	Yes
Client for NFS	Yes	Yes
Server for NFS	Yes	Yes
Server for PCNFS	Yes	Yes
Server for NFS Authentication	Yes	Yes
Gateway for NFS	Yes	No
Server for NIS	Yes*	No
Password Synchronization	Yes	Yes
Telnet Server	Yes	No°
Windows Remote Shell Service	Yes	Yes
User Name Mapping	Yes	Yes

Server for NIS can only be installed on a Windows 2000 Domain Controller with Active Directory, since the NIS information is stored in the directory.

°*The Telnet server that is installed with Windows XP is, according to Microsoft, almost identical to the one supplied with SFU, so it's not offered as an installation option. However, the SFU release notes tell how you can manually replace XP's telnet server with the SFU version if you wish.*

It is beyond the scope of this book to delve into every application that SFU 3.0 offers. Instead, in the following sections we'll look at some of the more important utilities provided by SFU 3.0 for file and print sharing, and describe how to install and configure those components. To start with, you must use the SFU 3.0 CD (or a downloaded setup package) to install at least one of the components. Any installation will by default install the MMC Console Snap-In used to manage the various components you choose, as well as a Help file and the release notes for SFU 3.0.

Installing Services For Unix (SFU) 3.0

SFU is easy to install. Insert the installation CD or run the downloaded installation program, and follow the standard setup wizard. You can use a Standard or Custom installation, depending on whether you want to install all or just some of the tools.

NOTE

The NFS components make use of the Name Mapping Server. If you choose NFS components, then you can enter the name of the Name Mapping Server, if you have previously installed that component of SFU. If not, just click Next and you can enter it at a later time. If this is the first time you are installing SFU components, and you are going to install the name server, then you'll be prompted to enter the name of the server that the SFU components are being installed on. For more information about installing the Name Mapping Service, select the product when you install SFU 3.0 and check out the help files.

Once you've installed the SFU files, you can then begin to manage the different components that are appropriate to your network.

Using MMC to Administer SFU 3.0

Click on Start, All Programs, and then Windows Services for Unix. Click on Services for Unix Administration menu option and an MMC console will pop up that allows you to centrally manage components of SFU that you installed.

In the left pane of the MMC you'll see the various components of SFU (see Figure 20.11). Clicking on a component will bring up options for configuring the component. The options available will be different for each component.

NFS

Using SFU, you can configure clients to use the NFS or PCNFS service. As discussed earlier in this chapter, NFS is an acronym for Sun's Network File System, and it has been implemented on many operating systems due to its usefulness.

When using PCNFS (PC network file system), the UIDs and GIDs that are used by the Unix NFS file system are transparent to the operating systems involved, so long as User Name Mapping Services (another component of SFU) is installed.

20

Figure 20.11
The SFU MMC utility allows you to configure the components that make up SFU.

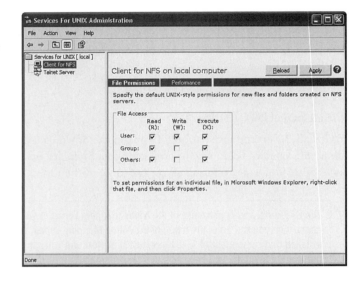

CAUTION

The PCNFS version of NFS is not a very secure version of NFS. While it allows PCs to use NFS file systems, it can present security problems in a network due to the form of encryption used for username and passwords. Do not use PCNFS on servers that contain mission-critical data.

The SFU 3.0 package contains several different components you can use for NFS, which are similar to the Unix connectivity products found in SFN 2.0. These are

- **Client for NFS**—This allows Windows XP (and other Windows clients) to access files on a Unix NFS file system server.

- **Gateway for NFS**—Allows a Windows 200x Server to operate as a gateway, offering Unix-based NFS files to Windows XP (and other Windows clients) as a file share.

- **Server for NFS**—This component will let you offer Windows directories to NFS clients.

NFS allows you to share files with remote systems regardless of the operating system. NFS has been implemented in so many different environments that, like FTP and Telnet, you'll find NFS most everywhere. It will either be part of the operating system or an add-on. Since Macintosh's newest operating system, OS X, also supports NFS using the IP protocol, this gives you another advantage for using NFS. The file sharing doesn't stop at just Unix. For example, many mainframe systems, such as OpenVMS, provide for support for NFS. This can be important in a shop that uses mainframe scale computers along with the servers and workstations used by many businesses.

INSTALLING GATEWAY FOR NFS

To use the gateway services for NFS you need to install it on a Windows 200x Server computer. This is one of the components of SFU that *does not* run on Windows XP or 2000 Professional.

The Gateway for NFS component allows you to use a Windows 200x Server to provide access for Windows clients to NFS file shares on a Unix network. Similar to the Gateway for NetWare service, the Gateway for NFS allows a single server to make the actual connections to the Unix file systems and offer them as file shares to Windows clients.

To install Gateway for NFS on Windows 200x Server after you have installed other SFU 3.0 components, use the following steps:

1. Click Start/Control Panel and then select the Add or Remove Programs icon or menu entry.
2. In the dialog box that appears, select Microsoft Windows Services for Unix.
3. Click the Change button, and then Next.
4. When the list of SFU components appears, expand the listing by clicking on the plus sign next to the NFS component. From the listing that expands, select Gateway for NFS and after that select Entire feature will not be available.
5. You can then click on Gateway for NFS, choose the local hard drive and click Next.

A wizard will prompt you through the remainder of the process. Once you've installed the gateway software, you can configure the file systems you want to offer through the gateway. First, start the service. You can do this from the Services for Unix Administration MMC. Right-click the Gateway for NFS entry and select Start. You can also use this method and click Stop to stop the service.

> **TIP**
>
> You can also use the command `nfsadmin gw <computername> start` to start the service from the Command Prompt, or from within a script file.

You will need to add the NFS servers that your gateway will access for clients. Double-click on My Network Places and then Network Neighborhood. Right-click on NFS Network and finally click on Add/Remove NFS LANs. You should then see a button labeled Add LAN. Click this, enter a name you want to use for this NFS connection, and then enter the IP address for the server that exports the NFS file system. Click OK. Depending on the configuration of your network, you may also have to enter the subnet mask for this IP address. Clients, such as Windows XP, can then map a network drive to the name you have given to this NFS file system.

20

INSTALLING CLIENT FOR NFS

To install the NFS client service on a Windows computer, use the same steps used for the gateway service. However, if you selected Gateway for NFS previously, then only Client for NFS will show up.

TIP

> There are many other command-line options you can use with the NFS client software. Use `nfsadmin /?` to get help text about other functions you can perform.

Before you can use the client you need to select a mapping server to use. In the Services for Unix Administration tool, click on Services for Unix and then the Settings tab. Enter the name of the User Name Mapping server to use for authentication and then click the Apply button. Note that before you can use the mapping service, you must first put your computer name in the `.maphosts` file running on the User Name Mapping server. For more information about the Name Mapping Server, see the documentation on the SFU 3.0 CD.

Once you've installed the client software and got it started, you will find that a new folder called "NFS Network" will be installed in My Network Places. This folder will contain a list of the NFS file systems available from Unix servers that you can access. However, you must first add NFS servers to this file. To add an NFS server

1. Double-click on My Network Places (or Network Neighborhood for older clients) and then double-click on Entire Network. You should see NFS Network. Click on it.

2. Click on Add/Remove NFS LANs, and then Add LAN.

3. Enter the information about the server (such as the IP address) and then click OK. If additional fields are present, then contact the Unix administrator for the information required to connect to the NFS server.

Once you've added one or more servers to your NFS LAN folder, you can map it to a network drive much like any other file share. Using Windows Explorer you simply select Map Network Drive from the Tools menu, enter a drive letter from the drop-down list, and then use the Browse button to locate the NFS server. You can also just enter the path to the share in the format *server:/path*. Finally, click the Finish button.

TIP

> You can also use the `mount` command from the Command Prompt to connect to NFS shares. Use `mount /?` to get the syntax for using this command.

INTERNETWORKING WITH NOVELL NETWARE

NetWare is the oldest PC network operating system still commonly used today. NetWare had the majority of the networking market share until Windows NT/2000 came along. While some think that NetWare will slowly go away, there are those who point to Apple, which was also predicted to vanish under the Microsoft steamroller, but which is still alive and kicking. Novell continues to vigorously develop and enhance NetWare. The widely used NetWare Directory Services (NDS) is now called the eDirectory. Many new features, such as the Internet Printing Protocol-based iPrint service, make NetWare an attractive alternative to Windows for enterprise networking.

Both Novell and Microsoft provide products and protocols that allow their systems to interact. These include Microsoft's Client for NetWare, Novell's various clients for different Windows operating systems, Microsoft's Gateway Services for NetWare, and an additional product from Microsoft named Services for NetWare.

As with Macintosh clients, there are several ways you can provide access to NetWare resources to Windows clients. These are listed in Table 20.4.

TABLE 20.4   WINDOWS/NETWARE INTERNETWORKING TECHNIQUES

Service	Hosted By	Used By	Technique
Print & File	NetWare Server	Windows	Install Microsoft Client for NetWare
			Or install Novell Client
			Or install Gateway Services for NetWare on Windows 200x Server
	Windows Server	Windows with Client for NetWare	Install Services for NetWare on Windows 2000 Server

You can have Windows clients directly access NetWare resources using either the Microsoft-supplied client package or a similar client package developed by Novell. The Microsoft client is reportedly more stable than the Novell client and is preferred in most cases. However, the Novell client provides application programs access to many specific NetWare networking services that the Microsoft client doesn't, and its use is required if you want to use many network applications that were specifically designed for use on Novell networks.

You can also use the Gateway Services for NetWare package on Windows 2000x Server, which acts as a proxy for Novell resources. In other words, the Windows server makes printers and volumes shared by Novell servers appear as if it is sharing them itself. As I discussed at the beginning of the chapter, this means that client computers don't need to be aware of the NetWare environment at all, although this comes with a performance penalty.

Finally, and this is going to seem a bit peculiar, you can install Services for NetWare on Windows 2000 Server, which shares Windows resources as if they were being offered by a NetWare server. The purpose of this is to insinuate Windows servers into a primarily Novell environment, with the goal of eventual replacement, and ultimately world domination (oops, did I say that?). In the initial stages of deployment, the installed Novell client base doesn't need to be reconfigured as the Novell servers are replaced. Services for NetWare also provides bidirectional synchronization between the Windows Active Directory and Novell's NDS. See www.microsoft.com/windows2000/sfn for more information.

20

N O T E

> At the time this book was written, Microsoft is not providing Gateway Services for NetWare or Services for NetWare for Windows Server 2003. This may change if there an outcry from customers, but my hunch is that it won't happen.

INSTALLING NOVELL'S CLIENT FOR WINDOWS 2000 AND XP

If you use software applications that depend on the Novell Application Programming Interface (API), you'll want to use the Novell Client on your Windows XP computers. The actual formal title of this software, at the time this book went to press, is Novell Client v4.83 including SP1 on Windows NT/2000/XP, and it's available in several national languages. You can get this software at the URL download.novell.com. Note that by the time you read this, there may be one or more updates to this client, so be sure to check for newer versions.

INSTALLING AND CONFIGURING THE NOVELL CLIENT

Once you've downloaded Novell's latest client for Windows operating systems, log on as a Computer Administrator and execute the file to unpack its contents and start the installation. This is a self-extracting file that will prompt you for a temporary directory to use to store the expanded files. When you have extracted the files to this location, execute the setup program to start the installation process. The setup program, called SETUPNW.EXE will be found using the following path:

temporary directory/WINNT/i386

where *temporary directory* is the folder you chose to extract the files to. Execute the NETUP-NW.EXE program to install the client software.

On reboot you will be presented with a Novell logo logon dialog, instead of the usual Microsoft logon dialog. Both require you to press Ctrl+Alt+Del to bring up the logon dialog box. You can use the Advanced button of Novell's logon box to specify information other than a username and password, such as the NDS tree and context as well as a server for older bindery servers. Enter the correct name and password that has been established on the server, or in NDS to continue. Your network administrator should be able to provide you with the bindery server, NDS tree context, and the username and password you will need.

20

N O T E

> The Welcome screen won't be displayed because the computer will most likely be a member of a domain, rather than workgroup, network.

N O T E

> In addition to enabling you to log on to the Novell network, you can also select to log on to the local workstation from the logon box. If you have an account on the workstation (such as an administrator's account) then you can logon and make changes to the workstation, but not to the Novell network.

After a NetWare client has been installed, you can access NetWare services in the same ways as Windows servers. The only difference, if you're used to the Novell way of naming resources, is that remote folders and files must be specified using standard Windows UNC format.

- NetWare users are familiar with the *server**volume*:*path**file* format—for example, MUNICH\SYS:PUBLIC\SYSCON.EXE.
- From Windows, the same file would be \\MUNICH\SYS\PUBLIC\SYSCON.EXE.

This format takes a bit of getting used to, and you must make some changes to existing batch files and programs. But beyond this small difference, you can treat NetWare resources just like Windows resources and therefore can do the following:

- Browse the network from My Network Places.
- Specify remote files or directories using standard UNC names.
- Make drive mappings using the Explorer's Tools menu.
- Make drive mappings from the command line by using the command net use.
- Print to Novell print queues by adding network printers with the Add Printer Wizard in the Printers and Faxes folder.

When locating a file, mapping a network drive, or just exploring the network, you can find a NetWare server in My Network Places or any other network browsing dialog. Expand Entire Network, and you'll notice two network branches: Microsoft Windows Network and NetWare or Compatible Network. By expanding the NetWare branch, you can see any available NDS trees or individual NetWare bindery servers.

You can drill down into shared volumes (for example, sys), folders, and files if you wish.

When you attach to a NetWare server, by default, your Windows login name and password are used to make the connection. You can use an alternate login name and password if you use the Map Network Drive Wizard, which is available from the Explorer's Tools menu. Having different account names and passwords on your Windows and Novell servers can be a bit confusing, however, so your network manager will probably try to make them match. You might need to manually update your passwords to keep them identical on the two server types, which I'll discuss in the next section.

INSTALLING AND CONFIGURING THE MICROSOFT CLIENT

If you don't need the Novell-specific client, you're probably best off using the Microsoft client, which is provided with Windows XP. Installing it is a simple matter:

1. From the Control Panel in classic view, select the Network Connections icon. From the new category view, select Network and Internet Connections, and then select Network Connections under the section titled "or pick a Control Panel icon."
2. Right-click on the network connection you want to use. Select Properties.

20

3. On the General tab of the properties pages that appear, click the Install button.

4. From the dialog box that appears, select Client. From the client selection list, select Client Service for NetWare and then OK.

When prompted, you can select to reboot the computer to finish the installation of the client.

INSTALLING GATEWAY SERVICES FOR NETWARE

To allow Windows XP clients (or other Windows clients) to access resources on a NetWare network without configuring them to use a NetWare client or NetWare protocols, you can install Gateway Services for NetWare (GSNW). GSNW allows a Windows 2000 server to act as a proxy to the NetWare servers, and Windows clients access NetWare resources through this server as though they were network shares on the Windows 2000 Server.

CAUTION

> If you have any version of the Novell Client for Windows operating systems running on the Windows 2000 Server computer, this client software should be removed before you attempt to install GSNW. Also, as with all services and protocols, you must be a member of the Administrators group to perform this function.

GSNW uses a *single* user account and group on a NetWare server to gain access to NetWare resources. For NetWare 5 and earlier versions, use the NWAdmin NDS utility or the SYSCON utility to create the user account and group. The group should be named NTGATEWAY, and the user account you create for the gateway must be made a member of this group. The NetWare account must be given the necessary trustee rights (permissions) to access the resources that the gateway will allow Windows clients to use.

GSNW requires the use of the NWLink protocol, and you can install the protocol before you begin the process of installing GSNW. You'll be prompted to install the protocol when you install and configure GSNW. In order to install GSNW you must have the administrative rights to create a share on the Windows 2000 Server computer. To install the service, use the following steps:

1. Click Start, Settings, and then Network and Dial-up Connections.

2. Right-click on the local area (LAN) connection icon for your network and select Properties. Select the General tab and then the Install button.

3. The dialog box Select Network Component Type will appear. Click on the Client entry, and then the Add button.

4. The dialog box Select Network Client will appear. Select Gateway (and Client) Services for NetWare and then the OK Button.

5. The Select NetWare Logon dialog box will appear. If you are establishing a gateway to a bindery-based NetWare server, enter the name in this dialog box. Otherwise, if you are creating a gateway that will use NetWare Directory Services (or the eDirectory),

then click on the Default Tree and Context button, and then enter the NDS tree and context names.

6. If you wish to run a login script when the Windows server connects, then select the Run Login Script check box.

7. Click the OK button. In order for this service to run, you will have to reboot the Windows server.

After the server has rebooted, you can do a quick check by issuing the following command:

```
net view /network:nw
```

This command should show the servers on the NetWare network that your gateway will have access to.

When deciding whether you should run a logon script and what kinds of trustee rights to grant to the account you create, be sure to only allow access to the data on the NetWare servers that your clients need in order to accomplish their jobs. There will be no distinction made between Windows users—all users coming through the gateway will use the single gateway user account. You can exercise limited control over the permissions granted to individual users by applying share permissions on the Windows server, as we'll discuss shortly.

CONFIGURING GATEWAY SERVICES FOR NETWARE

After you have installed GSNW, an icon for the service will appear in the Control Panel. You can use this icon to make changes to the configuration and manage additional capabilities of the software. In Figure 20.12 you can see the Gateway Service for NetWare dialog box.

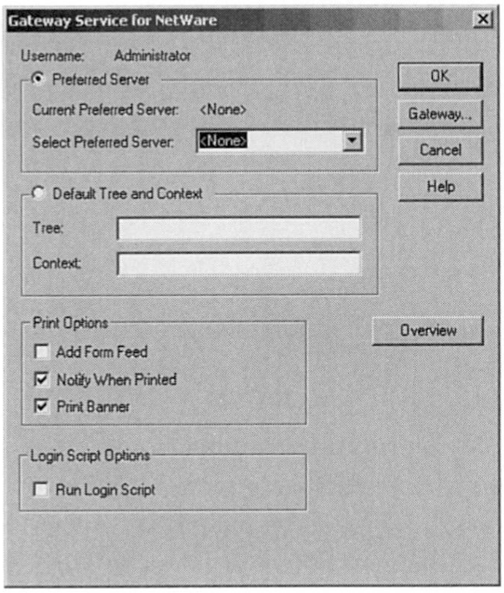

Figure 20.12
Manage GSNW using the Control Panel icon.

As you can see in this figure, you can configure or change the preferred server or NDS tree and context. You can also select a few print options and change whether or not to run a NetWare login script for the NetWare account that the gateway uses.

Before Windows users can begin to use the Gateway, it must be enabled. Use the Gateway button on the Control Panel GSNW icon to bring up the Configure Gateway dialog box, which is shown in Figure 20.13.

Figure 20.13
You can enable the Gateway for Windows users through this dialog box.

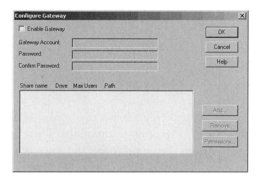

In this dialog box you must enter the NetWare user account name and the same password that was created for the NetWare user account. If the user account or password are changed on the NetWare side, then you'll have to use this dialog box to keep the user accounts and passwords in sync, or else the Gateway will not have access to the NetWare resources provided by the account.

CREATING WINDOWS FILE SHARES FOR NETWARE RESOURCES

Once you've entered this information, you can create file or printer shares that Windows clients use to connect to NetWare resources. In the Configure Gateway dialog box, click on the Add Button. In the New Share dialog box that appears, you can enter

- The network path for the data to be shared.
- A drive letter to use for the share.
- A name for the share.
- A numeric value to limit the number of simultaneous users of the share.

You are not limited to creating a single share. If NetWare servers are a large part of your network, then you will probably end up creating a number of shares, each pointing to different resources in the NetWare environment. Just use the Add button and create each share. When you return to the Configure Gateway dialog box you will see a listing of the shares created. You can also select a share and then click on the Permissions button to establish permissions (on the Windows side of the network) for the share. Note that these permissions can further limit, but not expand, the permissions (trustee rights) set on the

NetWare side. Thus, you have two points in the network that can be used to control access by Windows clients to resources on NetWare servers.

NOTE

> In addition to creating multiple shares for a single gateway, you can also create additional gateways, either on a single Windows 2000 server, or on separate servers. While you can set separate permissions on each network share you create, by creating additional gateways you can make connections to different servers, or different contexts in the NDS tree, so that shares can be more easily created in situations where the trustee rights (permissions) on the NetWare side of the network are different. To create an additional gateway, use the same process described in this section, but use a different user account name. Do not use the same user account name to create a new gateway, even if it is on another Windows 2000 Server.

Services for NetWare 5.0 (SFN)

Services for Netware (SFN) is an add-on product that shares Windows resources as if they were being offered by a NetWare server. It sells for around $150 retail, and you do not have to purchase SFN for each server; one copy can be used throughout the enterprise. SFN is a very inexpensive way to expand NetWare and Windows network connectivity. All of the components of the previous version of this product (SFN 4.0) are contained in the newer version.

SFN 5.0 consists of many useful components, some of which are discussed in detail in this chapter:

- **Microsoft Directory Synchronization Services (MSDSS)**—This tool allows you to synchronize the Active Directory with NDS, as well as migrate NDS information into the Active Directory should you choose to decommission NetWare NDS servers.

- **Microsoft File Migration Utility**—This utility can be used in situations where you want to move files from NetWare servers to Windows 2000 Servers. This tool can be used to migrate just a few files or directories, or all of the files currently supported on your NetWare network.

- **File and Print Services for NetWare 5**—This tool works in the opposite manner as Microsoft's gateway and client software for NetWare described earlier in this chapter. You can use FPSN to allow existing computers that use NetWare clients to access Windows file and print services as if they were being provided by NetWare servers.

- **File and Print Services for NetWare 4**—This tool was included in the previous version of SFN. It works in a similar manner as its version 5 counterpart, but allows NetWare 3.x clients to access services on a Windows NT 4.0 Server computer.

- **Directory Service Manager for NetWare**—This tool was included in the previous version of SFN. It allows Windows NT 4.0 domain controllers to interact with NetWare 2.x and 3.x bindery servers.

20

In the following section, we'll discuss the components of SFN that can be used with Windows XP.

First off, you'll need a copy of the Novell Client. See the section titled "Installing and Configuring the Novell Client" earlier in this chapter for the details. Install the Novell Client on the Windows 2000 Server that you'll use to run SFN.

Once the Novell client is installed, you can install MSDSS using the following steps:

1. Place the SFN 5.0 CD into your server's CD-ROM drive. View the CD in Windows Explorer.

2. Two folders will be displayed: FPNW and MSDSS. Open the MSDSS folder.

3. Double-click on the MSDSS icon found inside the MSDSS folder. The Windows Installer program will copy the appropriate files to your system and you will be prompted to reboot your computer.

Once you've rebooted the server you can then configure MSDSS.

CONFIGURING MSDSS SYNCHRONIZATION SESSIONS

MSDSS Synchronization copies user and group information back and forth between NetWare NDS (eDirectory) and Active Directory so that changes made in one directory system will be reflected in the other. To create a synchronization session, use the following steps:

1. Start the MSDSS utility: Click Start, Programs, Administrative Tools, Directory Synchronization. MSDSS will pop up as a Snap-in to the Microsoft Management Console (MMC).

2. In the left pane of the MMC you can right-click on MSDSS and select New Session. Or, you can select the MSDSS entry and from the Action Menu, click on All Tasks, and then New Session. Figure 20.14 shows this selection method.

Figure 20.14
MSDSS operates as a Microsoft Management Console Snap-In.

20

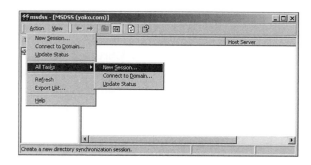

3. A New Session Wizard will appear and prompt you through the remainder of the process. In Figure 20.15 you can see that you first must select to perform a one-way or two-way synchronization, and also whether the Novell side of the synchronization uses NDS or Bindery security.

Figure 20.15
The New Session Wizard will prompt you for the type of synchronization to perform.

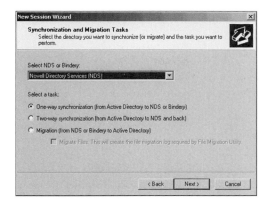

4. In Figure 20.16 you can see that the wizard next prompts you for the Active Directory container object that will be synchronized with NDS for this session. If you are not sure of the container object's name, use the Browse button to locate the container.

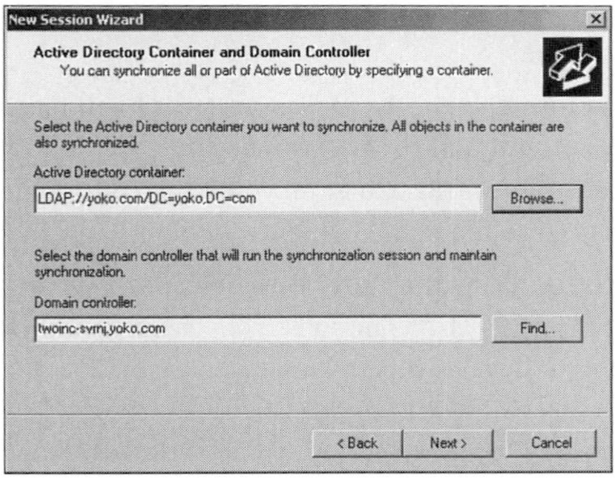

Figure 20.16
Select the Active Directory container object that will be used for this synchronization session.

5. The next screen of the wizard will enable you to enter the NDS container object that will be the other half of this synchronization session. You can enter the target in the field provided, or use the Browse button to locate the NDS container or the Bindery you wish to use for this session. You will be prompted to enter a NetWare username/password that has access to the target in order for the synchronization to work.

20

In order to make the synchronization a simple process, the wizard will then prompt you for a few more items. For example, it's not likely that both NDS and the Active Directory will contain the same object or container names. So, the wizard will prompt you to perform a reverse synchronization. This means that objects found in the NDS or bindery on the NetWare side of this process will be copied back to the Active Directory. This is useful if you are performing only a one-way synchronization. The Active Directory will then contain all of the objects currently in the directory, as well as those imported from NetWare. When the one-way synchronization process is run, objects that do not exist in the NetWare side of the process will be created.

There is still one problem that needs to be addressed for a one-way synchronization: Passwords. Windows, NDS, and the Bindery all use different methods to encrypt passwords for user accounts, and it's not possible to unencrypt them from one format so that they can be encrypted into another. Thus, while accounts can be copied from one system to another, passwords can't.

When performing a one-way synchronization, you can choose from several methods for populating the password field in the Active Directory for objects that will be imported during the reverse-synchronization:

- **Set passwords to blank**—For user objects, there will be no password required when a user logs in the first time. This may present a security problem. Once logged in, users can always set a password value, however.

- **Set passwords to the user name**—This is a little better than the first choice, but still not a very secure method. Again, users should be instructed to change their password after logging in the first time.

- **Set passwords to a random value**—A random password will be generated, as well as a file that shows the user account and the password generated. The file will be located in the directory %systemroot%\System32\Directory Synchronization\Session Logs. Look in the Event Viewer to get the file name, which should end in .pwd.

- **Set all passwords to the same value that you specify**—You can use the same password for all accounts. Since this also is not a terribly secure method, be sure to instruct users to log on and change the password as soon as possible.

Of the previous, setting the password to a random value is probably the best choice. The help desk (or its equivalent) can then use the file that is generated and contact each user using a secure method and let them know their new password.

The wizard will also present a screen that allows you to create static mappings between objects that exist in both directories, but which do not necessarily fall under the same container objects in both directories. By creating a list of static mappings, the session can locate the appropriate objects for propagating changes made to the directory. The last Wizard screen will let you give a name to the session. Click the Finish button to exit the wizard.

If you want to create a two-way synchronization, then simply make that selection in the dialog box shown in Figure 20.12. The following dialog boxes will be similar, but you'll have to provide the authentication information to allow access to the NetWare side of the connection.

If you are going to migrate NDS data to the Active Directory and then decommission the NDS servers, you can do this by selecting the Migration radio button (from NDS or Bindery to Active Directory). In addition, if you want to migrate files from NetWare servers to Windows 2000 servers, you should use the Migrate Files check box. This will create a file that can be used by the File Migration Utility to move the files from NetWare servers to Windows 2000 Servers. This file can be found in the directory `%systemroot%\Directory Synchronization\Session Logs`. The log file name will match the server name you used for creating the file.

The File Migration Utility that comes with SFN 5.0 can be used for migrating files to Windows, if you have decided to quit using NetWare servers in your network. By using the synchronization utility, you can continue to operate a heterogeneous network and manage NetWare and Windows clients in a very efficient manner. Thus, this tool can serve two purposes.

FILE AND PRINT SERVICES FOR NETWARE (FPNW)

Installing and configuring FPNW is a simple matter. Right-click on the icon for the local area connection you wish to use to bring up the properties pages for the connection. Click the Install button and then from the window that appears, select Service and then Add. When the Select Network Service dialog box appears, click on the Have Disk button. Insert the Services for NetWare CD into your CD-ROM drive and fill in the path using the drive letter of the CD-ROM, followed by \FPNW. Click OK and wait for files to be copied to your computer's disk drive.

The Install File and Print Services for NetWare dialog box will pop up and enable you to enter NetWare-specific information about the volume to create for NetWare users. For example, you will have to specify the disk drive and directory that will contain the SYSVOL directory, which is the name given to what would be the SYS: volume on a NetWare server. Choose this disk carefully. If using a FAT partition, then only share level security will be enforced. If using an NTFS disk volume, then you can enforce rights by the username/ password method. Since you can also use NTFS permissions on an NTFS volume, you can fine tune which files and directories are available to each user.

While FPNW can be installed on any Windows 2000 Server, there is a caveat: A special account called the FPNW Service Account is created, and requires a password. If you are going to use FPNW on domain controllers, this password should be the same on each controller.

When you have finished entering this information, reboot the server and the service will start.

After the reboot examine the SYSVOL directory and you will see several directories. They are

- **\LOGIN**—This directory holds the utilities that NetWare clients use to log in to the NT Server.
- **\MAIL**—User subdirectories are created here and may contain login scripts for users.

20

- **\PUBLIC**—Contains the following utilities: attach, capture, endcap, login, logout, map, setpass, and slist.
- **\SYSTEM**—Contains files used to support printing.

After the reboot, you will also see an FPNW icon in the Control Panel that you use to manage the service. Here you can set up print queues and view statistical information (such as the number of files open). There are three buttons:

- **Users**—Produces a display of the names, network address and login time for users. There are also buttons that can be used to send a message to users, or to disconnect one or more users.
- **Volumes**—The volumes you have set up to share with FPNW clients will be displayed using this button. Similar to the Users button, you will see information about users connected to each volume, the connection time and open files. And, there is a also a button that can be used to disconnect users.
- **Files**—Use this button if you want to see information about open files. You can see which user opened the file, information about file locking, and the path to the file. This button displays information about each open file, the user who opened it, locking information, and the path to the file. There is also a button that enables you to close one or all files.

Since FPNW management is done via the Control Panel icon, you can always create additional volumes when needed, in addition to managing existing volumes.

IBM HOST CONNECTIVITY

In the past, in order to allow connections to IBM AS/400 and mainframe hosts, you had to buy third-party software or Microsoft's SNA Server product. Microsoft has replaced SNA Server with a new product called Host Integration Server. You cannot install this product on Windows XP, but you can install it on a Windows 200x Server, where it can serve a large number of Windows XP clients. Both 3270 and 5250 IBM terminal client support is provided in this server product. Some of the main features include

- **Single Sign-On**—Just what you'd expect from a Windows-based network.
- **Password Synchronization**—Similar to the SFN 3.0 product, you can keep passwords on Windows 2000 Active Directory user accounts in sync with the user ID and password on IBM systems.
- **Virtual Private Network (VPN)**—You can use the VPN technology that is part of Windows 200x Server.

Host Integration Server can be broken down into several categories: Application Integration Services, Data Integration Services, Network Integration Services, and Administrative Services.

NOTE

Unlike Services for Macintosh, Host Integration Server isn't free, but you can download a free 120-day trial version for evaluation purposes.

APPLICATION INTEGRATION SERVICES

The COM Transaction Integrator for CICS and IMS (COMTI) is a service that provides a bridge between automation components and applications that reside on a mainframe computer, such as COBOL programs or Web-based applications. As far as a developer is concerned, these components are just automation servers that can be added to an application on a Windows computer. COMTI acts as an interface between these components and applications running on MVS. The value you gain from this is the massive computing power of the mainframe, along with its storage, and the ability to use the data generated on the mainframe in an application, such as a Web server on a Windows system.

The MSMQ-MQSeries Bridge is used to provide a connectionless store and forward bridge between Microsoft's Message Queue Server (MSMQ) and IBM's MQSeries.

In addition to these application services, you'll also find a Software Development Kit that can be used to create applications that make use of these services.

DATA INTEGRATION SERVICES

ODBC is Microsoft's Open Database Connectivity interface that allows application developers to interact with multiple database platforms. Data Integration Services provides an OLE DB Provider for access to AS/400 and VSAM (Virtual Storage Access Method) files, as well as a provider for DB2 databases. The OLE DB Provider for DB2 is implemented using IBM's Distributed Relational Database Architecture (DRDA), and can access all systems that are DRDA-compliant. This includes MVS, VSE, VM, OS/400, AIX RS/6000, Sun Solaris, HP-UX, Digital/Compaq (now HP) Unix, Windows NT, and OS/2. It is obvious that using this tool, application programmers can easily integrate data from many different sources by using a single interface.

THE SHARED FOLDERS GATEWAY

The Shared Folders Gateway Service allows users on computers that do not have the client software installed to access files on an AS/400 host computer. There are many other services and capabilities of Host Integration Server, which are beyond the scope of this chapter. Nevertheless, Host Integration Server provides a very comprehensive solution that will allow you to integrate IBM platforms into your network so that from the desktop to the mainframe, you can design and plan a solution for your site.

20

NAMING ON A MIXED NETWORK: DNS VERSUS HOST FILES

If you have a small LAN with mixed and matched computers, you're probably like me and have a chart of computer names and IP addresses posted on your wall—and not just computers, but routers, firewalls, monitored devices, and all manner of devices. Who knows? Soon the espresso machine might be wired in, too.

On a corporate or enterprise LAN, the LAN administrators will probably enter each device into the organization's Domain Name Service system, under your own default domain, so that you can type a command such as ping firewall instead of having to type ping firewall.mycompany.com or, worse, something like ping 192.168.56.102.

On a home or small office workgroup LAN, you probably don't have your own domain name server. Or, your network manager hasn't entered names for the devices you use most frequently (for example, ping espresso). On a heterogeneous network, your Macintosh and test-bed Linux machines probably aren't in any domain name list anywhere.

The hosts file can be the answer to this annoying situation. You can add entries to the file \windows\system32\drivers\etc\hosts to associate names with IP addresses. The Windows domain-name lookup system looks first in this "hosts" file before consulting the network, so you can add entries for your own workgroup's computers and devices, regardless of operating system.

The format is simple. Edit the file in Notepad. Add lines to the file, listing IP addresses at the left margin, followed by some whitespace (tabs or spaces), followed by one or more names. You can enter simple names or full domain names. Simple names are assumed to belong to your default domain.

My hosts file looks like this:

```
127.0.0.0 localhost lh
192.168.1.1 firewall fw
192.168.1.45 macone
```

The first entry is the default entry shipped with Windows. localhost stands for "my own computer" and is used for internal testing of the network software. I've added a second name, lh, because I'm lazy and would rather type ping lh than ping localhost.

I added the second entry myself to give a name to my network's firewall. I can now configure the firewall by typing **telnet firewall** or, on a lazier day, **telnet fw** rather than having to look up at that sheet on the wall and type a bunch of numbers.

Finally, there's an entry for my Macintosh computer, macone. This way, I can view its Web server's home page from Internet Explorer using http://macone rather than having to remember its IP address.

This file also serves as a sort of documentation of my network, as it records important IP addresses.

While the hosts file is very handy, there are two things that you have to watch out for:

1. You can't use the hosts file to record computers whose IP addresses are assigned automatically by a DHCP server. It's only for computers whose IP address is set manually.

2. You shouldn't use the hosts file to record the IP address of a computer you don't manage yourself. If its manager changes the computer's IP address without telling you, you won't be able to connect to this computer. Worst of all, you probably won't remember that you even *made* the hosts entry, so you'll spend a lot of time wondering what's wrong.

Therefore it's best to use the hosts file only for local computers that are manually configured, and stored in nobody's DNS system.

NOTE

Without a hosts file and a DNS server, you can still use computer names for *Windows* computers. For example, you can type **net use j: \\sumatra\share**, if one of your computers is named Sumatra. Here's why: If Windows can't resolve a computer name using the hosts file or the DNS system, it falls back on the Windows NetBIOS naming scheme.

This only works for Windows and Samba-equipped computers, however, so the hosts file is a real advantage on a mixed-vendor network. On a small network, I think it's worth using manual IP address assignments just so I can use a hosts file.

20

TROUBLESHOOTING YOUR NETWORK

Troubleshooting 101

When problems occur on a network, perhaps the hardest thing to do is decide where you should begin your troubleshooting efforts. In this chapter, we'll cover the basic logic behind network troubleshooting, and the software utilities to diagnose problems on a network. Some of these utilities are standard parts of the TCP/IP suite of protocols and applications, while others are specific to Windows-based operating systems.

The Importance of Preparation

Problems are eventually going to occur on any computer network. You'll be in a much better position to diagnose and repair these inevitable problems if you take some time to prepare *before* trouble occurs. Here are some of the ways you can prepare:

- Collect information about your network's organization so that you have a good "map" to work with.

- Keep up-to-date records of each computer's configuration settings, as well as any additional devices such as routers or switches.

- Perform basic diagnostic tests and record the results while the network is working so that you can detect differences when it is not.

- Maintain a file or bookshelf with all of the documentation for every piece of network hardware and software, including network adapters, routers, switches, storage devices, and so on.

- Keep a list of hardware and software manufacturer's Web sites, support resources, FAQ lists, and so on.

- Keep a log of all problems you encounter and their solutions, so you and others don't end up having to solve the same problem twice.

Knowing how your network is supposed to look and act when it's working is extremely valuable, and having adequate documentation is essential. Let's go over some of these points in more detail.

Document Your Network

To start with, it's important to have an up-to-date map of your network to solve problems, listing each component and its basic information: computer name, IP address, operating system, and so on. It's too easy to install a new workstation, server, or router, and forget to add it to a diagram of the network. But, if you have several users reporting that they can no longer reach a server, a map can quickly tell you if each of these users are connected to the same switch, or if their network segment is connected to the same router. A well-documented network is much easier to troubleshoot.

In addition to a diagram showing how your network devices are connected, it is also a good idea to store, in a database or perhaps a spreadsheet, settings for each computer, as well as important equipment such as routers and servers. If you have to replace equipment, it's

21

faster to configure it when you have the information written down and don't have to guess. It's easier than you might think. For example, to record Windows settings, you can take screen shots of the network dialog boxes using Alt+PrtScrn and paste the pictures into a Word or Wordpad document.

Another tool you should have close at hand is documentation for every bit of software and hardware device. While this may seem obvious, it does deserve a mention. If you have a large network, you probably don't use the same routers throughout the entire network. Are all the routers of the same type? Do they use the same version of the operating system? Are you an expert at the commands needed to configure every device?

PERFORM DIAGNOSTIC TESTS

Windows comes with several tools that can help you diagnose network problems, including ping, pathping, and tracert. However, unless you know what these programs report when your network is functioning correctly, it can be difficult to tell whether or not their results are indicating a problem.

As an example, I sometimes experience problems with my office's DSL line--it seems slow, or I can reach some Internet sites but not others. The first time this happened, I used the ping program to see if data was getting in and out of my office reliably, and it was. Ping reported that 100% of the test data I sent to the next-closest router at my ISP's office was returned, with a 120 millisecond (msec) round trip time. That would have sounded good, except that I'd done the ping test when there were no problems, and written the results down: the round-trip time should have been about 50 msec. Resetting the DSL modem by powering it off and back on fixed the problem--when it came back up, the round trip times were back in the 50 msec range, and the connection difficulties went away. Now, sometimes there really are problems out on the Internet that cause spotty Internet connections, but about once a month, the ping test tells me that it's my DSL modem.

NOTE

> It also never hurts to have baseline information about the usual network traffic on all segments of your network. You can use the Network Monitor tool that's part of Windows 200x Server to save historical records of this type of information. If your network seems slow, you can compare current statistics to past patterns; you may find that the problem is simply congestion, and that you need to beef up your network.

KEEP LOGS

I strongly suggest that you keep a log book in which you record all of the problems that do occur on your network, as well as how the situation was resolved. This type of documentation can find the solution to the current problem, as well as determine if there is some part of your network that needs rethinking if the same problem keeps cropping up. It's *really* hard to remember just what you did when that laptop wouldn't connect to the network last year--wasn't it something in the registry that you had to change? Or...?

21

STARTING THE ATTACK ON A NEW PROBLEM

When a new problem crops up, it helps to attack it in systematic way. The following steps should get you off in the right direction:

- When a new problem is reported, make an entry in your trouble log right away. For a home or small office, this could be a simple spiral-bound notebook kept by the computer; in a large corporation, it could be a database application shared by the entire company. In any case, it's good to get in the habit of starting the documentation process from the outset of the problem.

- When trying to solve a network problem, first find out what the specific symptoms are. Most users describe problems in terms of what they can't do or what isn't happening. But, "I can't get to the file server" doesn't give you much to work with. It helps to know what *is* happening. If you ask, "What happens when you *try* to get to the server?" and the answer is "Nothing, the screen is completely black and all the lights are out in my building," you're going to take a different tack than if they said, "It says my password has expired."

- The first thing to determine is where the problem lies; in fact, you should ask, "Is there really a problem at all?" Sometimes users are inadequately trained in the applications they use. Is the user perhaps trying to locate files (or other services) on the wrong server?

- If there *is* a problem, obtain accurate descriptions of the actual symptoms, of what *is* happening. Good questions to ask are along the lines of Can the user access some servers, but not others? Can other users on the same segment make connections while another user cannot? If the latter, then maybe the user has a computer that is misconfigured. If *nobody* can access a network resource, the problem is likely at the point the resource is shared, in an individual server or workstation. If *one* person can access the resource, you know the problem lies somewhere between the server and the user who can't.

- If something that worked before suddenly stops working, it could be that some piece of hardware has failed, but it's just as likely that that something was changed. Have security settings or user account changes been made in a server? Have there recently been changes made in the wiring closet that patches together network segments? Have router settings been changed recently? Has the particular user recently updated to a newer network adapter that is not properly configured? Is this a new user who may have incorrect settings for the network or applications?

DIAGNOSTIC TOOLS AND UTILITIES

There are several sorts of problems that you can encounter in a network:

- Pilot error: entering incorrect paths, filenames, or passwords.
- "Soft" problems that occur even with perfectly functioning network connectivity; these are problems such as inadequate security privileges on accounts to access network resources.
- "Hard" problems, the failure of network connectivity itself. These can be due to software configuration errors, or hardware failure.

Networks are built in layers, from the nitty-gritty of wiring and hardware up to the more abstract concepts of user permissions, and each layer depends on the ones below it. As I mentioned in the previous section, you can often determine where a problem is located by looking at the symptoms. If a network server won't give access because it says that the user's password is invalid or expired, it's clear that basic connectivity is working: The bad password is getting to the server, and the complaint is getting back. In a case like this, you can start your investigation at a higher "level." But, when you suspect that connectivity isn't working, or if you don't know where to start, you have to start at the bottom.

There are two basic kinds of tools to diagnose basic problems on a network using Windows XP. First, the TCP/IP protocol suite contains a number of command-line tools that test everything from basic network connectivity to checking whether name services are working correctly. Second, you can use GUI applications such as the Network Connections window and the Event Viewer to look for configuration problems that are causing problems on your network.

We'll start by looking at the TCP/IP utilities, which you can use to test basic network connectivity.

USING TCP/IP UTILITIES

Windows comes with a set of command-line utilities that were developed for use with the TCP/IP network protocol on which most Windows XP networks rely.

→ To learn more about the TCP/IO Protocol, **see** "TCP/IP in a Nutshell," **p. 604**.

PING

Ping is perhaps the simplest program you can use to begin diagnosing a network problem. The ping utility sends a small data packet (technically, an ICMP "ECHO REQUEST" packet) to a remote host and waits to see if a reply comes back (that is, if the remote host sends back an ICMP "ECHO REPLY" packet). This tests the most basic part of the network's infrastructure, much as a doctor's knee tap tests your reflexes.

21

If you use this utility on your LAN and find that you do not get a response from the computer you are trying to exchange data with, then there definitely is a problem. The `ping` utility won't tell you what the problem is, but it will tell you that something is wrong--your or the other computer may have an improper network configuration, a broken cable, a faulty adapter, or even a problem with a router in between. The basic information that `ping` gives you is that the packet isn't getting to the destination or the reply isn't returning to your computer. So, a communications breakdown has occurred in one or both directions between your computer and the remote computer.

Ping can tell you several other things about the path between your computer and the destination computer. First, the round-trip time between the two computers. Second, by using a "sequence number" field in the ICMP packet, `ping` can determine if some packets are being responded to with an ECHO REPLY packet, while others are being dropped. Dropped packets can indicate network traffic congestion somewhere along the path.

The simplest method for using `ping` is to use the command with the hostname of the computer you want to reach:

`ping <computername>`

This command uses default values for the size and number of packets to send (32 bytes, and four packets, respectively), and displays any replies that come back.

The following is an example of using the `ping` utility from a Command Prompt window:

```
C:\> ping mail.twoinc.com
Pinging mail.twoinc.com [24.120.30.6] with 32 bytes of data:

Reply from 24.120.30.6: bytes=32 time=292ms TTL=114
Reply from 24.120.30.6: bytes=32 time=273ms TTL=114
Reply from 24.120.30.6: bytes=32 time=272ms TTL=114
Reply from 24.120.30.6: bytes=32 time=261ms TTL=114
Ping statistics for 24.120.30.6:
    Packets: Sent = 4, Received = 4, Lost = 0 (0% loss),
Approximate round trip times in milli-seconds:

    Minimum = 261ms, Maximum = 292ms, Average = 274ms
```

In this example, the `ping` utility sent four echo requests to the computer named `mail.twoinc.com`, whose IP address was found in the DNS system as `24.120.30.6`. The list following the `ping` command shows the IP addresses of the computer system that sent back ICMP ECHO REPLY packets. And, looking at the time involved (less than 300 milliseconds, a small amount of time on the Internet) and looking at the TTL value, you can see that this was an easy target to locate and send data to and receive data from. The fact that four packets were sent and none were dropped also indicates that a good network path exists between the sending computer and the target computer.

NOTE

When you are using `ping` or `tracert` on the Internet, you may find that you do not get a response back even though the computer you are trying to `ping` does exist and is communicating properly. For security reasons, some network firewalls block ping echo requests received from the "outside world." For example, don't even bother trying `ping` www.microsoft.com. It doesn't work.

So, you can't count on using public servers as test targets to see if your Internet connection is working. You'll have to experiment to find public servers that will work for this. Your ISP's DNS servers will usually work. (Check *before* you have Internet problems!)

However, Windows-based computers generally *do* respond to ping requests, so `ping` is a good tool to use within your own network to check to see whether your computers can communicate.

Of course ping may tell you that no response is received from the remote system. For example:

```
Ping www.twoinc.com
pinging www.twoinc.com [24.120.30.52] with 32 bytes of data:
Request timed out.
Request timed out.
Request timed out.
Request timed out.
Ping statistics for 24.120.30.52:

    Packets: Sent = 4, Received = 0, Lost = 4 (100% loss),
```

In this situation, the `ping` utility attempted to send ICMP ECHO REQUEST packets to a destination four times, and each time the utility did not receive a reply from the target computer. This can indicate a problem that could be caused by the target computer (which we know existed at one time or another, because DNS has translated the name into an IP address). It could be that the computer is offline, or that a router or other device between the two computers is not functioning correctly. Remember that `ping` is just telling you that, for the moment, the network path between your computer and the host computer is not working as far as ICMP is concerned.

NOTE

For those who care about trivia, the name `ping` is derived from the original name Packet Internet Groper. Some compare it to a sonar "ping."

If you've determined that you can't reach another computer, it's time to step back and start checking your own computer, then any other intermediate computers or routers between you and your destination. You may have to use a process of elimination to find the problem.

To check to see if your own network adapter and TCP/IP protocol stack are working, type the command

`ping 127.0.0.1`

21

The IP address `127.0.0.1` is a special address reserved for this sort of test. If this command gets no replies, then most likely, you have a problem with your network adapter.

The second thing to check is your own computer's IP address. In the command prompt window, type the command

```
ipconfig
```

This will print out a list something like the following:

```
Windows IP Configuration

Ethernet adapter Local Area Connection:
        Connection-specific DNS Suffix  . : mycompany.com
        IP Address. . . . . . . . . . . : 192.168.0.101
        Subnet Mask . . . . . . . . . . : 255.255.255.0
        Default Gateway . . . . . . . . : 192.168.0.1
```

This indicates that my computer's network adapter has IP address `192.168.0.101`. If your network adapter has no IP address—that is, if it prints `0.0.0.0` or doesn't print at all—then you have a network configuration problem that has to be repaired. We'll discuss this shortly.

Use the `ping` command to attempt to ping your own computer's IP address; in my case this would be

```
ping 192.168.0.101
```

If you cannot ping your adapter's own TCP/IP address then your network adapter configuration needs to be checked and/or repaired, as we'll discuss shortly.

If `ping` indicates that your own computer appears to be working correctly, the next step is to ping other computers on your local network. Use the `ipconfig` command on other computers to determine their IP addresses (the command is `winipcfg` on Windows 9x and Me), and then use `ping` to see if they can be reached.

NOTE

> The IP addresses of all of the computers on your local network should be similar; for example, they should all start with the same set of digits. If they don't, then the network is not assigning IP addresses correctly, which we'll discuss shortly.

If you can ping your own computer but not one on your local network, then either *that* computer is misconfigured, or you have a hardware problem in the network adapters, cables, or hub.

`Ping` has additional command-line options that let you adjust how ping does its work. The full syntax for `ping` as implemented for Windows XP is:

```
ping [-t] [-a] [-n count] [-l size] [-f] [-i TTL] [-v TOS] [-r count]
     [-s count]  [[-j host-list] | [-k host-list]] [-w timeout] target_name
```

The square brackets `[ ]` indicate optional parts of the command line. The options are described in Table 21.1.

TABLE 21.1 OPTIONS FOR THE ping COMMAND

Option	Tells ping to...
-t	keep sending data to the specified host until stopped. Use Control-C to stop. You can also use Control-Break to stop and see current statistics and then continue pinging.
-a	display hostnames (if they can be resolved) instead of IP addresses.
-n <count>	send <count> echo requests to the specified host instead of the default 3.
-l <size>	send echo request packets with <size> bytes of data inside, instead of the default 32.
-f	set the Don't Fragment flag in the IP packet.
-i <TTL>	set the Time To Live value to the specified number of "hops." Each time an ECHO REQUEST packet traverses a router, this value is decremented by 1. If it reaches zero before reaching the destination, the packet is discarded.
-v <TOS>	use <TOS> as the Type Of Service. In most implementations of IPv4 this field is ignored.
-r <count>	record the route taken by the echo requests for for the first count hops.
-s <count>	record timestamps for the first count hops.
-j <host-list>	use loose source routing through the host-list.
-k <host-list>	specify a specific set of host names through which the packet will travel.
-w <timeoutvalue>	wait at most <timeoutvalue> milliseconds for replies to return, instead of the default 1000.

These options can come in handy in some cases:

- You can perform constant testing by adding the -t option. This is helpful if you're checking to see if there is a cable problem; adding -t to the command makes ping keep sending packets indefinitely while you're fooling around with cables and hubs, so you can see if the network starts working again.

- You can adjust the size of the data packets that ping sends with the -l option. For example, ping -l 1000 <servername> sends 1000 bytes of data in each echo request. If small packets get through but these larger packets don't, the problem is probably the network adapter hardware, configuration of network routers, the wide-area network connection, or in the case of broadband Internet connections, the wiring between your home and the ISP. In any case, it indicates a problem for a professional network technician.

If you can use ping to reach local computers but not more distant ones—for example, computers on the Internet or in other parts of your organization—you can use the tracert

21

command to see if you can reach the intermediate network routers between you and the computer you're trying to reach.

Tracert

If you can't ping another computer that is separated from your computer by a router, then you need to use the tracert to find out if the remote network and host can be reached. (If you are familiar with Unix, this the same as the traceroute utility found on most Unix systems.)

The tracert utility uses ICMP "echo request" messages, like ping, but doesn't directly target the destination computer at the start. What it does is send the "echo request" with a "time to live" value of one. As I mentioned in Chapter 16, "Introduction to XP Networking," the "time to live" number in an IP packet is used to prevent the packet from circling indefinitely in the case that routing tables have become messed up. Some clever programmer realized that the same mechanism could be used to map the route that data packets take across a TCP/IP network. When the test packet reaches the first router on its way to the intended destination, the router says, in effect, "Oooh, this packet has traveled too far, better send it back." The router then turns the packet around, and sends it back as "undeliverable," just as the post office would return a misaddressed letter. Recorded in the packet is the IP address of the router that sent it back. When this packet arrives back at your computer, the tracert program can see the IP address of the first router that was used to attempt to deliver the data to your selected host.

Then, tracert sends another ICMP "echo request," this time with a Time To Live value of *two*. This packet passes through the first router, but the second router returns it, and tracert thus learns the IP address of the *second* router in the path to the selected host.

As illustrated in Figure 21.1, when everything is working, tracert keeps sending packets with ever increasing Time To Live values, until it finally receives a packet from the intended target, and its job is done—it will have listed the IP addresses of each router between you and the host.

If there is a problem somewhere along the way, then you can look at the last listed router to start your troubleshooting efforts. It may be that the last router in the list is malfunctioning (or has bad information in its routing table), or it may be the router that *follows* it in the chain that is causing the problem. This is one reason why you should record these things while your network is working, so you know what to expect and so you know what is missing from the path that tracert prints out.

To run the tracert command, open a command-prompt window and type **tracert** followed by the IP address or hostname of the computer whose path you want to trace. However, there are other options you can use. The syntax for the tracert command is

```
tracert [-d] [-h maximum_hops] [-j host-list] [-w timeout] target_name
```

The options are listed in Table 21.2.

Figure 21.1
The traceroute command sends a succession of ICMP ECHO REQUESTS to trace a network path.

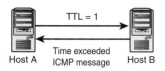

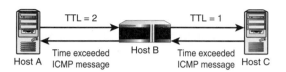

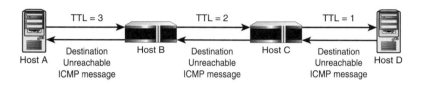

TABLE 21.2 TRACERT OPTIONS

Option	Tells tracert to...
-d	print IP addresses only and not try to resolve addresses into hostnames
-h <maximum_hops>	trace the path at most <maximum_hops> out from your computer
-j <host-list>	use loose source routing along <host-list>.
-w <timeout>	wait at most <timeout> milliseconds for replies.

Following is an example of using the tracert command on a Windows XP Professional computer:

```
c:\> tracert mail.twoinc.com
Tracing route to mail.twoinc.com [24.120.30.6]
over a maximum of 30 hops:

  1    522 ms    159 ms    189 ms   tnt1.white-horse.nj.da.uu.net [67.193.128.57]
  2    200 ms    199 ms    189 ms   67.193.130.173
  3    175 ms    189 ms    189 ms   229.at-2-1-0.HR1.NYC9.ALTER.NET [152.63.23.178]
  4    193 ms    199 ms    189 ms   0.so-0-0-0.XL1.NYC9.ALTER.NET [152.63.15.126]
  5    182 ms    159 ms    189 ms   0.so-2-1-0.XL1.NYC8.ALTER.NET [152.63.1.41]
  6    160 ms    189 ms    279 ms   0.so-5-0-0.BR4.NYC8.ALTER.NET [152.63.21.53]
  7    168 ms    189 ms    199 ms   204.255.169.126
  8    188 ms    199 ms    199 ms   ae0-52.mp2.NewYork1.Level3.net [64.159.17.34]
  9    237 ms    239 ms    249 ms   so-3-0-0.mp1.LosAngeles1.Level3.net [64.159.1.125]
 10    245 ms    259 ms    249 ms   gige8-1.hsipaccess1.LosAngeles1.Level3.net
➥[64.159.1.201]
 11    263 ms    259 ms    249 ms   unknown.Level3.net [166.90.145.14]
 12    372 ms    269 ms    259 ms   1000m.e2-8.bi8.cr.lvcm.com [24.234.1.233]
```

21

```
 13    260 ms    249 ms    249 ms  24.234.1.198
 14    270 ms    299 ms    249 ms  cm006.30.120.24.lvcm.com [24.120.30.6]

Trace complete.
```

This is an example of a working path. It also shows that on the Internet, there can be 10 to 20 routers in between you and the servers you use! On a typical corporate wide area network (WAN), there may be only one to five.

If the router at step 11 was not working, the last part of the printout might have looked like this:

```
  9    237 ms    239 ms    249 ms  so-3-0-0.mp1.LosAngeles1.Level3.net [64.159.1.125]
 10    245 ms    259 ms    249 ms  gige8-1.hsipaccess1.LosAngeles1.Level3.net
➥[64.159.1.201]
 11      *         *         *     Request timed out.
 12      *         *         *     Request timed out.
 13      *         *         *     Request timed out.
```

and so on, until you stopped the process by typing Ctrl+C, or until `tracert` gave up after the default 30 steps. In this case, you know that the problem is occurring somewhere in the Internet backbone network of Level3.net, where there is little or nothing you can do about the problem; unfortunate—but still useful—information.

PATHPING

There is still another utility that Windows XP offers which is sort of a cross between the `ping` utility and the `tracert` utility. It's the `pathping` utility. This utility allows you to do further research when trying to diagnose which routers are causing problems between your computer and the destination computer.

`Pathping` first uses `tracert`'s technique to determine the path between your computer and a remote host; it's a bit more sophisticated though, because it sends all of its probes at once and thus determines the path quite rapidly. It then sends a large number of ICMP "echo request" packets (100, by default) addressed to each of the routers along the path, and computes packet-loss and round-trip time statistics for each of them, again, all simultaneously.

The results can locate which router is the bottleneck in your network. It does this by letting you know which routers are causing the highest count of *dropped packets*, packets that a router discards because it is receiving them faster than it can forward them on. (Remember, TCP/IP is designed to tolerate lost data; but you don't want it to happen too often because retransmitting takes time.)

The syntax of this command under Windows XP is a little different than its Windows 2000 version:

```
pathping [-g host-list] [-h maximum_hops] [-i address] [-n] [-p period]
[-q num_queries] [-w timeout] [-P] [-R] [-T] [-4] [-6] target_name
```

The options, which are case sensitive, are listed in Table 21.3.

TABLE 21.3   PATHPING OPTIONS

Option	Instructs pathping to...
-g <hostlist>	use a list of routers with loose source routing. You can list certain routers that you want the packets to pass through, though the packets may also pass through other routers as they pass through the list. Separate up to 9 routers using commas.
-h <maxhops>	limit the number of hops (or routers) through which the packets are sent. The default is 30.
-i <address>	use the specified source address.
-n	list IP addresses rather than both IP addresses and hostnames. This can improve performance since it eliminates DNS lookups.
-p <period>	wait <period> msec between pings during the statistical sampling. The default is 3000, or 3 seconds.
-q <numberqueries>	test each router with <numberqueries> packets each. If not specified, 100 are sent.
-w <timeoutvalue>	wait at most <timeoutvalue> milliseconds for echo replies.
-P	determine whether *all* of the routers in the path support the Resource Reservation Protocol (RSVP).
-R	test each of the individual routers in the path for RSVP support.
-T	determine whether the routers in the path support Layer-2 priority tags.
-4	use the standard IPv4 protocol.
-6	use the IPv6 protocol.

The following listing shows an example of using this command:

```
pathping comcast.net
Tracing route to comcast.net [24.153.64.7]
over a maximum of 30 hops:
  0  winxpp1.sunrise.com [68.44.4.111]
  1  10.121.248.1
  2     *          *          *
Computing statistics for 50 seconds...
            Source to Here   This Node/Link
Hop  RTT    Lost/Sent = Pct  Lost/Sent = Pct  Address
  0                                            winxpp1.sunrise.com [68.44.4.111]
                              100/ 100 =100%   |
  1  ---    100/ 100 =100%     0/ 100 =  0%   10.121.248.1
                                0/ 100 =  0%   |
  2  ---    100/ 100 =100%     0/ 100 =  0%   winxpp1.sunrise.com [0.0.0.0]

Trace complete.
```

21

In this example you can see that a pretty good path exists between the Windows XP computer and the destination being tested. Of the 100 test packets sent, there was no loss. The Round Trip Time (RTT) column contains only dashes. This shows that the packets returned too fast to measure; usually this columns shows the average round trip time in milliseconds.

NOTE

> `pathping` only works well if each of the routers between your computer and the test target returns echoes; `pathping` stops probing the route if one of the routers won't return echoes.

CHECKING FOR INSTALLATION ERRORS

If the `ping` and `tracert` commands indicate that you are not able to communicate on the network, it's time to check the network configuration on your computer. Depending on your environment, you'll find that your computer was either manually configured, or used DHCP. For a small Windows 2000/XP network, another automatic form of address configuration can also be used: Automatic Private Internet Protocol Addressing (APIPA), although, as I explained in Chapter 17, "Building Your Own Network," I don't recommend using APIPA.

On a Windows XP Professional or Home Edition computer you can easily check your local area network (LAN) TCP/IP configuration. You can use the `ipconfig` command at the Command Prompt, or you can use several GUI tools, including

- The Event Viewer
- The Device Manager
- The Network Protocol, Services and Client Configuration
- The properties sheets for a Network Adapter
- The Computer Name tab on the System applet in the Control Panel

THE EVENT VIEWER

The Event Viewer is a very important diagnostic tool; one of the first to check, as Windows often silently records very useful information about problems with hardware and software in its Event Log. You can get to the Event Viewer using almost the same steps used to get to the Device Manager. Right-click My Computer, select Manage, and then click on Event Viewer. In Figure 21.2 you can see the Event Viewer window. In this figure, the tree view in the left pane has been expanded by clicking on the plus-sign to show the different types of log files that Windows XP keeps. For diagnostic purposes, you should check the System, Application, and Security logs in that order.

21

Figure 21.2
The Event Viewer might display important diagnostic information when you have network problems. View the System, Application, and Security logs.

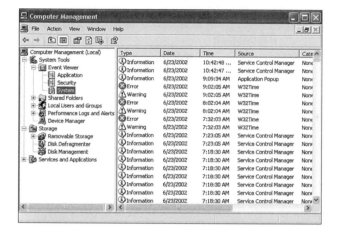

Log entries for serious errors are displayed with a red X circle; warnings appear with a yellow ! triangle. Informational entries are marked with a blue *I* and, as the name implies, are often not indicative of a problem. Instead, informational entries usually are made by services or applications when they start up or shut down, or when significant events occur; they usually indicate that something is actually working as it should.

However, entries that have a red or yellow icon indicate that something out of the ordinary has occurred. The default sorting of entries in the Event Viewer is to place the most recent entries at the top, but you can reverse this ordering by selecting Oldest First from the View Menu. Keep in mind that a single problem may be the source of another problem, and so on. Thus, don't depend on a single entry to help you in your troubleshooting efforts. Instead, look for related events.

The Source column in the error log indicates the Windows XP component that logged the event. These names are usually fairly cryptic. A few of the more common ones that are not obvious upon first glance are listed in Table 21.4.

TABLE 21.4   NETWORK SOURCES OF EVENT LOG ENTRIES

Source	Description
NetBT	Client for Microsoft Networks
MrxSmb	Client for Microsoft Networks
Browser	Name resolution system for Client for Microsoft Networks
Application Popup	(Can come from any system utility; these warning messages are usually significant)

21

continues

TABLE 21.4   CONTINUED

Source	Description
RemoteAccess	Dial-Up Networking
SMTPSVC	The SMTP mail transport service, part of Internet Information Services (IIS)
W3SVC	The WWW server component of IIS
SNMP	Simple Networking Monitoring Protocol, an optional networking component
IPNATHLP	Internet Connection Sharing
NWCWorkstation	Client for Novell Networks
NwlnkIpx	SPX/IPX Network transport layer
W32Time	Computer clock synchronization service
Dnsapi	DNS client component
Dnscache	DNS client component
atapi	IDE hard disk/CDROM controller

If you're at a loss to solve the problem even with the information given, check the configuration of the indicated component, or remove and reinstall it to see whether you can clear up the problem.

→ To learn more details about the Event Log, **see** "Event Viewer," **p. 1069**.

> **T I P**
>
> A problem with one network system usually causes other problems. Therefore, the oldest error message in a sequence of errors is usually the most significant; subsequent errors are just a result of the first failure. Because the Event Log is ordered most-recent-first, you might get the most useful information down a bit from the top of the list.

Just looking at the one-line entries in the Event Viewer might not give you a lot of information you need to troubleshoot a problem. So, when you see an entry that looks suspicious, double-click on the entry and a box will pop up showing additional information about the event. For example, in Figure 21.3, you can see that the Windows XP computer was unable to contact a domain controller. Notice also that the box has a hyperlink embedded in it that you can click on to get additional help via the Web.

You will also notice that on the right side of the box are up and down arrows. You can use these to look at other events without having to double-click on each one. Keep in mind that one event may be explained by a prior event. For example, if network connectivity cannot be established when the computer boots, you may find errors from many different applications, which are caused because they cannot use the network to perform their functions. So, when using the Event Viewer, don't just look at the most recent events. Look at others that you think might be the cause of the most recent events you are browsing through.

Figure 21.3
By double-clicking on an event in the Event Viewer, you can get additional details about the event record.

> **T I P**
>
> The real cause of your problem might reveal itself at system startup time rather than when you observe the problem. Reboot your system, and note the time. Then reproduce the problem. Check the Event Log for messages starting at the reboot time.

THE DEVICE MANAGER

Hardware problems with a network card will most likely be recorded in the Event Log. If you suspect that your network card is the culprit, and nothing is found in the Event Log, then you should check the Device Manager.

The easiest method for starting the Device Manager is to click Start, right-click My Computer, and select Manage from the menu that appears. Select Device Manager from the tree in the left-pane. In Figure 21.4 you can see that this will cause the right pane to display different categories of hardware installed on your computer. To view information about any network cards, just click on the plus sign next to the Network Adapters entry. This will expand the category to show one or more network adapters, depending on the configuration of your computer.

> **T I P**
>
> If you are an old-timer like me and prefer to use the Control Panel, you can get to the Device Manager by using the System applet (and clicking on the Device Manager button on the Hardware tab). Or, click on the Administrative Tools icon and then the Computer Management icon.

21

Figure 21.4
The Device Manager can help you quickly locate a malfunctioning hardware device.

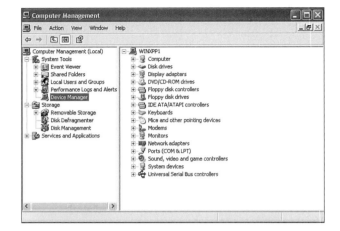

If you notice a yellow ! icon next to a device, then there is a significant problem with the device. It may be a hardware problem, an incorrect driver, or perhaps the device has been misconfigured (for example, is using an interrupt or I/O address that is also used by some other device, or is not operating at the correct network data rate).

NOTE
> Just because the Device Manager doesn't show a yellow ! next to a device doesn't mean that the device is functioning perfectly. It just means that Windows XP hasn't yet detected any hardware problems with the device, so you may need to investigate further.

If you see a device with the yellow ! icon, then double-click on the device and examine the explanation given by Windows XP about the device and the possible problem with the device.

If you suspect that the device is misconfigured, then you can examine the Properties page for the device. Right-click on the device and select Properties from the menu that appears. In Figure 21.5 you can see an example of the Properties page for a network adapter card.

On the General tab shown in Figure 21.5 you can see the manufacturer, the type of device, where it is located on the PCI bus (for PCI cards), and more importantly, you can see the box labeled Device Status. In this example it tells you that the device is working properly. However, if you don't see this text, then you can use the Troubleshoot button to start the wizard that will walk you through a series of dialog boxes that may help solve the problem. The dialog boxes the wizard displays at each step will depend on your answers to previous dialog boxes. Also, located at the very bottom of the General tab you can see a drop-down menu you can use to enable or disable a device.

21

Figure 21.5
You can view the properties of the devices attached to your computer while using the Device Manager.

Why would you want to disable a device? When troubleshooting one device, you may find that it conflicts with settings for another device. You can test this by disabling the other device and seeing if the device you are having problems with will then function. It will probably be then a simple matter to change some settings, such as the interrupt request line (IRQ) or I/O memory range used by one of the devices.

You can find additional information on the other tabs of the device's Properties pages:

- Advanced tab—Depending on the type of device, you may see several items here in a box labeled Property. In the case of a network adapter card you will usually just see a single entry named Line Speed. Off to the right side you'll see a drop-down menu that allows you to select the line speed. You should be sure you select the correct one. For example, the line speed(s) you'll find in this menu include 10Base-T as well as 100Base-T, and whether or not you are using full- or half-duplex. Check the documentation that came with the adapter! I've also noticed that some switches will not recognize a device with the correct speed selected! If so, select Auto-Negotiation from this drop-down menu, which will cause the card to exchange data with the switch to determine the correct network speed. This is a very common problem with both low-end switches for SOHO environments, as well as for enterprise switches that contain 20, 50, or more ports.

- The Driver tab will let you know the provider of the driver software. If this is a plug-and-play adapter that's on Microsoft's hardware compatibility list, then you'll probably see Microsoft here. Additional information includes the date of the driver and the version. Check the vendor's Web site for newer drivers that support additional capabilities! The buttons on this page include Driver Details, which basically just shows the directory path to the software driver, and the original manufacturer who wrote the software for Microsoft or another vendor. If you've downloaded new driver software from the vendor, then you can use the Update Driver button to install it. More importantly, should

21

something go wrong after you do this, the Roll Back Driver button can be used to return to the previous driver, which Windows XP doesn't delete when you install a new one. The last button on this page allows you to remove the driver. Use this if you are taking out an old card and installing a new one. This will free up the resources used by the old driver.

■ The Resources tab will help you most when trying to diagnose problems with the IRQs and I/O memory ranges discussed earlier. While some devices can share an IRQ, some cannot. At the bottom of this tab you'll see a box that will tell you if the device is having a resource conflict with another device. At the top you'll see a box showing the resources currently assigned to the device. When troubleshooting, write these down so you can compare to other devices and possibly make different selections in order to get both devices working properly.

■ On portable computers, there may be a power management tab. You generally will not need to work with these settings, but in some cases network cards may be set to shut off during periods of inactivity, and due to bad drivers fail to "wake up" properly when they're needed. You may want to be sure that your network adapter is not set to power down.

CHECKING YOUR NETWORK CONFIGURATION

If the Error Log and Device Manager report no obvious network problems, you should check to be sure that your computer or computers are configured properly; an incorrect setting can certainly mean the difference between networking and net-not-working. In this section, I'll describe several ways to check whether Windows is correctly configured. You'll notice that several of the tools provide the same information; you can check them all out and choose the tools that you like best.

IPCONFIG

If your computer can't communicate with other computers on your LAN, after you check the Event Log and Device Manager, you can use the `ipconfig` command-line utility to be sure your computer has a valid IP address. Check others on the LAN, too, to ensure that they do as well.

At the command prompt (which you open by choosing Start, All Programs, Accessories, Command Prompt), type the following command:

```
>ipconfig /all
```

The results should look something like this:

```
Windows IP Configuration
        Host Name . . . . . . . . . . . . . : AMBON
        Primary DNS Suffix  . . . . . . . : mycompany.com
```

21

```
        Node Type . . . . . . . . . . . . : Broadcast
        IP Routing Enabled. . . . . . . . : Yes
        WINS Proxy Enabled. . . . . . . . : No
        DNS Suffix Search List. . . . . . : mycompany.com

Ethernet adapter Local Area Connection:
        Connection-specific DNS Suffix  . : mycompany.com
        Description . . . . . . . . . . . : Realtek RTL8139(A) PCI Fast Ethernet
➥Adapter
        Physical Address. . . . . . . . . : 00-C0-CA-14-09-7F
        DHCP Enabled. . . . . . . . . . . : No
        IP Address. . . . . . . . . . . . : 192.168.0.101
        Subnet Mask . . . . . . . . . . . : 255.255.255.0
        Default Gateway . . . . . . . . . : 192.168.0.1
        DNS Servers . . . . . . . . . . . : 201.202.203.72
                                            201.202.213.72
```

The most important items to look for are the following:

- **Hostname**—This should be set to this computer's name in your organization's DNS server, or, if you don't have a DNS server, the computer name assigned for Windows networking.

- **IP address**—This should be set appropriately for your network. If your LAN uses Internet Connection Sharing, the address will be a number in the range 192.168.0.1 through 192.168.0.254. If your LAN uses DHCP for automatic configuration, your network manager can tell you whether the IP address is correct.

  If you see a number in the range 169.254.0.1 through 169.254.255.254, your computer is set for automatic configuration, but no DHCP server was found, so Windows has chosen an IP address by itself using the APIPA mechanism I mentioned earlier. If there *should* have been a DHCP server, or if you use Internet Connection Sharing or a hardware Internet Connection router, this is a problem. Restart the ICS computer or the router, and then restart your computer and try again.

- **Network mask**—This usually looks like 255.255.255.0, but other settings are possible. At the very least, all computers on the same LAN should have the same network mask.

Each computer on the same LAN should have a *similar* but different IP address, and the same network mask. If they don't, check your network configuration.

NETWORK CONNECTIONS SUPPORT TAB

You can use the Connection Status pages for your Local Area Network connection to view configuration information and possibly repair common configuration problems. Simply double-click on the particular network connection icon in Network Connections window and select the Support tab (see Figure 21.6). Note that you should double-click the network connection icon—don't right-click and select the properties page.

21

Figure 21.6
The Support tab
shows basic local area
network information.

Much of the information here is available by using the `ipconfig` command at the Command Prompt (`winipcfg` in previous versions of Windows). In addition to the information shown in Figure 21.6, the Details button will pop up the Network Connection Details display showing the following information:

■ Physical Address, also called the Media Access Control (MAC) address for the network adapter.

■ IP address and subnet mask assigned to the adapter.

■ Default gateway(s) configured for the adapter.

■ DHCP server and lease information, if the adapter was configured by a DHCP server.

■ DNS information, if one or more DNS servers are configured for use by the adapter.

■ WINS server information, if one or more WINS servers are configured for use by the adapter.

NETWORK CONNECTION REPAIR BUTTON

In the previous section, you'll note that on the Local Area Connection Status Support tab there is a button named Repair. This button can help solve some of the more basic problems that occur with Windows XP networking. You may also bring up this option if you see a balloon pop up from the system tray telling you that your IP configuration is invalid.

The following list describes the steps that the Repair function performs:

■ Renews the IP address lease, if the computer was configured by a DHCP server. Note that this does not release the lease and then try to obtain another lease. This is because if the original IP configuration information is released, and the DHCP server is down, then it would not be possible to obtain new configuration information! To avoid making things worse than they may already be, the renew option is used so that your computer will maintain its current configuration if the DHCP server cannot be contacted.

21

- Flushes the Address Resolution Protocol (ARP) cache. This makes Windows forget the hardware (MAC) addresses of any computers it's communicated with on the local network segment, and forces it to relearn these addresses. This will fix the communication problems that occur (for a few minutes) if two devices share the same IP address, or if one device is remove and another with the same IP address is installed.

- Flushes the DNS cache. This will clear all IP address/name associations remembered from recently obtained DNS lookups, and force Windows to look all names up again. This solves problems where computer IP addresses have changed but the DNS information has not yet timed out, and is the same as running the command-line utility `ipconfig /flushdns`.

- Reregisters DNS names. This will cause your computer's name and current IP address to be registered with the local DNS server, if it supports dynamic updating, so that other computers can find yours. This is the same as running the command-line utility `ipconfig /registerdns`.

- Clears the NetBIOS name cache, which is similar to the ARP cache, but which involves name translations for the NetBIOS protocol. After the cache is cleared, any entries in the `lmhosts` file that have the `#PRE` qualifier will be reloaded. This is the same as manually running the command-line utility `nbtstat -R`.

- Releases then reregisters NetBIOS names with WINS servers. If your network uses the Windows Internet Naming Services (WINS) services from Windows NT versions 3 or 4, Windows will register your computer's NetBIOS names. This is the same as running the command-line utility `nbtstat -RR`.

While these steps won't clear any permanent network configuration problems, they will correct most transient ones, and will do about as much good as rebooting your computer, in terms of getting back on the air.

NOTE

One thing Repair doesn't do is force a new election on the Windows Browser service, which is the service responsible for filling in the Network Neighborhood window. If Network Neighborhood isn't working, wait 20 minutes, and Refresh the window. If it still isn't working, reboot all of your computers.

NETWORK PROTOCOL, SERVICES, AND CLIENT CONFIGURATION

You should be sure that your Local Area Network connection is configured with all of the protocols and services necessary to use and share network files and printers.

To examine the properties of your LAN connection, open the Network Connections window. From the Category view, select Network and Internet connections, and from the next menu, select Network Connections. When the Network Connections page appears, right-click on the Local Area Connection icon and select Properties. In Figure 21.7 you can see the properties pages.

21

Figure 21.7
You can view the properties of your LAN connection.

In this figure you can see that the following basic components are installed:

■ Client for Microsoft Networks
■ File and Printer Sharing for Microsoft Networks
■ QoS Packet Scheduler
■ Internet Protocol (TCP/IP)

Be sure that the check box next to each of these items is checked.

If you are using a NetWare network from your Windows XP computer, please see "Joining a NetWare Network" in Chapter 17 for information about the protocols and services used in a legacy IPX/SPX NetWare environment. However, since most NetWare systems installed since 5.x use TCP/IP as a transport, you will probably not need to use the NWLink protocol (Microsoft's version of IPX/SPX). For the remainder of this section we'll examine the configuration using TCP/IP, which is the most prevalent protocol used in networks today, as well as the Internet.

To view the TCP/IP configuration, select the General tab shown in Figure 21.7, select Internet Protocol (TCP/IP), and then click on Properties. In Figure 21.8 you can see the properties pages for this protocol.

In most networks, a DHCP server (which will automatically configure a Windows client computer, or a Unix or Linux computer) will be used if you select the radio buttons Obtain an IP Address Automatically, and Obtain DNS Server Address Automatically. As discussed in Chapter 16, if your network uses a DHCP server, your computer will send out a request packet when it boots, and the DHCP server will provide an IP address and DNS address, along with other information needed to make your computer communicate with the LAN.

21

Figure 21.8
The TCP/IP Protocol properties page allows you to check that your network settings are entered correctly.

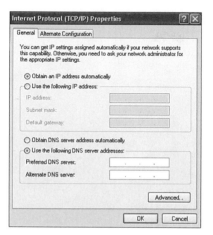

NOTE

If you use a broadband connection sharing router, or Windows Internet Connection sharing, then your network most likely uses the DHCP server provided by these services. Likewise, if you are on a medium- to large-scale corporate network, your network almost certainly uses DHCP.

If you do not have a DHCP server on your Windows XP network, and your network adapters are not manually configured but are still configured to obtain a network address automatically, then another feature of Windows XP called Automatic Private IP Addressing (APIPA) will kick in and cause the computers to select their own addresses. As I discussed in Chapters 16 and 17, I do *not* recommend that you rely on APIPA, as it can cause terrible performance slowdowns.

If you choose to assign static information for the Windows XP computer, you should verify that you have manually set the addresses used for Domain Name System (DNS) servers, as well as the default gateway. The *default gateway* is a router that forwards packets from your LAN to another LAN where your organizations main computers are located, or to the Internet.

NETWORK IDENTIFICATION

You can use the System Properties dialog to check and correct your computer's network name and workgroup or domain membership. Right-click My Computer and select Properties. Select the Computer Name tab to view your name and domain/workgroup settings, as shown in Figure 21.9. Be sure that

21

Figure 21.9
The System Properties dialog lets you verify or correct network identification information.

- Each computer has a different name.
- Each computer on your network uses the same domain or workgroup name.
- No computer uses the workgroup or network name as its computer name. For example, if your workgroup name is "TEST", no computer can use the name "TEST".

NETWORK DIAGNOSTICS WEB PAGE

Windows XP sports two comprehensive network diagnostic tools that perform basic checks on Windows's network software and hardware; one has a Web-based interface and one has a command-line interface. I'll discuss the command-line interface in the next section.

New to Windows XP is a Web-based tool called Network Diagnostics, which displays the results of a number of networking tests. There are three ways to bring up this tool:

- If you're logged on as a Computer Administrator, you can type **netsh diag gui** at the command prompt.
- View the URL hcp://system/netdiag/dglogs.htm or type this at the command prompt.
- Open the Help and Support Center, select Networking and The Web from the help topic list, then Fixing Networking or Web Problems, and finally Diagnose Network Configuration and Run Automated Networking Tasks.

To use the tool, select Set Scanning Options and check every box. Then select Scan Your System. A sample results page is shown in Figure 21.10.

21

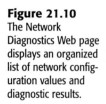

Figure 21.10
The Network Diagnostics Web page displays an organized list of network configuration values and diagnostic results.

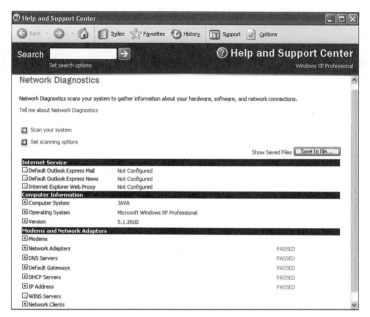

On this results page, the words PASSED or FAILED indicate the result of a test or set of tests. You may see a plus sign (+) next to a test. If so, you can click on this to expand the item to get more information. There's quite a bit of information here, so I'll outline the items that are most useful in diagnosing network problems.

- **Network Adapters**—Under Network Adapters, you can view a list of adapters, and under each adapter is its configuration information. This includes DHCP lease information, default gateways (which should read "Same subnet"), and the IP address or addresses.

- **DNS Servers**—Again, under DNS servers is a list of network adapters, and under each, a list of DNS Servers. The word PASSED indicates that the DNS server responded to ping tests.

- **Default Gateways**—Same deal again but this section lists the default gateway or gateways assigned for each network adapter, and the results of ping tests of each. If these say FAILED, you will be unable to send network traffic off of the local network segment as the router is down.

You can save the results of a diagnostics scan by clicking Save to File. Enter a file name and click OK. Saved files are created on your desktop, and if you are logged on as a Computer Administrator, a copy is placed in the directory `%systemroot%\pchealth\helpctr\system\netdiag` *in addition.*

21

Netsh

In addition to starting up the Web interface described in the previous section, the `netsh` command is a powerful tool for those who prefer to work in the Command Prompt when troubleshooting. In addition, you can include `netsh` commands in script files, so administrators can use this command to automate some processes to check Windows XP computer configurations on a periodic basis.

To start using `netsh` for diagnostics, use the following syntax:

```
netsh -c diag
```

After entering diag[nose] mode, you can use the following commands at the prompt:

- `connect`—This will connect you to a network resource, such as IE Proxy (to see if a connection can be made to the network proxy port used by Internet Explorer), IP host (to test a connection to a particular user-defined port), Mail (to test for a connection to the Outlook Express mail application), and News (to test for a connection to the Outlook Express news application). Use the command `connect help` to get a full list of the resources.

- `ping`—You can ping the following: network adapter; IP address for a local adapter, or for another computer; DHCP server; DNS server(s); default gateway; IE Proxy server; the loopback adapter; the Outlook Express mail or news server; and any WINS servers on the network.

- `show`—Use this command to display information about parts of your network configuration. You can issue commands such as `show adapter` to list all network adapters, `show dhcp` to display all known DHCP servers, and so on. `show test` tests connectivity to network resources such as DHCP and DNS servers and displays the results (it's does much the same thing as the Network Diagnostics Web page). Type **show** by itself to see a list of all possible items.

In addition to the previous commands and the subcommands associated with them, you can use the qualifiers `/p` to show all of the properties that have associated values and `/v` to show all properties, including those that do not have a value associated with them.

If you want to run all of the tests that would be run if using the default check boxes on the Web page, at the `netsh diag>` command prompt simply enter **show test**. And, as explained in the previous section, the command `netsh diag gui` can be used to start up the graphical Web page version of this application.

The importance of using this tool, especially by an experienced network administrator, should not be underestimated. You can get a lot of detailed information. For example, you can get the build number of the operating system, the boot device, and even more detailed information such as the free space in the paging files and total virtual memory size. For modems, you can get just about every configurable item the modem is capable of along with the current values. The same goes for network adapters.

21

TASK MANAGER NETWORKING TAB

The Performance Monitor gathers statistics about hundreds of items, called *counters*, that can assist you in troubleshooting how the operating system is performing. You can create reports or display real-time graphs for certain counters and can use this information to find out if a bottleneck exists in some resource that is causing your computer to run at less than the usual level you have grown to expect.

You can select counters in the Performance Monitor that can be used to examine network information, but using the Performance Monitor is not an easy task for the uninitiated. First, the overwhelming number of counters can make it difficult to select which ones you need to monitor. And unless you are very skilled in the operating system, and the environment in which it operates (including the applications that run on the computer), this can be a very difficult tool to use.

However, the Windows XP Task Manager, which is most usually used to kill misbehaving applications, has several new tabs added to it. One of these, as you can see in Figure 21.11, is the Networking tab.

Figure 21.11
You can view local area network rates and statistics on the Task Manager's Networking tab.

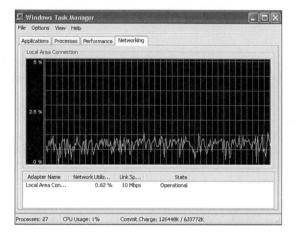

To bring up the Task Manager, just right-click on the taskbar and select Task Manager. Or, use Ctrl+Alt+Del. Then, click Task Manager and select the Networking tab.

On the menu bar at the top of the Task Manager, you will see several menus you can use to customize what data is presented, and how it is displayed. The view menu allows you to specify

- **Refresh Now**—This will clear any current data on the display and start any counters over at zero.

- **Update Speed**—This sets the time interval for updating the display. You can set this to High (1/2 second refresh rate), Normal (1 second), Low (2 seconds), or Paused (stops refreshing and leaves display as is).

21

- **Network Adapter History**—Use this to specify three kinds of data: Bytes Sent, Bytes Received and Bytes Total.
- **Select Columns**—This is perhaps the most important item on this menu. As you can see in Figure 21.12, you can choose from a wide variety of items that will be displayed on the screen underneath the graphical display.

Figure 21.12
The Select Columns option on the View menu allows you to decide what data to display beneath the graphical display.

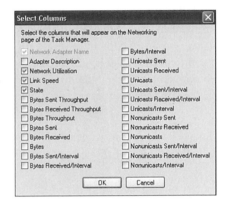

In Figure 21.12, you can see that only a few network counters are selected by default. You can use this dialog box to select a wider range of counters, and by picking and choosing different counters, you'll find it easier to narrow down problems on the network.

TIP

> Another interesting feature that you might find helpful when using the Network tab of the Task Manager is that you can place your cursor on the right side of the display and drag the side to expand the size of the window. This allows you to get a much larger display, so you can watch the counters that are being graphed over a longer period of time.

The Options menu also gives you some important configuration items that you might find useful:

- **Tab Always Active**—Selecting this option means that the Task Manager will continue to collect information while another tab in the Task Manager is selected. Thus, you won't lose information as you switch from one tab to another.
- **Show Cumulative Data**—This will cause cumulative data to be displayed, starting from the time you opened the Task Manager.
- **Auto Scale**—This selection sizes the graph based on the largest amount of traffic within a certain interval.
- **Reset**—This will reset the current display and all counters.
- **Show Scale**—For low bandwidth utilization, this option is useful since it will show the scale being used to display the data.

If you want to see a larger display just double-click on the graphical part of the display and the graphical display portion of the view will grow to take up the entire Task Manager window. Double-click again to return to a normal view. Since you can drag the edge of the Task Manager to create a larger window, you can get a very large, detailed display that can be useful in diagnosing network problems.

NETDIAG

Netdiag is a comprehensive network connectivity and configuration diagnosis tool included with the Windows XP Support Tools. It's similar to the netsh diag command, and can be used at the Command Prompt to display a bunch of information about the Windows XP computer's network configuration. It can also fix some DNS problems, although the netsh command (and its GUI equivalent) fix more problems than netdiag does. However, this is still a very useful tool.

You have to fetch it from your Windows XP Installation disk, as it's not installed with Windows XP by default. To install it, follow these steps:

1. Browse your Windows XP installation CD, and look for a folder named \SUPPORT\TOOLS.

2. Double-click setup.exe. If you are not currently logged on as a computer administrator, Windows will prompt you to enter the username and password of a computer administrator account.

3. Step through the installation program. When you get to the Custom Installation screen, click Optional Tools and select Entire Feature Will Be Installed on the Local Hard Drive. Then proceed with the installation.

When the support tools have been installed, you can run netdiag from a Command Prompt window.

NOTE

> While you're at it, you should take a look at the other utilities installed as part of the support tools. To view the tools' documentation, search for the file suptools.chm and open it. A list of the support tools can be found in Appendix B, "Windows XP Programs and Services."

To use netdiag, log on as a Computer Administrator and issue the command

`netdiag | more`

This will run the diagnostics and page the results through the more utility a screenful at a time. Press Enter to see each successive screen.

The output of netdiag is long—more than 180 lines on my computer—because it tests quite a number of network subcomponents. Scroll through the output looking for tests marked Failed. They help point you toward fixing a network problem. (If you are not logged on as

21

a Computer Administrator, some of the tests that `netdiag` performs will not work, and you will get more "Failed" notices than you should.)

If you have a Windows 200x Server-based domain network, you should refer any failed tests in the Global Results section to your network administrator because they indicate problems with your computer's domain membership.

The `netdiag` tool permits you to add any of several options to the command line:

- `/q`—This switch produces "quiet output," which means that it reports only those tests that produce an error.

- `/v`—This switch produces "verbose output," which gives an extensive list of the test data as each test performed.

- `/l`—An important switch that records the output from the tests. The filename is `NetDiag.log` and it will be found in the default directory from which you run the command.

- `/debug`—This will produce the most voluminous output (more than `/v`), showing the test data and reasons for the data displayed.

- `/d:<domainname>`—This will locate a domain controller for the domain specified by *domainname*.

- `/fix`—This switch will compare values stored on a DNS Server with values in the `hosts` file, and make repairs.

- `/DcAccountEnum`—This option enumerates domain controller computer accounts.

- `/test:<testname>`—This option runs only the test specified by *testname*. Use `netdiag` `/?` to get a list of the tests it will perform.

- `/skip<testname>`—This causes `netdiag` to skip the test indicated by *testname*.

When you view the output from `netdiag` you may see the word FATAL with the results of a test. This is an indication that a serious condition exists and you should fix it immediately. If you see WARNING, then a failure condition does exist, but can most likely be further investigated.

IS IT A HARDWARE PROBLEM?

If all of your software configuration checks out for the local network and you have eliminated routers or other equipment outside the local network, then you just might have a hardware problem. The components you need to check are

- **Network Interface Card (NIC)**—Also called a network adapter card.

- **Network cables**—Which include not only the cables that attach your computer to a hub or switch, but also any cables that are used to connect additional hubs or switches to the local network.

- **Hubs and Switches**—These devices sometimes fail, and there are tests you can use to make sure they are working correctly.

- **EMI or RFI Interference**—The best laid plans of mice and men don't take into account things like placing network cabling too close to sources of electrical noise such as an arc welder, which can degrade signals traveling down a copper wire.

CHECKING NETWORK ADAPTER CARDS

Most network adapter cards today are plug-and-play, and involve nothing more than physically installing them in a Windows XP computer and letting the operating system locate a driver for the adapter. If you have a newer adapter you might have to load the driver from the diskette or CD-ROM disc that comes with the adapter. Additionally, most adapters will have diagnostic software on the diskette or CD-ROM that can be used to detect problems with the adapter. Network adapters also will usually have one or possibly two small LEDs (lights) located so that you can see them when you look at the PCI slots on the rear of your computer. If you only have one LED, it's probably a link LED, which simply tells you that it is receiving a response from the hub or switch, and that a network path exists between the two. If the card has two LEDs the other is called the activity LED, and blinks when the card is transferring or receiving data.

First, check the LEDs. If the network cable (usually twisted-pair in today's networks) is plugged in firmly to the network card and the hub or switch, then the link LED should be lit. If not, then there is a problem with the adapter card, the hub, or the switch. You can check to see if it's a problem with the network adapter card by running the diagnostic program that comes with the card, or by moving the cable from the network adapter card to another computer that you know is functioning correctly on the network. If the cable works for the other computer, then try reseating your network card and insert the network cable and try again. If that fails, throw the card in the trash can and buy another! Network cards that operate at 10/100 Mbps today can be had for less than $25.00, more if you want one with extra features such as "wake on LAN."

CHECKING HUBS AND SWITCHES

Hubs and switches for small networks generally do not come with any kind of diagnostic software. Devices such as these used in larger networks, usually rack-mounted hardware with lots of sockets to attach computers, do come with management software that can be used to track down problem devices or ports. If so, check your documentation and find out what needs to be done to isolate a bad port or get a bad device replaced or repaired.

Small hubs and switches, which can be used in small office home office (SOHO) environments, or perhaps in a departmental setting in a larger network, are easier to check, since they usually have LEDs like network cards that can help you pinpoint problems. For example, when you plug a network cable into a hub or switch and a network adapter card, you should also see a link LED on the hub or switch. If your device has this LED and it doesn't light up, try moving the cable to a different port. If that works, then you may have a bad

21

port. You can also try swapping the cable with a port that is working to determine if you may have a problem with a cable.

Some switches have two other types of LEDs. Instead of a link LED, newer small switches have an LED that lights up if your connection is 100Mbps instead of 10Mbps. This LED takes the place of the link LED. If it is not lit, then there's a problem. Try moving the cable from a suspect port to a known good port. A second LED is often used on these newer switches to indicate whether the card is functioning at half- or full-duplex. This is an important thing to know, since full-duplex connections allow communications between your computer and the switch at the maximum speed in both directions. One of the problems some switches encounter, however, is determining which speed your network adapter card is using. I have found that setting the network adapter card's advanced settings for Link Speed to "auto-negotiate" will work when setting to the correct value sometimes does not work! This is especially true for network adapter cards that support full-duplex communications.

TESTING NETWORK CABLES

The cabling that glues all of your network devices together, from computers to switches to routers and so on, is something most network administrators take for granted. Once cables have been run to create the backbone of the network, and once the horizontal runs to each office or cubicle have been put in place, it's not unusual to go for years without encountering a network problem that can be traced to a bad cable.

The exception to this general rule is that last few feet where a cable connects the desktop computer to the faceplate on the wall; that is where most problems occur. It's best to run the cable directly from the faceplate on the wall, behind the desk, and then attach it to the computer's network card. For this connection, choose a cable length that doesn't leave a lot of extra cable lying around on the floor. Simply rolling a chair over a twisted-pair cable can impede performance, or make the cable unsuitable for any data transmission.

When installing horizontal cabling (the cables that run from the faceplate back to the wiring closet), be sure that the installer tests each cable. For a small amount of money you can buy a basic cable tester, which attaches to both ends of a cable and uses small LEDs to let you know that at least the cable can carry an electrical signal. However, while these inexpensive testers can check for reversed, shorted, or disconnected wires, they can't guarantee that the cable will perform properly at the level required to get a high-speed connection, such as that offered by Fast Ethernet (100Base-T). The same thing goes for backbone cables that connect wiring closets. While most backbone installations today use fiber optic cables, there are times when it is appropriate to use copper cabling, especially for short runs.

In addition to a simple cable tester, there are more expensive devices that run into the thousands of dollars, which are usually found only in a large enterprise. These kinds of devices test for problems other than simple wiring connectivity. Some of the more important tests that can be performed will help detect the following types of common problems:

21

- Cable lengths exceeding the EIA/TIA standards for cable used in backbone, horizontal, and work area connections for the network technology you are using (that is, 10Base-T, 100Base-T). For standard unshielded twisted pair networking, the maximum cable length is 200 meters.

- Inappropriate connectors or cable types, for example, using CAT-3 cable for 100BaseT networking.

- Kinks, shorts, or open connections in cables. The expensive devices can not only detect that there is a problem, they can tell exactly where the problem is, by measuring the amount of time that a signal pulse takes to travel through the cable.

- Missing terminators on old-fashioned coaxial cable wiring.

- Interference (EMI and RFI). Sources of interference include such common items as fluorescent lighting, microwave ovens (is there cabling running through the wall in your break room?), and power cables too close to network cables. Machinery that involves motors or transformers, such as that usually found on a factory floor, can introduce this kind of problem.

- NEXT (Near End Cross-Talk). Cross-talk occurs when one wire in the cable interferes with the signal in another wire in the cable. The twisting of the wires in standard network cables eliminates cross-talk to a great degree, but the number of twists per foot differs among the different cable types. And, you lose some of this twist protection where the wires are attached to the connector. NEXT is used to describe the cross-talk that can occur at the ends of a cable where the connector is attached. Untwisting a cable for more than 1/2 inch, for example, can cause problems in Category 5 cables.

As you can see, a number of problems associated with cabling and connectors can cause problems that only expensive devices can detect. In some cases you can troubleshoot these problems yourself by simply installing a new cable (such as at the point where the computer connects to the faceplate). If you use a contractor to install cabling, be sure you get written results of tests on all segments of the cable plant. By meticulously following the EIA/TIA standards for installation of your network wiring, you can usually prevent these problems altogether.

Fiber optic cables can be tested using a variety of methods, but two of the most common devices used are a power monitor and a time domain reflectometer (TDR). The power monitor is similar to a basic cable checker, but measures the strength of the light at the end of a cable. This measurement is made in decibels (dB) and can tell you the amount of signal degradation over the length of the cable. Things that can introduce loss of light in fiber optic cables include splicing (which should be kept to a minimum) and the connectors used at each end of the cable. An additional source of problems with fiber optic cabling is caused by not following the manufacturer's specification for the *bend radius*, which is the maximum number of degrees that the cable can be bent. This will vary from one manufacturer to another, but it is always a good idea to minimize the angle at which fiber optic cables are bent, especially in tight areas where there is little space.

21

NOTE

> An additional factor to consider with both fiber optic cabling as well as copper is the maximum length of cable used. For example, multi-mode fiber, which uses more than one beam of light, will lose signal strength of approximately 0.1dB for each 100 feet when using an 850nm light source, or 0.025dB when using a 1300nm light source. For single-mode fiber, which uses a smaller core to transmit light, as well as a single beam of light, you can cover much longer distances before the signal starts to degrade.

A TDR, which is a much more expensive device, can be used with both copper and fiber optic cabling. The TDR can perform a larger variety of tests than can a power meter. The *reflectometer* part of the name indicates that the device can detect reflections of light caused by imperfections in the cable. Thus, after proper calibration, the TDR can detect such things as excessive bending of the cable, bad connectors, and splices that were not performed very well. One interesting feature you can use a TDR for is to test cabling before you install it. The TDR can tell you if a spool of fiber optic cabling contains splices (not a good idea when you're buying new cable) and it can tell you the length of the cable. The ability to locate problems and tell you, within a few feet of where the problem lies, is one of the best features of using a TDR.

Other methods of testing cables are really methods used to test the network protocols themselves. The System Monitor or the Network tab on the Task Manager can be used to determine whether congestion is occurring on a particular network segment. Just compare the data obtained from one segment with that of another. If you have the same number of users on each cable segment, and they all make about the same usage of the network (which you can tell by keeping frequently updated base information), then you may have a cable problem.

PART V

SECURITY

CHAPTER 22

LOCKING DOWN YOUR COMPUTER

In this chapter

22

PREPARING FOR THE WORST

We all have elders who recall the days when one could leave one's front door unlocked and the keys in the car. Back then a movie cost a nickel and…well, that was a long time ago. It's a rough world out there now, and thanks to the Internet, there's a direct pathway for thieves, hoodlums, and miscreants of all stripes to reach right up to or into your computer. And if that's not bad enough, in a business setting you have to be further concerned that visitors, intruders, or even your own employees might get hold of information they're not entitled to.

There's nothing you can do that will absolutely, positively guarantee that your data will be safe and secure in all possible circumstances; people make mistakes, accidents happen, and besides, there are still plenty of security bugs still hiding in Windows, and way too much enthusiasm and energy on the part of hackers to find them. But, there are some steps you can take to help minimize the risks, the three most important of which are listed here:

■ Use all of the security features provided by Windows to their best advantage. Your front door has a lock—use it. Keeping Windows locked down not only helps thwart attacks by intruders, it also helps minimize damage from "friendly fire"; that is, from well-intentioned but incorrect system management actions by authorized users.

■ Keep your software and security measures up-to-date, to shorten the duration of your exposure to newly discovered security flaws and system bugs.

■ Back up your data frequently. If you don't have a backup system in place (using tape, writeable CD or DVD media, or a removable hard disk), *get one now!*

These topics are discussed all throughout this book. In this chapter, we'll pay special attention to several aspects of the first: keeping Windows locked down.

THE ADMINISTRATOR ACCOUNT

When you're logged in using a "Computer Administrator" account, you have permission to change any aspect of Windows, including any file, folder, or user account. This is exactly what you need when you're installing new hardware or software, managing user accounts, setting permissions on folders, or performing other system management tasks.

However, this *carte blanche* power is overkill for day-to-day work. While it may seem convenient, using the Administrator account poses several risks:

■ You might inadvertently delete a crucial file needed for system operation.

■ You might accidentally receive an email virus, or visit a Web page that has malicious script code embedded inside. Run from the context of an Administrator user account, the virus or script will have full run of your computer.

■ An untrained user logged on with an Administrator account can change system settings or otherwise misconfigure the system.

So, save the Administrator account for essential work only. Instead, create "Power User" or "Limited" users accounts for day-to-day use, even for a home computer used by one person only.

→ For instructions on controlling user account privileges, **see** "Managing Users Through the Microsoft Management Console Interface," **p. 418**.

> **TIP**
>
> When installing software and running some system management tools, you often don't have to even log on as the Administrator. You can use the Run As right-click option to run the installation or management program with Administrator privileges, while staying logged on with your normal account. (This works for just about everything except the network management.)

Furthermore, the Administrator account's powers make it the prime target of hackers who are trying to get control of your system. You *must* choose a complex, unusual password for the Administrator account, especially if your system is reachable over the Internet through Remote Desktop Connection. Use a password that contains uppercase letters, lowercase letters, and numbers, preferably using a word that isn't in the dictionary. Make a Password Reset diskette and store it in a secure location in case you forget this complex password.

> **TIP**
>
> One way to make a complex password is to join two words that you can easily remember, change the case of a couple letters, and turn some of the letters into numbers. For example, if the phrase "pricey meal" was something you could remember, you could use "PRic3y me8L" as a password.

On Windows XP Home Edition, your security options are more limited. The "Power Users" user account category doesn't exist, so you'll have to decide whether to accept the limitations of a "limited user" account versus the dangers of a Computer Administrator account. (You could solve this dilemma by upgrading to Windows XP Professional.) Also, you must boot your computer in Safe mode to obtain access to the Administrator account.

Is it still worth setting an Administrator password on Home Edition, even when several other user accounts are likely to have Computer Administrator Privileges? Yes! You should have passwords set on *every* account. This will at least prevent total strangers from being able to easily access your system.

To set an Administrator password, follow these steps:

1. Restart your computer. When Windows is first starting up, press F8.
2. From the startup menu, choose Safe Mode.
3. Log on to the Administrator account. Administrator should appear as a choice on the Welcome menu. If it doesn't, press Ctrl+Alt+Del twice, and then type **Administrator** in the login dialog box.
4. Open the Control Panel and select User Accounts.

22

5. Select the Administrator account and select Create a Password.

6. Enter the password twice, as requested. Do not lose or forget the Administrator password.

While you are in the User Accounts control panel, be sure that each account says "Password Protected." under the account name.

POLICIES, PERMISSIONS, AND COMPUTER MANAGEMENT

Windows has three distinct mechanisms that it uses to restrict the abilities of users (friendly or otherwise) to view and change files, folders, and settings. These are

- Access Control Lists (ACLs), which limit users' access to files, folders and registry settings.

- User Permissions, which control whether or not an account can perform certain operating system functions such as logging on at the computer, logging on over the network, or installing system services.

- Policies, which are registry settings whose values are used by a wide variety of system programs to "tune" the features and interface options made available to a given user. For example, policy settings can instruct the Control Panel not to display certain control applets. Another policy setting can instruct the Start Menu not to display the "Run" option. Policies are assigned by the local computer Administrator, or on a domain network by the domain administrator. Policies are available only on XP Professional.

ACLs are discussed elsewhere in this book: NTFS file security will be discussed later in this chapter, and is discussed further in Chapter 23, "Managing File Security." Registry security is discussed in Chapter 30, "Registry Maintenance and Repair." We'll discuss User Permissions and Policies in the next several sections.

NOTE

> The Policy mechanism is not available on Windows XP Home Edition. If you're working with XP Home Edition, you can skip ahead to the section titled "Hardware Security," on page 920.

THE MECHANISM BEHIND POLICIES

As you're undoubtedly aware, Windows stores most of its configuration information in the Registry, which is a database of sorts; it holds information organized in a hierarchy of keys and values, much in the same manner as a file system is organized by folders and files. The Registry contains information used to configure the system at large (the "Local Machine" section), and a section that contains information specific to a given user (the "Current User" section). The information in these sections is stored in a set of files called *hives*, with the Local Machine hive files stored in `\windows\system32\config`. The current user's hive is in the user's profile folder, for example, `\Documents and Settings\username\ntuser.dat`.

The policy system works by adding an extra hive file containing additional registry data that adds to and/or supersedes the entries stored in the standard hives. Figure 22.1 illustrates how this works. On an Active Directory network, this data is downloaded from a domain controller server; otherwise it is obtained from the Local Computer Policy set. The policy registry entries are secured with access control lists that prevent them from being directly altered, so in effect, data in the policy hive overrides data configured by the usual means (that is, settings made by standard configuration and control panel applets), and locks it in so that the computer user can't change it.

Figure 22.1
When looking up registry data, Windows checks the Policy data set first. Thus, registry entries set by the policy mechanism add to or supersede any entries set in the local registry hives.

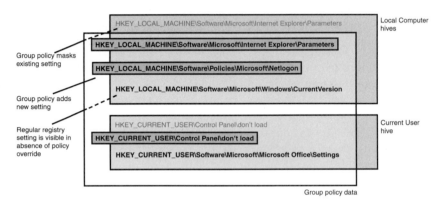

Windows constructs the policy set by "layering" in policy data. Policy data can come from several different sources, depending on the type of network that the computer belongs to and the type of user account with which the user logs on.

POLICY CONSTRUCTION ON AN ACTIVE DIRECTORY NETWORK

If the computer is a member of a domain network with Active Directory, when a user logs on with a domain user account, the full-blown Group Policy (GP) system comes into play. GP allows administrators to define policy items that apply to the computer, by virtue of its membership in the domain, in addition to policy that is applied based on the user's identity. Windows builds the effective policy (called the *Resulting Set of Policy*, or *RSoP*) by combining the per-user and per-computer policy settings from several sources, in this order:

1. Local Computer Policy.
2. Site Group Policy objects (sets), in the order specified by the Administrator.
3. Domain Group Policy objects, in the order specified by the Administrator.
4. Organizational Unit Group Policy objects, from the outermost container to the innermost container, with objects in each container applied in the order specified by the Administrator.

22

In other words, Windows starts with the policy settings defined by Local Computer Policy, and then adds in any site-specific policy settings. If the Site Policy includes items also defined by the Local Policy, the Site definitions replace the Local Policy definitions. Then in a similar fashion Windows adds in Domain policy, and finally Organization Unit policy, with definitions for the innermost container having the final say.

For example, Group Policy can be used to configure the outgoing SMTP mail server used by Outlook. The Default Domain policy definition might be used to select a master corporate mail server, while Organizational Unit objects representing regional offices would point to local mail servers. The idea is that configuring computers to use local servers provides the fastest, most efficient service, but if no regional definition applied to a given computer, the global definition would at least work.

If you think this sounds complicated, you're right. When different values for the same setting can appear in several different policy locations, it can be hard to predict what the final result will be. And, if the policy settings that permit and deny access to critical system features are misconfigured, the consequences can be severe. To help out, Microsoft provides with the Server versions of Windows a Resulting Set of Policy (RSoP) viewing tool that lets administrators test out policy setting changes before they go "live," so that they can be sure that users end up with the intended settings, restrictions and privileges.

Furthermore, Group Policy (GP) on an Active Domain network provides hundreds more options than are available just from XP's own Local Computer Policy settings. These extra options fall into several categories. On an Active Directory network, GP has

- Many more lockdown and restriction options than are available in XP's Local Computer Policy set. For example, GP provides settings that prevent Windows from giving access to the command prompt or the registry editor, and settings to independently enable and disable just about every item on the Start Menu and Task Manager.

- The ability to redirect the location of each user's My Documents folder and user profile folder so that these folders may be stored on a network server rather than on the local computer. This is a part of Microsoft's IntelliMirror initiative, which has as its goal the disposable computer—if a local workstation is lost, the user should be able to simply replace it with another and carry on with no data loss and no apparent difference in settings or configuration.

- The ability to designate software applications that should be made available to designated users and groups, or even automatically installed on users' computers.

Finally, one of the most significant features that full-blown Group Policy adds to the mix is the ability to delegate the ability to edit specific Policy settings and objects to sub-administrators and managers at various levels of the organization. So, while Group Policy is complex, it has a rather sensible and natural structure whose goal is not just the centralization of control, but also the distribution of control.

POLICY CONSTRUCTION ON A DOMAIN NETWORK WITHOUT AD

For a computer on a Domain-type network without Active Directory—that is, one run by Windows NT Server or Windows 2000 Server with Active Directory disabled—when a user logs on with a domain account, policy is constructed from two sources:

1. Local Computer Policy.
2. Policy template files (.adm files) stored in the domain user profile.

This is an old-fashioned but still widely used mechanism for implementing policy. As you can see, policy must be configured or at least disseminated on a per-user basis; this mechanism lacks the ability to define policy settings in the hierarchical manner afforded by Active Directory.

POLICY CONSTRUCTION ON A STANDALONE COMPUTER

On computers that are not part of a domain network (including those that are part of a workgroup network), or when a user logs on with a local computer account, Windows XP uses the Local Computer Policy settings only.

So, in terms of managing your own computer, you can look at the policy system this way:

■ If your computer is a member of a workgroup network, use the Administrator account to make Local Computer Policy setting changes in order to lock down your own computer. There are no other policies to worry about.

■ On a domain network, security is properly managed at the Server level. If your computer is a member of a Domain network (with or without Active Directory) and you're not a domain administrator, your Local Computer Policy will be overridden by your network administrator. You most likely can't—and probably don't need to—fuss with any of this yourself.

If you are a domain administrator in charge of managing Windows XP desktop computers, however, you do need to worry about this. The benefits of locking down most of the Windows configuration options are twofold: less need to configure individual computers, and less end-user mucking-about with the settings. You'll need to carefully weigh these benefits against the inevitable grumbling and chafing that the restrictions will produce.

SECURING WINDOWS XP WITH POLICY

The last section of this chapter lists all of the Local Computer Policy options available on a standalone Windows XP Professional computer. If you're not familiar with the policy options, I suggest that you skip ahead and scan through the listing to familiarize yourself with the scope of the available options—it's quite extensive.

The level of lock-down that you will need depends on the environment in which your computer will operate, as well as your tolerance for end-user configuration. For example, in a computer that is going to be made available for public access in a "kiosk" type setting, you would want to use the maximum level of control to prevent users from downloading software, obtaining access to the control panel, or running command-line programs of any kind. In other words, you'd want to use policy to disable virtually everything but the one program that you intend the public to run.

In an enterprise environment, you would probably want to disable access to network settings, prevent software installation, and prevent Microsoft Office, Internet Explorer, and Outlook or Outlook Express from executing macros delivered from outside your organization.

Local Computer Policy is managed through the Group Policy editor "aimed" at the local computer rather than at a domain controller.

On Windows XP Professional, to open the Group Policy Editor tool, log on as a Computer Administrator and select Start, Run, enter **gpedit.msc**, and press Enter.

NOTE

> If you're not logged on as a Computer Administrator, select Start, Run, and enter the command **runas /user:Administrator cmd**. In the new Command Prompt window, type **start gpedit.msc**.
>
> A subset of Local Computer Policy can be run from the Administrative Tools menu; the item is called Local Security Policy. However, this tool displays only a subset of the Local Computer Policy categories.

The editor displays policy categories in the left pane, using the standard Windows Explorer-type tree view shown in Figure 22.2.

Figure 22.2
The Local Computer Policy editor displays policy categories in the left pane and policy items in the right pane.

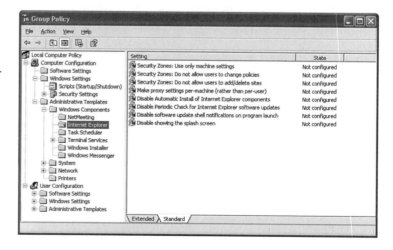

When you select a policy item, the policy editor displays a dialog box that lists the choices or data type required by each setting. In most cases, settings can take one of the following values:

- **Not Configured**—The policy item is not defined, so the system's standard configuration or settings will apply.
- **Enabled**—The policy restriction will take effect.
- **Disabled**—The policy restriction will not take effect. This setting is especially useful in full-scale Group Policy configurations to let a higher-priority policy turn off a setting enabled by a lower-priority policy. For example, the setting Prohibit Access to the Control Panel might be enabled by the domain policy (making the control panel inaccessible to most users), and then disabled for specific users or containers (restoring access to the control panel).

  However, this setting can still be useful even in the context of Local Computer Policy, as the Disabled value can undo a restriction set in the registry by normal means.

Some settings take numeric or string values, as illustrated in Figure 22.3. For example, Maximum Password Age takes a numeric value that determines the maximum number of days that a user may keep his or her password without changing it, while Primary DNS Suffix takes a string value that, if defined, overrides the DNS suffix set on the Computer Name of the System Properties dialog. On some policy items, you can select the Explain tab to view a detailed description of the policy and its purpose.

Figure 22.3
The edit dialog box for each policy setting explains what type of value the setting uses. Some policy settings have an Explain tag that contains a detailed description.

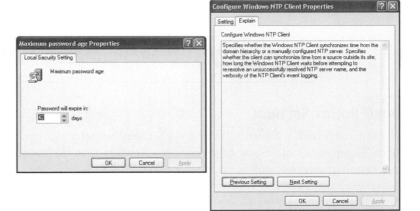

NOTE

> Online help can provide additional information about each setting. To obtain help, press F1 while using the Local Computer Policy editor. In the contents pane, open Security Settings, Concepts, Security Setting Descriptions, and then locate a particular policy item.

22

In the next several sections, we'll go over some important policy items that you may want to consider using to lock your Windows XP computer down against inadvertent or malicious tampering.

> **TIP**
>
> If you have several computers to configure and want to use the same settings on each, you may want to make a security template file and apply it to each computer. See "Security Templates" later in this chapter for the procedure.
>
> There's an added bonus: Security Templates provide several additional categories of policy settings beyond those listed in the following sections. I'll describe the additional settings in the Security Templates section.

SCRIPTS (STARTUP/SHUTDOWN) SETTINGS

The Scripts (Startup/Shutdown) section lets you name script files that are to be executed when the computer starts up and shuts down. By default these script files (.BAT or .CMD batch files, or .VBS or .JS Windows Script Host programs) are stored in `C:\WINDOWS\ system32\GroupPolicy\Machine\Scripts\Startup` and `...\Shutdown`.

> **CAUTION**
>
> These scripts run with SYSTEM (Administrator) privileges, so you must be sure that only Administrator users have write permissions in these directories!

These scripts can be used to install Security Templates (discussed later in the chapter), clean up temporary files, or perform other housekeeping duties.

> **NOTE**
>
> There is no guarantee that a shutdown script will actually run; a user might simply pull the computer's power cord.

PASSWORD POLICY SETTINGS

Under Computer Configuration\Windows Settings\Security Settings\Account Policies, the Local Computer Policy editor has two major categories that can be used to force users to use complex passwords and to change them periodically. As a practice, these settings can help ensure that your users will actually secure their accounts (although you can't stop them from writing their passwords on post-it notes stuck to the monitor). The most important settings are listed in Table 22.1. The items marked with an asterisk (*) are the most significant settings. Setting all of these will significantly increase your system's password security.

TABLE 22.1 IMPORTANT PASSWORD POLICY SETTINGS

Policy	Effect
Enforce Password History *	If you decide to enforce periodic password changes, you'll want to prohibit users from simply selecting the same password every time. Setting this policy to, say, 10 or more makes it more difficult for users to reuse passwords. (They could still change their password 11 times, and on the 11th time re-enter the original password, but they probably won't be aware that this is possible, and it's very inconvenient).
Maximum Password Age *	If greater than zero, the interval in days in which users will be forced to change their passwords.
Minimum Password Age	If greater than zero, the minimum number of days that must elapse between password changes. Can be used to prevent password reuse by cycling through several changes.
Minimum Password Length *	If greater than zero, the shortest permitted password. A value of 8 or more encourages strong passwords.
Password must meet complexity requirements *	If enabled, forces users to select passwords that (in principle) should be difficult to guess. The passwords will have to be 6 or more characters in length, not contain the user's logon name, and must contain characters in at least three of the following four categories: uppercase letters, lowercase letters, digits, and punctuation.
Store password using reversible encryption...	Lets Windows store recoverably encrypted versions of users' passwords. Should not be enabled unless required by specific system applications such as IAS (Internet Authentication System).

NOTE

The Security Settings group is the subset of Local Computer Policy that can be edited by the Local Security Policy editing tool on the Administrative Tools menu.

ACCOUNT LOCKOUT POLICY SETTINGS

Account Lockout Policy can be used to help fend off "dictionary" password attacks, in which a hacker or intruder tries one password after another in hopes of guessing the correct one.

22

When a lockout policy is enabled, the system calls a "time out" when a certain number of incorrect passwords are used against a user account, after which the account won't permit a logon until a certain time has passed.

I recommend that you enable the settings marked with asterisks. The relevant settings are listed in Table 22.2.

TABLE 22.2 ACCOUNT LOCKOUT POLICY SETTINGS

Policy	Effect
Account Lockout Threshold *	If greater than zero, sets the number of failed logon attempts needed to trigger a lockout. 3 to 5 would be a reasonable setting.
Account Lockout Duration *	Time in minutes that an account will be made unavailable. 10 would be a reasonable setting.
Reset Account Lockout Counter After *	Time in minutes between logon attempts for them to be considered consecutive and counted against the threshold. Use same value as duration.

AUDIT POLICY SETTINGS

Under Local Policies are three categories of policy items that control the majority of Windows's security features: Audit Policy, User Rights Assignment, and Security Options.

The Audit Policy settings let you record user actions that involve the exercise of privileges in the Security event log. You can record successful use of privileges, in order to create an audit trail of administrative actions; attempts to perform actions that require privileges the user does not possess, in order to track attempted hacking and privilege abuses; neither; or both.

By default, all audit items are set for No Auditing.

If you are most concerned about recording hacking attempts, set all of the policy items to Failure, except Audit Policy Change and Audit Account Management, which should be set to Success, Failure so that you can see if your auditing scheme has been compromised.

To maintain a more complete audit trail including authorized use of the computer, set all of the items to Success, Failure except Audit Directory Service Access, Audit Privilege Use, and Audit Process Tracking, which should be set to log Failure only—these items are used too frequently for it to be reasonable to record successful uses. If you do this, be sure to frequently check, save, and clear the Security log so that you don't fill the log and lose entries.

NOTE

> To audit successful and unsuccessful access to files, folders, registry entries, or printers, enable Audit Object Access for failure and/or success, and then enable auditing on the specific files, folders, registry keys or printers, using the Auditing tab on the items' Security properties page. You must be logged on as an Administrator to see the Auditing tab.

NOTE

> Audit Privilege Use, if enabled for success audits, does not by itself cause successful backup and restore events to be logged; you must also enable Audit: Audit use of Backup and Restore Privilege under Security Options, which is described in the next section.

TIP

> Auditing is especially useful when you need debugging access to files, folders, printers, registry keys, or Active Directory objects. Enable success and/or failure auditing for the objects of interest, attempt the operation that isn't working using the appropriate user account, and then log back on as Administrator and check the Security event log for a record of the failed access. The entries should tell you which files, keys, or permissions were lacking. When you've solved the problem, be sure to disable any auditing you no longer need, to avoid filling the Security log.

USER RIGHTS ASSIGNMENT SETTINGS

The User Rights Assignment settings are used by the Windows operating system (and the NT kernel underneath Windows) to determine what operating system functions may be performed by each user account. Since system and network services operate in the context of one or more user accounts, these permissions control the operation of Windows itself as well as what you would normally call a "user." These permissions can be assigned to individual users and also to security groups, which makes their administration somewhat easier.

NOTE

> While it's more natural to think about granting privileges to accounts and groups, User Rights Assignment works the other way around. Instead of checking off a list of privileges to be given to each account, you must list the accounts that are to receive each privilege.

For the most part, it is not necessary to make any changes to the User Rights Assignments. Windows preconfigures most of the settings, and the installation procedure for system services such as Internet Information Services (IIS) automatically grants the appropriate privileges to the IIS access accounts. The full list of privileges is listed in the last section of this chapter. Some of the more significant items are described in Table 22.3.

TABLE 22.3   USER RIGHTS ASSIGNMENT SETTINGS

Policy	Effect
Allow logon through Terminal Services	Determines which users may access the computer through Remote Desktop. Don't edit this list. The group "Remote Desktop Users" is preconfigured as a member, and when you select users through the Remote tab of the System Properties dialog, they are automatically added to this group.
Bypass traverse checking	This privilege lets users view folders to which they have read access even if they don't have read access to higher level folders. By default Everyone is granted this permission and it should stay this way.
Deny logon locally	Sets users (or groups) which are not allowed to log on to the computer. By default, Guest and the preconfigured SUPPORT_xxx account are listed here.
Deny access to this computer from the network	Sets users (or groups) that are not allowed to connect to the computer via File Sharing. By default, SUPPORT_xxx is listed, and if Simple File Sharing is disabled, Guest is listed as well. With Simple File Sharing enabled, Guest must not be listed here, as all network access is granted through the Guest account.
Shut down the system	By default, the Users group is listed here; you can prevent Restricted accounts from shutting down Windows by removing them from this list.

SECURITY OPTIONS SETTINGS

The Security Options policy group contains a large number of items grouped according to the system service they affect. The most significant of these are listed in Table 22.4. For maximum Windows security you may want to consider changing the settings marked with an asterisk (*).

TABLE 22.4   SECURITY OPTIONS SETTINGS

Policy	Effect
Accounts: Administrator account access	Can be used to disable access to the local Administrator account; useful on a domain network, but the local Administrator account is available when booting in Safe Mode regardless of this setting.
Accounts: Guest Account Status *	Can be used to disable local logon through the Guest account. Should be disabled.
Accounts: Limit local account use of blank passwords to console logon only *	Should remain enabled so that accounts with no password cannot log on using FTP, telnet, or Terminal Services. Best to (re-)enforce this through Group Policy if available.
Accounts: Rename administrator account *	You can use this policy to rename the Administrator account to another name; this account is a prime target for hackers, so renaming it can help thwart dictionary attacks on the account.
Audit: Shut down system immediately if unable to log security audits *	Enabling this option prevents a hacker from filling your security log with innocuous events and then proceeding to have at your system with no further activities recorded. If you do this, you must also configure the Event log not to overwrite security events.
Devices: Allow undock without having to logon *	Enabled by default; if disabled, requires users to log on before ejecting a laptop in a docking station that uses a software-controlled locking mechanism. You may or may not want to disable this setting.
Devices: Prevent users from installing printer drivers *	Enable to prevent "limited" users from installing printer drivers. Enabled, only Power Users and Administrators can install printer drivers. Enabling this helps prevent users from installing inappropriate or untrusted drivers, but may cause problems attaching to network printers; a Power User or Administrator must attach to a network printer first, in order to download the correct driver. Only then will other users be able to attach.
Devices: Restrict CD-ROM access to locally-logged on user only	If enabled, prevents CD and DVD drives from being shared on the network.

continues

TABLE 22.4 CONTINUED

Policy	Effect
Devices: Restrict floppy access to locally-logged on user only	If enabled, prevents floppy drives from being shared on the network.
Devices: Unsigned driver installation behavior *	Can be configured to allow, discourage, or prevent the installation of device drivers not bearing a Microsoft approval certification.
Domain Member: ...	These settings can be set by the Domain Administrator to ensure that communications between domain member and domain controller computers is always encrypted and signed.
Interactive logon: Do not display last user name	Enabled, this setting blanks the last user name from the logon dialog to avoid giving an intruder a valid logon name against which to start an attack.
Interactive logon: Do not require Ctrl+Alt+Del *	Should remain disabled so that a Trojan horse program can't be used to capture logon names and passwords from unwary users.
Interactive logon: Message text/title for users attempting to log on *	If set, these two settings are used to display a dialog box at each direct logon; the same text is also displayed by the FTP server upon logon. Can be used to display a legal disclaimer saying that activity will be monitored, and so on.
Interactive logon: Smart card removal behavior *	Determines whether Windows will ignore the removal of the smart card when smart card logons are used, or whether it should lock the workstation or force a logoff.
Microsoft Network client: Send unencrypted password to connect to third-party SMB servers *	By default this is disabled. It can be enabled to permit Windows to send passwords in unencrypted form to Samba and other non-Windows SMB-based sharing services. It should not be necessary to do this; current Samba servers support password encryption.
Network access:	Allow anonymous SID/Name translation
Network access: Do not allow anonymous enumeration...	Leave these settings disabled on XP Pro to prevent anonymous network users (and hackers) from obtaining valid user account and share names.

TABLE 22.4   CONTINUED

Policy	Effect
Network access: Do not allow Stored User Names and Passwords to save ... *	If enabled, prevents Windows from saving domain credentials entered when a user accesses resources under alternate usernames (for example, as the Administrator). This feature is a convenience, but a security risk.
Network access: Sharing and Security model for local accounts	This is the primary setting involved in enabling Simple File Sharing; however, you should use the Explorer Folder Options dialog to enable and disable Simple File Sharing as other settings are involved.
Network security: Do not store LAN Manager hash value on next password change *	If you don't need to access your computer's shares from Windows 9x/Me, enable this setting to prevent Windows from storing passwords in an obsolete and easily cracked encryption format. After making the setting change, change all defined passwords.
Recovery console: Allow floppy copy and access to all drives and all folders	If you preinstall the Recovery Console (and I suggest that you do), you may wish to enable this policy so that you can use the set command in the Recovery Console to gain access to your floppy drive. This gives you many more recovery and repair options.
Shutdown: Allow system to be shut down without having to log on	Not as useful as one might think. There's always the power plug.
Shutdown: Clear virtual memory page file *	Clears the page file upon system shutdown. The page file contains an image of the computer's memory and may potentially contain plaintext copies of passwords and encrypted files. This setting makes it somewhat less likely that a person who steals the computer could recover this plaintext data using a "disk doctor" type program.

PUBLIC KEY POLICIES SETTINGS

Under Public Key Policies and Encrypting File System, you may enter certificates to authorize recovery agents. The Encrypting File System is discussed in Chapter 23 under "File Encryption."

22

SOFTWARE RESTRICTION POLICIES SETTINGS

The Software Restriction Policies section lets you restrict certain programs and types of programs from being run on the computer. This control can be exercised by allowing or disallowing programs on a per-user, per file, per path, per-file-type, or per-Internet-zone basis.

This mechanism can be used, for instance, to make it impossible to run designated Windows maintenance and configuration programs unless the user possesses a smart card that contains a management-issued certificate. It can also be used to ensure that no downloaded, user-installed, or user-developed software can be run.

The Additional Rules list under Software Restriction Policies lets you define a set of rules by which each program that a user attempts to run is judged as Disallowed, in which case the program will not run under any circumstances, or Unrestricted, in which case the program will be run (so long as the user also has Execute permission with respect to a file stored on an NTFS-formatted disk).

By default, only one rule is defined when XP is installed, granting the Administrator account "unrestricted" access to all programs.

You can add additional rules. There are four types of rules:

- **Hash rules** identify a version of a specific file to be allowed or disallowed. *Hashing* is a term for deriving a numeric value (called a *signature* or *hash*) based on the contents of a file, its name, its creation date and time, and so on. When you mark a specific file as disallowed or unrestricted, Windows uses the file's hash value to be sure that the rule only applies to the specific version of the file that was selected when the rule was created.

    Hash rules are used to give "allowed" status to particular files in a folder that is otherwise marked "disallowed." The reason for using a hash value rather than just the file's name is that this prevents a hacker from replacing the designated file with a bogus version that would then be allowed to run.

- **Certificate rules** apply to specific users and/or bearers of specified certificates.
- **Path rules** apply to specific files, folders or file types.
- **Internet Zone rules** apply to files that were downloaded from Internet or intranet domains designated by Internet Explorer.

Several rules may apply to the same file. For example, one rule may disallow all .VBS script files, while another says that all files in C:\WINDOWS are unrestricted. To sort this out, Windows considers rules in the following fixed order, from highest to lowest precedence:

1. Hash rule. If a file is named by a hash rule, the rule's setting is used without further consideration.
2. Certificate rule. Per-user rules override all but hash rules.
3. Path rule of the form `drive:\folder\...\filename.extension`.
4. Path rule of the form `drive:\folder\...\*.extension`.

5. Path rule of the form `*.extension`.

6. Path rule of the form `drive:\folder\folder\...\`.

7. Path rule of the form `drive:\folder\` (in other words, more specific paths are considered first).

8. Internet zone rule.

If two rules of the same precedence end up referring to the same file, Disallowed wins out over Unrestricted.

A rule set can't completely prevent people from installing and running their own software. Even if you have access to full-blown Group Policy and turn off access to the command prompt, the Run command, and so on, dedicated users can still work around this. For example, they could write a macro in Microsoft Word to run an external program, and the Explorer-like Save As dialogs used by most applications can still be used to locate and launch programs. So, in most cases, Software Restriction isn't too helpful a lockdown tool.

Still, in the most restrictive environments such as kiosks, you can use these rules to help at least a bit. In this type of environment you would want to take the following steps:

- Define a rule making the root folder `c:\` "disallowed."
- Define a rule making the Windows folder (usually `c:\windows`) "unrestricted."
- Define a rule making the Program Files folder `c:\program files` "unrestricted." These first three rules will ensure that only normally installed software can be run.
- If desired, define additional rules to block non-essential specific program types, such as *.VBS, *.JS and so on.
- Use the NTFS file system so that the file system can be secured.
- Prevent the limited user account from writing to `c:\windows` or `c:\program files`. (This may cause problems with software that expects to write .INI files in these folders.)

Software Restriction policies can also be effectively used to block access to specific management programs that you want to prevent your users from using, such as mmc.exe, regedit.exe, and so on. The Administrator will still have access, granted by the certificate rule.

CAUTION

> If you decide to create Software Restriction rules, be very careful. You might make the system unusable. Be sure to leave the Administrator certificate rule alone, so that in the event you create a rule set that makes it impossible for regular user accounts to work, the Administrator can still log on to clean it up.

IP SECURITY POLICIES ON LOCAL COMPUTER SETTINGS

If your computer is a member of a secure network that uses IPSec encryption and authentication, you can adjust policy so that Windows will use the maximum security level available.

Normally, when connecting to another computer on the network, Windows will negotiate with the other computer to decide what security techniques to use. If both computers "prefer" to use encryption—which does take up a chunk of CPU power—then the connection will be encrypted. In high security environments, you may want to configure Windows to *require* encrypted communications. In this case, no connection will be made to a computer that doesn't support encryption.

Three policy sets are defined:

- **Client (Respond only)**—Can be selected if you want your computer to permit unsecured communications, and to let the computers decide whether or not to secure the connection.

- **Secure Server (Require Security)**—Can be selected if you want your computer to require encryption and authentication in all connections.

- **Server (Request Security)**—Can be selected if you want your computer to request, but not require security in all connections.

If desired, at most one of the policies should be enabled.

The policies are preconfigured for an Active Directory network. You can also add a custom policy for other network types, with rules specified with the following considerations:

- **Type of connection**—LAN, remote, or all connections.

- **Type of network traffic**—IP, ICMP, or specific protocol/IP address/Port values.

- **Filtering action for each traffic type**—Permit without security, request security, require security.

- **Authentication method(s)**—Kerberos V5 (Active Directory), Certificate, or preshared key. Several choices can be listed in order of preference.

- **Tunnel settings**—Specific IPSec tunnel endpoint or untunneled.

- **Internet Key Exchange details**—Integrity algorithm (MD5 or SHA1), Encryption type (DES or 3DES), Diffie-Hellman group (1 or 2), key regeneration interval. Several choices can be listed in order of preference.

WINDOWS COMPONENTS SETTINGS

Local Security Policy contains several sections of policies that let you selectively disable features of NetMeeting, Internet Explorer, the Task Scheduler, Terminal Services (Remote Desktop), Windows Installer, and Windows Messenger.

These settings are listed in Listing 22.1 at the end of the chapter; you may wish to browse through them to look for likely candidates for lockdown. Of particular interest are the Zone configuration restrictions under Internet Explorer; these settings let you lock down IE Zone security so that it cannot be modified by users.

NOTE

> Many more configuration options for these same components may be found under User Configuration\Administrative Tools\Windows Components.

22

SYSTEM SETTINGS

A large set of settings under Computer Configuration\Adminstrative Templates\System are meant primarily for use as Group Policy on an Active Directory network, to override the local computer users' and local computer administrator's ability to configure Windows. Of particular interest are the settings that configure Remote Assistance, which allow the domain administrator to designate accounts that can connect to member computers with Remote Assistance without even being asked, and the Windows Time Service setting which lets you designate the time servers to be used on the network. The Disable AutoPlay and Download Missing COM Components settings might be used to restrict the useful—but potentially risky—features.

NETWORK AND PRINTER SETTINGS

Network settings appear under Computer Configuration and User Configuration. These settings, again, are mostly useful only in an Active Directory environment as part of Group Policy, rather than as part of a Local Computer Policy for a standalone computer. The reason for this is that these settings can be used to "force" the configuration of network settings into member computers; these settings are simple enough to set up individually on non-Active Directory computers.

The settings are listed in Listing 22.1 at the end of the chapter. Of particular interest are the DNS Client settings, which you can use to force correct TCP/IP network client settings. The Offline Files and Network Connections sections can be used to disable or configure the Offline files feature, and can be used to disable Internet Connection Firewall, Internet Connection Sharing and bridging on member computers; this can be very helpful in preventing end-user network reconfiguration.

Printer settings can be used to enable and disable Web-based (IPP) printing, to force or prevent end-user installed printers from being published in Active Directory, and to configure a custom text message to be displayed on the Printers control panel page; for example to display your organization's technical support department contact information.

USER CONFIGURATION

More configuration options for these same components may be found under Local Computer Policy's User Configuration section. However, the User Configuration settings are really meant to be used on an Active Directory network where they can be assigned on a per-user basis (via domains and Organizational Unit containers). When set in Local Computer Policy on a non-AD computer, the settings apply to *all* users, limiting their usefulness somewhat.

22

However, you can still use the User Configuration settings on a non-AD network to lock down settings so that users can't modify them without Administrator privileges.

Of particular interest are the settings for Internet Explorer, Windows Explorer, and Windows Update. You can use these settings (and there are a *lot* of them) to disable or configure almost each individual feature of these programs.

SECURITY TEMPLATES

In the previous sections we discussed Local Computer Policy settings. If you have more than one computer to configure, you will find the process tedious and error-prone. The Security Templates system lets you store policy settings in a file that can then be deployed to multiple computers with relative ease.

One way to think of the difference between policies and security templates is that policies persist in the computer and work all the time; templates are "applied" to the computer as a "policy installation" procedure. And at the same time, security templates can be configured to reset file and registry permissions, can adjust Event Log size and overrun settings, and can set the startup options for system services.

A template file can contain one or more policy settings. When you apply the template to your computer, these settings are written to the Local Computer Policy database. You can apply more than one template file, if you desire; the settings simply accumulate and in the case of conflicting settings, the value from the last-applied template is used.

Windows comes with several predefined template files that you could use to perform a certain level of system lock-down without having to make any choices; you can also create your own template from scratch, or using one of the predefined templates as a starting point.

TIP

> You can view template files as text files with Notepad; they're stored in `\windows\security\templates`.

CREATING AND EDITING SECURITY TEMPLATES

You can run the Security Template editor from the Microsoft Management Console. Follow these cumbersome steps:

1. Log on as a Computer Administrator.
2. Click Start, Run, and enter `mmc`.
3. Click File, Add/Remove Snap-In.
4. Click Add, locate Security Templates in the Snap-in list, highlight it, and click Add.
5. Click Close, and then OK.
6. Double-click the title bar of the inner Console Root\Security Templates window to make it fill the MMC console window.

You can expand the list in the left hand pane to see the predefined templates, as shown in Figure 22.4.

Figure 22.4
The Security Templates editor displays a list of template files. Inside each template, you can configure any Group Policy items.

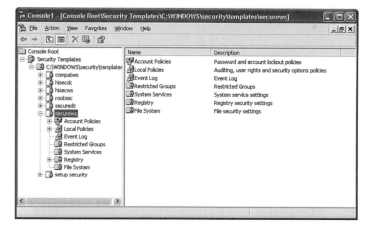

The predefined template files installed with Windows XP Professional are listed here:

- **compatws**—Relaxes file and registry permissions so that users in the "limited user" class (that is, user accounts that are members of the Users group but not the Power Users group) can run applications that require write permission in the Windows directory. You can apply this template to give "limited users" somewhat greater permissions rather than making them full-fledged "power users," which have the ability to install devices and so on.

- **securedc**—Intended to be applied only to domain controller servers, tightens security by restricting access by anonymous network connections and limits use of easily-cracked LanManager authentication.

- **hisecdc**—Intended to be applied only to domain controller servers, adds even tighter security measures than securedc; requires encryption and signing of network traffic.

- **securews**—Tightens network security of a domain member computer (workstation) by limiting use of LanManager authentication, enables signing/encryption of network traffic when requested by connected servers, and restricts access by anonymous network connections.

- **hisecws**—Tightens network security of a domain member even more than securews; enables requirement of signing/encryption of network traffic.

CAUTION

By default, the hisecws template removes all users from the Power Users group, in effect turning all but the Administrator account into "limited users." If you want to use the hisecws template's other settings, but don't want to mess up your Power User accounts, you may want to make a copy of this template and delete the Restricted Groups policy for Power Users. Restricted Groups are discussed later.

22

- **rootsec**—Resets NTFS file permissions on the hard drive containing Windows, and resets permissions on all subfolders and files. This template can be used if you accidentally mess up NTFS permissions so badly that Windows doesn't function properly for one or more users.

- **setup security**—Sets security and system options to the original "out of the box" defaults used when Windows is first installed. It's useful in a "disaster recovery" situation to restore correct permissions to the drive on which Windows is installed.

More detailed descriptions of the predefined templates are available in Windows online help. To view it, open the Security Templates editor, press F1, and locate Security Templates, Concepts, Predefined Security Templates in the contents pane.

If you decide to use a standardized set of policy settings to configure the computers in your organization, you may wish to create one or more additional template files of your own, by following this procedure:

1. Decide where to store the template file. You can store it in the default folder, or you can create a new template folder. To create a new folder, right-click Security Templates in the left pane, and select Create New Template Search Path.

2. Right-click the chosen template folder and select New Template. Enter a name for the template (don't add an extension; Windows will add the `.inf` extension automatically). You can also enter a description listing the purpose of the template. (You can later edit the description field by right-clicking the template name and selecting Set Description).

3. Open the tree view under the template name and make the desired policy settings.

4. Right-click the template name and select Save.

N O T E

> If you fail to save changes you've made to the template before you exit the Security Templates editor, it will prompt you with a list of altered templates.
>
> You can hold down the Ctrl key and select or deselect any of the listed template names; then click Yes to save the changes.

You can also create a new template using an existing template as a starting point. To do this, follow these steps:

1. Right-click the existing template and select Save As.

2. Enter a new name for the template and click Save.

3. Right-click the newly added template name in the left pane and select Set Description.

4. Edit the description text to describe the purpose of the new template.

5. Edit the templates policy settings as desired.

6. Right-click the template name in the left-hand pane and select Save.

You can then copy your template files to a network share or a floppy disk to distribute it to other computers.

TIP

> You can copy entire categories of template settings from one template to another. To copy the Account Policies, Local Policies, Event Log, Restricted Groups, System Services, Registry, or File System section, right-click the section title in one template and click Copy. Then right-click the same title in another template and click Paste.
>
> The paste operation *replaces* the entire section in the second template; it doesn't just add settings from the first template to those already in the second.

Security Templates can contain several additional categories of policy settings that do not appear in the Local Computer Policy editor. These settings are described in the next few sections.

EVENT LOG SETTINGS

Security Templates can be used to set limits on Event Log file size, to determine how the Event Log responds when one of its files is filled, and to control access to the Event log by anonymous network users.

There are four settings for each of the Event Log's three sections, which are named Application Log, Security Log, and System Log. The settings are listed in Table 22.5.

TABLE 22.5   EVENT LOG SETTINGS

Policy	Effect
Maximum xxx log size	Sets the maximum size for the log file section named "xxx". If selected, you can set a maximum file size in KB.
Prevent local guest group from accessing xxx log	If selected you can enable or disable the local guest account from viewing the log; the guest account is used for anonymous access when Simple File Sharing is enabled.
Retain xxx log	If selected, you can specify the minimum number of days events are kept in the log before being overwritten.
Retention method for xxx log	If selected, determines if and how the Event Log will overwrite data when the maximum file size has been reached. The options are Overwrite Events by Days, Overwrite Events as Needed, or Do Not Overwrite.

You don't want it to be possible for a hacker to fill the security event log with meaningless data; if this is possible, he or she can then work at will with no audit trail. Thus for maximum security you want to set a reasonably large size for the Security log (say 10000KB); select Do Not Overwrite Events for the Security log; enable the option Audit: Shut Down System Immediately If Unable to Log Security Audits under the Local Computer Policy section Computer Configuration, Windows Settings, Security Settings, Local Policies, Security Options; and finally enable failure auditing of logins and other privileged operations.

RESTRICTED GROUP SETTINGS

The Restricted Groups feature is used to specify which specific users are permitted to be members of various local security groups. When the template is applied to the computer (or, in the case of Group Policy, when Group Policy is refreshed on the workstation), any user not listed in groups with Restricted Groups policy is removed from the group. This mechanism can be used to prevent inappropriate users from being made members of, for example, the Administrators group. More precisely, it prevents users from remaining members of inappropriate groups after a policy refresh.

To add a Restricted Group, right-click the Restricted Group title in the left pane and select Add Group. Enter the group name or, to select from a list, click Browse, Advanced, and Find Now; then select a group name from the list.

Then, add the users and/or groups that should be members of this group by clicking Add in the group's properties page.

You can also list groups that this group should be made a member of.

CAUTION

When the template is applied, the users listed in the Restricted Group policy item will be added to the security group and *all other users will be deleted*. If you leave the user list blank, *all users will be removed from the group*. Be very careful, then, not to apply a Restricted Group policy to the Administrators group that doesn't include the Administrator account!

SYSTEM SERVICES SETTINGS

The items in the System Services section can be used to set the startup parameters for specific system services. This section lists all installed system services. When the Startup and Permission columns are listed as "Not defined," the template does not change the services' current settings.

However, you can define policy settings for any service or services, and can select from the standard startup options: Automatic (service starts when Windows boots), Manual (service starts only when an Administrator, Power User, or other service requests it), or Disabled (service will not start). You can also configure the service's security settings, which determine the user account under which the service is run.

CAUTION

Be careful about changing the user account used by preinstalled, standard Windows services—if you use an account that does not have the privileges required by the service, the service will not work.

Registry Settings

You can add registry key security settings to the template. When the template is applied to a computer, the security Access Control Lists for the designated registry keys will be updated.

To add a registry key to be updated, follow these steps:

1. Right-click Registry Settings in the left pane of the template editor and select Add Key.

2. Select the registry key from list displayed in the Add Key dialog. You can select a key at any level of the registry hierarchy. For example, MACHINE, MACHINE\ SOFTWARE, MACHINE\SOFTWARE\Microsoft, and so on. When you've selected the key, click OK.

3. Edit the Security list to assign the desired registry access permissions. For example, you may wish to add or remove the Everyone group, or you may wish to adjust whether or not the Users group has write permission on a given key.

4. Select how the changed permissions should be applied to the key. The choices are

   - **Propagate Inheritable Permissions to All Subkeys**—The permissions you've defined will be added to any already defined for any subkeys of the specified key.

   - **Replace Existing Permissions on All Subkeys with Inheritable Permissions**—The permissions you've defined will replace any already defined for all subkeys of the specified key.

   - **Do Not Allow Permissions on This Key to Be Replaced**—The policy will prevent other lower priority policies from modifying this key's permissions.

File System Settings

NTFS Permissions on files and folders can be updated by Security Template Policy in exactly the same manner as registry key permissions are updated. See the previous section, "Registry Settings," to see how to add permission policies (substituting the word "subfolder" for "subkey", as appropriate).

You can use File System template rules to enforce security settings appropriate to your environment. For example, you can use a policy rule to remove access by the group Everyone to the root folder of all hard drives, and then add Everyone just to specific folders.

Applying Security Templates

There are two ways to apply a security template to a computer's Local Security Policy. The first is through the Security Configuration and Analysis MMC snap-in, and the second is with a command-line program.

Using Security Configuration and Analysis

The graphical method of applying a template file is through the Security Configuration and Analysis tool. To run this program, follow these steps:

1. Log on as a Computer Administrator.
2. Click Start, Run, and enter **mmc**.
3. Click File, Add/Remove Snap-In.
4. Click Add, locate Security Analysis and Configuration in the Snap-in list, highlight it, and click Add.
5. Click Close, and then OK.
6. Double-click the title bar of the inner window to make it fill the MMC console window.
7. Select Action, Open Database.
8. In the Open Database dialog, enter a filename such as **local**, and click Open. This will create a new file.
9. In the Import Template dialog, locate the template file you wish to use and click Open.
10. Select Action, Analyze Computer Now.

The analysis tool will then compare the computer's current policy settings with those that would be in effect after the template is applied. You can browse through the policy list and look for changed settings. Settings that will be changed by the template will be listed with a red "x" over the policy name, as shown in Figure 22.5. The prospective new value for each policy is listed under Database Setting, and the current computer policy value is listed under Computer Setting. You can use this display to confirm that the template does what you want it to do.

Red X

Figure 22.5
Security Analysis and Configuration displays policies that would be altered by a template with a red X.

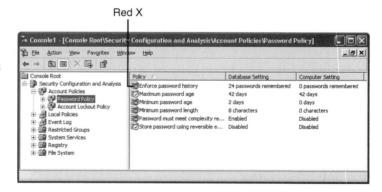

If you wish you can import additional templates by clicking Action, Import Template. The display will show the combined effect of the imported templates.

When you are sure that you want to apply the template, select Action, Configure Computer Now.

22

> **CAUTION**
>
> This action is not reversible! You may wish to use a test computer, and also perform a full backup before applying a template the first time.
>
> (You can delete templates from the Security Templates editor. However, this just deletes the template file; it can't undo the changes that an applied template has made to your computer.)

APPLYING TEMPLATES FROM THE COMMAND LINE

You can also apply security templates using the `secedit` command-line utility. The syntax for applying a template is

```
secedit /configure /db security.db /cfg templatefile
```

where `security.db` is the name of the security analysis database to create (it should not exist beforehand), and *templatefile* is the path to the desired template file. You can delete the file `security.db` after the program has run.

You must be logged on as a Computer Administrator to run this command. It writes a log file describing the actions it's taken in file `\windows\security\logs\scesrv.log`.

FILE, PRINTER, AND NETWORK SECURITY

Another important way to secure your system is to use the NTFS file system on your hard disks, which provides the ability to control access to files and folders on a user-by-user basis. This is important not only to protect your personal and corporate files from inappropriate browsing, but also to protect Windows itself. In addition to user-level security, NTFS supports encrypted files, for even greater security.

In addition to increased security, NTFS offers significantly increased reliability over the older FAT16 and FAT32 file systems; lost clusters after a crash or power failure just don't occur with NTFS.

> **NOTE**
>
> Windows XP Home Edition can also use NTFS, but doesn't provide direct access to its security features. You can gain access to the security features in Safe Mode, and through the `cacls` command-line utility, but this is for the most part not worth the trouble. Still, for the increased reliability, I recommend that you use NTFS even with XP Home Edition, unless you need to access your hard disks from other operating systems.

> **TIP**
>
> Access to file system security is also blocked with XP Professional when Simple File Sharing is enabled.

22

If NTFS was used when your computer was set up, unless you need to access your Windows disk volumes with other operating systems, you should seriously consider converting the disks to use NTFS.

MANAGING FILE SECURITY

In general, for the greatest security, you should follow the principle of granting access to objects only on an as-needed basis. Certainly, to use the system, every user needs read permission in \windows, \windows\system32, and \program files, for this is where application programs and Windows system programs reside. Each user must have full read and write permissions in his or her own profile folder (that is, the user's folder under \documents and settings). But, everything else should be considered on a case-by-case basis.

Managing this sort of security manually is quite difficult, and even dangerous: The Windows operating system itself must play by NTFS's security rules (it uses the account named SYSTEM), and if security is misconfigured, Windows can find itself unable to read system and driver files.

By default, upon installation (or after converting a FAT partition to NTFS) Windows configures security for the root folder, the \windows folder, the \documents and settings folder, and \program files. You don't need to change the security settings on these folders.

However, you should check and adjust the NTFS settings on any folders you create besides the standard root-level folders, on the Windows drive or on any other hard drives in your system.

NETWORK SECURITY

Network security is one of the most important areas to consider when making your system secure, for networks and the Internet in particular provide a means for tens to millions of other people to gain direct access to your computer. It's important enough that we've devoted all of Chapter 24, "Network Security," to this topic.

As a summary, however, here are the most important areas that you need to ensure are properly locked down:

- *Every* connection to the Internet *must* be secured with a firewall, with packet filtering, or with Network Address Translation (NAT, also called *masquerading*, or Internet Connection Sharing), to prevent hackers from gaining direct access to your computers through Windows File Sharing and the Remote Procedure Calls system. Firewalls, filters and NAT are discussed in Chapters 8, 17, and 24.

- If you use wireless networking, you *must* use the Wired Equivalency Privacy (WEP) scheme to provide at least minimal security on your wireless network. WEP is discussed in Chapter 17.

- If you don't *completely* trust every user on every computer connected to your local area network, you should not use Simple File Sharing. Simple File Sharing is discussed in Chapters 16 and 17.

- If you share folders on your computer, you should carefully consider whether or not to allow remote users to write to those folders. Sharing and sharing security is discussed in Chapter 18.

PRINTER SECURITY

You can manage security for printers—both local printers and those shared over the network—just as you can manage security for shared files and folders. In most environments, this is not a significant issue, as an unwanted print user would have to make an appearance to come get his or her printed output; this usually serves as a deterrent to abuse. Still, printers could conceivably be subject to denial of service attacks, and in any case, when you have to pay for ink and paper consumed, you should have some say over who gets to use it. If you have a printer with expensive consumables and are worried that a child, parent, coworker, or neighbor might take advantage of it, you can lock it down.

You can configure Printer security from the printer's property page. The Security tab, shown in Figure 22.6, lists authorized users and groups. When a user or group is selected, the lower part of the dialog shows what activities the user or group may perform.

Figure 22.6
A printer's Security properties page lets you determine who can use and manage the printer.

You must be logged on as a Computer Administrator or Power User to change these settings. There are four permission categories listed:

- **Print**—If checked, the user or group may send documents to the printer, and may cancel, pause, or resume their own documents.
- **Manage Printers**—If checked, the user or group may change the printers settings such as the port and default attributes, and may also modify printer security.
- **Manage Documents**—If checked, the user or group may cancel, suspend, or resume documents submitted by *other* users.
- **Special Permissions**—Displayed, but not applicable for printers.

22

By default, the group Everyone is given Print permission. If you wish to strictly control access to your printers, you may wish to select Everyone in the user list and uncheck Print in the bottom pane. You may then click Add to enter specific users to be given permission to use the printer.

FTP AND WEB SITE SECURITY

If you run a Web server and/or FTP server on your computer, especially one that is publicly accessible, you *must* be vigilant about managing security in the folders offered by the server. Very bad things can happen if you don't:

- Hackers could install and execute their own software on your computer, gaining control of and ransacking it, and could then use it to attack other computers on the Internet.
- Your hard drive might become a repository used to store and transfer pornography or worse.

It is absolutely crucial that you place the folders containing your Web server files (by default, this is the \inetpub folder, if you're using Microsoft's Internet Information Services) on a disk formatted with NTFS. It's best if this folder is on a different drive or partition than the one containing Windows, and preferably one used for nothing else at all.

FTP servers have special considerations, as FTP can be used to load foreign software onto your computer, where it could conceivably be run from the Web server, all from a remote location. Therefore, if anonymous FTP access is enabled, you *must not* grant Write permissions to the FTP folders.

For greatest security, you should also verify that Web server folders that have script or execute permissions are not writeable by anyone other than Administrator. This makes it impossible to publish scripts to your Web site using FTP or FrontPage, but significantly decreases the chances that someone can insert and the execute their own software on your computer.

→ To find more information about securing IIS, **see** "Safety First: Web Server Security," **p. 554.**

HARDWARE SECURITY

So far in this chapter we've focused on securing your computer through software. However, there are several security measures you can take through hardware.

To be sure, if someone can gain physical access to your computer, there isn't much you can do to prevent them from breaking into it...NTFS security is great, but if your disks are removed and installed in a computer on which the thief has Administrator privileges, all files that aren't protected by the Encrypting File System can be read.

So, if security is a concern, you should encrypt files that contain sensitive information. You must also take steps to prevent a thief from breaking into your account, which would give him access to your files. With physical possession of the computer, a hacker can simply try one password after another in an attempt to guess the correct one. So, you must choose a good, complex password that is not easily guessed, which doesn't appear in the dictionary, and which isn't easy to reach through iterative testing of all possible password combinations; in other words, use a long password with uppercase letters, lowercase letters, numbers, and punctuation.

If a creative hacker can break into your computer's Administrator account, even encrypted files can be fair game if the local administrator has a recovery certificate. (This is why, on enterprise and domain networks, a recovery certificate is never installed on a computer unless it's actually need to recover an encrypted file.)

→ To learn more about the Encrypted File System and encrypted file recovery, **see** "The Encrypted File System," **p. 1036**.

What you can do, however, is slow them down and possibly thwart the less sophisticated thief. In this section, we'll cover some of the ways you can do this.

BIOS PASSWORDS

One way an intruder can circumvent file system security is to access to your hard drive through another operating system. Stripped down versions of Linux, for example, can be put on a single floppy disk along with tools for reading NTFS- and FAT-formatted disks. These are valuable emergency recovery tools, but in the wrong hands, they're like skeleton keys.

To help prevent an intruder from booting an alternate operating system, you can disable your computer's ability to boot from floppy and CD drives, using the system BIOS setup screens. However, you must also secure this BIOS configuration by defining a setup password, so that the BIOS settings can't easily be changed. Your computer or motherboard instruction manual will tell you how to set a BIOS setup password.

If you want to do this, remember three things:

- This may not be welcome in an enterprise environment. Your tech support people probably won't appreciate it. (On the other hand, they may have already set up a BIOS setup password to prevent *you* from making this sort of change.)

- If you lose the password, you'll have to perform a "CMOS reset" on your motherboard. It's best if you record the password somewhere secure so this isn't necessary.

- This won't stop a determined intruder from opening your computer case and resetting the BIOS's CMOS memory himself, so this security measure is not all that solid.

(Personally, I always configure my BIOS to boot only from the hard drive and never from floppy or CD, to prevent viruses or other unexpected software from firing up when I boot my computer. I don't bother with a BIOS password, as my computer isn't bolted to the floor and could easily be made off with and attacked at someone's leisure.)

22

NOTE

> Some BIOS/hard drive combinations support a feature called *Drive Lock*, which makes a drive inaccessible unless it is the boot drive (where the installed operating system can enforce access control), or unless you supply a password. With Drive Lock a drive can't be viewed by booting an alternate operating system from CD, floppy, or another hard drive, and can add considerable security.

SMARTCARDS AND BIOMETRIC DEVICES

Windows XP and Windows 2000 support Smart Cards for user authentication. A Smart Card is a piece of plastic the size of a credit card, with an embedded microcomputer/ memory chip. This chip can be used to store a user certificate or another encrypted identification scheme. A computer equipped for Smart Card authentication is much harder to break into, as logon requires the presence of the card (as well as a PIN number), not just a password. Such systems are immune to the "dictionary" attack of simply guessing passwords, as well as the more benign but still unsafe practice of users sharing their passwords with one another.

Microsoft includes built-in support for several supported smart card manufacturers with Windows XP. Other manufacturers may be supported through add-on drivers. Readers are available with USB, PCMCIA, and RS-232 interfaces. Smart Cards are used primarily in a domain environment, as the default system uses a public-key certificate as the authentication mechanism. Some manufacturers sell smart card authentication systems that can be used on standalone workstations, but Microsoft does not endorse these systems.

Windows XP also supports biometric devices, which validate a user's identity by measuring a physical attribute such as a fingerprint or a retinal pattern. While these devices are fun and interesting, in my opinion they are neither as secure nor as useful as smart cards. They're less secure because they have a significant false positive rate (that is, they can be fooled by someone with a similar biometric pattern), and worse, a significant false negative rate (they'll occasionally deny you access to your own account). They're less useful because they simply identify you; they don't provide additional information such as a public key certificate. Such additional information would have to be stored on the computer, where it could be attacked, and we're back to square one on security.

PARANOIA

As you've seen in this chapter, you can take quite a few steps to keep people out of your computer and to protect your data. But, it's often the simplest thing that trips up the best laid plans. You can change your password every day, but if you keep it stuck to your monitor on a Post-It note, it's not worth much.

If you're truly concerned about keeping your information secure, you have to venture into an area of security I call "paranoia," where you take pains to cover up a few of the very small holes in Windows best security features. They're small, but they're still holes.

HIBERNATION FILE AND PAGING FILE SECURITY ISSUES

The Encrypted File System keeps your data encoded while it's on the hard disk, but it has to be converted back to cleartext (that is, its normal readable form) when you want to use it. The problem is, there are several ways that this data can get written to disk in plain form:

- The data is decoded in memory. However, Windows frequently copies data from memory to its *paging file*. If the memory copied to the paging file holds the unencrypted data from your encrypted file, and if the computer is shut off before this region of the paging file gets overwritten with other data, a clear copy of the encrypted file could be snooped out.

- If you put your computer into hibernation mode, all memory is written to a file called the hibernation file. Again, cleartext data from your encrypted file could be stored there.

- If you edit an encrypted file with a word processor, the word processor has to work with cleartext data, and it may write one or more temporary files containing this data. If the word processor or Windows crashes, the temporary files may be left on your hard disk indefinitely. Even after closing the word processor properly, in which case these files are deleted, the part of the disk that contained these files will still contain the cleartext data.

It sounds picky, but if your data is truly sensitive, this is a grim situation. There are several things you can do to help with the problem:

- Configure your word processor to store all temporary files in a particular folder, and be sure to mark that folder for encryption so that the temporary files will be encrypted too. If you use Word, be sure that "Autorecovery" files will be stored in an encrypted folder too. This way, whether the word processor shuts down normally or not, the temporary data on disk will be encrypted.

- Enable the Local Computer Policy or Group Policy item Shutdown: Clear Virtual Memory Pagefile, so that when Windows shuts down normally, it will zero out all information in the page file. This is discussed earlier in the chapter under "Security Options Settings."

- While you're at it, if you use the Offline Files feature to keep copies of sensitive files from other computers on your network, be sure that the offline file cache is encrypted. This can be set by policy under `Configuration\Windows Settings\Administrative Templates\Windows Components\System\Network\Offline Files`, with the policy Encrypt the Offline Files Cache. It can also be set in Windows Explorer under Tools, Folder Options, on the Offline Files tab.

- By default, Windows XP encrypts files with a 256-bit Advanced Encryption Standard (AES) key. If you want even stronger encryption, you can enable Triple DES (3DES) by editing Group Policy or Local Computer Policy. Under `\Computer Configuration\Windows Settings\Security Settings\Local Policies\Security Options`, enable policy System Cryptography: Use FIPS Compliant Algorithms for Encryption. (This setting will only apply to newly encrypted files and folders.)

- Do not use hibernation or suspend mode when you have been working with encrypted files. Instead, shut Windows down completely.

These measures will ensure that if your computer is stolen, there won't be cleartext data left on your disk for someone to extract.

You should also do what you can to avoid giving an intruder any information about what account names are available on the computer. It's hard to guess passwords, but it's harder to guess both user account names and passwords.

To this end, you should make the following settings:

- Disable the Welcome screen, so that user names are not displayed. You can do this from the User Accounts control panel, under Change the Way Users Log On or Log Off.
- Change the name of the Administrator account, as this is a prime target for hacking. You can rename the account from the Computer Management Administrative Tool, under Local Users and Groups.
- In Local Computer Policy (described earlier in the chapter), under `Computer Configuration\Windows Settings\Security Settings\Local Policies\ Security Options`, enable the policy Interactive logon: Do Not Display Last User Name so that the logon dialog will not show the name of the last user who logged on.

SYSTEM STARTUP KEY

You can configure Windows to require a password at boot time for further protection against abuse by thieves and intruders, through a security feature called *syskey*. By default, syskey is enabled on Windows XP and further encrypts the Windows password database (which stores only hashed passwords to begin with), so that cracking techniques can't be used to attempt to obtain account passwords. A startup key is required to access the encrypted password file.

You can ask syskey to store the startup key locally (that is, in the registry), to require a password to be typed on the keyboard, or to require a password stored on a floppy disk in order for Windows to boot. By default, the password is stored locally, so Windows boots without any additional password. To change this setting, log on as a Computer Administrator, select Start, Run and type `syskey`. Click Update to display the Startup Key dialog box shown in Figure 22.7.

This section lists the Local Computer Policy settings available for Windows XP Professional *without* domain membership; these settings can be used to enforce security and configuration by restricting access to configuration tools, and by overriding default values and settings made through the control panel and other normal means. Additional policy items are available when Group Policy is configured on a Windows 2000 Server domain controller, and more items still on a Windows Server 2003 domain controller.

Figure 22.7
The syskey program lets you specify a password that must be entered in order to boot Windows.

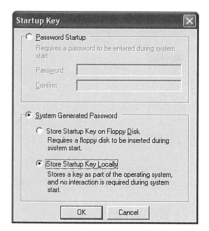

NOTE

These policy configuration settings are not available on XP Home Edition.

The items listed in Listing 22.1 follow the hierarchical scheme used by the Local Computer Policy editor. Some of these items are discussed earlier in the chapter under "Securing Windows XP with Policy." This section lists all of the items. We suggest that you scan this list to get a feel for the scope of control that the policy mechanism offers. Sections marked with an asterisk (*) are available only in Security Templates.

NOTE

Online help can provide additional information about each setting. To obtain help, press F1 while using the Local Computer Policy editor. In the contents pane, open Security Settings, Concepts, Security Setting Descriptions, and then locate a particular policy item. Some items have an Explain tab that provides a detailed description.

LISTING 22.1   LOCAL COMPUTER POLICY AND SECURITY TEMPLATE SETTINGS ON WINDOWS XP PROFESSIONAL

```
Computer Configuration
   Windows Settings
      Scripts (Startup / Shutdown)
         Startup
         Shutdown
      Security Settings
         Account Policies
            Password Policy
               Enforce password history
               Maximum password age
               Minimum password age
               Minimum password length
               Password must meet complexity requirements
```

continues

LISTING 22.1 **CONTINUED**

```
            Store password using reversible encryption for all users in the
                domain
    Account Lockout Policy
        Account lockout duration
        Account lockout threshold
        Reset account lockout counter after
    Kerberos Policy *
        Enforce user logon restrictions
        Maximum lifetime for service ticket
        Maximum lifetime for user ticket
        Maximum lifetime for user ticket renewal
        Maximum tolerance for computer clock synchronization
Local Policies
    Audit Policy
        Audit account logon events
        Audit account management
        Audit directory service access
        Audit logon events
        Audit object access
        Audit policy change
        Audit privilege use
        Audit process tracking
        Audit system events
    User Rights Assignment
        Access this computer from the network
        Act as part of the operating system
        Add workstations to domain
        Adjust memory quotas for a process
        Allow logon through Terminal Services
        Back up files and directories
        Bypass traverse checking
        Change the system time
        Create a pagefile
        Create a token object
        Create permanent shared objects
        Debug programs
        Deny access to this computer from the network
        Deny logon as a batch job
        Deny logon as a service
        Deny logon locally
        Deny logon through Terminal Services
        Enable computer and user accounts to be trusted for delegation
        Force shutdown from a remote system
        Generate security audits
        Increase scheduling priority
        Load and unload device drivers
        Lock pages in memory
        Log on as a batch job
        Log on as a service
        Log on locally
        Manage auditing and security log
        Modify firmware environment values
        Perform volume maintenance tasks
        Profile single process
        Profile system performance
```

LISTING 22.1 CONTINUED

22

```
        Remove computer from docking station
        Replace a process level token
        Restore files and directories
        Shut down the system
        Synchronize directory service data
        Take ownership of files or other objects
    Security Options
        Accounts: Administrator account status
        Accounts: Guest account status
        Accounts: Limit local account use of blank passwords to console
                logon only
        Accounts: Rename administrator account
        Accounts: Rename guest account
        Audit: Audit the access of global system objects
        Audit: Audit the use of Backup and Restore privilege
        Audit: Shut down system immediately if unable to log security
                audits
        Devices: Allow undock without having to log on
        Devices: Allowed to format and eject removable media
        Devices: Prevent users from installing printer drivers
        Devices: Restrict CD-ROM access to locally logged-on user only
        Devices: Restrict floppy access to locally logged-on user only
        Devices: Unsigned driver installation behavior
        Domain controller: Allow server operators to schedule tasks
        Domain controller: LDAP server signing requirements
        Domain controller: Refuse machine account password changes
        Domain member: Digitally encrypt or sign secure channel data
                (always)
        Domain member: Digitally encrypt secure channel data (when
                possible)
        Domain member: Digitally sign secure channel data (when
                possible)
        Domain member: Disable machine account password changes
        Domain member: Maximum machine account password age
        Domain member: Require strong (Windows 2000 or later) session
                key
        Interactive logon: Do not display last user name
        Interactive logon: Do not require CTRL+ALT+DEL
        Interactive logon: Message text for users attempting to log on
        Interactive logon: Message title for users attempting to log on
        Interactive logon: Number of previous logons to cache (in case
                domain controller is not available)
        Interactive logon: Prompt user to change password before
                expiration
        Interactive logon: Require Domain Controller authentication to
                unlock workstation
        Interactive logon: Smart card removal behavior
        Microsoft network client: Digitally sign communications (always)
        Microsoft network client: Digitally sign communications (if
                server agrees)
        Microsoft network client: Send unencrypted password to
                third-party SMB servers
        Microsoft network server: Amount of idle time required before
                suspending session
```

continues

LISTING 22.1 CONTINUED

```
            Microsoft network server: Digitally sign communications (always)
            Microsoft network server: Digitally sign communications (if
                  client agrees)
            Microsoft network server: Disconnect clients when logon hours
                  expire
            Network access: Allow anonymous SID/Name translation
            Network access: Do not allow anonymous enumeration of SAM
                  accounts
            Network access: Do not allow anonymous enumeration of SAM
                  accounts and shares
            Network access: Do not allow storage of credentials or .NET
                  Passports for network authentication
            Network access: Let Everyone permissions apply to anonymous
                  users
            Network access: Named Pipes that can be accessed anonymously
            Network access: Remotely accessible registry paths
            Network access: Shares that can be accessed anonymously
            Network access: Sharing and security model for local accounts
            Network security: Do not store LAN Manager hash value on
                  next password change
            Network security: Force logoff when logon hours expire
            Network security: LAN Manager authentication level
            Network security: LDAP client signing requirements
            Network security: Minimum session security for NTLM SSP based
                  (including secure RPC) clients
            Network security: Minimum session security for NTLM SSP based
                  (including secure RPC) servers
            Recovery console: Allow automatic administrative logon
            Recovery console: Allow floppy copy and access to all drives
                  and all folders
            Shutdown: Allow system to be shut down without having to log on
            Shutdown: Clear virtual memory pagefile
            System cryptography: Use FIPS compliant algorithms for
                  encryption, hashing, and signing
            System objects: Default owner for objects created by members of
                  the Administrators group
            System objects: Require case insensitivity for non-Windows
                  subsystems
            System objects: Strengthen default permissions of internal
                  system objects (e.g. Symbolic Links)
      Public Key Policies
         Encrypting File System
      Software Restriction Policies
         Enforcement
         Designated File Types
         Trusted Publishers
         Additional Rules
            Administrator  (default rule granting Administrator unrestricted
                  rights)
         Security Levels
            Disallowed
            Unrestricted
      IP Security Policies on Local Computer
         Client (Respond Only)
         Secure Server (Require Security)
         Server (Request Security)
```

LISTING 22.1 CONTINUED

```
Administrative Templates
    Windows Components
        NetMeeting
            Disable remote Desktop Sharing
        Internet Explorer
            Security Zones: Use only machine settings
            Security Zones: Do not allow users to change policies
            Security Zones: Do not allow users to add/delete sites
            Make proxy settings per-machine (rather than per-user)
            Disable Automatic Install of Internet Explorer components
            Disable Periodic Check for Internet Explorer software updates
            Disable software update shell notifications on program launch
            Disable showing the splash screen
        Task Scheduler
            Hide Property Pages
            Prevent Task Run or End
            Prohibit Drag-and-Drop
            Prohibit New Task Creation
            Prohibit Task Deletion
            Remove Advanced Menu
            Prohibit Browse
        Terminal Services
            Client/Server data redirection
                Do not allow clipboard redirection
                Do not allow smart card device redirection
                Allow audio redirection
                Do not allow COM port redirection
                Do not allow client printer redirection
                Do not allow LPT port redirection
                Do not allow drive redirection
                Do not set default client printer to be default printer in a
                    session
            Encryption and Security
                Always prompt client for password upon connection
                Set client connection encryption level
            Licensing
                Prevent License Upgrade
            Session Directory
                Session Directory Active
                Session Directory Server
                Session Directory Cluster Name
            Sessions
                Set time limit for disconnected sessions
                Set time limit for active sessions
                Set time limit for idle sessions
                Allow reconnection from original client only
                Terminate session when time limits are reached
            Temporary Folders
                Do not use temp folders per session
                Do not delete temp folder upon exit
            Terminal Services
                Client/Server data redirection
                Encryption and Security
                Licensing
```

continues

22

LISTING 22.1 CONTINUED

```
          Temporary folders
          Session Directory
          Sessions
          Keep-Alive Messages
          Limit users to one remote session
          Enforce Removal of Remote Desktop Wallpaper
          Limit number of connections
          Limit maximum color depth
          Do not allow new client connections
          Do not allow local administrators to customize permissions
          Remove Windows Security item from Start menu
          Remove Disconnect item from Shut Down dialog
          Set path for TS Roaming Profiles
          TS User Home Directory
          Remote control settings
        Start a program on connection
    Windows Installer
        Disable Windows Installer
        Always install with elevated privileges
        Prohibit rollback
        Remove browse dialog box for new source
        Prohibit patching
        Disable IE security prompt for Windows Installer scripts
        Enable user control over installs
        Enable user to browse for source while elevated
        Enable user to use media source while elevated
        Enable user to patch elevated products
        Allow admin to install from Terminal Services session
        Cache transforms in secure location on workstation
        Logging
        Prohibit User Installs
        Turn off creation of System Restore Checkpoints
    Windows Messenger
        Do not allow Windows Messenger to be run
        Do not automatically start Windows Messenger initially
System
    Disk Quotas
        Enable disk quotas
        Enforce disk quota limit
        Default quota limit and warning level
        Log event when quota limit exceeded
        Log event when quota warning level exceeded
        Apply policy to removable media
    Error Reporting
        Display Error Notification
        Report Errors
        Advanced Error Reporting settings
            Default application reporting settings
            List of applications to always report errors for
            List of applications to never report errors for
            Report operating system errors
            Report unplanned shutdown events
    Group Policy
        Turn off background refresh of Group Policy
        Group Policy refresh interval for computers
        Group Policy refresh interval for domain controllers
```

LISTING 22.1   CONTINUED

```
        User Group Policy loopback processing mode
        Group Policy slow link detection
        Turn off Resultant Set of Policy logging
        Remove users ability to invoke machine policy refresh
        Disallow Interactive Users from generating Resultant Set of Policy
            data
        Registry policy processing
        Internet Explorer Maintenance policy processing
        Software Installation policy processing
        Folder Redirection policy processing
        Scripts policy processing
        Security policy processing
        IP Security policy processing
        EFS recovery policy processing
        Disk Quota policy processing
    Logon
        Don't display the Getting Started welcome screen at logon
        Always use classic logon
        Run these programs at user logon
        Do not process the run once list
        Do not process the legacy run list
        Always wait for the network at computer startup and logon
    Net Logon
        DC Locator DNS Records
        Expected dial-up delay on logon
        Site Name
        Negative DC Discovery Cache Setting
        Initial DC Discovery Retry Setting for Background Callers
        Maximum DC Discovery Retry Interval Setting for Background Callers
        Final DC Discovery Retry Setting for Background Callers
        Positive Periodic DC Cache Refresh for Background Callers
        Positive Periodic DC Cache Refresh for Non-Background Callers
        Scavenge Interval
        Contact PDC on logon failure
        D Locator DNS Records
            Dynamic Registration of the DC Locator DNS Records
            DC Locator DNS records not registered by the DCs
            Refresh Interval of the DC Locator DNS Records
            Weight Set in the DC Locator DNS SRV Records
            Priority Set in the DC Locator DNS SRV Records
            TTL Set in the DC Locator DNS Records
            Automated Site Coverage by the DC Locator DNS SRV Records
            Sites Covered by the DC Locator DNS SRV Records
            Sites Covered by the GC Locator DNS SRV Records
            Sites Covered by the Application Directory Partition Locator
                DNS SRV Records
            Location of the DCs hosting a domain with single label DNS name
    Remote Assistance
        Solicited Remote Assistance
        Offer Remote Assistance
    Remote Procedure Call
        RPC Troubleshooting State Information
        Propagation of extended error information
    Scripts
```

22

continues

LISTING 22.1 CONTINUED

```
            Run logon scripts synchronously
            Run startup scripts asynchronously
            Run startup scripts visible
            Run shutdown scripts visible
            Maximum wait time for Group Policy scripts
        System Restore
            Turn off System Restore
            Turn off Configuration
        User Profiles
            Do not check for user ownership of Roaming Profile Folders
            Delete cached copies of roaming profiles
            Do not detect slow network connections
            Slow network connection timeout for user profiles
            Wait for remote user profile
            Prompt user when slow link is detected
            Timeout for dialog boxes
            Log users off when roaming profile fails
            Maximum retries to unload and update user profile
            Add the Administrators security group to roaming user profiles
            Prevent Roaming Profile changes from propagating to the server
            Only allow local user profiles
        Windows File Protection
            Set Windows File Protection scanning
            Hide the file scan progress window
            Limit Windows File Protection cache size
            Specify Windows File Protection cache location
        Windows Time Service
            Global Configuration Settings
            Time Providers
                Enable Windows NTP Client
                Configure Windows NTP Client
                Enable Windows NTP Server
    Network
        DNS Client
            Primary DNS Suffix
            Dynamic Update
            DNS Suffix Search List
            Primary DNS Suffix Devolution
            Register PTR Records
            Registration Refresh Interval
            Replace Addresses In Conflicts
            DNS Servers
            Connection-Specific DNS Suffix
            Register DNS records with connection-specific DNS suffix
            TTL Set in the A and PTR records
            Update Security Level
            Update Top Level Domain Zones
        Network Connections
            Prohibit use of Internet Connection Sharing on your DNS domain
                network
            Prohibit use of Internet Connection Firewall on your DNS domain
                network
            Prohibit installation and configuration of Network Bridge on your
                DNS domain network
            IEEE 802.1x Certificate Authority for Machine Authentication
```

LISTING 22.1 CONTINUED

```
Offline Files
    Allow or Disallow use of the Offline Files feature
    Prohibit user configuration of Offline Files
    Synchronize all offline files when logging on
    Synchronize all offline files before logging off
    Synchronize offline files before suspend
    Default cache size
    Action on server disconnect
    Non-default server disconnect actions
    Remove 'Make Available Offline'
    Prevent use of Offline Files folder
    Files not cached
    Administratively assigned offline files
    Turn off reminder balloons
    Reminder balloon frequency
    Initial reminder balloon lifetime
    Reminder balloon lifetime
    At logoff, delete local copy of user's offline files
    Event logging level
    Subfolders always available offline
    Encrypt the Offline Files cache
    Prohibit 'Make Available Offline' for these file and folders
    Configure Slow link speed
QoS Packet Scheduler
    Limit reservable bandwidth
    Limit outstanding packets
    Set timer resolution
    DSCP value of conforming packets
        Best effort service type
        Controlled load service type
        Guaranteed service type
        Network control service type
        Qualitative service type
    DSCP value of non-conforming packets
        Best effort service type
        Controlled load service type
        Guaranteed service type
        Network control service type
        Qualitative service type
    Layer-2 priority value
        Non-conforming packets
        Best effort service type
        Controlled load service type
        Guaranteed service type
        Network control service type
        Qualitative service type
SNMP
    Communities
    Permitted Managers
    Traps for Public community
Printers
    Allow printers to be published
    Allow pruning of published printers
    Automatically publish new printers in Active Directory
```

continues

LISTING 22.1   CONTINUED

```
        Check published state
        Computer location
        Custom support URL in the Printers folder's left pane
        Directory pruning interval
        Directory pruning priority
        Directory pruning retry
        Disallow installation of printers using kernel-mode drivers
        Log directory pruning retry events
        Pre-populate printer search location text
        Printer browsing
        Prune printers that are not automatically republished
        Web-based printing

User Configuration
   Software Settings
   Windows Settings
      Scripts (Logon/Logoff)
         Logon
         Logoff
      Security Settings
         Public Key Policies
            Enterprise Trust
      Internet Explorer Maintenance
         Browser User Interface
            Browser User Interface
            Connection
            URLs
            Security
            Programs
         Connection
            Connection Settings
            Automatic Browser Configuration
            Proxy Settings
            User Agent String
         Programs
            Programs
         Properties
            Programs
         Security
            Security Zones and Content Ratings
            Authenticode Settings
         URLs
            Favorites and Links
            Important URLs
   Administrative Templates
      Windows Components
         NetMeeting
            Enable Automatic Configuration
            Disable Directory services
            Prevent adding Directory servers
            Prevent viewing Web directory
            Set the intranet support Web page
            Set Call Security options
            Prevent changing Call placement method
            Prevent automatic acceptance of Calls
            Prevent sending files
```

LISTING 22.1 **CONTINUED**

```
        Prevent receiving files
        Limit the size of sent files
        Disable Chat
        Disable NetMeeting 2.x Whiteboard
        Disable Whiteboard
    Application Sharing
        Disable application Sharing
        Prevent Sharing
        Prevent Desktop Sharing
        Prevent Sharing Command Prompts
        Prevent Sharing Explorer windows
        Prevent Control
        Prevent Application Sharing in true color
    Audio & Video
        Limit the bandwidth of Audio and Video
        Disable Audio
        Disable full duplex Audio
        Prevent changing DirectSound Audio setting
        Prevent sending Video
        Prevent receiving Video
    Options Page
        Hide the General page
        Disable the Advanced Calling button
        Hide the Security page
        Hide the Audio page
        Hide the Video page
Internet Explorer
    Search: Disable Search Customization
    Search: Disable Find Files via F3 within the browser
    Disable external branding of Internet Explorer
    Disable importing and exporting of favorites
    Disable changing Advanced page settings
    Disable changing home page settings
    Use Automatic Detection for dial-up connections
    Disable caching of Auto-Proxy scripts
    Display error message on proxy script download failure
    Disable changing Temporary Internet files settings
    Disable changing history settings
    Disable changing color settings
    Disable changing link color settings
    Disable changing font settings
    Disable changing language settings
    Disable changing accessibility settings
    Disable Internet Connection wizard
    Disable changing connection settings
    Disable changing proxy settings
    Disable changing Automatic Configuration settings
    Disable changing ratings settings
    Disable changing certificate settings
    Disable changing Profile Assistant settings
    Disable AutoComplete for forms
    Do not allow AutoComplete to save passwords
    Disable changing Messaging settings
    Disable changing Calendar and Contact settings
```

continues

LISTING 22.1 CONTINUED

```
Disable the Reset Web Settings feature
Disable changing default browser check
Identity Manager: Prevent users from using Identities
Configure Outlook Express
Configure Media Explorer Bar
Internet Control Panel
    Disable the General page
    Disable the Security page
    Disable the Content page
    Disable the Connections page
    Disable the Programs page
    Disable the Privacy page
    Disable the Advanced page
Offline Pages
    Disable adding channels
    Disable removing channels
    Disable adding schedules for offline pages
    Disable editing schedules for offline pages
    Disable removing schedules for offline pages
    Disable offline page hit logging
    Disable all scheduled offline pages
    Disable channel user interface completely
    Disable downloading of site subscription content
    Disable editing and creating of schedule groups
    Subscription Limits
Browser menus
    File menu: Disable Save As... menu option
    File menu: Disable New menu option
    File menu: Disable Open menu option
    File menu: Disable Save As Web Page Complete
    File menu: Disable closing the browser and Explorer windows
    View menu: Disable Source menu option
    View menu: Disable Full Screen menu option
    Hide Favorites menu
    Tools menu: Disable Internet Options... menu option
    Help menu: Remove 'Tip of the Day' menu option
    Help menu: Remove 'For Netscape Users' menu option
    Help menu: Remove 'Send Feedback' menu option
    Disable Context menu
    Disable Open in New Window menu option
    Disable Save this program to disk option
Toolbars
    Disable customizing browser toolbar buttons
    Disable customizing browser toolbars
    Configure Toolbar Buttons
Persistence Behavior
    File size limits for Local Machine zone
    File size limits for Intranet zone
    File size limits for Trusted Sites zone
    File size limits for Internet zone
    File size limits for Restricted Sites zone
Administrator Approved Controls
    Media Player
    Menu Controls
    Microsoft Agent
    Microsoft Chat
```

LISTING 22.1   CONTINUED

```
             Microsoft Survey Control
             Shockwave Flash
             NetShow File Transfer Control
             DHTML Edit Control
             Microsoft Scriptlet Component
             Carpoint
             Investor
             MSNBC
     Windows Explorer
         Turn on Classic Shell
         Removes the Folder Options menu item from the Tools menu
         Remove File menu from Windows Explorer
         Remove "Map Network Drive" and "Disconnect Network Drive"
         Remove Search button from Windows Explorer
         Remove Windows Explorer's default context menu
         Hides the Manage item on the Windows Explorer context menu
         Allow only per user or approved shell extensions
         Do not track Shell shortcuts during roaming
         Hide these specified drives in My Computer
         Prevent access to drives from My Computer
         Remove Hardware tab
         Remove DFS tab
         Remove Security tab
         Remove UI to change menu animation setting
         Remove UI to change keyboard navigation indicator setting
         No "Computers Near Me" in My Network Places
         No "Entire Network" in My Network Places
         Maximum number of recent documents
         Do not request alternate credentials
         Request credentials for network installations
         Remove CD Burning features
         Do not move deleted files to the Recycle Bin
         Display confirmation dialog when deleting files
         Maximum allowed Recycle Bin size
         Remove Shared Documents from My Computer
         Turn off caching of thumbnail pictures
         Common Open File Dialog
             Items displayed in Places Bar
             Hide the common dialog places bar
             Hide the common dialog back button
             Hide the dropdown list of recent files
     Microsoft Management Console
         Restrict the user from entering author mode
         Restrict users to the explicitly permitted list of snap-ins
         Restricted/Permitted snap-ins
             Active Directory Users and Computers
             Active Directory Domains and Trusts
             Active Directory Sites and Services
             ADSI Edit
             ActiveX Control
             Certificates
             Component Services
             Computer Management
             Device Manager
```

continues

22

Listing 22.1 Continued

```
            Disk Management
            Disk Defragmenter
            Distributed File System
            Event Viewer
            FAX Service
            FrontPage Server Extensions
            Indexing Service
            Internet Authentication Service (IAS)
            Internet Information Services
            IP Security
            IP Security Policy Management
            IP Security Monitor
            Link to Web Address
            Local Users and Groups
            Performance Logs and Alerts
            QoS Admission Control
            Remote Desktops
            Removable Storage Management
            Routing and Remote Access
            Security Configuration and Analysis
            Security Templates
            Services
            Shared Folders
            System Information
            Telephony
            Terminal Services Configuration
            WMI Control
        Extension snap-ins
            AppleTalk Routing
            Certification Authority
            Connection Sharing (NAT)
            DCOM Configuration Extension
            Device Manager
            DHCP Relay Management
            Event Viewer
            Extended View (Web View)
            IAS Logging
            IGMP Routing
            IP Routing
            IPX RIP Routing
            IPX Routing
            IPX SAP Routing
            Logical and Mapped Drives
            OSPF Routing
            Public Key Policies
            RAS Dialin - User Node
            Remote Access
            Removable Storage
            RIP Routing
            Routing
            Shared Folders Ext
            Send Console Message
            Service Dependencies
            SMTP Protocol
            SNMP
            System Properties
```

LISTING 22.1 CONTINUED

```
        Group Policy
            Group Policy snap-in
            Group Policy tab for Active Directory Tools
            Resultant Set of Policy snap-in
            Group Policy snap-in extensions
                Administrative Templates (Computers)
                Administrative Templates (Users)
                Folder Redirection
                Internet Explorer Maintenance
                Remote Installation Services
                Scripts (Logon/Logoff)
                Scripts (Startup/Shutdown)
                Security Settings
                Software Installation (Computers)
                Software Installation (Users)
            Resultant Set of Policy snap-in extensions
                Administrative Templates (Computers)
                Administrative Templates (Users)
                Folder Redirection
                Internet Explorer Maintenance
                Scripts (Logon/Logoff)
                Scripts (Startup/Shutdown)
                Security Settings
                Software Installation (Computers)
                Software Installation (Users)
    Task Scheduler
        Hide Property Pages
        Prevent Task Run or End
        Prohibit Drag-and-Drop
        Prohibit New Task Creation
        Prohibit Task Deletion
        Remove Advanced Menu
        Prohibit Browse
    Terminal Services
        Start a program on connection
        Remote control settings
        Sessions
            Set time limit for disconnected sessions
            Set time limit for active sessions
            Set time limit for idle sessions
            Allow reconnection from original client only
            Terminate session when time limits are reached
    Windows Installer
        Always install with elevated privileges
        Search order
        Prohibit rollback
        Prevent removable media source for any install
    Windows Messenger
        Do not allow Windows Messenger to be run
        Do not automatically start Windows Messenger initially
    Windows Update
        Remove access to use all Windows Update features
    Windows Media Player
        Networking
```

continues

22

LISTING 22.1 CONTINUED

```
            Hide Network Tab
            Streaming Media Protocols
            Configure HTTP Proxy
            Configure MMS Proxy
            Configure Network Buffering
        Playback
            Prevent Codec Download
        User Interface
            Set and Lock Skin
            Do Not Show Anchor
    Start Menu and Taskbar
        Remove user's folders from the Start Menu
        Remove links and access to Windows Update
        Remove common program groups from Start Menu
        Remove My Documents icon from Start Menu
        Remove Documents menu from Start Menu
        Remove programs on Settings menu
        Remove Network Connections from Start Menu
        Remove Favorites menu from Start Menu
        Remove Search menu from Start Menu
        Remove Help menu from Start Menu
        Remove Run menu from Start Menu
        Remove My Pictures icon from Start Menu
        Remove My Music icon from Start Menu
        Remove My Network Places icon from Start Menu
        Add Logoff to the Start Menu
        Remove Logoff on the Start Menu
        Remove and prevent access to the Shut Down command
        Remove Drag-and-drop context menus on the Start Menu
        Prevent changes to Taskbar and Start Menu Settings
        Remove access to the context menus for the taskbar
        Do not keep history of recently opened documents
        Clear history of recently opened documents on exit
        Turn off personalized menus
        Turn off user tracking
        Add "Run in Separate Memory Space" check box to Run dialog box
        Do not use the search-based method when resolving shell shortcuts
        Do not use the tracking-based method when resolving shell shortcuts
        Gray unavailable Windows Installer programs Start Menu shortcuts
        Prevent grouping of taskbar items
        Turn off notification area cleanup
        Lock the Taskbar
        Force classic Start Menu
        Remove Balloon Tips on Start Menu items
        Remove pinned programs list from the Start Menu
        Remove frequent programs list from the Start Menu
        Remove All Programs list from the Start menu
        Remove and disable the Turn Off Computer button
        Remove the "Undock PC" button from the Start Menu
        Remove user name from Start Menu
        Remove Clock from the system notification area
        Hide the notification area
        Do not display any custom toolbars in the taskbar
    Desktop
        Hide and disable all items on the desktop
```

LISTING 22.1   CONTINUED

```
Remove My Documents icon on the desktop
Remove My Computer icon on the desktop
Remove Recycle Bin icon from desktop
Remove Properties from the My Documents context menu
Remove Properties from the My Computer context menu
Remove Properties from the Recycle Bin context menu
Hide My Network Places icon on desktop
Hide Internet Explorer icon on desktop
Do not add shares of recently opened documents to My Network Places
Prohibit user from changing My Documents path
Prevent adding, dragging, dropping and closing the Taskbar's toolbars
Prohibit adjusting desktop toolbars
Don't save settings at exit
Remove the Desktop Cleanup Wizard
Active Desktop
   Enable Active Desktop
   Disable Active Desktop
   Disable all items
   Prohibit changes
   Prohibit adding items
   Prohibit deleting items
   Prohibit editing items
   Prohibit closing items
   Add/Delete items
   Active Desktop Wallpaper
   Allow only bitmapped wallpaper
Active Directory
   Maximum size of Active Directory searches
   Enable filter in Find dialog box
   Hide Active Directory folder
Control Panel
   Add/Remove Programs
   Prohibit access to the Control Panel
   Hide specified Control Panel applets
   Show only specified Control Panel applets
   Force classic Control Panel Style
   Add/Remove Programs
      Remove Add/Remove Programs Programs
      Hide Change or Remove Programs page
      Hide Add New Programs page
      Hide Add/Remove Windows Components page
      Hide the "Add a program from CD-ROM or floppy disk" option
      Hide the "Add programs from Microsoft" option
      Hide the "Add programs from your network" option
      Go directly to Components Wizard
      Remove Support Information
      Specify default category for Add New Programs
   Display
      Remove Display in Control Panel
      Hide Desktop tab
      Prevent changing wallpaper
      Hide Appearance and Themes tab
      Hide Settings tab
      Hide Screen Saver tab
```

continues

22

Listing 22.1   Continued

```
        Screen Saver
        Screen Saver executable name
        Password protect the screen saver
        Screen Saver timeout
        Desktop Themes
            Remove Theme option
            Prevent selection of windows and buttons styles
            Prohibit selection of font size
            Prohibit Theme color selection
            Load a specific visual style file or force Windows Classic
    Printers
        Browse a common web site to find printers
        Browse the network to find printers
        Default Active Directory path when searching for printers
        Point and Print Restrictions
        Prevent addition of printers
        Prevent deletion of printers
    Regional and Language Options
        Restrict selection of Windows menus and dialogs language
Shared Folders
    Allow shared folders to be published
    Allow DFS roots to be published
Network
    Offline Files
        Prohibit user configuration of Offline Files
        Synchronize all offline files when logging on
        Synchronize all offline files before logging off
        Synchronize offline files before suspend
        Action on server disconnect
        Non-default server disconnect actions
        Remove 'Make Available Offline'
        Prevent use of Offline Files folder
        Administratively assigned offline files
        Turn off reminder balloons
        Reminder balloon frequency
        Initial reminder balloon lifetime
        Reminder balloon lifetime
        Event logging level
        Prohibit 'Make Available Offline' for these file and folders
        Do not automatically make redirected folders available offline
    Network Connections
        Ability to rename LAN connections or remote access connections
                available to all users
        Prohibit access to properties of components of a LAN connection
        Prohibit access to properties of components of a remote access
                connection
        Prohibit TCP/IP advanced configuration
        Prohibit access to the Advanced Settings item on the Advanced menu
        Prohibit adding and removing components for a LAN or remote access
                connection
        Prohibit access to properties of a LAN connection
        Prohibit Enabling/Disabling components of a LAN connection
        Ability to change properties of an all user remote access
                connection
        Prohibit changing properties of a private remote access connection
        Prohibit deletion of remote access connections
```

LISTING 22.1   CONTINUED

```
            Ability to delete all user remote access connections
            Prohibit connecting and disconnecting a remote access connection
            Ability to Enable/Disable a LAN connection
            Prohibit access to the New Connection Wizard
            Ability to rename LAN connections
            Ability to rename all user remote access connections
            Prohibit renaming private remote access connections
            Prohibit access to the Dial-up Preferences item on the Advanced
                  menu
            Prohibit viewing of status for an active connection
            Enable Windows 2000 Network Connections settings for Administrators
      System
         Don't display the Getting Started welcome screen at logon
         Century interpretation for Year 2000
         Configure driver search locations
         Code signing for device drivers
         Custom user interface
         Prevent access to the command prompt
         Prevent access to registry editing tools
         Run only allowed Windows applications
         Don't run specified Windows applications
         Turn off Autoplay
         Restrict these programs from being launched from Help
         Download missing COM components
         Windows Automatic Updates
         User Profiles
            Connect home directory to root of the share
            Limit profile size
            Exclude directories in roaming profile
         Scripts
            Run logon scripts synchronously
            Run legacy logon scripts hidden
            Run logon scripts visible
            Run logoff scripts visible
         Ctrl+Alt+Del Options
            Remove Task Manager
            Remove Lock Computer
            Remove Change Password
            Remove Logoff
         Logon
            Run these programs at user logon
            Do not process the run once list
            Do not process the legacy run list
         Group Policy
            Group Policy refresh interval for users
            Group Policy slow link detection
            Group Policy domain controller selection
            Create new Group Policy object links disabled by default
            Default name for new Group Policy objects
            Enforce Show Policies Only
            Turn off automatic update of ADM files
            Disallow Interactive Users from generating Resultant Set of Policy
                  data
         Power Management
            Prompt for password on resume from hibernate / suspend
```

CHAPTER 23

MANAGING FILE SECURITY

In this chapter

FILE SYSTEM (NTFS) SECURITY

Windows XP—like its Windows 2000 and Windows NT ancestors—can take advantage of the NT File System, or *NTFS*. Windows XP can also use FAT (File Allocation Table) or FAT32, but with the FAT formats, you lose the user-level file and folder security. With FAT formats, you also lose the ability to audit file and folder access, and you won't be able to utilize NTFS-based file encryption and compression—all of which we'll discuss in this chapter. On large drives, FAT has a greater percentage of slack (the wasted space due to increasing cluster sizes for larger drives), so you'll have better drive space utilization on an NTFS drive.

In case you couldn't tell by the above paragraph, I'm really trying to drive (yeah, I know…lame pun) you toward selecting NTFS over FAT. Not only will NTFS present you with all of the benefits noted previously, but if you select to format your drives using FAT, you would have no reason to read the rest of this exciting chapter. If you're interested in securing your system at all, then you *must* use NTFS.

→ This chapter focuses primarily on the security-related aspects of NTFS. For more in-depth coverage of the differences between NTFS and FAT formatted drives, refer to Chapter 25, "Managing Your Hard Disks," beginning on **p. 995**.

At the most basic level, NTFS security specifies which users or groups have access to modify, list, read, execute, write, or change access controls applied to files or folders. At a somewhat more intermediate level, we add an additional layer of file and folder access auditing that can be performed only against objects stored on an NTFS volume. At the advanced level, we see that NTFS provides a number of additional granular advanced access control settings under Windows XP, as well as an ability to encrypt files for added protection. We will discuss all of these features throughout this chapter.

COMPONENTS INVOLVED IN ACCESS CONTROL

Before we can really discuss the full access control process, we need to review the components that enable access control. The main items of concern are

- Users and Security Identifiers
- Objects and Containers (files and folders)
- Access Control Lists and Access Control Entries

USERS AND SECURITY IDENTIFIERS (SIDS)

User accounts and groups appear differently to humans and computers, and I'm not talking about binary versus ASCII. To you, your user name probably looks like some vague concatenation of your actual typed name, ID, or handle. You can clearly tell the difference between the Administrator account and the Guest account by glancing at the displayed names, "Administrator" or "Guest." But Windows XP doesn't see accounts quite the same way. To Windows XP, you're just another faceless, unpronounceable security identifier, or *SID*.

SIDs are unique, variable-length strings used by Windows XP to track an account. When you apply NTFS-based security to an object, or when you add a user object to a group object, it may appear to you that you're adding your human-readable account name to the object. In reality, Windows applies the SID, which the system will resolve to the display name for purposes of display via the GUI. By using SIDs instead of user-specified text strings for account tracking, you are able to rename a user account or change the account's displayed name without needing to re-establish group membership or modify object-specific security permissions simply to maintain a user's access.

For example, when Amy O'Brien marries Jeff Ferris and elects to change her last name because the apostrophe wreaks havoc on Web forms, the system administrator doesn't want to try to figure out all the resources Amy should be allowed to access. He just wants to rename the account and get on with other administrative duties. If account permissions were applied based on display name, this wouldn't be possible. But fortunately for our heroic system administrator, Windows XP uses SIDs, and renaming AO'Brien to AFerris doesn't change the SID.

Suppose the administrator were to accidentally delete the AO'Brien account and add a new account with the updated name. Obviously, this new account will not have any of the permissions from the original account, and everything will have to be configured from scratch. What about re-creating a new AO'Brien account, and then renaming the new account to AFerris? Well, unfortunately, you can't restore the permissions simply by creating a new account with the same name, because Windows will generate a different SID than the original account. For this reason, it is recommended to *disable* user accounts—rather than *delete* user accounts—when revoking access from a Windows XP environment. If you disable the account first, and later discover an error that requires re-enabling the account, you won't have to add the account name to all of the groups or objects to which rights were explicitly allowed or denied. Just don't forget to clean up the accounts after a suitably safe error-detection time has passed.

So if Windows XP uses unique SIDs instead of user names, does that mean you can have a duplicate user name? After all, the account will still be unique to the system, right? Well, even though the SID is different, the user is expected to enter the textual representation of the account when logging on. Since the system has no way to discern between different users other than this text-based account name entered at the logon screen, Windows will still not allow duplicate user names.

You usually won't need to worry about what SIDs are associated with accounts, but now and again it helps with certain authentication-related troubleshooting activities. If you're interested in the guts of Windows authentication, you may wonder how to translate account and group names into SIDs.

To resolve local or domain users and groups to their SIDs, you can use the command-line utility GETSID.EXE, available from Microsoft's Web site:

```
http://www.microsoft.com/windows2000/techinfo/reskit/tools/existing/getsid-o.asp
```

The GETSID tool was actually designed to compare the SIDs from two accounts. To use this tool to see the SID for a single account, you'll have to specify the account name twice:

```
Getsid \\%computername% accountname \\%computername% accountname
```

In addition to GETSID, you can use the WHOAMI.EXE utility from the Resource kit. To see the SID for the current user, the command is as follows:

```
whoami /user /sid
```

To see the SIDs for groups of the currently logged on user, the command is

```
whoami /groups /sid
```

IDENTIFYING COMMON SECURITY IDENTIFIERS

There are some common security identifiers that never vary in value, and others that have common prefixes and suffixes with a unique SID for the domain buried in the middle. A selection of these common SIDs is listed in Table 23.1. The SIDs with *domainSID* in the middle will show up with the same prefix and suffix, but *domainSID* will be replaced with the unique SID for the domain. This domain SID will be the same for all accounts or groups that use it.

TABLE 23.1 COMMON WINDOWS XP SECURITY IDENTIFIERS

Text Name	Security Identifier	Description
Everyone	S-1-1-0	This group includes all authenticated users, anonymous users, and guest users.
Network	S-1-5-2	This group contains all users connected to the system from somewhere other than the local console. You cannot override membership in this group.
Batch	S-1-5-3	This group contains all users who have logged on as a batch job.
Interactive	S-1-5-4	This group contains the locally logged-on user—the user interacting at the keyboard. You cannot manually add accounts to this group.
Service	S-1-5-6	This group includes all accounts that are currently logged on as a service. You cannot manually control accounts that belong to this group.
Anonymous	S-1-5-7	This group includes all users who are logged on anonymously. You cannot manually control membership to this group.
Authenticated Users	S-1-5-11	This group contains all authenticated users, logged on using valid accounts from either the local system or the domain. This is a dynamic group, and you cannot manually control the membership.

Text Name	Security Identifier	Description
Administrator	S-1-5-*domainSID*-500	This is the default administrator account. If on a local machine, this account has full control over the local machine. If in the domain, this account has full control over all systems joined to the domain.
Guest	S-1-5-*domainSID*-501	A user account, disabled out-of-the-box, for people who do not have individual accounts. This user account does not require a password.
Domain Admins	S-1-5-*domainSID*-512	Members of this global group are authorized to administer the domain. The Domain Admins group is automatically added to the Administrators group on all computers joined to the domain, including domain controllers. The Domain Admins group contains the Administrator account for the domain.
Domain Users	S-1-5-*domainSID*-513	This global group contains all user accounts in the domain.
Domain Guests	S-1-5-*domainSID*-514	By default, this global group contains only the default Guest account for the domain.
Domain Computers	S-1-5-*domainSID*-515	This global group includes all machines that have joined the domain.
Domain Controllers	S-1-5-*domainSID*-516	All domain controllers for the current domain are automatically added to this global group.
Administrators	S-1-5-32-544	Members of this built-in group have full control of the system on which the group is located. On a standalone system, the only default member of the group is the Administrator. When joining a system to the domain, the Domain Admins group is automatically added to the group.
Users	S-1-5-32-545	Members of this built-in group have limited (non-administrative) rights on the system. Newly created local users will automatically be added to this group. When joining a system to the domain, the Domain Users group is automatically added to this group.
Guests	S-1-5-32-546	The only default member of this built-in group is the Guest account. User profiles are deleted on logout for any members of the Guests group.
Power Users	S-1-5-32-547	By default, this built-in group has no members. Power Users can create local users and groups. Power Users cannot create users with greater privileges than those held by the Power Users group. Members of this group can install most programs, and create or delete file shares.

23

Seeing All Local SIDs

If you would like to see the SIDs for all local accounts on your system, you can use this quick VBScript:

```
Set objcol = _
    GetObject("WinMgmts:/root/cimv2").InstancesOf("Win32_UserAccount")

For Each i in objcol
    wscript.echo "Account: " & i.name & vbTab & "SID: " & i.sid
Next
```

OBJECTS AND CONTAINERS

In the previous section we discussed the user component of NTFS security, but we don't really gain much without applying access controls for those user groups to *objects* and *containers*. Objects, in the case of NTFS file system security, refer to individual files. Containers, as you may have guessed, refer to folders. A container can hold additional containers (subfolders) or objects (files), all of which can inherit permissions or have unique and explicitly defined permissions on a per-object basis.

ACCESS CONTROLS LISTS (ACLs) AND ACCESS CONTROL ENTRIES (ACEs)

While it would be an extremely cool feature, there is no way to look at a user's account and see a list of all files, folders, shares, or Registry keys that the user can access. Access controls are applied only to the objects or containers, and are implemented using Access Control Lists (ACLs, pronounced like "jackal" without the "j") containing Access Control Entries (ACEs). Viewing the security applied to a specific object will show you the ACL, containing an ACE for any permission specifically granted or denied to any user or group who has rights defined on or inherited by that object.

→ For details on security restrictions for network shares, see Chapter 24, "Network Security."

→ For more information on setting permissions for Registry keys, refer to Chapter 30, in the section titled "Registry Security" starting on **p. 1252**.

Microsoft's Platform SDK for Security defines ACLs and ACEs as follows:

■ **Access Control List (ACL)**—A list of security protections that applies to an object. An object can be a file, process, event, or anything else having a security descriptor. An entry in an ACL is an Access Control Entry.

■ **Access Control Entry (ACE)**—An entry in an Access Control List. An ACE contains a set of access rights and a security identifier (SID) that identifies a trustee for whom the rights are allowed, denied, or audited.

There are two types of access control lists:

■ **Discretionary Access Control List (DACL)**—The DACL is the access control list that specifies object access permissions for groups or users. In general, references to a file or folder's ACL are actually references to the Discretionary Access Control List.

■ **System Access Control List (SACL)**—The SACL specifies the object access actions that will be audited.

Now that you should be familiar with all of the main components that go into the Windows XP access control process, let's take a look at how they all play together.

HOW ACCESS CONTROL WORKS

When you attempt to access an object or container, Windows XP takes a look at your *access token*. This token contains a list of SIDs, including the unique user SID and the SIDs for each group to which a user belongs. If any of the SIDs associated with your account match any of the SIDs present in the DACL on the resource you are attempting to access, Windows XP evaluates the applicable ACEs to determine whether or not you should be allowed to interact with the resource.

Windows XP will check local ACEs before inherited ACEs, and Deny ACEs (which *prevent* a specified type of access) are evaluated before Allow ACEs (which, as the name suggests, *allow* a specific type of access). So, effective permissions are determined with the following priority, with the top line being highest priority, and the bottom line being the lowest:

- Local object Deny permissions
- Local object Allow permissions
- Inherited Deny permissions
- Inherited Allow permissions

When evaluating an access request, Windows XP will check to see if one of your SIDs match up with an ACE defined locally on the object. Then, Windows XP will evaluate whether or not the SID is denied the type of access you are requesting—such as reading, writing, or executing the file. If you are specifically denied access to perform the operation you are requesting, Windows XP stops processing the ACE right there. If a matching ACE is present but does not deny you access, then it must be granting a permission. Windows XP takes note of the permissions granted by the current ACE. If these permissions match those required to perform the operation requested against the object, access is granted and operation continues as normal. If Windows XP needs additional access permissions, it looks at the next ACE in the DACL until it has gone through all of the local ACEs.

Each ACE is cumulative. If the ACE that Windows XP just checked only grants you Read access, and the next ACE that Windows XP checks only grants you write access, you will have both read and write access against the object in question. If these are the only permissions required to perform the operation you were attempting, Windows XP will check no further. If you still don't have all of the access control permissions you need (and Windows hasn't already encountered a specific Deny ACE), the process will continue down the list of ACEs. If Windows XP reaches the end of the local object ACEs without accumulating the permissions required to perform the requested action against the object, then the ACE checking process will continue by running through all of the inherited ACEs until the proper permissions have been accumulated.

NEGATIVE PERMISSIONS

With NTFS permissions under the initial release of Windows NT 4.0, there was a special permission known as No Access. You may remember that No Access would always override specifically defined access permissions. With Windows NT 4.0 SP4, Windows 2000, and Windows XP, the general No Access permission went away, replaced instead with a Deny column, to granularly deny specific permissions to users or groups.

Using this negative permission model, you can configure a group to have full read/write access to all objects within a specific container, but still specify that a specific user or another group that may represent a subset of users in the first group are allowed only to read the files in the container, and they are specifically denied the ability to write to the container.

It can be a bit confusing to talk about it in such general terms, so here's an example. Let's say you have an Accounting group, and all user accounts that belong to the Accounting group need Read and Write access to the AccountingShare container. AccountingShare contains two subdirectories, AccountsPayable and AccountsReceivable. Everyone in the Accounting group should have Read access to all objects under the AccountingShare folder, but only the AccountingAR group should be able to write to the AccountsReceivable folder, and only members of the AccountingAP group should have write access to the AccountsPayable folder.

Under Windows XP, you can accomplish your desired security by configuring the Access Control Entries as follows:

- Grant the Accounting group Read and Write access permissions on the AccountingShare container. The permissions will propagate to the child objects by default.

- Deny the AccountingAR group the Write permission on the AccountsPayable container.

- Deny the AccountingAP group the Write permission on the AccountsReceivable container.

This would not have been possible under the initial provisions of Windows NT 4.0, as all rights were cumulative except for No Access, which always won. To accomplish the same thing in Windows NT 4.0, you would have had to apply access control permissions as follows:

- Grant the Accounting group Read and Write access permissions on the AccountingShare folder and select the option to apply the permissions to all child objects.

- Change the access permissions for the Accounting group to provide only Read access permissions on the AccountsPayable container.

- Grant the AccountingAP group the Write permission on the AccountsPayable container.

- Change the access permissions for the Accounting group to provide only Read access permissions on the AccountsReceivable container.

- Grant the AccountingAR group the Write permission on the AccountsReceivable container

Both solutions achieve the same results, but the ability to use negative permissions just makes things a little more straightforward. Well, at least it seems straightforward, until we have to consider container and object inheritance.

CONTAINER AND OBJECT INHERITANCE

Remember Windows NT 4.0? NT 4 used *static inheritance*, in which all child objects (such as files and subfolders) received a copy of their ACL from their parent object (the folder under which they were created). After an object was created, its ACL was in no way connected to the parent container. The ACL could be overwritten by an explicit copy operation from the parent object, but the ACLs were always separate, unrelated objects.

In contrast, Windows XP uses a *dynamic inheritance* model, meaning that any child object inherits ACLs applied to parent objects. Changes to a parent object's ACL will automatically propagate down to any child objects on which inheritance has not been blocked. ACEs that were previously added to the ACLs of child objects are not overwritten, but the inherited ACEs will be updated.

So what happens when a child object has an ACE and a change to a parent object's ACL introduces a conflicting ACE? Here's where things can really get confusing. As I mentioned under the heading "How Access Control Works," Windows XP will check local ACEs before inherited ACEs. None of the conflicting entries are overwritten or deleted, so it is possible to have an object-specific local ACE granting permission to a specific user, an inherited ACE granting a negative permission to the same user, and both ACEs will exist peacefully in the DACL for the object in question. At this point, it falls to Windows XP's access control processing to determine the effective permissions, as in the process previously described under the section, "How Access Control Works."

Again, it may help to explain this process using a specific example. Let's say you have a directory called TimeSheets. Within TimeSheets, you have a file named MattTime.XLS. The TimeSheets directory has an ACE denying Read access to the Bartenders group. Matt's user account is a member of the Bartenders group. The MattTime.XLS file has a local ACE granting Read and Write access to Matt's account, and the file is not blocking inheritance.

Even though a group to which Matt belongs is specifically denied access to the file, the Deny ACE is inherited. Since Matt's Grant ACE is defined locally, it will be processed first, and all required permissions will be available from the locally granted ACEs. Windows XP will never even process the inherited ACEs, and Matt will be able to open the file.

It is possible to *block inheritance* on an object, so the only applicable access permissions are the ones defined locally on the object. Changes to parent objects will not affect the ACE of an object with blocked inheritance. To see exactly how to enable inheritance blocking, refer to the third step of the walkthrough under the next section, "Managing File Permissions." In that step, we will be removing permission inheritance from the Parent_Folder container.

MANAGING FILE PERMISSIONS

Now that you've learned how NTFS file system access protection works, how do you actually implement it? Fortunately, it is much easier to use access permissions than it is to explain how they work.

→ Refer to Chapter 11 if you need assistance creating users and groups.

You'll need to perform the following steps on a Windows XP Professional machine, logged in as an account with local administrative privileges.

We'll start by creating some users. Add two local user accounts:

- LocalBoy
- LocalGirl

Next, create three groups:

- Boys
- Girls
- Ladies_and_Gentlemen

Add LocalBoy to the Boys group, add LocalGirl to the Girls group, and add both LocalBoy and LocalGirl to the Ladies_and_Gentlemen group.

Next, we need to add a container and object structure so we can examine inheritance. Create a folder and file structure on an NTFS-formatted volume as shown here (contents of the text documents are unimportant):

    📁 <Root of NTFS volume>
        📁 Parent_Folder
            📄 Child_Document_L1.txt
            📁 Child_Folder_L1
                📄 Child_Document_L2.txt
                📁 Child_Folder_L2
                    📄 Child_Document_L3A.txt
                    📄 Child_Document_L3B.txt

Now, to apply some access controls...

1. Right-click Parent_Folder and select Properties from the pop-up list.
2. Select the Security tab.

3. Click the Advanced button, and deselect Inherit from Parent the Permission Entries That Apply to Child Objects. Include These with Entries Explicitly Defined Here. When you uncheck the box, you will see a security dialog asking whether you wish to copy previously applied permissions, remove previously applied permissions, or cancel the operation. Select Remove. This will ensure that we're both starting with a clean slate.

4. Select Replace Permission Entries on All Child Objects with Entries Shown Here That Apply to Child Objects. Click OK, and you will see a Security confirmation dialog. Click Yes to continue. You will receive another Security dialog warning you that no one has been given rights to the object. We're about to fix that, so click Yes to continue.

5. You should now be back at the Security tab on the Parent_Folder Properties dialog. Click the Add button, and select the Ladies_and_Gentlemen group to add it to the DACL, and click OK. Click Allow for the permissions Modify, Read & Execute, List Folder Contents, Read, and Write, as in Figure 23.1.

Figure 23.1
Applying access permissions to Parent_Folder.

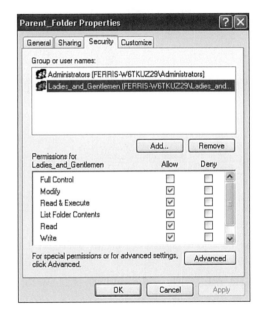

6. Click Add again, and select the local Administrators group. Click Allow for the Full Control permission. This will ensure that you still have the access required to complete the rest of the steps. Click OK.

7. Go into Parent_Folder, right-click Child_Folder_L1, and select Properties from the pop-up list.

8. Select the Security tab. You should see the same permissions in this window as you had under Parent_Folder, so we know inheritance is working.

9. Select the Ladies_and_Gentlemen group to add it to the DACL. Click Deny for the Write permission. Click OK. A confirmation dialog will appear. Click Yes to continue.

10. Go into the Child_Folder_L1 folder, right-click Child_Folder_L2, and select Properties from the pop-up list.

11. Select the Security tab. The ACE for Ladies_And_Gentlemen should be the combined permissions held by the parent folders, as shown in Figure 23.2.

Figure 23.2
Aggregate access permissions applied to Child_Folder_L2.

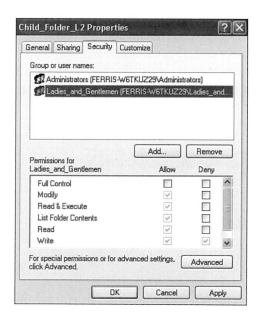

12. Click the Add button, and select the Girls group to add it to the DACL. Click Allow for the Write permission, and click OK.

13. Go into the Child_Folder_L2 folder, right-click Child_Document_L3A, and select Properties from the pop-up list.

14. Select the Security tab. Select the Girls group, and select Deny for all permissions.

15. Click the Add button, and select the Boys group to add them to the DACL. Click Allow for the Modify, Read & Execute, Read, and Write permissions, and click OK. Click Yes on the security confirmation dialog.

16. Right-click Child_Document_L3B and select Properties from the pop-up list.

17. Click the Add button, and select the Boys group to add them to the DACL. Click Deny for all permissions and click OK. Click Yes on the security confirmation dialog.

When you are finished, the local Administrators group should still have full control for all objects. The effective permissions on the objects and containers for LocalBoy and LocalGirl are reflected in Table 23.2.

TABLE 23.2   EFFECTIVE PERMISSIONS OF OBJECTS AND CONTAINERS

Object	Account	Effective Permissions
Parent_Folder	LocalBoy	Allow = MERLW
	LocalGirl	Allow = MERLW
Child_Folder_L1	LocalBoy	Allow = MERL
		Deny = W
	LocalGirl	Allow = MERL
		Deny = W
Child_Document_L1	LocalBoy	Allow = MERLW
	LocalGirl	Allow = MERLW
Child_Folder_L2	LocalBoy	Allow = MERL
		Deny = W
	LocalGirl	Allow = MERLW
Child_Document_L2	LocalBoy	Allow = MERL
		Deny = W
	LocalGirl	Allow = MERL
		Deny = W
Child_Document_L3A	LocalBoy	Allow = MERLW
	LocalGirl	Deny = MERLWF
Child_Document_L3B	LocalBoy	Deny = MERLWF
	LocalGirl	Allow = MERLW

Permissions Legend
M = Modify
E = Read & Execute
R = Read
L = List Folder Contents
W = Write
F = Full Control

In the previous walkthrough, you learned how to implement everything we've discussed so far. You blocked inheritable permissions on Parent_Folder, set inheritable permissions at two child container levels, set local access permissions on two documents, and implemented local object Allow permissions that took precedence over inherited object Deny permissions.

ISSUES WITH HOME EDITION

With Windows XP Home Edition, you are still able to use NTFS-formatted drives, yet there is no Security tab on file or folder objects during a normal logon session. Seems a little odd, especially since the files and folders can still have security permissions applied to them. You just have to be a bit sneaky about it.

There are two ways you can modify security permissions on an NTFS volume under Windows XP Home Edition. The first still uses the familiar Security tab GUI; you just have to sneak in through the back way to get there. To access the Security tab under Windows XP Home Edition, you must boot into safe mode and log on as the local administrator. Due to what is being called a "usability feature," Windows XP Home Edition will not allow you to log on as the local administrator unless you are in safe mode. Follow these steps to log on as the local administrator:

1. Reboot your system.

2. Immediately after the system POSTs (the Power On Self Test, where the system displays the BIOS screen, counts up through the memory, and so on), press the F8 key to access the Windows XP boot menu.

3. Select Safe Mode with Command Prompt and press Enter.

4. Select the proper installation at the screen showing your boot options. If this system only has one operating system on it, you should only see one entry. Press Enter.

5. When the system gets to the Sign-on screen, select the Administrator account. Unless you had previously configured a password for this account, it should not require one.

6. Access the Security tab for any file or folder by navigating to the object, right-clicking it, selecting Properties from the pop-up menu, and selecting the now-visible Security tab.

If you're looking for a way to manipulate access permissions without all the mucking about in safe mode, you could also try using the CACLS command from the command-line. Running CACLS from the command line without any arguments will display the following help listing:

```
Displays or modifies access control lists (ACLs) of files

CACLS filename [/T] [/E] [/C] [/G user:perm] [/R user [...]]
               [/P user:perm [...]] [/D user [...]]
   filename     Displays ACLs.
   /T           Changes ACLs of specified files in
                the current directory and all subdirectories.
   /E           Edit ACL instead of replacing it.
   /C           Continue on access denied errors.
   /G user:perm Grant specified user access rights.
                Perm can be: R  Read
                             W  Write
                             C  Change (write)
                             F  Full control
   /R user      Revoke specified user's access rights (only valid with /E).
   /P user:perm Replace specified user's access rights.
                Perm can be: N  None
                             R  Read
                             W  Write
                             C  Change (write)
                             F  Full control
   /D user      Deny specified user access.
Wildcards can be used to specify more that one file in a command.
You can specify more than one user in a command.
```

```
Abbreviations:
    CI - Container Inherit.
        The ACE will be inherited by directories.
    OI - Object Inherit.
        The ACE will be inherited by files.
    IO - Inherit Only.
        The ACE does not apply to the current file/directory.
```

For most purposes under Windows XP Home Edition, I recommend using Safe mode as the local administrator if you need to make any changes to any object access permissions.

VIEWING EFFECTIVE PERMISSIONS

To confirm the effective permissions for any group or user name against any object or container, follow these steps:

1. Right-click the object in question, select Properties from the pop-up menu, go to the Security tab, click the Advanced button, and select the Effective Permissions tab.

2. Click the Select button, enter the name of the user or group for which you wish to view effective permissions, and click OK.

3. The effective permissions for the selected user or group are displayed. Figure 23.3 shows the effective permissions for LocalBoy on object Child_Document_L3A. Note that you cannot change the effective permissions on this screen—it is for display only.

Figure 23.3
Effective Permissions for LocalBoy on object Child_Document_L3A.

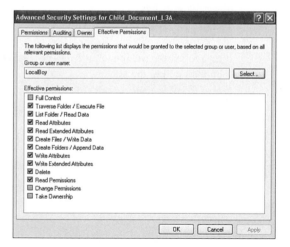

ADVANCED PERMISSIONS

There are a number of advanced permissions available under Windows XP. For the most part, you should be able to accomplish any day-to-day permission administration requirements using standard access control permissions. On the off chance that you do need to get more granular, you can access the advanced permissions dialog by right-clicking the target object or container, selecting Properties from the pop-up menu, going to the Security tab, and clicking the Advanced button. Click the Add button to add advanced permissions for a user not listed in the Permission entries table, or select a user and click Edit to change the advanced permissions for an existing user. Table 23.3 describes the advanced permission options.

TABLE 23.3   ADVANCED PERMISSION ATTRIBUTES

Permission	Description
Full Control	Contains all of the other access permissions listed in this table.
Traverse Folder/Execute File	If on a folder object, Traverse Folder allows or denies permission to move through folders to access other files and folders. If on a file object, Execute File allows or denies running a file.
List Folder/Read Data	If on a folder object, allows or denies permission to list the contents of the folder. If on a file object, allows or denies the ability to read a file.
Read Attributes	Allows or denies the ability to view file or folder attributes, such as System, Hidden, Read-Only, or Archive.
Read Extended Attributes	Allows or denies the ability to view extended attributes on a file or folder. Extended attributes vary by file type.
Create Files/Write Data	If on a folder object, allows or denies permission to create new files within the folder. If on a file object, allows or denies the ability to update or write to the file.
Create Folders/Append Data	If on a folder object, allows or denies permission to create new subfolders within the folder. If on a file object, allows or denies the ability to add data to the end of the file, but not change any existing parts of the file.
Write Attributes	Allows or denies the ability to change file or folder attributes, such as System, Hidden, Read-Only, or Archive.
Write Extended Attributes	Allows or denies the ability to edit extended attributes on a file or folder. Extended attributes vary by file type.
Delete Subfolders and Files	Allows or denies the deletion of subfolders or files, but not the object to which it is applied.
Delete	Allows or denies the deletion of the object to which it is applied.
Read Permissions	Allows or denies the ability to read permissions applied to the file or folder.
Change Permissions	Allows or denies the ability to change permissions applied to the file or folder.
Take Ownership	Allows or denies the ability to take ownership of the file or folder.

FILE ENCRYPTION

With NTFS-formatted drive volumes, you have the option to encrypt files or folders to further protect them from unauthorized access. Windows XP file encryption utilizes the Encrypting File System (EFS), available since Windows 2000. As you've learned from the earlier sections in this chapter, Windows XP provides access control mechanisms by which to grant or deny specific activities against files or folders. So why would encryption be necessary? Why would you need the extra layer of protection provided by encryption if access to the file already requires authentication?

Well, I'm glad I'm pretending you asked.

You see, even though Windows XP can restrict access based on user accounts or groups, it is still possible to get around the access restrictions. In fact, doing so can be quite simple. First, any user with local administrative privileges on the box can take ownership of the protected files or folders, giving them full control over the object. This can be done from the local system, or over the network. The only prerequisite is an account with administrative access to the machine. In most cases, you are likely not too concerned about your local administrators having access to your files. After all, if you trust someone enough to give them unrestricted control of your machine, they will hopefully not betray that trust by taking ownership of files to which you've denied them access.

A second method for gaining access to files or folders that have been protected only with access controls would take a bit more effort. This method, often used by individuals without administrative access to a system, involves removing the physical drive containing the desired data, installing the drive as a secondary drive in a system on which the user *does* have administrative access, and taking ownership of the files from the secondary drive on which the access permissions will be invalid. This method would require physical access to the system in order to remove the drive.

The third method, which takes quite a bit longer and can be destructive to the target system, involves reinstalling Windows XP on the system containing the access-restricted files. Since you are reinstalling the OS, this method requires physical access to the system. By reinstalling the operating system, the system configuration will be reset to an unmodified state, all local accounts will be gone, and the system will be as if applications were never installed. To prevent the deletion of the data files, you must not repartition or reformat the system during setup. During the GUI mode portion of setup, you will be prompted for a default administrator password. Using the Administrator account to log in to the newly reloaded system, you will be able to take control of the files.

As you can see, overriding access restrictions is not an impossible task. Fortunately, by using EFS, none of the above methods will work to gain unauthorized access to protected files. Any files protected with EFS are inaccessible gibberish to anyone accessing them without using either the original user account that encrypted the file, or the account of an EFS *recovery agent*, explained in the "Recovering Encrypted Files" section later in this chapter.

CAUTION

> Under Windows XP, you cannot use both NTFS encryption and NTFS compression on the same file or folder. You can have some encrypted and some compressed objects on the same system; it is just not possible to combine both encryption and compression applied to the same object or container. See "Compressing Files and Folders" in Chapter 25, **p. xxx**, for more information on NTFS compression.

PROTECTING FILES AND FOLDERS

Now that we've established *why* you'd want to use EFS, how do we actually use it? Enabling encryption is a fairly straightforward process:

TIP

> For the sake of manageability, I strongly recommend setting aside a single folder under which you will store your encrypted files, rather than individually encrypting multiple files or folders in various locations.

1. Select a folder that you wish to encrypt. I usually create a folder named Secure under my My Documents directory.

2. Move the documents containing your top-secret plans for global domination into the directory that you will be encrypting.

3. Right-click your selected directory and select Properties from the pop-up menu.

4. On the General tab, click the Advanced button.

5. There is no need to change any options under Archive and Index attributes. Under Compress or Encrypt attributes, select the option marked Encrypt Contents to Secure Data.

   Refer to Figure 23.4, and you will notice that the options to compress or encrypt appear as check boxes. This is a little misleading, because if you attempt to select both options, you will see that the check boxes behave like option buttons—you can select only one or the other, and never both. Click OK.

Figure 23.4
The check boxes to encrypt or compress are misleading. You can only select one, not both.

6. Click OK on the folder properties dialog, and you will see the confirmation box displayed in Figure 23.5. Select the bottom option and click OK.

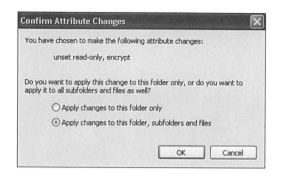

Figure 23.5
The top option changes the properties for the selected container, but affects none of the files or subfolders inside. The second option will encrypt everything contained under the Secure folder.

> **Confirm Attribute Changes**
>
> You have chosen to make the following attribute changes:
>
>   unset read-only, encrypt
>
> Do you want to apply this change to this folder only, or do you want to apply it to all subfolders and files as well?
>
> ○ Apply changes to this folder only
>
> ⦿ Apply changes to this folder, subfolders and files
>
>   [OK]   [Cancel]

7. An Applying Attributes progress box will be displayed while the contents of the selected folder are encrypted. The more data you have to encrypt, the longer this dialog will be displayed.

That's all it takes. Your files won't look any different to you. You can work with the files exactly like you did before. Their encrypted status will be completely transparent to you and any applications started under your security context.

You can perform the same operation on a single file, and the process is nearly identical. You will follow the same steps listed previously, except there will be no confirmation box as in Step 6.

Now that you have encrypted the contents of the Secure folder, open the folder under Windows Explorer. The file names of encrypted files, by default, should show up as green text. (Compressed files would show up as blue text.) Right-click one of the files within the encrypted folder, and select Properties. As before, click the Advanced button. You will notice that the Encrypt Contents to Secure Data option is enabled, and unlike before, so is the Details button. Click the Details button to view the list of users who can access the selected file. Figure 23.6 shows the resulting Encryption Details dialog.

MOVING AND COPYING ENCRYPTED FILES

Now that you know how to enable encryption, let's see what happens as we copy or move files or folders into and out of the encrypted directory:

> **TIP**
>
> If you are following along and you wish to confirm the encryption status of a file or folder, remember that you can check the status through the advanced file properties.

Figure 23.6
Users listed in the top box have transparent access to the file. If any users are listed in the bottom box, they are EFS recovery agents, enabled via the Group Policy setting for domain recovery agents.

- First and foremost, always remember that encrypted files must be stored on NTFS volumes. Copying or moving encrypted files or folders from an NTFS volume to a FAT volume will cause the files to decrypt, because FAT volumes do not support encryption.

- Files copied into an encrypted directory are automatically encrypted with the copy operation.

- Folders copied into an encrypted directory are automatically encrypted, as are any files or folders contained within.

- Moving an unencrypted file into an encrypted folder will automatically encrypt the file.

- Moving an unencrypted folder into an encrypted folder *will not* encrypt the folder or its contents.

- Copying an encrypted file to an unencrypted directory *will not* decrypt the file.

- Copying an encrypted folder to an unencrypted folder *will not* decrypt the folder or its contents.

- Moving an encrypted file to an unencrypted directory *will not* decrypt the file.

- Moving an encrypted folder to an unencrypted folder *will not* decrypt the folder or its contents.

DISABLING EFS FOR SELECTED FILES OR FOLDERS

If you copy or move an encrypted file or folder to a location where you intend to decrypt it or make it accessible to others, you must decrypt it by deselecting the encrypted option under the advanced file/folder properties:

1. Move the file or folder you wish to decrypt to the location where you wish to decrypt it.

2. Right-click the item and select Properties from the pop-up menu.

3. On the General tab, click the Advanced button.

4. Under Compress or Encrypt attributes, deselect the option marked Encrypt Contents to Secure Data. Click OK.

5. Click OK on the properties dialog. If you are decrypting a file, it will decrypt with no further input.

   If you are decrypting a folder, you will see the Confirm Attribute Change dialog box. Select the bottom option to apply the decryption request to the folder, all subfolders, and files. Click OK. The Applying Attributes progress box will be displayed while the contents of the secure folder are decrypted. The more data you have to encrypt, the longer this dialog will be displayed.

Suppose you would like to prevent a specific file or folder from ever getting encrypted. There are two ways to prevent files and folders from being encrypted. The first is to simply turn on the System attribute for the folders or files you don't want encrypted. Windows XP will not allow a system file to be encrypted.

The second method to prevent files or folders from getting encrypted is to add the following two lines to a `Desktop.ini` file in the directory containing the files that you do not want encrypted:

```
[Encryption]
Disable=1
```

If you are creating the Desktop.INI file from scratch, make sure you don't save it with a .TXT extension or it won't work. You can double-check by doing a directory list from the command line. If you try to encrypt a folder containing a `Desktop.ini` file with these entries, or if you attempt to encrypt any individual files at the same directory level as a `Desktop.ini` file containing these entries, you will receive the message displayed in Figure 23.7.

Figure 23.7
Trying to encrypt a file in a directory disabled for encryption.

DISABLING EFS IN A DOMAIN

If you are a domain administrator and you wish to disable EFS altogether on a selection of client systems in your domain, you can do so with a group policy setting.

→ Refer to the section titled "Policies, Permissions, and Computer Management" in Chapter 22, **p. 892**, for more information on creating Group Policy Objects and modifying Group Policy settings.

To disable EFS for an OU in your domain, follow these steps:

1. Start the Active Directory Users and Computers applet from Start, Settings, Control Panel, Administrative Tools, Active Directory Users and Computers. If you do not have the applet on your system, you must install the administrative tools by running ADMINPAK.MSI from the Windows 200x Server CD.

2. Navigate to the OU containing the computer accounts for which you wish to disable EFS. Right-click and select Properties.

> **TIP**
>
> You can apply this setting at the domain level, disabling EFS on all clients in your domain, or at an OU level, disabling EFS for computers with their computer accounts under the selected OU.

3. Click the Group Policy tab and either edit an existing GPO, or create a new one.

4. In the group policy editor, navigate to the following location:

   Default Domain Policy\Computer Configuration\Windows Settings\Security Settings\Public Key Policies\Encrypted Data Recovery Agents

5. Right-click the policy Encrypted Data Recovery Agents and select Delete Policy from the pop-up. Click Yes when asked to confirm.

6. Right-click the policy Encrypted Data Recovery Agents and select Initialize Empty Policy from the pop-up.

After the group policy settings are updated for any target system in the affected OU, you will no longer be able to encrypt files or folders on that machine. Using EFS in a domain *requires* a non-empty data recovery policy. By default, you would not have had any data recovery policy defined, resulting in a non-empty policy setting of *no policy*, rather than an empty policy. Users would still be able to encrypt files in this situation. After performing the previous steps, you will have created an *empty policy*, and an empty policy will prevent EFS from functioning on any systems to which the policy is applied. If you try to enable encryption on a system with an empty policy for the EFS recovery agent, you will receive an error message stating "There is no encryption recovery policy configured for this system," and the encryption attempt will fail.

MANAGING ENCRYPTED FILES ON A NETWORK

We just discussed disabling EFS throughout an entire domain, but what if you decide you want your domain users to be able to utilize EFS? There are a few things you need to take into consideration. For one thing, users will probably try storing encrypted files out on the network drives somewhere. This will work fine, as long as the network share supports EFS and participates in domain security for the same (or a trusted) domain as the user encrypting the files.

TIP

> You can access encrypted files stored on other systems or on network shares *only* if you are accessing the files with the *exact same* account credentials used to encrypt them. The account must have the same SID, not just the same username and password.

TIP

> Do you use roaming user profiles or folder redirection for the My Documents directory? If so, you can encrypt files and folders that will be cached to your local system, but you *must* be using NTFS-formatted drives on both your local system and the network shares on which your profile or My Documents folder are stored. If your local drive is not NTFS, the cached copy of your encrypted files will be unencrypted when they cache to your local system.

23

Another important consideration is your account troubleshooting practices. If your help desk is in the habit of re-creating user accounts to diagnose technical issues (never recommended, but trust me—it happens), realize that any files encrypted using EFS will be inaccessible to a user if their account is deleted and re-created.

RECOVERING ENCRYPTED FILES

In the event that a user manages to lose their EFS key—for example, if their user account is accidentally deleted (remember, best-practices are to disable accounts, not delete them), how can they go about recovering encrypted files? This sounds like a job for the Recovery Agent.

By default, Domain Administrators are automatically configured as Recovery Agents for all user accounts in a domain. Remember the policy we modified in the "Disabling EFS" section? It was under `Default Domain Policy\Computer Configuration\Windows Settings\Security Settings\Public Key Policies\Encrypted Data Recovery Agents`. You can add additional users or groups to this policy to enable additional Recovery Agents in your domain. In the event a user loses access to files encrypted using their domain account, the EFS Recovery Agents should be able to remove encryption from the file, restoring access for the unfortunate user.

If an administrator resets a user's password on a non-domain workstation, any EFS-protected files encrypted by the user will be lost. To prevent this sort of loss, Windows XP provides the ability to create a password reset disk. The password reset disk will allow a user to reset their own password without destroying EFS-protected files and folders.

→ Creation and utilization of a password reset disk is explained in Chapter 11, in the section "Local Accounts and Password Reset Disks," **p. 423**.

Before imaging a system containing files encrypted using the Encrypting File Service (EFS), you *must* decrypt the files. As a by-design security function, any encrypted files contained in a master disk image will be inaccessible and completely unrecoverable when applied to a new target system. There is no way to override this behavior.

→ Refer to Chapter 5, "Automated Installation and Network Deployment," for more information about SYSPREP.

23

FILE AND FOLDER AUDITING

Another feature found under the advanced security settings of objects stored on an NTFS volume is file and folder auditing. Auditing records information in the Windows Security Event log about users' successful and unsuccessful attempts to use files and system privileges. Auditing has two primary uses:

- To monitor attempts by users to access files and system services they're not authorized to use.
- To gather debugging information when a service or program fails to work as expected; auditing can help you find out what files the program can't access or what privileges the program lacks.

You can configure auditing on files or folders, but before auditing will log any entries into the Security log, you must enable an auditing security policy for the target machine. To do this

1. Start the Local Security Policy management console.
2. Select Local Policies, Audit Policy from the left pane.
3. Double-click the Audit object access policy from the right pane.
4. Select the check boxes for both Success and Failure and click OK.
5. Close the Local Security Policy console.

TIP

If you wish to enable auditing for a collection of computers in a domain, you can enable auditing through a Group Policy Object, instead of through the Local Security Policy.

Once auditing is enabled, you must enable auditing for specific files and folders, and you must specify the types of access you wish to log. To get to the Auditing tab

1. Right-click a file or folder for which you wish to enable auditing. Select Properties from the pop-up menu.
2. Select the Security tab.
3. Click the Advanced button.
4. Select the Auditing tab.
5. The Auditing tab lets you select specific users and access attributes—for example, Read, Write, Delete, or any other access permission as defined in Table 23.3 of the "Advanced Permissions" section earlier in this chapter. Click Add, enter the group name Everyone to log events for all users, and select the events for which you wish to capture audit logs. You can select to audit successes, failures, or both by checking the appropriate columns. In Figure 23.8, I've selected to audit both successful and failed attempts for a selection of access types for the selected folder, subfolder, and files.

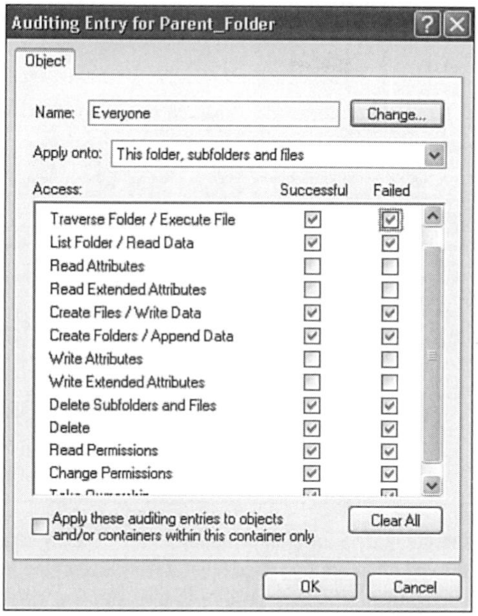

Figure 23.8
Selecting object access permissions that will generate audit log entries.

6. Once you've configured the auditing entries, click the OK button. Click OK to exit the advanced security settings dialog, and click OK once more to close the properties dialog for the folder or file to which you were configuring auditing.

NOTE

Remember, you can only audit files and folders on NTFS volumes. If it's FAT or FAT32, auditing won't work.

VIEWING AUDIT EVENTS

Once auditing is enabled and configured for a selection of objects, you'll be able to find the audit log entries in the Security log of the Event Viewer (Start, Run, EVENTVWR). Figure 23.9 shows the Event Viewer with both success and failure entries from my attempts to access the files as both the administrator (an account *with* access permission) and the jferris account (an account *without* access permission).

Double-clicking any of the events in the Security log will show details about the account attempting access, the type of access attempted, and the file against which an access attempt occurred. Figure 23.10 shows an example of the detailed view from a log entry in which a read attempt was denied.

Figure 23.9
Audit entries in the
Security Log of the
Event Viewer.

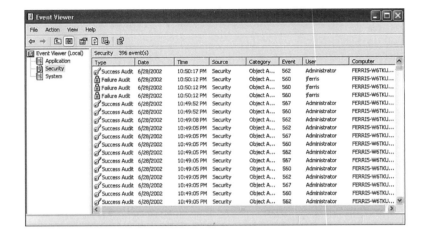

NOTE

Auditing can generate quite a lot of information in the Security Log. Be sure to examine, save and clear the log often enough to prevent it from becoming full. If you're using auditing to gather debugging information, be sure to turn auditing off after you've solved your problem. For more information about maintaining the Event log, **see** "Event Viewer," **p. 1069**.

Figure 23.10
Detailed view of a
Security log entry.
This is a Failure audit
entry, in which I
attempted to open the
file C:\Parent_Folder\
Child_Document_L1.
txt from within
Notepad with the
account jferris.

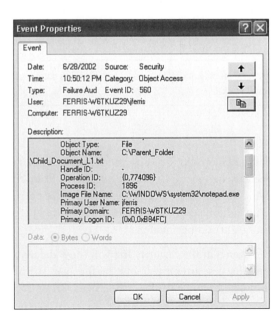

CHAPTER **24**

NETWORK SECURITY

In this chapter

NETWORK SECURITY—WHY BOTHER?

Ah, the Internet! Terabytes of information at my fingertips. Instant, online access to financial records, research papers, music, pictures, videos, applications, and games...almost anything I could ever imagine! Free, open, and available 24 hours a day, 7 days a week. I just can't believe so many people let me download these things right off of their home systems.

Let me be clear about something: The previous paragraph is not an admission of guilt. I don't scan the subnets late at night, looking for open networks and downloading personal files. But others do. I know, because my own network gets hit dozens of times per week. And you might be surprised what they can find with just a little bit of work.

In fact, numerous Web sites offer what amounts to prepackaged plans walking hacker wannabes through scanning and accessing systems. The accessibility of this information has led to a phenomenon referred to as *point-and-click hacking*. Take a look at www. attackportal.net to see just how easy it can be. Now that always-on broadband connections are so prevalent in homes and small offices, it really doesn't take much effort or intelligence to find open shares on personal machines.

If you are a computer user in a large corporation, you are probably protected by some combination of enterprise-level safety measures, which could include the following:

- Firewalls
- Intrusion detection systems
- Virus scanners
- Content filters

Enterprise-level protection is a broad topic a bit out of scope for this book. For in-depth coverage of enterprise security, take a look at some of these titles:

- *Inside Network Perimeter Security: The Definitive Guide to Firewalls, VPNs, Routers, and Network Intrusion Detection* from New Riders; ISBN 0735712328
- *The Concise Guide to Enterprise Internetworking and Security* from Que; ISBN 0789724200
- *Computer Security Basics* from O'Reilly & Associates; ISBN 0937175714

For those of you who are interested in protecting small offices or home machines, some of the integrated features of Windows XP offer protection from many threats. Fortunately, with a bit of effort, a little caution, and maybe a little money, you can protect yourself from the common pitfalls that could result in data loss, accidental exposure of personal data, or legal liabilities associated with failure to protect your company's network.

WHAT, ME WORRY?

Many have already taken some precautions to protect home or small office broadband networks, such as virus scanners and software or hardware firewalls. But for the majority of people using dial-up connectivity, the protective measures often stop at local virus scanners, leading to a false sense of security. Even virus scanners aren't foolproof; the virus definitions must be updated regularly to catch the latest risks, and often a time gap separates the discovery of a new virus and the release of virus definitions that detect the virus. In addition, viruses are only one aspect of the threats to your computer in today's online world. Other common types of attacks or vulnerabilities include the following:

- **Password Cracking**—Given a user account name, a cracker can attempt to guess a valid password for the account. Applications are available to automatically try a list of dictionary entries against specific user accounts, allowing crackers to effortlessly attempt password cracking against multiple systems. To defend against password cracking, always use passwords consisting of a combination of letters and numbers that have no personal significance and would not be found in a dictionary. To see audit passwords on your system and just how easy password cracking can be, take a look at L0phtCrack (now called LC4) at www.l0pht.com (also www.atstake.com).

- **Address spoofing**—If you have the Caller ID service on your telephone, you've no doubt looked at an inbound call, thought to yourself, "Telemarketer," and let the call go to the machine. What if you'd looked at the Caller ID and saw that it was a call from your parents? You'd probably answer the call. Well, imagine if telemarketers could monitor your phone line and figure out whose calls you answered, and whose calls you let go to the machine. Now, what if the telemarketers could make their calls look like they were coming from people you'd normally answer? This scenario is analogous to address spoofing. If your computer automatically trusts traffic from other systems, it might be possible for a hacker to send "spoofed" network commands into your machine that look like they are from the trusted machine. In addition, viruses (and sometimes spammers) often spoof the From address of email messages to make the message appear to be from a known individual.

- **Impersonation**—By tricking Internet routers or providing false entries in a domain name server, hackers can route Internet or network traffic to their own computer rather than the intended, legitimate destination. With a fake Web site in operation, a hacker could collect credit card numbers, usernames, passwords, or other information that might have been valid on the original destination. In fact, there are easier ways to impersonate another Web site that require less technical skill. If I sell Widgets by credit card to registered users of The Widget Network from my Web site www.buywidgets.net, and someone else comes along and registers www.buywidgets.com, that person could duplicate the appearance of my Web site. Users who mistyped the URL would assume it was the valid site and enter their usernames, passwords, and ordering information on the false site without ever knowing what they'd done until it was too late.

- **Packet sniffing**—This is adigital eavesdropping in which the traffic over your telephone line, network cable, or wireless signal is monitored and decoded to expose the content of unencrypted network packets.

- **Exploits**—Complex software has bugs, and you need to be prepared to patch those bugs as software vendors release fixes. If you don't patch the bugs, some of them could

24

leave your system vulnerable to *exploits*, a process intentionally designed to take advantage of a bug in such a way that a hacker can execute arbitrary code or perform some unwanted function on your computer without your permission. The Code Red and NIMDA viruses of 2001 took advantage of a buffer-overrun type of exploit. Patches that would have protected systems from both NIMDA and Code Red were available weeks ahead of the virus outbreaks. Had more administrators been applying the patches as suggested by any of the numerous security advisories, the damages from the viruses would have been significantly reduced.

- **Back doors**—Some software developers put special features into programs intended for the developer's use only, usually to help in debugging. These back doors often circumvent security features. If hackers discover these back doors, they might be able to take advantage of them to gain access to your system.

- **Open doors**—Imagine for a minute that you're a burglar. It's about 9:30 a.m., and you're strolling down the block, looking for houses that don't have any cars parked out front. You come across a house with the garage door open, and no cars parked inside. Not only that, but whoever lived there left in such a rush, they left the door open between the garage and the rest of the home. Now, some of the other houses might have left their front doors unlocked, but you'd still have to go around wiggling the doorknobs. On this house, there are no visible barriers to entry, so you just walk right on in. The same thing can happen with computers. A user can intentionally put a computer on the network with no password protection, open file shares, and no security measures, virtually inviting any passing-by hackers to come in and have a look around.

- **Viruses**—Viruses are still some of the most common security risks to computers today. Viruses used to spread primarily through floppy disks with boot sector infections, but now the delivery mechanism of choice is email. Viruses are small applications or scripts that are self replicating (just like a biological virus), and more often than not cause unwanted results on the systems on which they run.

- **Trojan horses**—Trojan horses are like viruses, except they usually masquerade as useful programs—a guise just to get the user to execute the Trojan, analogous to the Trojan Horse of classic Greek mythology—and are usually not self replicating. In fact, a Trojan Horse might even execute on your computer, displaying a neat little fireworks display or a funny little dancing baby, but in the background, the Trojan Horse is opening the door for the soldiers of the hacker who created it.

- **Social engineering**—Social engineering is the art of tricking people into giving you what you need to gain access to something you shouldn't have. For example, you're sitting at your desk, happily working away. Someone calls you on the phone and tells you he's upgrading your email server, but to move your account, he needs your username and password. If you give it to him, you've just fallen prey to social engineering.

- **Denial of service**—A denial of service usually involves flooding a system with false requests so that real requests cannot be processed. For a good example, read the write-up at www.grc.com/dos/grcdos.htm.

To evaluate your system's readiness against a few potential vulnerabilities, check out an online port scanner or run Microsoft's Baseline Security Advisor tool against your machine.

ONLINE PORT SCANNERS

To get a better idea of some of the possible ways into your computer, take a look at the free, online port scanner at the Gibson Research Corporation, www.grc.com. Go to the ShieldsUP link, and try both the Test My Shields and Probe My Ports options. This is by no means a comprehensive evaluation of all the possible holes in your network security, but if you are not behind a firewall, it will show you some of the most common high-risk configuration holes that hackers could use to gain access to your network.

Another online port scanning tool is available at www.dslreports.com/scan. This online port scanner takes about a minute to complete, and it provides a list of open TCP or UDP ports on your system.

MICROSOFT BASELINE SECURITY ADVISOR

For a Microsoft operating system-specific security evaluation, take a look at the Microsoft Baseline Security Advisor (MBSA), available as a free download from www.microsoft.com/technet/security/tools/Tools/MBSAhome.asp. MBSA can run a scan against your local system or against any remote system on which you have administrative access. MBSA will run on Windows 2000 or Windows XP and will output a report on hot-fixes, service packs, and vulnerabilities for

- Windows NT 4.0 SP4 (see the following note), Windows 2000, and Windows XP operating systems
- Office 2000 and Office XP
- SQL Server 7.0 and SQL Server 2000
- Internet Information Services (IIS) Server 4.0 and IIS Server 5.0
- Internet Explorer 5.01 or later

NOTE

> The MBSA tool can run against a remote machine running Windows NT 4.0 SP4 or greater, but the scan must be executed from a Windows 2000 or Windows XP system.

GENERAL SECURITY PRACTICES

So now you've seen some of the threats; what general practices can you use to protect yourself? Whether you're using a standalone system or a LAN, consider following these recommendations:

- Install a virus scanner, and update the virus definitions on a regular—daily, or at worst, weekly—basis.

- Disable the Outlook or Outlook Express preview pane.

- Use at least Medium security settings in Internet Explorer.

- Never run email attachments from unknown sources.

- Disable bridging in corporate environments to keep users from bridging secure networks to insecure networks.

- Never run email attachments, even from known sources, if you weren't expecting to receive them.

- Never share your password, not even with a system administrator or technician.

- If you don't use SNMP to monitor your network, disable SNMP.

- Never install IIS if you aren't hosting a Web server, FTP site, or other service that would require it.

CAUTION

Installing IIS is one of the easiest ways to open up your system to a whole new slew of attacks. Do not use IIS unless absolutely necessary.

- Don't install the optional "Simple TCP Services." They are unnecessary and leave your system open for additional denial-of-service attacks.

- In a corporate environment, don't allow people to use dial-up lines at their desks. They'll be able to connect to personal ISPs, overriding your enterprise security measures.

- Enable Macro Virus Protection in all Microsoft Office applications.

- Keep your system up-to-date with Automatic Updates, Windows Updates, Service Packs, and hotfixes for all applications. Pay particular attention to updates for the OS, Internet Explorer, Microsoft Outlook, and Microsoft Office.

- Keep the Guest account disabled (or, as it's called on the User Accounts control panel screen, "turned off").

- Don't install unnecessary applications. For applications you do install, regularly check the vendor's Web site for required patches.

- Sign up for security notification mailing lists to always be aware of new security risks and to take action in a timely manner.

NOTE

Some good sites at which you could sign up for security bulletins include these:

- Predictive Systems (www.predictive.com)
- NT Bugtraq (www.ntbugtraq.com)
- BindView's RAZOR (http://razor.bindview.com)
- CERT (www.cert.org)

- Use strong passwords on *every* account. Never use a blank password. Log out and lock your machine when you step away. Check Return to the Welcome Screen or Require Password when configuring your screen saver.

- Enable the Internet Connection Firewall on all connections that access the Internet (see the section "Making a Secure Internet Connection" later in this chapter), unless the connection is through your office LAN, and the LAN has a firewall or NAT router between it and the Internet.

→ For additional security in a networked environment, consider implementing security through *group policy*, as explained in Chapter 22, "Locking Down Your Computer."

MAKING A SECURE INTERNET CONNECTION

The safest way to completely secure your system from outside influences is to disconnect it from any and all networks on which you are not the only client. This includes corporate networks as well as the Internet. Unfortunately, that makes it difficult to get your email, surf the Web, and download virus updates. So your next best option is to make your system *appear* as if it were disconnected from the network by hiding behind a firewall. A firewall acts as a protective boundary against unexpected traffic or unauthorized connections between a trusted network, such as your computer or your LAN, and a distrusted network, such as the Internet.

Large corporate networks often use sophisticated, expensive hardware/software combinations to provide firewall services for the corporate LAN. For a single Windows XP computer or for a home or small office LAN, though, the three best options are these:

- XP's built-in Internet Connection Firewall (ICF)
- A hardware connection-sharing router/firewall
- Third-party firewall software such as BlackICE Defender and ZoneAlarm

In this section, I'll discuss some of the pros and cons of these three solutions.

INTERNET CONNECTION FIREWALL

Internet Connection Firewall (ICF) is a software firewall implementation included as a built-in feature of Windows XP networking. ICF can be enabled on any network adapter or dial-up connection on your system, although it is generally not recommended for use on a VPN connection because it often interferes with VPN connectivity. Although ICF can be enabled for any connection except the private connection of a machine enabled for Internet Connection Sharing (ICS), it should only be used on connections that connect directly to the Internet. Otherwise, you might interfere with desirable internal network functions such as file and printer sharing or remote administration.

24

ICF does a fine job of protecting your computer or LAN from most types of hacking attacks. Its three main advantages are that it's free, fall-down-the-stairs easy to set up, and designed to work with Remote Assistance and videoconferencing applications such as Microsoft Messenger and NetMeeting. It automatically opens the firewall to allow the peculiar incoming connection protocols for these applications. This last item is a big plus—you can't use Messenger video or Remote Assistance if you use other types of firewall services.

However, this openness is also ICF's Achilles Heel. Because holes in the firewall can be opened under software control, without a doubt Trojan horse and virus software has been or will be written to exploit it. If such a program somehow was allowed to run on your computer, it could instantly disable ICF. This is the biggest problem with ICF: On general principles, it's a bad idea to let a system guard itself. Just as they say that a doctor who treats himself has a fool for a patient, a computer that acts as its own firewall has…well, you get the point.

Finally, although ICF does protect you from incoming hacking attempts, you cannot use it to set up filters that block *outbound* connections on designated port numbers. Outbound filtering is a highly desirable tool to block designated protocols such as file sharing, regardless of whether the request comes from inside or outside your network.

HARDWARE CONNECTION SHARING/FIREWALL DEVICES

Network routers, hardware devices that intelligently transfer data traffic between separate networks, have been around for decades. Routers were once the exclusive domain of companies such as Cisco, AT&T, and Nortel Networks and used to cost thousands of dollars, but this is no longer true. The growing popularity of broadband Internet connections and the plummeting price of high-speed network electronics have given rise to a category of "consumer" level routers often called Cable/DSL sharing routers. These devices provide network address translation (NAT) service to offer Internet service to several computers using one broadband connection and often provide additional (if simple-minded) firewall capabilities based on port filtering. They are amazingly inexpensive for what they do: Ethernet versions now cost around $75 and 802.11b wireless versions can be had for less than $200.

CAUTION

If you use a wireless network, be sure to enable WEP security. For more information about configuring wireless networks, see the "Wireless Network Security" section later in this chapter.

Using these devices with a DSL or cable Internet connection provides several advantages. One is that they move the job of protecting your computer *out* of your computer. If the firewall somehow gets flooded or shut down by an attacker, the router might get shut down, but your computer will not be exposed to the attack. Because their software is much less complex than Windows', they're less likely to have bugs and exploits. And, although a failure of a software service such as ICF might not be noticed—you might surf away for days not knowing you're unprotected—if your external router fails, you'll notice that your Internet connection will go down. These devices also have low power consumption, so compared to leaving a Windows computer on and running ICS all the time, they save energy. Finally, sharing routers usually have the capability to filter all traffic on specific TCP/IP ports, so you can definitely block network traffic for sensitive network services such as file sharing and SNMP.

THIRD-PARTY FIREWALL SOFTWARE

Several companies offer add-on firewall software for Windows XP. The major offerings are as follows:

- ZoneAlarm and ZoneAlarm Pro by Zone Labs
- McAfee Firewall by Network Associates
- Norton Personal Firewall by Symantec
- Sygate Personal Firewall and Personal Firewall Pro by Sygate
- BlackICE PC Protection by Internet Security Systems

These products offer valuable features that hardware routers and Windows's ICF don't, including the following:

- Pop-up notification of unexpected incoming or outgoing connection attempts, which you can choose to permit or deny
- Detailed logging and analysis of suspicious network traffic, probes, and hack attempts
- Fine-grained configuration of incoming and outgoing data traffic on a per-port or even per-application basis
- Filtering by data content and suppression of pop-up and banner ads

Not all of the listed products offer all of these features, and not all of them work as well as you'd hope, so read up on the latest product reviews before investing or even trying one of these products. www.firewallguide.com/software.htm would be a good place to start.

The downsides to third-party products are that you have to go to some trouble to actually obtain and install them; they tend to be difficult to configure (and a misconfigured firewall is less than useless if it leaves you vulnerable without your knowledge); and many early releases of these products have gotten poor marks in the "plays well with others" category. In particular, some have had problems working with ICS.

On the other hand, a third-party firewall package can give you finely tuned control over network security and can provide much in the way of real-time, interactive notification of potential problems. In-your-face notification is a good thing when it comes to security.

An additional advantage of third-party firewall products is that these companies have a vested interest in making the product work correctly. Although Microsoft knows you're stuck with its products (and its track record on quality and bug-fixing reflects this), independent vendors have to make you happy (eventually).

MAKING THE CHOICE

Personally, for small networks, of the three alternatives we just discussed, I prefer a dedicated hardware-based firewall, such as the low-cost EtherFast Cable/DSL Router, part number BEFSR41 from Linksys (www.linksys.com). For complete firewall functionality including Stateful Packet Inspection, consider upgrading to the BEFSX41 EtherFast Cable/DSL Firewall Router with 4-Port Switch/VPN Endpoint. Stateful Packet Inspection tracks each connection passing through a firewall and examines both the header and the contents of the packet to ensure validity.

Although you lose the capability for NetMeeting/Messenger video and for incoming Remote Assistance, I like the added security offered by adding an actual physical device between my network and potential attackers. For even better protection, use both the hardware router and third-party firewall software. (Manufacturers seem to like the idea: Several hardware routers now come with coupons for discounted licenses for commercial software firewall products.)

Sometimes, though, a hardware-based firewall is not an option. If, for example, you...

> ...will be traveling and plugging into a broadband network in a hotel
>
> ...connect via wireless in an airport or conference center
>
> ...connect to a large corporate network (other internal users in your company can be a threat, too!)
>
> ...need to use NetMeeting or other videoconferencing software, or want to receive Remote Assistance connections from another Windows XP user

...you probably want to use the integrated Internet Connection Firewall included by default with Windows XP. As I stated earlier, ICF has some shortcomings, but as long as it's not compromised from the inside, it's good protection, and in any case, it's certainly better than nothing.

CONFIGURING A HARDWARE CONNECTION SHARING ROUTER

At least a dozen connection sharing router devices are on the market today, and I can't provide specific instructions for configuring them (although some discussion of the process can be found in Chapter 8, "Configuring Your Internet Connection"). If you've purchased one of these devices, you'll have to follow the manufacturer's installation and setup instructions.

When you configure the router, be sure to take the following security measures:

■ Change the routers from the manufacturer's default to a strong password using both letters and numbers.

- Disable management access to the router from "outside."
- If your network uses netlog or other network event monitoring, see if your sharing router can be configured to report significant events to your network logger.

After the router is configured and working, your network will be protected against most incoming hacking attacks through the router's network address translation (NAT) function. For additional security, you might want to configure port filtering to block several of the most risky network services. Table 24.1 lists the minimum ports to block; you might want to add others. Most routers have a limited number of port-filtering entries, so you'll want to choose the ports carefully and take advantage of the ability to enter ranges of numbers where you can.

TABLE 24.1 MINIMUM LIST OF TCP/IP PORTS TO BLOCK

Port or Port Range	Network Service
23	Telnet
137–139	Windows File Sharing
161–162	SNMP
445	Windows File Sharing

Of course, you need to leave these ports unblocked if you want to permit inbound connections from the Internet to your servers.

CONFIGURING AN INTERNET CONNECTION FIREWALL

Figure 24.1 illustrates three different ways you might use ICF:

- With a standalone dial-up or broadband connection (computer A)
- With a shared dial-up connection (computers B and C)
- With a shared broadband connection (computers D and E)

In each case, ICF is enabled only on the connection that attaches to the distrusted network. It is not enabled on the connections for inside the network because it would block the computers' ability to interact with each other on the network. When ICF is enabled on a network with multiple clients, ICS is also enabled to allow other client PCs access through the Internet-attached PCs network connection.

→ Refer to the Chapter 8 section, "Sharing Your Internet Connections," for information on configuring ICS.

Figure 24.1
Shown are three common ways you might connect to the Internet. ICF is used on the connections that go directly to the distrusted network.

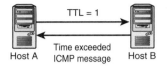

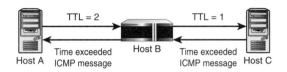

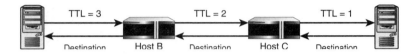

ENABLING INTERNET CONNECTION FIREWALL

ICF is available on Windows XP Home, Windows XP Professional, and Windows Server 2003, but it's not available on Windows XP 64-bit Edition. ICF must be enabled per-connection under Windows XP. To turn it on, follow these steps:

1. If you're using the Classic view, click Start, Settings, Control Panel, Network Connections. If you're using the XP Start Menu view, click Start, Control Panel, Network and Internet Connections. Then click Network Connections under the Control Panel Icons section.

2. Find the connection you use to connect to the Internet. Right-click the connection and select Properties from the pop-up menu.

3. Select the Advanced tab and check the Protect My Computer and Network by Limiting or Preventing Access to This Computer from the Internet check box.

4. Click OK.

That's all it takes. Some advanced settings will allow your system to respond to specific external requests, enable logging, or enable response to specific Internet Control Message Protocol (ICMP) requests (such as `Ping`) from external systems. These advanced options are accessed by clicking the Settings button on the Advanced tab from step 3. Just remember this before enabling any additional services or ICMP ports: The more external requests your system will pass, the more potential for an exploitable security hole.

ALLOWING SERVICE REQUESTS TO PASS THROUGH AN INTERNET CONNECTION FIREWALL

If you are enabling ICF on a system that provides a service to clients on the distrusted network (for example, hosting a Web server), you must configure ICF to pass the request. This can be accomplished as follows:

1. If you're using the Classic view, click Start, Settings, Control Panel, Network Connections. If you're using the XP Start Menu view, click Start, Control Panel, Network and Internet Connections. Then click Network Connections under the Control Panel Icons section.

2. Find the connection that has ICF enabled. Right-click the connection and select Properties from the pop-up menu.

3. Select the Advanced tab and click the Settings button.

4. On the Services tab, check any boxes for which this system provides services to external clients. For example, if you want for external clients to be able to connect to this system using Remote Desktop connections, select the option marked Remote Desktop.

5. When you enable this option, a Service Settings dialog box will open, containing the name of the local computer in the Name or IP Address of the Computer Hosting This Service box. If a different machine on your private network provides this service, enter that machine's name or IP address here, and click OK.

6. If the service you want to provide is not listed (for example, if you are providing a standard service on a nonstandard port), you must add it. First, let's assume you're hosting a Web server on Port 8080 on the local machine. Enabling the Web Server (HTTP) option won't do anything for you because your Web server isn't running on the standard port 80. To add this service, click the Add button on the Services tab.

7. Enter a description for the service in the Description of Service box. For this example, I'll call it Special Web Service.

8. Enter the current computer name in the box labeled Name or IP Address of the Computer Hosting This Service. Note again, if a different computer on your private network hosted this service, you would enter that system's name or IP address here.

9. Enter 8080 for both the External and Internal port numbers.

10. Because a Web server is a TCP-based service, select the TCP Option box. You should see the configuration depicted in Figure 24.2. Click OK.

11. Click OK on the Advanced Settings dialog and again on the properties for your connection.

LOGGING INTERNET CONNECTION FIREWALL REQUESTS

If you'd like to track and review the activities of the ICF, you can enable security logging. Security logging can save any activity logged by the firewall, including dropped packets or successful connections.

For example, if you are not allowing FTP services through your firewall, and an external connection attempts to connect to your machine on Port 21 (the standard FTP service port), ICF will drop the packets. If you have enabled logging for dropped packets, an entry will be made to the log.

Figure 24.2
Shown is what you'll see when adding a service to ICF.

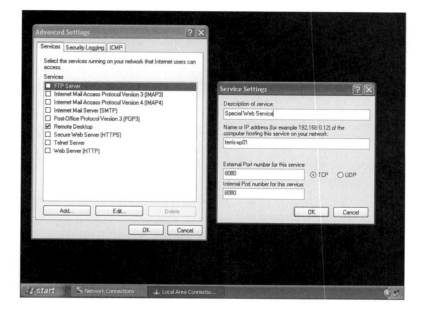

If you have enabled logging for successful connections and an internal user accesses a Web site over the connection with ICF enabled, an entry will be logged acknowledging the successful connection. Likewise, if the connection came from outside the network to the ICF box requesting a Web page, and if ICF was passing the Web Server service to an internal machine, the successful attempt would generate an entry in the log file.

ICF logging is not enabled by default. To turn it on, do this:

1. If you're using the Classic view, click Start, Settings, Control Panel, Network Connections. If you're using the XP Start Menu view, click Start, Control Panel, Network and Internet Connections. Then click Network Connections under the Control Panel Icons section.

2. Find the connection that has ICF enabled. Right-click the connection and select Properties from the pop-up menu.

3. Select the Advanced tab and click the Settings button.

4. Select the Security Logging tab. Figure 24.3 shows the dialog. Selecting Log Dropped Packets logs all dropped packets that originate from the private network or the Internet. Selecting Log Successful Connections logs all successful connections that originate from the private network or the Internet.

5. Click OK on the Advanced Settings dialog and again on the properties for your connection.

Figure 24.3
Shown is the Security Logging configuration panel.

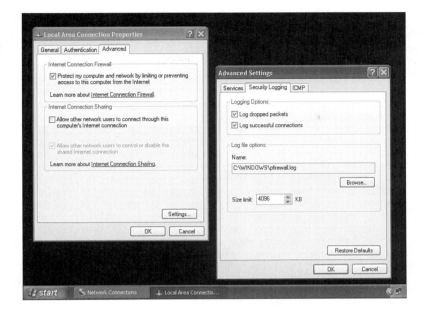

The log file is stored by default in C:\WINDOWS\pfirewall.log. You can change this location on the Security Logging configuration tab. This log file is stored in the W3C Extended Log File Format and can be viewed in a standard text editor such as Notepad.

The following listing shows a newly created log file after a user visits Microsoft's site and tries to ping the machine with ICMP echo disabled. Lines preceded with ### are comments I've inserted to explain what was going on when the entries were created.

```
###The following lines are created whenever a new log file is first started.
#Version: 1.0
#Software: Microsoft Internet Connection Firewall
#Time Format: Local
#Fields: date time action protocol src-ip dst-ip src-port dst-port size tcpflags
➥tcpsyn tcpack tcpwin icmptype icmpcode info

###The following lines resulted from a successful connection from my local
###machine to http://www.microsoft.com
2002-05-29 23:26:55 OPEN TCP 192.168.1.102 207.46.197.113 3015 80 - - - - - - - -
2002-05-29 23:26:56 OPEN TCP 192.168.1.102 207.46.197.113 3016 80 - - - - - - - -
2002-05-29 23:26:56 OPEN TCP 192.168.1.102 207.46.197.113 3017 80 - - - - - - - -
2002-05-29 23:26:56 OPEN TCP 192.168.1.102 207.46.197.113 3018 80 - - - - - - - -
2002-05-29 23:26:56 OPEN TCP 192.168.1.102 207.46.130.149 3019 80 - - - - - - - -
2002-05-29 23:26:56 OPEN TCP 192.168.1.102 207.46.197.113 3020 80 - - - - - - - -
2002-05-29 23:26:57 OPEN TCP 192.168.1.102 207.46.197.113 3021 80 - - - - - - - -
2002-05-29 23:26:57 OPEN TCP 192.168.1.102 207.46.197.113 3022 80 - - - - - - - -
2002-05-29 23:26:57 OPEN TCP 192.168.1.102 207.46.197.113 3023 80 - - - - - - - -
2002-05-29 23:26:57 OPEN TCP 192.168.1.102 207.46.197.113 3024 80 - - - - - - - -
2002-05-29 23:26:57 OPEN TCP 192.168.1.102 207.46.197.113 3025 80 - - - - - - - -
2002-05-29 23:26:57 OPEN TCP 192.168.1.102 207.46.197.113 3026 80 - - - - - - - -
2002-05-29 23:26:57 OPEN TCP 192.168.1.102 207.46.197.113 3027 80 - - - - - - - -
2002-05-29 23:26:58 OPEN TCP 192.168.1.102 207.46.197.113 3028 80 - - - - - - - -
2002-05-29 23:26:58 OPEN TCP 192.168.1.102 207.46.197.113 3029 80 - - - - - - - -
```

```
2002-05-29 23:26:58 OPEN TCP 192.168.1.102 207.46.197.113 3030 80 - - - - - - - - -
2002-05-29 23:26:58 OPEN TCP 192.168.1.102 207.46.197.113 3031 80 - - - - - - - - -
2002-05-29 23:27:46 CLOSE TCP 192.168.1.102 207.46.197.113 3015 80 - - - - - - - - -
2002-05-29 23:27:46 CLOSE TCP 192.168.1.102 207.46.197.113 3016 80 - - - - - - - - -
2002-05-29 23:27:46 CLOSE TCP 192.168.1.102 207.46.197.113 3017 80 - - - - - - - - -
2002-05-29 23:27:46 CLOSE TCP 192.168.1.102 207.46.197.113 3018 80 - - - - - - - - -
2002-05-29 23:27:46 CLOSE TCP 192.168.1.102 207.46.130.149 3019 80 - - - - - - - - -
2002-05-29 23:27:46 CLOSE TCP 192.168.1.102 207.46.197.113 3020 80 - - - - - - - - -
2002-05-29 23:27:46 CLOSE TCP 192.168.1.102 207.46.197.113 3021 80 - - - - - - - - -
2002-05-29 23:27:46 CLOSE TCP 192.168.1.102 207.46.197.113 3022 80 - - - - - - - - -
2002-05-29 23:27:46 CLOSE TCP 192.168.1.102 207.46.197.113 3023 80 - - - - - - - - -
2002-05-29 23:27:46 CLOSE TCP 192.168.1.102 207.46.197.113 3024 80 - - - - - - - - -
2002-05-29 23:27:46 CLOSE TCP 192.168.1.102 207.46.197.113 3025 80 - - - - - - - - -
2002-05-29 23:27:46 CLOSE TCP 192.168.1.102 207.46.197.113 3026 80 - - - - - - - - -
2002-05-29 23:27:46 CLOSE TCP 192.168.1.102 207.46.197.113 3027 80 - - - - - - - - -
2002-05-29 23:27:46 CLOSE TCP 192.168.1.102 207.46.197.113 3028 80 - - - - - - - - -
2002-05-29 23:27:46 CLOSE TCP 192.168.1.102 207.46.197.113 3029 80 - - - - - - - - -
2002-05-29 23:27:46 CLOSE TCP 192.168.1.102 207.46.197.113 3030 80 - - - - - - - - -
2002-05-29 23:27:46 CLOSE TCP 192.168.1.102 207.46.197.113 3031 80 - - - - - - - - -
###This is where I ceased communications to www.microsoft.com.
###The following lines are dropped packets resulting from trying to ping
###my ICF-protected workstation from another system on my network.
2002-05-29 23:30:00 DROP ICMP 192.168.1.5 192.168.1.102 - - 60 - - - - 8 0 -
2002-05-29 23:30:05 DROP ICMP 192.168.1.5 192.168.1.102 - - 60 - - - - 8 0 -
2002-05-29 23:30:10 DROP ICMP 192.168.1.5 192.168.1.102 - - 60 - - - - 8 0 -
2002-05-29 23:30:15 DROP ICMP 192.168.1.5 192.168.1.102 - - 60 - - - - 8 0 -
###As is standard, four PING attempts, dropped four times.
```

ALLOWING INTERNET CONTROL MESSAGE PROTOCOL CONNECTIONS

If you want to allow ICMP connections, follow this procedure:

1. If you're using the Classic view, click Start, Settings, Control Panel, Network Connections. If you're using the XP Start Menu view, click Start, Control Panel, Network and Internet Connections. Then click Network Connections under the Control Panel Icons section.

2. Find the connection that has ICF enabled. Right-click the connection and select Properties from the pop-up menu.

3. Select the Advanced tab and click the Settings button.

4. Select the ICMP tab, and configure the options to your liking. In Figure 24.4, I've enabled the option Allow Incoming Echo Request, so that this system will respond to ping commands. The available options are shown in Table 24.2.

5. Click OK on the Advanced Settings dialog and again on the properties for your connection.

Figure 24.4
The ICMP tab can allow the ICF-protected system to respond to ping requests.

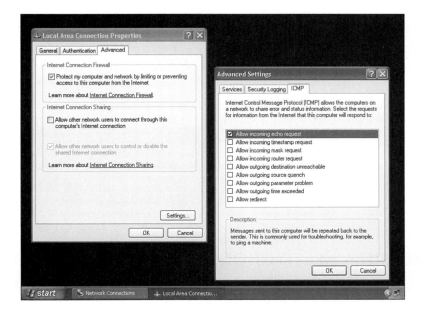

TABLE 24.2   ICMP CONFIGURATION OPTIONS UNDER ICF

Option	Description
Allow Incoming Echo Request	Messages sent to the ICF computer will be repeated back to the sender. This option is required if you want this system to respond to `ping` requests.
Allow Incoming Timestamp Request	Data sent to the ICF computer can be acknowledged with a confirmation message indicating the time the data was received.
Allow Incoming Mask Request	The ICF computer will accept and respond to requests for more information about the network to which it is attached.
Allow Incoming Router Request	The ICF computer will respond to requests for information about the routes it recognizes.
Allow Outgoing Destination Unreachable	Data sent over the Internet that fails to reach the ICF computer due to an error will be discarded and acknowledged with a `Destination Unreachable` message explaining the failure.
Allow Outgoing Source Quench	If the ICF computer's ability to process incoming data cannot keep up with the rate of a transmission, data will be dropped and the sending computer will be asked to slow down.

continues

TABLE 24.2 CONTINUED

Option	Description
Allow Outgoing Parameter Problem	When the ICF computer discards received data due to a problematic header, it will reply to the sender with a `Bad Header` error message.
Allow Outgoing Time Exceeded	When the ICF computer discards an incomplete data transmission because the entire transmission required more time than allowed, it will reply to the sender with a `Time Expired` message.
Allow Redirect	Data sent from the ICF computer will be rerouted if a more direct route exists.

SECURITY RESTRICTIONS ON NETWORK SHARES

As you probably know, Windows XP allows you to set security restrictions on shared resources. It is generally preferred to set Everyone to Full Control on the share and manage file permissions at the NTFS level to restrict user access. Naturally, your drives must be formatted as NTFS to do this. Setting permissions on the files, rather than on the shares, ensures the same level of access permissions for a particular group or individual, regardless of potentially conflicting or nested shares. In addition, setting permissions at the file system level ensures that a user or group will have the same access permissions whether they are accessing a system remotely or from the local keyboard.

→ Refer to Chapter 18, "Using the Network," for information on creating and managing shared network resources.

→ Refer to Chapter 23, "Managing File Security," for information on setting NTFS-level permissions for object and container access.

Most of what you need to know about protecting shares is covered in the earlier chapters. A few additional considerations are worth noting, however:

- Use hidden shares (share names ending with a dollar sign [$]) whenever possible.

- Review configured shares on a regular basis, and delete those that are no longer needed.

- Never connect a system with shares to the Internet without placing the system behind a firewall or enabling the ICF.

- Remember: Administrators, Server Operators, and Power Users all have rights to create shares. Don't add users to these groups unless you trust them with this permission.

- Never set shares at the root level of the drive. Default shares available only to administrators are at the root level of every hard disk drive. For example, the C drive will be shared as C$, and the D drive will be shared as D$.

WIRELESS NETWORK SECURITY

Another major security hole in many networks has come about from the recent explosion in wireless networking with 802.11b and 802.11a devices.

→ Refer to the "Wireless Networking" section in Chapter 17, "Building Your Own Network," for more information about setting up wireless networks.

With wireless networking, unencrypted data packets are being broadcast through the air, where they're just waiting to be picked up by drive-by hackers. In addition, if your wireless connection is not secured, it might be possible for someone to connect to your wireless access point as if he were a legitimate client on your network. After that, he would have access to any unprotected resources on your network, which could include such items as your corporate intranet. In addition, after someone is connected to your network, he can bypass your security precautions that isolate your internal trusted network from the unsecured free-for-all chaos of the Internet.

NOTE

In some urban areas, guerilla network hackers are even placing discrete marks on sidewalks and signposts where unsecured networks have been found. This isn't a joke—wireless network security is a big problem.

Just for fun, try driving around your own neighborhood looking for unsecured wireless access. You can try using the automatic wireless configuration features of Windows XP, or for a slightly more advanced tool, take a look at www.netstumbler.com. With NetStumbler on my Pocket PC, I was able to find *five* unsecured wireless networks within two blocks of my house.

If you are a network administrator in an office, you can use the same technique to see if any users have set up unauthorized rogue wireless access points and have them running unsecured on your network.

WIRED EQUIVALENT PRIVACY

Fortunately, you can gain a small degree of protection by disabling broadcast associations on your wireless access points and enabling Wired Equivalent Privacy (WEP) encryption. When WEP is enabled, a wireless client device authenticates itself to the wireless access point by using a shared secret key. All clients who use the same access point will have an identical key. Key length is usually 40-bit or 128-bit. After a client has connected to the wireless access point using WEP, all traffic between the client and the access point is encrypted using an RC4 cipher tied to the WEP key.

Unfortunately, WEP encryption was broken early in the wireless technology lifecycle. For details on the vulnerability, see the write-up by the SANS Institute at http://rr.sans.org/wireless/equiv.php.

To configure WEP on your system, go to your Network Connections panel. Right-click the connection associated with your wireless card, and select Properties. Then select the

Wireless Networks tab, and click the Add button under Preferred Network. Enter the WEP key associated with the wireless network in the requisite blank, as shown in Figure 24.5.

Figure 24.5
Shown are dialogs for enabling WEP. My wireless network is the one with the SSID of AAWUG (for Austin Area Wireless Users Group). The other network IDs were both picked up as broadcast SSIDs from inside my home office.

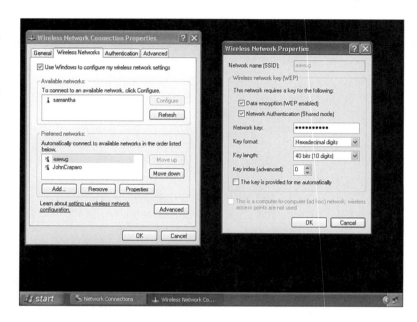

802.1x

IEEE 802.1x is a port-based standard for network access control. 802.1x authentication is able to provide authenticated access to 802.11-based wireless networks and to wired Ethernet devices, meaning you can perform authentication before providing a connection to anything on the network other than the systems providing authorization. 802.1x allows for the use of industry-recognized security and encryption standards over 802.11 wireless connections, providing significantly more secure communications than WEP-based encryption.

To break it down a little further, 802.1x allows a network client to connect to a restricted port. The EAP traffic is exchanged for authentication, and if the authentication is successful, the client's port is changed to "Authorized." Then the client can communicate to other systems on the network. The client has a connection to the network right out of the gate, but until it's authorized, the port only allows authentication traffic to pass, and nothing else.

NOTE

For a background of the 802.1x implementation within Windows XP, refer to the "Wireless 802.11 Security with Windows XP" whitepaper at
www.microsoft.com/windowsxp/pro/techinfo/administration/
wirelesssecurity/default.asp.

Setting up 802.1x security requires quite a bit more than a change of configuration to a local system. It requires a certificate infrastructure, an active directory, Internet authentication services, an authentication protocol (such as RADIUS), and more. Refer to the Enterprise Deployment of IEEE 802.11, "Using Windows XP and Windows 2000 Internet Authentication Service" (www.microsoft.com/WindowsXP/pro/techinfo/deployment/wireless/default.asp) for a full implementation guide for 802.1x.

After you have an 802.1x infrastructure in place, you must enable 802.1x authentication for the network connection that will use it. To do this:

1. Click Start, Control Panel (if you're using Category view, click Network and Internet Connections), and then click Network Connections under the Control Panel Icons section.

2. Right-click the connection for which you are enabling 802.1x, and select Properties from the pop-up menu.

3. Select the Authentication tab. Select the Enable Network Access Control Using IEEE 802.1x check box, and select the proper EAP type for the infrastructure that is supporting your 802.1x implementation.

4. If you are using certificate-based authentication, click the Properties button to select whether to use a smart card or a locally stored certificate. You can also opt to validate the server certificate by selecting a trusted root certificate authority from the drop-down box. Figure 24.6 shows the 802.1x properties box.

Figure 24.6
Use these dialog boxes to configure a network connection for 802.1x.

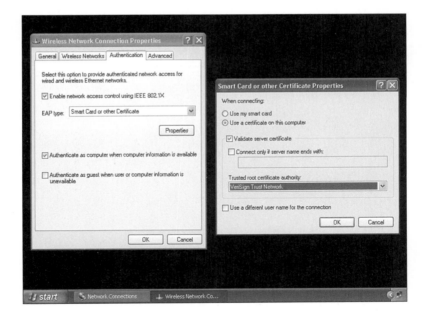

5. Click OK on any remaining open windows.

PROTECTING WIRELESS NETWORKS WITH VPNS

An interesting emerging best practice in wireless network implementation involves the creation of a separate physical network to host the wireless infrastructure. Clients on the wireless network are then logically treated just like systems out on the Internet. They are isolated from corporate resources just like Internet clients, and accessing the corporate network requires logging in using a standard VPN connection. In addition to requiring a valid username and password in the domain before allowing a connection, all traffic to corporate resources will be encrypted between the client and the VPN server. This protects data from wireless network sniffers.

24

MANAGEMENT, MAINTENANCE, AND REPAIR

CHAPTER 25

MANAGING YOUR HARD DRIVES

In this chapter

DISK FORMATTING AND STORAGE OPTIONS

When you think of formatting a hard drive, whether brand new to a computer or existing equipment, you may not really put much thought into it. After all, what really is there to think about? You just tell Windows to format the drive (or alternatively use the format command) and off you go, right? If only it were that easy. In the old days (we're talking really old, like DOS days), you could get away with that little thought. You used fdisk to partition a drive and then formatted your partitions, and boom, you were in business. As much as Windows XP makes your life easier, it also adds difficulty in that you must make more choices now than ever before. What's worse is the fact that the choices you make early will affect your computer's capabilities later on.

The first and perhaps most important choice you'll have to make when working with new hard drives is what file system you will use on the hard drive. Windows XP contains many features that require the use of the NTFS file system, even though you can still successfully run Windows XP on a FAT- or FAT32-formatted hard drive. Formatting with NTFS is an irreversible procedure—there's no going back. Formatting a drive with FAT or FAT32 allows you the choice of converting to NTFS at a later date, although that again is a one way process. You do gain one advantage when installing Windows XP on a FAT or FAT32 hard drive, in that you can uninstall the operating system so long as you have not converted the hard drive to NTFS, but more on that later.

While the choice of the file system is the most important decision you will typically have to make, it's not the only one. There are a few other decisions:

- Whether to use advanced features that gang hard drives together for faster throughput, such as *striping*.

- Whether to use the traditional *Basic* storage approach or newer *Dynamic* storage features. Dynamic Disks, among other things, provide a couple means of joining individual drives (or portions of drives) to effectively create very large logical drives from smaller ones. The use of dynamic storage or basic storage is entirely up to you and has little to no effect on the operations of Windows XP.

- The last major consideration that you need to be aware of is NTFS file compression and EFS encryption. While the configuration of these actually occurs after all of the other steps of configuring a hard drive, you need to plan for them early on lest you find yourself out of luck when the time comes and cannot implement NTFS encryption or file compression. NTFS file compression and EFS encryption will be addressed later in this chapter in the "NTFS File and Folder Compression" section and the "The Encrypting File System" section.

In the following sections, we will look at each major hard drive consideration. We will start with an overview of each item and then drill down to a more detailed coverage of your options and why one may be better than another.

CHOOSING YOUR FILE SYSTEM: NTFS OR FAT

It's no secret that Windows XP was built to run on an NTFS-formatted volume. With the exception of share permissions, the rest of Windows XP's native security and management features rely on NTFS for their availability. While Windows XP will run on FAT or FAT32 (as will Windows 2000 and Windows Server 2003), you will want to give careful consideration to performing new installations onto a FAT formatted hard drive. But what if you are working in a situation where you still need to provide for the use of a legacy operating system, such as Windows 98? In this case, you will definitely need to stay with the FAT or FAT32 file system you have in place.

TIP

> **Just Say No to FAT16**
>
> Stay away from the FAT (FAT16) file system if at all possible in Windows XP. Support for the FAT file system in Windows XP pretty much exists for backward compatibility with Windows 95 and older versions of Windows, and was not intended to be the primary file system for Windows XP.

Table 25.1 outlines some of the features and differences between the FAT16 and FAT32 file systems. Table 25.2 outlines some of the features and differences between the NTFS 4.0 (prior to Windows NT 4.0 SP4) and NTFS 5.0 file systems.

25

TABLE 25.1   FEATURES OF THE FAT16 AND FAT32 FILE SYSTEMS

Feature	FAT16	FAT32
File allocation table size	16 bit	32 bit
Maximum volume size	4GB (best is 2GB or less)	2TB (limited to 32GB in Windows 2000)
Maximum file size	2GB	4GB
Operating systems supported	MS-DOS, all versions of Windows	Windows 95 OSR2, Windows 98, Windows Me, Windows 2000, Windows XP
Maximum number of supported volumes	26	26
Supports NTFS 4.0/5.0 features?	No	No

TABLE 25.2   FEATURES OF THE NTFS 4.0 AND NTFS 5.0 FILE SYSTEMS

Feature	NTFS 4.0	NTFS 5.0
Maximum volume size	32GB	2TB
Maximum file size	32GB	Limited by volume size
Operating Systems supported	Windows NT 4.0, Windows 2000, Windows XP	Windows 2000, Windows XP, Windows NT 4.0 (minimal support)
Maximum number of supported volumes	Unlimited number of volumes using spanning or striping. Maximum of 26 volume letters assigned.	Unlimited number of volumes using spanning, striping, or mount points. Maximum of 26 volume letters assigned.

As I previously alluded to, some of the best features in Windows XP will not work without an NTFS-formatted hard drive. Some of the key features that you may want to make note of before deciding against using the NTFS file system include

- **NTFS file and folder permissions**—Using NTFS permissions, you can control access to every file on an NTFS volume. Thanks to permissions inheritance (a default option), permissions applied at the root of a volume will flow downward to all child objects. You can configure permissions at each level of the directory structure to meet your needs for allowing and/or preventing access to files and folders. However, don't get NTFS permissions confused with share permissions—they are two entirely different items, each requiring consideration both individually and as a pair.

- **The Encrypting File System**—Using a public/private key pair, EFS provides strong cryptographic encryption of files and folders that is extremely resistant to attack and compromise. Should the user's private key be lost, a Designated Recovery Agent can decrypt the file and deliver it back to the user for re-encryption with a new set of keys. EFS is completely transparent to the user and in Windows XP supports multiple user access to an encrypted file. The only down side to using EFS is that you can't use it and NTFS compression at the same time on the same file or folder.

- **File compression**—The NTFS file system supports encryption on both files and folders. NTFS uses a lossless compression algorithm which ensures that no data is lost when compressing and decompressing data. This is in contrast to *lossy* compression algorithms (for instance, .jpg images file compression) in which some data is lost each time data compression and decompression occur. As previously mentioned, compression is mutually exclusive with EFS encryption.

- **Disk space quota management**—Using disk quotas allows you to control the amount of data that users can store on your NTFS volumes. Quota control is on a per-volume basis and can be configured with custom quotas for select users as desired. The disk quota system allows you to determine when users are nearing their limits and automatically prevents usage after a user has reached their defined quota limitation.

- **Volume mount points**—You can finally escape the 26-volume limit on a computer by using volume mount points. Think of it as mapping a path to a hard drive or CD-ROM to a folder on an NTFS volume; thus a new hard drive you've installed to hold user data can be mounted as C:\UserDocs or whatever name you choose. An example of how volume mount points physically work is shown in Figure 25.1. Figure 25.2 shows the before and after view from Windows Explorer—the logical side to how volume mount points function. Creating volume mount points will be discussed in the "Creating Mounted Drives" section later in this chapter.

- **Sparse file support**—Very large files that are created by applications that actually contain very little nonzero data. NTFS can allocate only the required disk space to the file that is taken up by nonzero data, thus greatly saving hard drive space. A common example of a sparse file would be a large database file with many available, but empty fields.

- Some other noteworthy NTFS features that will not be expounded upon here include reparse points, change journals, and distributed link tracking.

Figure 25.1
The volume point from a physical perspective.

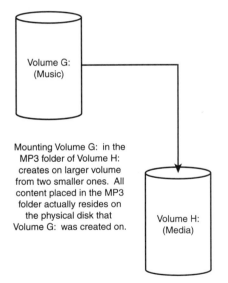

Mounting Volume G: in the MP3 folder of Volume H: creates on larger volume from two smaller ones. All content placed in the MP3 folder actually resides on the physical disk that Volume G: was created on.

NOTE

Hardcore NTFS Information

For additional information on the features of the NTFS file system and how they work, you may find the MSDN article at http://msdn.microsoft.com/library/en-us/fileio/sys_538t.asp interesting.

Figure 25.2
The volume point from a logical perspective.

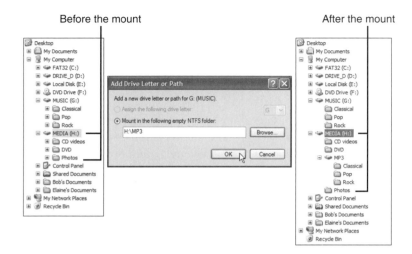

So, as you can see, the NTFS file system is far superior in every way to legacy file systems such as FAT16 or FAT32. Whatever your choice for a file system ends up being, be sure that you have put adequate forethought and planning into the decision so as to anticipate future changes.

STORAGE TYPES: WHAT'S BEST FOR YOU?

Dynamic storage is a fantastic new storage type that was introduced with Windows 2000 and carried forward into Windows XP Professional. Dynamic storage, however, is something that is not to be taken lightly...a recurring theme around here, eh?

> **NOTE**
>
> Dynamic disks are not supported in Windows XP Home Edition.

Basic storage is just that—basic. It's the same plain vanilla storage scheme that we have been using since the earliest version of DOS. Unfortunately, with basic storage you have a limited amount of configuration options available to you when trying to design fault-tolerant arrangements or those that can easily be reconfigured to meet your changing demands and expectations. Enter the dynamic storage system.

Basic storage uses partition tables to divide up the space on a hard drive. You can create a maximum of four primary partitions or three primary partitions and one extended partition on a basic disk. Primary partitions can be marked as active (that is, you can boot the computer from them) and extended partitions can be further split up into logical drives. Sounds confusing, doesn't it? With dynamic storage, all of these arcane and confusing limitations are removed. Dynamic disks are divided into volumes, which can be resized and extended almost at will to accommodate almost any situation that you may encounter. Thus the name "dynamic."

Figure 25.3 shows an example of a basic disk with three primary partitions and one extended partition that contains three logical drives.

Figure 25.3
A sample basic disk configuration.

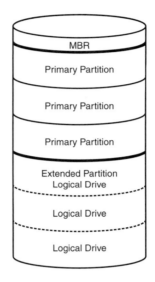

CAUTION

You cannot share a dynamic disk with another operating system, so dynamic disks are out if you have a dual-boot configuration—even if the other installation is Windows XP Professional.

Dynamic storage volumes allow you the following options when divvying up disk space:

- **Simple volumes**—Pretty much the same as a basic storage partition, simple volumes utilize disk space from only one disk.

- **Spanned volumes**—Utilize multiple disks (between two and thirty–two) to create a single volume. Spanned volumes provide no fault tolerance, however, and therefore if one disk fails the entire set will be lost. Spanning volumes provides a quick and easy way to add more room to a volume that is running low. Figure 25.4 shows how a spanned volume works on the physical level.

- **Striped volumes**—Utilize multiple disks to write data across each disk in 64KB sequential stripes. Once the stripe has been written to the first disk in the set, the next disk is written and so forth. Striped volumes, however, provide no fault tolerance and therefore if one disk fails the entire set will be lost. Disk striping is commonly known as RAID-0. Striping volumes improves the overall disk I/O performance of a computer by distributing disk I/O requests over multiple disks. Striping writes to all disks so that data is added to all disks at the same rate.

Figure 25.4
Dynamic disks in a
spanned volume.

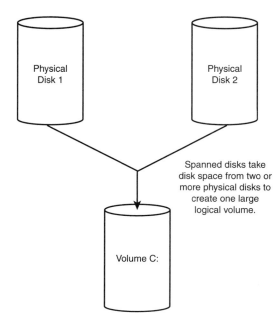

Spanned disks take
disk space from two or
more physical disks to
create one large
logical volume.

25

NOTE

No RAID Here

You'll notice an absence of mirrored volumes or RAID-5 volumes from the list above due to the fact that Windows XP Professional doesn't support them. You'll need a Windows 2000 Server or Windows 2003 Server to use them.

You can convert basic disks to dynamic disks with no data loss, provided that you meet the following requirements. Should you decided at a later time, however, that you want to revert a dynamic disk back to a basic disk, you will lose all data contained on that dynamic disk—just a small point to keep in the back of your mind!

- Master Boot Record (MBR) disks must have at least 1MB of free space available at the end of the disk for the dynamic disk database to be created.

- Dynamic storage cannot be used on removable media. Removable media can only use basic storage with primary partitions.

- Hard drives on portable computers can't be converted to dynamic storage. This is because portable computers typically contain only one hard drive, so the benefits made available by dynamic storage couldn't be utilized.

- The sector size on the hard drive must be no larger than 512 bytes in order for the conversion to be able to take place. Use the `fsutil`, `fsinfo`, or `ntfsinfo x:` command to determine the sector size, where x: is the volume in question.

DISK MANAGEMENT

Garnering a full understanding of these exciting and powerful Windows XP disk management options is crucial before you begin tinkering, obviously. Unfortunately, even after you've mastered the meaning of the new terms, mentally churned through the ramifications of your choices, and are ready to take a plunge or two, you'll have to figure out how to execute those plans. Even if you have experimented with hard disks, older DOS and Windows operating systems, third-party apps such as Partition Magic, and so on, you should still prepare yourself to be a bit confused at first.

Windows XP essentially takes the disk management methods first introduced in Windows 2000 and then improves upon them. Thus, your primary means of performing disk configuration and management will be via the Disk Management console. Additionally, you can use several command-line utilities to perform disk management and maintenance tasks. These various tools will be explored in some depth in the next sections.

MASTERING THE DISK MANAGEMENT CONSOLE

Regardless of what file system or storage types you have in place on your hard drives, all routine maintenance and configuration is done from one place: the Disk Management console, as shown in Figure 25.5.

Figure 25.5
The Disk
Management console.

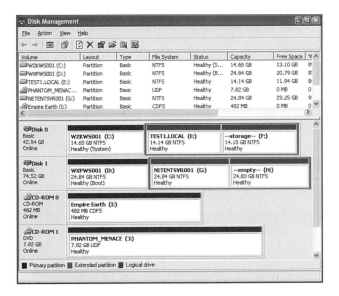

You can open the Disk Management console in any one of three different ways, as outlined in the list below.

- From within the Computer Management console: Click Start, Programs, Administrative Tools, Computer Management (or right-click on My Computer and choose Manage). Then, from within the Computer Management console, expand the Storage node and then select Disk Management.

- From the command line: Type `diskmgmt.msc`. (This will produce the single console shown in Figure 25.3.)

- From the command line: Type `MMC`. From the empty console, add the Disk Management snap-in. (The advantage here is that you can save this custom console, something lacking from the pre-created console discussed previously.)

No matter which way you use to get to the Disk Management console, the same functionality is provided. The following are just some of the tasks that can be performed using the Disk Management console:

- Create new partitions and logical drives.

- Create new volumes.

- Determine disk size, file system, disk health, and other pertinent information. This can easily be done by looking at each volume in the Disk Management console as shown in Figure 25.5.

- Format volumes and partitions.

- Assign drive letters or paths to hard drives and removable storage drives. This can be done by right-clicking on the volume of concern and selecting Change Drive Letter and Paths.

- Mount and unmount drives.

- Upgrade basic storage to dynamic storage.

- Extend the size of dynamic volumes.

Some of the more tasking evolutions from the list below are discussed in more detail in the following sections.

CREATING NEW PARTITIONS AND LOGICAL DRIVES

To create a new partition or logical drive from the Disk Management console, follow these steps:

1. Open the Disk Management console as discussed previously.

2. To create a new partition, right-click an unallocated region of a basic disk, and select New Partition. To create a logical drive, right-click in an extended partition, and select New Logical Drive.

3. Follow the onscreen prompts in the New Partition Wizard.

If you want to create a new partition or logical drive from the command line, such as part of a script, use the procedure here:

1. Open a command window by clicking Start, Run and entering **cmd** into the Run box. Click Enter.

2. Type **diskpart**.

3. Type **list disk**. Write down what disk number you wish to create the partition or logical drive on.

4. Type **select disk x**, where *x* is the disk you identified in the previous step.

5. Enter one of the following commands:

    ■ create partition primary [size=n] [offset=n] [noerr]

    ■ create partition extended [size=n] [offset=n] [noerr]

    ■ create partition logical [size=n] [offset=n] [noerr]

NOTE

> You must be logged in with administrative credentials to create partitions or logical drives.

The root level commands create partition primary, create partition extended, and create partition logical will be explained at the end of this chapter in the "Advanced Disk Management from the Command Line" section. The modifiers to these root level commands are explained in Table 25.3.

25

TABLE 25.3   EXPLANATION OF THE CREATE PARTITION MODIFIERS

Modifier	Description
size=n	The size of the partition in megabytes (MB). If no size is given, the partition continues until there is no more unallocated space in the current region. The size is cylinder snapped; the size is rounded to the closest cylinder boundary. For example, if you specify a size of 500MB, the partition would be rounded up to 504MB.
offset=n	The byte offset at which to create the partition. If no offset is given, the partition will start at the beginning of the first free space on the disk. For master boot record (MBR) disks, the offset is cylinder snapped; the offset is rounded to the closest cylinder boundary. For example, if you specify an offset that is 27MB and the cylinder size is 8MB, the offset is rounded to the 24MB boundary.

CREATING NEW SIMPLE VOLUMES

To create a new simple volume from the Disk Management console, follow these steps:

1. Open the Disk Management console as discussed previously.

2. Right-click the unallocated space on the dynamic disk on which you want to create the simple volume, and then click New Volume.

3. In the New Volume Wizard, click Next and then click Simple. Follow the onscreen prompts to complete the process.

You can also create simple volumes from the command line as follows:

1. Open a command window by clicking Start, Run and entering **cmd** into the Run box. Click Enter.

2. Type **diskpart**.

3. Type **list disk**. Write down what disk number you wish to create the partition or logical drive on.

4. Type **create volume simple [size=*n*] [disk=*x*]**, where *n* is the size of disk in MB and *x* is the disk you identified in the previous step.

> **NOTE**
>
> You must be logged in with administrative credentials to create volumes.

You can create other types of volumes on dynamic disks in much the same fashion.

FORMATTING DISKS AND VOLUMES

Formatting storage media is a fairly common task you can easily accomplish using the Disk Management console. Windows XP supports formatting numerous kinds of media, partly due to its excellent multimedia support. You can format hard drives, removable storage media (such as ZIP drives), and DVD-RAM disks to name a few of your options.

> **NOTE**
>
> **Formatting Removable Storage**
>
> Although you can format removable media from within the Disk Management console, you most likely won't. Instead it's more likely that you will use Windows Explorer, simply because it's easier to get to an Explorer window and because many of the advanced Disk Management console tools for fixed drives don't apply to removable storage.

Windows XP is fairly intelligent and self-protective (which reminds me of more than one bad sci-fi movie I've seen), and thus it will not allow you to format the system or boot partitions from within the Disk Management console. Those options will be grayed out. (Of course, as with all things, this too can be defeated by using the command line, so be careful with the command-line approach.) To begin the process of formatting a hard drive or removable media device, right-click the volume (or unallocated space) of interest from within the Disk Management console and select Format, which opens the window shown in Figure 25.6. Depending on how large the volume to be formatted is, you will have the choice to format it as FAT16, FAT32, or NTFS.

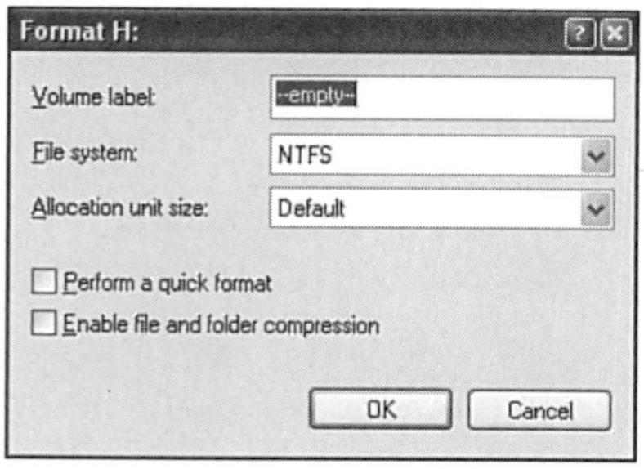

Figure 25.6
Formatting a hard
drive.

Format H:	?☒
Volume label:	--empty--
File system:	NTFS ⌄
Allocation unit size:	Default ⌄
☐ Perform a quick format	
☐ Enable file and folder compression	
	OK Cancel

N O T E

> **Working with Floppy Disks**
>
> We haven't mentioned standard floppy disks. Does anyone use them anymore? I have a huge pile of them sitting around gathering dust, and even a PC or two with no floppy drive. But formatting a floppy is a need I have once in a while. From within the GUI, the only way to format standard floppy disks is using Windows Explorer. Standard floppy disks are formatted using a special file system called FAT12, incidentally.

Formatting removable media such as DVD-RAM or ZIP disks follows the same process, except that you will not have the choice of file systems; all removable media (other than floppies) are formatted with the FAT (which is really to say FAT16) file system.

Remember that in order to convert a basic disk to dynamic later on, be sure to select 512 bytes as the sector size. In most cases, this is the smallest size available (due to the physical construction of the hard drive itself) and will be selected by Windows XP automatically if the Allocation Unit Size setting is left as Default, as seen in Figure 25.6.

The other options available to you during a format operation are fairly simple, but still deserve some mention.

- The volume label can be a descriptive name that you use to readily identify the volume. You should keep the label as short as possible and avoid using the following reserved characters: < > : " / \ | * ? + and . as they will cause problems when accessing volumes over the network. Note that Windows XP will not stop you from using the characters for a volume name—you have to do that for yourself.

  If a disk is formatted with the FAT file system, the label can contain up to 11 characters. If the disk is formatted with the NTFS file system, the limit is 32 characters.

- The file system will be a choice of FAT16, FAT32, or NTFS as previously mentioned.

- Selecting to perform a quick format removes files from the disk but does not scan the disk for bad sectors. You should only use this option if the disk has been previously formatted and is known to not have any damage to it.

- Selecting the last option, Enable File and Folder Compression, will configure the newly formatted volume for file and folder compression. Remember that this will prevent you from later using EFS encryption unless compression is removed.

25

Of course, should you need to format drives from the command prompt, you still can. The `format` command has the following syntax:

```
format volume [/fs:filesystem] [/v:label] [/q] [/a:unitsize] [/c]
```

The parameters for the `convert` command are outlined in Table 25.3.

TABLE 25.3   PARAMETERS FOR THE format COMMAND

Parameter	Description
volume	Specifies the mount point, volume name, or drive letter of the drive you want to format.
/fs:filesystem	Specifies the file system to use: FAT, FAT32, or NTFS. Floppy disks can use only the FAT file system.
/v:label	Specifies the volume label. If you omit the /v command-line option or use it without specifying a volume label, format prompts you for the volume label after the formatting is completed.
/q	Performs a quick format. Deletes the file table and the root directory of a previously formatted volume but does not perform a sector-by-sector scan for bad areas.
/a:unitsize	Specifies the cluster size, also known as allocation unit size, to use on FAT, FAT32, or NTFS volumes. If *unitsize* is not specified, it will be chosen based on volume size.
/c	NTFS only. Files created on the new volume will be compressed by default.

NOTE

You must be logged in with administrative credentials to format basic and dynamic volumes.

CREATING MOUNTED DRIVES

To create a mounted drive from the Disk Management console, follow these steps:

1. Open the Disk Management console as discussed previously.

2. Right-click the partition or volume you want to mount, and then click Change Drive Letter and Paths.

3. To mount a volume, click Add. Click Mount in the following empty NTFS folder and enter or browse to the empty folder. To unmount a volume, click it and then click Remove.

You can also create mounted drives from the command line as follows:

1. Open a command window by clicking Start, Run and entering **cmd** into the Run box. Click Enter.

2. Type **diskpart**.

3. Type **list volume**. Write down what simple volume you are mounting in an empty folder.

4. Type **select volume** *n*, where *n* is the simple volume you identified in the previous step.

5. Type **assign [mount=*path*]**, where *path* is the simple volume you identified in the previous step.

> **NOTE**
>
> You must be logged in with administrative credentials to mount drives.

The various root level commands that can be used with diskpart are explained at the end of this chapter in the "Advanced Disk Management from the Command Line" section.

CONVERTING BASIC DISKS TO DYNAMIC DISKS

To convert a basic disk from the Disk Management console, follow these steps:

1. Open the Disk Management console as discussed previously.

2. Right-click the basic disk you want to convert and select Convert to Dynamic disk. Follow the onscreen prompts to complete the process. Looking at Figure 25.5, the area to click in is that area on the left side of each disk in the bottom frame.

You can also convert basic disks from the command line as follows:

1. Open a command window by clicking Start, Run and entering **cmd** into the Run box. Click Enter.

2. Type **diskpart**.

3. Type **list disk**. Write down what basic disk you want to convert to dynamic.

4. Type **select disk** *n*, where *n* is the basic disk you identified in the previous step.

5. Type **convert dynamic**.

> **NOTE**
>
> You must be logged in with administrative credentials to convert basic drives to dynamic drives.

The various root level commands that can be used with diskpart are explained at the end of this chapter in the "Advanced Disk Management from the Command Line" section.

25

EXTENDING SIMPLE VOLUMES

To extend a dynamic volume from the Disk Management console, follow these steps:

1. Open the Disk Management console as discussed previously.
2. Right-click the simple or spanned volume you want to extend and click Extend Volume. Follow the onscreen prompts to complete the process.

You can also extend a simple volume from the command line as follows:

1. Open a command window by clicking Start, Run and entering `cmd` into the Run box. Click Enter.
2. Type `diskpart`.
3. Type `list volume`. Write down what simple volume you want to extend onto another disk.
4. Type `select volume` n, where n is the simple volume you identified in the previous step.
5. Type `extend [size=x] [disk=d]` where x is the size in MB you want the extended disk to be and d is the disk you want to extend the simple volume onto.

NOTE You must be logged in with administrative credentials to extend simple volumes.

A few things to keep in mind when attempting to extend volumes:

- You cannot extend a system volume or a boot volume.
- You cannot extend striped volumes.
- You cannot extend a dynamic volume that was upgraded from a basic volume to a dynamic volume in Windows 2000 if you've upgraded to Windows XP.
- You cannot extend a simple volume onto additional dynamic disks to create a spanned volume. Spanned volumes cannot be mirrored or striped.
- If you extend a spanned volume, you cannot delete any portion of it without deleting the entire spanned volume.

The various root level commands that can be used with `diskpart` are explained at the end of this chapter in the "Advanced Disk Management from the Command Line" section.

RESIZING BASIC DISKS

If you are using basic storage on your disk drive and you decide that you need to adjust your partition layout after it has been initially created, you have three possible means to this end: You can use the `diskpart` utility, you can delete and re-create partitions, or you can use a third-party utility such as PartitionMagic.

Using the extend command within the diskpart utility, you can add more space to existing primary partitions and logical drives as long as you meet the following requirements:

- The basic volume must be formatted with NTFS.

- You can extend a basic volume using space from the same physical hard disk only (unlike dynamic volumes). The basic volume must be followed by contiguous unallocated space.

- You can extend a logical drive only within the contiguous free space that exists in the partition that contains the logical drive.

If you meet all of the aforementioned requirements, you can extend a basic disk as follows:

1. Open a command window by clicking Start, Run and entering **cmd** into the Run box. Click Enter.

2. Type **diskpart**.

3. Type **list volume**. Write down what volume you want to extend.

4. Type **select volume** *n*, where *n* is the volume you identified in the previous step.

5. Type **extend [size=n]**, where *n* is the extended size of the volume in MB.

NOTE

> You must be logged in with administrative credentials to extend basic drives.

If working from the command line is not your thing, and you are not ready to perform mass deletions (as required by the third method), then you may want to consider using a third-party disk utility, such as PartitionMagic from PowerQuest. PartitionMagic allows you to redesign your partition table graphically within the Windows XP GUI and then on the subsequent restart performs the required actions to carry out your wishes. Figure 25.7 shows PartitionMagic 7.0 during the planning phase—as mentioned before, the actual reconfiguration of the partition table would occur during the subsequent restart of the computer. Notice that I have, in this example, decreased the size of drive H: from 25GB to 14GB, and therefore I will have leftover, unallocated space at the end of the disk after the change has been applied. I could just as easily increase the size of a volume to extend it into unallocated space.

NOTE

> Find out more about PartitionMagic at the PowerQuest Corporation Web site, located at http://www.powerquest.com/partitionmagic/.

25

Figure 25.7
Using PartitionMagic to reconfigure partitions. Note the unallocated space following volume H:. I could later extend volume H: into this space using the diskpart command or by using Partition Magic.

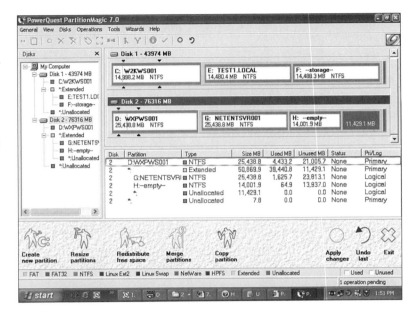

If you choose not to use either of the other methods presented, you can still resize your basic disks, with no out-of-pocket cost. It is more laborious, however. You'll need to back up all pertinent data on the partition(s) in question, delete the partitions, and then re-create them sized to your liking. After formatting the new partitions, you can then restore your data onto them.

If you are running with dynamic storage volumes, then resizing your volumes is an easy process. You simply right-click on the volume that you want to extend and select Extend Volume. This will bring up the Extend Volume Wizard, which will allow you to enter the size you want to extend the volume to. After the wizard has finished, which is a relatively quick process, you will have a volume that is now larger...all without a restart of the computer or the time-intensive process of copying and recopying all of the files in that volume. Quite a time saver.

CONVERTING THE FAT16/FAT32 FILE SYSTEMS TO NTFS

Should you make the decision to upgrade your file system from FAT16 or FAT32 to NTFS, you will need to perform the upgrade from the command line by using the convert command. The convert command has the following syntax:

```
convert [volume] /fs:ntfs [/v] [/cvtarea:FileName] [/nosecurity] [/x]
```

The parameters for the convert command are outlined in Table 25.4.

TABLE 25.4   PARAMETERS FOR THE convert COMMAND

Parameter	Description
volume	Specifies the drive letter (followed by a colon), mount point, or volume name to convert to NTFS.
/fs:ntfs	Required. Converts the volume to NTFS.
/v	Specifies verbose mode; that is, all messages will be displayed during conversion.
/cvtarea:FileName	Specifies that the Master File Table (MFT) and other NTFS metadata files are written to an existing, contiguous placeholder file. This file must be in the root directory of the file system to be converted. Use of the /CVTAREA parameter can result in a less fragmented file system after conversion. For best results, the size of this file should be 1KB multiplied by the number of files and directories in the file system; however, the convert utility accepts files of any size.
	You must create the placeholder file using the fsutil file createnew command prior to running convert. convert does not create this file for you. convert overwrites this file with NTFS metadata. After conversion, any unused space in this file is freed.
/nosecurity	Specifies that the converted files and directory security settings are accessible by everyone.
/x	Dismounts the volume, if necessary, before it is converted. Any open handles to the volume will no longer be valid.

CAUTION

Converting to NTFS and Uninstalling Windows XP

Converting your existing FAT or FAT32 volume to the NTFS file system will preclude you from uninstalling Windows XP Professional at a later date. This is no big loss of freedom if you are upgrading from Windows 2000 or NT, since those upgrades are not reversible anyway. But if you hoped to return to Windows 98 or Me, for example, since they don't read NTFS, it's obvious why uninstallation would be problematic. This sort of limitation is one reason why people who deal with multiboot scenarios stick with FAT-based disks, as discussed earlier in this book (see Chapter 4, "Installing Windows XP for Multi-booting").

Of course, you'd still be able to manually erase the Windows XP system files and install something else on the disk, such as Linux, so long as the Linux or other installer could read and write on an NTFS-formatted partitions. There are some Linux NTFS drivers around, although the consensus is that NTFS is problematic for Linux.

During the conversion process, you will be warned about the loss of uninstallation capability. See http://www.microsoft.com/technet/prodtechnol/winxppro/proddocs/uninstall_windowsxp.asp for more information about uninstalling Windows XP.

As shown in Figure 25.8, the bare minimum required to execute the process is the following command:

```
convert x: /fs:ntfs
```

Where *x:* is the volume to be converted. You will need to have the current volume name handy, as Windows uses this as a sort of checkpoint to ensure that you are really ready to convert the file system to NTFS.

Figure 25.8
Converting a FAT32 volume to NTFS.

25

NOTE

New and Better convert

Unknown to most people, the convert command has quietly received an upgrade from the Windows 2000 version. Using the convert command in Windows 2000 would produce a volume that did not have the default NTFS permissions settings that you would get after installing Windows itself. The version of convert that comes with Windows XP fixes this problem by automatically applying the correct default permissions to all folders. When used with the /cvtarea switch to create an unfragmented MFT, there is virtually no difference anymore between a volume converted to NTFS during setup of Windows or by using the convert command.

CONVERTING THE NTFS FILE SYSTEM TO FAT16/FAT32

Reversion from NTFS to FAT16 or FAT32 is not supported by Windows XP; however using a third-party disk utility such as Partition Magic will allow you to perform this task.

CAUTION

Saying Goodbye Is Hard to Do

You will lose all security permissions assigned to the volume after the conversion to FAT16 or FAT32. If the volume will be accessed across the network, share permissions may still be applied for limited security.

Additionally, you will lose all other features that are based on the NTFS file system, such as EFS encryption, after you convert the volume to FAT16 or FAT32.

From within Partition Magic, right-click the volume to be converted from NTFS and select the Convert option, which opens the dialog box shown in Figure 25.9. From here you can configure the conversion process.

Figure 25.9
Converting an NTFS volume to FAT32.

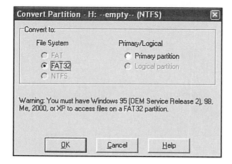

HARD DRIVE CLEANING

It may seem that after getting your hard drives set up and configured to your liking that all of your work is done. Nothing could be further from the truth, unfortunately. Over time, as I'm sure you know, Windows systems do accumulate hundreds and possibly thousands of unnecessary files and folders on your hard drives. Not only do these files and folders waste valuable space, they can slowly degrade system performance. In this section, I am going to blow the top off of some of Windows's secrets and show you how to keep your hard drives slim and trim.

TEPORARY FILES—TO BE ELIMINATED AT ANY COST

Windows XP likes to store its temporary files in three places, more often than not. That is not to say that some rogue program will not deposit some temporary files in another location; just that in most cases you can look in three places to find the dead wood you've been collecting on your system. These three places are

- **%USERPROFILE%\Local Settings\Temp**—Here you will typically find temporary files that were not properly cleaned up by the application that created them.
- **%USERPROFILE%\Local Settings\Temporary Internet Files**—Here you find the cache used by applications such as Outlook and Internet Explorer.
- **%SYSTEMROOT%\Temp**—Another dumping ground that some applications like to use for their temporary files.

Figure 25.10 shows where you can find the majority of your dead wood, in this case for the built-in Administrator account.

Figure 25.10
Locating your tempo-
rary files.

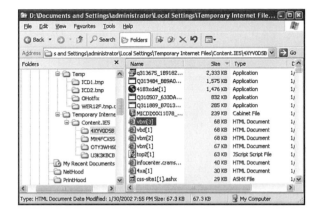

In the next two sections we will look at two methods for cleaning up temporary files: the
GUI-based Disk Cleanup utility and a command-line-based script you can use.

USING THE DISK CLEANUP UTILITY

The easiest way to help clean the dead wood from your hard drives is to use the Disk
Cleanup utility on a regular basis. The Disk Cleanup utility is launched by clicking Start,
Programs, Accessories, System Tools, Disk Cleanup. You can also launch it by right-clicking
on a drive icon in any Explorer window and choosing Properties, Disk Cleanup. After Disk
Cleanup has scanned the selected volume, you will be presented with the results display as
shown in Figure 25.11.

Figure 25.11
The analysis results
window.

TIP

> **A Few Files Short of a Full Cleanup**
>
> A little known fact about the Disk Cleanup utility is that it only reports temporary files that are older than seven days old. These are the files covered in the "Temporary Files" section of the display. These files that are less than seven days old can only be deleted by directly working with the folder in which they are located. See the "Taking Things into Your Own Hands" section later in this chapter.

Temporary files build up very quickly if not taken care of. The best way to use the Disk Cleanup utility is a combination of two separate tricks. The first thing you will need to do is to make use of two undocumented switches for the Disk Cleanup utility that can be accessed from the command line. The second thing you will do is to schedule the Disk Cleanup utility to run automatically, using advanced settings of your choice, thus purging your hard disk of specific types of unwanted types of files on a regular basis. To stealthily perform both of these actions, just follow the steps below.

The biggest advantages to using the Disk Cleanup utility in this fashion are that cleanup is automated, and thus out of your mind, and also that you have additional configuration options, as shown in Figure 25.12.

Figure 25.12
Additional configuration settings available.

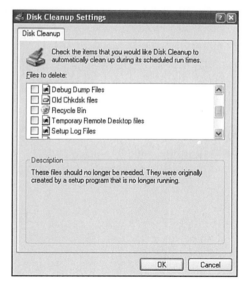

25

1. Start the Disk Cleanup utility from the command line by opening a command window and typing `cleanmgr /d x /sageset:n`, where *x* represents the drive letter you want to run the Disk Cleanup utility on and *n* is any number between 1 and 65535. The `/d` switch is mandatory in this method, as it allows you to specify the drive letter to be cleaned. The `/sageset:n` value provides a means for you to create multiple pre-configured Disk Cleanup instances, each with the specific drives and options selected

that you desire. Which value you choose for the /sageset:*n* value doesn't matter; it is only used to store your settings in the Registry to allow you to run Disk Cleanup with those options again in the future.

2. After pressing Enter, the hard disk will grind a bit. Then up will pop the Disk Cleanup Settings dialog. Select the settings you want to apply to the Disk Cleanup utility and click OK to save these settings into the registry. You can click on each option to read a description of it. Note that choosing to compress files that are not often used could take a while, during which time the compression occurs.

3. Create a shortcut to cleanmgr /sagerun:*n*, where *n* is the number you chose previously in Step 1.

4. Using the Scheduled Task Wizard (Start, Settings, Control Panel, Scheduled Tasks), create and configure a scheduled task to run daily or weekly using the shortcut you created in Step 3.

NOTE

You will probably want to create a Disk Cleanup setting and shortcut for each drive on your system.

See Chapter 29, "Automating Routine Tasks," for more information on scheduling tasks.

TAKING THINGS INTO YOUR OWN HANDS

I mentioned earlier the odd behavior of the Disk Cleanup utility—it doesn't consider temporary files less than seven days old. So, the question that may come to mind is "How do you get rid of these files?" As with most management tasks in Windows, there is a way to do this manually. To start the process of locating and removing these files, close all open programs. Then open a Run window by clicking Start, Run. Enter %TEMP% and then click OK. Now you can delete any files left in this folder. I use a script to perform this task for me and schedule it as well. The script that I use is presented below.

```
cd %temp%
del *.* /f /s /q
exit
```

To use a script such as this, follow these steps:

1. Open Notepad and enter the text as shown in three separate lines.

2. Save the file in a convenient location, such as the Desktop with a name ending in .bat, such as deltemp.bat.

3. Run the batch file by double-clicking on it.

While this script does an excellent job of removing all files, it will not remove the folders located in the %temp% directory. This will have to be done by hand. The modifiers used with the del command are outlined here:

- *.*—Specifies all files to be deleted. * is a wildcard that can be used to specify any value. For example, if you put *.doc, then only files with the .doc extension would be deleted.

- /f—Forces the deletion of read-only files.

- /s—Specifies the deletion of files from all subdirectories.

- /q—Runs the script in quiet mode, preventing the prompting for permission to delete when using the global wildcard *.* as discussed previously.

NOTE

Where Exactly Is TEMP?

The global variable %TEMP% is typically defined as the %USERPROFILE%\Local Settings\Temp location, which changes depending on which user is logged in. If you want to clean out all users' Temp folders in one fell swoop, you will have to hard-code in the directory paths as appropriate. Otherwise, you could create a script for each user, which could be set to run when that user logs in to the system.

CAUTION

You want to be careful not to run the script unless all programs are closed, however, or you might erase currently open temp files relating to documents the user is working with. Remember, XP can log users in and out without closing their apps and documents, so switching users doesn't necessarily give you the green light.

USING THE SEARCH UTILITY TO LOCATE UNWANTED FILES

It is not too uncommon to acquire several dozen or even several hundred large media files on your computer over time. These files add up fast to take away hard drive space. Searching for them by using an advanced search can help you quickly and easily give your hard drive some extra room.

To begin the search, launch the Search utility by clicking Start, Search, For Files and Folders. Select the drive or drives you want to search. Next select the file type you want to search for. Place a check in the Type check box and select a file type from the drop-down listing. Figure 25.13 shows a search I've configured on my D: drive looking for MP3 files.

You can also perform advanced searches by configuring several search criteria such as date and size. You also have the option to configure even more advanced searches by searching in hidden folders, system folders, and using other options by placing a check in the Advanced Options check box.

Figure 25.13
Searching with
advanced options.

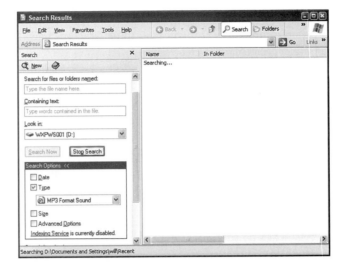

CAUTION

Don't arbitrarily delete a file if you do not know what its function is! Also, the times where you would need to delete files from system folders are few and far between.

USING THIRD-PARTY DISK TOOLS TO EXAMINE DISK SPACE

There are hundreds of third-party disk tools out there to perform dozens of different functions. One of my favorites is SizeExplorer, which provides you with a fast and powerful way to determine exactly where the space on your hard drives is being used. Figure 25.14 shows one of the reports available from SizeExplorer.

Figure 25.14
Using SizeExplorer.

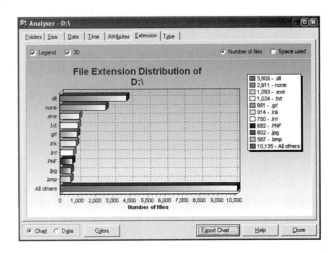

25

TIP

> For more information on SizeExplorer, visit the SizeExplorer Web site located at
> `http://www.sizeexplorer.com/`.

REMOVING THE HIBERNATION FILE

One of the nicest features of Windows XP for portable computer users is the Hibernation option. By placing your portable computer into Hibernation, you can save your current session onto the hard drive and power down the computer. When you resume the session, you are presented with your session exactly as you left it...definitely a boon for users who must frequently power down their systems. Of course, some desktop computers support hibernation also, but this is obviously not as useful for a desktop system.

As nice a feature as Hibernation is, it eats up a chunk of hard drive space equal to the amount of RAM installed in the computer. While portable computer users must accept this fact if they want to make use of Hibernation, desktop users do not need to let Windows chew up this hard drive space—which it will do by default on an ACPI-compatible computer.

TIP

> ### It's Cool to Hibernate
>
> Some desktop users might really like the hibernation feature. Why? For starters, resuming from hibernation is quicker than rebooting. Secondly, although system standby is a good option for desktop users (and resumes even faster than hibernation does), it has its drawbacks: Most specifically, in the case of power outage, hibernating is more secure than standby, since a computer in hibernation does not rely on system power to keep the system state intact. It's recorded on the hard disk. When the power comes back on, the entire session (including open files and applications) is restored from the hibernation file, and the user can continue right where he or she left off.

Figure 25.15 shows the hiberfil.sys file, which is the file used by Windows XP during hibernation. As you might have guessed, this machine has 256MB of RAM installed.

Figure 25.15
The hibernation file:
hiberfil.sys.

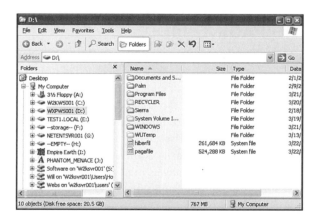

NOTE

> **Viewing the hiberfil.sys File**
>
> The hibernation file (as well as the paging file discussed later) is a hidden, protected system file. You will need to enable display of these files from Windows Explorer by clicking Tools, Folder Options, and switching to the View tab. From the View tab, you will need to select Show Hidden Files and Folders and also unselect Hide Protected Operating System Files.

If you do not intend to use hibernation on your computer (this is usually only applicable to desktop workstations and servers), you can reclaim this disk space that has been automatically allotted to the hiberfil.sys file. In order to reclaim this space, you must disable hibernation on the computer.

In order to reclaim the space automatically allotted to the hiberfil.sys file, we can disable Hibernation. Hibernation is controlled from the Power Options applet, which is opened by clicking Start, Settings, Control Panel, Power Options. Once the applet is open, switch to the Hibernate tab and uncheck the Enable Hibernation option, as shown in Figure 25.16. Voilà! An instant savings in hard drive space used, without requiring a reboot.

Figure 25.16
Disabling hibernation on a desktop system.

25

OPTIMIZING THE PAGING FILE

Did you notice the pagefile.sys file that was shown in Figure 25.15? This 512MB of space (on that particular system at least) is the space that has been allotted to the paging file. The paging file is a hidden, protected system file located in the boot partition of your Windows XP computer. Commonly referred to as the *swap file* by earlier versions of Windows, the paging file acts as an extension to your computer's installed physical RAM. Together, the physical RAM and the paging file comprise the virtual memory your computer has to work with. By default, the paging file is sized at 1.5× the amount of RAM you have installed in your computer and can expand dynamically as required. The paging file shown in Figure 25.15 is actually a manually configured paging file for 2× the amount of RAM installed. Don't fret; we're going to get to that very soon!

When it comes to manipulating the paging file, there are two major things you should take into consideration:

- Do you have more than one physical hard drive in your computer? If so, you can create a second paging file to increase disk I/O performance. Note that I did not say to remove the paging file from the volume on which Windows XP Professional is running—you'll see why soon.

- Do you want to prevent decreased disk I/O performance due to dynamic resizing? If so, then you may want to configure a manually sized paging file.

Configuration of the paging file in Windows XP is handled from the Advanced tab of the System applet and is fairly straightforward. To access the Virtual Memory page (see Figure 25.17), click the Settings button in the Performance area of the Advanced Tab of the System applet. From the Performance Options window, switch to the Advanced tab and then click the Change button.

Figure 25.17
Configuring the paging file.

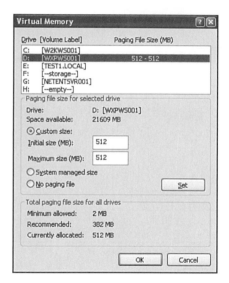

CREATING A SECOND PAGING FILE

If you've got more than one physical hard drive (as opposed to logical drives, which are simply partitions or volumes on a physical drive), you can benefit from creating a second paging file on one or more of your other physical drives. Creating a paging file in a location other than the boot partition (the partition that Windows XP is running from) can result in better computer performance and better management of disk space.

When a computer has only one paging file configured, there is a constant competition between read requests and write requests due to the read/write heads moving constantly back and forth from the location on the hard drive where the paging file is located to other locations and so forth. Additionally, paging files located on boot partitions commonly suffer from excessive fragmentation as the paging file expands dynamically (more on this in a bit). This type of fragmentation is so great at times, that not even running the Disk Defragmenter multiple times can correct the fragmentation.

Windows, by design, uses the paging files that are located on less frequently accessed partitions over the paging files on the more heavily accessed boot partition. An internal algorithm is used to determine which paging file to use for virtual memory management.

To create a second paging file on a separate physical drive, you simply need to select the drive, select Custom Size, and enter the size as shown in Figure 25.18 where I've configured a second 512MB paging file.

Figure 25.18
Configuring a second paging file.

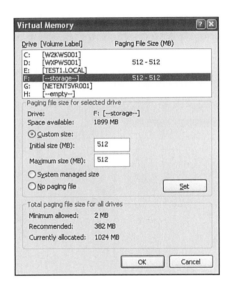

CAUTION

Paging File No-No's

You can resize and relocate the paging file, but don't completely remove it. Completely removing the paging file may render your computer unable to boot.

If you completely remove the paging file from the boot partition, Windows cannot create a dump file (memory.dmp) in which to write debugging information in the event that a kernel mode STOP error message occurs.

MANUALLY CONFIGURING THE PAGING FILE SIZE

As I have already alluded to, the paging files shown in Figures 25.17 and 25.18 are manually configured for a custom size of 512MB for both the Initial size and the Maximum size. There is a valid reason for this.

Microsoft recommends that you make your paging file 1.5× the RAM installed, although the general rule of thumb is generally to size it at 1.5× to 2.5× the RAM installed. For a 256MB system, 512MB is right in the middle of the range, at 2× the amount of installed RAM. Although all versions of Windows have the capability to dynamically resize the paging file if left in System managed size (the default), there is a definite downside to this. The resizing process is extremely CPU intensive and tends to eat up processor cycles like crazy. To avoid this from happening, you can opt to manually configure a paging file with the same value set in both fields (as shown in Figure 25.18). Since the paging file never has to be resized, system performance increases and more cycles can be allotted to applications.

Creating and deleting paging files on other volumes, other than the boot partition, will not normally require a restart of the computer. Changing paging file configuration for the boot partition will always require a restart of the computer to complete the process. It's usually best to perform the restart as soon as possible after changing the paging file size. Also, it's usually not a good idea to change the paging file more than one time before restarting the computer. I've seen quite a few strange things happen to computers due to people "playing" with the paging file, so don't take any chances you don't have to.

DEFRAGMENTING FOR GREATER SPEED

Not too long ago, the average hard drive was smaller than 1GB and the FAT16 file system was king. As time passed, larger hard drives and more efficient file systems, such as FAT32 and NTFS, were introduced. With the NTFS file system came the untruth that an NTFS drive never got fragmented. The absence of a built-in defragementation utility in Windows NT 4.0 only added to this myth. Even today, with the super large hard drives in use and the extremely efficient NTFS 5.0 file system, disk fragmentation is a problem still.

Windows XP continues the positive trend begun in Windows 2000 with the inclusion of a "lite" version of Executive Software's Diskeeper for performing disk defragementation. You can access the Disk Defragmenter utility from any one of the following three methods.

- From within the Computer Management console: Start, Programs, Administrative Tools, Computer Management. From within the Computer Management console, expand the Storage node and then select the Disk Defragmenter tool.
- From the command line: Type `dfrg.msc`.
- From the command line: Type `MMC`. From the empty console, add the Disk Defragmenter snap-in.

TIP

Check out the full version of Diskeeper at `http://www.executivesoftware.com/diskeeper/diskeeper.asp`.

No matter which way you launch the GUI version of the disk defragmenter; your options are the same.

If you do not have the time to waste by performing defragmentation when not required, you can simply run an analysis on a volume by clicking the Analyze button. When the analysis is complete, you will receive a report similar to the one shown in Figure 25.19. From here you can quickly determine the necessity for defragmentation, the amount of fragmentation and the most fragmented files.

Figure 25.19
The analysis results window.

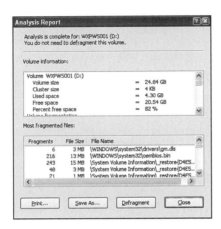

Should you decide to perform the defragmentation, click the Defragment button and watch the progress as shown in Figure 25.20.

Figure 25.20
Defragmenting a volume.

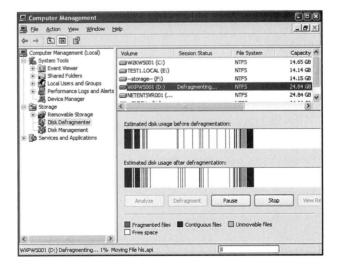

Defragmenting a volume is an extremely CPU- and hard drive- intensive operation. While defragmentation is in progress, you should avoid using the computer as much as possible. As with the Disk Cleanup utility, the true power of the Disk Defragmenter comes when you create a scheduled event for it and allow it to run weekly during a low-usage time, such as Sunday mornings. See Chapter 29 for more information on scheduling tasks.

Although you can perform disk deframentation from within the GUI, you may find instances where you would rather do it from the command line. In these cases, you defragment a volume by using the defrag command, which has the following syntax:

```
defrag volume [/a] [/v] [/f]
```

The parameters for the defrag command are outlined in Table 25.5.

TABLE 25.5   PARAMETERS FOR THE defrag COMMAND

Parameter	Description
volume	The drive letter or a mount point of the volume to be defragmented.
/a	Analyzes the volume and displays a summary of the analysis report.
/v	Displays the complete analysis and defragmentation reports.
/f	Forces defragmentation of the volume regardless of whether it needs to be defragmented.

TIP

Defrag Advanced Options

If you want to perform defragmentation across the network, you will either have to acquire a fully functional defragmentation utility such as Diskeeper, or use a script that executes the defragmenter locally on each computer.

A few points should be kept in mind when attempting to perform disk defragmentation:

- A volume must have at least 15% free space for defrag to completely and adequately defragment it. Defrag uses this space as a sorting area for file fragments. If a volume has less than 15% free space, defrag will only partially defragment it.

- You cannot defragment volumes that the file system has marked as "dirty." A volume that is marked as dirty may be in an inconsistent status, which will require the chkdsk utility to be run to verify the consistency of the volume. A volume could be marked as dirty if it is online and has outstanding changes that must be made at the next successful startup or if the volume is corrupt.

- You cannot run the defrag command and GUI Disk Defragmenter utility simultaneously. On this same note, you cannot defragment more than one volume at a time.

RECYCLE BIN MANAGEMENT

The Recycle Bin is something that rarely gets any notice. While this is usually not a problem, if you have multiple volumes in use or are running tight on drive space, you may want to pay some attention to this often overlooked part of Windows.

There are a few extremely important things that need to be understood about the Recycle Bin. Getting a good grasp on these will prevent you from any surprises or problems when working with deleted files.

- Files that are deleted off of network volumes, across the network, are gone forever. These files do not make use of the Recycle Bin.
- Files that are deleted off of removable media such as floppy disks and ZIP drives are not recoverable via the Recycle Bin.
- Files that are deleted off of a local volume from the command line using the `del` command are also gone forever.
- By default, each volume on a computer has 10% of its total space reserved for use by the Recycle Bin; this space can add up quickly, especially if you have several large volumes on your computer.

Let's dive in a little deeper now, and see how we can take control of the Recycle Bin and make it work the way we want to.

SETTING RECYCLE BIN USAGE LIMITS

The first thing you will want to consider doing if you have multiple volumes, or a single large volume, is to customize the size of the reserved area that is set aside for the Recycle Bin. As I previously mentioned, Windows will set aside 10% of each volume for usage by the Recycle Bin. Figure 25.21 shows the Recycle Bin properties window, from which you can change the settings to your liking.

Figure 25.21
Configuring Recycle Bin usage limitations.

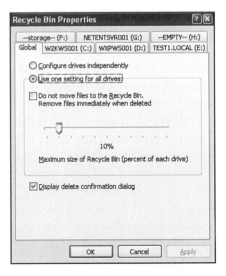

By selecting to configure all drives independently, you can set the amount of space used to your liking or even disable usage of specific volumes. You also have the choice of preventing files from being placed in the Recycle Bin at all if you desire; however I would not recommend this setting, as you remove the capability of reclaiming a file you deleted by accident and later want to reclaim. Removing the check mark from the Display Delete Confirmation Dialog option will suppress the display of the standard "are you sure" warning typically received when deleting a local file from within the Windows GUI.

WHERE ARE RECYCLE BIN FILES REALLY STORED?

In order to make the Recycle Bin work, the files you place into it must be kept somewhere before actually being deleted, right? But where are they kept? That is the question. Any files that you have deleted locally from within the Windows GUI are placed into a special location, called the Recycler, which is a hidden, read-only system folder located in the root of every volume. Figure 25.22 shows the Recycler folder.

Figure 25.22
The hidden, read-only system Recycler folder.

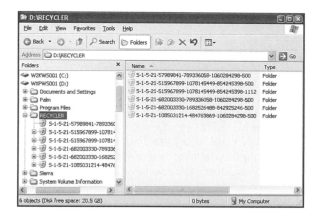

NOTE

> **Showing the Recyler**
>
> In order to be able to view the Recycler folder, you will need to enable support for this. From Windows Explorer, click Tools, Folder Options and switch to the View tab. From the View tab, you will need to select Show Hidden Files and Folders and also unselect Hide Protected Operating System Files. Click OK to close out the window. You will now be able to see the Recycler folder, as well as several other hidden files and folders.

Inside the Recycler folder, you will find another folder for each and every volume on your computer that has space reserved for the Recycle Bin—so, by default, the number of folders here will be equal to the number of volumes you have. As you can see in Figure 25.23, I have six volumes on my computer.

Figure 25.23
The Recycle Bin
unmasked.

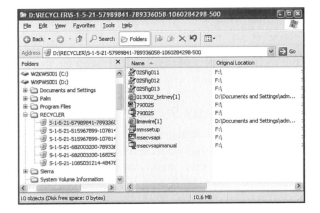

NOTE

New Math?

The math involved here can get a bit tricky, so let's do a quick overview of how the Recycler folder and the Recycle Bins themselves work. I have six volumes on my computer. Opening the Recycler folder on each of these six volumes shows six individual Recycle Bins, so you might at first assume that I actually have six identical copies of the Recycler folder and a total of thirty-six Recycle Bins on my computer. This is not the case. The Recycler folder you see is a replica no matter which volume you are looking at it from. So, if I were to examine the Recycler folder located on the C: drive, it in fact is the same one I would see if I looked at the Recycler folder located on the E: drive. The "Secrets of the Recycle Bin" section later in this chapter discusses this also, but from a network perspective.

These "Recycle Bins" certainly have strange names though...or do they? Not really, as these are Security Identifiers (SIDs) that identify each individual object. In this case, unlike most all other cases, these objects are displayed with their SIDs instead of a friendly name. If you empty the Recycle Bin from your desktop, all Recycler folders will also be emptied...and the contents of the Recycle Bin removed from your computer.

SECRETS OF THE RECYCLE BIN

The Recycle Bin is really quite a mystery and seems to have its secrets fairly closely guarded. There are, however, a couple secrets that I've been able to uncover that you may find both useful and interesting.

- You can include the Recycle Bin in your search parameters by selecting the "Search hidden files and folders" option of the Search Companion.

- You cannot encrypt the Recycle Bin. Attempting to encrypt the actual SID folders in the Recycler folder will fail outright, although it will appear that you are allowed to encrypt the contents—in reality, no encryption will be applied. So beware—items sitting around in your Recycle Bin will not be hidden very thoroughly from prying eyes should someone decide to restore them.

- You can compress the Recycler folder and all SID subfolders if you choose.

- You cannot unset the read-only properties of the Recycler folder or any SID subfolders.

- If multiple users place files in the Recycle Bin, files visible are limited to those deleted by the currently logged-in user.

- You can share the Recycler folder and allow for access to it across the network, however this is a moot point as the only Recycle Bin contents a user will ever see is their own, regardless of what Recycle Bin or Recycler folder they look at.

- You can restore files out of the Recycle Bin to a different location than they were deleted from by selecting the file(s) and then clicking Edit, Move to Folder.

TIP

Not Your Momma's Recycle Bin

For advanced Recycle Bin management, check out a program called Undelete from Executive Software, http://www.executivesoftware.com/. It provides a means for replacing the Recycle Bin with a similar, but more advanced system that can give you a second chance to recover erased files.

COMPRESSING FILES AND FOLDERS

25

Native file and folder compression is one of the many benefits of using the NTFS file system, as discussed briefly earlier in the chapter. The compression algorithm used by NTFS is a lossless one, which results in no data loss during the compression or decompression routine. Windows XP, however, has another trick up its sleeve when it comes to compression.

Realizing the fact that data compressed on your local hard drives using NTFS compression does you no good when you have to transmit it via email or removable media, Microsoft has included support for reading and writing ZIP files natively within Windows XP...without requiring the use of any third-party compression products, such as the ever-popular WinZIP by WinZip Computing, Incorporated. Both of these compression features will be examined further in the next sections.

NTFS FILE AND FOLDER COMPRESSION

File and folder compression is an integral part of the file system when using NTFS on your computer's hard drives. However, this useful feature comes at a price: You cannot simultaneously have EFS encryption and NTFS compression enabled on the same file or folder. Another caveat to using compression is that uncompressed file size values are used for computing disk quota usage.

Should you decide to make use of NTFS compression, enabling it is a simple procedure. Compression can be managed from within Windows Explorer or alternatively from the command line by use of the compact command. Follow the procedure outlined below to compress a folder (containing subfolders and files) from within Windows.

1. Open Windows Explorer and select the folder to be compressed.

2. Right-click the folder and select Properties. Click the Advanced button to open the Advanced Attributes window, as shown in Figure 25.24.

3. Select Compress Contents to Save Disk Space and click OK.

4. Click OK again to close the Properties page.

5. You may be presented with a dialog box asking you whether you want to apply the changes to the selected folder or to the selected folder, subfolder, and all files. Make your selection and click OK one last time to complete the process.

Figure 25.24
Compressing a folder.

NOTE

Confusing Check Boxes

Although you would think that the check boxes for Compression and Encryption shown in Figure 25.24 work like normal check boxes (you could select one, both, or neither of them), this is not the case. These check boxes function like modified radio buttons in that you can only select one or the other or neither—but never both at the same time.

Compressing a previously encrypted file or folder (or vice versa) will result in the encryption attribute being removed and the compression attribute being applied. This is what the dialog box in Step 5 of the procedure is alerting you to among other things.

TIP

Colors of the Rainbow

If you have enabled it, you will now see this folder and its files and subfolders displayed with blue text. From Windows Explorer, click Tools, Folder Options, and switch to the View tab. Scroll down the list of options and select the Show Encrypted or Compressed NTFS Files in Color option. Click OK to close out the window. You will now be able to see compressed files in blue and EFS-encrypted files in green. This option does not have any effect on compressed (zipped) files, however.

Moving and copying compressed files works like this:

■ Moving an uncompressed file or folder to another folder on the same NTFS volume will result in the file or folder remaining uncompressed, regardless of the compression state of the target folder.

- Moving a compressed file or folder to another folder results in the file or folder remaining compressed after the move, regardless of the compression state of the target folder.
- Copying a file to a folder causes the file to take on the compression state of the target folder.
- Overwriting a file of the same name causes the copied file to take on the compression state of the target file, regardless of the compression state of the target folder.
- Copying a file from a FAT folder to an NTFS folder results in the file taking on the compression state of the target folder.
- Copying a file from an NTFS folder to a FAT folder results in all NTFS-specific properties being lost.

MANAGING NTFS COMPRESSION FROM THE COMMAND LINE

Windows provides for management of NTFS compression from the command line via the compact command, which has the following syntax:

```
compact [{/c|/u}] [/s[:dir]] [/a] [/i] [/f] [/q] [FileName[...]]
```

The parameters for the compact command are outlined in Table 25.6.

TABLE 25.6 PARAMETERS FOR THE compact COMMAND

Parameter	Description
/c	Compresses the specified directory or file.
/u	Uncompresses the specified directory or file.
/s	Specifies that the requested action (compress or uncompress) be applied to all subdirectories of the specified directory, or of the current directory if none is specified.
/a	Displays hidden or system files.
/i	Ignores errors.
/f	Forces compression or uncompression of the specified directory or file. This is used in the case of a file that was partly compressed when the operation was interrupted by a system crash. To force the file to be compressed in its entirety, use the /c and /f parameters and specify the partially compressed file.
/q	Reports only the most essential information.
FileName	Specifies the file or directory. You can use multiple file names and wildcard characters (* and ?).

25

COMPRESSED (ZIPPED) FOLDERS IN WINDOWS XP

If you do not have any third-party compression utilities installed on your Windows XP computer, you will be able to make use of a new feature of Windows—the reading and writing of ZIP files. Files and folders that are compressed using the compressed (zipped) folders feature remain compressed on both FAT and NTFS drives and can be moved to any drive, volume, or folder on any computer without having their compression affected. These files are particularly well suited for transmission via the Internet and as email attachments. Files created with this option can be opened by any third-party application that supports ZIP files such as WinZip or StuffIt.

Files can be directly accessed from within these compressed archives without decompressing them (Windows will decompress the file in the background for you). Compressed (zipped) folders created using this option will be displayed as a folder with a zipper on it, as shown in Figure 25.25.

Figure 25.25
Compressed folders in Windows XP.

To open a zipped folder, just click on it. A new window opens, showing the contents of the "folder." You can then view and use files within the zipped folder as you normally would, with some restrictions. Keep in mind that the files are stored within a compression scheme that is not as transparent to the operating system as NTFS encryption. Therefore, editing the files does not tend to work well. For example, opening a Word .doc file stored in a zipped folder and then editing and attempting to save the file will result in a "read only" error message from Word. You'll be asked to save the file in another location. Saving directly from an app into a pre-existing zipped folder is not an option, since Save As dialogs will not display the zipped folder target. Therefore, the way to work with zipped folders is to do one of two things:

- Since Explorer-style drag and drop works with zipped folders, you can simply drag and drop any file(s) you want to work with into a regular Explorer folder. Then save your work on the file(s) there, and drag back into the zipped folder if you want to, for safe keeping, emailing, and so on. *It may help to see what you're mailing, as well as the relationship between the zipped folder and the rest of the hard disk's folder structure, by clicking on the Folders button in the toolbar.*

- Notice that you'll see an Extract All Files command at the top of the Explorer Bar of a zipped folder. Clicking on this command runs a wizard that will walk you through the process of decompressing and pulling out the files into another folder.

TIP

> To send a zipped folder to an email recipient, just right-click on it and choose Send To, Mail Recipient.

TIP

> To easily zip some files or folders, select them in an Explorer window. Then right-click on them and choose Send To, Compressed (zipped) folder.

Compressed (zipped) folders can be protected, if desired, with a password. To protect a zipped folder with a password, first open the folder. From the File menu, select Add a Password and enter the password twice. Click OK to accept the password. Keep the following points in mind when working with compressed folders:

- If you copy over a file in a compressed folder that has a password, the password will not be applied to that file.
- If you add a new file in a compressed folder that has a password, the password will not be applied to that file.
- Passwords are applied to an entire compressed folder, not to individual files or subfolders. If some files are not password protected, you will need to remove the password from the folder and then reapply it to the folder.
- To compress individual files using compressed folders, create a compressed folder and then move or copy the files to that folder.

NOTE

> The compressed (zipped) folders feature is not available on Windows XP Professional 64-Bit Edition.

NOTE

> Although it is possible to have a compressed (zipped) folder also being NTFS compressed, it is a waste of effort. You can only compress a file once, and thus if you place a compressed (zipped) folder inside of an NTFS compressed folder, no extra compression occurs.

25

THE ENCRYPTING FILE SYSTEM

One of the single largest improvements in Windows XP over Windows 2000 is in the area of the Encrypting File System. EFS in Windows XP provides the following new features:

- More than one user can be allowed access to an encrypted file.
- Offline files can now be encrypted.
- Data Recovery Agents (DRAs) are not required, but still recommended.
- The triple-DES (3DES) encryption algorithm is available, replacing the DESX algorithm.
- A password reset disk can be used to reset a user's password.
- Encrypted files can be stored in Web folders.

NOTE

> Remember that in order to use EFS encryption, you must using the NTFS file system on your hard drive.

EFS works by using a public-private key pair for each user and a per-file encryption key to encrypt and decrypt data on the fly. When a user selects to encrypt a file, EFS will generate a file encryption key (FEK) that is used to encrypt the data. The FEK is then encrypted with the user's public key and the encrypted FEK is stored with the file that has been encrypted. When a file is decrypted, EFS decrypts the FEK using the user's private key and then decrypts the data using the decrypted FEK.

NOTE

> EFS encryption is not available in Windows XP Home Edition.

Should you decide to make use of EFS encryption, enabling it is a simple procedure. Encryption can be managed from within Windows Explorer or alternatively from the command line by use of the cipher command. Follow the procedure outlined below to encrypt a folder (containing subfolders and files) from within Windows.

1. Open Windows Explorer and select the folder to be encrypted.
2. Right-click the folder and select Properties. Click the Advanced button to open the Advanced Attributes window, as shown in Figure 25.26.
3. Select Encrypt Contents to Secure Data and click OK.
4. Click OK again to close the Properties page.
5. You may be presented with a dialog box asking whether you want to apply the changes to the selected folder or to the selected folder, subfolder, and all files. Make your selection and click OK one last time to complete the process.

Figure 25.26
Encrypting a folder.

EFS and Multiple Users

As mentioned earlier, one of the improvements to EFS in Windows XP Professional is the ability to allow multiple users to have access to an encrypted file. Once you have encrypted the file of your choice, the process to add additional authorized users is extremely simple. To start the process, open the Advanced Attributes window again and click the Details button, which will open the Encryption Details window as shown in Figure 25.27. You can choose to add additional users by clicking the Add button. Any user to be added must possess a valid EFS certificate. You cannot add users to an encrypted folder, only to encrypted files.

25

Figure 25.27
Adding users to an encrypted file.

Preventing Users from Using EFS

In Windows 2000, removing the Default Recovery Agent would prevent the use of EFS encryption. Even with the removal of the DRA from a Windows XP Professional computer (or from the domain in a Windows 2000 Server domain), you can still use EFS. Not a good situation if you were hoping to prevent users from using EFS. The change in behavior from Windows 2000 to Windows XP Professional is due to the upcoming change in behavior of Windows Server 2003 Certificate Authorities. These Server CAs will store both public and (now) private keys, thus eliminating the need for a DRA. A new Group Policy option in Windows Server 2003, called "EFSConfiguration" will be the key to preventing Windows XP Professional clients from being able to use EFS. When the value of this object is set to 1 in the local computer's Registry, Windows XP Professional computers will refuse to encrypt files.

In order to prevent encryption on a computer-by-computer basis, you will need to edit the Registry as outlined in the following steps:

1. Start the Registry Editor by typing **regedit** in a Run dialog box (Start, Run).

2. Expand the keys until you arrive at the HKEY_LOCAL_MACHINE\ SOFTWARE\Microsoft\Windows NT\CurrentVersion\EFS subkey, as shown in Figure 25.28.

3. Right-click on the right pane and select New, DWORD Value.

4. Enter **EfsConfiguration** for the value name and **1** for the value data to disable EFS.

5. Restart the computer to complete the process.

Figure 25.28
Disabling EFS on the local Windows XP computer.

My Computer\HKEY_LOCAL_MACHINE\SOFTWARE\Microsoft\Windows NT\CurrentVersion\EFS

TIP

> If you want to prevent users from encrypting only certain folders, you can do so by creating a file named desktop.ini that contains the following data:
>
> ```
> [Encryption]
> Disable=1
> ```
>
> Save this file in each folder you want to prevent encryption; it will affect all subfolders of the root level folder it is saved in.

Should you need to disable EFS on all Windows XP Professional computers and don't want to edit the Registry, you can do so by creating a custom ADM template and adding it to the

Administrative Templates for a Group Policy. See `http://www.mcpmag.com/backissues/ columns/article.asp?EditorialsID=391` for more information on disabling EFS across all of your Windows XP Professional computers.

MANAGING ENCRYPTION FROM THE COMMAND LINE

Should you need to manage EFS encryption from the command line, you can do so using the following syntax.

```
cipher [{/e|/d}] [/s:dir] [/a] [/i] [/f] [/q] [/h] [/k] [/u[/n]] [PathName [...]]
| [/r:PathNameWithoutExtension] | [/w:PathName]
```

A typical command using ciper might look something like this: `cipher /e /s:h:\myfolder /i /f`, where the target of the encryption was the myfolder directory on the volume H:, as shown in Figure 25.29.

Figure 25.29
Using EFS encryption from the command line.

The parameters for the `cipher` command are outlined in Table 25.7.

TABLE 25.7 PARAMETERS FOR THE `cipher` COMMAND

Parameter	Description
/e	Encrypts the specified folders. Folders are marked so that files that are added to the folder later are encrypted too.
/d	Decrypts the specified folders. Folders are marked so that files that are added to the folder later are encrypted too.
/s: dir	Performs the selected operation in the specified folder and all subfolders.
/a	Performs the operation for files and directories.
/i	Continues performing the specified operation even after errors occur. By default, `cipher` stops when it encounters an error.
/f	Forces the encryption or decryption of all specified objects. By default, `cipher` skips files that have been encrypted or decrypted already.

continues

25

TABLE 25.7   CONTINUED

Parameter	Description
/q	Reports only the most essential information.
/h	Displays files with hidden or system attributes. By default, these files are not encrypted or decrypted.
/k	Creates a new file encryption key for the user running cipher. If you use this option, cipher ignores all of the other options.
/u	Updates the user's file encryption key or recovery agent's key to the current ones in all of the encrypted files on local drives (that is, if the keys have been changed). This option only works with /n.
/n	Prevents keys from being updated. Use this option to find all of the encrypted files on the local drives. This option only works with /u.
PathName	Specifies a pattern, file, or folder.
/r:PathNameWithoutExtension	Generates a new recovery agent certificate and private key, and then writes them to files with the file name specified in *PathNameWithoutExtension*. If you use this option, cipher ignores all of the other options.
/w:PathName	Removes data on unused portions of a volume. *PathName* can indicate any directory on the desired volume. If you use this option, cipher ignores all of the other options.

→ To learn more about securing your computer, see Chatper 22.
→ To learn more about securing your files, see Chatper 23.
→ To learn more about securing your network, including EFS issues on the network, see Chapter 24.

BACKUP FOR SAFETY

The last major part of taking care of your hard drive is ensuring that your data is fault tolerant by means of properly planned and performed backups. There are five types of backup that you can perform on your systems, and although they are pretty much common knowledge, they deserve a quick review before we move on.

- **Normal backup**—Copies all selected files and marks each file as having been backed up (the archive attribute is cleared). Only the most recent copy of the backup file is required to perform restoration.

- **Incremental backup**—Copies only those files created or changed since the last normal or incremental backup; the archive attribute is then cleared. Using normal and incremental backups, you will require the last normal backup and all incremental backups in order to perform restoration.

- **Copy backup**—Copies all selected files but does not mark each file as having been backed up (the archive attribute is not cleared). Copy backups have no effect on any other type of backup operation.

- **Daily backup**—Copies all selected files that have been modified the day the daily backup is performed; the archive attribute is not cleared in this case.

- **Differential backup**—Copies files created or changed since the last normal or incremental backup; clears the archive attribute.

The backup utility in Windows XP has undergone some changes from its predecessor in Windows 2000. No longer will you be creating an ERD (Emergency Repair Disk)—this has been replaced by the new and improved ASR (Automated System Recovery) function. The other major change to the Windows XP Backup utility is that it supports Volume Shadow Copy. Figure 25.30 shows the Backup utility in advanced mode.

Figure 25.30
Backup utility.

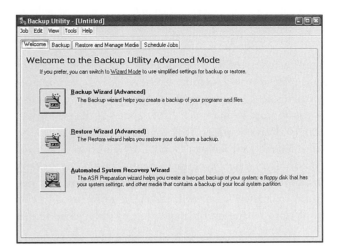

THE NEW FEATURES

Using the volume shadow copy, an instant copy of the original volume is created at the time the backup is initiated. Data is then subsequently backed up to the backup media from this shadow copy instead of the original files. This new technology provides a means to back up open files that were in use at the time of the backup being initiated. Using volume shadow copy, files that would normally be skipped during the backup are instead backed up in their current state (at the time of the shadow copy creation) and thus appear closed on the backup media. Any applications that are running during the backup process can continue to run during the backup process. After the backup has been completed, the shadow copy is deleted. The volume shadow copy feature requires the NTFS file system to be in use and can be disabled if desired (although I can't imagine why you'd want to), by clicking the Advanced button after completing the configuration of a backup job, as shown in Figure 25.31.

Figure 25.31
Disabling the volume
shadow copy option.

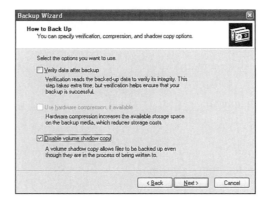

NOTE

You cannot disable the volume shadow copy option when performing a backup of the system state data.

Automated System Recovery (ASR) is an advanced restoration option of the Backup utility that can be used to restore your system if other disaster recovery methods fail or are not available for use. Using ASR, you can restore the Operating System back to a previous state, which will allow you to start Window XP Professional in the event that other methods do not work. You should always consider ASR your last resort for recovery, after Safe Mode, the Recovery Console, and Last Known Good Configuration. You should make a point to keep your ASR media up to date as you make configuration changes to your computer in order to minimize the amount of recovery required should you ever need to use ASR. To use the ASR Wizard to create a set of ASR media, you only need to click on the Automated System Recovery Wizard button on the main page of the Backup tool, as shown in Figure 25.30.

Using Windows Backup

The Backup utility provided in Windows XP, ntbackup.exe, is again a "lite" version of a commercially available third-party solution. In this case, the Backup utility has been provided by Veritas Software. Although limited in its ability, the included Backup utility, when used properly, can provide you with all of the functionality you should need for small networks or workgroups. If you have a larger network, you will want to place some serious thought into acquiring an enterprise backup solution, such as Backup Exec or NetBackup.

Using the Backup utility consists of three distinct processes: creating one or more backup configurations, scheduling backups to occur automatically, and performing restorations.

NOTE

Find out more about Veritas Software's full-featured products at
`http://www.veritas.com/.`

CREATING THE BACKUP CONFIGURATIONS

The Windows Backup utility makes it extremely simple to create a backup configuration. The basic steps to create the configuration are outlined here, although your options and decisions will vary depending on how your system and backup media devices are configured.

1. Start the Backup Wizard by clicking Start, Programs, Accessories, System Tools, Backup. If you get the wizard-based screen shown in Figure 25.32, click the Advanced Mode link to switch to Advanced mode.

Figure 25.32
The Backup or Restore Wizard.

2. Start the Backup Wizard by clicking the Backup Wizard (Advanced) button from the main page of the Backup utility.

3. Click Next to dismiss the opening page of the Wizard. From the What to Back Up page, select the scope of the backup. Click Next; if you choose to back up selected files and folders, proceed to step 4, otherwise skip to step 5.

4. From the Items to Back Up page, choose the files and folders to back up and click Next.

5. From the Backup type... page, choose the backup filename and location and click Next.

6. To configure advanced options, including scheduling and disabling volume shadow copy, click Advanced and proceed to step 7. If you want to perform this backup immediately, click Finish.

7. From the Type of Backup page, select the type of backup you want (the default is Normal) and click Next.

8. From the How to Back Up page, select your preferences as they relate to verification and volume shadow copy and select Next.

9. From the Backup Options page, select whether to append or overwrite existing data and select Next.

10. From the When to Back Up page, select when you want to perform this backup and click Next. If you selected Now, then click Finish to start the backup.

11. If you selected Later, then you will be able to configure scheduling options. When you have completed setting all scheduling options, click Next. Enter the user name and password information when requested (ensure this user has permissions to perform backups). Click Finish to complete the procedure.

Additionally, you can choose to create a backup configuration manually; however you will still make all of the same decisions as when using the Backup Wizard.

Scheduling Your Backups

Managing a backup schedule is very easy in Windows XP. Simply switch to the Schedule Jobs tab from the Backup utility advanced view (see Figure 25.28). Each day on the calendar will show what type of backup is scheduled for that day. Holding the cursor over a backup will display the backup name. You can edit the backup properties, including rescheduling the backup by clicking it. You can also create new backup configurations by clicking the Add Job button. Figure 25.33 shows the backup schedule I have in place on one of my Windows XP Professional computers.

Figure 25.33
Scheduling backup jobs.

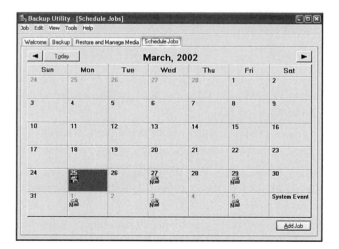

D-Day: Performing the Restoration

Should the day actually come that you need to put your backup system to the test, the actual process of performing the restoration is a relatively easy task in Windows XP Professional—as long as you are ready for the task. The basic steps to perform a restoration are outlined here, although your options and decisions will vary depending on how your system and backup media devices are configured.

1. Start the Backup Wizard by clicking Start, Programs, Accessories, System Tools, Backup. If you get the wizard-based screen shown previously in Figure 25.30, click the Advanced Mode link to switch to Advanced mode.

2. Start the Backup Wizard by clicking the Restore Wizard (Advanced) button from the main page of the Backup utility.

3. Click Next to dismiss the opening page of the wizard.

4. From the What to Restore page, select the media and files to restore. If your media is not listed, click the Browse button to locate it. After making your selections, click Next.

5. To configure advanced options, such as changing the restoration location, click Advanced and proceed to step 6. Otherwise, click Finish to start the restoration.

6. From the Where to Restore page, select the restoration location for the files and click Next.

7. From the How to Restore page, select your option in regards to overwriting existing files and click Next.

8. From the Advanced Restore Options page, select the options you want and click Next.

9. Click Finish to start the restoration.

The following list provides some additional help when deciding which advanced restore options to choose.

- **Restore Security**—Restores security settings for each file and folder.

- **Restore Junction Points, and Restore File and Folder Data Under Junction Points to the Original Location**—Restores junction points on your hard disk as well as the data that the junction points point to. If you are restoring a mounted drive, and you want to restore the data that is on the mounted drive, you must select this check box. If you do not select this check box, you will only restore the folder containing the mounted drive.

- **Preserve Existing Volume Mount Points**—Prevents the restore operation from writing over any volume mount points you have created on the partition or volume you are restoring data to.

- **Restore Removable Storage Database**—Restores the Removable Storage database and deletes the existing Removable Storage database. If you are not using Removable Storage to manage storage media, you do not need to select this option.

NOTE

> **Form of a Junction Point!**
> A junction point is a physical location on a hard disk that points to data located at another location on your hard disk or another storage device. Junction points are created when you create a mounted drive.

USING THE REMOVABLE STORAGE MANAGER

The Removable Storage Manager provides an easy way for you to keep track of all of your removable storage media attached to the computer. This media can be of any type, such as changers, jukeboxes, CD-ROM drives, and so on. The Removable Storage manager provides many control options for you in order to help you manage your removable storage media easier and with less effort.

The Removable Storage manager will help you by labeling, tracking, and cataloging all media inserted into your removable storage drives. It additionally can be used to control library devices, slots, and doors—it can be used to inject and eject media.

By itself, the Removable Storage manager does not perform any backup or restoration functions, but instead works with your backup and restoration software to allow for the efficient sharing and usage of your removable storage media. The Removable Storage manager can automatically move media between media pools as required providing the amount of storage required by each application that is interfacing with it; however, it does not provide any volume management functions such as media siding or striping, nor does it provide any file management services, as previously mentioned.

In order for the Removable Storage Manager to function properly, you must have all of your removable media devices connected to the same computer that is running the data management application; Removable Storage Manager cannot support multiple computers connected to the same library or storage device.

You can open the Removable Storage console in any one of three different ways:

- From within the Computer Management console: Start, Programs, Administrative Tools, Computer Management. From within the Computer Management console, expand the Storage node and then select the Removable Storage manager.
- From the command line: Type `ntmsmgr.msc`.
- From the command line: Type `MMC`. From the empty console, add the Removable Storage snap-in.

Figure 25.34
The Removable
Storage Manager.

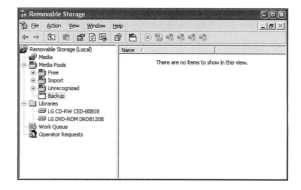

As you can see, I have no exotic removable storage on this machine—it is but a simple work-station. My CD-ROM and DVD-ROM drives show up, however, as removable storage since they fit the guidelines.

N O T E

See the Windows XP Professional Resource Kit at `http://www.microsoft.com/technet/prodtechnol/winxppro/reskit/prdg_dsm_fpdt.asp` for more information on the Removable Storage Manager.

WHAT'S NEW IN WINDOWS XP PROFESSIONAL 64-BIT EDITION?

Working with the 64-bit edition of Windows XP Professional affords you some additional disk-management considerations above and beyond those found in the regular 32-bit Windows XP Professional version that most of us will be using. Itanium-based systems running Windows XP 64-bit Edition can make use of a new partitioning style called the Globally Unique Identifier Partition Table, or GPT for short.

GPT disks have the following features, which are unavailable on any other version of Windows XP:

- GPT disks can support partitions up to 18 exabytes in size.
- GPT disks can support up to 128 partitions per disk.
- GPT disks do not contain a standard system partition; instead they reserve 1% of the total disk space (up to 100 MB maximum) for what is called the EFI System partition. This partition contains the required files to start Windows XP 64-bit Edition.
- GPT disks contain a Microsoft Reserved Partition (MSR), which is either 32MB or 128MB (depending on total disk size), and is responsible for ensuring system components are guaranteed space to allocate new partitions for their own use as required.
- GPT disks that are basic disks contain primary partitions.
- EFI System partitions and MSR partitions count against the 128 total partitions limit.
- GPT disks that are dynamic disks contain an LDM Data partition, which contains all data volumes on the drive.

For more information on GPT disks, see `http://www.microsoft.com/technet/prodtechnol/winxppro/reskit/prkb_cnc_helm.asp` from the Windows XP Professional Resource Kit.

N O T E

Disk management for GPT disks is conducted from the Disk Management tool, just the same as for MBR disks.

25

ADVANCED DISK MANAGEMENT FROM THE COMMAND LINE

Although it is often easier (and safer) to carry out management options from within the Windows GUI, sometimes it becomes necessary to work from the command line. Some people, the die-hards like myself, prefer the command line as we've been used to using it for so long. Another extremely useful and valid reason for working from the command line comes into play when using scripts and batch files to execute configuration changes automatically—even from across the network. Command-line support for disk management in Windows XP Professional is superb to say the least and two new tools, `fsutil` and `diskpart`, give you power like never before.

CAUTION

> **Super Powers**
>
> When I say "power like never before," that should give you some indication of just how dangerous misusing these tools can be. Don't make any changes without first thoroughly researching and understanding what you are doing. You'll be sorry if you rush in without adequate preparation beforehand. Don't say I didn't warn you....

25

fsutil

The `fsutil` utility is command line tool new in Windows XP that has multiple uses and a large potential for causing irreparable damage to your system. Microsoft recommends that only experienced users work with the `fsutil` command, and thus you must have administrative privileges to use it. The `fsutil` tool can be used to perform many FAT- and NTFS file system-related tasks such as managing reparse points, managing sparse files, dismounting a volume, or extending a volume.

Working with the `fsutil` tool is somewhat similar to working with the `netsh` command in that it is context-specific. When I say context-specific, I mean that each root level command has several subcommands that are dependent on the root level command—they won't work if not used after the root level command. However, the `fsutil` tool is not like `netsh` in that it *does not* require you to place the focus on an object before working with it. As we will see later in this section, the `diskpart` command does function this way.

The root level commands for the `fsutil` command are outlined in Table 25.8. Within each of these root-level commands are several subcommands, some of which I will discuss in the sections following the table.

TABLE 25.8 RootLevel Commands for the `fsutil` Command

Command	Description
behavior	Queries, changes, enables, or disables the settings for generating 8.3 character-length filenames.
dirty	Queries whether a volume's dirty bit is set. Sets a volume's dirty bit.
file	Finds a file by security identifier, queries allocated ranges for a file, sets a file's short name, sets a file's valid data length, sets zero data for a file, or creates a new file.
fsinfo	Lists all drives, queries the drive type, queries volume information, queries NTFS-specific volume information, or queries file system statistics.
hardlink	Creates a hard link. A hard link is a directory entry for a file. Every file can be considered to have at least one hard link. On NTFS volumes, each file can have multiple hard links, and thus a single file can appear in many directories (or even in the same directory with different names).
objectid	Manages object identifiers, which are used by Windows XP to track objects such as files and directories.
quota	Manages disk quotas on NTFS volumes in order to provide more precise control of network-based storage.
reparsepoint	Queries or deletes reparse points, which are NTFS file system objects that have a definable attribute containing user-controlled data, and are used to extend functionality in the input/output (I/O) subsystem.
sparse	Manages sparse files.
usn	Manages the update sequence number (USN) change journal, which provides a persistent log of all changes made to files on the volume.
volume	Manages a volume. Dismounts a volume or queries to see how much free space is available on a disk.

25

The basic context of the `fsutil` command can generally take on four different formats, as shown in the bulleted list. Of course, this is not an absolute rule, as some of the root level commands do not require the use of a behavior modifier to accomplish their function.

- fsutil *rootlevel_command* create *subcommand* [*optional_value]*
- fsutil *rootlevel_command* delete *subcommand* [*optional_value]*
- fsutil *rootlevel_command* query *subcommand* [*optional_value]*
- fsutil *rootlevel_command* set *subcommand* [*optional_value]*
- fsutil *rootlevel_command* track *subcommand* [*optional_value]*

The following sections will explore some of the subcommands available for use with each root level command of the `fsutil` utility.

TIP

> **For a Complete Listing of `fsutil` Commands**
>
> For more complete information on the `fsutil` command, which is beyond the scope of this chapter, be sure to visit TechNet at `http://www.microsoft.com/TechNet/prodtechnol/winxppro/proddocs/fsutil.asp`.

THE behavior COMMAND

To query the file system behavior for writing 8.3 character-length file names, type

```
fsutil behavior query disable8dot3
```

A returned value of 0 indicates that 8.3 character-length filenames are being written, while a returned value of 1 indicates that they are not. Assuming that we received a value of 0 and wish to disable the writing of 8.3 character-length file names, we would type

```
fsutil behavior set disable8dot3 1
```

THE dirty COMMAND

To query the system for the dirty bit status on volume D, type

```
fsutil dirty query D:
```

The returned value will either be "Volume - D: is NOT Dirty" or "Volume - D: IS Dirty". If you wanted to set the dirty bit on volume E to force chkdsk to run at the next restart of the computer, type

```
fsutil dirty set E:
```

THE file COMMAND

To find all files saved by user will on volume D by his SID, type

```
fsutil file findbysid will D:\
```

THE fsinfo COMMAND

To query a computer about all drives installed, type

```
fsutil fsinfo drives
```

To query a computer for the drive type for a specific drive, type

```
fsutil fsinfo drivetype C:
```

To query a computer for information about a specific drive, type

```
fsutil fsinfo volumeinfo C:
```

THE hardlink COMMAND

To create a new hardlink (directory entry) to a file, type

```
fsutil hardlink create NewFilename ExistingFilename
```

Creating additional hardlinks is useful if you want to list a file in multiple directories, without actually having multiple copies of the file. Each hardlink is simply just a pointer to the actual file. Deleting a hardlink does not delete the file itself, unless all hardlinks (including the first one, which is created when the file is first created) are deleted.

THE objectid COMMAND

The objectid command is used to manage object identifiers (also known as OIDs), which are internal objects used by the Distributed Link Tracking (DLT) Client service and File Replication Service (FRS) to track other objects such as files, directories, and links. Object identifiers are invisible to most programs and should never be modified. With that having been said...

To query an object identifier on a file, type

```
fsutil objectid query D:\Temp\dump.txt
```

To set an object identifier, type

```
fsutil objectid set ObjectID BirthVolumeID BirthObjectID DomainID PathName
```

The values for the objectid set command are

- *ObjectID*—A file-specific 16-byte hexadecimal identifier that is guaranteed to be unique within a volume. It is used by the Distributed Link Tracking (DLT) Client service and the File Replication Service (FRS) to identify files. Any file that has an ObjectID also has a BirthVolumeID, a BirthObjectID, and a DomainID. When you move a file, the ObjectID may change, but BirthVolumeID and BirthObjectID remain the same, which enables Windows XP to always find a file, no matter where it has been moved.

- *BirthVolumeID*—A 16-byte hexadecimal identifier that indicates the volume on which the file was located when it first obtained an ObjectID. This value is used by the DLT Client service.

- *BirthObjectID*—A 16-byte hexadecimal identifier that indicates the file's original ObjectID (note that the ObjectID may change when a file is moved). This value is used by the DLT Client service.

- *DomainID*—A 16-byte hexadecimal domain identifier that is not currently used and must be set to all zeros.

- *PathName*—Specifies the drive letter (followed by a colon), mount point, or volume name.

25

CAUTION

> **Alarm Bells Should Be Going Off...**
>
> I would recommend, very strongly, to just avoid the `objectid` command altogether. You'll be much happier for it; trust me.

THE quota COMMAND

To query the quota status on a specific volume, type

```
fsutil quota query D:
```

To query for quota violations on a specific volume, type

```
fsutil quota violations D:
```

THE reparsepoint COMMAND

Reparse points are NTFS file system objects that have a definable attribute containing user-controlled data, and are used to extend functionality in the input/output (I/O) subsystem. Reparse points are used for directory junction points and volume mount points. They are also used by file system filter drivers to mark certain files as special to that driver.

To query about the reparse point data associated with a file or folder identified by a specific handle, type

```
fsutil reparsepoint query PathName
```

To delete a reparse point from the file or folder identified by a specific handle, type

```
fsutil reparsepoint delete PathName
```

CAUTION

> **Danger, Will Robinson!**
>
> The `reparsepoint` command, much like the aforementioned `objectid` command, is one that is best left untouched. Bad things can happen here.

THE sparse COMMAND

To mark a large file as being sparse (and therefore to save space), type

```
fsutil sparse setflag D:\Data\file.mdb
```

To query a large file, looking for sparse areas, type

```
fsutil sparse queryrange D:\Data\file.mdb
```

THE usn COMMAND

The update sequence number (USN) change journal provides a persistent log of all changes made to files on the volume. As files, directories, and other NTFS objects are added, deleted, and modified, NTFS enters records into the USN change journal, one for each volume on the computer. Each record indicates the type of change and the object changed. New records are appended to the end of the stream. Programs can consult the USN change journal to determine all the modifications made to a set of files. The USN change journal is much more efficient than checking time stamps or registering for file notifications. The USN change journal is enabled and used by the Indexing Service, File Replication Service (FRS), Remote Installation Service (RIS), and Remote Storage.

To query USN data for volume D:, type

```
fsutil usn queryjournal D:
```

To create a USN change journal for volume D:, type

```
fsutil usn createjournal m=1000 a=100 D:
```

Where m is the maximum size (in bytes) the change journal is allowed to use and a is the size, in bytes, of memory allocation that is added to the end and removed from the beginning of the change journal.

To read the USN data for a file in the temp folder on drive C, type

```
fsutil usn readdata D:\Data\file.mdb
```

CAUTION

> ### Deleting a Change Journal...
>
> ...is not only a very resource-intensive task that may continue into the next successful restart of the computer, but can also cause problems if other applications are actively attempting to use the change journal. Generally, you will be best to avoid deleting a change journal from your computer.

25

THE volume COMMAND

To dismount a mounted volume on drive D, type

```
fsutil volume dismount D: VolumePathname
```

To query the free space of a volume on drive D, type

```
fsutil volume diskfree D:
```

diskpart

The diskpart utility allows for the management of objects such as disks, partitions, and volumes from the command line. Working with the diskpart tool is extremely similar to working with the netsh command. Before you can actually execute a diskpart command on an object, you must first give the desired object the focus by selecting it. Once a specific object has the focus, all commands entered after that will be executed on that object until another object is given the focus. Because of this difficult and structured method, the diskpart tool is best used from within a script, instead of interactively from the command line.

The root-level commands for the diskpart command are outlined in Table 25.9. Within each of these root-level commands are several modifiers that control how the command is executed. I've placed the `list` commands and the `select` commands out of order at the beginning of the table, as they are the key to making `diskpart` work for you.

TABLE 25.9   ROOTLEVEL COMMANDS FOR THE `diskpart` COMMAND

Command	Description
list disk	Displays a list of disks and information about them. The disk marked with an asterisk (*) has focus.
list partition	Displays the partitions listed in the partition table of the current disk.
list volume	Displays a list of basic and dynamic volumes on all disks.
select disk	Selects the specified disk and shifts the focus to it.
select partition	Selects the specified partition and gives it focus. If no partition is specified, the `select` command lists the current partition with focus.
select volume	Selects the specified volume and shifts the focus to it. If no volume is specified, the `select` command lists the current volume with focus.
active	On basic disks, marks the partition with focus as active. This informs the BIOS or Extensible Firmware Interface (EFI) that the partition or volume is a valid system partition or system volume.
add disk	Mirrors the simple volume with focus to the specified disk.
assign	Assigns a drive letter or mount point to the volume with focus. If no drive letter or mount point is specified, then the next available drive letter is assigned. You cannot assign drive letters to system volumes, boot volumes, or volumes that contain the paging file. In addition, you cannot assign a drive letter to an Original Equipment Manufacturer (OEM) partition or any GUID Partition Table (GPT) partition other than a basic MSDATA partition.
break disk	Breaks the mirrored volume with focus into two simple volumes. One simple volume retains the drive letter and any mount points of the mirrored volume, while the other simple volume receives the focus so you can assign it a drive letter. By default, the contents of both halves of the mirror are retained. Each half becomes a simple volume. If you use the `nokeep` parameter, you will retain only one half of the mirror as a simple volume. The other half will be deleted and converted into free space.

Command	Description
clean	Removes any and all partition or volume formatting from the disk with focus.
convert basic	Converts an empty dynamic disk into a basic disk.
convert dynamic	Converts a basic disk into a dynamic disk.
convert gpt	Converts an empty master boot record (MBR) basic disk to a GUID partition table (GPT) partition style disk. Only works on Itanium-based computers running Windows XP Professional 64-bit Edition.
convert mbr	Converts an empty GPT partition style disk to a basic disk. Only works on Itanium-based computers running Windows XP Professional 64-bit Edition.
create partition efi	Creates an Extensible Firmware Interface (EFI) system partition on a GPT disk. After the partition has been created, the focus is given to the new partition. Only works on Itanium-based computers running Windows XP Professional 64-bit Edition.
create partition extended	Creates an extended partition on the current drive. After the partition has been created, the focus automatically shifts to the new partition.
create partition logical	Creates a logical drive in the extended partition. After the partition has been created, the focus automatically shifts to the new logical drive.
create partition msr	Creates a Microsoft Reserved (MSR) partition on a GPT disk. Only works on Itanium-based computers running Windows XP Professional 64-bit Edition.
create partition primary	Creates a primary partition on the current basic disk. After you create the partition, the focus automatically shifts to the new partition. The new partition will not automatically receive a drive letter.
create volume raid	Creates a RAID-5 volume on the specified dynamic disks. After you create the volume, the focus automatically shifts to the new volume. *Not applicable to Windows XP.*
create volume simple	Creates a simple volume. After you create the volume, the focus automatically shifts to the new volume.
create volume stripe	Creates a striped volume on the specified disks. After you create the volume, the focus automatically shifts to the new volume.
delete disk	Deletes a missing dynamic disk from the disk list.

25

continues

TABLE 25.9   CONTINUED

Command	Description
delete partition	On a basic disk, deletes the partition with focus. You cannot delete the system partition, boot partition, or any partition that contains the active paging file or crash dump (memory dump).
delete volume	Deletes the selected volume. You cannot delete the system volume, boot volume, or any volume that contains the active paging file or crash dump (memory dump).
detail disk	Displays the properties of the selected disk and the volumes on that disk.
detail volume	Displays the disks on which the current volume resides.
exit	Exits the diskpart utility.
extend	Extends the volume with focus into the next contiguous unallocated space.
help	Displays a list of the available commands.
import	Imports a foreign disk group into the local computer's disk group. The import command imports every disk that is in the same group as the disk that has focus.
online	Brings an offline disk or volume with focus online.
rem	Provides a way to add comments to a script.
remove	Removes a drive letter or mount point from the volume with focus. If the all parameter is used, all current drive letters and mount points are removed. If no drive letter or mount point is specified, then diskpart removes the first drive letter or mount point it encounters.
rescan	Locates new disks that may have been added to the computer.
retain	Prepares an existing dynamic simple volume to be used as a boot or system volume.

On an x86-based computer, creates a partition entry in the master boot record (MBR) on the dynamic simple volume with focus. To create an MBR partition, the dynamic simple volume must start at a cylinder aligned offset and be an integral number of cylinders in size.

On an Itanium-based computer, creates a partition entry in the GPT on the dynamic simple volume with focus.

Several examples of the diskpart command in action were illustrated in these sections earlier in this chapter:

- Creating new partitions and logical drives
- Creating new simple volumes

- Creating mounted drives
- Converting basic disks to dynamic disks
- Extending simple volumes

Figure 25.35 shows the process I went through to gather some information about one of the volumes on my computer.

Figure 25.35
Querying a volume for basic information using diskpart.

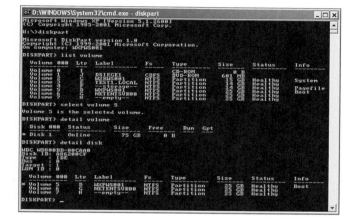

There are quite a few other tasks that can be performed using the diskpart command. For a full explanation of all diskpart commands and modifiers, see the TechNet article at http://www.microsoft.com/TechNet/prodtechnol/winxppro/proddocs/DiskPart.asp.

25

CHAPTER 26

USING THE COMPUTER MANAGEMENT CONSOLE

In this chapter

MICROSOFT MANAGEMENT CONSOLE (MMC) BACKGROUND

Introduced in a crude form in Windows NT 4.0, honed to perfection in Windows 2000, and carried over to Windows XP, the Microsoft Management Console (MMC) is the easiest way to manage your Windows computer from within the Graphical User Interface (GUI). Its simplicity and power, combined with its ability to delegate responsibility, make MMC an ideal management tool for any size organization.

But what is MMC? Many people think that it's a management tool in and of itself. This is not quite true. MMC is simply a shell that serves as a place to put, or "snap in," one or more of several dozen available management tools such as the Event Viewer, Disk Defragmenter, Group Policy Editor, and Internet Services Manager, to name just a few. MMC snap-ins can manage Windows XP computers as well as Windows 2000 Professional, Server, and 2003 Server computers, and can manage the local computer or remote computers across a network. MMC provides these various tools with a consistent look and feel.

A set of tools that is useful to keep together as a group is called a *console*. Windows comes with a few preconfigured consoles, and you can create your own by adding your favorite snap-ins to a blank MMC window. The familiar Computer Management program that appears when you right-click My Computer and select Manage (shown in Figure 26.1) is in fact an MMC console prepopulated with a set of useful management snap-ins.

Figure 26.1
The Computer Management program is actually an MMC console. Plug-ins are listed in the left pane, and the selected plug-in interacts with you in the right pane.

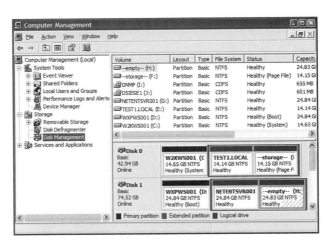

Before we get into the discussion of the preconfigured consoles available to you, let's look at the standard snap-ins, discussed in the next section, "Building a MMC Console," that you can expect to find installed on just about any Windows XP computer. These snap-ins can be added to an empty MMC shell or to any existing custom console that you may have previously created.

NOTE

> The 64-bit versions of Windows XP come with two versions of MMC: MMC32 runs snap-ins compiled for Win32, and MMC64 runs snap-ins built for Win64. For the most part, Windows will automatically choose which version of MMC to run. You can force Windows to run one version or the other by adding /32 or /64 to the mmc command line. For more (incredibly obtuse) information about this, open MMC, click Help, Help Topics, then search for "Win64, MMC Version Determination."

BUILDING AN MMC CONSOLE

You can manage many Windows components through the standard "Computer Management" console that's predefined when you install Windows. However, there are several reasons you might want to construct your own console:

- You frequently use MMC snap-ins that don't appear in Computer Management, such as the Certificate Management tool.

- You manage computers on your network and want quick access to their management tools.

- You want to manage Windows 2000/2003 Servers using snap-ins such as the Active Directory Users and Groups tool.

To create a new console, enter the command mmc from the command prompt, or press Windows+R, and then enter mmc into the Run box. Figure 26.2 shows an empty shell waiting to be customized with the snap-ins that you require.

Figure 26.2
The empty MMC shell—management launching point.

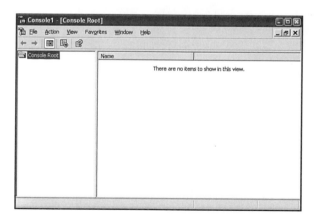

Then, to add snap-ins, click File, Add/Remove Snap-in to open the page shown in Figure 26.3.

26

Figure 26.3
Click Add to add snap-ins to your custom console.

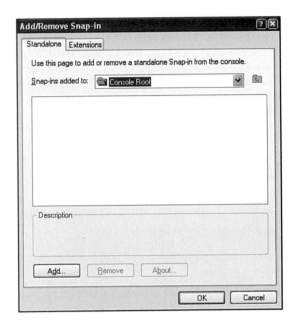

Then, click the Add button to open the Add Standalone Snap-in page shown in Figure 26.4. Choose the snap-in you want and click Add. Depending on the snap-ins that you place in your console, you may be presented with some additional options, such as which account, computer, or user the snap-in will be targeted to.

Figure 26.4
Choose a snap-in to add to a custom console.

If you manage networked computers and servers, you might want to add a given snap-in several times, once for each important machine. Figure 26.5 shows such a console configured to manage services on my computer and all of the servers on my network. (More on this in the next section.)

Figure 26.5
A custom console can give you quick management access to several computers on your network.

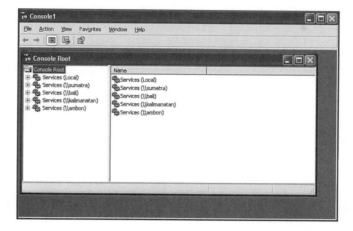

When you have finished adding all of the snap-ins you want to place in this console, click Close and then OK to return to the console.

You can add the snap-ins shown in Table 26.1 to a Windows XP Professional computer by default. You can additional snap-ins by installing the Admin Pack, by copying .MSC files from another computer, or by installing some third-party applications.

NOTE

If you have a Domain and/or Active Directory network and would like to perform administrative tasks from a Windows XP Professional computer, see MSKB #Q304718 at http://support.microsoft.com/default.aspx?scid=kb;EN-US;q304718 for information about the Adminpack.msi file. (As Windows XP Home Edition computers cannot be members of a Domain network, they can't be used to manage Domain servers.)

In most cases, you can't simply copy an .msc file from a Server computer to an XP Pro computer to get an added management function, as most .msc files are simply XML text files that make reference to software components (COM objects) that must be installed separately.

26

TABLE 26.1   DEFAULT SNAP-INS AVAILABLE

Snap-in	Purpose	Covered in Chapter...
ActiveX Control	Allows you to add an ActiveX control to your console, such as an Excel spreadsheet.	This chapter
Certificates	Allows you to browse the contents of the certificate stores for yourself, a service, or a computer.	This chapter
Component Services	Component Services (COM+) management tool.	This chapter
Computer Management	Computer management and related system tools, a collection of multiple snap-ins.	This chapter
Device Manager	Allows you to list and configure hardware devices on a computer.	27
Disk Defragmenter	Allows you to defragment your computer's hard drives to improve performance.	25
Disk Management	Provides tools and utilities for disk and volume management.	25
Event Viewer	Displays event logs.	26
Folder	Allows you to create a folder in the list of snap-ins, in which you can organize other snap-ins.	26
FrontPage Server Extensions	Manages the extensions; this option appears only if you've installed Internet Information Services (IIS).	15
Group Policy	Allows you to edit Group Policy Objects that can be linked to a Site, Domain, or Organizational Unit in the Active Directory or stored on a computer.	22
Indexing Service	Provides fast and flexible searching on file contents and properties.	6, 12
Internet Information Services	Manages Internet Information Services components (Web, FTP, and SMTP servers).	15
IP Security Monitor	Allows you to monitor the IP Security status.	26
IP Security Policy Management	Allows you to configure Internet Protocol Security (IPSec) Administration. Manages IPSec policies for secure communication with other computers.	26
Link to Web Address	Allows you to add a shortcut to a Web page, for example, to a Web-based software and hardware management tool.	26

Snap-in	Purpose	Covered in Chapter...
Local Users and Groups	Allows you to manage Local Users and Groups	11
Performance Logs and Alerts	Configures performance data logs and alerts.	26
Removable Storage Management	Catalogs removable media and manages automated libraries.	25
Resultant Set of Policy	Allows you to view the Resultant Set of Policy for a user on a machine.	26
Security Configuration and Analysis	Allows you to provide security configuration and analysis for Windows computers using security template files.	22
Security Templates	Provides editing capabilities for security template files.	22
Services	Starts, stops, and configures Windows services.	26, Appendix B
Shared Folders	Displays shared folders, current sessions, and open files.	18
SIDWalker Security Manager	A tool used to help migrate Windows NT 4 domains to Windows 2000/2003.	(not covered)
Terminal Services Connections	Lets you build a list of computers that you wish to access through Terminal Services (Remote Desktop).	22
WMI Control	Allows configuration and control of the Windows Management Instrumentation (WMI) service.	26

26

If you think it will help organize things, you can create groups of plug-ins in subfolders, for example, one for one each of your network's servers. Start by adding Folder items to an empty MMC console. Then, select a folder under Snap-ins Added To, and add snap-ins to it. When you've finished adding snap-ins to each of the folders and have dismissed the Add Plugins dialog, you can right-click and rename the folders to something useful, such as "Server X" and "Server Y".

SAVING CONSOLE SETUPS

Once you've configured your custom console, you can use it and then just close the MMC window, or you may save the configuration for future use. If you want to distribute the configured console file for use by others, before saving the console, you may want to first set the console mode. This lets you simplify the MMC user interface to make the console more user-friendly. There are four console modes available to choose from:

- **Author mode**—Allows access to all MMC functionality, including the ability to add or remove snap-ins, create new windows, and navigate the entire console tree.
- **User mode-full access**—Allows the user all window management commands and full access to the console tree, but prevents the adding or removing of snap-ins or changing the console properties.
- **User mode-limited access, multiple window**—Prevents the user from opening new windows in the console. This also prevents users from accessing areas of the console tree that were not visible when the console file was saved. Multiple child windows are allowed, but the user cannot close them.
- **User mode-limited access, single window**—Similar to user mode-limited access, multiple window except that in this case only a single window is allowed, thus the controls for working with multiple windows are not present.

The more restricted console modes have simpler user interfaces; the unnecessary menu items disappear. To set the console mode, click File, Options to open the Options page. Normally, MMC saves personalized changes to the console view.

- If you want users to see the same initial view every time they open the console, check Do Not Save Changes to This Console.
- If you want to prevent end-users from altering the console display at all, even without saving those changes, uncheck Allow the User to Customize Views.

Once you have configured your desired options, click OK to close the Options page.

Finally, to save the console definition, click File, Save, and give the console a name. The extension should always be `.msc`. By default the console will be saved in the Administrative Tools folder in the Start Menu of the currently logged in user, although you can easily change this. You can put the .msc file in a shared network folder for convenient access from any computer.

NOTE

In order to allow each user to make his or her own personalized modifications to the console view, MMC saves a customized version of user-mode consoles in each user's profile folder, in the folder `Application Data\Microsoft\MMC\`*xxx*, where *xxx* is the name of the console without the .msc extension.

When you open an MMC console, MMC checks to see if a customized version of the selected .msc file exists in this profile folder, and if so, it uses the private copy. MMC is smart enough to know whether the customized version belongs to a different console file that just happens to have the same name. If this is the case, it opens the selected original .msc file.

Once the console file has been saved, you can fire up your predefined set of tools in any of the usual ways:

- Double-click the .msc file's icon.

- Create a shortcut to the .msc file on your desktop, Quick Launch bar, or Start Menu.

- Type **start *drive:/path/xxx*.msc** at the command prompt, where *xxx* is the name you gave the file. If the file is in the current directory or in your search path, you can omit the drive and path.

MANAGING REMOTE COMPUTERS

The true coolness of MMC is that you can use it to connect across a network to remote computers in order to manage them. You will, of course, need to know the computer name and possess the required Administrator credentials to connect and perform remote administration.

There are three ways to tell Windows which remote computer you wish to manage. The first way is to choose a computer when you add snap-ins to a custom console. As I mentioned in the previous section, some snap-ins prompt you to choose which computer the snap-in is to manage. An example of this is shown in Figure 26.6, where I can choose to connect to a remote computer for Group Policy management. If you check Allow the Selected Computer to Be Changed When Launching from the Command Line, you can alter the target computer for all snap-ins by specifying an alternate computer name when you start MMC—which I'll discuss in a moment.

Figure 26.6
Some snap-ins let you select the computer to be managed.

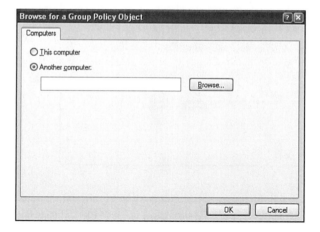

The second way to connect to a remote computer is to right-click on the name of a snap-in in the left pane of an open MMC console, and select Connect To Another Computer from the context menu. Figure 26.7 shows a management connection being made to one of my Windows 2000 servers.

Figure 26.7
You can ask an active MMC console snap-in to connect to a remote network computer.

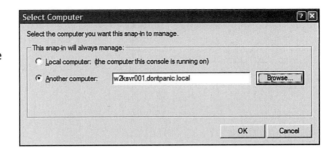

Finally, if you check Allow the Selected Computer to Be Changed... when you add snap-ins to the console window, you can select the target computer by opening the console .msc file from the command prompt or a shortcut with a command line like this:

```
mmc /computer=computername drive:path\xxx.msc
```

For example

```
mmc /computer=sales_server n:\consoles\mytools.msc
```

will open the "mytools.msc" console with the snap-ins aimed at sales_server. This is a clumsy thing to have to type directly, but it is useful if you create shortcuts using this sort of command line. The advantage of this setup is that you can arrange one console file with all of the necessary snap-ins, and then make multiple shortcuts to it, one for each server. Figure 26.8 shows a folder I set up with shortcuts to manage all of my office's servers.

Figure 26.8
You can create shortcuts to several different computers using the /computer= command-line option.

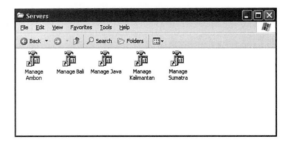

TIP

MMC considers specifying a computer name on the command line as making a change to the .msc file. To avoid getting the "Do you want to save changes?" prompt every time you use the console, select File, Options, change the Console Mode from Author to one of the limited versions, and check Do Not Save Changes to This Console, then save the console file.

THE COMPUTER MANAGEMENT CONSOLE

Windows XP comes preconfigured with several consoles, each containing one or more snap-ins. If the administrative tasks you need to perform can be addressed by using one of these preconfigured consoles, you can get right to work without having to create a customized console. In fact, you've probably used these consoles many times without knowing that MMC was part of the picture.

This section looks at the console that you have probably already used the most: the Computer Management Console, shown previously in Figure 26.1. To bring it up, right-click My Computer and select Manage. You can also get to it by clicking Start, All Programs, Administrative Tools, Computer Management, or from the Control Panel by selecting Performance and Maintenance, Administrative Tools, Computer Management.

Snap-in Confusion

The Computer Management console is actually just another snap-in itself. What makes it unique is that it contains several other snap-ins—the most commonly used ones, in one location for easy management. All of the snap-ins in the Computer Management console are available for use individually when creating custom consoles. Additionally, you can select the Computer Management snap-in and all of its tools in one swell foop, when building a custom console.

EVENT VIEWER

The Event Viewer, shown in Figure 26.9, is the convenience store of Windows monitoring. I say this because assuming you have the correct permissions, you can quickly get in, see what you need, and get back out. As you will see later when we discuss the Performance console, it is the powerhouse of computer monitoring.

26

Figure 26.9
The Event Viewer records many useful pieces of information about your computer's operation.

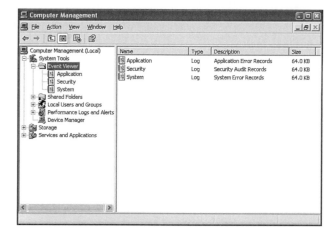

TIP

You can also access the Event Viewer snap-in by entering `eventvwr.msc` from a command prompt or by clicking Start, All Programs, Administrative Tools, Event Viewer.

The first thing you should notice about the Event Viewer is that it has three logs created in it by default with the installation of Windows XP Professional or Home Edition. Windows 2000 Servers and Windows 2003 Servers have these three and usually several others, depending on their purposes and the services running on them. From Figure 26.10, you can see a portion of the Application Log on my laptop computer—yes indeed, there are quite a few Errors logged there, but that is to be expected when you take a domain-based client computer out on the road!

Figure 26.10
Event entries written to the Application Log can give you a good idea of what is going on with your Windows XP computer.

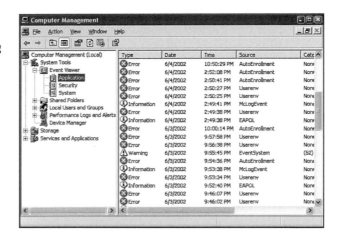

Looking at Figure 26.10, you can see three types of entries: Error, Warning, and Information. These three types of log entries, along with two others not yet seen, are discussed in detail in Table 26.2.

TABLE 26.2 WINDOWS EVENT TYPES

Event Type	Description
Error	Indicates a serious problem that has occurred, such as a loss of data or degradation in usability or reliability. A service that fails to load or a Domain Controller that is unavailable for contact will cause an Error event. More often than not, you will receive an onscreen warning concerning the Error event.
Warning	Indicates that a less serious event has occurred which should not normally have an immediate adverse effect on the computer. Low disk space or failure to contact a time server in a domain environment can cause a Warning event.

Event Type	Description
Information	Indicates the successful completion of a task or the successful operation of an application, device, or service. Many occurrences will create an Information event, such as the starting of a network service or the loading and configuring of a driver.
Success Audit	Indicates that an action that was configured for success auditing was attempted and was successful. Auditing can monitor access to files or folders, logging on to the network, use of privileges, and so on.
Failure Audit	Indicates that an action that was configured for failure auditing was attempted and was unsuccessful. Failure audit events can be used to identify users who are attempting to gain access to files or privileges for which they are not authorized.

As I previously mentioned, there are three logs created on a Windows XP Professional and Home Edition computers. They are

- **Application log**—Contains events logged by applications or programs running on the computer. For example, a program might record a file error in the application log. A program's developer decides which events to record.

- **System log**—Contains events logged by Windows system components. For example, the failure of a driver or other system component to load during startup is recorded in the System log. The event types logged by system components are predetermined by Windows and can't be changed by users or administrators.

- **Security log**—Records security events such as valid and invalid logon attempts as well as audit events related to resource use such as creating, opening, or deleting files. The administrator can specify which events will be recorded in the Security log by enabling specific logging actions.

The EventLog service starts automatically early in the bootup process. All users of a computer can view the Application and System logs, but only administrators can gain access to the Security logs.

Security Logging and Auditing

By default, security logging is turned off and must be enabled through Group Policy. The administrator can also set auditing policies in the Registry that cause the system to halt when the security log is full. Auditing and the use of the Security Log are discussed in Chapter 25, "Managing Your Hard Disks."

When working with the Event logs, you have a handful of things you can do, all of which are designed to make the Event Viewer flexible and easy to use. To access these common tasks, select the relevant log and right-click it. Select your desired action from the context-menu choices. Some of the more common tasks include

- To open a saved log file, select Open Log File. This comes in handy if you've saved and cleared out Event Logs.

26

- To save a log file for archival purposes, select Save Log File As. You will need to select from three file types: .EVT, .TXT, or .CSV. If you plan on opening the log later in the Event Viewer, you should save it in .EVT format. If you save a log in .TXT (plain text) or .CSV (comma-delimited) format, you will import the data into a spreadsheet or database for further processing. Logs that are not saved in .EVT format will lose all of their binary data.

- Clicking New Log View simply creates a copy of the selected log, allowing you to create a custom view of it without changing the view of the original.

- After you've archived a log, you can Clear All Events in the log to start with a clean slate again.

- Export List is a nice feature that allows you export a log file to a text file for easy transport and viewing in any text editor.

The last major option of concern on the context menu is the Properties selection. As with most other Properties options, this one allows you to perform some custom configuration on the selected Event Log. Figure 26.11 shows the General tab, from which you can configure most of the basic options for a log.

Figure 26.11
The General tab of the log Properties page allows you to configure how logging is to occur.

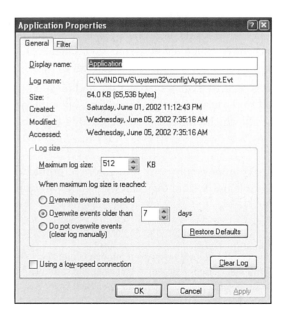

By default, the maximum log size is capped at 512KB. You can enter a custom size to suit your needs. You may also want to configure how Windows reacts when the maximum log size is reached. By default, the log files can be overwritten once they are greater than seven days old. If you don't plan on archiving log files at least weekly, you may want to either choose a longer interval or disable automatic overwriting of the logs altogether.

CAUTION

A common hacker trick is to do something improper, and then flood the log with innocuous entries to flush out any record of their misdeeds. On important servers, then, it's a common security practice to disable automatic overwriting of the security log. However, if you disable the overwriting of old events and your log grows to the maximum configured size, the logging of new events will not occur. Always pay careful attention to your logs when you have selected to manually clear log entries.

From the Filter tab, shown in Figure 26.12, you can cut down the list of displayed events in order to help you quickly locate the precise information you are looking for in the log. As shown, you can filter by any of the attributes stored in an event: type, source, category, ID, user, computer, or date range. I usually find it useful to filter by event type or event ID, if known.

Figure 26.12
The Filter tab allows you to configure what events will be displayed in your logs.

PERFORMANCE MONITOR AND PERFORMANCE LOGS AND ALERTS

The Performance Logs and Alerts snap-in is available in the Computer Management console and in customized consoles you've built yourself. This tool lets you view recorded performance data, and configure management alerts to be sent when system measurements stray from preset bounds.

If you type `start perfmon.msc` at the command line, or choose Start, All Programs, Administrative Tools, Performance, you'll get a console with Performance Logs and Alerts, plus an additional and more useful tool: the System Monitor, which plots system activity in real-time, as shown in Figure 26.13. For some strange reason, System Monitor is not available as a selection when building custom consoles.

Figure 26.13
The Performance console is the powerhouse of performance monitoring.

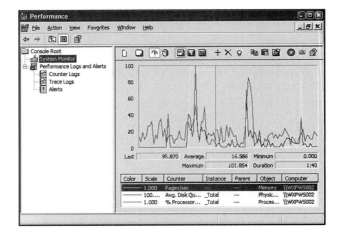

Whether you are looking for real-time graphical views or a log you can peruse at your convenience, the Performance console can provide the type of data you need to evaluate performance and recommend system modification if necessary.

Monitoring performance begins with the collection of data. The Performance console allows you various methods of working with data, although all methods use the same means of collecting data. Data collected by the Performance Monitor is broken down into objects, counters, and instances.

An *object* is the software or device being monitored, such as memory or processor.

A *counter* is a specific statistic for an object. Memory has a counter called `Available Bytes`, and a processor has a counter called `% Processor Time`.

An *instance* is the specific occurrence of an object you are watching; in a multiprocessor server with two processors, you will have three instances: `0`, `1`, and `Total`.

The primary difference between using the System Monitor and Counter Logs/Trace Logs is that you typically watch performance in real-time in System Monitor (or play-back saved logs), where you use Counter Logs and Trace Logs to record data for later analysis. Alerts function in real-time by providing you with (you guessed it) an alert when a user-defined threshold is exceeded. Collecting data and displaying it will be discussed at length in the "Using System Monitor" section. Counter Logs, Trace Logs, and Alerts will be discussed in great detail in the "Using Performance Logs and Alerts" section later in this chapter.

USING SYSTEM MONITOR

The System Monitor (shown previously in Figure 26.13) enables you to view statistical data either live or from a saved log. You can view the data in three formats: graph, histogram, or report. Graph data is displayed as a line graph; histograms are displayed as bar graphs; and reports are text-based and show the current numerical information available from the statistics.

The basic use of the System Monitor is straightforward. You decide which object/instance/counter combinations you want to display and then configure the monitor accordingly. At that point, information begins to appear. You can also change the properties of the monitor to display information in different ways.

To add counters to the Performance Monitor, click the "+" icon, which is the eighth icon from the left in the System Monitor; this opens the Add Counters dialog box shown in Figure 26.14. At the top of the dialog box is a set of radio buttons with which you can obtain statistics from the local machine or a remote machine. This is useful when you want to monitor a computer in a location that is not within a reasonable physical distance from you. Under the radio buttons is a pull-down list naming the performance objects that can be monitored. Which performance objects are available depends on the features (and applications) you have installed on your server. Also, some counters come with specific applications. These performance counters enable you to monitor statistics relating to that application from the Performance Monitor.

Figure 26.14
Using the Add Counters dialog box to add counters to the System Monitor.

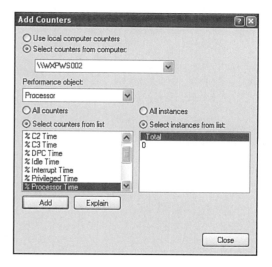

Under the performance object is a list of counters. When applied to a specific instance of an object, counters are what you are really after, and the object just narrows down your search. The counters are the actual statistical information you want to monitor. Each object has its own set of counters from which you can choose. Counters enable you to move from the abstract concept of an object to the concrete events that reflect that object's activity. For example, if you choose to monitor the processor, you can watch for the average processor time and how much time the processor spent performing non-idle activity. In addition, you can watch for %user time (time spent executing user application processes) versus %privileged time (time spent executing system processes).

To the right of the counter list is the instances list. If applicable, instances enumerate the physical objects that fall under the specific object class you have chosen. In some cases, the instances list is not applicable. For example, there is no instances list with memory. In cases where the instances list is applicable, you may see multiple instance variables. One variable represents the average of all the instances, and the rest of the variables represent the values for the first physical object (number 0, 1, and so on). For example, if you have two processors in your computer, you will see (and be able to choose from) three instance variables: Total, 0, and 1. This enables you to watch each processor individually and to watch them as a collective unit.

You can make several modifications to the System Monitor to improve how it functions in your environment. The properties enable you to change the look, the data source, and how the data is to be displayed.

To access the properties for the System Monitor, right-click the graph and select Properties from the menu that appears. The properties window is shown in Figure 26.15.

Figure 26.15
The General property tab allows you to customize the display.

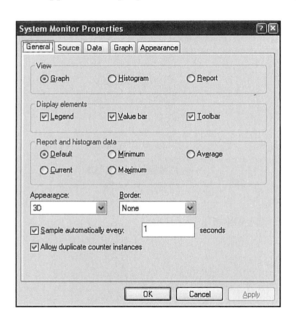

USING PERFORMANCE LOGS AND ALERTS

Using the Performance Logs and Alerts section of the Performance Monitor, you can log counter and event trace data. Additionally, you can create alerts triggered by performance that can notify the administrator of critical changes in monitored counters. The following three items are located in the Performance Logs and Alerts section of the Performance Monitor:

- **Counter logs**—Enable you to record data about hardware usage and the activity of system services from local or remote computers. You can configure logging to occur manually or automatically based on a predefined schedule. If you desire, continuous logging is available, but it consumes large amounts of disk space quickly. You can view the logs in System Monitor or export the data to a spreadsheet or database program, such as Microsoft Excel and Microsoft Access, respectively.

- **Trace logs**—Used to record data as certain activity, such as disk I/O or a page fault, occurs. When the event occurs, the provider sends the data to the log service.

- **Alerts**—Can be set on a specific counter defining an action to be performed when the selected counter's value exceeds, equals, or falls below the specified setting. Actions that can be set include sending a message, running a program, and starting a log.

COUNTER LOGS

Although the System Monitor is useful for immediate analysis of a performance problem, it is not very useful as a real-time tool for bottleneck analysis. To understand how resources are used on your computer, you need to examine data collected over a long period of time so you can view periodic spikes in usage in the proper context. It's best not to use the System Monitor in real-time mode when determining system performance and the need for upgrades; you would have to sit in front of the console for long periods of time recording the current statistical results. Instead use *counter logs* that take the same information that is captured by the System Monitor and, instead of displaying it in a graph, record it in a file. You can set the log to run and then come back to it in a week (or a month) to see general trends. After the log has been created, you can use the System Monitor in a static mode to look at the data collected by the log.

When configuring a counter log, you have the same choices for monitoring as you do with the System Monitor. You can choose specific objects, as well as counters and instances associated with those objects. However, unlike System Monitor, you can use logs to log all counters and instances for a specific object. This is a good feature to use when you do not know, or do not have available, the counters you want to monitor when you set up the log. In addition, you can also choose the interval at which to poll the system for information; this is something you should experiment with to determine what interval setting gives you the best data capture with the least amount of excess data created.

One of the advantages of logging is that it can be configured to automatically start and stop itself at specific times and on specific days. If all you are interested in logging is system performance between 1:00 a.m. and 5:00 a.m., you can set the log to begin at 1:00 a.m. and then turn itself off at 5:00 a.m. Meanwhile, you're asleep at home.

You can configure as many simultaneous logs as you like. Logging does not create much system overhead, and as a result, it does not really affect the results you get from the logging process. What you do need to be careful of is how much data you collect and where you put the collected data. It is recommended that when you log, you create a partition that contains nothing but log data. In this way, if the log fills the disk, the only thing it affects is logging. It will not choke out any other applications or the operating system itself.

When you create a log, you will see a dialog box with three property sheets. On these property sheets, you can configure the data to capture, the place to put the data, and the schedule by which to run the logging process.

26

Sample Counter Log

For your convenience, a sample log configuration has been created for you, and it is installed automatically on your computer. You can activate it and begin logging right away, even if you do not fully understand the logging process. This sample log, named "System Overview," can be found in the Counter Log node of the Performance Logs and Alerts section of Performance Monitor. To start it, simply right-click it and select Start. The icon will change from red to green once the log has been started.

As you can see in Figure 26.16, the General properties tab enables you to configure the log with the counters you want to track and the interval at which you want to collect information. To add counters, click the Add Counters button. The dialog box that appears is the same as what you saw when you added counters to the System Monitor. Besides adding counters, you can set the interval at which information is gathered. The interval can be set as high as 999,999, and the units can be set to seconds, minutes, hours, or days. Despite the large number of possible interval settings, the interval can never exceed 45 days. The rule of thumb is generally that the longer you are going to run the log, the larger the interval should be to prevent your log file from getting too large. However, sometimes you might want to log for a long time but still use short intervals to get finely generated data.

Figure 26.16
The General property tab allows you to select add counters and set the sampling interval.

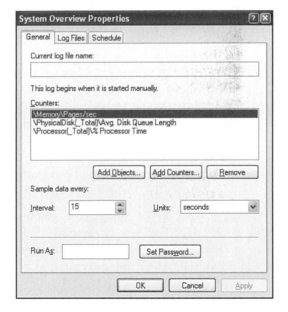

TRACE LOGS

The difference between a trace log and a counter log is the trigger that causes data collection. With a counter log, the trigger of data collection is a time interval. If you set the time interval to 10 seconds, you will get data every 10 seconds whether or not there is any change to the data from the last interval. With a trace log, the trigger of data collection is the occurrence of an event. For example, if you want to track user logins, you can set Active

Directory or the Local Security Administrator (depending on whether you are tracing domain or local account logons) to watch for the event. When a user log in occurs, the trace process collects the data.

Trace logs are one of those deep, dark secrets that no one seems to talk about much in the Windows world. We can put the discussion about Trace Logs to rest by saying this: Trace logs were never intended to be used by the average (or even somewhat advanced) user; they are provided for developers to perform specialized monitoring through the use of custom-made tools. No utilities are provided with Windows XP for reading the .ETL files created by the trace log, thus a parsing tool is required to interpret the trace log output. Developers can create such a tool using application programming interfaces (APIs) provided on the Microsoft Web site at http://msdn.microsoft.com/.

ALERTS

Over the long term, you probably do not want logging enabled all the time. This will necessitate that you check the system periodically to ensure that it is working efficiently and that potential problems are not sneaking up on you. However, you can let Windows keep an eye open for potential problem by configuring alerts. Alerts can notify you or perform a preconfigured action when a performance monitor counter crosses a specified threshold. For example, if you decide that disk utilization greater than 80% is a potentially serious condition, you can configure an alert to watch for disk utilization crossing this threshold. When this threshold is reached, an action you configure occurs, such as sending an email notification. Email alerts, for example, are very powerful tools, especially with the advent of text messaging–capable pagers and cell phones that can receive these email messages. You'll never be out of the loop now!

The alert configuration dialog box consists of three pages: General, Action, and Schedule. Schedule is just like the Schedule page for counter and trace logs, so it will not be discussed further here.

The General page lets you configure multiple counters and the thresholds for each (see Figure 26.17). In addition, you can configure the polling interval.

The Action page is used to configure what happens in response to an alert; there are a variety of possible responses. The default is to write a message to the application log (accessible from the Event Viewer console). In addition (or alternatively), you can have a message sent to a specific computer in the form of a pop-up window. You can also have the Performance Monitor begin a specific counter log (thus making the alert a trigger for starting the collection of data about a specific set of circumstances). Finally, you can have the Alert run a program of your choice. While Windows doesn't come with any programs that are particularly useful for Alert notification, you could purchase or write such a program yourself. You could write an executable program, batch file, or Window Script Host script to send an email, ring a pager, or perform some other response action.

26

Figure 26.17
The General property tab allows you configure what to monitor and when to alert you.

The advantage of using these command-line arguments is that you do not have to reconfigure the exact information sent to a program that is executed. All you configure is the type of data; then the alert controls the specific data based on the current time or the trigger value. You could write a Visual Basic, C++, or Java program that accepts the parameters you send to it.

SERVICES

Services are the backbone of any operating system. They are applications that start automatically, run in the background, and provide critical system features to users. These features include such things as network browsing, print spooling, and DHCP lease acquisition. New to Windows XP, services also provide us with the Internet Connection Firewall, Fast User Switching, and Volume Shadow Copy to name a few. The Windows service can be thought of as the equivalent of a Unix "daemon" application. Figure 26.18 shows the Services snap-in, from which you can manage the services available on your computer.

TIP

You can also access the Services snap-in by entering *services.msc* from a command prompt or by clicking Start, All Programs, Administrative Tools, Services.

Table 26.3 provides a listing of the default services that are installed on a typical Windows XP Professional computer. The actual services installed on your computer may vary due to the components that are actually installed.

Figure 26.18
The Services snap-in allows you to monitor and change the status of services.

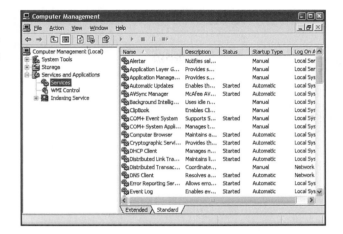

TABLE 26.3   DEFAULT WINDOWS XP PROFESSIONAL SERVICES

Service	Startup Type	Log On As
Alerter	Manual	Local Service
Application Layer Gateway	Manual	Local Service
Application Management	Manual	Local System
Automatic Updates	Automatic	Local System
Background Intelligent Transfer Service	Manual	Network Service
ClipBook	Manual	Local System
COM+ Event System	Manual	Local System
COM+ System Application	Manual	Local System
Computer Browser	Automatic	Local System
Cryptographic Services	Automatic	Local System
DHCP Client	Automatic	Local System
Distributed Link Tracking Client	Automatic	Local System
Distributed Transaction Coordinator	Manual	Network Service
DNS Client	Automatic	Network Service
Error Reporting Service	Automatic	Local System
Event Log	Automatic	Local System
Fast User Switching Compatibility	Manual	Local System
Fax	Automatic	Local System
FTP Publishing	Automatic	Local System

26

continues

Table 26.3   Continued

Service	Startup Type	Log On As
Help and Support	Automatic	Local System
Human Interface Device Access	Disabled	Local System
IMAPI CD-Burning COM	Manual	Local System
Indexing Service	Manual	Local System
Internet Connection Firewall (ICF)/Internet Connection Sharing (ICS)	Manual	Local System
IPSEC Services	Automatic	Local System
Logical Disk Manager	Automatic	Local System
Logical Disk Manager Administrative Service	Manual	Local System
Messenger	Automatic	Local Service
MS Software Shadow Copy Provider	Manual	Local System
Net Logon	Automatic	Local System
NetMeeting Remote Desktop Sharing	Manual	Local System
Network Connections	Manual	Local System
Network DDE	Manual	Local System
Network DDE DSDM	Manual	Local System
Network Location Awareness (NLA)	Manual	Local System
NT LM Security Support Provider	Manual	Local System
Performance Logs and Alerts	Manual	Network Service
Plug and Play	Automatic	Local System
Portable Media Serial Number	Automatic	Local System
Print Spooler	Automatic	Local System
Protected Storage	Automatic	Local System
QoS RSVP	Manual	Local System
Remote Access Auto Connection Manager	Manual	Local System
Remote Access Connection Manager	Manual	Local System
Remote Desktop Help Session Manager	Manual	Local System
Remote Procedure Call (RPC)	Automatic	Local System
Remote Procedure Call (RPC) Locator	Manual	Network Service
Remote Registry	Automatic	Local Service
Removable Storage	Manual	Local System

26

Service	Startup Type	Log On As
Routing and Remote Access	Manual	Local System
Secondary Logon	Automatic	Local System
Security Accounts Manager	Automatic	Local System
Server	Automatic	Local System
Shell Hardware Detection	Automatic	Local System
Simple Mail Transfer Protocol (SMTP)	Automatic	Local System
Smart Card	Manual	Local Service
Smart Card Helper	Manual	Local Service
SSDP Discovery	Manual	Local Service
System Event Notification	Automatic	Local System
System Restore Service	Automatic	Local System
Task Scheduler	Automatic	Local System
TCP/IP NetBIOS Helper	Automatic	Local Service
Telephony	Manual	Local System
Telnet	Manual	Local System
Terminal Services	Manual	Local System
Themes	Automatic	Local System
Uninterruptable Power Supply	Manual	Local Service
Universal Plug and Play Device Host	Manual	Local System
Upload Manager	Automatic	Local System
Utility Manager	Manual	Local System
Volume Shadow Copy	Manual	Local System
WebClient	Automatic	Local Service
Windows Audio	Automatic	Local System
Windows Image Acquisition (WIA)	Manual	Local System
Windows Installer	Manual	Local System
Windows Management Instrumentation	Automatic	Local System
Windows Time	Automatic	Local System
Wireless Zero Configuration service	Automatic	Local System
WMI Performance Adapter	Manual	Local System
Workstation	Automatic	Local System
World Wide Web Publishing	Automatic	Local System

26

The startup type determines whether the service starts automatically (Automatic) upon Windows XP booting or must be manually (Manual) started by the user or by another service or application. The log on account is really of little concern, as all three of the accounts used (Local System, Local Service, and Network Service) are special accounts created by and for the explicit use of the operating system. You will not be able to locate these accounts should you go looking for them in the Local Users and Groups snap-in.

The following common tasks can be performed on each service from the Services snap-in:

- Start, stop, pause, resume, or restart the service. Restarting a service stops it and then immediately starts it again. It's like "rebooting" the service. This can be especially useful in cases where you need to restart a service that either is not working or is consuming 100% of the CPU doing nothing (I have seen the Printer Spooler service do this), or to clean up settings (for example, restarting the DNS Client clears stale entries from the local DNS cache).

- Set the startup type to automatic, manual, or disabled. This can be useful in cases where you want to prevent a service from starting automatically for one reason or another.

- Define the login account used for the service. This is most useful when you are configuring additional third-party services or services for a very specific task where you want to confine the service to an account that has only the specific privileges it requires to perform its function.

NOTE

> If you specify an account and password to be used by a service, and later change the account's password, you must come back to the Services snap-in and re-enter the logon password for the service.

- Enable or disable the service in each of the computer's hardware profiles.
- Configure recovery actions to be performed on the failure of the service. This is the list of other services that a given service requires to do its job, and the list of services that depend on this service to do their jobs. Disabling a service will disable any dependent services.
- View the service's dependency tree.

You can perform these tasks on the local or a remote computer, provided you have the appropriate credentials (that is, providing you are using a Computer or Domain Administrator account).

NOTE

> To administer services on the local computer, you must be logged on as at least a Power User, or you must use Run As to specify a Computer Administrator or Power User account—right-click Services on the Administrative Tools menu to do this. If you are connecting to a remote computer you can specify an account when you make the remote connection.

You can manage services from the command line as well. If you find that you perform the same management tasks over and over, it can be easier and quicker to use a batch file than to poke around with the GUI. A classic case of this would be to restart stuck print spools across the network from the convenience of your desktop. See Chapter 29, "Automating Routine Tasks," for more information on managing services with scripts and batch files.

WMI CONTROL

Windows Management Instrumentation (WMI) is the Microsoft-specific implementation of WBEM, an industry initiative to establish standards for accessing and sharing management information over an enterprise network. WMI is used by network management tools, such as Microsoft Systems Management Server (SMS) and Microsoft Operations Manager (MOM), to help manage and control computers over the network. WMI can also be used with custom scripts or programs to retrieve configuration details about a remote computer and to affect changes as desired.

WMI, however, is not just used for network management of computers. Three snap-ins on the Computer Management console make use of WMI to do their jobs: System Properties, System Information, and Services. Also, Windows Script Host programs can use WMI's ability to get its fingers into nearly every aspect of Windows.

The WMI Control snap-in is unique compared to the rest of the snap-ins in the Computer Management console in that it has no options that can be directly configured from the console. To work with the WMI Control snap-in, you must right-click the snap-in and select Properties. Figure 26.19 shows the WMI Control Properties page.

Figure 26.19
The WMI Control
Properties page.

TIP

You can also access the Services snap-in by typing `wmimgmt.msc` from a command prompt or by clicking Start, All Programs, Administrative Tools, Services.

Working with the WMI Control is not usually done except by highly trained and prepared developers and administrators. It's not recommended that you perform any configuration changes here without adequate preparation and planning. For more information on WMI, see the MSDN section on it located at `http://msdn.microsoft.com/library/en-us/` `wmisdk/wmi/wmi_start_page.asp`.

SNAP-IN ROUND-UP

For the rest of the snap-ins that are not covered elsewhere in this chapter or in other chapters, you will find valuable information in the next sections. The following snap-ins will be covered here:

- ActiveX Control
- Certificates
- Component Services
- Folder
- IP Security Monitor
- IP Security Policy Management
- Link to Web Address
- Resultant Set of Policy
- Terminal Services Connections

As these are individual snap-ins, you will be using them in a custom MMC console. Looking back at the beginning of this chapter, you can open a blank MMC console by typing **MMC** from the command line. From there, you can add snap-ins in any combination and order that you require.

THE ACTIVEX CONTROL SNAP-IN

Placing (or snapping-in) the ActiveX Control snap-in is a bit different than any of the other snap-ins. But then again, when you consider what you are actually doing, this makes perfect sense: You're adding general-purpose Windows software plug-ins, rather than one of the more narrowly defined set of MMC tools.

Selecting to add the ActiveX Control to your custom console will open the Insert ActiveX Control Wizard. Click Next to dismiss the standard opening screen and get down to business, as shown in Figure 26.20.

Figure 26.20
Adding an ActiveX Control to your console...more than a hundred to choose from.

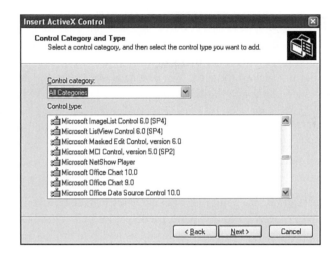

While an in-depth discussion of all of the ActiveX controls and their uses would take much more space than we have available here, let me present you with an example console I've configured using two ActiveX controls: Calendar Control 10.0 and the Microsoft Outlook View Control. Figure 26.21 shows my customized ActiveX console in action. From this console I have both a simple calendar and the contents of my Outlook Inbox to work with, all in one small and simple tool.

Figure 26.21
One possible use of the ActiveX Control snap-in.

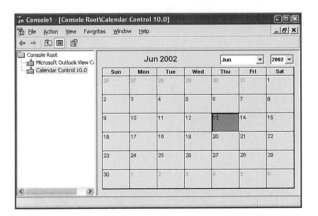

26

Of course, there are literally thousands of different possible custom consoles you could create using all of the various ActiveX items. This is an area where you will want to enlist the help of a subject matter expert, usually a programmer familiar with ActiveX, if you plan on using it a great deal in a custom console.

THE CERTIFICATE SNAP-IN

Have you ever purchased an item from an online retailer or used EFS encryption to protect a file on your computer? Chances are that you have—and you've been using digital certificates without giving it a second thought. Digital certifications are the house keys and photo ID of the digital world. Although digital certificates based on the X.509 standard are very robust and flexible, they have seen two major uses over the past few years as security has become paramount in the digital world. Digital certificates are commonly used for verification of identification and the establishment of a trusted relationship between two computers, two users, or a computer and a user. Can you see now how certificates have become a part of your life that you are happy having around—even if you never knew they were there?

As you might expect, there are a number of certificates installed on your Windows XP Professional computer, even more if you are participating in a Windows 2000 Active Directory domain that has a Certificate Authority established on the network. Attempting to add the Certificate snap-in to a custom MMC console opens the Certifications snap-in dialog box, asking you to make a choice of what the Certificates snap-in is going to focus on. You can choose from creating a snap-in that is focused on your user account, the service account, or the computer account. Most commonly, you will want to work with the certificates associated with your user account.

Figure 26.22 shows the Certificates snap-in in place in the custom console—this one was created to manage the digital certificates for my user account.

Figure 26.22
The Certificates snap-in, targeted on my user account.

26

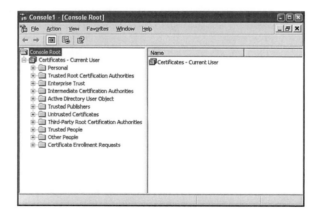

EXPORTING CERTIFICATES

As a general rule of thumb, you should consider exporting your certificates (or at least your EFS encryption certificate) to a floppy disk. This is done to safeguard the certificate (and associated private key) against loss should disaster strike. Some other reasons why you may want to export a certificate include copying it for use on another computer or moving it permanently to another computer. The process of exporting a certificate is not too difficult, provided you have a basic understanding of the process and the choices you will be required to make along the way.

When it comes to exporting (or importing) certificates, you have the following file format choices available to you:

- **PKCS #12**—Public Key Cryptography Standard #12 (also called PFX) is the industry standard format when dealing with the transfer of certificates and their corresponding private keys. The PKCS #12 format is the only one that Windows XP will support for exporting both a certificate and the private keys.

- **PKCS #7**—The Public Key Cryptography Standard #7 format is a slightly older format that allows you to transfer a certificate and all of the certificates in the certification path. PKCS #7 also allows you to associate attributes with a signature, such as a countersignature or signing time.

- **DER Encoded Binary X.509**—The Distinguished Encoding Rules (defined by ITU-T X.509) is a cross-platform standard for encoding objects (certificates and messages) for transfer between different computing systems. This format will be typically used when dealing with non-Windows 2000 (or Windows 2003) Certificate Authorities.

- **Base64 Encoded X.509**—This format is used extensively in Secure/Multipurpose Internet Mail Extensions (S/MIME) for providing cryptography for email systems. All MIME clients can decode Base64 data, which is stored in ACSII text, so this format is also suitable for use with non-Windows 2000 (or Windows 2003) Certificate Authorities and systems.

If you plan on exporting your certificate for use on another Windows computer, you should use the PKCS #7 format due to its support for moving the entire certificate chain. If you plan on exporting your certificate (and private keys) for archival purposes, you will need to make use of the PKCS #12 format. Transferring certificates to a non-Windows computer will require the use of one of the X.509 standards.

The actual process of exporting your certificates is a fairly simple one. Simply locate the certificate that you want to export, right-click on it, select All Tasks, and then select Export. Proceed through the pages in the Certificate Export Wizard and you're done. A few notes about exporting certificates:

- If the certificate you want to export was issued by a Windows 2000 Certificate Authority, the private keys can only be transferred if the certificate was requested via the Advanced Certificate Request certification authority page and the Mark keys as exportable option was selected (see Figure 26.23). Alternatively, you can also export private keys with EFS and EFS recovery certificates.

- Unless you are given the option to remove the certificate, and you actually select it, the original certificate will remain in the certificate store. If you select to remove the certificate after successful exportation, it will be removed. Likewise, if you are not given the option to remove it, you can remove it manually later.

26

- Do not select the Enable Strong Protection option if the target computer is not running Internet Explorer 5 or later on Windows NT 4.0 SP4 or better. If you do not meet these requirements, you will experience compatibility issues when attempting to later import your certificate.

Figure 26.23
Requesting a certificate from a Windows 2000 Certificate Authority using advanced options.

The most common reasons for exporting certificates are to prevent their loss should the certificate store be lost (such as fire or flood) or to transfer them to a new computer. Extreme care should be taken when handling the removable media containing your certificate and private keys, as this is the digital equivalent of your house keys. If you are exporting a certificate (and keys) for archival purposes, be sure to place the media in a safe and secure location, such as a safe deposit box or some other off-site location.

IMPORTING CERTIFICATES

The process of importing a certificate file varies from one operating system to the next, however here we will be examining the importation of a certificate file on a Windows XP Professional computer. By double-clicking the certificate file, you will open the Certificate Import Wizard; alternatively, you can right-click the folder you want to place the certificate into (within the Certificates snap-in) and select All Tasks, Import. If the certificate you are attempting to import has a set of corresponding private keys, you will of course need the password that goes with the certificate file. Also, you should select to mark the private keys as exportable in the event you should need to export the certificate and private keys again in the future.

When prompted for the location to place the imported certificate, it's usually best to leave the default selection enabled unless you know specifically where the certificate should be placed.

26

THE COMPONENT SERVICES SNAP-IN

The Component Services snap-in, shown in Figure 26.24, is an advanced snap-in that is usually only used by system administrators or developers to deploy and administer COM+ programs from or to automate administrative tasks using a scripting or programming language. Additionally, developers can use the Component Services snap-in to configure component and program behavior, such as security and participation in transactions, and to integrate components into COM+ programs.

Figure 26.24
The Component Services snap-in—not for the typical user!

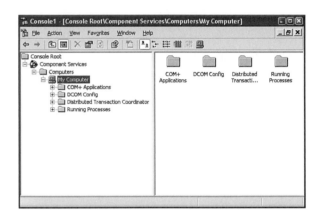

At this time, some definitions might be useful:

- Component Object Model (COM) is a software architecture that was developed by Microsoft. COM can be compiled into either self-standing programs or add-on components that can be unplugged from a program without having to recompile the program. COM serves as the foundation to other core Windows features, such OLE (Object Linking and Embedding), ActiveX, and DirectX.

- COM+ is a set of services based on extensions to Microsoft Transaction Server (MTS) and the Component Object Model (COM) that provide improved threading and security, transaction management, object pooling, queued components, and application administration and packaging. COM+ is fully backward-compatible with COM, so existing applications will not be lost.

- The Distributed Component Object Model (DCOM) specifies how components behave and communicate over Windows-based networks. Using DCOM, you can distribute COM components for a single application over multiple computers. You can also run an application distributed across two or more computers (for load balancing and redundancy) with the distribution invisible to user.

As I previously mentioned, the Component Services snap-in is not a place where you are likely to find yourself as a typical user. Administrators and developers can make use of the Component Services snap-in for the administration and configuration of COM components

26

and COM+ applications. However, if you decide to pay a visit to Component Services land, Table 26.4 will be of value to you in deciphering the variety of icons you will encounter.

TABLE 26.4   COMPONENT SERVICES ICON LEGEND

Icon	Description
	Component Services administrative snap-in
	COM+ library application
	Disabled COM+ library application
	COM+ server application
	Disabled COM+ server application
	COM+ service application
	Disabled COM+ service application
	COM+ proxy application
	COM+ component
	Disabled COM+ component
	64-bit COM+ component
	Disabled 64-bit COM+ component
	Process that is running
	Process that is undergoing recycling
	Process that is paused
	Listing of current transactions
	Data about current and aggregate transactions
	COM+ application partition
	COM+ interface
	COM+ method
	COM+ user

Icon	Description
![]	COM+ security role that has been assigned to a user
![]	COM+ subscription

If you want to read further on COM and COM+, be sure to visit the COM home page, located at http://www.microsoft.com/com/.

THE FOLDER SNAP-IN

While not truly a snap-in in the truest sense (in that it doesn't provide any management functionality), the Folders snap-in is a great organizational tool that anyone creating custom consoles will want to make use of. As shown in Figure 26.25, I've created a custom console and organized it using folders.

Figure 26.25
A custom console organized using folders.

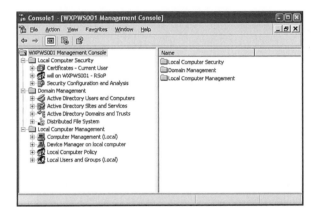

The only real catch to using folders and snap-ins is that you must ensure you place the snap-ins into the correct folder. Figure 26.26 depicts the location selection option you will have when adding new snap-ins. When one or more folders have been added to a console, you can now choose where new snap-ins will be located in the console. The easiest way to create a customized console using folders is to create the folders first, then add snap-ins to them. You can rename the folders once you have placed them into your console.

THE IP SECURITY MONITOR SNAP-IN

Monitoring the status of your IPSec implementation is a natural need, especially if you are implementing IPSec on your network. The IP Security Monitor snap-in, shown in Figure 26.27, provides you with a means to monitor all aspects of IPSec on your computer.

26

Figure 26.26
Selecting the location to place a new snap-in.

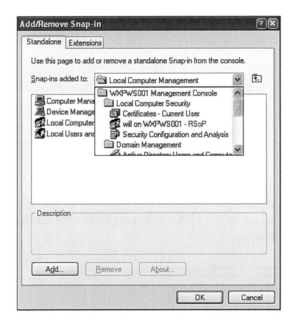

26

Figure 26.27
The IP Security Monitor snap-in allows you to monitor the status of IPSec on your computer.

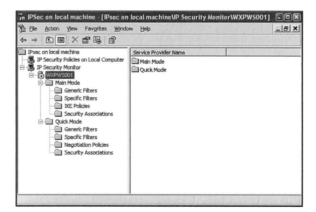

Navigating through each of the nodes, you can view information about the current state of IPSec on your computer. By right-clicking on the computer name under IP Security Monitor and selecting Statistics, you can get a concise listing of statistics (see Figure 26.28) that gives an administrator or power user a quick glimpse at what is going on with IPSec.

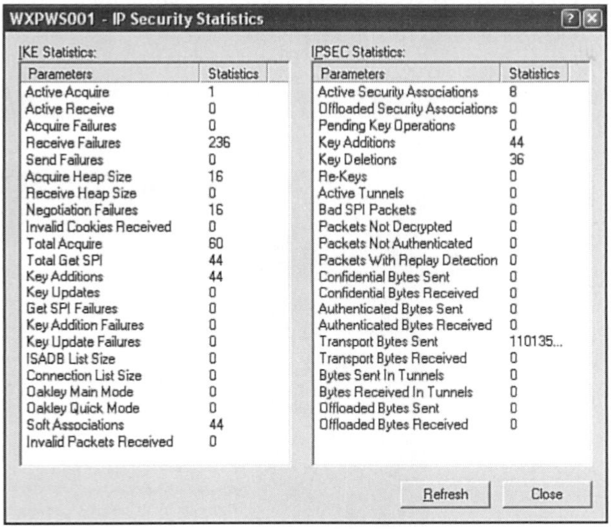

Figure 26.28
Getting IPSec statistics, useful for monitoring and troubleshooting IPSec.

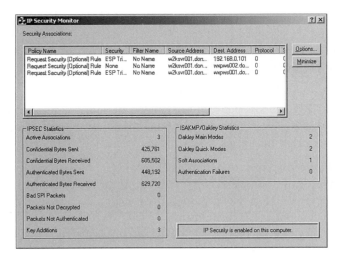

There is nothing to configure from the IP Security Monitoring snap-in—it is provided only for your convenience in monitoring the local computer (or remote computers you have selected to add to the display). If you plan on performing detailed monitoring or analysis of IPSec on the network, you will want to make use of the ipsecmon.exe utility, part of Windows 2000 Server (see Figure 26.29).

Figure 26.29
Using the Windows 2000 Server ipsecmon.exe utility to get detailed information on IPSec.

26

THE LINK TO WEB ADDRESS SNAP-IN

The Link to Web Address snap-in (see Figure 26.30) does just what it sounds like it should—it allows you to quickly add a link to a Web page into your custom console. These are useful on a Management console because so many services and hardware devices these days—from routers to email servers—use Web-based management. You could also use this capability to add links to often-used support Web sites.

Figure 26.30
Web page links can link to Web-based management tools and support sites.

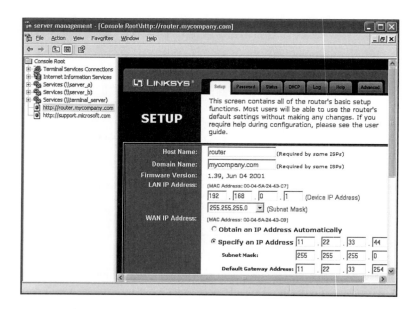

26

THE RESULTANT SET OF POLICY SNAP-IN

The Resultant Set of Policy (RSoP) snap-in (see Figure 26.31), is a new addition to Windows XP Professional that goes a long way toward helping you determine what the net effect of Group Policy applied at different levels is on a specific user and computer combination. Its use on a domain network is beyond the scope of this book, but I can give you a brief overview of its use and purpose.

One twist with working with the RSoP snap-in comes when you try to add it to your console. You are asked to choose between Logging Mode and Planning Mode, with Planning Mode not being available (it's reserved for future use). Just select Logging Mode and click Next to move onto the next page.

When you add this snap-in to your console, you will be presented with an option page asking you to choose how to implement the snap-in. At the time of this writing, "Planning Mode" was not yet available. Getting down to business with the RSoP snap-in, you can quickly see what a boon it is to administrators who need to quickly see what the net result of all Group Policy Objects (GPOs) are on a user and computer combination.

Figure 26.31
RSoP configured to look at my user account.

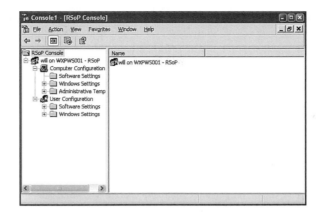

A quick review on Group Policy implementation would be helpful when using the RSoP snap-in. Group Policy settings are processed in the following order:

- **Local**—Each computer has one (and only one) Local GPO. It is always processed first.

- **Site**—Site GPOs are processed after the Local GPO. As there can be more than one Site level GPO, the order of processing can be specified. Site GPOs can overwrite settings in the Local GPO.

- **Domain**—Domain GPOs are processed after the Site GPOs. As there can be more than Domain-level GPO, the order of processing can be specified. Domain GPOs can overwrite settings in Site and Local GPOs.

- **Organization Unit(OU)**—GPOs linked to the current user's (and computer's) Organizational Unit are processed last. The GPO linked to the OU highest in the Active Directory organization is processed first, followed by GPOs linked to child OUs. Each GPO can be overwritten by the GPO that is processed after it. When more than one GPO is linked to a specific OU, they are processed in the order specified. OU GPOs overwrite all lower level GPOs.

There are two options that you should be aware of that can be used to affect the way that Group Policy Objects are processed:

- **Block inheritance**—Any Site, Domain, or Organizational Unit can be configured to block the inheritance of Group Policy from above except in cases where the No override setting has been previously configured.

- **No override**—Any Group Policy Object linked to a Site, Domain, or Organizational Unit can be configured to No override. This will prevent its policy settings from being overwritten by any child container's GPO.

With that (very) short introduction about how Group Policy Objects are processed and applied to a user and computer, you can get down to the business of analyzing the Resultant Set of Policy that is applied to a user and computer combination. If when looking at the

RSoP display you see things that don't look right to you, be sure to make a note of it so that you can go back and look at your Group Policy Objects and determine where the problem lies. Of course, using the RSoP snap-in is only truly useful in organizations where you have your Windows XP Professional computers participating in a Windows 2000 Active Directory domain; otherwise the only GPO will be the Local GPO and the use of the RSoP snap-in will not be required.

Using RSoP

When using the RSoP snap-in, you will not be able to actually modify any of the Group Policy settings. Of course, if you had another MMC console open with the appropriate Group Policy snap-in then you could edit settings as you identified a need to. After making changes, you would need to refresh Group Policy (using gpupdate on Windows XP or secedit on Windows 2000) and wait for it to propagate.

TERMINAL SERVICES CONNECTIONS

The Terminal Services Connections snap-in lets you view Remote Desktop connections within an MMC console. The Terminal Services facility (now called Remote Desktop) can be used to connect to Windows NT 4 Terminal Services Edition, Windows 2000 Server versions, Windows XP Professional, and Windows 2003 Server versions. It's a great way to manage and work with remote computers.

The snap-in version of the Remote Desktop client lets you build a list of computers that you use frequently. Using this tool, as opposed to the standard Remote Desktop Client program, the remote computer's desktop display will appear within the management console window, as shown in Figure 26.32, and you can instantly switch back and forth between any number of remote computer connections by clicking on computer names in the left pane.

26

Figure 26.32
The Terminal Services Connection gives you instant Remote Desktop connections to any number of computers.

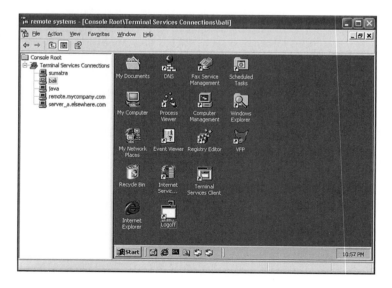

To configure the list of remote computers and servers, build a console with the Terminal Services Connections snap-in. Right-click the Terminal Services Connections item in the left pane and select Add New Connection. Enter the server's DNS name (for remote computers), IP address, or NetBIOS name (for computers on your local LAN). Click OK to save the computer name. You can add as many names as you wish.

> **NOTE**
>
> There are fields into which you can type a logon name, domain, and password to have Terminal Services log on automatically. As of Windows XP Service Pack 1, this feature does not appear to work. Actually, for security's sake I recommend that even if it did work you shouldn't take advantage of this. Anyone having access to your computer would automatically gain access to the other computers.

Once a computer name has been entered into the Termanal Services Connections list, you can request a specific desktop window size by right-clicking the computer name and selecting Properties. There are three properties tabs:

- **General**—Lets you modify the connection's computer name or IP address, and set automatic logon information (supposedly).
- **Screen Options**—Lets you set the size of the virtual desktop on the remote computer. You can choose between Expand to Fill MMC Result Pane, a list of standard sizes such as 800×600, or a custom size.
- **Program**—Lets you specify a program to execute automatically upon login, and its working directory. This program is run *instead* of the standard Windows desktop program (explorer.exe) and when this program exits, you are logged out and disconnected.

After making any desired configuration changes, connect to a given computer by clicking its name in the list in the left pane. If a logon screen doesn't appear within a few seconds, right-click the name and select Connect. Once connected, you can use the remote computer as if you were sitting at its screen and keyboard. Local disks, serial ports, printers, and sound adapters are *not* available, however; for that, you have to use the full-blown Remote Desktop client, which is discussed in Chapter 19, "Windows Unplugged: Remote and Portable Computing."

While you're connected, you can use your own mouse and keyboard to control the remote computer. Some standard Windows keyboard shortcuts are changed, in order to distinguish between those intended for your computer and those intended for the remote computer. Table 26.5 lists these alternate keyboard shortcuts.

> **NOTE**
>
> There are differences between these shortcuts and those available in the full Remote Desktop client.

26

TABLE 26.5 KEYBOARD SHORTCUTS FOR TERMINAL SERVICES CONNECTIONS

To Send This to the Remote Computer...	Type This on Your Local Computer	Function
Ctrl+Alt+Del	Ctrl+Alt+End	Task Manager
Alt+Enter	Ctrl+Alt+Break	Switch between windowed and Full Screen mode
PrintScreen	Ctrl+Alt+Numpad -	Active window to clipboard
Alt+PrintScreen	Ctrl+Alt+Numpad +	Entire remote desktop to clipboard
Alt+Tab	Alt+PageUp	Switch applications
Alt+Shift+Tab	Alt+PageDown	Switch applications
Alt+Esc	Alt+Insert	Cycle through applications
Windows	Alt+Home	Start Menu
Alt+Space	Alt+Delete	Window control (system) menu

You can switch between any number of computers by selecting the names in the left pane, and you can connect to several at once.

To disconnect from a remote computer, log out using the Start menu on the remote desktop. You can also disconnect without logging out—leaving your applications running—by right-clicking the computer name in the left-hand pane and selecting Disconnect.

ADVANCED SNAP-INS

Of course, the snap-ins we've discussed up to this point do not represent all possible options. They are, as I stated, the set of snap-ins that you can expect to see on a typical Windows XP Professional installation. If you install the Admin Pack, you will gain the following additional snap-ins, which are used to manage Windows 2000 and 2003 Server services and facilities from an XP Pro workstation:

- Active Directory Domains and Trusts—Allows you manage the trust relationships between Windows 2000 and 2003 Server domains.
- Active Directory Schema—Allows you to modify the Active Directory Schema.
- Active Directory Sites and Services—Allows you to create sites and manage the replication of Active Directory.
- Active Directory Users and Computers—Allows you to manage users, computers, groups and other objects in the Active Directory.
- Certification Authority—Allows you to manage Certificate Authorities on the network.
- Cluster Administrator—Allows you manage the Cluster Service, which lets a group of servers act as one, to provide "high availability" service.
- DHCP—Allows you to manage the Dynamic Host Configuration Protocol service.

- Distributed File System (DFS)—Allows you to manage the Distributed File System implementation on your server.

- DNS—Allows you to manage the Domain Name System Server service.

- Internet Authentication Service (IAS)—Allows you to configure services to authenticate remote users connecting to your network.

- Network Load Balancing Manager—Allows you manage the Network Load Balancing service, another part of a "highly available" server solution.

- Remote Storage—Allows you to manage the Remote Storage system, which moves infrequently accessed data to archival storage media such as tape and optical.

- Routing and Remote Access—Allows you manage dial-up and VPN connections to your network.

- WINS—Allows you to manage the Windows Internet Naming system service.

You may also find additional MMC snap-ins and pre-configured consoles available for download from the Microsoft Web site and from Windows Update at `http://windowsupdate.microsoft.com`. Additionally, some third-party software and hardware manufacturers provide MMC snap-ins to manage their products. You can mix and match these add-on snap-ins with Windows snap-ins to create your own custom consoles.

26

CHAPTER 27

MANAGING HARDWARE DEVICES

In this chapter

UNDERSTANDING DEVICE DRIVERS

In order to solve device driver problems, it is necessary to understand the concepts behind device driver management. This chapter will help you learn what a device driver is, how it functions, and how you can utilize that knowledge to manage device drivers and solve problems relating to them. Let's start by looking at the basic concepts.

An operating system consists of many different components, each of which performs a specific task. The most important component is the kernel. The kernel is a relatively small set of core operating instructions that all system components rely on to perform their larger tasks. If we were to compare a computer operating system to a person, we might say that the kernel of the operating system performs a similar function as the brain of a person. All processing, in one fashion or another, is routed through the kernel and either operated on or passed to another function for additional post processing.

If we take this analogy a bit further, then device drivers might be considered part of the nervous system. Device drivers usually consist of two components. There is the small core level software component that functions as an interface between the kernel and the hardware and operates in kernel mode. There are also one or more pieces of software that function as an interface between higher level software and the underlying hardware that operates in user mode. Separating software to run in kernel mode or user mode is a means of protecting the operating system from poorly written code. This separation enhances the operating system reliability. To understand kernel mode vs. user mode, it might be helpful to look at a graphical representation of the two operating modes as shown in Figure 27.1.

The dark line in the picture illustrates the boundary between software that operates in user mode and software that operates in kernel mode. Kernel mode software is considered trusted software that has higher privileges than user mode software. Kernel mode software may directly communicate with other kernel mode components and in some cases directly to the underlying hardware. User mode software, on the other hand, is generally considered non-trusted software and is where the bulk of applications operate. So, when you start Windows Media Player, it runs in user mode. When Media Player attempts to play a music CD, it makes software requests that are in turn handled by user mode processes that are processed by lower level routines that eventually talk to a device driver that accesses the CD player.

Device drivers are not written ad-hoc. They do need to follow a specification that describes how the device driver will function in a Windows environment. The technical term for this specification is called the Windows Driver Model (WDM) and is our next subject to review.

Figure 27.1
The Windows XP driver model kernel and user mode.

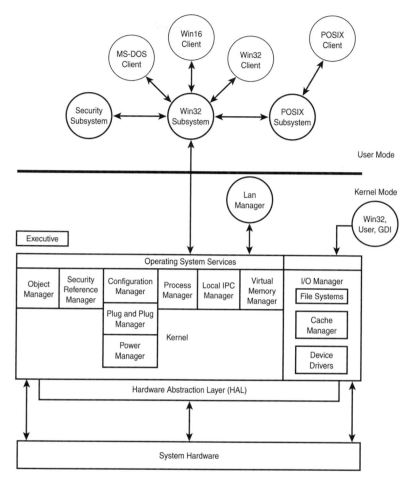

WINDOWS DRIVER MODEL

Most Windows XP device driver error messages will reflect an understanding of what a device driver is and how it operates. Knowing more about device drivers in general will provide a greater understanding of where the device driver has failed and help you solve problems. Consider the following example.

You install a new sound card in your computer. After booting the computer, you install the OEM drivers as described in the documentation. You reboot as required by the driver installation program, but after you log on to the computer, you do not hear any welcome greeting as you expected. Puzzled, you examine the Device Manager listing and see a yellow exclamation mark next to the sound card's device driver and an error code 12 (This device cannot find enough system resources that it can use...). Using this error code and message you can determine there is some type of resource (usually an interrupt) conflict that needs to be corrected before you can use the device. You could correct the situation by removing the conflicting device, attempting to manually assign resources, or possibly reconfiguring the BIOS to free up a resource (turn off a serial port for example to free up an interrupt for the sound card to use).

Computer hardware often falls into many different categories. Windows Driver Model device drivers, however, fall into only three different types, which include

- **Bus Driver**—A bus driver communicates with an input/output bus and provides per slot device independent functionality. Some of the more common bus drivers include drivers for PCI, AGP, USB, PC Card, Cardbus, SCSI, ISA, serial, parallel, and other low level interfaces.

- **Function Drivers**—A function driver communicates with a specific hardware component and provides device functionality. This type of driver is what most people mean when they discuss device drivers. Sound cards, network cards, video cards, and so on all have a function driver that converts a Windows API call to a specific function on the attached hardware.

- **Filter Drivers**—A filter driver filters (limits) input/output requests for a device, device class, or bus. Filter drivers can occur at the bus level (filtering ACPI power management requests for example), low level (filtering mouse acceleration, stylus gestures for example), or high level (filtering keyboard commands or implementing a third party security method for example).

The generic driver described in Figure 27.2 is a representation of a complex driver utilizing the highest layering of driver types. Not all drivers contain all seven layers as displayed. Layers displayed as a dashed line are optional components. These layers may be grouped, from the top down, into five function components that include

- Upper-level class and device filters. These drivers are usually provided by independent hardware vendors and are considered optional components.

- A function driver is required. It is the primary driver for the hardware device. A function driver is generally provided by the device manufacturer.

- Lower-level class and device filters are considered optional components. They usually modify the behavior of a device. These drivers are usually provided by independent hardware vendors. There is no set limit on the number of low level filters for a specific device.

- Bus filters are considered optional components. A bus filter provides additional functionality to a bus and is usually provided by an independent hardware vendor.

- Bus drivers. A Bus driver is a required component and is used to communicate with an input/output bus controller, bridge, or adapter. Windows XP includes many bus drivers for common bus types. Third parties may provide additional bus drivers for a proprietary or nonstandard bus.

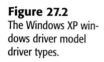

Figure 27.2
The Windows XP windows driver model driver types.

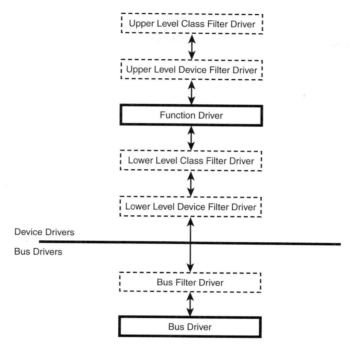

At a bare minimum, a Windows Driver Model driver requires a function driver and a bus driver. For many devices, Microsoft has already provided a bus driver; therefore, only a function driver may be provided by the manufacturer.

INSTALLING HARDWARE DEVICES

Device driver management in Windows XP has been vastly simplified. It now utilizes a similar interface to that of Windows 98 or Windows Me instead of that provided in prior versions of Windows NT. This simplified interface has both its good points and its bad points. On the good side is its consistency with prior versions of Windows. If you know how to manage devices there, you will know where to look to manage devices in Windows XP. On the bad side, however, is the irksome inability on ACPI (Advanced Configuration and Power Interface) compliant computers to override Windows XP's Plug and Play settings and use the BIOS, rather than the operating system, to configure devices. Windows XP will disable most ACPI BIOS settings for a device and configure the device to use the resources it deems proper.

An ACPI-compliant computer consists of hardware and software devices that provide device configuration and power management integration with the operating system. You can read more about ACPI at the Intel Web site at `http://www.intel.com/technology/iapc/acpi/faq.htm`. This integration with the operating system can make it easier to configure your computer's devices. On the other hand, when the ACPI integration goes awry, you are

27

left with fewer choices, and in some cases no choice, to configure the device manually. If you were able to use the BIOS to specify the configuration of the device, you may have been able to provide a usable configuration that would work under Windows XP. Unfortunately, that option is no longer available.

TIP

> The Plug and Play setting on your computer should only be configured to No/Disabled for a Non-ACPI compliant BIOS. Windows XP will disregard the setting on an ACPI compliant BIOS and use ACPI to configure the devices on your system.

INSTALLING NEW DEVICES

Installing a device in Windows XP, for the most part, is an easy process. The only time you should encounter difficulties is if a resource conflict exists, you have a poorly written device driver, or have a version conflict. While these problems do occur—just check the news-groups to see how often—most users continue to operate day to day without problems. There are two basic methods of installing a new device on your computer. These can be categorized as internal or external devices. For an internal device you must power off the computer, install the device, power up the computer, start Windows XP, then walk through the device manager wizard and install your device drivers. For an external device, Windows XP is already started, so it is just a matter of plugging in the device and walking through the wizard to install your device driver software.

NOTE

> Some software packages do not provide a Windows installable device driver on floppy or CD. Therefore the usual method of running the wizard and having it detect your device driver will fail. For this type of software package, the proper way to install the device driver is to install the package before you connect the device. This will preinstall the driver. The device manager wizard will then automatically detect the device and install the correct driver.

PLUG AND PLAY

Part of the functionality of the Device Manager wizard is to configure the device's resources for proper operation. Windows XP uses Plug and Play (PnP) to determine the available resources and assign a non-conflicting resource to the device. The method Windows XP uses differs slightly based on the computer's compliance to the ACPI specification. For an ACPI-compliant system, Windows XP uses the following method:

1. The function driver for the bus that the device is plugged into detects that a new device has been connected.

2. The bus driver then notifies Windows XP's PnP subsystem that its list of devices has changed.

3. The Windows PnP subsystem then queries the bus driver for a current list of devices attached to the bus.

4. The Windows XP PnP subsystem then compares the list provided by the bus driver with the old list and determines if a new device has been added or an old one removed.

5. The Windows XP PnP subsystem then determines the resources required by the new device and begins to configure it.

6. The Windows XP PnP subsystem then checks the registry to determine if the device has already been installed and configured. If not, the subsystem then stores information about the device in the registry.

7. The Windows XP PnP subsystem then attempts to find the function and filter drivers for the device and if found loads them.

8. The Windows XP PnP subsystem assigns the allocated resources to the device and if needed issues an input/output request packet (IRP) to start the connected device.

On non-ACPI-compliant systems, the BIOS is responsible for Plug and Play configuration as follows:

1. Determines if any ISA PnP devices are installed.

2. Creates a list of resources allocated to non-PnP devices.

3. Maintains a list of previously allocated resources in non-volatile storage or memory.

4. Selects and enables input and output devices required for system startup.

5. If the device is a boot device, the BIOS initializes the device ROM.

6. Allocates resources to non-configured devices.

7. Activates appropriate devices.

8. Initializes any detected option ROMs.

9. Starts the bootstrap loader.

Do keep in mind that on a non-ACPI-compliant computer, you have control over system resource allocation assuming that your BIOS, like most non-ACPI-compliant BIOSes, provides for manual resource allocation. You can choose to manually reserve interrupts or DMA channels for specific ISA devices. You can manually assign interrupts for specific AGP/PCI slots. You can even specify what devices (serial, parallel, USB, and so forth) to enable.

FORCING DETECTION

Sometimes Windows does not properly detect your device. Or it was previously detected, but no device driver was installed. If no driver was installed, the device will be listed in the Device Manager in the Unknown Device section. There are two ways to force redetection of this device. The simple way is to select the device listed in the Unknown Device section, right-click it, and choose Uninstall from the pop-up menu to remove it. Then right-click the computer entry and choose Scan for Hardware Changes from the pop-up menu. Alternatively, you can select the unknown device, right-click it, choose Properties from the pop-up menu, and then click the Device Driver button. Both of these methods will invoke the Device Manager Wizard.

27

INSTALLING OLDER DEVICE DRIVERS

Before installing an older driver for your device, you should check for new versions. The very first place you should check is the Windows Update Web site. You can search the Windows Update web site as part of the Device Manager Wizard. If you don't find a driver there, try the manufacturer Web site. If you don't know what the manufacturer Web site is, try one of the following Web sites:

```
http://www.driversplanet.com/
http://www.driverzone.com/
http://www.driverguide.com/
http://www.windrivers.com/
```

If you still can't find a newer certified Windows XP driver you can try to install either a Windows Driver Model (WDM) driver or a Windows 2000 driver. This usually requires a manual install using the following steps:

1. Select the device in Device Manager and click Properties.
2. Click the Update Driver button to start the Hardware Update Wizard.
3. Enable the Install from a list or specified location (Advanced) radio button.
4. Click the Next button.
5. Click Don't Search. It will choose the Driver to Install radio button.
6. Click the Next button.
7. Click the Have Disk button.
8. Click the Browse button and choose the disk and directory where the driver is located.
9. Click the OK button.
10. Select the appropriate device and click the Next button.
11. Click the Finish button.

REPLACING HARDWARE

Sooner or later, everyone has to replace some hardware on his or her computer. It might be the replacement of a malfunctioning network card, a disk drive that is starting to fail, or just installing a faster video card. If your version of Windows XP is not part of an Open License or Enterprise purchase, then you may find that when you have replaced a new piece of hardware, your installation will require that you reactivate Windows XP to continue to use it.

WINDOWS ACTIVATION

Windows Product Activation (WPA) was created by Microsoft to discourage casual copying of Microsoft products. Due to security reasons, Microsoft is not providing information on exactly what type of hardware is used to create the hardware key contained in your Windows XP product ID. Nor is Microsoft providing information on exactly how many changes are allowed before the product will be required to be reactivated. What is important to know is that if you change your hardware sufficiently, you may be required to reactivate it.

NOTE

> During my expedition into Windows Product Activation, I came across a couple Web sites with some interesting information. For the curious, and technical minded, take a look at the Fully Licensed home page at http://www.licenturion.com/xp/. You'll find an in-depth discussion of the Installation ID and hardware key, as well as an application to examine the Installation ID.

TIP

> If you need to move your current copy of Windows XP to new hardware, there is a Microsoft-supported method using NTBACKUP to back up and restore a computer. The basic details are provided at
> http://support.microsoft.com/default.aspx?scid=kb;en-us;Q314070.

USING DEVICE MANAGER

Windows XP uses the Device Manager to manage devices. This applet is very similar to that provided in Windows 98 or Windows Me. It can also be accessed from the Computer Management application in the Administrative Tools menu folder, or, more commonly, as a standalone applet from the Control Panel System applet's Hardware properties page as shown in Figure 27.3.

Figure 27.3
The Windows XP
Device Manager
Applet.

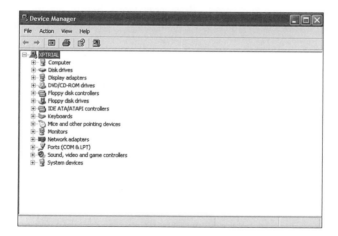

VIEWING DEVICES

As you can see, devices are categorized into types. Each type has a + next to it that can be expanded to show the devices contained within the type. When a type has been expanded, the + changes to a –. If this interface looks familiar, it should, as the Windows Explorer uses the same methodology.

The default view, as shown in Figure 27.5, is Devices by Type. However, you can also view devices in the following formats:

- **Devices by connection**—This view lists devices based on their connection to each other. It may be useful to determine how multiple devices are connected to an external bus (USB or PCMCIA), for example.

- **Resources by type**—This view lists devices by the type of resource (Direct Memory Access [DMA] channel, Input/Output ports, Interrupt Request [IRQ], or Memory).

- **Resources by connection**—This view lists devices by the resource (Direct Memory Access [DMA] channel, Input/Output ports, Interrupt Request [IRQ], or Memory) and how they are connected.

CONFIGURING DEVICES MANUALLY

Sometimes, a device will fail to function after being configured by Windows XP's PnP subsystem. This usually occurs because the device requires a resource that is not used by any other device. Windows XP will allow you to manually configure a device, so long as it is not configured as an ACPI-compliant device, but it takes a little work to get there. You can accomplish this task by following these steps:

1. Open the Device Manager.
2. Select the device.
3. Right-click the device and choose Properties from the pop-up menu. A General device property page, similar to that shown in Figure 27.4, will be displayed.

Figure 27.4
The General device properties page in the Windows XP Device Manager.

4. Select the Resources property page as shown in Figure 27.5.

Figure 27.5
The Resources device properties page in the Windows XP Device Manager.

5. Clear the Use Automatic Settings check box.

6. Choose an alternate configuration in the Setting Based On list box. If no alternate configuration will work, you can then manually select a resource and click the Change Setting button to manually assign a resource.

7. Repeat Step 7 for each resource in question.

8. Click the OK button to save your changes.

> **N O T E**
>
> Not all devices can be manually configured. Even if Windows XP displays a Use Automatic Settings check box and allows you to disable it in order to manually configure a device, it's possible that Windows XP will not allow you to manually assign a resource and you are therefore limited to alternate configurations. In some cases, the alternate configuration will also not provide a non-shared resource and cause a device failure. Should that occur, you may be forced to disable devices in the BIOS (unused serial or parallel ports, USB, and so on) to provide a free resource for the device.

TROUBLESHOOTING PROBLEM DEVICES

The key to troubleshooting devices is interpreting the generic, or esoteric, message Windows XP Device Manager provides. Between the message the Device Manager provides, the event log, and the information displayed in the following sections, I hope to provide you with the relevant information to resolve the problem.

> **N O T E**
>
> For each error code below, there are three sections of text: the *displayed message*, the *meaning*, and the suggested resolution.

27

ERROR CODE 1—DEVICE NOT CONFIGURED CORRECTLY

DISPLAY MESSAGE

This device is not configured correctly. (Code 1)

MEANING

This message usually indicates that no software (driver) has been installed for the peripheral or that the peripheral has a resource conflict.

RECOMMENDED RESOLUTION

Open the device in question using the Device Manager and change to the Driver property sheet. Click the Driver Details button. If no driver has been installed then click the Update Driver button. This will invoke the Hardware Update Driver Wizard and walk you through installing a driver for the device.

If you are unable to find a suitable device driver using the wizard, then you will need to install a driver manually using your OEM-supplied software. Usually this means executing a program (often called Setup.EXE or Install.Exe) that will install a compressed driver on the computer and invoke the Add New Hardware Wizard to automatically detect, configure, and install the appropriate driver. Once the driver has been successfully installed the device should work as expected.

ERROR CODE 2—BUS CONFLICT DETECTED

DISPLAY MESSAGE

Windows could not load the driver for this device because the computer is reporting two *<type>* bus types. (Code 2)

where *<type>* is ISAPNP, PCI, BIOS, EISA, or ACPI.

Or

The <type> device loader(s) for this device could not load the device driver. (Code 2)

MEANING

This error message occurs when a device loader fails to load a device driver. In the case of the first message, the error occurs at the root bus (ISA, PCI, AGP, and so on) device, and in the case of the latter message after the root device driver has loaded.

RECOMMENDED RESOLUTION

If you see a message concerning a root device (first message format) then check with your manufacturer for a replacement BIOS. If the second format message occurs, you should obtain a replacement driver from your manufacturer or install a previous version driver.

ERROR CODE 3—CORRUPTED DEVICE DRIVER

DISPLAY MESSAGE

The driver for this device might be corrupted, or your system may be running low on memory or other resources. (Code 3)

Or

The driver for this device might be bad, or your system may be running low on memory or other resources. (Code 3)

MEANING

This message indicates that some type of error (disk error, virus infection, and so forth) has changed the contents of the driver file and corrupted it, or that there are insufficient memory resources available for the device driver to function properly.

RECOMMENDED RESOLUTION

First determine which problem is the most likely. To do so, open the Task Manager and check your memory resources. If they do not appear low, then most likely you have a corrupted driver. If the memory resources are low, you can free up some memory by closing applications, reconfiguring the Performance Options (open the System control panel applet, select the Advanced property sheet, and configure the Visual Effects to Adjust for best performance), or installing additional memory.

To replace a corrupted driver, first remove the existing one by selecting it in the Device Manager. Right-click the driver, and then choose Uninstall from the pop-up menu. Reboot your computer. Depending on the device in question and its installation/removal program, Windows XP may prompt you for a driver diskette or reinstall the previous driver. If prompted for a driver diskette, insert the disk and install a new copy of the driver. If the previous driver was installed, you can replace it if needed by right-clicking the device in Device Manager and selecting Update Driver from the pop-up menu.

ERROR CODE 4—BAD DEVICE DRIVER

DISPLAY MESSAGE

This device is not working properly because one of its drivers may be bad, or your registry may be bad. (Code 4)

MEANING

This message often occurs when the registry information for the driver is corrupted or if the .inf file contains an incorrect format field.

27

Recommended Resolution

First remove the driver by right-clicking it in Device Manager and choosing Uninstall from the pop-up menu. Then reinstall it by choosing Scan for Hardware Changes from the Action menu. If that fails, check with the manufacturer for an updated .inf file and/or driver. If no updated driver is available, you can manually inspect the .inf file, looking for possible text fields that are coded as binary fields, and replace the binary field type with the appropriate text type and try and reinstall the driver.

Error Code 5—Unknown Resource Requested

Display Message

The driver for this device requested a resource that Windows does not know how to handle. (Code 5)

Meaning

This message occurs when a device driver requests a resource type that Windows XP does not know how to provide.

Recommended Resolution

Remove the driver by right-clicking it in Device Manager and choosing Uninstall from the pop-up menu. Then reinstall it by choosing Scan for Hardware Changes from the Action menu. If the same message appears, contact the manufacturer for an updated device driver.

Error Code 6—Device Driver Resource Conflict

Display Message

Another device is using the resources this device needs. (Code 6)

Meaning

This message occurs when Windows XP detects a resource conflict between two separate devices.

Recommended Resolution

Verify that the resources requested by the device are available using the Device Manager or System Information tool (WinMSD.EXE). If another device is using the requested resources, you can resolve the problem by disabling the conflicting device, reconfiguring either the conflicting device or the failed device using the Device Manager, or reconfiguring the conflicting or failed device using your BIOS configuration program.

Error Code 7—Reinstall Device Drivers

Display Message

The drivers for this device need to be reinstalled. (Code 7)

Meaning

This is a generic error message displayed by Windows XP when the operating system is unable to configure the device and no specific user actions are available to resolve the error.

Recommended Resolution

Determine whether the device is working properly. If it is working, then ignore the error message. If the device is not working, then obtain a replacement driver from your device manufacturer or install a previous working version of the driver.

Error Code 8—Missing or Corrupted Device Driver

Display Message

This device is not working properly because Windows cannot load the file *<name>* that loads the drivers for the device. (Code 8)

where *<name>* is the system DevLoader that cannot be found.

Or

This device is not working properly because Windows cannot find the file *<name>* that loads the drivers for the device. (Code 8)

where *<name>* is the DevLoader that is missing.

Or

This device is not working properly because the file *<name>* that loads the drivers for this device is bad. (Code 8)

where *<name>* is the name of the DevLoader.

Or

Device failure: Try changing the driver for this device. If that doesn't work, see your hardware documentation. (Code 8)

Meaning

These error messages occur when a device loader fails to load the appropriate device driver. In the case of the first two messages, if the *<name>* begins with an asterisk (*) then it is a system driver that failed to load. If the driver *<name>* does not contain an asterisk then the file is missing. The third message indicates that the file does exist, but may be corrupted. The final version of the message indicates that a software registry key is missing, empty, or corrupt.

RECOMMENDED RESOLUTION

Remove the driver by right-clicking it in Device Manager and choosing Uninstall from the pop-up menu. Then reinstall it by choosing Scan for Hardware Changes from the Action menu. If the same message appears, determine whether the driver exists. If you cannot find the driver and it is a system driver (denoted by an asterisk in the name), reinstall Windows XP. If the file is missing, reinstall the driver. If the file exists, try to reinstall the driver using your original driver disk to replace a possibly corrupt file. If the problem is registry-related and reinstalling did not resolve the problem, you may be able to resolve the problem by deleting the root registry key for the device, rebooting, and then reinstalling the device.

CAUTION

> Although we assume that you are an experienced user, we'd be remiss if we didn't warn you about the dangers of mucking around with the registry. Modifying the registry should not be attempted by those who are unaware of the consequences. At the very least, make a backup of the registry key before you delete it in case you need to restore it. It's also a good idea to make a System Restore Point (see "Using System Restore" later in this chapter).

ERROR CODE 9—DEVICE NOT WORKING

DISPLAY MESSAGE

This device is not working properly because the BIOS in your computer is reporting the resources for the device incorrectly. (Code 9)

Or

This device is not working properly because the BIOS in the device is reporting the resources for the device incorrectly. (Code 9)

MEANING

This message indicates a discrepancy between the resources the hardware device reports as being required and the resources specified by Windows XP or the device driver. The most likely cause is a corrupted, or incorrect, registry key or value.

RECOMMENDED RESOLUTION

Remove the driver by right-clicking it in Device Manager and choosing Uninstall from the pop-up menu. Then reinstall it by choosing Scan for Hardware Changes from the Action menu.

ERROR CODE 10—UNABLE TO START DEVICE

DISPLAY MESSAGE

This device cannot start. (Code 10)

Or

This device is either not present, not working properly, or does not have all the drivers installed. (Code 10)

MEANING

This error message indicates that the device driver failed to start properly when Windows XP attempted to load it.

RECOMMENDED RESOLUTION

This generic error message has many potential reasons for occurring.

First the peripheral may not be installed correctly. To check for this possibility, remove the peripheral in question and physically reinstall it. If the peripheral is an internal peripheral on the PCI or ISA bus, clean the copper contacts using an eraser before reinstalling it. If the peripheral is connected via a cable, verify that all cable connections are clean, not damaged, and that the cables themselves are not routed by any device that may cause interference (power supply, monitor, speakers, and so on).

Second, the peripheral may have a resource conflict. Verify that the resources requested by the device are available. This can be accomplished using the Device Manager or System Information tool (WinMSD.EXE). If another device is using the requested resources you can resolve the problem by disabling the conflicting device, reconfiguring either the conflicting device or the failed device using the Device Manager, or reconfiguring the conflicting or failed device using your BIOS configuration program.

Finally, the device driver may not be installed correctly, or the wrong device driver (such as one designed for a prior version of Windows) may be installed. To resolve the former, first uninstall the device driver then reinstall it as described previously for Error Code 3. If the latter, remove the driver and have Windows XP redetect and install the appropriate driver using the Add New Hardware wizard. If Windows XP does not install a device driver, then the driver in question is almost certainly not the correct driver. In that case you should either use the OEM driver diskette with a valid Windows XP driver, or go online to the manufacturer Web site and download the appropriate Windows XP compliant driver.

27

ERROR CODE 11—DEVICE DRIVER BLOCKED

DISPLAY MESSAGE

Windows stopped responding while attempting to start this device, and therefore will never attempt to start this device again. (Code 11)

MEANING

This message indicates that when Windows XP loaded the device driver, the device driver did not return control of the computer back to it in a timely fashion. Therefore Windows XP will no longer attempt to load the device driver.

RECOMMENDED RESOLUTION

This is a serious error. The best solution is to attempt to find a replacement driver from the manufacturer. If that is not possible, remove the driver by right-clicking it in Device Manager and choosing Uninstall from the pop-up menu. Then reinstall it by choosing Scan for Hardware Changes from the Action menu. If the system still hangs, either roll back the driver to a previous known working version (see "Using Driver Rollback" later in this chapter) or disable the device driver (right-click the device and choose Disable from the pop-up menu).

ERROR CODE 12—INSUFFICIENT FREE RESOURCES

DISPLAY MESSAGE

This device cannot find enough free resources that it can use. If you want to use this device, you will need to disable one of the other devices on this system. (Code 12)

MEANING

This message usually indicates a resource (I/O port, interrupt, or DMA channel) conflict has occurred. It can also occur if a required resource was not allocated to the device.

RECOMMENDED RESOLUTION

First verify that the BIOS is not disabling a required interrupt or DMA channel or not reserving a resource for a legacy device. Resource problems of this type usually fall into three categories:

1. Failed USB devices—If this is the case, verify that interrupts have not been disabled for the USB controller in the BIOS.
2. Failed PCI devices—If this is the case, verify that the requested interrupt or DMA channel has not been reserved for a specific legacy (ISA) device.
3. Failed legacy devices—If this is the case, verify that the required interrupt or DMA channel has been reserved by the BIOS for the device.

It is also possible to resolve the problem by disabling a conflicting device, or removing it physically from the computer.

ERROR CODE 13—DEVICE NOT PRESENT

DISPLAY MESSAGE

This device is either not present, not working properly, or does not have all the drivers installed. (Code 13)

MEANING

This error message specifies that the device driver was unable to find the associated hardware.

RECOMMENDED RESOLUTION

If the hardware is a removable device and is not attached, connect the device and restart the computer. If the device is attached, but not found, check for a resource conflict using the Device Manager or System Information tool (WinMSD.exe). If no resource conflict is being reported, perhaps removing the driver by right-clicking it in Device Manager and choosing Uninstall from the pop-up menu, and then reinstalling it by choosing Scan for Hardware Changes from the Action menu will resolve the problem.

ERROR CODE 14—RESTART COMPUTER

DISPLAY MESSAGE

This device cannot work properly until you restart your computer. (Code 14)

MEANING

This message usually means that the device driver is a boot-time device driver and requires that the computer be restarted before the device driver can load.

RECOMMENDED RESOLUTION

Reboot the computer. If the driver fails to start, use the previous error codes to diagnose potential problems.

ERROR CODE 15—RESOURCE CONFLICT DETECTED

DISPLAY MESSAGE

This device is causing a resource conflict. (Code 15)

MEANING

This message indicates that two or more devices are using the same hardware resources causing a resource conflict.

27

RECOMMENDED RESOLUTION

Verify that the resources requested by the device are available. This can be accomplished using the Device Manager or System Information tool (WinMSD.EXE). If another device is using the requested resources, you can resolve the problem by disabling the conflicting device, reconfiguring either the conflicting device or the failed device using the Device Manager, or reconfiguring the conflicting or failed device using your BIOS configuration program.

ERROR CODE 16—UNABLE TO IDENTIFY DEVICE RESOURCES

DISPLAY MESSAGE

Windows cannot identify all the resources this device uses. (Code 16)

Or

Windows could not identify all the resources this device uses. (Code 16)

MEANING

This message means that Windows XP could not determine, or allocate, all required resources for the peripheral. The device may therefore only function partially. As an example, consider a sound card that obtains the required resources for wave file playback (interrupt, DMA, and I/O port), but fails to obtain the required I/O port for the midi synthesizer. In this example, the sound card would be able to play wave files, audio CDs, and so on but fail to play any requested midi sound files.

RECOMMENDED RESOLUTION

Open the device in question in Device Manager. Change to the Resources property sheet. Look for a resource with a question mark next to it in the Resource settings field. If you see a question mark, select that resource and manually assign a non-conflicting resource.

ERROR CODE 17—MULTIFUNCTION DEVICE CONFIGURATION ERROR

DISPLAY MESSAGE

The driver information file *<name>* is telling this child device to use a resource that the parent device does not have or recognize. (Code 17)

where *<name>* is the .inf file for the device.

MEANING

This message indicates that the device in question is a multifunction device and that the associated information configuration file (.inf) is improperly specifying how Windows XP should split and allocate the resources to be used by the device.

RECOMMENDED RESOLUTION

Remove the driver by right-clicking it in Device Manager and choosing Uninstall from the pop-up menu. Then reinstall it by choosing Scan for Hardware Changes from the Action menu. If the error reoccurs, obtain a new driver from the manufacturer, roll back the driver, or disable the driver.

ERROR CODE 18—REINSTALL DEVICE DRIVER

DISPLAY MESSAGE

Reinstall the drivers for this device. (Code 18)

Or

The drivers for this device need to be reinstalled. (Code 18)

MEANING

This message means that Windows detected some type of problem (missing driver file, unloadable driver file, and so forth).

RECOMMENDED RESOLUTION

Open the Device Manager, select the device in question, right-click the device, and choose Update Driver from the pop-up menu. This will invoke the Hardware Update Driver Wizard and walk you through installing a driver for the device.

ERROR CODE 19—BAD REGISTRY

DISPLAY MESSAGE

Windows cannot start this hardware device because its configuration information (in the registry) is incomplete or damaged. To fix this problem you can first try running a troubleshooting wizard. If that does not work, you should uninstall and then reinstall the hardware device. (Code 19)

Or

Your registry may be bad. (Code 19)

MEANING

This message means that some type of registry-related problem was detected by Windows XP while trying to start the device in question. This problem may occur if more than one service attempts to use a specific device, if a service subkey is unable to be accessed (possibly missing or corrupt, incorrect permissions, and so on), or if the driver name is unable to be accessed (corrupt, missing, incorrect permissions).

27

RECOMMENDED RESOLUTION

To resolve this problem try the following:

1. Open the Device Manager. Select the device in question. Right-click it and choose Properties. Click the Troubleshoot button on the General property sheet to start the troubleshooting wizard. The wizard may be able to restore the missing or damaged registry keys.

2. Uninstall the driver. Reboot. Reinstall the driver.

3. Reboot the computer and use the Last Known Good option to restore a previously working registry.

4. Reboot the computer in Safe Mode and use a previous System Restore point to restore a previously working registry.

CAUTION

> It is possible to manually modify the registry to restore, rebuild, or change permissions on a registry key or value. However, doing so should only be attempted by those familiar with the registry editor and sufficiently knowledgeable about the registry.

ERROR CODE 20—UNABLE TO LOAD DRIVER FOR DEVICE

DISPLAY MESSAGE

Windows could not load one of the drivers for this device. (Code 20)

MEANING

This error message occurs when the VxD (Virtual Device Driver) loader returns an unknown result.

RECOMMENDED RESOLUTION

Remove the driver by right-clicking it in Device Manager and choosing Uninstall from the pop-up menu. Then reinstall it by choosing Scan for Hardware Changes from the Action menu. If the error message still occurs, obtain a replacement driver, roll back the driver, or disable the driver.

ERROR CODE 21—REMOVING DEVICE

DISPLAY MESSAGE

Windows is removing this device. (Code 21)

MEANING

This message means that Windows XP is currently attempting to remove the device in question.

27

RECOMMENDED RESOLUTION

Wait for 15 seconds or so. If the device still appears, reboot the computer.

ERROR CODE 22—DISABLED DEVICE

DISPLAY MESSAGE

This device is disabled. (Code 22)

Or

This device is not started. (Code 22)

MEANING

This message means the device was previously disabled by a user using the Device manager.

RECOMMENDED RESOLUTION

Open the Device Manager. Right-click the device in question and choose Enable from the pop-up menu.

ERROR CODE 23—DISPLAY ADAPTER NOT FUNCTIONING

DISPLAY MESSAGE

This display adapter is not functioning correctly. (Code 23)

Or

The loaders for this device cannot load the required drivers. (Code 23)

MEANING

The first type of message usually indicates that the primary display adapter in a dual display environment is not functioning properly. The second type of message indicates that the device driver did not inform Windows XP that the device was ready to be started.

RECOMMENDED RESOLUTION

In the first case, try removing the primary and secondary adapters if needed, display adapters in Device Manager, and restart the computer to redetect and reinstall the appropriate device drivers.

In the second case, try removing the driver by right-clicking it in Device Manager and choosing Uninstall from the pop-up menu. Then reinstall it by choosing Scan for Hardware Changes from the Action menu. If the error message still occurs, obtain a replacement driver, rollback the driver, or disable the driver.

27

ERROR CODE 24—DEVICE NOT PRESENT

DISPLAY MESSAGE

This device is not present, is not working properly, or does not have all its drivers installed. (Code 24)

MEANING

This message usually means that the peripheral is not correctly installed, is malfunctioning, or needs an updated driver. This message may also be displayed if the device has been marked for removal by Windows XP. Once the driver has been removed, the message will no longer be displayed.

RECOMMENDED RESOLUTION

There are several reasons for this error message to occur.

First, the peripheral may not be installed correctly. To check for this possibility, remove the peripheral in question and physically reinstall it. If the peripheral is an internal peripheral on the PCI or ISA bus, clean the copper contacts using an eraser before reinstalling it. If the peripheral is connected via a cable, verify that all cable connections are clean, not damaged, and that the cables themselves are not routed by any device that may cause interference (power supply, monitor, speakers, and so on).

Second, the peripheral may have a resource conflict. Verify that the resources requested by the device are available. This can be accomplished using the Device Manager or System Information tool (WinMSD.EXE). If another device is using the requested resources, you can resolve the problem by disabling the conflicting device, reconfiguring either the conflicting device or the failed device using the Device Manager, or reconfiguring the conflicting or failed device using your BIOS configuration program.

Finally, the device driver may not be installed correctly. To resolve the problem, first uninstall the device driver by right-clicking it in Device Manager and choosing Uninstall from the pop-up menu. Then reinstall it by choosing Scan for Hardware Changes from the Action menu.

ERROR CODE 25—SETTING UP DEVICE DRIVER

DISPLAY MESSAGE

Windows is in the process of setting up this device. (Code 25)

MEANING

This error message usually only occurs during the initial setup of Windows XP during the first or second reboots. It usually indicates an incomplete file copy.

RECOMMENDED RESOLUTION

Restart the computer. If that fails to resolve the situation, reinstall Windows XP.

ERROR CODE 26—DEVICE DRIVER FAILED TO LOAD

DISPLAY MESSAGE

Windows is in the process of setting up this device. (Code 26)

MEANING

This error message occurs when a device driver fails to load properly.

RECOMMENDED RESOLUTION

Restart the computer. If that fails, then uninstall the device driver by right-clicking it in Device Manager and choosing Uninstall from the pop-up menu. Then reinstall it by choosing Scan for Hardware Changes from the Action menu. If the problem persists, obtain a new driver from the manufacturer, rollback the current driver, or disable it.

ERROR CODE 27—UNSPECIFIED RESOURCES FOR DEVICE

DISPLAY MESSAGE

Windows can't specify the resources for this device. (Code 27)

MEANING

This error message occurs when Windows XP detects a conflict in the information for the device stored in the registry. An example of such a conflict would occur if the configuration file (.inf) for the device contained information specifying that the resource is hardwired when the registry information specifies that the device is software configurable.

RECOMMENDED RESOLUTION

Remove the device driver by right-clicking it in Device Manager and choosing Uninstall from the pop-up menu. Then reinstall it by choosing Scan for Hardware Changes from the Action menu. If the problem persists, obtain a new driver from the manufacturer, rollback the current driver, or disable it.

27

ERROR CODE 28—NO DEVICE DRIVER INSTALLED

DISPLAY MESSAGE

The drivers for this device are not installed. (Code 28)

MEANING

This message indicates that no device drivers have been installed for the device in question.

RECOMMENDED RESOLUTION

Install the device driver as described for error code 1.

ERROR CODE 29—DEVICE DISABLED BY BIOS

DISPLAY MESSAGE

This device is disabled because the firmware of the device did not give it the required resources. (Code 29)

Or

This device is disabled because the BIOS of the device did not give it the required resources. (Code 29)

MEANING

This message means the peripheral is disabled in the peripheral's BIOS.

RECOMMENDED RESOLUTION

Refer to the online screen message provided by the peripheral's BIOS (as an example, a message will be displayed to press Ctrl-A to access the BIOS for an Adaptec controller) or refer to the peripheral documentation to enable the device.

ERROR CODE 30—REAL-MODE DEVICE INTERRUPT CONFLICT

DISPLAY MESSAGE

This device is using an Interrupt Request (IRQ) resource that is in use by another device and cannot be shared. You must change the conflicting setting or remove the real-mode driver causing the conflict. (Code 30)

MEANING

This error message occurs when two or more devices request the same interrupt. This error may also occur when a real-mode device driver is loaded in the autoexec.bat or config.sys file that uses the same interrupt.

RECOMMENDED RESOLUTION

If a real-mode driver is present, remove it. If no real-mode driver is present, verify that the resources requested by the device are available. This can be accomplished using the Device Manager or System Information tool (WinMSD.EXE). If another device is using the requested resources, you can resolve the problem by disabling the conflicting device, reconfiguring either the conflicting device or the failed device using the Device Manager, or reconfiguring the conflicting or failed device using your BIOS configuration program.

ERROR CODE 31—DEVICE DRIVER NOT LOADED

DISPLAY MESSAGE

This device is not working properly because Windows cannot load the drivers required for this device. (Code 31)

Or

This device is not working properly because <device> is not working properly. (Code 31)

MEANING

This message means that Windows was unable to load the device driver.

RECOMMENDED RESOLUTION

Follow the same procedure as outlined for Error Code 10.

ERROR CODE 32—SERVICE DISABLED

DISPLAY MESSAGE

A driver (service) for this device has been disabled. An alternate driver may be providing this functionality. (Code 32)

Or

Windows cannot install the drivers for this device because it cannot access the drive or network location that has the setup files on it. (Code 32)

MEANING

This message means that Windows XP has determined that the driver has been disabled in the registry, most likely through manual intervention (that is, disabling the device driver using the registry editor or choosing disabled in the Device Manager).

Or

Windows XP cannot locate the drivers for the device to install them. The most likely reason for this is that the drivers are stored on inaccessible media (floppy, CD-ROM, or shared network drive).

RECOMMENDED RESOLUTION

If the driver is actually a service, you can edit the startup value in the registry by using the Service MMC snap-in to resolve the problem. For a device, you can either uninstall, and then reinstall the driver as described for Error Code 18, or edit the registry directly and change the start type.

27

Or

If the problem is caused by inaccessible media, locate the floppy or CD-ROM, or map the appropriate network share and provide Windows XP with the location of the missing driver.

ERROR CODE 33—UNKNOWN DEVICE CONFIGURATION

DISPLAY MESSAGE

Windows cannot determine which resources are required for this device. (Code 33)

MEANING

This message means that Windows XP could not determine the required resources to start the device driver.

RECOMMENDED RESOLUTION

Follow the procedure outlined for Error Code 16. If that method fails, you should attempt to reconfigure the device's resource allocation using the supplied OEM documentation. If manual resource allocation is not possible, contact the vendor for additional hands-on technical support. If technical support is unavailable, or unable to resolve the problem, consider replacing the hardware.

ERROR CODE 34—MANUAL DEVICE CONFIGURATION REQUIRED

DISPLAY MESSAGE

Windows cannot determine the settings for this device. Consult the documentation that came with this device and use the Resource tab to set the configuration. (Code 34)

MEANING

This message means that Windows XP could not determine the required resources to start the device driver.

RECOMMENDED RESOLUTION

Follow the procedure outlined for Error Code 16 and manually allocate the resources.

ERROR CODE 35—DEVICE NOT SUPPORTED BY BIOS

DISPLAY MESSAGE

Your computer's system firmware does not include enough information to properly configure and use this device. To use this device, contact your computer manufacturer to obtain a firmware or BIOS update. (Code 35)

MEANING

This message means the BIOS on your computer does not support the peripheral.

RECOMMENDED RESOLUTION

Obtain an updated BIOS from your computer manufacturer and replace the outdated BIOS.

ERROR CODE 36—IRQ MISCONFIGURATION

DISPLAY MESSAGE

This device is requesting a PCI interrupt but is configured for an ISA interrupt (or vice versa). Please use the computer's system setup program to reconfigure the interrupt for this device. (Code 36)

MEANING

This message means that Windows XP is unable to utilize the requested interrupt for the specified device.

RECOMMENDED RESOLUTION

Use your BIOS configuration program to release the interrupt. The most likely cause is an interrupt was reserved for an ISA peripheral that is no longer in use. Or a PCI slot was assigned a specific interrupt that is required for an ISA device. In either case, a conflict has been created that must be resolved before the device can be utilized.

ERROR CODE 37—UNABLE TO INITIALIZE DEVICE DRIVER

DISPLAY MESSAGE

Windows cannot initialize the device driver for this hardware. (Code 37)

MEANING

This error means that the device driver returned a failure status from its initialization routine.

RECOMMENDED RESOLUTION

Remove and reinstall the device driver as described for Error Code 1. If that fails, you should visit the OEM Web site and attempt to obtain an updated driver.

ERROR CODE 38—DEVICE DRIVER STILL IN MEMORY

DISPLAY MESSAGE

Windows cannot load the device driver for this hardware because a previous instance of the device driver is still in memory. (Code 38)

Meaning

This error means a previous driver that was removed is still in memory and a newer, or replacement, version cannot be loaded to replace it.

Recommended Resolution

Reboot the computer. This should flush the existing driver and allow the newly installed driver to replace it.

Error Code 39—Corrupted or Missing Device Driver

Display Message

Windows cannot load the device driver for this hardware. The driver may be corrupted or missing. (Code 39)

Meaning

This message means that Windows XP could not load the driver because the driver file is inaccessible (not present or incorrect permissions), is corrupt, is located on a bad sector on the disk (I/O subsystem problem), or the driver is trying to load another driver that fails to load.

Recommended Resolution

You should first scan your hard disk for errors using CHKDSK or third-party disk utility. Then replace the driver as described for Error Code 1.

Error Code 40—Bad Service Key

Display Message

Windows cannot access this hardware because its service key information in the registry is missing or recorded incorrectly. (Code 40)

Meaning

This error means that Windows XP has determined that registry data (keys or values) are corrupt, missing, or inaccessible.

Recommended Resolution

Follow the procedure outlined for Error Code 19.

Error Code 41—Hardware Not Found

Display Message

Windows successfully loaded the device driver for this hardware but cannot find the hardware device. (Code 41)

MEANING

This error means that Windows XP was able to successfully load the device driver, however the device driver was unable to find, or access, the actual hardware peripheral. This error usually occurs when Windows XP cannot detect a legacy (non–plug and play) hardware device.

RECOMMENDED RESOLUTION

If the peripheral was previously removed, uninstall the driver by opening up the Device Manager. Right-click the device and choose Uninstall from the pop-up menu.

If the peripheral is still installed, remove the device driver as described previously, then attempt to reinstall the device driver by right-clicking the Computer icon in the Device Manager and selecting Scan for Hardware Changes from the pop-up menu.

If the device driver fails to load, attempt to obtain a newer driver from the manufacturer.

ERROR CODE 42—DUPLICATE DEVICE DETECTED

DISPLAY MESSAGE

Windows cannot load the device driver for this hardware because there is a duplicate device already running in the system. (Code 42)

MEANING

This error message occurs when a Windows XP bus driver incorrectly creates a duplicate child device. It may also occur when a serial device is detected at a new location before the old location has been deleted.

RECOMMENDED RESOLUTION

Reboot the computer to reload the driver. If the error continues, obtain a new driver from the manufacturer.

ERROR CODE 43—DEVICE REPORTED PROBLEMS

DISPLAY MESSAGE

Windows has stopped this device because it has reported problems. (Code 43)

MEANING

This message means that the device driver informed Windows XP that the hardware device has encountered a critical error. Critical errors of this nature should be logged in the System or Application event log.

27

RECOMMENDED RESOLUTION

Restart the computer. If the error continues, use the logged entries to determine the cause of the error. Often these messages will provide sufficient information to resolve the problem. If not, use the logged messages in conjunction with the Microsoft Knowledgebase to attempt to resolve the problem. If that fails, request help from the manufacturer.

ERROR CODE 44—DEVICE SHUTDOWN

DISPLAY MESSAGE

An application or service has shut down this hardware device. (Code 44)

MEANING

This message means that an application or service has informed Windows XP that the hardware device has encountered a critical error. Critical errors of this nature should be logged in the System or Application event log.

RECOMMENDED RESOLUTION

Follow the procedure described previously for Error Code 43.

ERROR CODE 45—DEVICE NOT CONNECTED

DISPLAY MESSAGE

Currently, this hardware device is not connected to the computer. (Code 45)

MEANING

This message means that Windows XP has detected that the peripheral has been removed from the system.

If Device Manager is configured to show hidden devices then any previously attached, but currently not present, devices are displayed in the device manager list and assigned this error code.

TIP

> Forcing non-present devices to be displayed requires that you set an environment value before using the "Show Hidden Devices" switch. That variable is
>
> `devmgr_show_nonpresent_devices = 1`
>
> Set it in the System Manager Environment variables for permanent use or run it via a command line.
>
> See `http://support.microsoft.com/default.aspx?scid=kb;en-us;241257` for more details.

RECOMMENDED RESOLUTION

To resolve the problem, reconnect the peripheral. Otherwise, this is an information message and should not be considered a problem.

ERROR CODE 46—UNABLE TO ACCESS DEVICE

DISPLAY MESSAGE

Windows cannot gain access to this hardware device because the operating system is in the process of shutting down (Code 46).

MEANING

This message means that Windows XP is in the process of shutting down the system and is therefore unable to access the requested peripheral.

RECOMMENDED RESOLUTION

Reboot the computer and the device should function as expected.

This is an information message and should not really be considered a problem.

NOTE

This error code will only be displayed when Driver Verifier is enabled and all applications have already been shut down.

ERROR CODE 47—DEVICE PREPARED FOR REMOVAL

DISPLAY MESSAGE

Windows cannot use this hardware device because it has been prepared for "safe removal", but it has not been removed from the computer (Code 47).

MEANING

This message means that the user has requested that Windows XP unload the device driver for the peripheral prior to physically removing the device (PC-Card, USB device, and so on).

27

RECOMMENDED RESOLUTION

Reload the device driver by either removing and reinserting the peripheral, or restarting the computer.

ERROR CODE 48—DRIVER STARTUP BLOCKED

DISPLAY MESSAGE

The software for this device has been blocked from starting because it is known to have problems with Windows. Contact the hardware vendor for a new driver. (Code 48)

MEANING

This message means that Windows XP has a known incompatibility with the device driver in question and has prevented it from loading.

RECOMMENDED RESOLUTION

Obtain a Windows XP–compatible device driver from the manufacturer and install it as described in the procedure for Error Code 1.

ERROR CODE 49—REGISTRY SIZE LIMIT EXCEEDED

DISPLAY MESSAGE

Windows cannot start new hardware devices because the system hive is too large (exceeds the Registry Size Limit). (Code 49)

MEANING

This error means that the System registry hive has exceeded its maximum size as specified in the registry.

RECOMMENDED RESOLUTION

1. Open the Device Manager. Choose Show Hidden Devices from the View menu. Uninstall any unused devices.

2. The registry hive limitation in Windows XP is based on the amount of physical memory (RAM) installed in the computer. To resolve the error, add additional physical memory (RAM) to the computer to provide additional space for the registry hive. For more information on this, check

   ```
   http://msdn.microsoft.com/library/default.asp?url=/library/en-us/sysinfo/
   base/registry_storage_space.asp.
   ```

3. As a last resort, reinstall Windows XP.

CAUTION

Modifying the registry should only be attempted by those familiar with the registry editor and sufficiently knowledgeable about the registry.

USING DRIVER ROLLBACK

If after installing a device driver you find that the driver did not work, has caused system instability, or caused another problem, you can easily replace it with the previous driver using driver rollback. You can accomplish this task by following these steps:

1. Open the Device Manager.

2. Expand the device type to display the device driver that is not functioning.

3. Select the device.

4. Right-click the device and choose Properties from the pop-up menu. The General device property page will be displayed.

5. Select the Driver property page as shown in Figure 27.6.

Figure 27.6
Rolling back a driver using the Windows XP Device Manger.

6. Click the Driver Rollback button.

7. You will be prompted for confirmation that you want to replace the existing driver with a previous version.

8. Click the OK button to install the previous version of the driver, or Cancel to continue using the existing driver.

9. Click the Close button to return to the Device manager.

27

USING SYSTEM RESTORE

Sometimes, installing a device driver causes such severe instability that you want to restore your system to a previously known good state. In the old days, the only way to do this was to restore your system from a backup. Today, however, Windows XP has a System Restore application that can be used to restore a previous configuration of Windows XP. When you install a new piece of hardware, Windows XP creates a restore point. You can also manually create one by following these steps:

NOTE

It's worth noting that XP's System Restore does not back up documents or user files, only system files. If you want a backup utility that makes it possible to recover your work documents and files in the same way that System Restore does with system files, check out the coverage of Roxio's GoBack, in Chapter 6, "Setting Up Important System Services."

1. Open the System Restore application from the System Tools folder located in the Accessories folder on the All Programs menu. The System Restore application, shown in Figure 27.7, will be displayed.

Figure 27.7
The System Restore Application.

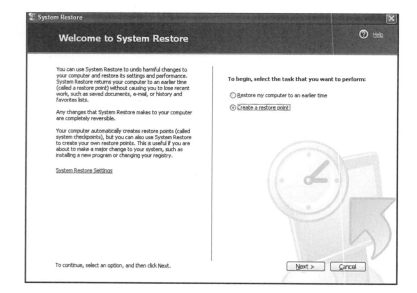

2. Select the Create a Restore Point radio button and click the Next button.
3. Specify a description for the restore point in the Restore point description field as shown in Figure 27.8.
4. Click the Create button.
5. The Restore Point will be created. When finished, click the Close button to close the application.

Assuming your computer will boot into normal mode or safe mode, and you either manually created a System Restore Point, or Windows XP created one for you when you installed your device driver, you can restore a previous configuration. Just follow these steps:

1. Open the System Restore application from the System Tools folder located in the Accessories folder on the All Programs menu.

Figure 27.8
Specifying the description for a System Restore Point.

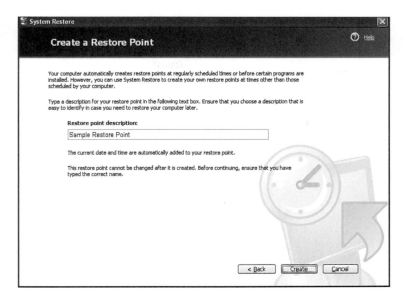

2. Select the Restore My Computer to an Earlier Time radio button and click the Next button.

3. Choose the month, and then select the restore point, as shown in Figure 27.9 to restore.

Figure 27.9
Choosing a System Restore Point to restore.

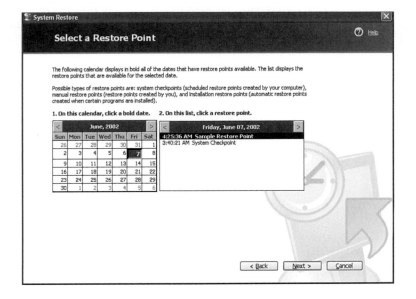

4. Click the Next button.

5. The Confirm Restore Point dialog, as shown in Figure 27.10, will be displayed.

Figure 27.10
Installing a System
Restore Point.

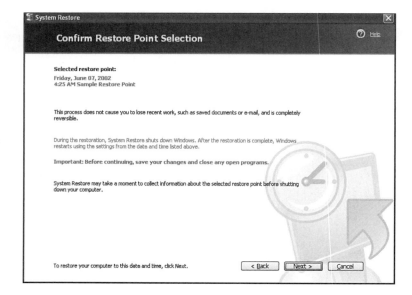

6. Click the Next button to install the system restore point and reboot your computer.

NOTE

System Restore will create a restore point every 24 hours if the system is left on. If the computer is shut down, a restore point is created when the computer is restarted, provided the most recent restore point was created more than 24 hours ago.

CHAPTER 28

CONFIGURING WITH THE CONTROL PANEL

NAVIGATING THE WINDOWS XP CONTROL PANEL

Upon first opening the Control Panel in Windows XP, you may be dismayed at the radical change in appearance, as shown in Figure 28.1.

Figure 28.1
The Control Panel in Windows XP category view.

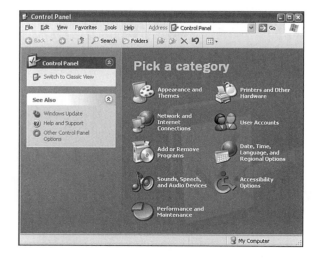

As you can see, your options have been subdivided into nine different categories, although three of these directly launch a specific applet. The nine categories and their included Control Panel applets are outlined in Table 28.1.

TABLE 28.1   CONTROL PANEL APPLETS BY CATEGORY

Category	Applets
Appearance and Themes	Display, Folder Options, Taskbar, and Start Menu
Network and Internet	Connections Internet Connections, Network Connections
Add or Remove Programs	Opens the Add or Remove Programs applet
Sounds, Speech, and Audio Devices	Sounds and Audio Devices, Speech
Performance and Maintenance	Administrative Tools, Power Options, Scheduled Tasks, System
Printers and Other Hardware	Game Controllers, Keyboard, Mouse, Phone and Modem Options, Printers and Faxes, Scanners and Cameras
User Accounts	Opens the User Accounts applet
Date, Time, Language, and Regional Options	Date and Time, Regional and Language Options
Accessibility Options	Opens the Accessibility Options applet

28

NOTE

> **Missing Applets?**
>
> You might have noticed that not all Control Panel applets were covered in Table 28.1. You can view the Mail and Speech applets, along with any third-party applet, by clicking Other Control Panel Options.

This approach, known as category view, was designed to make things easier for you when configuring and managing your computer. Whether or not this holds true depends on your opinion of what is easier. I personally prefer the Classic view as it makes working with the Control Panel quicker, easier, and more intuitive to me. You can change the viewing configuration of the Control Panel by clicking Switch to Classic View. The Control Panel in Classic view is shown in Figure 28.2.

Figure 28.2

The Control Panel in Classic view. Note that you may have additional icons not shown here or you may not have all of these icons (particularly the Java Plug-in and VirusScan) depending on your installed applications.

NOTE

> **Classic View Please**
>
> If you have selected Use Windows Classic Folders from the Folder options applet, the Control Panel will be displayed in Classic view.

Table 28.2 gives a brief overview of the Control Panel applets available.

28

TABLE 28.2   CONTROL PANEL APPLETS

Applet (Command to Open)	Icon	Description	For More Information, see Chapter...
Accessibility Options (access.cpl)		Allows you to adjust the computer's settings for vision, mobility, and hearing disabilities.	10
Add Hardware (hdwwiz.cpl)		Allows you to install and troubleshoot hardware devices attached to your computer.	27
Add or Remove Programs (appwiz.cpl)		Allows you to install and remove applications and Windows components. Also, Service Pack 1 allows you to "hide" Microsoft middleware applications such as Internet Explorer and Outlook Express from view.	9
Administrative Tools (control admintools)		Opens a folder that provides additional tools for performing administrative tasks on your computer. The Administrative Tools can also be accessed directly from the Start Menu if enabled from the Taskbar and Start Menu Properties page.	26
Date and Time (timedate.cpl)		Allows you to set the date, time, and time zone settings for your computer. Windows XP computers that are not part of a Windows 2000 domain have a new feature here that provides for the synchronization of the date and time via an Internet time server.	28
Display (desk.cpl)		Allows you to change the appearance of the desktop, screen saver, fonts, and colors of your computer.	10
Folder Options (control folders)		Allows you to change the display of files and folders, modify file extensions, and configure offline folders.	12
Fonts (control fonts)		Allows you to add, change, and manage fonts installed on your computer. The Fonts applet is discussed in more detail later in this chapter.	28

28

Applet (Command to Open)	Icon	Description	For More Information, see Chapter...
Game Controllers (joy.cpl)		Allows you to add, remove, and configure game controllers attached to your computer, such as game pads and joysticks. The Game Controllers applet is discussed in more detail later in this chapter.	28
Internet Options (inetcpl.cpl)		Allows you to manage Internet Explorer display and configuration settings.	14
Keyboard (control main.cpl,@1)		Allows you to customize your keyboard settings, such as character repeat rate and cursor blink rate. The Keyboard applet is discussed in more detail later in this chapter.	28
Mail		Allows you to configure the Outlook settings for your mail accounts.	14
Mouse (main.cpl)		Allows you to customize the mouse settings on your computer, such as double-click speed and mouse pointers. The Mouse applet is discussed in more detail later in this chapter.	28
Network Connections (ncpa.cpl or control netconnections)		Allows you to create, delete, and configure connections to other computers and services. Allows you to manage all installed network adapters on your computer.	8
Phone and Modem Options (telephon.cpl)		Allows you to configure your telephone dialing rules and modem options.	8
Power Options (powercfg.cpl)		Allows you to configure power settings for your computer, including Standby and Hibernation.	6
Printers and Faxes (control printers)		Allows you to add, remove, configure, and manage printers and faxes on your computer.	7
Regional and Language Options (intl.cpl)		Allows you to customize the display of text, numbers, dates, and currencies for different regions. The Regional and Language Options applet is discussed in more detail later in this chapter.	28

continues

28

TABLE 28.2 CONTINUED

Applet (Command to Open)	Icon	Description	For More Information, see Chapter...
Scanners and Cameras (control scannercamera)		Allows you to add, remove, and configure scanners and digital cameras attached to your computer.	14, 27
Scheduled Tasks (control schedtasks)		Allows you to add, remove, and configure scheduled tasks to run automatically on your computer.	29
Sounds and Audio Devices (mmsys.cpl)		Allows you to configure installed sound devices and microphones on your computer. Allows you to change the sound scheme settings on your computer.	28
Speech (control speech)		Allows you configure options for text-to-speech and speech recognition on your computer.	10
System (sysdm.cpl)		Allows you to perform advanced configuration of your computer, including performance, startup and shutdown, hardware management, and automatic updates. The System applet is discussed in more detail later in this chapter.	28
Taskbar and Start Menu (rundll32.exe shell32.dll, Options_RunDLL 1)		Allows you to customize the taskbar and Start menu for your computer.	10
User Accounts (nusrmgr.cpl)		Allows you to configure user accounts and settings for the user accounts on your computer.	11
Wireless Link (irprops.cpl)		Allows you to configure Infrared port properties if you have a wireless network connection. This is not installed unless needed, but can be found in the %systemroot%\Driver cache\I386\ Driver.cab file.	28

TIP

> **Control Panel Easy Access**
>
> To show the Control Panel in My Computer, open the Folder Options applet. From the View tab, select the Show Control Panel in My Computer check box. A Control Panel icon will now appear in the My Computer folder. If you would like Control Panel applet access directly from a flyout menu off of the Start button, right-click the Start button, choose Properties, click the Start Menu tab, click Customize, and then choose the Start menu style you want. Click the Customize button. You'll find an option in the resulting dialog box from which you can expand the Control Panel menu. (The final option you choose differs in name depending on whether you set the Start menu to Classic or XP style.)

Most of the applets in the Control Panel have been covered in other chapters of this book, as indicated in Table 28.2; however, some still remain and thus we will perform an applet round-up of sorts in this chapter. The applets we will be exploring in greater detail include

- Date and Time
- Fonts
- Game Controllers
- Keyboard
- Mouse
- Regional and Language Options
- Sounds and Audio Devices
- System
- Wireless Link

DATE AND TIME

The Date and Time applet has received a nice and very useful feature in Windows XP—but you'll only get to see it if your computer is not part of a Windows 2000 Active Directory domain environment. Figure 28.3 shows the new (and improved) Date and Time applet.

Looking at the Date and Time applet, the first thing that you notice is that there is an extra tab: Internet Time. The other two tabs, Date & Time and Time Zone, perform the same tasks they have since Windows 95.

From the Date & Time tab you can set the date and time your computer stores in CMOS and uses for date/time stamping of all files and system actions.

28

Figure 28.3
The Date and Time applet.

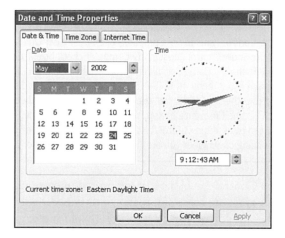

The Time Zone tab allows you to select the time zone your computer is located in and also allows Windows XP to automatically update the system time for changes in Daylight Savings Time.

The Internet Time tab, shown in Figure 28.4, is the real exciting part of this applet. This tab, however, only appears when you are not participating in a Windows 2000 Active Directory domain. In a Windows 2000 Domain environment, the Kerberos security system protocol requires all domain member computers to be time-synchronized. Typically the PDC Operations Master computer is delegated the function of being the authoritative time server for a Windows 2000 Active Directory domain.

TIP

Setting Up the Windows Time Service

For more information on setting up the Windows time service, see the following Knowledge Base articles:

- MSKB #Q224799 located at `http://support.microsoft.com/ default.aspx?scid=kb;EN-US;q224799`.

- MSKB #Q216734 located at `http://support.microsoft.com/ default.aspx?scid=kb;en-us;Q216734`.

- MSKB #Q314054 located at `http://support.microsoft.com/ default.aspx?scid=kb;en-us;Q314054`.

28

Figure 28.4
The Internet Time tab
of the Date and Time
applet.

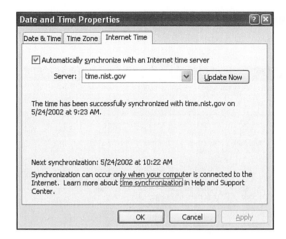

To enable your non-domain computer to take advantage of the Internet Time feature, place a check in the Automatically Synchronize with an Internet Time Server check box. By default, you can choose from a time server in the Microsoft domain or a time server provided by the National Institute of Standards and Technology (NIST). Time synchronization occurs once per hour automatically, although you can force synchronization at any time by clicking the Update Now button.

Should you want to use an additional time server, simply enter the new time server name into the Server list and click the Update Now button to synchronize your computer using the new time server. You can only add one additional time server to the time server list, however.

TIP

> **Public Time Servers**
>
> A list of public time servers can be found at `http://www.ntp.org`.

Fonts

The Fonts applet has been around, largely unchanged, since Windows 95. It actually might be a stretch to call this an applet, since it is really nothing more than a customized Windows Explorer window. The Fonts window is shown in Figure 28.5.

From this window, you can perform a multitude of tasks related to managing the fonts installed on your computer. The tasks that you can perform from the Fonts window are

- Install new fonts.
- Delete existing fonts.
- View and/or print font samples, as shown in Figure 28.6.

28

- Determine fonts that are similar to a selected font, as shown in Figure 28.7.
- View font properties.

Figure 28.5
The Fonts window.

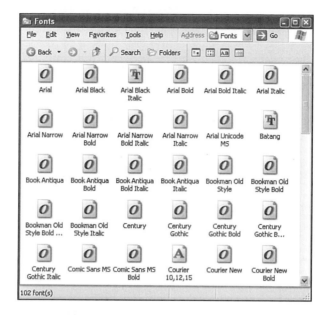

Figure 28.6
Viewing fonts.

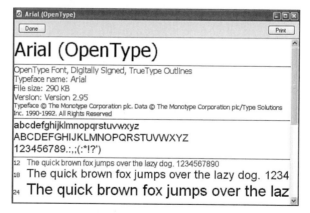

The Fonts window will most likely go unused on your system unless you are using your computer for desktop publishing or something similar, but it's there if and when you need it.

Figure 28.7
Viewing fonts by similarity.

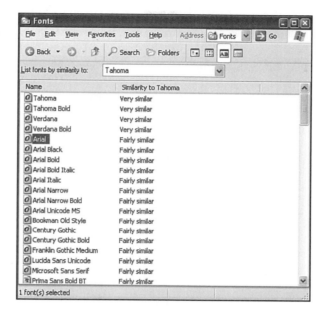

GAME CONTROLLERS

The Game Controllers applet (see Figure 28.8) is a relatively unknown applet that has been around, largely unchanged, since Windows 95. The only real change to the Game Controllers applet is the addition of additional controllers to the prepopulated list. Most of the popular controllers are listed here, and those that aren't will either include their own software for installation or can be added by using the Custom selection.

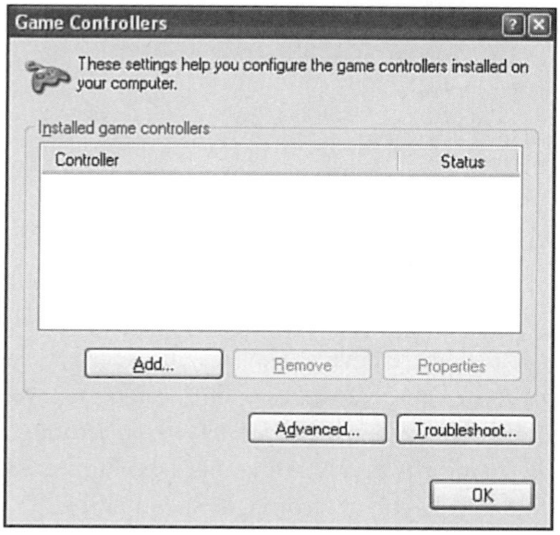

Figure 28.8
The Game Controllers applet.

28

To begin the process of adding a new game controller, click the Add button as seen in Figure 28.8. This will open a new dialog box (as shown in Figure 28.9), similar to installing other hardware, where you will be able to either select your controller from the list or manually add a controller not on the list by clicking Custom (see Figure 28.10).

Figure 28.9
Adding a new game controller.

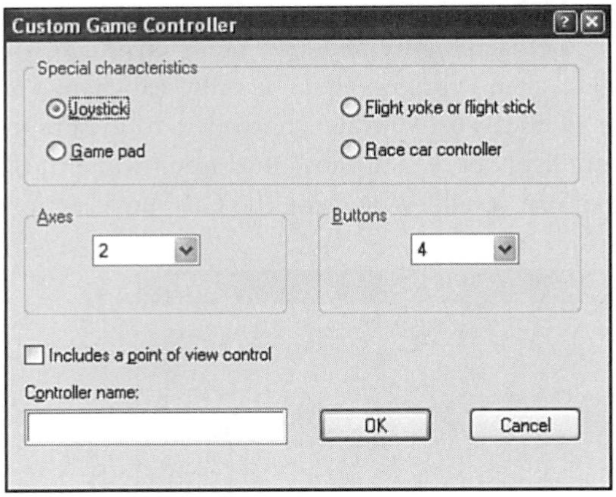

Figure 28.10
Adding a custom game controller.

KEYBOARD

The keyboard is one of those hardware devices that we all use every day and most of us never give a second thought to it. Either it works or it doesn't. Believe it or not, the keyboard does have some configurable options associated with it, although they are all done from within Windows itself. Using the Keyboard applet (see Figure 28.11), you can configure the following options for your keyboard from the Speed tab:

- *Repeat Delay*—The amount of time that elapses before a character begins to repeat when you hold down a key.

- *Repeat Rate*—The speed at which a character repeats when you hold down a key.

- *Cursor Blink Rate*—The speed at which the cursor (or insertion point) will blink.

The repeat delay and repeat rate settings can be tested in the test area in the middle of the page so that you can verify the settings are acceptable to you. The blink rate setting is observed next to its slider bar.

Figure 28.11
The Keyboard applet.

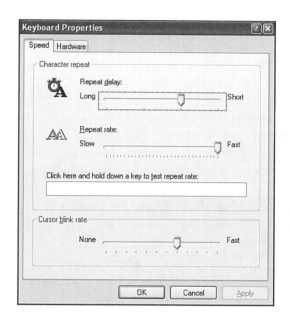

The Hardware tab of the Keyboard applet allows you to perform troubleshooting and maintenance tasks on the keyboard. Clicking the Troubleshoot button opens the Keyboard troubleshooter in a new Help and Support Center window. Clicking the Properties button opens the standard hardware Properties window (identical to the one opened from the Device Manager) from which you can examine and work with the keyboard drivers as required.

NOTE

Regionalized Keyboard Layouts

If you want to configure a regionalized keyboard layout, see the Regional and Language Options applet, which is covered later in this chapter.

28

MOUSE

The mouse is another one of the those hardware devices that we use every day and oftentimes pay little attention to, although it has some pretty neat configuration options that bear some looking into. If you have a standard (no frills) mouse installed on your system, you will most likely only have the five tabs discussed here. If you do not have a wheel mouse, then you will most likely only have four tabs. Also, you may very likely have additional tabs if you have a specialty mouse or touchpad, such as on a portable computer.

The Buttons tab (shown in Figure 28.12) allows you to configure the behavior of your mouse buttons with the following options:

- *Switch Primary and Secondary Buttons*—If you are right-handed and the left mouse button is your primary mouse button, clear this check box. If you are left-handed and the right mouse button is your primary mouse button, select this check box. This setting is really only useful if you have a generic mouse that is not shaped to fit the left hand.

- *Double-click Speed*—Used to adjust the amount of time allowed between clicks when you double-click the primary mouse button.

- *Turn on ClickLock*—Select this to lock a mouse or trackball button after a single-click, enabling you to select or drag without continuously holding down the mouse button.

Figure 28.12
The Buttons tab of the Mouse applet.

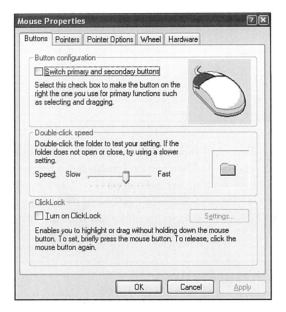

From the Pointers tab (see Figure 28.13), you can select predefined mouse pointer schemes or customize the mouse icons to your liking. I personally prefer the Dinosaur's theme.

28

Figure 28.3
The Pointers tab of
the Mouse applet.

The Pointer Options tab (shown in Figure 28.14) allows you to configure the behavior of
your mouse pointer with the following options:

- *Select a Pointer Speed*—Can be used to adjust the distance that your mouse pointer will
  move respective to the distance that the mouse or trackball has moved.

- *Enhance Pointer Precision*—Controls whether the enhanced pointer precision control is
  turned on or off. When turned on, you have more control over the pointer when moving small distances on the screen.

- *Automatically Move Pointer to the Default Button in a Dialog Box*—Forces the mouse to
  automatically snap to the default button in the dialog box which has the focus, such as
  OK, Cancel, or Apply.

- *Display Pointer Trails*—Adds a trail to the mouse pointer, making it easier to see.

- *Hide Pointer While Typing*—Removes the pointer from view when you are typing; the
  pointer will remain hidden until the mouse is moved.

- *Show Location of Pointer When I Press the CTRL Key*—Shows the location of the mouse
  pointer when you press the CTRL key by placing a set of collapsing concentric rings
  around it.

The Wheel tab (see Figure 28.15) controls how a scroll mouse behaves. The Roll the Wheel
One Notch to Scroll option defines how far a page scrolls when you roll the wheel one
notch. You can scroll a specific number of lines or an entire screen.

28

Figure 28.14
The Pointer Options tab of the Mouse applet.

Figure 28.15
The Wheel Options tab of the Mouse applet.

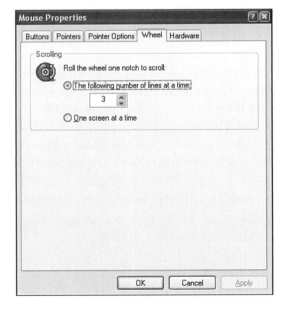

The Hardware tab of the Mouse applet allows you to perform troubleshooting and maintenance tasks on the mouse. Clicking the Troubleshoot button opens the Mouse troubleshooter in a new Help and Support Center window. Clicking the Properties button opens the standard hardware Properties window (identical to the one opened from the Device Manager) from which you can examine and work with the mouse drivers as required.

28

REGIONAL AND LANGUAGE OPTIONS

The Regional and Language Options applet is probably one that will mostly go unnoticed. For those that will actually make use of it, it will prove to be quite useful. Using the Regional and Language Options applet, you can control that format that Windows uses to display dates, times, currencies, numbers, and numbers with decimal points. In addition to specifying display options, you can also configure your computer to use any of a large number of input languages and text services, such as different keyboard layouts, Input Method Editors (IME), and handwriting/speech recognition programs. When switched to another input language, some programs (such as Microsoft Word) often offer special features such as fonts and spell checkers designed for that language.

Although Windows XP installs support for most input languages by default, it does not automatically install the East Asian languages such as Chinese and Japanese or the complex right-to-left languages such as Hebrew or Georgian. You can install these languages from the Windows XP Professional setup CD-ROM if desired.

NOTE

> **The Windows XP Multilingual User Interface Pack**
>
> To change the language used for menus and dialog boxes, you will require the Windows Multilingual User Interface Pack. This also holds true for most applications, such as Microsoft Word, which requires the Office Multilingual User Interface Pack in order to show the user interface or help system in a different language.

From the Regional Options tab (see Figure 28.16), you can configure display properties such as date and time format, as well as setting the location to be used for regional content from certain Internet services.

- *Standards and Formats*—Determines the way you want programs to display dates, times, currencies and numbers. An example of the selected method will be shown. Additionally, you can customize the settings if you desire.

- *Location*—Determines what country or region you will receive local content for via your Web browser, although this selection only affects certain providers.

From the Languages tab (see Figure 28.17), you can add or remove the languages and methods you want to use to enter text. To add additional languages, you must have administrative permissions. Once installed, languages will be available to all users of the computer.

28

Figure 28.16
The Regional Options tab of the Regional and Language Options applet.

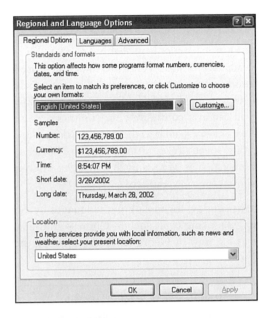

Figure 28.17
The Languages tab of the Regional and Language Options applet.

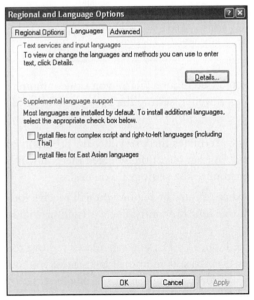

- *Text Services and Input Languages*—Allows you to add or remove input languages and text services for use on your computer. Input languages are the languages that you use to enter and display text. Clicking the Details button here opens the window shown in Figure 28.18, from which you can configure input languages and all means of providing input including the keyboard, handwriting recognition devices, and speech recognition devices.

■ *Supplemental Language Support*—Allows you to install the language files for those languages that are not installed on Windows XP by default, such as East Asian or complex right-to-left languages.

Figure 28.18
The Text Services and
Input Languages
page.

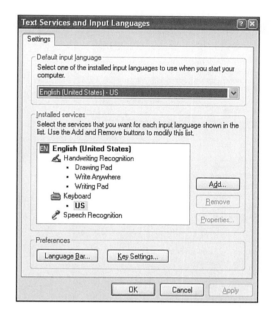

CAUTION

Go Easy on the Languages...

Although you can conceivably select as many different languages as you like, it's best if you only install the files you need. Language files are loaded into memory during startup and will consume system resources. Additionally, the East Asian language selection will require about 230MB of disk space on your hard drive.

The Advanced tab of the Regional and Language Options, like many other Advanced tabs, contains all of the settings and configuration options that didn't fit in anywhere else. In this case, you have configuration controls for non-Unicode programs.

■ *Language for Non-Unicode Programs*—Allows you to configure language support for older programs that do not support Unicode encoding. Configuring this option will allow menus and dialog boxes to display properly.

■ *Code Page Conversion Tables*—Allows you to select the page conversion tables that are currently installed on your computer. By adding (selecting) a conversion table, Windows is able to interpret the letters and other characters used in that program and convert them to and from Unicode.

■ *Default User Account Settings*—Allows you to select whether the settings you have made in Regional and Language Options apply to all new user accounts created on this computer.

28

NOTE

Only members of the Administrators group can install or remove code page conversion tables.

Figure 28.19
The Advanced tab of the Regional and Language Options applet.

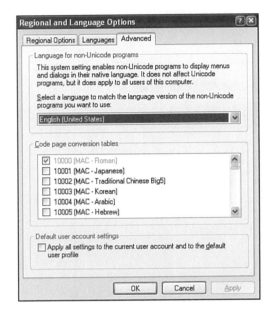

WORKING WITH A MULTI-LANGUAGE COMPUTER

Although you now know how to set up a multi-language computer, you may be wondering why this is done. Two instances where having multiple input languages configured would be helpful include

■ In a company that works in multiple languages, such as French and English or English and Spanish.

■ A shared computer in a dorm room where each student has a different primary language other than English.

Of course, there are many other situations that would require the use of a multi-language computer. Once you've gotten multiple languages configured on your computer, you can easily switch between them by configuring the options found on the Text Services and Input Languages page (shown in Figure 28.18). By using the Language Bar and Key Settings buttons, you can configure methods to switch between languages.

Additionally, if you have more than one language configured on your Windows XP computer, you can easily switch between them by turning on the Language Bar. To turn on the Language Bar, right-click an empty area of your Taskbar and select Toolbars, Language Bar.

SOUNDS AND AUDIO DEVICES

The Sounds and Audio Devices applet is a fairly simple and intuitive applet that you can use to configure and manage sounds and sound devices attached to your computer. Although the applet has five tabs by default, it is possible that you may have additional tabs if your sound card has extra configuration options associated with it.

The Volume tab (see Figure 28.20) allows you to perform basic volume and device configuration. You can control the volume of your speakers and whether or not to display a control icon in the taskbar for quick access to the Sounds and Audio Devices applet. Additionally, you can control individual speaker volumes and select the arrangement that matches your speakers, such as 5.1 Surround, and so on.

Figure 28.20
The Volume tab of the Sound and Audio Devices applet.

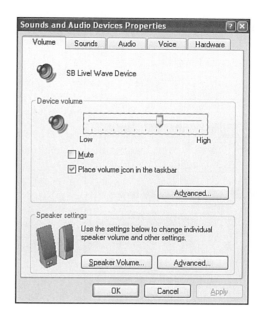

The Sounds tab (see Figure 28.21) allows you to configure sounds for your computer from pre-defined or customized sound schemes.

From the Audio tab (see Figure 28.22), you can configure and customize the devices to be used for playback of WAVE and MIDI files as well as the device to be used for recording.

The Voice tab (see Figure 28.23) allows you to configure voice playback and recording options for your computer.

Figure 28.21
The Sounds tab of the Sound and Audio Devices applet.

Figure 28.22
The Audio tab of the Sound and Audio Devices applet.

The Hardware tab allows you to perform troubleshooting and maintenance tasks on all installed audio-enabled devices and codecs. Selecting an item from the list and clicking the Troubleshoot button opens a troubleshooter in a new Help and Support Center window. Clicking the Properties button opens the standard hardware Properties window (identical to the one opened from the Device Manager) from which you can examine and work with the drivers as required.

28

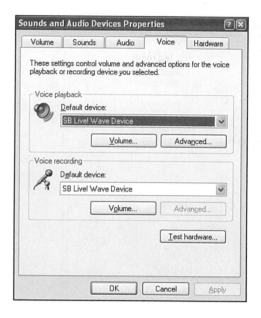

Figure 28.23
The Voice tab of the Sound and Audio Devices applet.

SYSTEM

Of all the Control Panel applets, the System applet is by far the most useful, versatile, and dangerous. As with most things in life, power has its price and in this case the power you have to configure your computer via the System applet also gives you the power to completely muck it up. The System applet in Windows XP has undergone a facelift from the Windows 2000 version, with the addition of the System Restore, Automatic Updates, and Remote tabs.

OLD TAB ROUNDUP—GOOD AS GOLD

As seen in Figure 28.24, the General tab of the System applet is just that—general. From here you can get a quick snapshot of the basic configuration of the computer. Some computers will also have a Support button that can be clicked to provide support contact information.

From the Computer Name tab (see Figure 28.25), you can enter a computer description (a Windows first), configure the computer's name (used to create the fully qualified domain name of a computer in a domain environment), and control the computer's membership in your workgroup or domain. Entering a descriptive name makes it easier to tell which computer is which when looking at computer accounts in the My Network Places folder, shown in Figure 28.26.

28

Figure 28.24
The General tab of the System applet.

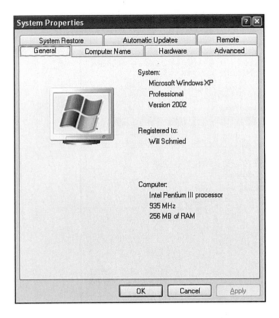

Figure 28.25
The Computer Name tab of the System applet.

The Hardware tab (see Figure 28.27) provides a wealth of configuration and control options to you. From here you can invoke the Add Hardware Wizard, configure Driver Signing, open the Device Manager, or configure hardware profiles for your Windows XP computer.

28

Figure 28.26
Computer description displayed in My Network Places.

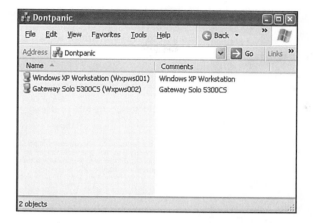

Figure 28.27
The Hardware tab of the System applet.

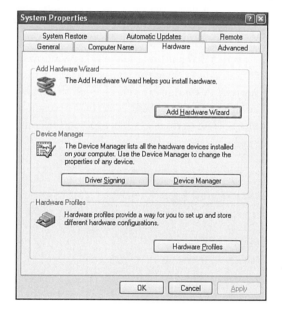

The Add Hardware Wizard (see Figure 28.28) allows you to not only add new hardware to your computer, but also to perform troubleshooting on hardware devices that are not functioning properly. Chapter 27, "Installing, Removing, and Managing Hardware Devices," covered the addition of new hardware to your computer.

28

Figure 28.28
The Add New
Hardware Wizard.

Digitally signed drivers are a way Microsoft uniquely marks Windows drivers so you can guarantee that a particular driver comes from the source that it claims to and that it has passed Microsoft's testing process. A vendor can release their drivers without Microsoft's digital signing, but unsigned drivers haven't been tested by Microsoft and might be more prone to cause system problems. The options available to you for configuring Driver Signing (see Figure 28.29) include

Figure 28.29
Setting Driver Signing
options.

■ *Ignore*—Directs the system to proceed with the installation even if it includes unsigned files. You have no protection from poorly written drivers when the Ignore option is selected; as a result, it is not recommended that you configure Driver Signing with the Ignore option.

- *Warn*—Notifies the user that files are not digitally signed and lets the user decide whether to stop or to proceed with the installation and whether to permit unsigned files to be installed. Driver Signing is set to Warn by default; however, it is not recommended to keep this setting in a production environment.

- *Block*—Directs the system to refuse to install unsigned files. As a result, the installation stops, and none of the files in the driver package are installed. This is the recommended setting for a production environment, and will guarantee the highest level of protection for client machines against poorly written device drivers.

Additionally, if you are logged in to the computer with Administrative privileges, you can set the Driver Signing selection to be the default for all users of the computer.

Even though it is easy to see the benefit of using only digitally signed drivers, in some cases you may have no other choice but to install and use unsigned drivers. Situations such as this typically arise when you are attempting to use a very old piece of hardware that is no longer in production or a very new piece of hardware that has not been tested by the Microsoft hardware quality labs. In either case, should you decide to use a hardware device that does not have digitally signed drivers, you should test the device driver in a lab environment for some time to ensure it functions properly before rolling it out into a production environment. If you don't have a lab and a production environment—that is, it's just you and one or a few computers—you can deploy the driver to the smallest number of computers and watch them carefully for signs of trouble. Should the installation go south, you can usually take advantage of another Windows XP new feature: Driver Rollback, as discussed in Chapter 27.

The Device Manager is largely unchanged from Windows 2000 and was discussed in detail in Chapter 27; hardware profiles were discussed in detail in Chapter 6, "Setting Up Important System Services."

The Advanced tab (see Figure 28.30) allows you to configure many options that didn't quite fit in anywhere else:

- Performance options such as visual effects, processor scheduling, memory usage, and virtual memory. Performance options are covered in detail later in this chapter in the "Performance Options" section.

- User Profiles options that deal with the profiles stored on your computer. From the User Profiles page, you can manage the profiles stored on your computer. You can delete, rename, copy, or change the type of profiles. The User Profiles page is covered in greater detail in Chapter 11, "Creating and Managing User Accounts."

- Startup and Recovery options deal with computer startup, failure, and debugging options. Startup and Recovery Options are covered in detail later in this chapter in the "Startup and Recovery Options" section.

- Environment Variables options allow you to configure user and system environment variables that are used on your computer. Environment Variables are covered in detail later in this chapter in the "Environment Variables" section.

28

■ Error Reporting options provide configuration controls for how your computer should report errors to Microsoft. Error Reporting is covered in detail later in this chapter in the "Error Reporting" section.

Figure 28.30
The Advanced tab of the System applet.

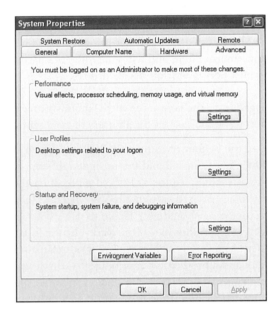

TIP

> **Who's Been Using My Computer?**
> Over the years, I have found the best use for the User Profiles page is to keep an eye on who has logged in to a workstation in a domain network. From here you can easily see who has been on the computer, how much space they are using, and if desired, delete their local profile from the computer.

PERFORMANCE OPTIONS

The Performance Options page is full of configurable items. From the Visual Effects tab, shown in Figure 28.31, you can configure many special visual effects for your Windows XP Professional computer. You have options to configure such visual effects as animated windows, fading menus, sliding menus, and many other visual effects. In most cases, you will be just fine selecting the Let Windows Choose What's Best for My Computer option.

The Advanced tab, shown in Figure 28.32, provides you with some rather esoteric and advanced controls that affect the behavior of your computer in regards to memory usage and processor usage.

28

Figure 28.31
The Performance Options page, Visual Effects tab.

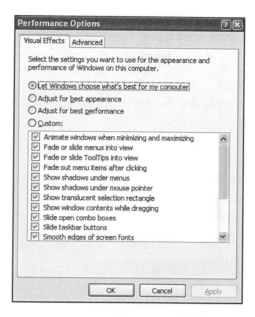

Figure 28.32
The Performance Options page, Advanced tab.

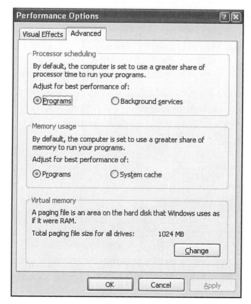

The Processor scheduling options allow you to configure your computer to give more resources either to programs or background services running on your computer. Typically, servers are configured with the Background Services option and all other computers are configured with the Programs option. The default value for this setting is Programs, and typically does not need to be changed in Windows XP Professional.

28

The Memory Usage options allow you to configure your computer to manage memory usage in much the same way as discussed previously with processor usage. Typically, servers are configured with the System cache option—this is also a good choice for workstations that have programs requiring a large system cache. The Programs option is applicable to workstations and results in faster program speed. The default value for this setting is Programs, and typically does not need to be changed in Windows XP Professional.

The Virtual memory options refer to configuration options for the paging file. Configuring the paging file is discussed at length in Chapter 25, "Managing Your Hard Disks."

STARTUP AND RECOVERY OPTIONS

Windows XP Professional has some useful options hidden on the Startup and Recovery page (see Figure 28.33), accessible by clicking the Settings button in the Startup and Recovery area of the Advanced Tab. From here you can perform the following tasks:

Figure 28.33
Configuring Startup
and Recovery options.

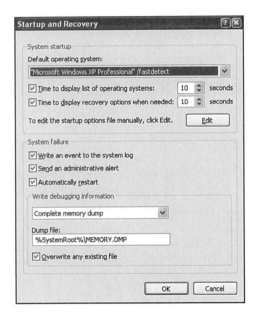

- Set the default operating system to load at computer startup. Editing the boot.ini file is discussed in Chapter 4, "Installing Windows XP for Multibooting."
- Configure the order that all operating systems will be shown in on the boot menu. Editing the boot.ini file is discussed in Chapter 4.
- Configure the amount of time (in seconds) that the boot menu and advanced startup options should be displayed before the default selection is forced. Editing the boot.ini file is discussed in Chapter 4.
- Configure what actions to carry out in the event of a system fault, such as notifying the administrator or restarting the system.

- Configure the detail level (if any) of logging that should occur when Windows stops unexpectedly.

- Configure the file name and location for the dump file and whether or not it can be overwritten.

When choosing what level of logging to perform, you have the following three options available to you:

- *Write an event to the system log*—Tells Windows to write information to the System Log when the computer stops unexpectedly.

- *Send an administrative alert*—Tells Windows to send a control alert to administrators when the computer stops unexpectedly.

- *Automatically restart*—Tells Windows to automatically restart the computer when it stops unexpectedly.

When choosing what level of logging to perform, you have the following three options available to you:

- *Small Memory Dump*—Records the smaller set of data that is useful in helping you determine why the system stopped unexpectedly. A paging file of at least 2MB is required on the boot partition for small memory dumping to function. Additionally, the dump file will be stored by default in the %SystemRoot%\Minidump folder.

- *Kernel Memory Dump*—Records only the data that was stored in kernel memory, which results in faster logging when the system stops unexpectedly. This will require a paging file with anywhere from 50MB to 800MB of space on the boot volume (depending on the amount of installed RAM) for a kernel memory dump to function. The dump files will be stored by default as %SystemRoot%\MEMORY.DMP.

- *Complete Memory Dump*—Records the entire contents of the system RAM when the system stops unexpectedly. This will require a paging file on the boot volume at least as big as the amount of RAM installed in the computer. The dump files will be stored by default as %SystemRoot%\MEMORY.DMP.

NOTE
You must be logged on as a member of the Administrators group to set recovery options.

The file name and location for dump files should not normally be changed, although you can enter any valid local location should you want to. You can also have new dump files overwrite existing dump files except in the case of Small memory dumps, which are saved sequentially in the %SystemRoot%\Minidump directory.

28

ENVIRONMENT VARIABLES

The Environment Variables page (see Figure 28.34) allows you to view, modify, and customize the environmental variables your profile and your computer use. The window is split into two halves, with the top half for the currently loaded profile and the bottom half for the system as a whole.

Figure 28.34
Configuring Environment variables.

The most common use for working with the Environment Variables (for the non-programmer) is to reassign the location of the TEMP directory, and thus I will use that as an example. To change the location of the TEMP directory, you can see that you will need to change two system environmental variables (shown in Figure 28.32). To change an existing variable, select it and then click Edit. Enter the changes and click OK to complete the process. You can also add new variables or remove existing variables as desired.

If you are not logged on as administrator to the local computer, the only environment variables you can change are user variables. If you make changes to the environment variables, Windows saves the changes in the registry so they are available automatically the next time you start your computer. If you have any programs open that depend on the modified environment variables, you should close them and then reopen them after you have made your changes to allow the new settings to take effect.

ERROR REPORTING

The Error Reporting page (see Figure 28.35) is a new addition to Windows XP, although one that most people may not particularly like. Error Reporting was designed to provide feedback to Microsoft about system and program errors that are occurring on Windows XP computers. The goal was to provide a centralized collection location for all user-reported errors so that over time more information will be available to you in regards to specific errors that you may experience—after all, other people are likely having the same errors.

Figure 28.35
The Error Reporting
page.

Error Reporting is used for both system (Blue Screen Of Death) errors and program errors. When a program error occurs, you will be notified of the error and prompted to either send or not to send the collected information to Microsoft—of course this only works if you have an active Internet connection at the time the error occurs. Figure 28.36 shows a typical Error Reporting notification dialog.

Figure 28.36
An error has
occurred!

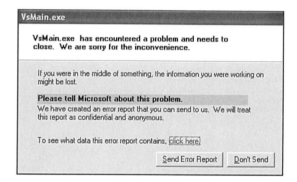

Should a system error occur, also known as a STOP error or a Blue Screen of Death (BSOD), then the error dialog box will be shown on the subsequent restart of the computer.

By default, error reporting is enabled for both the operating system and selected applications. You can select the programs to be monitored by clicking the Choose Programs button. Should you, like me, want to disable error reporting, you have the option.

NEW TAB ROUNDUP—NEW CHOICES, NEW PROBLEMS

With Windows XP, three new tabs make their appearance in the System applet: System Restore, Automatic Updates, and Remote.

System Restore is a new feature in Windows XP, although most people may find it a new pain in the butt. The idea behind System Restore is that every now and then (daily and

28

before software installations), Windows takes a snapshot of your computer and provides you a means to roll-back to a previous state if something goes awry. Think of it as the poorman's backup. The good thing about System Restore is that it's on by default and requires no configuration. Additionally, System Restore does not touch the My Documents directory, so your data files should always be safe from any changes made during a System Restore restoration action. The downside to System Restore is that it's on by default, using 12% of each and every volume for restore points. Additionally, you must be able to log in successfully to Windows in order to perform a roll-back using System Restore. You can either turn off monitoring for all volumes or turn off monitoring selectively on volumes of your choice. Additionally, you can configure the allowable space for System Restore from 1% to 12% of the total volume space. One last point to keep in mind: When you disable System Restore on a volume, all restore points on that volume are permanently lost.

Figure 28.37
The System Restore tab of the System applet.

CAUTION

System Restore and Viruses

Current anti-virus solutions cannot clean infected files that may reside in the System Restore directory. Should you become infected with a virus, worm, Trojan, or other hostile executable, you must disable System Restore in order to purge restore points from your computer that could potentially be infected. Once you are certain that you computer has been cleaned of all hostile code, you can then enable System Restore again.

Automatic Updates is another new and not-so-welcome feature found in Windows XP. When you are online, Windows will automatically search for and download (depending on your settings) updates for your computer from the Windows Update site. It's pretty easy to see how, in a domain network environment, this sort of thing could very easily get out of hand. More often than not you will probably end up disabling Automatic Update. Windows was not the first product to offer this type of functionality, however, as it's been in use for years in anti-viral applications such as McAfee Virus Scan and Norton Anti-Virus. You must be logged in with Administrative privileges in order to change the Automatic Update setting. (Automatic updates in an enterprise or networked setting are covered in detail in Chapter 33, "Managing Windows XP in an Enterprise Setting.")

Figure 28.38
The Automatic Updates tab of the System applet.

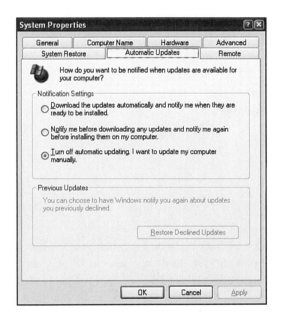

The third new tab in the System applet, the Remote tab (see Figure 28.39), deals with controlling how the computer may be used for Remote Assistance and Remote Desktop sessions. You have the option to allow or disallow Remote Assistance requests to be sent from the computer, as well as selecting whether or not a validated remote assistance connection can take control of the computer. In regards to Remote Desktop, you can add to a list of authorized users who are allowed to make a Remote Desktop connection with the computer. The user account that you created during the installation of Windows XP is included in the list of authorized Remote Desktop users by default. Remote Assistance is covered in more detail in Chapter 14, "Internet Applications."

28

Figure 28.39
The Remote tab of the
System applet.

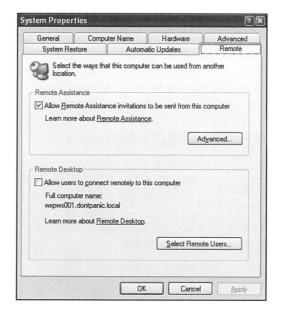

WIRELESS LINK

If your computer is equipped with an Infrared port, then you will have this last applet in your Control Panel. Most desktop systems do not have an IR port, and about roughly half of all portable computers currently have an IR port. Infrared ports are used by devices like digital cameras and Personal Digital Assistants (PDAs), such as a Palm or Handspring.

The Infrared tab (see Figure 28.40) allows you to configure some basic IR port items such as indicating when IR devices are active or playing a sound when an IR device is near. Additionally, you have control over how files are transferred and where incoming files are placed on your computer.

The Image Transfer tab (see Figure 28.41) deals primarily with the transfer of images from a digital camera to your computer via the IR port.

The Hardware tab of the Wireless Link applet allows you to perform troubleshooting and maintenance tasks on the IR port. Clicking the Troubleshoot button opens the Wireless Link troubleshooter in a new Help and Support Center window. Clicking the Properties button opens the standard hardware Properties window (identical to the one opened from the Device Manager) from which you can examine and work with the IR port drivers as required.

28

Figure 28.40
The Infrared tab of the Wireless Link applet.

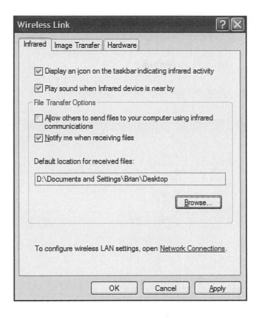

Figure 28.41
The Image Transfer tab of the Wireless Link applet.

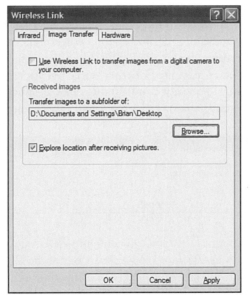

ADVANCED CONTROL PANEL OPTIONS VIA GROUP POLICY

In most cases where you have many computers to tend to, you will not want just any user to be able to use the Control Panel. After all, it is the virtual keys to the kingdom—a lot of

28

good and bad can be done from within. Fortunately for us, Group Policy makes it a snap to keep people out of specific applets or the entire Control Panel, as you see fit. The Group Policy objects of concern here are located in the User Settings node in the Control Panel folder as shown in Figure 28.42.

→ For details on working with the group policy editor, **see** "Understanding Group Policy" **p. 19** on the CD.

Figure 28.42
Controlling the
Control Panel via
Group Policy.

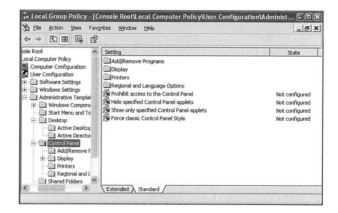

The sure-fire way to lock out all access to the Control Panel and all of its applets is to enable the Prohibit Access to the Control Panel option. When users try to access an applet from any method, they will receive an error dialog box like the one shown in Figure 28.43. Access to Control Panel applets is prevented whether the access attempt was made from the command line, from the Control Panel, or from a right-click context menu (such as from the Desktop), so it's a pretty good solution that's quick and easy to implement.

Figure 28.43
Control Panel lockout.

You do, however, have some options that you can configure via Group Policy, although they will not have quite as dramatic an effect on keeping users out of the Control Panel. You can enable the Hide Specific Control Panel Applets option or the Show Only Specified Control Panel Applets option and provide the required information if you simply want to show or hide specific applets. This will not prevent users from accessing the applets via any other means, however, so keep this in mind—not a very secure option. Control Panel applets can be found in the %SystemRoot%\System32 folder with the extension of .cpl, as shown in Figure 28.44.

28

Figure 28.44
Locating the Control
Panel applets.

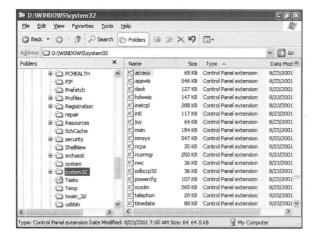

You can explicitly prevent users from using the Add or Remove Programs applet or the Display applet by configuring the appropriate options for those applets from the folders shown previously in Figure 28.42.

NOTE

Group Policy in Action

Group Policy is a powerful tool, especially for enterprise IT department staff who need to ensure that hundreds or thousands of user computers match approved and planned corporate configurations. Group Policy is one of several enterprise administration features covered in Chapter 33.

28

AUTOMATING ROUTINE TASKS

SAVING MORE THAN TIME

As a software author and consultant, I spend a lot of time moving files around, pushing data through various applications, and managing networks and computers. A few years ago I came to the conclusion that for many of these tasks, Windows's graphical user interface does *not* save me time or trouble. In fact, it can be a big drag.

Here's an example. Take a folder with 50 files named "file1.dat", "file2.dat", "file3.dat" and so on. Now, change their extensions to ".txt": "file1.txt", "file2.txt", and so forth. If you have to do this with Windows Explorer, right-clicking and retyping each name one by one, by the time you reach file7, you'll be about ready to scream. Yet, in a Command Prompt window, you can do this by typing `ren *.dat *.txt`. Start to finish, it takes about 5 seconds.

This one example shows that the old-fashioned command prompt is still useful in a practical, everyday way. Even better, you can type commonly used sequences of commands into files called *scripts* or *batch files*, and use them to perform repetitive or complex tasks with just a few keystrokes or mouse clicks. This is actually a very old-fashioned concept, but it's incredibly useful even today. Master it, and you'll be able to run computational circles around users who are stuck with just the mouse and GUI.

Increased productivity isn't the only benefit of using batch files and scripts. These command files also serve as a form of documentation, as they describe in concrete terms how to perform a given task.

As an example, suppose one of your day-to-day tasks is creating new user accounts for your office network. This might involve creating a user account, assigning a password, creating a shared folder on the network, assigning access privileges, configuring applications, and creating a mail system account. Using the spiffy Windows GUI, this task might take you 15 minutes for each account. You might forget one step and end up with a frustrated and confused user. If you're out of the office on the day that a new employee appears, the person filling in for you might not remember the nuances and steps correctly. In this case, the result will be several frustrated and irritated people. You can probably imagine similar scenarios involving your own daily tasks—installing a new computer, introducing a new customer to your business, setting up for a new semester at a school, ending an accounting quarter, and so on.

If you take the time to write a script or batch file to perform this sort of task, you'll not only have a tool to do the job the right way every time it's needed, but the script itself is a written record of what the task involves. Whether you or your colleagues use it, it will function correctly. And, in six months, after you've forgotten the details yourself, the script is there to remind you. From a business perspective, this sort of security can more than compensate for the initial investment of time it takes to learn how to script, and to write and test an automated application.

In this chapter, I'll touch on the two most common tools for automating tasks in Windows XP: Windows Script Host and the batch file language. Batch files let you use command-line programs to manipulate files, manage Windows, and control application programs.

Windows Script Host is a more modern tool that lets you write your own programs to manage Windows and networks in a very detailed way. Scripts can process data, move files, send email, and can even work Word and other application programs like a player piano.

In only a few pages, I can't teach you everything you need to know about automation. I'll give you an overview and walk through a few examples. My hope is that if you're not already familiar with these tools, this chapter will inspire you to go on and learn more.

NOTE

A good place to learn more about automation is Brian's book *Windows XP Under the Hood, Hardcore Windows Scripting and Command Line Power*, published by Que.

WINDOWS SCRIPT HOST

In the last decade or so, Microsoft has worked diligently to provide ways for programmers to gain access to the internal functions of commercial applications like Word and Excel and of Windows itself. The approach is based on a technology called the Common Object Model, or COM, which lets a properly designed program share its data and its functional capabilities with other programs—any other programs, written in any other programming languages. If you've ever written macros for Word or Excel, you've worked with scripting and COM. One product of these efforts is Windows Script Host, or WSH, which provides a fast and easy way to write your own management and utility programs.

HOW WSH WORKS

The Windows Script Host program itself does almost nothing. Rather, all of the real work is done by other software components that WSH recruits to do your bidding, as illustrated in Figure 29.1. Windows Script Host doesn't even know how to interpret the programming language that your script is written in—it depends on a "scripting engine" to read and follow your instructions. And the real work of most scripts is done by *objects*, which are separate software components that represent real-world items—data, files, folders, networks, Windows user accounts, system services and so on. I'll talk more about objects shortly.

Figure 29.1
Windows Script Host acts as an intermediary between your script program, a scripting language engine, and other program components called objects.

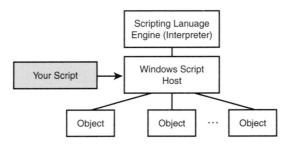

29

Windows XP comes with engines for two different scripting languages:

- VBScript, which is nearly identical to the Visual Basic for Applications (VBA) macro language used in Word and Excel.
- JScript, Microsoft's version of the JavaScript language, which is widely used to make Web pages interactive. (JavaScript, by the way, is not the same thing as Java. Java is another programming language altogether, and it's not used by Windows Script Host.)

In addition, you can download and install other language engines. If you have a Unix or Linux background, for example, you might want to use the Perl, Python, or TCL scripting languages. You can get free WSH-compatible versions from ActiveState Corporation at www.activestate.com.

If you are already versed in one of the scripting languages I've mentioned, by all means, use it. If you don't already know a scripting language, VBScript is probably the best one to start with, as you can also use it to write macros for Microsoft's desktop applications.

NOTE

Later in the chapter, I'll give you a very quick tour of VBScript. If you've never seen it before, you might want to skip ahead and read that section before continuing here with the ins and outs of creating and running scripts.

CREATING SCRIPTS

Scripts are stored as plain text files, which you can edit with Notepad or any other text file editor. Script filenames can end in any of the extensions listed in Table 29.1.

TABLE 29.1 SCRIPT FILENAME EXTENSIONS

Extension	Description
.vbs	Script written in VBScript.
.js	Script written in Jscript.
.pls	Script written in ActiveState PerlScript.
.pys	Script written in ActiveState ActivePython.
.wsf	Windows Script File, a more sophisticated script file format. WSF files contain one or more script programs with special instructions written using XML markup.
.wsc	Windows Script Component file, which contains custom object programs written in a scripting language.
.vbe	Encrypted VBScript script.
.jse	Encrypted JScript script.

NOTE

> I don't have room here to discuss WSF files, WSC files, or script encryption, but I do discuss these topics in my book *Windows XP Under the Hood*.

29

To create a script file, choose a descriptive name, something like "WorkSummaryReport" perhaps, and add the extension that corresponds to the language you'll be using.

As an example, I'll write a script using VBScript, which I'll call "hello.vbs". If you want to try it yourself, follow these steps:

1. Open a Command Prompt window by clicking Start, All Programs, Accessories, Command Prompt.

2. The command prompt window opens on the default directory \Documents and Settings*your_user_name*. If you want to create the script in another folder, you will need type in a **cd** command to change directories. For the purposes of this example, we'll skip that and use the default directory.

3. Type the command **notepad hello.vbs**. When Notepad asks if you want to create a new file, click Yes.

4. Type in the text

   ```
   wscript.echo "Hello, this message comes from a script"
   ```

5. Save the script by clicking File, Save. You can leave the Notepad window open, or close it with File, Exit.

6. Bring the Command Prompt window to the foreground.

7. Type **wscript hello.vbs** and press Enter.

If everything works, you should see the dialog box shown in Figure 29.2. Click OK to close the message dialog.

Figure 29.2
The sample script displays a simple text message.

On the other hand, if VBScript (or whatever language engine you are using) finds a glaring error in the script program—for example, a missing comma or an extraneous line of text—instead of the message box, you may be treated to an error message like that shown in Figure 29.3.

In this case, VBScript is saying that the script has a problem on its seventh line (to find this, you'll need to view the script file in Notepad and press the down arrow key 6 times).

Figure 29.3
If the scripting engine finds a glaring error, it will display a descriptive message.

To fix a problem or to change how a script works, you need to edit the script file again and alter its contents. For the sample script we created, you can type **notepad hello.vbs** again to edit the script. Or, you can locate the file in Windows Explorer, right-click it, and select Edit.

> **TIP**
>
> You can save yourself the trouble of using the Command Prompt each time you want to create a new script by adding a script template to Windows Explorer's "New" context menu. To do this, download and install the TweakUI Powertoy for Windows XP from www.microsoft.com. Create an *empty* script file with the name script.vbs. Locate the script file in Windows Explorer. Run TweakUI from the Control Panel, and select the New tab. Drag the script file's icon from Window Explorer into the list in TweakUI. Now, you can select any folder, and right-click New, VBScript Script File. Rename the file, then right-click it and select Edit to start entering its contents.
>
> You might also want to install the Command Prompt Here powertoy—it lets you open a command prompt in any folder from an Explorer view.

At this point, before describing how to run and debug scripts, I'll present a brief introduction to VBScript.

INTRODUCTION TO VBSCRIPT

VBScript is based on the Visual Basic programming language, and is nearly identical to Visual Basic for Applications (VBA), which is used to create macros (prerecorded instructions) for Microsoft Word, Excel, and many other applications. VBScript is a full-fledged programming language. Even if you've never written a computer program, you can probably pick up enough VBScript to get by, just by reading and toying with working scripts that other people have written.

In this section, I'll give you a *very* brief overview of VBScript. For a full treatment, you can buy any of several books on the topic (see the end of this chapter for some ideas), you can download detailed references from Microsoft's Web site at msdn.microsoft.com/scripting, or you can scour the Web, where you'll find innumerable sites that discuss and share scripts.

In any case, if you want more details about VBScript as a programming language, you can read the next section; otherwise, you can skip ahead to the section on Objects.

VARIABLES AND EXPRESSIONS

VBScript is a programming language with all of the expected features: variables, flow-of-control statements, and user-defined functions and subroutines. VBScript programs can work with several different types of data, which are listed in Table 29.2.

TABLE 29.2   VBSCRIPT DATA TYPES

Type	Description
Integer	"Whole" numbers such as -2, 0, 1 and 47
Floating Point	Fractional numbers like 100.34 and -3.5
String	Text such as "ABCD" and "summary file.doc"
Boolean	The values True and False
Date	A number that represents a date, such as March 2, 2003
Date-Time	A number that represents a date and time such as March 2, 2003 7:09:39 p.m
Object	A block of data managed by another program; we'll discuss objects shortly

Table 29.3 lists some examples of the way you can specify values in a VBScript program.

TABLE 29.3   LITERAL VALUE FORMATS IN VBSCRIPT

Literal Values	Interpretation
123	Decimal integer 123
&H12AB	Hexadecimal integer 12AB (decimal 4779)
&O177	Octal integer 177 (decimal 127)
1.234	Floating point number 1.234
"abc"	String "abc"
#March 2, 2003#	The date March 2, 2003. This is the preferred format for specifying dates
#3/2/2003#	Date interpreted according to your Windows Locale settings. In the U.S., this means March 2, 2003. Most everywhere else, this means February 3, 2003. (Avoid entering dates in this format if you plan to distribute your script internationally!)
#March 2, 2003 19:09:39#	The date-time March 2, 2003 at 7:09:39 PM
True	Boolean value True
False	Boolean value False

You can assign values of any type to any variable, using VBScript statements like these:

```
filename = "c:\myfiles\report.doc"      ' string value
nfiles = 0                              ' integer numeric value
cutoff_date = #January 1, 2003#         ' date
```

You can make calculations with variables and literal values using the standard mathematical symbols + (addition), - (subtraction), * (multiplication), and / (division), as in these statements:

```
nfiles = nfiles+1                                        ' add one to nfiles
price = unit_cost * num_items * (1 - percentdiscount/100) ' compute net price
fullpath = foldername + "\" + filename + ".doc"          ' join strings
```

When adding (joining) strings, however, it's best to use the ampersand (&) symbol, as this makes it clear to both VBScript and other people looking at the script that the program is dealing with text rather than numbers. The last example could also have been written:

```
fullpath = foldername & "\" & filename & ".doc"          ' join strings
```

VBScript Functions

VBScript provides a large complement of built-in *functions*, which can help you perform complex calculations. Functions can take string or numeric values called *arguments*, do something with the argument values, and return a result value. For example, the sqrt function calculates the square root of a numeric value, and it's used like this:

```
side_c = sqrt(side_a*side_a + side_b*side_b)
```

When it encounters this statement, VBScript calculates the value of side_a*side_a + side_b*side_b, gives this value to sqrt, and stores the value returned by sqrt in variable side_c.

There are a total of 97 functions listed in Microsoft's VBScript reference. A bare handful are listed in Table 29.4, to give you an idea of what's available.

TABLE 29.4 SOME OF VBSCRIPT'S BUILT-IN FUNCTIONS

Function	Description
CStr(*value*)	Converts any type of value or expression into a string representation. For example, cstr(4-6) returns the string "-2".
Date()	Returns the current date as a date value.
Day(*date*)	Returns the day of the month (a number from 1 to 31) of the given date value. For example, Day(Date()) returns the current day of the month.
Hour(*time*)	Returns the hour of the day (a number from 0 to 23) of the given time or date-time value. For example, Hour(Now()) returns the current hour.

Function	Description
InStr(*string1***,** *string2***)**	Returns the starting position of *string2* if it occurs within *string1*, or 0 if *string2* is not present. For example, InStr("abcd", "bc") returns 2.
InStr(*start***,** *string1***,** *string2***)**	If three arguments are specified, the first is a number that indicates the position within *string1* to begin the search. For example, InStr(3,"abcabc","a") returns 4.
InStrRev(*string1***,** *string2***)** **InStrRev(***start***,** *string1***, _** *string2***)**	Like InStr, but searches starting at the right end of the string. For example, InStr("a.b.c", ".") returns 4.
LCase(*string***)**	Returns the string expression with all the characters in lowercase. For example, LCase("My Name") returns the string "my name".
Len(*string***)**	Returns the length of the string in characters. For example, Len("ABC") returns 3.
Mid(*string***,** *start***)**	Returns the remainder of the string starting at position *start*. For example, Mid("ABCD", 3) returns "CD".
Mid(*string***,** *start***,** *length***)**	Like the previous version, but returns at most *length* characters. For example, Mid("ABCD", 3, 1) returns "C".
Now()	Returns the current date and time as a date-time value.
UCase(*string***)**	Returns the string value with all the characters in uppercase. For example, UCase("Apple") returns "APPLE".

As I mentioned, there are many more functions provided with VBScript to help you slice and dice text strings, perform numerical calculations, and format results.

INPUT AND OUTPUT

If necessary, scripts can prompt you for input. You may want to do this, for example, before having a script overwrite an existing file. VBScript comes with a function named MsgBox that you can use to display simple messages, and also to query the person using the script with simple yes/no type answers.

MESSAGE BOX INPUT

You can display a simple message with a statement like this:

```
MsgBox "The time is " & Now(), vbOKOnly, "Current Time"
```

This statement gives the MsgBox function three values. The first is the text to display, the second is a special value that tells what button or buttons to display, and the third defines the message box's title. If you place this statement in a script file, called perhaps showtime.vbs, and type the command **showtime** in the Command Prompt window, VBScript will display the dialog box shown in Figure 29.4.

Figure 29.4
You can control a message box's text, title, and buttons.

When you read the VBScript documentation, you'll see the MsgBox function described this way:

MsgBox(_prompt_[, _buttons_[, _title_[, _helpfile_, _context_]]]**)**

The parts in boldface are meant to be typed literally. The words in italics are placeholders—you're meant to insert your own program's information there. And the square brackets [and] are not meant to be typed in at all; they enclose parts of the program statement that are optional. When you omit optional arguments, VBScript will act as if you had specified some value called the _default value_. The function's documentation will describe what default values are assumed if you omit arguments.

What this means for MsgBox is that there are four ways you can use the function, shown in these four examples:

```
' Display the time using the default button (OK) and default title ("VBScript")
MsgBox Now()

' Display the time, and explicitly ask VBScript to display just an OK button
MsgBox Now(), vbOKOnly

' Display the time, choose the buttons, and set the title
MsgBox Now(), vbOKOnly, "Current Time"

' Display the time, choose the buttons, set the title, and specify a help file
' and help subject number; this adds a Help button as well as the OK button.
MsgBox Now(), vbOKOnly, "Current Time", "myscript.hlp", 1
```

You can also omit arguments in the middle of the list, in which case VBScript uses the default values for the missing items, as in this example:

```
' Display the time and set the title;
' let VBScript supply the default VBOKOnly argument
MsgBox Now(), , "Current Time"
```

You can use any of these versions in your scripts.

MsgBox is actually a function that can return a numeric value that tells you which button was pressed. If you want to use MsgBox to select how your script should behave, you must enclose the arguments to MsgBox in parentheses, and then you can use MsgBox() as a numeric value. Here's an example that displays a question with Yes and No buttons, and performs an action only if the Yes button gets clicked:

```
                        ' display a msgBox asking if it's OK to delete the file
if MsgBox("Do you want to delete the file?", vbYesNo) = vbYes then
    file.Delete       ' delete the file only if the user clicked Yes
end if
```

Now, how are you supposed to know to type vbYesNo in order to get Yes and No buttons, and how do you know that the MsgBox function will return the value vbYes if the user clicks Yes? You have to refer to the VBScript documentation, which you can download from www.microsoft.com, or which you can find in the appendix section of most books on scripting. Table 29.5 shows how this might look.

TABLE 29.5   MSGBOX BUTTON ARGUMENT CONSTANTS

Constant	Value	Description
vbOKOnly	0	Display **OK** button only
vbOKCancel	1	Display **OK** and **Cancel** buttons
vbAbortRetryIgnore	2	Display **Abort**, **Retry**, and **Ignore** buttons
vbYesNoCancel	3	Display **Yes**, **No**, and **Cancel** buttons
vbYesNo	4	Display **Yes** and **No** buttons
vbRetryCancel	5	Display **Retry** and **Cancel** buttons
vbCritical	16	Display "Critical Message" icon
vbQuestion	32	Display "Warning Query" icon
vbExclamation	48	Display "Warning Message" icon

The value returned by VBScript depends on which button the user clicks. These possible values are also described in the VBScript documentation and are listed in Table 29.6.

TABLE 29.6   MSGBOX RETURN VALUES

Constant	Value	Description
vbOK	1	OK button or Enter key
vbCancel	2	Cancel button, or Esc key
vbAbort	3	Abort button
vbRetry	4	Retry button
vbIgnore	5	Ignore button
vbYes	6	Yes button
vbNo	7	No button

29

29

If you want the message box to display an icon along with the text, you can *add* in one of the three icon values, as in this example:

```
' tell them they may be in trouble and give the option to quit
if MsgBox("The hard disk is nearly full. Do you want to proceed?", _
        vbYesNo+vbQuestion) = vbNo then   ' if they choose No,
    wscript.quit                          ' cancel the script
end if
```

The result is shown in Figure 29.5

Figure 29.5
Message box with a
warning icon added.

In your VBScript programs, for the `button` argument to `MsgBox`, you can use a named constant such as `vbOKOnly`, or the corresponding numeric value. I suggest that when possible you use named constant values rather than numeric values, as it makes the script easier to read. To see what I mean, compare the previous script sample to this equivalent version:

```
if MsgBox("The hard disk is nearly full. Do you want to proceed?", 36) = 7 then
    wscript.quit                          ' if they choose No, cancel the script
end if
```

The numbers 36 and 7 do work, and VBScript doesn't care either way, but it sure makes it difficult for us mere humans to understand what this script is doing.

TEXT INPUT

If you want to ask the user a question whose answer has to be typed in, you can use the `InputBox` function. `InputBox` is much like `MsgBox`, except that it displays a text entry field into which the script user can type. It's used like this:

```
variable = InputBox(prompt[, title [, defaultvalue]])
```

where *prompt* is the question that you're asking the user to answer, *title* is the title to display at the top of the dialog box, and *defaultvalue* is the value to fill into the box before the user types anything. You can omit *title* and/or *defaultvalue*. Here's an example:

```
fldr = InputBox("Enter folder to be cleaned up:", "Cleanup Script", "C:\TEMP")
```

You might use this at the start of a script that deleted .TMP and .BAK files, for instance.

FLOW OF CONTROL

In most scripting tasks, the script program will have to take different actions depending on the circumstances it finds itself in. For example, a script to print out the contents of your floppy disk drive would have to take one course of action if it found that there was no disk inserted in the drive, and another if a disk was present. Then, the number of files on the floppy disk is variable, so the script program will have to have a way to print one entry for each file that it finds. Similarly, a script that was intended to back up different sets of files on different days of the week would have to have a way of running some commands on Monday, and different commands on Tuesday.

Programming languages use *flow of control* statements to describe these sorts of tasks. The most basic is the if statement, which in VBScript looks like this:

```
if expression then
    statements that are to be run if the expression is true
    .
    .
    .
else
    statements that are to be run if the expression is false
    .
    .
    .
end if
```

where *expression* is a VBScript expression or variable that evaluates to the Boolean value True or False. The else part of the if statement is optional. Examples of if statements are shown here:

```
if number_of_files = 0 then
    wscript.echo "No files were found"
else
    wscript.echo "There are files on the disk"
    .
    .
    .
end if

if (today = "Wednesday") or (today = "Friday") then
    wscript.echo "Backing up D drive"
    .
    .
    .
end if
```

If your program might encounter one of several different situations, you can extend the if statement to test several conditions in sequence with the elseif statement:

```
if expression then
    statements that are to be run if the first expression is true
elseif expression then
    statements that are to be run if the second expression is true
elseif expression then
    statements that are to be run if the third expression is true
else
    statements that are to be run if no expression is true
end if
```

29

Another commonly used statement is `do while`:

```
do while expression
    statements to execute if expression is true
    .
    .
    .
loop
```

This is a lot like `if`, but if the expression is True, after executing the statements VBScript goes back and tests the expression again. If the expression is still True, it executes the statements again, and repeats this over and over until finally the expression turns out to be False. This kind of statement is useful when reading information from a file, for example, where you don't know in advance how much information you'll find. The `do while` expression can check to see if you've reached the end of your input file, and VBScript will repeat the statements as long as there is still more data to read.

You'll see practical examples of these and other flow-of-control statements in this chapter, and you can read all about them in the full VBScript documentation.

VBSCRIPT FORMATTING

As I mentioned earlier, you can type VBScript programs using Notepad or any other text file editor. VBScript programs can be typed in uppercase, lowercase, or any mixture; VBScript doesn't care. For example, the statements

```
MYAGE = 43
myage = 43
MyAge = 43
```

or

```
WScript.Echo "hello, world"
wscript.echo "hello, world"
```

are all the same to VBScript. However, text strings that are used as data *are* case sensitive. The two statements

```
wscript.echo "Hello, world"
wscript.echo "hello, world"
```

are not the same. As data, "Hello" and "hello" are as different as "Hello" and "Jello".

VBScript also ignores any so-called *whitespace*: blank lines, blank spaces, and tabs in the text of your script programs. For example, to VBScript, the program

```
myhometown="Smallville"
myage=20
for yearsold = 1 to myage
wscript.echo "When I was", yearsold, "I lived in", myhometown
next
```

is the same as

```
myhometown = "Smallville"
myage      = 20
```

```
for yearsold = 1 to myage
    wscript.echo "When I was", yearsold, "I lived in", myhometown
next
```

However, the extra spaces in the second version make the script easier for you and me to read, so it's worth taking the extra time to type scripts this way.

To make your scripts even easier for others to understand, you should add *comments* to describe what the script is doing, how to use it, and any other helpful background information you think is useful. This will even help you, after some time has passed and you're rusty on the details of how a particular script works. VBScript ignores anything after a single quote symbol ('), so you can enter comments like this:

```
' cleantemp.vbs - this script deletes all .TMP and .BAK files
' from the folder C:\TEMP

set fso = CreateObject("Scripting.FileSystemObject") ' create helper object

for each file in fso.GetFolder("c:\temp").Files        ' scan files in c:\temp
    extn = ucase(fso.GetExtensionName(file.Name))      ' get file extension in
                                                       ' upper case to match TMP
                                                       ' as well as tmp
    if (extn = "TMP") or (extn = "BAK") then           ' if this type is unwanted
        wscript.echo "Deleting", file.Name             ' print a message
        file.Delete                                    ' and delete the file
    end if
next                                                   ' get next file to examine
```

Finally, sometimes you'll have to type very long commands. You can make them easier to read and edit by breaking them into multiple lines. However, you have to tell VBScript that you're doing this as normally, each separate line in the script file is looked at as a separate instruction. If you end a line with an underscore character (_), VBScript assumes that the next line is part of the same command. So, instead of writing

```
wscript.echo "There are", n_bytes_free, "bytes on", drive_type, "drive",
drive_letter
```

you can write

```
wscript.echo "There are", n_bytes_free, "bytes on", _
    drive_type, "drive", drive_letter
```

NOTE

> In this book, from time to time I'll have to type script statements this way because of the limited width of the printed page. If you type in any of the scripts listed in this chapter, you can type them with the underscores and line breaks intact, or you can omit the trailing underscore and continue typing the next line's text where the underscore was.

OBJECTS

VBScript is an *object-oriented* language. *Objects* are add-on components that extend a programming language's intrinsic capabilities. In the most general sense, objects are little program packages that manipulate and communicate information. They're a software representation of something tangible, such as a file, a folder, a network connection, an email message, or an Excel document. Windows comes with hundreds of built-in objects that you can use in scripting.

Your script program interacts with objects through features called *properties* and *methods*. Properties are data values that describe the attributes of the thing the object represents. Methods are actions you can use to alter or manipulate whatever it is that the object represents.

For example, a file on your hard disk has a size, a creation date, and a name. So, these are some of the properties a `File` object would have. You can rename, delete, read, and write a file, so a `File` object would provide methods to perform these tasks.

Because each programming language has a unique way of storing and transferring data, objects and the programs and scripts that use them must have some agreed-upon, common way of exchanging data. Microsoft uses what it calls the *Component Object Model (COM)*, which I mentioned earlier. Objects based on COM can be used by any compatible language, including VBScript, JScript, C, C++, C#, Visual Basic, Perl, Object REXX, and so on. COM objects may at times also be called *ActiveX Objects, Automation Objects*, or *OLE* objects.

VBScript and COM take care of all the details of managing and communicating with objects. All you have to worry about is learning about their properties and methods, which in programming jargon is called their *interface*. Figure 29.6 shows the interface of a hypothetical `File` object. Each separate copy of an object in a program is called an *instance* of the object. (Here's how to think if it: If you had triplets, you'd have three instances of the "child" object.)

Figure 29.6
This hypothetical `File` object has properties and methods that a script program can use to manipulate a real file on the hard disk.

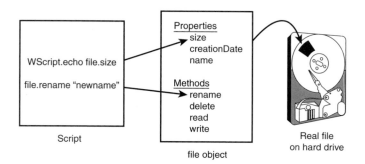

USING OBJECTS IN VBSCRIPT

In VBScript, you can create an instance of an object using the `CreateObject` function. Objects are stored in variables, but there is a trick: you must use the `set` keyword to tell VBScript that you are working with an object. Here's an example:

```
set fso = CreateObject("Scripting.FileSystemObject")
```

This statement asks VBScript to create an instance of the object called Scripting.FileSystemObject, which is an object provided with Windows Script Host with properties and methods that help you work with the files and folders on your computer. The CreateObject function returns an instance of this object type, which is stored in variable fso. The set keyword tells VBScript that variable fso is being assigned an object and not a normal number or string value.

Here is another small script example that shows objects in use:

```
1|   set fso = CreateObject("Scripting.FileSystemObject")
2|   set drivelist = fso.Drives
3|   for each drv in drivelist
4|     if drv.IsReady
5|       wscript.echo drv.DriveLetter, "has", drv.FreeSpace, "bytes free"
6|     end if
7|   next
```

I'll explain each of the lines of this script one by one.

1. This statement creates a Scripting.FileSystemObject object, and stores it in a variable named fso.

2. This statement gets the value of the Drives property from the Scripting.FileSystemObject instance we created in step 1, and stores this value in variable drivelist. The Drives property returns a special type of object (which is why this statement uses set) called a *collection*. A collection is a list of one or more separate objects. In this case, it is a collection of Drive objects, each of which represents a drive on your computer. The collection will contain one Drive object for each floppy, CD, DVD, Zip, and network drive attached to your computer.

3. This special version of VBScript's for statement tells VBScript to execute all of the program commands between the lines with for and next once for each of the objects in the drivelist collection. Each time through, the variable drv will contain one of the Drive objects in drivelist. This for statement lets you scan through each of the objects in the collection without knowing in advance how many there are.

4. At this point of the program, variable drv contains an instance of a Drive object. The Drive object has properties and methods that let you check on a drive's free space, volume name, and so on. This statement uses the object's IsReady property to be sure that the drive is online and, in the case of removable disks, has a disk inserted. The property returns True if the drive is okay, and False if it is offline or empty. Thus, the if statement will only execute statement 5 if the drive is online.

5. This statement uses the Drive object's FreeSpace property to get the number of free bytes on the drive. The wscript.echo command, which we used in earlier examples, uses the predefined wscript object to print out the number of free bytes, and the other text on the statement.

6. End if ends the block of commands that depend on the if statement in line 4.

7. Next ends the block of commands that are executed with each turn of the for loop.

Try this script yourself; type the script into a file named `freespace.vbs` (without the numbers at the left), and type the command **cscript freespace.vbs** to see the results. On my computer, this printed the following lines:

```
C: has 15866540032 bytes free
D: has 27937067008 bytes free
F: has 335872000 bytes free
H: has 460791808 bytes free
```

BUILT-IN OBJECTS

In the previous section, we touched on the `Scripting.FileSystem` and `Drive` objects. There are actually hundreds of objects provided with Windows. Several of them are supplied as part of Windows Script Host. In this section, I'll go over a few methods and properties of the most important of these. However, in this chapter I only have room to give you a small taste of their capabilities. There are many more functions that these objects can perform.

Scripting.FileSystemObject

The `Scripting.FileSystemObject` object gives you access to the drives, files, and folders on your computer. It also provides some helpful methods that let you construct and deconstruct the parts of filenames.

This object has a property named `Drives`, which returns a collection of Drive objects; each of these describes one of the drives physically attached to your computer or connected via the network. Earlier in this chapter under "Using Objects in VBScript," I showed you how this can be used.

`Scripting.FileSystemObject` also has several methods, which you can use as tools to locate information on the disk or to manipulate filenames. I'll show you a few examples of these methods.

The `FileExists` method returns True if a specified file exists, or False otherwise. A script that depended on finding a particular input file might use this method:

```
set fso = CreateObject("Scripting.FileSystemObject")

' be sure required file exists. If it doesn't, say so and stop the script
if not fso.FileExists("C:\data\script-input.dat") then
    MsgBox "The file c:\data\script-input.dat does not exist"
    wscript.quit
end if
```

The `GetFolder` methods returns a `Folder` object that represents a specific folder on your hard drive. You can then examine the properties of the `Folder` object; for example, its `Files` collection and its `Subfolders` collection. Here is an example of a script that uses these objects to list all of the files on your C drive:

```
' script to list all of the files on the C drive:

set fso = CreateObject("Scripting.FileSystemObject")   ' create helper object
list fso.GetFolder("C:\")                              ' list contents of C:\
```

29

```
' subroutine that lists the contents of a specific folder.
' The argument to the subroutine is a Folder object
sub list (folder)
    on error resume next          ' if there is a permissions error,
                                  ' just ignore the file or folder

    for each file in folder.Files ' scan all of the files first and
        wscript.echo file.Path    ' print each file's full path and name
    next

    for each subfolder in folder.Subfolders ' then scan each subfolder and
        list subfolder                       ' list the subfolder's contents
    next
end sub
```

`Scripting.FileSystemObject` is one of the most useful tools in VBScript, so you should spend some time learning about all of its methods and properties.

WScript.Shell

The `Wscript.Shell` object helps you locate user-specific folders such as My Documents and the Desktop, creates shortcuts, and can access the environment and the Registry.

The object's `Environment` property serves three purposes: It can retrieve information from the current environment, it can set the default environment variables that every user receives at logon, and it can set personalized defaults for the user who runs the script. I'll just discuss the first use in this chapter.

You can use `Environment` to get information from environment variables such as USER-NAME, which is set to the current user's logon name, and PATH, the program search path. The following sample script shows how this works.

> **NOTE**
>
> One usual thing in this script is the set of four quotation marks. In VBScript, to place a quotation mark inside a string you have to double it up, so `" " " "` is a string consisting of a single quotation mark.

```
set shell = CreateObject("WScript.Shell") ' create shell helper object
                                          ' show username from the environment
wscript.echo "Username:", shell.Environment("process").Item("USERNAME")
                                          ' get the search path
path = shell.Environment("process").Item("path")

' break path into an array of folder names where separated by semicolons

dirs = split(path, ";")              ' (built-in function 'split' does this)

for each dir in dirs                 ' scan each item in the array
    if left(dir,1) = """" then       ' if first character of folder name is a
        dir = mid(dir, 2)            ' quote, remove the first character
    end if
    if right(dir,1) = """" then      ' if last character is a quote, likewise
```

```
        dir = left(dir, len(dir)-1) ' remove the last character
    end if

    wscript.echo "Search path folder:", dir    ' display the folder name
next
```

WSHShell's GetSpecialFolder property lets you get the actual full path—including drive letter—for user-specific folders such as the Desktop, My Documents, and Start menu. This is a neat trick and spares you having to try to guess where Windows placed these folders. The property actually returns a collection of several special folder objects, but you can ask it to return the path to a specific folder as a string by giving it the name of the desired folder. Here's a script that shows how this works:

```
set shell = CreateObject("WScript.Shell")    ' create shell helper object

wscript.echo "User's Desktop folder:", shell.SpecialFolders("Desktop")
wscript.echo "All Users desktop:   ", shell.SpecialFolders("AllUsersDesktop")
wscript.echo "My Documents folder: ", shell. SpecialFolders("MyDocuments")
```

Here is the full list of folder names you can request from SpecialFolders:

AllUsersDesktop	NetHood
AllUsersStartMenu	PrintHood
AllUsersPrograms	Programs
AllUsersStartup	Recent
Desktop	SendTo
Favorites	StartMenu
Fonts	Startup
MyDocuments	Templates

The AllUsers... versions return the paths to the special folders in the All Users user profile; items placed in these folders appear in everyone's Start menu, Desktop, Startup folder, and so on. The other folders are user-specific and are located in your own user profile folder.

WScript.Network

The WScript.Network object lets you work with network connections to other computers. It lets you create and delete network drive mappings, and add and remove remote network printer icons in your Printers folder.

The object's EnumNetworkDrive property returns a collection of string values, with two items for each network drive mapped on the computer that is running the script. The items are

Element 0	Drive letter of first network drive
Element 1	UNC Share name of first network drive
Element 2	Drive letter of second network drive
Element 3	UNC Share name of second network drive

and so on. Since the information in this collection is arranged in pairs, the normal way of stepping through a collection using `for each` will not work. Instead, we have to use the `Length` and `Item` properties that every collection provides. `Length` tells us how many items are in the collection, and `Item` lets us retrieve a specified item from the collection. The following sample script uses this technique to display your computer's current network drive mappings:

```
set wshNetwork = CreateObject("WScript.Network") ' create network helper object

set maps = wshNetwork.EnumNetworkDrives  ' get collection describing mappings
for i = 0 to maps.Length-2 step 2        ' step through collection by twos
    wscript.echo "Drive", maps.item(i), "is mapped to", maps.item(i+1)
next
```

When I put this script into file `showmaps.vbs` and typed the command **cscript showmaps.vbs**, the output looked like this:

```
Drive M: is mapped to \\server\officefiles
Drive S: is mapped to \\server\email
Drive W: is mapped to \\server\inetpub
```

The `WScript.Network` object also lets you create and delete drive mappings. You might want to do this in a script that has to run a program that depends on a particular network drive letter. The script can use `EnumNetworkDrives` to see if the drive mapping already exists, and if it does not, it can create the mapping.

To create a drive mapping we can use `WScript.Network`'s `MapNetworkDrive` method. This method takes three arguments:

`drive_letter`	A string, the drive letter to map.
`path`	A string, the UNC path to the shared folder you want to use. For example, `"\\server\officefiles"`.
`update_profile`	A Boolean value. If True, the mapping will be saved in your user profile so that it will be re-created the next time you log on. If False, the mapping will not be saved.

We have to consider that the drive we want to use may already be mapped to another network share. In this case, before we can establish the desired mapping we have to delete the current one. We can use the `RemoveNetworkDrive` method, which also takes three arguments:

`drive_letter`	A string, the drive letter to delete.
`force`	A Boolean value. If True, the mapping is deleted even if another application is using the drive. If False, the mapping will not be deleted if the drive is in use; instead the script will stop with an error message.
`update_profile`	A Boolean value. If True, the mapping is removed from your user profile so that it won't be reestablished the next time you log on. If False, the mapping will be deleted now, but will not be deleted from your profile.

Here is a script that uses these methods to ensure that drive letter M: is mapped to \\server\officefiles:

```
required_drive = "M:"                              ' drive letter we need
required_path  = "\\server\officefiles"            ' network path that we need

set wshNetwork = CreateObject("WScript.Network") ' create network helper object

is_mapped  = False    ' this will be set True if the drive is already mapped
is_correct = False    ' this will be set True if the mapping is already correct

set maps = wshNetwork.EnumNetworkDrives   ' get collection describing mappings
for i = 0 to maps.Length-2 step 2         ' step through collection by twos
                                          ' is this the drive we're looking for?
    if ucase(maps.item(i)) = ucase(required_drive) then
        is_mapped = True                      ' yes: drive is already mapped
                                              ' mapped to the correct path?
        if ucase(maps.item(i+1)) =  ucase(required_path) then
            is_correct = True                 ' yes: mapping is already correct
        end if

        exit for    ' no need to look at any more drives; break out of the loop
    end if
next

if not is_correct then                    ' if drive mapping is not set up
    if is_mapped then                     ' if currently mapped, delete old mapping
        wshNetwork.RemoveNetworkDrive required_drive, True, True
    end if                                ' now, map drive to desired share
    wshNetwork.MapNetworkDrive required_drive, required_path, True
end if

' Now, at this point we can be sure that the drive is
' mapped to \\server\officefiles
```

The WScript.Network object can also manage icons for network printers in your Printers and Faxes folder. The three most useful methods for this purpose are

- AddWindowsPrinterConnection—Installs a network printer icon
- RemovePrinterConnection—Deletes a network printer icon
- SetDefaultPrinter—Sets a network printer to be the user's default printer

In the most basic usage, these three methods take as their argument the UNC share name of a network printer.

Here's an example script that installs an icon for the printer \\sumatra\EpsonColor:

```
set wshNetwork = CreateObject("WScript.Network")
wshNetwork.AddWindowsPrinterConnection "\\sumatra\epsoncolor"
```

Unlike local printers, which once installed are available to all users on the computers, network printers are installed per-user. To ensure that every user automatically received the same set of network printer icons, you could use the AddWindowsPrinterConnection and

`SetDefaultPrinter` methods in a logon script to install appropriate printers based on logon name, location or other attributes.

NOTE

On an Active Directory domain network, you can also force printer installation through Group Policy. On a small workgroup network, it is probably sufficient to let Windows automatically locate all shared network printers.

WScript OBJECT

The WScript object is predefined by Windows Script Host; that is, there is a predefined variable named wscript that you can use in your scripts without having to use CreateObject.

Here are a few examples of ways you can use the WScript object in your scripts.

The WScript.Sleep method pauses your script for some number of milliseconds. You can use this if you wrote a script whose job it was to email any files that were dragged into a particular network folder. This script would run constantly waiting for work to do, but to keep it from bogging down the computer on which it's run, you could use Sleep to make it run only every 30 seconds:

```
' script to scan for files in the shared folder \\server\workfolder

set fso = CreateObject("Scripting.FileSystemObject")
do while True
    set files = fso.GetFolder("\\server\workfolder").Files
    for each file in files
        commands that would process then move or delete each files found
        .
        .
        .
    next
    wscript.Sleep 30000      ' pause 30 seconds to wait for more files to appear
loop
```

The WScript.Quit method exits the script immediately. You can use this method to stop the script if a problem is encountered and you don't want the script program to go on. You can specify a numeric *exit status* if you want, which is useful if you run the script from a batch file and want to signal the problem to the batch file. Here is an example of using Quit:

```
' script to copy all files from the floppy disk to the hard disk

set fso = CreateObject("Scripting.FileSystemObject") ' create helper object

if not fso.GetDrive("A:").IsReady then               ' if drive is not OK
    MsgBox "There is no disk in the floppy drive"    ' pop up warning message
    wscript.Quit 2                             ' and terminate script with errorlevel 2
end if

for each file in fso.GetFolder("A:\").Files          ' scan each file on drive
    fso.CopyFile file.FullPath, "C:\incoming files"  ' copy each to c: drive
next
```

WScript also gives you access to the command-line arguments used when your script was run; that is, the items placed on the command line after the name of the script file. I'll discuss command-line arguments later in the chapter.

SYSTEM OBJECTS

Objects pervade Windows. In addition to those I mentioned in the previous section, the ones provided with Windows Script Host, many Windows services and applications use objects to expose their internal functions and data. In this section, I'll give a few illustrations of how these objects can help you automate your processing and management tasks.

THE CDO MESSAGING (EMAIL) OBJECTS

Windows XP comes with a set of objects collectively called the *Collaboration Data Objects*, or *CDO*. CDO objects can be used to send email from scripts, with text and HTML formatted messages and file attachments. Here are a few reasons you might want to send email from a script:

- To automate your workflow; you can drag files onto a desktop script to automatically mail them to a colleague
- To report the results of scripts that are run unattended by the Task Scheduler
- To distribute the results of scripts that generate reports, such as disk-space utilization summaries for all users on a network

CDO is fairly complex and there's not enough room here to describe its ins and outs. However, I can show you a script that sends an email to a specific person, containing as attachments every file named on the script's command line. You might use this to forward completed documents to a coworker. With a shortcut to this script on your desktop, all you have to do is drag and drop your documents onto the shortcut to send the files on. If you want to use this script, you'll have to change the names of the sender and recipient, and change the name of the SMTP mail server to the one used on your network.

```
' mailfiles.vbs - mails files named on command line (or dragged onto
' shortcut) to the specified user.

if WScript.arguments.count <= 0 then        ' no files were specified
    MsgBox "Usage: mailfiles filename..., or drag files onto shortcut"
    WScript.quit 0
end if

const cdoSendUsingPort = 2                   ' standard CDO constants
const cdoAnonymous     = 0

sender     = "brian@mycompanyxyz.com"        ' sender of message
recipient  = "sheila@mycompanyxyz.com"       ' recipient of this message
mailserver = "mail.mycompanyxyz.com"         ' name of SMTP server

set msg  = CreateObject("CDO.Message")       ' create objects
set conf = CreateObject("CDO.Configuration")
set msg.configuration = conf
```

```
With msg                                ' build the message
    txt = ""
    nfiles = 0                          ' count of files attached
    for each arg in WScript.arguments   ' treat each argument as a
        .AddAttachment arg              ' file to be attached
        txt    = txt & vbCRLF & arg     ' list filename in message text too
        nfiles = nfiles+1
    next
    if nfiles = 1 then plural = "" else plural = "s"
    .to       = recipient               ' address the letter
    .from     = sender
    .subject  = nfiles & " File" & plural & " for you"
    .textBody = "File" & plural & " attached to this message:" & vbCRLF & txt
End With

prefix = "http://schemas.microsoft.com/cdo/configuration/"
With conf.fields                        ' set delivery options
    .item(prefix & "sendusing")         = cdoSendUsingPort
    .item(prefix & "smtpserver")        = mailserver
    .item(prefix & "smtpauthenticate")  = cdoAnonymous
.update                                 ' commit changes
End With
on error resume next    ' do not stop on errors
msg.send                ' deliver the message
errn = err.number       ' remember error status
on error goto 0         ' restore normal error handling

if errn > 0 then        ' report results with a message box
    MsgBox "Error sending message"
else
    MsgBox "Sent " & nfiles & " file" & plural & " to " & recipient
    ' (future development: at this point it might be useful to have
    ' the script move the files to an "already sent" folder)
end if
```

WINDOWS MANAGEMENT INSTRUMENTATION

Windows Management Instrumentation or *WMI* is a system service that provides objects that represent every aspect of a Windows computer system, from the hardware components up to the highest level system services. Some of these objects, like the ones that describe system hardware, are informational only: They have properties that describe the system, but you can't change the information. Other objects can be used to manage the system. You can use WMI to start and stop system services, monitor and stop applications, create drive mappings, share folders, and, with the appropriate updated WMI drivers installed, even manage system services such as Internet Information Services, Microsoft Exchange, and the Domain Name service on Windows 200x Server.

WMI is complex and takes a bit of getting used to. If you are a network or system manager, however, it's worth getting to know, as it can help you automate many time-consuming monitoring, installation, and maintenance tasks.

Here are three examples of WMI scripts. The first is called shownetconfig.vbs. It lists each of the network adapters in your computer and shows their IP addresses information. If you

29

add a computer name or names to the command line, this script will list the information for other computers on your network. (However, this will often not work unless you are on a domain network and have administrator privileges.)

```
' display network adapter TCP/IP configuration of any computer on the LAN
' Usage: shownetconfig [computername ...]

set loc = CreateObject("WBemScripting.SWbemLocator") ' create WMI helper object

if wscript.Arguments.Length = 0 then   ' if no arguments on command line
    check "localhost"                   ' examine computer running the script
else                                    ' otherwise
    for each name in wscript.Arguments  ' check each name on command line
        check name
    next
end if


' subroutine "check" displays the network adapters and IP address info for
' the computer whose name is passed in the argument 'name'

sub check (name)
    wscript.echo
    wscript.echo "Network adapters on " & name & ":"

    on error resume next                ' don't quit script if error occurs
                                        ' get WMI network adapter objects
    set adapters = GetObject("winmgmts:{impersonationlevel=impersonate," &_
        "authenticationlevel=pkt}!" &_
        "//" & name & "/root/CIMV2:Win32_NetworkAdapterConfiguration")

    errno = err.number                  ' get error information, if any
    msg   = err.description
    on error goto 0                     ' go back to normal stop-on-error

    if errno <> 0 then                  ' if there was an error, print info
        wscript.echo "Connect to", name, "failed"
        wscript.echo msg
        exit sub                        ' and quit working on this computer
    end if

    for each card in adapters.Instances_    ' list info for each adapter
        if card.IPEnabled and not isnull(card.IPAddress) then
            wscript.echo " ", card.Caption  ' print adapter make/model

            for each addr in card.IPAddress ' list IP addresses (1 or more)
                wscript.echo "    IP Addr ", addr
            next
            for each addr in card.DefaultIPGateway  ' and gateway address(es)
                wscript.echo "    Gateway ", addr
            next                        ' and MAC address
            wscript.echo "    MAC Addr", card.MACAddress
            wscript.echo
        end if
    next
end sub                                 ' end of subroutine
```

On my computer, the output of this script looks like this:

```
Network adapters on localhost:
  [00000001] SMC EZ Card 10/100 PCI (SMC1211TX)
    IP Addr   192.168.0.101
    Gateway   192.168.0.1
    MAC Addr  00:FF:12:34:0E:14
```

NOTE
> Due to to a bug in WMI, this script can fail with an error message if your computer is sharing its Internet connection and the connection is not up.

The second sample WMI script lists the status of each system service installed on your computer. This script file can be named showservices.vbs.

```
set services = GetObject("winmgmts:{impersonationlevel=impersonate," &_
      "authenticationlevel=pkt}!" &_
      "/root/CIMV2:Win32_Service")      ' get services WMI info

for each svc in services.Instances_       ' display information for each service
    wscript.echo svc.name, "State:", svc.State, "Startup:", svc.StartMode
next
```

On my computer, the first few lines of output from this script look like this:

```
Alerter State: Running Status: OK Startup: Auto
ALG State: Stopped Status: OK Startup: Manual
AppMgmt State: Stopped Status: OK Startup: Manual
Ati HotKey Poller State: Stopped Status: OK Startup: Auto
AudioSrv State: Running Status: OK Startup: Auto
```

As a final example, this script locates all running instances of the Windows Notepad program and terminates them.

```
set processes = GetObject("winmgmts:").ExecQuery(_
    "select * from Win32_Process where Name='notepad.exe'")

for each process in processes    ' scan objects representing Notepad instances
    process.Terminate            ' and terminate each instance
next
```

You can see that this is powerful medicine, but it can be exceptionally useful if you are developing or testing software applications.

Active Directory Scripting Interface (ADSI)

ADSI provides a way to view and administer the Windows Active Directory on a domain network. Like WMI, it's a complex yet rich programming tool that lets you manage the most complex networks using scripting tools. At the end of this chapter under "Getting More Information" I'll list some ADSI scripting resources.

APPLICATIONS (FOR EXAMPLE, WORD)

Many Windows applications provide objects that you can use from scripts. As I mentioned earlier in the chapter, Microsoft Office applications such as Word and Excel use a scripting language that is very similar to VBScript. And, in fact, you can start to manipulate Microsoft Office applications from VBScript just as easily as you can using these applications' macro facilities.

For example, this script lists the entire contents of your C: drive, formatting the listing into an Excel spreadsheet:

```
' script to list all of the files on the C drive into a spreadsheet

set fso    = CreateObject("Scripting.FileSystemObject") ' create helper object

set excel     = CreateObject("Excel.Application")        ' open instance of Excel
excel.visible = True                                      ' make it visible
set workbook  = excel.Workbooks.Add                       ' create empty workbook
set worksheet = workbook.Worksheets("sheet1")             ' and select a worksheet

nfiles = 0                                                ' we have no files yet
list fso.GetFolder("C:\")                                 ' list contents of C:

totalrow = nfiles+2                                       ' total the file sizes
worksheet.Cells(totalrow, 1).Value     = "Total"
worksheet.Cells(totalrow, 1).Font.Bold = True
worksheet.Cells(totalrow, 2).Value     = "=sum(B1:B" & ltrim(str(nfiles)) & ")"
worksheet.Cells(totalrow, 2).Font.Bold = True

set worksheet = nothing             ' release the worksheet
set workbook  = nothing             ' and the workbook
set excel     = nothing             ' release Excel but leave it running


' -------------------------------------------------------------------
' subroutine to list the contents of a specific folder.
' The files inside are placed into the excel spreadsheet
' and all subfolders are listed as well
' -------------------------------------------------------------------

sub list (folder)
    on error resume next            ' if there is a permissions error,
                                    ' just ignore the file or folder

    for each file in folder.Files        ' scan all of the files first
        nfiles = nfiles + 1                  ' count one new file
        worksheet.Cells(nfiles, 1).Value = file.Path   ' put name in column 1
        worksheet.Cells(nfiles, 2).Value = file.size   ' put size in column 2
    next

    for each subfolder in folder.Subfolders        ' then scan each subfolder
        list subfolder
    next
end sub
```

This script shows how you can mix the functions of Windows Script Host and other applications. You could extend this concept and, for instance, use WMI to automatically produce a spreadsheet of all network adapter information on your network.

As another example, in my consulting work I recently had a need to automatically convert Microsoft Word documents to Rich Text Format (RTF). To do this, I wrote the following script, which examines an input folder and for each Word document (.doc file) it finds, it creates a corresponding .RTF file in an output folder, if one does not already exist.

```
indir  = "C:\documents\in"                          ' directory for .DOC files
outdir = "C:\documents\out"                         ' directory for .RTF files

const wdFormatRTF = 6                               ' save format constant

set fso = CreateObject("Scripting.FileSystemObject") ' create helper object
set oWord = Nothing                                 ' no instance of Word yet

for each file in fso.GetFolder(indir).Files         ' scan the input folder
    docfile = file.Path                             ' get full pathname
    extn = lcase(fso.GetExtensionName(docfile))     ' and get extension

    if extn = "doc" then                            ' if this is a .doc file,
                                                    ' build .rtf filename
        rtffile = fso.BuildPath(outdir, fso.GetBasename(docfile)) & ".rtf"

        if not fso.FileExists(rtffile) then         ' if rtf file doesn't
                                                    ' exist yet, make it
            Wscript.Echo " ... converting", docfile, "to rtf"

            if oWord is Nothing then   ' if Word not running yet, start it
                set oWord = CreateObject("Word.Application")
                oWord.Visible = True   ' probably best to make it visible
            end if

            ' manipulate Word into saving our file as RTF
            oWord.Documents.Open docfile            ' open file, save as RTF
            oWord.ActiveDocument.SaveAs rtffile, wdFormatRTF, False, "", False
            oWord.ActiveDocument.Close False        ' close
        end if
    end if
next

if not oWord is Nothing then                        ' if we started a copy of Word
    oWord.Quit                                      ' close it
    set oWord = Nothing                             ' and release the object
end if
```

With the script, I simply drag documents into the folder C:\documents\in, double-click the script's icon, and the RTF files magically appear in C:\documents\out. Now, converting Word documents into RTF might not be something you have to do every day, but if you had to convert a few hundred of them a day as I did, a script like this saves hours of time.

EXECUTING SCRIPTS

After creating a script file, you can run it by double-clicking the file in Windows Explorer, or through a shortcut to the script file. But Windows being what it is, you may suspect that there are at least a half dozen other ways to do the same thing. Indeed, there are.

You can also run scripts from the command line by typing the base name of the script file, without the file extension. For example, after creating the sample script that I discussed earlier in the chapter, you can type `hello` at the command prompt, and Windows will run the script.

WINDOWED VERSUS COMMAND-LINE SCRIPTS

At this point, I need to explain that there are two versions of Windows Script Host: a "windowed" version named `wscript`, and a command-prompt version named `cscript`. The main difference between the two is how messages from the script are displayed to you. The windowed version displays messages through pop-up dialog boxes, as shown in Figure 29.2. The command-line version displays text in the Command Prompt window, as shown in Figure 29.7.

Figure 29.7
The command-line version of Windows Script Host displays output in the Command Prompt window.

```
C:\Documents and Settings\bknittel>cscript hello.vbs
Hello, this message comes from a script

C:\Documents and Settings\bknittel>
```

NOTE

> For more advanced script programmers, the command-line version can read from the standard input and write to the standard output, so scripts run with cscript can be used with redirection and pipes.

For the most part, you can use either version to run your scripts. The windowed version `wscript` is nice when you've created a script that does most of its work silently, and only displays a message when it finishes or runs into trouble. For most scripting work, however, the command-line version is more useful.

It's cumbersome to type `wscript` and `cscript` every time you want to run a script, so you can tell Windows which version to use whenever you type a command line containing just the script's filename, or when you double-click a script file icon. To do this, open a command-prompt window and type one of the following two commands:

`cscript //H:cscript`   To make `cscript` the default script processor

`cscript //H:wscript`   To make `wscript` the default processor

Afterward, when you run a script without specifying `wscript` or `cscript` explicitly, Windows will use the selected version.

COMMAND-LINE ARGUMENTS

When you write scripts to do a job such as emailing files or adding user accounts, you'll have to tell the script which files to mail, or what username to add. You could build this sort of information into the script, but you'd have to change the script every time you wanted to change the names of the files, or user, or whatever.

Instead, you can write your script in such a way that it gets the names of the things it's to work on through the command line. For example, I might write a user-account script so that I could type a command like

```
makeuser jsmith elee mfritz
```

to instruct the script to create three user accounts with the given names. These bits of data—specified at the moment that you run the script—are called *command-line arguments*. You can specify command-line arguments by typing directly at the command prompt, or you can enter them in the "Target" field of a shortcut to a script, as shown in Figure 29.8.

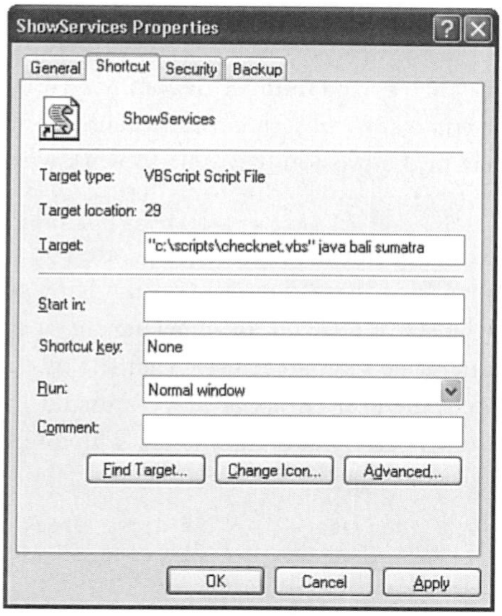

Figure 29.8
You can add com-
mand-line arguments
to a shortcut's defini-
tion.

TIP

If you create a shortcut to a script file on your desktop, Windows will let you drag file icons and drop them onto the script shortcut. Windows will then run the script with the dropped file name or names added as command-line arguments. You can use this to great advantage, for example, if you use scripts to email files to a coworker, move files to a special folder, or whatever else you need to do with files on a regular basis. It's very convenient.

The command-line arguments used when you start a script are made available through properties of the predefined object variable wscript. Its property Arguments is a collection that contains all of the command-line arguments. This collection itself has two properties of interest to us here: Length and Item. The Length property tells how many command-line arguments were specified when the user started the script. The Item property lets you retrieve individual arguments by number, starting with 0, up to Length-1. Here is a sample script that you can use to see how command-line arguments work:

```
wscript.echo "Number of arguments:", wscript.Arguments.Length

for i = 0 to wscript.Arguments.Length-1
    wscript.echo "Argument #", i, "-", wscript.Arguments.Item(i)
next
```

If you put this into a file named, for example, showargs.vbs and type the following command at the command prompt

```
showargs "first argument" second third
```

the output is

```
Number of arguments: 3
Argument # 0 - first argument
Argument # 1 - second
Argument # 2 - third
```

You can write your scripts that require a fixed number of command-line arguments which each have a specific meaning, or you can write scripts that accept a variable number of arguments, and use a loop like the one in the previous example to work with however many were entered.

If you write a script that uses command-line arguments, there are two things you can do to make life easier for the script users. First, have the script verify that a sensible number of arguments were specified when the script was run, by checking the .Length property. If the number isn't reasonable, print a message telling the user what she or he should have entered, and stop the script. Also, if the user enters /? as a command-line argument, do the same thing. Suppose a script requires exactly two arguments. The following sample script shows a good way to check for correct usage.

```
if wscript.Arguments.Length <> 2 then usage     ' if not 2 args, print error msg
if wscript.Arguments.Item(0) = "/?" then usage ' likewise if first arg is /?

   .
   .
   .

(rest of script uses wscript.Arguments.Item(0) and
wscript.Arguments.Item(1) for some purpose)

   .
   .
   .
```

```
' subroutine "usage" prints the correct command line syntax & stops the script
sub usage
    wscript.echo "Usage: myscript filename1 filename2"
    wscript.echo
    wscript.echo "Filename1 is the name of the file we want to process"
    wscript.echo "Filename2 is the name of the file we will create"
    wscript.quit
end sub
```

In this example, there is a script subroutine at the bottom of the script file that displays the correct command-line usage and the halts the script. If any part of the script determines that there is something wrong with the arguments, using the name usage as a VBScript command will run the subroutine and show the user what he or she should have typed. This is the way that most Windows command-line programs work, and it's good style to make your scripts behave the same way. Here's what it looks like in the Command Prompt window in use:

```
C:\Documents and Settings\bknittel>myscript /?
Usage: myscript filename1 filename2

Filename1 is the name of the file we want to process
Filename2 is the name of the file we will create
```

MAKING SCRIPTS AVAILABLE

If you want to make your Windows-based scripts convenient to use (those scripts that you want to run with wscript, or those that create no output), you can put shortcuts to them on your desktop or in your Start menu. If you want to make shortcuts available to everyone who uses your computer, follow these steps:

1. Put the script files in a folder that is available to everyone, such as C:\Documents and Settings\All Users\Scripts.

2. Right-click the Start button, and select Explore. Locate \Documents and Settings\All Users\Start Menu\Programs.

3. Create a folder named Scripts inside Programs, and open that folder.

4. Create shortcuts to the script files into the Scripts folder, or drag them in from elsewhere.

Once you've created a script shortcut, you can edit to make it explicit that you want to run the script with wscript or cscript. To do this, follow these steps:

1. Right-click the shortcut and select Properties.

2. Click in the Target field, and press the Home key to move the cursor to the beginning of the filename.

3. Type cscript or wscript, followed by a space, as shown in Figure 29.9. You may also change the default directory, if desired.

Figure 29.9
Add `cscript` or
`wscript` before the
shortcut Target name
to explicitly run a
script in console or
windowed mode.

> **Shortcut to test.vbs Properties**
>
> General | Shortcut | Compatibility | Security | Backup
>
> Shortcut to test.vbs
>
> Target type: Application
>
> Target location: system32
>
> Target: wscript "C:\Documents and Settings\bknittel\test
>
> Start in: "C:\Documents and Settings\bknittel.JAVA"
>
> Shortcut key: None
>
> Run: Normal window
>
> Comment:
>
> Find Target...   Change Icon...   Advanced...
>
> OK   Cancel   Apply

   4. Click OK to save the changes.

It's a bit of work setting these up, but once you're done, these scripts will be available to anyone simply by clicking Start, All Programs, Scripts.

If you want to share scripts with other users on your network, place the script files in a shared folder. Users can run the scripts by clicking on the icons for these files. It's a bit trickier making shortcuts to files on the network. Unless you are positive that everyone will have the same drive letter mapped to the same shared folder, you need to create shortcuts to these files using full UNC paths, for example `\\bali\shared_scripts\cleandisk.vbs`. It's best if you create these shortcuts once, and place *them* in a shared folder that other people can drag to their Start menu or desktop, rather than asking each person to try to make the shortcuts themselves (their success rate usually turns out to be fairly low).

If you want to be able to execute scripts from the Command Prompt window, in any folder you happen to be working with, you should put your scripts in a folder that is in the Windows PATH list. This is a list of folders that Windows searches whenever you type a command's name. I suggest that you create a folder specifically for scripts, and then add this folder to the PATH.

If you want to create scripts for your own use, but not make them available to other people who use your computer, follow these steps.

   1. Create a private folder for command-line scripts in your profile folder, which is usually named something like `C:\Documents and Settings\`*YourUserName*. I created a folder named `C:\Documents and Settings\bknittel\scripts`.

   2. Click Start, right-click My Computer, and select Properties.

3. Select the Advanced tab and click Environment Variables.

4. In the *top* pane, if there is not a line labeled Path, click the upper New button, and enter the name Path in the Variable Name box, as shown in Figure 29.10. You can use upper- or lowercase. Then, click inside the Variable Value box and proceed with Step 5.

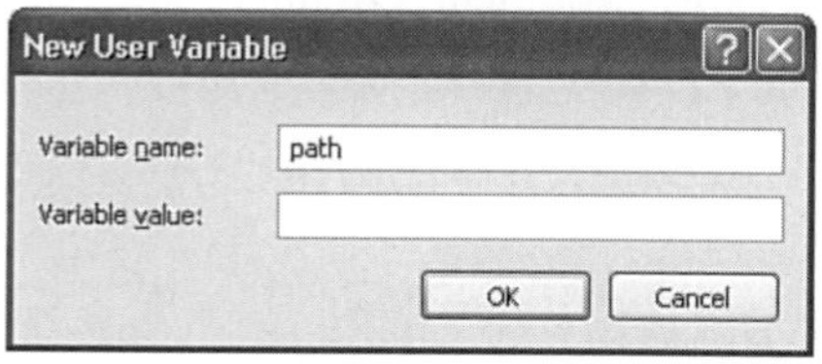

Figure 29.10
Creating a PATH entry.

If there is already an entry labeled Path in the top pane, select it and click Edit. Press the End key to move the cursor to the end of any existing text, and then add a semi-colon, as shown in Figure 29.11.

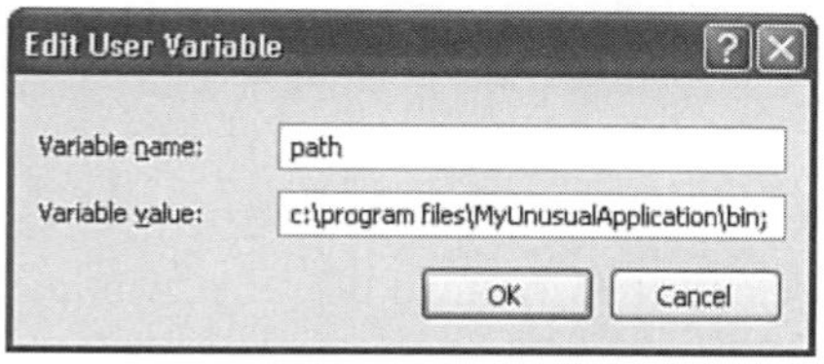

Figure 29.11
Adding a new entry to an existing PATH list.

5. Add the full path to your scripts folder to the variable value, including the drive letter, and enclose it all in quotes. If you have placed it in your profile folder, you can use the shortcut `"%USERPROFILE%\scripts"`, as shown in Figure 29.12.

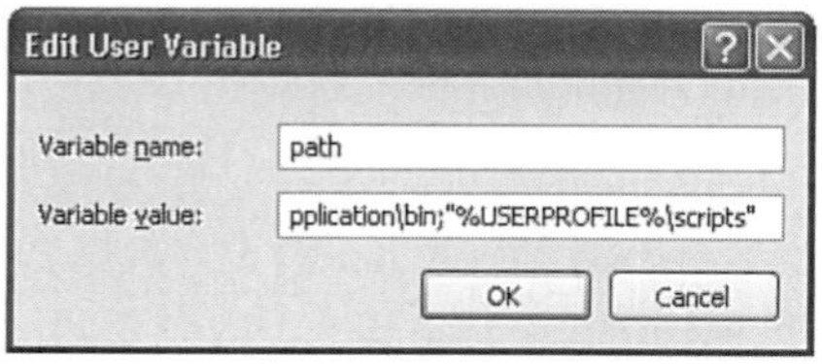

Figure 29.12
Adding a script folder name to the path.

6. Click OK, and then OK again to close the dialogs.

Now, whenever you open a new Command Prompt window, Windows will be able to locate your script files by name.

Alternatively, if you want to make the scripts available to everyone who uses your computer, follow these steps instead:

29

1. Create a public folder for command-line scripts, for example, `C:\program files\ scripts`.
2. Log on as a Computer Administrator user.
3. Click Start, right-click My Computer, and select Properties.
4. Select the Advanced tab and click Environment Variables.
5. In the *bottom* pane, select the line labeled Path and click Edit.
6. Press the End key to move the cursor to the end of the existing text, add a semicolon, and then the full path to your scripts folder including the drive letter, all closed in quotes, as shown in Figure 29.13. Click OK, and then OK again to close the dialogs.

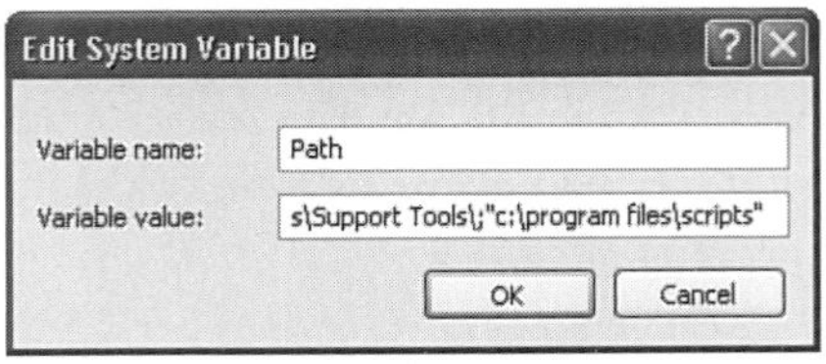

Figure 29.13
Adding a folder to the system Path.

Edit System Variable

Variable name: Path

Variable value: s\Support Tools\;"c:\program files\scripts"

7. Log off and back on.

Now, whenever you or anyone else opens a Command Prompt window, Windows will be able to locate script files stored in the public folder. For example, if you move the sample script `hello.vbs` that I discussed earlier in the chapter into the scripts folder, you can open a command-prompt window and type **hello**. This is very useful with scripts that, for example, scan the current directory and delete temporary files.

DEBUGGING SCRIPTS

Even for an experienced programmer, the chances of having a script work correctly the first time that it is run are amazingly small. Finding out what's wrong with a buggy program is more art than science, but if you enjoy puzzles, it can actually be the most fun part of programming.

The easiest way to debug a problematic script is to watch what is going on inside the script as it runs. You can do this with a tool called a *debugger*, a program that displays the contents of a script program as it runs, lets you start and stop the script or step through it line-by-line, and lets you view the values stored in variables.

As installed, Windows XP doesn't come with a debugger. If you have installed Microsoft Visual InterDev or .NET Studio, then an "Active Debugger" was installed as part of that package. I won't describe those tools here, as if you have them, you are probably already very familiar with them.

If you don't have a Microsoft development product, and you plan on writing scripts, you should download the free Windows Script Debugger. Visit `msdn.microsoft.com/scripting`, select Downloads in the left column, and select Microsoft Windows Script Debugger. (You'll have to be logged on as a Computer Administrator to install this.)

Once the debugger is installed, you can step through a script by running the `cscript` or `wscript` command with `//X` as the first command-line argument. For example, here is the command to debug the script `bad.vbs`.

```
cscript //X bad.vbs
```

You'll see a window like the one shown in Figure 29.14.

Figure 29.14
The Windows Script Debugger displays the contents of your script as it runs.

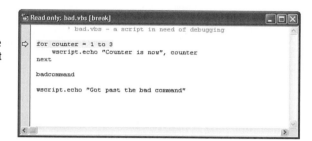

As the script runs, a yellow pointer shows the script statement that is next to be processed. In the figure, because I've just started the debugger, the pointer is on the first actual script command after the comment and blank line.

Now, you can walk your script through its paces one step at a time, or you can tell it to run ahead to a particular point and stop. Although you can use the debugger's menus to do this, you'll find it much easier to use if you learn the keyboard shortcuts listed in Table 29.7.

TABLE 29.7 WINDOWS SCRIPT DEBUGGER FUNCTION KEYS

Key	Action
F8	Steps the script ahead one statement at a time. If the script calls a script subroutine or function, the debugger will "step into" the subprogram and stop at its first line.
Shift+F8	Similar to F8 but "steps over" any subroutines or functions.
F9	Click the cursor in any of the script's program lines and press F9 to set or clear a *breakpoint* in the line. A breakpoint stops the program in its tracks when the program reaches the marked line. This is very useful if you want to see what happens at a certain point in the program and don't want to step to that point one line at a time—just set a breakpoint and press F5.
F5	Lets the program run ahead full speed until it either ends, encounters a serious error, or encounters a breakpoint.
Ctrl+Shift+F8	If the program is inside a script subroutine for function, this shortcut lets the script run until the current subprogram returns.

29

Besides letting you step through your script, the debugger also lets you view and modify the contents of variables inside the script. This is the debugger's most valuable feature. Click View, Command Window to display the command window, as shown in Figure 29.15.

Figure 24.15
The Command Window lets you view and alter variables, and execute subprograms manually.

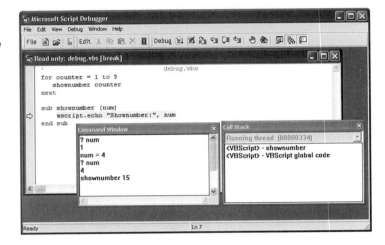

The Command window lets you do three things to help you debug your program:

■ You can display the value of any variable by typing a question mark followed by the variable name and the Enter key. In Figure 29.15, I requested the value of variable `num`, and the debugger displayed `1`.

■ You can alter the value of a variable by typing an assignment statement, as you can see in the figure where I changed the value of `num` from 1 to 4. You can use this ability when your script has made a mistake and you'd like to continue debugging. While you can't fix the program itself while the debugger is running, you may be able to get a bit more information out of your debugging session by correcting the variables and continuing.

■ You can call any subroutine, function, object method, or property by typing an appropriate program statement. Use ? to call and display function values; for example ? `mid("ABC",2)`. To call subroutines, just type the subroutine name and any arguments, as shown in Figure 29.15. In the figure, I called subroutine `shownumber` with argument `num = 15`.

BATCH FILES

While Windows Script Host is the most powerful tool for creating your own helpful programs, it's also useful to know how to use the batch file language. Batch files let you take advantage of the hundreds of command-line programs supplied with Windows. While the batch file language is less powerful than VBScript, it has variables, primitive functions, and rudimentary flow-of-control commands, so it does qualify as a programming language.

A batch file, at the very simplest level, is just a list of command-prompt commands typed into a file whose extension is .BAT or .CMD. When you enter the name of a batch file at the command prompt, Windows looks for a file with this name in the current directory and in the folders of the search PATH that I discussed earlier under "Making Scripts Available." Then, it treats each of the lines in the batch file as a command, and runs it as if you'd typed the commands by hand. At this simplest level, then, a batch file can be a big help if you find yourself typing the same commands over and over.

BATCH FILE BASICS

On every computer I own, I make a folder named `c:\bat` to hold my batch files and scripts, and I put this folder in the PATH. Since this folder is in the PATH, any script or batch file in it is available whenever I'm using a Command Prompt window.

Since I use the Command Prompt window a lot, I also like to make batch files with one- or two-letter names, which contain commonly used commands.

For example, if I'm working for a client named "XYZ Corporation" and I have this client's files in a folder named `d:\data\xyz project`, I'll probably have a frequent need to have a Command Prompt window open in this folder. So, I'll create a batch file named `c:\bat\xyz.bat` with this one line inside:

```
cd /d "d:\data\xyz project"
```

(Adding `/d` to the `cd` command sets both the current drive and the current directory.) Now, whenever I open a Command Prompt window, I can type `xyz`, and Windows will instantly switch to the right drive and directory. This may sound trivial, but it's a real timesaver.

Another command I use frequently is one to test whether my network's DSL connection is working correctly. Whenever I run into an Internet glitch, I find myself typing the command

```
ping 65.104.11.1
```

which tests the "gateway" address for my Internet service provider—if the ping command can reach this address, it means that my Internet connection is working, and any connectivity problems must be out there on the Internet. This command went into the file `c:\bat\dsl.bat`; now I can just type `dsl` to instantly test my line without having to go look up that darned number.

Of course, batch files can contain more than one command, but the principle remains the same: If you find yourself entering the same command or sequence of commands over and over, put them into a batch file to save wear and tear on your fingers.

Batch files become even more useful when you start using command-line arguments. Anything you type on the command line after the name of the batch file can be used to insert filenames and so on into the commands in your batch file. Anywhere that `%1` appears in a batch file, the characters `%1` are replaced with the first extra word on the command line. Likewise, `%2` gets replaced with the second argument on the command line, and so on.

For example, if I created a batch file named `bf.bat` with this line inside:

```
notepad c:\bat\%1.bat
```

and then typed

```
bf ibm
```

at the command prompt, Windows would see this as

```
notepad c:\bat\ibm.bat
```

and would run Windows Notepad to edit the file `ibm.bat`. Now I have a batch file that will let me easily edit any batch file in the folder `c:\bat`. It's not exactly rocket science, but you can see that with longer sequences of commands, this can really save time and trouble.

Here are a few other batch file basics:

- Normally, Windows prints out each line of a batch file as it reads through it; this is called *echoing* the commands. It can be ugly. You can suppress echoing of any line in the batch file by starting the line with an at sign (@); this is removed from the command line before it's run.

- You can permanently disable echoing in a batch file with the command `echo off`; this way you don't have to start each command with `@`. But to keep this command from being echoed before it takes effect, you do need to use `@` with just this command. This is why many batch files start with the line `@echo off`.

- Any lines that start with the words `rem` or `remark` are treated as comments, not commands.

- If you have a batch file that isn't doing what you expect it to do, change the batch file's first line to `rem @echo off`. Now, with this command disabled, when you run the batch file, the commands will echo as they're encountered, and you can see where it's going astray. When it's fixed, remove the word `rem` to make it quiet again.

- Wherever they occur in the batch file, the sequences `%1`, `%2`, `%3`, and so on are replaced with the first, second, and third command-line arguments, and so on. You can use this to specify filenames and other information at the time you run the batch file, rather than having this information hard-wired in.

- If the user types fewer command-line arguments than you expect, these command-line substitution sequences are replaced with nothing; that is, they disappear. For example, if you run a batch file with the command `mybatch one two three`, `%3` will be replaced by `three`, but `%4` will silently disappear.

- If you enter the name of an environment variable surrounded by percent signs, Windows replaces this sequence with the value of the environment variable. For example, `%USERNAME%` will be replaced with the logon name of the user running the batch file. (Environment variable names aren't case sensitive, so `%username%` does the same thing.)

- There are many predefined environment variables that can provide information such as the current user's logon name, the current date and time, and the user's home and profile directories. See the Windows Help and Command Center entry titled "Command Shell Overview" for more information.

- There is a way to extract just part of an environment variable or command-line argument. For information and examples, search the Help and Support Center for "Using batch parameters" (view the entry titled "Using Batch Parameters") and "variable substitution" (view the entry titled "For"). The discussion of batch parameter substitution applies to command-line parameters as well as batch parameters. The "For" command page has a section titled "Variable Substitution," which applies to environment variable substitution as well as the for variable.

- If you need to use the percent sign itself in a command, you need to type %% for each one you need, to indicate that you aren't calling for a replacement like the ones mentioned previously. Each %% is replaced with a single %.

If this sounds convoluted, you're catching on. Batch file programming is convoluted and rarely elegant.

> **TIP**
>
> There is a wealth of online documentation about the command prompt environment and commands. After reading this chapter, check out the following Windows Help and Support Center topics:
>
> Command Shell Overview
>
> Environment Variables
>
> Using Batch Parameters
>
> Using Batch Files
>
> Using Command Redirection Operators
>
> Cmd
>
> Command-Line Reference
>
> Then, open a command prompt window and type the following commands
>
> ```
> help cmd
> help set
> help for
> help if
> ```
>
> and so on.

BATCH FILE PROGRAMMING

So far, I've described how you can place simple sequences of commands into a text file that Windows will interpret line by line. The batch file programming language has other constructs that let you perform commands repeatedly and let you test conditions and take different actions depending on the findings. Here they are in a nutshell.

THE SET STATEMENT

The set statement sets environment variables. The basic form is

```
set variable=value
```

where *variable* is the name of the environment variable you wish to set, and *value* is the text you want to assign to the variable. Many environment variables are predefined by Windows (type the command **set** with no argument to see the entire list), and you can define more in your batch files to hold information.

There are two additional ways you can use the set command. If you precede the variable name with /a, the set command treats the *value* part of the command as an arithmetic expression using numbers, environment variable names, and mathematical operators. The numeric result is turned into its text representation. Thus, this batch file

```
set nfiles=0
set /a nfiles=nfiles+1
set /a nfiles=nfiles+1
echo Nfiles = %nfiles%
```

prints

```
Nfiles = 2
```

The command

```
set /p variable=promptstring
```

lets your batch file prompt the user for the value to assign to an environment variable. For example, you can use a statement such as

```
set /p filename=Please enter the filename:
```

to get the name of a file that the batch file is to work with; then, later in the batch file, %filename% will be replaced with whatever the user typed.

> **TIP**
>
> I can't show blank spaces in this book, but you should put a space after the colon at the end of the prompt string; it makes the prompt look better when the script runs.

THE If STATEMENT

The If statement lets you execute commands if some condition is true, and if you want, other commands if the condition is false. The If statement can compare strings, test to see whether files exist, and check the error status reported by the previous program run by the batch file. The basic If statement takes this form:

```
if condition command
```

where *condition* specifies something that can be determined to be true or false; the *command* is run if the condition is true. *Command* can be any command-line statement.

Condition can be one of the following:

exist `filename`

is true if the specified file exists. If the *filename* contains wildcards, the condition is true if any file matches the filename.

not exist `filename`

is true if the specified file does not exist; or if a wildcard is used, if no matching file exists

`string1 == string2`

is true if *string1* exactly matches *string2*. If you are testing to see whether an environment variable or command-line argument matches some specific value, it's best to enclose both strings with some character such as " or / so that, in the event that the environment variable or argument is blank, there will be something present in the `if` statement at the appropriate spot. For example, you can use the statement

`if /%1/ == /debug/ then echo on`

to turn on command echoing in your script. If you don't specify a command-line argument, then the command turns into `if // == /debug/ then echo on`, in which case the two strings are not equal and the `echo on` command is not used. Without the /'s, the command would look like `if == debug then echo on` which is not valid.

`not string1 == string2`

The reverse of `string1 == string2`; the command is run only if the strings are not equal.

`string1 compareop string2`

A more advanced string comparison. `Compareop` can be any of the following words, to perform any of the following comparisons:

EQU	exactly equal
NEQ	not equal
LSS	less than
LEQ	less than or equal to
GTR	greater than
GEQ	greater than or equal to

If both of the strings contain only digits, the comparison is made numerically. Otherwise the comparison is made alphabetically.

`/I string1 compareop string2`

Like `string1 compareop string2`, but the string comparison is not case sensitive. In most cases, you should use `/I` so that your script is not sensitive to the case of filenames or input.

29

Here are more involved versions of the `if` statement that let you execute more than one command, or let you run alternate commands if the condition tested is not true:

```
if condition (command1 && command2 && ...])

if condition (
    command1
    command2
    .
    .
    .
)

if condition (command) else (alternatecommand)

if condition (
    command1
    command2
    .
    .
    .
) else (
    alternatecommand1
    alternatecommand2
    .
    .
    .
)

if condition1 (
    .
    .
    .
) else if condition2 (
    .
    .
    .
) else if condition3 (
    .
    .
    .
) else (
    .
    .
    .
)
```

TIP

> You must be very careful if you use environment variables in multiple-line `if` or `for` statements. All of the lines are read at once, and all environment variables inside % signs are replaced *immediately,* so `set` commands that modify these variables inside the block of command statements will not take effect immediately. If you need to modify and use environment variables inside a group of statements in an `if` or `for` command, place the command `setlocal enabledelayedexpansion` at the top of your batch file, and inside the compound command, enclose environment variable names with exclamation points instead of percent signs, like this:

```
setlocal enabledelayedexpansion
.
.
.
if condition (
    set var=value
    command !var!
)
```

THE Goto STATEMENT

You can use the goto statement to tell Windows to jump to another part of the batch file and start reading commands from that point. The format of the command is

```
goto label
```

which directs Windows to look for a line in the batch file that starts with :label. *Label* can be any word. The special version goto :EOF tells Windows to jump to the end of the batch file, which ends it. (You can also have a batch file stop in its tracks with the command exit /b.)

THE Call STATEMENT

Batch files can contain subroutines, which let you run another batch file or jump down to a label, run a series of commands, and then return to the point that you started. It looks like this:

```
call anotherbatch xxx
call anotherbatch yyy
call anotherbatch zzz
```

This script invokes a different batch file named anotherbatch three times, with different command-line arguments. Inside the called batch file, %1 and the other command-line argument items refer to the arguments on the call command, not the command-line arguments used with the original batch file.

You can use call within the same batch file if you wish. It looks like this:

```
call :mysub xxx
call :mysub yyy
call :mysub zzz
... other batch file commands
goto :EOF

:mysub
... subroutine's batch file commands; use %1 to pick up xxx, yyy and zzz
goto :EOF
```

THE For STATEMENT

The basic for statement repeats a command once for every item that appears in a list. It looks like this:

```
for %%v in (list) do command
```

29

where *v* is a single-letter environment variable that is to be set to the names found in the list; *list* is a list of file or folder names, or even just plain words, separated by spaces or semicolons. If an item in the list contains the characters ? or *, Windows replaces the item with any filenames matching the item using * and ? as wildcards. *Command* is a command to be run once for each item in the list. In *command*, %%v will be replaced with the items. (The % sign has to be doubled up in `for` commands.)

Here's an example. In a batch file

```
for %%v in (a;b;c) do echo %%v
```

will print

```
a
b
c
```

You can have the `for` loop run several commands for each item in the list by using parentheses:

```
for %%v in (list) do (
    command 1
    command 2
    .
    .
    .
    command n
)
```

TIP

> You must to be very careful if you use environment variables in a multiple-line `for` statement. See the note under the `if` command, earlier in this section. Alternatively, have the `for` command call a subroutine, like this:
>
> ```
> for %%v in (list) do call :sub %%v
> .
> .
> .
> goto :EOF
>
> :sub
> echo Working with file %1...
> set var=%1
> .
> .
> .
> ```

On Windows XP, the `for` command has several options that let it automatically scan for directories, step its variable through a range of numeric values (like the `for` statement in VBScript), and more. Also, you can use special characters to indicate that Windows is to extract only part of a filename matched by a `for` statement. For more information, type **help for** at the command prompt, or view the Windows Help and Support Center entry for "Command-Line Reference A-Z"; then select For.

BATCH FILE TIPS

Table 29.8 lists several short batch files that I put on every computer that I use. These short command scripts take advantage of the batch file programming techniques discussed in this chapter, and let me edit files, change the path, view a folder with Explorer, and so on, simply by typing a couple of letters followed by a folder or filename. They don't involve fancy programming, but they can save you a significant amount of time.

TABLE 29.8   USEFUL TINY BATCH FILES

Filename	Contents and Purpose

ap.bat	`@echo off`
	`for %%p in (%path%) do if /%%p/ == /%1/ exit /b`
	`set path=%1;%path%`
	Adds the named folder to the PATH if it is not already listed (lasts only as long as Command Prompt window is open).
	Example: `ap c:\test`

bat.bat	`cd /d c:\bat` Makes `c:\bat` the current directory, when you want to add or edit batch files and scripts. Example: `bat`
bye.bat	`@logout` Logs off from Windows. Example: `bye`
e.bat	`@if /%1/ == // (explorer /e,.) else explorer /e,%1` Opens Windows Explorer in Folder mode to view the named directory, or the current directory if no path is entered on the command line. Example: `e d:`
n.bat	`@start notepad %1` Edits the named file with Notepad. Example: `n myfile.vbs`

COMMAND-LINE MANAGEMENT TOOLS

One of the main reasons people write scripts and batch files is to help maintain and administer Windows and Windows networks. Where Windows Script Host has a host of objects that help you perform management tasks, the batch file language has only command-line programs to work with.

In this section, I'll outline a few of the command-line programs provided with Windows XP that can help you perform routine maintenance and administrative tasks from the command line and from batch files.

TIP

> The Windows 2000 Professional and Windows 2000 Server Resource Kits come with a CD containing almost 200 additional management and maintenance command-line utilities—it's an indispensable tool for Windows XP administrators.

THE net use COMMAND

I discussed the `net` command in Chapter 18, "Using the Network," under "The Net Command," so I won't repeat its description here. Here I'll show you how the `net use` subcommand, which can create and delete network drive mappings, is useful in writing batch files.

I often write small batch files to help move files around on my network; for example, to back up important files, or to publish files on a Web server. I use `net use` in these batch files to make sure that the network drive mappings I need are set up correctly. You can also use `net use` in logon scripts to ensure that required network mappings are made correctly each time users log on.

For example, if a batch file wanted to use drive R: to copy files to a shared folder named `\\bali\officefiles`, you could put the following command in the batch file:

```
net use r: \\bali\officefiles
```

We probably don't want the batch file to continue if the drive mapping can't be made and the `net use` command fails, which might happen if the network server is down. Luckily, the `net` command—like most command-line programs—sets the batch file `errorlevel` to a value of 1 or higher if it can't complete its job, so we can write the command this way, in order to stop the batch file in the event of a problem:

```
if errorlevel 1 (
    echo Unable to create mapping for drive R:, can't proceed
    pause
    exit /b
)
```

However, the `net use` command will also fail if drive R: is already in use when you start the batch file, even if it's connected to the desired shared folder. So, before attempting to create a network mapping, the batch file should delete any preexisting connection with a command like this:

```
net use r: /delete
```

There's one last potential problem: If there was no preexisting drive mapping, *this* command will print an error message. In this case, however, we don't really care if it does, as it's not really a problem. To avoid seeing the error message, we can redirect this command's output to the NUL file—a black hole built into Windows; information written to file NUL is simply discarded. The delete command should be written as

```
net use r: /delete >nul 2>nul
```

to discard messages written to the standard output and to the standard error output. Putting it all together, this is how a batch file should set up a network drive mapping:

```
@echo off
net use r: /delete >nul 2>nul
net use r: \\bali\officefiles
if errorlevel 1 (
    echo Unable to create mapping for drive R:, can't proceed
    pause
    exit /b
)
```

After this, the batch file can use drive R: to copy files at will with programs such as copy, xcopy, or if you have the Windows 2000 Resource Kit, robocopy. Then, at the end, you would probably also want to delete the drive mapping at the end of the batch file, although that is optional.

Here's an actual batch file I use on my network to back up any account's My Documents folder to a network server:

```
@echo off

rem *** set up drive R to point to \\server\backups
net use r: /delete >nul 2>nul
net use r: \\server\backups
if errorlevel 1 (
    echo Unable to create mapping for drive R:, can't proceed
    pause
    exit /b
)

rem *** copy the current user's My Documents folder to the network
rem *** folder, inside subfolders named for this computer and user

set fromfolder="%USERPROFILE\My Documents"
set tofolder="R:\%COMPUTERNAME%\%USERNAME%"

xcopy %fromfolder% %tofolder% /H /K /R /E /D /I /Y

rem *** remove the drive mapping
net use r: /delete
```

THE sc COMMAND

sc is called the Service Controller program, and for good reason. sc can manage just about every aspect of installing, maintaining, and modifying system services and device drivers on local and networked Windows XP computers. It's another command with a huge number of options, which you can list by typing **sc** /?. It has so many options that after printing the /? help information, it prompts you to see whether you want to view additional information about its query and queryex subcommands. Here, I'll focus on how sc is useful in batch files.

The basic format of an sc command is as follows:

sc [*computername*] *command* [*servicename* [*option* …]]

If the *computername* argument is omitted, sc operates on the local computer. There is no provision for entering an alternate username or password, so you'll need to be logged on as Administrator or use the runas command if you want to do more than view the installed services.

LISTING INSTALLED SERVICES

The command sc queryex (or sc *computername* queryex) prints a long list of installed services along with their current status. A typical service listing looks like this:

```
SERVICE_NAME: Dhcp
DISPLAY_NAME: DHCP Client
        TYPE               : 20  WIN32_SHARE_PROCESS
        STATE              : 4   RUNNING
                                 (STOPPABLE,NOT_PAUSABLE,ACCEPTS_SHUTDOWN)
        WIN32_EXIT_CODE    : 0   (0x0)
        SERVICE_EXIT_CODE  : 0   (0x0)
        CHECKPOINT         : 0x0
        WAIT_HINT          : 0x0
        PID                : 844
        FLAGS              :
```

The most useful parts of this listing are detailed in Table 29.9.

TABLE 29.9   USEFUL FIELDS IN THE sc queryex PRINTOUT

Field	Description
SERVICE_NAME	The "short" name for the service. This name can be used with the sc or net command to start and stop the service.
DISPLAY_NAME	The "long" name for the service. This name is displayed in the Services panel in Windows Management.
STATE	The service's current activity state.
PID	The service's process identifier number.

You can add type= driver or type= service (with a space after the equals sign) to the sc queryex command to limit the listing to just drivers or just services.

STARTING AND STOPPING SERVICES

System managers occasionally need to start and stop services for several reasons: to reset a malfunctioning service, to force a service to reinitialize itself with new startup data, or to temporarily stop a service while other services are being maintained. You can manage services using the GUI Windows Management tool, but when you have to perform this sort of task frequently, it's more convenient to use a batch file. For instance, I use a batch file to stop and restart my company's mail server after I make changes to its configuration file. Typing the batch file's name ("downup," in case you're curious) is much easier than navigating through Computer Management.

29

To use sc to start and stop services on a local or remote computer, you must know the service's "short" name. The easiest way to find a service's short name is to use sc queryex to get the listing of all service names, as I described previously. Then, you can put the command

```
sc stop servicename
```

or

```
sc \\computername stop servicename
```

into a batch file to stop a service on the local computer or on a remote computer. Likewise, you can use the command

```
sc start servicename
```

or

```
sc \\computername start servicename
```

to start the service. A stop command followed by a start command is the most useful combination, as it lets you restart the service to recover from a crash or a hung condition. My mail server's downup.bat batch file contains:

```
sc stop SMTPRS
sc stop SMTPDS
sc stop POP3S
sc start SMTPRS
sc start SMTPDS
sc start POP3S
```

which restarts the receiver, delivery, and post office services that are used in my mail system. This is another of those convenience batch files that I discussed earlier; it's must easier to type downup than to spend a minute or two poking at the Services management tool.

NOTE

> sc has many other commands that let you install and configure services as well as interrogate their operational status and dependency lists. The installation commands can be especially useful if you need to deploy services in an enterprise environment.

USING THE TASK SCHEDULER

To save even more time and trouble, you can have Windows run batch files and WSH scripts for you, on a scheduled basis. The Task Scheduler lets you enter commands to be run on an hourly, daily, weekly, or other schedule. You can use scheduling to perform disk cleanups, backups, reports, software installation, or any other task that you want to occur (a) when you're not around, or (b) even if you forget to do it by hand.

29

NOTE

> When a scheduled batch file or script runs, unless you're logged on at the time with the same username as you use to run the scheduled task, you won't see anything on your screen. You won't see any error messages, and you won't be present to type in any information or click on any dialog boxes. So, programs that are to run under the Task Scheduler must be completely debugged, and must require no interaction at all.
>
> To help ensure this, if you are scheduling a Windows Script program, you should explicitly use the `cscript` command. That is, enter the command as `cscript scriptfilename.vbs` rather than just the script file name.

SCHEDULED TASKS

Scheduled Tasks, which I prefer to call the Task Scheduler, is found in the Control Panel and in the Start menu under All Programs, Accessories, System Tools, Scheduled Tasks.

TIP

> The Task Scheduler can not only run a program based on time and date, it can also run scripts or programs when the system boots, when a user (any user) logs on, or when the system is idle. How is this different from putting a script or program in the Startup group for All Users? For one thing, the Task Scheduler lets you specify the security context—the logon name and password—to use for this task. For example, whenever a user logs on, you can have the Scheduled Tasks run a program with Administrator privileges to record information in a protected file.

After you define the tasks to run, the Task Scheduler service sits in the background, checking the computer's system clock, and when a predetermined time for a task rolls around, runs it as though executed by the specified user. The Task Scheduler service automatically starts each time the computer boots. By itself, it does not significantly affect system performance, although the tasks it runs can.

NOTE

> Obviously, the computer has to be up and running in order to run a task, so if you schedule a disk cleanup for 4 a.m., be sure you leave the computer on. If you turn on the system at 4:01 a.m., you'll have missed the execution. The scheduler will not inform you of missed launchings; you'll have to view the information in the Last Run Time column within the Scheduled Tasks window to figure it out for yourself.

SETTING UP A SCHEDULED TASK

To schedule a task, follow these steps:

1. Run Scheduled Tasks by choosing Start, All Programs, Accessories, System Tools, Scheduled Tasks. If you have previously scheduled tasks, they will appear in the list.

2. Click Add Scheduled Task to invoke a wizard that walks you though adding a new task. Click Next to see a list of installed programs (see Figure 29.16). If the program isn't

listed in the resulting list (it won't be if you are scheduling a script or batch file), click the Browse button to find it. For system-related applications, the most likely browse locations are in \windows or \windows\system32. For application programs you've installed, try the Program Files subfolders. For scripts or batch files, browse to the folder in which you stored them.

Figure 29.16
The Scheduled Task Wizard's program selection page.

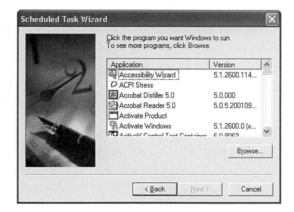

3. Click Next, and choose how often you want the program to run (see Figure 29.17). Click Next again, and then specify applicable time options, such as time of day, as required.

Figure 29.17
The Scheduled Task Wizard's execution schedule page.

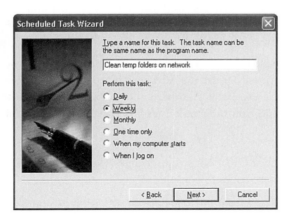

4. Click Next, enter the user name and password to use when running this task (typically, your account, or Administrator). After a username and password are set, another user cannot cancel or delete the task unless that user has the correct permissions. If you are working with a user account without a password, don't type in anything in the password field. If your computer is a member of a domain network, you can enter a username in the form *domainname**username*, or *computername**username*, to use a domain or local account, respectively.

N O T E

If you later change the password of the account you use for a scheduled task, you will have to come back to the Task Scheduler screen, select the task(s), choose Properties, and re-enter the password. Windows doesn't automatically change this for you, and if you forget, you won't be notified—the scheduled task just won't run.

5. Click Next. If you are running an application, script, or batch file that needs command-line arguments, or if you want to set advanced options such as "Don't run if the computer is running on batteries," check Open Advanced Properties for This Task When I Click Finish.

   You should always check this if you're scheduling a Windows Script Host script.

6. Click Finish to close the wizard. The task is then added to the list and will execute at the preassigned time.

If you chose to open the task's advanced properties upon clicking Finish, its dialog box now opens. To open this dialog box manually, open the Scheduled Tasks applet, right-click the task in question, and choose Properties. The three tabs on this dialog box enable you to modify it as follows:

- From the Task tab on the Properties dialog, you can enter command-line arguments for a batch file, script, or other application, and you can select the working directory in which the application is run, as shown in Figure 29.18. You can also disable the task temporarily without completely deleting it by clearing the Enabled check box.

  If you're scheduling a Windows Script Host script, you should insert the word `cscript`, followed by a space, before the script file name, as illustrated in the figure. This will ensure that the script is run using the non-interactive command-line script interpreter.

- Use the Schedule tab to change the task's timing. You can change the scheduled time using the options present, or use the Advanced button to access more advanced scheduling options. There is also a check box that allows you to enable multiple schedules for the task; this would let you run a task Tuesdays at 9:00 and Fridays at 11:00, for instance.

When you're finished, click OK to save your changes. Now that you've established a task, though, there are still more issues to consider.

If you want to remove a task from the Scheduled Tasks list, right-click it, and choose Delete. Choosing Delete here doesn't remove the executed application from your hard disk, it just removes the task from the list of tasks to be executed.

To use controls that affect all tasks in the Scheduled Tasks applet, use the commands on the Advanced menu from the main Scheduled Tasks window's menu bar. You'll see a number of useful items there, as shown in Table 29.10.

Figure 29.18
Enter command-line arguments on the Task properties sheet.

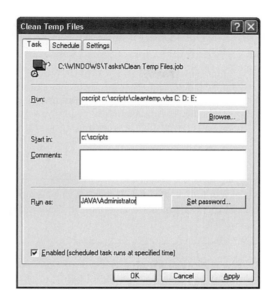

TABLE 29.10	ADVANCED SETTINGS FOR THE SCHEDULED TASKS
Option	**Description**
Stop Using Scheduled Tasks	This option turns off the scheduler, preventing it from running any added tasks. The scheduler won't start automatically the next time you start Windows XP. To reactivate it, you have to open the Scheduled Tasks and choose Start Using Scheduled Tasks.
Pause Scheduled Tasks	This option temporarily suspends added tasks in the task list. This capability is useful if you are running a program whose operation could be slowed down or otherwise influenced by a scheduled task. To resume the schedules for all tasks, choose Advanced, Continue Scheduled Tasks. If a task's execution time is now past, it will run at the next scheduled time.
Notify Me of Missed Tasks	If a task can't complete for some reason, a dialog box pops up, letting you know what was missed. For example, if the computer was turned off when a task should have been run, you'll be told of this situation when you boot up next.
AT Service Account	The Scheduled Tasks runs any commands scheduled using the at command-line utility, which is a carryover from Windows NT. By design, commands scheduled by at all run under the same login account. This option lets you specify which account is to be used. You can leave it set to the default LocalSystem setting, or you can turn on This Account to specify a user account.

continues

29

TABLE 29.10   CONTINUED

Option	Description
View Log	This option brings up a text file in Notepad, listing tasks completed, date, and other information about the tasks. Note that some tasks listed in the log might not appear in the Scheduled Tasks list. This omission can result from system tasks initiated by other services such as synchronization (such as Web page subscriptions and offline folders).

TIP

> You can run one of your tasks immediately by right-clicking the task in question and choosing Run. You can quickly reach Scheduled Tasks through Windows Explorer by going to the `\windows\tasks` folder.

You can view scheduled tasks on a remote computer by opening My Network Places, opening the computer in question, and then opening the Scheduled Tasks folder. You need Administrator privileges to view the settings on a remote machine. If you want to edit settings remotely, the requirements are even greater: You can edit tasks on a remote computer running Windows 95 or later, Windows NT 4.0, Windows 2000, or Windows XP only if that remote computer has remote Registry software installed and has not deleted the boot drive's administrative share.

Unlike under Windows 2000, Windows XP tasks do not have task-level ACLs. However, if the user account defined as the "run as" account does not have access to the executable, the task will not be able to run.

NOTE

> If you are familiar with the old `at` command-line utility from Windows NT, you'll be happy to know that it still works in Windows XP. Commands scheduled with `at` appear in the Scheduled Tasks's list, as well as the list of commands that `at` displays. It's one and the same list. However, if you modify the command within Scheduled Tasks, it will no longer appear in the list displayed by `at`.
>
> There is also an updated command-line interface to the task scheduler, named `schtasks`. For information type
>
> `schtasks /? | more`
>
> in a command-prompt window.

GETTING MORE INFORMATION

This chapter has barely scratched the surface of what you can do with scripting, batch files, and automation. I hope that you'll check out my book *Windows XP Under the Hood, Hardcore Windows Scripting and Command Line Power*, published by Que. It contains tutorials, handy reference sections, and many more examples.

Some other books I've found helpful are

- *Windows Management Instrumentation (WMI)*, by Ashley Meggitt and Matthew M. Lavy (New Riders)
- *WMI Essentials for Automating Windows Management*, by Martin Policht (Sams)
- *Windows NT/2000 ADSI Scripting for System Administration*, by Thomas Eck (New Riders)

In addition, there are numerous Web sites devoted to scripting and automation. Some of the sites I've found useful are listed in Table 29.11.

TABLE 29.11   WEB RESOURCES FOR SCRIPTING AND AUTOMATION

Web Site or Newsgroup	Description
msdn.microsoft.com/scripting	The official Microsoft site.
communities.msn.com/windowsscript	Extensive FAQs, examples, links, and articles.
www.serverguys.com	Articles and examples with an emphasis on Active Directory Service Interface (ADSI) and Windows Management Instrumentation (WMI).
www.win32scripting.com	Archives of *Windows 2000 Magazine*'s articles on scripting. Good questions and answers in the FAQ section.
www.winguides.com/scripting	Nifty online reference for VBScript and WSH.
www.sapien.com	Purveyors of a nifty $150 script editing program called PrimalScript. Definitely beats using Notepad.
Newsgroups: microsoft.public.scripting.wsh microsoft.public.scripting.vbscript microsoft.public.win32.programmer.wmi microsoft.public.adsi.general microsoft.public.platformsdk.adsi	Public newsgroups hosted by Microsoft. A great place to scout for scripting ideas, and to post any questions you have. While you won't get tech support from Microsoft employees here, the community of visitors seem to do a good job of answering questions and giving advice.

There are hundreds of others. If you find other particularly useful scripting resources, let me know by dropping me a line through the guestbook at www.helpwinxp.com.

CHAPTER 30

REGISTRY MAINTENANCE AND REPAIR

In this chapter

THE REGISTRY IN A NUTSHELL

The Windows XP Registry is the central repository in which Windows and most properly written Windows applications store all configuration information, including such items as these:

- Hardware settings
- Software configuration information
- User settings to build the user profile
- Licensing and registration information
- Application usage histories
- Recently accessed file lists
- Software associations to identify which application opens a file based on the file's extension

Long ago, in the days when 8088s through 80386s still roamed the earth, every program with settings to maintain did so through an INI file. Windows stored most of the basic start-up and system configuration information in either SYSTEM.INI or WINDOWS.INI. Now, almost all functions that were once handled by the INI files are managed through the Windows Registry. Now and again, you will still stumble across the errant INI file if you dig around for a couple of seconds. On a clean installation of Windows XP Professional, for example, I found 161 INI files scattered throughout the drive after having logged on as the local administrator.

For most of your daily tasks with Windows XP, you will never need to crack open the Registry. Almost everything you'll ever need to configure that shows up in the Registry can be handled through a Control Panel applet or through built-in option screens included with applications. Sometimes, however, you might find yourself troubleshooting an issue that requires manual tweaks to a Registry setting. It could happen because of an underdeveloped configuration interface, an undocumented setting discovered through a TechNet article, a virus that modified your Registry settings, or an improperly written or corrupted device driver setting. This chapter helps you navigate the Registry with confidence when called upon to diagnose such issues.

STRUCTURE OF THE REGISTRY

The Registry is a specialized database consisting of *hives*. Hives are the physical files that combine to form the five top-level keys. Strangely, according to the Windows XP Glossary, hives are so named for their resemblance to the cellular structure of a beehive.

Physically, the hives are simply a collection of files and related change logs that are all stored in one of two locations. Most hive files can be found in the *%systemroot%*\System32\Config folder. In this location are the following files that correspond to Registry hives:

- default and default.LOG

- SAM and SAM.LOG

- SECURITY and SECURITY.LOG

- software and software.LOG

- system and system.LOG

Two additional hive file pairs do not show up in this directory. The first pair holds the majority of user preference-related settings. This file pair is named ntuser.dat and NTUSER.DAT.LOG and can be found under each user profile, stored by default in the %systemdrive%\Documents and Settings\username folder.

The second pair, UsrClass.dat and UsrClass.dat.LOG, can be found a bit deeper under each user profile in the %systemdrive%\Documents and Settings\username\Local Settings\ Application Data\Microsoft\Windows folder. This second pair holds the list of keys that *add to* and *override* systemwide settings that are specified in the HKEY_CLASSES_ROOT key. This feature makes it possible for users to have individualized document type/application associations (which used to be applied throughout the system) and for individual users to have customized application and ActiveX/COM object installations.

NOTE

> You can see a complete listing of the full paths to all currently loaded Registry hives under HKEY_LOCAL_MACHINE\SYSTEM\CurrentControlSet\Control\hivelist
>
> If you examine this key, you might notice multiple instances of ntuser.dat and UsrClass.dat. If so, it is either because you are running Windows XP in standalone or workgroup mode with multiple users actively logged in, or because there is a nonsystem service account running in the background.

Logically, each top-level key contains a plethora of hierarchically related keys, subkeys, values, and data. The top-level keys (in order of appearance) are as follows:

- **HKEY_CLASSES_ROOT (HKCR)**   This contains file association data. For example, when you click on a file ending in .TXT, the .TXT subkey contains the information that tells Windows to display the file using NOTEPAD.EXE. HKEY_CLASSES_ROOT builds itself by combining the values from HKEY_LOCAL_MACHINE\Software\Classes, which contains systemwide default application associations, and from HKEY_CURRENT_USER\Software\Classes, which contains user-specified preferences for application associations. If any keys appearing in both locations are in conflict, the settings specified under HKEY_CURRENT_USER will win. HKCR also contains the configuration information for COM and ActiveX objects and document type/MIME type associations.

- **HKEY_CURRENT_USER (HKCU)**   This references the subsection of HKEY_USERS pertaining to the currently logged on user. This hive is a duplicate of the user-specific subkey under HKEY_USERS.

- **HKEY_LOCAL_MACHINE (HKLM)** This stores all hardware and machine-specific setup information for your computer. For example, this key lists every device driver to load, all of your hardware's settings, all services and service configurations, and any software setup and configuration data that is common to all users.

- **HKEY_USERS (HKU)** This contains a subkey for each user of the computer. Under each user's key, Windows stores user-specific information such as file locations, display preferences, software preferences, and recently accessed file lists.

- **HKEY_CURRENT_CONFIG (HKCC)** This is a shortcut to `HKEY_LOCAL_MACHINE\System\CurrentControlSet\Hardware Profiles\Current`. The subkeys in this location represent the hardware configuration that is specific to your currently selected hardware profile.

The section "Inside the Main Registry Keys" later in this chapter drills down a little deeper into these keys.

NOTE

When referencing the Registry via a script or command-line utility—as well as in much of the documentation available for the Registry—the parent Registry hives are often referred to only by their three- or four-letter standard abbreviations. The accepted abbreviations are listed in parentheses behind their associated full names in the preceding list.

The primary interface to the Registry, the Registry Editor, displays a representation of the Registry using an interface that is similar to the familiar layout of folders and files as viewed through Windows Explorer. Figure 30.1 shows a view of the Registry, accessible by clicking Start, Run, and opening `REGEDIT.EXE`.

Figure 30.1
The Registry and its parts: pure, unfiltered access to all your system's deepest configuration options.

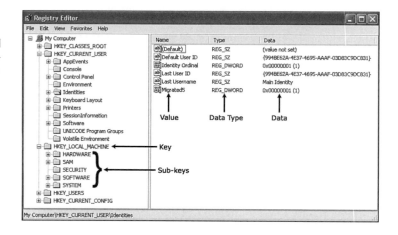

In Figure 30.1, the left pane contains the five top-level keys. The status bar along the bottom displays the full path of the currently selected key. I've expanded the HKEY_CURRENT_USER and HKEY_LOCAL_MACHINE keys to show the first round of subkeys beneath each. The right pane shows a sample of Registry values with their associated data types and data. The data is also sometimes referred to as the setting because this is the part of the Registry most commonly modified through the Registry Editor. Occasionally, you need to add new Registry values. Seldom do you need to add a new Registry subkey. And in case you're wondering, it is impossible for you to add a new top-level Registry key.

The five main data types in the Registry are as follows:

- **REG_DWORD**   This is a single hexadecimal or decimal number.
- **REG_BINARY**   This is a block of binary data displayed in the REGEDIT interface in hexadecimal format.
- **REG_SZ**   This is a plain-text string of alphanumeric characters.
- **REG_MULTI_SZ**   This is similar to REG_SZ, but it can contain multiple strings of text.
- **REG_EXPAND_SZ**   This is similar to REG_SZ, but the string can contain environment variables such as %SYSTEMROOT% or %USERNAME%.

INSIDE THE MAIN REGISTRY KEYS

In the section, "Structure of the Registry," you were introduced to the five top-level Registry keys. This section drills down into those keys a bit deeper, discussing exactly what types of things you can find under each.

HKEY_CLASSES_ROOT

HKEY_CLASSES_ROOT is made up of the contents of HKEY_LOCAL_MACHINE\Software\Classes combined with the contents of HKEY_CURRENT_USER\Software\Classes. Entries specified in the latter override conflicting entries specified in the former. This type of conflict can occur when the user specifies preferences that differ from the system's default settings. The first thing you will probably notice if you expand this key under the Registry Editor is a list of file extensions. These subkeys tie a file type (as defined by the file extension) to an application program that can interact in some way with that type of file.

You should not edit these settings directly. Stick to the file association configuration accessible through Windows Explorer by selecting Tools, Folder Options, File Types. Table 30.1 further explains the types of subkeys under HKEY_CLASSES_ROOT.

30

TABLE 30.1 DIGGING IN TO HKEY_CLASSES_ROOT

Subkey	Description
* through .zzz	For each listed file extension, the default value assigns a name to the file type. The named file type shows up again as HKEY_CLASSES_ROOT\<name>. For example, the (Default) value of the .txt subkey specifies a name of txtfile. Scrolling down in HKEY_CLASSES_ROOT, you find the txtfile subkey. Under txtfile\shell, you see the commands (open and print, for example) that are available for interacting with text files.
	Some file types have OLE handlers with a subkey of PersistentHandler. PersistentHandler contains a Class ID. Continuing with the .txt example, the Class ID is {5e941d80-bf96-11cd-b579-08002b30bfeb}. This Class ID shows up again under the CLSID subkey.
filetype	Each named file type (such as txtfile in the previous example) contains information such as the default icons for the listed filetype, as well as commands available for interacting with the file. In some cases, you will find a CLSID subkey. If so, you can follow this to the HKCR\CLSID\<specified ID> subkey.
CLSID	This contains a subkey that corresponds to the CLSID subkey for each registered file type containing a Class ID. The subkeys point to the proper application handler for the named Class ID.
MIME	Subkeys under HCKR\MIME\Database\Content Type list registered Multipart Internet Mail Extension (MIME) types, which Windows uses to identify the file type of downloaded Internet content received in Web pages and email.

HKEY_CURRENT_USER

HKEY_CURRENT_USER is essentially a shortcut to the subkeys of the HKEY_USERS key associated with the currently logged in user. The subkeys under HKEY_CURRENT_USER contain user-specific settings, preferences, and application options that are unique to the current user.

Table 30.2 further explains a selection of subkeys under HKEY_CURRENT_USER. I don't describe all of the subkeys, but I do explain some of the more interesting ones.

TABLE 30.2 SETTINGS AVAILABLE UNDER HKEY_CURRENT_USER

Subkey	Description
Environment	The Environment subkey contains user-specific environment variables. These variables can be viewed and set through the GUI by right-clicking on My Computer, Properties, selecting the Advanced tab, and clicking the Environment Variables button. The user-specific variables are in the top section of the page.
Network	Subkeys under the Network subkey are the drive letters and LPT ports that are mapped to network resources under the currently logged in user account. The RemotePath value specifies the actual resource to which the parent subkey is mapped.

Subkey	Description
Software	The Software subkey contains user-specific software settings for Windows and installed applications. This subkey also includes many entries corresponding to software manufacturer names for applications installed on your system. You can find a similar subkey under HKEY_LOCAL_MACHINE.
Volatile Environment	This subkey contains numerous dynamic environment variables that are specific to the current user during the current session. Values under this subkey include LOGONSERVER, HOMEDRIVE, HOMEPATH, and other similar settings.

HKEY_LOCAL_MACHINE

The HKEY_LOCAL_MACHINE key contains information that is specific to the computer. These settings persist regardless of the logged in user. Table 30.3 breaks down the first level of subkeys found within HKEY_LOCAL_MACHINE.

TABLE 30.3   SETTINGS AVAILABLE UNDER HKEY_LOCAL_MACHINE

Subkey	Description
HARDWARE	This subkey contains information about the computer's hardware configuration, including all settings that are assigned for plug-and-play devices. This section has no user-configurable settings.
SAM	This subkey contains part of the Windows Security Account Manager database. This subkey appears empty because it doesn't contain user-configurable settings, and only Windows is allowed to view the information.
SECURITY	The SECURITY subkey, like the SAM subkey, contains part of the Windows Security Account Manager database. This subkey also appears empty, for the same reasons as the SAM subkey.
SOFTWARE	The SOFTWARE subkey contains systemwide software settings for Windows and installed applications. This subkey also includes many entries that correspond to software manufacturer names for applications that are installed on your system. There is a similar subkey under HKEY_CURRENT_USER.
SYSTEM	This subkey contains CurrentControlSet, which holds the current settings for your active hardware and services. In addition, many ControlSet00# entries maintain previous configuration sets as backups in the event that a recently made change causes problems with your system.

HKEY_USERS

HKEY_USERS contains a subkey for each user on the system, as well as a .DEFAULT entry that is used in the creation of new local computer account profiles. It is only used when creating a new profile because the .DEFAULT entries for domain accounts come from the domain servers, not from this local subkey. The remaining subkeys for the individual users are represented as alphanumeric *security identifiers (SIDs)*, the unique identifying value generated by Windows for tracking and referencing the individual user accounts.

NOTE

> The `.DEFAULT` entry under `HKEY_USERS` also stores the profile used when no one is currently logged on to the workstation, such as when waiting at the logon screen. For example, to change the prelogon background from NT Blue to a sleek techno-black, you would change the `HKEY_USERS\.DEFAULT\Control Panel\Colors\Background` from `0 78 152` to `0 0 0`. Note that you would not see this particular modification on a stand-alone system using the Welcome screen because the Welcome screen hides the background desktop color under a full-screen bitmap.

The subkeys for a specific user appear under `HKEY_CURRENT_USER` and `HKEY_CLASSES_ROOT` when that user is actively logged in.

NOTE

> If you would like to figure out which accounts tie to which SIDs, a Resource Kit utility named `GETSID.EXE` allows you to resolve a username to an account SID on any machine. You can download `GETSID.EXE` from Microsoft's Web site at `http://www.microsoft.com/windows2000/techinfo/reskit/tools/existing/getsid-o.asp`.
>
> If you would like to see the SIDs for all local accounts on your system, you can use this quick `VBScript` program. Put the following lines into a file named `listsids.vbs`:
>
> ```
> Set objcol = _
> GetObject("WinMgmts:/root/cimv2").InstancesOf("Win32_UserAccount")
>
> For Each i in objcol
>     wscript.echo "Account: " & i.name & vbTab & "SID: " & i.sid
> Next
> ```
>
> Then, at the command prompt, type the line `cscript listsids.vbs`.

HKEY_CURRENT_CONFIG

The `HKEY_CURRENT_CONFIG` key contains information that Windows uses to initialize during the system boot process. This is a virtual key containing linked data from a number of other Registry locations. You never need to modify anything under this key.

BACKING UP AND RESTORING THE REGISTRY

Before diving into Registry modifications, I'll talk about backing them up. Now, I'll admit, I've been working with computers for many years. I *know* the importance of backing up before starting major work, and I believe I've completed a full backup on one of my personal systems maybe twice in the past 15 years. So what you do with this information is up to you, but trust me—a little up-front time creating a backup saves you a great deal of time reinstalling if something goes awry.

→ If your Registry gets really botched up and you don't happen to have a backup handy, all might not be lost. Read about the Recovery Console in Chapter 32, "Crash Recovery," for some suggestions on hard-core ways to deal with Registry corruption.

BACKING UP AND RESTORING THE REGISTRY

You can back up the Registry in Windows XP in five ways: You can back it up as part of a regular disk backup; you can selectively back up portions of the Registry by exporting the keys with the Registry Editor; you can create a System Restore Point; you can use the command-line application REG.EXE; or you can use a special-purpose Registry backup program.

REGISTRY BACKUP AND RECOVERY WITH WINDOWS BACKUP

As you might remember from the section "Using Windows Backup" (Chapter 25, **p. 1042**), Windows XP includes a simple, straightforward backup and restore utility to back up your entire system, including data files, system files, and Registry files. To back up only the Registry using the NTBACKUP utility included with Windows XP Professional, follow these steps:

1. Click Start, Run, and type ntbackup in the open box. Click OK.

2. If the backup utility starts in the wizard interface, click the Advanced Mode option in the body of the main paragraph to take you out of the wizard and display the tabbed Backup Utility interface.

3. Select the Backup tab and select the System State option in the tree in the left pane. The System State is composed of the Registry, the boot files, the Active Directory files, and the certificates.

4. Enter a backup media or filename in the designated box. You should see something similar to what is displayed in Figure 30.2. Note that if you don't have a backup device, your only option is to back up to a filename.

Figure 30.2
The tabbed interface of the Windows XP Backup Utility application.

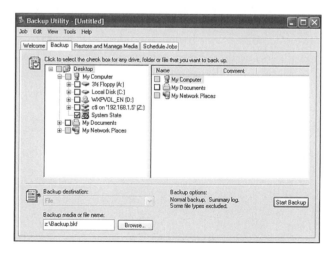

5. Click the Start Backup button. You are then prompted for a backup description. Select the option to Replace the Data on the Media with This Backup.

6. Click the Advanced button and uncheck the option to Automatically Backup System Protected Files with the System State. This ensures that you're grabbing only a backup of the Registry and cuts your backup file down from 1GB to somewhere between 10 and 50MB, depending on your Registry size. Click OK, and then click Start Backup.

7. The Backup Progress dialog displays. When the job completes, click Close.

If you'll be making modifications to this system, you should keep the resulting backup file on a separate location, such as a network drive or some sort of removable media. The backup won't do you much good if something happens to the system where you're storing it and you can't get to the file.

To restore the Registry from a backup made with ntbackup, follow these steps:

CAUTION

> *Do not* follow along with this procedure on a properly functioning system. This is a drastic procedure meant only for recovering from Registry-related disasters and should not be attempted unless necessary or if you are working on a lab machine specifically set up to test this process.

1. Click Start, Run, and type ntbackup in the open box. Click OK.

2. If the backup utility starts in the wizard interface, click the Advanced Mode option in the body of the main paragraph to take you out of the wizard and to display the tabbed Backup Utility interface.

3. Select the Restore and Manage Media tab.

4. Select Tools, Options, Always Replace the File on My Computer because your Registry files already exist. Click OK.

5. In the right pane, expand the list of cataloged backups until you find the one you want to restore. If you do not see your backup job in the list, click Tools, Catalog a Backup File, and enter the location for the backup file in the resulting box. Select the applicable backup set and select System State in the left pane as shown in Figure 30.3.

6. Click Start Restore. A dialog warns you that System State is always restored to the current location. Because that's what you want to happen, click OK.

7. Click OK on the Advanced Options dialog.

8. Confirm the proper name and location of the backup set, and then click OK.

9. When the restore completes, you must restart the system to successfully load the restored Registry files.

Figure 30.3
Restoring the System
State through the
Windows XP Backup
utility.

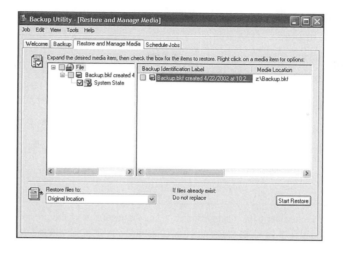

EXPORTING AND IMPORTING REGISTRY FILES WITH THE REGISTRY EDITOR

The Registry Editor that is included with Windows XP allows you to selectively export anything from a single subkey to an entire Registry key. If you're performing significant modifications, this is a good way to ensure that you can figure out what the original values were if you need to roll back your changes.

To back up a key including all subkeys and values, follow these steps:

1. Click Start, Run, type **regedit**, and click OK.
2. Select the key you want to back up from the list in the left pane.
3. Select File, Export.
4. In the common file dialog, select a directory and enter the filename where you would like to save the exported Registry entries.

CAUTION

> The default extension for an exported Registry file is .REG. Double-clicking on a .REG file automatically imports the file into the Registry after providing a single confirmation box. To prevent accidental Registry imports, save exported Registry files as text files, with the .TXT extension.

5. Select Selected Branch in the Export Range option box, and click Save.

Because this is a plain-text file, you can open it in Notepad to see the contents. I often use this method to make limited Registry changes on a single system, export the change as a .REG file, move the file to other target systems, and import the settings to those machines.

Importing a Registry file exported through the Registry editor is just as straightforward as exporting:

1. Click Start, Run, type **regedit**, and click OK.

2. Select File, Import.

3. In the common file dialog, enter the filename containing the data you want to import.

4. Select Open.

Importing a Registry setting through the Registry Editor overwrites existing keys or values and adds missing keys or values, but it does *not* delete extra keys or values that are not contained in the Registry file. You can use a Registry file to explicitly specify subkeys or values to delete. I show you how in the section "Deploying Registry Settings with .REG Files," later in this chapter.

NOTE

> Remember when I suggested changing the extension of the previous Registry file from .REG to .TXT so you wouldn't accidentally import the settings? You can use the inverse to enable a two-step, REGEDIT-free Registry file import. Simply rename the Registry file you want to import with a .REG extension. Then double-click the Registry file to quickly import the contents of the file into your Registry. You can't back out of the import after you've confirmed it exists, so ensure you know what you're importing before you run the REG file.

CREATING A SYSTEM RESTORE POINT

A system restore point allows you to restore your computer to a previous state, rolling back changes to device drivers, system files, and Registry entries. By creating a manual restore point before foraging into the Registry, you can make changes and easily roll them back if something doesn't work.

→ For more information on manually creating and reverting to System Restore Points, **see** Chapter 6, "Setting Up Important System Services," **p. 201**.

COMMAND-LINE BACKUP AND RESTORE USING REG.EXE

A command-line Registry manipulation tool called REG.EXE is included with Windows XP. This tool is useful for selectively backing up or restoring specific Registry subkeys. Numerous functions are available in REG.EXE, including Registry exporting and importing.

NOTE

> You can do quite a few things using REG.EXE. Use the command REG /? for a complete usage syntax of the REG.EXE command.

To back up a Registry key using REG.EXE, use the following syntax:

```
REG EXPORT Rootkey\Subkey File
```

For Rootkey, you can use the abbreviations HKLM, HKCU, HKCR, HKU, or HKCC. Subkey must be the full name of a Registry key under the selected root. File is the name of the file to which you want to save the exported data.

To restore a Registry key using `REG.EXE`, use the following syntax:

`REG IMPORT File`

When importing, `File` can be any `REG` file created with `REG EXPORT`, created with an export from `Regedit`, or created manually with a text editor.

BACK UP AND RESTORE THE REGISTRY USING A THIRD-PARTY REGISTRY BACKUP PROGRAM

Third-party tools are available specifically for working with the Registry. Although most commercially available backup software packages that can back up the Registry are generally a safe bet, I do not recommend third-party applications that are dedicated solely to dealing with the Registry. If the only actions performed by these third-party utilities were backing up and restoring the Registry, I might change my tune, but often added features, such as Registry cleanup, Registry defragmentation, and Registry tuning are included. The Registry is such a core component of your system, and automated tuning of this nature so potentially risky, that I can't recommend such actions in good conscience.

30

EDITING THE REGISTRY

CAUTION

> Editing the Registry can change the configuration of your system. Therefore, by nature, it is a potentially destructive task. Do not directly manipulate the Registry when using the GUI will suffice, and never blindly fiddle with the Registry unless you are willing to accept the potential consequences.

Occasionally, you might need to manually edit data in the Registry. As mentioned earlier in this chapter, Windows XP includes a Registry Editor, `REGEDIT.EXE`, which you can use to view and edit the Registry.

CAUTION

> I've said it before, and I'll say it again: Before you make changes to your Registry, make a backup. Refer to the section "Registry Backup and Recovery with Windows Backup," earlier in this chapter, to make a backup of your Registry using `ntbackup`.

Because the Registry is not a place for mere mortals, you won't find a shortcut to the Registry Editor under the program menus. You won't even find it in the Control Panel or under Administrative Tools. To open the Registry Editor, click Start, Run, type **regedit** in the Open field, and click OK. You already explored the Registry Editor interface earlier in this chapter in the "Structure of the Registry" section (**page xxx**), when you viewed the default Registry keys. No differences in the interface exist when viewing or editing Registry entries.

What tasks might you perform when editing the Registry? Through the Registry Editor, you can do the following:

- Add, delete, or rename Registry keys.
- Add new values and value data.
- Delete existing values.
- Change value data for existing values.
- Search the entire Registry for key names, value names, or value data.

You can perform all these tasks by selecting the proper location among the keys or values and selecting a function from the Edit menu of the Registry Editor.

To change the data associated with a value, double-click the value and change the value data in the resulting dialog. Keep in mind that all changes are final. There is no Undo. Many changes take place immediately; others require a restart of an associated application or a reboot of the system. If you delete a key, the only way to put it back is to manually re-add it or restore it from backup.

NOTE

> If you need to edit the Registry of a system other than your own, you can connect to a Registry over the network. In the Registry Editor, simply click File, Connect Network Registry, and enter the computer name for the remote system in the resulting dialog. To perform this function, you must be an administrator on both the machine you are working from and on the machine to which you are trying to connect.

REGISTRY SECURITY

Under Windows 2000, viewing or modifying security on the Registry involved the use of a separate, somewhat clunkier Registry Editor interface invoked with `regedt32.exe`. Fortunately, Windows XP does away with the `regedt32` interface and integrates access control into `regedit.exe`.

Registry security uses an access control interface similar to what you would see when managing NTFS or network share security settings.

NOTE

> It's quite rare that you would need to adjust permissions on registry keys. About the only time I've had to do this is when an application program's installer adds registry keys with read/write permission granted only to administrator. If you want to run the application from normal user accounts, you have to adjust the security settings on the application's keys, usually under `HKLM\Software\`*`manufacturer`*. If you suspect this sort of problem is going on with your system, I suggest that you contact the manufacturer's technical support department before trying to change anything.

CAUTION

I know I sound like a broken record with all these warnings, but changing security on Registry keys can be just as dangerous as editing or deleting keys. Don't do it if you don't have to.

To view or change the security permissions applied to a Registry key—and you can only apply permissions at the key/subkey levels; you can't apply as granularly as to a single name value within a key—follow these steps:

1. Open regedit and drill down to the key you want to view or modify.
2. Select the key.
3. Select Edit, Permissions.

You should see the Security tab displayed in Figure 30.4.

Figure 30.4
Registry key permissions settings.

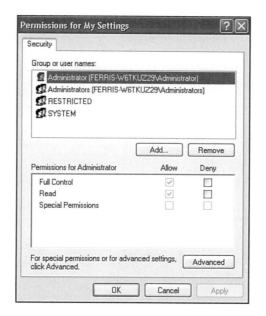

As you can see from Figure 30.4, only three general permissions are available for Registry keys. Full Control does just what it says and grants full control, including the ability to read, write, or modify values within the key. Read, again, does exactly what you might expect—users with Read permissions can read associated subkeys and values but cannot modify them. Special Permissions is not nearly as intuitive as the other two. I explain this in just a bit, but for now, look again at Figure 30.4. Notice how the entire Allow column is grayed out, as is the Deny box for Special Permissions. This is because this Registry key is *inheriting* permissions from the parent key. To change these keys, you must click the Advanced button and deselect the option marked Inherit from Parent the Permission Entries That Apply to Child Objects. This permission inheritance is similar to container and object inheritance explained in Chapter 23, "Managing File Security."

To see the breakdown of Special Permissions, click the Advanced button, and then click the Effective Permissions tab. When you first visit the tab, the Group or User Name box is blank. Click the Select button, enter a valid account name for an account with access to the machine you're working on, and click OK to see the effective permissions for the selected account. Figure 30.5 shows the result.

Figure 30.5
Registry key Effective Permissions dialog.

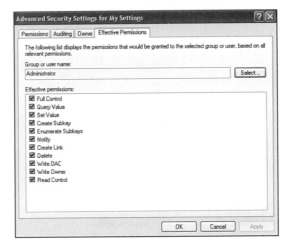

As with most NTFS-type security permissions, all of the special access permissions listed in Figure 30.5 can be audited for success or failure through the Auditing tab of the Security Settings dialog.

→ For more information on NTFS-type permissions, **see** "File System (NTFS) Security" **p. 946**.

DEPLOYING REGISTRY SETTINGS

Because it wouldn't be very practical to go running around your entire organization logging in to systems and manually changing individual Registry keys, and because you can't really trust the users to successfully navigate the Registry Editor on their own, you need to have some ways to easily change Registry settings with little to no user interaction.

DEPLOYING REGISTRY SETTINGS WITH .REG FILES

The easiest method for distributing Registry settings is through the use of a REG file. You saw how to export and import REG files earlier in this chapter, in the section "Exporting and Importing Registry Files with the Registry Editor" (**p. xxx**), but in that section you were exporting an entire Registry key. Let's take a look at using REG files to deploy a limited group of settings.

In the earlier example, we selected the top-level Registry key and exported the entire thing to a REG file. If you viewed the resulting file in the Registry editor, you probably noticed fairly significant and unruly content. That is because the REG file contained all keys, subkeys, values, and data in the branch of the Registry that you exported. Let's manually create a REG file that adds a key and some values to HKEY_CURRENT_USER. Create the following file in a plain-text editor, such as Notepad:

```
Windows Registry Editor Version 5.00

[HKEY_CURRENT_USER\My Settings]
@="Platinum Edition"
"IfYouKeepPickingAtIt"="ItWillNeverHeal"
"Author"="Jeff Ferris"
"TheAnswerIs"=dword:0000002a
```

Save this file as mysettings.reg. To import the settings, follow these steps:

1. Double-click the mysettings.reg file.

2. You see a pop-up confirmation message that asks Are you sure you want to add the information in c:\mysettings.reg to the registry? Click Yes to import the file.

3. You then receive a confirmation box stating Information in C:\mysettings.reg has been successfully entered into the registry. Click OK.

After you import the REG file, open the Registry Editor (Start, Run, regedit). Expand HKEY_CURRENT_USER, and you should see a subkey named My Settings that contains values as displayed in Figure 30.6.

Figure 30.6
The Registry key and values created by mysettings. reg.

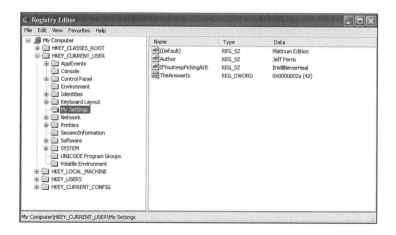

NOTE

Importing a REG file by double-clicking it is pretty straightforward, but what about those two confirmation boxes? What if you don't want your users to know that you are importing Registry settings? And what's more, you don't want them having an opportunity to reject the setting by clicking No on the confirmation dialog. Fortunately, you can silently install a Registry file from the command line using the following command:

continues

continued

```
regedit /s filename.reg
```
Add a line like the above to a logon or startup script, and you can quickly, easily, and silently deploy Registry settings to users and computers throughout your environment.

30

Deploying Registry settings using REG files overwrites existing keys, values, or data and adds missing keys, values, or data. REG files do *not* delete extra keys, values, or data that are in the Registry but not in the Registry file. To delete information in the Registry, you must use regedit, remove the key using a script (as demonstrated in the next section), or explicitly define the keys or values you want to delete within the REG file. To demonstrate, I show you how to manually create two REG files to manipulate values created under the HKEY_CURRENT_USER\My Settings key created earlier in this section.

First, delete the IfYouKeepPickingAtIt value. Create the following file in a plain-text editor, such as Notepad, and save the file as WhackOneValue.reg:

```
Windows Registry Editor Version 5.00

[HKEY_CURRENT_USER\My Settings]
"IfYouKeepPickingAtIt"=-
```

Notice the minus (-) sign where the data normally goes for the IfYouKeepPickingAtIt value. This directs the Registry Editor to delete the associated name and data pair when you run or import the REG file. After you run WhackOneValue.reg, open the Registry Editor. You no longer find the IfYouKeepPickingAtIt value under HKEY_CURRENT_USER\My Settings. Note that if you had the Registry Editor open when you ran the script, you might need to press F5 to refresh the display before seeing the effect of the script.

Next, delete the entire My Settings key. Create the following file in Notepad and save the file as WhackMySettings.reg:

```
Windows Registry Editor Version 5.00

[-HKEY_CURRENT_USER\My Settings]
```

Notice the minus (-) sign in front of HKEY_CURRENT_USER. This directs the Registry Editor to delete the following key when you run or import the REG file. After you run WhackMySettings.reg, open the Registry Editor. You no longer find the My Settings key under HKEY_CURRENT_USER. Again, if you had Registry Editor open when you ran the script, you might need to press F5 to refresh the display before seeing the effect of the script.

DEPLOYING REGISTRY SETTINGS WITH VBSCRIPT

Managing the Registry with VBScript is amazingly straightforward using the RegRead, RegWrite, and RegDelete methods against the WScript.Shell object.

NOTE

For full downloadable Windows Scripting Host documentation in the Windows Help File format, see the Microsoft Developers Network Scripting resources at http://msdn.microsoft.com/scripting.

The following code listing creates a new Registry subkey named *My Key* under the HKEY_CURRENT_USER key. The script uses the RegWrite method to populate the default value, plus three additional values under the new subkey. Each new value is populated with data. After populating the key, values, and data, the script displays the data values by reading the Registry with the RegRead method. Enter the following lines of code into a plain-text editor, such as Notepad, and save the file as addkey.vbs.

```
Set myReg = CreateObject("WScript.Shell")
key =   "HKEY_CURRENT_USER\"

'Write the keys
myReg.RegWrite key & "My Script\", "Platinum Edition"
myReg.RegWrite key & "My Script\IsCool", "True"
myReg.RegWrite key & "My Script\Author", "Jeff Ferris", "REG_SZ"
myReg.RegWrite key & "My Script\TheAnswerIs", 42, "REG_DWORD"

'Read the keys
WScript.Echo "Default Value: " & myReg.RegRead(key & "My Script\")
WScript.Echo "IsCool Value: " & myReg.RegRead(key & "My Script\IsCool")
WScript.Echo "Author Value: " & myReg.RegRead(key & "My Script\Author")
WScript.Echo "TheAnswer Value: " & myReg.RegRead(key & "My Script\TheAnswerIs")
set myReg = Nothing
```

After you run addkey.vbs, open the Registry Editor (Start, Run, regedit). Expand HKEY_CURRENT_USER, and you should see a subkey named *My Script*, containing values as displayed in Figure 30.7.

Figure 30.7
The Registry key and values created by addkey.vbs.

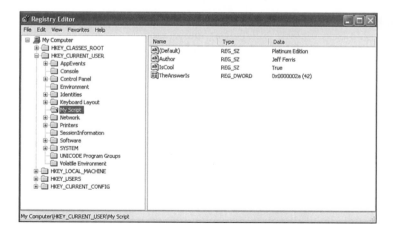

To demonstrate the use of the RegDelete method—and to clean up the useless Registry key created previously—create a delkey.vbs script containing the following five lines.

```
'Delete the keys
Set myReg = CreateObject("WScript.Shell")
key =   "HKEY_CURRENT_USER\"
myReg.RegDelete key & "My Script\"

Set myReg = Nothing
```

After you run `delkey.vbs`, open the Registry Editor. You no longer see the `My Script` key under HKEY_CURRENT_USER. If you had Registry Editor opened when you ran the script, you might need to press F5 to refresh the display before seeing the effect of the script.

Because `startup`, `shutdown`, `logon`, and `logoff` scripts can all be written using VBScript, the previous samples give you an easy way to deploy scripted changes to the Registry of any systems on which you control the related script policies.

CAUTION

> Often, deploying settings through the `startup`, `shutdown`, `logon`, or `logoff` scripts is your only way to distribute Registry edits now that REG and VBS files effectively function as a sort of poor man's virus for virus authors who can't afford compilers. You definitely don't want to get your users in the habit of opening VBS or REG attachments from their email. In fact, many corporate email scanners automatically delete attachments of these types, and Outlook XP automatically blocks both types of attachments. Therefore, a user might not even be able to open or run VBS or REG files if you don't deploy them through the system scripts.

DEPLOYING REGISTRY SETTINGS WITH GROUP POLICY

As mentioned in the previous section, you can add Windows Scripting Host scripts to the `startup`, `shutdown`, `logon`, or `logoff` script sections of a Group Policy object, allowing for automated deployment of script-based Registry changes to any systems to which the Group Policy settings are applied. But more than that, you should recognize that the core technology on the local workstation responsible for the proper application of Group Policy is the Registry. Nearly all Group Policy settings made in a Group Policy Object are implemented by way of a change somewhere in the Registry. Group Policy just provides an interface in an organized, easily navigated, context-sensitive help–enabled, hierarchical management interface, sparing you from the countless nights you'd need to spend making and debugging the same changes by manually digging through the Registry.

Group Policy can be configured locally through the Local Policy manager, or it can be applied to users or computers through a site, domain, or organizational unit (OU) container using Active Directory. After a Group Policy has been configured, systems receive the update to the settings either at the next reboot or the next time the local security policy requests an update (usually no longer than eight hours).

To illustrate the relationship between Group Policy and the Registry, Table 30.4 lists a selection of common Group Policy settings and their associated Registry keys.

TABLE 30.4 GROUP POLICY SETTING TO REGISTRY VALUE MAPPING

Group Policy Setting	Registry Value
User Configuration\AdministrativeTemplates\ Desktop\Active Desktop, **Active Desktop Wallpaper**	HKCU\Software\Microsoft\ Windows\CurrentVersion\ Policies\System, Wallpaper & WallpaperStyle
User Configuration\AdministrativeTemplates\ Desktop\Active Desktop, **Disable Active Desktop**	HKCU\Software\Microsoft\ Windows\CurrentVersion\ Policies\Explorer, NoActiveDesktop
Computer Configuration\ Administrative Templates\System, **Turn Off Autoplay**	HKLM\Software\Microsoft\ Windows\CurrentVersion\ Policies\Explorer, NoDriveTypeAutoRun
User Configuration\AdministrativeTemplates\ Start Menu & Taskbar, **Remove Logoff on the Start Menu**	HKCU\Software\Microsoft\ Windows\CurrentVersion\ Policies\Explorer, StartMenuLogOff
User Configuration\AdministrativeTemplates\ Start Menu & Taskbar, **Turn off personalized menus**	HKCU\Software\Microsoft\ Windows\CurrentVersion\ Policies\Explorer, Intellimenus
User Configuration\Administrative Templates\ System, **Prevent access to registry editing tools**	HKCU\Software\Microsoft\ Windows\CurrentVersion\ Policies\System, DisableRegistryTools
User Configuration\Administrative Templates System, **Don't run specified Windows applications**	HKCU\Software\Microsoft\ Windows\CurrentVersion\ Policies\Explorer, DisallowRun
User Configuration\Administrative Templates\ Control Panel\Display, **Password protect the screen saver**	HKCU\Software\Policies\ Microsoft\Windows\ Control Panel\Desktop, ScreenSaverIsSecure

HACKING THE REGISTRY

Okay, I *know* I've told you over and over in this chapter that you shouldn't dink around with the Registry unless absolutely necessary because your changes can't be easily undone and some mistakes could keep your system from booting. That said (again), you *can* implement many useful hacks through careful manipulation of the Registry. Several such modifications are scattered throughout this book as part of coverage of other topics. And sometimes a registry hack turns up that doesn't quite qualify under the "unless absolutely necessary" litmus test, but it is fairly useful, so I'll tell you about it anyway.

CREATE YOUR OWN PROGRAM ALIASES

I don't know about you, but I have a *lot* of programs showing up under my Start, Programs menu—so many, in fact, that I often have trouble quickly finding programs that I'm trying to run. Windows XP's Start Menu personalization feature helps a little by putting a selection of frequently run programs right on the initial Start bar, but I have a few more favorite applications than can fit in that small amount of space.

Frequently, to save time, I just press the Windows key + R to pop up the Run box, then type a program name in the box and click OK. For example, to open calculator, I know the executable name is `calc.exe`, so I type `<Windows key + r>, calc`, press Enter, and Calculator opens. But some programs are a little harder to remember. Take Microsoft Word, for example. I can never remember if the executable name is `word.exe`, `winword.exe`, or `msword.exe`. It turns out that the proper thing to type is `winword`, but about 50% of the time, I try `word` first.

It sure would be nice if I could somehow create an alias so that `word` would open Microsoft Word, and, with a minimal amount of Registry fiddling, I can! The following assumes you've installed Microsoft Office XP:

1. Open the Registry Editor (Start, Run, `regedit`).
2. Navigate to `HKEY_LOCAL_MACHINE\SOFTWARE\Microsoft\Windows\CurrentVersion\App Paths`.
3. Right-click the App Paths key and select New, Key. The key is created with the name `New Key #1`. Rename the key to `word.exe`.
4. Double-click the (Default) value, and set the data to the full path to `winword.exe` on your system. On my machine, I found it in `C:\Program Files\Microsoft Office\Office10\Winword.EXE`.
5. Exit the Registry Editor.
6. Test the new setting by typing `<Windows key + r>, word`. Press Enter. Microsoft Word should start.

You can use similar steps to create program aliases for any applications on your system.

CHANGE THE *MY COMPUTER* LABEL TO SOMETHING USEFUL

For any of you who regularly use a keyboard, mouse, and video (KMV) switch to flip between computers, or for those of us with multiple logins (for example, one regular user, and one with administrative rights), I'm sure you're familiar with the associated identity crisis that comes along with switching systems too often. You suddenly find yourself wondering, "Which computer is this, and who did I log in as?" Well, the following Registry tweak helps minimize that confusion by changing the *My Computer* label on the My Computer icon to read *Username on Computername*.

1. Open the Registry Editor (Start, Run, `regedit`).
2. Navigate to `HKEY_CLASSES_ROOT\CLSID\{20D04FE0-3AEA-1069-A2D8-08002B30309D}`.

3. Rename the `LocalizedString` value to `OldString`.

4. Right-click in the right pane and select New, Expandable String Value to create a new value of type `REG_EXPAND_SZ`. Name the new value `LocalizedString`.

5. Set the data for the new value to `%username%` on `%computername%`.

6. Exit the Registry Editor.

Now click on the Desktop and press F5 to refresh. Your My Computer label should now reflect your current username and computer name.

If, by some chance, this does not work, it might be because the computer name has already been changed for the currently logged on user. If this is the case, you can correct the issue by deleting the `HKEY_CURRENT_USER\Software\Microsoft\Windows\CurrentVersion\Explorer\CLSID\` `{20D04FE0-3AEA-1069-A2D8-08002B30309D}` key.

NOTE

A quick way to find the `HKEY_CURRENT_USER\Software\Microsoft\` `Windows\CurrentVersion\Explorer\CLSID\{20D04FE0-3AEA-1069-A2D8-` `08002B30309D}` key is to right-click My Computer, select Rename, and enter a name that is not likely to be found anywhere else in the Registry, such as `RubberChicken`. Now, in the Registry Editor, search for the data value of `RubberChicken`. It should be in the key you're looking for.

SPEED UP OUTLOOK WHEN CONNECTING OVER DIAL-UP OR VPN

If you use Outlook over dial-up or VPN to connect to an Exchange server to access your corporate email, you're really going to love this final hack. I noticed an extremely slow initial connection time for Outlook 2000 and Outlook XP whenever I tried to connect over a VPN. For the longest time, I attributed the problem to the link speed. After all, a significant difference exists between wired Ethernet and a cable modem.

Then my company installed a wireless network. To access corporate resources over the wireless network, I had to log in to the VPN servers. The initial connection to Outlook was still extremely slow, but I was connected at 11Mbps and shouldn't have really noticed a problem. I started digging around in TechNet to look for a way to optimize Outlook communication and stumbled upon this lightly documented Registry tweak:

1. Open the Registry Editor (Start, Run, `regedit`).

2. Navigate to `HKEY_LOCAL_MACHINE\SOFTWARE\Microsoft\Exchange\Exchange Provider`.

3. Double-click the entry named `Rpc_Binding_Order`.

4. The default value data of this entry is `ncalrpc,ncacn_ip_tcp,ncacn_spx,ncacn_np,` `netbios,ncacn_vns_spp`. Change it to `ncacn_ip_tcp,ncalrpc,ncacn_spx,ncacn_np,` `netbios,ncacn_vns_spp`. (Just swap the first and second entries.) This change tells Outlook to attempt to communicate over TCP/IP before attempting communication over remote procedure call (RPC). Before making the change, I had to wait for the

RPC communication attempt to time out, after which the system would attempt to communicate over TCP/IP. This often created a wait of 30 seconds or more.

5. Exit the Registry Editor.

Since making this change, Outlook XP has successfully connected to my Exchange server in around 7 seconds, even when using a dial-up or VPN connection. Compared to the 30 seconds it was taking prior to the change, this minor change led to significant performance improvement.

30

CHAPTER **31**

TROUBLESHOOTING COMMON WINDOWS XP PROBLEMS

In this chapter

TROUBLESHOOTING SYSTEM AND APPLICATION PROBLEMS

It's going to happen. Your system will freeze up or you'll be staring at a big blue screen or your application will stop responding, and suddenly you'll find yourself scrambling to figure out what just went wrong. Maybe you'll think that it has to do with the new driver you installed or the application you loaded. Or maybe you'll scratch your head wondering what exactly just happened.

Luckily, Windows XP includes an assortment of tools that allow you to troubleshoot system Stop errors and application faults that affect your ability to work efficiently and effectively. Your strategy can include anything from submitting dump files for analysis to viewing application and system error messages. By accessing the various types of information about your system, you can identify the source of the problem and begin to arrive at a solution.

ANALYZING DUMP FILES

If you receive a Stop error, one option you have is to analyze the dump file that's created after the Stop error occurs when you reboot your system. A *Stop error* refers to a severe error that occurs in the operating system that causes the system to stop functioning properly. A *dump file* is a file that contains system information that was in memory when the error occurred. When a Stop error occurs, system memory information is "dumped" to the file. You can analyze the dump file manually, or you can send the mini dump file to Microsoft for analysis.

Kernel debuggers are available for you to manually analyze a dump file. The debugger allows you to view the contents of the file, which contains data from your computer's memory. For example, the Kernel Debugger tool (Kd.exe) is a command-line utility that you can use to analyze a memory dump, or you can use the WinDbg Debugger tool (Windbg.exe) to do the same thing, but WinDbg Debugger uses a GUI interface. You can obtain both tools from the Microsoft Debugging Tools Web site (www.microsoft.com/ddk/debugging).

→ For more information about Stop errors and analyzing dump files, **see** Chapter 32, "Crash Recovery," **p. 1287**.

TIP

> The Dumpchk.exe command-line utility allows you to check a dump file. Dumpchk displays basic information about the file and verifies all the listed virtual and physical addresses. This information can provide you details about the Stop error and the address of the driver that called the exception. The Dumpchk utility is available on the Windows XP installation CD-ROM. You must install the Support Tools by running the Setup.exe file in the Support\Tools folder.

You also have the option of sending your mini dump file to the Online Crash Analysis Web site at Microsoft. The file is part of an error report that you submit to the site. You can submit a report automatically through the Error Reporting service, or you can submit it manually by accessing the site directly. For more information about the Error Reporting service and the Online Crash Analysis Web site, see the "Reporting System and Application Errors" section later in this chapter.

USING EVENT VIEWER

Event Viewer allows you to view logs that can help you identify system and application problems. When designated events occur in an application or in the OS, an event message is added to the appropriate log (Application, Security, or System). This is particularly useful for troubleshooting problems with applications, drivers, services, or other components.

Event Viewer is a Windows XP administrative tool. If your Start menu is set up to display the Administrative Tools link on the Start menu (which is always my preference), you can open Event Viewer by clicking Start, pointing to Administrative Tools, and then clicking Event Viewer. If you see an error or warning message displayed, double-click the message to view information about that event. Figure 31.1 shows the details of an error event that occurred in Windows Explorer.

Figure 31.1
Event Properties dialog box for a Windows Explorer error event.

As you can see, the log entry (in the Application log) includes information about the type of event, the source of the event, when it occurred, which executable file was the faulting application, and binary data that can be used by programmers and support technicians to help troubleshoot the problem.

→ For more information about using Event Viewer, **see** Chapter 26, "Using the Computer Management Console," **p. 1059**.

Application and system events are configured to automatically trigger an event message, and, for the most part, you can't control which events are included in these logs. However, you can configure whether Stop error events are recorded in the System log. To configure this option, open the System utility in Control Panel, select the Advanced tab, and click the Settings button in the Startup and Recovery section of the tab. The Write an Event to the System Log check box, shown in Figure 31.2, determines whether a Stop error event is recorded in the System log. This option is enabled by default.

Figure 31.2
Startup and Recovery
dialog box.

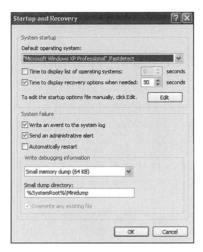

TIP

You can also add events to your System log that record the reasons for computer shut-downs and restarts. When you enable the Shutdown Event Tracker feature, the Shutdown Event Tracker dialog box appears whenever certain events related to shutdowns and startups occur; for example, when you manually shut down your computer or after power is disconnected and the computer is restarted. You're then given the option to indicate whether the shutdown was scheduled (planned), unscheduled (unplanned), or unexpected. The event is then recorded in the System log, which you can view in Event Viewer.

To enable the Shutdown Event Tracker function, you must change a value in the registry. Open the ShutdownReasonUI value in HKEY_LOCAL_MACHINE\SOFTWARE\Microsoft\ Windows\CurrentVersion\Reliability, and change the value data from 0 to 1. (You can change it back to 0 whenever you want to disable this feature.)

VIEWING SYSTEM INFORMATION

Another resource that you can use to troubleshoot hardware and software problems is System Information. System Information is a great tool for viewing a variety of information about your system. The tool displays information like an MMC console; by default, there is one main node—System Summary—and four subnodes beneath the main one—Hardware Resources, Components, Software Environment, and Internet Settings—as shown in Figure 31.3. Additional nodes might be added when you install other applications, such as Office XP.

You can access System Information by typing **msinfo32** in the Run dialog box and then clicking OK. You can also launch it from the Start menu or through the Help and Support Center.

Figure 31.3
System Summary
node of System
Information.

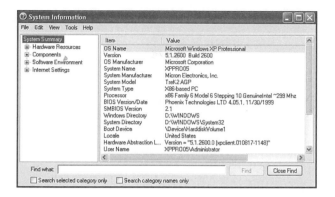

NOTE

You can also use the Systeminfo command-line utility to view some information about your current environment. However, this utility doesn't provide nearly as much information as System Information. The details that Systeminfo provides are comparable to what you'd find by selecting the System Summary node of System Information.

In System Information, you can view current or historical system information, search for specific components, or connect to additional diagnostic tools such as Dr. Watson or the DirectX Diagnostic Tool. You can also use the information in each of the nodes to identify possible problems within your system. Table 31.1 provides a brief description of each of these nodes and points out specific features that might be useful in troubleshooting problems on your system.

TABLE 31.1   NODES IN SYSTEM INFORMATION

Node	Description
System Summary	Shows basic information about such components as your processor, BIOS version, system type, and memory. Having the BIOS version number can be handy if you need to update your BIOS.
Hardware Resources	Includes information about hardware-specific settings, such as DMAs, IRQs, and memory. The Conflicts/Sharing node provides information about shared and conflicting devices. This information can be helpful in determining problems with a specific device.
Components	Displays information about all the major devices in your system, including details such as I/O ports, IRQ channels, and drivers. The Problem Devices node is useful when troubleshooting your system because it lists all devices not loading or initializing properly.

continues

TABLE 31.1 CONTINUED

Node	Description
Software Environment	Displays a variety of information about software-related settings, including details about drivers, environment variables, running tasks, loaded modules, services, program groups, startup programs. In the Software Environment node, you can determine whether a specific process is running, what version driver is being used, or whether a service is running or stopped. You can also view application error reports, which are discussed in more detail later in this chapter.
Internet Settings	Includes information about your Internet Explorer settings.

Note that some applications will add additional nodes to System Information. For example, Microsoft Office will add the Applications node.

> **TIP**
>
> Device Manager also provides information about the hardware on your system and shows you whether any devices are not working properly. Unlike System Information, Device Manager also allows you to change configuration settings and update device drivers. You can access Device Manager by opening the System utility in Control Panel, selecting the Hardware tab, and clicking Device Manager. Despite Device Manager's expanded functionality, you might want to start with System Information because it gives you an excellent overview of your entire system, unless you're relatively certain that the problem you're having is hardware-related.

→ For more information about managing hardware devices and using Device Manager, **see** Chapter 27, "Managing Hardware Devices," **p. 1103**.

USING THE SERVICES ADMINISTRATION TOOL

The Services administration tool is an MMC snap-in that includes the information that you can view through the System Summary\Software Environment\Services node in System Information. However, the Services utility also allows you to choose between Extended and Standard views; start, stop, pause, and resume services; and view and modify the properties of specific services. The properties include general information about the service, logon and recovery options for the service, and details about service dependencies.

When troubleshooting a problem, the Services tool is useful for determining whether a service has been stopped or paused, which can explain why a specific component on your system might not be responding. In addition, many of the services include recovery options that allow you to set how the computer should respond after the first failure, second failure, and subsequent failures.

→ For more information about the Services administration tool, **see** Chapter 26, "Using the Computer Management Console," **p. 1059**, and Chapter 32, "Crash Recovery," **p. 1287**.

USING DR. WATSON

Dr. Watson for Windows is a handy little utility that allows you to view and log information about application errors. When you set up Windows XP, Dr. Watson is installed in your system folder and runs automatically when an application error occurs. However, you can open Dr. Watson manually and change the default settings. The changes that you make are stored in the registry at HKEY_LOCAL_MACHINE\SOFTWARE\Microsoft\DrWatson.

To open Dr. Watson, type **drwtsn32** in the Run dialog box, and click OK. The Dr. Watson for Windows dialog box appears, as shown in Figure 31.4.

Figure 31.4
Dr. Watson for
Windows dialog box.

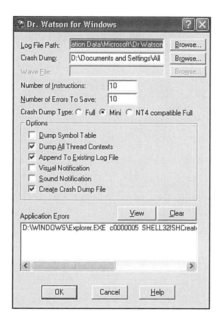

31

In this dialog box, you can configure where log and dump files are saved, what type of information they will contain, and how you'll be notified when an error occurs. You can also view error log files or clear errors from the list. By default, Dr. Watson creates a log file (Drwtsn32.log) and crash dump file (User.dmp) when an error occurs and stores them in the Documents and Settings\All Users\Application Data\Microsoft\Dr Watson folder. The User.dmp file is a binary crash dump file that can be loaded into a debugger.

To view an error log, select the error from the Application Errors list, and then click View. In the Log File Viewer window, you can view information about which program caused the error, the error that occurred, system information when the error occurred, programs and services running when the error occurred, modules that the program loaded, and other types of information that can be used by support professionals to identify the problem. The lists of tasks and modules can be used to duplicate the conditions that existed when the error occurred.

For more information on configuring Dr. Watson and working with log files, click the Help button in the Dr. Watson for Windows dialog box and search for Dr. Watson in the Help and Support Center.

USING THE DIRECTX DIAGNOSTIC TOOL

DirectX APIs allow Windows XP to take advantage of acceleration technologies used by newer video, audio, and input devices. The APIs enhance multimedia performance and enable compatibility with these devices. The DirectX Diagnostic Tool displays information about your system's DirectX components and drivers, allows you to test DirectX components, and allows you to save that information to text files.

To open the DirectX Diagnostic Tool, type **dxdiag** in the Run dialog box, and click OK. The DirectX Diagnostic Tool window appears, as shown in Figure 31.5.

Figure 31.5
System tab of the DirectX Diagnostic Tool window.

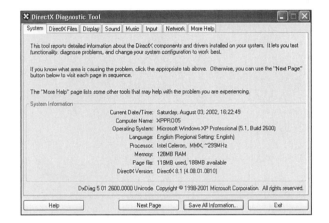

In the DirectX Diagnostic Tool, you can view, test, and save information related to audio, video, controller, input, and network devices. The DirectX Diagnostic Tool window includes eight tabs; each tab supports various types of functionality. You can also save the diagnostic information collected from all the tabs (by clicking Save All Information). Table 31.2 describes each of the tabs in the DirectX Diagnostic Tool window.

TABLE 31.2 TABS IN THE DIRECTX DIAGNOSTIC TOOL WINDOW

Tab	Description
System	Displays information about your computer, OS, processor, memory, page file, and DirectX version.
DirectX Files	Lists DirectX files installed on your computer. The information includes the file name, version, attributes, language, date, and size.

Tab	Description
Display	Provides information about the display device and drivers and whether DirectDraw, Direct3D, and AGP Texture acceleration are enabled or available. You can disable any feature that's available, and you can test DirectDraw and Direct3D.
Sound	Provides information about the display device and drivers. You can change the sound acceleration level and test DirectSound.
Music	Provides music port information and whether Default Port acceleration is available. You can disable Default Port acceleration if it's available, and you can test DirectMusic.
Input	Lists the input devices and drivers on your system.
Network	Lists the registered DirectPlay service providers and applications. You can also test DirectPlay.
More Help	Provides links to additional troubleshooting tools: DirectX Troubleshooter, Sound Troubleshooter, System Information, and the DirectDraw Override option.

31

At the bottom of most of the tabs is a Note text box. This area displays information specific to the tabs. The best message to see down there is "No problems found"; however, you should look for warnings in this section about files marked as Beta, Debug, Outdated, or Unsigned. You should always make sure that you're using the most recent version of a DirectX file.

USING THE SYSTEM CONFIGURATION UTILITY

The System Configuration Tool is a convenient utility that allows you to make temporary changes in the way your system starts up. For example, you can disable services or startup programs, modify the System.ini file, or change your boot options.

You must be logged on to your system as an administrator to use the tool and make these changes. To open the System Configuration Utility, type **msconfig** in the Run dialog box, and click OK. The System Configuration Utility window appears, as shown in Figure 31.6.

Figure 31.6
General tab of the System Configuration Utility window.

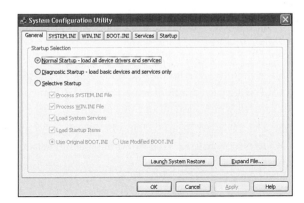

The System Configuration Utility window includes six tabs, three of which correspond to specific startup files (System.ini, Win.ini, and Boot.ini). Table 31.3 describes each of the six tabs and how they can be modified to change the way your system starts up.

TABLE 31.3 TABS IN THE SYSTEM CONFIGURATION UTILITY WINDOW

Tab	Description
General	Provides three types of startup options: Normal, Diagnostic, and Selective. Diagnostic startup starts Windows XP in safe mode. Selective startup includes options that correspond to the other tabs. If you select an option, the corresponding file, services, or applications are processed.
SYSTEM.INI	Allows you to disable and enable specific services in the System.ini file, reorder those services, add new services, or edit existing ones.
WIN.INI	Allows you to disable and enable specific services in the Win.ini file, reorder those services, add new services, or edit existing ones.
BOOT.INI	Allows you to customize the Boot.ini file, check boot paths, change the order of operating systems, change the default operating system, and select boot options.
Services	Allows you to disable and enable services running on your system. You can also hide Microsoft services so that only third-party services are listed.
Startup	Allows you to disable and enable startup programs on your system.

Selecting options on one tab affects options on other tabs. For example, if you clear the Process SYSTEM.INI File check box on the General tab, all options on the SYSTEM.INI tab are cleared. If you select the Normal Startup radio button on the General tab and then clear an option on the SYSTEM.INI tab, the General tab will be changed so that the Selective Startup radio button is selected and the Process SYSTEM.INI File check box will show a green box in it, rather than a check mark. This indicates that only some options are selected.

The easiest way to understand how options are selected in the System Configuration Utility is to look at the startup selections on the General tab:

- If you select the Normal Startup radio button, all options are selected on the SYSTEM.INI, WIN.INI, Services, and Startup tabs.
- If you select the Diagnostic Startup radio button, all options are cleared on the SYSTEM.INI, WIN.INI, Services, and Startup tabs.
- If you select the Selective Startup radio button, all options are selected on the SYSTEM.INI, WIN.INI, Services, and Startup tabs unless you clear individual options under that radio button, in which case all options on the corresponding tab are cleared.
- You cannot clear the Use Original BOOT.INI radio button. You must make changes directly on the BOOT.INI tab to clear that radio button and select the Use Modified BOOT.INI radio button.

C A U T I O N

> If you clear the Load System Services check box on the General tab, the System Configuration Utility disables Windows XP services, such as the Event Log service and the Plug and Play service, and deletes the restore points used by the System Restore service. Do not clear this check box if you need to retain your restore points.

Implementing Boot Logging

Boot Logging is another tool that you can use to troubleshoot your system. Boot Logging records all files that were loaded or not loaded during startup so you can determine whether any of these files might be causing problems. There are two methods that you can use to enable boot logging:

- Modify the Boot.ini file by adding the /bootlog parameter to the Windows XP entry in the [operating systems] section of the file.

- Restart your computer and, when prompted, press F8. Select Enable Boot Logging from the Windows Advanced Options menu.

When you enable boot logging, all startup files are logged into the %windir%\Ntbtlog.txt file. The log contains two types of entries: those files that were loaded and those that were not loaded. For example, if the NDProxy.sys file is loaded, it will appear as follows in the Ntbtlog.txt file:

```
Loaded driver \SystemRoot\System32\Drivers\NDProxy.SYS
```

And if it does not load, it will appear in the following manner:

```
Did not load driver \SystemRoot\System32\Drivers\NDProxy.SYS
```

From this information, you can troubleshoot what files might not be loading correctly when Windows XP starts up. This information can also help you determine whether critical system files are corrupted or missing. To determine whether an unloaded file is corrupted, check for files with a time stamp that doesn't match the OS installation date or check for zero byte files. You can also compare the unloaded files to the same files on another Windows XP computer or on the installation CD-ROM. You might also want to try running the System File Checker (Sfc.exe) command-line utility to inspect your system files.

Another troubleshooting strategy that you can use the Ntbtlog.txt file for is to compare which files are loaded in normal mode as opposed to safe mode. This allows you to see which services run in normal mode only. From there, you can experiment with adding one service at a time to determine which service might be causing problems. If you start your system in safe mode and an Ntbtlog.txt file already exists, the new boot log entries are appended to the existing file.

31

REPORTING SYSTEM AND APPLICATION ERRORS

When trying to find information about a system or program error, you have the option to report your error directly to Microsoft. Windows XP supports two methods for reporting errors to Microsoft:

- Error Reporting service
- Online Crash Analysis Web site

USING THE ERROR REPORTING SERVICE

The Error Reporting service monitors your system for OS and application errors and allows you to report them to Microsoft. If similar problems have been reported and information is available about the error, you'll be directed to this information. In addition, you'll be able to track your report on the Online Crash Analysis Web site.

By default, the Error Reporting service is configured to start automatically when you start Windows XP, and error reporting is enabled on the OS and all programs. To modify this configuration, open the System utility in Control Panel, select the Advanced tab, and click Error Reporting. The Error Reporting dialog box appears, as shown in Figure 31.7.

Figure 31.7
Error Reporting dialog box with Error Reporting enabled.

In the dialog box you can enable error reporting on the operating system and on programs running on your system. If you want to monitor specific programs, click Choose Programs to open the Choose Programs dialog box. The dialog box allows you to monitor all programs, Microsoft programs, Windows components, or individual programs. You can also designate specific programs to be omitted from the monitoring process.

Once Error Reporting is enabled, you'll receive a message alert each time Windows XP detects an error of a monitored system. If a Stop error has occurred, you won't receive the message alert until after you've restarted your computer in safe mode or normal mode and have logged on to Windows XP.

The message alert gives you the option of reporting the problem to Microsoft. If you select this option, a report is sent to Microsoft over an SSL connection. In some cases, you might be prompted for additional information about the problem or your system.

NOTE

> You must be connected to the Internet to be able to transmit error reports to Microsoft.

Once you've submitted an error report to Microsoft, you'll be provided a link to resources related to the problem, such as patches, updated drivers, or Microsoft Knowledge Base articles, depending on what's available. You'll also be directed to the Online Crash Analysis Web site (oca.microsoft.com), where you can track the report's progress. To check a report's status, you must have a valid .NET Passport account, which you can get at the Microsoft Passport Web site (www.passport.com). The Online Crash Analysis Web site is discussed in more detail below.

The Error Reporting service monitors your system for kernel mode errors and user mode errors. Kernel mode errors are the Stop errors you see when you're suddenly faced with a blue screen (the Blue Screen of Death). These are the errors that result in dump files being created on your system's hard disk. User mode errors, on the other hand, are those you see when an application hangs or generates an error. The OS keeps operating, but the application, at the very least, usually needs to be restarted. The method that the Error Reporting service uses to generate an error report depends on whether it is a kernel mode error or a user mode error.

31

KERNEL MODE REPORTING

When a Stop error occurs, Windows XP displays a Stop message that includes information about the error and writes information to the paging file—Pagefile.sys—which, by default, is located on the root directory of your system drive. Depending on how your system is configured, you must then either restart your computer, or it will restart automatically.

TIP

> When a Stop error occurs, you should record the information provided on the blue screen error message. However, if your computer is configured to restart automatically after a Stop error, you might not have enough time to write down all the details. You can disable the automatic restart feature by opening the System utility in Control Panel, selecting the Advanced tab, and clicking the Settings button in the Startup and Recovery section on the tab. When the Startup and Recovery dialog box appears, clear the Automatically Restart check box and click OK.

If your computer is restarted in safe mode or normal mode, Windows XP creates a memory dump file based on the information in Pagefile.sys. You can configure your system to create one of three types of dump files:

- **Small memory dump**—Consists of the least information and uses only 64KB of disk space. Sometimes referred to as mini dump files.

- **Kernel memory dump**—An intermediate size file that contains kernel memory information only. The file can be as large as 800MB.

- **Complete memory dump**—A file that contains the complete contents of the physical memory. The file will be the size of the physical RAM plus 1MB.

You can configure your system to use any one of these three types of dump files. To set up the type of dump file and its location, open the System utility in Control Panel, select the Advanced tab, and click the Settings button in the Startup and Recovery section. When the Startup and Recovery dialog box appears, select the type of file and enter the location of where it should be saved.

Windows XP creates a small memory dump file (mini dump) if a Stop error occurs, even if you've configured your system to create a kernel or complete dump file. The Error Reporting service sends the mini dump to Microsoft when it submits its error report. By default, the mini dump file is stored in the %systemroot%\Minidump folder and assigned a unique name that is based on the date (for example, Mini073102-01). The file includes stop error information, a list of drivers running on your system, and information about the process and thread that stopped.

NOTE

When you restart your computer after a Stop error has occurred, you're prompted to report the problem to Microsoft. After this event, Windows XP might begin to prompt you each time you restart your computer, even if there was no error during the previous session. This problem occurs because a flag has been set in the paging file saying that a mini dump file needs to be written. To resolve this problem, you must download a file from the Microsoft Web site or re-create the paging file. For information on how to resolve this issue, see Microsoft Knowledge Base article Q317277.

USER MODE REPORTING

The main difference between user mode reporting and kernel mode reporting is that user mode doesn't use a mini dump file. Instead, it uses information gathered when an application fault occurs. You still receive a message alert after the application fails, and you can send a report to Microsoft, but you don't have to configure any file settings or worry about rebooting your computer in safe mode or normal mode. As long as Error Reporting is configured for the programs you want to monitor, you're set to go.

You can view a list of errors recorded by the Error Reporting service in System Information. To access System Information, open the Run dialog box, type **msinfo32** in the Open textbox, and click OK. When the System Information window appears, expand the Software Environment node and click Windows Error Reporting. A list of errors is displayed in the details pane.

USING THE ONLINE CRASH ANALYSIS WEB SITE

The Online Crash Analysis site (oca.microsoft.com) allows you to send your mini-dump file—by submitting an error report—to Microsoft so that they can analyze your Stop error. To submit an error report, simply go to the Web site, click Submit an event report, and follow the on-screen instructions.

To use the Online Crash Analysis Web site, you must ensure that both JavaScript and cookies are enabled in Internet Explorer. You can submit your report anonymously, or you can provide your name, email address, and phone number so you can be kept informed of the status of and future developments about your error message. In order to check the status of your report, you must have a valid .NET Passport account.

Once you do submit your report, Microsoft tries to do the following:

- Determine the cause of the Stop error
- Categorize it according to the type of error
- Send you information related to the error

Microsoft prioritizes error reports based on the number of people who have been affected by the Stop error. You can check the status of your report by clicking Status and then following the onscreen instructions. For more information about Online Crash Analysis, visit the site and view the home page, the privacy information, and the frequently asked questions.

TROUBLESHOOTING INTERNET CONNECTIVITY PROBLEMS

Along with the proliferation of Internet usage has come remarkable strides in Internet-related technology. Applications and hardware are more powerful, a lot more reliable, and usually more user-friendly, making connecting to the Internet easier than ever. Yet the Internet—and our ability to connect to it—involves a complex system of domain namespaces, user authentication, power supplies, servers, protocols, routers, switches, cables, connections, modems, ISPs, and of course, properly configured home or business computers that allow us to connect our machines to the rest of the world. Sounds simple, right? Fortunately, Windows XP makes access to the Internet easier than ever. Yet even with today's sophisticated software, it's just a matter of time before you run into Internet connectivity problems, and when these problems do occur, the places to look are your hardware, your software configurations, and your TCP/IP connections.

➔ For more information about configuring and troubleshooting your Internet connection, **see** Chapter 8, "Configuring Your Internet Connection," **p. 275**.

TROUBLESHOOTING YOUR HARDWARE

I remember one time I started having trouble with a computer on my network. I could ping other systems, but I couldn't access any network resources. My requests seemed to time out before I could get what I needed. I spent hours pinging computers, switching hubs, checking connections, verifying permissions, reconfiguring TCP/IP, and even editing HOSTS and LMHOSTS files. Finally, as a last resort, I decided to switch the LAN cable on that computer, and suddenly everything worked. It didn't matter that I had no trouble prior to that time, or that the odds of a cable suddenly going bad are probably about a million to one. The point is that the cable stopped working correctly.

In today's world of more reliable hardware (and the software to support it), it's important to remember that a device can go bad and that whenever a connectivity problem does arrive, you should suspect your hardware as well as any other component in your system.

You've no doubt heard the urban legend about the product support technician who received a call from a gentleman who could not get his computer to work. After asking the customer a number of questions, the support tech determined that the problem was not with the computer, but with the fact that the computer was not plugged in.

I'm not suggesting that, should you run into connectivity problems, your solution will be quite so obvious. At the same time, it never hurts to ask yourself those questions whose answers might provide you with quick and easy solutions:

- Do you have power to your external modem? Is it plugged in? Turned on? Is the power light on?
- Are your network and phone cables properly connected? Do they work? Have they been recently tested?
- Do the indicator lights work properly on your modems, hubs, and network cards? Do they flicker when you send and receive data?
- Does your phone line have a dial tone? Can you make calls on that line?

The best way to test any of these devices is to try them in a working situation. For example, if you connect a phone to the line that connects to your computer and you can call out on that line, you can usually assume that the phone line and cable are not the cause of your problem.

NOTE

> If your modem makes screeching sounds for about 15 seconds and then disconnects you, or if you can contact your ISP but not establish a connection, your modem might be incompatible. Check with your ISP for information about compatibility.

In addition to checking external devices, you should check Event Viewer for information about connectivity problems related to your hardware. As I mentioned earlier in this chapter, Event Viewer allows you to view logs that can help you identify system and application problems. Look for warning and error messages related to your modem or network adapter.

→ For more information about using Event Viewer, **see** Chapter 26, "Using the Computer Management Console," **p. 1059**.

You should also check Device Manager if you're experiencing Internet Connectivity problems. Device Manager provides you with information about the hardware that's installed on your computer. You can use Device Manager to determine whether your hardware is work-ing properly, change your hardware configurations, identify and update device drivers, roll back a driver, or troubleshoot problems. Pay particular attention to the devices listed beneath the following nodes: Modems, Network adapters, Ports (COM and LPT), and Universal Serial Bus controllers.

If you see a device marked with a warning icon (a yellow circle with an exclamation point in it), you'll need to try to determine why you're receiving this warning. There are several rea-sons why a device might not be working:

- The device driver is incorrect or it has failed.

- The power has failed, is turned off, or is inadequate.

- Hardware resources conflict with each other.

To determine why a device is not working properly, you should view its properties. To do this, right-click the device and click Properties. You can then view information about the device and its driver, launch the Troubleshooter to try to find out the cause of a problem, modify configuration settings, run diagnostic tests, change port settings, update or roll back drivers, and modify resource settings.

31

TIP

> If you install a new modem on your system and Windows XP appears to be trying to use the old modem, you might have to delete the listing for the old modem from Device Manager. Go into Device Manager, expand the Modems node, right-click the old modem, and click Uninstall.

→ For more information about managing your hardware devices and using Device Manager, **see** Chapter 27, "Managing Hardware Devices," **p. 1103**.

TROUBLESHOOTING YOUR SOFTWARE CONFIGURATIONS

If you're troubleshooting your Internet connection and you're confident that your hardware is not the problem, you should start looking at your software configurations. Where you look depends on the type of Internet connection that you use. However, regardless of which type it is, be sure that you've checked the basics. For example, are you using the correct user name and password? Does your ISP require that a domain name be included with your user name?

You should also make sure that any applications you're using to access Internet resources are set up correctly. This can include your browser and email programs. For example, you can configure various connection options in Internet Explorer and Outlook.

If you're using a dial-up connection for Internet access, you'll first want to check the prop-erties for that connection. To view the properties, right-click the dial-up connection and click Properties. In the Properties dialog box, verify that you're dialing the right phone number, using the correct prefixes, and connecting with the proper modem. Also review your security and networking settings to be certain that they're set up correctly.

If you're using a broadband connection, you'll want to look at the properties of that connection. You should make certain that you're using the right device, protocols, and services. If you're using an external modem, you'll have to verify that the modem is also configured properly. Many of these settings will be specific to your ISP, so be sure to review any documentation you received when you set up your account.

→ Chapter 8, "Configuring Your Internet Connection," includes extensive information about troubleshooting your dial-up and broadband connections, **see p. 275**.

TROUBLESHOOTING TCP/IP CONNECTIVITY

TCP/IP, often considered the backbone of the Internet, is a suite of protocols and services that allow computers and other devices from around the world to communicate with each other and exchange data. In order for your computer to make that connection to the rest of the world, your TCP/IP settings must be configured correctly, and you must be able to establish TCP/IP connections at every point between you and your destination.

Before you can establish connectivity with other computers over the Internet, you must ensure that TCP/IP is properly configured on your computer. In most cases, you'll need to configure these properties to obtain your IP addressing information automatically, as shown in Figure 31.8.

Figure 31.8
Internet Protocol
(TCP/IP) Properties
dialog box.

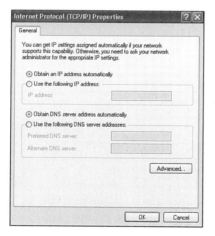

In order to troubleshoot TCP/IP connectivity, you should understand how TCP/IP is set up on your system. TCP/IP properties are configured for the individual connections. Once the connection is configured, the TCP/IP properties are assigned to the device that is used for the connection. For example, suppose you use a dial-up connection to communicate over the Internet via a modem. Before you can do that, your TCP/IP will have to be properly configured for that connection. If you were to configure the connection to be assigned an IP address automatically, the modem would receive an IP address from your ISP when you logged on to their system.

To configure TCP/IP, open the properties for the specific connection and find the listing for Internet Protocol (TCP/IP). For a broadband or dial-up connection, Internet Protocol

(TCP/IP) is listed on the Networking tab of the Properties dialog box. For a LAN connection, it's listed on the General tab. Once in the correct tab, select the Internet Protocol (TCP/IP) listing and click Properties. From there, you can configure the appropriate settings for your device. Be sure to consult your ISP's documentation to ensure that you configure the correct settings.

In addition to ensuring that TCP/IP is configured correctly, you can use TCP/IP utilities to troubleshoot your Internet connections. TCP/IP includes a number of utilities that allow you to verify TCP/IP configuration settings, connections, and routes. Some of these utilities allow you to run commands on remote computers, display the status of a print queue, or transfer files to and from remote computers. You can use several of these utilities specifically for the purpose of troubleshooting your TCP/IP connections. Table 31.4 providesan overview of these utilities.

TABLE 31.4   TCP/IP UTILITIES

Utility	Description
ipconfig	The ipconfig utility is always a good place to start whenever you're troubleshooting your Internet connection. This utility displays the current TCP/IP addressing information for network adapters and active dial-up connections on your computer. If the IP address, default gateway, or subnet mask appear incorrect, you've located at least one possible source of your problem. The utility is particularly useful if you receive addressing information automatically. This way you can see what IP addressing information has been assigned to the device.
ping	The ping utility allows you to verify your connections to routers, default gateways, and computers on the Internet. It's a quick way to determine whether or not you're able to connect to a specific computer. For example, if you can ping a computer on the Internet, you know that your hardware is working correctly and that your TCP/IP settings are correct. It also tells you that any routers between you and your destinations are working correctly.
tracert	The tracert command, like ping, sends packets to remote hosts. As it does this, it reports connectivity between each router in the path between you and the host. If you know that your Internet connection and computer are working, but you can't reach some or all sites, tracert can help you identify where the problem might be. When you run tracert, it first tests your network's gateway. If this is successful, it goes out to your ISP. If a problem occurs after two or three more connections, the problem is probably with your ISP. If you get past that, then there may be an Internet outage somewhere. One drawback with tracert is that many sites use firewalls, which block out tracert packets. In these instances, your request will time out for those segments.
pathping	The pathping utility is similar to tracert, except that it tests router connections more intensely. The utility first determines the route (sending only one packet per hop, rather than three, as is done by tracert), and then sends 100 ping packets to each router in the path. It then provides you with the number of lost packets and the average round-trip time for each hop.

31

For further information on these and other TCP/IP utilities, search for the utility in the Help and Support Center. You can search either on the utility name or you can simply type in `TCP/IP utilities`.

TROUBLESHOOTING POWER MANAGEMENT PROBLEMS

Windows XP supports several levels of power management. On systems that are fully compliant with the Advanced Configuration and Power Interface (ACPI) specification, the operating system manages most power-related functions. ACPI is installed on your system (during setup) only if all components are in compliance. On systems that are not ACPI-compliant but use an Advanced Power Management (APM) BIOS, Windows still provides power management, but it is not as extensive as an ACPI-based system. If ACPI and APM are not supported, Windows can still support some power management functions, but they are very limited.

You can configure power options in the Power Options Properties dialog box (shown in Figure 31.9). To access the dialog box, double-click the Power Options icon in Control Panel. The dialog box will not appear the same on all computers, depending on which type of power management is supported and whether you're on a desktop or laptop.

Figure 31.9
Power Options Properties dialog box.

The Power Options Properties dialog box shown in Figure 31.9 is for a laptop computer that supports the ACPI specification. To determine whether your system is using ACPI, open the Device Manager, and expand the Computer node. If ACPI is being used, there will be an entry named Advanced Configuration and Power Interface (ACPI) PC beneath the Computer node.

If your system does not support ACPI but supports APM, an APM tab will be included in the Power Options Properties dialog box. If your computer does not support ACPI or APM, ACPI will not appear in Device Manager, an APM tab will not be available in the

Power Options Properties dialog box, and the dialog box will include only limited functionality.

→ For more information about power management, **see** Chapter 6, "Setting Up Important System Services," **p. 201.**

Two important features supported by ACPI and APM are standby and hibernation. Unfortunately, these are the two areas in which you're most likely to experience problems related to power management. When your system is entering or exiting standby or hibernation, the following events might occur:

- You won't be able to leave standby or hibernation mode.
- You'll receive an error or Stop message when entering or exiting standby or hibernation mode.
- Your system will run differently after exiting standby or hibernation mode.

Any of these problems can be related to hardware, firmware, or software.

TROUBLESHOOTING HARDWARE COMPONENTS AND THEIR DRIVERS

Your hardware and its drivers must be ACPI-compliant or support recent revisions in APM standards. You'll have to verify with the manufacturer that your components support advanced power management and don't predate newer standards. Out-of-date devices and drivers can often cause incompatibility problems and can prevent your system from entering or resuming from standby or hibernation.

Audio and video devices are especially susceptible to disrupting power management. If a problem occurs, you should check for Windows XP updates for your drivers. However, if you find that you need to update multiple drivers, install one at a time and then test your system after each update.

Be especially careful with third-party drivers that are unsigned. A driver must support power management before it can be certified, so an unsigned driver can be the source of your power management problems. You may find it necessary to uninstall the software that installed the third-party driver. In some cases, adding a device that does not support advanced power management techniques can make certain options in the Power Options Properties dialog box unavailable.

TROUBLESHOOTING FIRMWARE

If firmware is out-of-date, you may experience power management problems. These can be the result of outdated system firmware (your BIOS) or the firmware in peripheral devices. In either case, you should check with your system's manufacturer to determine whether an updated version of the firmware is available.

If you need to update your system's BIOS, you are of course better off with firmware that is ACPI-compliant. If an ACPI-compliant BIOS is not available and your system is using

APM-based BIOS, you may have to disable APM to eliminate startup problems such as Stop errors or instability.

If you believe that your peripheral firmware is the cause of the problem, first check to see whether the software package you received with the peripheral includes diagnostic software that allows you to verify which version of firmware is installed. You can then check whether a newer version is available. Updates are often available for modems, CD-ROM drives, SCSI adapters, and video adapters. Remember, if you need to update more than one device, do it one at a time so you can see the effect of the update.

TROUBLESHOOTING SOFTWARE

Incompatible software can cause power management problems on your system. Certainly if your problems start to occur after you've installed new software, you're being given a pretty important clue. And if you uninstall the program and your problems go away, you can pretty much assume that the software itself is causing your problems, or it's the device drivers installed by the program.

If you suspect a problem with your software, you'll need to contact the manufacturer to determine whether any patches or product updates are available, or whether there are updated drivers. In the mean time, you might be able to get by simply by shutting down the program before your system goes into standby or hibernation mode. If this doesn't work, you might have to uninstall the program if it's causing you problems you can't live with.

Third-party programs that are associated with imaging devices, such as scanners and cameras, are more likely to cause power management problems than other types of software; however, these are not the only devices to be concerned with. For example, some CD-ROM mastering software developed for earlier versions of Windows might appear to be functioning properly but can in fact be incompatible with advanced power management features. What complicates situations like this is the fact that an error message might not correctly describe the problem. The message might tell you that standby failed and then point you to the device driver for your CD-ROM drive, rather than to the mastering software.

NOTE
> Some Direct3D screensavers, such as the 3D Flowerbox, 3D Flying Object, or 3D Text, might prevent your system from entering into standby or hibernation mode. The problem has to do with the timer used by ACPI to determine when to implement standby or hibernation mode. You can work around this either by selecting a different type of screensaver or by downloading a fix from Microsoft. For more information, see Knowledge Base article Q306676.

USING THE MICROSOFT KNOWLEDGE BASE

One of the most valuable resources that you have for troubleshooting problems on your system is the Microsoft Knowledge base. The Knowledge Base comprises a set of articles that provide solutions to various technical problems, explain how to perform product-related tasks, and answer commonly asked support questions.

You can search the Knowledge Base by going to the Microsoft support Web site (http://support.microsoft.com/default.aspx) and clicking the Search the Knowledge Base link. When you define your search criteria, you can select a Microsoft product; search for a specific topic, keyword, phrase, or article ID; select how the search will be conducted (for example, search the exact words as entered); limit how many articles are returned in a result set; determine which parts of the articles should be searched (the entire article, the title, or just the article ID); or define the date range based on when the articles were last modified.

Knowledge Base articles are each assigned an article ID (for example, Q234019, which is the article "Media Player Invalid File Format Error Message"). Being able to search by article ID is useful because various types of documentation refer to an article ID when suggesting sources of additional information.

You can also search the Knowledge Base by error message. In the Search for textbox, type the exact wording of the error message, including the error number, and if appropriate, select a product from the Select a Microsoft Product drop-down list. In addition, if you know the name of a file that you want to download, enter the file name in the Search for dialog box.

T I P

> I have found that sometimes when I'm searching for information on a specific topic, it helps to not select a product. Occasionally, an issue can apply to more than one product, or the information provided in an article for one product can help you find a solution to a problem you've run into in another product. This is particularly true with products in the same family, such as Windows 2000 and Windows XP.

In addition to the article ID, each Knowledge Base article includes the date the article was last modified, the products that the article applies to, and information about the issue that the article addresses. At the bottom of each article, you'll find a list of keywords that are related to products and subjects. Product Support Services use these keywords for tracking and sorting; however, you can use them to find groups of articles about similar topics.

For more information about using the Microsoft Knowledge Base, review the information on the Knowledge Base search page. If you're a TechNet subscriber, the Knowledge Base is included in your monthly Technical Information CD. This is more efficient and easier to search (in my opinion), but it's not always as up to date as the Web site.

31

CHAPTER 32

CRASH RECOVERY

In this chapter

RECOVERING WHEN THE SYSTEM FAILS

If you believe in Murphy's law that "if anything can go wrong, it will," then you already understand why Microsoft includes the ability to create a core dump in its operating systems. A *core dump* is that mysterious blue screen with white characters that you see when a Windows operating system, such as XP, has a system failure. It's also referred to jokingly as the "Blue Screen Of Death" (BSOD). A core dump includes specific information about a problem that Windows XP is unable to deal with on its own.

NOTE

The official Microsoft name for the BSOD seems to be "Bug Check," though they use a few different terms, and in conversation the Softies (software programmers at Microsoft) mostly seem to just use "Blue Screen."

TIP

If you're a network manager, you will probably want to test your computers' ability to recover from crashes and to properly report crashes to the event log or to your network monitoring system. You can manually cause a blue screen crash for testing purposes by opening the registry key

```
HKEY_LOCAL_MACHINE\System\CurrentControlSet\Services\i8042prt\
Parameters
```

and adding a DWORD value named CrashOnCtrlScroll with the value 1. Hold down the right Ctrl key and press Scroll Lock twice to crash Windows XP. It goes without saying, but we have to say it anyway: Before you do this you should be sure that you don't have any unsaved documents open and that the computer isn't running any critical applications. And, you'll probably want to delete the registry value or set it to 0 before deploying Windows XP in your organization. Unfortunately, this trick doesn't work with USB keyboards. Check out Microsoft Knowledge Base Article Q244139 for more details.

Core dumps are not the only result of incompatible hardware, faulty device drivers, or buggy software. Nor do all problems result in a core dump. In this chapter we will examine some of the most likely problem areas, such as system recovery, and provide possible solutions. Besides understanding core dumps, we need to interpret the BSOD information in order to diagnose the problem and to fix it. We'll also study methods to deal with application-specific issues. For example, you will learn how to use the Windows compatibility modes, Windows 95, Windows 98/Me, Windows NT 5 with Service Pack 5, or Windows 2000, to provide the correct emulation environment for your legacy applications and determine where Windows stores its temporary data files so you can recover data from crashed applications. Finally, we will look at methods to repair a Windows XP installation using the recovery console or the installation CD-ROM.

A core dump is primarily used by three types of people:

- **Windows XP device-driver developer**—This person writes kernel-mode device drivers for Windows XP and usually has a very intimate knowledge of the kernel. The developer generally spends quite a bit of time debugging the device driver.

- **Professional support technician**—This person determines the cause of a problem to prevent future occurrences of the same problem. Microsoft employees who are tasked with solving the problem of a reoccurring system crash on a server usually fit this profile.
- **The system administrator or IT professional**—Or in other words…You. While you might not get deeply involved in the process of dissecting core dumps to resolve them using a kernel debugger, you might want to get more involved but lack the knowledge of how to accomplish this goal. This chapter can help you gain such knowledge and improve your problem-solving skills.

Sometimes, you just need common sense to solve a problem. For example, you just installed new software or hardware and the computer reboots a blue screen. Chances are the new software or hardware is the cause of the failure, since you introduced something new to the system. Most times, you'll choose the Last Known Good option at system startup, and the computer will once more boot without a problem. However, to determine with certainty the cause of the problem, you really need to understand more about the information that a core dump provides.

T I P

> It might be worth noting that if the user logs in, they lose the ability to use Last Known Good.

32

INTERPRETING THE BLUE SCREEN OF DEATH

When a core dump occurs, it means Windows XP encountered an error it could not handle. If you enabled the Recovery option to write debugging information to a dump file, then a file called MEMORY.DMP will be placed in the SystemRoot directory, as well. You can change the location where the dump file will be written by altering the recovery settings, but this is the default location. This dump file size may vary, depending on the options you have chosen, and will contain a copy of memory of various system components, or the entire system memory, at the time the error occurred. If you choose a Complete memory dump and have a computer with 64MB of RAM, then your MEMORY.DMP file will be 64MB in size. We'll learn the options for reviewing a dump file in the section titled "Examining a Memory Dump File" later in this chapter. For now, let's concentrate on core dumps.

SETTING YOUR RECOVERY OPTIONS

Specifying your recovery options is performed through the Control Panel System applet. The recovery options are accessible by opening Control Panel, System applet, then Advanced, and clicking the Settings button next to Startup/Recovery. This will display the Startup and Recovery properties sheet shown in Figure 32.1. Within this property sheet, you can specify the following System failure settings:

Figure 32.1
The Startup and
Recovery property
sheet.

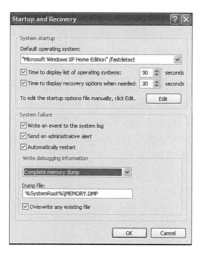

■ **Write an Event to the System Log**—Specifies to insert a copy of the stop message, not the complete dump, into the system event log when a stop message is encountered.

■ **Send an Administrative Alert**—Specifies to send an alert to the administrator that a stop message was encountered along with a copy of the stop message. To use this option, the Alerter and Messenger services must be running on both computers.

■ **Automatically Restart**—Specifies to reboot the computer after writing the dump file or, if no dump file was selected to be written, then shortly after the core dump screen has been displayed.

Within the Write debugging information group you may specify the following settings:

■ **Choose a Dump File Type of**
  • **(none)**—No dump file will be created.
  • **Small Memory Dump (64K)**—Creates the smallest possible dump file containing the most relevant information regarding the stop error.
  • **Kernel Memory Dump**—A dump containing kernel memory only.
  • **Complete Memory Dump**—A dump file containing everything in memory.

■ **Dump File**—Specifies to write a dump file to the specified file in the specified location.

■ **Overwrite Any Existing File**—Specifies to write a new dump file over a previous version, if it exists.

NOTE

The Overwrite Any Existing File option is only available if a Kernel Memory Dump or Complete Memory Dump is selected. The default is a Small Memory Dump.

By default, the Small Memory Dump option is enabled when you install Windows XP. I always recommend enabling the Kernel Memory Dump options on a computer that is encountering problems. When a stop error occurs, you will want to know why, so you can prevent the error from reoccurring. If the error cannot be resolved locally and you need to call in Microsoft Product Services and Support (PSS), creating a Complete Memory Dump is a better choice. A Microsoft PSS person can use that information to diagnose the problem and offer possible resolutions.

When a core dump happens, a blue screen with white text similar to the text shown in Listing 32.1 will appear. The core dump message shown in Listing 32.1 occurred on a desktop computer. I forced this error to occur by physically removing the bootable hard disk drive while trying to copy several megabytes of files. This is not something that would normally occur in a working system unless you accidentally pull a disk drive cable out while working on your system.

LISTING 32.1   THE CONTENTS OF A FORCED CORE DUMP

```
A problem has been detected and Windows has shutdown to prevent damage
To your computer.

KERNEL_STACK_INPAGE_ERROR

If this is the first time you have seen this Stop error screen
Restart your computer. If this screen appears again, follow these steps:

Check to make sure new hardware or software is properly installed.
If this is a new installation, ask your hardware or software manufacturer for
any Windows updates you might need.

If the problem continues, disable or remove any newly installed hardware
or software. Disable BIOS memory optimizations such as caching or shadowing.
If you need to use Safe Mode to remove or disable components, restart
your computer, press F8 to select Advanced Startup options, and then select
Safe Mode.

Technical Information:
*** STOP: 0x00000077 (0xC000000E, 0xC000000E, 0x00000000, 0x001F5000)

Beginning dump of physical memory
```

Like most core dumps, the one in Listing 32.1 is composed of four parts:

- The first part is the stop error code (often referred to as a Bugcheck) and it's the most important part of the core dump. If you enabled the recovery option to write a system event when a stop error occurs, it will include this first part of the core dump. Even if you enable the recovery option to write a system event, however, you should always write down the stop error code, its parameters, and, if available, the base address and driver that caused the problem.

32

NOTE

The error indicated in Listing 32.1 by the **STOP: 0x00000077 (0xC000000E, 0xC000000E, 0x00000000, 0x001F5000) KERNEL_STACK_INPAGE_ERROR** is a kernel stack in page error that indicates that the kernel attempted to read a page from the paging file but did not succeed. This is not surprising, because there was no hard disk in the computer at the time. The first parameter is a status code. The second is an I/O status code. To interpret either code requires a copy of the Windows XP Device Driver Kit (DDK). The third parameter specifies the paging file that the kernel tried to access. In this case, it tried to access the first paging file (the first paging file is zero, the second is one, and so on). The fourth parameter is an offset into the paging file that indicates the page that was trying to be read.

- The second part of the core dump is the recommended user action. This is usually a fairly generic, or common sense, message. The message usually has two parts. The first part usually states that if this is the first time the error has occurred, just restart your computer and ignore the error. The second part, however, often provides useful information concerning the most common cause of the error.

- The third part of the core dump is the driver information. This part, if present (not shown in the previous listing), usually includes the base address where the driver was loaded and a date time-stamp for the driver file. The base address helps isolate the cause of the error because some stop errors list an address that caused the error to occur. If this address falls within the base address of a driver, then that driver might be the cause of the error. The date time-stamp points out a version conflict that might have caused the error to occur. *It's worth noting that that the Date/Time stamp isn't in the expected human-readable format.*

- The fourth part of the core dump, when present (not shown in the previous listing), is the debug port and dump status information block.

It really helps to have a listing of the kernel mode error messages. After all, if you can understand the message, you might be able to correct the problem. The next section describes a variety of error messages you might encounter.

CAUTION

While I have done my best to translate the error messages into plain English and point out specific instances of what might cause them, I have to warn you that some of them are only for the technically advanced user, such as developers who regularly write device drivers.

KERNEL MODE ERROR MESSAGES

Windows XP includes so many different error messages that the only people who have a complete list are probably its developers. It's doubtful that even the device driver kit (DDK) has all the kernel mode error messages defined. The error messages that follow are those that have been defined and made available by Microsoft. Each is followed by some explanatory text. Be warned that this list is not comprehensive. However, it includes all the error messages I could find or have seen personally over the years.

APC_INDEX_MISMATCH (0x00000001)

Specifies that a kernel internal error occurred. This error is often caused by a file system driver that improperly enters or leaves a critical section.

IRQL_NOT_LESS_OR_EQUAL (0x0000000A)

Specifies that an attempt was made to access pageable memory at a process internal request level (IRQL) that is too high, or an attempt was made to access an area of memory with insufficient privileges. This error is usually caused by device drivers using improper address-es. *This error can also mean that the kernel-mode process or driver tried to access a memory location it doesn't have permissions to.*

If the kernel debugger is available, you can use it to get a stack back trace and determine the offending driver. The first parameter specifies the memory address that was referenced. The second parameter specifies the IRQL. The third parameter specifies a read operation (if zero) or a write operation (if one). The fourth parameter specifies the application address that referenced the memory.

NOTE

> In NT 4, application addresses can be used in troubleshooting because you always had a stack dump listing the addresses of the appropriate drivers. However, with Windows XP that type of dump rarely occurs. Stack traces that list possible memory locations aren't available without a debugger.

TIP

> The IRQL_NOT_LESS_OR_EQUAL error can also be caused by a resource conflict for a hardware device. So, it pays to check your installed hardware for any interrupt, I/O, DMA, or memory address (ROM BIOS/RAM buffer) conflicts.

KMODE_EXCEPTION_NOT_HANDLED (0x0000001E)

Acts as the default exception handler and is invoked if no other driver handles the exception. It can be a fairly common error message on a system with hardware that is seriously incom-patible with Windows XP. Another possible cause of this problem could be virus related. It may therefore be a good idea to scan for a virus on your next reboot. Assuming you can boot the system.

The exception address usually relates to a driver or service that caused the problem. Always make a note of this address as well as the file date of the offending driver or image that con-tains this address. You can use this information to determine if your problem was created by a version conflict (for example, installing an older version of the file). The first parameter specifies the exception code that was not handled. If you have the Windows XP DDK, you can examine NTSTATUS.H for a possible cause of the error. The second parameter speci-fies the address at which the exception occurred. The third parameter specifies parameter 0 of the exception. The fourth parameter specifies parameter 1 of the exception.

32

TIP

> If you look at the driver list on the bottom of the screen, you might find a file system driver (NTFS.SYS, FASTFAT.SYS, and so forth) or network driver (such as RDR.SYS). If you do, this often indicates a problem with the file system on the computer. Sometimes, Windows XP's auto-check cannot detect or repair a file error. If you are able to boot the system, then, from a command prompt, issue the CHKDSK *Drive*: /F command where *Drive* is the drive letter of one of your volumes. Repeat this command for each volume on your system. This procedure will run a more thorough scan of your hard disk and attempt to repair any errors it encounters. If you have a SCSI disk drive, you might also want to use the /R parameter, which will perform a low-level scan and attempt to replace any bad sectors found on the hard disk drive.
>
> Another commonly found error code is 0x80000003. This error code means that a hard-coded breakpoint or assertion was hit, but the system was booted with the /NODEBUG switch. This problem should not occur often. If it does, make sure a debugger is connected, and the system is booted with the /DEBUG switch. On non-Intel systems, if the address of the exception is 0x0BFC0304, then the bug code is the result of a cache-parity error on the CPU. Contact the hardware manufacturer for additional technical support if this problem occurs frequently.

KERNEL_APC_PENDING_DURING_EXIT (0x00000020)

Specifies that a file system driver or network redirector was written incorrectly. Third-party software redirectors are often the cause of this error because they do not always receive the heavy-duty testing of the base redirectors included with Windows XP. The first parameter specifies the address of the APC found pending during exit. The second parameter specifies the thread's APC disable count. The third parameter specifies the current IRQL.

FAT_FILE_SYSTEM (0x00000023)

This code specifies that an error occurred on a FAT volume.

NTFS_FILE_SYSTEM (0x00000024)

This code specifies that an error occurred on an NTFS volume.

CDFS_FILE_SYSTEM (0x00000026)

This code specifies that an error occurred while accessing a CD-ROM volume.

TIP

> File system errors are rare occurrences. Should you find yourself in this position, check the Microsoft Knowledge Base. For example, if you receive an error on an NTFS volume, you can specify STOP *FileSystemHexCode ErrorCode* within your query, where *FileSystemHexCode* would be 0x00000024 and the *ErrorCode* is the first parameter of the stop message. This might help determine whether your error is a known error and whether it has been fixed in a service pack or hot fix.

INCONSISTENT_IRP (0x0000002A)

Specifies that an I/O Request Packet (IRP) was encountered that was in an inconsistent state. This means that some field(s) of the IRP were inconsistent with the remaining state of the IRP. The first parameter specifies the address of the IRP that was found to be inconsistent.

PANIC_STACK_SWITCH (0x0000002B)

Specifies that the kernel mode stack was overrun or corrupted. This error usually occurs if the kernel mode driver consumes too much stack space.

DATA_BUS_ERROR (0x0000002E)

Generally, specifies that a parity error occurred in the system memory. It can also be due to faulty L2 cache or video memory, or even, in rare cases, by a cracked or damaged system board. This error can also be caused by a device driver accessing a 0x0000008XXXXXXX address that does not exist. The first parameter is the virtual address that caused the fault. The second parameter is the physical address that caused the fault. The third parameter is the processor status register (PSR). The fourth parameter is the faulting instruction register (FIR).

TIP

> If hard disk damage occurs from a virus, it can generate a DATA_BUS_ERROR. Therefore, if you can boot your system after receiving a DATA_BUS_ERROR it's a good idea to run a virus scanner to see if your computer is infected.

32

PHASE0_INITIALIZATION_FAILED (0x00000031)

Specifies that the system initialization failed early in the boot process. The kernel debugger is required to determine the cause of the error because this code tells you almost nothing about the root cause of the problem. The most likely cause is a hardware malfunction.

PHASE1_INITIALIZATION_FAILED (0x00000032)

Specifies that the system initialization failed during the boot process. The first parameter specifies the Windows XP status code that describes why the system thinks initialization failed. If you have the DDK, the second parameter indicates the location within INIT.C where phase one initialization failure occurred. The INIT.C file is a series of initialization instructions. If you can read C code, you can use this error code to determine the possible cause of the error. You can download the DDK from Microsoft at http://www.microsoft.com/ddk/.

NO_MORE_IRP_STACK_LOCATIONS (0x00000035)

Specifies that a higher-level driver has attempted to call a lower-level driver through the IoCallDriver() interface, but there are no more stack locations in the packet. So, the lower-level driver could not access the parameters passed to it by the higher-level driver. If you encounter this error, it is almost certainly caused by the manufacturer of the device driver. The first parameter contains the address of the IRP. *This is a pretty serious error. If this one pops up there is almost certainly going to be memory corruption and maybe data loss.*

DEVICE_REFERENCE_COUNT_NOT_ZERO (0x00000036)

Specifies that a device driver has attempted to delete one of its device objects from the system, but the reference count for that object was nonzero, which means that there are outstanding references to the device. If you encounter this type of problem, it is usually caused by a bug in the calling device driver, and you should contact the manufacturer for additional support. The first parameter specifies the address of the device object.

MULTIPROCESSOR_CONFIGURATION_NOT_SUPPORTED (0x0000003E)

Specifies that the system has more than one processor, but they are asymmetric in relation to one another rather than symmetric. To be symmetric, all processors must be of the same type and level. Trying to mix two Pentium processors with different *steppings (different microcode revision levels)*, for example, could cause this error. Additionally, on x86 systems, floating-point capabilities (ability to do mathematical calculations using a decimal point) must be present on all or no processors.

NO_MORE_SYSTEM_PTES (0x0000003F)

Specifies that the system has run out of Page Table Entries (PTE). This error can occur if the system is sustaining a high order of I/O operations causing fragmentation, or depletion, of the PTE storage. It can also occur from a device driver that does not manage memory allocations correctly, or from large kernel memory allocations from an application.

TIP

> If the error occurs due to insufficient PTE storage, you can edit the registry and increase the number of available PTEs. To do so, locate the HKEY_LOCAL_MACHINE\SYSTEM\ CurrentControlSet\Control\Session Manager\Memory Management key. Examine the PagedPoolSize and SystemPages values. If PagedPoolSize is not 0, change it to to 0. If SystemPages is not 0, assign a value of 40000 for systems with 128MB or less, or a value of 110000 for systems with 128MB to 256MB. It is not recommended to increase the value any higher without Microsoft technical support consultation.

MUST_SUCCEED_POOL_EMPTY (0x00000041)

This code specifies that a request for a nonpaged pool memory resource could not be fulfilled. Generally speaking, this error has two possible causes: First, the error may be caused by a driver or service that is leaking memory. To determine which driver or service may be at fault, first make sure you have installed the latest service packs and updates. Then disable all third-party drivers and services. Reenable them one at a time and monitor the nonpaged memory pool using the Performance Monitor. Any heavy spikes on the chart when a specific driver or service has been enabled will point to the offending driver or service. The second possible cause is insufficient physical RAM on your system. The documentation included with the product should indicate its memory requirements. If your physical memory falls within the amount required by the manufacturer, then either there is a bug in the product or you have other applications running (such as SQL Server) that are using too much of the nonpaged memory pool. If the latter is the case, you must add additional RAM or reconfigure the service to use less memory. If kernel debugger is available, you can use the VM command to list the size of the various memory pools. The first parameter specifies the size of the request that could not be satisfied. The second parameter specifies the number of pages used in a nonpaged pool. The third parameter specifies the number of pages that could not be provided by the nonpaged pool. The fourth parameter specifies the number of pages available.

MULTIPLE_IRP_COMPLETE_REQUESTS (0x00000044)

Specifies that a device driver has requested that an I/O Request Packet (IRP) be completed, but the packet has already been completed. Determining the device driver that caused the problem is difficult, because the tracks of the first driver have been covered by the second. The driver stack for the current request, however, can be found by examining the DeviceObject fields in each of the stack locations. The first parameter specifies the address of the IRP.

CANCEL_STATE_IN_COMPLETED_IRP (0x00000048)

Specifies that an IRP that is to be canceled has a cancel routine specified in it. This means that the packet is in a state in which the packet can be canceled. However, the packet no longer belongs to a driver, as it has entered I/O completion. This usually indicates either a driver bug or more than one driver accessing the same packet. The first parameter specifies the pointer to the IRP.

PAGE_FAULT_WITH_INTERRUPTS_OFF (0x00000049)

Specifies that a request to load a page from the virtual memory pool failed because interrupts have been disabled. It should be treated similar to an IRQL_NOT_LESS_OR_EQUAL (0x0000000A) error code.

FATAL_UNHANDLED_HARD_ERROR (0x0000004C)

Specifies that a hard error occurred during the system boot. The following are some common examples:

- **0x218**—Specifies that a necessary registry hive file could not be loaded. The hive file could be corrupted or missing. The Emergency Repair disk might be required to recover from this situation. The device driver might have corrupted the registry data while loading it into memory, or the memory where the registry file was loaded is not actually physically present. This last condition could be caused by an incorrect configuration on a computer with an EISA bus. In this case, examine the EISA configuration. The EISA

32

configuration utility must be properly configured to recognize that there is 16MB of RAM or more.

- **0x21A**—Specifies that either Winlogon or CSRSS (Windows) terminated unexpectedly. The exit code provides more information. Usually the exit code is C0000005, meaning that an unhandled exception crashed either of these processes.

- **0x221**—Specifies that a device driver is corrupted, or a system DLL was determined to be corrupted. Windows XP does its best to check the integrity of drivers and important system DLLs. If a corrupted file is detected during the load process, a message box might be displayed with the offending DLL listed. If the error occurs during the boot process, a blue screen might be displayed with the name of the corrupted file. The error will occur any time XP loads a system-required DLL that is corrupted. Reinstalling the OS is not always necessary, but might be the only way out. If you happen to have another OS on the same machine, you could boot into that, then compare the offending file to the original on CD/disk to be sure it isn't corrupted. The tricky part there is that if the hard disk containing the suspect OS is formatted NTFS, you have to be able to read that NTFS partition. You might also be able to boot the machine from a floppy or CD and compare the files, but this can be tricky as well.

NO_PAGES_AVAILABLE (x0000004D)

Specifies that no free pages are available to continue operations. The first parameter is the number of dirty pages (a page with modified data). The second is the number of physical pages on the computer. The third is the extended commit value in pages. The fourth specifies the total commit value in pages. If this error occurs, the most likely cause is insufficient memory or a page file setting that is too low to accommodate your system requirements. Either increase the size limit of your page file or add additional physical memory (preferred).

PFN_LIST_CORRUPT (0x0000004E)

Specifies that the error is caused by corrupted I/O driver structures. If the first parameter is one, then the second parameter specifies the ListHead value that was corrupted, and the third parameter specifies the number of pages available. The fourth parameter should be zero. If the first parameter is two, then the second parameter is the entry in the list that is being removed, while the third parameter is the highest physical page number, and the fourth parameter is the reference count of the entry being removed. This error may be caused by faulty RAM or motherboard.

PAGE_FAULT_IN_NONPAGED_AREA (0x00000050)

Specifies that an application, or operating system component, requested data that was not in memory. This error often occurs from faulty memory (main, cache, and so on) or applications (remote control or virus scanning software). The first parameter indicates the memory address where the fault occurred. The second parameter is 0 for a read operation and 1 for a write operation. (To be more specific, it's written out as a 32-bit hex value: 0x00000000 and

0x00000001.) That parameter specifies the type of access that was being performed when the error occurred. The third parameter, if not 0, is the instruction address that referenced the address in the first parameter. The fourth parameter is reserved for future use.

REGISTRY_ERROR (0x00000051)

Specifies that something has gone wrong with the registry. The first and second parameters specify where the bug code occurred. The third might be a pointer to the hive, and the fourth might be the return code from the HvCheckHive system call if the hive is corrupted.

NOTE

> Should your system fail to boot due to a corrupted registry, don't panic. There is hope for recovery. So long as you have made at least one Restore Point, you can use the technique provided in the Knowledge Base article Q307545 at
> `http://support.microsoft.com/search/preview.aspx?scid=kb;`
> `en-us;Q307545` to restore a previous snapshot of your registry.

TIP

> The REGISTRY_ERROR error can also indicate that the registry received an I/O error while trying to read one of its files. This means the error could be caused by hardware problems or file system corruption. The error can also occur because of a failure in a refresh operation used only by the security system (if resource limits are encountered during the refresh operation). If you see this error code, note whether the machine is a PDC or BDC. Determine how many accounts are in its security account manager (SAM) database, whether it can be a replication target, and whether the volume where the hive files reside is nearly full. This can be useful in determining the root cause. If the computer is a replication target, for example, and disk space is low on the SystemRoot partition, then the lack of disk storage could be the cause of the problem.

FTDISK_INTERNAL_ERROR (0x00000058)

Specifies that your system was booted from a mirrored set when the slave (shadow) drive is more up-to-date than the master (original) partition. This error might occur, for example, when you boot from the slave drive while the master is offline (perhaps it crashed). Or this error could occur when you boot from a revived Primary drive in a RAID 1 configuration after you have booted and run from the shadow drive for some period of time. In that case, when you revive the primary drive and reboot (from the primary drive) there could be data on the shadow drive that isn't on the primary (the data written while the primary was down). One solution is to boot from a Fault Tolerance boot diskette and go through the steps to break and re-create the mirror. Otherwise you might lose the data that's only on the shadow drive. Another solution is to shut down the system, wipe the mirror set flag using the FT disk utilities, set the slave drive as a master, and then boot the system. If the drives are to be remirrored, then the new drive (usually the drive failed because it was bad) can be configured as a slave drive and then a new mirror set can be created.

CONFIG_INITIALIZATION_FAILED (0x00000067)

Specifies that the registry could not allocate the memory pool needed to contain the registry files. This error should never occur in reality because it is early enough in system initialization that there should always be plenty of space in the paged pool. If it does occur, the most likely cause is faulty RAM. Parameter one should be five, and parameter two indicates the location in NTOS\CONFIG\CMSYSINI that failed.

IO1_INITIALIZATION_FAILED (0x00000069)

Specifies that initialization of the I/O system failed for some reason. There is usually no other information available. Generally, this error occurs because Setup made some incorrect decisions about the installation of the system or the user has reconfigured the system. Usually, the only way to resolve this error is to reinstall Windows XP, or to restore the previous hardware configuration.

PROCESS1_INITIALIZATION_FAILED (0x0000006B)

Specifies that a process failed to initialize early in the boot process. Parameter one specifies the status code that suggests why the Windows XP initialization failed, while parameter two specifies the location in NTOS\PS\PSINIT.C where the failure was detected.

> **TIP**
>
> The PROCESS1_INITIALIZATION_FAILED error can be caused by incompatibilities in the I/O subsystem. It is often seen on computers that have an older BIOS that does not support drives with greater than 1024 cylinders. It can also be related to generic drive geometry problems or incompatible software.

CONFIG_LIST_FAILED (0x00000073)

Specifies that one of the core system hives is corrupted or unreadable. The hive can be either SOFTWARE, SECURITY, or SAM. Parameter one is usually set to five, parameter two is usually set to two, parameter three is the index of the hive in the list, and parameter four is a pointer to a UNICODE_STRING containing the file name of the hive.

BAD_SYSTEM_CONFIG_INFO (0x00000074)

Specifies that the error might indicate that the SYSTEM hive loaded by the OSLOADER/NTLDR was corrupted. This is unlikely, however, because OSLOADER checks a hive to make sure it is not corrupted after loading the hive. This error can also indicate that some critical registry keys and values are not present in the hive. Rebooting and using the Last Known Good option might correct the problem. If that fails, you probably will need to reinstall or use the Emergency Repair Disk.

> One possible reason this error may occur is that a user attempts to install a previous version of Windows when Windows XP is already installed, in an attempt to dual-boot Windows XP and a previous version of Windows (such as Windows 2000). Previous versions of Windows are unaware of Windows XP and were not designed to load Windows XP.

CANNOT_WRITE_CONFIGURATION (0x00000075)

Specifies that the SYSTEM hive files (SYSTEM and SYSTEM.ALT) cannot be grown to accommodate additional data written into the hive between registry initialization and phase one initialization (when the file systems are available). Usually, this error means there are zero bytes of free space available on the drive, although it could be caused by trying to store the registry on a read-only device.

PROCESS_HAS_LOCKED_PAGES (0x00000076)

Specifies that a device driver is not cleaning up completely after an I/O operation. The first parameter is zero. The second parameter lists the process address. The third parameter is the number of locked pages. The fourth parameter is either a pointer to the driver stacks or zero if there aren't any driver stacks.

KERNEL_STACK_INPAGE_ERROR (0x00000077)

Specifies that the requested page of kernel data could not be read. This error is usually caused by a bad block in a paging file, a disk controller error, a loose disk cable, or improper termination of a SCSI chain. In rare cases, it is caused by running out of resources; specifically, the nonpaged pool with a status code of c000009a. If the first and third parameters are zero (0), then the second parameter is the stack value and the fourth parameter is the signature address on the kernel stack. If the first parameter is non-zero, then the second parameter is an I/O status code, the third parameter is the page file number, and the fourth is an offset into the page file.

TIP

> If you receive a KERNEL_STACK_INPAGE_ERROR error and the first and third arguments are both zero, then the stack signature in the kernel stack was not found. This error is usually caused by bad hardware. An I/O status of c000009c (STATUS_DEVICE_DATA_ERROR) or c000016a (STATUS_DISK_OPERATION_FAILED) normally specifies that the data could not be read from the disk due to a bad block. Upon rebooting the system, auto-check will run and attempt to map out the bad sector. If the status is c0000185 (STATUS_IO_DEVICE_ERROR) and the paging file is on a SCSI disk device, the cabling and termination should be checked. This error may also be caused by two devices (one of which is a disk device) sharing the same IRQ.

MISMATCHED_HAL (0x00000079)

Specifies that the HAL revision level and HAL configuration type do not match that of the kernel or the machine type. This error probably occurs because the user has manually updated either NTOSKRNL.EXE or HAL.DLL. Or, the machine has a multiprocessor HAL and a uniprocessor kernel, or the reverse. Parameter one specifies the type of mismatch that can be one of the following:

- The PRCB release levels mismatch (for example, something is out of date). If this is the case, parameters two and three are one of the following:
  - 2—Release level of NTOSKRNL.EXE
  - 3—Release level of HAL.DLL
- The build types mismatch. If this is the case, parameters two and three are one of the following:
  - 2—Build type of NTOSKRNL.EXE
  - 3—Build type of HAL.DLL, where the build types can be one of the following:
    - 0—Free multiprocessor-enabled build
    - 1—Checked multiprocessor-enabled build
    - 2—Free uniprocessor build
- The Micro Channel Architecture (MCA) mismatch. MCA computers require a MCA-specific HAL. If this is the case, parameters two and three are one of the following:
  - 2—Machine type as detected by NTDETECT.COM, where a value of 2 means the computer is MCA.
  - 3—Machine type that HAL supports, where a value of 2 means the HAL is built for MCA.

KERNEL_DATA_INPAGE_ERROR (0x0000007A)

Specifies that the requested page of kernel data could not be read. This error is commonly caused by a bad block on the hard drive under the paging file. The first parameter specifies the lock type (either 1, 2, or 3) OR the PTE address. The second parameter is always an I/O status code. The third parameter specifies the current process OR a virtual address. The fourth specifies the virtual address that could not be paged in.

INACCESSIBLE_BOOT_DEVICE (0x0000007B)

Specifies that during the initialization of the I/O system, the driver for the boot device (or the boot device itself) might have failed to initialize the device that the system is attempting to boot from. Or, the file system that is supposed to read the device might have either failed its initialization or simply not recognized the data on the boot device as a file system structure. Check that the disk controller is working and compatible. In the case of the driver failing to initialize, the first argument is the address of a Unicode string data structure that is the ARC name of the device from which the boot was being attempted. In the case of the file system not initializing or being recognized, the first argument is the address of the device object that could not be mounted.

TIP

> If the INACCESSIBLE_BOOT_DEVICE error occurs during the initial setup of the system, then the error might have occurred because the system was installed on an unsupported disk or SCSI controller. If this is the case, try to upgrade the BIOS firmware, locate any possible driver updates, and check for possible IRQ or I/O conflicts. This error can also be caused by the installation of a new SCSI adapter or disk controller or by repartitioning the disk with the system partition. If this is the case, on x86 systems, the BOOT.INI file must be edited, and, on ARC systems, Setup must be run.

INSTALL_MORE_MEMORY (0x0000007D)

Specifies that you need to add additional RAM. The first parameter specifies the number of physical pages found, the second the lowest physical page, the third the highest physical page, and the fourth should be zero.

UNEXPECTED_KERNEL_MODE_TRAP (0x0000007F)

Specifies that a trap occurred in kernel mode—either a kind of trap that the kernel is not allowed to have or catch (a bound trap), or a kind of trap that is always instantly fatal, such as a double fault. The first parameter is the number of the trap (0x8, for example, is a double fault).

NMI_HARDWARE_FAILURE (0x00000080)

Specifies that the HAL is reporting a hardware problem that the OS can't overcome, and that the user should call their hardware vendor for support.

32

MBR_CHECKSUM_MISMATCH (0x0000008B)

Specifies that the master boot record checksum that the system calculates does not match the checksum passed in by the loader. This usually indicates a virus has infected the boot sector. The first parameter is the disk signature from the MBR, the second is the MBR check sum calculated by OSLOADER, and the third is the MBR checksum calculated by the system.

PP0_INITIALIZATION_FAILED (0x0000008F)

Specifies that the phase zero initialization of the kernel mode Plug And Play Manager failed.

PP1_INITIALIZATION_FAILED (0x00000090)

Specifies that the phase one initialization of the kernel-mode Plug And Play Manager failed.

UP_DRIVER_ON_MP_SYSTEM (0x00000092)

Specifies that a uniprocessor-only driver is loaded on a multiprocessor system with more than one active processor. Parameter one specifies the base address of the driver.

INVALID_KERNEL_HANDLE (0x00000093)

Specifies that the kernel code (server, redirector, or other driver) attempted to close a handle that is not a valid handle. The first parameter specifies the handle that was passed to NtClose. If the second parameter is zero, it means that a protected handle was closed. If the second parameter is one, it means an invalid handle was closed. If you have a security dongle (a device connected to the serial or parallel port) attached to your computer, it may be the cause of this error. If such is the case, boot into Safe Mode and uninstall the software for the device or rename the device driver to prevent it from loading.

KERNEL_STACK_LOCKED_AT_EXIT (0x00000094)

Specifies that a thread exited while its kernel stack was marked as not swappable.

INVALID_WORK_QUEUE_ITEM (0x00000096)

Specifies that the kernel attempted to remove a queue item that contained a null parameter. This message usually indicates a device driver that incorrectly utilizes worker thread work items.

BOUND_IMAGE_UNSUPPORTED (0x00000097)

Specifies that MmLoadSystemImage was called to load a *bound image* (an image linked to a specific DLL). Bound images are not supported in the kernel. To resolve the problem, make sure BIND.EXE was not run on the image in question.

INVALID_REGION_OR_SEGMENT (0x00000099)

Specifies a device driver called ExInitializeRegion or ExInterlockedExtendRegion with an invalid set of parameters.

SYSTEM_LICENSE_VIOLATION (0x0000009A)

Specifies that a violation of the software license agreement has occurred. This can often be caused by attempting to change the product type of an offline system or attempting to change the trial period of an evaluation unit of XP. If the first parameter is set to

- **0**—An offline product type change was attempted. The second parameter should be set to 1 if the product is Windows 2003 Server or 0 for Windows XP Professional. The third parameter should be a partial serial number, and the fourth parameter should be the first two characters of product type from the product options.

- **1**—An offline change of the evaluation time period to a Windows XP evaluation version was attempted. The second parameter should be the registered evaluation time, the third parameter should be a partial serial number, and the fourth should be a registered evaluation time from an alternate source.

- **2**—The setup key could not be opened. The second parameter specifies the status code associated with the open key failure.

32

- **3**—The SetupType value from the setup key is missing. Therefore, the GUI setup mode could not be detected. The second parameter should specify the status code associated with the key lookup failure.
- **4**—The SystemPrefix value from the setup key is missing. The second parameter should then be the status code associated with the key lookup failure.
- **5**—Offline changes were made to the number of licensed processors. The second parameter should be a status code, the third should be the invalid value found in licensed processors, and the fourth should be the officially licensed number of processors.

UDFS_FILE_SYSTEM (0x0000009B)

Specifies that an error occurred on a UDF volume. (CD-ROM and DVD-ROM volumes)

MACHINE_CHECK_EXCEPTION (0x0000009C)

A fatal machine check exception has occurred. The parameters vary based on the processor type. If the processor has the ONLY MCE feature available (the Intel Pentium, for example), then the first parameter specifies the low 32 bits of P5_MC_TYPE MSR. The second parameter is zero. The third parameter is the high 32 bits of P5_MC_ADDR MSR. The fourth parameter is the low 32 bits of P5_MC_ADDR MSR. If the processor also has the MCA feature available (Intel Pentium Pro, for example), the first parameter is the MCA bank number. The second parameter is the address field of MCi_ADDR MSR for the MCA bank that had the error. The third parameter is the high 32 bits of MCi_STATUS MSR for the MCA bank that had the error. The fourth parameter is the low 32 bits of MCI_STATUS MSR for the MCA bank that had the error. There is nothing to be done about this error, other than knowing that it is defined.

DRIVER_POWER_STATE_FAILURE (0x0000009F)

Occurs when a device driver is in an inconsistent or invalid power state. This error message generally occurs during a shutdown, hibernation, suspend, or resume request.

If the first parameter is 1, then parameter 2 is a pointer to the device object and parameter 3 and 4 are reserved. The most likely cause of the problem is a device object that is being released from memory has an incomplete power request pending.

If the first parameter is 2, then parameter 2 is a pointer to the target device object, parameter 3 is a pointer to the device object, and 4 is reserved. The most likely cause of the problem is that the device object completed an I/O request for a system power state, but failed to call PoStartNextPowerirp. Should this error occur, check for an updated driver from the manufacturer.

If the first parameter is 3, then parameter 2 is a pointer to the target device object, parameter 3 is a pointer to the device object, and parameter 4 is the I/O request packet. The most likely cause is a faulty device driver that did not set the I/O request packet as pending or complete it. Once more, your best bet here is to check with the manufacturer for an updated device driver.

32

> **TIP**
>
> If the DRIVER_POWER_STATE_FAILURE error occurs frequently, the Microsoft Knowledgebase article Q266169 "How to Troubleshoot Problems with Standby Mode, Hibernate Mode, and Shutting Down Your Computer in Windows 2000" at `http://support.microsoft.com/default.aspx?scid=kb;[LN];Q266169` may provide assistance in resolving the issue.

ATTEMPTED_WRITE_TO_READONLY_MEMORY (0x000000BE)

Specifies that a device driver attempted to write to a read-only memory location. This error generally occurs after installing a faulty device driver. Recovery can be attempted by rolling back the driver, removing the driver, or using the Last Known Good. The first parameter is the virtual address of the write attempt. The second parameter is the contents of the PTE (Page Table Entry). The third and fourth parameters are reserved.

BAD_POOL_CALLER (0x000000C2)

Indicates that a faulty device driver, or kernel mode process, attempted to allocate a memory pool of zero bytes, allocate a memory pool that does not exist, attempt to free a memory pool that has already been freed, or attempt to free a memory pool at too high an IRQL. This error generally occurs after installing a faulty device driver. Recovery can be attempted by rolling back the driver, removing the driver, or using the Last Known Good. Additional causes include failing or defective hardware and some types of software (virus scanner, back-up, incompatible system service, and so on).

DRIVER_UNLOADED_WITHOUT_CANCELING_PENDING_OPERATIONS (0x000000CE)

Occurs when a faulty device driver exits without canceling a pending operation. The first parameter is the address of the memory being referenced. The second is a 0 for a read, or 1 for a write operation. The third, if non-zero, is the address of the instruction that referenced the memory. The fourth parameter is reserved. Recovery can be attempted by rolling back the driver (if listed), removing the driver, or using the Last Known Good.

DRIVER_IRQL_NOT_LESS_OR_EQUAL (0x000000D1)

Specifies that an attempt was made to access pageable memory at a process interrupt request level (IRQL) that is too high. This error is usually caused by device drivers using improper addresses. The first parameter specifies the memory address that was referenced. The second parameter specifies the IRQL. The third parameter specifies a read operation (if 0) or a write operation (if 1). The fourth parameter specifies the driver address that referenced the memory.

DRIVER_USED_EXCESSIVE_PTES (0x000000D8)

May occur if a device driver requests large amounts of kernel memory when insufficient page table entries (PTEs) exist. Parameter one, if not null, is a pointer to the name of the driver. Parameter two, if not null, is the number of PTEs in use by the offending driver. The third parameter is the number of free system PTEs available. The fourth parameter is the total number of system PTEs.

THREAD_STUCK_IN_DEVICE_DRIVER (0x000000EA)

Indicates a problem with a device driver that is causing the system to wait in a paused state indefinitely. Possible causes include drivers attempting to write to the video memory and waiting for the video card to return to an idle state. The most likely resolution to the problem is to obtain an updated video driver from the manufacturer or use a built-in video driver provided by Windows XP. There are four parameters. The first is a pointer to a thread object that is stuck in an infinite loop. The second is a pointer to a DEFERRED_ WATCHDOG object. The third is a pointer to a graphics device interface supplied context. The fourth, if not null, includes additional debugging information.

UNMOUNTABLE_BOOT_VOLUME (0x000000ED)

Occurs when a kernel mode I/O subsystem component attempts to load a boot volume and the attempt fails. This error may occur on systems using high throughput (ATA 66/100) disk drives with IDE cables not conforming to the ATA 66/100 specification (80 strands wide and 18" in length). The first parameter is the device object of the boot volume. The second parameter is the status code from the file system device driver indicating why it failed.

HARDWARE_INTERRUPT_STORM (0x000000F2)

Specifies that the operating system kernel detected a level interrupt device (usually PCI/AGP devices) that failed to release an interrupt request (IRQ). This error may indicate a faulty device driver or an attempt to share an IRQ between edge (AT) and level (PCI/AGP) devices. (Edge and Level are two classifications of devices differentiated by the kinds of interrupts that trigger them.) Resolution may be possible by reserving the IRQ used by the edge (AT) device in the system BIOS and forcing the PCI/AGP device to use another IRQ. Other possible solutions include removing the offending driver or hardware device.

STATUS_SYSTEM_PROCESS_TERMINATED (0xC000021A)

Occurs when the operating system switches into kernel mode and a user mode subsystem (Winlogon, Client Server Runtime Subsystem CSRSS) has been compromised and can no longer provide security. This error may indicate a faulty third-party application, modification of system files permission levels that prevent the system from accessing required files, or incompatible system files. Recovery can be attempted by removing the offending software using the Last Known Good, driver rollback (see Chapter 27 "Managing Hardware Devices."), or by restoring the applicable permissions to system files.

TIP

One of the causes of this error is incompatible backup/restore software. Should you encounter this error, check your backup software to make sure it is Windows XP-compatible. If not, upgrade it or replace it.

STATUS_IMAGE_CHECKSUM_MISMATCH (0xC0000221)

Occurs when a system file is corrupted. If the error occurred due to newly installed software, recovery may be attempted by rolling back the driver, uninstalling the software, or restoring the original file from your installation media. This error can also be caused by a disk read error, faulty memory, or a faulty page in the page file (bad disk block).

Examining a Memory Dump File

The next step in the process of getting down and dirty with a core dump is to examine the MEMORY.DMP file. While this might not always prove useful to you, it will prove useful to the Microsoft technical support person you call when trying to solve a recurring problem that you cannot solve yourself. So, let's take a look at the available tools and see what you can find in a dump file.

NOTE

> Remember that there are three kinds of memory dumps: Complete, Kernel, and Small. The size and location of the memory dump file can be set via the System applet in Control Panel, Advanced tab. However, basically the bulk of useful information relevant to an administrator is the same as that provided by the blue screen error message. Using a memory dump is just another way to obtain this information, assuming the user rebooted without writing it down.

Why Bother with Dissecting Core Dumps?

For most people—even the most advanced users—dissecting a core dump isn't going to be helpful unless you are a software developer. Only the most technical-minded developers ever bother with a core dump. The main reason for discussing the core dump thus far is to obtain the stop error code and to prepare a dump file to be sent out to your technical support personnel. This technical support contact might be a hotshot device driver developer within your own organization, or it might be a member of the Microsoft Product Support Service (PSS) group. In either case, you can save a great deal of time and effort by verifying the dump file before you send it out.

Of course Windows XP doesn't always produce a core dump when something goes wrong. Instead of core dumps, you're more likely to encounter problems with legacy applications malfunctioning, which we'll discuss in the next section.

Before you can use a dump file, you need to set up your computer to read it. This requires that you install the debug symbol files on to your computer. These symbol files must also exactly match the build of Windows XP that you are trying to debug. Which means, if you installed a service pack onto Windows XP, then you need to install the debug symbols from the service pack, as well. The symbol files and debug tools are available for download from

`http://www.microsoft.com/ddk/debugging/`

The symbol files are in a self-extracting archive. The only choice the user has to make is to accept the default location, or to change it.

32

TIP

> An alternative to using locally installed symbols is to use the Microsoft Symbol Server. The Microsoft Symbol Server is a computer on the Internet that contains the currently available symbol files. A debugger that uses the Microsoft Symbol Server will download symbol files from the server to a local directory on an as-needed basis. This can save a significant amount of local disk storage and assure that you are using the most current symbol file. Using the Microsoft Symbol Server requires a computer with a direct Internet connection. Directions for using the Microsoft Symbol Server can be found at
> `http://www.microsoft.com/ddk/debugging/symbols.asp.`

NOTE

> The Microsoft Web Resources includes a wealth of useful knowledge and tools. It is located at `http://www.microsoft.com/windows/reskits/webresources/`. Also, you may want to check out the Microsoft Symbol Server which is a handy tool for anyone with a live Net connection:
> `http://www.microsoft.com/ddk/debugging/symbols.asp.`

If you are a Windows XP developer and familiar with the Windows XP APIs, then you can use the Windows XP kernel debugger to examine the memory dump file.

Before you can use the kernel debugger, you have to set an environment variable to inform the debugger where the symbol files are located. You can accomplish this with the command

```
SET _NT_SYMBOL_PATH=C:\WINNT\SYMBOLS
```

if you installed the symbols into the default path. Otherwise, you will need to change the path for the `set` command. Once you have done this, you can load the dump file using the Windows Debugger (WinDbg.EXE) and choosing Open Crash Dump from the File menu. You can also use the Kernel Debugger in command-line mode by opening a command prompt, changing the directory to the location of the KD.EXE executable (by default that is C:\Program Files\Debugging Tools for Windows), and executing the following command:

```
kd -z DumpFileName
```

where *DumpFileName* is the location of the dump file to load.

Once you have loaded a dump file, in WinDbg or KD you can issue the `.bugcheck` command to display the bug check (stop error) code and data. For more detailed information about the error, use the `!analyze` command in WinDbg and a listing similar to that provided in Listing 32.1 will be displayed, as you see in Figure 32.2. The `!analyze -v` command will display a text-based error code (MANUALLY_INITIATED_CRASH), the hex stop code or bugcheck (e2), and any parameters.

Figure 32.2
A sample stop error being viewed in WinDBG.

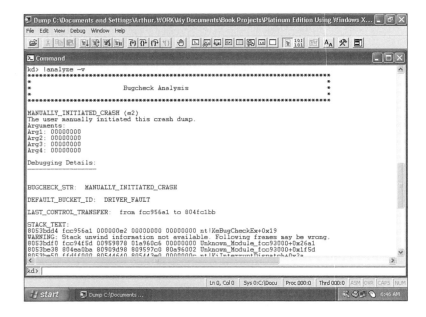

FIXING MALFUNCTIONING LEGACY APPLICATIONS OR SERVICES

Just because you are using Windows XP doesn't mean that all of your applications are Windows XP-ready. In fact, most users have more legacy applications than they do Windows XP-certified applications on their computer. There is no guarantee that legacy applications will run properly under Windows XP. Problems range from minor display-related problems to major application crashes including general protection faults and loss of associated data.

Since most users are unwilling to give up their legacy applications, Microsoft included legacy compatibility modes to improve your chance of running your favorite legacy application. Legacy services that have problems running under Windows XP should be upgraded as soon as possible to officially compatible Windows XP versions. If that isn't possible, and the fault is minor, you may be able to use the service recovery features to automatically recover and continue to use the service. Should you be in the position of running an application when it crashes and burns, knowing where the application stores its temporary data file may allow you to recover all, or part, of the data. If an application stops responding, it may be useful to know how to terminate it. In the next four sections, we will examine each of these options in more detail.

When an application crashes, you are presented with a dialog similar to that shown in Figure 32.3. This dialog can be useful in many ways. You can use the supplied information to send to your developers to aid them in their debugging efforts. Or you can send it as a report to Microsoft so that Microsoft can attempt to resolve the problem or relay the information to the manufacturer of the application.

Figure 32.3
A crashed application
dialog box.

Before you do, you may want to examine the data yourself to ease your mind concerning the information sent to Microsoft. The specific information provided to Microsoft is similar to that provided by the old Dr. Watson report. You can view this data yourself by following the onscreen *click here* links. The basic data that is included is

- **Exception Information**—This data includes the exception code, exception flags, a record, and address location of the exception.
- **System Information**—This data includes the version of Windows, a CPU vendor code, a CPU version code, a CFP feature code, and a CPU AMD feature code.
- **Module X**—This data includes specific information about the application or module that crashed and any other modules loaded in memory. It includes the application name, image base address (where it is located in memory), image size, checksum, time date stamp, and version information (signature, structure version, file version, product version, flag masks, flags, operating system, file type, sub type, file data).
- **Thread X**—This data lists assembler register and stack data for each thread running on the computer.

Using Compatibility Modes

Windows XP includes several different runtime environments tailored to more closely emulate Windows 95, Windows 98/Me, Windows NT 4 with service pack 5 installed, and Windows 2000. If your application has display-related problems, then the compatibility display options may provide a solution to allow your legacy application to operate. There are two ways to configure the compatibility modes. First, you can use the Windows XP Program Compatibility Wizard. Secondly, you can manually configure the application's compatibility mode though a shortcut to the application. The shortcut can reside on the desktop or Start menu.

NOTE

One of the advantages the Program Compatibility Wizard provides is the ability to install the application and use the Windows XP Migration DLLs to replace incompatible files, move files to new locations, or move registry subkeys and entries during the application setup. It can therefore be useful to remove the application and then reinstall it using the Program Compatibility Wizard.

To use the Program Compatibility Wizard follow these steps:

1. Select the Program Compatibility Wizard by clicking Start, All Programs, Accessories.
2. Click Next to begin the wizard and follow the onscreen prompts.

In case you didn't know it, all application shortcuts let you easily configure them to run in a specific compatibility mode. To manually configure the compatibility mode of a shortcut on your Start menu, Desktop, Quick launch bar, and so on, follow these steps:

1. Right-click the shortcut and choose Properties from the popup menu.
2. Select the Compatibility tab, and the property sheet displayed in Figure 32.4 will appear.

Figure 32.4
The Windows XP Compatibility Mode Property Sheet.

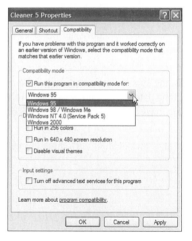

3. In the Compatibility mode group, check the Run This Program in Compatibility Mode check box.
4. From the drop-down list box (also shown in Figure 32.4), select the appropriate emulation environment.

TIP

> Choosing the most appropriate emulation environment can be difficult. The best way to determine the most likely mode is to refer to the program documentation and view the system requirements. If the application is a Win16 (16-bit application) designed for Windows 95, choose Windows 95 instead of Windows 98/Me. If the application is a Win32 (32-bit application) designed for Windows NT or Windows 2000, choose the Windows NT or Windows 2000 environments. If the application fails to operate correctly, try another option in the list and run the app again. Sometimes, even though an application will run fine under a specific operating system (for example, on a machine that really has, say, Windows 98 installed), it may not run properly using the Windows 98 compatibility mode in XP or any of the other emulation environments.

5. Click the OK button and run the application.

TIP

> If the application runs, but there are some display anomalies, repeat the above steps, and modify the Display settings. For applications, mostly games, designed to run in VGA mode, enable the Run in 640×480 screen resolution checkbox. If the application requires a 256-color palette, enable the Run in 256 Colors check box. If you see menu aberrations, enable the Disable Visual Themes check box.

APPLICATION COMPATIBILITY TOOLKIT

Microsoft supplies a special Application Compatibility Toolkit (ACT) on the XP CD to aid both application developers and IT professionals in making their applications usable with XP. You'll find the toolkit in the \Support\Tools directory of the Windows XP CD. There's a later release of the toolkit available online at www.microsoft.com/windows/appexperience. (The application has an easily findable link in it for easy updating, as well.)

ACT contains several tools for developers and IT professionals to aid in rendering older applications workable on the XP platform. There are also extensive overview and help files that discuss many aspects of application compatibility and workarounds for older programs. These tools help you fine tune the environment settings for older applications so they can run with a minimum of fuss, crashing, or failure to execute.

One of the programs for IT pros is called QFixApp (Quick Fix App). It makes short work of testing close to 200 environment fixes (known as "shims") on a given app, to determine their effectiveness. When invoked, Qfixapp.exe first reads the %SystemRoot%\windows\apppatch\sysmain.sdb database to produce a list of available fixes. When you choose an application to fix, the adjusted settings (called the AppFix) will be applied to the app, if found.

TIP

> See Microsoft Knowledge Base Article 294416 for more info about using QfixApp.

Another IT application, called the Compatibility Administrator Tool, includes a database of predefined fixes for known applications (see Figure 32.5). By examining the predefined fixes for specific apps, you can try matching a set of those to a similar program you may be having trouble with, and apply those using QFixApp.

Figure 32.5
The Compatibility Administrator Tool.

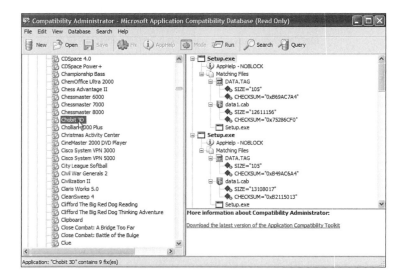

Windows NT used to be known for being a bit irksome by not running older Windows and DOS apps peaceably. With these tools, however, you stand a better chance than ever of keeping your legacy programs going until they can be updated. Using these tools will take some research, but can pay off in the long run. Of course, first try running your apps using the various preset environments via the shortcut properties, as explained in the previous section, since that's a much easier fix than digging into these IT tools.

USING SERVICE RECOVERY MODES

Unfortunately, there is no compatibility mode for services like there is for applications. Services that fail to operate correctly, that cause data loss or system instability should be upgraded immediately. If an upgrade is not available, they should be uninstalled or disabled. If the error is minor, however, and the only outward sign of incompatibility is the occasional service failure where the service stops executing, you can use the Service Recovery feature to automatically restart the service. To configure the Service Recovery Options, follow these steps:

1. Select the Services shortcut from the Administrative Tools folder in the Control Panel to launch the Services MMC.

2. Right-click the service in the Name column and choose Properties from the pop-up menu.

3. Select the Recovery tab to display the Recovery property sheet as displayed in Figure 32.6.

Figure 32.6
Configuring a service's recovery mode.

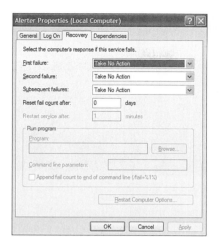

4. For the First, Second, and Subsequent failures list box select one of the following choices for each entry:

   • Take No Action: Do nothing.

   • Restart the Service: Restarts the service.

   NOTE

   > The Reset Fail Count After *x* Days entry is used to specify a time (in days) to reset a failure count back to zero. The Restart Service After *x* Minutes entry is used to delay restarting the service for the specified time. Often this option is used in conjunction with a batch file, user-specified application, or other error-checking routine to provide time for the process to finish executing before restarting the service.

   • Run a Program: Enables the Run program group and allows you to run a user-specified program, specify a command line to pass to the program, and if desired enable a fail count switch parameter to be passed to the application.

   • Restart the Computer: Restarts the computer if the service fails.

5. Click the OK button and save the service recovery settings.

FINDING WINDOWS TEMPORARY FILES

If the worst happens, and your application terminates unexpectedly while working on a document, there is a good chance that you will have lost the data since the last time you saved the document. You can often recover this data without a great deal of work. You just need to know where to look for the data file used by the application. Usually data is stored in a temporary location specified by the Temp or TMP environment variables. The easiest way to locate these absolute paths is to run the set command from a command prompt. The output from such a command is displayed in Figure 32.7. Notice the temp and tmp variables in the listing.

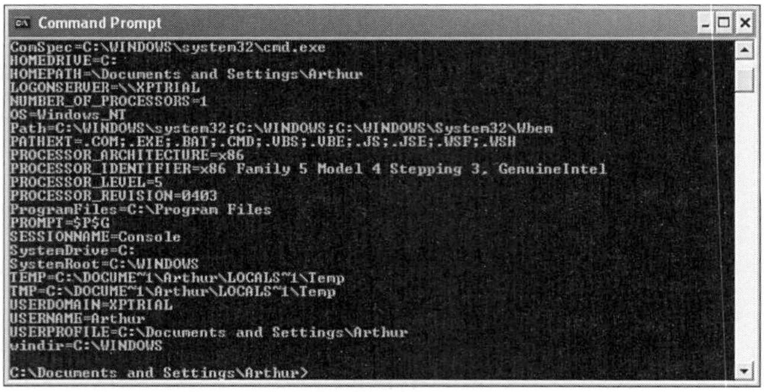

Figure 32.7
Determining the absolute path for temporary files.

As you can see from the preceding output, the default temporary directory is stored in the individual user profile directory. The environment variable uses short (8.3) filenames. The actual directory path is C:\Documents and Settings*UserName*\Local Settings\Temp where *UserName* is the logon name of the current user. The temporary directory can be overridden by modifying the `temp` and `tmp` environment variables using the Control Panel System applet.

> **NOTE**
>
> If you upgraded your Windows XP installation from a previous version of Microsoft Windows, then your temporary directory setting from your autoexec.bat file may have been migrated as well.

Some applications do not use the default temporary directory as specified by the environment variables. Instead they use a custom application specific directory. Usually, the application will provide a GUI interface to allow you to choose, or modify, the temporary directory. Some applications, such as Microsoft Outlook and Outlook Express, store their permanent data (like your personal folder file) in subdirectories of the user profile path. So, if you do not see the data in the Temporary directory previously mentioned, look in

`C:\Documents and Settings\`*UserName*`\Application Data/`*Company Name*`/`*Application Name*

or

`C:\Documents and Settings\`*UserName*`\Local Settings\Application Data\`*Application Name*

where *UserName* is the logon name of the current user, *Company Name* is the name of the company that developed the application (such as Microsoft), and *Application Name* is the name of the program (such as Outlook).

> **NOTE**
>
> The Application Data directory described previously is a hidden directory. It will not be viewable in Windows Explorer unless you enable the Show Hidden Files and Folders option. You may access this option by choosing the Folder Options command from the Tools menu in Windows Explorer. Then change to the View property sheet and look under Hidden Files and Folders.

TERMINATING AN APPLICATION THAT DOESN'T RESPOND

Just because an application no longer appears to be responding to your input commands via the mouse or keyboard, that doesn't necessarily mean the application has stopped responding. It may be that the application is just taking a long time to process previous inputs. A Windows application processes Windows messages (input via keyboard or mouse) in a message loop. So long as messages continue to be processed by the application, Windows XP considers the application to be responding properly. When an application stops responding to messages, however, Windows XP will assume the application is not responding and change its status accordingly. You can determine the status of running applications by using the Task Manager as shown in Figure 32.8.

Figure 32.8
Checking the status of an application with the Task Manager.

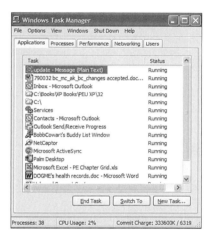

When an application stops responding, it still continues to use system resources. These resources include CPU cycles, memory, and possible temporary disk storage. The preferred method to terminate an application is to click the Close button (X in the upper right hand corner of the application), because if the application is still processing Windows messages it will terminate itself and release all system resources. If the application is not responding to messages, the End Task dialog will be displayed allowing you to terminate the application.

Even though you can terminate a non-responding application in this fashion, it is not recommended except as a last resort. Terminating a task in this fashion will recover some, but rarely all, system resources that were in use by the application. Temporary disk storage will almost never be released properly, which means that you will need to manually delete the temporary files used by the application.

An alternative method of terminating an application is by using the Task Manager. You can launch the Task Manager by pressing Ctrl-Alt-Del and clicking the Task Manager button or by right-clicking the Taskbar and selecting Task Manager from the pop-up menu. To terminate an application, just select it in the Task and Status window of the Task Manager and click the End task button.

REPAIRING WINDOWS XP

If you are reading this section, then most likely you are preparing for the worst, or the worst has already happened. Hopefully, you're doing the prudent thing by preparing for the inevitable failure. There are basically three methods you can use to repair, or in extreme cases, rebuild Windows XP. These methods are

- Using the Recovery Console
- Using the installation CD-ROM
- Using a third-party recovery application

NOTE

> Before you try any other method to repair your Windows XP installation, you should try one of the three available Safe Mode alternatives. Use Safe Mode if you have your installation media available and can boot into GUI mode without problems. Use Safe Mode with Networking if you can boot into GUI mode and your installation media resides on a network. Use Safe Mode with Command Prompt if you are unable to boot into GUI mode.

USING THE RECOVERY CONSOLE

The Recovery Console provides a subset of the Windows XP operating system environment. Its purpose is to allow recovery of a corrupted, or otherwise inaccessible, operating system when you are unable to boot using Normal Mode or Safe Mode. It can be accessed by booting from the installation CD-ROM, as shown in Figure 32.9, or on an x86 system, from the Advanced Options boot menu.

Figure 32.9
Accessing the Recovery Console from the Windows XP installation CD-ROM.

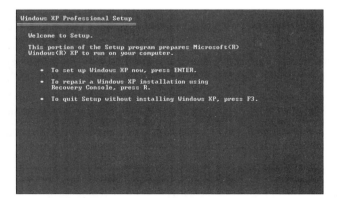

NOTE

> The boot menu option for the Recovery Console is only available if the Recovery Console has been installed as an available boot option. Installing the Recovery Console can be accomplished by inserting your installation CD-ROM and executing the following command:
>
> `CDRomDriveLEtter\I386\WINNT32 /CMDCONS`
>
> You must be logged in to Windows as an Administrator to run the above command.

The Recovery Console provides limited access to the NTFS file system. You can use the Recovery Console to run a limited number of command-line applications to perform basic troubleshooting and maintenance tasks. The commands you may execute while using the Recovery Console are displayed in Table 32.2.

CAUTION

> To gain access to the file system, the Recovery Console will prompt you for the local computer's administrator account password. It will then authenticate this password using the current password stored in the SAM registry hive. If this hive is damaged, you may be unable to log on to the local file system and run the recovery console.

TABLE 32.2   THE RECOVER CONSOLE COMMANDS

Command	Description
Attrib	Changes file, or directory, attributes.
Batch	Executes a series of commands stored in a text file.
Bootcfg	Scans your hard disk and adds, or repairs, your boot.ini file.
CD or Chdir	Changes directories.
ChkDsk	Checks a volume for disk errors and repairs them.
Cls	Clears the screen.
Copy	Copies a single file from one location to another.
Del or Delete	Deletes file(s).
Dir	Displays the contents of a directory or subdirectory.
Disable	Disables a service or driver.
DiskPart	Manages hard disk drive partitions.
Enable	Enables a service or driver.
Exit	Closes the Recovery Console and reboot your computer.
Expand	Decompresses a compressed file.
FixBoot	Rewrites the boot sector on your hard disk drive.
FixMbr	Rewrites the master boot code on the Master Boot Record (MBR).

continues

32

TABLE 32.2 CONTINUED

Command	Description
Format	Formats a volume.
Help	Displays Recovery Console Help information.
ListSvc	Lists installed services on your computer.
Logon	Detects and logs on to a Windows XP installation.
Map	Lists all available drive letters.
Md or MkDir	Creates a directory.
More or Type	Displays the contents of a file.
Rd or RmDir	Removes a directory.
Ren or Rename	Renames a single file.
Set	Sets an environment variable.
SystemRoot	Sets the current working directory to the Windows XP installation directory (usually C:\Windows).

To run the Recovery Console

1. Choose the Recovery Console from the boot menu.
2. You'll be asked which Windows installation you want to log in to. Point to the one you want to repair.
3. You'll be prompted to enter your administrator password.

Once you have successfully launched the Recovery Console (it's nothing fancy; you just see a typical DOS prompt, incidentally), and have access to the local file system, you can begin to repair your computer. Keep in mind that you can only use the commands displayed in the previous table within the Recovery Console. As an example, consider the problem of a boot-time device driver that causes the system to reboot when loaded. A boot-time driver will most likely still load in Safe Mode and also cause the system to reboot when loaded. Removing this driver can be accomplished by using the Recovery Console. For this example, assume the boot-time driver Beep is causing a system-related problem and needs to be disabled. Disabling a driver or service can be performed by issuing these commands in the recovery console:

1. Execute the `LstSvc` command to list the services and drivers on your system.
2. Press the Space bar to list the next screen of services and drivers.
3. Repeat step 2 until you see the Beep (or your service or driver name) driver listed.
4. Press the Esc key to stop the list of services or drivers and return to a command prompt.
5. Execute the command `Disable Beep`.

6. You will be presented with a message informing you that the service startup status has been changed and listing its previous state so you can record it for later use.

7. Exit the Recovery Console and restart the system.

To enable a service or driver—for this example, we will once again use the Beep driver—you can follow these steps:

1. Execute the LstSvc command to list the services and drivers on your system.

2. Press the Space bar to list the next screen of services and drivers.

3. Repeat step 2 until you see the Beep (or your service or driver name) driver listed.

4. Press the Esc key to stop the list of services or drivers and return to a command prompt.

5. Execute the command Enable Beep SERVICE_SYSTEM_START.

CAUTION

> The Enable command has four startup types. These are SERVICE_BOOT_START, SERVICE_SYSTEM_START, SERVICE_AUTO_START, SERVICE_DEMAND_START. You should use the same startup value as originally assigned to the service or driver to avoid potential startup problems. If you are unsure of the startup type, supply no startup type and the default type that was previously recorded by the system will be used.

6. You will be presented with a message informing you that the service startup status has been changed and listing its previous state so you can record it for later use.

7. Exit the recovery console and restart the system.

Another method of stopping a service or device driver from loading that will not change the registry is to simply rename it. This can be accomplished with the following commands:

1. Execute the CD C:\WINDOWS\SYSTEM32\DRIVERS command.

2. Execute the REN *Driver*.SYS *Driver*.ORG command where *driver* is the name of your device driver. This will rename the device driver file to a new name. As Windows will be unable to find the driver, it will be unable to load it and therefore the offending driver will no longer prevent the system from starting. A message will be displayed and recorded in the event log that the driver failed to load at system startup.

3. Exit the recovery console and restart the system.

REPAIRING WINDOWS WITH THE INSTALLATION CD-ROM

Repairing Windows XP with the installation CD-ROM is not something to attempt unless it is your last recourse. Repairing an installation from the original CD-ROM may mean loss of data, reinstalling all service packs and updates, and at the very least a significant amount of your time. If you must attempt a recovery of a failed installation, before you proceed you should decide what you want to accomplish. Is your most important consideration your

32

data? If so, the first thing you should do is attempt to recover your file system and copy the data to a safe location. Only after you have copied your data should you attempt a system recovery.

By now, I expect you are asking "how do you recover your file system so you can copy your data?" Well, there are several ways you can recover the file system. First, if you have more than one Windows XP computer, you can remove your existing drive on the failed system and add it to the computer that is working (typically as a slave drive on the first IDE channel). Once installed you can run ChkDsk or a third-party disk recovery tool (such as Symantec's Norton Disk Doctor) to scan the disk for errors and correct them. Once corrected, you can then copy the data to a safe location. Second, if no other Windows XP system is available, you can try a dual installation. A dual installation just means installing another copy of Windows XP on a separate disk partition, or a separate disk drive if you have two drives available. If you do not have two disk drives, or two partitions, you could try to use Partition Magic, or a similar disk utility, to modify your partition table and free up sufficient space (about 2GB) for a dual installation.

TIP

> Should your system fail to boot due to a corrupted registry, don't panic. There is hope for recovery. So long as you have made at least one Restore Point, you can use the technique provided in the Knowledge base article Q307545 at `http://support.microsoft.com/search/preview.aspx?scid=kb;en-us;Q307545` to restore a previous snapshot of your registry.

If a dual installation is not possible, and you have no other Windows XP computer to use to recover the data, then you have to accept the possible loss of data for repair options. The first choice is to use the Recovery Console as described previously. If that fails, then you can attempt to repair your existing installation by reinstalling Windows XP over the current installation. When you do, you will be given the chance to repair the existing installation or perform a new install. A repair will attempt to recover your existing installation by replacing system files, but will use your existing registry. Therefore, your user accounts will remain and your NTFS permissions should be recoverable as well. A new installation, if performed in the same directory, will erase your existing installation, but will leave your data intact unless you repartition or reformat the disk drive.

TIP

> If your data is especially important, it may be worthwhile to pay for a third party recovery service. One of the most well known recovery services is provided by OnTrack. For more information check out their Web site at `http://www.ontrack.com/`.

REPAIRING WINDOWS (AND DATA FILES) WITH GOBACK 3

Funnily, this section started as a note, and then it grew so long and exciting that I had to make it into a larger section. Here's why. If system protection and restoration is what you're after, a program to seriously check out is GoBack, from Roxio at www.roxio.com. GoBack is a truly inexpensive (cheap, cheap, cheap) security blanket. It's only about $50. Here's the scoop on it, and why you should check it out.

In addition to all the other MS OSes, it supports Windows XP Home and Professional. Think of it as XP's System Restoration feature, but on steroids. System Restore isn't designed to restore anything but system files themselves. GoBack can work even if Windows won't boot, without a boot or restore disk. GoBack protects those as well as the rest of your files and settings.

GoBack inserts itself between Windows and your hard disk, monitoring all changes. It watches your hard disk for any changes made to files on it, and keeps a journal of them in a separate pre-allocated area of the HD (defaulting to 10 percent of the total HD size). "Safe points" are created during your working day, allowing a range of choices if recovery should be necessary. For example, application installations trigger safe points, as do system bootups. Periodic time lapses will also trigger the creation of a safe point. These time lapses can be very small indeed, typically when the hard disk isn't accessed for even a few seconds. Figure 32.10 shows the splash screen options for the program.

Figure 32.10
GoBack 3.1 Deluxe
might save your day.

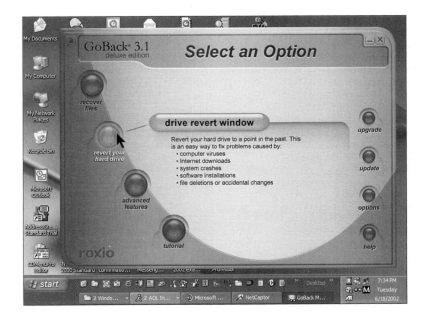

32

Whenever something funky such as a virus, driver conflict, or crash happens, you just reboot your computer and go into GoBack from a boot menu. Now you have a butt-saving ability to revert your entire PC to a time a few minutes, hours, or days ago when everything worked. Pick one of the offered safe points, wait through a few minutes of rewriting and rebooting, and it's as if the trouble never happened. You can return your hard drive to the way it was at any time in the recent past, recover deleted or overwritten files, even those emptied from the Recycle Bin.

When you open the main GoBack applet, a huge and impressive list showing restore points appears on the left with a calendar and a clock to better spot the day you want to go back to (see Figure 32.11). The list shows every file and folder that was modified with the date and time. Roxio seems to have thought of every possible recovery scenario. For example, when you revert your system to its condition two hours previous, the program pops up a list of files that changed during the period you just wiped out and it lets you recover any work you did during that time.

Figure 32.11
GoBack's listing of Safe Points and file actions that occurred between them. You can restore to any safe point.

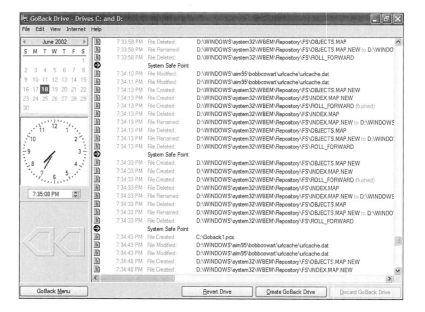

Another useful option displays an Explorer window with a virtual disk that represents a prior state of your system, so you can drag files from the older disk into the current version (see Figure 32.12).

If you edit documents a lot (and who doesn't?), the GoBack Deluxe extension to the Explorer shell is a definite plus. The Explorer context menu for any document file will show an option called "Show Revisions." Clicking on this brings up a list of versions of the file with date stamps. Just open the revision you want. This command alone is worth its weight in gold to us writers!

Figure 32.12
GoBack can create virtual drives that display in Windows Explorer, have drag and drop capability, and whose contents consist of previous versions of all modified files.

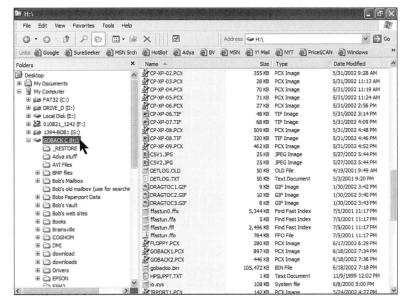

GoBack is ideal for public-access PCs or kiosks in computer labs, classrooms, libraries, and training centers where the ability to revert the system automatically to a clean condition at regular intervals is a boon.

Obviously, if your hard disk is completely hosed and you don't even get the boot menu, things get a little more complicated, but this happens much more rarely than some simpler mess caused by installing an errant application, or by an application crashing and messing up yesterday's almost-perfect document anyway. If worse comes to worst, and if your HD won't boot, you can start up GoBack from a floppy.

Password protection, included with the Deluxe Edition only, could be useful for corporate IT types. This protection option can keeps end-users from accessing historic information (or deleted files) logged by GoBack away from prying eyes.

By logic, the program must increase CPU overhead a bit, yet it was virtually undetectable in tests. Journaling of HD changes is deferred until the safe-point drive isn't being used by other programs, so perhaps that is partly the explanation. Since it mainly tracks writes, GoBack doesn't impact read times during most activities.

What are the gotchas? Only three we could discover:

- GoBack won't work with third-party multi-boot managers such as PowerQuest's BootMagic. Even still, it works smoothly with the multi-boot option built in to Windows NT and 2000, and XP if the following is true: Only two operating systems are used and one is Windows 9x/Me and the other is Windows NT 4.0/2000/XP.

- GoBack does not protect removable media, such as floppy, Zip, FireWire drives, and so on. Only drives recognized by a system's BIOS are monitored and restorable.

- GoBack is not compatible with some advanced features of Windows NT/2000/XP usually associated with servers. Examples include multiple processors, volume sets, dynamic disks, and striping.

TIP

> In cases where the data is very valuable, specialized services can take your hard drive and recover the data using forensic techniques, even from severely damaged hard drives. They're generally pretty expensive, but if the data is critical they may be your only hope as a last resort.

RECOVERING IF YOUR ADMINISTRATOR PASSWORD IS LOST

If you are unfortunate enough to be in the position of having a lost or forgotten Administrator password, do not give up all hope. There are several potential recovery methods available to you. First, if you are using Windows XP Professional and are a domain member, just ask your network administrator to reset your Administrator account password. He can do this locally on your computer or remotely via the network. Second, if you have more than one account on your computer with administrative privileges, then you can reset the password yourself. You can use the User Accounts applet located in the Control Panel. Or you can use the Local Users and Groups folder of the Computer Management application. The Computer Management application is located in the Administrative Tools group in the Control Panel. Both provide a means to reset a specific user account.

If you do not belong to a domain, or have a second account with administrative privileges, then it is more difficult to recover the password. A few methods that can resolve the problem are those that restore a previous SAM registry hive to a time when you know the Administrator password. This can include a tape, or disk, backup. Or system recovery disk. Or a Password recovery disk.

The first method described previously requires that you have a prior backup of your system, one that includes a copy of the registry. The second method can be used with the Automated System Recovery (ASR) wizard, but also requires that you have previously configured your system to restore itself using the ASR wizard. The third method also requires that you use a previously created recovery diskette. As you can see, all of these methods require that you consider the possibility of a lost password before the problem occurs. If you have not performed one of these tasks now, I suggest you do so immediately. Making a backup to disk, or invoking the ASR wizard, can be performed using the built-in backup application located in the System folder of the Accessories folder on the Program menu. Creating a password recovery disk can be accomplished by the following steps:

1. Open the Control Panel.
2. Launch the User Accounts applet.

3. Select the user account.

4. In the Related Tasks window, select Prevent a Forgotten Password. The Forgotten Password Wizard will be invoked.

5. Click the Next button.

6. Insert a blank formatted disk in the A: drive. Then click the Next button.

7. Specify the current password for the account when prompted. Then click the Next button.

8. When the disk has been created, click the Next button.

9. Click the Finish button. Then place your password reset disk in a safe location.

CAUTION

> Be sure to place your recovery diskette in a safe and secure location, as anyone with access to it can use your diskette to reset your password and log on to your computer.

To use your newly created password recovery disk, just follow these steps:

1. Attempt to log on to the account, but supply an incorrect password. At this point you will be prompted to use the Reset Password Wizard to reset your password.

2. Click the Use Your Password Recovery Disk link.

3. Insert your diskette and click the Next button.

4. Supply a new password and hint and click the Next button.

5. Click the Finish button.

6. Log on using your new password.

32

INDEX

SFU (Services for Unix), 831

software blocking, 907

volumes, creating, 1006

administration tools, CD:134–CD:140

administrative accounts, privileges, 417

Administrative Options Accessibility Options dialog box, 383

Administrative Tools, displaying, 410, 420

Administrative Tools applet (Control Panel), 1144

Administrator accounts
passwords, Setup Manager and, 178
security risks, 890–892
Welcome screen and, 412
XP User Management interface, capabilities, 421–422

Administrator log in, UPS installation, 207

Administrator passwords, setting, 891

Administrators Pak (NTFS recovery utilities), 432–433

ADSI (Active Directory Scripting Interface), VBScript, 1207

advanced support tools, CD:173

Advanced tab
Device Manager, 869
Modem Properties sheets, 294–296
printer properties, 249

advertisements, stopping in Internet Explorer, 516–517

alerts, 1079–1080

Alerts (Performance Logs and Alerts MMC snap-in), 1077

aliases (applications), creating with Registry, 1260

All Programs Start menu, 361
pinning applications, 362

Allow Incoming Echo Request (ICMP option), 987

Allow Incoming Mask Request (ICMP option), 987

Allow Incoming Router Request (ICMP option), 987

Allow Incoming Timestamp Request (ICMP option), 987

Allow META REFRESH (IE security setting), 500

Allow Outgoing Destination Unreachable (ICMP option), 987

Allow Outgoing Parameter Problem (ICMP option), 988

Allow Outgoing Source Quench (ICMP option), 987

Allow Outgoing Time Exceeded (ICMP option), 988

Allow paste operations via script (IE security setting), 501

Allow Redirect (ICMP option), 988

Alt-Tab replacement utilities, 332

Alternate Configuration tab (TCP/IP properties), 100

Always On Top item (Start menu), 388

answer files, naming, 182

Answer Mode (fax property), 271

antivirus software, 216
System Restore, 1174

AOL Instant Messenger URL protocol, 495

APC_INDEX_MISMATCH (kernel mode error message), 1293

APIPA (Automatic Private IP Addressing), 614–615, 875

APM (Advanced Power Management), 227

appearance, configuration, 372–374

Appearance and Themes category (Control Panel), 1142

AppleTalk, 604
network printers, 714
printer support (Windows 2000), 816–817

applets
Control Panel, 1144, CD:143
location of within categories, 1142
Date and Time, 1147–1149
Fonts, 1149–1150
Game Controllers, 1151–1152
Keyboard, 1152–1153
Mouse, 1154–1156
Power Options, disabling hibernation, 1022
Regional and Language Options, 1157–1160
Sounds and Audio Devices, 1161–1162
System, 1163–1168
Automatic Updates feature, 1174
Environment Variables, 1171–1172
Error Reporting, 1172–1173
paging file optimization, 1023
Performance Options, 1168, 1170
Remote feature, 1175

I

I/O (input/output), VBScript
message box input, 1189–1192
text input, 1192

IBM hosts, networking compatibility, 813, 846
application integration services, 847
data integration services, 847
Shared Folders Gateway Service, 847

ICF (Internet Connection Firewall), 311, 977–978
adding services, 311
configuring, 981
allowing ICMP connections, 986–988
allowing service requests, 982–983
enabling, 982
logging requests, 983–984, 986
disabling, 225
Network Setup Wizard and, 225
shortcomings, 313
troubleshooting, 320

ICMP (Internet Control Message Protocol), 605
connections, allowing in ICF, 986–988

ICS (Internet Connection Sharing), 600
Discovery and Control service, 663–664
Internet services availability and, 678
IP addressing, 661
Remote Desktop and, 795
securing networks and, 667
troubleshooting, 320, CD:170
VPN access and, 781

Idle tab Synchronization Settings dialog, 751

IE 6.0 (Internet Explorer), features, 43

IE (Internet Explorer), 494
ActiveX controls
finding damaged, 514–515
fixing damaged, 515–516
properties, 515
security considerations, 516
advertisements, stopping, 516–517
Authenticode, 511–512
Autocomplete, configuring, 509–510
Autosearch, 512–513
selecting provider, 513–514
Privacy control, 502, 504–509
Search Assistant, configuring, 514
security, 497
configuring security zones, 497–498, 500–502
security precautions, 976
troubleshooting, CD:171
updating, 497
Windows Update and, 202

IEEE-1394 port, networking and, 643

IEEE 1394a, networking ports, 306

if built-in command, CD:68, CD:72
conditional processing, CD:82–CD:83, CD:93–CD:94
checking for files and folders, CD:94
checking program success, CD:94–CD:95
extended if command, CD:95–CD:96

if command (CMD), comparison testing, CD:96–CD:97

if statement
batch files, 1222–1225
VBScript, 1193

IIS (Internet Information Server)
advantages of, 552
files comprising, CD:149–CD:151
folder attributes, 569–570
folders, sharing, 573–574
Indexing Service, installing, 575–577
installation, 556–558
interactive site scripting, 579–582
limitations under XP Professional, 552
log files, 574
MIME types and, 568–569
online documentation, 571
overview, 552, 570–571
printer management, 571
remote computing and, 806
Remote Desktop and, 571–572
security
limiting risk, 554
overview, 554–555
precautions, 976
services, 553–554
FrontPage Server Extensions, 560–562
FTP management, 564
management interface, 559
SMTP management, 565–566
WWW service, 558–559
shared connections, configuring, 577–578
snap-in, 553
Web server
configuring, 562–563
executing programs, 569
Web sites
configuring, 572–573
creating content, 566
home pages, 568
mapping folders, 567
Windows Update importance of, 558

i.Link, networking ports, 306

K

Kd.exe (Kernel Debugger tool), 1264

keep printed documents option (printers), 251

Kelly's XP Korner Web site, CD:176

Kerberos, support for, 602

Kernel Debugger tool, 1264, 1309

Kernel memory section, Performance tab of Task Manager, 391

kernel mode error codes, 1293–1308

Kernel mode error reporting, 1275–1276

Kernel mode errors, 1275

KERNEL_APC_PEND-ING_DURING_EXIT (kernel mode error message), 1294

KERNEL_DATA_INPAGE_ ERROR (kernel mode error message), 1302

KERNEL_STACK_ INPAGE_ERROR (kernel mode error message), 1301

KERNEL_STACK_ LOCKED_AT_EXIT (kernel mode error message), 1304

Keyboard applet (Control Panel), 1145, 1152–1153

keyboard combinations, Ctrl+Alt+Delete, 387

keyboard shortcuts
Remote Desktop, 800
Terminal Services Connections MMC snap-in, 1099
Windows Script Debugger, 1217

keys
EFS, 1036
Registry
exporting and importing, 1249–1250
hiding last logged-on user, 410
HKEY CLASSES ROOT key, 1243–1244
HKEY CURRENT CON-FIG key, 1246
HKEY CURRENT USER key, 1244–1245
HKEY LOCAL MACHINE key, 1245
HKEY USERS key, 1245–1246
security settings, changing, 1252–1254
top-level, 1241
URLs and, 495
Welcome screen accounts, 412

KMODE_EXCEPTION_ NOT_HANDLED (kernel mode error message), 1293

Knowledge Base, 1284–1285

L

label built-in command, CD:65

lagging on, biometric authentication, 413–414

LAN (Local Area Network), ICF (Internet Connection Firewall) and, 978

language, changing for menus and dialog boxes, 1157

languages
adding, 1157
performance issues, 1159
MUI (Multilingual User Interface) Pack, 195, 197

LANs (Local Area Networks)
NAT, 566
troubleshooting connections, 873–875

laptop computers
Device Manager, power management tab, 870
dynamic disks, 1002
hardware profiles, 230
power management, troubleshooting, 1282–1283

Last Known Good feature, 48

Last Used On date, meaning of, 329

launching
applications, CD:132
New Connection Wizard, 276

Launching programs and files in an IFRAME (IE security setting), 500

LDP.EXE (support tool), CD:174

legacy applications
Application Compatibility Toolkit (ACT), 1313–1314
compatibility, 1310–1311
compatibility modes, 1311–1313
Service Recovery, 1314–1315

legacy device drivers, installing, 1110

legal issues, licensing, 173
multiple installations, 174–175

licenses, 173
auditing, CD:29
copying media, 485
GNU, 822
multiple installations, 174–175
Web site, 174

LILO (Linux boot loader), 154–155

How can we make this index more useful? Email us at indexes@quepublishing.com

T

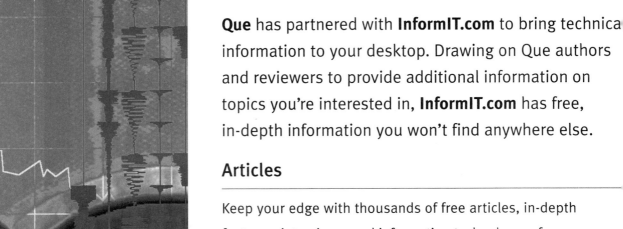

informIT

www.informit.com

Your Guide to Information Technology Training and Reference

Que has partnered with **InformIT.com** to bring technical information to your desktop. Drawing on Que authors and reviewers to provide additional information on topics you're interested in, **InformIT.com** has free, in-depth information you won't find anywhere else.

Articles

Keep your edge with thousands of free articles, in-depth features, interviews, and information technology reference recommendations – all written by experts you know and trust.

Online Books

Answers in an instant from **InformIT Online Books'** 600+ fully searchable online books. Sign up now and get your first 14 days **free**.

POWERED B

Safar

Catalog

Review online sample chapters and author biographies to choos exactly the right book from a selection of more than 5,000 titles.

As an **InformIT** partner, **Que** has shared the knowledge and hands-on advice of our authors with you online.
Visit **InformIT.com** to see what you are missing.

RUNNING THE CD INCLUDED WITH THIS BOOK

This CD-ROM is optimized to run under Windows 95/98/Me/NT/2000/XP using the QuickTime Player version 6 (or greater), from Apple. The CD-ROM is not designed to run on a Mac. If you don't have the QuickTime Player installed, you must install it, either by downloading it from the Internet at http://www.quicktime.com or by running the Setup program from the CD-ROM. If you install from the Web, it's fine to use the free version of the QuickTime player. You *do not* need to purchase the full version.

To install QuickTime player from the CD-ROM, follow these steps:

1. Insert the CD. A menu should appear onscreen. Choose *Install Quicktime 6 for Windows*.
2. If the menu does not appear, then
3. Run Windows Explorer.
4. Browse to the CD-ROM.
5. Open the QuickTime folder.
6. Double click on QuickTimeInstaller.
7. Follow the setup instructions onscreen.

RUNNING THE CD IN WINDOWS 95/98/ME/NT/2000/XP

The CD included with this book will run on machines meeting the following specifications, though performance will be enhanced on PCs with more RAM and processing power.

Minimum Requirements:

- QuickTime 6 Player
- Pentium II P300 (or equivalent)
- 64MB of RAM
- 8X CD-ROM drive
- Windows 95, Windows 98, Windows 2000, Windows Me, Windows NT 4.0 with at least Service Pack 4, and Windows XP (both Home and Professional Editions, with or without Service Pack 1 or later)
- 16-bit sound card and speakers

This presentation can run directly from the CD and should start automatically when you insert the CD in the drive. If the program does not start automatically, your system might not be set to automatically detect CDs. If this is the case, be sure that the Auto Insert Notification option is selected for your CD-ROM drive. Your system should now auto-run the CD when it is inserted into the drive.

NOTE

> Occasionally some XP computers have trouble recognizing the QuickTime movie files. Please click on Help on the CD's menu (or use Windows Explorer to open the file *help.htm* and read the troubleshooting section called "The CD will not run").

You may also manually start the lessons by right-clicking the CD icon, choosing Explore, opening the CD-ROM folder, and double-clicking startnow.exe. Follow the onscreen instructions.